Retailing

CANADIAN EDITION

DALE M. LEWISON | UNIVERSITY OF AKRON
D. WESLEY BALDERSON | UNIVERSITY OF LETHBRIDGE

Prentice Hall Canada Inc., Toronto,
Ontario

This effort is dedicated to my wife, Jacqueline;
my parents, Selmer and Helen Lewison;
my daughter, Ana Maria;
and my sons, Mac and Tyler.
– D.L.

Special thanks to my family
for their patience during the process and
to my grandfather, Alfred Ririe—a lifelong retailer,
for providing opportunity and interest in the field.
– W.B.

Canadian Cataloguing in Publication Data

Lewison, Dale M.
Retailing

Canadian ed.
ISBN 0-13-095073-4

1. Retail trade. I. Balderson, D. Wesley (David Wesley), 1948- . II. Title.

HF5429.L487 1999 658.8'7 C97-932820-9

ISBN 0-13-095073-4

Publisher: Patrick Ferrier
Acquisitions Editor: Mike Ryan
Developmental Editor: Amber Wallace
Senior Marketing Manager: Ann Byford
Production Editor: Andrew Winton
Copy Editor: Valerie Adams
Production Coordinator: Deborah Starks
Permissions/Photo Research: Susan Wallace-Cox
Cover Design: Verve
Cover Image: Bill Heinsohn
Page Layout: B.J. Weckerle

Original English Language edition published by Prentice-Hall, Inc.
Upper Saddle River, New Jersey

3 4 5 CC 02

Printed and bound in The USA.

All cases in the book were prepared as a basis for class discussion rather than to illustrate either effective or ineffective handling of an administrative situation.

Brief Contents

Contents

Preface

Lewison's *Retailing* is seventeen years old. Preparation of the first edition started in 1979, and it was published in 1982. The Canadian edition of *Retailing* continues the tradition of being one of the most comprehensive and contemporary texts on the subject of retailing. To keep pace with the dynamic retail marketplace, *Retailing*, Canadian Edition, has been adapted to the Canadian market and updated with respect to new retailing formats, emerging retail trends, current retail practices, and innovative retail strategies. The adaptation examines the most contemporary issues, explores many of the more challenging problems, and investigates the myriad of changes that Canadian retailers must struggle with as they enter the twenty-first century.

TEXT ATTRIBUTES

Retailing, Canadian Edition, builds upon the many strengths of the five previous U.S. editions.

- *High Adaptability.* The Canadian edition is easily adapted to courses in either Principles of Retailing or Retail Management. Although all chapters incorporate issues involving problem solving and decision making, the first fourteen chapters represent an extensive survey of the principles of retailing and have a more tactical and operational thrust. The last four chapters deal with retail strategies and have a more strategic and theoretical focus. For Principles of Retailing courses, the first fourteen chapters constitute complete coverage of the topics relevant to an introductory course. For a Retail Management course, all eighteen chapters represent one of the most all-encompassing treatments available.

- *Comprehensive Coverage.* The Canadian edition Provides the most comprehensive coverage of the subject of Canadian retailing on the market today. Both the *breadth* (the number of different subjects) and the *depth* (the extensiveness of a discussion on any given subject) of coverage have rarely been matched in any other source. The Canadian edition discusses all key retailing concepts and subjects with an appropriate level of detail. The organizational structure of the text enables teachers and/or students to eliminate those discussions that are not relevant to their individual circumstances and interests.

- *Superior Organization.* The Canadian edition is a systematic and highly structured investigation of the field of retailing. It carefully guides the reader from one topic to another through the use of extensive subtitling, visual representations (see "Chapter Organizers"), lead-in paragraphs, and summary exits. The organizational arrangement is the ultimate in "tell them what you are going to tell them" (for example, chapter objectives, chapter outlines, opening vignettes, organizational graphics), "tell them" (for example, chapter titling, content), and "tell them what you told them" (for example, chapter summary, key terms and concepts, review questions, review exams). The overall organizational framework of the text is portrayed and discussed in Chapter 1.

- *Contemporary Content.* *Retailing*, Canadian edition not only covers all of the traditional retailing subject matter, it also provides comprehensive coverage of those contemporary issues that are emerging as key determinants of future retailing success. Global retailing, ethical business practices, total quality management, superior customer service, quick-response procurement systems, relationship retailing, strategic alliances, micromerchandising, and portfolio retailing are but a few of the more contemporary issues examined in the Canadian edition. To support the contemporary content coverage, present-day examples of high-profile retailers (for example, Wal-Mart, The Bay, Sears, Toys R Us, and Canadian Tire) are used to illustrate many concepts. These examples enhance understanding of text material, increase reader enjoyment, and provide real-world perspectives.

• *Extensive References.* The text is supported by extensive lists of Canadian references, with both academic and trade sources. In addition to traditional sources of retail information, many nontraditional references are used to add different perspectives and to create a certain sense of uniqueness. As well as exposing students to the wide range of information sources available, the extensive referencing can provide students with the leads they need for continuing study and can even spark their interest to initiate further study.

• *Quality Reproduction.* The text's larger size (almost 8 1/2 by 11 in.) heightens its readability. The four-colour treatment of photos greatly enhances the text's visual presentation.

• *Supportive Pedagogy.* *Retailing* uses an extensive list of pedagogical tools (see the "Pedagogical Features" section) to enhance the learning environment of the text. Equally important is the quality of those tools. The style, detail, and structure of each learning aid are all designed to make the text as student friendly as possible. They provide a quick, convenient, and effective means for furthering the student's understanding of course content. Many of the pedagogical supports help to promote experiential learning by giving the students an opportunity to apply and practice what they have learned.

• *Supportive Supplements.* The Canadian edition provides both students and instructors with an extensive support package (see the "Supplements Package" section) designed to assist them in successfully carrying out their respective tasks.

PEDAGOGICAL FEATURES

• *Chapter Outline* previews the important topics covered in each chapter and helps students organize their approach to the chapter and subject matter.

• *Learning Objectives* guide students' reading of the chapter and help students to identify the key concepts and issues to be discussed and learned.

• *Opening Vignettes* of Canadian retailers, help spark students' interest and establish the tone of the chapter's subject matter.

• *Chapter Organizers* visually organize the chapter or part of a chapter and help to give students a picture of the relationships that exist among various chapter concepts and topics.

• *"The World of Retailing"* is a special feature that highlights contemporary issues in retailing. Business ethics, retail technology, politically correct retailing, and international retailing are the focal points.

• *"Retail Strategies and Tactics"* is another type of feature. These focus students' attention on interesting and different decision-making and problem-solving issues that retailers face.

• *Visual Aids* are extensive. Photographs, graphics, tables, and drawings illustrate, explain, and summarize important information and relationships. A four-colour photo essay insert provides thought-provoking captions and real-world retailing examples.

• *Chapter Summary* provides a concise review of the chapter's key topics.

• *Key Terms and Concepts* enable students to check their awareness and understanding of the retailer's language.

• *Review Questions* focus students' attention on the important questions that are addressed in the chapter and help prepare students for essay exams.

• *Review Exam* provides students an opportunity to take practice "true or false" and "multiple-choice" quizzes.

• *Investigative Projects* present structured opportunities for students to expand their skills through field studies, library searches, and survey assignments.

• *Strategic and Tactical Cases* mix tactical and strategic problems, as well as operational and managerial issues faced by well-known retailers. Cases are presented in one convenient location in Appendix B.

• *Weblinks,* exciting and useful Internet sites are integrated throughout the text and are easily identifiable by the Weblinks Icon.

SUPPLEMENTS PACKAGE

Retailing, Canadian Edition, is accompanied by a complete supplements package.

• *The Instructor's Manual with Video Guide* contains a detailed lecture outline of each chapter designed to assist the instructor in making effective in-class presentations. The instructor's package also includes informative case notes for both the Case Appendix and the CBC Video Cases integrated throughout the text, and answers to the end-of-chapter discussion questions.

• *The Test Item File* contains over 1000 multiple-choice, true/false, and short essay questions. Each question is rated by level of difficulty and includes a text page reference. It is available in both printed and electronic formats.

• *Prentice Hall Custom Test* The Prentice Hall Custom Test merges the Test Item File with a powerful software package in the Windows platform. With the Prentice Hall Custom Test's user-friendly test-creating abilities, you can create tailor-made, error-free tests quickly and easily. The Custom Test allows you to create an exam, administer it traditionally or online, and evaluate and track student's results—all with the click of the mouse.

• *Transparency Resource Package* Over 100 transparency masters, including figures, graphs, and key concepts featured in the text, are available in printed format and electronically in PowerPoint 4.0.

• *Prentice Hall Canada/CBC Video Library* Prentice Hall Canada and the CBC have worked together to bring you seven segments from the CBC series *Venture*. These programs have extremely high production quality and have been chosen to relate directly to chapter content. Please contact your Prentice Hall Canada sales representative for details.

ACKNOWLEDGMENTS

The Canadian edition of *Retailing* has been prepared with the assistance of several people. Thanks goes to undergraduate assistants Jennifer Byers and Patti Balderson. Cases were contributed by Shilpa Stocker, Peggy Cunningham, and me. Many companies responded positively to requests to use materials about their organizations. In this regard we thank the Hudson's Bay Company, Dylex, mmmuffins, Home Hardware, Sears Canada, West Edmonton Mall, Costco, United Furniture Warehouse, Provigo, and Molly Maid. In addition, we thank many publishing companies for allowing permission to reprint parts of articles appearing in their publications. These are duly noted as sources for the excerpt.

I am grateful to the following reviewers for their comments: Theresa Champion, Niagara College; Marilyn Drews, Camosun College; Adam Finn, University of Alberta; Charlene Hill, Capilano College; Bob Jershy, St. Clair College; Pat Kolodziejski, Mohawk College; and Wayne McIntyre, Algonquin College.

I thank the staff at Prentice Hall for their assistance with this project. Pat Ferrier initiated the interest in doing the work and Amber Wallace, Andrew Winton, and Valerie Adams assisted in its completion.

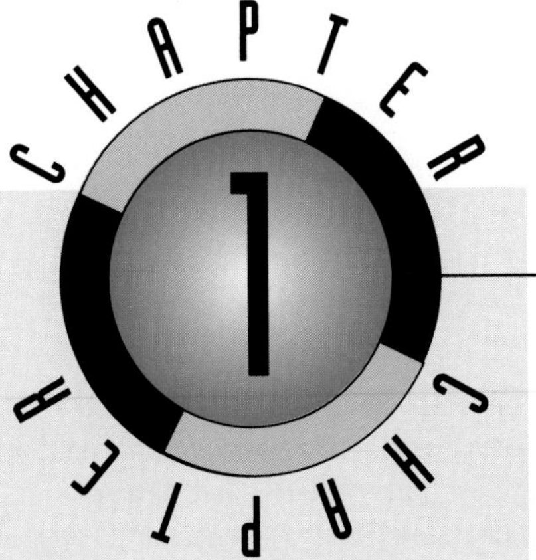

The Complex Nature of the Retail Industry

Outline

Objectives

To appreciate the complexities of operating a retail business

To understand the role of the retailer as a key link in the chain that connects the producer/wholesaler with the final consumer

To distinguish retailers and their activities from other marketing institutions

To delineate the marketing channel of distribution and to discern the relationships between the retailer and other channel participants

To understand the marketing and retailing concepts and to appreciate how these operating philosophies should direct the retailer's activities

To discuss the retailer's problem of striking a balance between the customer's merchandising needs and the retailer's performance needs

To explain what merchandising factors are involved with offering the right product, in the right quantities, in the right place, at the right time, at the right price, by the right appeal, with the right service

To identify the role of operating and financial ratios in establishing performance standards for retailers

To outline the major components of the right retailing plan

Retail Vignette

Hudson's Bay Company

The Hudson's Bay Company, incorporated in 1670, is generally acknowledged as the first retailer in Canada. Much of the commercial buying, selling, and trading in western Canada prior to Confederation was carried out by this organization. Today the Hudson's Bay Company, through its two major divisions, the Bay and Zellers, is Canada's largest retailer. This level of growth has been a result of retailing success, but is also a result of aggressive expansion in the acquisition of other retail chains. During the first half of the twentieth century, the Hudson's Bay Company was content to follow a relatively conservative course while other chains, such as Eaton's and Simpsons (Sears did not come to Canada until 1952), were growing rapidly. It wasn't until the early 1970s, when the majority ownership of the Hudson's Bay Company was transferred from England to Canada, that a more expansionist strategy was implemented.

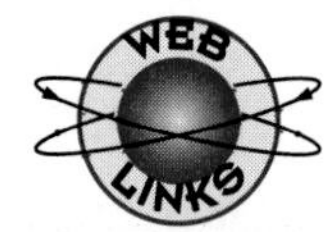

Hudson's Bay Company
www.sd35.bc.ca/Schools/ac/FL/hbc.html

In the 1970s the Hudson's Bay Company added significant real estate assets to its already large holdings in retailing and oil and gas. It was also during the 1970s that the Hudson's Bay Company began to pursue a greater market share of the Canadian retail industry. In 1978 it purchased Zellers, a successful Montreal discount department store chain of 200 stores for $170 million. Then in 1979 the Hudson's Bay Company purchased the Simpsons chain of Toronto in a much publicized battle that included Simpsons management and Sears Roebuck of the United States. The sixteen Simpsons stores cost an estimated $367 million. Shortly after the Simpsons purchase, in a dramatic turn of events, control of the Hudson's Bay Company itself was purchased by the Ken Thomson empire.

The decade following these corporate transactions proved very difficult for the Hudson's Bay Company. The acquisitions of Zellers and Simpsons and the expansion of the Bay division had been financed by borrowed money. The recession of 1981 and the simultaneous run-up of interest rates caught the Hudson's Bay Company in the classic squeeze; sales were off and competition forced gross profit down while interest costs soared. Management was slow to react and failed to differentiate between Simpsons and the Bay, with the result that they were competing for the same customer. As a result, the Hudson's Bay Company endured four years of losses from 1982 to 1985.

Following a management change in 1985, new strategies were adopted by the company. Department store retailing was identified as the core business and all other businesses were sold or disposed of. These included real estate and petroleum subsidiaries, wholesale and fur divisions, and even the Northern Stores division where the company had its roots. The marketing strategies of the three retail divisions were refocused with Zellers aimed at the middle to low segment of the market, the Bay at the broad middle, and Simpsons (reduced to the Toronto area) at the middle to upscale segment. The improving profits enabled the company to raise additional equity which, together with cash from the sale of assets, was used to reduce debt and interest charges.

By 1990–91, despite another recession, a turnaround had been achieved. Zellers, whose strategies included everyday low prices, tough expense management, a frequent shopper program, and Club Z, had become the most successful of the Canadian discount department stores. The Bay returned to profitability by emphasizing higher margin soft goods, employing high-tech computer programs to control inventory, revitalizing its downtown stores, and absorbing Simpsons a casualty of the recession.

By 1990, after five years of downsizing, the Hudson's Bay Company was financially strong enough to purchase the 51-store Towers chain and merge it with Zellers.

Effective in June of 1993, the Hudson's Bay Company acquired Woodward's Ltd. This resulted in a net addition of 11 Bay and 10 Zellers stores, which significantly improved their competitive positions in both British Columbia and Alberta.

The purchase of the Woolco chain by Wal-Mart Stores in 1994 signalled a new era of retail competition in Canada for the Hudson's Bay Company. Although it had been affected by Wal-Mart's move to Canada, it has made strategy adjustments and has emphasized its strengths to remain very competitive and retain its position as the number-one retailer in Canada. In the spring of 1997, the Hudson's Bay Company hired William Fields, a former Wal-Mart executive, as its new president and chief operating officer. Mr. Fields's background and experience is expected to assist the Hudson's Bay Company in meeting the challenge of global retailing which now characterizes Canadian retailing.

Printed with permission of Hudson's Bay Company Ltd.

Canadian Retailing—An Industry in Transition

Retailing in Canada is a very dynamic industry. Retailers range from large sophisticated chains to small independent operators. In Canada, retailing tends to be more diversified and mature than in most other countries. Retail sales in Canada in 1996 were $216.6 billion and are growing by over 2 percent per year.[1] Currently, however, the retail industry in Canada is in a state of transition. A recession in the early 1990s, changing consumer demographics and tastes, new retail formats, increased foreign competition, increasing operating costs, new technology, and taxes have all had an adverse effect on sales and profits of retailers in the country. Many retailers are demonstrating that it is still possible to be successful in such an environment by employing well thought out strategies and skillful execution. It is hoped that the information presented and discussed in this book will provide a background to enable the prospective or current retailer to cope with the dynamic nature of the industry.

Retailing—A Local Type of Business

There is ongoing consolidation in every sector of retail. Bigger companies are grabbing greater market share in virtually every sector of retail. With a growing diversity of consumer demographics and lifestyles, targeting consumers will be more challenging than ever. Micromarketing will become the key to reaching fragmented markets. This trend is already under way. Retailing is a local type of business. The large chains that run centralized, standardized merchandising and marketing operations ignore the reality of the local nature of retailing.[2]

Retailing—More for Less

Consumers demand it. Retailers must deliver it. From the consumer's perspective, more for less comes in the form of more quality, function, fashion, innovation, service, information, convenience, consistency, and selection . . . for less money, time, effort, or risk. From the retailer's perspective, delivering more for less means dealing in former contradictions: Optimizing in-stock position but owning less inventory; providing more service, but paring payroll; raising quality, but lowering prices; having all the right stuff, but working with fewer vendors. These were yesterday's paradoxes. They are today's playing field. Tomorrow they may not be good enough.[3]

The focus of this introductory chapter is an overview of the problems and decisions facing the retail manager. Based on the old adage that "a problem well defined is a problem half solved," Chapter 1 identifies and describes the key issues examined in the remaining seventeen chapters of this textbook. Figure 1–1 outlines the topics to be covered in our initial examination of the complex nature of the retail industry.

Figure 1–1

The complex nature of the retail industry

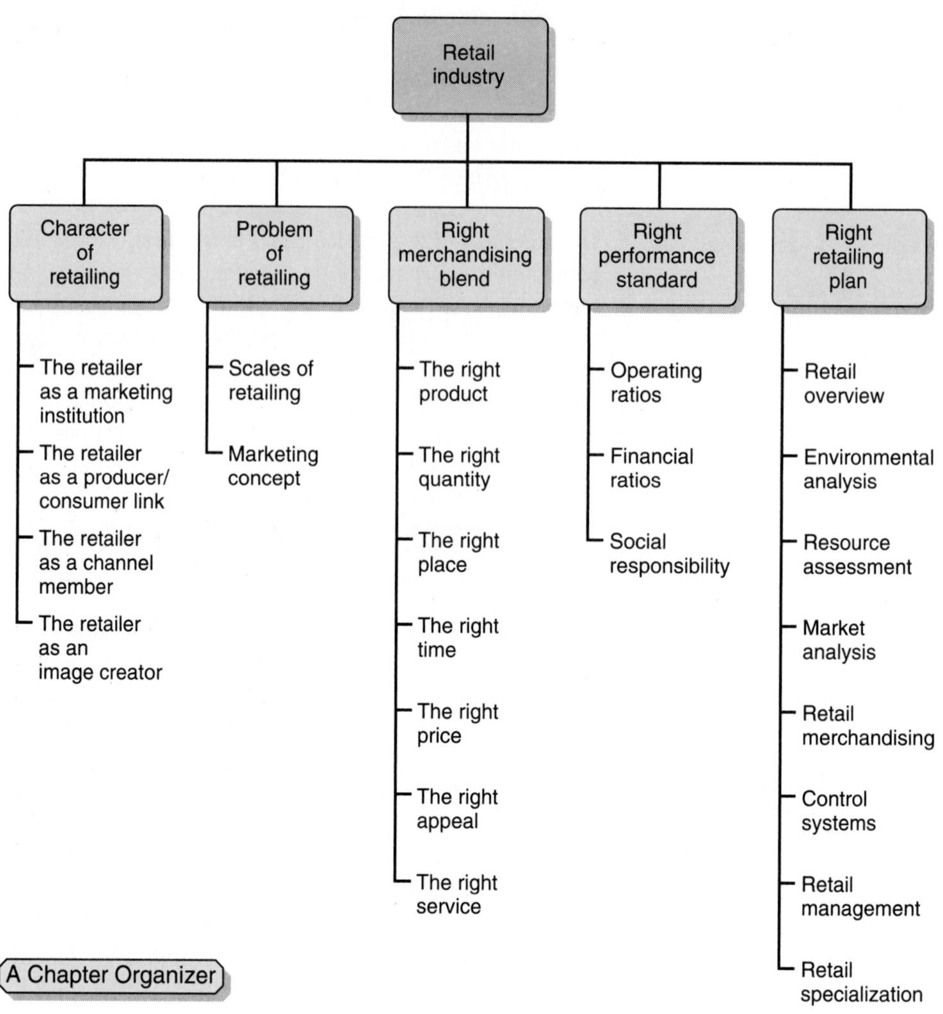

The Character of Retailing

The Retailer as a Marketing Institution

The many definitions of retailing all share the same basic thought: **Retailing** is the business activity of selling goods or services to the final consumer. A **retailer** is any business establishment that directs its marketing efforts toward the final consumer for the purpose of selling goods or services. Using this definition, a retail organization can be classified as a goods retailer or a services retailer. As illustrated in Figure 1–2, the core business of a **goods retailer** is the selling of goods (for example, apparel, appliances, foodstuffs) supported by appropriate complementary services (for example, alterations, installations, bagging). The sale of services (for example, hairstyling, insurance, medical care) represents the core business of a **services retailer**. Hair spray, financial brochures, and prescription medicine are examples of complementary goods that might be sold or given as complements in support of the sale of these services. A real-world example is Hampton Inns, which provides a free continental breakfast (complementary goods) to each of its registered guests (core service).[4]

The key words in our definition of retailing are "the final consumer." A business selling the same product to two different buyers may in one instance perform a retailing

Figure 1–2

The definition of retailing

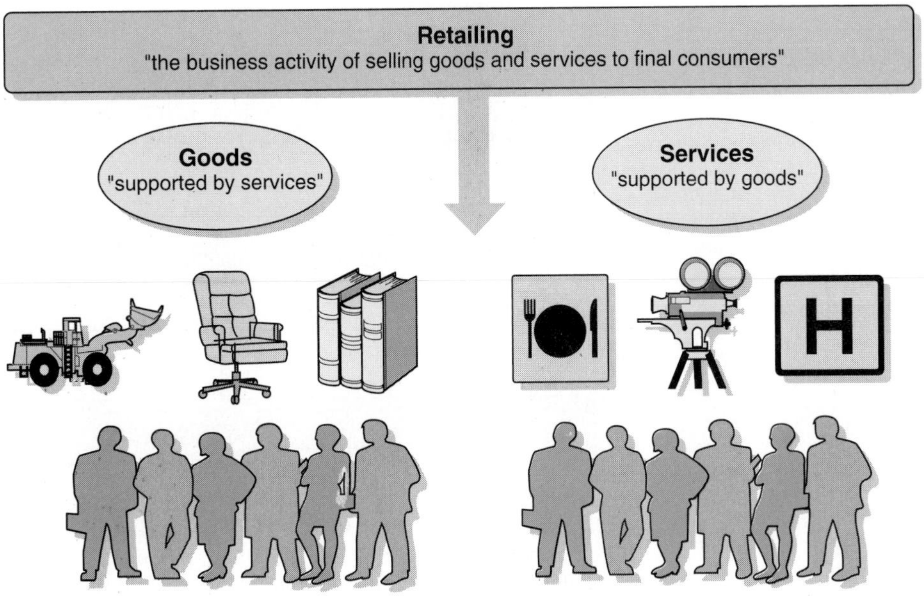

Retailing
"the business activity of selling goods and services to final consumers"

Goods
"supported by services"

Services
"supported by goods"

activity but not in the other. As an example, assume that you buy a chandelier to hang in your living room. In this case, the lighting company has made a retail sale. On the other hand, assume that a home builder walks into the same store, purchases the same chandelier, and installs it in a home he or she is building. In this case, the lighting company did not make a retail sale, because the chandelier was not sold to the final consumer (user) of the product. A decorator who advises a homeowner on how to decorate a home is making a retail service sale. If that same decorator advises a hospital on how to decorate its lobby and waiting room, he or she would be making a business sale. Thus, a sale is a retail sale when the ultimate consumer purchases the product. For example, Sally's Beauty Supply, a division of Alberto Culver, sells a variety of hair-care products to walk-in customers at one price and to registered beauticians at a 20% to 25% discount.[5]

What distinguishes a retail sale from other types of sales is the buyer's reason for buying. If the buyer purchases the product for personal use, the sale is considered a retail sale. If the buyer purchases the product for resale at a profit or to use in a business, the sale is not a retail sale; instead, it is a business sale. Therefore, retailing may be defined as all activities in the marketing process that result in offering for sale goods and services to individuals or organizations for purposes of ultimate consumption.

Most retailers tend to focus a vast majority of their resources on making retail sales, which is why they are retailers. Occasionally retailers, in an effort to expand, lose sight of their main target market. Several Canadian retailers have gotten sidetracked and have neglected their core business in the past by moving into financial services, other merchandise categories, and real estate. Recognizing this mistake, some are re-focusing their strategy to their core customer and the original market.[6]

The Retailer as a Producer/Consumer Link

As marketing institutions, retailers act as links between producers and consumers by directing their efforts at overcoming a series of discrepancies between what is ideal for the producer's production process and what is needed by consumers in their consumption activities. These discrepancies are identified as assortment, quantity, space, and time gaps (see Figure 1–3).

An **assortment gap** is the discrepancy that occurs because producers must produce and sell a limited line of identical or nearly identical products, whereas consumers want to choose from a wide selection of products. This limited assortment on the part of producers stems from the need to realize the economies of scale associated with the mass production process. Retailers help bridge the assortment gap by buying the limited product

Figure 1–3

The retailer as a producer/consumer link

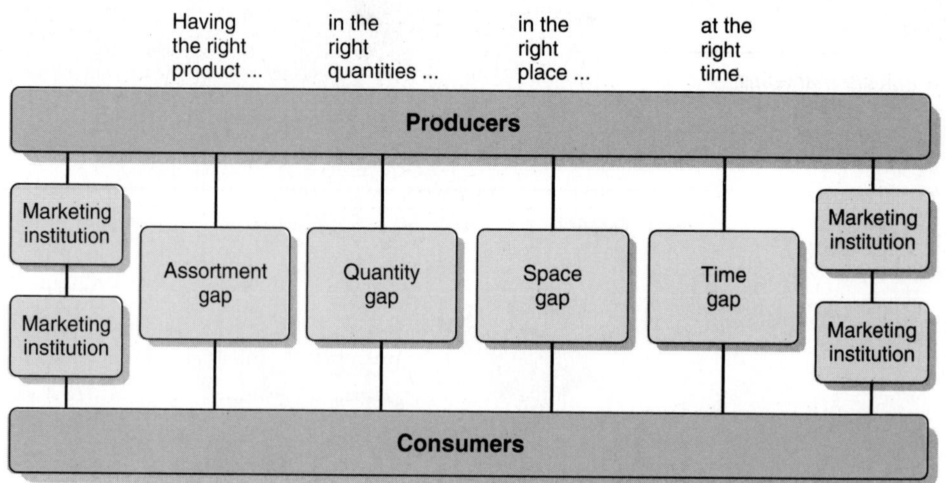

line offering of several different producers/wholesalers, creating product selection by combining these lines, and offering them for sale to the consumer. Hence, by engaging in this **accumulating** and **assorting process**, retailers can collect and merchandise product groupings that create greater customer satisfaction.

A **quantity gap** develops from economies of scale in production that require producers to produce and sell in large and often bulky quantities. However, consumers need to buy in small individual units because of low rates of consumption, limited storage space and transportation capabilities, and restricted funds available for making purchases at any given time. To overcome this discrepancy in selling and buying quantities, retailers buy in large quantities from producers/wholesalers, perform "break-in-bulk" functions, and sell smaller quantities to other intermediaries (that is, case lots) and consumers (that is, individual units). This **allocation process** is vital in meeting the quantity demands of the marketplace.

Points of production and points of consumption are likely to be characterized by spatial separation. Retailers assist in bridging the **space gap** by creating **place utility**. To do this, they buy products from many different producers in many different areas and transport these products to a place that is centrally and conveniently located with respect to consumers. Neighbourhood, community, and regional shopping centres, as well as the central business districts (CBDs) of major metro areas, are all good examples of places that retailers utilize to enhance the place utility of the producer's product offering.

A **time gap** occurs when producers must produce on a continuous, long-run basis (that is, staple products) or at certain appropriate times (that is, seasonal products), whereas consumers want to consume products at particular times that may or may not coincide with production requirements. An additional "in-transit" time gap results from the time needed to overcome the distance between points of production and consumption. This time gap is bridged in part by retailers adding **time utility** through purchasing products as they are produced and transporting and storing these products at various places until consumers need them. Finally, retailers add time utility by extending credit. Consumers who have the opportunity to "buy now and pay later" can realize immediate gratification of their needs.

The Retailer as a Channel Member

Retailers are referred to as *middlemen* or *intermediaries*. Both references suggest that retailers occupy a position "in the middle of" or "between" two other levels. Retailers do, in fact, occupy a middle position between the consumption level and the wholesale or production level of the marketing channel of distribution. They purchase, receive, and store products from producers and wholesalers to provide consumers with convenient locations for buying products. As shown in Figure 1–4, retailers are part of a chain called

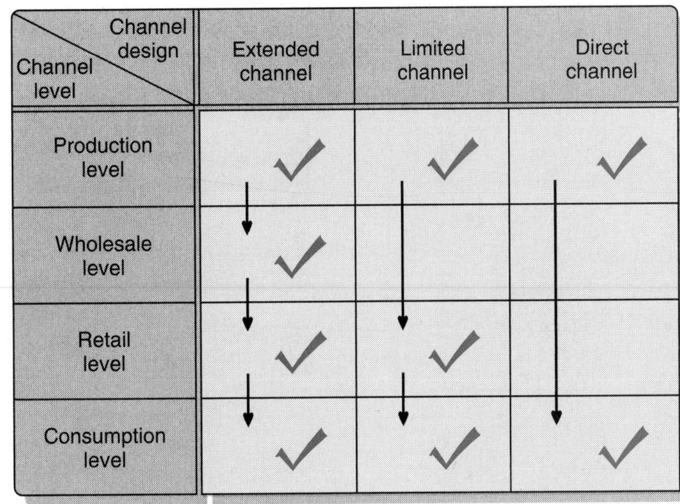

Channel design
Channel level
Extended channel
Limited channel
Direct channel
Production level
Wholesale level
Retail level
Consumption level

Figure 1–4

Alternative marketing channel structures

a **marketing channel**—a team of marketing institutions that directs a flow of goods or services from the producer to the final consumer. Generally, the team consists of a producer, one or more wholesalers, and many retailers.

The marketing channel can be described as a multilevel structure made up of channel teams whose interactions coordinate channel flows through channel teamwork. To facilitate our understanding of the marketing channel, we examine each major component of this system: (1) channel levels, (2) channel teams, (3) channel interactions, (4) channel flows, and (5) channel teamwork.

Channel Levels Marketing channels can be characterized by several structural designs defined by the inclusion or exclusion of various intermediaries. The producer has a number of alternative channel structures to reach consumers. As Figure 1–4 illustrates, there are three basic channel structures: extended, limited, and direct.

The first alternative is to use an **extended channel** by marketing through both wholesalers and retailers. In this case, producers rely on wholesalers to reach retailers that, in turn, will stock their products and sell them to final consumers. Because there usually are fewer wholesalers than retailers in a marketing channel, this option enables the producer to spend less time and money cultivating the necessary channel contacts to reach the ultimate consumers.

The second alternative for a producer is the **limited channel**, that is, to use only retailers, thereby eliminating the wholesaler. A growing number of producers of such products as automobiles, furniture, appliances, and other big-ticket items are using the limited channel. Also, manufacturers of "perishable" products such as clothing (which goes out of style quickly) and fresh and frozen foods (which spoil rapidly) frequently use a limited channel. Packard Bell pioneered selling home computers through department stores and big electronics chains at a time when the rest of the personal computer (PC) makers focused on direct sales to businesses or sold by mail to final consumers.

The third alternative is the **direct channel**. In this case, the producer eliminates both the retailer and the wholesaler. By using door-to-door, television, magazine, Internet, or direct-mail selling techniques, these producers market directly to final consumers.

Although a producer may choose not to use another team member in the channel, it can never eliminate the functions that must be performed at each channel level. In other words, *it can eliminate the retailer but not the retail level and the retail functions*. Thus, producers that sell directly to consumers have taken over, but not eliminated, retailer operations at the retail level. Such producers become both wholesalers and retailers.

Channel Teams Channel teams include both full- and limited-member institutions supported by facilitating nonmember institutions. Membership in the marketing channel

Figure 1–5

Interactive tasks performed by the channel team

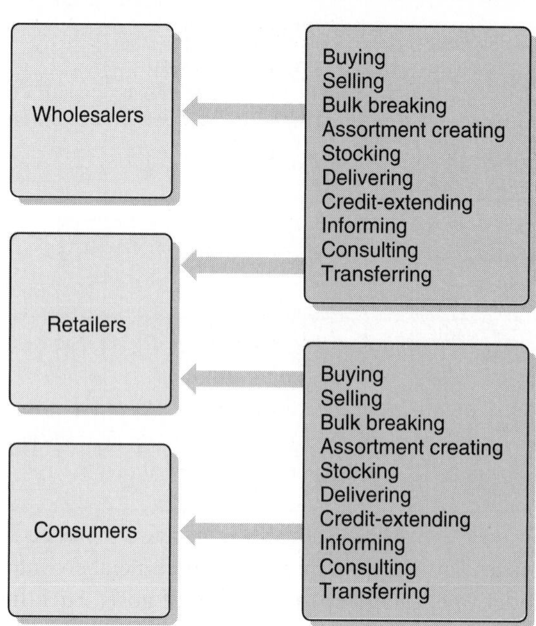

team is based on the nature of an institution's transactional involvements and whether members assume title to the goods involved in the transaction. A **full-member institution** is a wholesaler or retailer directly involved in the purchase and/or sale of products and that takes title to the products involved in the transaction. Merchant wholesalers and nearly all retailers have full membership in the channel team. **Limited member institutions** are marketing intermediaries with a direct involvement in purchase/sales transactions that do not take title to the involved product. Agent wholesalers hold limited team membership, as do retailers when they engage in consignment selling.

Several organizations provide a wide range of support functions. These **nonmember facilitating institutions** assist the team effort by providing specialized advertising, research, transportation, storage, financial, risk-taking, and/or consulting services. These facilitators neither take title to goods involved in a transaction nor become directly involved in the sale and/or purchase of those goods.

Channel Interactions Interactions between participants within the marketing channel of distribution can take several forms. As intermediaries, wholesalers and retailers must successfully complete several tasks for each other and their clientele to accomplish distribution and transactional functions most efficiently and effectively. These interactive tasks include buying, selling, breaking bulk, creating assortments, stocking, delivering, extending credit, informing, consulting, and transferring titles and payments (see Figure 1–5).

Channel Flows A marketing channel can be likened to a pipeline or conduit that guides the movement of entire marketing programs among channel participants. Although the flow of physical goods is the channel flow most commonly recognized by the general public, other types of flows are equally important to delivering a successful marketing effort. The five major types of channel flows are as follows:

1. **Physical flow**—the actual movement of a physical product from one channel participant to another
2. **Ownership flow**—the transfer of title (right of ownership and usage) from one channel participant to another
3. **Information flow**—the two-way communication of useful data between channel participants

4. **Payment flow**—the transfer of monies from one channel participant to another as compensation for services rendered and/or goods delivered
5. **Promotion flow**—the flow of persuasive communication directed at influencing the decisions of consumers (consumer promotion) and other channel participants (trade promotion)

In most channel structures retailers are directly involved in each flow and play a key role in channel flow management.

Channel Teamwork As a social interactive system, the marketing channel is subject to the behavioural processes inherent in all such systems. The behaviour of each channel participant affects all other participants—hence the need for channel teamwork. Good teamwork results in a cooperative spirit and a coordinated effort; poor teamwork nets channel disruptions and conflict. From the retailer's perspective, good relationships with customers require that the retailer give employees and channel members equal attention. To ensure good teamwork the channel of distribution must be integrated. **Channel integration** is the process of incorporating all channel members into one channel system and uniting them under one leadership and one set of goals. Such firms as Firestone, Singer, and The Gap are examples of manufacturers with vertically integrated distribution channels.

Channel integration ends the segregation of intermediary operations and their functional tasks. As Figure 1–6 shows, channel integration can take the form of a highly integrated vertical marketing system or a modestly integrated conventional marketing channel. A vertical marketing system is "a professionally managed and centrally programmed network, pre-engineered to achieve operating economies and maximum market impact."[7] The advantage of this type of system is that it enables the channel team to achieve technological, managerial, and promotional leverages by integrating and synchronizing the five channel flows.[8] A **vertical marketing system** can be established using persuasive administrative powers, legally binding contractual agreements, and partial or total ownership of channel members.

In a vertical marketing system, each channel member assumes the functions and tasks that will best support the entire channel system. As a team member, the retailer operates

Figure 1–6

Forms of channel integration

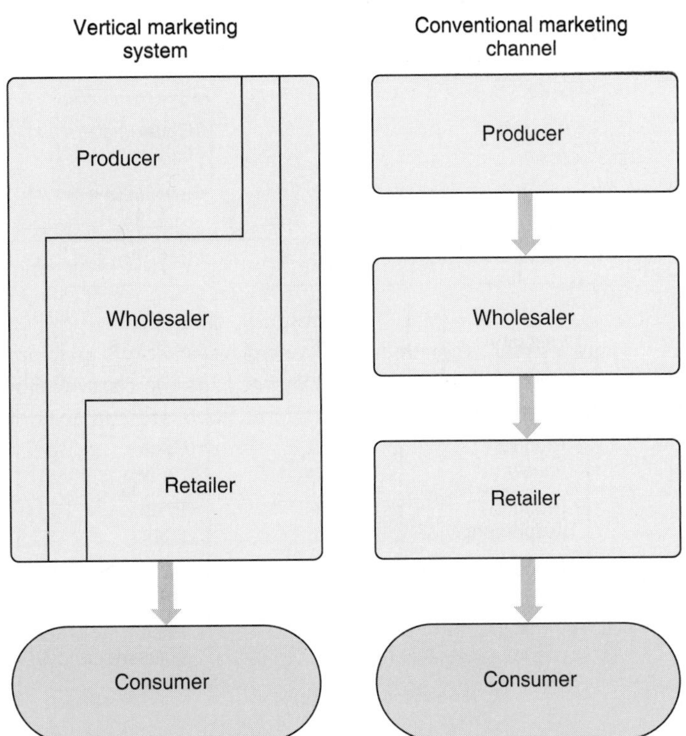

within the retail level of distribution and provides most of the teamwork at that level. Some, however, engage in operations at the wholesale and even the production levels of the marketing channel.

A **conventional marketing channel** is a loosely aligned, independently owned and operated channel team. The chief advantage of this type of arrangement is the freedom each member has in conducting business. The disadvantages of conventional channels include (1) the failure to achieve economies of scale, (2) the instability of the arrangement as a result of the ease of channel entry and exit, and (3) the limited levels of cooperation as a result of the greater autonomy of participating members.

The Retailer as an Image Creator

Retailing is an image-creating activity. Consumers often evaluate and select retailers on the basis of the image they project; hence, retailers must cultivate and communicate the right retail image. An **image** is a mental picture that forms in the human mind as a result of many different stimuli; it is an individual's perceptions of people, places, and things. **Retail image** can be defined as the impression, personality, or mental picture that is called to mind when a consumer is asked to describe or characterize a particular retail operation. Retail images are delineated by a complex blend of functional (factual) qualities and psychological (emotional) attributes. As such, it represents an overall composite of how consumers see and what they feel about a given retailer. Figure 1–7 illustrates some of the components that consumers use in formulating their mental impressions of what they think about the retailer and its activities.

The image portrayed by a retailer is important for several reasons. First, consumers are exposed to vast amounts of sensory data that they are unable or unwilling to analyze and organize. To simplify their lives as consumers, shoppers develop mental snapshots of retailers and use these general images to make judgments regarding the worth of various retail offerings and decisions as to whether to patronize one retailer over another. "In the current economic environment, the consumer's perception of the retailer and what a retailer stands for has become the single biggest reason for selecting to shop a particular store. The successful retailers will be the ones that can stand on their own as a reason to shop it and to do this they must broaden the perception of who they are and what they stand for."[9]

It is the consumer's perceived image of the retailer that determines store patronage; therefore, the retailer must ensure that the image being perceived is the one it wishes to

Figure 1–7

The components of a retail image

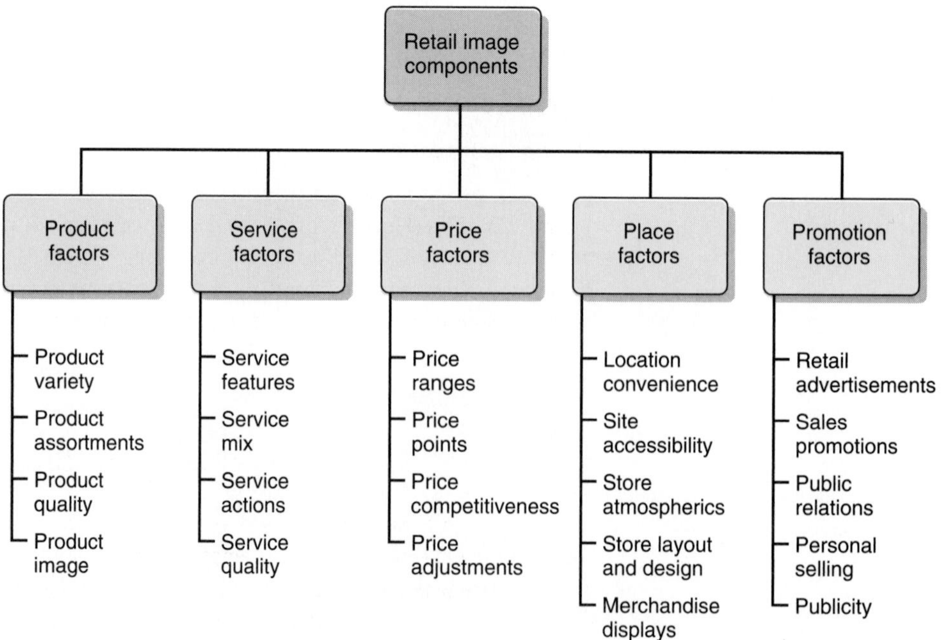

communicate. A clear, distinctive, and consistent image can be a vital factor in determining the retailer's ability to attract and hold customers. For years, Sears had a fuzzy image ranging from a traditional mass merchandiser to collection of specialty stores within a store. Recent efforts by the retailer have clarified its image as a "moderate-price department store."[10]

Images are equally important because consumers have a tendency to patronize the retailer whose image is closest to the image they have of themselves. For example, consumers who view themselves as thrifty are more comfortable shopping in a store they perceive as offering lower prices in a more spartan environment. The "fried" in Kentucky Fried Chicken was limiting the Colonel's growth in the fast-food market, where health-conscious consumers' fear of cholesterol, sodium, and fat is creating an unhealthy image of frying. The firm replaced its original name with just the initials KFC.[11]

The closer the firm's retail image is to the consumer's self-image, the greater the likelihood that the store will be successful in attracting and satisfying a certain class of consumers. Footlocker stores cater to the young, active, and athletic consumer, and interior design, merchandise assortment, and personnel reinforce that image.

Finally, the retailer's image is an important tool that a company's management uses to help differentiate itself from other retailing organizations. Retail image assists the consumer in making comparisons among retailers. Unfortunately, most retailers are not well positioned. "Marketing research shows that consumers are unclear on most retailers' positioning strategies. Consumers are not clear what the companies stand for—how they are different from competitors."[12] This "positioning" strategy encourages shoppers to think in relative terms about retailers and their offerings. Canada's department stores are currently adjusting their strategies to provide a more clearly focused image to the consumer.[13] Retailers are positioned in the consumer's mind as having (1) higher or lower prices, (2) better or poorer service, and (3) greater or lesser selection.

The Problem of Retailing

The Scales of Retailing

The retailer's problem is how to maintain a proper balance between the ability of the firm's merchandising programs to meet the needs of targeted consumers satisfactorily and the ability of the firm's administrative plans to meet the retailer's need to operate effectively and efficiently. Just as the scales of justice must judge the rights and responsibilities of two disputing parties, the "scales of retailing" must weigh the product and service needs of the customer against the operational and financial needs of the retailer. A successful retail business strikes a balance between the customer's merchandising needs and the retailer's performance standards (see Figure 1–8). High-performance retailers have "adopted the seemingly contradictory goals of lowering operating expenses while increasing ability to serve the customer. They have accomplished these dual objectives by minimizing costs, eliminating non-value-adding steps, and optimizing business processes."[14]

The Marketing Concept

The **marketing concept** is the philosophy that the overall goal of every business organization is to satisfy consumer needs at a profit. A firm adopting the marketing concept, however, strives to sell what the customer wants. "It is the willingness to recognize and understand the consumer's needs and wants and a willingness to adjust any of the marketing mix elements [product, price, place, promotion] . . . to satisfy those needs and wants."[15] The marketing concept, then, stresses keying supply to demand rather than keying demand to supply. Companies that respond and listen to customer needs not only have

Retail Strategies and Tactics

The Store to End All Stores

Today's shoppers want value. They have less money to shop than their parents did. Twenty-five years ago, Canadian families spent more than 80% of their income on consumption. Today, thanks largely to increasing taxes and slightly higher savings rates, that proportion has slid to about 72%. Real family income, in fact, never mind disposable income, has been falling since 1989, and sits today at about the same level as it was in 1980.

Today's shoppers want convenience. These days, 69% of mothers with children under 16 years of age work outside the home. As companies downsize, the demands on the workers remaining increase. Statistics Canada reports that 1.3 million Canadians work extra hours every week, and that the portion of the workforce putting in a 50-hour week, now 13.5%, has, on average, been higher in the last five years than in the preceding decade. By the time parents pick up their children at daycare, commute home over congested highways, and feed the family, they have precious little time for shopping.

Jody Martin, a consultant with Stillerman Jones & Co. Inc. in Indianapolis, studies shopping patterns in malls and can quantify the change. The average trip to the mall now lasts 71 minutes, down from 90 in 1982. The number of stores visited is down to 2.6 from 3.6. But the average expenditure per trip is rising slightly faster than inflation. What all that means, says Martin, is that shoppers are becoming more efficient than ever. Although she doesn't study Canada, it's a safe bet that the same is true here. "The day is gone when people regularly went shopping for something to do," she says.

What Wal-Mart has done is figure how business operates and how consumers think, and learned to manipulate both. The story behind its success often begins and ends with its distribution and inventory systems. Wal-Mart's checkout scanners feed instantaneous inventory information, via the company's own satellite, back to its distribution centres. Products zip through on high-speed conveyers, few spending more than 48 hours in the warehouse. Most of the stores are within a day's drive and many get daily inventory replenishment.

Source: Mark Stevenson, Canadian Business, *May 1994, 22–23.*

Figure 1–8

The scales of retailing

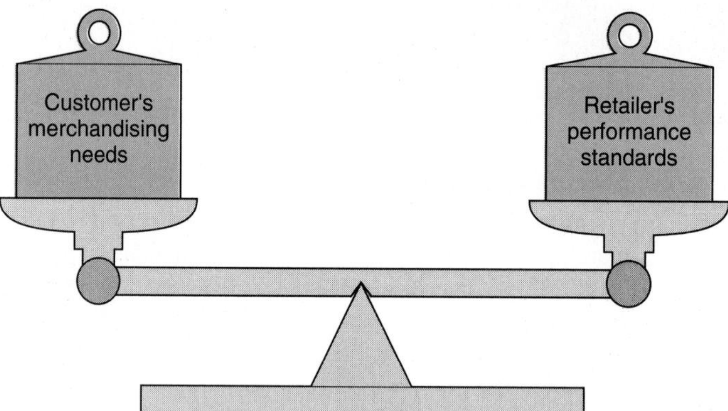

satisfied customers but also develop strong relationships that lead to customer loyalty, better market feedback, and a basis of differentiation that is difficult to match.[16] "Happy customers should exhibit at least one of three measurable characteristics: loyalty (retention rates), increased business (share of wallet), and insusceptibility to your rivals' blandishments (price tolerance)."[17]

The equally important objective in addition to customer satisfaction is, of course, profit. Without profit, the firm cannot stay in business to satisfy anyone's needs. Retailers that adopt the marketing concept are neither exclusively customer driven nor exclusively profit driven; rather, they seek a workable balance between these two important goals (see Figure 1–8).

For the retailer, more so than any other marketing institution, adoption of the marketing concept is an immediate problem. The retailer is the first to reap the benefits of consumer satisfaction but also the first to bear the brunt of consumer dissatisfaction. As one retail industry expert describes, "satisfaction means that customers come back." Research indicates that most dissatisfied customers never complain to the company; instead, 60 to 90 percent of them simply switch stores or brands. "It's very common for companies to lose 15% to 20% of their customers each year. Simply cutting this defection rate in half would more than double most retailers' growth rate right out of the box. By retaining just 5% more customers on average, a retailer can potentially increase profits by as much as 100%."[18]

A high level of customer satisfaction is an integral part of the retailer's program of **relationship retailing**—the operational philosophy that all of the retailer's activities be directed at establishing and maintaining intimate customer relationships by focusing on the specific needs of a targeted customer base. Customer-intimate retailers do not pursue one-time transactions; rather, they cultivate long-term relationships by specializing in satisfying unique needs, which they recognize through an intimate knowledge of the customer.[19] While relationship retailing focus helps satisfy current retail customers, do more business with existing customers, and attract new customers, it also recognizes that not all customers are equal. In most retail businesses a small proportion of customers account for the overwhelming portion of the revenues and profits.[20] Hence, a basic tenet of relationship retailing is to target carefully those consumers whose needs the firm is uniquely qualified to meet.

Because it costs five times as much to attract a new customer as it does to retain an existing one, it makes sense for a store to try to ensure customer satisfaction. It has also been documented that customers become more profitable to the retailer over time; hence, **retention retailing** (holding onto customers over time) is vital to the retailer's long-term

Retail Strategies and Tactics

Customer Loyalty: Benefiting from the Flywheel Effect

Customer loyalty is a behavioural concept. It reflects how customers act and react to a retailer's market offering. Loyal customers exhibit nonrandom behaviour toward the retailer over an extended period of time. Customer loyalty suggests consistent, frequent, and biased behaviour toward a retailer. Customer loyalty is about building strong and lasting relationships. The real magic of a successful customer loyalty strategy is the **flywheel effect**—customer loyalty begets more customer loyalty, and the resulting benefits can be enormous. The flywheel effect starts with loyal customers who represent more repeat sales, which leads to improved market share, which results in lower cost structures and better profit margins. Higher profits mean more profit sharing, which leads to higher job satisfaction and employee retention. Loyal employees provide better customer service, which leads to greater customer loyalty. Both Wal-Mart and Home Depot have used this model to build the largest chains within their respective retailing industries—discount stores and home centres. The basic flywheel effect and its strategic implications can be modelled as shown at left:

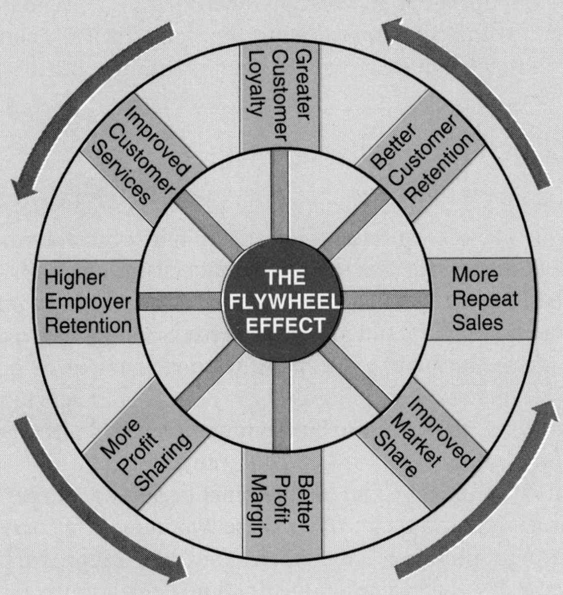

Adapted from Rahul Jacob, "Customers: Why Some Are More Equal Than Others," Fortune, September 19, 1994, 215–24. Also see Jill Griffin, Customer Loyalty (New York: Lexington Books, 1995), 1–18; and Patricia Sellers, "Can Home Depot Fix Its Sagging Stock?" Fortune, March 4, 1996, 139–46.

success.[21] Happy customers who have been provided superior customer satisfaction are more profitable because they involve

- less wasted motion—retailers know what customers want and they focus their resources on providing it;
- a greater price advantage—happy customers are less price-sensitive and are typically willing to pay a little extra for the additional satisfaction they obtain from a retailer;
- lower transactional costs—repeat sales are easier and faster than first-time sales, hence greater transactional efficiency;
- higher transaction sizes—loyal customers tend to buy higher-margin goods because they are less deal oriented; and
- lower communication costs—satisfied customers are valuable word-of-mouth promoters.[22]

Satisfying the customer at a profit is not a simple task. It is no longer a fad and is even beyond trend status. Customer satisfaction has become a way of life in the corporate world today, much the same way "information technology" and "strategic planning" have before it. "In a price-crazed environment, sellers are learning that the economies of customer retention are more compelling than ever. In an unusually faddish era, building customer loyalty is one business precept that will not go out of fashion."[23] By definition, then, the solution to the marketing concept—and to the problem of retailing—involves developing the right merchandising blend and setting the right performance standards.

The Right Merchandising Blend

The right **merchandising blend** is a mixture of merchandising ingredients capable of satisfying those consumers who comprise the retailer's target market. The number of successful blends and their correct ingredients is as numerous as the number of potentially viable target markets. A right blend would include some combination of all of the following seven ingredients: Offering the right product, in the right quantities, in the right place, at the right time, at the right price, by the right appeal, with the right service. The right blend is thus the one that satisfies both customer and retailer before, during, and after the sales transaction has been completed.

The Right Product

What makes an item the **right product** is a unique composite of four product elements known as the total product concept. The **total product concept** recognizes that a product is more than just the tangible object offered for sale. Retailers that sell "things" will soon discover that there is no one to sell them to. To be successful, the retailer must act on the premise that a product is more than just its functional and aesthetic features; the concept also incorporates the various service features and psychological benefits conveyed by the product. In essence, the total product concept acknowledges the need for retailers to market every one of a product's dimensions. The relationship among a product's many facets is illustrated in Figure 1–9.

A product's **functional features** include the tangible elements of size, shape, and weight, together with its chemical and/or biological makeup. Functional features are extremely important because they determine to a large extent how well the product will actually perform the functions it was designed to accomplish. Mentadent, a tooth cleaner dispensed from a bulky double-chamber pump, mixes baking soda with peroxide to pro-

Figure 1–9

The total-product concept

Levi Strauss
www.levi.com

duce fizz and supposedly cleaner teeth. Although Mentadent does not even look like toothpaste and costs almost twice as much as other premium brands, it is now the third-largest selling toothpaste.[24] If a product cannot clean and polish, or brighten and freshen, or cool and heat—in short, if it cannot perform the basic function it was designed to do—then all other aspects of the product are severely diminished. Procter & Gamble's over-the-counter pain medicine Aleve, which provides 8- to 12-hour dosage, lets users go through a workday or a night's sleep without needing to take a second dose—a functional feature popular with arthritis sufferers.[25] "Wrinkle-free cotton slacks now account for more than 60% of the $2 billion men's cotton pants category. The Big 3 players—Farah USA's Savane line, Haggar Apparel Co. and Levi Strauss & Co.'s Dockers—all plan to expand the wrinkle-free concept into shirts and shorts."[26]

The **aesthetic features** of a product are elements that appeal to the five senses. Consumers have strong preconceived ideas about an item's aesthetic features. If a product does not look, smell, feel, sound, and/or taste "right," its merchandising qualities have been substantially reduced or eliminated. The restyled 1996 Ford Taurus, with its sculptured, curvey look, is a bold design departure that Ford dealers hope will continue Taurus's record of being North America's most popular automobile. From the front end, with its softer, rounded line with oval headlights and a sculptured hood to the stylish rounded rear window, oval taillights, and tapered rear fenders, the aesthetic features of the Taurus create a different look that consumers may or may not find appealing.[27]

Service features are "extras" that include delivery, alterations, installation, repairs, warranties, returns, adjustments, wrapping, telephone and mail ordering, or any other service that consumers want for purchase satisfaction. A retailer must determine which service features are *required* for the purchase decision and which are simply *desired* by the customer as an added product dimension. These requirements and desires then are incorporated into the retailer's product-service mix. The surge in dual-income families, for instance, and the corresponding rise in careerism should suggest to the retailer that time-saving conveniences are fast becoming a required, not desired, part of the total product offering. As the average family faces more stress and less time, the retailer wants to avoid contributing to that stress and to assist the customer in freeing up time by offering shopping services.

When consumers buy products, they seek something more than the physical product: They expect to benefit in some way from the purchase. The expected **psychological benefits** that consumers derive from buying, using, and possessing the product are essential to the consumer's need satisfaction. Consumers buy products to be beautiful, safe, thin, comfortable, and noticed; to gain prestige, recognition, security, independence, and love; or to obtain a host of other benefits. "Adults buy colour printers thinking they'll use them for work, but the colour applications often end up primarily as a plaything for the kids. Parents are convinced that children who hand in colourized school reports get better grades."[28] Retailers that recognize that a product's psychological endowments are as important as, if not more important than, the product itself will have considerably more to sell to their customer than just a physical product.

The Right Quantity

The **right quantity** is the exact match between the consumer's buying and using needs and the retailer's buying and selling needs. Customer factors the retailer must consider in determining the right quantity are the number of units and the size of units. For some consumers, a single unit is the right quantity; for others, multiple-unit packages are the right quantity. When Quaker Oats acquired Snapple, one of its first actions was to improve the beverage's packaging. Snapple can now be purchased in 12-packs, 4-packs, and plastic 32- and 64-ounce bottles.[29] On the one hand, smaller unit packages have gained in popularity

The World of Retailing

International Retailing

Neither the Right Quantity nor the Right Place

Wal-Mart's Value Club shoppers in Hong Kong seem to be voting for better locations, smaller product sizes, and products more familiar to Chinese households by spending fewer dollars and visiting the stores less often than Value Club managers probably would like.

Wal-Mart's joint venture with C.P. Pokphand may be in trouble. Perhaps the warehouse club format cannot be transferred directly to the Hong Kong environment without modifying it.

It may be that warehouse clubs have little to offer Hong Kong customers, who seem to place a premium on convenience, high-quality service, and store atmosphere. These customer values combined with the distinctive features of Hong Kong's crowded urban environment—high cost of prime retail space, small living quarters with insufficient storage, limited number of parking spaces, relatively few autos, and traffic congestion—imply that the fundamental nature of warehouse clubs is incompatible with Hong Kong.

Because Value Club outlets are located away from the public transportation backbone, shoppers would have to spend more on taxis or buses. They *may* realize that the lower price at the store would be offset by the higher transportation costs.

Compounding the location problem is the traditional practice of Chinese housewives shopping every day to bring home the freshest food for their families. The most convenient places for them to shop are the stores on the way home from work or those in their apartment complexes. It is worth a few extra dollars at the checkout counter to avoid carrying bulky products from the warehouse store on a bus.

Many products available at Value Club are just not those that Hong Kong households commonly use. If the products came in smaller packages, shoppers might be willing to try them. But they would not want to risk wasting money and losing face by throwing out a large amount of a new product they did not like.

Products also are a problem for at least two more reasons. First, families of five often live in 400 sq. ft. [approx. 40 m^2] apartments with extremely limited storage space and small refrigerators. There may be nowhere to store a gallon of cooking oil except on the floor, and a gallon of orange juice may not even fit in the refrigerator. Second . . . [petite] Asian women are not able to accurately pour a small amount from a large bottle of cooking oil or soy sauce into meals they are cooking.

Source: Neil Herndon, "Hong Kong Shoppers Cool to Wal-Mart's Value Club," Marketing News, *November 20, 1995, 11.*

as the average household has decreased in size; on the other hand, the sale of bulk packages has increased as consumers look for savings during tougher economic times.

Products come in many sizes: small, medium, large, and extra-large; short, regular, and long; king, queen, and regular; individual and family. "The operative word in televisions these days is BIG. Consumers are attracted to big screen television sets—26 in. or larger, and they are willing to part with big bucks to get what they want."[30] The right size women's dress shoe is one that does not cause bunions, calluses, corns, ingrown toenails, or pinched nerves. In a comfortable women's dress shoe, the heel should be no higher than 6 cm and the length should be 1–2 cm longer than the longest toe.[31]

Retailers know that the "size" labels they carry affect the kind of clientele they attract and the sales they make. Consider fashion retailing for full-figured women. "Women with ample figures could not find much to wear, but now they are one of the fastest-growing segments of the fashion business. Antels and Penningtons are specialty store chains emphasizing this target market, and department stores such as Eaton's, The Bay, and Sears have separate departments with clothing for the full-figured woman.

The retailer's decision about quantity is in many ways more critical than the consumer's. A retailer that does not purchase enough merchandise risks stockouts and therefore lost sales. Purchasing too much merchandise causes overstocking and subsequently higher inventory carrying costs and very likely reduced profit margins if markdowns are necessary. Buying the proper quantity therefore leads to customer satisfaction and higher retail profits.

The Right Place

A retailer trying to determine the **right place** should consider the following place factors in making the decision: (1) market area, (2) market coverage, and (3) store layout and design.

Market Areas

A **market** is a geographic area where buyers and sellers meet to exchange money for products and services. The right marketplace for retailers is the area containing enough people to enable retailers to satisfy consumer needs at a profit. The retailer's marketplace can range from one block to several hundred miles. To find the "right" market area, the retailer must consider (1) regional markets, (2) local markets, (3) trading areas, and (4) site.

Regional Markets. For the retailer, the **regional market** may be the entire nation or a certain part of the country. Chain retailers, however, must evaluate different parts of the country to determine where to locate new stores. Many chain retailers face the decision of whether to expand into or increase their representation within various parts of Canada.

Local Markets. At the level of **local markets**, retailers must determine the right town and the right part of town. Some retailers may be less concerned with total population and more with the size and demographic composition of a segment of the population. In some cases, a smaller town might be a preferred local or second-tier market if it represents a better competitive environment. For example, The Brick, an Edmonton-based operator of consumer electronics and furniture superstores, has expanded into smaller cities such as Lethbridge, Alberta. Sears is expanding its network of smaller Dealer Stores (hardware, appliances, home electronics) in small communities.[32]

Trading Area. When the right local market has been chosen, the retailer must determine the right **trading area**, that is, shopping area or shopping centre. Some retailers go it alone, relying on their own abilities to draw customers—a convenience food store located near a residential neighbourhood, for example. Other retailers rely on the drawing power of a cluster of stores. They believe that by grouping together in shopping centres or associating with anchor stores (such as department stores, discount houses, and supermarkets), they can create the "right" place. For the Voyageur Restaurant, a family restaurant chain across Canada, the right trading area is incorporated into its "Trans Canada Highway" strategy. The plan calls for restaurants to be located on a major highway and within the immediate vicinity of a major shopping centre.

The World of Retailing

Retail Technology

Information Superhighway: All Roads Lead to "Marketspace"

The **information superhighway** is an emerging, intelligent, robust global infrastructure that allows the interactive exchange of information in any form, independent of the user's origin or destination. In other words, it is a set of communication paths, or channels, with the potential to greatly extend traditional modes of communicating and to provide interaction with wider audiences than ever before. The origins of these channels can be seen today in the form of standard telephone lines, the cable television network, the international network of networks called the Internet, and its daughter application, the World Wide Web.

Retailers can use the information superhighway, both inside and outside organizations and supply chains, as a technology tool in the following ways:

- To improve speed, efficiency, and ease of communication; streamline processes by shortening the communications loop; and increase productivity. This includes internal and external communications (such as orders, invoices, regulatory information) with suppliers, customers, government regulators and others
- To interact with new customers and create "virtual communities" outside the firm (for example, through advertising to a highly specialized consumer group)
- To serve as a distribution network, providing for interactive remote shopping and purchase of products and services by consumers

Retailers must think about a different sort of marketplace—a **"marketspace"**—that is served by the information superhighway. The traditional components of value can be organized into three categories: content, context, and infrastructure. Content is the substance of the transaction, or what product is offered for sale. Context is the environment within which the transaction occurs, or how the content is delivered. Infrastructure is the collection of services and facilities that enables the transaction to occur successfully.

In the conventional marketplace, the three components are almost always inextricably intertwined. In the electronic marketspace, these components are disaggregated, creating new opportunities to add value.

Bernard F. Mathaisel and Jeff Kvaal, "Information Superhighway: Road to the Future," in Retail *i.t. Technology: It's in the Bag. Ernst & Young's 14th Annual Survey of Retail Information Technology (New York: Retail Industry Services, Ernst & Young LLP, 1995), 42–43.*

Gap
www.gap.com

Site Location. For the freestanding retailer, the right **site** enables the store to intercept customers on their way to work or on their way home; is readily accessible to consumers from the standpoints of approaching, entering, and exiting; and is visible to passing consumer traffic. Such nationally known apparel chains as Talbots, Gap, and Eddie Bauer are setting up shop on the main streets of suburban Canada. Lower cost structures, greater customer convenience, and higher awareness levels are some of the more common reasons cited for the return to Main Street.[33] The Tobu Department Store, one of Japan's largest stores (twenty floors and 83 600 m^2 of space), "is built over the west exit of the Ikebukuro station, one of Tokyo's busiest commuter stations. It is the transit point for seven train and subway lines, and serves an average of 2.83 million people per day."[34] The Ikebukuro site has to be one of the world's best interceptor locations. Within a shopping mall, the right site may be on the ground floor or at one end of the mall, or it may be a location within the mall that attracts customers who are compatible with the retailer's operations. For example, high-end specialty retailers such as Braemar and Cleo might be near an upscale department store (for example, Holt Renfrew).

Market Coverage

A saturated marketplace makes the market coverage decision a vital part of the retailer's survival and growth strategy."[35] The right place may be every place, a few places, or a single place. As part of the "right place" decision, retailers must decide whether they want intensive, selective, or exclusive market coverage (Figure 1–10).

Intensive Market Coverage. With **intensive market coverage** the retailer selects and utilizes as many retail outlets as are justified to obtain "blanket" coverage of an entire

Figure 1–10

Planning the right market area coverage

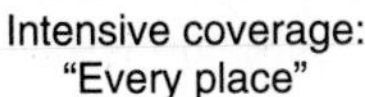

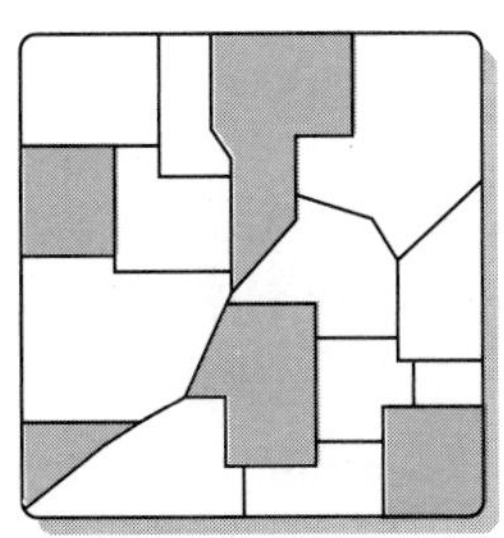

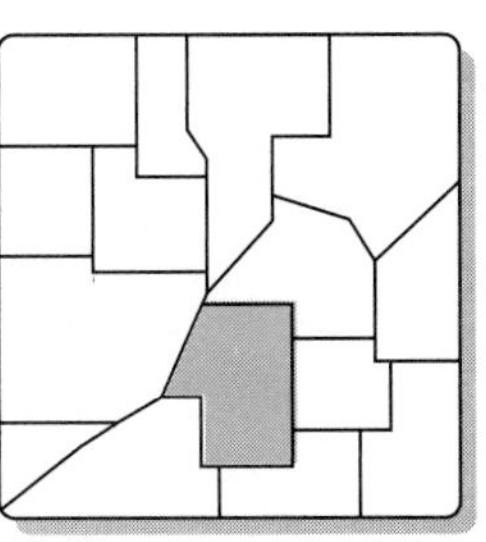

Intensive coverage: "Every place"

Selective coverage: "A few places"

Exclusive coverage: "A place"

market area. Generally, convenience goods retailers use an intensive market strategy. (*Convenience goods* are products and services consumers want to purchase with a minimum of effort; examples are snack foods and soft drinks.) Because the retailer that employs an intensive coverage strategy must try to serve *all* customers within a given market area, the right place is *every place.*

Selective Market Coverage. When a retailer sells shopping goods, the logical strategy is **selective market coverage.**[36] (*Shopping goods* are products that consumers want to compare for style, price, or quality before making a purchase decision—such as clothing, furniture, appliances.) The number of outlets the retailer establishes in the selective coverage strategy should equal the number of market segments served. Generally speaking, many chain retailers such as apparel and department stores follow a selective market coverage strategy by locating an outlet in each of the major shopping malls within a given city or metro area. In this case, the right place is the *select* place.

Exclusive Market Coverage. In an **exclusive market coverage** strategy, the retailer elects to use one location to serve either an entire market area or some major segment of that market. An exclusive strategy is ideal for retailers that sell specialty goods. (*Specialty goods* are those that consumers are willing to put forth considerable effort to obtain.) Specialty goods manufacturers often enter into exclusive arrangements with certain retailers. The advantages to manufacturers are more intense selling efforts on the part of their retailers and an exclusive, high-quality image for their products.

By the same token the exclusive retailer enjoys some advantages: (1) the retailer's store image is enhanced because of the exclusive merchandise, and (2) no *direct* competition exists for the brands of merchandise carried. For these retailers the right place is *a* place. Many specialty stores dealing in well-known, prestigious products such as Mercedes-Benz, Jaguar, and Steuben Glass use this form of market coverage. Giorgio Armani, the fashion designer who pioneered the natural look in clothes, follows his exclusive distribution policy of *dare e togliere* (to give and take away). To maintain Armani as an elite brand, the company ruthlessly controls distribution of all licensed products by limiting both the number of outlets and the type and amount of merchandise each outlet receives.[37]

Store Layout and Design Store layout and design are two essential elements to consider in creating the right shopping atmosphere for the chosen target market. The retailer should consider (1) floor location, (2) shelf position, (3) in-store location, and (4) display location.

Floor Location. In some department stores the right place in a store for a product, department, display, event, or activity may be either the basement, the first floor, or the top floor. The right floor is the one that is most consistent with where customers think things should be and where the retailer can provide the level of service consumers expect.

Shelf Position. Retail merchandisers and marketers generally agree that **eye-level merchandising** reaps the greatest rewards. "Retailers believe consumers are more apt to buy clothes that appear in full size and colour assortments. So they put their most complete lines at eye level where shoppers see them first. Lower racks show 'broken' assortments that are missing some colours and sizes."[38] The type, amount, and location of shelf space within a store make up one of the retailer's most valuable resources. How the retail manager merchandises the store's shelf space will have a significant impact on sales and profits; it will also influence customer satisfaction with the store shopping experience.

In-Store Location. The right place within a store for a product, a customer service, or a display is the one that best conforms to customer in-store traffic patterns. The right place therefore might be either in front, in back, along the sides, or in the centre. The in-store layout of most supermarkets, for example, is based on the **ring of perishables principle.**[39] Food retailers know that consumers purchase their perishables (eggs, milk, butter, meat, vegetables, and so on) every week. By placing perishables in a ring around the store (sides and back), supermarket retailers can draw customers into other sections of the store. According to the Food Marketing Institute, a supermarket's perimeter is where the bulk of its profit originates.[40] Supermarkets using this technique greatly increase the chance that customers will pass by and purchase other products and make impulse purchases.

Another strategy some retailers use is the **attractors and interceptors strategy**. Many department stores place merchandise such as men's suits, better women's wear, and other big-ticket items in the back of the store to act as attractors, drawing customers through the entire length of the store. In the process, customers are intercepted by departments carrying complementary product lines, such as shirts, scarves, and jewellery. It is the strategy of "getting them coming and going." By sprinkling specialty departments and services throughout the store, retailers can guide the shopper around the store while creating more opportunities for cross-merchandising.

Display Location. Retailers use displays to draw attention to their product offerings. Whether at the end of an aisle, at the checkout stand, or in a freestanding location near high-traffic areas, the right place is the "visible" place for these special displays. Some retailers are increasingly recognizing that their selling space is valuable real estate and a valuable asset in their negotiations with vendors. For example, most major supermarket chains now are demanding that manufacturers pay "slotting allowances" (fees for displaying new product lines) and other charges. Stores are "looking to make money not just by selling products to consumers, but by renting shelf space to manufacturers."[41]

Within the display itself, "right is also right": the best position within a display is the right side. This bias is based on the belief that most consumers view a display from right to left; so right is "right" because it is the first place consumers look.

The Right Time

The **right time** to sell is when consumers are willing to buy. Because time affects different types of consumers differently, retailers must develop retailing strategies that coincide with consumer buying times. With two-income families approaching 50 percent, time is a commodity that has become scarce, which leads to "time-buying" behaviour. While people can try to earn more money, they cannot get more time; so they must use time differently. By trading dollars for time-saving goods and services and by shopping in time-efficient stores, consumers are doing just that. The typical discount store shopper today spends only forty minutes per shopping trip, down from two hours ten years ago. The number and length of mall shopping trips have also been sharply curtailed.

To survive in today's time-compressed world, retailers need to get their customers in and out quickly and efficiently. People are willing to buy time to make life simpler. Some particular times that retailers consider in developing time strategies are (1) calendar times, (2) seasonal times, (3) life times, and (4) personal times.

Calendar Times

In the category of calendar times, retailers consider times of the day, week, month, and year. Because consumers' behaviour is largely geared to these times, any one may be an opportune time for the retailer. Whether morning, noon, afternoon, or evening, many retailers have businesses with daily peak periods. Restaurants, for example,

holds more potential for creating a competitive advantage than does product quality."[54] **Customer service** incorporates all the features, acts, and information that augment the customer's ability to realize the potential value of a core product or service.[55] This definition suggests several relationships that must be clarified. As shown in Figure 1–13, total customer service is a function of two components: customer service features and actions.

First, customer service involves augmenting service extras the retailer should provide. **Customer service features** can be defined as the number and type of service extras offered to the customer and the terms and conditions under which services are provided. The sum total of all service features is the retailer's **customer service mix**. Customer service features such as delivery and installation, alteration and repair, wrapping and packaging, returns and adjustments, transactional and informational assistance, credit and layaway, parking and toting, complaint resolution, and store hours are all complementary services that could enhance the customer's perceived value of the original purchase of either a core product (for example, apparel) or core service (for example, hairstyling). The Bay and other Canadian department stores have increased their efforts in the area of customer service in response to the introduction of Wal-Mart into the Canadian market.[56]

Second, customer service equally involves how all these extra service features are to be performed. **Customer service actions** deal with how customer services are performed and how customers are treated, assisted, and served. Stanhome Inc. (formerly Stanley Home Products), the direct seller of collectable figurines and decorative plates, arrange cruises and parties at which collectors can swap figurines while being entertained by celebrity performers. They also sponsor seminars, membership clubs, and newsletters for collectors.[57]

As illustrated in Figure 1–13, **customer service quality** is defined by the nature and level of the retailer's customer service actions. Friendliness, politeness, willingness, trustworthiness, responsiveness, dependability, reliability, security, and approachability of the service provider are all attributes that define customer service actions and the quality of those actions. "Service can go way beyond exceeding expectations. Service can be superb, graceful, beautiful, divine, and wonderful."[58] With the expansion of the downscale market due to weak economic conditions, more retailers are looking downscale (lower-wage market) without looking down (lower-level service). The downscale shopper aspires to a better way of life and is entitled to seek small indulgences when it comes to quality products and services.[59]

Finally, it is not sufficient to offer all the required service features supported by superior service actions. The retailer must effectively communicate to the customer the extent of the services package by providing information that enables the customer to fully

Figure 1–13

The right service

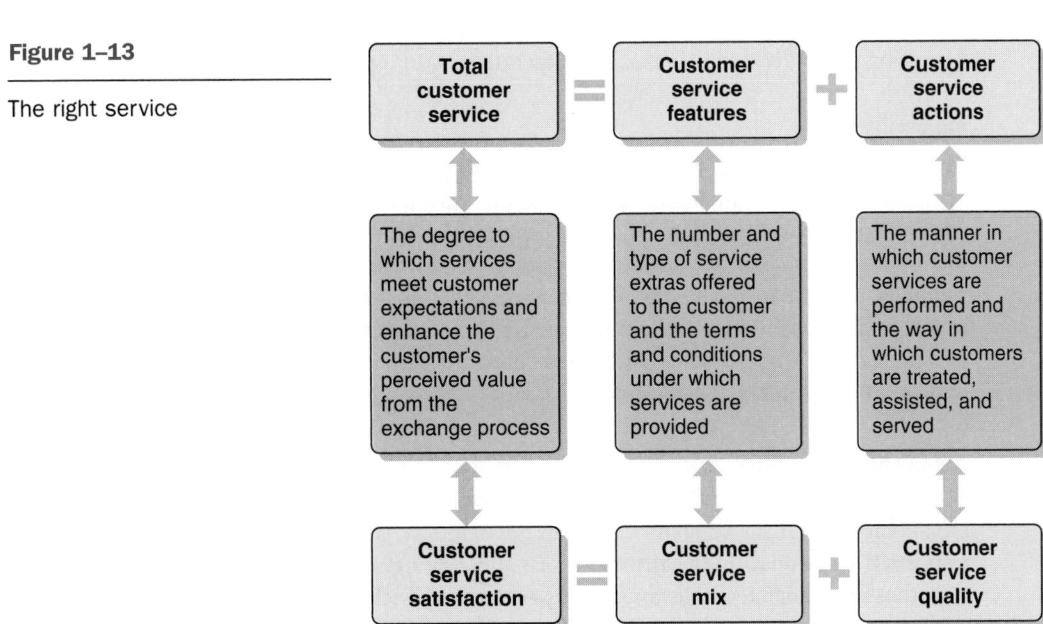

perceive the uniqueness and quality of the retailer's service offering. The **right service** is the one that provides the customer with the right package of service features supported by the right level of service actions.

Having discussed those elements of the right merchandising blend, let us now examine the other half of the equation for a successful retail organization—the right performance standards.

The Right Performance Standards

Retailers must have some means by which to judge both the operational and financial performance of their firms; they need the **right performance standards**. Several operating and financial ratios can aid their judgment. These ratios concisely express the relationship between elements in the income statement and the balance sheet. Because these ratios have gained wide acceptance, they have become trade standards by which retailers can judge their individual performances against national and trade norms. These standard ratios are published annually by private firms such as Dun & Bradstreet and trade organizations such as the Retail Council of Canada.

Within individual retail organizations, historic comparisons can be made between current and past ratios. The availability of these external and internal standards helps each retailer assess the firm's operating efficiency and financial ability. Ratio analysis provides a "snapshot" of the relative health of the retailer's operating and financial condition and serves as a control to identify conditions deviating from established norms. The right performance standards are not limited to judgments regarding the retailer's efficiency and profitability. Responsible retailers hold themselves accountable for all the firm's actions and their impact on other individuals and society.

Operating Ratios

Retailers compute some ratios to gain insight into the firm's operating performance. Retailers use **operating ratios** to compute relationships between elements in the income statement. Ratio computations simply divide one element of the income statement (for example, operating profit) by another element (for example, net sales; see Figure 1–14). A standard practice is to convert ratios into percentages by multiplying the results by 100. Of particular concern to most retailers are operating ratios involving net sales (that is, operating profit divided by net sales). Operating ratios are discussed further in Chapter 14.

Financial Ratios

Financial ratios identify relationships among elements of a balance sheet or between a balance sheet element and an element in the income statement (see Figure 1–14). The most widely used financial ratios are those reported by Dun & Bradstreet. These key performance measurements help the retailer make meaningful comparisons between the firm's financial performance and the national median performance of similar retailers. These ratios are also useful in establishing realistic financial objectives. The ratios of retailing are used as basic reference points and not as absolute guidelines for judging financial performance levels for a given retail firm.

Social Responsibility

Social responsibility is the retailer's acceptance of the obligation to consider operating efficiencies, financial returns, customer satisfaction, and societal well-being as equally important in evaluating the firm's performance. Being socially responsible is the recognition that retail management must be as concerned with the more qualitative dimensions of consumer and societal benefits as well as the quantitative measures of sales, expenses,

Figure 1–14

Computing performance standards

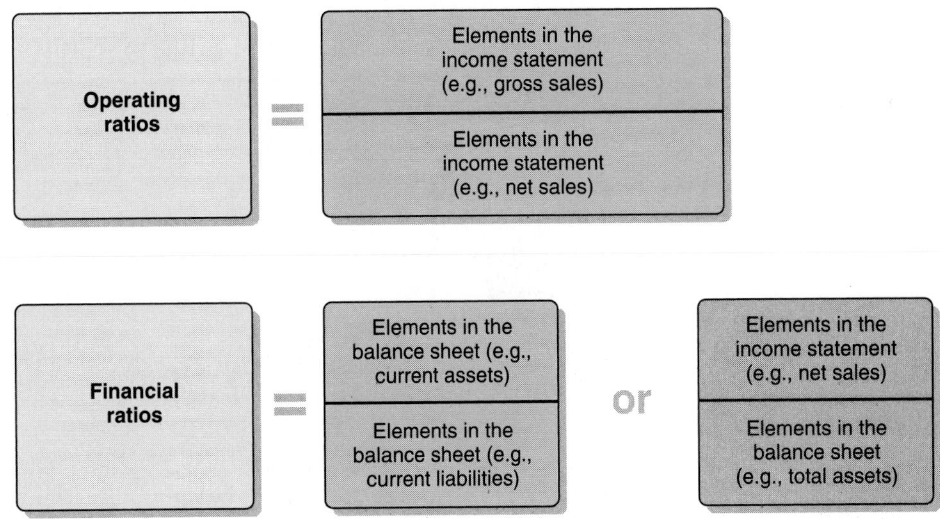

Safeway
www.safeway.com

profits, and returns by which operational and financial performance is traditionally measured. Social responsibility issues range from a host of environmental concerns (for example, pollution, recycling) to concerns for the welfare of the general public (for example, unemployment, the homeless). Sears sponsored a Phil Collins tour in which part of the proceedings were donated to the homeless. It also donated a percentage of its credit card sales to the cause of the homeless.[60] Canada Safeway supports health, social services, education, youth, and amateur sport as part of a community support program.[61] Typically, social responsibility issues also include fair and equitable treatment of customers, employees, competitors, suppliers, shareholders, and any other relationships involving the retailer and its management.

The Right Retailing Plan

The right retailing plan addresses the operational questions of why, what, when, where, and how specific retail business activities are to be accomplished. It also describes the organizational structure of this text. The retailing process can be viewed as a sequential series of activities and decisions organized into eight parts. Figure 1–15 illustrates the eight-part structure of this text and the content (chapters) covered in each part.

Part I, "Retail Overview," provides a general description of the retail industry and its various components. The problems and decisions that create the complex nature of the retail industry are discussed in this chapter (Chapter 1). A general survey of the strategies and tactics of various types of competing retail formats is examined in Chapter 2.

Part II, "Environmental Analysis," examines the uncontrollable environments surrounding each retail operation. Chapter 3 discusses the impact on retailers of the dynamic changes in the demographic makeup of the population, the social fibre of society, the economic structure of consumer markets, and the development and application of new operating technologies. A review of consumer buying behaviour (what, how much, which, why, how, and where consumers buy) is presented in Chapter 4. Chapter 5 looks at the legal and ethical aspects of retail decisions and actions.

Part III, "Resource Assessment," is an essential element of any retail plan. Human resource management (Chapter 6) and store facilities management (Chapter 7) are its focus. Part IV, "Market Analysis," examines the geographic dimension of retailing. Identifying, evaluating, and selecting regional/local markets and trading areas and retail

Figure 1–15

Developing the right retailing plan

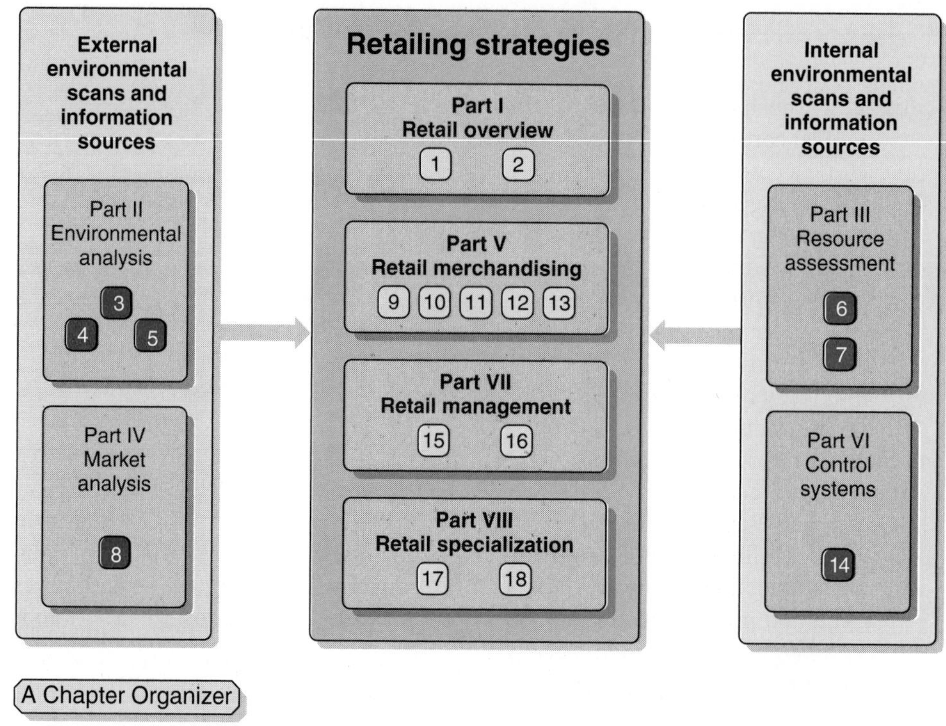

site locations (Chapter 8) are the issues treated in this fourth stage of the retail planning process.

Part V, "Retail Merchandising," deals with managing the merchandise process. The making of merchandise decisions, the planning of merchandise strategies, the evaluating of merchandise offerings, and the creating of merchandise plans are covered in Chapter 9. The buying, ordering, and handling of merchandise are discussed in Chapter 10. Chapter 11 considers the setting and adjusting of retail prices. The retailer's customer service programs and its personal selling efforts constitute the discussion offered in Chapter 12. Finally, the retailer's customer communications program is outlined in Chapter 13.

Part VI, "Control Systems," deals with all the issues facing management as it attempts to gain the necessary information to control and manage the retail organization. Chapter 14 explores the issues of financial, inventory, and expense management.

Part VII, "Retail Management," examines the strategic retail management process (Chapter 15) and explores the theories, practices, and trends in adaptive retail behaviour (Chapter 16).

Part VIII, "Retail Specialization," investigates two specialized forms of retail operations. Chapter 17 inspects the unique operating aspects of service retailing, and Chapter 18 surveys the global dimensions of international retailing. Figure 1–15 will help you organize the vast subject matter called retailing. Also note that in the lower left-hand corner of Figures 1–1 and 1–15 is the inscription "A Chapter Organizer." Throughout the text, you will find more of these chapter-organizing diagrams to assist you in identifying the major topics to be covered in the chapter or some section of it. Each organizer is also a guide to how the chapter is set up and an overview of the relationships among various chapter topics.

Summary

Retailing is the business activity of selling goods and services to the final consumer. A retailer can be either a goods retailer (selling a core good supported by services) or a services retailer (selling a core service supported by goods). As an institutional marketing and distribution link between producers and consumers, retailers play an essential role in overcoming the assortment, quantity, space, and time gaps that separate consumers from producers. Retailers are members of the marketing channel of distribution; hence, they are involved with directing the flow of goods and services between producers and consumers. The marketing channel can be described as a multilevel structure (extended, limited, and direct channel) made up of channel teams (full, limited, and facilitating team members) whose interactions (buying, selling, transferring titles and payments) coordinate channel flows (physical, ownership, information, payment, and promotion) through channel teamwork (channel integration). The retailer is also viewed as a mental image by which consumers judge retailers.

The basic task of retailing is to balance the product service needs of the consuming public with the financial and operational needs of the retailer. The marketing concept describes this as satisfying customer needs at a profit. This balancing act can also be stated as finding the right merchandising blend to ensure the right performance standards.

Elements of the right merchandising blend include offering the right product (functional, aesthetic, and service features, together with the product's psychological benefits), in the right quantities (number and size of units), in the right place (market areas, market coverage, aid store design), at the right time (calendar, seasonal, life, and personal times), at the right price (profitable, competitive, customer-satisfying prices), by the right appeal (message, audience, and media), with the right service (features and actions). Performance standards can be expressed in terms of operating ratios, financial ratios, and social responsibility.

Student Study Guide

Key Terms and Concepts

accumulating process *p. 6*
aesthetic features *p. 15*
allocation process *p. 6*
assorting process *p. 6*
assortment gap *p. 5*
attractors and interceptors strategy *p. 20*
channel integration *p. 9*
conventional marketing channel *p. 10*
customer service *p. 25*
customer service actions *p. 25*
customer service features *p. 25*
customer service mix *p. 25*
customer service quality *p. 25*
direct-action message *p. 24*
direct channel *p. 7*
emotional approach p. 24
exclusive market coverage *p. 19*
extended channel *p. 7*
eye-level merchandising *p. 19*
financial ratios *p. 26*
flywheel effect *p. 13*
full-member institution *p. 8*
functional features *p. 14*
goods retailers p. 4
image *p. 10*
indirect-action message *p. 24*
individual customer market/audience *p. 24*
information flow *p. 8*
information superhighway *p. 18*
intensive market coverage *p. 18*
limited channel *p. 7*
limited-member institution *p. 8*
local market *p. 17*
logical approach *p. 24*
market *p. 17*
market/audience niche *p. 24*
market segmentation *p. 24*
marketing channel *p. 7*
marketing concept *p. 11*
marketspace *p. 18*
mass market or audience *p. 24*
merchandising blend *p. 14*
nonmember facilitating institutions *p. 8*
operating ratios *p. 26*
ownership flow *p. 8*
patronage appeal *p. 24*
payment flow *p. 9*
physical flow *p. 8*
place utility *p. 6*
price appeal *p. 24*
product appeal *p. 24*
promotion flow *p. 9*
psychological benefits *p. 16*
quantity gap *p. 6*
regional market *p. 17*
relationship retailing *p. 13*
retail image *p. 10*
retailer *p. 4*
retailing *p. 4*
retention retailing *p. 13*
right appeal *p. 23*
right audience *p. 24*
right media *p. 24*
right message *p. 23*
right performance standards *p. 26*
right place *p. 17*
right price *p. 22*
right product *p. 14*
right quantity *p. 16*
right service *p. 26*
right time *p. 20*
ring of perishables principle *p. 20*
selective market coverage *p. 19*
service features *p. 15*
services retailers *p. 4*
site *p. 18*
social responsibility *p. 26*
space gap *p. 6*
target market or audience *p. 24*
time gap *p. 6*
time utility *p. 6*
total product concept *p. 14*
trading area *p. 17*
vertical marketing system *p. 9*

Review Questions

1. What is retailing? How do retailers differ from other members of the marketing channel of distribution (wholesalers and producers)?
2. Distinguish a goods retailer from a services retailer.
3. Describe the retailer's role as a link between producers and consumers. What gaps does the retailer overcome?
4. Characterize the three basic alternative channel structures that retailers use to reach the consumer.
5. Characterize the five types of channel flows that must be effectively managed to ensure successful retailing operations.
6. Why is channel teamwork important? How is it achieved?
7. Identify the three reasons why the retailer should be extremely careful to cultivate the right retail image.
8. Define the marketing concept. How does it relate to the problem of retailing.
9. Describe the total-product concept and the features and benefits that constitute it.
10. What quantity is the right quantity? Provide an original example for each of the factors considered by the retailer in determining the right quantity.
11. Outline the geographic dimensions of regional and local markets, trading areas, and site locations.
12. Compare and contrast intensive, selective, and exclusive market coverage.
13. Identify the four types of time categories. Provide two examples of merchandising strategies for each category that retailers use to meet the needs associated with different consumer buying times.
14. When is a retail price right for both the consumer and the retailer?
15. The right appeal equals the right message plus the right audience plus the right media. Briefly characterize each element of this equation.
16. Describe the two components that compose the total customer service concept.
17. What are the right performance standards?

Review Exam

True or False

_____ 1. If a buyer purchases a product from a retailer for purposes of reselling the product at a profit or using it in a business, the sale is still considered a retail sale.

_____ 2. Retailers differ from wholesalers in that retailers tend to use variable prices, whereas wholesalers tend to use a one-pricing policy based on some form of discounting structure.

_____ 3. The marketing concept stresses matching supply to demand rather than matching demand to supply.

_____ 4. Exclusive market coverage is most appropriate when merchandising specialty goods.

_____ 5. Customer satisfaction is the most important factor in determining the right price.

_____ 6. Social responsibility is something that a retailer should be concerned with; however, retail management should not be held accountable for social causes because the only realistic responsibility of managers is to ensure customer satisfaction at a profit.

Multiple Choice

_____ 1. The marketing channel alternative in which the producer elects to market directly to the retailer and thereby eliminate the independent wholesaler from the channel team is the _____ channel.

a. limited
b. extended
c. selected
d. direct
e. extensive

_____ 2. The advantage of the _____ marketing system is that it allows the channel team to achieve technological, managerial, and promotional leverages through integrating and synchronizing the five channel flows.

a. conventional
b. historic
c. traditional
d. vertical
e. none of the above

_____ **3.** Which of the following is not one of the ingredients of the "right blend"?
a. the right product
b. the right appeal
c. the right time
d. the right profit
e. the right price

_____ **4.** The best part of any selling season is the _____ season when retailers can sell goods at full markup.
a. postperiod
b. beginning
c. middle
d. end
e. aftermath

_____ **5.** If the retailer elects to emphasize the rightness of its store facilities, its location, and its operating hours, then the retailer is attempting to make a(n) _____.
a. patronage appeal
b. product appeal
c. price appeal
d. combined appeal
e. emotional appeal

_____ **6.** Operating and financial ratios are beneficial to retailers because they can _____.
a. be used for historic comparisons
b. be used to determine operating efficiency and financial ability
c. provide a "snapshot" of the retailer's operating and financial health
d. serve as a control to identify deviations from established norms
e. do all of the above

Student Application Manual

Investigative Projects: Practice and Application

1. Briefly describe what would constitute for you the right quantity, place, time, price, appeal, and service dimensions for each of the following products: (1) undergarments, (2) your favourite magazine, (3) watch, (4) a fun evening, and (5) God.

2. Several retail institutions have arisen over the years, have become very successful for a time, and then started to fade. County Supermarkets is one such example. Established in 1970, County Supermarket experienced a steady growth in sales for fifteen years. The last few years, however, have seen sales level off. Profits dropped in 1990 for the first time ever. Management is worried. You have been called in to analyze the situation. Using the information discussed in this chapter, what advice might you give?

3. Harry Rosen, the 75-year-old clothier of upscale men's clothing, built its business by focusing on 55-year-old men who wear three-button Harry Rosen suits and only visited the store twice a year. This specialty focus and a strong image for quality goods and services had proven to be a successful strategy for decades. However, during the early 1990s, a significant image problem surfaced in that younger generations tended to regard the Harry Rosen look as something for dad's generation. To grow and become more profitable, Harry Rosen needs to revise its existing strategy or develop a new strategic thrust. What would you recommend?

Endnotes

1. *The Daily*, Statistics Canada, February 20, 1997, 11.
2. Chad Rubel, "Fewer companies seen holding more retailing power in 2005," *Marketing News*, November 20, 1995, 5.
3. Elaine Pollack, "Raising the Bar: Keys to High-Performance Retailing," *Chain Store Age Executive*, January 1994, 2MH.
4. Pauline Yoshihashi, "Limited-Service Chains Offer Enough to Thrive," *The Wall Street Journal*, July 27, 1992, B1.
5. Amy Feldman, "When Lenny Met Sally," *Forbes*, February 13, 1995, 62.
6. Sean Silcoff, "The Emporiums Strike Back," *Canadian Business*, September 26, 1997, 54.
7. Bert C. McCammon, Jr., "Perspectives for Distribution Programming," in *Vertical Marketing Systems*, ed. Louis P. Bucklin (Glenview, IL: Scott, Foresman, 1970), 43.
8. *Ibid.*
9. Cyndee Miller, "Study Says Consumers Perceive Stores as Brands," *Marketing News*, August 8, 1991, 25.
10. "Sears: In With the New . . . Out With the Old," *Fortune*, October 16, 1995, 96.
11. Christopher Power and Mark Landler, "And Now, Finger-Lickin' Good for Ya?" *Business Week*, February 18, 1991, 60.
12. Kevin J. Clancy and Robert S. Shulman, "Marketing—Ten Fatal Flaws," *Retailing Issues Letter* (copublished by the Center for Retailing Studies, Texas A&M University and Arthur Andersen & Co.), November 1995, 3.
13. Ian McGugan, "Eaton's on the Brink," *Canadian Business*, March 1996, 46.
14. Pollack, "Raising the Bar: Keys to High-Performance Retailing," 5MH.
15. Franklin S. Houston, "The Marketing Concept: What It Is and What It Is Not," *Journal of Marketing*, 50 (April 1986): 86.
16. Michael Silverstein, "World-Class Customer Service Builds Consumer Loyalty," *Marketing News*, August 19, 1991, 11.
17. Thomas A. Stewart, "After All You've Done for Your Customers, Why Are They Still NOT HAPPY?" *Fortune*, December 11, 1995, 182.
18. Sandra J. Skrovan, "Reengineering for Revenue: Developing Closer Relationships," *Chain Store Age*, August 1995, 8A.
19. Michael Treacy and Fred Wiersema, "How Market Leaders Keep Their Edge," *Fortune*, February 6, 1995, 89. Also see Joshua Levine, "Relationship Marketing," *Forbes*, December 20, 1993, 232, 234.
20. Peter A. Doherty, "The Time Has Come for Customer Relationship Marketing," *Chain Store Age*, August 1995, 9A.
21. Jill Griffin, *Customer Loyalty, How to Earn It, How to Keep It* (New York: Lexington Books, 1995), 11. Also see Richard G. Barlow, "Relationship Marketing—The Ultimate in Customer Services," *Retail Control* (March 1992): 30.
22. Milind M. Lele and Jagdish N. Sheth, *The Customer Is Key* (New York: Wiley, 1991), 24–27.
23. Rahul Jacob, "Why Some Customers Are More Equal Than Others," *Fortune*, September 19, 1994, 215. Also see Howard Schlossberg, "Customer Satisfaction: Not a Fad, but a Way of Life," *Marketing News*, June 10, 1991, 18.
24. Zachary Schiller, "The Sound and the Fluoride," *Business Week*, August 14, 1995, 48.
25. Joseph Weber, "Painkillers Are About to O.D.," *Business Week*, April 14, 1994, 54.
26. Jennifer DeCoursey, "Haggar, Farah, Levi's Iron Out the Wrinkles," *Advertising Age*, March 6, 1995, 12. Also see Susan Reda, "Marketing Magic," *Stores*, January 1994, 44, 46; and Susan B. Garland and Richard S. Dunham, "Pumping No-Iron Slacks," *Business Week*, February 7, 1994, 30–31.
27. Kathleen Kerwin, "The Shape of a New Machine," *Business Week*, July 24, 1995, 60–66.
28. Damon Darlin, "Here's One for Your Xmas list," *Forbes*, September 15, 1995, 190.
29. Zina Moukheiber, "He Who Laughs Last," *Forbes*, January 1, 1996, 43.
30. "Bigger Is Better in TV Market," *Stores*, December 1995, 38.
31. John Pierson, "Man Walked on Moon, Why Can't Man Make a Women's Dress Shoe That Doesn't Hurt?" *The Wall Street Journal*, January 10, 1996, B1.
32. David P. Schulz, "Home Centers Cultivate Rural Market," *Stores*, December, 1995, 29–30.
33. Mitchell Pacelle, "More Stores Spurn Malls for the Village Square," *The Wall Street Journal*, February 16, 1996, B1.
34. Penny Gill, "Japan's Tobu: A Rising Star," *Stores* (June 1992): 28.
35. Mary Kuntz, "Reinventing the Store," *Business Week*, November 27, 1995, 87.
36. Ryan Mathews, "The Ties That Bind Can Also Strangle," *Progressive Grocer*, October, 1995, 25.
37. Joshua Levine, "Dare e Togliere (Give and Take Away)," *Forbes*, October 28, 1991, I 15–I 18.
38. "Tricks the Stores Use to Sell," *Consumer Reports*, November 1994, 717.
39. Stephen Bennett, "Masters of the Perimeter," *Progressive Grocers*, November 1995, 41.
40. Richard Gibson, "Planning Supermarkets to Maximize Temptation," *The Wall Street Journal*, May 9, 1991, B1.
41. Lois Therrien, "Want Shelf Space at Supermarket? Ante Up," *Business Week*, August 7, 1990, 60.
42. Lisa Gubernick, "Butterless Popcorn," *Forbes*, July 20, 1992, 44.
43. Jeanne Whalen, "Retailers Aim Straight at Teens," *Advertising Age*, September 5, 1994, 8. Also see Jeanne Whalen and Leah Rickard, "Stores Brace for Fall Shopping," *Advertising Age*, August 7, 1995, 33.
44. Jennifer DeCoursey, "Monster Event for Marketers," *Advertising Age*, October 16, 1995, 1.
45. Christie Brown, "The Body-Bending Business," *Forbes*, September 11, 1995, 197.
46. "Make the Store Work for You," *Consumer Report*, November 1994, 216.
47. Leonard Berry, "Stores with a Future," *Retailing Issues Letter* (copublished by Center for Retailing Studies, Texas A&M University and Arthur Andersen), March 1995, 3.
48. Bill Saporito, "Why the Price Wars Never End," *Fortune*, March 23, 1992, 68–74, 78.
49. "Every Day Low Prices—The New Improved Version," Marina Strauss, *Globe and Mail*, March 30, 1996, B10.

50. Lori Bongiorono, "Dollar Days for the Cartier Crowd," *Business Week*, August 21, 1995, 53.

51. D. Kirk Davidson, "Merchants: Stick to Your Merchandising," *Marketing News*, April 13, 1992, 4.

52. Mary Kuntz, "Extra-Strength Aspiration," *Business Week*, May 1, 1995, 46.

53. "The Power of Emotional Retailing," *Stores*, January 1996, MM3.

54. Earl Naumann, *Creating Customer Value* (Cincinnati: Thomson Executive Press, 1995), 77.

55. William H. Davidow and Bro Uttal, *Total Customer Satisfaction: The Ultimate Weapon* (New York: Harper & Row, 1989), 22.

56. Silcoff, "The Emporiums Strike Back," *Canadian Business*, Sept. 26, 1997, 58.

57. Matthew Schifrin, "Okay, Big Mouth," *Forbes*, October 9, 1995, 48.

58. Tom Peters, "Service or Perish," *Forbes ASAP*, December 4, 1995, 142.

59. Brian Bremner, "Looking Downscale—Without Looking Down," *Business Week*, October 8, 1990, 62, 66–67.

60. Lisa Gubernick and Robert La Franco, "Charity as a Commodity," *Forbes*, September 26, 1994, 119.

61. Pat Price, "Community Support," *Grocer Today*, April 1997, 14.

The Competitive Behaviour of Retail Institutions

Outline

The Nature of Competitive Retail Strategies
Retail Strategy
Forms of Retail Competition
Levels of Retail Competition
Retailer Classification

Retail Formats that Utilize Merchandise Selection as Their Distinctive Competitive Strategy
Specialty Store Retailing
Department Store Retailing

Retail Formats that Utilize Merchandise Pricing as Their Distinctive Competitive Strategy
Discount Retailing
Superstore Retailing
Off-Price Retailing

Retail Formats that Utilize Operational Structure as Their Distinctive Competitive Strategy
Chain Store Retailing
Contractual Retailing
Warehouse Retailing

Retail Formats that Utilize Time/Place Convenience as Their Distinctive Competitive Strategy
Food Retailing
Vendor Retailing
Direct Selling

Retail Formats that Utilize Direct Marketing as Their Distinctive Competitive Strategy
Direct-Mail Retailing
Mail-Order Retailing
Direct-Response Retailing

Retail Formats that Utilize Core Services as Their Distinctive Competitive Strategy

Summary

Student Study Guide
Key Terms and Concepts
Review Questions
Review Exam

Student Application Manual
Investigative Projects: Practice and Application

Endnotes

Objectives

To identify and discuss the four major types of retail competition

To review the various types of competitive strategies used by retailers to gain a comparative advantage

To recognize the different types of retail formats that the retailing community comprises

To identify the organizational and operational traits that characterize each type of retail format

To discuss the principal product, price, place, and promotional strategies each type of retailer employs

To discuss the competitive advantages and disadvantages that each retail format enjoys

To describe the operational and merchandising strengths and weaknesses that accrue to each retail format and to outline how they affect the format's ability to compete

Retail Vignette

Dylex Ltd.

Dylex is one of Canada's leading specialty retailers, with 642 stores across the country selling mainstream fashions and family merchandise under such well-known names as BiWay, Braemar, Fairweather, Thrifty's, and Tip Top.

The company was established in 1967 when Wilfred Posluns and James Kay formed a corporation to purchase one of Canada's best-known retail chains: Tip Top Tailors. After more than two decades of expansion in both Canadian and U.S. markets, Dylex was threatened by substantial debt levels in the early 1990s. Consequently, on January 11, 1995, Dylex and eleven related companies were granted an Order from the Ontario Court providing protection from creditors, and allowing Dylex to effect a financial and operating restructuring under the Companies' Creditors Arrangement Act (CCAA).

Dylex
www.dylex.com

As a result, Dylex closed 190 underperforming stores across Canada, and their restructuring plan met with approval from all outside parties. Dylex emerged from the CCAA on May 31, 1995.

Following Dylex's emergence from the CCAA, a new executive team was brought on board: Elliott Wahle, as President and Chief Executive Officer; Graeme Eadie, as Executive Vice-President and Chief Financial Officer; and Jeffrey Sarfin, as Executive Vice-President, Corporate Operations. In February of 1996 the team presented a three-part strategy outlining its plans to refocus the company by repositioning its core retailing divisions, selling non-strategic businesses and assets, and implementing a program to take advantage of economies of scale.

In conjunction with the plan, the company purchased the 25 percent minority interest in San Remo Knitwear, and all the shares of Braemar Apparel Inc. In addition, Dylex divested itself of its remaining shares of The Wet Seal, Nu-Mode Dress, John Forsyth Company, Harry Rosen, and Club Monaco (the latter in connection with an initial public offering). All of the company's businesses are now wholly owned.

In fiscal 1997, Dylex experienced its most profitable year since 1988, with net earnings of $22.9 million on sales of $1.2 billion. Dylex's capital structure has improved significantly; the company is now a focused and integrated retailing organization with virtually no debt. Dylex is well under way in reducing the operating cost structure and leveraging the available economies of scale. Management believes that the company has established a solid foundation for its core retail divisions, allowing them to leverage Dylex's many advantages into improved profitability.

- Women's wear
  - Braemar/Braemar Petites (61 stores)—Sportswear and classically styled fashion coordinates for women.
  - Fairweather (73 stores)—Fashionable women's clothing and accessories.

- Menswear
  - Tip Top Tailors (125 stores)—Quality men's clothing, sportswear, and accessories.

- Family stores
  - BiWay (274 stores)—Basic apparel, food, health and beauty aids, toys, housewares.
  - Thrifty's (109 stores)—Denim and other casual wear and accessories.

Printed with permission of Dylex.

Overstoring—Too Many Stores and Too Few Customers

North America is overstored. Too many stores compete for too few customers. Intertype competition (competition among similar retailers) has never been more intense than it is today. Yet, for most retailers an even bigger challenge is intratype competition (competition among dissimilar retailers). Overstoring hurts mediocre retailers far more than excellent retailers. High-performance retailers, such as Wal-Mart, Costco, and Home Depot, just keep growing. Mediocre retailers with no special competence, no special flair, struggle to survive. The central implication of overstoring is that the level of retailing effectiveness required for survival continues to rise.[1]

Disintermediation—There Are Many Roads to the Marketplace

Disintermediation, or the bypassing of traditional channels for delivery of goods and services in the marketplace, is the cornerstone of the modern economy. No delivery channel is fixed or safe, for any product or any profession. Doctors face "medical McDonalds" and storefront optometry, paraprofessionals and homeopaths, aromatherapy, and health clubs. Lawyers face do-it-yourself wills, and ministers are up against 12-step, self-help programs. Discounters, warehouses, TV shopping and catalogues are just a few of the choices of delivery channels available. Everyone is getting into everyone else's business, and leveraging delivery channels through joint ventures and crossover marketing.[2]

Re-Storing—Succeeding in a Sea of Change

Creative retailers are combining with the brutal pressures of the marketplace to drive out the slow, the old-fashioned, and the inefficient. Familiar formats that have endured for decades—supermarkets, hardware stores, discount stores, travel agencies, car dealerships—are being transformed or superseded. From vast megastores to tiny one-product kiosks, new kinds of outlets are springing up that look nothing like the stores of ten years ago. There is a sea of change in the configuration of retailing. The innovative retailers are the ones that are taking market share from everyone else. Not all the new formats will succeed, but as retailers grapple with change, these innovators point the way to the "re-storing" of North America.[3]

> Today's retailing landscape is starkly different from the past. It is tougher to get and keep customers. It is harder to design a business model that works for both customers and shareholders. Retail sales are shrinking as a share of gross domestic product. Spending is shifting from goods to services. Time- and budget-tight consumers are shopping less, visiting fewer stores, and spending more purposefully. The industry is overstored. Competition is intensifying. Power is concentrated among fewer, bigger, and stronger players.[4]

One of the most dramatic developments in today's world of retailing is the number of alternative types of stores available to consumers. With many market areas being overstored (the capacity to retail exceeds the capacity to consume), successful retail operations can only be achieved by offering shoppers something better, different, or extra.

This chapter is a survey of both the structure of retail competition and the broad spectrum of competitive approaches to the retail marketplace. Specifically, the chapter reviews the nature of competitive retail strategies and the various types of retail formats and their distinctive competitive strategies (see Figure 2–1). Based on operating and merchandising characteristics, the strengths and weaknesses of each format are examined in light of the retailer's ability to compete, survive, and grow.

Figure 2–6

Six distinctive competitive strategies used in classifying retail groups

Retail Formats That Utilize Merchandise Selection as Their Distinctive Competitive Strategy

The retailer's merchandise selection is defined by the firm's total **product mix**—the full mixture of products offered to the consumer. **Product variety** (the number of different product lines) and **product assortment** (the number of different product items stocked within each product line) defines this total product mix concept. By focusing on a carefully constructed product variety and assortment combination, retailers can develop a retail format that offers certain distinctive competitive advantages (see Figure 2–7).

Specialty Store Retailing

The merchandising and operating strategies of the specialist are directed at serving the needs of a more targeted and homogeneous market segment. Specialty stores are based on a merchandising concept that creates a distinctive image for the retailer. "Every successful specialty retailing format starts with a unique idea that strikes consumers as new, fresh, and different. Retail ideas become ego expressions of the people involved in creating, nurturing, and developing them. A retail idea reflects a particular approach to product selection, display, merchandising store design, and customer service."[12] The **specialty store retailer** attempts to serve all consumers in one or a limited number of market segments. To accomplish this targeting effect, specialty retailers "specialize" in the merchandise they offer a consumer; they become "focused merchandisers."

The specialty store concept exhibits a wide range of merchandising and operating strategies. Specialty retailers vary according to (1) the type, selection, and quality of merchandise; (2) the range of price lines; and (3) the size, design, and location of stores. Specialty retailers are classified on the basis of the nature and structure of their merchandise selection.[13] The available selection of merchandise ranges from the very narrowly defined product line of the classification retailer to the wider selection of the products merchandised by the category specialist. Figure 2–8 characterizes the various types of specialty retailers.

Classification Retailers **Classification retailers** are stores that focus on a single product class (e.g., socks) or a few product classes that are highly related (e.g., big and tall men's apparel). The classification retailer uses a "focus format" in which it directs its attention to meeting the selective product needs of a very limited segment of the consumer market. As shown in Figure 2–8, the degree of focus is what distinguishes one classification retailer from another.

Superspecialist. The most sharply focused of all specialty retailers, the **superspecialist** offers an extremely narrow product line variety (a single merchandise class) supported by

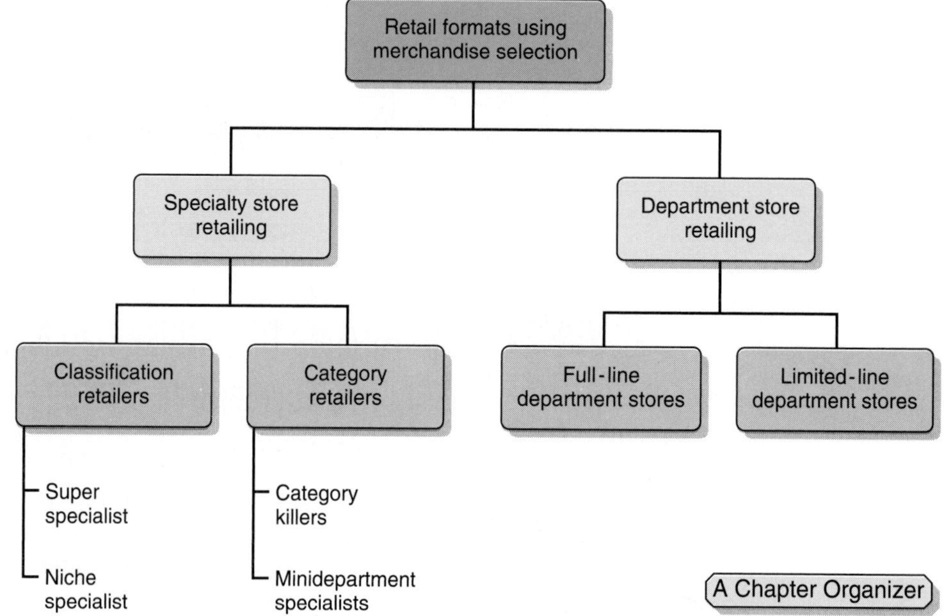

Figure 2–7

Retail formats based on merchandise selection

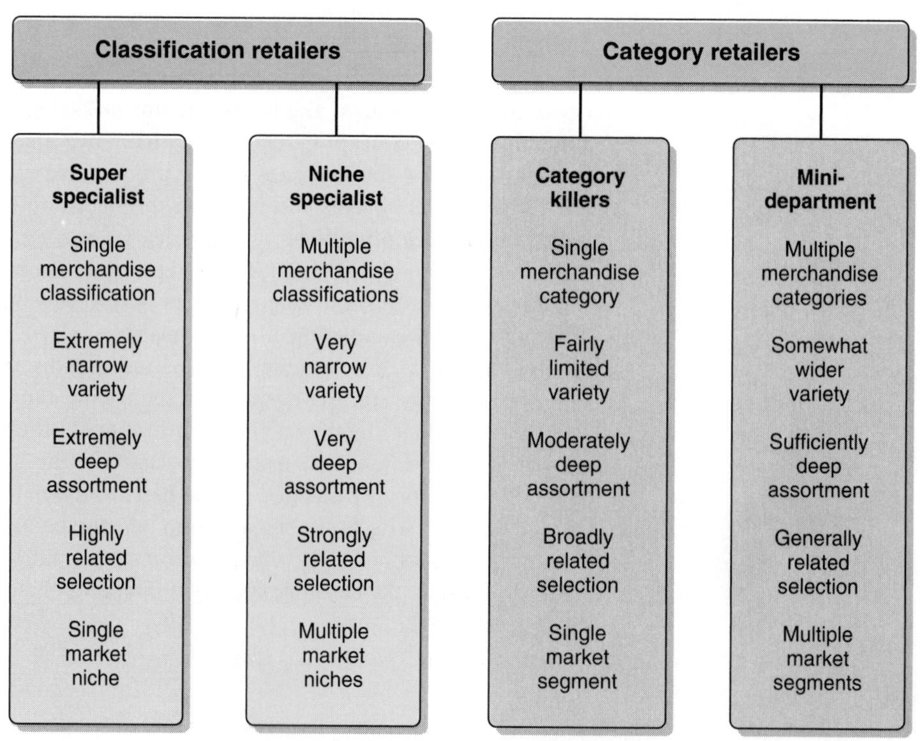

Figure 2–8

Types of specialty retailing

a deep assortment of product items (brands, sizes, models, colours, styles, and prices). The superspecialist typically serves a single market niche—a group of consumers who have a very specific need for particular product items that are comparable and substitutable. A one-stop comparison shopping experience for a narrowly defined class of merchandise is the distinctive competitive advantage enjoyed by the superspecialist format. Sunglass Hut is such an example, with several kiosks in Canada's large shopping malls.

Niche Specialist. The **niche specialist** attempts to serve multiple market niches by offering a strongly related selection of merchandise that can be described in terms of its very narrow variety of product lines (a few merchandise classes) supported by a relatively deep assortment of individual product items within each merchandise class. The Flag Shops, created in Vancouver by Doreen Braverman, is a successful chain of stores specializing in flags and accessories.[14] "Nichers" differ from superspecialists in that they offer a few more product lines but provide a little less selection of items within each line. By satisfying almost all of the consumer's needs for a few merchandise classifications, the niche specialist builds customer loyalty and obtains a strong competitive position in the marketplace. Bath and body stores like The Body Shop, specialize in bath gels, body lotions, massage oils, and aromatherapy.[15]

Category Retailers **Category retailers** sell one or more categories of merchandise (broadly related product lines) to one or more market segments. The typical category retailer's total product selection is made up of several merchandise classifications. Category retailers are "power formats" that use their expanded selection of merchandise together with their size, merchandising muscle, and operational efficiency to either dominate the market for a product category or assume at least a market leader position within the product category. As identified in Figure 2–8, category retailing can be divided into two formats: category killers and mini-department retailers.

Category Killers. A **category killer** specializes in a single merchandise category (a fairly limited variety of merchandise).[16] However, by offering a moderately deep assortment of brands, styles, models, and prices in all of the merchandise classes that make up the category, these jumbo-size stores can meet most or all of the needs of their target markets. Satisfying the needs of an entire market segment for an entire merchandise category translates into a dominant market position and a distinctive competitive advantage. The growth of category killers in Canada has adversely affected the performance of other retail formats.[17] Future Shop (consumer electronics), Pacific Linen (towels, bedding, bathroom accessories), Fanny's Fabrics (fabrics), Chapters Book Stores, Blockbuster (videos), Office Depot (office supplies), Petsmart (pet food), and Sportchek (sporting goods) are all examples of category retailers that have the killer instinct. This "big box" retailing format is spreading to other product categories—home decorating, pet food, and baby items.[18]

Mini-Department Retailers. A **mini-department retailer** is a retail format that pursues a product line extension strategy to better serve existing market segments and to target new customer groups. Mini-department specialty retailers offer several generally related categories of merchandise (a somewhat wider variety than the standard specialty store) that are supported by a sufficiently deep assortment of product items within each merchandise category.

Specialty Store Operations The complexity of the **specialty store** industry is portrayed in Figure 2–9. Specialty retailers specialize in just about every type of product available on the open market. Some specialists offer personal merchandise for the individual consumer and his or her home; others focus on consumer recreational and entertainment activities or the customer's need for various accessories (see Figure 2–9a). As discussed earlier, the merchandise selection offered by specialists can range from one or more product classifications to several product categories (see Figure 2–9b).

Figure 2–9

Profile of the store retailer: (a) merchandise type, (b) merchandise selection; (c) merchandise quality, (d) price lines, (e) store size, (f) store design, and (g) store location.

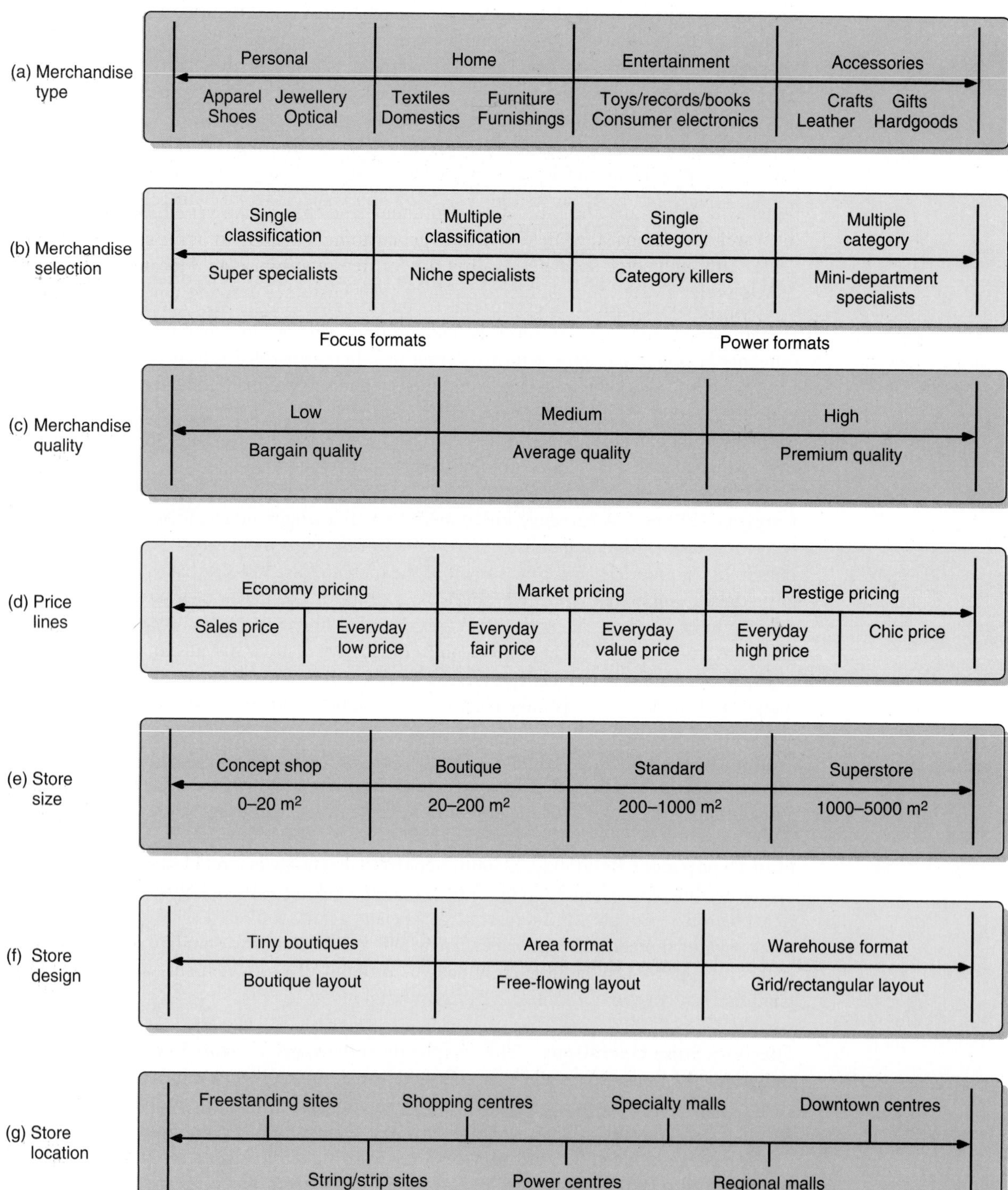

Specialty retailing covers the entire length of the merchandise quality continuum (see Figure 2–9c). At the low end of the continuum are one-price retailers. These specialty apparel retailers offer mostly bargain-quality merchandise at bargain prices. Premium-quality merchandise is well characterized by the English tailor of conservative Savile Row and the avant-garde men's shops on London's Floral Street.

As illustrated in Figure 2–9d, retailer specialists utilize the complete complement of pricing alternatives: (1) low economy prices in terms of sales promotional pricing and everyday low-pricing policies; (2) market pricing that stresses fairness and value (that is, an acceptable relationship between price and merchandise quality); and (3) prestige pricing in the form of everyday high prices to top-of-the-line chic prices. In this case, psychic value as delivered by the store and/or product image is as important a price determinant as is a more functional assessment of product worth (see Figure 2–9d).

Specialty stores range in size from small concept (lifestyle) shops of less than 20 m^2 that depend on other retailers for customer traffic generation to huge superstores of more than 1000 m^2 that are capable of being destination stores with the ability to attract and hold their own clients (see Figure 2–9e). Store designs include upscale, exclusive tiny boutiques with luxurious and intimate environments and the spartan yet efficient environs of the warehouse format that are designed to get customers in and out of the store (see Figure 2–9f). Although some specialty retailers opt for freestanding isolated locations, most specialists prefer clustering together to enhance their customer drawing power and to allow comparison shopping and one-stop shopping opportunities (see Figure 2–9g).

Department Store Retailing

Department stores have been slowly reclaiming some of the market share they have lost over the last two decades.[19] The department store industry is in transition. "An industry shakeout has left fewer, stronger players. A number of leaner, more responsive companies have moved quickly to gain market share by acquiring chains. As market share concentrates among fewer players, these companies are also moving to collapse divisions and eliminate costly redundancies. Department stores are beginning to more closely resemble mass chains, with similar strategies and structures."[20] The restructuring and repositioning of the department store industry over the last ten years has redefined the traditional department format in a broader context. Today's department store has eliminated many of the departments that made it a traditional department store. No longer can consumers pick up a new outfit or accessory, and then stroll to the next aisle or floor to shop for a new refrigerator or other "white goods," a compact disc, a book, sewing notions, or fabric.[21]

The traditional definition of the **department store** identified it as a large retailing institution that carries a wide variety of merchandise lines with a reasonably good selection within each line. In the past, a breakdown of department store merchandise resulted in an even split between hard goods and soft goods. Today, department stores have become largely soft-goods retailers: 80 percent soft goods and 20 percent hard goods. This lack of variety has led many retail watchers to describe department stores as large-space specialty stores, multidepartment soft-goods stores, and specialty department stores.

Full-Line Department Stores

Full-line department stores offer a wide variety of merchandise categories in a departmentalized framework. Whereas larger merchandise departments are typically defined by categories of merchandise, smaller departments, special concept shops, and boutiques are often created on the basis of merchandise classifications. A mix of hard and soft goods is still a basic merchandising strategy of the full-line store: however, that mix has been reformulated to place a much stronger emphasis on soft goods. The Bay, Sears, and Eaton's all operate as full-line department stores.

Limited-Line Department Stores

Limited-line department stores stock a limited variety of merchandise categories and classifications (mostly soft goods and hardware) but function with a fashion orientation, full markup policy, and operate in stores large enough to be shopping centre anchors. Limited-line department stores would include such specialized department store chains as Holt Renfrew.

Department Store Operations Regardless of the nature of individual department store chains, what distinguishes the department store format is its organizational structure, specifically the high degree of "departmentalization." From an operational standpoint, most of the basic functions of buying, selling, promoting, and servicing are conducted entirely or at least in part at the department level. Also, accounting and control procedures are organized on a departmental basis. The advantages of this type of organization are that it allows both *functional* (buying, selling, and so on) and *merchandise* (apparel, shoes, and so on) specialization, while gaining the economies of scale associated with a large retailing operation. Figure 2–10 lists Canada's top department stores by market share.

The product strategy of department stores is to offer a wide selection of brand-name and designer-label merchandise within those product categories and classifications stocked by the store. To differentiate themselves from competitors, department stores are becoming more focused in their merchandising approach. Department stores have refocused on their most defendable niches—upscale apparel and home furnishings. Within those niches, they are trying to differentiate their merchandise better.[22] Department stores are defining the economic level of the customer they want to attract, identifying the fashion attitudes of each target segment, and developing merchandising programs to satisfy the various lifestyle needs of these customers. Sears has targeted a loyal middle-class clientele by focusing on national brands at promotional prices instead of designer goods at prestige prices. While Eaton's targets the high-end business, The Bay targets fashion customers in the middle by being a little more fashion-forward but staying very promotional. Canada's three major department stores are currently in the process of redefining their strategies to better compete with new competition and changing times.[23]

"With factory-outlet malls and off-price stores now flooded with designer clothes and other national brands, department stores are using house brands to present exclusive merchandise, and to address lifestyle and demographics of their customers."[24] Besides enabling the retailer to offer an exclusive merchandise collection, private labels afford the opportunity to realize higher profit margins—30 percent to 40 percent more. Department stores avoid some of the vicious markdown cycle that is common with branded products because consumers cannot directly compare prices on private brands. Although private labels add an extra dimension to the merchandise mix, they are not the cure for what ails some department store organizations.

Department stores usually are high-margin operations. Because of the high operating expenses (30 to 40 percent of sales) stemming from the store's organizational structure, service offering, physical facilities, and high-risk merchandise, margins between merchandise costs and retail selling prices must be substantial to ensure a fair profit. Department stores normally appeal to middle- and upper-income consumers. To appeal to such a diverse group of consumers, some department stores have multiple pricing points. "Promotional" prices are directed at the lower- to middle-income consumer; "regular" prices appeal to those who want neither the lowest nor the highest priced merchandise;

Figure 2–10

Canada's department stores

Source: Company annual reports as reported by Canadian Press in Lethbridge Herald, *September 19, 1997, B10.*

Company	Market share % 1994	Market share % 1996
Wal-Mart	16	24
Zellers	24	23
Sears	20	18
The Bay	17	15
Eaton's	14	12
Kmart	9	8

and "prestige" prices are aimed at the upper-income consumer who desires the best. These good, better, and best price lines not only enable the department store to project a broad price appeal but also help consumers make price and quality comparisons. While upscale department stores, such as Eaton's, focus their attention on the middle and upper pricing points, Sears directs most of its attention to the middle-price lines. The place strategy of most department stores has been to locate in an "anchor" (end) position at one or more major suburban shopping centres. The exterior and interior motifs of the average department store are designed to create a prestigious image. The department store's principal promotional appeals are product selection and quality, service offerings, and shopping atmosphere. Each of these appeals is directed toward enhancing a unique image for the department store. Both product and institutional advertising are an integral part of the department store's strategy to influence potential consumers favourably.

Retail Formats That Utilize Merchandise Pricing as Their Distinctive Competitive Strategy

Price is a powerful motivator of consumer behaviour. Various retail formats have been able to utilize this motivating force effectively to gain a distinctive advantage over competing formats. Figure 2–11 charts the three price-oriented formats of discount, superstore, and off-price retailing.

Discount Retailing

The concept of discount retailing has its origins in the variety store industry. The idea of offering many different lines of low-price merchandise was at the heart of the "dime store" strategy. The nation's largest discount chains, Wal-Mart and Zellers, had their beginnings as variety store operations. After a brief examination of variety store operations, we look in depth at the traditional discount store format.

Figure 2–11

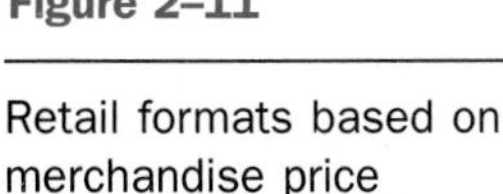

Retail formats based on merchandise price

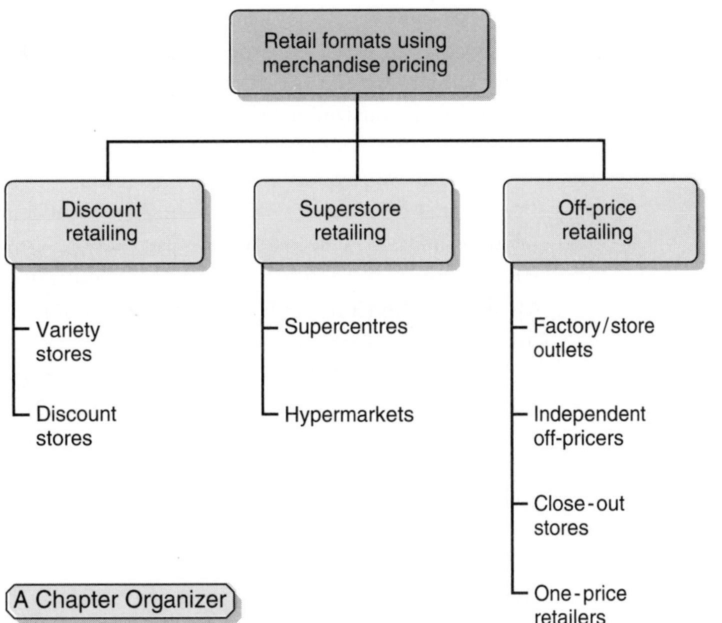

Variety Store Retailing The **variety store** format involves offering a wide variety (hence the name) of inexpensive merchandise at reasonable prices in a self-service store. Traditionally, the variety store offers a very limited selection within each product line, its competitive strategy being to offer a little bit of everything. Over the last two decades, the variety store format has almost become extinct. To survive, variety stores are sticking to the fundamentals of a basic mix of inexpensive goods, convenient neighbourhood and community centre locations, personal and friendly customer attention, and a little nostalgia for the good old days that dime stores represent.

Discount Store Retailing Discounting is a mature retail industry with limited geographical expansion potential. Growth in the discount sector will come by taking business away from other retailing formats (for example, supermarkets, department stores).[25] **Discount stores** are retailing institutions that sell a wide variety of merchandise (full line) at less than traditional retail prices; hence, they are often referred to as **full-line discount stores**. The largest players in the discount format in Canada are Wal-Mart and Zellers.

Targeted to meet the needs of the economy-minded consumer, the discount store uses mass-merchandising techniques that enable it to offer discount prices as its major consumer appeal.[26] The discount store sells brand-name (national or manufacturers' brands) and private-label merchandise at prices that consumers easily recognize as lower than traditional prices. The full-line discounter carries a fairly wide variety of hard and/or soft goods. Discount store customers generally come in for hard goods (soap, batteries, cosmetics), but it is soft goods (apparel, sheets, towels) that generate the best profits for discounters like Kmart. Hence, part of the discounter's strategy is to attract customers (with attractive prices on hard goods) into the store in hopes of making additional unplanned sales of soft goods.

In its drive for high turnover, the typical discounter stocks only the most popular brands, styles, models, sizes, and colours, along with its own private labels. In general, the product strategy of the full-line store is to carry many different product lines but limit the amount of selection within each line.

A few nationally well-known brands in key areas are an integral part of the discounter's product strategy. In selling national brands, the discounter takes advantage of the fact that consumers know the going price for various products. Selling national brands below the manufacturer's suggested retail price greatly enhances the store's discount image. This image helps the discounter convince the general public that its large selection of private labels is also a good value. To further enhance its image, Kmart has edged a bit upscale with some celebrity tie-ins—a fashion line of women's apparel under the Jaclyn Smith label, for example.

The discounter's service offering is limited to services necessary to run the operation. Traditionally cash-and-carry businesses, most major discount chains now offer credit services. Operated largely as a self-service business, discount stores do use sales personnel in departments where customers require sales assistance (jewellery, cameras, and so on). Store personnel also include those who staff information booths, return and credit approval desks, layaway counters, and checkouts.

Conventional discounters select suburban locations convenient to the large, middle-class consumer market; discount houses frequently serve as anchors for community shopping centres and, in some rare cases, as the major anchors of regional shopping centres. The typical discounter operates out of a modern one-story building ranging in area from 6000 to 15 000 m^2, depending on the local market size. Many discount stores create a carnival-like environment through their store decor and special sales events. Centralized checkout areas are a prominent part of all discount operations. Some leased departments (see page 55) and high-ticket item departments have localized checkouts.

Most discount stores are aggressive advertisers. Discounters use a broad message appeal highlighting variety, selection, and especially price. Newspapers are the discounter's principal medium, but television and radio advertising are increasing. Another key promotional strategy discounters use to inform and persuade the consumer is the point-of-purchase display. Bargain tables, bins, and stacks greet consumers as they enter, check out, and exit. End-of-aisle and main-aisle displays intercept shoppers as they travel through the store.

Superstore Retailing

Although the term **superstore retailing** can refer to any store that is bigger than one would expect to find selling a particular product line, in this discussion **superstore retailers** are huge combination supermarkets and discount general merchandise stores that stock and sell a complete selection of food products together with a wide variety of hard and soft goods at deep discount prices. Superstores can be differentiated into two size categories: the large supercentres and the jumbo hypermarkets.

Supercentres **Supercentres** are large combination supermarket/discount stores that typically range in size from 10 000 to 20 000 m^2 with more than 20 checkout stands and are open 24 hours. "About one-third of the selling area is dedicated to food and two-thirds of the store's space is devoted to general merchandise."[27] Wal-Mart's Super Center Stores stock 65 000 SKUs (stock keep units) and operate with gross margins of 18 percent. Kmart's Super Kmart stores are combination stores that devote about 2000 m^2 to grocery merchandise and 8500 m^2 to general merchandise. For busy people with families, the supercentre provides a convenient one-stop shopping opportunity.[28] Kmart emphasizes cross-merchandising as a distinct feature. Toasters are above the fresh baked breads, kitchen gadgets are across from produce, and infant centres have everything from food to clothing. "Cross-merchandising gets people to shop the entire store. It encourages the flow of traffic so that the shopper is aware of all of the departments throughout the Super Kmart."[29] Wal-Mart is also committed to developing the supercentre format. Wal-Mart supercentres combine groceries, general merchandise, and a wide range of services including pharmacy, dry cleaning, portrait studios, photo finishing, hair salons, and optical shops.[30]

The supercentre concept is being extended, modified, and adopted by retailers that have not been associated with this type of format. For example, multibrand auto dealers operate auto malls selling many competing brands under one roof.

Hypermarkets They were supposed to be the ultimate in one-stop shopping: cavernous stores with acres of floor space, scores of checkout lines, and oodles of merchandise and services—groceries, toys, videos, furniture, sporting goods, banking, fast food, and more—all crammed under one roof. But "hypermarkets," a can't-miss idea in the late 1980s, have enjoyed limited success.[31]

Hypermarkets are huge combination stores averaging 25 000 m^2. To succeed, this "mall without walls" concept must become a destination-type store capable of attracting customers from a 100-kilometre radius. A self-service retailer with central checkouts (typically fifty or more) and a sophisticated system of materials handling, the hypermarket attempts to underprice traditional retailers by as much as 20 to 40 percent. To enhance its drawing power, hypermarkets incorporate cafés, video stores, beauty salons, eye-care, and pharmacies.

Off-Price Retailing

Off-price retailers are specialty retailers that sell soft goods and/or hard goods at price levels 20 to 60 percent below regular retail prices. There are five general types of off-price operations: (1) factory outlets, (2) store outlets, (3) independent off-price outlets, (4) closeout stores, and (5) one-price retailers.

Factory Outlets **Factory outlets** are direct manufacturers' outlets where producers sell their own seconds, overruns, and pack-aways from last season. Many of these factory outlet stores also buy outside goods to supplement their merchandise mix.

Store Outlets **Store outlets** are direct retailers' outlets where retailers sell their own overstocks, shopworn goods, and odd-lot sizes and colours.With the growth of off-price retailing, many manufacturers and retailers realized that it was better to get into the business of off-price retailing than to continue as a willing supplier to a competitive retail format.

Independent Off-Price Outlets **Independent off-price outlets** are retail operations that buy seconds, irregulars, cancelled orders, overages, or leftover goods from manufacturers or other retailers and offer them to consumers at substantially discounted prices. Winners is the largest independent off-price retail chain in Canada. A key concept in this retailer's strategy is selling designer labels and branded merchandise; consumers know the price is an "off-price" if they can make price comparisons on like goods. Merchandise mixes often include product lines in which the brand name would fail to meet the standard of having a "national status." The independent's mode of operation can be described as follows:

- Low buying prices, often lower than for conventional discounters and lower than could be expected on the basis of quantity discounts.
- A high proportion of established, often designer, brands from manufacturers that seek the highest prices they can get for distressed and leftover merchandise, overruns, and irregulars
- Merchandise often of higher quality than that usually found in "discount stores"
- A changing and unstable assortment in that the customer cannot confidently predict exactly what the retailer will have on a given day—a major factor distinguishing off-pricing from simple discounting
- Customer services varying from minimal to extensive, sometimes including wrapping, exchange, refunds, and credit card acceptance
- Variety ranging from very narrow (for example, men's suits) to very broad (for example, family apparel)

One explanation for the ability of independent off-price outlets to obtain favourable terms is that they tend to pay promptly and do not ask for such extras as advertising allowances, return privileges, and markdown adjustments.[32] On the selling side, independent off-price retailers strive to keep their overhead low to maintain lower margins. Operating expenses are reduced by operating out of modest facilities located in strip malls, where rent is half that charged by large shopping centres.[33]

Closeout Stores Another variation of the off-price retailer is the **closeout store**—an outlet that specializes in retailing a wide variety of merchandise obtained through closeouts, retail liquidations, and bankruptcy proceeds (for example, Liquidation World). The merchandise mix depends on buying opportunities; an 80/20 product mix (hard to soft goods) is common. The typical closeout store layout lacks organization; searching for bargains is part of the traditional appeal of shopping for closeout merchandise.[34] Like other off-price outlets, closeout stores strive to keep operating expenses at a minimum. Failure to control expenses has a fast and damaging effect on profitability and long-run survival.[35]

One-Price Retailers **One-price retailers** offer all merchandise (for example, overruns, odd lots, cancelled orders, closeouts) at a single, fixed price. The Buck or Two Store chain is an example of the firms operating this type of off-price operation. "Because the stores buy opportunistically, the merchandise constantly changes. Customers say searching for that pearl of a product makes shopping more fun and more challenging."[36] The one-price clothing chains are (1) working best in smaller communities; (2) offering "true value" at discount prices in order to gain return trade; (3) favouring the $1, $6, $8, and $9 price points; and (4) selecting strip centre locations.[37]

Retail Formats That Utilize Operational Structure as Their Distinctive Competitive Strategy

By enhancing the operational capabilities of their retail enterprise, chain stores, contractual retailers, and warehouse retailers gain competitive advantages in attracting and holding significant numbers of consumers. Operational enhancements involve lowering operating expenses, which in turn result in lower retail prices. More effective operations also result in improved customer service. Figure 2–12 outlines those retail formats that focus on operational efficiencies.

Chain Store Retailing

A **chain store** is any retail organization that operates multiple outlets, offers a standardized merchandise mix, and utilizes a centralized form of ownership and control. Technically, any retail organization that operates more than one unit can be classified as a chain. However, the *Census of Business* considers chains as retail organizations that operate eleven or more units. A working compromise is to refer to chain organizations as *small* (two to ten units) or large (eleven or more units) *chains*. Another criterion for classifying a chain is that each unit in the chain must sell similar lines of merchandise. The third criterion is that there must be a central form of ownership and control. With central ownership, the parent organization has control over all operating and merchandising aspects of the entire chain of stores.

Technically, a chain store organization could be a multiunit operation of specialty stores, discount outlets, department stores, or food markets. The most commonly thought-of chains are the large general merchandise firms operated by Sears, The Bay, and Eaton's or the large specialty store chains such as Gap or Toys R Us.

Economies of scale are an important part of the chain's central buying policies. By buying in large quantities, often directly from the manufacturer, chain stores can acquire merchandise at the lowest costs in the retailing industry. Several additional advantages accrue to chain store operations. First, by operating a large number of stores within a particular market, chains can exert substantial control over their stores and achieve economies of scale through a centralized distribution system. The result is high turnover rates and few stockouts and overstocks. Second, chains can spread risk over many different stores in many different markets. Third, chain organizations obtain benefits from ver-

Figure 2–12

Retail formats based on operational structure

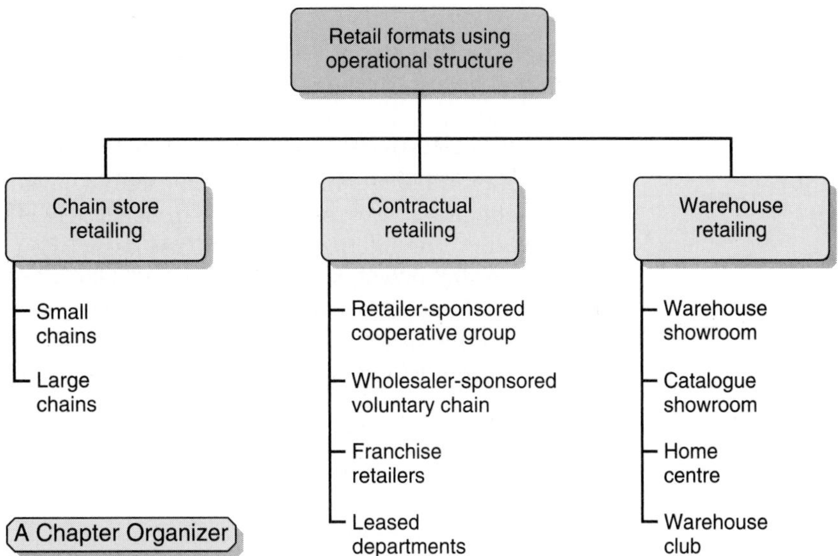

tically integrating their channels of distribution. Finally, national and regional chain operations enjoy the advantage of a high level of consumer recognition.

Chain stores usually promote both their store image and their individual products. Generally, chains promote the standardized nature of their operations and therefore the consistency (product quality, customer service, and so on) of their offerings from store to store. Many chains stress the reliability of buying from a large national or regional firm. Finally, with multiple locations within a given market, chain stores can effectively use the most expensive media (television) and exposure time (prime time). When Sears rolls out a merchandising program for a new line like Canyon River Blues or Arizona blue jeans, it can amortize its advertising costs over a large, national sales base.[38]

Contractual Retailing

Retailers often attempt to achieve economies of operations and an increased market presence by integrating their operations with other retailers and wholesalers. By entering into contractual arrangements, retailers can formalize the rights and obligations of each party in the contract. The terms of the contract can, and often do, cover all aspects of the retailer's product, place, price, and promotional activities. Contractual retailing exists in several forms, but the four most common are (1) retailer-sponsored cooperative groups, (2) wholesaler-sponsored voluntary chains, (3) franchised retailers, and (4) leased departments.

Retail-Sponsored Cooperative Groups The **retail-sponsored cooperative group** is a contractual organization formed by many small independent retailers and usually involves the common ownership of a wholesaler. Originally formed to combat competition from large chain organizations, this type of contractual system enables the small independent to realize economies of scale by making large-quantity group purchases. The contractual agreement usually requires individual members to concentrate their purchases of products from the cooperative wholesaler and, in turn, receive some form of patronage refund. Associated Grocers is a large food wholesaler having cooperative contractual arrangements with independent food retailers.

Wholesaler-Sponsored Voluntary Chain The **wholesaler-sponsored voluntary chain** is a contractual arrangement in which a wholesaler develops a merchandising program that independent retailers voluntarily join. By agreeing to purchase a certain amount of merchandise from the wholesaler, the retailer is assured of lower prices. These lower prices are possible because the wholesaling organization can buy in larger quantities with the knowledge that it has an established market. The Independent Grocers Alliance (IGA) and Provigo are both food wholesalers that sponsor voluntary chains. Home Hardware and True Value have both built strong cooperative relationships with their retailing partners.

Franchise Retailers Franchising in Canada experienced rapid growth during the 1960s and 1970s. During the 1980s, however, growth became stagnant as many markets became saturated. The 1990s have seen another upsurge in the popularity of franchising, as many services have been adapted to the franchising system of operations.[39] A franchise system is a form of retailing in which a parent company (franchisor) obtains distribution of its products, services, or methods through a network of contractually affiliated dealers (franchisees). The International Franchise Association defines **franchising** as "a continuing relationship in which the franchisor provides a licensed privilege to do business, plus assistance in organizing, training, merchandising, and management in return for a consideration from the franchisee."[40] In other words, what the franchisor offers the franchisee is a patterned way of doing business that includes product, price, place, and promotional strategies.

In practice, this means that the franchisee is the owner of his or her own business, distributing the goods or services of the franchisor and paying for that privilege through an initial fee and/or a percentage of future sales or profits. Though the franchisee owns the business, the franchisor usually exercises control over some aspects of its operation to ensure conformity to the franchisor's proven methods and standards for products, services, quality, and methods.

In return for the fees and royalties paid by the franchisee, the franchisor may provide some or all of the following services: (1) location analysis and counselling; (2) store development, including lease negotiations; (3) store design and equipment purchasing; (4) initial employee and management training and continuing management counselling; (5) advertising and merchandising counsel and assistance; (6) standardized procedures and operations; (7) centralized purchasing with consequent savings; (8) financial assistance in the establishment of the business; (9) an exclusive territory in which to operate; and (10) the goodwill and recognition of a widely known brand or trade name.

Franchisors expect franchisees to conform to the business pattern and also to provide them with some form of compensation for their right to use the franchise. Franchisor compensation usually involves either one or a combination of the following:

1. **Initial franchise fee**—A fee that the franchisor charges up front for the franchisee's right to own the business and to receive initial services.
2. **Royalties**—An operating fee imposed on the franchisee's gross sales.
3. **Sales of products**—Profits the franchisor makes from sales to the franchisee of raw and finished products, operating supplies, furnishings, and equipment.
4. **Rental and lease fees**—Fees that the franchisor charges for the use of its facilities and equipment.
5. **Management fee**—A fee that the franchisor charges for some of the continuous services it provides the franchisee.[41]

Among the primary advantages of owning a franchise unit are that it usually requires less capital to set up a franchise than it would to start up independently, it is often unnecessary to possess knowledge about a particular type of business because of franchisor training programs, and business risk is frequently reduced because of the recognition and goodwill of the franchisor's name and product as well as the initial and continued help the franchisor provides in running the business.

Franchising, however, should not be considered an easy and failure-proof way to financial success. The franchisee faces a number of disadvantages. First, the relationship between the franchisor and franchisee usually involves control over many aspects of the franchisee's business operations, and some owners find that this overly inhibits their creativity and independence. Second, to acquire a blue-chip franchise such as a McDonald's or Pizza Hut requires considerable financial resources and high royalty payments. Third, the success of each franchise unit is dependent on the workings of the parent company, and even the best managers can find their business—and investment—jeopardized if trouble develops in the franchisor's operations. Finally, experts urge those thinking of purchasing a franchise to remember that it is usually much more a full-time job than an investment, with most new owners finding themselves putting in well above an average work week.

Today, there are franchise companies involved in almost every type of retail business area, from hairdressing to mufflers, as evidenced by Magicuts joining Midas shops on the scene. New franchises follow new trends: The growing desire to stay home is leading to several franchising formats that are homebound—home food delivery services, home improvement, home maintenance, and home entertainment businesses are thriving.

Franchise companies can be divided into two main types. The first, product or **tradename franchises**, is characterized by franchised dealers that carry one company's product line and identify their business with that company and product. Examples of this type include automobile dealers, gasoline stations, and soft drink bottlers. These types of operations are often referred to as *manufacturer-sponsored* and *wholesaler-sponsored* (see Figure 2–13).

The second type is called **business format franchising**, or a *service firm–sponsored retailer*, a business system in which the franchisee carries not only the

Figure 2–13

Types of franchising systems

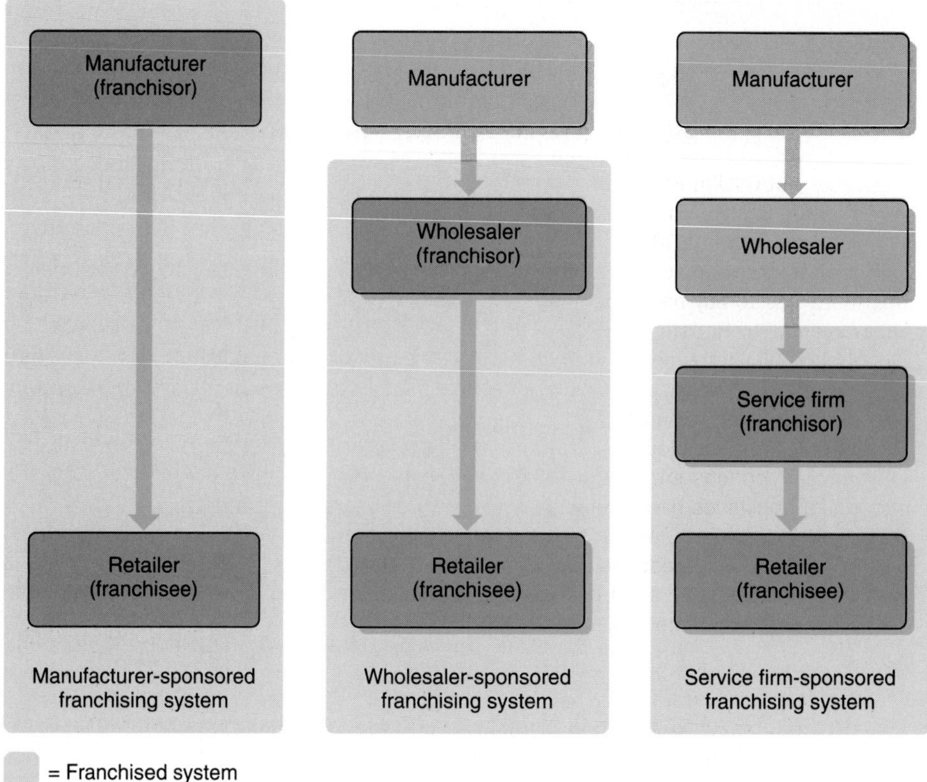

franchisor's products and trade name but the entire business format itself, from merchandising to store design (see Figure 2–12).

> The realization that detailed management systems can be replicated to strict specifications was central to the development of the business format franchising. Typically, the relationship between franchisor and franchisee includes product sourcing, and sometimes supply, marketing and merchandising, strategies and plans, operational manuals and standards, and quality control provisions supported and enforced by the parent company.[42]

Most aspects of the franchisee's operations are coordinated to ensure a certain and consistent image designed to appeal to particular market segments. This category includes restaurants (McDonald's), auto repair shops (Midas), personal and business services (H&R Block), and many others, and it is increasing at a much greater rate than product franchises. This growth in services franchising has led the industry to achieve sales of close to $90 billion and to account for nearly 50 percent retail sales in Canada.[43]

The hierarchical arrangement of the best franchising opportunities would generally reflect the following rankings:

1. soda bottlers and beer distributors
2. car dealers and gas stations
3. fast-food outlets
4. convenience stores
5. auto-service shops
6. marginal product and service operations.[44]

Retail Strategies and Tactics

Fight at the Food Counter

In the late 1980s Jim Robertson headed up C Corp. Inc., a Provigo operating company with operations that included a chain of more than 100 Red Rooster convenience stores in Western Canada, primarily in Alberta. One of his jobs there was to buy back some of the autonomous, freewheeling Red Rooster franchises and open more tightly controlled Winks franchises. Whenever a Red Rooster lease would come up for renewal, Robertson would offer the owner a stricter franchise agreement. For example, where the former Red Rooster leases were for as long as 10 years with options for additional 5-year periods, the new Winks franchises had maximum terms of three years; and where the old Red Rooster franchisees had a great deal of leeway to act independently, Winks franchises were rigidly governed by a set of rules and restrictions that became known simply as "the program."

"It just devastated the personal initiative and entrepreneurship that built the franchises in the first place," says a former Red Rooster owner. "Overnight, it destroyed whatever goodwill those stores had built up."

In the franchisees' eyes, however, the program was the problem. In addition to establishing lease and advertising rates, it sets the price at which franchisees bought their groceries from suppliers, and the price at which they sold goods to the end customer. By squeezing those margins, they argued, Loeb [Provigo's grocery chain] was in a position to siphon profits out of the stores and into the corporation—shifting the profit centre, in other words, from the retail level to the wholesale level. Then, when margins became insupportable and stores began to lose money, the franchisees claimed, Loeb could move in, buy out the impoverished franchises at fire-sale prices and install corporate managers whose success would not hinge on retail profitability.

Loeb vehemently disputes this interpretation of events. Narrow retail margins are simply a sign of the times, Robertson argues, the result of a hypercompetitive grocery industry rather than a Loeb conspiracy. "That loaf of bread you could sell for $1.20, you can now sell for only $1—that $0.20 is obviously going to come out of the gross profit of the business," he says. "That is a function of what is going on in the market right now."

Source: Mark Anderson, Canadian Business, *February 1997, 69–70.*

The top two categories and the best operators in categories 3 and 4 are almost untouchable (costs are prohibitive in that most prospective buyers have insufficient startup capital) or unbuyable (most, if not all, new franchises are awarded to existing franchisees who have successful track records). Unfortunately, most of the current action is at the bottom of this hierarchy. Although good franchising arrangements can be found, a potential franchisee must carefully investigate and evaluate all aspects of the franchisor's business pattern. With the average age of the Canadian population rising and the increasing number of two-earner families, forecasters see further creation of franchise opportunities in such areas as maid services, repair and home remodelling, carpet and other cleaning services, and various maintenance functions. One of the fastest growing Canadian personal service franchises is Magicuts, owned by Bryan Laborsky.[45] Franchises specializing in business services are expected to grow at an even faster rate, a product of the so-called age of information and the increasing preference of many firms to contract out functions they once performed internally. Growth is expected to come in franchises supplying services for businesses such as accounting, advertising, packaging and shipping, consulting, security, personnel, and copying and printing. Canada's leading franchising companies are shown in Figure 2–14.

Leased Departments **Leased departments** are retailers that operate departments (usually in specialized lines of merchandise) under contractual arrangements within conventional retail stores. Many supermarkets and department stores, for example, lease space to outside organizations to sell magazines (as in supermarkets) and auto supplies and shoes (as in many department and discount stores). The most frequently leased-out departments are beauty salons, books, cameras, candy, costume jewellery, electronics, family shoes, fine jewellery, furs, and photo. New additions to this type of retailing are the Tim Hortons/Wendy's, and Chapters/Starbucks combinations. The lessor usually

Figure 2–14

Canada's leading franchisors

Source: D. Wesley Balderson, Canadian Entrepreneurship and Small Business Management, *Third Edition, Prentice Hall Canada 1998, 205.*

Franchise	Gross revenue ($ thousands)	Parent	Type of business
Canadian Tire	$3 771 300	Billes family	Retail hardware
Metro-Richelieu Inc.	3 160 200	Widely held	Convenience food
A&P Co.	2 467 772	A&P U.S.	Food retailer
McDonald's Restaurants	1 695 100	McDonald's Corp.	Fast food
Speedy Muffler King	637 400	Goldfarb Corp.	Auto repair

furnishes space, utilities, and basic in-store services necessary to the lessee's operation. In turn, the lessee agrees to provide the personnel, management, and capital necessary to stock and operate a department with carefully defined merchandise. Generally, the contract calls for the lessee to pay the lessor either a flat monthly fee, a percentage of gross sales, or some combination of the two. A rapidly growing trend in the subleasing of space is the **in-store vendor shop**—an area in the store that is stocked, merchandised, staffed, and managed by a single vendor. In-store vendor shops range from high-fashion boutiques within specialty department stores to auto repair service areas within discount stores. Although leased departments are becoming more popular, potential for conflict between the lessee and store owner abound due to differences in the objectives of both parties.[46]

Warehouse Retailing

The typical warehouse retailing operation combines warehouse and showroom facilities. In some cases, these facilities are located in separate but adjacent areas; in others, the warehouse and showroom are combined into one large physical structure. Generally, the warehouse retailer uses warehouse principles to reduce operating expenses and thereby offer discount prices as a primary customer appeal. Four types of warehouse retailers can be identified: (1) warehouse showroom, (2) catalogue showroom, (3) home centre, and (4) warehouse club (see Figure 2–12).

Warehouse Showrooms

The **warehouse showroom** is generally a single-line hard-goods retailer that stocks merchandise such as furniture, appliances, or carpeting. To help the consumer make price comparisons with conventional home furnishing retailers, the warehouse showroom typically stocks only well-known, nationally advertised brands. These retailers set up sample merchandise displays in showrooms so potential consumers can get an idea of what the products will look like in their homes. After making a selection, consumers immediately receive the merchandise in shipping cartons from the completely stocked adjacent warehouse. Most warehouse retailers offer credit, delivery, and installation services. Warehouse retailers provide these services at an additional fee over the selling price. Warehouse showroom locations usually are freestanding sites near major traffic intersections.

Catalogue Showroom

The **catalogue showroom** is a warehouse retailer featuring hard goods such as housewares, small appliances, jewellery, watches, toys, sporting goods, lawn and garden equipment, luggage, stereos, televisions, and other electronic equipment at a discount. The distinguishing feature of the catalogue showroom is that a merchandise catalogue is combined with the showroom and an adjacent warehouse as part of the retailer's operation. By adding a catalogue of products to showroom products, the retailer provides consumers with both an in-store and at-home method of buying merchandise. As with the warehouse showroom, the catalogue showroom features nationally branded merchandise that facilitates consumer price comparisons with conventional hard-goods retailers.

For consumers, the typical shopping trip to a catalogue showroom involves: (1) filling out an order form using the merchandise/price code found on either the showroom price tag or in the catalogue, (2) ordering and paying for merchandise at a cashier's desk, and (3) retrieving the merchandise at a pickup desk. Best Products is updating the format by: (1) making some products available right on the shelves so customers can serve themselves, (2) providing computer ordering stations throughout the store, and (3) using hand-held wireless computers that enable employees to place orders. The pickup desk is directly connected to an adjacent warehouse containing a complete stock of merchandise. Recently closed Consumers Distributing was the best known Canadian catalogue showroom.

Home Centres The modern **home centre** combines the traditional hardware store and lumber yard with a self-service home improvement centre. The typical merchandise mix includes a wide variety and deep assortment of building materials, hardware, paints, plumbing and heating equipment, electrical supplies, power tools, garden and yard equipment, and other home maintenance supplies. Some home centres have also expanded their merchandise offerings to include household appliances and home furnishings. Home centres usually have large showrooms that display sample merchandise (large, bulky items) and complete stock (small, standardized items). "Warehouses usually average 100,000 square feet of selling space, with an additional 10 000 to 15 000 square feet [approx. 1000–5000 m^2] outside devoted to lawn and garden. Size varies widely, however, as units range from 85 000 to 150 000 square feet [approx. 15 000 m^2]."[47] Higher ceilings in these "big box stores" create considerably greater potential for vertical merchandising than would be possible in more traditional facilities. Consumers purchase showroom sample merchandise by placing an order at the order desk, and clerks pull the order from adjacent warehouse stocks. Customers simply serve themselves with showroom stock. A recent innovation in this format has been the introduction of the drive-through concept; customers simply follow a well-marked auto aisle through a covered yard, select and load their order, and pay at the end of the yard before exiting.[48]

While appealing to all home owners, the home centre has been particularly successful in appealing to the "do-it-yourselfers" (DIYers). By providing customers with information on materials and equipment and by offering how-to services, home centres have developed a strong customer following. Home centres also sell to "buy-it-yourselfers" (BIYers), who purchase the materials themselves but hire the work to be done, and to professionals (small contractors and remodellers) who often buy wholesale. Recently, home centres have been developing more programs that target professionals:

> As warehouse home centre store growth begins to saturate the do-it-yourself market, the professional/business market will afford the greatest opportunities for future growth. Many operations have begun to offer services designed to attract these customers, such as a separate contractors' entrance and desk, early morning hours, job site delivery, fax-in orders, special orders, credit accounts, and blueprint estimating.[49]

Home Depot is the industry's number one player, with stores ranging from 7000–15 000 m^2. Outlets stock about 30 000 different items of building materials, home improvement and repair products, and lawn and garden supplies.[50] Canada's top ten home centre chains are shown in Figure 2–15.

Warehouse Clubs **Warehouse clubs** are no-frills, deep-discount warehouse outlets that cater to customers who have joined the club in order to obtain merchandise at 20 to 40 percent below prices at supermarkets and discount stores. Most warehouse clubs have a two-tiered membership plan: (1) wholesale/business members who must be operators of small businesses and (2) group members who pay membership fees and purchase goods about 5 percent above the ticket price. Wholesale/business members represent 30 to 35 percent of club memberships but account for 65 to 70 percent of sales; group members compose 65 to 70 percent of the memberships but generate only 30 to 35 percent of sales. However, group membership fees represent significant revenues for the wholesale club.[51] The principal retail mix strategies are as follows:

Figure 2–15

Top 10 home centres

Source: "Top Canadian Home Centre Retailers," Hardware Merchandising Magazine, *Maclean Hunter Publishing Ltd., May 1997, 22.*

Company	1996 retail sales ($ millions)	1995 retail sales ($ millions)	# of stores in 1996	# of stores in 1995
Canadian Tire Corp., Toronto	4 700*	4 500*	425	424
Home Depot, Scarborough, Ont.	1 000[1]	721	24	19
Beaver Lumber, Markham, Ont.	680	660	140	133
Reno Depot, Montreal	433	388	11	11
Revelstoke Home Centres, Langley, B.C.	380	320	36	34
Cashway Building Centres, Port Hope, Ont.	265	245	56	55
Lansing Buildall, Etobicoke, Ont.	150*	N/A	9	9
Kent Building Supplies, Saint John, N.B.	145*	130*	16	16
Lumberland Building Materials, Burnaby, B.C.	120[2]	130*	17[2]	17
Windsor Building Supplies, Surrey, B.C.	120	120	62	64

*Estimated sales

[1]Estimated sales based on Molson Companies (shareholder) year end March 31, 1997.

[2]Lumberland prior to January '97 purchase by Revelstoke Home Centres.

Retail Strategies and Tactics

Home Depot Builds Tough Competition

A few years ago, Ken Plourde knew of at least 10 lumber stores in Toronto's east end. But the ranks have since dwindled to his own store, Danforth Lumber Co., and just one other. Two words explain the mortality rate: Home Depot.

The Atlanta-based superstore chain's expansion into Canada "consolidated the market quite a bit," says Mr. Plourde, who runs his 20-year-old family business with his brother Doug. The brothers have managed to hang on, he says, by extending hours, offering personalized service, expanding inventory and staying competitive on pricing.

Competition is tight these days for lumber and home-supply retailers. Price conscious do-it-yourselfers are willing to drive out of their way to pay less for a sheet of drywall or a two-by-four. They want more advice and selection. Retailers have had to become more savvy to survive. The good news is that for those building retailers that do make it, house-proud consumers seem more willing to spend money at their stores than at other retail outlets.

At Danforth Lumber, Mr. Plourde agrees that home owners are willing to spend more money and take on bigger projects. But they also have a keen eye for a deal. "I've never seen customers as demanding as they are today." Mr. Plourde says his affiliation with Home Hardware has helped respond to these demands. The dealer-owned network operates a central buying and warehouse system, which brings costs down and allows access to a wider selection of goods without carrying a lot of inventory. He also goes out of his way to hunt down special requests from customers, especially contractors, who still account for about 50 to 60 percent of his business.

Source: Elizabeth Church, Globe and Mail, *September 2, 1996, 13–14.*

- **Product mix**—The basic approach is to keep it simple by stocking a limited variety of high-turnover product lines supported by a limited assortment (3000 to 4500 SKUs) of the top-selling brands.
- **Service mix**—Cash-and-carry business with limited hours and no amenities (for example, no bathrooms).
- **Place mix**—Large (10 000 m^2) facilities (warehouse) located along high-traffic arteries where costs are lower and access is easy.
- **Price mix**—Rock-bottom wholesale prices that produce paper-thin gross margin profits (10 to 11 percent).
- **Promotional mix**—Minimal advertising (less than 0.5 percent of sales) supported by minimal sales support, visual merchandising, and sales incentives.

To keep their business growing, Price/Costco (a Kirkland, Washington–based operation) has intensified its focus on business customers.[52]

Retail Formats That Utilize Time/Place Convenience as Their Distinctive Competitive Strategy

Consumers are pressed for time and financially squeezed—hence their demand for more convenience and better value. For the contemporary consumer, both time and place convenience has become an essential part of the merchandising mix of any retailer selling goods and services that are required and purchased on a frequent and regular basis. Food retailers fall into this group of convenience-oriented retailers. Other retail operations survive by being present when and where the customer needs them; vendor-based retailing represents this group of convenience retailers. Direct selling—contacting (visiting or telephoning) customers at their place of residence or work—usually provides a high level of place convenience. If the contact is made at the right time under the right circumstances, time convenience is also welcomed by the customer. Figure 2–16 charts the various types of retailers that use time and place convenience as a key merchandising tool.

Figure 2–16

Retail formats based on time/place convenience

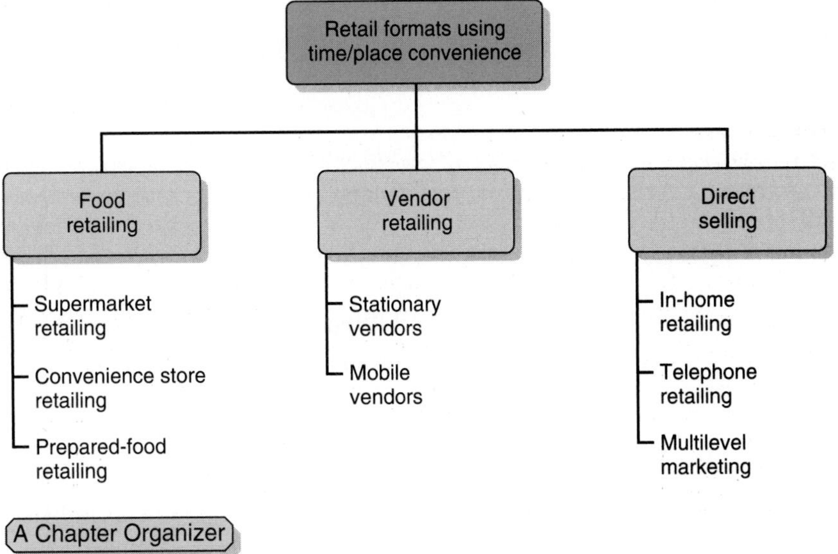

Food Retailing

Supermarkets, convenience stores, and fast-food restaurants stress time and place convenience as an essential success ingredient for their merchandising and operating mix. Given the perishable nature of most of the food industry's product lines and the limited amount of time available for food-related shopping, an emphasis on convenience as a distinctive competitive strategy is very appropriate.

Supermarket Retailing No one definition of a **supermarket** exists because of the wide range of business formulas used in this industry. Figure 2–17 lists the top supermarket operations in Canada. The products offered by a supermarket include a relatively broad variety and complete assortment of dry groceries, fresh meats, produce, and dairy products. Basic food lines have been supplemented by a variety of prepared food lines (the deli department) and nonfood lines. By adding prepared foods, the supermarkets hoped to limit the threat posed by the fast-food restaurants. The addition of "carry-out services" and "eating-in areas" for such foods as deli products, fresh bakery products, and fast-food restaurant lines (for example, hamburgers, hot dogs, chicken, tacos, fish) represents a direct effort to obtain a large share of this eating-out business.

By broadening their merchandise lines to include nonfood products, supermarkets have successfully increased sales and profits. With large numbers of customers moving through these stores each week, this product strategy has resulted in numerous sales of convenience and shopping goods. Today, a supermarket's upgraded and upscale operations include such nonfood lines as prescription drugs, small appliances, linens, auto accessories, books, magazines, clothing, flowers, and housewares. Many supermarkets have added such services as dry cleaning, postal, banking, tailoring, medical, dental, insurance, and legal services.

Supermarkets tend to be low-margin operations that depend on high stock turnover rates to sustain profits. Operating out of clean, modern facilities (an extremely important patronage motive for most food shoppers), the supermarket is basically a self-service operation supported by such services as parking, cheque cashing, fast checkout, and bagging. Although some supermarkets accept credit cards[53] and offer tote services to automobiles, cash-and-carry is the preferred method of doing business. Most supermarkets are attempting to capture sales and avoid pure price competition by offering premium private labels.[54]

Today, two general price strategies dominate the supermarket industry: the *high–low* pricing strategy and the everyday low-pricing strategy. The high–low strategy is a promotional pricing strategy in which advertisements of loss or low-price leaders (products sold below or at cost) are used to attract consumers into the store, where it is hoped they will

Figure 2–17

Canada's top supermarkets/ food retailers

Source: Canadian Business Performance 500, *Special Annual Issue, June 1997, 150–175.*

Company	1996 sales ($millions)	Income ($millions)
Loblaws	9 847.5	173.7
Oshawa Group Ltd.	6 383.5	55.2
Provigo Inc.	5 832.5	38.8
Canada Safeway Ltd.	4 733.7	157.4
Westfair Foods Ltd.	3 352.9	90.6
Metro-Richelieu Inc.	3 266.0	61.0
Empire Co. Ltd.	2 915.2	42.1
Great Atlantic & Pacific Co. of Canada Ltd.	2 372.3	N/A
Southland Corp. Ltd.	745.7	N/A
Calgary Co-operative Association Ltd.	537.6	17.3

purchase the rest of their weekly shopping list at full markup prices. The *everyday low-pricing* strategy maintains low price levels on all items at all times in hopes of developing store loyalty and a steady return trade. Canada has seen a decline in consumer purchases at supermarkets during the last few years as more people eat at restaurants and purchase food from warehouse retailers and department stores such as Wal-Mart.[55] This has increased the competition for the food seller in Canada and has spelled disaster for some supermarkets.[56]

Convenience Store Retailing The modern-day version of the corner "Mom and Pop" grocery store is the **convenience store**—an outlet that offers time convenience by being open longer and during the inconvenient early morning and late-night hours, as well as place convenience by being a small, compact, fast-service operation close to consumers' homes and workplaces. The basic premise of the convenience store is capturing fill-in or emergency trade—when the consumer has forgotten to purchase a needed product during the planned weekly trips to the supermarket or has unexpectedly run out of a needed product before the next planned supermarket trip. Because these stores are frequently located between the consumer's home and the nearest supermarket, they serve as effective "interceptors" of fill-in and emergency trade.

Convenience stores carry both food and nonfood merchandise lines. Like supermarkets, convenience stores have broadened their basic product mix to include a wider variety of groceries, prepared foods, snacks, and nonfood items and services.[57] Product assortments within each line are limited. Major national brands dominate the product line, although some of the major chain organizations offer private labels. Because they provide time and place utilities, convenience stores typically charge appreciably higher prices than other stores. Some convenience chains, however, have altered their product-service mix to compete with supermarkets. Fresh produce and bakery products together with prepared foods are the three common product line enhancements that convenience stores are using to intercept supermarket traffic. Convenience stores are also teaming up with fast-food operators such as Taco Bell, Burger King, McDonald's, Subway, Pizza Hut, and KFC to broaden their appeal to the time-stressed consumer.[58]

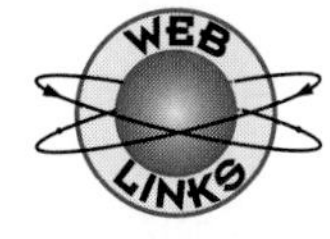

Subway
www.subway.com

From a promotional viewpoint, the store's sign is the most important weapon in the war to attract consumers. The convenience store's facilities include buildings that range from 100–300 m² and parking areas that accommodate five to fifteen cars. Store layouts are designed to draw customers throughout the store to increase impulse purchasing. The largest convenience store chains in Canada are shown in Figure 2–18.

Prepared-Food Retailers Changes in the North American lifestyle (for example, dual-career families, smaller and single households) have created a large demand for the convenient consumption of food products and services. North Americans now spend about one-half of their food dollars on prepared foods.[59] Prepared-food retailers can be categorized into two operating formats: (1) fast-food retailers and (2) sit-down restaurants.

Fast-Food Retailers. **Fast-food retailers** offer a limited selection of prepared foods with quick response service (that is, a short time span from placing the order to serving the customer). Typically, fast-food outlets offer a specialized menu featuring a main entrée, the most common specialties being hamburgers (McDonald's, Burger King, Wendy's, A&W),

Figure 2–18

Top Canadian convenience store chains

Source: Canadian Business Performance 500, *Special Annual Issue, June 1997, 150–175.*

Company	Sales ($millions)	Employees
Southland Canada Inc. (7-11)	745.7	5 500
Silcorp Ltd. (Mac's, Mike's Marts)	633.8	7 000
Alimentation Couche-Tard Inc.	368.6	1 828

chicken (KFC), pizza (Domino's, Pizza Hut), roast beef (Arby's, Rax), submarine or hero sandwiches (Subway), and tacos and burritos (Taco Bell). In recent years, some major specialty chains have extended their menus in order to expand their market appeal and grow their businesses. Initially, product extensions were new items within their current specialty (for example, different types of pizza). Recently, new product additions have been menu items taken from competitive specialties (for example, Pizza Hut and Domino's adding chicken wings).

Although price competitiveness will remain a driving force in obtaining customer patronage, fast-food retailers are exploring strategies involving nonprice competition. Taco Bell plans to develop over 200 000 "points of access" by the year 2000, including airport carts, convenience stores, schools, and theatres.[60] Another growth vehicle is to develop dual-branded tandem units. For example, Pepsico, parent of KFC, Taco Bell, and Pizza Hut, plans to open 100 KFC/Taco Bell units, and recently Tim Hortons/Wendy's units have opened.[61]

Sit-Down Restaurants. The **sit-down restaurant** business is frequently segmented into three basic types: (1) midscale family restaurants and cafeterias such as Denny's; and (2) casual dining houses such as the Olive Garden, Kelsey's, and Earl's; and (3) fine-dining, white-tablecloth restaurants that are typically locally owned and operated. Faced with shrinking margins, increasing food costs, additional operating expenses, and unit saturation, sit-down restaurants are dropping prices, revamping menus, offering meal combinations, enhancing the dining environment, and using other value-enhancement tactics (for example, live music, free parking, quick seating). "As an aging baby boom generation weaned on fast food decides to sit down, chains with an informal atmosphere and moderate prices offer a logical step up."[62]

With the demise of conspicuous consumption comes opportunities in the middle market. Casual dining is currently enjoying the fastest growth rate.[63] This format represents a compromise between the high prices of fine dining and the plainness of the midscale family restaurant; it represents something special without special prices. The theme restaurant business is enjoying considerable success.

One potential growth area for all restaurants is the off-premises consumption of prepared foods, consisting of takeouts, drive-throughs, and delivery. In this expanding segment of the food business, sit-down restaurants, fast-food retailers, supermarkets, and convenience stores are all competing to provide good-quality food and the means of transporting that quality to the customer's intended destination.

Vendor Retailing

A vending operation is a sales process that involves an exchange process between the customer and a vending machine or between a customer and individual vendor. Both types of vending are directed at providing quick accessibility at and when the customer wishes to buy.

Stationary Vendors Vending machines are the principal example of **stationary vendors**, which are similar to convenience store retailing in that they usually serve the fill-in, emergency, and after- or off-hours needs of consumers. Products that vending machines dispense are small, branded, and standardized products of low-unit value. Candies, soft drinks, hot beverages, snacks, and cigarettes are the most popular vending machine items. Nonfood products frequently sold by vending machines include life insurance policies for air travel, postage stamps, newspapers, health and beauty aids, and some novelty items.

One of the most significant developments in the use of vending machines is in the field of entertainment. Jukeboxes, pinball machines, and electronic games have greatly expanded the sales potential of vending operations. "Now that nearly everyone is comfortable with automatic teller machines, many businesses and government agencies figure [North] Americans are ready to retrieve information and order products via computer kiosks."[64] Services such as job listings, reservations, directions, and a host of other information-based tasks are now being handled by computerized vending machines.[65]

Mobile Vendors **Mobile vendors** represent that vast army of travelling retailers that take their goods and services to the point of sale and consumption. The beer vendor at the ballpark, the hot dog vendor outside the office building, the newspaper vendor on the street corner, the jewellery kiosks in the shopping mall, the refreshment stand in the airport, and the flower stand along the road are all examples of the mobile vendor making a living by intercepting consumers in the right place at the right time. Mobile merchandising is becoming increasingly common as established retailers attempt to expand their businesses. Pizza Hut, KFC, and Dairy Queen are banking on mobile units to increase their sales and market exposure over the next decade.

Direct Selling

Direct selling is direct-to-customer marketing through personal explanation and demonstration of products and services. This person-to-person contact can be accomplished through face-to-face selling at the customer's home or over the telephone.

In-Home Retailing **In-home retailing** (for example, door-to-door) is the direct-selling approach of making personal contacts and sales in the consumer's home. This form of retailing offers the consumer the ultimate in place convenience and, if the salesperson makes an appointment, an equal amount of time convenience. In-home retailing is a highly personalized form of service that lets customers try the product in a home setting before buying. It saves the consumer the time and effort of going to the store, searching for needed merchandise, and waiting in checkout lines.

In-home retailing also offers the seller certain advantages, including (1) no direct competition because the seller presents its products in "isolation" in the home, where consumers cannot make direct comparisons with similar products; (2) avoidance of uncontrollable intermediaries; and (3) elimination of investments in stores and other facilities, because sales representatives are compensated on a commission basis and pay their own expenses.

The in-home method of retailing exists in three principal forms: the cold canvass, the established territory or route, and the party plan. The *cold-canvass method* involves soliciting sales door to door without either advanced selection of homes or prior notice to potential consumers of an intended sales call. Vacuum cleaners, magazines, and books are some of the more common products sold by the cold-canvass method.

The *established territory method* assigns salespeople to prescribed geographic areas, in which they must make their door-to-door sales and delivery calls at regular, predetermined time intervals. The best-known user of the established territory method is the cosmetics retailer Avon. Recently, Avon has extended its product lines to include apparel items on the belief that it can sell clothes by offering customers both the convenience and low price of catalogue shopping and the attention of a personal shopper.[66]

The *party plan method* of at-home retailing requires a salesperson to make sales presentations in the home of a host or hostess who has invited potential customers to a "party." Usually, the party plan includes various games and other entertainment activities in which participants receive small, inexpensive gifts. Closing the sale occurs when the salesperson takes orders from the people attending the party. As a reward for holding the party, the host or hostess receives either cash or gifts from the salesperson. Tupperware makes extensive use of the party method in selling its plastic containers.

Telephone Retailing In recent years, telephone retailing, or **telemarketing**—the selling of goods and services through telephone contact—has helped some retailers increase service satisfaction by providing greater customer convenience. For customers who want to avoid traffic congestion and parking problems, telephone shopping is a desirable alternative. In Canada, it is estimated that 100 000 companies use telemarketing to generate an estimated $3.1 billion in sales.[67]

Telemarketing operations assume one of two forms: inbound or outbound. *Inbound telemarketing* involves the retailer motivating the customer to call the retailer. This form of telemarketing usually relies on a toll-free 800 number. "Its main applications are taking orders, receiving requests for literature, and servicing customers. Order processing and customer service frequently involve cross-selling [of complementary product lines] or upgrading initial sales [to better quality, more quantity, and higher prices]."[68] Also experiencing increased traffic are 900 numbers, which require the caller to pay for the call. Political polls, socialization, sports information, and charitable causes are some examples of services that are sold on 900 numbers by charging the fee to the caller's telephone bill.

Outbound telemarketing involves the retailer calling the customer. A fast and efficient sales method, telephone retailing can be used to presell (initial call to create awareness and arouse interest), sell (second call to gain trial and confirm sale), and postsell (follow-up call to check on customer satisfaction with the sale).[69] According to Telecom Canada, the primary reasons companies establish telemarketing programs are customer service, increased sales, order efficiency, and decreased costs.[70]

Multilevel Marketing **Multilevel marketing** is a direct-selling format in which a hierarchical network of distributors is created to sell and distribute a wide variety of goods and services. This retailing approach is distinguished by the fact that each distributor in the network is not only seeking to make retail sales of goods and services to final customers but is also looking for distributors to join his or her distribution network.[71] By recruiting and training new distributors, the recruitor becomes a master distributor who either earns sales commissions and bonuses on the retail sales of all distributors within the network or buys goods and services from the parent company and resells them to each distributor in the network.[72]

The pyramidal character of the multilevel marketing approach is shown in Figure 2–19. As illustrated, if one individual recruits two distributors, who in turn recruit two distributors, and this recruiting process continues through four levels, the original (or master) distributor would have thirty members from which to earn commissions or to which profitable sales can be made. The harder each member of the network recruits, the deeper and wider the sales pyramid becomes. For those who get in early and develop and maintain an extensive network of distributors, the rewards can be substantial; for those who enter the network later and at lower levels, the rewards are often limited.

Past abuses by some firms employing illegal "pyramid marketing schemes" have created problems for this method of direct selling. Undue sales pressure, lack of full disclosure of rights and responsibilities, misleading sales presentations, questionable product quality, slow order fulfillment, illegal pricing practices, and unfair commission structures all created a poor image and an unsettling legal environment for pyramid-style selling. Aggressive government action in the 1980s against illegal operations and the establishment of guidelines by direct-marketing trade organizations have created a favourable atmosphere for this unique marketing effort.

Figure 2–19

Four-level multilevel marketing organization

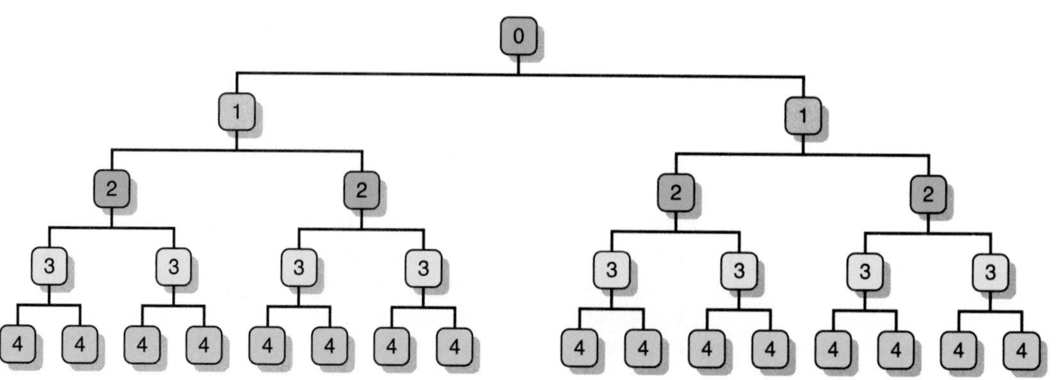

Amway, a manufacturer and distributor of a vast array of goods and services, is the second largest door-to-door sales operation in the world. Although the lion's share of money earned by Amway distributors is pocketed by 2 percent of the sales force (those at the top of the network), "Amway goes a crucial step beyond mere money. It offers its recruits membership in a community of like-minded people—entrepreneurial, motivated, upwardly mobile people who believe in their country, in God, and their family."[73] Forever Living Products International sells a wide range of products that contain extract of aloe. In this multilevel marketing company, a new salesperson "keeps 48% of the $14.95 retail price of an aloe gel jug. The manager who recruited her gets a bonus of 13% of the retail price from the company. The manager's percentage shrinks as the salesperson sells more cases, however, the salesperson and manager also get bonuses based on sales from any new recruits brought in by the salesperson."[74] The average Amway distributor in North America will net around $780 a year in bonuses and markups from selling Amway products.[75]

Retail Formats That Utilize Direct Marketing as Their Distinctive Competitive Strategy

Direct marketing involves retailers that do not use conventional store facilities as part of their standard mode of operation.[76] As defined by *Direct Marketing Magazine*, **direct marketing** is an interactive system (between seller and buyer) of marketing that uses one or more advertising media (for customer exposure) to effect a measurable response (an inquiry) and/or transaction (an order). The major retail users of direct marketing in Canada are magazines, book and record clubs, oil companies, and department stores.[77]

As shown in Figure 2–20, direct-marketing retailers employ a marketing practice called **database marketing**, which uses a computerized database (a list of customers together with interrelated data capable of meeting the marketing information needs of the retailer) to design direct-marketing programs to individual target markets. The basic operating structure is very direct; the retailer uses a database to identify target markets and to develop tailored merchandising offers that are communicated to the consumer through such nonpersonal media as television, radio, newspapers, magazines, or direct mail. Consumer responses (inquiries, orders) are typically transmitted back to the retailer via the mail, telephone, or cable (see Figure 2–20).[78]

In some cases, direct-marketing activities are designed to solicit a store visit by the consumer. The major distinctive competitive strategy of the direct-marketing retailer is to take the "store" (for example, catalogue) to the customer rather than wait for the customer to come to the retailer (that is, store). Figure 2–20 identifies the principal types of retail formats using a direct-marketing approach: direct-mail, mail-order, and direct-response retailers. What distinguishes one direct-marketing format from another is the type of communication medium used by the retailer and the type of response mechanism available to the consumer.

Direct mail utilizes only postal services to communicate the offer to the consumer, who in turn responds by mail or telephone. The commercial message (the offer) is most often presented in the form of a letter, brochure, or catalogue. **Mail order** communicates its offer of goods and services through television, radio, newspaper, and magazine advertisements, but orders are fulfilled by mail or telephone. Like mail order, **direct response** uses both broadcast and print media to communicate with the consumer; however, they differ in that consumers may use additional response mechanisms (cable) to place orders or make inquiries. Figure 2–21 charts in detail the particular forms that comprise these three formats.

Figure 2–20

A profile of direct-marketing operations

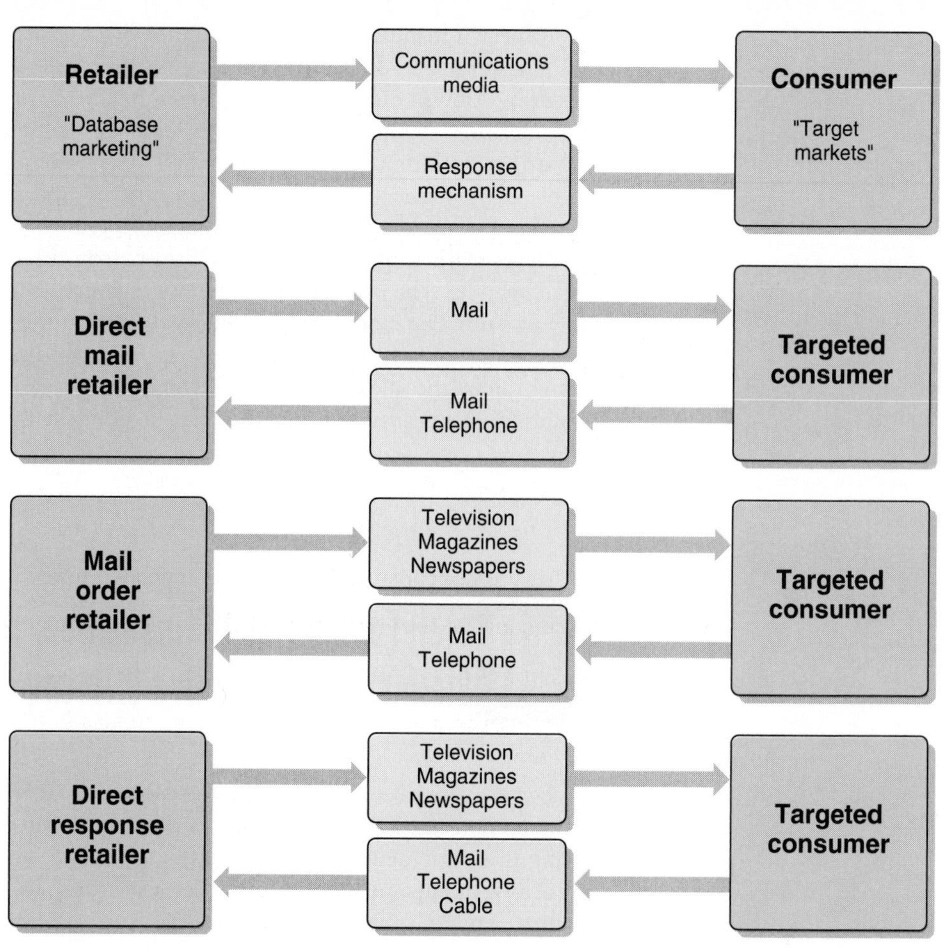

Figure 2–21

Retail formats based on direct marketing

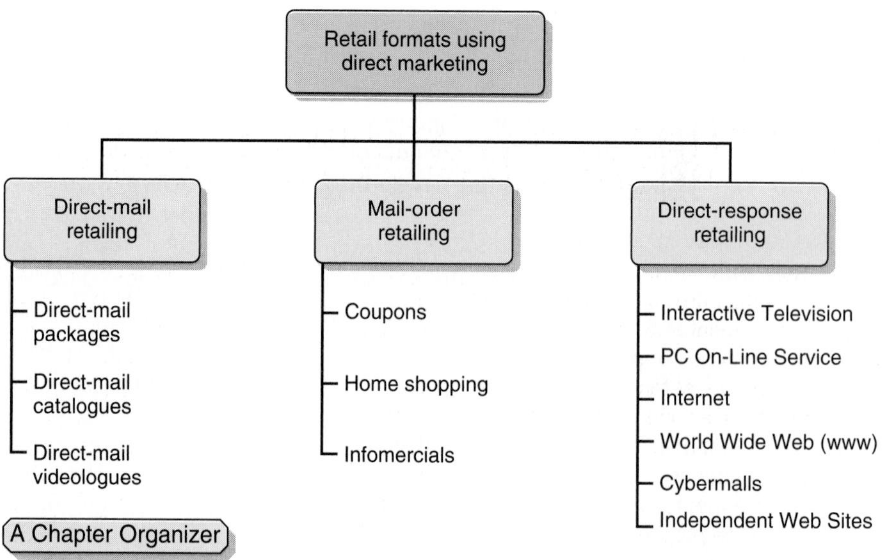

Direct-Mail Retailing

Direct-mail operations differ tremendously in the variety and assortment of merchandise lines they offer the customer. The three forms of direct-mail retailing are packages, catalogues, and videologues.

Direct-Mail Packages The basic direct-mail package consists of four components: (1) the outer envelope, (2) the letter, (3) the brochure, and (4) the order form. Each of these components has an important role to play in obtaining the customer's patronage.[79]

First impressions are important in personal relationships; they are even more important in the success of a direct-mail sales effort. The first thing that the customer sees is the outer envelope. If the customer is to be exposed to the rest of the package, the outer envelope must do its job: which is to invite the customer to open the package. That invitation is accomplished using several techniques:

- Place a selling proposition on the envelope.
- Note that the package's contents were requested.
- Print teaser copy on the envelope to create interest.
- Personalize the envelope with the customer's name.
- Add a personal message.
- Entice the customer by using a peek-in window or show-through envelope that reveals part of the offer inside.
- Use official- or professional-looking envelopes to resemble first-class mail and valuable contents.[80]

The letter presents the selling proposition to the customer, which typically includes a description of the product and its benefits, the terms and conditions of sale, the reasons and rationale for accepting the retailer's proposition, and the services and extras that support the retailer's offer. Although the letter's message (what to say) is crucial to the acceptance of the offer, the tone of the letter (how to say it) is equally important. Experts generally believe that a more personal tone is more likely to produce favourable results. Like

Retail Strategies and Tactics

Sears: No More Big Books but Lots of Little Books

Recognizing that it was impossible to sell all things to all people through the mail, Sears discontinued its 100-year-old general merchandise catalogue in 1993. A year and a half later, Sears re-entered the catalogue business with a lineup of thinner niche catalogues targeted to specific consumer groups. By setting up joint ventures and alliances through licensing agreements with several specialty catalogue companies (Hanover Direct), Sears and its partners now mail over 150 million catalogues. Partnering arrangements call for Sears to lend its powerful name to each catalogue and to provide partner access to its extensive database of 24 million credit card customers. In turn, alliance partners develop and produce specialty merchandise catalogues, handle catalogue mailings, fulfill orders, and manage customer follow-ups. Workwear, power and hand tools, plus sizes, health care, and home furnishings are a few of the market niches being targeted by Sears and its partners. This strategy enables Sears to exploit its strengths in database marketing and to pursue a low-cost, low-risk opportunity to take advantage of the growing catalogue business. Sears' catalogue operations employ about 20 people, down from 19 000 employees. Sears and its partners expect to mail 250 million catalogues by the year 2000.

Adapted from Laura Loro, "Hanover Fortifies Its Brand Portfolio," Advertising Age, November 20, 1995; 22; Jeanne Whalen, "Less Is More for Neiman Marcus Catalogs," Advertising Age, November 11, 1995, 52; Julie Tilsner, "Strategies for the New Mail Order," Business Week, December 19, 1994, 82–83; Howard Rudnitsky, "Growing Pains," Forbes, 58; and Jason Hudson, "Nonstore Retailing: Paper Remains King," Chain Store Age, *August 1995, 27A.*

any good sales presentation, the letter should open with a strong message (a compelling patronage motive for the customer) and close by asking for the sale.

In print advertising terms, if one views the outer envelope as the headline and the letter as the copy, then the brochure carries the direct-mail retailer's logo and provides the illustrations that build comprehension of the offer and provides the distinctive "signature" of the retailer. Through art, drawings, and photos, the brochure supports and enhances the offer made in the letter. These interesting and attention-getting brochures often emphasize the innovative nature of the product, the quality of the merchandise, the quickness of the service, and/or the good value of the offer.

"Asking for the sale" is the cornerstone of any sales proposition—in this case, getting the customer to fill out and mail or telephone in the order. The order form should be simple and quick to fill out and readdressed with the postage prepaid. Response rates indicate customer acceptance and determine customer satisfaction at a profit.

Direct-Mail Catalogues **Catalogue** operations use specially prepared catalogues that present the retailer's merchandise with words and pictures. Basic product assortment (sizes, colours, materials, styles, models, and so on) and pricing information are included along with directions stating how to use the order blanks provided. Modern catalogue operations allow the customer to place orders by mail or telephone. In addition, catalogue operations offer a variety of delivery arrangements such as mail, parcel post, or express service. Though plagued by rising paper and postage cost, the catalogue is expected to continue as a growth industry due to the time-stressed nature of the two-earner family.[81] Figure 2–22 shows the extent of the catalogue industry in Canada.

Direct-Mail Videologues **Videologues**, the next wave of catalogue shopping, are shop-at-home videotapes. With VCRs in 85 percent of homes, the opportunities for direct selling through videologues are extensive.[82] Customers either receive the video for free by mail or pay a fee that is credited toward any purchase. A third distribution alternative is to make the videologues available free to customers through video stores; however, the video

Figure 2–22

The catalogue industry in Canada

Source: 1995 Catalogue Age survey, conducted by Catalogue Age of Stamford, CT, as reported in James Polluck, "Lists of Opportunity," Marketing, *May 26, 1995, 14–15.*

	1992	1993	1994
Number of catalogues	550	570	620
Total sales	$1.98 billion	$1.88 billion	$1.84 billion
Nature of catalogue:			
Consumer	64%	62%	52%
Business-to-business	8%	28%	17%
Combined (consumer/business)	28%	17%	31%
Catalogue sales by dollar volume:			
Less than $1 million	66%	42%	66%
$1 million to $2.9 million	15%	14%	13%
Annual circulation:			
Less than 100 000	56%	56%	81%
100 000 to 250 000	17%	8%	4%
Frequency per year:			
Once	70%	52%	51%
Twice	10%	17%	21%
3 or more times	12%	32%	27%

must be returned to the video store. Videologues can be produced to reflect product usage, consumers' lifestyles, or any other merchandising theme. Their twofold sight and sound appeal provides a competitive edge over the sight-oriented printed catalogue. One of the most recent developments in the catalogue industry is the use of CD-ROM; L.L. Bean, and Lands' End are among the leading catalogue retailers offering goods and services on CD-ROM catalogues.[83]

Mail-Order Retailing

Direct marketers make extensive use of both print media (newspapers and magazines) and broadcast media (television and radio) in offering the consuming public a wide range of goods and services. Consumers are asked to respond to the offer by mail or telephone. To encourage immediate response, mail-order retailers typically offer some type of deal (for example, reduced price, free merchandise, extended terms) if the consumer responds within a defined time. Dell Computer and Gateway 2000 have become heavyweights in the retail computer industry by appealing to the best PC customers—those who are experienced business clients and knowledgeable consumers looking for the most cutting-edge and expensive models.[84] There are a vast number of mail-order formats; this discussion features one print format (coupons) and two broadcast formats (home shopping and infomercials).

Coupons The coupon form of mail-order retailing involves using magazine and newspaper advertisements to attract customers and mail-in coupons designed to close the sale. Advertisements featuring special merchandise or offering unique services together with response coupons are placed in magazines and newspapers that appeal to specific market segments. By tailoring the coupon offer to the needs and behaviours of carefully chosen consumer groups, this mail-order format can greatly increase the chance of a positive response.

Home Shopping Home shopping combines two of North America's favourite pastimes: watching television and going shopping. A value-oriented retailing operation, home shopping is a business format in which

1. merchandise items are displayed, described, and demonstrated on television;
2. customers order the merchandise by calling a toll-free number;
3. customers pay for the order by credit cards, cash on delivery, or cheque;
4. the retailer (home shopping network) delivers the merchandise by United Parcel Service (UPS) or some other parcel post company; and
5. the retailer typically offers money-back guarantees if merchandise is returned within thirty days.

The big two of the home shopping format are QVC (Quality, Value, Convenience) Network and the Home Shopping Network.[85] QVC Network considers itself the class act; its practice employs a slower, softer sell of items that include national brands such as Craftsman tools and Sony electronics. The Home Shopping Network utilizes a more aggressive, hard-sell format. Both networks are using celebrity endorsements to boost sales—QVC has Joan Rivers and Angie Dickinson selling costume jewellery, and Ivana Trump, Connie Stevens, and Suzanne Somers typify the HSN celebrity hawkers.[86] MTV Network has launched "The Goods," a series of half-hour and hour programs which target its 18- to 49-year-old audience of its three networks: MTV (Music Television), VH1, and Nickelodeon's Nick-at-Nite.[87]

Infomercials **Infomercials** are thirty-minute ads that mix information and entertainment with sales presentations. "The format is standard: A celebrity or upbeat host pushing a product, then three breaks to call attention to the toll-free number to buy the product—all neatly wrapped up in a 30-minute package."[88] The infomercial format is a focused selling effort that has found success in merchandising weight-loss products and services, money-making plans, kitchen utensils and gadgets, skin care products, stop-smoking offers, and personal and professional development programs.[89] HealthRider exercise equipment, Psychic Friends Network, Jake's Hip & Thigh Machine, Murad Skin Care, and Curashine Car Polish are some of the top-grossing infomercials.[90] "Infomercials offer marketers two things a regular commercial can't: a way to stand out from the cacophony of short spots, and a way to measure results by the number of viewers who call the 800 number usually featured."[91] The infomercial format is being tested by such store retailers as Sears. Craftsman Rob Grip and Kenmore Supreme air cleaner are two products that Sears has successfully sold using infomercials.[92]

Direct-Response Retailing

Electronic shopping—via interactive television or personal computer—is still in the early stages of growth and not likely to reach critical mass until sometime after the turn of the century. "Right now, technology is advancing faster than people's ability to absorb it, so it is difficult to gauge the retailer's and the consumer's learning curves and levels of acceptance."[93] A "battle of the boxes" is shaping up in which interactive television and the PC are fighting for the consumer's time and money. "As new technology brings the capabilities of television and personal computers closer together, by adding computing power to TVs and sound and video via networks to PCs, the two devices will compete more directly for the time and money of [North] American consumers."[94] Convenience, safety, customization, and efficiency are four customer patronage factors that will continue to drive the development of electronic retailing.

Interactive Television **Interactive television** is an electronic retailing format in which merchandise is displayed on a television screen and can be ordered by pressing keys on a special set-top box or on a touch-tone telephone that is connected directly to the retailer. A set-top box is a navigation device that helps viewers to sort through hundreds of channels to find a particular program. It also sends commands or orders back down the cable and is vital to the effectiveness of interactive television.[95] Both cable and telephone companies are developing new systems for enabling customers to interact with their television and control its product/service offerings.[96] Some describe it as the next technological revolution:

> It could transform the humble television set into a powerful new medium, through which viewers sitting at home could order videos, pick their own camera angles for TV sports, play games with other viewers, buy and sell products—and train the set to pick only the fare they want and air it when they feel like watching.[97]

Many supporters of interactive television believe that its ultimate attraction as a retailing format may lie in its heritage as an entertainment vehicle. By cross-marketing entertainment services and shopping, interactive television might be able to gain an advantage over computer-based electronic retailing.

PC On-Line Services **PC on-line services** are interactive electronic systems in which data and graphics are transmitted from a computer network over telephone or cable lines and displayed on a subscriber's computer-terminal screen. These subscription services offer a shopping experience whereby the customer selects from a series of choices, called menus, that are displayed on the screen. For example, a shopper narrows down the choice by selecting from a menu of product lines and product items (brands, styles, sizes, colours, prices, and so on). In this form of electronic shopping, "browsing" will take on a whole new meaning. "Consumers may use their computers to comparison shop among various retail outlets for selection, price, and availability."[98] Order placement and payment are handled by computer or telephone transactions.

In addition to at-home shopping, on-line providers offer subscribers a wide selection of services including news, weather, sports, financial, and consumer information; at-home

Retail Strategies and Tactics

Cyber Shopping: Hot Trend or a Lot of Hype?

Many of us are old enough to remember the days of milkmen, bread trucks, and, yes, even home delivery of groceries. Now, as the song goes, everything old is new again, and home shopping is all the rage—or is it? While many grocers have continued to offer telephone shopping and home delivery over the years, new distribution channels are emerging that could change the face of grocery retailing forever. A groundswell of applications driven by the so-called "new media"—kiosks, interactive television, and, most significantly, the ubiquitous Internet—threatens to engulf the unwary retailer.

But despite the proliferation of new distribution channels, the jury remains out on the viability of electronic commerce. Sure, it's fun and even informative to surf the "Net," but is anyone actually using the medium to buy goods and services? According to a recent survey by A.C. Nielsen Canada and Nordicity Group Ltd., more than 487 000 Internet users have made at least one purchase on-line; more than half of those electronic consumers said they would definitely shop on the Internet again, citing convenience as the main reason for cyber shopping. And while this figure represents only a tiny percentage of the total population in Canada, the survey also reveals that approximately 20% of Canadians have already launched themselves into cyberspace, making it "one of the fastest growing communications and marketing mediums," according to a press release from Nielsen.

Source: Sally Praskey, Canadian Grocer, *April 1996, 11–13.*

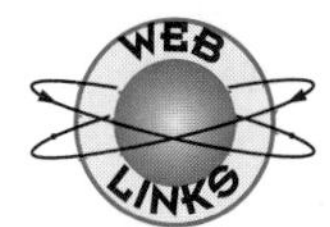

Compuserve
www.compuserve.com

America Online
www.aol.com

banking, reservations, and travel information; electronic encyclopedias and magazines, videocoupons and educational/instructional games; directories; real estate and employment listings; home energy management; security, medical, and fire monitoring; and electronic mail/messaging.[99]

The three leading PC on-line services are CompuServe, America Online, and Prodigy. Although each of these services has substantially increased the total number of subscribers, only a small percentage of those who are on-line shop on-line. Slick new graphics, easier navigation systems, a wide range of services, standardized software, and a more user-friendly gateway to the Internet are some of the changes that on-line providers are making to attract new customers and keep existing subscribers.[100] CompuServe's Electronic Mall has over 170 cataloguers, direct marketers, and consumer products companies on-line with its subscribers.[101]

Internet By using the Internet, the whole world becomes one marketplace. The **Internet** is an international computer-based electronic channel through which millions of people communicate, perform research, find entertainment, and buy and sell products and services. "Internet users may send individual e-mail, contribute e-mail to discussion groups, participate in real-time conversations with other Internet users, transfer data files to and from one another, and take advantage of a host of other services."[102] What makes the Internet fundamentally different from commercial on-line services is the fact that it is owned by no one. When a network (currently there are more than 49 000 networks worldwide that make up the Internet) joins the Internet, it retains control and ownership over itself.[103] "The Internet works because all the participating networks agree on certain communications protocols regarding how packets are sent and received, how e-mail is addressed, and so on."[104]

The Internet is composed of three major parts or subsets. The **Usenet Newsgroup** is the Internet's bulletin boards, where messages are posted for any other interested party. **E-mail** is the electronic mail capability of the Internet, which allows direct communications between two or more parties. The final Internet subset is the World Wide Web; because of its importance to retailers it is discussed independently of the Internet.

World Wide Web The **World Wide Web** (WWW) is a vast repository of documents that are linked together. Its nonlinear design enables users or "surfers" to jump from topic

Figure 2–23

Clicking your way around the Web

The World Wide Web is a software scheme that's making the Internet easy to use. Just click with a mouse on graphical buttons and you can browse through thousands of multimedia documents, or Web "pages," stored all over the world. The name Web reflects the fact that each document is linked invisibly to related documents in other computers. Using a Web browser program such as Netscape in your PC, here's how you might access information about the latest products from the Bata organization, one of Canada's most successful companies.

1. Tap into the Bata Company by clicking on Net Search in the Netscape browser. (The Bata home page will appear as shown opposite.)
2. Click on "History" to learn about the company.
3. Click on "World" to find where Bata's nearest factory is.
4. Click on "Brands" to identify Bata's brands and models of merchandise.
5. Click on "Sites" to find Bata's retail locations near you.

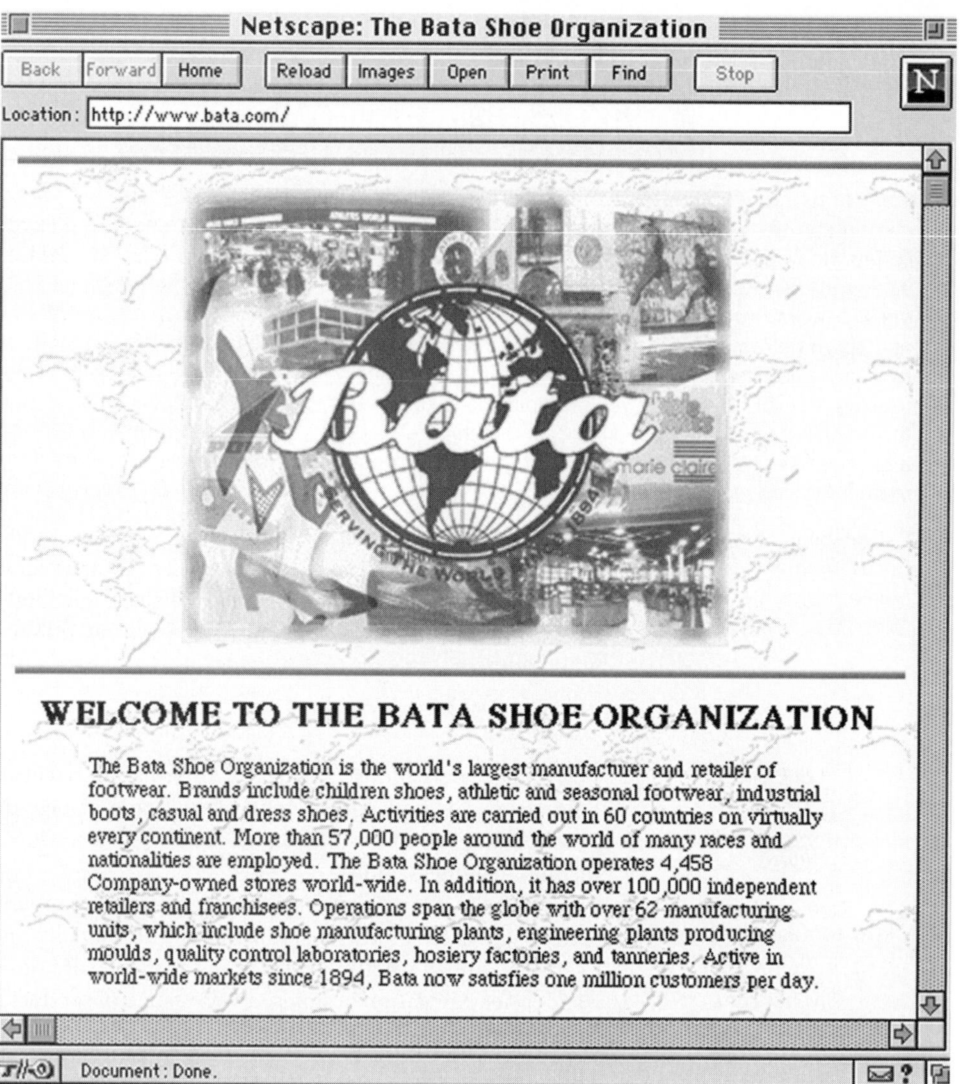

to topic and site to site. The Web is accessed by computer, which is connected to the Internet by a modem and a special "browsers" software package (for example, Netscape, Mosaic).[105] The major on-line services are also providing access to the Web. Figure 2–23 provides an illustration of how one can browse the World Wide Web.

The World Wide Web is unique in that it permits point-and-click access to information worldwide.

> The Web also contains audio and even video files that can be downloaded with a simple point and click of the mouse. Because of these robust multi-media capabilities, many companies and individuals have found that the World Wide Web is an excellent place to begin selling goods and services. Internet merchants can display products, give and collect detailed information, show product demonstrations and take payments.[106]

Convenience is a big factor in attracting customers. "In a physical store, customers must wander around trying to find items and expert advice is often at the end of a long line—if it can be had at all. Several on-line stores offer 'search engines'—or software built into the Web pages—that allow customers to search the stores electronic warehouse. The next step is offering 'intelligent agents'—essential electronic to-do lists—that search several stores so that customers can compare selections and prices without having to visit each site themselves."[107] Additional software enables the Web shopper to shop in three-dimensional space, which starts to capture the real feel of a store.[108] Opinions vary as to the potential impact of the Web on the retailing industry. One expert believes that nonstore retailing will account for 55 percent of total retail sales by 2010. Others feel that nonstore retailing formats will account for little more than its current 15 percent of total sales. In either case, the Internet is "the place to be today if you want to learn how to do business in the 500-channel future. The Internet is where [retailers] are going to learn what it takes to gain people's attention in a crowded, confused, and conflicting electronic environment."[109] The place to be on the Internet if you are a retailer may well be a "cybermall."

Cybermalls **Cybermalls** are individual networks on the Web that are created by local service providers with enough marketing and technical know-how to establish an electronic buying and selling environment. Cybermalls on the Web can take on different configurations; they can be large or small, broad or specialized, national or international. Cybermalls are international marketplaces: a Canadian shopper can access a cybermall in Paris or Sydney as easily and quickly as a electronic mall in Toronto or Vancouver. Finding a particular cybermall can be confusing; however, most cybermalls can be found by accessing a directory known as The Hall of Malls. Marketplace MCI (general merchandise), Internet Shopping Network (general merchandise), Surfin' UTC (information centre), Cybershop (home furnishings), and Virtual Vineyard (California wines) are a few select examples of cybermalls that are currently in operation.[110]

Independent Web Sites **Independent Web sites** are do-it-yourself shopping addresses created by retailers who do not want to be part of any cybermall. These individually controlled and managed Web sites enable the retailer to create a shopping environment that is not constrained by the look and feel of a cybermall. The principle limitation of this approach to Internet marketing is access—creating awareness among Web surfers and shoppers of the site's address and its shopping opportunities. Wal-Mart Stores is an example of a traditional store-based retailer who has opened shop on the World Wide Web.[111] Recently the former owner of Mark's Work Wearhouse, a successful workwear chain in western Canada, established an Internet shopping company called Mark's Market.[112] A retailer does not have to be large to establish a shop on the Web. Several small and specialized booksellers are experimenting with doing business electronically by setting up a **home page** on the Internet. "A home page is to an on-line business what a sign is to a storefront business."[113]

Retail Formats That Utilize Core Services as Their Distinctive Competitive Strategy

As discussed in Chapter 1, the sale of services represents the core business for many service retailers. Figure 2–24 illustrates the four major categories of service retailers and identifies the major types of formats under each category. Because Chapter 17, "Service Retailing," is devoted to describing the merchandising and operating nature of this special type of retail business, this discussion is limited to the descriptions in Figure 2–24.

Figure 2–24

Retail formats based on core services

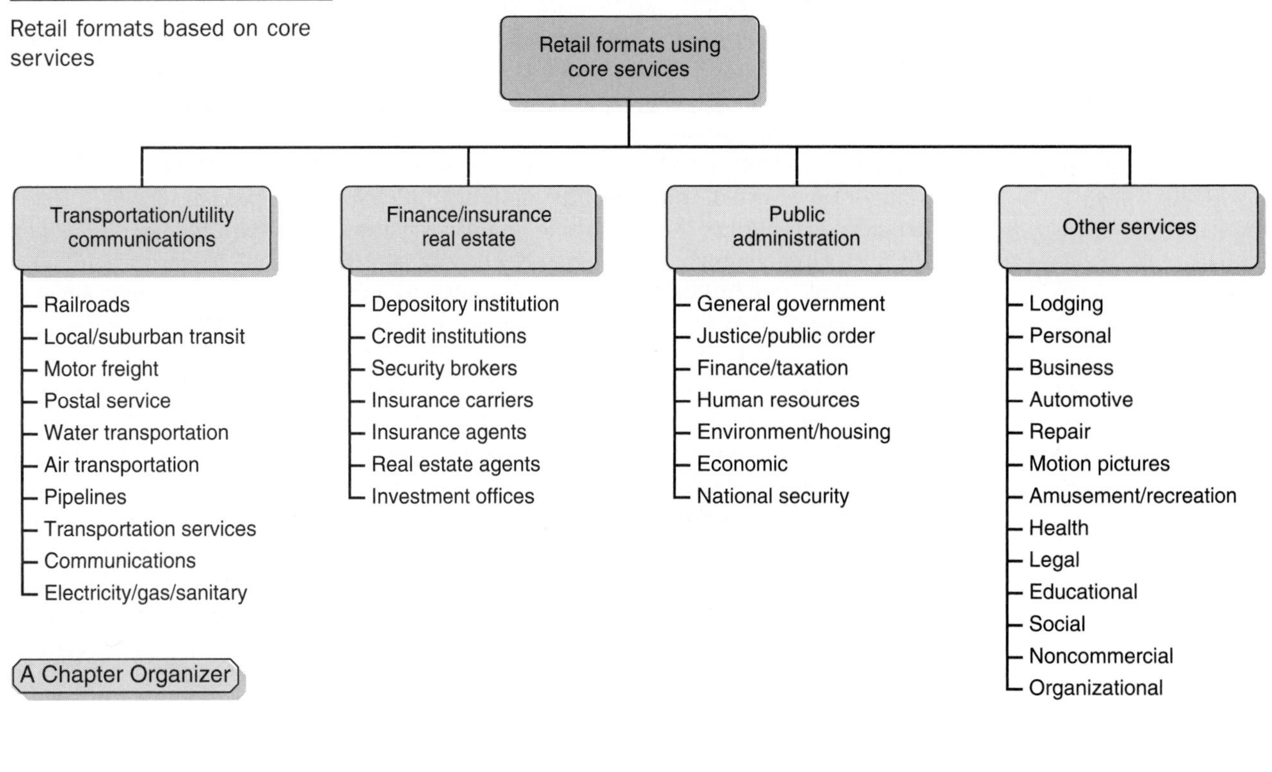

Summary

Retailers compete with one another by using different retail formats to gain advantages in order to better serve target markets. The retailer must operate in a very complex competitive environment. Retail competition can take one of several forms: intratype, intertype, vertical, and systems. Retailers also face different levels of competition as defined by the number, size, and quality of competitors.

The diversity and complexity of business formats found within the retailing industry preclude any one classification system that clearly differentiates each type of retailer. However, retail formats can be characterized by their distinctive competitive strategy; six such strategies are described in this chapter to classify the merchandising and operating formats of contemporary retailers. The various types of retailing institutions are distinguishable on the basis of merchandise selection, merchandise pricing, operational structure, time/place convenience, direct marketing, and core services. Depending on the variety of the retailer's merchandise selection, retailers are classified as either specialty store retailers (classification or category retailers) or department stores (full-line or limited-line department store operations). Retail operations that use merchandise pricing strategies to distinguish themselves include discount retailing (variety stores and full-line discounters), superstore retailing (supercentres and hypermarkets), and off-price retailing (factory outlets, store outlets, independent off-price outlets, closeout stores, and one-price retailers).

Gaining an operational advantage in serving consumer markets is the strategic focus of chain stores (large and small). Some retailers try to formalize their operating relationships with suppliers and other retailers by entering a contractual arrangement (retailer-sponsored cooperative group, wholesaler-sponsored voluntary chain, franchising organization, and leased department). Other retailers tend to stress a certain method of operation (warehouse showrooms, catalogue showrooms, home centres, and warehouse clubs). Having the right product in the right place at the right time is the strategic differentiation of the convenience retailer.

Retail formats that stress time/place convenience include food retailers (supermarkets, convenience stores, and prepared-food retailers), vendor retailing (both stationary and mobile), and direct-selling operations (in-home retailing, telephone retailing, and multilevel marketing). Retailers that use the direct-marketing format hope to gain a competitive advantage by serving the consumer directly through the three related retailing methods: direct mail (packages, catalogues, and videologues), mail order (coupons, home shopping, and infomercials), and direct response (interactive television, on-line service providers, and the Internet).

Student Summary Guide

Key Terms and Concepts

business format franchise *p. 53*
catalogues *p. 68*
catalogue showroom *p. 56*
category killers *p. 43*
category retailers *p. 43*
chain store *p. 51*
classification retailers *p. 42*
closeout store *p. 50*
competitive advantage *p. 37*
convenience store *p. 61*
cybermalls *p. 73*
database marketing *p. 65*
department store *p. 45*
direct mail *p. 65*
direct marketing *p. 65*
direct response *p. 65*
direct selling *p. 63*
discount store *p. 48*
e-mail *p. 71*
factory outlets *p. 49*
fast-food retailers *p. 61*
franchising *p. 52*
full-line department store *p. 45*
full-line discount store *p. 48*
home centre *p. 57*
home page *p. 73*
hypermarkets *p. 49*
in-home retailing *p. 63*
in-store vendor shop *p. 56*
independent off-price outlet *p. 50*
independent Web site *p. 73*
infomercials *p. 69*
interactive television *p. 70*
Internet *p. 71*
intertype competition *p. 38*
intratype competition *p. 38*
limited-line department stores *p. 45*
leased department *p. 55*
mail order *p. 65*
mini-department retailers *p. 43*
mobile vendors *p. 63*
multilevel marketing *p. 64*
niche specialist *p. 43*
off-price retailer *p. 49*
one-price retailer *p. 50*
PC on-line services *p. 70*
product assortment *p. 41*
product mix *p. 41*
product variety *p. 41*
retail format *p. 37*
retail strategy *p. 37*
retailer-sponsored cooperative group *p. 52*
sit-down restaurants *p. 62*
specialty store *p. 43*
specialty store retailer *p. 41*
stationary vendors *p. 62*
store outlet *p. 49*
supercentre *p. 49*
supermarket *p. 60*
superspecialist *p. 42*
superstore retailers *p. 49*
systems competition *p. 38*
target market *p. 38*
telemarketing *p. 63*
trade-name franchise *p. 53*
Usenet Newsgroup *p. 71*
variety store *p. 48*
vertical competition *p. 38*
videologues *p. 68*
warehouse clubs *p. 57*
warehouse showroom *p. 56*
wholesaler-sponsored voluntary chain *p. 52*
World Wide Web *p. 71*

Review Questions

1. What is a retail strategy? Diagram and describe its components.
2. Identify the four forms of retail competition. Illustrate and describe each form of competition and provide two nontext examples of each type.
3. What distinguishes specialty store retailing from other forms of retailing? Describe the key merchandising strategies employed by the various specialty retailers.
4. Develop a profile of the operational and merchandising strategies of department stores.
5. Compare and contrast the merchandising tactics of the full-line discounter and the off-price retailer. How are they alike and how do they differ?
6. Profile the two types of superstore retailers.
7. What three criteria must a retail organization meet in order to be classified as a retail chain?
8. What is contractual retailing? Describe the four types of contractual retailers.
9. Describe the similarities and differences of the various types of warehouse retailers.
10. Food retailers are fighting for North America's $500 billion budget. Describe the competitive strategies now being used by food retailers to capture and hold market share.
11. What are the customer and retailer advantages and disadvantages of in-home shopping? Do the advantages and disadvantages vary with the form of in-home retailing?
12. Diagram a multilevel marketing organization. How does this type of organization differ from more traditional retail organizations?
13. What are the operational differences among direct mail, mail order, and direct response?

Review Exam

True or False

______ **1.** Intertype competition exists between two or more retailers using different types of business formats to sell the same type of merchandise.

______ **2.** Specialty store retailers typically stock a limited variety of product lines with a limited assortment or selection within each line.

______ **3.** To appeal to both middle- and upper-income consumers, many department stores use two or three pricing points for most merchandise lines.

______ **4.** A major reason that full-line discount stores sell brand-name merchandise at below-market prices is to enhance their discount image.

______ **5.** The hypermarket is a general merchandise warehouse retailer that stocks and sells food products, as well as a wide variety of hard and soft goods.

______ **6.** The World Wide Web is a network of telemarketers who use special telephone systems to market their goods and services.

Multiple Choice

______ **1.** The best description of the market strategy aims of a specialty retailer is to serve ______.
a. all consumers in one or a few markets
b. all consumers in many markets
c. some consumers in many markets
d. some consumers in one market
e. everyone all of the time

______ **2.** The advantages of a ______ store organization are that it allows functional (buying, selling) and merchandise (apparel, furniture, jewellery) specialization, while gaining the economies of scale associated with larger retailing operations.
a. franchised
b. contractual
c. warehouse
d. departmentalized
e. horizontal

______ **3.** A specialty retailer that sells hard and/or soft goods at discount prices significantly (20 to 60 percent) below regular retail prices is referred to as a(n) ______.
a. off-price retailer
b. conventional discounter
c. discount-department store
d. low-ball retailer
e. fashion mart

______ **4.** In recent years, supermarkets have added such nonfood lines as prescription drugs, small appliances, linens, and housewares to their traditional product mix. This process is referred to as ______.
a. trading up
b. opening the door
c. scrambling
d. hit-and-miss merchandising
e. trading out

______ **5.** The franchisor compensation method that involves imposing an operating fee on the franchisee's gross sales is called a(n) ______.
a. royalty
b. rental fee
c. management fee
d. initial franchise fee

______ **6.** The ______ approach to at-home retailing involves door-to-door sales and delivery calls at regular and predetermined time intervals.
a. cold-canvass
b. hot-pavement
c. party plan
d. back-door
e. established territory

Student Application Manual

Investigative Projects: Practice and Application

1. Identify three franchising opportunities by locating advertisements in the *Globe and Mail* or some other newspaper or magazine. Answer each ad and obtain the franchise prospectus and other information regarding the franchisor's offer. Compare and contrast the three opportunities. What are the strengths and weaknesses of each opportunity? Which one offers the best opportunity? Justify your choice.

2. To compete in today's dynamic retailing environment, specialty retailers in many product categories are considering upsizing their stores to "superstore" or "category killer" status. What are the advantages and disadvantages of upsizing? What market conditions would increase the likelihood of success? Describe any other conditions that would contribute to a successful upsizing of a specialty store.

3. The average Web user is 35 years old with an income of $69 000. More than 80 percent of Web users are male. Most are rather inexperienced and access the Web through one of the on-line services. What opportunities does this information suggest to a retailer who is considering the Web as a business address? What are the limitations? What are the marketing implications of this information?

Endnotes

1. Leonard L. Berry, "Stores With a Future," *Retailing Issues Letter* (copublished by the Center for Retailing Studies, Texas A&M University and Arthur Andersen, March 1995), 1.
2. Edith Weiner, "The Fast Approaching Future," *Retailing Issues Letter* (copublished by the Center for Retailing Studies, Texas A&M University and Arthur Andersen, July 1994), 1.
3. Mary Kuntz, "Reinventing The Store," *Business Week*, November 27, 1995, 86.
4. Elaine Pollack, "Raising the Bar: Keys to High-Performance Retailing," *Chain Store Age Executive*, January 1994, 2MH.
5. See Carolyn Thompson, "Only the Strongest Discount Retailers Survive," *Marketing News*, October 23, 1995, 7.
6. Michael Treacy and Fred Wiersema, "How Market Leaders Keep Their Edge," *Fortune*, February 6, 1995, 88.
7. See Sandra Block, "Goodyear Protects Its Dealers," *Akron Beacon Journal*, January 24, 1995, D8; Stuart Drown, "Goodyear Steps on the Gas," *Akron Beacon Journal*, January 29, 1995, C1; and Dana Milbank, "Consumer-Goods Makers, Growing Wary of Big Chains, Try to Forge Small Links." *The Wall Street Journal*, June 29, 1991, B1.
8. Stephen Baker and Keith L. Alexander, "Is General Nutrition Headed For Civil War?" *Business Week*, November 21, 1994, 58.
9. Susan Chandler, "Kids' Wear Is Not Child's Play," *Business Week*, June 19, 1995, 118.
10. See Susan Reda, "1995 NFR Gold Medal Award Winner, Charles Lazarus, Chairman of Toys R Us," *Stores*, January 1995, 131–144; Kate Fitzgerald, Competitors swarm powerful Toys R Us," *Advertising Age*, February 2, 27, 1995, 4; and Seth Lubove, "The Growing Gets Tough," *Forbes*, April 13, 1992, 68.
11. Alan Stewart, "Competition in Today's Retail Market," *Retail Exchange* (newsletter of the Institute of Retail Management, Brigham Young University, Fall 1995), 1.
12. Gordon Segal, "Crate & Barrel: Success Develops from a Unique Idea," *Retailers on Retailing, Lessons from the School of Experience* (Arthur Andersen & Co, SC, 1994), 85.
13. See J. Douglas Eldridge, "Hard Lines Specialty Stores: A Banner Year in 1994," *Chain Store Age*, August 1995, 31A–33A.
14. See D. Wesley Balderson, *Canadian Entrepreneurship and Small Business Management*, 3rd Edition, McGraw-Hill Ryerson Ltd., 1997, 314.
15. Leah Rickard, "Bath Stores Soaking It Up," *Advertising Age*, June 6, 1995, 1.
16. See "Growing Like Blockbusters, Video Update Expands by Acquisition," *Chain Store Age*, January 1996, 80–81. Also see Lore Groghan, "My Three Angels," *Financial World*, March 14, 1995, 32–33.
17. Dawn Walton, "It's Dog Eat Dog," *Globe and Mail*, July 21, 1997, B1.
18. Kuntz, "Reinventing the Store," 88.
19. Susan Chandler, "Gloomy Days Are Here Again," *Business Week*, January 8, 1996, 103.
20. Sandra J. Skrovan and Steven M. Robinson, "Department Stores: Reengineering a Mature Industry," *Chain Store Age*, August 1995, 25A.
21. "Rating the Stores," *Consumer Reports*, November 1994, 713.
22. Susan Chandler, "An Endangered Species Makes a Comeback," *Business Week*, November 27, 1995, 96.
23. Ian McGugan, "Eaton's on the Brink," *Canadian Business*, March, 1996, 46.
24. Teri Agins, "Big Stores Put Own Labels on Best Clothes," *The Wall Street Journal*, September 26, 1994, B1.
25. Sandra J. Skrovan and Tereska Buzek, "Discount Department Stores: Growing Fashion and Food," *Chain Store Age*, August 1995, 21A.
26. See Heikki Rinne and William R. Swinyard, "Segmenting the Discount Store Market: The Domination of the 'Difficult Discounter Core,' " *The International Review of Retail, Distribution, and Consumer Research*, April 1995, 123, 146.

27. Leah Rickard, "Supercenters Entice Shoppers," *Marketing News*, March 20, 1995, 10.

28. Zina Moukheiber, "The Great Wal-Mart Massacre, Part II," *Forbes*, January 22, 1996, 44.

29. Chad Rubel, "Discount Stores Battle Each Other with Supercenters," *Marketing News*, January 16, 1995, 1.

30. "Supercenters Providing Super Opportunity," *Chain Store Age*, August 1995, 4B.

31. Laurie M. Grossman, "Hypermarkets: A Sure-Fire Hit Bombs," *The Wall Street Journal*, June 25, 1992, B1.

32. Howard Rudnitsky, "The King of Off-Price," *Forbes*, January 31, 1994, 54.

33. Nancy Rotenier, "Ambience it Ain't," *Forbes*, August 15, 1994, 110.

34. See Michael Selz, "Consolidated Stores Discovers Bigger Isn't Always Better," *The Wall Street Journal*, January 18, 1990, B2.

35. William P. Barrett, "Pic 'N' Run," *Forbes*, October 12, 1992, 48.

36. Christina Duff, " 'Single-Price Stores' Formula for Success: Cheap Merchandise and a Lot of Clutter," *The Wall Street Journal*, June 30, 1992, B1.

37. See Gretchen Morgenson, "Shades of Frank W. Woolworth," *Forbes*, December 9, 1991, 41–43.

38. Sharon Edelson, "Stores Developing the Big Brands," *Womens Wear Daily*, January 17, 1996, 18.

39. John Southerst, "How To Succeed In Franchising," *Globe and Mail*, June 17, 1996, B12.

40. U.S. Department of Commerce, *Franchise Opportunities Handbook* (Washington, DC: U.S. Government Printing Office, November 1986), xxix.

41. Louis W. Stern and Adell I. El-Ansary, *Marketing Channels* (Englewood Cliffs, NJ: Prentice-Hall, 1992), 355.

42. William A. Baltz, "Franchising: A Powerful Strategy for Growth in Retailing," *International Trends in Retailing* (Chicago: Arthur Andersen and Andersen Consulting, Spring 1991), 51–69.

43. Southerst, "How To Succeed In Franchising," *Globe and Mail*, June 17, 1996, B12.

44. Andrew E. Serwer, "Trouble in Franchise Nation," *Fortune*, March 6, 1995, 116.

45. Southerst, "How To Succeed In Franchising," *Globe and Mail*, June 17, 1996, B12.

46. Robert Williamson, "Entrepreneur Fights For His Coffee Rights," *Globe and Mail*, May 16, 1996, B9.

47. Robert E. Lusch and Deborah Zizzo, "Warehouse Home Centers and Wholesalers: The Battle for the Business Customer," *International Trends in Retailing* (Chicago: Retail Distribution Industry Groups of Arthur Andersen and Andersen Consulting, July 1995), 64.

48. "All That's Missing Are the Carhops," *Chain Store Age Executive*, July 1992, 29–30.

49. Lusch and Zizzo, "Warehouse Home Centers and Wholesalers: The Battle for the Business Customer," 65.

50. See Matthew Schifrin, "Goofus and Gallant," *Forbes*, December 18, 1995, 115–17. Also see Cyndee Miller, "Big Chains Battle for Market Share in Home Improvement," *Marketing News*, September 28, 1992; also see Jacqueline S. Gold, "Feet of Clay?" *Financial World*, March 17, 1992, 30–33.

51. James M. Degen, "Warehouse Clubs Move from Revolution to Evolution," *Marketing News*, August 3, 1992, 8.

52. Louise Lee, "Warehouse Clubs Embrace Marketing to Fill the Aisles," *The Wall Street Journal*, November 17, 1995, B4.

53. Carrie Goerne, "Buying Groceries on Credit," *Marketing News*, September 28, 1992, 1.

54. Jacqueline Pollok, "Supermarkets: Caught in the Crossfire," *Chain Store Age*, August 1995, 17B.

55. Statistics Canada, *Family Food Expenditures in Canada*, 1994.

56. Casey Mahood, "New Competition Upsets Grocery Industry Cart," *Globe and Mail*, June 2, 1997, B1.

57. Jerry Parks, "Shoppers Turning to Convenience Stores," *Advertising Age*, June 19, 1995, 3.

58. Frank Badillo, "Convenience Stores: The Road to Growth," *Chain Store Age*, August 1995, 24A.

59. Judith Waldrop, "Eating-Out, Going Up?" *American Demographics* (January 1992): 55.

60. Jeanne Whalen, "Satellites, No-Frills, Tandems Feed Fast-Food," *Advertising Age*, September 27, 1995, 36. Also see Jeanne Whalen, "Pizza Hut Topping Its Rivals," *Advertising Age*, October 9, 1995, 1.

61. *Ibid.*

62. Don L. Boroughs, "Serving up Hot Profits," *U.S. News & World Report*, November 28, 1995, 84.

63. Barbara Caplan, "The Consumer Speaks—Who's Listening?" *Retailing Issues Letter*, (co-published by the Center for Retailing Studies, Texas A&M University and Arthur Andersen, July 1993), 4.

64. Evan I. Schwartz, "The Kiosks Are Coming, the Kiosks Are Coming," *Business Week*, June 22, 1992, 122.

65. Sandra Siwolop, "Vending-Machine Technology Pushes Electronics Frontier," *The New York Times*, July 17, 1994, 7.

66. Tumiko Ono, "Going Door to Door with Palazzo Pants," *The Wall Street Journal*, September 8, 1995, B1.

67. James Denmark, *Direct Line to Profit* (Toronto: Grosvenor House Press Inc., 1991), 17.

68. Herbert Katzenstein and Williams S. Sacks, *Direct Marketing*, 2nd ed. (New York: Macmillan, 1992), 307.

69. *Ibid.*, 312.

70. Telecom Canada, "Telemarketing in Canada," Ottawa, June 1990.

71. See Gini Graham Scott, *Success in Multi-Level Marketing* (Englewood Cliffs, NJ: Prentice-Hall, 1992), 1026.

72. See Stephanie N. Mehta, "Visions of Wealth and Independence Lead Professionals to Try Multilevel Marketing," *The Wall Street Journal*, June 23, 1995, B1. Also see Stephanie N. Mehta, "Not Taught at Harvard: Multilevel Marketing," *The Wall Street Journal*, December 19, 1995, B1.

73. Paul Klebnikov, "The Power of Positive Inspiration," *Forbes*, December 9, 1991, 246.

74. Christopher Palmeri, "The Aloe Juice Man," *Forbes*, August 14, 1995, 100.

75. Klebnikov, "The Power of Positive Inspiration," 245.

76. See John J. Burnett and Michael McCollough, "Assessing the Characteristics of the Non-Store Shopping," *The International Journal of Retail, Distribution, and Consumer Research*, October, 1994, 443–463.

77. See Keith Tuckwell, *Marketing in Action*, Prentice Hall, 1996, 587.

78. See Scott Hample, "Fear of Commitment," *Marketing Tools*, January/February, 1995, 6–10.

79. Herbert Katzenstein and William S. Sachs, *Direct Marketing*, 2nd ed. (New York: Macmillan, 1992), 242.

80. *Ibid.*, 242–44.

81. Howard Rudnitsky, "Growing Pains," *Forbes*, February 27, 1995, 59.

82. Junu Bryan Kim, "Marketing with Video," *Advertising Age*, May 22, 1995, S1.

83. Jason Hudson, "Nonstore Retailing: Paper Remains King," *Chain Store Age*, August 1995, 29A. Also see Calmetta Y. Coleman, "Spiegel Catalog to Publish CD-ROM Version . . . Again," *The Wall Street Journal*, February 15, 1996, B4.

84. Peter Burrows, "The Computer Is in the Mail (Really)," *Business Week*, January 23, 1995, 76–77. Also see Paul E. Eng, "The PC Is Not in the Mail," *Business Week*, July 11, 1994, 42.

85. Dan Sweeney, "Electronic Retailing: Does It Have a Future?" *Chain Store Age*, October 1995, 73.

86. Sharon Edelson, "Fashion Reevaluates Flickering Fortunes of TV Home Shopping," *Women's Wear Daily*, November 11, 1995, 9.

87. Chad Rubel, "Home Shopping Network Targets Young Audience," *Marketing News*, July 17, 1995, 13.

88. Chad Rubel, "Infomercials Evolve as Major Firms Join Successful Format," *Marketing News*, January 2, 1995, 1.

89. Howard Schlossberg, "Once Fodder and Filler, Infomercials Now Attract Mainstream Advertisers," *Marketing News*, January 20, 1992, 1, 6.

90. Kim Cleland, "Infomercial Audience Crosses over Cultures," *Ad Age International*, January 15, 1996, 18.

91. Mark Landler, "The Infomercial Inches toward Respectability," *Business Week*, May 4, 1992, 175.

92. Laura Bird, "Sharper Image's New Gadget: Infomercials," *The Wall Street Journal*, August 19, 1995, B6.

93. Susan Reda, "Interactive Shopping: Will Consumers Catch up With Technology?" *Stores*, March 1995, 21.

94. Don L. Boroughs, "Battle of the Boxes," *U.S. News & World Report*, September 12, 1994, 69.

95. *Ibid.*, 72.

96. Howard Schlossberg, "Interactive TV Forges Ahead," *Marketing News*, October 28, 1991, 1, 6.

97. "Age of Interactive TV May Be Nearing as IBM and Warner Talk Deal," *The Wall Street Journal*, 21, 1992, Al; also see Joanne Lipman, "Interactive TV Entices Many Marketers, but So Far Hype Outpaces Technology," *The Wall Street Journal*, August 25, 1992, B1.

98. Robert J. Untracht, "Endpaper: The Electronic Retailing Revolution," *Retail i.t., Technology: It's in the Bag* (Ernst & Young's 14th Annual Survey of Retail Information Technology, September 1995), 46.

99. See Gary Robins, "On-Line Service Update," *Stores*, February 1990, 24–31.

100. Paul M. Eng, "Prodigy Is in That Awkward Stage," *Business Week*, February 13, 1995, 90.

101. "Retailers on the Internet: Seeking Truth Beyond the Hype," *Chain Store Age*, September 1995, 40.

102. "Internet Shopping: New Competitor or New Frontier?" Supplement to *Stores*, Sponsored by Mastercard International, *Stores*, February, 1996, MC4–MC5.

103. "Retailers on the Internet: Seeking Truth Beyond the Hype," 37.

104. *Ibid.*

105. *Ibid.*, 38.

106. "Internet Shopping: New Competitors or New Frontier?" MC5.

107. Joan E. Rigdon, "Blame Retailers for Web's Slow Start as a Mall," *The Wall Street Journal*, August 16, 1995, B1.

108. Joan E. Rigdon, "Coming Soon to the Internet: Tools to Add Glitz to the Web's Offerings," *The Wall Street Journal*, August 16, 1995, B1.

109. "Retailers on the Internet: Seeking Truth Beyond the Hype," 38.

110. *Ibid.*, 40.

111. See John W. Verity, "The Internet: How It Will Change the Way You Do Business," *Business Week*, November 14, 1994, 80–88.

112. John Heinzl, "Blumes Brothers Differ on Dylex Bio," *Globe and Mail*, August 30, 1997, B7.

113. Dom Del Prete, "Booksellers Test Cyberspace Marketplace," *Marketing News*, January 15, 1996, 8.

The Dynamic Character of Retail Environments

Outline

Population/Demographic Patterns and Trends

Geographic/Economic Patterns and Trends

Social/Cultural Patterns and Trends

Physical/Natural Patterns and Trends

Technological/Informational Patterns and Trends

Summary

Student Study Guide

Student Application Manual

Endnotes

Objectives

To understand the nature of population studies and to determine who consumers are and how many there are

To describe the major population and demographic trends and to assess their impact on retailing practices

To recognize the dynamic character of the geo-economic environment, the changing nature of the sociocultural landscape, and evolving patterns in the physical/natural scene

To appreciate the advances in new and emerging technologies and to understand their retailing applications

To provide examples of how environmental conditions impact consumers' buying behaviour

To describe how key environmental patterns and trends influence retail merchandising and operating strategies

Retail Vignette

Loblaw

Loblaw Companies Limited is Canada's largest food distributer. In 1996, about 63 percent of its sales of $9.8 billion were at the retail level through its own stores, and the remainder was through wholesaling to franchised accounts. The company serves stores across Canada and in the U.S.

Loblaw has attempted to remain competitive with the warehouse supermarkets by establishing combination stores that retail many nonfood items within the confines of the supermarket. Named "The Real Canadian Superstore," "The Super Centre," and "The Real Atlantic Superstore," these stores have been successful across Canada.

Loblaw
www.loblaws.ca

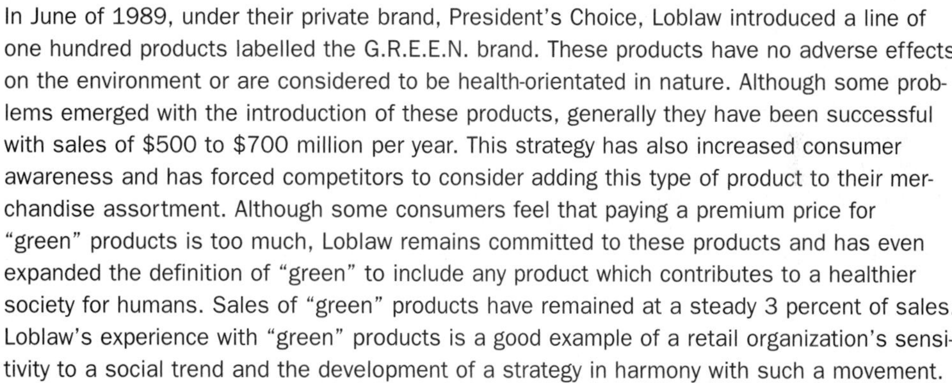

In June of 1989, under their private brand, President's Choice, Loblaw introduced a line of one hundred products labelled the G.R.E.E.N. brand. These products have no adverse effects on the environment or are considered to be health-orientated in nature. Although some problems emerged with the introduction of these products, generally they have been successful with sales of $500 to $700 million per year. This strategy has also increased consumer awareness and has forced competitors to consider adding this type of product to their merchandise assortment. Although some consumers feel that paying a premium price for "green" products is too much, Loblaw remains committed to these products and has even expanded the definition of "green" to include any product which contributes to a healthier society for humans. Sales of "green" products have remained at a steady 3 percent of sales. Loblaw's experience with "green" products is a good example of a retail organization's sensitivity to a social trend and the development of a strategy in harmony with such a movement.

Source: Loblaw's Annual Report, *1996;* Canadian Business Performance 500*; and Loblaw's 75th Anniversary Publication, 1996.*

Down-Aging: Life Begins at Forty

The refusal to be bound by traditional age limitations is the trend [known as] Down-Aging: redefining down what appropriate age-behaviour is for your age. A profound new phenomenon in the culture, it is the result of more than an unprecedented concern with health and longevity. The same baby-boom bunch that once said, "Don't trust anyone over thirty," now says, with equal militancy, "Life begins at forty."[1]

Inequality: Going Against the Notion of Fairness

Until recently, most economists thought inequality was a result, not a cause, of slow growth. That view lost its luster in the 1980s, when the big shocker was that the country got richer and those on the bottom did not. If this trend persists, it could tarnish North America's image as a land of opportunity, although there is still more economic mobility in Canada than in most countries.

Technology: Downing the "Downtime" and Upping the "Uptime"

It used to be said that the advent of computers would bring about a new leisure class. The computers arrived, but the leisure got lost. Instead of providing people with more "downtime," computers upped the "uptime." Laptop computers, computer "notebooks," and other technological devices such as fax machines and cellular telephones make it possible for many people to work virtually every waking minute.[2]

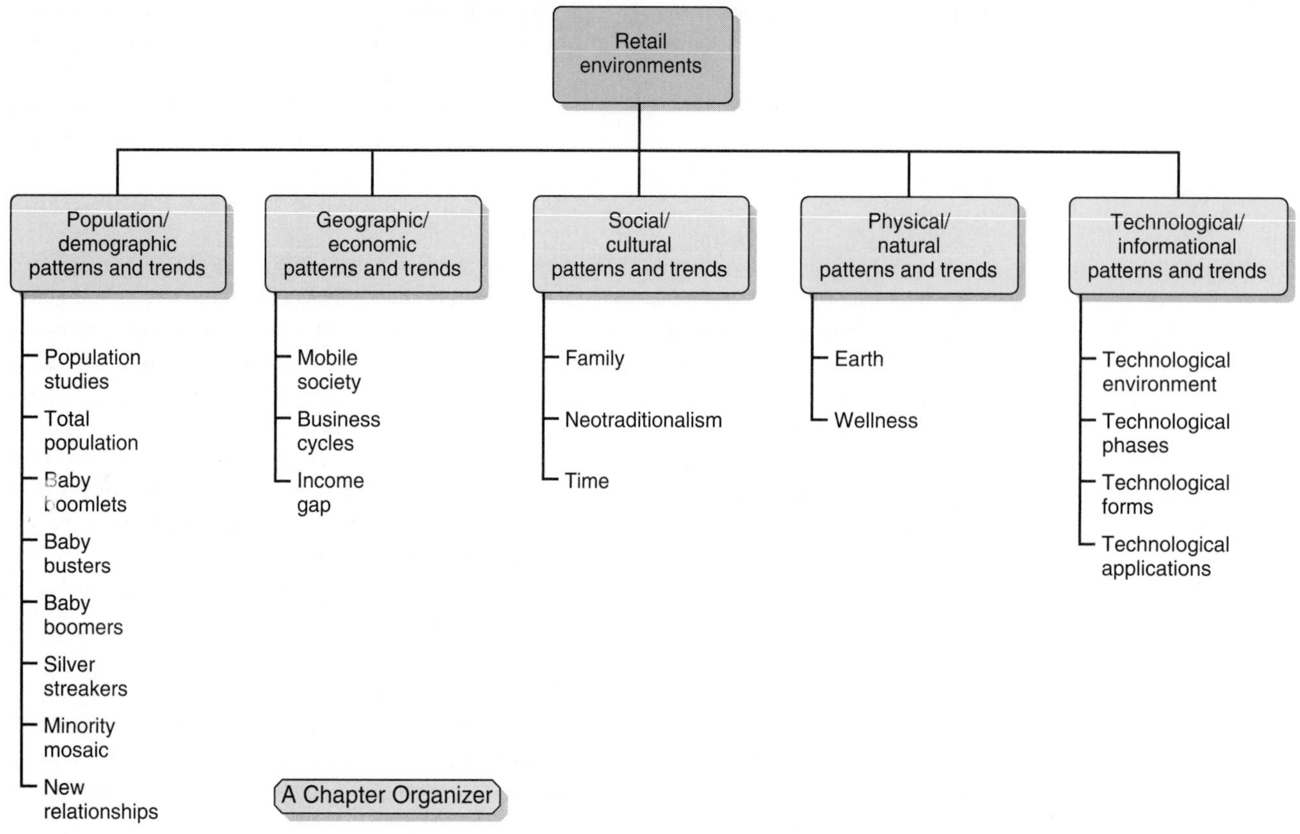

Figure 3–1

The dynamic character of retail environments

The 1980s and early 1990s constituted an era of upheaval and turmoil as well as a time of growth and progress. Change and adaptation were the watchword and will continue to be for the foreseeable future. High-performance retailers will be those organizations that correctly identify and totally appreciate the dynamic environmental changes that have occurred in the past and that will continue to emerge in the future. Figure 3–1 identifies the various environments about which the retailer must be concerned but that are typically beyond the control of any given retailer. Hence, adaptive strategies and flexible operations are essential ingredients for tomorrow's successful retailing format.

This chapter examines each of the environmental forces previewed in Figure 3–1. Rather than burying readers under a blizzard of facts and figures about each of the retailer's operating environments, the following discussions focus on several pronounced and emerging patterns and trends within each environment. Each discussion also covers ideas for adaptive strategies that retailers might employ in meeting the challenges of a dynamic marketplace.

Population/Demographic Patterns and Trends

Population Studies: The Quiet Revolution

The Canadian population is undergoing a quiet revolution that will have a profound effect on how retailers conduct business far into the next century. A study of the population and demographic patterns and trends is designed to answer two important questions for the retailer. First, population studies answer the question, How many ultimate consumers are there? Remember from Chapter 1 that it is the final or ultimate customer that is the focus of the retailer's merchandising efforts. The actual and potential market for any particular retailing format is determined in part by **total population**—the total number of persons residing in an area at a given time. However, not all persons within an area would be interested in what each retailer has to offer. Therefore, as in all good sales efforts, retailers need to qualify those segments of the total population that are actual customers or have the potential of becoming patrons. Demographic analysis is the first step in the retailer's efforts in identifying and qualifying actual and potential customers.

Second, demographic studies answer the question, Who are ultimate consumers? **Demography** is the study of characteristics and statistics that are used to describe a population. As illustrated in Figure 3–2, each person can be characterized in terms of age, sex, race/ethnicity, religion, **family** structure, education, employment, occupation, and income. These individual characteristics can be aggregated into relatively homogeneous profiles of population groupings that represent market segments. When these segments have been identified, described, and qualified, the retailer has the opportunity to tailor merchandising efforts to one or more of them. Figure 3–3 illustrates the market segmentation process. Demographic analysis also contributes to the process of making estimates of the sales potential of each targeted market (see Chapter 8). An analysis of changes in the nation's population and demographic profile reveals patterns that transform perceptions of the "average Canadian," the "typical Canadian family," the "standard household," the "middle class," or the "middle aged." Whereas national demographics reveal the "big picture," local demographics provide insights at the retail market level.

Total Population: More People but Smaller Markets

World population will leap from 5.6 billion in 1992 to 8.3 billion by 2025—the vast majority (93%) of new births will be in poor countries. This tremendous rise in the number of earth's residents will make population one of the most significant factors on the global scene for the next 30 years.[3]

> Recent scientific studies confirm that the Earth's basic resources are vastly greater than what are needed to feed even the 10 billion people who are almost certain to inhabit the planet by the middle of the next century. The real threat is not that the Earth will run out of land, topsoil, or water but that nations will fail to pursue the economic trade and research policies that can increase the production of food, limit environmental damage and ensure that resources reach the people who need them.[4]

For retailers, the sheer size of the world's population is enough to ensure that many retail operations will take on global dimensions in the pursuit of growth objectives.

Figure 3–2

The demographic makeup of a population

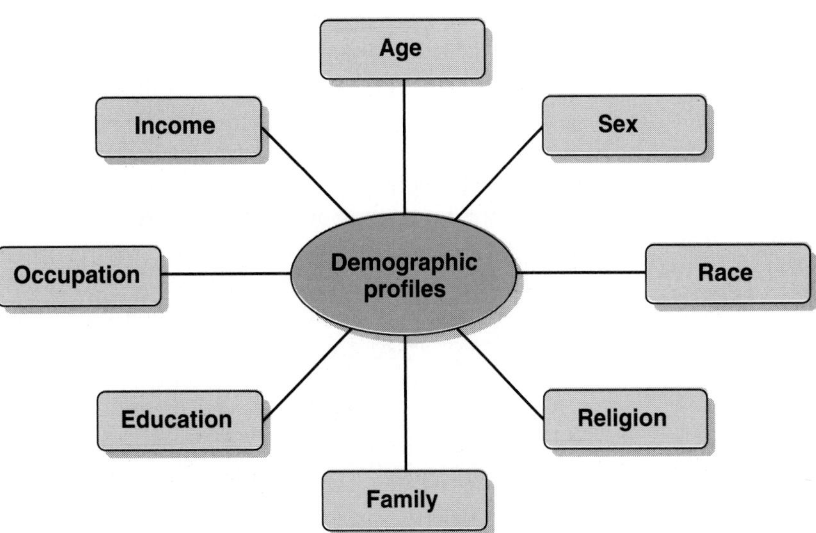

Figure 3–3

The market segmentation process

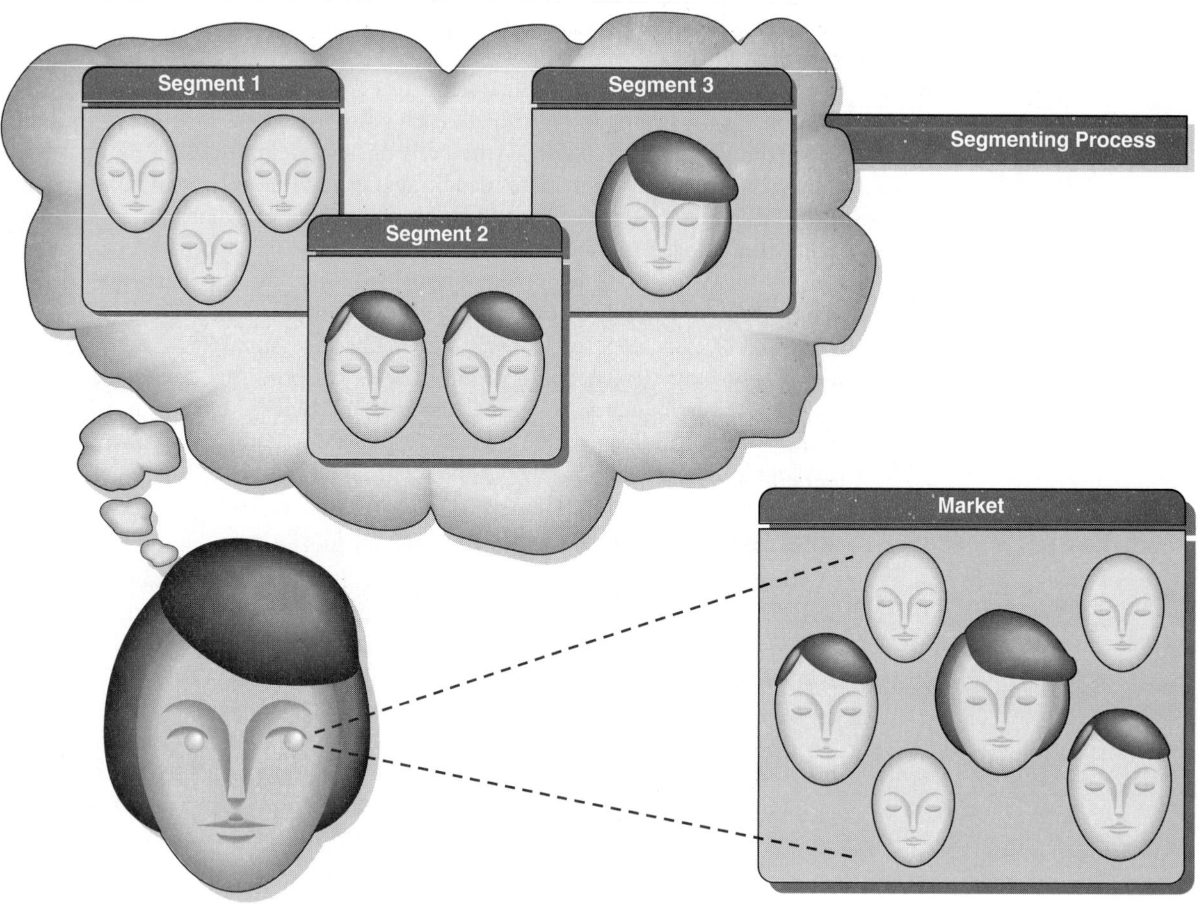

The total population of Canada was approximately 30 million in 1996. That number is expected to increase to 31.9 million by 2001, 33.7 million by 2006, and 37.1 million in 2016.[5] As illustrated in Figure 3–4, births and immigration are net contributors to a nation's population, whereas death and emigration reduce the total population. The birth rate between 1989 and1993 (baby boomlet) was the largest since the end of the legendary baby boom (1960–1964) and currently stands at 12.7 per 1000 while the death rate is 7.2 per 1000. This difference plus a positive net immigration indicates continued strong growth in the Canadian population in the future.[6] These factors, the renewal of the baby boom (increase in birth rates), the emergence of the "gray market" (longer life spans), and the rebirth of ethnic markets (immigration from new countries of origin) have conspired to fracture the old mass market and create the new "focused market." As described by one author, "[M]arket fragmentation is the retailing watchword of the 1990s."[7]

The ebb and flow of Canadian population growth has and will continue to have profound merchandising and operating implications. As each new population wave breaks

Figure 3–4

The determinants of total poulation

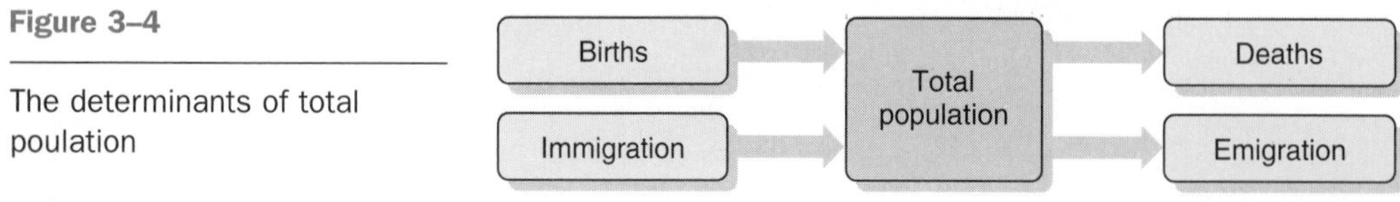

over the retailing system, new target market opportunities emerge that require continuous and innovative adjustments. Retailers react to these population changes by (1) altering product selections, (2) enhancing store atmospherics, (3) changing pricing structures, (4) modifying promotion programs, (5) improving customer services, (6) providing more conveniences, (7) changing the store's image, (8) offering better value, and (9) creating a hassle-free shopping experience.

Babies: "There's Gold in Them There Diapers"

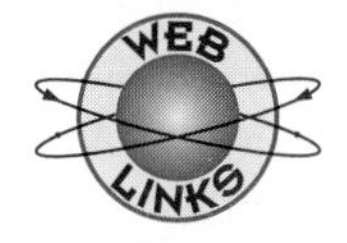

Comark
www.comark.com

The "four and under set" represents a large market in Canada. Babies have become a status symbol to those dual-career couples who have waited to have children and are thus able to spend more money on them when they do arrive. In 1996 there were almost 2 million babies (aged zero to four years) in Canada.[8] The significance of this increase in first time births lies in the fact that first time babies require new cribs, strollers, changing tables, furniture, car seats, room decorations, and other capital goods beyond the normal purchases of clothing, diapers, baby food, and formula that is required for all babies regardless of their place in the family.

A "baby as doll" phenomenon has spawned a whole new industry. Catering to the whims and wishes of well-to-do parents and grandparents, a number of upscale retail chains have developed in-store boutiques or separate retail outlets to capture part of this lucrative market. Baby Club is a chain in the Comark group which caters to this market.

Kids: Marketing Clout and the Power of Influence

Spending on and by children 4–12 years of age is one of the fastest-growing sectors of the economy and likely to remain vigorous for some years. The robustness of the **kids market** (about 4 million in Canada) can be attributed to the following factors:

- More "**boomlets**" are being added to the market as more boomers start their families.
- Thirty-something parents have more money to spend and give to their children in a quest to build an even better baby.
- The well-equipped kid has become something of a status symbol in some social circles.
- Some working parents try to compensate for the lack of quality time with the children by providing an abundance of quality products.[9]
- Well-heeled, gift-giving grandparents add greatly to the market—they account for about 30 percent of buying for children.

The kiddie market has attracted a wide variety of specialty store formats, from large chains with a general market appeal to superspecialists targeting a well-defined market niche. Kids' retailers are increasingly directing more of their merchandising effort at children as opposed to their parents. Stores are designed with child-friendly environments (e.g., smaller-size display units, more manageable groupings of merchandise, bright and colourful decors), interactive activities, and large-screen video monitors to involve kids in the shopping experience. Some stores even have a separate pint-sized entrance of their own. The fact that children can play and shop in a controlled setting has obvious appeal to security-conscious parents. Lad and Lassie is a Canadian chain which targets this kiddie market.

When developing merchandising programs for the boomlet market, retailers should keep in mind the following attitudes that govern children's shopping behaviour. Kids are

- shoppers with distinct preferences regarding where they like to shop;
- very fashion-conscious and place intense emphasis on brand-name merchandise;
- strongly influenced by peers in their choices of where to shop and what to buy;

- more comfortable visiting the same store over and over again;
- able to recognize and make judgments on what constitutes good value; and
- willing to earn and spend their own money for goods and services they want.[10]

Children exert influence on almost every aspect of family spending, from the food they eat and the type of clothes they wear to the purchase of the family automobile and the vacation destinations the family chooses. One study reveals that "a child makes requests an average of 15 times during a single trip to the grocery store. The average parent will buy 50 percent of those items."[11] The child consumer is quite sophisticated, they often know what products they want, they have preference brands, and they have a fairly good understanding of what constitutes value.

Teens: Spenders and Trendsetters

The ranks of teenagers have started to grow again. Teenagers in Canada reached over 4 million in 1996 and are expected to reach 5.5 million by 2011.[12] The emerging teen market is different from its predecessors in that (1) multiculturalism is an established part of their environment, (2) nontraditional family structures (for example, single and divorced parents) are the norm for one-third of this population group, (3) gender-blending has blurred the traditional roles of males and females, and (4) the split between the haves and have-nots is becoming more pronounced.[13]

The teen market is a consumer segment too powerful, too influential, and too profitable for retailers to ignore. Teens represent a major marketing opportunity for several reasons:

- **Teens have real spending power.** Teenage boys spend an average of $44 a week of their own money while girls average about $34 a week.
- **Teens spend family money.** In two-earner and single-parent families, teens assume greater responsibility for household shopping.
- **Teens influence household spending.** Teens impact household spending when they (1) accompany their parents to the store, (2) encourage parents to buy certain products or preferred brands, (3) serve as sources of information for such purchases as stereos, computers, fashion, and other trendy merchandise, and (4) ask for gifts and other special occasion purchases.
- **Teens are trendsetters.** Teens are society's trendsetters in that they tend to be early adopters of a wide range of new products. Teens are very experimental in fashion, music, computer games, social ideas, and new attitudes.
- **Teens are future spenders.** Forward-thinking retailers recognize that this teen market will become the largest adult market ever in the very near future.
- **Teens are a growing market.** The teen market will expand up through 2011, when it peaks at about 5.5 million potential customers.[14]

According to one survey, department stores ranked number one with teens because of the breadth of their fashion selection. Specialty stores were the next most popular type of outlet, followed by sporting goods stores.[15] "One of the keys to targeting the teenage market is to create an environment where teens feel comfortable. Generally, teens want to shop in stores that have young salespeople, brand-name products, and reasonable prices. They want the shopping experience to be fun and the merchandise to fit in with their lifestyle."[16]

Xers: Busters and Boomerangers

Sandwiched between the massive baby-boom generation and their offspring (babies, kids, and teens) is the comparatively smaller population group known as the **X-generation** or **baby busters**—those young adults born between 1965 and 1976. The X-generation was

The World of Retailing

International Retailing

Teens: The First Truly Global Consumer?

Teens around the world are living very parallel lives and show remarkably similar attitudes and shopping patterns and share universal taste in food and fashion. Both "hip-hop" fashion (the loose-fitting urban street wear featuring baggy jeans, sweat shirt, hiking boots, and baseball cap worn backwards) and the "grunge" look (the outdoor, back-to-the-basics style of dress characterized by torn jeans, flannel shirts, and hiking boots) gained a high level of acceptance and acclaim from the international teen market. Another teen uniform that has enjoyed global acceptance consists of baggy Levi's or Diesel jeans, T-shirts, Nikes or Doc Martens, and leather jackets. Additional signs of the homogenization of the world teen market include (1) the international tone of entertainment as set by American movies and music, (2) the unifying effect and popularity of MTV and its music videos, news, and socially conscious programming, (3) the popularity and acceptance of global brands, and (4) the acceptance of sports as the second universal language and the exporting of home sports into the worldwide arena through international leagues and the Olympics.

At the same time, teenagers have a deep-seated need and pride for their individual roots and cultural heritage. Although there are certain fundamental values and behavioural patterns that young people around the globe share, sufficient cultural differences exist so that it is extremely difficult to speak in one voice throughout the world. Although some global marketers elect to serve the world market with minor adjustments in a single business format, many international marketers feel that global marketing is a fallacy. While it may be a popular idea that represents cost efficiencies, only prestige brands or retailers can attain the acceptance levels needed to purse a global strategy. For most brands and retailers appealing to the teenage market, an international approach to this world market is needed in which marketing programs are tailored to the individual preferences and expectations of each cultural area.

Adapted from Paula Dwyer, "The Euroteen (and How to Sell to Them)," Business Week, April 11, 1994, 84; Cyndee Miller, "Teens Seen as the First Truly Global Consumers," Marketing News, March 27, 1995, 9; and Shawn Tully, "Teens: The Most Global Market of All," Fortune, May 1994, 90–97.

created "during the era of the Pill, legalized abortion, liberalized divorce, and a stampede of women into the labour force. For these and other reasons, baby busters are comparatively few in number" (4.2 million).[17] The impact of this low ebb in the age wave will be felt in one way or another throughout the first half of the next century. The exact nature of this generational impact is uncertain, as demographers and retailers are just now focusing their attention on this often-overlooked segment of the market.

Xers are a very different type of Canadian. They tend to be cautious, conformist, and pro-business and aspire to the traditional values of career, home, and family.[18] Hence, goods and services retailers whose operating and merchandising formats cater to these values will find distinctive but smaller market segments. Although the busters should have less competition for entry-level jobs, the boomers have all but clogged the channels of upward mobility in the leaner and meaner business organization.

Baby busters have developed several coping techniques to neutralize the economic shortcomings facing their generation. Two of the more important strategies include postponing marriage and household formation (for example, getting an apartment). More than half of the 18- to 24-year-olds are becoming "boomerangers"; that is, they are returning home to live with their parents.[19] In targeting the Generation X market, the retailer should emphasize leisure activities, family entertainment, economical and functional clothing, small and portable apartment furnishings and appliances, and smaller, more economical automobiles.[20] For a savvy and skeptical group, hype and image are out and product value is in.[21] "Any product or service that feeds the need of young, single Xers to stay in touch and in control at the same time will do well. The future is bright for carphones, beepers and pagers, answering machines, computer mail, fax machines. These are necessities—not luxuries—to Generation X."[22]

Boomers: Life Begins at Forty

The 10 million Canadians born between 1946 and 1964 not only are the largest generation, but they are set to become the longest-lived population group in the history of Canada.[23] On January 1, 1996, the first **baby boomers** turned 50 years old.[24] As the millennium nears, no demographic trend holds more importance to the retailer than the middle-aging of the boomers. The occupants of this middle-age bulge in the population time line can be described as being better educated, marrying less and divorcing more, having fewer children, swelling middle-aged ranks, and possibly never catching up with their parents in wealth accumulation.

As baby boomers enter their peak earning years, this age wave will have a profound impact on all aspects of retailing. The clear and unmistakable implication is that retailers must respond to this powerful mass of mature consumers well into the twenty-first century. Like all generations, baby boomers present a collection of many different marketing segments; it would be a serious mistake for retailers to think of them as one targetable consumer group that can be reached by one or a few mass-merchandising programs. As seen in Figure 3–5, there is within-group variance between mature, middle, and young boomers in their lifestyles and buying behaviour. Also evident in Figure 3–5 is the variance in lifestyles and buying behaviour between boomer consumers and preboomer babies and postboomer busters.

Nevertheless, one theme that is or will be central to the baby-boom generation is middle age; all boomers will either enter, occupy, and/or exit the middle-age years during the 1990s. This discussion focuses on the concerns and behaviours that characterize the middle years and briefly examines some of the more pronounced and interesting profiles of this dominant segment of the retail market.

- **Extended longevity.** Middle-aged consumers will defy the age markets traditionally associated with maturity. Extended longevity has greatly altered the what, when, where, and how boomer consumers get married, raise children, buy a home, decide to retire, go to college, rest from work, and try to relax. Midlife consumers could well experience several varying mini–life cycles instead of one generally defined pattern of living. The baby-boom generation is a moving target. Moving with it is the key to survival and growth for many retailers.

- **Balanced lifestyles.** Middle-aged boomers will seek ways to balance work, family, and recreation. Dominant themes in the 1990s will be raising families, quality of life, and productive work: Each will play an important part in the boomer's concept of the good life. They will be looking at product technologies and personal services to assist them in obtaining and maintaining a balanced lifestyle.[25]

- **Less materialism.** The boomers are outgrowing their youthful materialism and focusing more on home and family. Conspicuous consumption of prestige products did not prove to be the route to happiness. Boomers are turning back to cooking, gardening, do-it-yourself home improvements, hiking, reading, and other serenity-seeking activities. Retailers who are attuned to this soul-searching and back-to-the-basics activities will benefit.

- **Wellness awareness.** Age and predisposition will converge to heighten middle-aged consumers' interest in health (for example, avoiding high blood pressure, caring for an injury) and wellness (for example, nutrition, exercise). Because of boomers' skeptical nature and high educational level, they will assume an assertive role in maintaining their health. As charter members of the youth society, boomers will redefine what middle age means. It will be more vigorous, active, casual, attractive—in short, more youthful.

- **Gender blender.** Middle-aged men and women will become increasingly similar in the marketplace. Retailers will have to adapt to the converged attitudes, expectations, and buying habits of a more androgynous male/female. Women

Babies	Boomers	Busters and boomlets
■ **World War I babies** (born 1910–1919). Due to the impact of the Stock Market Crash and Great Depression, they remain overly cautious about spending money on all but basic necessities. ■ **Roaring '20s babies** (born 1920–1929). Experiences take priority over possessions, with spending on travel, entertainment, friends, and family remaining high and spending on personal apparel declining. ■ **Depression babies** (born 1930–1939). Spending today is on children's college, upgraded home furnishings, big domestic cars, and travel and entertainment as well as other luxuries; but during the next decade, focus will shift dramatically from status spending on husband's career to status spending on retirement. ■ **World War II babies** (born 1940–1945). Polarized between traditional, achievement-oriented households that have remained intact, and those whose dreams slipped away (often divorced females), spending now is on kids, upgraded home furnishings, travel and entertainment, and autos.	■ **Mature boomers** (born 1946–1950). Ambivalent toward materialism, they feel guilty about spending, but like nice things, indulging their own children as they were once indulged. During the coming years, their spending will shift toward maintaining their fantasies. ■ **Mid-boomers** (born 1951–1957). Less ambivalent about material goods, the women in this cohort know they deserve nice things, especially when they work hard for their money, and spend more than any other cohort's females on apparel. In contrast, many men in this group could care less about making a fashion statement and prefer practical, functional apparel. During the next decade, spending will shift from individual to family needs, and consumers will become more price conscious while still demanding quality. ■ **Young boomers** (born 1958–1964). Dramatically different from their older siblings, they are today focused on making money and spending it on themselves, buying "apartment furniture," home entertainment products and selected luxuries. During the next decade, their spending will accelerate along with their incomes, as they buy career wear and buy and furnish homes.	■ **Mature busters** (born 1965–1970). Largely peer driven and highly media impacted, their spending will increase dramatically with their first "real" job earnings. In the coming years, they will spend on furnishing apartments, on children, on sporting goods, and on work-related items like wardrobes, transportation, and PCs. ■ **Young busters** (born 1971–1976). Still in their key developmental years, they spend not only what they earn, typically from part-time work, but also influence family spending. In the next decade, they will spend on first cars, apartment furnishings, entry-level work clothes, and electronic gadgets. ■ **Mature boomlets** (born 1977–1982). Highly indulged by their boomer parents, and typically children of dual working parents, this cohort has more money, more responsibilities, and more influence on household spending than previous cohorts had at comparable ages. By 2000, many will still influence family spending and will spend on tuition and books, consumer electronics, food, and personal items. Apparel expenditures will still be geared toward leisure wear.

Figure 3–5

Consumer cohorts

Source: Adapted from "Cohorts Study: Age Matters," Stores *(November 1989): 36. Copyright © National Retail Federation, Inc., New York, New York.*

will be just as important in the workplace as men, and men will assume equally significant roles in the home and life of the family.

- **Educated consumer.** Middle-aged consumers will be experienced shoppers with considerable buying experience and product information. Boomers will seek, demand, and expect product and service quality; experience has taught them to recognize and value this quality.[26] As very experienced buyers, these middle-aged consumers will patronize those retail formats offering the best combination of price, selection, quality, and service. Boomers will also be less inclined to follow fads or buy on impulse; rather, they will be aggressive evaluators of products and services. The old patronage reasons of indulgence and luxury have been replaced with the hardnosed realities of quality, value, and service.[27]
- **Midlife crisis.** Middle-aged consumers will place greater emphasis on convenience and comfort. Convenience is essential to time conservation, which is very important to the boomer who might be experiencing a "midlife crisis."

Comfort in terms of both physical and psychological dimensions are important to the consumer who might be seeking a warm, safe, and hassle-free environment. Time and place convenience together with quality form utility, which will continue to be extremely important patronage reasons to be considered by retailers. Physically, this aging population group will be battling baby boomer sag. Both Sears and The Bay are increasing the amount of space devoted to shapewear (corsets, girdles, waist cinchers, control panties, and push-up bras).[28]

- **Gaining control.** Middle-aged consumers will be looking for ways to increase their sense of control. With middle age comes a sense of vulnerability and heightened awareness of risks.[29] Diminished physical capacities, impending retirements, and loss of loved ones are all occurrences that contribute to feelings that one has lost control over events that shape one's life. Risk-reduction goods and services that give the consumer a sense of control over physical and financial affairs will flourish. In the purchase of automobiles, for example, safety-conscious boomers are willing to buy such costly options as airbags and antilock brakes.
- **Life experiences.** Middle-aged consumers will be increasingly interested in purchasing experiences rather than things. The age of accumulation will be replaced by the age of involvement. Products and services will be judged on the basis of how well they create a desirable experience or enrich the quality of the consumer's life. The quest for vivid experiences should be one focus of the retailer's merchandising efforts.

Silver Streakers: The Mature and the Restless

The elderly population is currently the fastest growing demographic group in Canada. Nationally, people aged 50 years and older make up 24 percent of the population. The mature, **fifty-plus market** is large (more than 7 million) and is getting larger; Figure 3–6 illustrates the growth of the market. By the year 2011 this market will comprise 34 percent of the population.[30]

Although increased numbers are certainly a major factor in the growth potential of the mature market, an even more significant factor is the fact that people 50 years of age and older already control 75 percent of the nation's wealth and half of the discretionary income.

While the fifty-plus market is the most lucrative one, there is a great deal of variance of wealth among members of the mature market.

Because so many mature consumers do not act their age, it can be difficult to understand what they want. Today's fifty-plus consumers, or **silver streakers**, do not act like grandparents; rather, they pursue a wide range of interests and activities as they go through the various stages of aging. In addition to the time spent on home, family, and personal care, mature consumers spend their substantial free time watching television, participating in religious worship, reading a variety of materials, participating in sporting and other gaming activities, travelling, attending educational or entertainment events, visiting,

Figure 3–6

Growth of the fifty-plus market in Canada

Source: Statistics Canada, CANSIM Matrix 6900.

Year	Millions of people	% of population
1996	7.2	24
2001	8.9	28
2006	10.4	31
2011	12.1	34

and conversing. According to one mature market expert, "When it comes to marketing to the mature market, think in terms of how they feel, not how they are or look."[31]

Mature consumers exhibit heavy expenditure patterns in the following product and service categories: (1) leisure travel and home entertainment, (2) second homes and home furnishings, (3) luxury and domestic automobiles, (4) cosmetics and bath products, (5) lawn and garden products, (6) clothing and accessories, (7) stocks, bonds, and mutual funds, (8) recreation and sporting goods, (9) health clubs and health foods, and (10) medicines and medical supplies.

"The elderly have more time to shop, [have] more disposable income, are smarter than younger buyers, [are] more concerned about quality and price and [are] more likely to remember being satisfied with a retailer. They go to stores in search of many things: fashion, fitness, and fun."[32] In reality, mature consumers have needs in just about all product/service classifications and categories. What they require is modest product-service modifications (for example, larger-print books, more fully cut apparel, more leisurely paced activities). As shoppers, the fifty-plus market "demands quality in what it buys, and courteous, efficient, informed service when it buys. The older consumer opts for quality over all other attributes, tends to buy fewer items of a higher quality, and is not so much price-sensitive as value-sensitive. The consumer expects to get what they pay for, whether the absolute price is higher or lower."[33] Of particular interest to retailers is the fact that mature consumers will exhibit a high degree of store loyalty to those retailers that continue to meet their needs.[34]

Minority Mosaic: More People, More Diversity, and More Important

Historically, Canada's minority populations, in contrast to those in the U.S., have tended to retain their cultural and ethnic identities. This has allowed for the retention of their subcultural traditions and values. Such additional traits as customs, language, and religion which are maintained make the ethnic segment of the market a potentially important market for the retailer. On the one hand, the retailer can more easily target a particular group. On the other, a large chain may need to provide alternative strategies within their market to meet the needs of such homogenous groups. Figure 3–7 illustrates the ethnic diversity that exists in Canada.

As the French-Canadian market is by far the largest, a detailed discussion of this market follows.

Figure 3–7

Canadian population's home language by region

Source: 1995 Executive Report, Canadian Grocer, *5.*

	English	French	Italian	German	Chinese	Importance of five languages
National	62.2	24.5	1.7	1.6	1.6	91.6
Newfoundland	98.7	0.4	—	—	0.1	99.2
Maritimes	82.3	16.0	—	0.2	0.1	98.6
Quebec	9.0	83.3	1.8	0.3	0.4	94.7
Ontario	77.5	4.7	2.9	1.5	2.1	88.7
Manitoba	76.1	4.5	0.5	6.0	0.8	87.9
Saskatchewan	85.2	2.0	0.1	0.6	0.1	88.0
Alberta	83.5	2.1	0.5	2.9	2.1	91.1
British Columbia	81.4	1.4	0.8	2.5	4.4	90.5

The French-Canadian Consumer Over one quarter of the Canadian population is of French ethnic background with its own distinct and separate culture and lifestyle. Over 90 percent of the French-Canadian population lives in Quebec, but other significant segments of this market are located in Ontario and New Brunswick, in counties adjacent to Quebec.

The French-Canadian market possesses some unique consumer behaviour characteristics which retailers should not ignore. Some of the more relevant of these are listed below.

- Traditional values such as family and community are much stronger in Quebec. Quebecers believe a career is a priority, but not at the expense of family life and having children. As well, relationships are important to Quebecers, who believe a single person cannot have a satisfying, enjoyable life and who consider marriage without children incomplete.
- Quebecers watch 26 hours of television a week and prefer made-in-Quebec television shows. The Canadian average is 22.6 hours a week and displays a definite preference for shows produced in the United States.
- Quebecers prefer home-grown magazine titles such as *Croc, L'actualité, filles d'aujourd'hui, Style*, and *Elle Québec*. Such magazines have tapped the essential pulse of Quebecers; they delight in reading about themselves.[35] English Canadians in other regions prefer national titles such as *Chatelaine* and *Maclean's*.
- Quebecers are lovers of good food and restaurants. An intimate dinner for two or with a group of friends ranks as the most popular leisure activity. Quebecers have a higher level of attendance at the cinema, live theatre, and concerts, compared to people in other provinces. Quebecers dine out frequently, make it more of an occasion, and spend more money than their counterparts in the rest of Canada.[36]
- Quebecers prefer small, specialty stores where service is more personalized; in other regions a preference for larger stores is the norm.[37] When it comes to fashion purchases, younger age groups overspend, while older, traditional shoppers spend less than their counterparts in other provinces.
- Quebecers view shopping as an experience and the store as a brand with an individual personality based on the owner or owner's family. Value and quality come first. Price is secondary and is linked closely to perceived value. Price tends to be more important in other regions. For this reason, Quebecers are less inclined to buy generic and private label brands, compared to consumers in other regions.
- French-speaking Quebecers are quality-conscious, have higher expectations of products, and express low tolerance for those not meeting expectations. Quebecers are also more brand loyal. If a brand makes them feel good, they are less likely to switch brands.[38]

Some retailers have experienced difficulties as a result of the above-mentioned characteristics. Loblaws, Canada's largest supermarket chain, recently cancelled plans to expand into Quebec partly due to the differences in this market.[39] Wal-Mart made some serious errors in Quebec as part of their takeover of the Woolco chain,[40] and Mark's Work Wearhouse was required to alter its strategy before entering this market.[41]

Other Ethnic Groups Almost one-quarter of the Canadian population is of single or mixed ethnic heritage other than English or French. This ethnic population tends to congregate in close-knit communities in Canada's larger cities. Figure 3–8 illustrates this for Vancouver, Toronto, and Montreal. This figure also shows that the ethnic market is projected to grow much faster in the future than the rest of the population.

32. Anne L. Balazs, "Positioning the Retail Shopping Center for Aging Consumers," A summarized article from 1994 *Journal of Marketing Research* published in *Retailing Review* (published by the Center For Retailing Education and Research: University of Florida, Spring 1995), RR10.

33. Stephani Cook, "Riding the Silver Streak," *Retailing Issues Letter* (published by Arthur Andersen & Co. in conjunction with the Center for Retailing Studies: Texas A&M University, September 1989), 2.

34. See Thomas S. Gruca and Charles D. Schewe, "Researching Older Consumers," *Marketing Research* (September 1992): 18–23.

35. Penny Stevens, "Quebec's Divisions Regional, Not Linguistic," *Marketing*, March 22, 1993, 20.

36. "Quebec Focus: Leisure Activities," *Marketing*, November 29, 1993, 26.

37. Jacques Mercier, "Marketers Must Respect Differences in Quebec's Consumers," *Marketing*, November 16, 1992, 18.

38. Patti Summerfield, "Statistics Reveal Unique Profile," *Strategy*, November 30, 1992, 25, 33.

39. George Condon, "Does Anyone Think It's Premanent," *Canadian Grocer*, January 1994, 5.

40. Adam Finn, "The Americans Are Coming," *The Edge*, Fall 1994, 23.

41. Grace Casselman, "Masters of the Niche," *Canadian Retailer*, May/June 1997, 11.

42. Jennifer Lynn, "Approaching Diversity," *Marketing*, July 3, 1995, 11.

43. Warren J. Keegan, Sandra B. Moriarty, Thomas Duncan, and Stanley Paliwoda, *Marketing*, Canadian ed. (Scarborough: Prentice-Hall Canada Inc., 1995), 213.

44. *Ibid.*

45. Matthew Schifrin, "Goofus and Gallant," *Forbes*, December 18, 1995, 117.

46. Jeanne Whalen and Jane Hodges, " 'You Do It' Taps the Hardware Side of Sears," *Advertising Age*, October 9, 1995, 41.

47. See Sandra Forsythe, Sara Butler, and Robert Schaffer, "Surrogate Usage in the Acquisition of Women's Business Apparel," *Journal of Retailing* (Winter 1990): 446–69.

48. Diane Crispell, "Dual-Earner Diversity," *American Demographics*, July 1995, 32.

49. *Ibid*, 35.

50. Statistics Canada, 1996 Census, Catalogue #93-357-XPB.

51. Statistics Canada, Catalogue #93-375-XPB.

52. Faith Popcorn, *The Popcorn Report* (New York: HarperBusiness, 1992), 53.

53. See Kenneth M. Johnson and Calvin L. Beale, "The Rural Rebound Revisited," *American Demographics*, July 1995, 46–55.

54. Statistics Canada.

55. Statistics Canada.

56. See Jack Kasulis, "The Frugal Family of the Nineties," *Retailing Issues Letter* (published by Arthur Andersen & Co. and the Center for Retailing Studies: Texas A&M University, September 1991), 1–4.

57. Peter Francese, "America at Mid-Decade," *American Demographics*, February 1995, 24.

58. *Ibid.*

59. Statistics Canada, Catalogue #91-213.

60. Christopher Farrell, "Where Have All the Families Gone?" *Business Week*, June 29, 1992, 91.

61. Leah Haran, "Families Together Differently Today," *Advertising Age*, October 23, 1995, 1, 12.

62. "Fast Forward to 2045," *Advertising Age*, July 31, 1995, 32.

63. See G. Christian Hill, "The Myth of Multimedia," *The Wall Street Journal*, June 19, 1995, 6; Lornet Turnbill, "Intelligent Homes Can Do Everything but Dishes," *Akron Beacon Journal*, October 24, 1992, A6.

64. Mitchell Pacelle, "Makers of Automated-Home Systems See a Future of TVs Talking to Thermostats," *The Wall Street Journal*, September 28, 1992, B1.

65. Carol Farmer, "The Less Decade: Dream or Nightmare?" *International Trends in Retailing* (Arthur Andersen, July 1995), 50.

66. John Heinzl, "Sears Canada Profit Plunges," *Globe and Mail*, January 30, 1996, B11.

67. Leonard L. Berry, "Stores with a Future," *Retail Issues Letter* (copublished by the Center for Retailing Studies, Texas A&M, and Arthur Andersen, March 1995), 3.

68. R. Fulton Macdonald, "Shake, Rattle & Roll: The Coming Retail Revolution," *Retail Control* (April/May 1992): 25.

69. See "Store," *Grocer Today*, January/February 1996, 19.

70. Patrick Brethour, "Goldspring Chills Forzani With $2.8 Million Loss," *Globe and Mail*, September 12, 1996, B1.

71. Marina Strauss, "It's Wait Till Next Season For Weather Weary Retailers," *Globe and Mail*, September 23, 1996, B3.

72. Peter Stisser, "A Deeper Shade of Green," *American Demographics*, March 1994, 26.

73. *Ibid*, 27.

74. "Wal-Mart's New Green Initiative," *Chain Store Age Executive*, May 1995, 186. Also see "Leading the Crusade into Consumer Marketing," Fortune, February 12, 1990s, 50; and Kevin Helliker, "Wal-Mart Will Open Store that's Helpful to the Environment," *The Wall Street Journal*, August 8, 1992, B5.

75. Patrick Carson, "Green Is Gold," *International Trends in Retailing* (Chicago: Arthur Andersen and Andersen Consulting, Summer 1992), 37, 48.

76. See Suzanne Oliver, "Seeds of Success," *Forbes*, August 15, 1994, 88; Susan Reda, "Higgins Natural," *Stores* (July 1992): 29–30; Pat Sloan, "Where, O Wear, Can You Get 'Green' Garb?" *Advertising Age*, June 8, 1992, 3, 50; and Cyndee Miller, "Levi's, Esprit Spin New Cotton into Eco-Friendly Clothes," *Marketing News*, April 27, 1992, 11.

77. See Chad Rubel, "Help those who can't help themselves to salt," *Marketing News*, January 1, 1996, 15; David Stipp, "New Weapons in the War on Fat," *Fortune*, December 11, 1995, 164–174.

78. See Neil Gross and Peter Coy, "The Technology Paradox," *Business Week*, March 6, 1995, 76–84.

79. This discussion of technological forms is based on Dale Achabal and Shelby McIntyre, "Emerging Technology in Retailing: Challenges and Opportunities for the 1990s," in *The Future of U.S. Retailing*, ed. Robert A. Petersen (New York: Quorum Books, 1992), 90–92.

80. *Ibid*, 91.

81. *Ibid*, 93.

82. See Toddi Gutner Block, "Riding the Wave," *Forbes*, September 11, 1995, 182–83.

83. Jonathan Berry, "Database Marketing," *Business Week*, September 5, 1994, 59.

84. See Gary Robins, "Wireless POS Systems," *Stores* (February, 1994): 47–48.

85. "From the Store to the Door," *Akron Beacon Journal*, November 22, 1995, B7.

86. Bruce Fox, "Bizarre Idea Gets a Second Chance," *Chain Store Age* (May 1991): 145.

87. Louise Lee, "Garment Scanner Could Be a Perfect Fit," *The Wall Street Journal*, September 20, 1994, B1.

88. "Mastering the Computer Revolution: What the Retail Executive Needs to Know," *Chain Store Age Executive* (October 1991): 1A–20A.

89. See "Price Chopper Quiets Backroom Chaos," *Chain Store Age Executive* (January 1990): 76–80. Also see Bruce Fox, "RF Seen as Key to Value City MIS Upgrade," *Chain Store Age Executive* (February 1992): 43–44.

90. Renee Rouland, "Image Technology: A New Retail Vision," *Discount Merchandiser* (March 1990s): 54.

91. "Retail Technology," *Chain Store Age Executive* (August 1989): 133. Also see "Hype Is Gone, But Job of Expert System Remains," *Chain Store Age*, October 1995, 66.

92. Kathy Chin Leong, "Store Systems Help Retailers Give Shoppers What They Want," *Computerworld*, November 28, 1988, 68.

93. Bill Stack, "Small Firms Can Reap Huge Gains with Electronic Data Interchange," *Marketing News*, April 1, 1991, 19. Also see Gary Robins, "EDI: Small Independents Stay in Step," *Stores* (March 1992): 38–39.

94. Gary Robins, "Auto ID: Retailers and Vendors Gear Up,." *Stores* (May 1991): 40–44.

95. Russell Mitchell, "The Smart Money Is on Smart Cards," *Business Week*, August 14, 1995, 68–69. Also see Stephen Kindel, "Smart Cards," *Financial World*, January 19, 1993, 47.

Figure 1–1

Retail businesses focus on goods or services.

Figure 1–2

Retailers create product assortments.

Figure 1–3

What image do you have of this retailer in terms of product selection, pricing practices, service offerings, and store atmospherics?

Figure 1–4

In terms of your personal preferences, what are the most important functional, aesthetic, service, and psychological features associated with the purchase of this automobile?

Figure 1–5

End-of-aisle displays are special displays designed to increase sales of displayed merchandise.

Figure 1–6

Price advertisements are direct-action messages that encourage consumers to react immediately to the retailer's appeal.

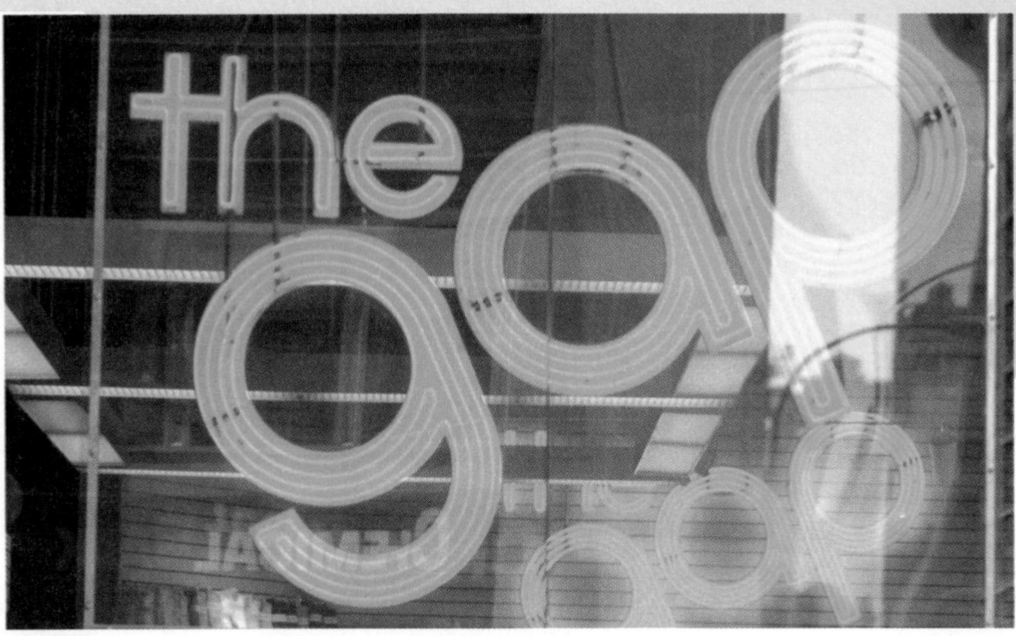

Figure 2–1

Specialty retailers target a select group of customers by developing a focused assortment of product lines. Which customer group is being targeted by this specialty retailer?

Figure 2–2

Do the benefits of belonging to a franchising organization outweigh the costs associated with being a franchisee? Which franchising system provides the best cost/benefit ratio?

Figure 2–3

A home centre is a warehouse retailer that targets both the professional builder and the amateur do-it-yourselfer.

Figure 3–1

Canadian consumers are a diverse group of people who have different needs and preferences and exhibit a wide range of shopping behaviours. How important is it to treat each of these diverse groups as a separate market segment? Is it possible to treat them as one large group and effectively employ mass marketing strategies?

Figure 3–2

How important is the kids' market? Should kids' stores be designed for kids or their parents? What role do children play in the buying process?

Figure 4–1

Which of these items do you consider to be convenience products, shopping products, and specialty products?

a

b

c

Figure 4–2

Describe your attitude with respect to this retailer.

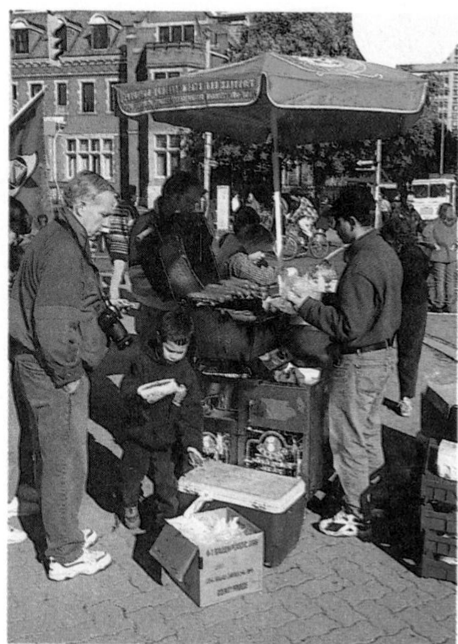

Figure 4–3

Retailer vendors provide a high level of place convenience by taking their business to the customer. In your opinion, what kind of future does this type of retailing have?

Chapter five 5

Figure 5–1

What aspects of this business operation are regulated by local officials?

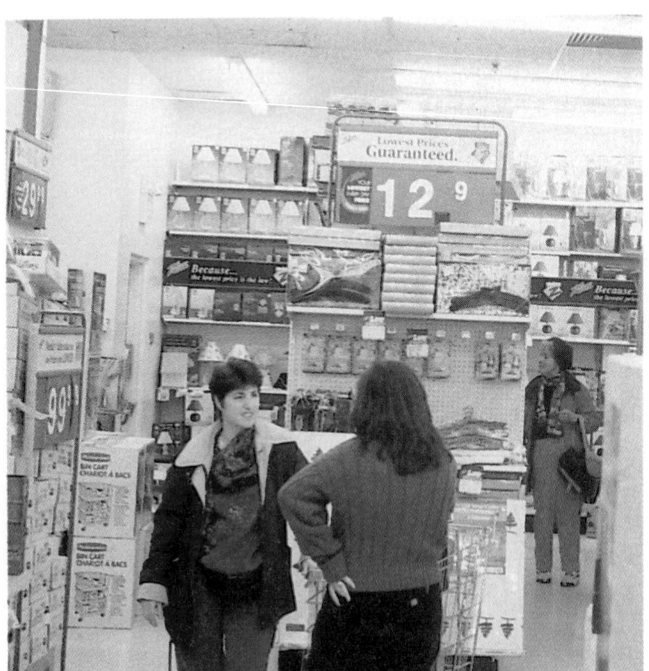

Figure 5–2

Would reading a guarantee impact your buying decision? Why or why not?

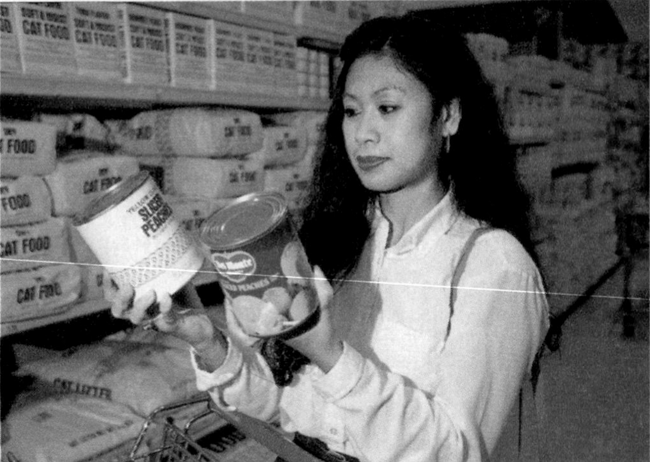

Figure 5–3

Competitive-price comparsions must be made on identical products. Do these price comparisions meet Federal guidelines on identical product comparsions?

Chapter six 6

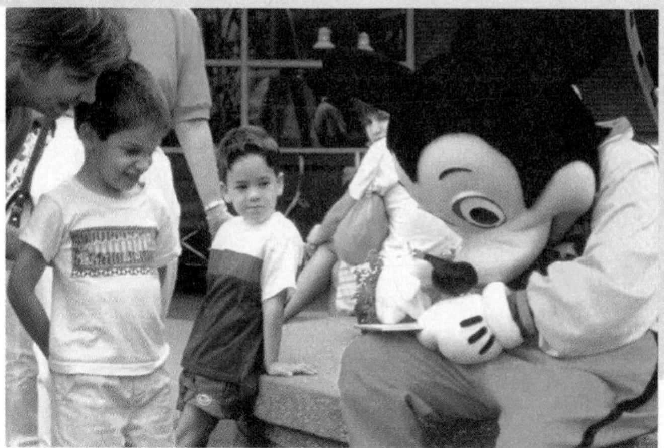

Figure 6–1

Employees of Walt Disney World are carefully integrated into a customer-oriented service culture that is generally recognized as one of the best organizational cultures in the world.

Figure 6–2

New computer-assisted training methods have great potential for increasing the retailer's labour productivity.

Chapter seven 7

Figure 7–1

Which of these store exteriors best communicates what the store is all about? Which exteriors make a positive impression? Are there any negative impressions communicated by these stores?

a

b

c

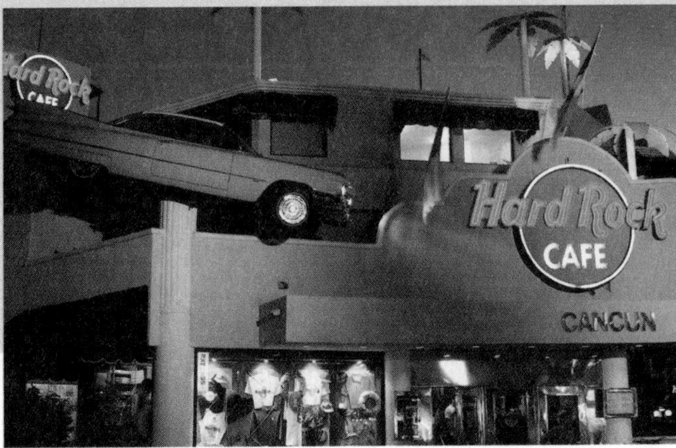

Figure 7–2

Why are people attracted to theme restaurants? What are some of the ways in which these restaurants use store decors to enhance the dining experience?

Figure 7–3

Are these storefronts (or display windows) effective in attracting the attention of passing consumers? Which front (or window) is the most effective? Why?

a

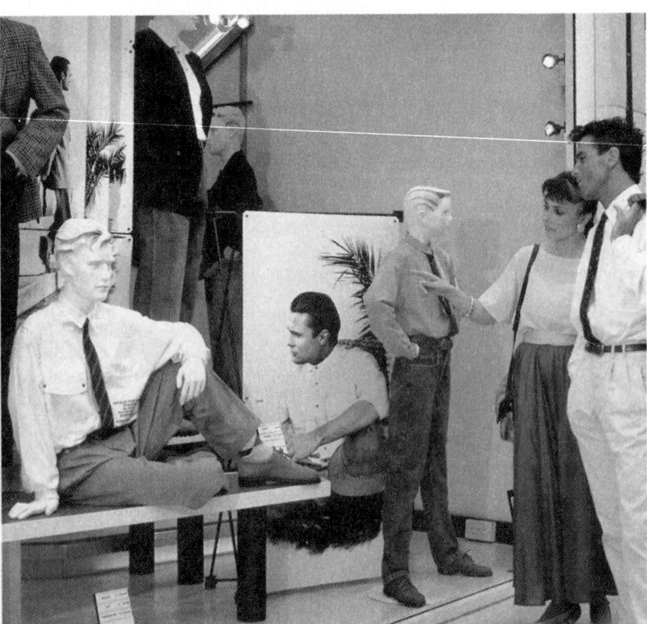

b

Chapter eight 8

Figure 8–1

An important trend in shopping centre development is the restoration, preservation, and conversion of manufacturing plans, railroad stations, shipping docks, warehouses, and other interesting structures into specialty shopping malls.

Figure 8–2

The community convenience center is a highly accessible strip mall located along a major traffic artery or at the intersection of two thoroughfares.

Figure 8–3

Recreational and entertainment activities are becoming an essential part of the total shopping experience at most regional shopping clusters.

Figure 8–4

Specialty attraction malls provide for interesting and unique shopping experiences.

Figure 8–5

Central and secondary court areas within shopping areas are used to overcome the tunnel effect and create an entertaining place to shop.

Chapter nine 9

Figure 9–1

A product line is any grouping of related products in which the relationship is important to the consumer.

Figure 9–2

A merchandise classification (e.g., paper products) is a specific line of products in which items are directly comparable and substitutable. It is at this level within a product line that comparison shopping occurs.

Figure 9–3

Many retailers are aggressively selling private-label brands in an attempt to improve profit margins.

a

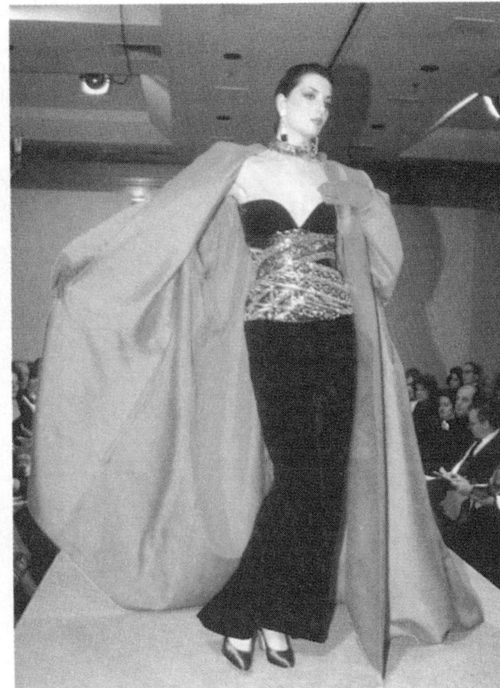

b

Figure 9–4

What is fashion? Who decides what is fashionable? What factors do you consider when you make judgments on whether or not an apparel item is the appropriate fashion on you?

Figure 10–1

Regional apparel marts provide local store buyers within a region an alternative source of supply that is more convenient and economical than travelling to central markets.

Figure 10–2

Scanning is the most effective way of collecting inventory data. Hand-held scanners that read bar codes are used to identify both the product and its manufacturer.

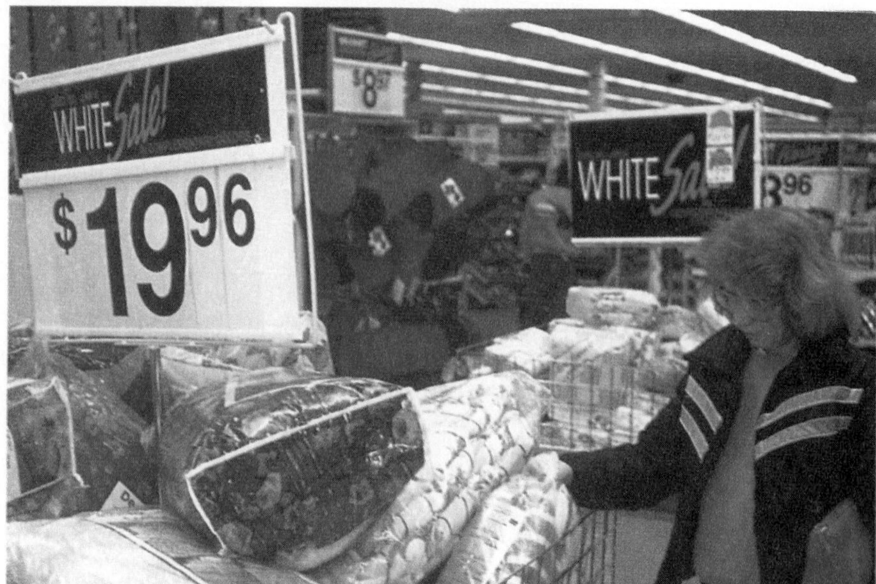

Figure 10–3

Bulk marking is one way retailers cut labour costs by avoiding the extra cost of marking each individual item. What are some of the problems that might arise from using this marking method?

Chapter eleven 11

Figure 11–2

Odd pricing promotes the image of a bargain price.

Figure 11–1

Wal-mart is able to maintain its price leadership role because of its low cost operating structure. What are some of the ways in which Wal-mart lowers its operating costs?

Chapter twelve 12

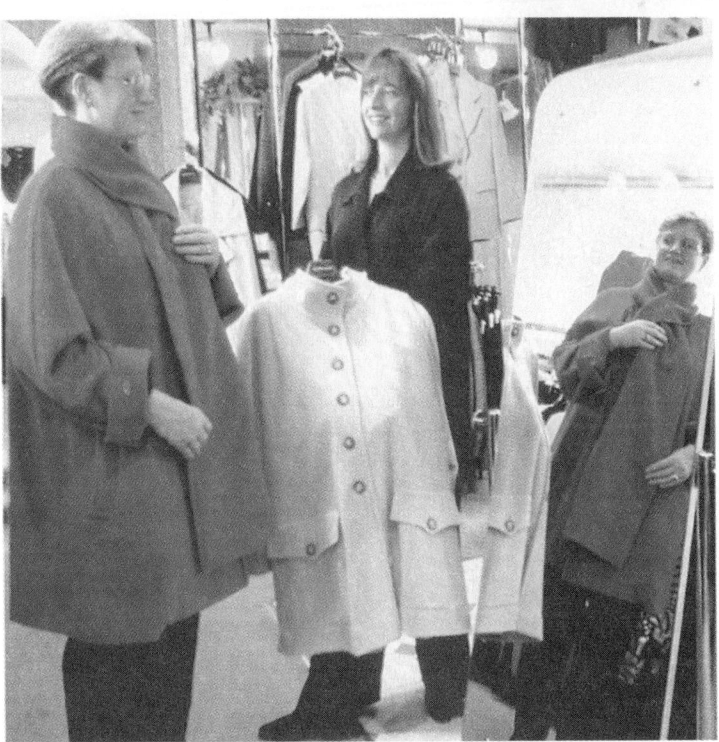

Figure 12–1

Relationship selling requires that the retailer's sales associates closely interact with the customer and build a lasting rapport.

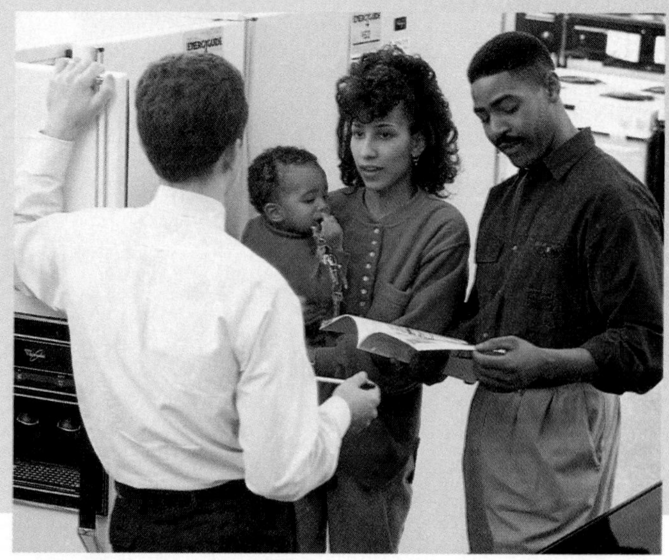

Figure 12–2

Providing customers with information and assistance greatly enhances the likelihood of a successful sales transaction.

a

b

Figure 12–3

How would you describe the salesperson-customer similarity situation in each of these situations? Is similarity very important in building good customer rapport?

Figure 13–1

Sign advertising can be an effective and relatively inexpensive way for retailers to draw attention to themselves. Which of the signs below is most effective in communicating its message?

a

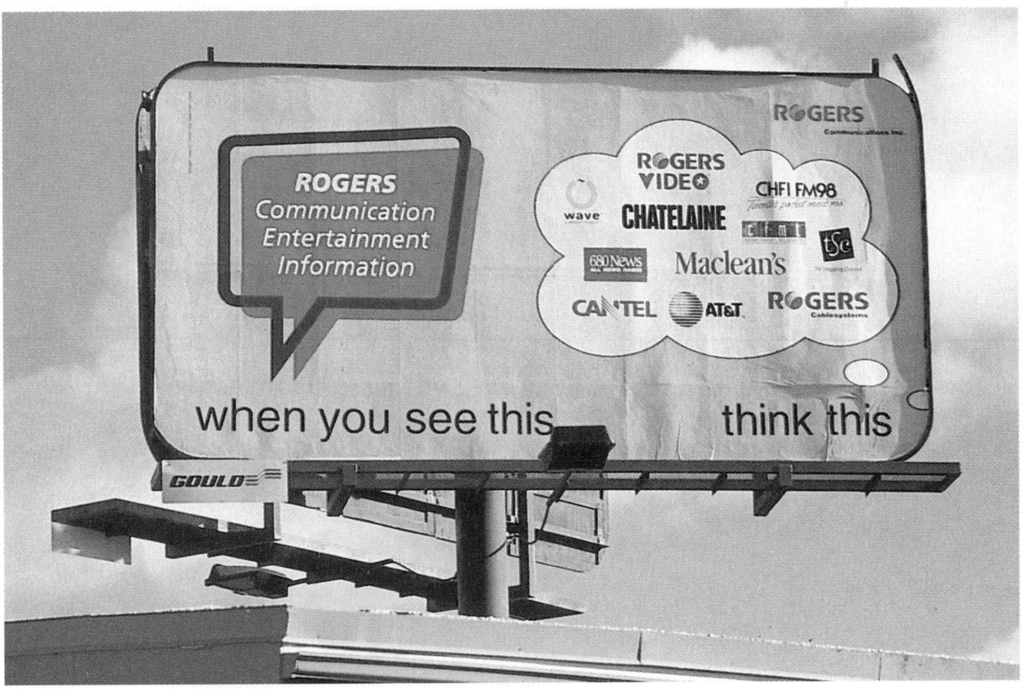

b

Figure 13–2

Is transit advertising an effective means for the retailer to gain exposure and create awareness? Why or why not?

a

b

The Buying Behaviour of Consumers

Outline

Objectives

To understand the concepts of product tangibility, durability, and availability, and their impact on consumer buying behaviour

To explain the concept of market potential and discuss the elements of the market potential equation

To compare the individual and household buying centres

To describe the psychological, personal, and social factors that influence consumer buying behaviour

To outline and discuss the five stages of the consumer buying process

To identify and discuss the various buying scenes

Retail Vignette

Mmmarvellous Mmmuffins

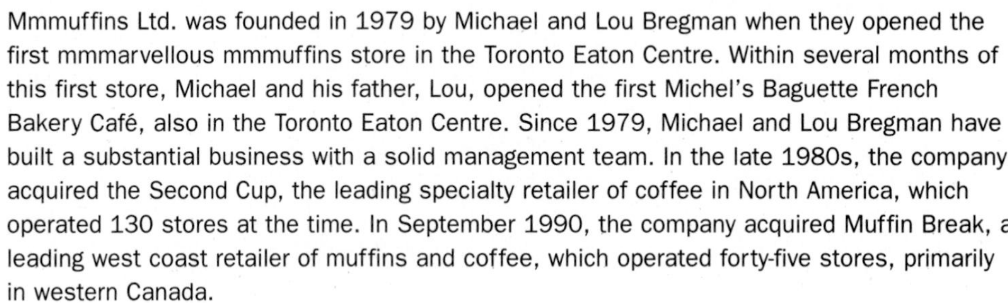

Richmont Food Services, a privately held company, is the largest specialty food retailer in Canada and operates three separate food concepts: mmmarvellous mmmufffins, Muffin Break, and Michel's Baguette French Bakery Café. Mmmuffins has grown rapidly since its founding in 1979, both through internal growth and by acquisition, with system-wide sales budgeted to exceed $60 million in the fiscal year of 1997.

As of 31 December 1997, 97 percent, were franchised and the rest were company-operated. Store operations are well dispersed geographically.

mmmuffins
www.mmmuffins.com

Mmmuffins Ltd. was founded in 1979 by Michael and Lou Bregman when they opened the first mmmarvellous mmmuffins store in the Toronto Eaton Centre. Within several months of this first store, Michael and his father, Lou, opened the first Michel's Baguette French Bakery Café, also in the Toronto Eaton Centre. Since 1979, Michael and Lou Bregman have built a substantial business with a solid management team. In the late 1980s, the company acquired the Second Cup, the leading specialty retailer of coffee in North America, which operated 130 stores at the time. In September 1990, the company acquired Muffin Break, a leading west coast retailer of muffins and coffee, which operated forty-five stores, primarily in western Canada.

In all of its operating businesses, mmmuffins distinguishes itself from other food service establishments and other franchised operations by delivering value to its customers through exceptionally high quality products and excellent customer service. To deliver this commitment to quality and customer satisfaction, mmmuffins puts a strong emphasis on franchising. The company believes that owner-operators who are carefully selected and well trained have a greater likelihood of succeeding than a store manager. Mmmuffins views its franchisees as its "valued customers" and, through its support office, provides its franchisees with substantial marketing, purchasing, merchandising, leasing, and construction support.

Over the past 17 years, mmmuffins has continuously refined the operation of its businesses and developed uncompromising standards of operation. A franchisee becomes part of a proven retail chain with a refined store concept and successful operating systems and procedures in place. Mmmuffins maintains a tight quality control of its product offerings through detailed standardized recipes, which are developed and tested in a centralized product development centre at the support office. As well, mmmuffins maintains tight control of procurement of supplies. The result has been consistent attainment of industry leading measures.

Printed with the permission of mmmuffins.

Shopping Experiences: Seeking Situational Value

Retailers continue to think that consumers want quality, service, style, and selection. We say to retailers that what we want is "an experience." An experience can be driven toward the maximization of efficiency or an experience can be driven toward entertainment. Retailers who recognize that this bipolar orientation toward the foraging process exists and build strategies around either or both of these concepts will be tapping into the underpinnings of our motives.[1]

Changing Values: Experiences, Not Things

Changing values will determine what customers spend their money on. Categories that are insignificant today will grow exponentially. Sadly for retailers, most of these new categories are not about things one buys; instead, they are about experiences one has—travel, education, health, and relationships. In short, experiences are the things people are coming to value the most. The consumer values experiences and thus finds many stores endlessly boring. The consumer values taste and time; the retailer ignores both too often.[2]

Customer Satisfaction: Creating the Accustomed Shopper

A customer is a person who becomes accustomed to buying from you. The custom is established through purchase and interaction on frequent occasions over a period of time. Without a strong record of contact and repeat purchase, this person is not your customer; he or she is your "buyer." A true customer is "grown" over time.[3] Many Canadian retailers have adjusted their strategies in an attempt to meet consumer demand and to respond to competitive pressures.[4]

The previous chapter considers consumers as groups and previews the impact of this group behaviour on the retailer's operating and merchandising efforts. In this chapter, the focus is on the individual consumer and how he or she acts as a person and interacts within various groups (for example, family, peer groups). As suggested above, consumer markets are becoming more individualistic—hence the need to examine the buying behaviour of individuals.

Consumer **buying behaviour** is the manner in which consumers act and react to various situations involving the purchase of a good or service or the acceptance of an idea. Effective retailing requires an appreciation of the buying behaviour of consumers. Retailers must understand their customers better so that they can both respond to as well as anticipate their needs. Retailers require such buying behaviour information as what and how much consumers buy, who does the buying, and how and where consumers buy (see Figure 4–1). This section examines the ultimate consumer act of buying and the situations and influences that affect the consumer's choice of retailers and their products and services.

Figure 4–1

The buying behaviour of retail consumers

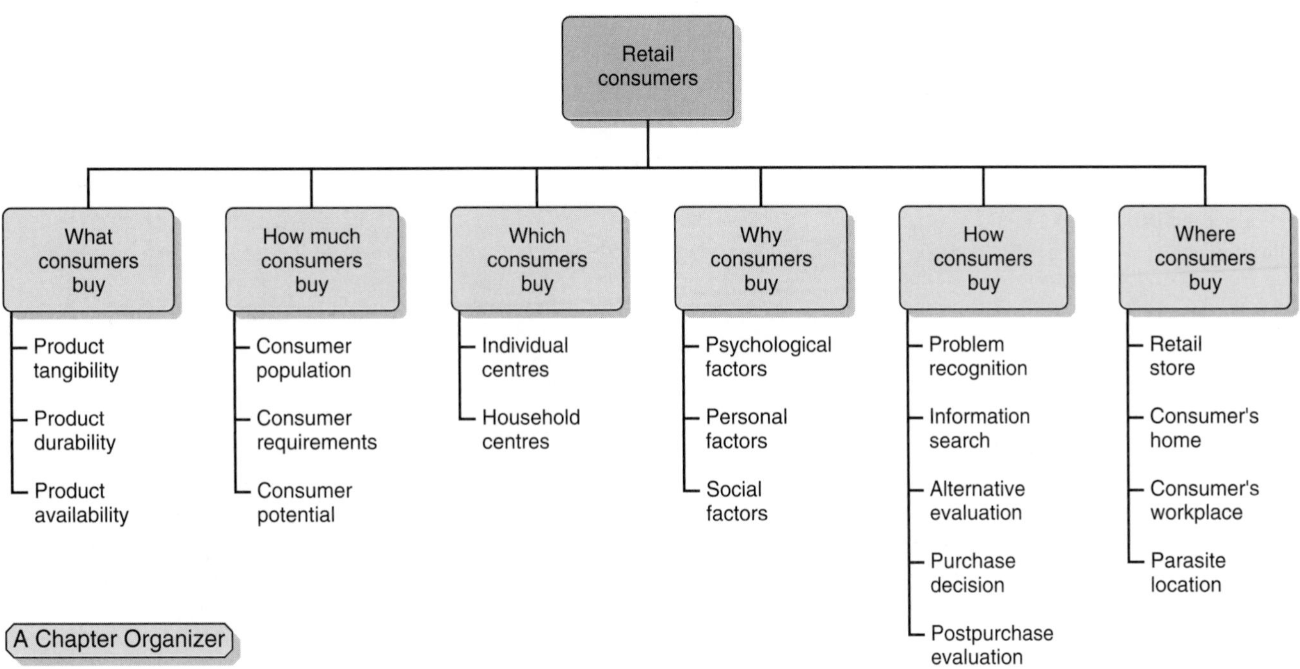

What Consumers Buy

"What do consumers buy?" is the first question that must be answered if we are to gain an understanding of consumer buying behaviour. Consumers buy products. **Products** are bundles of benefits capable of satisfying consumer wants and needs. A product can be anything that can be offered to a market as a need and want satisfier. Consumers have benefit expectations that must be realized in buying, using, and possessing products. Successful products are those that provide the tangible and/or intangible features necessary to realize the consumer's expectations of benefits. To enhance our conception of what a product is, marketers have developed several classifications based on various product and/or buyer behaviour dimensions. Let us look at the dimensions of tangibility, durability, and availability (see Figure 4–2).[5]

Product Tangibility

Tangibility is the degree to which an item has physical and material properties capable of being perceived. The sense of touch is generally considered to be the deciding factor in determining tangibility. Tangible products can be held, hefted, and felt; intangible products cannot.

Product tangibility ranges from goods to services to ideas (see Figure 4–2a). **Goods** are tangible items defined by their size, shape, and weight together with their chemical and/or biological makeup. This book is a good example, as is the chair you are sitting in. As discussed in Chapter 1, **services** are largely intangible activities that typically involve the application of human skills within a consumer problem-solving context. A service may or may not be associated with the sale of a good. Services range from personal services like hairstyling and massages to professional services such as medical attention and legal advice, from household services of housekeeping and gardening to automotive services of maintenance and repair, from recreational services of amusement parks and campgrounds to cultural services of plays and concerts. **Ideas** are concepts and ways of thinking about a particular event or situation. These highly intangible products are often extensions of the

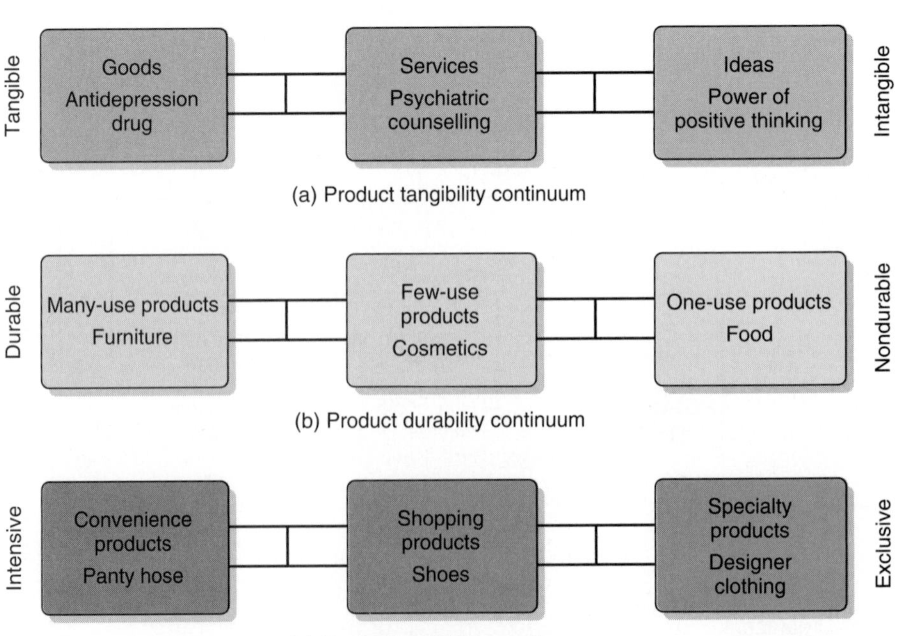

Figure 4–2

Product classification: (a) product tangibility continuum, (b) product durability continuum, (c) product availability continuum

opinions, attitudes, and interests of the person marketing the idea. Ideas are often categorized as business, religious, political, social, or personal expressions of conceptual thinking.

Product Durability

Durability is the capability of something to endure or to last. **Durables** are products that are capable of surviving many uses,[6] such as automobiles, appliances, and home furnishings. During recessionary times, consumers tend to stretch the life of durable products by holding onto them; consumers become more of an owner than a user of durable products. An economic recovery is often signalled by a pickup in the sale of durable products.

Nondurables are perishable products that are used up in one or a few uses. Food products represent one of the largest categories of nondurables. Faddish goods, services, and ideas with a limited useful life are all products that lack durability. Given the relatively short product life cycle of most nondurables, consumer shopping patterns tend to be characterized by frequent and regular purchase behaviour. Fresh, new, unique, modern, current, and fashionable are some of the product traits that the retailer should be concerned with when merchandising nondurables. Given the time sensitivity of these limited-life products, operational efficiency that promotes rapid turnover is essential to the generation of acceptable profit levels. Figure 4–2b illustrates the continuum of product durability.

Product Availability

Product availability is a means of classifying products on the amount of effort the consumer is willing to exert to obtain a particular good, service, or idea (see Figure 4–2c). **Convenience products** are those that the consumer is not willing to spend time, money, and effort in locating, evaluating, and procuring. In the future more goods and services will be treated as convenience goods, in which easy and quick availability will be paramount in the consumer's buying behaviour.

Consumers expect convenience products to be readily and consistently available. If a particular convenience product or brand is not available, the consumer will switch brands as well as stores. Bread, milk, cigarettes, and soft drinks are all traditional examples of convenience goods. However, in today's fast-paced world, just about any product might be treated as a convenience good given the right circumstances (for example, an emergency). Dry cleaning and automotive maintenance are typical convenience services; emergency medical care is a not-so-typical example of a convenience service.

The sale of many types of convenience goods is often the result of impulsive consumer behaviour. **Impulse goods and services** are products that consumers purchase as a result of a strong and often irresistible urge. Impulse purchases are sudden and spontaneous actions taken without much deliberation. Sensory stimulation (sight, smell, sound, taste, and touch) is the trigger for initiating these unplanned purchases. Retailers can substantially increase sales (by as much as 30 percent) by carefully constructing store atmosphere and layout to encourage consumers to make impulsive purchases at a convenient time.[7] Although North Americans are heavy users of batteries, the prominent end-of-aisle and checkout displays of batteries attest to the fact that consumers treat this product as an impulse item.[8]

Shopping products are products for which consumers want to make price, quality, suitability, and/or style comparisons. Because there is not much difference between one 100-MHz machine and another, PC retailers attempt to differentiate their computers by adding software and to create comparisons other than price. In such cases, the comparison shopping behaviour of PC buyers is directed as much at these add-ons as it is at the computer itself.[9] Consumers are willing to spend considerable amounts of time, money, and effort in obtaining shopping goods; therefore, these goods can be distributed selectively. What constitutes shopping products varies from one consumer to another. However, we usually think of clothing, furniture, household goods, and automobiles as shopping goods; and hair care, recreation and entertainment, and selective dental and

Retail Strategies and Tactics

The Store to End All Stores

Wal-Mart's move north is part of an industry revolution that will, no doubt, see some small merchants fold, some main streets suffer, and perhaps even a national chain or two go bust. But Wal-Mart will not destroy Canadian retailing. It will only help destroy mediocre retailers, and there's a big difference. Smart merchants who control their operations with the same kind of precision and who learn to understand their business and their customers as thoroughly, will thrive.

Wal-Mart will do to Canadian retail what the Japanese did to the North American auto industry—make it better. While North American automakers were puzzling over their odd operating techniques, or insisting that what North Americans wanted was North American cars, the Japanese were giving buyers what they really wanted—small, cheap, fuel-efficient cars that held together. Giving consumers what they want, rather than assuming they will take what is offered, is Wal-Mart's genius too. What the company has tapped into, and the warehouse clubs and the category killers have picked up on, is a consumer zeitgeist that has changed radically in the past decade.

Wal-Mart has redefined the retail experience. It has figured out that, in a discount store, price is the first priority. What busy customers want in the way of service is not fawning sales clerks, but convenience. They want stores that are big and bright and well laid out. They want a broad selection of products, and they want them in stock and on the shelves when they get there. They want to get in and out fast. As management guru Peter Drucker put it last summer: "What customers—at least a good many of them—want is not shopping that is enjoyable, but shopping that is painless."

Source: Mark Stevenson, The Store to End All Stores, Canadian Business, *May 1994, 21.*

medical services require some comparison shopping. In a similar vein, people shop around for ideas by attending different lectures, churches, and other events.

Specialty products are those for which the consumer's buying behaviour is directed at obtaining a particular good, service, or idea without regard to time, effort, or expense. Consumers will not accept a substitute; therefore, they will expend whatever effort is required to procure the product. An example might be a specific branded good such as Lagerfeld cologne, a company product line such as Royal Copenhagen figurines, or a non-allergenic pillow. For many skiers and bicyclists, a specialized pair of Oakley sunglasses are worth extra effort to find.[10] For the individual who is willing to travel to and wait for a particular hairstylist and pay whatever the price, that service is a specialty service. Given the insistent character of the consumer, specialty products tend to be exclusively distributed in a limited number of outlets.

How Much Consumers Buy

Consumer Population

Viewed from the perspective of the individual consumer, the question of how much he or she buys is a function of his or her needs and desires plus the ability, willingness, and authority to buy. Taking a broader market perspective, how much consumers will buy in total is the problem of determining **market potential**—a market's total capacity to consume a given good, service, or idea. As seen in Figure 4–3, market potential equals the total consuming population in a market plus its consumption requirements and potential. Let us examine each of these elements of the market potential equation.

A market's total capacity to consume is, in part, a function of the total number of consumption units that make up that market. Therefore, the first step in determining market

Figure 4–3

The determinants of market potential

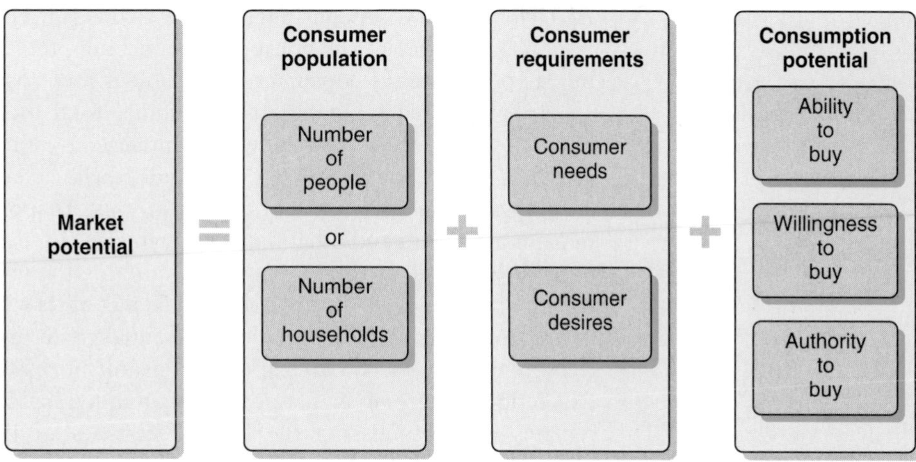

potential is to obtain an accurate count of the number of consumption units. However, before consumption units can be counted, they must be defined, depending on the type of product that is the focus of the market potential determination. The number of people is the most appropriate population count when market potential is being determined for such personal goods and services as clothing and accessories, health and beauty aids, or medical and legal services. On the other hand, a count of the number of households or "the number of residential units" probably is more indicative of a market's consumption capacity for hardware and household goods, furniture, and appliances, lawn and garden equipment, or plumbing and heating services. Although these population figures are important, they must be qualified in terms of their likelihood of a purchase now or in the near future.

Consumer Requirements

Prerequisites to the consumer buying process are needs and desires; they motivate and direct the buying activities of consumers. Although the distinction between needs and desires is open to debate, the main difference is in their essentiality: **Needs** are essential physiological or psychological requirements necessary to the general physical and mental welfare of the consumer, and **desires** are more akin to wishes, in that they are conscious impulses toward objects or experiences that hold promise of enjoyment in their attainment. However, the attainment of desires is less essential to the consumer's well-being than is the satisfaction of needs. A consumer may have a desire for a luxury automobile when the need is simply for reliable transportation (a midsize car). As baby boomers get older, the conflicts between their desires—to look young, to be comfortable, and to protect a natural appearance—should increase. Careful redesign and relabelling of products can help to ease the discomfort. Girdles that are renamed "body shapers" and described in terms of the "one-minute diet" and "instant slimmer" give the customer an easy choice between buying the product or embarking on a diet.[11]

Consumer Potential

Consumers must distinguish between having a need or desire for a product and buying it. Many consumers have product needs (for example, a new toaster) that go unsatisfied and desires (for example, a new Porsche) that go unfulfilled. The essential difference between needing or desiring a product, service, or idea and buying it is the consumer's ability, willingness, and authority to purchase it. With respect to product purchases, the list of what each of us would like to buy is far more extensive than the list of what we are willing and able to buy.

Ability to Buy A consumer's ability to buy is his or her **buying power—**the financial resources available to the consumer for making purchases. The determining elements of buying power are the consumer's spendable income, asset position, and available credit.

There are many expressions of income. **Total income** refers to the total amount of money received from salaries, wages, interest investments, pensions, and profit-making activities. Unfortunately, not all of an individual's or family's total income is available for spending as the individual or family pleases. **Disposable income** is the income that remains after taxes and other required payments (for example, Canada Pension Plan) have been deducted from total income. It is the total amount of money that is available for spending and saving. Although disposable income is an appropriate and useful expression of available income for the retailer of essential goods and services, it is not a useful tool in examining the capacity of a market to consume nonessential or luxury goods and services. **Discretionary income** is that portion of an individual's or family's disposable income that remains after purchasing the basic necessities of life (food, clothing, and shelter). Consumers are free to purchase whatever they want with their discretionary income. Marketers of many recreation, entertainment, household, automotive, and personal products are dependent on the amount of discretionary income consumers have for satisfactory sales volumes.

Credit and assets are the second and third buying power determinants. **Credit** is (1) the borrowing power of a consumer, (2) an amount of money that is placed at a consumer's disposal by a financial or other institution, and (3) a time allowed for payment for goods and services sold on trust. Consumers obtain credit through the use of credit cards, installment loans, and open-credit accounts. **Assets** are anything of value that is owned by an individual. Homes, automobiles, household goods, and recreation equipment together with various financial investments are the major assets held by the typical consumer. The role of assets in determining buying power is twofold: (1) they can be converted to cash, and (2) they are a major factor in determining the amount of credit that creditors are willing to extend.

Willingness to Buy A consumer may have a need and the ability to satisfy that need yet, for a number of reasons, may be unwilling to make a purchase decision. As consumers, our willingness to buy a product is related to the many influences that affect us and the way in which we make purchase decisions.[12] Many concerned parents, influenced by their belief that they need to give their kids an "edge," are buying educational toys in record numbers. Taking advantage of this willingness to buy are several new toy store chains specializing in educational toys and learning materials. Psychologically, we may or may not be motivated to make a purchase, or our perception of a product is such that we do not feel it is capable of meeting our needs. From a personal standpoint, a product must generally be congruent with our self-image and lifestyle. For example, college-educated households are much more likely to buy personal, financial, and entertainment services than households with less education. Fear has proven to be an important factor in one's willingness to buy—"Fear of unemployment, fear that higher taxes and health costs will make it impossible to balance the family budget, fear of crime, and fear, quite simply of being unable to cope."[13] On the other hand, our willingness to buy may be based on whether a product meets our "belongingness" need to be accepted by our family, peer groups, or social class.

Authority to Buy Even with the ability and willingness to buy, a certain degree of authorization must be present before a consumer will finalize the purchase decision. Authority to buy can be either formal or informal. Formal authorization consists of the consumer meeting various eligibility requirements such as age, residency, and occupation constraints. Minors cannot legally purchase alcoholic beverages. Many social and professional organizations make their products available only to members of certain occupations.

Informal authorization for making purchases is an expected courtesy when the purchase can be classified as being of major importance (special occasion or expensive) and involving more than one person. For example, when either a husband or wife is considering the purchase of a new automobile, the other partner expects to be consulted before the purchase is made.[14] Likewise, how, when, and where to take the family vacation is a decision for which informal approval and/or input is expected from all family members.

Which Consumers Buy

A pertinent question in any study of buying behaviour is, Who does the buying? To answer this question, marketers have developed the concept of a buying centre. A **buying centre** is a basic unit of consumption that engages in the buying process. In consumer products marketing, the basic consumption units tend to be either individuals or households. *Individual buying centres* are individuals who buy goods and obtain services for their own consumption with little or no regard for the needs or opinions of others. Household buying centres involve purchases made for a household by one of its members on the basis of collective needs and influenced by most or all household members.

The distinction between individual and household buying centres is important in studying buyer behaviour and developing merchandising programs that are appropriate to that behaviour. In the following sections, we look at the influences on the individual and household buying behaviour and the processes that are employed in making purchases by these two types of buying centres.

Why Consumers Buy

Why do consumers buy what, when, where, and how they buy? Marketers, like psychologists, do not fully understand the "whys" of human behaviour. Although we have a fair understanding of which factors influence behaviour, our knowledge of how those factors interact to influence behaviour is limited. The human mind is often compared to a "black box"; we know the inputs (stimuli) and the outputs (responses) but not the inner workings (processes) of the mind with respect to the transformation of inputs and outputs. Nevertheless, by detecting patterned buying responses that emerge from planned marketing stimuli, retailers can draw inferences about the processing system of the human mind. One viewpoint on the nature of retailing is that it is the art and science of creating and delivering a package of stimuli (products, prices, promotions, and places) that is capable of producing consistent patterns of buying behaviour.

In this section we explore the many interacting factors that affect buying behaviour and serve as a basis for formulating marketing strategies and tactics. Figure 4–4 is an overview of the major determinants of the buying behaviour of the ultimate consumer.

Psychological Factors

The field of psychology has contributed greatly to the marketer's quest for explanations to the "whys" of consumer behaviour. Motivation, perception, learning, and attitude are four major psychological factors that influence consumers in the determination of their buying choices.

Motivation Preceding any action, including buying, is the mental process of **motivation**. Motivation starts with stimulated needs that lead to aroused tensions and results in goal-directed actions (see Figure 4–5). A basic tenet of psychology is to "look behind the behaviour." What retailers have found when they have examined the buying choices of

Figure 4–4

The determinants of consumer buying behaviour

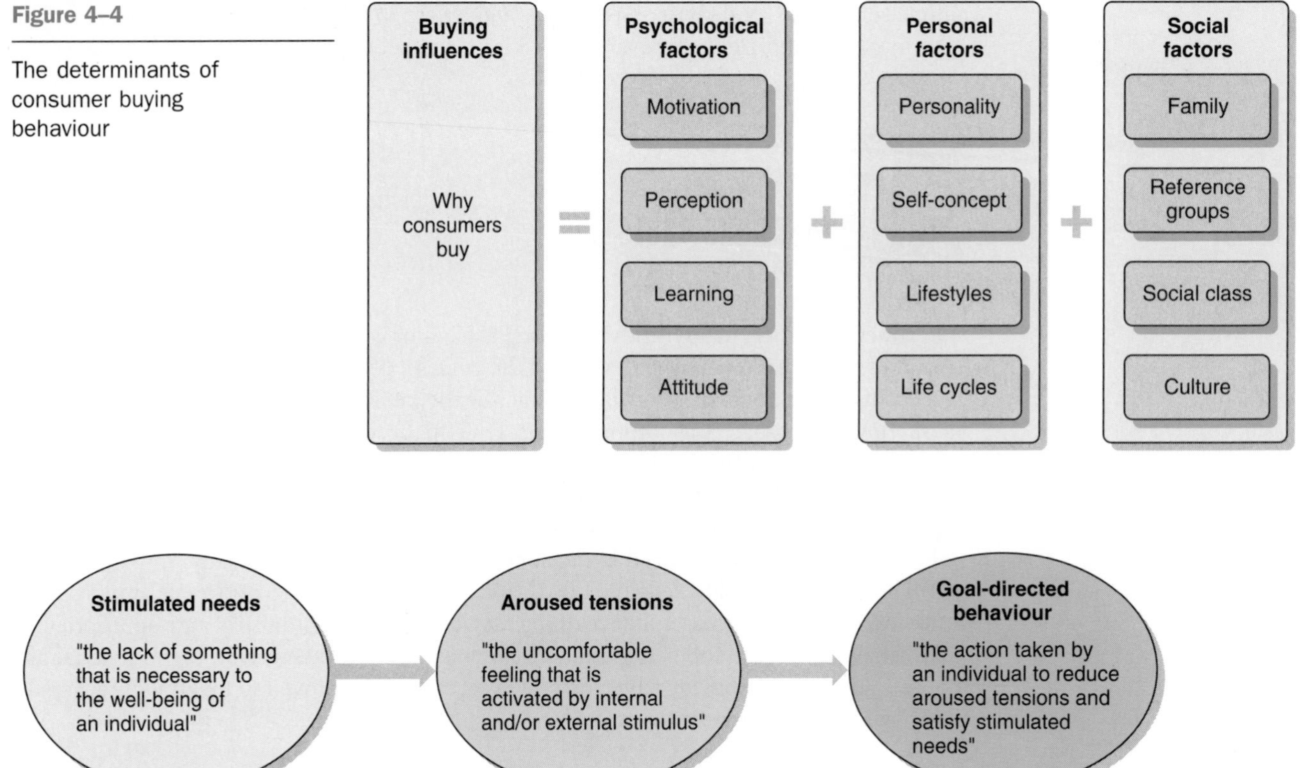

Figure 4–5

The motivation process

consumers are unsatisfied needs. As described previously, a need is the lack of something necessary to the well-being of the individual. Needs are the basic sources of buyer behaviour, but they must be stimulated before the consumer is driven to action.

Activation of a need is the result of some internal or external stimulus that arouses tensions. A headache is an internal stimulus that creates an uncomfortable feeling (an aroused tension), activating the goal-directed action of taking aspirin for relief from the headache (the need). An external stimulus might be a department store advertisement announcing the arrival of the latest fall fashions; this cue may stimulate our need to be noticed as a contemporary dresser, thereby promoting the action of purchasing something distinctive to wear. Canadian Tire and Zellers have used "Buy Canadian" campaigns as a motivational force.

Zellers
www.hbc.com

Having portrayed motivation as a needs-based process, we now require a further explanation of the nature and intensity of human needs. Needs have been categorized in a variety of ways; one of the more widely accepted need classification schemes is that of the psychologist Abraham H. Maslow (see Figure 4–6). According to Maslow, human needs are hierarchical and can be rank-ordered on the basis of their motivational power. Lower-order needs, those that are related to our physiological well-being, are basic innate needs that must be satisfied before higher-order needs can emerge as strong motivators of our behaviour. Higher-order needs are learned needs that are largely psychological in nature. Although higher-order needs are secondary to physiological needs, once these basic needs are satisfied, psychological needs will emerge as extremely important motivators of consumer behaviour. Let us explore Maslow's hierarchy of needs.

Physiological needs are life-sustaining and creature comforts that must be reasonably satisfied before the search for fulfillment of higher-order needs. Food, fluids, shelter, rest, waste elimination, and clothing are all basic to the physiological well-being of the individual. The casual look in men's and women's clothing meets a definite physiological need. North Americans are getting fatter, and casual clothing is a more "forgiving look," providing much greater comfort.[15] In reading this text, for example, your thirst for knowledge

Figure 4–6

Maslow's hierarchy of needs

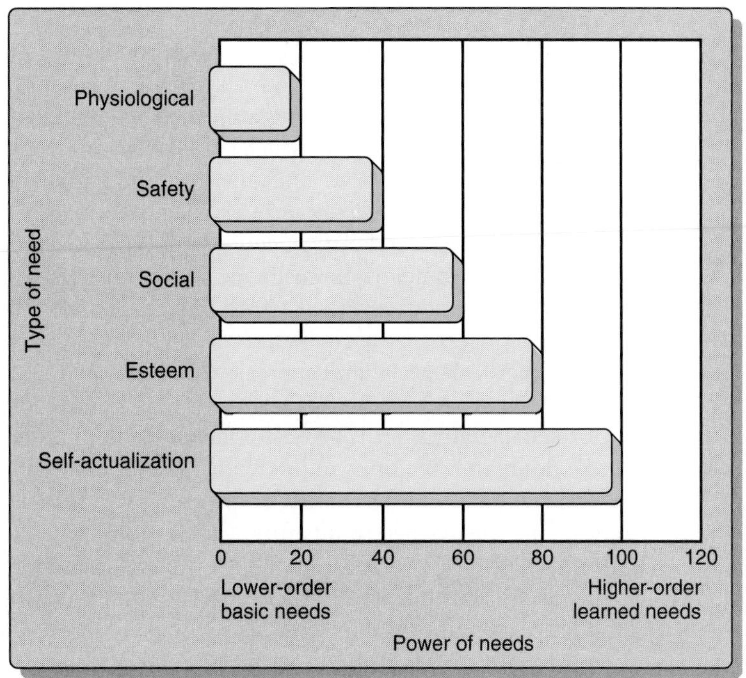

and an A on the next exam may be secondary to your need for sleep if you were out partying half the night. On the other hand, if you are well rested, your concern (aroused tension) over improving your grade point average (need) may encourage you to review this chapter several times in order to earn a B or better on the next exam (goal-directed action). However, one thing you can be sure of: After you have satisfied either or both of these needs, other needs will arise (for example, getting a date for the weekend).

Safety needs are satisfied by feelings of security and stability. To be secure, a person must feel free from physical harm or danger. Product and service retailers that focus on the need for protection include those that sell smoke or burglar alarm systems, insurance and retirement plans, exercise and health programs, warranties and guarantees, and caffeine-free, sugar-free, and salt-free foods and beverages. SAFE-T-MAN is a four-kilogram inflatable mannequin marketed to women who must drive solo and elderly persons who live alone.[16] Sears has created Sears Security Stores in about one-third of its sites; this store-within-a-store is a collection of security- and safety-related goods.[17] To facilitate the consumer's sense of security, manufacturers and retailers often produce and stock products containing such seals of approval as "CSA approved" (Canada Standards Act) or "recommended by the Canadian Dental Association." Consumer risk reduction can be a powerful force in attracting new customers and maintaining loyalty of existing shoppers. Timothy Eaton's famous policy "goods satisfactory or money refunded" has been adopted by many retailers to reduce purchase risk. Wendy's has regained lost market share and strengthened its image by focusing its management on the importance of providing "consistency" in all aspects of its fast-food business; giving customers what they expect is a very powerful security message.[18]

Stability is an equally important factor in meeting the need for safety. Generally, people feel more secure when there is a reasonable amount of order and structure in their lives. The often-heard expressions "I need to simplify my life" or "I need to get organized" are directed at obtaining relief from the tensions that are aroused by an unstructured, unorganized, and chaotic lifestyle. Simplification and organization are both excellent concepts to be used by retailers in developing product lines, designing store and display layouts, creating advertising appeals, and establishing pricing points.

As social creatures, we all have **social needs**—the desire for love, belongingness, affection, and friendship. Because of our relatively affluent society, social needs have become powerful motivators of our behaviour and influential organizers of our perceptions. Capitalizing on this need to "be accepted" or "fit in," retailers structure many merchandising strategies around the need for satisfying relationships with family, friends, peers, and reference groups. Social need gratification influences where we live, what we wear, which organizations we belong to, which stores we patronize, and how much we are willing to pay.

Esteem needs involve consumer aspirations regarding prestige, recognition, admiration, self-respect, success, and achievement. An individual who seeks to fulfill esteem needs wants to "stand out" as contrasted to the social need to "fit in." In satisfying esteem needs, a consumer is more likely to (1) purchase "limited edition" merchandise; (2) patronize distinctive outlets; (3) respond to individualist retail promotions; and (4) react in a less price-sensitive manner. The retailer's task in meeting esteem needs is to make the consumer feel special and appreciated.

"Doing what you are capable of doing" is a phrase that summarizes an individual's need for **self-actualization**. The desire for self-fulfillment is the highest-order need; it reflects the desire to reach one's full potential as an individual—"what you can be, you must be." The real luxury in the market of the future will be experiential and not necessarily a possession. This change results from "possession proliferation"; consumers own more goods but are forced to work harder, longer hours, under more stress. More consumers want few goods of better quality in order to free up time to enjoy life's experience. "Voluntary simplicity" is a growing movement based on the belief that both making and spending less money can be rewarding in itself.[19] A good example of an industry directed toward helping consumers realize their potential are the numerous motivational books, tapes, seminars, television infomercials, and programs designed to provide the means for realizing self-actualization.

Perception How motivated consumers act out the buying process is determined, in part, by their perceptions of the buying situation. **Perception** is the process by which consumers attach meaning to incoming stimuli by forming mental pictures of persons, places, and objects. An individual's perception is how he or she views the world. Black & Decker is attempting to alter the perception of its power tools among novices and do-it-yourselfers. The company is introducing a new cordless-tool line decked out in designer jade green.[20] Black & Decker hopes to create the impression that this line of tools is not only safe and convenient but also easy to use. The basic perceptual process consists of three stages: receiving, organizing, and interpreting stimuli (see Figure 4–7). *Stimulus reception* is accomplished through the five senses: sight, sound, taste, touch, and smell. For most people, the sense of sight is the most used and developed sense mode, a fact that retailers should keep in mind when planning all aspects of their retailing mix. Exposure is the key to receiving stimuli; perception follows exposure. A major tactic in any retailing program is the inclusion of plans for gaining buyer exposure for the firm's product offering.

Figure 4–7

The perception process

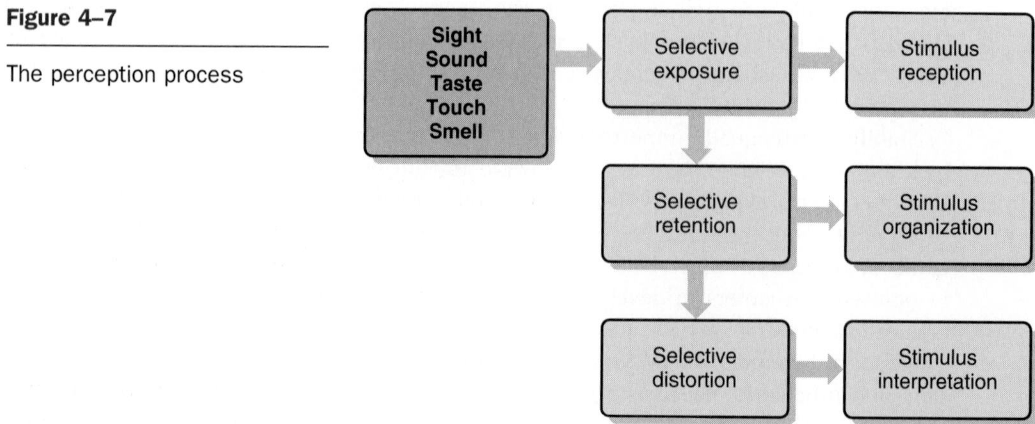

Stimulus organization is a mental data processing system in which incoming stimuli (data) are organized into descriptive categories. Received stimuli must be simplified through organization if they are to be mentally converted into meaningful information that can be useful in problem solving, that is, making purchase decisions. Individuals vary greatly in their ability to receive, store, and organize stimuli mentally; hence, their interpretations of stimuli exhibit equal variance.

Stimulus interpretation is the process of assigning meaning to stimuli. When the consumer attaches meaning to something he or she has sensed, the perceptual process is completed. Interpretation of stimuli is accomplished by the mental comparison of what is sensed to what the individual knows or feels from previous experience.

Selectivity is a natural phenomenon occurring within the perceptual process of receiving (selective exposure), organizing (selective retention), and interpreting (selective distortion) stimuli. What you see (hear, feel, taste, and smell) is what you get. What consumers actually perceive is almost always vastly different from the actual stimuli presented. The selectivity of perception is a key factor in explaining why different people have different perceptions of the same stimuli. **Selective exposure** is the act of limiting the type and amount of stimuli received and admitted to awareness. It is a screening process that enables us to select only the stimuli that interest us. "[North] Americans who share a strong preference for television, books, or other kinds of media are likely to have similar demographic characteristics. People who share a preference for media are also likely to share preferences for certain products."[21] Retailers use this consumer tendency to favour a certain media type in segmenting markets, identifying regional and local markets, making merchandising decisions, and planning promotional programs.

Selective retention is the act of remembering only the information that an individual wants to remember. "Consumers do not pay attention to advertising the way they used to. The average [North American] adult is already bombarded with 3000 marketing messages a day, so it is well-nigh impossible to get any one pitch noticed or remembered amid all the clamour."[22] Individuals tend to retain information that is consistent with their feelings, beliefs, and attitudes. Conflicting information is likely to be forgotten. To be effective, the retailer's persuasive communications must target consumers by developing message content (that is, what to say) and message presentations (that is, how to say it) that speak to the selected consumer's field of experiences.

Selective distortion is the act of misinterpreting incoming stimuli to make them consistent with the individual's beliefs and attitudes. By changing incoming information, people can create a harmonious relationship between that information and their mind-set and avoid the tension that results from not having one's beliefs supported by new inputs. For example, if we like a particular retail store because of its friendly sales personnel, we might distort the fact that its higher prices are not competitive. The selectivity of perception places a considerable strain on the retailer that must get messages admitted to awareness without being misinterpreted or forgotten.

Learning The logical extension of the motivational and perceptual process is learning. A considerable amount of human behaviour is learned. **Learning** is the process of acquiring knowledge through past experiences. Behavioural psychologists view learning as a stimulus-response mechanism in which drives, cues, and responses interact to produce a learned pattern of behaviour. A **drive** is whatever impels behaviour; it arises from a strongly felt inner need that requires action. A fear of failure, for example, may drive an insecure individual to work longer and more efficiently. **Cues** are external stimuli that direct consumers toward specific objects that can satisfy basic needs and reduce drives. To illustrate, an advertisement promoting a new book on time management is likely to catch the attention of an unsure individual who is looking for ways to improve his or her work efficiency. **Responses** are the actions taken to reduce a cue-stimulated drive. In a buying situation, these actions typically include identifying, trying, evaluating, and selecting purchase alternatives. To continue the example, our fearful individual may respond by visiting the bookstore and may or may not decide to buy the book after previewing it.

The extent to which an individual learns from this stimulus-response mechanism is influenced by three factors: reinforcement, repetition, and participation. **Reinforcement** is the comparing of anticipated results with the actual results experienced from a chosen response. If actual results compare favourably with anticipated results, response reinforcement occurs and learning takes place. As described by one retailing executive, if customers are treated like royalty every time they visit a store, actual treatment equals expected treatment, and the result is that royal customers become loyal customers.[23] Reinforcement could also take the form of return and allowance policies that confirm the retailer's intent to correct product deficiencies.

Repetition is the act of repeating a past experience. Learning is enhanced by performing the same action several times. The concept of repetition in learning has many applications in retail merchandising. In the area of store layout, for example, shoppers learn the store and where things are by developing an in-store travel pattern that they repeat each time they visit the store. Over time these shoppers become very comfortable and more efficient with their in-store trip behaviour, and any changes in store layout will force these repeat shoppers to relearn the store and new locations of items on their shopping list, a process not likely to be greeted with much enthusiasm.

Repetition is also extremely important in developing the retailer advertising program. Given the high degree of advertising clutter, retailers are generally better able to reach their target audiences by presenting a simple message repeated many times. Repetitive ads tend to be more memorable and effective in communicating to consumers positive images about retailers and their market offerings.

Participation is the active involvement in the learning process. An active role in any activity generally results in the acquisition of more knowledge about that activity. Free samples, trial sizes, and demonstrations are participation devices used in guiding the consumer's learning process toward the retailer's products. The key for the retailer in utilizing participation as a learning enhancement is to actively involve the customer's five senses. If the customer can see it, feel it, smell it, taste it, and/or hear it, he or she is bound to learn more about it. The retail store must encourage customer involvement with the merchandise and the buying process. Buying is not an act of observation; it is one of action.

From the perspective of the retailer, the ultimate goal of the learning process is initial store patronage and continuing store loyalty. When the customer has learned that the retailer's offering meets or exceeds expectations (customer satisfaction), the retailer should do whatever is reasonable to strengthen the customer's learned behaviour.[24] Retailers must concentrate on those key satisfaction factors that are pivotal in the customer's learning process. By reinforcing and repeating key satisfaction factors and involving the customer in the merchandising effort, retailers can have a significant impact on what the customer learns about its operational and merchandising programs.

Attitudes An **attitude** is a valuative mental orientation that provides a predisposition to respond in a certain fashion. People use their attitudes as valuative mechanisms to pass judgment (that is, good or bad, right or wrong) and as orientation mechanisms to focus that judgment on particular persons, places, things, or events. Attitudes can perform an important simplification function of the buying process by providing the consumer with a preset way to respond to the object of the attitude. For example, if Bob thinks that department stores are overpriced, he can avoid shopping there. One recent study suggests that "[North] Americans are experiencing doubts about their collective and individual futures. And in recognizing these doubts and fears, [they] have moved from an attitude of invincibility to a deep and unsettling sense of vulnerability."[25] Assuming the study's results are valid, how might retailers incorporate this attitudinal change into their merchandising efforts? Reliability, stability, responsibility, dependability, and credibility are all strong messages and appropriate actions that could counter feelings of vulnerability.

What is the makeup of an attitude? Figure 4–8 portrays the three basic components of an attitude: cognitive, affective, and behaviour. The **cognitive component** consists of what the consumer believes about an object on the basis of available information and knowledge. Essentially, a cognition is what is known about the object and its attributes. Feelings, not beliefs, are the focal point of the **affective component**—the emotions a consumer feels about an object. Emotions such as fear, surprise, sadness, anger, joy, and disgust are extremely important because they serve as fuel for drives that impel buying and other

Figure 4–8

The components of an attitude

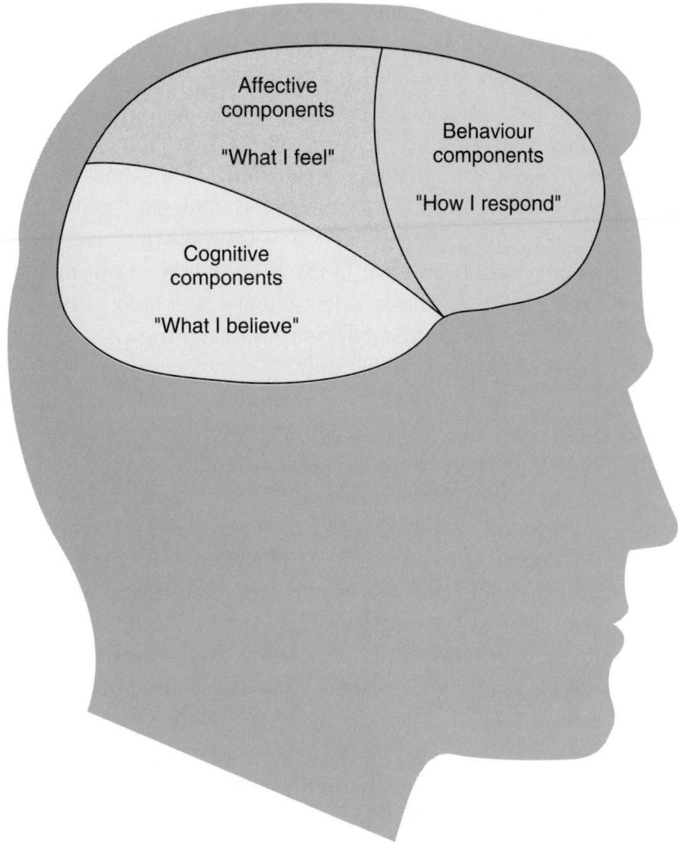

types of behaviour. When not in suit and tie, the North American male often adopts what etiquette authority Letitia Baldrige calls the "bathrobe attitude," defined thus: "I am comfy and that's all that counts."[26] The third element of an attitude, the **behaviour component**, is the predisposition to respond in a certain way to the object on the basis of one's beliefs and feelings. The strength of the consumer's beliefs and feelings about a particular object will determine the degree to which the consumer is predisposed to act. Nevertheless, if the consumer believes that discount stores offer the best overall value, his or her tendency is to patronize discount stores unless that belief system is altered.

Attitude formation is the result of past experiences. For example, consumers who grew up during the Depression view spending money very conservatively; they believe in saving for that inevitable rainy day. Consumers who experienced both the Depression and the post–World War II boom years prefer to save some and spend some. The baby-boom generation developed its attitudes during a prosperous postwar period; its approach was spend it all and then some. Recent economic downturns and changing lifestyles have required the boomers to cultivate more conservative attitudes toward consumption.

Attitudes are learned through interactions with family members and a wide range of peer and reference groups. People often adopt the prevailing attitudes of their associates. The learning of an attitude takes one of several forms: (1) trial and error (purchasing and using a product), (2) visual observation (watching a product demonstration), and (3) verbal communication (listening to the product opinions of others). Through involvement in trial and error, visual observation, and verbal communication experiences of consumers, retailers can influence attitude formation.

Personal Factors

An individual's personality, self-concept, lifestyle, and position in the life cycle are all personal factors that affect that individual's buying behaviour (see Figure 4–4). We continue our exploration of the whys of consumer behaviour by discussing each of the four personal factors.

Personality Everyone has a personality; unfortunately, there is considerable disagreement as to what it is and to what extent it influences buying behaviour. Because of its complex nature, **personality** is perhaps best defined in general terms: a general response pattern used by individuals in coping with their environment. For example, an individual may be positive or negative, pessimistic or optimistic, aggressive or passive, independent or dependent, sociable or unsociable, and friendly or withdrawn. Logically, the existence of a particular personality trait will affect an individual's buying behaviour. For example, a person with a pessimistic personality will approach buying situations with a considerable amount of doubt, whereas an optimistic individual will be more impulsive and confident about buying choices. Market researchers, however, have been largely unsuccessful in their efforts to find significant statistical relationships between personalities and buying behaviour.

Self-Concept Who are we? One answer to that question is that we are what we perceive ourselves to be—that is, our **self-concept**, or the set of perceptions we have of ourselves within a social context.[27] Each individual has a general awareness of his or her capabilities and attributes and how they are perceived within a social setting. "The '80s were defined by work and things: 'You are what you do,' or 'You are what you own.' The '90s, on the other hand, are much more about 'You are who you are.' "[28] The optimal lifestyle arrangement for most baby boomers is a more even blend of work, home, and recreation; they are just as likely "to define themselves as mothers and fathers, wind-surfers and skiers, as to talk about themselves as accountants and lawyers, carpenters and secretaries."[29] The self-concept consists of four parts: the real self, the ideal self, the looking-glass self, and self-image.

As illustrated in Figure 4–9, our self-image is to some extent a composite of the real, ideal, and looking-glass selves. The importance of the self-concept to retailers in understanding consumer behaviour is twofold: First, consumers often purchase products and/or brands that they feel support and reinforce their self-concept; and second, consumers never consciously purchase products that are incompatible with their self-concept. For example, "Ms. Conservative" pictured in Figure 4–9 may purchase a blue blazer with gray slacks because it is consistent with each of her "selves"; such an apparel selection would enable this individual to fantasize about being a swinging single (what she would like to be) while preserving the image as an average (what she really is) and ordinary (what others see her as) person.

One major way retailers use the self-concept is in the creation of advertising appeals. By directing an advertising message to such self-images as the "homebody," "good provider," "budding scholar," and "professional," the retailer has an additional tool for targeting selected consumer markets, developing product lines, planning price tactics, and designing store layouts.

Figure 4–9

The four parts of the self-concept

Lifestyles Some people lead an active life; others are more sedentary. Some people's lives are centred on their home and family; others are centred on jobs, organizations, hobbies, or events. A consumer's lifestyle affects what, when, where, how, and why he or she buys. **Lifestyle** can be defined as the way consumers live. It is a patterned style of living that stems from the individual's needs, perceptions, and attitudes; as such, it represents a behavioural profile of the individual's psychological makeup. How consumers choose to live is also a reflection of the influences exerted by family members, peers, and other groups. Most experts agree that the 1990s lifestyle will be one of "balancing personal desires with family responsibilities. Balancing the wish to spend with the need to save. Balancing aspirations against limited resources."[30] Both conforming and nonconforming lifestyles are behavioural reactions to what are expected and accepted modes of living. The casual lifestyle is a trend that most experts predict will become more of the norm rather than the exception. Dress-down days will be seven days a week by the year 2000.[31]

Lifestyle analysis (psychographics) is an attempt by marketing researchers to develop consumer profiles based on consumers' ways of living. Lifestyle profiles are composite pictures of the consumer's **activities, interests, and opinions (AIO)**, together with their demographic makeup. Figure 4–10 identifies a commonly used enumeration of AIO variables. To develop lifestyle profiles, consumers are asked to respond to a multitude of AIO statements by indicating their degree of agreement or disagreement with those statements (see Figure 4–11). By finding patterned responses to AIO statements (for example, strong agreement with all statements that reflect favourably on work-oriented activities, job-related interests, and pro-business opinions), the retailer can better identify market segments and target marketing programs.

Lifestyle analysis tends to be special-purpose research; that is, it is directed at determining lifestyle profiles relative to a particular market, product, or retailing program. Psychographic descriptions of the entire population are available from two commercial sources: (1) VALS—Values and Lifestyles Program, a product of SRI International and the most widely used description (see the Retail Strategies and Tactics box p. 136), and (2) Compusearch and Prizm-Canada, which seek to predict macrosocial changes by monitoring changes in consumer attitudes. Local psychographic profiles may be available from local television and radio stations, as well as research and consulting concerns that operate on the local level.

Life Cycle Are you single, married, widowed, or divorced? Are you with or without children? Are you young, middle-aged, or elderly? These are some of the factors that determine which stage of the life cycle you are in. The **life cycle** is a description of the changes that occur in an individual's demographic, psychographic, and behaviouristic profile during his or her lifetime. The life cycle starts with the singles stage and ends with the retired solitary survivor of a family. The nine stages of the life cycle and their key demographic, psychographic, and behaviouristic elements are portrayed in Figure 4–12.[32] The differences in buyer behaviour can often be explained by practical considerations. Families with children buy toys, large families buy large-sized packages, and empty-nest families are in a position to more easily afford the purchase of luxury products and services.

Figure 4–10

The dimensions of lifestyle

Source: Joseph T. Plummer, "The Concept of Life-Style Segmentation," Journal of Marketing *38 (January 1974); 34. Reprinted from the* Journal of Marketing, *published by the American Marketing Association, Chicago, IL, 60606.*

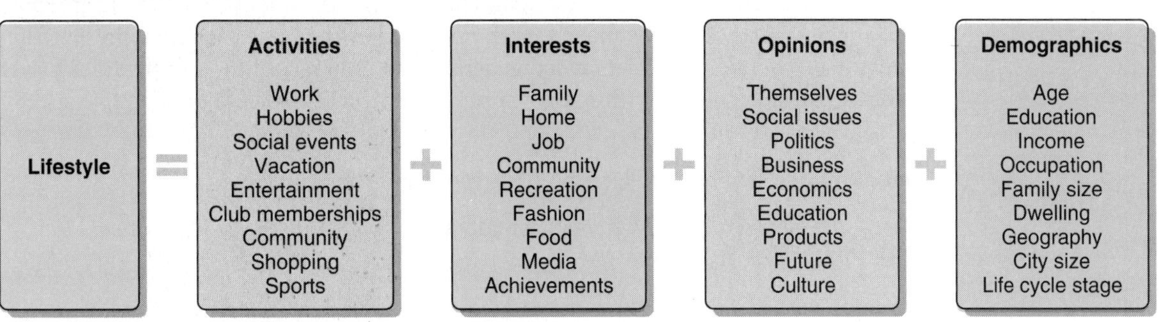

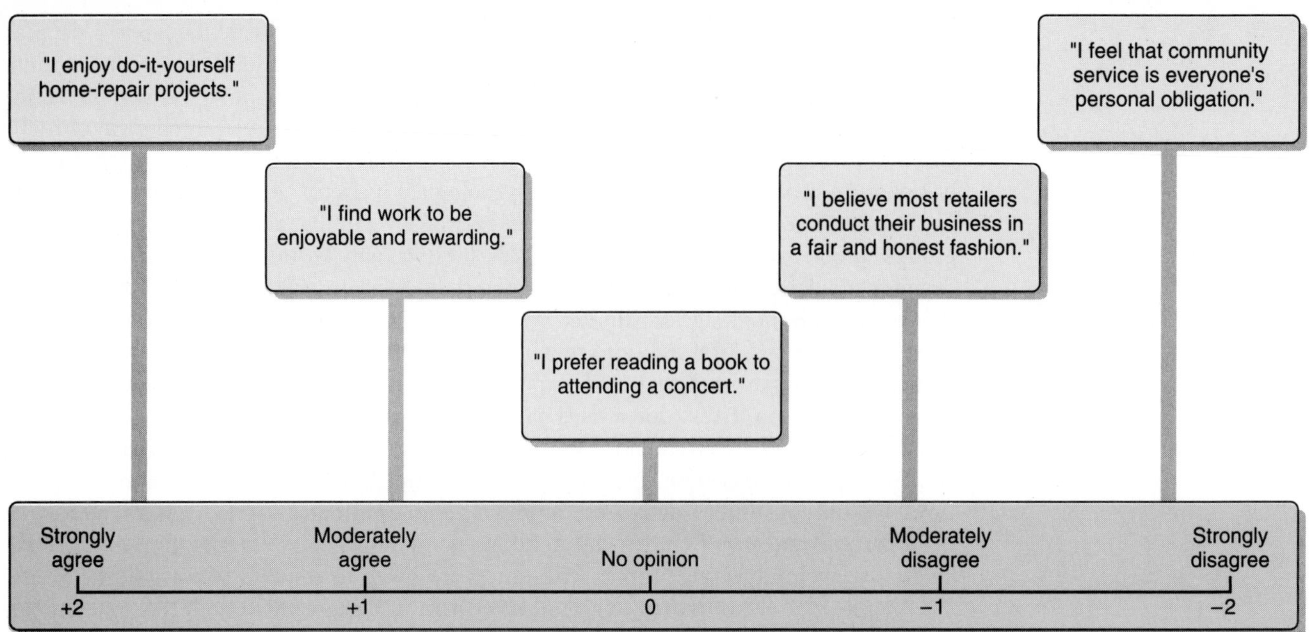

Figure 4–11

AID (activities, interests, and opinions) statements

Social Factors

Conformity to group expectations is a basic element of human behaviour. Much of what we do is directed at gaining acceptance from other people; so it is with our buying behaviour. We buy certain products, select particular brands, and patronize certain stores because we want the approval and support of others. The importance of group influences on individual buying behaviour is great. The following discussion examines the impact of the family, reference groups, social class, and culture on our individual buying behaviour (see Figure 4–4).

The Family A family can be described in terms of the *nuclear family*, consisting of a father, mother, and their children, or as the *extended family*, which includes the nuclear family plus grandparents, aunts, uncles, and cousins. Regardless of how the family unit is defined, it represents one of the most important social factors affecting our buying behaviour.[33] *Family influences* on individual buyer behaviour stem from childhood. Consciously or unconsciously, we adopt many of our parents' attitudes, values, morals, and ways of doing things. These basic orientations remain with us long after we have left our family of origin.

As we establish a new family by getting married and having children, the influences of our spouse and children assume a primary role of importance in the acquisition of new orientations and the development of new behavioural patterns. The role of the family and the occurrences of integrative family buying behaviour are expected to increase into the 21st century; this elevated family role is the result of the baby boomers' baby boomlet (see Chapter 3).

Family buying roles are a key issue in understanding consumer behaviour. From a merchandising perspective, a consumer is often not an individual but a family represented by an individual. Therefore, retailers must recognize and understand the various roles played by various family members within a given purchase situation. The following five specific roles have been identified:

1. **Initiator**—the family member who first recognizes the problem
2. **User**—the family member who will actually use or consume the product or service
3. **Decision maker**—the family member who decides what will be bought and at what time, place, and source

Figure 4–12

The life cycle process

Source: William D. Wells and George Gubar, "Life Cycle Concept in Marketing Research," Journal of Marketing Research *3 (November 1966): 362.*

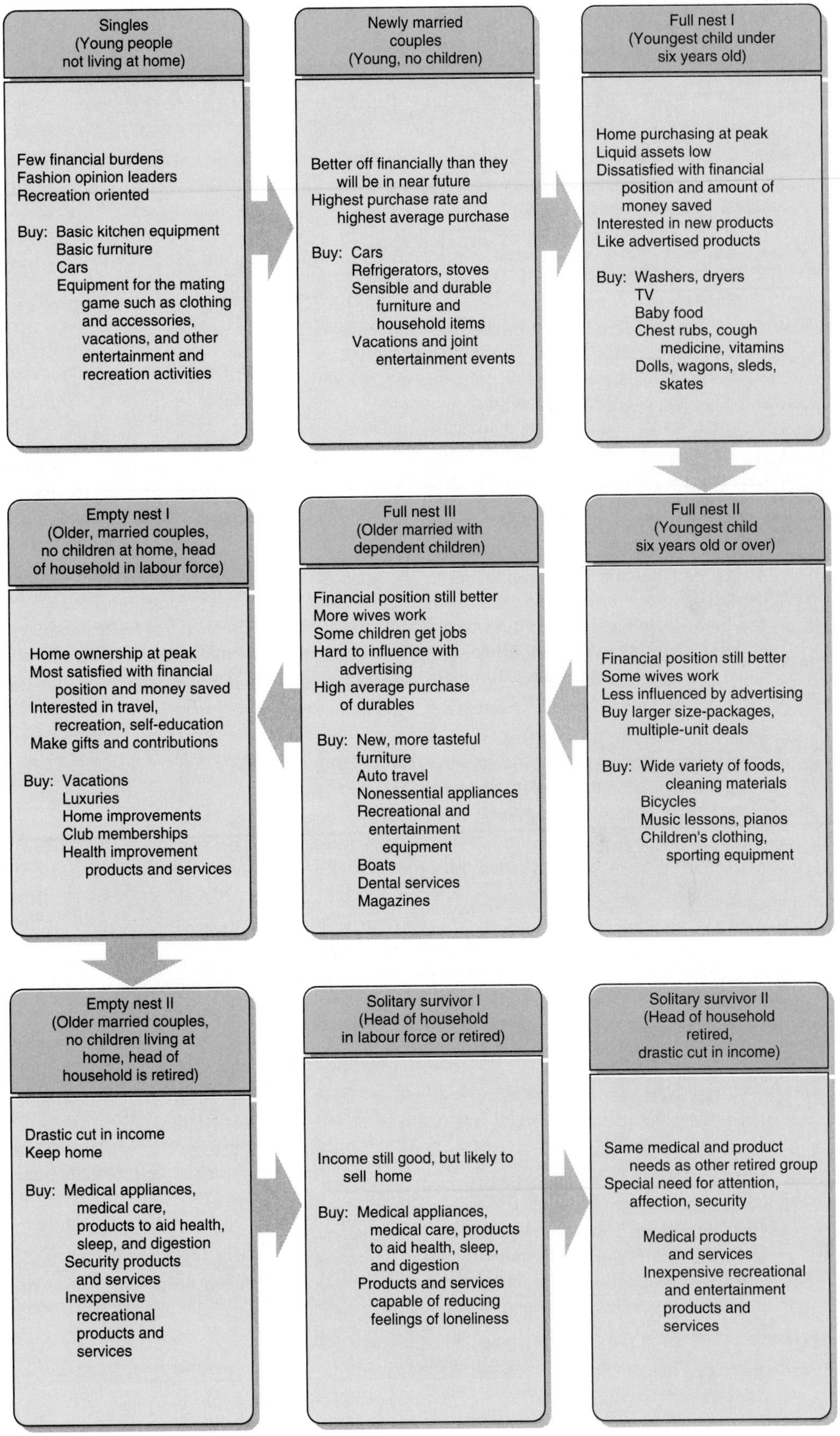

Singles (Young people not living at home)

Few financial burdens
Fashion opinion leaders
Recreation oriented

Buy: Basic kitchen equipment
Basic furniture
Cars
Equipment for the mating game such as clothing and accessories, vacations, and other entertainment and recreation activities

Newly married couples (Young, no children)

Better off financially than they will be in near future
Highest purchase rate and highest average purchase

Buy: Cars
Refrigerators, stoves
Sensible and durable furniture and household items
Vacations and joint entertainment events

Full nest I (Youngest child under six years old)

Home purchasing at peak
Liquid assets low
Dissatisfied with financial position and amount of money saved
Interested in new products
Like advertised products

Buy: Washers, dryers
TV
Baby food
Chest rubs, cough medicine, vitamins
Dolls, wagons, sleds, skates

Full nest II (Youngest child six years old or over)

Financial position still better
Some wives work
Less influenced by advertising
Buy larger size-packages, multiple-unit deals

Buy: Wide variety of foods, cleaning materials
Bicycles
Music lessons, pianos
Children's clothing, sporting equipment

Full nest III (Older married with dependent children)

Financial position still better
More wives work
Some children get jobs
Hard to influence with advertising
High average purchase of durables

Buy: New, more tasteful furniture
Auto travel
Nonessential appliances
Recreational and entertainment equipment
Boats
Dental services
Magazines

Empty nest I (Older, married couples, no children at home, head of household in labour force)

Home ownership at peak
Most satisfied with financial position and money saved
Interested in travel, recreation, self-education
Make gifts and contributions

Buy: Vacations
Luxuries
Home improvements
Club memberships
Health improvement products and services

Empty nest II (Older married couples, no children living at home, head of household is retired)

Drastic cut in income
Keep home

Buy: Medical appliances, medical care, products to aid health, sleep, and digestion
Security products and services
Inexpensive recreational products and services

Solitary survivor I (Head of household in labour force or retired)

Income still good, but likely to sell home

Buy: Medical appliances, medical care, products to aid health, sleep, and digestion
Products and services capable of reducing feelings of loneliness

Solitary survivor II (Head of household retired, drastic cut in income)

Same medical and product needs as other retired group
Special need for attention, affection, security

Medical products and services
Inexpensive recreational and entertainment products and services

Retail Strategies and Tactics

Lifestyles Segmentation Using the VALS 2 System

Marketing research has produced a large number of different lifestyle profiles designed for a specific product or company. A more universal lifestyle typology was developed by SRI International, a nonprofit think tank. They developed the original VALS system, which grouped individuals on the basis of their values (VA) and lifestyles (LS). VALS 2 is a revision of the earlier system and divides consumers into eight groups as defined by their psychological makeup or self-orientation (that is, patterns of attitudes and activities that help people reinforce, sustain, or even modify their social self-image) and their available resources (that is, education, income, self-confidence, health, eagerness to buy, intelligence, and energy level). The eight VALS 2 customer segments are as follows:

- *Actualizers*—Successful, sophisticated, active, "take-charge" people with high self-esteem and abundant resources. They are interested in growth and seek to develop, explore, and express themselves in a variety of ways—sometimes guided by principle, and sometimes by a desire to have an effect, to make a change. Their possessions and recreation reflect a cultivated taste for the finer things in life.
- *Fulfilleds*—Mature, satisfied, comfortable, reflective people who value order, knowledge, and responsibility. Most are well educated and in, or recently retired from, professional occupations. Content with their careers, families, and station in life, their leisure activities tend to centre around their homes. Although their incomes allow them many choices, they are conservative, practical consumers, concerned about functionality, value, and durability in the products they buy.
- *Believers*—Conservative, conventional people with concrete beliefs and strong attachments to traditional institutions: family, church, community, and the nation. They follow established routines, organized in large part around their homes, families, and social or religious organizations. As consumers, they are conservative and predictable, favouring domestic products and established brands.
- *Achievers*—Successful career- and work-oriented people who like to, and generally do, feel in control of their lives. They value structure, predictability, and stability over risk, intimacy, and self-discovery. They are deeply committed to their work and families. As consumers, they favour established products that demonstrate their success to their peers.
- *Strivers*—Seek motivation, self-definition, and approval from the world around them. They are striving to find a secure place in life. Unsure of themselves and low on economic, social, and psychological resources, they are deeply concerned about the opinions and approval of others. They emulate those who own more impressive possessions, but what they wish to obtain is generally beyond their reach.
- *Experiencers*—Young, vital, enthusiastic, impulsive, and rebellious. They seek variety and excitement, savouring the new, the offbeat, and the risky. Still in the process of formulating life values and patterns of behaviour, they quickly become enthusiastic about new possibilities but are equally quick to cool. They are avid consumers and spend much of their income on clothing, fast food, music, movies, and video.
- *Makers*—Practical people who have constructive skills and value self-sufficiency. They live within a traditional context of family, practical work, and physical recreation and have little interest in what lies outside that context. They experience the world by working on it (for example, building a house, canning vegetables) and have sufficient skill, income, and energy to carry out their projects successfully. They are unimpressed by material possessions other than those with a practical or functional purpose.
- *Strugglers*—Strugglers' lives are constricted. Chronically poor, ill educated, low skilled, without strong social bonds, aging and concerned about their health, they are often despairing and passive. Their chief concerns are for security and safety. They are cautious consumers; while they represent a very modest market for most products and services, they are loyal to favourite brands.

By targeting one (for example, Experiencers) or a limited number of lifestyle segments (for example, Fulfilleds, Believers), the retailer can create a customer focus through a carefully constructed mix of product lines, pricing points, service offerings, store environments, and promotional appeals.

Source: Adapted from Penny Gill, "New VALS 2 Values and Lifestyles Segmentation," Stores *(November 1989): 35.*

4. **Decision influencer**—the family member who has input to affect the choice of the decision maker
5. **Purchasing agent**—the family member who actually visits the store and makes the purchase

To be effective, a merchandising program must take into account each family member and his or her respective role. For example, the retailer's persuasive and informational advertising might be directed at (1) the initiator to create awareness, (2) the user to provide reinforcement, (3) the decision maker and decision influencer to develop comprehension and conviction, and (4) the purchasing agent to guide shopping trip behaviour.

Pizza Hut
www.pizzahut.com

Role specialization in family buying is common in most families. Children play an extremely important role as influencers. For example, children visiting fast-food restaurants typically bring adults, doubling or tripling the meal ticket. This importance of children in the family's decision to eat out helps to explain why PepsiCo's Taco Bell and Pizza Hut divisions are vying for some of the family traffic now flowing into McDonald's and Burger King.[34] Although some purchase decisions are made jointly or independently, other purchases are dominated by either the husband or wife. Canadian department stores have made menswear departments more appealing to females as they recognize that many females make purchases for their spouses.[35] With the increase of working mothers, many teens are taking on the adult buying roles of decision maker and purchasing agent. As the purchase decisions become more diffused, people within the household are playing it safe in terms of buying a brand they trust, because everyone else in the household will agree it is a good purchase decision, as opposed to buying a generic or unknown brand.

Reference Groups Reference groups provide individuals with a "frame of reference" in making such purchase decisions as what and where to buy. A **reference group** is a group that serves as a model or standard for an individual's behaviour and attitudes. An individual may develop associations with such reference groups as friends, colleagues, coworkers, clubs, and associations.

Reference group influences on purchase behaviour vary by product and brand. Purchases of highly conspicuous and visible products such as clothing, furniture, and automobiles are strongly influenced by reference groups. If the brand name, style, or design is uniquely conspicuous, reference group influences become an important decision factor. From preschool to high school, kids have long felt the pressure to dress a certain way and wear particular labels. Currently, some schools are experimenting with using a

Retail Strategies and Tactics

Kids Have Say in Household Purchases

Children at home are driving the market for computers and other modern household gadgets. Kids and keyboards are a natural fit, Statistics Canada said in an annual survey of ownership of household facilities.

The survey also shows that families with kids register the highest ownership of time-saving and leisure equipment like microwaves, dishwashers, VCRs, compact disc players, and more than one colour TV set.

"The trend was most pronounced where both parents were present, due not only to their higher incomes and associated purchasing power, but also due to the high proportion of families in which both parents worked," the agency said. Among households with incomes of $70 000 or more, 65 percent owned computers.

Dwellings with children are also mere likely to have modems and be hooked to the Internet. About 21 percent of these homes had modems and 9.4 percent use the Internet, compared with rates of 15.5 percent and 7.5 percent for households without kids. "Increasing use of computers in the classroom and higher computer literacy among the young are likely two factors contributing to this trend," the agency said.

Source: Staff, Lethbridge Herald, *February 13, 1997, B7.*

school uniform that would eliminate the pressure to be product- and brand-correct. Shoes (Nike and Reebok), jeans (Levi's and Lee), and jackets (NFL or other sports leagues) are some of the right stuff that kids and parents are pressured into buying to gain peer group acceptance. The "retro" look is the outcome of an antisneaker sneaker movement in which nostalgic styles from the 1960s and 1970s are enjoying a new life cycle. In one sense, it is a backlash to the aggressive marketing tactics of Nike and Reebok, in which sport celebrity endorsements attempt to create peer pressure in the purchase decision of footwear. Not surprisingly, it is Generation Xers who do not like being overmarketed to who are driving the retro trend.[36]

Social Class Canadians can be classified according to such variables as income, occupation, education, and residence. Using such criteria, social scientists have developed societal, rank-ordered groupings of individuals and families known as **social classes**. The higher the class rank, the higher the status (greater prestige) of the class. A widely used classification scheme of social classes is that developed by W. Lloyd Warner. His scheme consists of six levels ranging from upper-upper class to lower-lower class (see Figure 4–13).

Several generalizations can be made regarding the marketing implications stemming from our social class groupings. For instance, upper-upper-class consumers typically do not engage in conspicuous consumption; rather, they tend to be governed by conservative tastes and a selective buying process. They represent potential markets for unique and expensive products (for example, "originals" in fashion apparel). Patronage motives tend toward personalized services and individualistic merchandising at exclusive retailers.

Lower-upper-class consumers engage in conspicuous consumption of a provided range of highly visible personal, recreational, and household products and services. This buying behaviour is often directed at impressing lower social classes. A primary consideration of lower-upper-class purchasing behaviour is social acceptability of their peer class and the acceptance of the upper-upper class; in other words, much of this class's buying behaviour is directed at achieving status. The conspicuous consumption of the 1980s and early 1990s is being replaced by a more conservative consumption attitude—a reverse snobbery of conspicuous bargain hunting.

Upper-middle-class consumers are quality-conscious purchasers of products that are acceptable to the upper class; hence, they tend to be cautious consumers of prestigious products that communicate "who they are" to others. On the other hand, they also tend

Figure 4-13

The staircase of social classes

Source: Adapted from W. Lloyd Warner, American Life, Dream and Reality *(Chicago, University of Chicago Press, 1953).*

Upper-upper— 1.5 percent of the population; society's aristocracy; the social elite; inherited wealth; reside in older, fashionable neighbourhoods; membership in most prestigious country clubs; children attend elite private preparatory schools and colleges.

Lower-upper—1.5 percent of the population; society's new rich; successful professionals; high-level business executives; successful entrepreneurs; educated at public universities; send children to private elite universities; active in civic affairs

Upper-middle—10 percent of the population; career-oriented professionals such as physicians, lawyers, and engineers; best educated social class; quite status conscious; reside in prestigious neighbourhoods

Lower-middle—30 percent of the population; society's white-collar workers such as office workers, clerks, teachers, and salespeople; most conforming, hard working, religious, and home- and family-oriented of all social classes

Upper-lower—33 percent of the population; largest social class; blue-collar factory workers and skilled tradesmen; live a routine, day-to-day existence; not particularly status conscious; very security conscious; do not typically expect to rise above their present social station

Lower-lower—25 percent of the population; unskilled worker; chronically unemployed worker; poorly educated; slum-dweller; unassimilated; ethnic minority groups; rural poor; reject middle-class values and standards of behaviour to be venturesome in their willingness to try new products and seek out new places to shop. For the upper-middle class, their home is the centre of their personal and social life and therefore is a focus for their buyer behavior. Home Depot and Canadian Tire are retailers of housewares and furnishings that target this home-centred social class.

Lower-middle-class consumers focus a considerable amount of buying behaviour around maintaining a respectable home in a do-it-yourself context. They tend to be quite value-conscious in that they seek an acceptable relationship between lower prices and good quality. Standardization is a key factor in their buying behaviour; they therefore purchase products of standard design from traditional retail operations. Discount stores, superstores, off-price retailers, and other price-oriented retailers offering basic selections of both branded and private-label merchandise in a convenient, one-stop shopping format are the stores of choice for these economically strapped consumers.[37]

Retail Strategies and Tactics

Class Distinctions: Understanding the Middle Class

Class Distinctions: You are what you choose

		Lower Middle	Middle	Upper Middle
Car	1980s	Hyundai	Chevrolet Celebrity	Mercedes
	1990s	Geo	Chrysler minivan	Range Rover
Business shoe (men)	1980s	Sneakers	Wingtips	Cap toes
	1990s	Boots	Rockports	Loafers
Business shoe (women)	1980s	Spike-heel pumps	Mid-heel pump	High-heel pumps
	1990s	High-heel pumps	Dressy flats	One-inch pumps
Alcoholic beverage	1980s	Domestic beer	White wine spritzer	Dom Perignon
	1990s	Domestic lite beer	California Chardonnay	Cristal
Leisure pursuit	1980s	Watching sports	Going to movies	Golf
	1990s	Playing sports	Renting movies	Play with computers
Hero	1980s	Roseanne Barr	Ronald Reagan	Michael Milken
	1990s	Kathie Lee Gifford	Janet Reno	Rush Limbaugh

Source: Kenneth Labich, "Class in America," Fortune, *February 7, 1994, 116.*

Retail Strategies and Tactics

Mass Merchandisers Winning Shoppers

Aggressive promotion and uncertain economic conditions are causing a "fundamental shift" to mass merchandisers and warehouse club stores, according to a new survey of consumer shopping trends. The shift in spending patterns has come primarily at the expense of drug stores and convenience stores, but larger grocery stores are also feeling the heat from the push by such large retailers as Zellers, Wal-Mart, and Price/Costco.

The survey also suggests shopping patterns are changing. In the 36 weeks leading up to March 2, 1996, the number of shopping trips to warehouse clubs was up 21 percent over the corresponding period in 1995, and up 11 percent at mass merchandisers. The number of trips increased by only 3 percent at grocery store chains, was unchanged at drug stores and fell by 14 percent at convenience stores.

Supermarket chains have responded with an array of price options—such as discount stores offering generic products, house brands, and bulk purchases. Drug-store chains, which are no longer permitted to sell tobacco goods—a product that helped pull in shoppers—have responded by adding more packaged foods.

Cox said the shift away from supermarkets and convenience store shopping reflects "a blurring of channels. Mass merchandiser clubs are selling and promoting a lot of goods that at one time were found almost exclusively at grocery stores. Price is also a growing factor in shopping decisions. Much of that has to do with uncertain economic conditions and worry about high unemployment.

"Whoever is offering good product at low price is going to be a winner in the marketplace," said Len Kubas, president of the consulting firm that bears his name. "But one of the things that many people are finding is that you need more than just the low price. You need something that is going to attract the customers on a more frequent basis. And in North America, food is probably the most frequently purchased item that we buy."

Source: James Walker, Financial Post, *July 6, 1996.*

Upper-lower-class consumers are less concerned with purchasing products that enhance status and are more concerned with buying goods and services for personal enjoyment. In comparison to other classes above them, this class spends a lower portion of their incomes on housing and a higher proportion of their income on household goods. They tend to be impulsive buyers yet remain loyal to previously bought brands that they believe to reflect good quality. As heavy users of credit, this class is hesitant to try new retail outlets.

Lower-lower-class consumers use credit extensively and impulsively to purchase highly visible products of a personal nature (for example, clothing, beauty aids). Reduced income levels and the lack of mobility due to a higher level of dependence on public transportation prevents this class of consumer from engaging in extensive comparison shopping activities. Hence, they prefer well-known brands and local stores with credit programs.

Culture The final social influence on our behaviour is the cultural environment in which the consumer lives. **Culture** is the sum total of knowledge, attitudes, symbols, and patterns of behaviour that are shared by a group of people and transmitted from one generation to the next. Cultural traits include (1) profound beliefs (for example, religious), (2) fundamental values (for example, achievements), and (3) customs (for example, ladies first). Because cultural environmental influences are a major determinant of human behaviour, it is essential for the retailer to adapt and conform merchandising programs to the cultural heritage of its chosen markets. Canadian retailers must be aware of dominant cultural trends of the mainstream market[38] as well as any important subcultural characteristics which might affect their success.[39]

How Consumers Buy

Being loved and accepted, overcoming loneliness and insecurity, and gaining status and prestige are all problems that consumers attempt to solve in part by engaging in buying activities. Individuals make purchase decisions by passing through the five stages of what we call the consumer buying process. The **consumer buying process** is the sum total of the sequential parts of problem recognition, information search, alternative evaluation, purchase decision, and postpurchase evaluation (see Figure 4–14). The duration and extent to which an individual gets involved in any one stage of the buying process varies greatly depending on such factors as urgency of need, frequency of purchase, importance of purchase, and so on. A description of each stage is presented in the following discussion; see if you can recognize these stages in your own buying behaviour.

Stage 1: Problem Recognition

A felt discrepancy between an ideal state of affairs and the actual state of affairs starts the consumer's buying process by creating an awareness that a problem exists. Problem recognition is, then, a feeling that things are not what they should be. Internally felt physiological and psychological needs are tension-producing stimuli that create an awareness that something is lacking. In addition, external cues attract and direct the consumer's attention toward the recognition that he or she is unsatisfied with the current state of affairs. Exposure to the retailer's stores, products, advertisements, merchandising incentives, personal selling efforts, and price structures are all potential reminders to consumers of unfulfilled needs and wants.

Depending on importance, cost, knowledge, and/or experience factors, there are three types of problem-solving situations: extensive, limited, and routinized problem solving. **Extensive problem solving** involves a buying situation in which the consumer is considering the purchase of an important and costly product under the unfavourable circumstances of having no knowledge or experience with the product. First-time purchases, once-in-a-lifetime purchases, and highly infrequent purchases are all buying situations

Figure 4–14

The consumer buying process

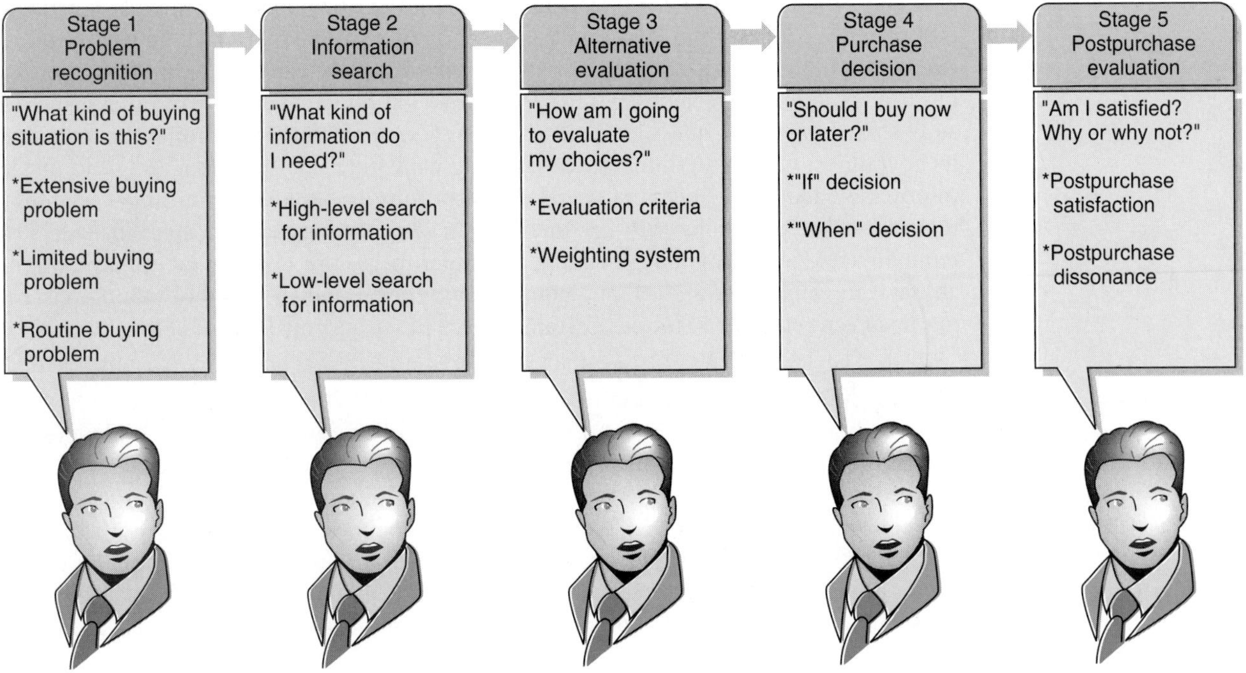

that require extensive consumer effort to achieve a satisfactory solution. Providing useful and readily available information and reducing risk and uncertainty of the purchase are key variables to be considered by the retailer when developing merchandising tactics to assist the consumer faced with an extensive problem-solving situation.

Limited problem solving occurs when the consumer has some knowledge and experience with purchasing and using the product under consideration. The problem may involve an important purchase and/or costly product. In either case, the buyer is able to limit the range of considerations (for example, brands, sizes, colours, materials) because of existing knowledge and previous experience. The retailer's task is to discover which limited decision factors are being used in making product selections, then to use these selective factors as focal points in developing appropriate product, price, distribution, and promotion strategies.

Routinized problem solving involves making the same purchase decision time after time. Consumers purchase many products frequently and regularly. Typically, these purchases tend to involve products of lower importance and cost that arise as repurchase needs. The typical weekly grocery list represents this type of purchase. Consumers simply repeat a previous purchase decision with little thought or deliberation because they feel there is no reason to change.

Stage 2: Information Search

Gathering information and gaining experience make up the second stage of the consumer buying process. Consumers who seek information about products and services tend to be better educated and more affluent than the average consumer. Not only do they realize the value of a good information search, but they also have the know-how and the money to conduct one.

A *low-level information* search involves an increased awareness of readily available information. The consumer pays closer attention to advertisements, store displays, sales pitches, and the comments of others in an effort to gather additional information to supplement existing product knowledge. To enhance the lower-order search for information, retailers are now experimenting with store entrance video kiosks that provide the customer with a store map and help locate specific items through an interactive touch-screen display. The same kiosk can also act as an ATM for cash withdrawals. Sears has installed "mini-kiosks" that will "enable customers to place catalogue orders, inquire about service and credit, check on the status of their car in the auto centre, or send a message to the store manager."[40]

A *high-level information search* consists of a conscientious effort to seek out and gather new and supplementary information from new and existing sources. It involves actively talking with, reading from, and observing information sources that will be useful for an extensive problem-solving situation. Extensive information searches might involve one or more of the following techniques: (1) surveillance—conducting in-store reconnaissance of store shelves, displays, and signage in search of additional details regarding the store and its operations; (2) counterintelligence—talking with store sales personnel to glean inside information about new incoming merchandise or future sales; (3) networking—establishing personal relationships with key information sources (for example, store managers or retail buyers); (4) researching—reading consumer magazines, product labels, promotional literature, and governmental and commercial reports; and (5) word of mouth—listening to current customers, former customers, and other informed sources.[41]

Stage 3: Alternative Evaluation

Product, brand, and store information must be processed before it is useful in the evaluation of purchase alternatives. Consumers use a variety of criteria in deciding which store to patronize and which product to buy, including selection, price, quality, service, value, and convenience. In times past, value was quality at almost any price; today, it is quality at the right price. What evaluation criteria would you use in purchasing a tube of toothpaste, a desk lamp, a winter coat, a colour television, and a new automobile? A comprehensive list of valuative criteria consumers use in purchasing these products is far too

Figure 4–15

Product, brand, and store evaluation criteria

- I. Product evaluation criteria
  - A. Functional features
    1. Size
    2. Shape
    3. Weight
    4. Material
    5. Workmanship
  - B. Aesthetic features
    1. Colour
    2. Texture
    3. Odour
    4. Taste
    5. Sound
    6. Style
  - C. Service features
    1. Delivery
    2. Alteration
    3. Installation
    4. Warranty
    5. Maintenance
  - D. Psychological features
    1. Prestige
    2. Image
    3. Acceptability
    4. Safety
    5. Security
    6. Uniqueness
- II. Merchandising evaluation criteria
  - A. Price features
    1. Selling price
    2. Perceived value
    3. Credit terms
  - B. Place features
    1. Convenience
    2. Availability
    3. Prestige
  - C. Promotional features
    1. Labels
    2. Logos
    3. Packages
- III. Personal evaluation criteria
  - A. Compatibility considerations
    1. Substitutive
    2. Complement
    3. Different
  - B. Appropriateness considerations
    1. Lifestyle
    2. Life cycle
  - C. Other considerations
    1. Durability
    2. Suitability
    3. Quality

complex and extensive to enumerate fully here; however, a general list of potential evaluation criteria is presented in Figure 4–15.

Criteria do not carry the same weight or have the same importance in deciding on a purchase. In some cases we are simply interested in having the product do what it was designed to do (for example, clean and polish, cool or heat); therefore, we place greater weight on the functional features of the product. In other cases, our needs may be more social in character; hence, we emphasize the psychological features of the product or brand and the personal considerations of the product or brand's appropriateness to our lifestyle and circle of friends. Many consumers are responding well to private-label jeans because they perceive these labels as representing good value; hence Sears' success with Canyon River Blues. On the other hand, those consumers who have to have jeans that say Calvin are making the jean purchase decision with more emphasis on the psychological benefits of the product.[42] In essence, for a given purchase, criteria are subjectively weighted along an importance scale ranging from not important to very important.

Stage 4: Purchase Decision

The purchase decision is actually two decisions: *if* and *when*. The "if" decision deals with the issue of whether to make a purchase. On the basis of the previous evaluation stage, the consumer may decide that there are several products, brands, or stores capable of resolving the problem identified in the first stage of the buying process—the **buy decision**. On the other hand, the consumer may conclude that of the known alternatives evaluated, none meet minimum expectations for need satisfaction—the **no-buy decision**.[43] A no-buy decision terminates the current cycle of the buying process; the consumer can either dismiss the problem or start the buying process anew with hopes of gaining a different perspective on the problem.

The "when" decision involves deciding whether to make an immediate purchase or to wait until some future date. A **decision to proceed** with the purchase may stem from urgently felt needs, currently available opportunities, and other circumstances that mediate against delaying the decision. A **decision to postpone** a purchase is frequently associated with a high level of perceived risk. The consumer becomes anxious because of the importance, cost, and/or uncertainty of the decision.

Stage 5: Postpurchase Evaluation

Purchasing a product does not end the consumer buying process. After a purchase has been made, the consumer proceeds to re-evaluate the decision in an attempt to judge whether he or she made the right (that is, best or acceptable) decision. Essentially, the postpurchase evaluation stage consists of comparing the actual performance of the product/service or the actual experience with the store against the expected or hoped-for performance or experience.[44]

The basic question to be answered by the consumer in the postpurchase evaluation stage is: "Did the product or store relieve aroused tensions stemming from felt needs?" In other words, "Did the product or store solve the problem?" An affirmative answer promotes *postpurchase satisfaction* and encourages the consumer to repeat the purchase behaviour at the same outlet when the same or a similar problem arises. A negative answer results in *postpurchase dissonance*—being dissatisfied with the purchase and the process that led to it. One of the most anxiety-provoking and least satisfying retail experiences for most people is the purchase of a new automobile. Car buyers rarely feel comfortable with how much they paid, how they were treated, and what they bought. This postpurchase doubt is a serious problem for the car manufacturers and their dealer networks.[45] To relieve the feelings of uneasiness associated with an unsatisfactory product, the consumer may engage in a variety of actions: (1) discard the product and write it off as a bad experience; (2) obtain some type of an allowance from the retailer, thereby increasing the product's perceived value; (3) return the product to the retailer and attempt to improve on their purchase decision process; or (4) write the retailer off as a poor place to shop.

Often consumers have mixed feelings regarding their purchases—a mild case of postpurchase dissonance. In such cases they attempt to confirm a right, or at least acceptable, decision by (1) seeking positive comments from others, (2) distorting information so that it fits the purchase decision, and (3) emphasizing positive information and de-emphasizing negative data.

Where Consumers Buy

The final buyer behaviour issues to be considered are buying scenes—where consumers buy. A **buying scene** is the actual place where consumers complete a purchase transaction. There are four possible buying scenes: (1) a retail store, (2) a consumer's home, (3) a consumer's workplace, and (4) a parasite point of consumption.

North Americans make a majority of their purchases by visiting a retail store or responding to in-home marketing efforts. Although a consumer's workplace is a place of production, not consumption, some retailers (for example, hairstylists, food vendors) have had success by providing the consumer with a high level of time and place convenience. Avon is following women to work, so that for some sales representatives 50 percent of their business is generated through offices. Snap-on Tool Corporation uses step vans to take its products to the customer.

Convenience is also the key to successfully marketing a limited number of products at "parasite" scenes (for example, newspaper stand at a restaurant, hot dog vendor at a football game, magazine rack at an airport). Rapidly growing examples of this retail format are the pushcart market and temporary, seasonal tenants found in various malls, marketplaces, and airports. Blimpie International, a franchiser of sandwich shops, is expanding beyond its traditional locations; Blimpie shops can be found on university campuses, golf courses, convenience stores, bowling alleys, casinos, hospitals, and airlines.[46] The Body Shop, the health and beauty aids retailer, has renovated an 18-wheeler into a travelling store that visits mall locations, college campuses, and areas without Body Shop locations.[47]

Retail Strategies and Tactics

Today's Consumer: A Moving Target

Numerous research studies confirm that the consumer of the nineties is very different from the consumer of the seventies and eighties. A research study conducted in 1994 by Kubas Consultants of Toronto concluded that consumer emphasis on value was so intense that it outdistanced variety, selection, and customer service as the primary motivator of where to shop. Consumers describe value as some combination of quality and price that meets their individual needs. In their search for value, they perceive that manufacturers and retailers offer them less value. Such an attitude was revealed in a 1994 study conducted by the Grocery Products Manufacturers of Canada. Six out of ten grocery shoppers believed they were getting less for their grocery dollar. The report said there is no clear reason why grocery shoppers think this way; it may be their perceptions of value are changing with increases in their standards of value and their expectations.

The same study revealed that two-thirds of all shoppers purchase store brands (rather than national brands) and that more and more consumers are using discount coupons to save money. Another study, conducted by the Canadian Council of Grocery Distributors in 1992, found that 28 percent of Canadians switched supermarkets in the past year solely to find better prices.

The attitudes and perceptions identified above are largely based on economic shifts in the past three decades. The seventies and eighties were characterized by protectionism, mass production and industrialization, and inflation and prosperity. These were times when consumers spent more freely. In contrast, the nineties is a decade of free trade, information, disinflation, and recession. This contrasting economic environment has a direct impact on consumers' attitudes and outlook. Modern consumers face higher rates of unemployment, longer working hours with static salaries, declining housing values, higher government debt, and rising taxes. If this looks and sounds like doom and gloom, it is! There is little wonder that consumers are moving to generic brands, larger sizes and bulk packs, grey market or knockoff products, and alternative forms of retailing (for example, warehouse outlets, price clubs, and direct home shopping). Consumers are demanding more for less money.

Source: Adapted from Keith Tuckwell, Canadian Marketing in Action, *Prentice Hall Canada Ltd., 1995, 185.*

Summary

Buying behaviour is the manner in which consumers act and react to various situations involving the purchase of a good or service or the acceptance of an idea. The dimensions of consumer buying behaviour include understanding what, how much, which, why, how, and where consumers buy. What do consumers buy? Consumers buy products—bundles of benefits capable of satisfying consumer wants and needs. Products are viewed in terms of their tangibility (goods, services, or ideas), durability (durables and nondurables), and availability (convenience, shopping, and specialty products).

How much do consumers buy? The answer is a function of an individual's needs and desires together with the individual's ability to buy (the financial resources—income, credit, assets—that are available to the consumer), willingness to buy (psychological, personal, and social reasons for buying), and authority to buy (formal and informal authorization). Buying centres deal with the issue "Who does the buying?" A buying centre is a basic unit of consumption that engages in the buying behaviour. Basic consumption units tend to be either individuals or households.

"Why consumers buy" is a topic of concern in any discussion of buying influences. The major influences of consumer buying behaviour include psychological, personal, and social factors. Motivation, perception, learning, and attitudes are the four major psychological factors that influence consumers in the determination of buying choices. An individual's personality, self-concept, lifestyle, and position in the life cycle are all personal factors that have an impact on his or her buying behaviour. Conformity to group expectations (family, reference group, social class, and culture) is the basic premise behind the impact of social factors on consumer buying behaviour.

The buying process is the sum total of the sequential art of problem recognition, information search, alternative evaluation, purchase decision, and postpurchase evaluation. In other words, the buying process answers the question "How do consumers buy?"

"Where consumers buy" is described in terms of the four buying scenes. A buying scene is the actual place where consumers complete a purchase transaction; it can be at a retail store, a consumer's home, a consumer's workplace, or a parasite point of consumption.

Student Study Guide

Key Terms and Concepts

activities, interests, and opinions (AIO) *p. 133*
affective component *p. 130*
assets *p. 124*
attitude *p. 130*
behaviour component *p. 131*
buy decision *p. 144*
buying behaviour *p. 119*
buying centre *p. 125*
buying power *p. 124*
buying scene *p. 145*
cognitive component *p. 130*
consumer buying process *p. 141*
convenience products *p. 121*
credit *p. 124*
cues *p. 129*
culture *p. 140*
decision to postpone *p. 144*
decision to proceed *p. 144*
desires *p. 123*
discretionary income *p. 124*
disposable income *p. 124*
drive *p. 129*
durables *p. 121*
esteem needs *p. 128*
extensive problem solving *p. 141*
family buying roles *p. 134*
goods *p. 120*
ideas *p. 120*
impulse goods and services *p. 121*
learning *p. 129*
life cycle *p. 133*
lifestyle *p. 133*
limited problem solving *p. 142*
market potential *p. 122*
motivation *p. 125*
needs *p. 123*
no-buy decision *p. 144*
nondurables *p. 121*
participation *p. 130*
perception *p. 128*
personality *p. 132*
physiological needs *p. 126*
products *p. 120*
reference group *p. 137*
reinforcement *p. 129*
repetition *p. 130*
responses *p. 129*
routinized problem solving *p. 142*
safety needs *p. 127*
selective distortion *p. 129*
selective exposure *p. 129*
selective retention *p. 129*
self-actualization *p. 128*
self-concept *p. 132*
services *p. 120*
shopping products *p. 121*
social classes *p. 138*
social needs *p. 127*
specialty products *p. 122*
total income *p. 124*

Review Questions

1. Define "product." Develop a graphic presentation of the various product classifications. Provide a description of each product class.
2. Distinguish between a need and a desire. Provide several examples from your own life of a current need and a future desire.
3. Describe the determinants of consumer buying power.
4. What is a buying centre? Profile the two types of buying centres.
5. Identify the elements of the motivational process. Distinguish between the various types of needs that direct individual consumer behaviour.
6. How is perception accomplished? Delineate between the various forms of selectivity that are portrayed in the perception process.
7. Discuss the stimulus-response mechanisms inherent in the learning process.
8. What are attitudes used for? Describe the components that make up an attitude.
9. Who are we? Identify and define the four parts of the self-concept.
10. Lifestyle profiles are composite pictures of what factors? How do lifestyles affect buying behaviour?
11. Portray the various roles that various family members might play relative to a given purchase situation.
12. Social classes are defined in terms of what criteria? How do social classes affect buying behaviour?
13. Outline the various stages of the consumer buying process.
14. Where do consumers buy?

Review Exam

True or False

______ 1. If a tangible good is a product, then an intangible service cannot be a product.

______ 2. Durables are perishable products that are used up in one or a few uses.

______ 3. Discretionary income is the income that remains after taxes and other required payments have been deducted from total income.

______ 4. Selective retention is the act of remembering only that information the individual wants to remember.

______ 5. The AIO variables in lifestyle profiles are attitudes, influences, and opportunities.

______ 6. Upper-upper-class consumers often engage in conspicuous consumption to meet their need to gain recognition.

Multiple Choice

______ 1. The determining elements of consumer buying power are the consumer's ______.
a. spendable income
b. asset position
c. available credit
d. a and c
e. a, b, and c

______ 2. Andy Lloyd enjoys shopping stores that allow him the freedom to find those products that enhance his individuality and his need to be what he wants to be. In this case, Andy is expressing his need for ______.
a. safety
b. love
c. belongingness
d. esteem
e. self-actualization

______ 3. A retailer's store sign, newspaper advertisement, and point-of-purchase display serve as a(n) ______ to guide individuals in their buying behaviour.
a. need
b. motive
c. cue
d. attitude
e. road map

______ 4. Mike sees himself as a budding scholar who forgoes conspicuously expensive clothing and

instead buys goods and services for mental enhancement. What part of the self-concept is being expressed by Mike in this case?
a. real self
b. looking-glass self
c. ideal self
d. self-image
e. hopeful self

______ **5.** A ______ is a group that serves as a model or standard for an individual's behaviour and attitude.
a. social class
b. subculture
c. reference group
d. culture
e. society

______ **6.** From past experience, Ted Lewis knows that he wants steel-belted radial tires. However, he is not sure which brand is best, what would constitute a fair price, and which retailer offers the best service. Ted Lewis is faced with a(n) ______ problem-solving situation.
a. extensive
b. limited
c. exclusive
d. routinized

Student Application Manual

Investigative Projects: Practice and Application

1. Classify each item on the following list of products as to its (a) product tangibility, (b) product durability, and (c) product availability.

meat	pencil
pet food	film
furniture	business suit
electricity	prescription drug
church service	haircut
auto insurance	concert
legal advice	college course
movie	candy bar
air conditioner	wedding ring
textbook	gasoline

2. Determine your ability to buy by estimating your buying power.
3. Consult the list of products in project 1. Which products do you purchase to meet (a) physiological needs, (b) safety needs, (c) social needs, (d) esteem needs, and (e) self-actualization needs?
4. Describe specific examples of your selective perception in terms of your selective exposure, retention, and distortion.

Endnotes

1. "Fast Forward to 2045," Advertising Age, July 31, 1995, 33. Also see Melanie Rigney, "Shoppers Crave Experiences," *Advertising Age*, July 10, 1995, 21.
2. Carol Farmer, "The Less Decade: Dreams or Nightmare," *International Trends in Retailing* (Arthur Andersen, July 1995), 55.
3. Jill Griffin, *Customer Loyalty, How to Earn It, How to Keep It* (New York: Lexington Books, 1995), 30.
4. Mark Stevenson, "Virtual Mergers," *Canadian Business*, September 1993, 20.
5. See Martin L. Bell, "Some Strategy Implications of a Matrix Approach to the Classification of Marketing Goods and Services," *Journal of the Academy of Marketing Sciences*, 14 (Spring 1986): 13–20.
6. See Kim P. Corfinan, Donald R. Lehmann, and Sarah Narayanan, "Values, Utility, and Ownership: Modeling the Relationships for Consumer Durables," *Journal of Retailing*, 67 (Summer 1991): 184–204.
7. See Jon M. Shapiro, "Impulse Buying: A New Framework," in *Developments in Marketing Science*, Vol. XV, ed. V.L. Crittenden (Chestnut Hill, MA: Academy of Marketing Science, 1992), 76–80.
8. See "Impulse Shoppers Rule Battery Business," *Stores* (December 1995): 36–37.
9. Gary McWilliams, "PCs: The Battle for the Home Front," *Business Week*, September 25, 1995, 112.
10. Josh McHugh, "Who's Hiding behind Those Shades?" *Forbes*, October 23, 1995, 66–70.
11. Patricia Braus, "Boomers against Gravity," *American Demographics* (February 1995): 54–55.
12. "The Future of Spending," *American Demographics* (January 1995): 12–19.

13. Walter F. Loeb, "Innovative Retailing: An Urgent Need for the Nineties," *Retailing Issues Letter* (copublished by the Center for Retailing Studies: Texas A&M University and Arthur Andersen, March 1994), 1.

14. See Cynthia Webster, "Toward Furthering the Explanation of Relative Influence in Husband/Wife Decision Making: A Qualitative Approach," in *Developments in Marketing Science*, Vol. XV, ed. V.L. Crittenden (Chestnut Hill, MA: Academy of Marketing Science, 1992), 105–9.

15. Christie Brown, "Dressing Down," *Forbes*, December 5, 1994, 115–56.

16. Kelly Shermach, "Scared Consumers Shop for Personal Safety," *Marketing News*, January 16, 1995, 1. Also see Alex Taylor III, "Cars that Beat Traffic," *Fortune*, February 20, 1995, 64–72.

17. Jeffre D. Zbar, "Fear!" *Advertising Age*, November 14, 1994, 18.

18. Joseph Basralian, "Ground Game," *Financial World*, January 17, 1995, 40–42.

19. G. Pascal Zachary, "When Shopping Sprees Pall, Some Seek the Simple Life," *The Wall Street Journal*, May 24, 1995, B1.

20. Fara Warner, "Black & Decker Adopts New Drill In Campaign for Do-It-Yourselfers," *The Wall Street Journal*, July 5, 1995, B6.

21. Robert Maxwell, "Videophiles and Other Americans," *American Demographics* (July 1992): 48.

22. Mark Landler, "What Happened to Advertising," *Business Week*, September 23, 1991, 68.

23. Mervin Morris, Alan Gold, and Annye Camara, "Creating a Company," *Retail Issues Letter* (co-published by Arthur Andersen & Co. and Center for Retailing Studies: Texas A&M University, 1992), 2.

24. Joshua Levine, "How'm I Doin'?" *Forbes*, December 24, 1990, 106, 109.

25. Joe Schwartz, "Hard Times Harden Consumers," *American Demographics* (May 1992): 10.

26. Graham Button, "No Bathrobes, Please," *Forbes*, November 6, 1995, 130.

27. See Tanuja Srivastava and Paul J. Hensel, "Self-Concept in Marketing: An Integrated Theoretical Update," in *Marketing Perspectives for the 1990s*, ed. Robert L. King (Richmond, VA: Southern Marketing Association, 1992), 6–9.

28. Farmer, "The Less Decade: Dream or Nightmare," 52.

29. Ken Dychtwald and Greg Gable, "Portrait of a Changing Consumer," *Business Horizons* (January–February 1990): 64.

30. John J. Shea, "Retail: Managing in Turbulent Times," *Retail Control* (June/July 1992): 10.

31. Jean E. Palmieri, "Federated's Lundgren to NRF Session: Distinctive Products Were Key to Sales, *Women's Wear Daily*, January 17, 1996, 2, 22.

32. For a review of some of the limitations of the life cycle concept, see Laurie Lofland and Nabil Y. Razzouk, "Revisiting the Family Life Cycle: Modifications and Implications," in *Developments in Marketing Science*, Vol. XV, ed. V.L. Crittenden (Chestnut Hill, MA: Academy of Marketing Science, 1992), 43–47.

33. See Scott D. Roberts, Patricia K. Voll, and Keren Ami Johnson, "Beyond the Family Life Cycle: An Inventory of Variables for Redefining the Family as a Consumption Unit," in *Developments in Marketing Science*, Vol. XV, ed. V.L. Crittenden (Chestnut Hill, MA: Academy of Marketing Science, 1992), 71–75.

34. Jeanne Whalen, "PepsiCo's Fast-Food Units up Kid Effort," *Advertising Age*, December 18, 1995, 3.

35. Sean Silcoff, "The Emporiums Strike Back," *Canadian Business*, September 26, 1997, 54.

36. Geoffrey Smith, "Sneakers that Jump into the Past," *Business Week*, March 1995, 71.

37. See Greg J. Duncan, Timothy M. Smeeding, and Willard Rodgers, "The Incredible Shrinking Middle Class," *American Demographics* (May 1992): 34–38.

38. Mark Stevenson, "The Store To End All Stores," *Canadian Business*, May 1994, 22.

39. "Does Anyone Think It's Permanent?" *Canadian Grocer*, January 1994, 1.

40. "Retailers Turn to Kiosks: Improve Customer Service via Automation," *Chain Store Age Executive* (April 1992): 42.

41. See Elizabeth M. MacDonald, "The Year of the Roboshoppers," *Money* (February 1991): 98–100, 102.

42. Mark Tosh, "Discounters Score with Private Labels," *Women's Wear Daily*, January 17, 1996, 18.

43. Christina Duff, "Six Reasons Women Aren't Buying as Many Clothes," *The Wall Street Journal*, February 11, 1994, B1.

44. See Richard A. Spreng and Andrea L. Dixon, "Alternative Comparison Standards in the Formation of Consumer Satisfaction/Dissatisfaction," in *Enhancing Knowledge Development in Marketing*, ed. Robert P. Leone and V. Kumar (Chicago: American Marketing Association, 1992), 85–91.

45. Keith Naughton, "Revolution in the Showroom," *Business Week*, February 19, 1996, 71.

46. See William R. Swinyard and David B. Whitlark, "The Effect of Customer Dissatisfaction on Store Repurchase Intentions: A Little Goes a Long Way," *The International Journal of Retail Distribution and Consumer Research* (July 1994): 329–44.

47. Leah Rickard, "Body Shop Taps Truck to Reach Grass Roots," *Advertising Age*, May 1, 1995, 46.

The Legal and Ethical Aspects of Retail Decisions

Outline

Objectives

To understand and respect the legal complexities under which the retailer must operate

To understand and appreciate the legal framework establishing the lawful limits within which retailing activities must be conducted

To identify and discuss the legal aspects of retail competition

To distinguish and profile the legal aspects of retail store operations

To recognize and describe the legal aspects of retail merchandising

To acknowledge and judge the ethical nature of various behaviours and issues

Retail Vignette

Home Hardware

How does a small independent retail hardware store compete with large chains like Canadian Tire and Wal-Mart? Many such retailers in Canada have found a way. It involves forming a retailer-owned cooperative run like a franchise, which can achieve many of the economies of scale that the larger organizations enjoy.

Home Hardware
www.pagemaker.com/_home/overview.html

Home Hardware Stores Limited is a prime example of such an organization. Home Hardware was established in 1963 by Walter Hachborn. Hachborn himself owned an independent hardware store in St. Jacobs, Ontario. Beginning as a 16-year-old employee, he learned the business and eventually purchased the store with two partners 10 years later. By the late 1950s, however, he was concerned by the continual erosion of the competitive position of his store and other small independents to the large chains. Having noticed the success of dealer co-ops in the U.S. and Europe, Hachborn attempted to organize several independent hardware retailers into such a co-op. After some difficulty he was successful in convincing 108 dealers in southern Ontario that such an organization would allow them to better compete with the fast-growing chains. Each dealer paid $1500 for equity ownership in return for the many benefits of being part of a larger organization. Lower pricing of quality products was a growing consumer buying trend in hardware products, and the combined buying power of several independents acting together was one way of accomplishing this.

The result of the establishment of Home Hardware has been nothing short of phenomenal. There are (as of 1997) close to 900 dealer-owners across Canada. Sales to independent Home Hardware dealers reached $984 632 000 which translates to approximately $1.5 billion at retail. Dealers have currently invested close to $150 million in the organization. As expected by Hachborn when Home Hardware was established, the organization has allowed member-dealers to be price-competitive with the large chains. Home Hardware has also been able to develop state-of-the-art computerized distribution facilities to serve its members. The distribution warehouse in St. Jacobs, Ontario, now covers 75 000 square metres and similar but smaller facilities have been constructed in Wetaskiwin, Alberta; Debert, Nova Scotia; Elmira, Ontario; and a paint manufacturing facility has been constructed in Burford, Ontario.

Home Hardware has also been responsive to consumer demand in establishing their own credit system (Homecard) and by branching into building materials, furniture, and work clothing.

Hachborn continues as president of Home Hardware (even though he is beyond normal retirement age) and regularly crosses the country meeting with dealers. Mr. Paul Straus is the present executive vice-president and general manager of the organization.

Printed with the permission of Home Hardware.

Right Is Right and Wrong Is Wrong

Right actions lead to right results. Wrong actions lead to wrong results. Wrong actions cannot lead to right results. Intuitively, we think people know what is right. But we also know the tendency is to try to get your way by hook or crook. These forces are battling each other: the desire to do the right thing versus the desire to get an advantage and elevate oneself somehow.[1]

Good Business Sense

Legal and ethical business conduct is a pragmatic, no-nonsense, bottom-line way of running your business for the long-term welfare of everyone involved.[2]

Thou Shalt, Thou Shalt Not

Ethics is more than pontification. It is more than platitudes and thou shalt nots. It is more than public relations. The study of ethics is a process of reasoning and thinking about actual problems. It is not haphazard. It is more than the statement "When in doubt do right." Ethics is about decision making.[3]

Ethics Is Not a Box

Ethics is not a box that can be checked after every employee has been through an ethics training program or has acknowledged reading the code of conduct. Ethics has to do with the basic culture and operating values of an organization—the pride and satisfaction employees find in their work, the attention to quality in production, the degree to which suppliers and customers are treated fairly and honestly—all of which impinge on the company's overall reputation and success.[4]

Legal and ethical business practices stem from a corporate culture that demands, promotes, and supports behaviour that conforms to the laws of the land and the codes of the profession. In this chapter, we examine the legal structure in which the retailer must operate. Chapter 5 also takes an in-depth look at (1) how to compete effectively within the legal limits prescribed by law, (2) which legal limitations govern the retailer's operational practices, (3) why certain merchandising strategies are legal and others are illegal, and (4) which business behaviours are within and which fall outside acceptable ethical standards (see Figure 5–1).

Figure 5–1

The legal and ethical aspects of retail decisions

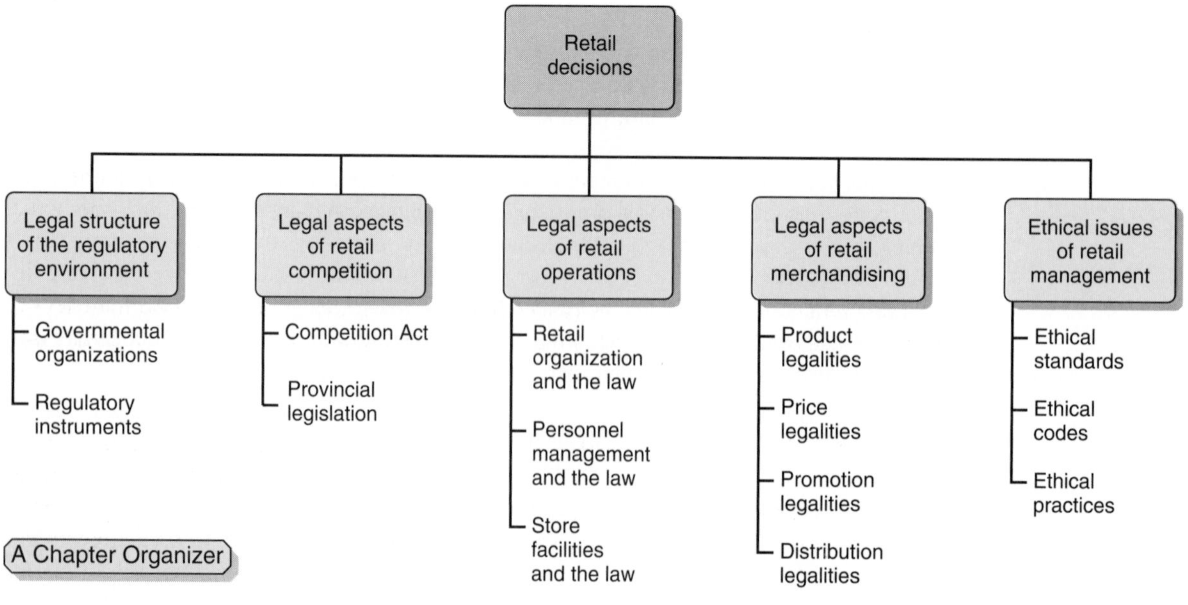

The Legal Structure of the Regulatory Environment

The regulatory environment is the framework that establishes the lawful limits within which retailing and other business activities must be conducted. As a result of an increasingly complex business and social climate, various governmental bodies try to modify or control the retailer's activities through statutory measures and regulatory instruments.

The intent of such regulatory measures is to protect companies from unfair competition, to protect consumers from unfair business practices, and to protect the interest of society against unrestrained business behaviour. In Canada, retailers are subject to legislation and regulation from three levels of government—federal, provincial, and municipal. In general, each level of government legislation addresses a different aspect of retail regulation. There are, however, areas of overlap in this regulation which require an understanding by retailers.

Federally, the legal environment for retailers is controlled by one of three bureaus within the department of Industry Canada. The **Bureau of Competition Policy** enforces the rules that govern and promote the efficiency of a competitive Canadian marketplace. It seeks to ensure that monopolies are not created, that competition is not affected negatively, and that business practices are carried out in a fair manner. The Bureau of Consumer Affairs attempts to promote a safe, orderly, and fair marketplace for consumers and businesses through the administration of several pieces of legislation designed to protect consumers. The Bureau of Corporate Affairs provides a regulatory framework for the business community in Canada by administering laws relating to the conduct among businesses and the encouragement of economic development.

Each provincial government in Canada has established a consumer affairs department (or equivalent) which administers legislation governing aspects of the sales transaction or of activities closer to the point of sale. This more closely relates to the seller of goods or services and is of significant relevance to retailers.

Municipal or local governments usually administer regulations relating to the retail operations such as licensing, zoning, and hours of operation.

The Legal Aspects of Retail Competition

Retail competition involves the actions of one retailer against other retailers in obtaining resources and the patronage of consumers. Competitive actions include both the actual operation of the store and retailers' merchandising strategies and tactics. Governments make laws to ensure that these competitive actions are conducted under equitable rules and circumstances. What is fair or equitable is naturally open to interpretation; generally, the court system and various governmental regulatory agencies make such interpretations.

Federal Competition Act

The dominant legislation in Canada that relates to retail competition is the **Competition Act**, which is administered by the Federal Bureau of Competition Policy of Industry Canada. The purpose of the Competition Act is to maintain and encourage competition in Canada, to ensure that small and medium-sized businesses have an equitable opportunity to participate in the Canadian economy, and to provide consumers with product choice and competitive prices.

Figure 5–2

Examples of violations of the Competition Act relating to restraints of competition

Source: Competition Act, News from the Competition Bureau, *Industry Canada, Issues 1, 2, 3, 1996.*

- September 6, 1991—Union Carbide Canada Ltd. and Canadian Oxygen Supply were fined $1.7 million and $700 000 respectively for conspiring to fix prices in the market for compressed gas.
- September 13, 1991—Liquid Air Ltd. and Liquid Carbonic Inc. were fined $1.7 million each for conspiring to fix prices in the market for compressed gas.
- July 16, 1996—New Oji Paper Co. Ltd. was fined $600 000 for conspiring to fix prices in the fax paper industry.
- November 6, 1996—Sherbrooke, Quebec, Driving Schools were fined $10 000 for being involved in price fixing and predatory pricing.

The Competition Act traces its roots back the Combines Investigation Act, which was enacted in 1889. The original legislation was not very effective because of the difficulty in prosecuting those charged. Offences had to be treated as violations of criminal law, and the government had to prove guilt "beyond any reasonable doubt." This legislation, however, did prevent two kinds of retailing activity: price-fixing by competitors and misleading price advertising. As a result of the weaknesses in the Combines Investigation Act, revisions were made in 1975 (Bill C-2) and 1986 (the current Competition Act). The specific practices which the Competition Act regulates will be discussed later in this chapter. It contains both criminal and noncriminal provisions relating to its regulations and has proved to be fairly effective in preserving competition in the retail marketplace. Examples of some of the recent convictions of Canadian retailers through the Competition Act are described in Figure 5–2.

Provincial Legislation

All provincial governments in Canada have enacted legislation which is intended to ensure that an unfair advantage is not obtained by a retailer. While there is some variation among provincial laws, the majority relate to deceptive or unfair trade practices which are of particular relevance to most retailers. Additionally, the province of Quebec has passed legislation banning advertising directed toward children and ensuring that the pre-eminence of the French language is maintained. Relevant provincial statutes will be discussed later in this chapter.

The Legal Aspects of Retail Operations

Government regulations and controls extend to all aspects of the physical operations of the store. In "running" the store, the retailer must follow laws pertaining to its organizational structure, personnel, and physical facilities. Figure 5–3 charts the major legal considerations in operating a retail business.

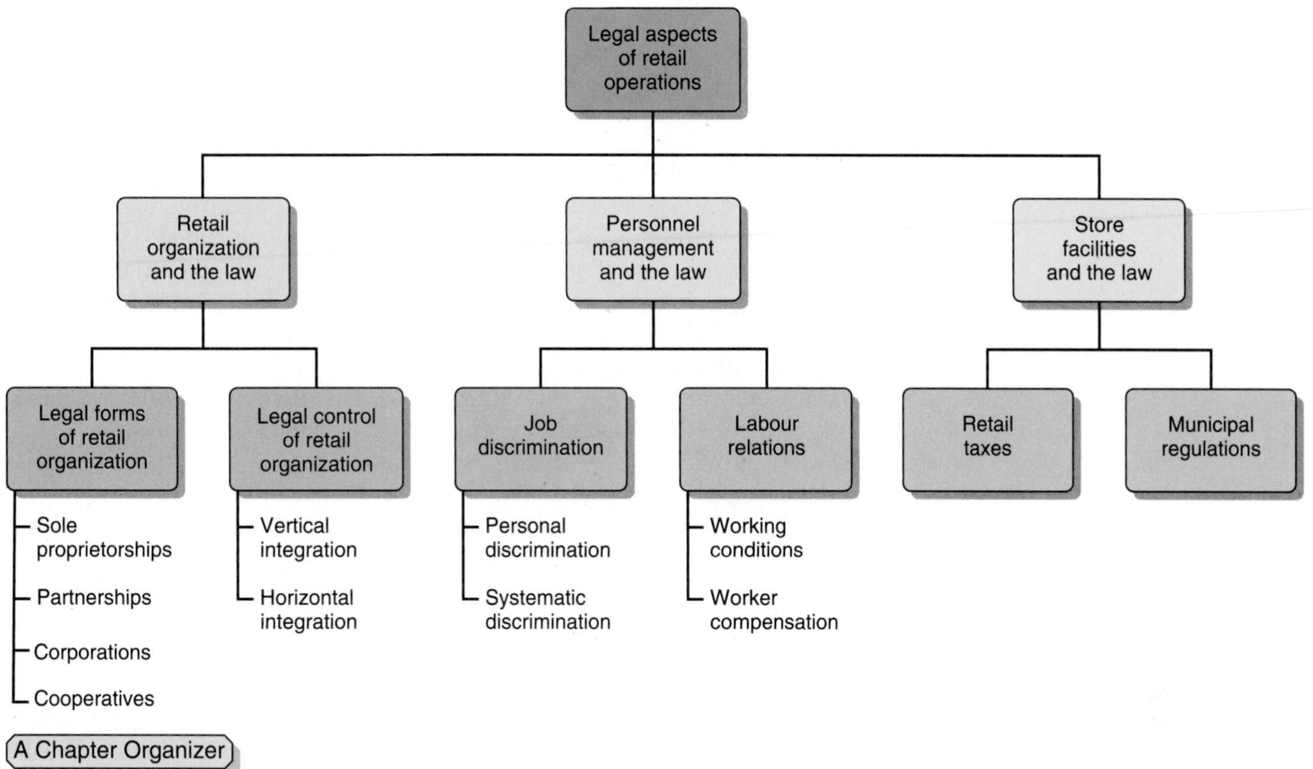

Figure 5–3

Legal aspects of retail operations

Retail Organization and the Law

In establishing, expanding, contracting, and discontinuing a retail business, the law imposes certain restrictions and controls. The influence of the law plays an especially important role in store organization.

The Legal Forms of Retail Organization Business organizations are created as different types of legal entities that have distinct advantages and disadvantages. Canadian corporate law recognizes four basic forms of retail business organization: the sole proprietorship, the partnership, the corporation, and the cooperative.

Sole Proprietorship. The **sole proprietorship** is a business owned and managed by a single individual. It is perhaps the most simple form of business organization to organize and operate. As the owner both owns and manages the retail operation, individual control is assumed over all aspects of the business. Provincial legislation may require that a proprietorship be registered with the government, particularly if the name of the business is not the same as that of the proprietor. For example, if Mary Solasky wishes to start a business called Super Shoe Store, she would have to register the name with the government. Although this is not an expensive procedure, the registration will serve to protect the name from others using it and must be renewed periodically.

Although a proprietorship is flexible and easy to set up, it does have a number of disadvantages. First, because the business is merely an extension of the owner, the owner is fully liable for all debts or legal judgments incurred by the business. For example, if a customer were to slip in Mary Solasky's Super Shoe Store and successfully sued the business for damages, then Mary would be personally liable. Of course, this assumes that no insurance coverage exists. This unlimited liability has caused many retailers to shy away from the proprietorship form of business organization, particularly when the risks that a business faces may not be insurable.

A second disadvantage of a proprietorship is that, legally, the business ceases to exist when the proprietor or owner dies. Depending on certain legal arrangements, this could mean that a growing business may have to be sold or terminated in the event of the owner's death.

Finally, the proprietorship form of a business may find more difficulty obtaining financing than one that is incorporated, and could have some tax disadvantages.

Partnership. A **partnership** may be defined as two or more persons carrying on a joint business venture with a view to making a profit. In many respects, a partnership is very similar to a proprietorship except that it allows more than one person to operate the business. Certain professional bodies only allow their members to operate businesses in the partnership form. Lawyers and chartered accountants fall into this category. Partnerships allow a pooling of skills and financial resources among the partners. In most provinces, partnerships must register with the government in a manner similar to that of a proprietorship.

The rights and obligations of the partnership are very similar to those of a proprietorship. Each of the partners is individually and jointly liable for the debts incurred by the business. In addition, if there is no partnership agreement to the contrary, the business would have to be closed or sold in the event of the death of one partner.

In order to protect the partners against problems that may occur during the operation of the business, such as death or a partner disagreement, many partnerships have an agreement that specifies the conditions and procedures to be followed in the event of the death of one partner, the resignation of one partner, or the admittance of a new person into the partnership. For instance, an agreement may allow for the continuation of the business in the event of a partner's death, providing that a settlement from the deceased partner's share of the business goes to that partner's estate. An additional problem that some partnerships face is the possibility of disagreements between the partners. Such problems plagued the early days of the Dylex chain of clothing stores.[5]

Corporation. A **corporation** is a separate, artificial, and legal entity authorized by the government. As a legal entity, it has a number of rights and obligations that render it distinct from the proprietorship or partnership. The **liability** of a corporation is limited to the assets of the corporation itself. If Mary Solasky incorporated Super Shoe Store Limited and, in turn, was sued by a customer who slipped and fell in her store, the customer could only recover damages equal to the assets owned by the corporation. Mary's personal assets, such as her house, car, and furnishings, could not be taken. There are some exceptions to this rule—for example, when an individual personally guarantees a corporation debt or when an individual was grossly and personally negligent in his or her actions. In most cases, however, the liability of the corporation is limited to the assets of the corporation only.

Compared to a proprietorship or partnership, transfer of ownership within the corporation is relatively easy. Ownership in a corporation is generally determined through the issuance of shares. These shares may be transferred from one person to another, but restrictions in the transfer of shares may exist for private corporations. The Corporations Act of a province or the Canada Business Corporations Act may restrict the transfer of shares, but these restrictions do not usually hinder an individual seeking to bring family members into the retail business.

Contrary to the proprietorship and the partnership, a corporation maintains continuity after the death of a shareholder. Since the ownership in a corporation is acquired through the purchase of shares, when the shareholder dies, the shares may be transferred as part of the assets of the estate. In most cases, this will not affect the operation of the corporation. Theoretically, the corporation can exist forever unless its charter or certificate is revoked by the issuing authority.

An incorporated company allows separation of ownership and management which may have a number of advantages. For example, a chain store could be run by one owner who may have several stores in different cities. Such an arrangement would make it physically impossible for the owner to operate all the stores simultaneously. As a result, management of any or all stores may be delegated to individuals or groups of individuals.

One disadvantage of incorporating a company includes the time, effort, and expense for the group of people who wish to obtain a charter. Recent changes to incorporation legislation, both provincially and federally, have made incorporation easier and have allowed the existence of "one person corporations." Now, for a relatively small fee, it is easy for an individual to incorporate a company where he or she is the sole owner, director, and officer.

Corporations can be recognized when the words "Limited," "Corporation," or "Incorporated" (or the abbreviations "Ltd.," "Corp.," or "Inc.") follow their names.

Cooperative. Although **cooperatives** are not a frequently used form of organization in the retailing industry, there are a number of large retail co-ops in the supermarket and agricultural retailing sectors (particularly in the Atlantic and Western provinces), as well as in hardware retailing. Federated Coop is the largest supermarket chain in Saskatchewan, while Coop supermarkets in Alberta and the Atlantic provinces rank second in sales in those areas.[6]

In most respects, the cooperative is similar to an incorporated company. A distinguishing feature, however, is that in a cooperative (which needs a minimum of six members) each member or individual has only one vote, whereas in a corporation each voting share has a vote.

Legal Control of Retail Organization There are legal guidelines and restrictions on gaining ownership and control of retail organizations through the use of various financial strategies—namely, mergers, acquisitions, and leverage buyouts. The law places limitations on any retailer's attempts to integrate (that is, to incorporate smaller business units into a larger unit) vertically or horizontally. The size and structure of a marketing channel and the means and methods used in creating a channel of distribution are subjected to a legal review.

Vertical Integration. The combining of two types of marketing institutions from different levels within a channel of distribution constitutes the marketing channel strategy known as **vertical integration**. Examples of vertical integration are the combining of a retailer and a wholesaler or a retailer and a producer. A restraint of trade issues could arise if the new combination (for example, retailer/producer) prevented competing retailers from having access to the producer's products or an acceptable substitute. The same combination could also be considered illegal if it prevented competing producers from having access to a market area because of the lack of acceptable and competitive retail outlets.

Horizontal Integration. The absorption of one marketing channel member by another member within the same channel level is an act of **horizontal integration**. For example, when one retail organization (for example, a department store chain) merges with another retailer (for example, a specialty store chain), a horizontally integrated retailing organization has been formed. This integration of direct or indirect competitors is very likely to be scrutinized by regulatory agencies of the federal government. As might be expected, horizontal integration of retail competitors can be seen as a possible attempt at (1) gaining regional or local market area control by reducing competition or (2) achieving a dominant market position by becoming the largest and strongest retail distributor within a market area. This is an area which has been investigated thoroughly by the Canadian government due to the trend of large U.S. retail chains expanding into Canada. Recently, Indigo Books and Music, a fledgling Canadian book megastore, was refused a merger with American book superstore Borders because it was felt that it would be too damaging to Canadian booksellers.[7]

Vertical and horizontal integration are accomplished through mergers, acquisitions, and leverage buyouts. A **merger** occurs when one firm (for example, a retailer) completes the **acquisition** of the stocks and assets of another firm (for example, a retailer or producer).[8] **Leverage buyouts (LBOs)** are financial integrative strategies in which the acquisition is financed through the sale of high-return bonds (junk bonds) and the support of bank loans. Both the bonds and loans are secured by the firm's assets.

Vertical and horizontal integrations using the financial strategies of mergers, acquisitions, and LBOs are regulated by the federal Competition Act.

Personnel Management and the Law

The law protects the retail employee in a variety of ways. A store's personnel manager must be acquainted with the legal environment surrounding job discrimination, working conditions, and various compensation requirements.

Job Discrimination Equal employment opportunity is considered a human right in Canada. Legislation relating to job discrimination is found at both the federal and provincial government levels.

Federally, the Canadian Human Rights Act prohibits discrimination in employment on the basis of race, sex, colour, origin, religion, or ethnic background. Each of the provincial governments has passed legislation concerning human rights in the workplace that retailers should be aware of. These "Bills" or "Codes of Human Rights" are administered by provincial Human Rights Commissions; this type of provincial legislation has jurisdiction over businesses not federally owned or regulated. As with its federal counterpart, these provincial regulations are designed to ensure that discrimination does not occur in the workplace.

Labour Relations Numerous legal requirements govern the relationships between retailers and their employees, particularly with respect to conditions under which the employees work. Of importance to the retailer are wage and hour requirements, restrictions on the use of child labour, provisions regarding equal pay, workers' compensation, unemployment benefits, and the Canada Pension Plan.

Both federal and provincial governments administer a considerable amount of legislation related to employment standards and labour relations. At both levels of government, there are ministries of labour that have the main responsibility in this field of regulation. In addition, both levels of government have legislation that allows for the establishment of unions and collective bargaining agents in the form of provincial Labour Relations Acts and the federal Canada Labour Code. The Canada Labour Code also deals with many aspects of fair labour standards, labour relations, dismissal procedures, severance allowances, and conditions of work. Each of the provinces similarly enforces statutes covering employment standards. These regulations govern such matters as:

- Minimum wage rates
- Hours of work
- Overtime
- Holidays and leaves
- Termination notices
- Employment of young people
- Information requirements on the statement of earnings and deductions

Employment safety and health programs help reduce absenteeism and labour turnover. Most provinces have passed Industrial Safety Acts that are designed to protect the health and safety of workers. These laws govern matters such as sanitation, ventilation, and dangerous machinery. In addition to legislation, provincial governments, as well as employers, provide programs and training designed to accomplish a similar purpose.

Workers' Compensation is an employee accident and disability insurance program required under provincial law. It covers the employee who is accidentally injured while working or who is unable to work as a result of a disease or injury caused by a particular occupation. While these programs vary among provinces, they generally provide for medical expenses and basic subsistence during the period of disability. Employers help pay for the program through assessment from the Workers' Compensation Board. The assessment rates, which many provinces have recently increased, represent a substantial operating expense, so they must be planned for and managed with considerable care.

Store Facilities and the Law

Retail Taxes Government legislation requires retailers to collect consumer taxes on merchandise which they purchase. Federally, retailers collect the Goods and Services Tax which is currently 7 percent. The retailer is required to remit this tax to the federal government and ensure the accurate administration of the GST.

Most provinces (with the exception of Alberta) also levy some form of provincial sales tax. The retailer usually is required to obtain a permit or licence from the ministry of revenue and collect sales tax on behalf of the government. This sales tax is remitted periodically to the ministry of revenue, and, in many cases, the government allows retailers to retain a portion of what they collect, as an administration fee for processing the tax. The rate of sales tax varies from province to province. In addition, exemptions that exist for certain types of goods in one province may not exist in another province. Retailers should check their own provincial regulations.

While sales tax is the major provincial control with which most retailers have to contend, other regulations also require attention. For example, in Ontario, retailers who rent video tapes need special permission from the Theatres branch; motor vehicle retailers require licensing and special certification by the government; pharmacies require certification not only by the government but, in some cases, by the provincial College of Pharmacists as well.

Municipal Regulations Several local or municipal regulations have direct bearing on the retailer's facilities and operations. Local or municipal government regulations relating to the retail industry generally are confined to such areas as licensing, zoning, hours of operation, smoking by-laws, property taxes, and building codes. For example, one of the issues of current debate relates to Sunday openings of retail stores. Generally, jurisdiction has been left to the municipal governments by the provinces. Significant implications exist in terms of operating costs and competitiveness in relation to this question.

Municipal authorities also tend to exercise an especially strong influence over retail food establishments. For instance, a municipality may exercise a licensing system for restaurants and other food-services establishments. Also, health inspectors may be

Retail Strategies and Tactics

Retailers Assail Sales Tax Concessions

The federal government and three Atlantic provinces tried to soften some of the most contentious aspects of their tax harmonization scheme [in January 1997], but businesses say the changes simply make a bad situation worse and will cause consumer chaos. The new rules did little to appease retailers and other businesses that still argue tax-inclusive pricing will impose unfair costs and bewilder consumers across the country.

The concessions on tax-inclusive pricing come less than three months before Ottawa merges the federal Goods and Services Tax with the provincial sales tax in New Brunswick, Nova Scotia and Newfoundland to create a 15-percent harmonized rate. But under federal guidelines issued [in January 1997], the government will not begin full enforcement of the tax-inclusive pricing rule until August 1. That will create a confusing four-month phase-in period, during which a few retailers may comply while many others will not, [Vice President of the Retail Council of Canada, Peter] Woolford warned.

Retailers have waged a fierce lobbying campaign to get Ottawa to abandon tax-inclusive pricing altogether, or at the very least, delay it for a year while the costs of the measure are studied. They say burying the tax will cost the industry $100 million a year—costs that consumers will have to bear.

And not just retailers are upset. All federally regulated industries—including airlines, banks, and phone companies—will have to start burying the GST in any posted prices right across the country on April 7 [1997].

Source: Barrie McKenna, Globe and Mail, *January 18, 1997, B1.*

employed to make periodic and sometimes unannounced inspections. (Any store that sells wine, beer, or liquor may require a licence from provincial liquor licensing authorities.)

Through the above means, all levels of government can exert strong controls on retailing. It is important for all retailers to acquaint themselves with the particular laws and regulations governing their operations. Government offices and bureaus often provide useful information and booklets to retailers outlining the requirements that they must meet in order to be licensed or certified under various provincial and municipal acts. The time spent in studying these requirements may help in ensuring the success of a retail store.

The Legal Aspects of Retail Merchandising

Offering the right product at the right price with the right appeal in the right place must be accomplished in the "right" way. The legal aspects of merchandising are outlined in Figure 5–4.

Product Legalities

As a reseller of products, the retailer assumes three major responsibilities: product guarantees, product warranties, and product liability. Meeting these responsibilities can help a retailer establish a reliable reputation.

Product Guarantees A **product guarantee** is a policy statement by the retailer expressing general responsibility for the products sold. It is a performance pledge that the retailer offers to the customer. Both goods and services retailers view guarantees as a means to distinguish themselves in a crowded market in which customers expect retailers to stand behind what they sell. Some retailers offer very broad guarantees, such as "complete satisfaction or your money back." This "money back" guarantee, introduced by Timothy Eaton with his first department store, has become policy for many retailers.

Figure 5–4

Legal aspects of retail merchandising

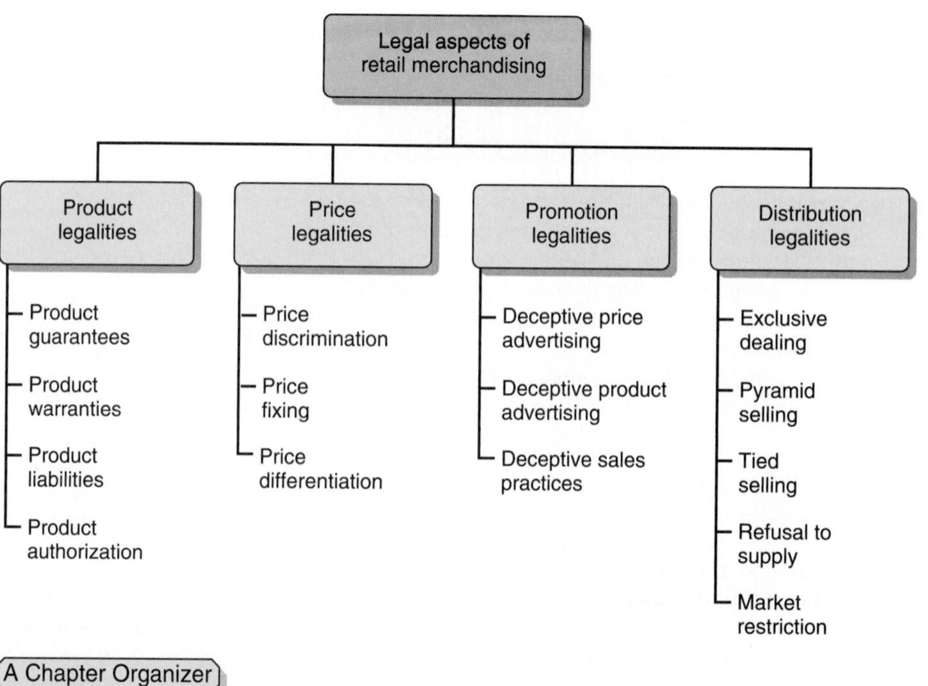

Consumers should remember, however, that it is not their legal right to return merchandise for a refund unless it is explicitly stated by the retailer. Others limit their guarantee statements to certain aspects of the product (for example, six months from date of purchase). Often consumers and retailers disagree about what is guaranteed; "consumers interpret satisfaction to apply not only to the products they acquire but also to the shopping experience that results in these acquisitions."[9] One of the hallmarks of a good guarantee is that it is convenient and painless to invoke. If guarantees require bureaucratic or confusing actions in order to obtain the benefits, they will dissuade people from cashing in on the offer.

Product Warranties A **product warranty** is a specific statement by the seller of the quality or performance capabilities of the product, and the exact terms under which the seller will take action to correct product deficiencies. It represents one method by which producers and retailers attempt to reduce the customer's perceived risk in making a major product purchase. Reliability, trustworthiness, and honesty are some of the image attributes that the retailer hopes to instill in the customer by offering a product warranty program.

Full and Limited Warranties. **Full warranties** represent total coverage on any product defects; the producer or the retailer will either repair the defect or replace the product without charge to the customer. **Limited warranties** place limitations on the responsibilities of the producer and seller to correct any product deficiency. Goodyear issued the ultimate warranty challenge on the Infinitred, a new long-wearing tire designed to outlast competitors' 80 000-mile tire. Goodyear will offer free replacement to drivers if the tires wear out within three years; after three years, Goodyear will offer replacements for half price for as long as drivers own their cars.[10]

Extended warranties are add-on service contracts between sellers and buyers in which the seller agrees to repair (parts and/or labour) or reimburse the customer for the cost of repairs for select product components that fail during the contract period. They are referred to as "extended" because they provide more comprehensive coverage of the physical product for a longer period of time than does the original factory warranty. Automobiles, recreation vehicles, lawn and garden equipment, and appliances are all products for which retailers frequently attempt to sell extended warranties. Warranty limitations must be conspicuously and clearly stated on each product or package.

Retail Strategies and Tactics

Money Back Guarantees

Retailers often sell products that consumers cannot fully evaluate before purchase. Books, compact discs, household appliances, restaurant meals and services such as hair cuts are examples. Marketing such "experience products" can be problematic. Before purchasing these goods, potential buyers must estimate the product's potential attractiveness. Realizing the risks involved, they may withhold purchases or deduct their willingness to pay, and as a result mutually beneficial exchanges with the retailer may be perceived.

One way to assure consumers about product quality is explicit manufacturer quality warranties. Such warranties, however, may not be sufficient for all buyers' satisfaction because of different tastes. Consumers may find a product to be unsatisfactory, not because of its inherent quality, but because of a design that does not suit their tastes. A recording of classical music may receive excellent reviews for sound quality, but a customer may dislike it because of the slow tempo, for example. Retailers are in a better position than manufacturers to match products to consumers because they can communicate with them at their stores. Many retailers allow customers to exchange products they dislike, and many give a full refund to unsatisfied customers through a "money back guarantee."

Source: Scott Davis, Eitan Gerstner, and Michael Hagerty, "Money Back Guarantees in Retailing: Matching Products to Consumer Tastes," Journal of Retailing, *71 (Spring 1995): 1.*

Expressed and Implied Warranties. **Expressed warranties** are written and verbal statements that the seller makes to consumers about a product and performance and that the retailer is legally obligated to honour. Although written statements of fact are expressed in fairly specific terms and subject to precise interpretation, verbal statements of fact and promises are more difficult to interpret. A fine line distinguishes verbal promises from mere sales talk. Often the distinction is made on the basis of whether the statements made during a sale are an expression of opinion or fact. Courts have recognized the difference between "puffery" and promise. To avoid being charged with engaging in unfair competitive acts, the retailer must be careful that its sales puffery is not construed as a legally binding promise of product performance.

Implied warranties are the sellers' implied or "intended" promises of product performance, even though they were not actually expressed in either written or oral form. Under the Sale of Goods Act, every sale is subject to a warranty of merchantability and a warranty of title. The *warranty of merchantability* implies that all merchandise that retailers offer for sale is fit for the purpose for which it is sold. A clothes dryer that scorches clothes, for example, is not fit for its intended purpose. The *warranty of title* implies that the seller has offered the buyer a free and clear title to the product. Consumers have the right to assume that they own the product and have full use of it without fear of repossession. That assumption is not valid, however, when the consumer elects to purchase an item from a questionable source (for example, a car from "Midnight Auto Sales").

The most significant piece of federal legislation regarding warranties is the Competition Act. This act greatly strengthens consumers' rights by substantially increasing the responsibilities of retailers and other sellers of products under warranty.

Product Liabilities The retailer, as well as the manufacturer, can be held liable for an unsafe product. The retailer's **product liability** can result from either failing to inform the customer of the dangers associated with using the product; misrepresenting the product as to how, when, and where it should be used; or selling a product that results in injury because of its failure to meet warranty standards. In developing warranty statements, such absolute terms as "unbreakable, harmless, foolproof, or anything else-proof should be avoided. The term *safer* is preferable to *safe*, and *minimal maintenance* is preferable to *maintenance-free*."[11] In Canada, the federal **Hazardous Products Act** prohibits the sale of hazardous products and also requires warning labels for potentially dangerous products. For retailers of food, the federal **Food and Drugs Act** prohibits the sale of any food which contains any harmful substances or was manufactured under unsanitary conditions.

Product Authorization Branded or labelled products are often made, sold, and/or distributed in fashion that is not approved by the owner of the **trademark**—a product's distinctive mark, word, picture, or design.

Lee Jeans
www.leejeans.com

NHL
www.nhl.com

Unauthorized merchandise, or counterfeit goods, are goods that have illegally used a registered trademark in order to deceive consumers into thinking that the merchandise was produced by the original manufacturer. Favourite targets of unauthorized merchandise include high-profile products like jeans (Levi's, Lee) and athletic shoes (Nike, Reebok), popular fashion labels (Anne Klein, Ralph Lauren), high-priced items like jewellery (Rolex watches), personal items (Mont Blanc fountain pens), and sports-licensed casual wear bearing such trademarks as the National Hockey League (NHL). The unauthorized use of trademarks represents an illegal infringement on the trademark. In Canada, trademarks are registered with the Commissioner of Patents, a department of the federal government in Ottawa. Searches may be conducted with this office to ensure that the trademark used is legally protected. The **National Trademark and True Labelling Act** also provides for a minimum Canadian Standards (C.S.A.) for many goods sold in Canada. Retailer's that knowingly or unknowingly distribute and sell unauthorized merchandise may be participating in an illegal marketing activity.[12]

Price Legalities

The most regulated aspect of a retailer's merchandising program is pricing. Government regulations influence prices that the retailer pays the supplier, prices the retailer charges customers, the conditions under which prices are set or adjusted, and the impact of the retailer's prices on the competitive structure of the marketplace.

Price Discrimination In a very broad sense, **price discrimination** covers many situations involving pricing arrangements under various buying and selling circumstances. The law recognizes both illegal and legal price discrimination. *Illegal pricing* potentially exists when different prices are offered or received under similar circumstances or when similar prices are offered or received under different circumstances. *Price discrimination* can be legally justified when different prices are offered or received under different circumstances. Obviously, the degree of the price differential, the exact nature of the circumstances, and their effects on all parties involved determine the precise legalities of the situation.

When a supplier treats one retailer unequally or differently from the way it treats other retailers, the first retailer becomes a potential victim of price discrimination. As defined by Section 34 of the Competition Act, pure discrimination occurs when a supplier charges different prices to competitors purchasing like quantities of goods. Price discrimination against retailers can result when a supplier treats one retailer differently from others, with respect to product characteristics, quantity discounts, special allowances, and special services. Another provision of the Competition Act relating to retail pricing includes the practice of "double ticketing," wherein a consumer is allowed to pay the lowest price if two or more prices are found on the merchandise.

Price Fixing **Price fixing** is any agreement to establish retail prices at a certain level or to stipulate the terms and conditions of sale (for example, fixed customer charges for alterations, delivery, layaway, service contracts). Price fixing agreements can be made between various members of the same marketing channel or between members in one marketing channel and competitors operating a different channel of distribution.

Vertical Price Fixing. The collaboration between a retailer and a wholesaler or manufacturer to set retail prices at an agreed-on level is the practice of **vertical price fixing**. The most common form of vertical price fixing is **resale price maintenance agreements**. Resale price maintenance is considered an illegal activity by Section 38 of the Competition Act.

Price maintenance occurs when a businessperson:

- by making a threat, a promise or an agreement, attempts to influence upwards, or to discourage the reduction of, the prices charged by another business person, such as a customer or competitor;
- refuses to supply a product to, or discriminates against, another businessperson because of that other person's low pricing policy; or
- attempts to induce a supplier to engage in price maintenance.

Manufacturers or distributors that make suggestions regarding resale prices should state clearly that their business customers are under no obligation to accept the suggested prices. This can be done simply by including the statement "Dealers may sell for less" in price lists or advertisements.

Any company or individual that produces, sells, rents, or provides a product can be subject to the price maintenance provisions of the Competition Act. (A "product" can be an article or a service.)

The following are examples of possible violations of the price maintenance provisions:

- a retailer threatens to stop doing business with a supplier unless that supplier agrees to stop providing products to discounters;

- a credit card company attempts to stop businesses from offering lower prices to customers who purchase with cash rather than on credit;
- a supplier cuts off a retailer for selling below "suggested" resale prices;
- a construction firm offers a competitor money to induce that competitor to submit a high price quote to a government purchasing agency.

Horizontal Price Fixing. **Horizontal price fixing** involves a verbal or written agreement between competing retailers to establish and charge a fixed retail price for one or more merchandise lines. For example, if all the major appliance dealers (for example, category killers) within a city agreed to follow fixed price guidelines and to charge a set price for home delivery, each party to the agreement would be part of a horizontal price fixing scheme. Court cases have established that price fixing between competitors is a collusive practice that limits competition and, therefore, is a restraint of trade and a violation of the Competition Act. Although competitive price audits (shopping the competition) are necessary to develop effective merchandising plans, they should be conducted by personal in-store observation of price tags and not through information exchanges with managers of competing stores.

Bid-Rigging. **Bid-Rigging** is an agreement whereby one or more bidders refrain from submitting bids in response to a call for bids or tenders, or whereby bidders submit bids which they have agreed upon or arranged secretly. Bid-rigging is a serious crime that eliminates competition among your suppliers, thereby increasing your costs and harming your ability to compete. Whether this occurs on government projects or in the private sector, these increased costs are ultimately passed on to the public. Bid-rigging is a criminal offence under Canada's Competition Act and is a form of price-fixing. Firms and individuals convicted of bid-rigging, at the discretion in court, face fines or imprisonment for up to five years, or both. The offence of bid-rigging is committed only if the parties to the agreement do not make the agreement known to the person requesting the bids or tenders before such bids or tenders are made.

Price Differentiation Retailers can also be engaged in an illegal pricing practice when price differences among stores are not justified by different cost structures. **Predatory pricing** is a pricing tactic in which the retailer charges customers different prices for the same merchandise in different markets in order to eliminate competition in one or more of those markets. Such pricing practices are illegal except under Section 34 of the Competition Act, when the firm can show that operating expenses (for example, rent, utilities, security, maintenance), distribution charges (for example, transportation, handling), and selling costs (for example, wages, commissions, store promotions) are greater in the market that is being charged the higher prices.

Promotion Legalities

Freedom of speech for the retailer is not without its limitations. Numerous laws govern what retailers may communicate to their customers and how they may communicate it. The principal legal vehicles through which the federal government regulates promotional activities are Section 36 of the Competition Act, the **Consumer Packaging and Labelling Act**, the Precious Metal Marking Act, and the Textile Labelling Act. Additionally, the provincial government **Trade Practices Legislation** governs deceptive marketing in each province. Together these laws make it illegal for a retailer to engage in any misleading or unfair method of promotion or unfair or deceptive act or practice in commerce.

Deceptive Price Advertising The following practices are viewed as illegal price advertising by the Competition Act:

- Charging the higher of two or more prices appearing on products.

- Confusing "regular price" with "manufacturer's suggested listed price," or a like term. They are often not the same.
- Using "regular price" in an advertisement unless it is the price at which the product is usually sold.
- Using the word "sale" or "special" in relation to the price of a product unless a significant price reduction has occurred.
- Increasing the price of a product or service to cover the cost of a "free" product or service.
- Selling a product above its advertised price.

Provincial Trade Practices legislation relating to price advertising may include (a) representing an item as "on sale" or a certain percentage "off" when this is not true; (b) giving an estimate or quotation of the price of goods and services which is materially less than the final price, and the supplier has completed the transaction without the consumer's consent; and (c) advertising the price, but giving less prominence to the total price than any part of the goods and services.

Deceptive Product Advertising **Deceptive product advertising** involves making a false or misleading claim about the physical makeup of the product, the appropriate uses for the product, or the benefits from using the product, as well as using packages and labels that tend to mislead the customer about the exact contents, quality, or quantity of the package. The Competition Act prohibits the following types of misleading statements about the product:

- Not fully and clearly disclosing all material information in the advertisement.
- Implying that you have reasonable quantities of a product advertised at a bargain price, when only a limited quantity is available.
- Using illustrations that are different from the product being sold.
- Making a performance claim before you can prove it, even if you think it is accurate. Testimonials usually don't amount to adequate proof.

In addition, the Consumer Packaging and Labelling Act provides a set of rules to ensure that full information is disclosed by the manufacturer, packer, or distributor. It requires that all prepackaged products bear the quantity in both French and English, and in metric as well as traditional Canadian standard units of weight, volume, or measure. The act also requires the name and address of the manufacturer to be placed on the label. The **Textile Labelling Act** and the **Precious Metals Marking Act** require information regarding the percentage makeup of the components of these types of products.

Provincial Trade Practices legislation frequently regulates the following deceptive product advertising practices:

- Goods or services (or the supplier) advertising that they have a certain sponsorship, approval, performance, characteristics, accusations, ingredients, quantities, components, uses, or benefits that they do not have.
- Representation that the goods are of a particular standard, quality, grade, style, or model if they are not.
- Representation that the goods have been used to an extent that is different from the fact.
- Representation that the goods are new if they are not.
- Representation that the goods or services are available for a reason that is different from the fact.

Deceptive Sales Practices The law also places restrictions on several kinds of personal selling that constitute **deceptive sales practices**. One is called **bait and switch**. The "bait" is an advertised low price on a product that the retailer does not really intend to sell. The "switch" involves personal selling techniques that induce the customer to buy a higher-priced product that will provide the retailer with greater profits. These selling techniques involve (1) making disparaging remarks about the product, (2) either failing to stock the product or planning a stock-out, (3) refusing to show or demonstrate the product to the consumer on some false pretense, or (4) denying credit arrangements in conjunction with the sale of the product. To protect the consumer, most provincial trade practice laws enforce retailers to make good any "bait" offer extended to customers.

A legal issue related to sales transactions involves **deceptive credit contracts**. In Canada, credit transactions are regulated by provincial governments. Most provinces have enacted **credit legislation** which requires that retailers must give borrowers a disclosure statement detailing the exact terms of their contract. Terms such as loan amount, finance charges, annual percentage rate, miscellaneous charges, number of payments, amount of each payment, and description of any property held by the lender as security must be

Retail Strategies and Tactics

The Perils of Bait and Switch

In 1994, Multitech Warehouse (Manitoba) Direct Inc. was convicted on charges of bait and switch selling. One of the witnesses in the case was a former employee. The employee was featured in a Multitech advertisement that offered a 14-inch television for $249. He testified that these were his instructions about selling this item: "The items in this ad were hammered or spiked. There was a joke around the store that they had a six-inch spike through them, and if we were to sell that product, we might as well go home, because, you know we weren't supposed to." In later testimony, the employee did say that the item was in stock occasionally. "It would trickle in every once in a while."

He also stated that employees were discouraged from selling the item. When specifically asked if he would sell the item at the sale price, the answer was "No." He indicated that only if a customer would yell and scream or otherwise create a problem or a scene would the staff actually sell the bargain-priced item.

It should be pointed out that there is a difference between the practice of "upselling," and bait and switch. There is nothing wrong with upselling—that is, advertising a product at a bargain price and trying to sell customers a more profitable product when they come into the store. However, according to the Competition Act, if a customer cannot be upsold and wants the advertised bargain price product, the obligation is on the retailer to provide that product.

Multitech did have a rain-cheque policy, but it was a joke among employees. According to the employee witness, some rain-cheques were thrown in the garbage when the customer left the store. One particular customer was even offered a rain-cheque when the store had four televisions in stock. When the customer asked when the product would arrive in the store, the employee said, "We're not sure if it's even coming in. We can't guarantee that." The appeal judge described Multitech's rain-cheque policy as a "run-around."

In rendering a decision, the judge stated: "The evidence convinces me that they had a specific policy of advertising products at very advantageous or bargain prices to attract customers and had a further specific policy of not supplying those advertised bargain-priced products or reasonable substitutes or giving any meaningful rain-cheque when the customer was not upsold to a more expensive item . . . the obligation is on the retailer to supply the product when advertised . . . or to offer a rain-cheque or a substitute product. . . ."

To summarize, the law specifically requires that reasonable quantities be on hand when an item is advertised on sale. What is reasonable depends on the type of product on sale, the nature of the market in which the advertiser caries on business, the type and size of the advertiser's business, the geographic location, and the method of advertising. Although there are a numerous laws and factors to consider when goods are offered on sale, ignorance of the law will not protect the advertiser. Often, consumers unwittingly get sold up or fall prey to bait-and-switch advertising tactics. Consumers who challenge retailers hold the key to abolishing such practice.

Source: Adapted from Eric Swetsky, "Broken Promises," Marketing, *April 11, 1994, 26.*

clearly stated in the disclosure statement. The same information must be included in credit advertising. Provincial governments also regulate the activities of collection agents.

Other trade practices which are deemed to be illegal by provincial trade practices legislation are the following:

- The subjection of the consumer to undue pressure by a supplier to enter into a consumer transaction.
- The entering into a consumer transaction by a supplier, where the consumer's ability is such that he or she is not reasonably able to understand the character or nature of the transaction.
- The supplier entering into a transaction where he or she knows that there is a defect in the goods or that any or all of the services cannot be provided.
- A representation by the supplier such that a consumer might reasonably conclude that the goods are available in greater quantities than they are available.

As there is some variation and frequent changes in provincial trade practices legislation, retailers should consult their Provincial Consumer Affairs Department to verify whether the above and other provisions mentioned in this chapter are in effect in their province.

Distribution Legalities

Retailers often enter into agreements with suppliers that might give them a competitive edge in the marketplace. These agreements are legal under some circumstances but illegal under others. Some of these competitively advantageous but potentially illegal arrangements are exclusive dealings, pyramid selling, tied selling, refusal to supply, and market restriction.

Exclusive Dealings **Exclusive dealings** are arrangements between retailers and suppliers in which the retailer agrees to handle only the supplier's products or no other products that pose direct competition. The Competition Act makes exclusive dealing arrangements illegal in Canada. Exclusive dealing, which may exist in franchise agreements, distribution relationships, or dealer agreements, occurs when a supplier requires or induces a customer to deal only, or mostly, in certain products. However not all restructure practices are harmful to competition. In some situations, these practices may enhance the distribution of a product to the benefit of users.

Pyramid Selling **Pyramid selling**, a form of multi-level marketing, is illegal under the Competition Act. Illegal multi-level marketing schemes include (a) the exaggeration of earning potential by disclosing nonrepresentative compensation earned by participants, (b) compensation for recruitment, (c) inventory leading (product sold to recruits in commercially unreasonable amounts), (d) required purchases as a condition of participation in a plan, and (e) failure to provide participants with a right to return a product on reasonable commercial terms.

Tied Selling **Tied selling** exists when a supplier, as a condition of supplying a particular product, requires or induces a customer to buy a second product. It may also occur when the supplier prevents the customer from using a second product with the supplied product. The Competition Act regulates tied selling.

Refusal to Supply Sellers have two commercial freedoms: (1) the right to select their own buyers (for example, dealers or retailers) according to their own evaluation criteria and methods and (2) the right to announce, in advance, the circumstances under which the firm might refuse to deal with a buyer. In other words, sellers have the right to form a preferred channel of distribution by asserting a **refusal to supply** with any given buyer. However, under certain circumstances, if a business refuses to supply another business the

Competition Act may apply. When all of the following requirements under the refusal to supply provisions of section 75 of the act are met:

- The would-be customer shows that the business has been substantially affected, or that the customer is unable to carry on business because he or she cannot obtain adequate supplies of a product on usual trade terms.
- The inability to obtain adequate supplies must result from a lack of competition among suppliers.
- The would-be customer must be willing and able to meet the supplier's usual trade terms.
- The product must be in ample supply.

Market Restriction **Market restriction** occurs when a supplier requires the customer to sell the specified products in a defined market (for example, by penalizing the customer for selling outside that defined market).

The exclusive dealing, tied selling, and market restriction sections of the Competition Act may apply when the following conditions are met:

- The conduct is engaged in by a major supplier or is widespread in a market. A firm with less than 35 percent of market share is not generally considered to be a major supplier.
- The conduct in question constitutes a practice.
- The restrictive practice discourages a firm's entry into, or expansion into, the market; in other words, you must show an exclusionary effect.
- The practice has substantially lessened competition or is likely to do so.

Retail Strategies and Tactics

Fight at the Food Counter

It was . . . an all too typical scenario in the final weeks of a bitter, five-month war between Loeb, a 114-store Ontario and Quebec grocery chain owned by Montreal food industry giant Provigo Inc., and 22 of its franchise stores; a war that blew wide-open last June [1996], when 21 franchisees launched a $205 million breach-of-contract suit against their franchiser partner. (The other franchisee had filed suit in May.) Loeb, which had $1.8 billion in sales in 1995 and a 10% share of the Ontario grocery market, responded by invoking a 90-day "termination without cause" clause (two of the litigants' contracts did not include that clause). Hostilities then escalated. The conflict finally ended in the last days of November in at least a partial victory for the franchisees, when the two sides reached an out-of-court settlement and Loeb purchased the embattled businesses. But even now the fallout lingers.

At the heart of the dispute was the franchisees' contention that Loeb was pricing them out of business, as part of a master plan to convert Loeb from a franchise network to a corporate-owned chain. Loeb denied the allegations, maintaining that while it does have a plan to replace some of its franchises with corporate-owned stores, a complete conversion is not its goal. It also argued that it had the contractual right to set prices as it saw fit, and that franchisees unwilling or unable to work within the Loeb framework were free to exercise their own 90-day exit clauses and leave.

Either way, the implications could go much further than anyone expected. By underlining the inherent inequities that characterize many franchiser/franchisee relationships, the dispute may end up contributing directly to legislation that, in Ontario at least, will help level the playing field. While prosecuting their civil suit, Loeb franchisees lobbied strenuously for the introduction of such legislation.

Source: Mark Anderson, Canadian Business, *February 1997, 68.*

The Ethical Aspects of Retailing

Is the marketing concept of "customer satisfaction at a profit" a sufficient guideline for conducting an honest, fair, and equitable retail business? For most retail organizations, the answer is clearly "no." The reason for this negative response lies in the reality that retailers are part of a much larger environment that incorporates the competing interest of shareholders, managers, employees, vendors, and the community, as well as the needs and wants of the firm's customers. Although being customer-focused is almost an absolute credo for most retailers, customers' wants and needs can and often do conflict with society's long-run interest. "History teaches that the marketer who has his eyes only on the bottom line will not last in the long run, although he might make a profit in the short run."[13] Successful retailers keep their eye on all of the firm's stakeholders—all individuals who have a stake in any aspect of the firm's business. Figure 5–5 organizes our discussion of the ethical issues facing the retail manager.

Ethical Standards

It is the retail firm's organizational culture that guides its employees and managers in determining right from wrong, fair from unfair, loyal from disloyal, trustworthy from untrustworthy, and a host of other ethical value distinctions. **Ethics** can be defined as "a system or code of conduct based on universal moral duties and obligations which indicate how one should behave. **Values** are core beliefs or desires which guide or motivate attitudes and actions."[14] Not all values involve ethics. Ethical values such as honesty, fairness, and loyalty involve the notion of moral duty and "reflect attitudes about what is right, good, and proper rather than what is pleasurable, useful, or desirable."[15] Values such as happiness, fulfillment, pleasure, personal freedom, and being liked and respected are all ethically neutral because they deal with matters other than moral duty and obligation.[16]

Today's lapses in ethical conduct by individuals within organizations "are more often motivated by the most basic of instincts—fear of losing their jobs or the necessity to eke out some benefit for their companies. If it means fudging a few sales figures, abusing a competitor, or shortchanging the occasional customer, so be it."[17] Breaches in moral and ethical conduct usually start with minor infractions and progress to more serious transgressions over time. Judging the morality of a particular action can be approached by using either relative or absolute standards.

Figure 5–5

Ethical isues in retail management

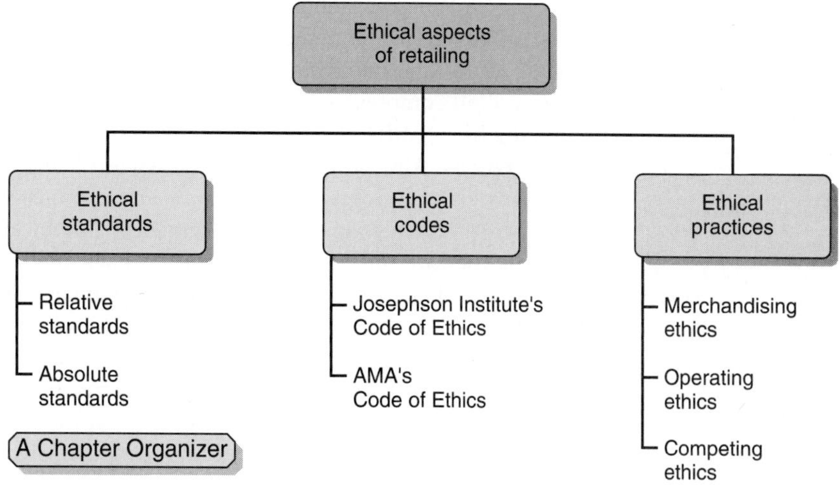

Relative Standards In using *relative* standards, the retailer judges the morality of an act on the basis of the particular circumstances surrounding the action. Because there are no absolutes when using relative standards, ethical behaviour involves making judgments using subjective, situational, and culturally determined criteria. This relative type of situation ethics comes in two basic forms:

- **Utilitarianism**—"Judges not the act itself but the consequences of the act. If the result means a net increase in society's happiness or welfare, then the act is believed to be morally right . . . akin to saying that the end justifies the means."[18]
- **Intuitionism**—"Decision is right if the individual's intuition or conscience tells him [or her] that it is right. If the person's sixth sense or gut feeling says that it is okay, that his [or her] motives are good, and that he [or she] doesn't intend to hurt anyone, then he [or she] can go ahead with it."[19]

Absolute Standards Absolute standards are rigid rules that clearly state whether an act is right or wrong; using these standards constitutes ethical behaviour and is clear regardless of the circumstances surrounding the situation.[20] These timeless truths are typically based on religious teachings; for example, the Bible has provided fixed permanent guidelines that have evolved into the Judeo-Christian value system. Such rules as "Do unto others as you would have them do unto you" (the Golden Rule or Rule of Reciprocity), "Thou shall not lie," and "Thou shall not steal" provide direct answers that appeal to some decision makers. The Mary Kay Corporation, the direct marketer of health and beauty aids, was founded on the Golden Rule and promotes the concept that one's priorities should be faith, family, and career.[21]

Ethical Codes

The government has provided much legislation to create a competitive business climate and protect the customer. An alternative to government control is self-regulation, under which an industry attempts to provide guidelines for the conduct of its members. Such organizations as the Retail Council of Canada and the Canadian Direct Sellers Association are examples. The Canadian Broadcasting Association, whose members include major television networks and radio stations across the country, has a code of ethics that helps govern the conduct of its members in terms of protecting the consumer against deceptive trade practices such as misleading advertising. Similarly, the Advertising Standards Council, the self-regulatory arm of the Canadian Advertising Foundation, has established the Canadian Code of Advertising Standards for its members to follow.

Another well-known self-regulatory group is the Better Business Bureau (BBB). This organization is a voluntary alliance of companies whose goal is to help maintain fair business practices. Although the BBB has no legal power, it does try to use "moral suasion" to get members to comply with its regulations. However, there are critics of self-regulation. These critics complain that there are two basic problems with self-regulation: noncompliance by members and lack of enforcement power.

As can be inferred from the preceding discussion, developing a practical and operational code of ethics or establishing a set of principles for ethical decision making can be an important but complex task. "Some 90% of North America's largest corporations have now adopted written codes of ethics that prescribe what is and is not acceptable in their day-to-day operations. Almost one-third of the biggest firms have designated an ethics officer."[22] An effective ethics program "has become an insurance policy against huge court fines that are so egregious they are themselves arguably unethical. Companies get off lightly if they can show they are not only against sin but have taken steps to prevent sinning and catch sinners."[23] Studies have drawn the following similar conclusions regarding the implementation of an ethics program for business organizations: (1) codes of ethics must be more than legal or public relations ploys—they must be useful, understandable, and practical; (2) visible signs of support for ethical behaviour must be forthcoming from management, with the moral tone of corporate conduct being set at the top; (3) there is no single approach to business ethics that is ideally suited to a particular organization; and (4) top management must champion its demand for the highest ethical posture for its company.[24] "Successful enterprises are inevitably based on a network of trust binding management, employees, shareholders, lenders, suppliers, and customers—akin to the network that Japanese call *keiretsu*. When companies slop into shoddy practices, these crucial relationships start to deteriorate."[25] Retailers also understand that if they collectively do not adhere to a set of ethical practices, public pressure may eventually result in government legislation governing the practice, such as was the case in Ontario with new franchise legislation.[26]

Retailers can implement ethics programs by adopting an already established ethics code. The Code of Ethics governing all members of the American Marketing Association is presented in Figure 5–6; it represents a code of behaviour for a particular profession or trade. Figure 5–7 presents twelve ethical principles that business executives should follow in making decisions.

Figure 5–6

American Marketing Association Code of Ethics

Source: "AMA Adopts New Code of Ethics," Marketing News, *September 11, 1987, 1, 10.*

Responsibilities of the Marketer

Marketers must accept responsibility for the consequences of their activities and make every effort to ensure that their decisions, recommendations, and actions function to identify, serve, and satisfy all relevant publics, customers, organizations, and society.

Marketers' professional conduct must be guided by:

1. The basic rule of professional ethics; not knowingly to do harm;
2. The adherence to all applicable laws and regulations;
3. The accurate representation of their education, training, and experience; and
4. The active support, practice, and promotion of this Code of Ethics.

Honesty and Fairness

Marketers shall uphold and advance the integrity, honour, and dignity of the marketing profession by:

1. Being honest in serving consumers, clients, employees, suppliers, distributors, and the public;
2. Not knowingly participating in conflict of interest without prior notice to all parties involved; and
3. Establishing equitable fee schedules including the payment or receipt of usual, customary, and/or legal compensation for marketing exchanges.

Rights and Duties of Parties in the Marketing Exchange Process

Participants in the marketing exchange process should be able to expect that:

1. Participants and services offered are safe and fit for their intended uses;
2. Communications about offered products and services are not deceptive;
3. All parties intend to discharge their obligations, financial and otherwise, in good faith; and
4. Appropriate internal methods exist for equitable adjustment and/or redress of grievances concerning purchases.

continued

Figure 5–6 (continued)

It is understood that the above would include, but is not limited to, the following responsibilities of the marketers:

In the area of product development and management,

- Disclosure of all substantial risks associated with product or service usage;
- Identification of any product component substitution that might materially change the product or impact on the buyer's purchase decision;
- Identification of extra-cost added features.

In the area of promotions,

- Avoidance of false and misleading advertising;
- Rejection of high-pressure manipulations or misleading sales tactics;
- Avoidance of sales promotions that use deception or manipulation.

In the area of distribution,

- Not manipulating the availability of a product for purpose of exploitation;
- Not using coercion in the marketing channel;
- Not exerting undue influence over the reseller's choice to handle a product.

In the area of pricing,

- Not engaging in price fixing;
- Not practising predatory pricing;
- Disclosing the full price associated with any purchase.

In the area of marketing research,

- Prohibiting selling or fundraising under the guise of conducting research;
- Maintaining research integrity by avoiding misrepresentation and omission of pertinent research data;
- Treating outside clients and suppliers fairly.

Organizational Relationships

Marketers should be aware of how their behaviour may influence or impact on the behaviour of others in organizational relationships. They should not demand, encourage, or apply coercion to obtain unethical behaviour in their relationships with others, such as employees, suppliers, or customers. Marketers should:

1. Apply confidentiality and anonymity in professional relationships with regard to privileged information;
2. Meet their obligations and responsibilities in contracts and mutual agreements in a timely manner;
3. Avoid taking the work of others, in whole or in part, and representing this work as their own or directly benefiting from it without compensation or consent of the originator or owner; and
4. Avoid manipulation to take advantage of situations to maximize personal welfare in a way that unfairly deprives or damages their organization or others.

Figure 5–7

Josephson Institute ethical principles for business executives

Source: Michael Josephson, "Ethical Principles for Business Executives," Ethical Decision Making in the Trenches *(Marina del Rey, CA: Joseph and Edna Josephson Institute for the Advancement of Ethics, 1989), 3. Copyright © The Joseph and Edna Josephson Institute for the Advancement of Ethics, Marina del Rey, CA.*

Ethical values, translated into active language establishing standards or rules describing the kinds of behaviour an ethical person should and should not engage in, are ethical principles. The following list of principles incorporates the characteristics and values that most people associate with ethical behaviour. Ethical decision making systematically considers these principles.

I. *Honesty.* Ethical executives are honest and truthful in all their dealings and they do not deliberately mislead or deceive others by misrepresentations, overstatements, partial truths, selective omissions, or any other means.

II. *Integrity.* Ethical executives demonstrate personal integrity and the courage of their convictions by doing what they think is right even when there is great pressure to do otherwise; they are principled, honourable, and upright; they will fight for their beliefs. They will not sacrifice principle for expediency, be hypocritical, or unscrupulous.

III. *Promise-Keeping and Trustworthiness.* Ethical executives are worthy of trust, they are candid and forthcoming in supplying relevant information and correcting misapprehensions of fact, and they make every reasonable effort to fulfill the letter and spirit of their promises and commitments. They do not interpret agreements in an unreasonably technical or legalistic manner in order to rationalize noncompliance or create justifications for escaping their commitments.

IV. *Loyalty.* Ethical executives who are worthy of trust demonstrate fidelity and loyalty to persons and institutions by friendship in adversity, support, and devotion to duty; they do not use or disclose information learned in confidence for personal advantage. They safeguard the ability to make independent professional judgments by scrupulously avoiding undue influences and conflicts of interest. They are loyal to their companies and colleagues and if they decide to accept other employment, they provide reasonable notice, respect the proprietary information of their former employer, and refuse to engage in any activities that take undue advantage of their previous position.

V. *Fairness.* Ethical executives are fair and just in all dealings; they do not exercise power arbitrarily, and do not use overreaching nor indecent means to gain or maintain any advantage nor take undue advantage of another's mistakes or difficulties. Fair persons manifest a commitment to justice, the equal treatment of individuals, tolerance for and acceptance of diversity, and they are open-minded; they are willing to admit they are wrong and, where appropriate, change their positions and beliefs.

VI. *Concern for Others.* Ethical executives are caring, compassionate, benevolent, and kind; they live the Golden Rule, help those in need, and seek to accomplish their business objectives in a manner that causes the least harm and the greatest positive good.

VII. *Respect for Others.* Ethical executives demonstrate respect for the human dignity, autonomy, privacy, rights, and interests of all those who have a stake in their decisions; they are courteous and treat all people with equal respect and dignity regardless of sex, race, or national origin.

VIII. *Law Abiding.* Ethical executives abide by laws, rules, and regulations relating to their business activities.

IX. *Commitment to Excellence.* Ethical executives pursue excellence in performing their duties, are well informed and prepared, and constantly endeavour to increase their proficiency in all areas of responsibility.

continued

Figure 5–7 (continued)

X. *Leadership.* Ethical executives are conscious of the responsibilities and opportunities of their position of leadership and seek to be positive ethical role models by their own conduct and by helping to create an environment in which principled reasoning and ethical decision making are highly prized.

XI. *Reputation and Morale.* Ethical executives seek to protect and build the company's good reputation and the morale of its employees by engaging in no conduct that might undermine respect and by taking whatever actions are necessary to correct or prevent inappropriate conduct of others.

XII. *Accountability.* Ethical executives acknowledge and accept personal accountability for the ethical quality of their decisions and omissions to themselves, their colleagues, their companies, and their communities.

Ethical Practices

The following illustrations of business practices are presented as actions that some retailers engage in that raise the following ethical question: How would you judge these practices? Does it make a difference if you use relative or absolute standards? Would they be consistent with the codes of ethics discussed previously?

- A department store that maintains interest rates on its proprietary (in-house) credit card at 21 percent when the prime rate drops to 7 or 8 percent.
- A specialty retailer that brings in merchandise at an artificially high price so that a larger planned markdown can be advertised in order to draw in more customers.
- A direct-mail marketer that offers new customers introductory prices that are lower than those prices offered to loyal existing customers.
- A convenience store that encourages gambling by selling lottery tickets.
- An off-price retailer that uses lie detector tests in screening potential employees when some studies indicate that such tests are often only 65 percent accurate.
- A video store chain that records your viewing habits (listing the type and frequency of the videos you rent) and your demographic profile and sells this valuable market information to direct marketing organizations.[27]
- A telemarketer that uses an auto dialer that spews unsolicited recorded messages, making it impossible to hang up until they are finished.[28]
- A mass merchandiser that initiates an incentive compensation plan to increase sales that encourages an environment of aggressively selling to customers more products and services than needed by the customer.[29]
- A discount store retailer that charges a lay-away cancellation fee of as much as 20 percent of the purchase price of the merchandise, or a merchant whose lay-away policy involves customers forfeiting their money and their merchandise if they do not meet payment deadlines.[30]
- A retailer promoting the commercialization of primary and secondary education by providing free merchandise to reward students for meeting regular achievement goals.[31]
- A direct-mail environmental protection marketer whose paperback book has two versions of things you can do to save the earth: One version, for the general market, has as its first recommendation to stop junk mail. The other version,

for active environmentalists, has as its first recommendation to stop unwanted junk mail.[32]

- An in-home retailer of cosmetics pulling a late-night raid of a competitor's dumpster in an attempt to gain information to fend off takeover advances by the competitor.[33]
- A specialty retailer that sends its employees to buy up large quantities of merchandise that a competitor sells at or close to costs (low or loss leader prices).

Have you found any clear-cut cases of unethical behaviour? Which ones? Which issues would you consider to be in the "grey area"—not unethical but not very professional? Why?

Summary

Legal considerations are an integral part of the retailer's daily operations. The retailer must consider the legal aspects of retail competition, store operations, and retail merchandising within the legal environment created by legislative departments of federal, provincial, and municipal governments.

The legal aspects of competition deal with various governmental bodies' attempts to correct present restraints on trade and prevent probable trade restraints and unfair trade practices. The major law dealing with maintaining a competitive environment is the Competition Act.

The legal forms of store organization (proprietorship, partnership, cooperative, and corporation); the legal control of retail organizations (vertical and horizontal integration); the laws governing personnel management (job discrimination and labour relations); and the restrictions on store facilities and store operations (tax laws and municipal regulations) are all central legal issues in store operations.

The legal aspects of merchandising require the retailer to carefully consider the legalities of its product, price, promotion, and distribution mix. Product guarantees, warranties, liability, and authorization are four of the more important legalities associated with the product offering. Price discrimination in terms of product characteristics, quantity discounts, and special allowances or services—together with vertical or horizontal price fixing, price solicitation, and price differentiation—are the retailer's chief legal concerns regarding price decisions. Deceptive price and product advertising and deceptive sales practices are illegalities of promotion that retailers must avoid. Finally, the laws pertaining to distribution call for careful consideration of exclusive dealings, bid-rigging, tied selling, refusal to supply, and the use of market restrictions.

Ethical behaviour is based on a system or code of conduct that is derived from a universal moral duty or obligation. Honesty, fairness, and loyalty are ethical values that help an individual determine what is right, good, and proper. Retail businesses use both relative and absolute approaches in judging the morality of a particular action. Many trade associations and individual companies develop specific codes of ethics to help their members act within ethical guidelines.

Student Application Manual

Key Terms and Concepts

acquisition *p. 157*
bait and switch *p. 166*
bid-rigging *p. 164*
Bureau of Competition Policy *p. 153*
Competition Act *p. 153*
Consumer Packaging and Labelling Act *p. 164*
cooperative *p. 157*
corporation *p. 156*
credit legislation *p. 166*
deceptive credit contracts *p. 166*
deceptive product advertising *p. 165*
deceptive sales practices *p. 166*
ethics *p. 169*
exclusive dealings *p. 167*
expressed warranties *p. 162*
extended warranties *p. 161*
Food and Drugs Act *p. 162*
full warranties *p. 161*
Hazardous Products Act *p. 162*
horizontal integration *p. 157*
horizontal price fixing *p. 164*
implied warranties *p. 162*

intuitionism *p. 170*
leverage buyouts (LBOS) *p. 157*
liability *p. 156*
limited warranty *p. 161*
market restriction *p. 168*
merger *p. 157*
National Trademark and True Labelling Act *p. 162*
partnership *p. 156*
Precious Metals Marking Act *p. 165*
predatory pricing *p. 164*
price discrimination *p. 163*
price fixing *p. 163*
product guarantee *p. 160*
product liability *p. 162*
product warranty *p. 161*
pyramid selling *p. 167*
refusal to supply *p. 167*
resale price maintenance agreements *p. 163*
retail competition *p. 153*
sole proprietorship *p. 155*
Textile Labelling Act *p. 165*
tied selling *p. 167*
trademark *p. 162*
Trade Practices Legislation *p. 164*
unauthorized merchandise *p. 162*
utilitarianism *p. 170*
values *p. 169*
vertical integration *p. 157*
vertical price fixing *p. 163*
workers' compensation *p. 158*

Review Questions

1. What actions define the retailer's legal environment?

2. What is the main principle of the Competition Act?

3. Compare and contrast the legal and operational advantages and disadvantages of proprietorship, partnership, cooperative, and corporate forms of retail organization.

4. What taxes are of relevance to a retailer?

5. Why do municipal governments enact zoning ordinances? What are the benefits and limitations for the retailer?

6. What is the general jurisdictional difference between federal and provincial legislation in Canada?

7. Compare and contrast product guarantees and product warranties.

8. What are the two basic types of warranties? Describe each type.

9. Under what conditions can the retailer be held liable for an unsafe product?

10. What is price discrimination? When is price discrimination illegal?

11. To avoid charges of deceptive price advertising when using former and competitive-price comparisons, which practices should the retailer follow?

12. What is deceptive product advertising? What is the major weapon the government uses in correcting false claims regarding product benefits? Explain.

13. What information is required to be included on the package under the Consumer Packaging and Labelling Act?

14. Describe the sales practice of bait and switch. When is it illegal?

15. Compare and contrast the distribution arrangements of exclusive dealings, tied selling, and market restrictions. When are they illegal?

16. When is multi-level marketing illegal?

17. Is the marketing concept of "customer satisfaction at a profit" a sufficient guideline for judging the ethics of business practices? Why?

18. Describe the two approaches for judging the morality of a particular business action.

Review Exam

True or False

______ **1.** A major advantage of a general partnership over a sole proprietorship form of organization is that the partnership represents a substantially reduced financial liability for each partner in the organization.

______ **2.** Before using training, education, and experience to justify wage differentials between employees, the retailer should be able to prove that these factors have a direct bearing on job performance.

______ **3.** Retailers can be held liable for unsafe products if they fail to inform the consumer of the dangers associated with using the product.

______ **4.** If the retailer wishes to make competitive price comparisons on products that are similar but not identical, then the advertisement must make it clear to the consumer that the price comparison is being made on comparable and not identical products.

______ **5.** Exclusive dealing arrangements between retailers and suppliers are generally viewed as a per se violation of the law.

______ **6.** Ethics can be defined as an individual's core beliefs or desires that guide or motivate attitudes and actions.

______ **7.** Applying the Golden Rule or the Rule of Reciprocity is an example of using situational ethics to judge behaviour.

Multiple Choice

_____ **1.** The Competition Act was enacted to protect consumers and businesses from ____.
a. restraints on trade
b. unfair trade practices
c. none of the above
d. both a and b

_____ **2.** The unintentional and inadvertent discrimination resulting from policies, practices, and decision-making criteria that negatively affect protected classes is termed ____ discrimination.
a. personal
b. organizational
c. social
d. systematic
e. pragmatic

_____ **3.** The warranty of ____ is the implied warranty that all merchandise offered for sale by the retailer is fit for the purpose for which it was sold.
a. liability
b. title
c. merchantability
d. performance
e. price

_____ **4.** Price discrimination is legal when ____.
a. different prices are offered under similar circumstances
b. different prices are received under similar circumstances
c. similar prices are received under different circumstances
d. different prices are offered under different circumstances
e. none of the above

_____ **5.** A retailer may be charged with predatory pricing if ____.
a. customers are charged different prices for the same product in different markets to eliminate competition in one or more of those markets
b. a fixed retail selling price is established for a particular product line within a market area
c. a brokerage allowance is obtained from suppliers, giving retailers an unfair purchase price advantage
d. financial, distribution, and marketing powers are used to gain lower prices from sellers

_____ **6.** Which of the following criteria would best represent the utilitarianism view of ethical behaviour?
a. My conscience tells me it is right.
b. Thou shalt not lie.
c. The end justifies the means.
d. Do unto others as you would have them do unto you.

Student Application Manual

Investigative Projects: Practice and Application

1. Obtain the product guarantee statement from three retailers. Analyze each statement to determine your view of the legal obligations of the retailer regarding its responsibility for the products it sells. Then interview the store manager to ascertain his or her view of the store's product guarantee obligations. Does the store manager's view match your view? Explain. How might any differences be reconciled?

2. Identify three or four potential examples of deceptive retail price advertisements by surveying your local newspaper. Describe how the advertisement might be deceptive. Visit the local store and investigate how the retailer supports the advertising claim. Was the advertisement deceptive? Was it legal or illegal? Explain. If it was legal, was it ethical? Explain your answer.

3. Are retail price-matching policies (promising to match the lowest advertised prices a shopper can find) legal? Critics question the fairness of a policy that allows retailers to make deals with certain vocal customers, while charging loyal customers higher prices. Do you agree? Describe the ethics of this practice.

4. One of North America's fastest-growing supermarket chains has been criticized for some of its expansion tactics. The firm employs part-time labour that it pays at the lowest possible rates. Because of high turnover, most of its labour force never qualifies for the firm's employee benefit plan. Extremely low labour costs enable the chain to be very competitive. Hence, it has been able to squeeze out many of its competitors. Customers benefit because in all of its market areas, the chain has been able to substantially lower the total price of a market basket of food. Evaluate the ethics of this behaviour using both the relative and absolute approaches to judging behaviour.

Endnotes

1. Dan Cordtz, "Always Do the Right Thing," *Financial World* (Fall 1994): 42.
2. Hershey H. Friedman and Lina Weiser Friedman, "Framework for Organizational Success," *Journal of Business Ethics*, 7 (March 1988), 220.
3. Lawrence B. Chonko, *Ethical Decision Making in Marketing*, (Thousand Oaks, CA: Sage Publications, 1995), x.
4. Dave Perry, "Reinforcing Business Ethics in a Recession," *Retail Control* (November 1991): 36.
5. Kenneth Kidd, "The Fall of the House of Dylex," *Report on Business*, September 1995, 57.
6. See Canadian Grocer 1997 Executive Report, *Canadian Grocer*, 1997, 16.
7. Margaret Feldstein, "Bookish Indignation," *Time*, September 28, 1997, 40.
8. Bernard Wysocki Jr., "Improved Distribution Not Better Production, Is Key Goal in Mergers," *The Wall Street Journal*, August 8, 1995, A1.
9. Sandra L. Schmidt and Jerome B. Kernam, "The Many Meanings (and Implications) of 'Satisfaction Guaranteed'," *Journal of Retailing*, 61 (Winter 1985): 89.
10. Stuart Drown, "Goodyear Bets Tires Will Last a Lifetime," *Akron Beacon Journal*, February 6, 1996, A1. Also see Emily Nelson, "Goodyear Hopes to Drive Home Lifetime Guarantee on New Tires," *The Wall Street Journal*, March 7, 1996, B12.
11. Paula Mergenbagen, "Product Liability: Who Sues?" *American Demographics* (June 1995): 52.
12. *Ibid.*, 91. Also see Joshua Levine and Nancy Rotenier, "Seller Beware," *Forbes*, October 25, 1993, 170, 173.
13. Geoffrey P. Lantos, "An Ethical Base for Marketing Decision Making," *Journal of Business and Industrial Marketing*, 2 (Spring 1987): 13.
14. Michael Josephson, *Ethical Decision Making in the Trenches* (Marina del Rey, CA: Joseph & Edna Josephson Institute for the Advancement of Ethics, 1989), 1.
15. *Ibid.*
16. *Ibid.*
17. Kenneth Labich, "The New Crisis in Business Ethics," *Fortune*, April 20, 1992, 167.
18. See Geoffrey P. Lantos, "An Ethical Base for Marketing Decision Making," *U.S. News & World Report*, March 20, 1995, 61–66.
19. *Ibid.*, 15–16.
20. Don L. Boroughs, "The Bottom Line on Ethics," *U.S. News and World Report*, March 30, 1995, 61.
21. Richard C. Bartlett, "Mary Kay's Foundation," *Journal of Business Strategy* (Fall 1995): 16–19.
22. Dan Cordiz, "Ethicsplosion!" *Financial World* (Fall 1994): 58.
23. Nick Gilbert, "1-800-22 Ethics," *Financial World* (Fall 1994): 22.
24. See Patrick E. Murphy, "Creating Ethical Corporate Structures," *Sloan Management Review* (Winter 1989): 1–7; and Patrick E. Murphy, "Implementing Business Ethics," *Journal of Business Ethics* (1988): 907–15.

25. Kenneth Labich, "The New Crisis in Business Ethics," *Fortune*, April 20, 1992, 167.

26. John Southerst, "Why Regulation Rattles Retailers," *Globe and Mail*, March 3, 1997, B7.

27. Michael W. Miller, "Coming Soon to Your Local Video Store: Big Brother," *The Wall Street Journal*, December 26, 1990, 9, 12.

28. See Mary Lu Carnevale, "FCC Adopts Rules to Curb Telemarketing," *The Wall Street Journal*, September 18, 1992, B1, B10; "New Laws Aimed at Telemarketing Abuse," *Marketing News*, August 3, 1992, 10; and Michael W. Miller, "Lawmakers Are Hoping to Ring out Era of Unrestricted Calls by Telemarketers," *The Wall Street Journal*, May 28, 1991, B1, B4.

29. See Gregory A. Patterson, "Sears Is Dealt a Harsh Lesson by States," *The Wall Street Journal*, October 2, 1992, B7A; and Rick Gallagher, "Compensation," *Stores* (August 1992): 6.

30. Francine Schwadel, "For Many Budget-Conscious Consumers, Layaways Can Turn into Throwaways," *The Wall Street Journal*, July 12, 1992, B1, B2.

31. Ann De Rouffignac, "Scholl Contest Helps Concerns Promote Brands," *The Wall Street Journal*, July 3, 1992, B1–B2.

32. Michael W. Miller, " 'Greens' Add to Junk Mail Mountain," *The Wall Street Journal*, May 13, 1991, B1.

33. Wendy Zellner and Bruce Hager, "Dumpster Raids? That's Not Very Ladylike, Avon," *Business Week*, April 1, 1991, 32.

Video Case for Part 2

Harry Rosen Stores

Harry Rosen is the founder of the chain of high-fashion menswear stores that carry his name. As a teenager, Rosen was a sales clerk at the Slack Shop in Toronto. After high school, he worked in production at Tip Top Tailors, and in 1954, at the age of 23, he and his brother borrowed $500 to open their own store on Parliament Street in Toronto. In 1961, the brothers moved their store to Richmond Street, which was at that time an unproven retail district. The store was so successful that, in 1969, Rosen sold his interest in the store to Wilfred Posluns, one of his customers and co-founder of the Dylex chain of stores.

But Rosen missed the day-to-day running of his own stores, and in 1976 he bought back 49 percent of the operation from Dylex and as a partner began to oversee the expansion of the Harry Rosen chain, which now includes 22 men's stores with annual sales of more than $100 million and profits of $1.2 million. Then in 1996, due to financial troubles and restructuring, Dylex Ltd. sold all of its shares (51 percent) back to Harry Rosen through an investment company which Rosen controls.

Harry Rosen stores have always followed a very segmented market approach by attempting to capture the upper-income executive male in search of high-quality, higher-priced merchandise. In order to preserve this high-quality image, Rosen developed its own private label, which has been used on an increasing percentage of its merchandise.

Concerned with stagnant sales in the mid-1990s, Harry Rosen decided to broaden the chain's customer base by reaching out to younger men. To assist in doing this, Mr. Rosen had extensive customer research done and changed advertising agencies. The result was an attempt to make the name "a little less stuffy" and cash in on the move to casual Fridays, direct advertising more at women (who shop for men), and use other media besides newspapers. The newspaper ads took on a different approach with large full-page pictures of well-known men and the queston "What will ______ be wearing today?"

In commenting on the future of the retail industy amid greater competition and a changing consumer, Harry Rosen responds, "Big box stores are a fact of life, but the independent menswear retailer will still strive because of the nature of the customers. Service is where you've got to concentrate."

Recently, Harry Rosen has shown that he is serious about service, as he has established an in-store retailing information system (RIS) which gives salespeople on-the-spot information about customers—so that any repeat customers get personal treatment in any store. Rosen points to the fact that the number of clients in the system has tripled in three years as proof of the program's success.

Questions

1. Discuss the advantages and disadvantages of segmenting a retail market using Harry Rosen as an example.
2. Discuss the potential consequences of Rosen's attempt to broaden his target market.
3. Discuss the costs and benefits of the new RIS that Rosen has established.

Source: "Harry Rosen Stores," Venture *609 (September 22, 1996; 13:06).*

Part three 3

Resource Assessment

Retail Organizations and Human Resource Management

Outline

Organizational Culture
Core Culture
Surface Culture
Diverse Subculture

Organizational Management
Organizational Elements
Organizational Principles
Organizational Structures

Human Resource Management
Position Statement
Personnel Recruitment
Personnel Selection
Personnel Training
Personnel Supervision
Personnel Evaluation
Personnel Compensation

Summary

Student Study Guide
Key Terms and Concepts
Review Questions
Review Exam

Student Application Manual
Investigative Projects: Practice and Application

Endnotes

Objectives

To understand the impact of an organization's culture on the behaviour of its members

To discuss how organizational objectives provide a focus for the tasks that must be accomplished by the organization

To describe the five basic principles of organization and explain their role in creating an effective retail business

To diagram the five basic types of organizational structures and describe the circumstances under which each type of structure is used to organize the retailer's business

To plan and conduct an effective retail personnel recruitment and selection process

To specify and describe the different procedures used in training and supervising store personnel

To outline and describe the various methods for evaluating and compensating retail employees

Retail Vignette

Home Depot

Home Depot was founded in 1978 in Atlanta, Georgia. It has been credited with being the leading innovator in bringing the "category killer" retail format to the home improvement industry. The success of this strategy is evident by Home Depot's growth. Since 1978, Home Depot has passed the $20 billion sales figure and currently operates over 550 stores in North America, making it the number one retailer in the world in its category.

Home Depot continues to grow at 20 percent per year and has recently expanded to Latin America.

Each Home Depot store stacks approximately 40 000 to 50 000 different kinds of building materials, home improvement supplies, and lawn and garden products. Layouts follow the grid approach with wide aisles and a neat, clean, and efficient interior. Home Depot combines economies of scale inherent in a warehouse format with a level of customer service unprecedented among warehouse-style retailers.

Home Depot
www.homedepot.com

Information systems play an important role in increasing efficiency and allowing employees to spend more time serving customers.

In February of 1994, Home Depot entered the Canadian market with the purchase of Aikenheads Home Improvement Warehouses. Steven Bebis, who helped establish Aikenheads, was installed as the President of Home Depot's new Canadian Division. In March 1996, Annette Verschuven succeeded Steven Bebis and became the new President of Home Depot Canada, coming from the same position at Michaels Canada. Led by her aggressive approach, Home Depot Canada plans to open 76 stores by the year 2001. Home Depot Canada stores maintain their Canadian identity by retaining Canadian employees, purchasing from Canadian manufacturers as much as possible, and staying involved in community relations. The company has a formal corporate giving and community investment program with a projected budget of approximately $10.3 million for fiscal 1997.

One of Home Depot's areas of strength is with its management of human resources. The company values communication with employees, provides attractive financial packages, and makes a considerable investment in training and counselling programs.

Recently, Home Depot has improved its distribution networks to get merchandise more quickly into the hands of its customers. It has increased store space for products which show higher growth potential, such as flooring, millwork, and paint. This continual monitoring and improvement has led to increased sales and sales per square foot each year. In the words of President and Chief Operating Officer, Arthur M. Blank, "Our aisles are more shoppable, our customers are greeted and helped more quickly, and they are finding it more convenient to shop at Home Depot."

Printed with permission of Home Depot Canada.

Cross-Functional Teams: Revamping the Retail Organization

More firms will organize around business functions. Traditional organizational charts, organized around functions, will give way to ones organized around business processes (like cross-functional teams) that can create value for the consumer almost always at lower cost.[1]

Employee Turnover: Finding the Right Match

Employee turnover in retailing is expensive, frustrating, and time-consuming. But retailers cannot seem to stop the revolving door. Turnover is actually a symptom of a more fundamental problem, which begins long before retailers notice employees coming and going at an alarming rate. Basic skills and competencies were sufficient employment criteria in the age of the assembly line, when little creativity or judgment were required. Retailing—or any job in which interactive skills are a factor—requires a precise matching of individual styles to company, coworker, and customer.[2]

Merchant Employees: Creating the Right Chemistry

What sets us [Wal-Mart] apart is that we train people to be merchants. We let them see all of the numbers—sales figures, profit, and shrinkage. They know their costs, their markup, their overhead, and their profit. It is a big responsibility and a big opportunity, but nobody gets anything out of just standing around and going through the motions. How can you expect people to do their best job, if you do not give them the tools to do it with? When people know you are counting on them, that you trust them, that you believe in their ability to do a good job, then they give it their best shot. The most important thing in any retail business is having the right chemistry and the right attitude on the part of the folks who deal with the customers.[3]

People make a successful business! However, organization is essential to any group of people having a common purpose or goal: Organization is the binding force that coordinates, channels, and propels the group toward its stated mission.[4] An understanding of the formal and informal organizational culture is a prerequisite to any study of organizational structures and interactions. This chapter begins with a look at the basic concept of organizational culture. Organizing the retail enterprise and the managerial issues involved in that process are reviewed in the second section of this chapter. Human resource management as seen from the viewpoint of the retail staffing process constitutes the focus of study in the last section of this chapter. Figure 6–1 is a pictorial organization of the topics to be discussed in this chapter.

Organizational Culture

Organizational culture is a set of key values shared by all or most members of a retail organization. An organization's culture is the unwritten policies and guidelines that help individuals understand organizational functioning and thus provide them with norms for behaviour in the firm.[5] These values are incorporated into various traditions that are passed from older to new employees. Disney World's Magic Kingdom theme park in Orlando, Florida, incorporates a set of values into its culture known as the "pixie dust" formula. Each employee is indoctrinated into the Disney service culture, where they are told that they are not just employees but pivotal "cast members" in a "show" designed to make the resort unreal. This culture is passed on from trainers (facilitators) to new cast members' training, support, and benefits.[6] Recreational Equipment, Inc. (REI), a large consumer-owned retail cooperative specializing in high-quality outdoor gear, has its unorthodox corporate culture shaped by the mountain climbers, ski racers, bike racers, kayakers, and trekkers that constitute a large portion of the firm's employees.[7]

Figure 6–1

Retail organization and human resources

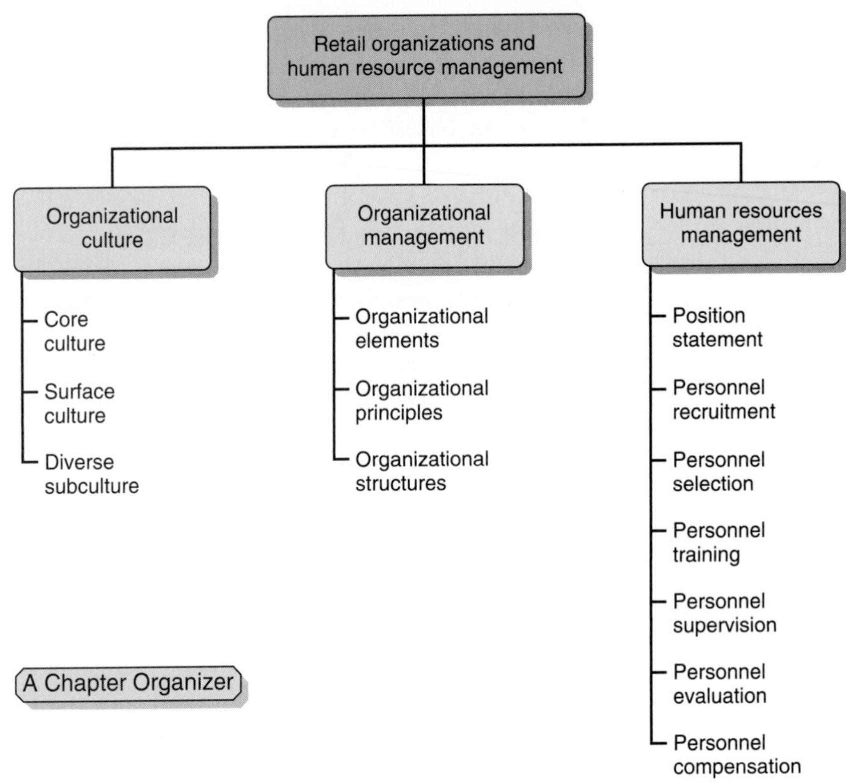

Retail Strategies and Tactics

The Gospel According to Wal-Mart

Canadian retailers have been looking for clues to Wal-Mart's almost mythical success since the caravan from Arkansas rolled across the border. The giant retailer has mesmerized suppliers, walked the tightrope with margins and pulled incredible profits out of the hat. But wizardry with numbers doesn't tell the whole story. As Bruce West, president of Wal-Mart Canada, will tell you, "it all boils down to people, and there's nothing magical in that."

Almost every angle on pricing is being used by Canadian retailers to lure customers. So much so that customer service is perhaps the last area in which retailers can distance themselves from competitors. Sam Walton saw it coming, and concluded that the key to customer service is staff motivation. Walton understood that minimum wage with no prospects does not inspire staff to go out of their way for customers or the company. As a result, Wal-Mart has one of the most progressive employee packages of any mass merchandiser in the world. In Canada, it is up to Bruce West to ensure that Wal-Mart employees are happy from the ground up. He calls it partnership.

According to West, to motivate employees, you must involve them on every level of the operation. Give them responsibility, recognition, and a share of the profits, and you have a successful partnership that gets results on the sales floor. He outlines a number of employee programs that he refers to as "part ownership."

Source: Paula Anderton and Elena Opasini, Centre Magazine, *March–April 1995, 13–15.*

Figure 6–2

Levels of retail organizational culture

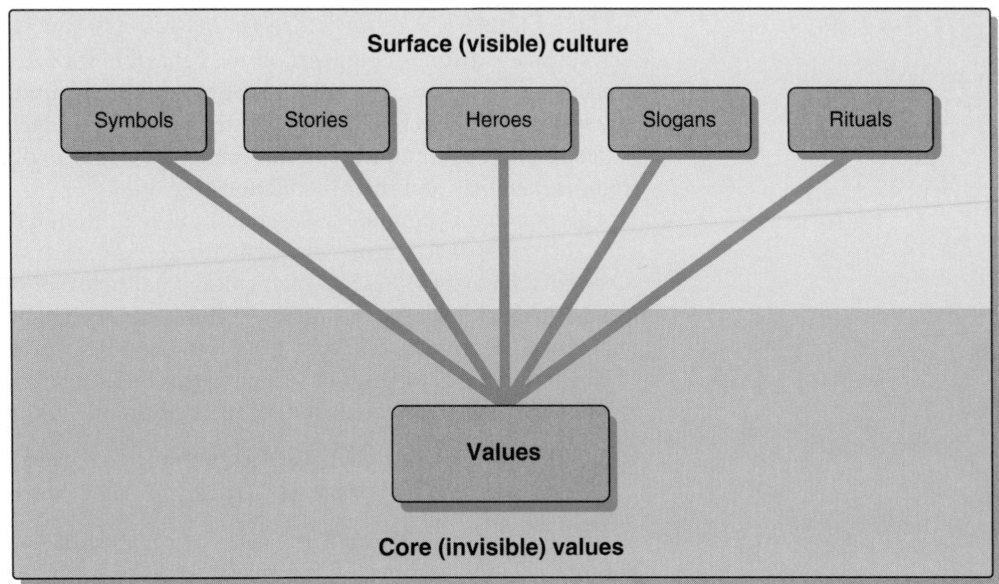

A company's culture is almost as obvious to its customers—and to its competitors—as the merchandise shown in its selling floors. It is displayed most obviously by the behaviour of salespeople in their face-to-face contacts with customers. It is the little things that matter in the treatment of customers and employees; a smile can make a big difference in a company's culture and its effectiveness. As illustrated in Figure 6–2, there are two levels of culture in the retail organization: the core culture and the surface culture.

Core Culture

The **core culture** is the basic value system underlying the retailer's organization. It is the invisible foundation that supports the observable behaviour of the surface culture (see Figure 6–2). As defined in Chapter 4, **values** are deep beliefs and understandings that guide and motivate the attitudes and actions of organizational members who share them. The organizational core culture represents informal norms that bind the retail organization together and gives meaning and direction to the day-to-day behaviour of its members.

Core cultures determine which behaviour is appropriate, which problems take priority, and which strategies are supported. From the viewpoint of employees, characteristics of healthy corporate cultures include the following: (1) It is a fun and enjoyable place to work, (2) Employees are allowed to make a mistake, (3) Employees are treated fairly, (4) Employees take pride in their work and feel they are making a contribution, and (5) Employees feel that they have responsibility for and control over their own work.[8] A **dysfunctional corporate culture** is "one whose shared values and behaviour are at odds with its long-term health."[9] For example, a retailer may celebrate the star salesperson even if that person neglects the nonselling activities related to customer service that are key to building customer loyalty and return trade.[10]

Delta Hotels
www.deltahotels.com

Delta Hotels have established a program to provide business services, such as fax machines, photocopiers, computers, and other office accessories, to their business guests to provide superior customer service.[11] Even though culture is less explicit than the organization's rules and procedures, it is a powerful force influencing how retailers solve problems, make decisions, and achieve goals. "In a world where many people find little satisfaction in the paycheques they receive from big companies . . . visions of financial independence are often compelling. But Amway [direct marketer] goes a crucial step beyond mere money. It offers its recruits membership in a community of like-minded people—entrepreneurial, motivated, upwardly mobile people who believe in their country, in God, and in the family."[12]

Surface Culture

The **surface culture** is composed of the behavioural environment and each personal relationship that one can observe and hear by walking around the organization. It is the manifestations of the internal cultural patterns that have emerged from the core culture. The surface culture communicates both formally and informally what the organization expects from its members and their interactions.

This communication process is accomplished through the use of (1) symbols—objects, acts, or events that convey the right image; (2) stories—histories and tales of special accomplishments; (3) heroes—recognition and praise of outstanding performers; (4) slogans—succinct expressions of key values and beliefs; and (5) rituals—planned and unplanned ceremonies celebrating special occasions and activities (see Figure 6–2).

The following list identifies several examples of retail organizations and their attempts at communicating the core values of their corporate culture:

- Symbols: McDonald's golden arches, although smaller than they once were, are well-known and have even served as the name for a new entry, the "Arch Deluxe."
- Stories: Eaton's stories of "no questions asked" money-back guarantees give employees and customers confidence regarding the importance of the customer.
- Heroes: "Mr. Sam" is Sam Walton, the late founder of Wal-Mart and a continuing influence within the firm's corporate culture. Some of the corporate legacies left by Sam Walton include a much-admired tradition of encouraging innovation and risk taking, a policy of treating employees as business partners, and a belief that businesses have the responsibility of giving something back to the community.[13]
- Slogans: Chiseled into a granite slab in the front of Stew Leonard's dairy store in Norwalk, Connecticut, is the slogan "Rule 1: The customer is always right. Rule 2: If the customer is ever wrong, reread Rule 1." Living up to this operating philosophy has made Stew Leonard's one of the most successful and talked-about food stores in the eastern United States.
- Rituals: Amway is one of the largest North American direct selling organizations, whose army of part-time sales associates need continuous motivation. Amway's rallies typically resemble a mix between a rock concert and a religious revival meeting. The evenings are often kicked off with inspiring music—the theme from Rocky or Chariots of Fire—followed by much hand holding, singing, swaying, and listening to testimonials. Amway chants and inspirational speeches last into the early-morning hours. A set of shared beliefs reinforced by myths, icons, and documents is the means by which Amway distributors are bound together.[14]

Diverse Subculture

As is the case with any social group, retail organizations have **subcultures**—groups of individuals within the organization that have similar values and beliefs based on one or more attributes shared by all of its members. Some of the more commonly identified subcultures within a retail organization are those based on (1) occupation—retail buyers and sales associates; (2) generation—mature employees and younger ones; (3) location—home office personnel and individual store personnel; (4) gender—female and male sales associates; and (5) ethnicity—French-Canadian, Anglo-Canadian, white, black, and Asian employees.

From a managerial perspective, subcultures must be recognized, not standardized. Although subculture diversity can promote territorial friction and personal conflicts, it also brings a broader and deeper perspective to the retailer's problem-solving and decision-making capabilities. "The whole point of managing diversity is to draw on the uniqueness of each employee. If people feel they must censor what they say and how they act, the major benefit of diversity is lost."[15] Given the diversity of the retailer's operating and merchandising environments (review the description in Chapter 3), considerable advantages accrue to the retailer that can draw upon managers and coworkers from dissimilar backgrounds. Different subcultural groups have different strengths and capabilities, and retail management must learn how to harness the best of what each group has to offer the organization. Experts tend to agree that the most successful diversity initiatives are all inclusive and comprehensive in scope. Sears uses a five-pronged program to diversify management; it involves "work and family issues, accessibility to equal opportunity in the workplace, diversity education, minority and female vendor sourcing and diversity market focuses."[16] Equally important to the long-term welfare of the retail organization is the creation of a work environment that respects individual differences and disdains the narrow-minded behaviour of intolerant people. Personnel evaluation, promotion, and compensation methods should be structured in such a way as to accommodate a diverse workforce.

Organizational Management

Although retailers exhibit several core and surface cultures, all retail firms utilize certain common organizational elements and principles in creating an organizational structure that is appropriate to a particular type of retailing format. The specific issues and concerns of organizational management are identified in Figure 6–3.

Organizational Elements

The particular organizational structure a retail firm adopts depends on several factors, including (1) the type of merchandise offered, (2) the variety and assortment of the merchandise stocked, (3) the type and number of customer services performed, (4) the type and number of locations used, (5) the availability and quality of personnel employed, and (6) the legal requirements and/or restrictions. Given this array of influential factors, the firm's organization must centre on specific organizational objectives and tasks.

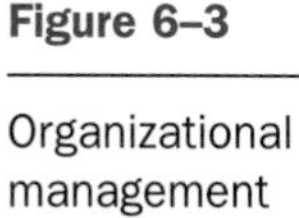

Figure 6–3

Organizational management

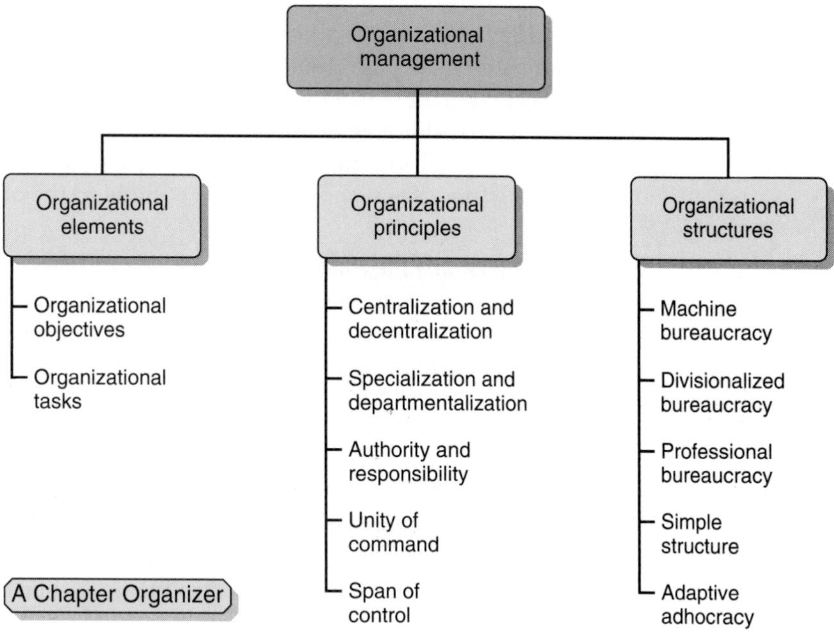

Figure 6–4

Levels of organizational objectives

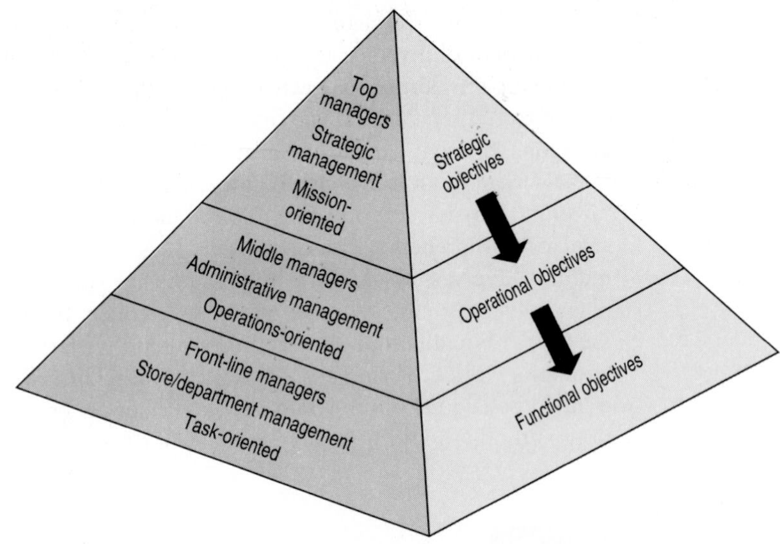

Organizational Objectives In retailing, the firm's organizational foundation focuses on achieving the firm's objectives. Establishing well-defined organizational objectives is an important step because it forces the retailer to think through what the firm is trying to accomplish, where the firm is going, and how the firm intends to get there. In addition, organizational objectives provide a realistic orientation to the retailer's planning process as well as a means of evaluating the firm's past performance and its current status.

Three levels of organizational objectives correspond to the three general levels of retail management (see Figure 6–4). **Strategic objectives** are general, long-term goals that the retail firm intends to pursue. Essentially, a strategic objective identifies an overall mission that the firm's management wishes to realize. **Operational objectives** are general, long-term operational requirements necessary to achieve a strategic objective. They establish the general framework within which a particular merchandising or operating function can be identified. **Functional objectives** are specific task objectives that identify a specific function and how it is to be accomplished. The unique value of functional objectives is their quantifiability, which makes them especially useful in planning, executing, and controlling a particular retailing activity. Functional objectives are developed to identify specific sales, profit, and operating results for each division, store, and department.

Organizational Tasks In developing the retail organization, the retailer must identify and assign the numerous tasks necessary to realize the firm's stated organizational objectives. Figure 6–5 lists the basic types of organizational tasks inherent to any retail organization. Although the list of tasks in Figure 6–5 can help a retailer develop a general organizational structure, a more detailed description of tasks must be made in assigning responsibilities and authority to each position in the organization.

Organizational Principles

There are five basic principles of organization that every retailer should consider in establishing a retail organization: (1) centralization and decentralization, (2) specialization and departmentalization, (3) lines of authority and responsibility, (4) unity of command, and (5) span of control.

Centralization and Decentralization **Centralization** is the organizational principle of concentrating decision-making authority within the central corporate office. A highly centralized organization is one in which corporate managers assume the responsibility for making key merchandising and operating decisions. The organizational principle of **decentralization** involves the delegation of decision-making authority and

responsible for all the physical operations of the store that are not directly assigned to one of the other divisions. Major tasks include facilities development and maintenance; customer services and assistance; receiving, checking, marking, and stocking of incoming merchandise; store security; and general store housekeeping. Many department stores create a five-function organization by establishing a personnel division, equal in status to the other four divisions. Other functional activities that retailers might consider for separate divisional status are distribution, real estate and construction, and catalogue operations.

Geographic Divisionalized Bureaucracy. A retail organization using the **geographic divisionalized bureaucracy** is one in which the retailer organizes tasks and assigns jobs on the basis of where those tasks and jobs are performed. Large specialty store chains that operate many outlets spread out all over the country often form organizational structures with several levels and various degrees of local market specialization (see Figure 6–11). The Home Depot, for instance, is organized geographically. Because there are differences in buying behaviour between one geographic area and another in the home-improvement field, Home Depot is organized into separate divisions in order to effectively merchandise to regional customers.

When department stores began to "branch out" into other geographic areas, they necessitated several changes in the basic Mazur Plan. These new organizational arrangements for department store chains included the geographic restructuring of their functional divisionalized bureaucracies. The three most common modifications were the main-store approach, the separate-store approach, and the equal-store approach. Figure 6–12 describes each of these modifications. However, while specialty retailers are becoming more decentralized, department stores are doing just the opposite. New technology is allowing Eaton's and The Bay to centralize inventory buying and control and achieve savings in order to meet new competition.[28] An unusual form of geographic divisionalized

Figure 6–11

A geographic divisionalized bureaucrcy

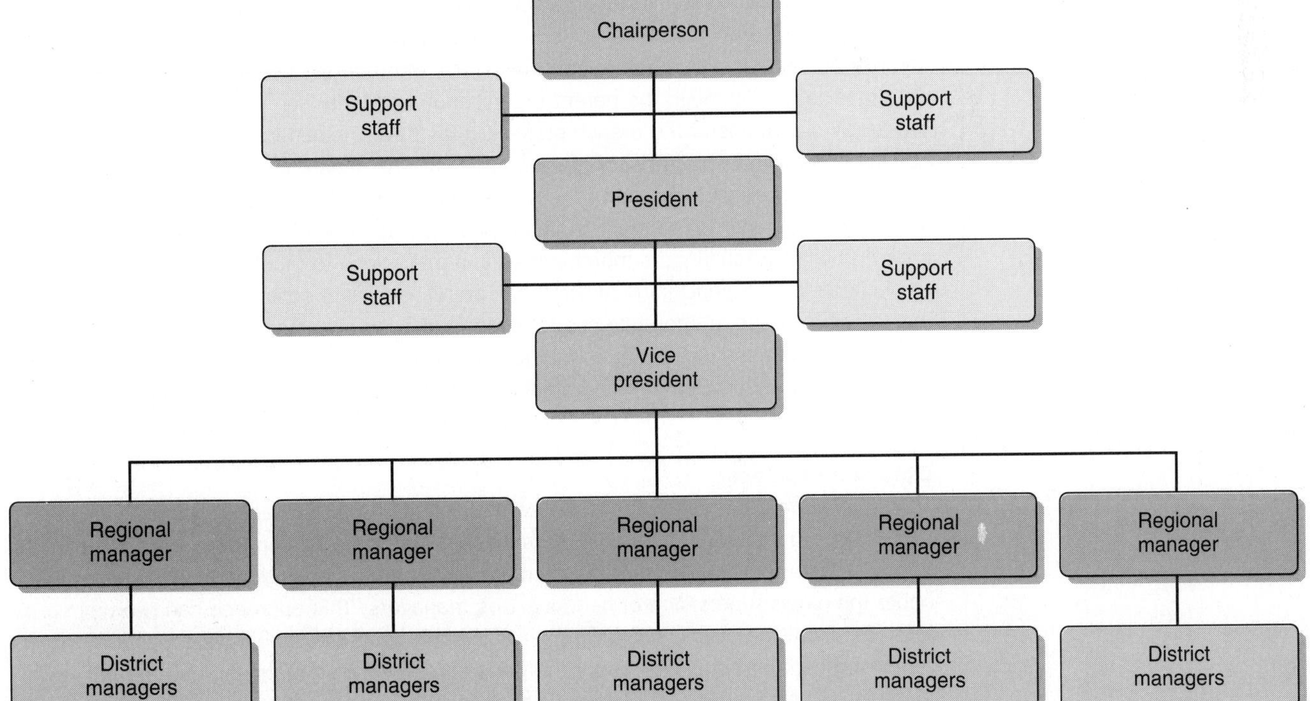

bureaucracy is practised by Sears, which has split its Home Group division into separate "off-the-mall" (freestanding Sears Hardware Stores) and "on-the-mall" business units.[29]

Product Divisionalized Bureaucracy. In the **product divisionalized bureaucracy**, the retailer organizes the store by product line. This divisionalized bureaucracy is centred on task and job specialization to meet the consumers' buying needs for certain products. For

Figure 6–12

Geographic restructuring of the department store's functional divisionalized bureaucratic organization

Main-store approach

With the main-store approach, the parent organization (the main store) exercises control over branch stores. Main-store managers of finance, general merchandise, promotion, and operations are responsible for supervising the same functions in the branch stores as at the main store. Under this organizational plan, main-store buyers and their assistants are responsible for securing merchandise for the main store and all branches. Sales activities in the main store are under the direct supervision of buyers, whereas sales activities in all branch stores are the responsibility of branch sales managers. Used by department stores in the initial stages of expansion, the main-store approach is most appropriate when (1) there are only a few branches; (2) customer preferences and the merchandise mix are fairly similar for the main and branch stores; (3) branch stores are located near the main store; and (4) main-store management and supporting staff can comfortably supervise branches without over-extending themselves.

Separate-store approach

The separate-store approach to branch department store organization treats each branch as an independent operation with its own organizational structure of managers, buyers, and sales personnel. Under this plan, branch-store management assumes both the merchandising responsibilities of buying and selling and the routine responsibilities of operating the branch store. Each branch has its own store manager as well as personnel, merchandise, and operations managers, who operate separately from the parent organization. Although the parent organization has little direct involvement in the day-to-day operations of the branch store, it does have the general responsibilities of serving in an advisory and policy making capacity. The separate-store approach generally is used by department stores that have four to seven branches approximately the size of the main store. The major advantage of this approach is that each branch has great flexibility in tailoring its merchandise and operations to meet the needs of its local clientele. The principal disadvantages are (1) a loss in economies of scale in buying, (2) an increase in operating costs because of additional management and staff needs, (3) increased difficulties in maintaining a consistent image from store to store, and (4) increased problems of coordination (for example stock transfers and promotion activities).

Equal-store approach

The equal-store approach emphasizes centralization of authority and responsibility. Under the equal-store plan, all major managerial functions are controlled from a central headquarters. The finance, merchandise, promotions, and operations functions are under the direct supervision of headquarters managers. This approach has two unique features. First, the buying and selling functions are separated; the buying function remains a centralized activity under the general merchandise manager, and the selling function becomes a decentralized activity under the manager of stores. Second, all stores (main and branches) are treated equally as basic sales units. The equal-store plan attempts to combine the advantages of centralized buying (economies of scale) with the advantages of localized selling (target market selling).

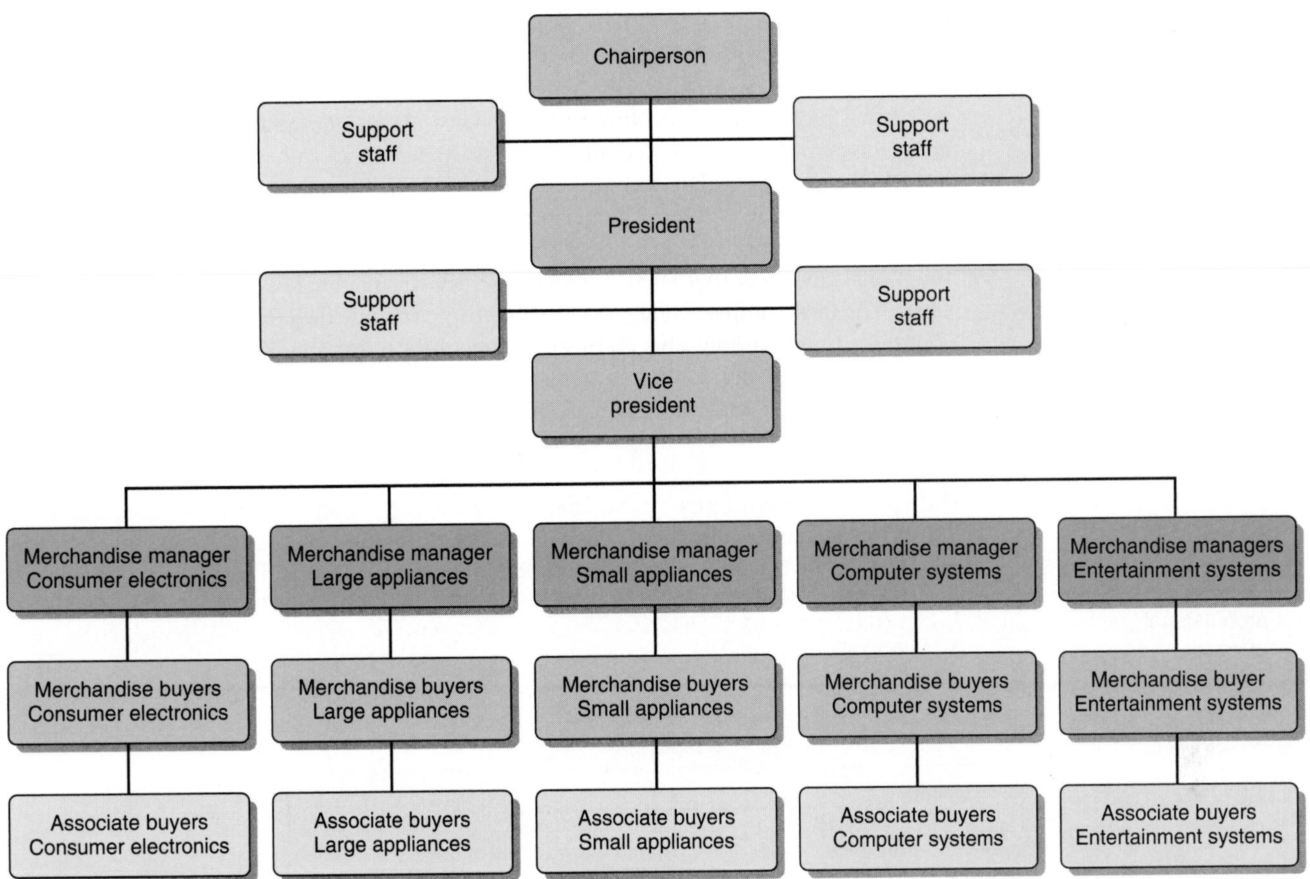

Figure 6–13

A product divisionalized bureaucracy

many shopping and specialty goods, for example, consumers think, shop, and buy in terms of product categories. For example, a specialty store conglomerate might organize its business by developing different retailing formats with different product mixes that are capable of targeting different target markets. Figure 6–13 illustrates a home centre superstore that has organized its operations around such product categories as consumer electronics, large appliances, small appliances, computer systems, and entertainment systems.

Professional Bureaucracy Service organizations that utilize a large number of highly skilled and trained professional employees are organized into a **professional bureaucracy**—a flat hierarchical structure with a limited number of middle managers and a large technical support staff who assist the organization's professionals by performing administrative functions. Figure 6–14 visualizes the structure of a professional bureaucracy at a university. As a highly decentralized organization, professionals (for example, deans, heads, faculty) make decisions and solve problems within their area of expertise (for example, arts, sciences, engineering, business, education). For any retail service enterprise (for example, medical establishment, law office, personal care firm), the professional bureaucracy is a common choice for structuring an organization in such a fashion that allows professionals considerable freedom in meeting their responsibilities while providing a formal relationship between various operating units.

Simple Structure. The **simple structure** is a flat organization with a single top manager and few if any middle managers or support staff. As this "lean" structure suggests, nonmanagerial employees perform most of the functions and tasks under the direct supervision of the top manager. The simple structure is an adaptive organization that gives the top manager centralized control while permitting individual workers considerable latitude and authority in completing their responsibilities. Small independent retailers and entrepreneurs are most often organized in this fashion.

Many retailers began business as a one-person, owner-operator enterprise in which the individual had the responsibility and authority for all organizational tasks. As the firm grew, the owner-operator hired additional store personnel to handle the increasing number of complex tasks that accompany a larger, more formal organizational structure. As illustrated in Figure 6–15, the owner-manager has the overall managerial responsibility for planning, executing, and controlling the firm's strategic initiatives. The two most common functional divisions that small retailers use are the merchandising and operations divisions. The merchandise manager's responsibilities include developing and buying the merchandise mix, planning and controlling inventories, creating and managing price, promoting, and devising selling strategies. The responsibilities of the operations manager involve personnel and facilities management, information and financial systems control, and store security.

Adaptive Adhocracy The **adaptive adhocracy** is an organizational structure that limits vertical management while promoting horizontal working relationships in accomplishing the firm's objectives. The distinction between line and staff positions becomes

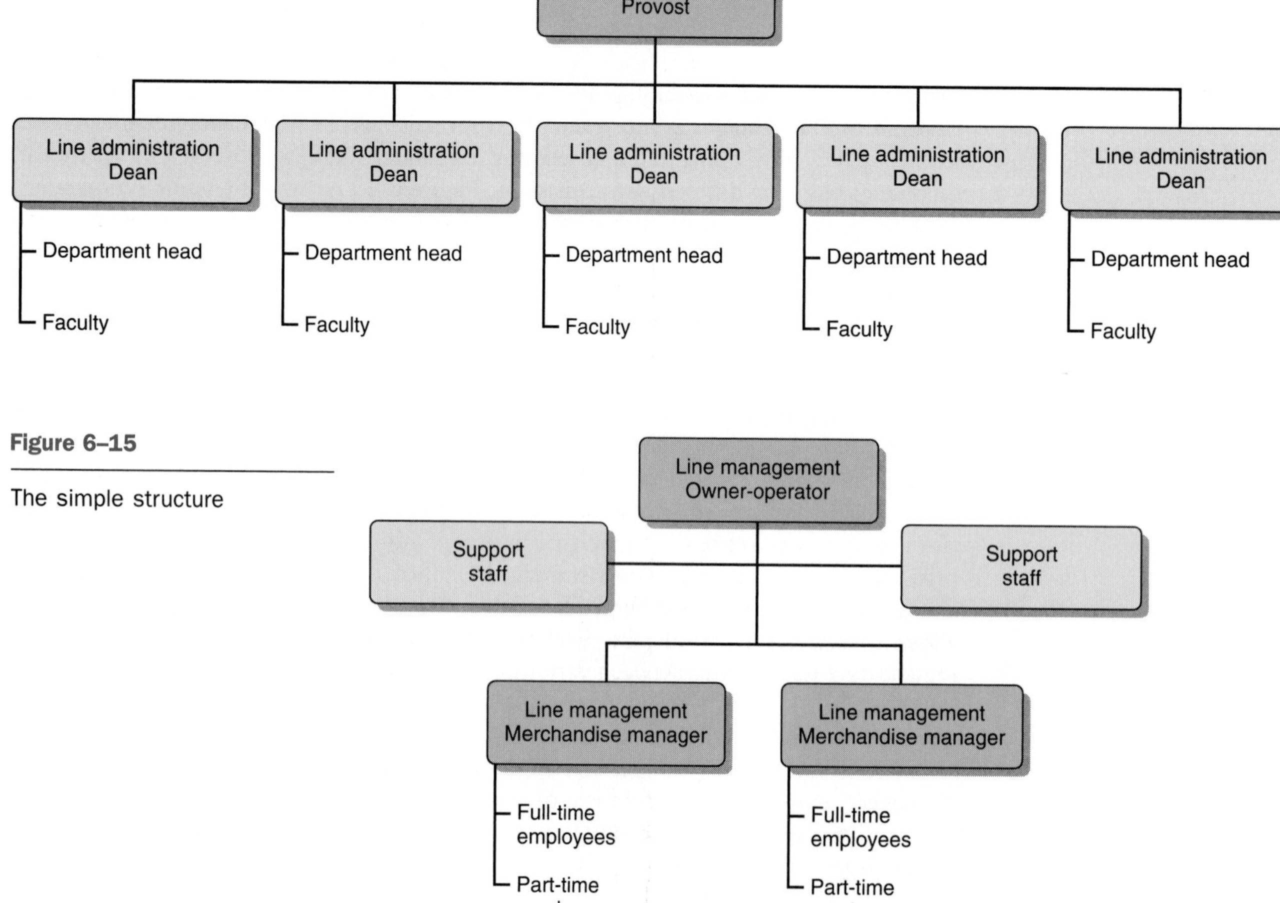

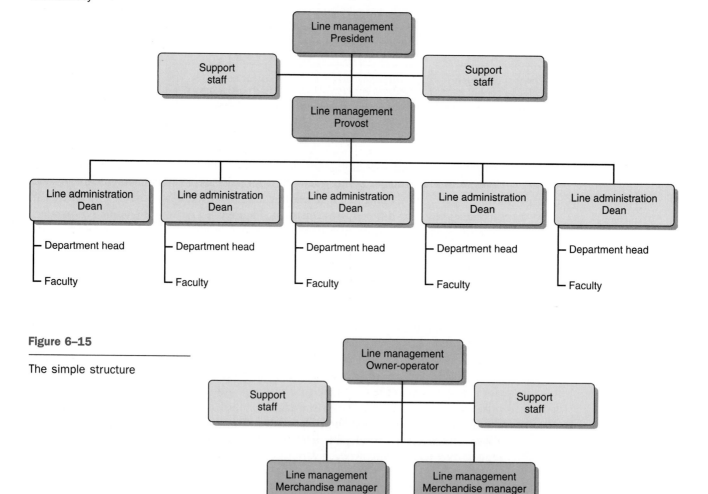

Figure 6–14

The professional bureaucracy

Figure 6–15

The simple structure

Figure 6–16

The adaptive adhocracy

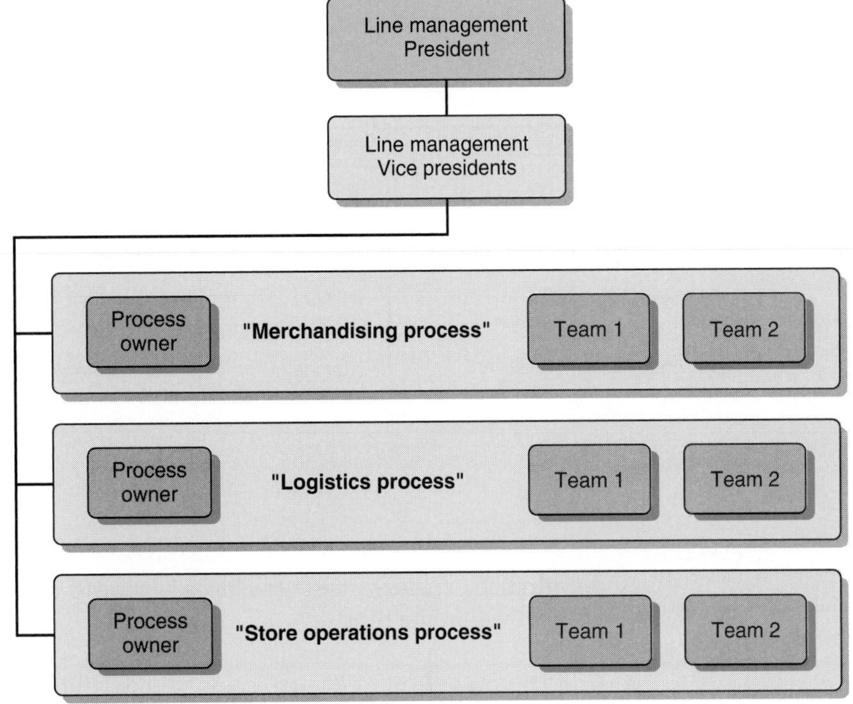

blurred as employees are grouped into teams on which individual expertise is directed at accomplishing a multifunctional project. The use of a horizontal organization requires that teams be the main building blocks of the retail organization. Supervisory roles are limited by making the team manage itself. Each team is held accountable for measurable performance goals and each team member is rewarded on the basis of team results, not just individual performance.[30] This highly decentralized and informal organization is illustrated in Figure 6–16.

Human Resource Management

As a labour-intensive business, retailers must manage their human resources carefully in order to realize financial objectives (for example, control labour expenses), operational objectives (for example, improve labour productivity), and marketing objectives (for example, attain customer satisfaction and loyalty). Retail staffing is a serious problem for most retailers because of the large number of part-time employees, stressful working conditions, high labour turnover rates, and shrinking skilled labour pool.[31] A shortage of qualified people will be one of the biggest problems that retailers must overcome. The human resource issue is even more serious when one considers the high visibility of most retail employees and their key role in dealing with the customer.

Having examined the issues surrounding the organization of the retailer's human resources, let us turn our attention to the process of staffing the retail firm. Figure 6–17 illustrates the seven steps of the staffing process.

Position Statement

The first step in the retail staffing process is a careful assessment of the firm's total human resource needs. Given the key role played by retail employees at all levels within the

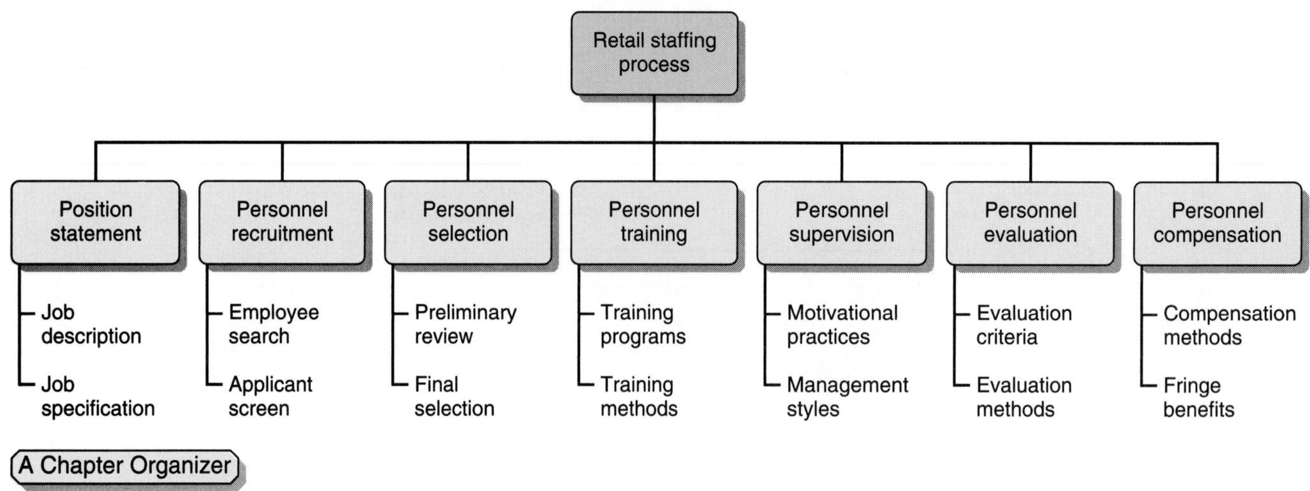

Figure 6–17

The retail staffing process

organization, retailers must develop a complete description and specification of each position within the firm.

Job Description The first action in the staffing process is to develop a well-defined, clearly expressed **job description**. Not only does this action force the retailer to determine its personnel needs carefully, but it also provides the potential employee with a means of evaluating the job. Before writing a job description, the retailer should conduct a job analysis to determine (1) specific job performance objectives and standards; (2) the tasks, duties, and responsibilities of the job; and (3) the skills, aptitudes, experience, education, and physical abilities that potential employees must possess to meet the minimum job requirements.

After the job analysis is completed, the retailer can write a job description containing the following items: (1) the job title (for example, sales representative, assistant store manager); (2) the job location (for example, store, department); (3) the job position and relationships with the firm's organizational structure (that is, identify superiors and subordinates, if any); and (4) job description (that is, duties and responsibilities). Figure 6–18 presents a typical job description for a sales manager position.

Job Specification To meet federal, provincial, and local regulations on hiring practices, many retailers provide potential employees with a written job specification. A **job specification** clearly states the minimum qualifications a person must have to obtain the job. Qualification criteria include education and training requirements and/or basic knowledge and skill requirements.

Because of recent legislation, retailers must recognize that they might be asked to prove that their qualifying criteria are directly related to successful performance in the positions outlined in their job descriptions. To avoid costly lawsuits, they must establish the validity of the relationship between job success and the stated job qualifications. Before filling any position, the retailer should protect itself by gathering evidence that the job qualifications actually enable an employee to meet job expectations. The retailer must avoid certain illegal conditions for employment in writing job qualifications, such as any requirement related either directly or indirectly to the applicant's race, age, creed, colour, sex, religion, or ethnic origin.

With today's labour shortage, many retailers are now writing job specifications that are designed to attract a class of workers that might previously have been overlooked or undervalued. One such group is older workers, who are proving to be an excellent source of reliable and productive associates.

Figure 6–18

A typical job description

Job title:	Sales Manager
Job location:	Men's Shoe Department Walnut Valley Branch Selmer's Department Stores
Job position:	Reports to Assistant Store Manager
Job description:	Achieve sales goals by setting and maintaining customer service standards, training and motivating a professional sales staff, and maintaining merchandise presentation standards.

Job objectives:

1. Work as a partner with the merchandise analyst to develop sales plans and to reach sales goals within the area of responsibility.
2. Ensure that the store's customer service standards and policies are maintained.
3. Train, develop, motivate, and appraise the sales associates working within the area of responsibility.
4. Work as a partner with the merchandise analyst and assistant store manager in developing stock assortments and quantities.
5. Verify that the appearance and presentation of merchandise on the selling floor adhere to the visual merchandising guidelines.
6. Ensure that selling services provide appropriate floor coverage to meet or exceed productivity goals.
7. Communicate with the branch store coordinator, assistant store manager, and merchandise analyst concerning floor presentation.
8. Ensure that advertised merchandise is properly priced, ticketed, and displayed, and ensure that sales associates are aware of this merchandise.
9. Control merchandise inventories, including but not limited to receiving, pricing, transfers, price changes, security, and damages.
10. Conduct all stock counts.
11. Supervise the control of sales register media and cash register shortage.
12. Shop the competition.
13. Input information into major sale résumés.
14. Disseminate all pertinent information to all sales associates including night contingents.
15. Ensure the correct documentation of time sheets within the area.
16. Implement credit promotions and other programs in the area.

Personnel Recruitment

Recruiting is the active search for qualified employees. The astute manager recruits personnel by aggressively seeking lists of qualified prospects, screening large numbers of applicants, and maintaining a pool of prospective employees.

Employee Search Several internal and external sources can provide the names and general backgrounds of prospective employees. Internal sources include lists of current and past employees as well as employee recommendations. Current employees should not be overlooked if they possess the necessary qualifications for the job. Promotions and transfers are not only a means of finding qualified persons but also a way to improve employee morale by demonstrating that advancement is possible within the firm. Past employees with satisfactory service records are an internal source of prospective employees that retailers often overlook. By maintaining files on past employees (full- and part-time), the personnel manager has access to prospective employees who could be productive immediately with minimal training. The third internal source is employee recommendations. Frequently, the firm's employees know of friends, relatives, and acquaintances who are in the job market and have the necessary skills and training to fill a position.

External sources of prospective employees come from advertisements, employment agencies, educational institutions, and unsolicited applications. Advertisements in newspapers, trade publications, and professional papers and journals are common methods of attracting applicants. These printed media frequently devote sections to employment opportunities at certain times or in particular issues. Private and public employment agencies are also sources of prospective employees. Two advantages of using employment agencies are that they provide initial screening for a large number of prospects and that they maintain the retailer's anonymity during the initial stages of the recruiting process. Before using the services of a private or government employment agency, the retailer should determine the agency's fee structure and which party is responsible for paying the fee—the employer or the employee.

The third external source of prospective employee is educational institutions. Career counsellors at most high schools often can provide a list of suitable prospects for part-time and entry-level positions. Placement offices at colleges and universities are always eager to supply retailers and other businesses with the names and qualifications of prospective employees for low- and middle-management positions.

Walk-ins and mail-ins represent *unsolicited applications* that retailers should keep on file and periodically review when a job becomes available. One additional external source of employees is pirating—hiring an employee who works for a noncompeting retailer. The major advantage of pirating is the retailing experience the prospective employee undoubtedly has. However, the retailer should proceed cautiously when hiring another retailer's employee. Potential employees which exhibit disloyalty to current employers may also demonstrate the same sense of loyalty to any new employer. Legal ramifications and ethical considerations should also be examined prior to any pirating activity.

Applicant Screen In the screening process, personnel managers examine the applicant's qualifications to determine whether the person has the requisite background and capabilities to perform the job. The most common criteria retailers use in the initial screening process are educational background, ability to communicate in verbal and written forms, experience in working with people, and knowledge, experience, or skills to perform a particular activity (for example, typing). Other screening criteria retailers use indirectly and subjectively are personal appearance, general attitude, motivation, and personality. "As companies emphasize the emotional content of frontline jobs, they are delving even deeper into the psychological makeup of the people they pick to fill them."[32] Disney, Goodyear, and the Cleveland Cavaliers basketball team employ a "life themes" approach (identifying a person's passions and then matching him or her to the right position) to evaluating prospective employees.[33]

Personnel Selection

From the list of qualified applicants, the retailer must select the individual best suited to the job. Matching job requirements to employee attributes is the first point of the selection step of the staffing process. In finding the best match, the retailer conducts a preliminary review of each applicant by gathering as much information on the prospective employee as possible before making the final selection.

Preliminary Review

Application Forms. All retailers should require each prospective employee to complete an application form as a prerequisite for further processing. Application forms provide the retailer with preliminary information on each applicant and (1) serve as a means of checking minimum qualifications during initial screening, (2) provide basic information to guide the interviewer during the personal interview process, (3) allow a preliminary check on the applicant's ability to follow instructions, and (4) provide background information for a permanent record if the applicant is hired. The typical application form provides space for the applicant's name, address, telephone number, employment history (when and where the applicant has previously worked, levels of compensation, and reasons for leaving previous jobs), formal education and training, and demographic information allowed by government regulations. The application form also usually includes space for a list of personal references. Although the retailer should carefully review all the information on the application form, special attention should be given to omissions and job changes. What is not on the application form could be as important as what is on it. The retailer should seek clarification of all omissions on application forms. Frequent job changes without good cause can also reveal something about the applicant's character and work ethic.

Reference Checks. After the retailer has initially screened prospective employees' application forms and eliminated those who are unqualified, the references of the remaining prospects should be contacted. Although most references that the applicants list are favourably biased, they do give the retailer a way to verify the accuracy and completeness of the applicant's form. Telephone calls to references normally provide more complete and honest evaluations than do letters, mainly because of the immediate and personal two-way communication telephone conversations allow. Telephone contact gives the retailer a chance to ask questions about issues of particular concern. To reinforce reference checks, many retailers contact former employers, teachers, and other individuals who might have specific knowledge of the applicant's character and abilities. Some retailers even check applicants' credit by calling local credit bureaus.

Personal Interviews. Retailers use personal interviews to question and observe applicants in a face-to-face situation. Formal, highly structured interviews have the advantage of establishing the relative roles of each party in the interview, permitting a controlled interviewing environment, and facilitating complete, effective information gathering. Informal, unstructured interviews help the applicant relax, talk freely, and act naturally, thereby enabling the interviewer to view the applicant in an unguarded state. Most retailers prefer to compromise by injecting enough formality and structure into the interview to promote efficiency but not enough to create undue tension in the applicant.

The number of interviews usually depends on the level of the position to be filled. When retailers are filling upper-level managerial positions, they normally interview each applicant several times; for entry-level positions, one interview generally suffices. Many retailers find it advantageous to have the applicant interview with several of the firm's managers so they can elicit several opinions of the applicant's qualifications.

The personal interviewing process should fully comply with provincial and federal equal employment opportunity regulations. Questions asked in the interview must be job related and necessary to judging the applicant's qualifications and abilities. To avoid charges of discrimination, the retailer should construct a list of questions to use in the interviewing process and have the store's legal department review it for any possible discriminatory inquiries.

Testing Instruments. Some retailers use tests to evaluate prospective employees. Applicants are asked to take pencil-and-paper tests to demonstrate their abilities to handle a job. Although the validity and usefulness of these instruments has been debated, many retailers believe they provide valuable insights into a person's qualifications for employment.

Retailers use two general types of instruments to evaluate their applicants: psychological tests and achievement tests. **Psychological tests** are instruments designed to measure an applicant's personality, intelligence, aptitudes, interests, and supervisory skills. **Achievement tests** are questionnaires designed to measure a person's basic knowledge and skills, such as the ability to do basic arithmetic computations or to operate cash registers or computers. Regardless of which tests are used, the retailer needs trained personnel to administer and interpret the results. Generally, retailers prefer achievement tests to psychological tests because they are easier to administer and interpret. Also, most retailers believe that achievement tests are more valid than psychological tests because the statistical relationship between the skills they measure and job success is stronger—a particularly important consideration in light of recent court rulings regarding equal employment opportunities.

Final Selection Ultimately, the retailer must make a final selection among the qualified applicants. No absolute, totally objective method can determine the most qualified person; rather, the final selection is largely a subjective choice based on all available information. An experienced personnel manager with good intuition is perhaps one of the most valuable assets a firm can have for selecting employees who will make a significant contribution over an extended period. Objective tests, experience, and good personal judgment are the tools a personnel manager needs to make the final selection.

Some of the most often cited reasons for rejection of an applicant include that he or she (1) will adapt poorly to work environment, (2) has inadequate reading and writing skills, (3) has no work experience, (4) demonstrates deficient calculation skills, (5) has poor verbal skills, and (6) failed a medical or drug test.

Personnel Training

Nike
www.nike.com

The fourth step in the staffing process is employee training. Training programs are needed not only for new employees but also for existing employees to update their knowledge and skills. Training should help both the employer and employee reach mutually beneficial goals. Nike Town, a company-owned and -operated store dedicated to the promotion of all of Nike's product lines, staffs its store with dedicated athletes—amateurs and college team players. "Before hitting the sales floor, each one is trained for three months at the 74-acre Nike World campus. There the staff is lectured and then quizzed on Nike history, technology, and products."[34]

Training Programs

Organization Orientation. **Organization orientation** is a program that either initiates new employees or updates old ones on the general organizational structure of the firm and its policies, rules, and regulations. It also acquaints employees with the company's history, objectives, and future expectations. Essentially, an organization orientation program makes employees aware of what the firm is trying to accomplish and how it plans to accomplish it. One aim of this program is to improve employees' morale and to make them feel they are members of the "team."

> Disney has overhauled its approach to orientation, putting less emphasis on policies and procedures and more on emotion. Traditions, the two-day initial training session attended by all new cast members, is part inculcation, part encounter group. Guided by two unfailingly upbeat cast members, neatly dressed neophytes seated at round tables in a classroom discuss their earliest memories of Disney, their visions of great service, their understanding of teamwork.[35]

Functional Training. **Functional training** is a program that develops and expands the basic skills and knowledge employees need to perform their jobs successfully. Starbucks, the Seattle-based chain of trendy coffee shops (which was established in Canada in the mid-1990s), recruits its "baristas" (coffee makers) from college campuses and trains them in the art and lore of coffeemaking.[36] Training sessions on selling techniques, customer service procedures, and inventory control are three examples of functional training directed at improving basic employee skills. Increasing employees' knowledge of the company's product lines and helping them to understand customer purchase motives are examples of knowledge-oriented, functional training.

On-the-Job Training. On-the-job **training** is a decentralized approach that occurs on the sales floor, in the stockroom, or in any other work environment where employees are performing their jobs. The trainee usually is under the direct supervision of the department manager or some other designated person responsible for handling the training program. Both specialty and department store training programs rely heavily (70 to 80 percent of training time) on on-the-job training and much less on a class/lecture format.

Off-the-Job Training. **Off-the-job training** is conducted in centralized training classrooms away from the employees' work environment. In centralized classrooms, the trainer can use learning aids such as films, demonstrations, and role playing under controlled conditions, allowing the employee to focus on the learning experience without interruption.

Training Methods

Individual Training. In the **individual training method** employees "train" themselves. One individual training method is the "on your own" approach, in which the employee is put on the job and expected to learn by trial and error, observation, and asking questions. In essence, this sink-or-swim approach includes no formal training. Although the retailer bears no training costs in the short run, the total costs in the long run could be substantial because of potential low employee productivity, high employee turnover, employee errors, and dissatisfied customers because of improper service.

Programmed Learning. An alternative training method is **programmed learning**, which relies on a highly structured format in either written (paper-and-pencil) or machine (mechanical and computer) form. Employees (1) study a unit of material; (2) respond to a series of questions (true/false, multiple choice, fill-in-the-blank, and so on) on the material they have read; (3) receive immediate feedback on their performance in answering the questions; and (4) continue to repeat the first three steps until they master the material. After the employees achieve an acceptable competence level on a unit of material, they move on to the next level of instruction. Repetition is the key to programmed learning.

Sponsor Training. The **sponsor training method** uses an experienced employee to assume part or all of the responsibility for training a new employee. Most retailers believe that this one-on-one approach is the best method for teaching new employees the basic

The World of Retailing

Retail Technology

High-performance retailers striving to deliver superior personal service to their customers have established hiring, training, and incentive programs to improve the overall calibre of store employees. Leading retailers establish their development priorities at the top and take a personal approach in communicating them to the store.

Using a VSAT satellite technology to carry live broadcasts of the company's founding visionaries, Home Depot motivates and develops its employees through the "Breakfast with Bernie and Arthur" television show, broadcast quarterly on Sunday mornings prior to store openings.

Bernard Marcus, Home Depot's chairman and CEO, and Arthur Blank, president, discuss chain growth plans, recap quarterly performances, and answer questions from store employees who phone in. New ideas for improving operations are shared among the stores.

In addition, Home Depot also produces and broadcasts over 100 training programs, including "Welcome Aboard," a show for new stores intended to get them fired up as they open for business.

Source: Bill Jacobs, "Operating Stores: High Octane Execution," Chain Store Age Executive *(January 1994): 21MH. Reprinted by permission. Copyright Lebhar-Friedman, Inc., 425 Park Ave., New York, NY 10022.*

skills of selling, buying, promotion, and so forth. The sponsor's responsibilities also extend to introducing the employee to fellow workers, evaluating the employee's progress, and providing advice on the employee's problems and concerns. Successful sponsor training programs involve sponsors who volunteer for the assignment and are compensated for their efforts with money or time off.

Group Training. The **group training method** involves the simultaneous training of several employees through lectures (or discussion, films, or slides), demonstrations (for example, on sales or marking and stock presentations), case studies (for example, verbal and written problem-solving situations), role playing (for example, a sales or customer complaint situation), computer simulations, and interactive videos. Large retailers use group training in centralized training facilities with specialized personnel. The advantage of group training is the low cost of training several employees at one time; the principal drawback is the lack of individual attention.

Executive Training. **Executive training programs (ETPs)** are educational sessions directed at supervisors, managers, and executives. Common among large department store and chain organizations, ETPs are designed to recruit personnel who have executive potential and to provide them with the opportunity to gain management experience. The typical ETP is a step-by-step training procedure in which the executive trainee gains practical management experience by progressing from low- to higher-level management positions.

Many large retail organizations also have special executive development programs for new and existing employees with extensive educational backgrounds and experience. These programs normally include orientation programs, project assignments, executive seminars, and sponsorship programs with one of the firm's top executives. Many companies also encourage a wide range of self-development activities.

Retail Strategies and Tactics

Hamburger University

The first class of the day has begun at Hamburger University, McDonald's Corp.'s 80-acre training facility in Oak Brook, Illinois.

Hamburger U mixes personnel and management classes that could easily rank with those at a premier graduate school of business. Positive mental attitude activities promote personal bonding: games, rewards—bachelor's degree in Hamburgerology at graduation—as well as those loud "good mornings."

The result is the acknowledged best fast-food franchise management training in the business.

As a franchiser, McDonald's relies on consistency and quality of service to protect its trademark and maintain sales. With a worldwide network of 14 000 restaurants in more than 70 countries, McDonald's uses Hamburger U as its upper-level training ground for managers, owner-operators, suppliers, and corporate executives.

Despite its name, Hamburger U is not where employees learn to flip hamburgers, mix shakes, or fry potatoes.

Admission requirements to Hamburger U include 2000 hours of in-store and regional training.

The building has test kitchens, lecture halls, auditoriums, and "team rooms," all equipped with the latest in technology. "Test answers are punched into small computer pads sitting in front of students; instructors know immediately if most of the class has caught on to a concept."

Videos, slide projector banks, lighting controlled from the instructor's podium, and rear-screen projection video capability are available to give the lectures zing.

In the team rooms an instructor can monitor three tables of eight students each, but the groups are separated by sliding panels. Each tries to solve a problem, based on real restaurant experiences, and then is evaluated on how well they did.

Ellen Shubart, "Hamburger U Gives Them Taste of Job," Advertising Age, *March 13, 1995, 29.*

Personnel Supervision

Supervision is the process of directing, coordinating, and inspecting the efforts of store employees to attain both company and individual goals. Effective supervisors can successfully satisfy the needs of the retailer (such as high-quality job performance, company loyalty, satisfactory profits) and the needs of the employee (such as fair treatment, a decent standard of living, a chance for advancement). The key to good supervision is knowing how to motivate employees.

Motivational Practices **Motivation** is the drive that moves people to act. Employees are driven to excel in a variety of ways. Some employees are motivated by money, others by praise, and still others possibly by the promise of free time to spend with their families. Good motivators coach people for improvement, publicly praise good performance, and celebrate success.[37]

Money can be a strong incentive for employee productivity, but it may not be enough. The link between pay and performance is more complex than the simple equation that incentive pay increases employee motivation and performance. That employees are motivated mainly by direct compensation is one of the great myths of retailing. A meaningful job in a positive work environment is described by one retailing expert as a stronger motivational force for many retail employees.[38] The supervisor must discover the key that motivates each employee.[39]

Satisfiers. **Satisfiers** are employment factors that produce pleasurable reactions within people's work lives. Frederick Herzberg found that the primary employment satisfiers were a challenging job, recognition of achievement, a responsible position, a chance for advancement, and professional and personal growth.[40] Additional job attributes that employees find important are (1) a pleasant work environment, (2) an opportunity to learn, (3) flexible scheduling, (4) compatible coworkers, (5) job security, (6) variety of work assignments, (7) training programs, (8) limited job stress, and (9) a good benefits package. In essence, motivation factors are conditions that enhance the employee's personal needs for self-esteem and self-actualization.

Dissatisfiers. **Dissatisfiers** are employment factors that make workers unhappy with their job, which lead to high turnover and weak performance. Over-supervision, poorly developed work rules, undesirable working conditions, restrictive company policies, and inadequate wages and fringe benefits are common examples of dissatisfiers. In general, dissatisfiers are closely associated with an individual's physiological and security needs. Given Herzberg's findings, the answer to how to motivate is to eliminate conditions that generate dissatisfiers and initiate programs and policies that promote satisfiers.

Retail Strategies and Tactics

Wal-Mart: A Hyperproductive Culture

Wal-Mart's biggest long-term competitive advantage is its hyperproductive culture, and senior executives are justly concerned about sustaining it. This unique amalgam is one part Southern Baptist evangelism, one part University of Arkansas Razorback teamwork, and one part IBM hardware. Wal-Mart gets everyone, from CEO to clerk, to work like a dog for relatively low wages and then brag about it. The voluble Soderquist [vice chairman and chief operating officer] clams up only when you ask him how much vacation he took last year. But the relentless work ethic also makes people rich, at least in the long run, because compensation for everyone includes stock. We have always been cheap, and we have always been very performance driven. It is a very conflicting thing.

Source: Bill Saporito, "And the Winner Is Still . . . Wal-Mart," Fortune, *May 2, 1994, 65.*

Management Styles **Autocratic Management.** Autocratic management relies on centralized authority and control to attain the firm's mission and goals. **Autocratic leaders** assume that employees are lazy, passive, self-centred, and irresponsible. Therefore, autocratic managers believe that the most effective management style is one that utilizes *legitimate power* (the ability to influence employees due to their position within the management hierarchy and the authority granted to it), *reward power* (the ability to influence employees due to the manager's prerogative to bestow various types of rewards—promotion, compensation, and work conditions), and *coercive power* (the ability to influence employees due to the manager's authority to extend various types of punishment—poor work schedules, undesirable work assignments, lower compensation rates, and lack of support). With these assumptions, autocratic managers maintain that they must closely supervise and control their employees to motivate them to work toward company goals and assume responsibilities.

Autocratic retailers subscribe to the school of thought that views economic inducements as the primary means of employee motivation. Under an autocratic management system, employees are managed from the human relations perspective of McGregor's Theory X.[41] According to Douglas McGregor, autocratic leaders holding Theory X make the following assumptions:

- Employees are not creative, so their work assignments must be highly structured. They need to be told what to do and how to do it.
- Employees are not responsible; therefore, they must be closely supervised. A narrow span of control is needed to ensure adequate supervision.
- Employees are not adaptive; thus job assignments must be carefully defined. Employees are recruited to fit a carefully constructed job description.

Retail Strategies and Tactics

Home Depot

Home Depot is a good place to shop because it's a good place to work. That, according to Steven Bebis, is the key to their success. "We encourage two way feedback between associates and management," says Bebis. "We listen to them, train and develop them, and treat them with respect." This respect includes a number of financial plans designed to help associates invest their money. Bebis describes the Share The Success program, which includes such options as Home Depot stock and purchase plans, bonuses and RRSP accounts, all aimed at cutting the employee in on Home Depot's success. One stock purchase plan allows an associate to buy 20 percent of their income in Home Depot stock at a 15 percent discount. Home Depot associates don't scrape by on a salesclerk's pittance or worry about making commissions. Dedication is expected and rewarded. And, as Bebis says, "Becoming stock holders makes a big impact on how they deal with customers."

Bebis also emphasizes self-image when describing a good employee. "When you work in an organization that's leading edge you often have a lot of self-respect," he says.

Home Depot's policy of acknowledging experience on the pay scale means seasoned employees can count on being compensated and appreciated for their value. Sales positions are considered careers at Home Depot so there are no casual positions. The only part-time employees work at the cash-outs at peak times, and even they receive full benefits. There's no "joe-job" atmosphere here because employees are taken seriously. Bebis claims 25 percent of company time is spent training and developing people, and attributes a full 50 percent of his time to that task. This is backed up by an extensive off-the-job support system for employees. The Caring, Assisting and Responding to Employees program, or C.A.R.E., is a resource available to help Home Depot staff solve personal problems ranging from day care to financial difficulties. In addition, a wellness coordinator works in every store to address health and well-being issues, including prenatal care, smoking cessation, and AIDS awareness. But what does Home Depot expect in return?

Source: Staff, Centre Magazine, *November–December 1994, 8–9.*

- Employees lack ambition; therefore, adequate job performance is achieved only by continuous motivation using authority, rewards, and punishments.

Some retailers consider that an autocratic style is the only way to motivate people in the lower-level positions of their stores. This type of "boss-centred" leadership style typically produces satisfactory performances when management is present to make decisions and supervise employee actions. Competitive, not cooperative, relationships among individual employees as well as various operating units are common within an autocratic management system; everyone is trying to obtain the favour of the autocratic leader.

Democratic Management. A more contemporary view of motivation and supervision is the democratic management approach, which relies on delegated authority to subordinates and voluntary participation by employees in the achievement of mutually beneficial goals and objectives. **Democratic leaders** influence subordinates through the use of *expert power* (the ability to influence employees by the manager's special knowledge, expert skills, and unique experiences) and *referent power* (the ability to influence employees by the manager's strong personality, which gains the respect and admiration of subordinates and in turn creates the desire on the part of employees to emulate the manager). Retailers

Retail Strategies and Tactics

Total Quality Management

Total quality management is the philosophy of meeting and exceeding customer expectations through a systematic process that involves both associates and managers at all levels assuming responsibility for continuous improvement in the firm's day-to-day merchandising and operating activities. It is a set of tools and techniques designed to improve a retailer's effectiveness and efficiency. Retailers that want to initiate a company-wide total quality management program must operationalize the following precepts:

- *Customer focus:* Retailers must create a customer focus by identifying quality goals and standards that direct the firm's attention toward customer satisfaction.
- *Top priority:* Senior managers continuously communicate that the first goal is "quality is job one."
- *Prevention, not correction:* They must inspire an action orientation of "do it right the first time every time."
- *Total participation:* Everyone, including managers, workers, suppliers, customers, and stockholders must support and participate in all of the company's quality initiatives.
- *Teamwork and cooperation:* Cross-departmental teams cooperate to solve problems and recommend actions that will improve the total quality output of the retailer in both goods and services.
- *Empowerment and information:* Retailers must recognize that employees want to succeed but need hard data and the freedom to make fact-based decisions analytically.

A total quality management program provides the benefits of greater customer satisfaction, reduced operating expenses, increased employee involvement, decreased employee turnover, better business relationships, improved working environment, and enhanced public relations.

Having used the creed of total quality management to save themselves, some retailers may well feel they do not need to keep going to church. Although total quality management may not be receiving the amount of press it once did, good-quality products and service have become a given in today's highly competitive marketplace. The "sins" of poor quality will quickly catch up with any retailer who fails to provide expected quality in all aspects of the business.

Sources: Adapted from Martha T. Moore, "Is TQM Dead?" USA Today, *October 17, 1995, B1; Michael J. O'Connor, "Can a System that Brought Revolutionary Change in a Car Factory Work in a Retail Store?"* International Trends in Retailing *(New York: Arthur Andersen & Co, December 1994), 45–56; Philip B. Crosby,* Quality Is Free: The Art of Making Quality Certain *(New York: McGraw-Hill, 1979); Tom Peters,* Thriving on Chaos *(New York: Knopf, 1987); Allan J. Magrath, "Marching to a Different Drummer,"* Across the Board *(June 1992): 53–54. Also see Jay Mathews and Peter Katel, "The Cost of Quality,"* Newsweek, *September 7, 1992, 48–49; and Gilbert Fuchsberg, "Total Quality Is Termed Only Partial Success,"* Wall Street Journal, *October 1, 1992, B7.*

that support this view believe that providing employees with a favourable work environment can create a situation in which employees will attain job satisfaction and their personal goals by directing their efforts toward the firm's needs. Wal-Mart's "servant leadership" style of management identifies the role of an executive as providing what workers need to serve the customer—merchandise, capital, information, and inspiration—and then get out of the way.[42]

McGregor's Theory Y describes this light-handed approach and the belief that close supervision and control are unnecessary because employees will assume their responsibilities and, in part, supervise themselves if a desirable social and psychological environment is present. The democratic leader believes that motivated employees are capable of self-direction and self-control.[43] In addition, given the freedom of a democratic management style, employees will solve problems and make decisions with imagination, ingenuity, and creativity.

To heighten associates' sense of mission, Wal-Mart executives "expect managers for each of the 34 departments within a typical Wal-Mart to run their operations as if they were running their own businesses."[44] Wal-Mart has 250 000 entrepreneurs in all its stores running their part of the business. The previously discussed satisfiers are the keys to creating this desirable social and psychological condition. Within this kind of working environment, less supervision produces better job performance.

Personnel Evaluation

The sixth step in the store staffing process is the development of personnel evaluation procedures. Each store employee, regardless of position or level, should be periodically evaluated. The purposes of personnel evaluations are to (1) determine compensation, (2) recommend or deny promotions and transfers, and (3) justify demotions and terminations. Conducted constructively, personnel evaluations can be used to motivate employees, improve store morale, generate information for planning purposes, encourage employee self-development, and improve communications between the employee and employer. In developing the store's personnel evaluation methods and procedures, the retailer should decide when, what, and how to evaluate.

A smart retailer evaluates personnel continuously. It would be unfair to judge an employee's contribution and performance at the end of an arbitrary time period, such as the end of the fiscal year. Instead, retailers should provide their employees with immediate feedback on their progress. "When workers have reasonable productivity standards to meet and they are given instant feedback on whether the standards are being met, the

The World of Retailing

Business Ethics

Stretch Goals: How Far Is Too Far?

A "stretch goal" is an extremely ambitious goal that most individuals do not know how to reach. Stretch goals are performance targets that management sets for its managers and employees in an attempt to get more output just by demanding more output. It is a management approach that says "We are not going to give you more people, or money, or physical space; we are not going to give you more of any resource, so your solution is going to have to involve to work smarter, get out of the box, and be creative." Managers and employees achieve stretch goals by the only means possible—by stretching their work hours using their personal and family time. By working evenings, weekends, and vacation times, managers and employees strive to reach the lofty objectives at the expense of their families, friends, and personal health. Stress and burnout can be the result of the ever-increasing drive to improve productivity and to gain competitive advantage.

Using stretch goals has been successful in getting people to perform their jobs in more creative and effective fashion, but are they an ethical management practice? How far can management stretch its stretch goals before they cross over the fairness line? Can stretch goals be justified? How and under what conditions?

Adapted from Strat Sherman, "Stretch Goals: The Dark Side of Asking for Miracles," Fortune, *November 13, 1995, 231.*

likelihood that they will meet or exceed standards is dramatically increased."[45] This informal feedback, however, should also be accompanied by an established, formal evaluation in which employees receive a detailed account of their job performance. Formal evaluations tell employees exactly what their status is. It is not unusual for new employees to be evaluated weekly or monthly. Established lower-level employees, however, are typically evaluated on a formal basis every six months, and annual evaluations for upper-level management and executive personnel are the norm.

Evaluation Criteria Retailers have learned that the most important employee factors to evaluate are performance-demonstrated skills and personal attributes. These factors relate most closely to employee success. Examples of such characteristics appear in Figure 6–19.

In selecting evaluation criteria and their respective measuring instruments, the retailer must consider the legal ramifications of each decision and the influence of any labour union that might be involved. It is often a good policy to seek advice regarding the legality of the employee evaluation system. In areas where labour is unionized, management should consult with appropriate union representatives before formulating evaluation methods and procedures.

Evaluation Methods Retailers use a variety of methods for evaluating store personnel; the method used depends on the degree of objectivity and formality that the retailer wants. Figure 6–20 identifies several objective employee evaluation methods, which are based largely on factual and measurable criteria, and subjective methods, which are based on the evaluator's perceptions, feelings, and prejudices. Formal methods are regularly scheduled evaluations; informal methods follow no set schedule, and the criteria and procedures may or may not be known to the employee.

Formal Objective Method. **Formal objective employee evaluations** include performance records and management by objectives (MBO) procedures. Performance records are

Figure 6–19

Personnel evaluation criteria

Performance characteristics	Personal attributes
Job knowledge	Enthusiasm
Quality of work	Loyalty
Quantity of work	Dependability
Organizing capabilities	Leadership
Supervision requirements	Maturity
Promptness	Stability
Peer relationships	Creativity
Customer relations	Honesty
Analytical abilities	Initiative

Figure 6–20

Personnel evaluation methods

Degree of objectivity / Degree of formality	Objective	Subjective
Formal	Performance records MBO (management by objectives)	Rating scales checklist
Informal	Professional shoppers	Intuition

quantitative measures of the employee's performance and include such varied statistics as (1) total sales dollars, (2) total number of sales transactions, (3) number of customer complaints, (4) number of merchandise returns and their dollar value, (5) number of times an employee is absent or late for work, and (6) net sales per working hour or per hourly wage. Ivana Trump holds the Home Shopping Network's record for sales per minute (U.S.$74 000).[46] By comparing the employee's performance against the store average for any one of these criteria, the retailer can identify above-, at-, and below-average performers.

The MBO procedures set measurable performance objectives for employees that should match their job descriptions. Employees are then evaluated on how well they achieved their objectives. Using MBO procedures has the advantage of drawing the employee into the evaluation process, thereby encouraging self-development and self-evaluation. The employee is asked to (1) set objectives in specific terms, (2) determine the method of accomplishment, (3) set an accomplishment time frame, and (4) determine the measure of accomplishment.

Formal Subjective Methods. Checklists and rating scales constitute two common **formal subjective employee evaluations**. The typical checklist procedure involves identifying and listing several criteria in an organized fashion on a form that lends itself to quick and convenient evaluations. The evaluator may weight the individual criterion according to its importance (see Figure 6–21). Typical rating scales are (1) satisfactory or unsatisfactory; (2) below average, average, or above average; and (3) poor, fair, average, good, and excellent.

Retail Strategies and Tactics

Snoops in the Shops

Dressed in his dark overcoat, Nicholas Samson looks like any other affluent urban Christmas shopper on a quest for silk lingerie or the latest electronic gizmo. But last week, Samson, a professional "mystery shopper," was on the prowl for customer service rather than gifts, when he visited a photography store in a suburban Toronto mall. Samson headed to the camera counter and waited behind a row of customers already being served. His gaze lingered on three young female salesclerks giggling together at an adjacent counter. They ignored him. Although the company's service standard calls for customers to be greeted within 30 seconds of entering the store, almost two minutes had passed since Samson arrived. Just then, a salesclerk appeared and capably answered Samson's detailed inquiries about cameras. The clerk was knowledgeable, helpful, and pleasant—which, a few minutes later, sitting on a bench in the mall, Samson duly noted as he filled out a multi-point report card on the store's performance. The grade: 80 out of a possible 100. "On the whole, I thought it was pretty good service," said Samson. "But I'm still kind of ticked off about those girls ignoring us."

In Samson's case, his written reports, along with similar ones from other stores in the chain, are forwarded to head office management each month. They, in turn, send the reports to the appropriate store managers who then inform staff members of the results. Samson, whose company employs about 600 shoppers across the country, says that many of his 50 retail clients offer some type of incentive reward to individual employees who have provided particularly good service, says Samson, whose firm is just one of several in Canada that specialize in such shop-floor research, the current trend is to emphasize the positive. "We like to say that we're catching people doing something right," he says.

The benefits of mystery shopping are threefold. First, Samson says that store management learns what areas need work across their chain. For instance, in the case of the photography store, the clerk neglected to follow company policy and offer Samson a protection plan that would insure the camera against future damage. In addition, mystery shopping puts employees on alert that their treatment of customers could be monitored at any time. But above all, it can reduce "shrinkage," the industry euphemism for employee theft. According to retail industry estimates, Canadian retailers lose about $2.75 billion a year—or $7.5 million a day—to theft, about one-third of it by employees. Samson's partner Howard Crabtree says that a decade ago, when the pizza chain he used to work for broadly publicized a new policy of using mystery shoppers in their largely unmonitored takeout restaurants, their revenues suddenly jumped by as much as 40 percent at some stores. Says Crabtree: "Just knowing that someone was paying attention made all the difference."

Source: Brenda Dalglish, Maclean's Magazine, *December 19, 1994, 28.*

Figure 6–21

A formal subjective employee evaluation form

Source: Norman M. Scarborough and Thomas W. Zimmerer, Effective Small Business Management *(New York: Merrill/Macmillan, 1984), 521–523.*

Employee's name ____________________ Date ____________________

Employee's title ____________________ Supervisor ____________________

Instructions: Please review the performance of the employee whose name is listed above on each of the following items. In order to guide you in your rating, the five determinants of performance have been defined.

Rating Points

5 Outstanding
A truly outstanding employee whose achievements are far above acceptable. Has consistently performed far beyond established objectives and has made significant contributions beyond current position. Requires minimal direction and supervision. (Relatively few employees would be expected to achieve this level.)

4 Superior
An above-average employee whose performance is clearly above acceptable. Has usually performed beyond established objectives and, at times, has made contributions beyond responsibilities of present position. Requires less than normally expected degree of direction and supervision.

3 Average
A fully acceptable employee who consistently meets all requirements of position. Has consistently met established objectives in a satisfactory and adequate manner. Performance requires normal degree of supervision and direction. (The majority of employees should be at this level.)

2 Below average
A somewhat below-average employee whose performance, while not unsatisfactory, cannot be considered fully acceptable. Generally meets established objectives and expectations, but definite areas exist where achievement is substandard. Performance requires somewhat more than normal degree of direction and supervision.

1 Unacceptable
A far-below-average employee whose performance is barely adequate to meet the requirements of the position. Generally performs at a level below established objectives with the result that overall contribution is marginal. Performance requires an unusually high degree of supervision. (This level is considered acceptable only for employees new to the job.)

Job criteria — Points

1. Amount of work. Consider here only the *quantity* of the employee's output. ____________
   Supervisor's comments:
2. Quality of work. Consider how well the employee does each job assigned. Include your appraisal of such items as accuracy, thoroughness, and orderliness. ____________
   Supervisor's comments:
3. Cooperation. How well does this employee work and interact with you and co-workers for the accomplishment of organization goals? ____________
   Supervisor's comments:
4. Judgment. Consider this employee's ability to reach sound and logical conclusions. ____________
   Supervisor's comments:
5. Initiative. The energy or aptitude to originate action toward organization goals. ____________
   Supervisor's comments:

continued

Figure 6–21 (continued)

6. Job knowledge. How well does the employee demonstrate an understanding of the basic fundamentals, techniques, and procedures on the job? ________
   Supervisor's comments:
7. Interest in job. Does the employee demonstrate a real interest in the job and the organization? ________
   Supervisor's comments:
8. Ability to communicate. How well does this employee exchange needed information with others in the work group and with supervisors? ________
   Supervisor's comments:
9. Dependability. Consider the employee's absences, tardiness, punctuality, timeliness in completing job assignments, and the amount of supervision required. ________
   Supervisor's comments:
10. Adaptability. Consider the degree to which this employee demonstrates adjustment to the varying requirements of the job. ________
    Supervisor's comments:

Total points ________

Supervisor's general comments:

Instructions: After you have rated the employee and made whatever comments you feel are pertinent to each criterion and the overall evaluation, schedule a meeting to review each item with the employee. An employee wishing to make comments about the evaluation should be asked to do so in the following space.
Employee's comment:

Date: ________________

Supervisor present (name): ________________________________

Employee's signature ________________________ Date: ________

Notice to employee: Signing the form does not imply that you either agree or disagree with the evaluation.

Given the subjective character of these ratings, many retailers prefer to have several supervisors rate each employee. The average of these ratings forms the basis for the employee's evaluation. When using rating scales, retailers should recognize the *central tendency effect*—the tendency of evaluators to rate everyone at or near the midpoint of the scale.

Informal Objective Method. The most common **informal objective employee evaluations** in retailing is to employ professional or mystery shoppers. Professional shoppers are people who wander into a store to "shop" for merchandise in a "typical" way. Actually, they are professional investigators who attempt to learn how a retailer's employees behave toward them. This evaluation method should not be the basis of employee evaluation but a supplement to the retailer's assessment of employees' job performance.

Informal Subjective Method. **Informal subjective employee evaluations** have no structure and rely heavily on the supervisor's intuition. Although a supervisor's feelings and perceptions might represent a correct evaluation of an employee, the lack of objectivity and formality leaves such a method open to criticism by both employees and outside concerns. A constant danger in using intuition as an evaluation method is the "halo effect" or the "good old boy syndrome." An employee who is a good person is not necessarily contributing effectively to the firm's efforts; in fact, such considerations often lead to other employees' accusations of favouritism.

Regardless of the method used to evaluate store personnel, employees should be made aware of the method (its criteria, measurements, and procedures), given feedback after each evaluation, and permitted to appeal the evaluation.

Personnel Compensation

Equitable compensation is an integral part of the retailer's staffing process. A well-designed compensation package is not only an important factor in rewarding past performance but also a critical incentive for future performance.[47] Compensation methods include the straight-salary plan, the straight-commission plan, the salary plus commission plan, and the salary plus bonus plan. "Long-term incentives (for primarily top-level management), annual bonuses (for mid-level management), and short-term incentives (for sales personnel) are becoming more important in all retail compensation practices.

Compensation Methods

Straight-Salary Plan. The **straight-salary plan** is a fixed amount of compensation for a specified work period such as a day, week, month, or year. For example, an employee's salary might be set at $320 per week or $8 per hour. Retailers typically use straight-salary plans when a job involves a considerable amount of customer service and nonselling time, such as stocking, receiving, clerking, and checking out. For the retailer, the straight-salary plan offers the advantages of easy administration and a high level of employer control. Under the straight-salary plan, the retailer can expect employees to engage in nonselling activities such as stocking and housekeeping. For the employee, the straight-salary plan has a known level of financial security and stability. The disadvantages of this plan for the retailer are (1) limited incentives to increase employee performance, (2) fixed costs that result in a high wage cost/sales ratio, and (3) lack of downward salary adjustments during periods of sales decline.

Home Depot prefers the straight-salary plan because management wants employees to take the time to provide the do-it-yourself home repair customer with the information and products necessary for that novice to be successful in his or her home repair projects.[48] Using straight salary allows for comparison of employee wages. This proved problematic for Safeway in Alberta, as employees were able to easily recognize the disparity in wages between full-time and part-time workers.[49]

Straight-Commission Plan. During the early 1990s, a quiet revolution swept through specialty and department store retailing. To boost sales and upgrade service, major retail chains converted thousands of hourly sales employees to commission pay.

Under a **straight-commission plan**, a store employee receives a percentage of what he or she sells. The commission percentage is either fixed (for example, 5 percent on all sales) or variable (for example, 6 percent on high-margin lines and 3 percent on low-margin lines). Retailers usually calculate an employee's commission on the basis of net sales (gross sales dollars minus dollar value of returned merchandise).

The major advantage of a straight-commission plan is the monetary incentive it creates for employees; however, this incentive often causes several problems. Salespeople on commission often become overly aggressive in trying to make a sale. By exerting undue pressure on the customer to buy now (as opposed to later, when a different salesperson might be serving the customer), the sale could be lost to the retailer forever. Also, commission sales tempt many salespeople to practise trading up the customer to more expensive merchandise or to sell merchandise or service that is not needed. Sears's commission policy in its automotive centres created a situation in which service managers and mechanics recommended and sold unnecessary repairs and services in order to boost their commissions. Sears reached out-of-court settlements with several consumer protection agencies. This type of aggressive commission selling leads to a large number of returns, lost sales, and most importantly, lost credibility and goodwill with the store's clientele. A cooperative supervision plan is needed to ensure that abuses do not occur.

For the commissioned salesperson, the straight-commission plan has the weaknesses of financial insecurity and instability. To overcome these limitations, many retailers have established "drawing accounts" that allow employees to draw a fixed sum of money at regular intervals against future commissions.

Salary Plus Commission. As the name implies, the **salary plus commission plan** provides employees with a salary and a commission. There are several variations to this plan. The straight salary/single commission variation uses a base salary (for example, $200 per week) plus (1) a single commission (for example, 0.5 percent) on all net sales up to the sales quota and a larger commission (for example, 2 percent) on all sales in excess of sales quota or (2) a commission only on net sales that exceed the quota. As a general rule, the base salary constitutes the greatest share of the employee's total compensation. To offer greater sales incentive, however, a retailer can increase the commission rate to make commission income a significantly higher proportion of the employee's total income.

The strengths of this plan are that it provides employees with financial security and stability while helping the retailer control and motivate personnel. Although the combination plan is more difficult to administer, its benefits generally outweigh its costs.

Salary Plus Bonus. A popular method for compensating middle-management personnel (such as department managers, store managers, and buyers) is the **salary plus bonus plan**, which involves a straight monthly salary supplemented by either semiannual or annual bonuses for exceeding performance goals. Performance goals and related bonuses are usually set by upper management for each operating unit and are typically expressed in the form of increased sales or profits, decreased operating costs, or some other measure of the operating unit's productivity. The most common problems associated with the salary plus bonus plan are employees' difficulty in understanding such plans and administrators' difficulty setting up the performance criteria and measurement instruments to make the systems work.

Fringe Benefits The employee's total compensation package also includes fringe benefits, which vary greatly from one retail firm to another. In recent years, fringe benefits like health care have become more important in the retailer's efforts to attract and keep qualified personnel. Fringe benefits are much more important for middle- and upper-level positions than for entry-level positions. As unionization of lower-level personnel becomes more common, however, benefit packages at that level will become more significant.

Among the most popular fringe benefits are (1) insurance programs covering life, health, accident, and disability; (2) sick leave; (3) personal leave time; (4) holiday leave and paid vacations; (5) pension plans; (6) profit sharing; (7) employee discounts; (8) recreation facilities; (9) coffee breaks; (10) employee parties; (11) child or elder care; (12) financial planning; (13) tuition reimbursement; (14) professional development and retraining; (15) family counselling; (16) flex-time and job sharing; and (17) team sponsorships.

Every associate who has been with Wal-Mart at least one year and who works at least 1000 hours is eligible for the company's profit-sharing plan. Using a formula base of profit growth, Wal-Mart contributes a percentage of every eligible associate's wages to his or her profit-sharing plan, which the associate can take when leaving the company, in cash or Wal-Mart stock.[50] As more women enter the labour force, child care is becoming an important benefit in attracting and retaining productive employees. On-site day-care centres, child-care allowances, and cooperative day-care centres are some recent additions to the benefit packages currently being reviewed by retailers.

Fringe benefits are becoming a more important form of compensation in today's leisure-oriented society, with the goal of making employees happy, content, and loyal to the store. Examples of such benefit packages include savings and profit-sharing programs, pension plans, no-cost life insurance, medical and dental insurance, paid vacation, and merchandise discounts. Additional perks for company executives might include club memberships, company cars, financial counselling, and spouse travel.

Collective Agreements Certain retail industries (for instance, some multi-unit grocery stores and department stores) have staff members who belong to a union. The relationship between the employer and the employee is then governed by a **collective agreement**, which is made between the employer and the union. Usually this agreement specifies such matters as rates of pay, benefits, hours of work, discipline procedures, and evaluation procedures. The specific details of collective agreements are too varied to be discussed here. However, for the retailer whose employees are unionized, it is important to know and abide by the provisions of the collective agreement. Failure to do this can result in an action by the union, such as a strike, work stoppage, or work slowdown. These types of events usually receive wide publicity in the media, and this can reflect negatively on the retail establishment. Some of Canada's larger retailers have experienced challenges in this area. Safeway Company received damage to its image and market share during a recent strike in Alberta.[51] Wal-Mart, which has always claimed little need for unionization due to its superior benefits, has recently been faced with unionization of one of its stores in Ontario.[52]

Summary

Organizational culture is a set of values shared by all or most members of the retail organization. It exists at two levels: the core or invisible level and the surface or visible level. Core culture is the basic value system underlying the retailer's organization; it represents informal norms that bind the organization together and gives meaning and direction to the behaviour of its members. Surface culture is a reflection of the internal cultural patterns that have emerged from the core culture and are communicated through the use of symbols, stories, heroes, slogans, and rituals. Depending on occupation, generation, location, gender, and other variables, organization cultures have subcultures that consist of individuals with similar values and beliefs that may vary from other subcultural groups. Good retail managers take advantage of the different strengths of these diverse groups by incorporating them into the decision-making and problem-solving processes.

The organization of a retail enterprise is centred on specific organizational objectives and tasks. In retailing, the firm's organization is directed at accomplishing certain strategic, operational, and functional objectives. Also, retailers must organize in such a manner that the basic operational tasks of planning and controlling the product, price, promotion, and place can be facilitated readily.

The retailer should consider several basic principles of organization in developing the structure of the firm. Of particular interest are the organizational principles of centralization and decentralization, specialization and departmentalization, lines of authority and areas of responsibility, unity of command, and span of control.

Many retailers prepare charts to illustrate their form of retail organization. Some retail organizational structures are characterized by a limited number of levels (horizontal organizations), while others incorporate many levels of organization (vertical organizations). Organizational structures can be viewed on a continuum from bureaucratic organizations (highly structured vertical arrangements) to adaptive organizations (loosely structured horizontal arrangements). Following this continuum, the five basic retail organizational designs are the machine bureaucracy, divisionalized bureaucracy, professional bureaucracy, simple structure, and adaptive adhocracy.

The staffing process consists of seven steps. The first is the position statement, which involves developing job descriptions and writing job specifications; the second step, recruiting store personnel, includes both an employee search and an applicant screening. The third step in the staffing process is personnel selection. From the list of qualified applicants, the retailer selects individuals best suited to the job by carefully reviewing application forms, personal interviews, reference checks, testing instruments, and other examinations.

Training store personnel is the fourth step in the staffing process. It requires the retailer to know what to train (organization orientation and functional or task training), where to train (on or off the job), and how to train (individual, programmed learning, sponsor, or group training methods). Executive training programs are sessions directed at store supervisors, managers, and executives.

The fifth step is personnel supervision. An important supervising task is motivation. One method of motivating employees is to eliminate conditions that generate job dissatisfaction and to initiate programs that promote satisfaction. Supervising can be approached using the contrasting management styles of the autocratic leader or the democratic leader.

Evaluating store employees constitutes the sixth step in the staffing process. The retailer must address such issues as when, what, and how to evaluate personnel. Finally, the retailer must determine the type of compensation system to use. Alternatives are the straight-salary plan, straight-commission plan, salary plus commission plan, and salary plus bonus plan, all of which might involve various fringe benefits.

Student Study Guide

Key Terms and Concepts

achievement tests *p. 205*
adaptive adhocracy *p. 200*
adaptive organization *p. 193*
autocratic leaders *p. 210*
bureaucratic organizations *p. 193*
centralization *p. 188*
collective agreement *p. 219*
core culture *p. 185*
decentralization *p. 188*
democratic leaders *p. 211*
departmentalization *p. 190*
dissatisfiers *p. 209*
divisionalized bureaucracy *p. 196*
dysfunctional corporate culture *p. 185*
executive training programs (ETP) *p. 208*
flat organizational structure *p. 192*
formal objective employee evaluations *p. 213*
formal subjective employee evaluations *p. 214*
functional divisionalized bureaucracy *p. 196*
functional objectives *p. 188*
functional training *p. 206*
geographic divisionalized bureaucracy *p. 197*
group training method *p. 208*
horizontal organizational structure *p. 192*
individual training method *p. 207*
informal objective employee evaluations *p. 216*
informal subjective employee evaluations *p. 216*
job description *p. 202*
job specification *p. 202*
line relationships *p. 191*
lines of authority *p. 190*
lines of responsibility *p. 190*
machine bureaucracy *p. 193*
Mazur Plan *p. 196*
motivation *p. 209*
off-the-job training *p. 207*
on-the-job training *p. 207*
operational objectives *p. 188*
organization orientation *p. 206*
organizational charts *p. 192*
organizational culture *p. 183*
product divisionalized bureaucracy *p. 198*
professional bureaucracy *p. 199*
programmed learning *p. 207*
psychological tests *p. 205*
salary plus bonus plan *p. 218*
salary plus commission plan *p. 218*
satisfiers *p. 209*
simple structure *p. 199*
span of control *p. 192*
specialization *p. 190*
sponsor training method *p. 207*
staff relationships *p. 191*
standardization *p. 194*
straight-commission plan *p. 217*
straight-salary plan *p. 217*
strategic objectives *p. 188*
subcultures *p. 186*
supervision *p. 209*
surface culture *p. 186*
tall organizational structure *p. 192*
unity of command *p. 192*
values *p. 185*
vertical organizational structure *p. 192*

Review Questions

1. Depict the core culture of a retail organization. What does it represent?
2. How do retailers communicate the core values of their corporate cultures?
3. What are the three levels of organizational objectives? Define each and describe its relationship to the general levels of retail management.
4. Compare and contrast the organizational principles of centralization and decentralization. What are their relative advantages and disadvantages?
5. Describe the organizational principles of specialization and departmentalization. How can specialization and departmentalization be accomplished?
6. What is the principle of unity of command? Why is the principle important?

7. What is span of control? Is there an ideal span of control? Describe the guidelines for determining it.

8. Compare and contrast the pros and cons of vertical and flat organization structures.

9. Outline the characteristics of a bureaucratic organization and an adaptive one.

10. Which type of retailer would utilize a machine bureaucracy form of organization?

11. Identify and delineate the various types of divisionalized bureaucracy.

12. Diagram the adaptive adhocracy.

13. Name the internal and external sources of prospective employees.

14. List the relative advantages of a formal, highly structured interviewing process and the informal, unstructured method of interviewing.

15. What two general types of testing instruments are used to evaluate applicants? Describe each type. Which instrument is generally preferred? Why?

16. Describe the two types of training needed by both old and new employees.

17. How do on-the-job and off-the-job training differ?

18. What methods are available to the retailer for training employees? Briefly describe each method.

19. What are satisfiers and dissatisfiers? How do they affect employee motivation?

20. Compare and contrast autocratic and democratic styles of management.

21. What are the advantages of the straight-salary compensation plan? What problems result from the monetary incentive created by the straight-commission plan?

22. How does the straight salary/single commission plan differ from the straight salary/quota commission plan?

Review Exam

True or False

______ 1. Operational objectives are general statements of long-term operational requirements that are necessary to achieve a strategy objective.

______ 2. Line managers are typically specialists whose primary function is to assist staff managers in realizing their objectives.

______ 3. Where tasks are highly centralized in one location, the supervisor's span of control can be broadened.

______ 4. The organizational structure of department stores is flatter and more generalized than small, independent retail organizations.

______ 5. A machine bureaucracy is best described as a flat hierarchical structure with a limited number of middle managers and a large technical support staff who assists the organization's professionals.

______ 6. Democratic leaders assume that employees are lazy, passive, and self-centred; therefore, the only way to make employees productive is to give them a great deal of freedom.

Multiple Choice

______ 1. A ______ clearly states the minimum qualifications a person must have to obtain the job.
a. job description
b. job analysis
c. job specification
d. job objective
e. rack jobber

______ 2. Applicant's ______ should not be requested on the retailer's application form.
a. name, address, and telephone number
b. employment history
c. formal education and training
d. complete demographic makeup
e. list of references

______ **3.** Which of the following is not an advantage of a formal, highly structured personal interview situation?

a. It establishes the relative roles of each party in the interview.
b. It permits a controlled interviewing environment.
c. It allows the applicant to be viewed in an unguarded state.
d. It facilitates complete, effective gathering of information about the applicant.

______ **4.** Group training methods involve the simultaneous training of several employees through the use of ______.

a. lectures
b. demonstrations
c. case studies
d. role-playing activities
e. all of the above

______ **5.** The democratic leader uses ______ to influence subordinates to work toward mutually beneficial goals.

a. expert power and reward power
b. coercive power and expert power
c. full power and unlimited power
d. intimidation and warnings
e. referent power and expert power

______ **6.** The "halo effect" or the "good old boy syndrome" is a constant danger associated with the ______ employee evaluation method.

a. informal-subjective
b. formal-subjective
c. informal-objective
d. formal-objective

Student Application Manual

Investigative Projects: Practice and Application

1. Obtain an organizational chart from a department store chain and a specialty store chain. Classify each store as to their organizational structure using the bureaucratic to adaptive continuum. Compare and contrast the two organizational charts. What are the strengths and weaknesses of each organizational form? On the basis of organizational structure, which organization would you most prefer as a career path? Why?

2. Obtain and analyze three retail job descriptions from your local newspaper or from the personnel director for a local retailer. Judging from the advertised job description, has the retailer made a careful determination of personnel needs, and does the retailer provide the potential employee with the means to evaluate the job as a potential source of employment?

3. Assume you are the manager of a sporting goods store and are responsible for conducting the initial personnel interviews of all applicants for the assistant department manager's position. Develop a list of prospective questions that you would ask each applicant. Explain your reason for asking each question, as well as what answers you would view favourably for each.

4. Obtain employee evaluation forms and procedures from a local retailer, then classify them as to their objectivity and formality. Assess the forms and procedures as to their effectiveness as employee evaluation instruments and their fairness to the employee.

Endnotes

1. Tom Rubel, "Moving Ahead: Blueprints for the Future," *Chain Store Age Executive* (January 1994): 27MH.

2. Terri Kabachnick, "Turning the Tide against Turnover," *Retailing Issues Letter*, (copublished by the Center for Retailing Studies: Texas A&M University and Arthur Andersen, September 1995), 1.

3. Sam Walton, "The Wal-Mart Partnership," *Retailers on Retailing* (Arthur Andersen: International Trends in Retailing, 1994), 142–43.

4. See Brian O'Reilly, "The New Deal—What Companies and Employees Owe One Another," *Fortune*, June 13, 1994, 44–52.

5. Cynthia Webster, "Marketing Culture and Marketing Effectiveness in Service Firms," *Journal of Service Marketing* 9 (2, 1995): 6.

6. Antonio Fins, "It's Not Easy Making Pixie Dust," *Business Week*, September 18, 1995, 134.

7. Bruce Fox, "Distribution Center Upgrade Planned by REI," *Chain Store Age Executive* (April 1961): 55.

8. Morty Lefkoe, "Unhealthy Business," *Across the Board* (June 1992): 30.

9. Thomas A. Steward, "Rate Your Readiness to Change," *Fortune*, February 7, 1994, 106.

10. See Michael Treacy and Fred Wiersema, "How Market Leaders Keep Their Edge," *Fortune*, February 6, 1995, 96.

11. See "Delta Debuts Business Zone," *Strategy*, October 3, 1994, 12.

12. Paul Klebnikov, "The Power of Positive Inspiration," *Forbes*, December 9, 1991, 246.

13. See Kevin Helliker, "Wal-Mart's Store of the Future Blends Discount Prices, Department Store Feel," *The Wall Street Journal*, May 17, 1991, B1, B8; Peter Annin, "The Reluctant Chairman," *Newsweek*, May 25, 1992, 67; and Mel Redman, "The Dynamics of Team Building," *Chain Store Age* (December 1995): 146.

14. Klebnikov, "The Power of Positive Inspiration," 246. Also see Linda Grant, "How Amway's Two Founders Cleaned Up," *U.S. News & World Report*, October 31, 1994, 77.

15. Faye Rice, "How to Make Diversity Pay," *Fortune*, August 8, 1994, 79.

16. Marianne Wilson, "Diversity in the Workplace," *Chain Store Age Executive* (June 1995): 22.

17. Kenneth Kidd, "The Fall of the House of Dylex," *Report on Business Magazine*, September 1995, 54.

18. Wendy Zellner, "Mr. Sam's Experiment Is Alive and Well," *Business Week*, April 20, 1992, 39.

19. "Sears: In with the New . . . Out with the Old," *Fortune*, October 16, 1995, 98.

20. See Stephanie Strom, "Sears Tries to Dress for Success," *Akron Beacon Journal*, November 16, 1992, DI, D4; and Francine Schwadel, "Sears to Slash 600 Salary Posts, Salespeople Pay," *The Wall Street Journal*, February 13, 1992, C9.

21. Robert Williamson, "Eaton's Has Changes in Store," *Report on Business*, July 29, 1993, B1.

22. See John R. Schermerhorn, *Management for Productivity* (New York: John Wiley & Sons, 1992): 311–12.

23. Ronald Henkoff, "Service Is Everybody's Business," *Fortune*, June 27, 1994, 48.

24. See Susan Caminiti, "What Team Leaders Need to Know," *Fortune*, February 20, 1995, 93–100.

25. See Henry Mintzberg, "The Structuring of Organizations," in *The Strategy Process: Concepts, Contexts, and Cases*, ed. James Brian Quirm, Henry Mintzberg, and Robert M. James (Englewood Cliffs, NJ: Prentice Hall, 1988), 300–303.

26. Schermerhorn, *Management for Productivity*, 313.

27. See Paul M. Mazur, *Principles of Organization Applied to Modern Retailing* (New York: Harper & Row, 1927).

28. Ian McGugan, "Eaton's on the Brink," *Canadian Business*, March 1996, 66.

29. "Sears Roebuck Makes Management Changes Tied to Store Strategy," *The Wall Street Journal*, October 4, 1995, B8.

30. John A. Byrne, "The Horizontal Corporation: It's About Managing Across, Not Up and Down," *Business Week*, December 20, 1993, 76–77.

31. Kevin Helliker, "Retailing Chains Offer a Lot of Opportunity, Young Managers Find," *The Wall Street Journal*, August 8, 1995, A2, A10.

32. Ronald Henkoff, "Finding, Training, and Keeping the Best Service Workers," *Fortune*, October 3, 1994, 120.

33. *Ibid.*

34. Kerry Hannon, "The 1992 Store of the Year," *Money* (December 1991): 86.

35. Henkoff, "Finding, Training, and Keeping the Best Service Workers," 118.

36. Dori Jones Yang, "The Starbucks Enterprise Shifts into Warp Speed," *Business Week*, October 24, 1994, 77.

37. Redman, "The Dynamics of Team Building," 146.

38. Chad Rubel, "Treating Coworkers Right Is the Key to Kinko's Success," *Marketing News*, January 19, 1996, 2.

39. Ginger Woodard, Nancy Cassill, and David Herr, "The Relationship between Psychological Climate and Work Motivation in a Retail Environment," *The International Review of Retail*, Distribution and Consumer Research 4 (July 1994): 297–314.

40. Frederick Herzberg, "One More Time: How Do You Motivate Employees?" *Harvard Business Review*, 46 (January–February 1968): 53–62.

41. See Douglas McGregor, "The Human Side of Enterprise," in *Leadership and Motivation: Essays of Douglas McGregor*, ed. W.G. Bennis and E. Schein (Cambridge, MA: MIT Press, 1966).

42. Bill Saporito, "And the Winner Is Still . . . Wal-Mart," *Fortune*, May 2, 1994, 68.

43. See Robert F. Lusch and Bernard J. Jaworski, "Management Controls, Role Stress, and Retail Store Manager Performance," *Journal of Retailing*, 67 (Winter 1991): 397–421.

44. Sarah Smith, "Leaders of the Most Admired," *Fortune*, January 29, 1990, 46.

45. "System Boosts Productivity—Immediate Feedback on Job Performance," *Chain Store Age Executive* (June 1992): 42.

46. Dyan Machan, "Ivana's Revenge," *Forbes*, November 7, 1994, 41.

47. "Store Manager Pay Jumps," *Stores* (December 1995): 26–27.

48. See Chuck Hawkins, "Will Home Depot Be 'the Wal-Mart of the '90's?" *Business Week*, March 19, 1990, 124. Also see Walecia Konrad, "Cheerleading, and Clerks that Know Awls from Augers," *Business Week*, August 3, 1992, 51.

49. Patricia Lush, "Wage Disparity Plagues Safeway," *Globe and Mail*, October 9, 1996, B6.

50. Kevin Helliker, "Falling Profit Marks End of Era at Wal-Mart," *The Wall Street Journal*, January 18, 1996, B1. Also see "The Secret of Wal-Mart's Success," *Money* (July 1992): 24; and Sam Walton with John Huey, *Made in America* (New York: Doubleday, 1992).

51. Andrew Nikiforuk, "Why Safeway Struck Out," *Canadian Business*, September 1997, 28.

52. John Heinzl and Marina Strauss, "Wal-Mart's Cheer Fades," *Globe and Mail*, February 15, 1997, B4.

Store Facilities Management

Outline

Store Environment
Store Image
Store Atmospherics
Store Theatrics

Exterior Store Design
Store Position
Store Architecture
Store Marquee
Store Frontage

Interior Store Design
Store Aesthetics
Space Planning
Store Layout

Visual Merchandising
Display Types
Display Concepts
Display Content
Display Arrangement

Store Security
Customer Theft
Customer Fraud
Employee Theft
Supplier Theft
Felony Theft

Summary

Student Study Guide
Key Terms and Concepts
Review Questions
Review Exam

Student Applications Manual
Investigative Projects: Practice and Application

Endnotes

Objectives

To appreciate the physical and psychological impact that store facilities have on customer attraction, employee morale, and store operations

To distinguish design features vital in creating a desirable store image, building a stimulating store atmosphere, and staging an entertaining store theatre

To identify and explain the major considerations in planning store exteriors capable of stopping, communicating with, and attracting customers

To specify and discuss the key features of the store's interior and their role in creating an inviting, comfortable, and convenient facility

To discuss the unique contribution of visual merchandising in the retailer's customer communication program

To plan and construct an effective in-store display

To identify and discuss the various types and causes of retail security problems and outline the methods and techniques directed at detecting and preventing criminal activities

Retail Vignette

Sears

When the majority ownership of a store changes, new methods, such as "tracking studies," are sometimes needed to carry out new goals.

Sears Canada has had an interesting and colourful history. On September 18, 1952, a partnership agreement was signed between Simpsons Limited of Toronto and Sears, Roebuck and Co. of Chicago for the formation of a new Canadian catalogue order and retail company to operate under the name Simpsons-Sears Limited. The company was incorporated under the laws of Canada by Letters Patent dated September 17, 1952.

Sears Canada
www.yellowpages.ca/sears

In December 1978, the Hudson's Bay Company acquired Simpsons Limited, and in doing so, gained approximately 35 percent of the outstanding shares of Simpsons-Sears Limited. As a result of this acquisition, the federal government required that Simpsons-Sears Limited and Simpsons Limited operate as two separate companies and that all shared facilities and services be discontinued.

Plans to change the company's name to clarify its identity originated in 1979, shortly after the Bay's acquisition of Simpsons Limited, and was finalized in late 1983. Approval was given at the May 16, 1984, shareholders' meeting to officially change the corporate name to Sears Canada Inc., effective May 31, 1984.

With majority ownership now originating in the U.S. and the name changed to Sears Canada, the company followed the lead of its U.S. parent by beginning a massive overhaul of existing stores, a return to the middle-income consumer, and a "right goods in the right environment at the right price" philosophy. One technique that enabled Sears to effectively carry out this new mandate involved the use of "tracking" studies wherein sales of different types of merchandise are monitored closely in an attempt to always have in stock the best-selling merchandise.

In 1991, Sears Canada acquired five Simpsons and two Hudson's Bay retail store locations in the Toronto market. This expansion doubled the presence of Sears in the greater Toronto area, further strengthening its market share in one of Canada's largest retail markets.

Today, Sears Canada Inc. is the largest single retailer of general merchandise in Canada. The company has approximately 110 department stores, 12 outlet stores for merchandise liquidations, and over 1700 catalogue stores. This giant retailer services all 10 provinces and both territories. Its two core businesses, retail and catalogue shopping, together employ approximately 39 000 regular and part-time employees across Canada.

The Sears Canada credit card now has more cardholders than any other single retail credit card issuer in Canada, and almost half the households in Canada have one or more major appliances displaying the Sears Kenmore brand name. In 1992, Sears Canada issued 47.5 million copies of its catalogue.

Sears Canada Inc. is now considering creating offshoot specialty businesses such as automotive and home repair services as a way to grow—rather than adding many more traditional department stores, chairman and chief executive officer Paul Walters says.

Sears Canada's blueprint for growth entails setting up "off-mall" businesses in specialty sectors such as home renovations, hardware supplies and auto parts, rather than adding significantly more traditional stores, he said. The strategy is patterned on a similar path taken by Chicago-based parent Sears Roebuck and Co. and has already had some success in Canada in separate furniture stores, he said. "We're looking at a tremendous number of growing options," Mr. Walters said.

In 1996, Sears began investing heavily in remodelling their stores, reducing the number of suppliers, and increasing its emphasis on soft goods and fashion merchandise. The major promotional theme of this effort is to show "the softer side of Sears." Early results show that this strategy may be paying, as 1996 profits were $34.3 million on sales of $3.9 billion.

Printed with permission of Sears Canada Inc.

The Nordstrom Way

Nordstrom [a successful regional department store chain in the northwest United States] wants to make it as easy as possible for customers to circulate and shop through the entire store, and for sales associates to help them do just that. Departments are designed, and merchandise better organized, edited, and more clearly defined by lifestyles so that the presentation is instantly understood and a wardrobe can be more quickly assembled by the entrepreneurial salespeople who implement customer service the Nordstrom way. Store layouts typically resemble a wheel. The hub is the escalator well and the spokes are the marble aisles that lead directly back to each of the thirty or so departments. The subtleties and details make the shopping experience easy and convenient. Aisles provide ample room for customers to browse and give shoppers the freedom to circle the store and plunge into the centre of each individual department.[1]

Sticky Fingers

Customer and employee theft are increasing fairly dramatically across the industry. There just seems to be more criminal activity from gangs and from organized theft rings. To keep a lid on costs, many retailers have cut back on sales staffs, leaving fewer workers to supervise customers and other employees. Wages in the industry have remained low, while the

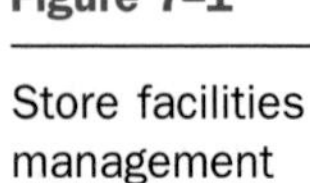

Figure 7–1

Store facilities management

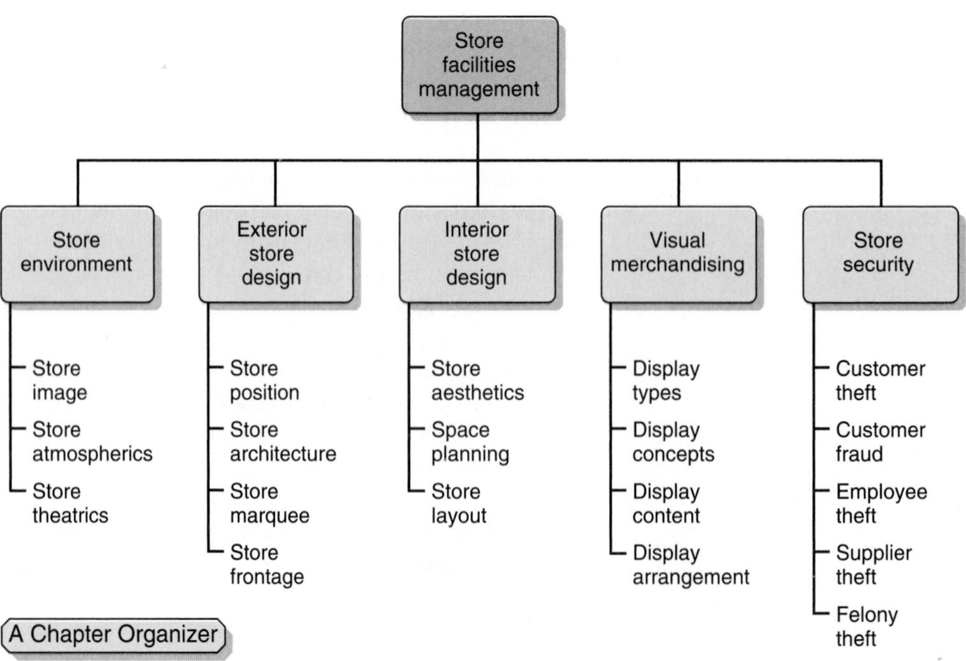

use of part-timers has risen—leading to lower employee loyalty and higher theft, some retail observers contend. Financial instability or breakneck growth only exacerbate a retailer's potential for theft problems.[2]

A store and its immediate area create the environment within which a retailer must operate. It is an environment that either attracts or repels potential customers. A good store planner will conduct a continuous inquiry into the consumer's visual, tactile, and spatial consciousness. It is also the environment in which the retailer must find a way of operating effectively, efficiently, and securely. Therefore, the retailer must make a concentrated effort to ensure that the store's environment is conducive to both retail operations and consumers' shopping needs.

The importance of the store and its environment becomes evident when one realizes that three out of four customer purchase decisions are finalized while consumers are in the store inspecting the merchandise. Store facilities management requires the creation of a motivating store environment, an inviting store exterior, an engaging store interior, an exciting merchandise presentation, and a comforting, safe store. Figure 7–1 outlines the major concerns of the store facilities manager.

Store Environment

In creating and designing a store's environment, the retailer must consider its physical and psychological impacts on customer attraction, employee morale, and store operations. Store operations and customer shopping are both enhanced by a well-planned and well-designed shopping scene.

A store's physical environment is a composite of the tangible elements of form as reflected in the way land, building, equipment, and fixtures are assembled for the convenience and comfort of both customers and retailer. Equally important is the store's psychological environment—the perceived atmospheric setting the retailer creates. In essence, a store's psychological environment is the mental image of the store produced in the customers' minds. A store's effectiveness and uniqueness lie in the retailer's ability to plan, create, and control both the store's physical and psychological setting. The psychological impressions a store makes on consumers depend on the store's image, atmospherics, and theatrics (see Figure 7–2).

Store Image

A **store image** is the store's personality. It is how the consumer sees the store as well as what the consumer feels about the store. It is important, therefore, that retailers know and plan what they want the consumer to see and feel. Because image represents to the consumer a composite picture of the retailer, it is one of the most powerful tools in attracting and satisfying consumers. The visible and tangible nature of a store makes it a key factor in the retailer's image-creating efforts.

Creating an image, however, is a difficult task. As described in Chapter 1, an image is a mental picture that forms in the human mind as a result of many different stimuli. Of interest to us in this chapter are the emotions and reactions that can be generated by the retailer's physical facilities—the store's exterior and interior—as well as how the retailer presents the firm's total offering of merchandise and creates a safe and secure shopping experience.

External Impressions Externally, the position of the store on the site, its architectural design, its storefront, and the placement of signs, entrances, and display windows all contribute to the store's image. The external features of a retail store and its immediate environment can be an important vehicle for nonverbal communication. The importance of communicating the right impression is based on the belief that the store's personality

Figure 7–2

The store's environment

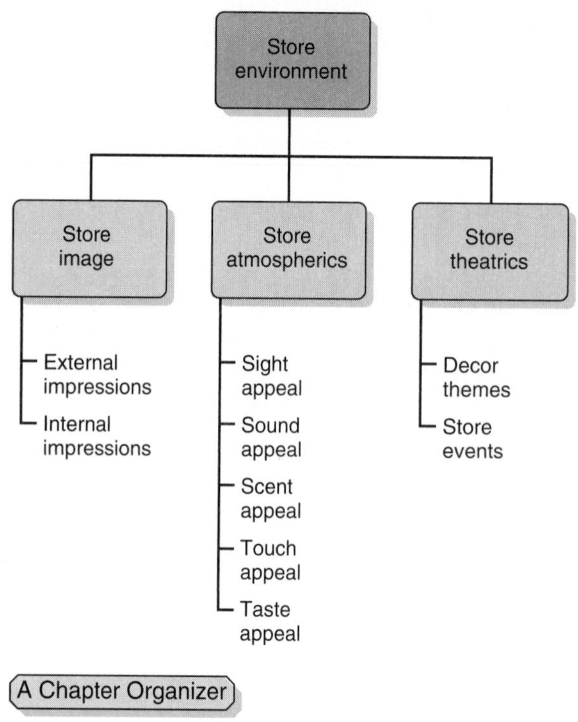

helps "position" one retailer against others, thereby facilitating the store selection process for consumers. Communicating the right impression, then, is a problem of how best to use the external attributes of the store to make the right impression by conveying to consumers what the retailer wants them to see and feel. Because the store's exterior is one of the first things seen by the consumer, it is often the first impression the consumer has of the retailer—and first impressions are extremely important in the cluttered and competitive world of retailing. Paul Smith, the English designer, makes his stores his trademark. Each store starts with quirky windows that attract attention and generate interest. "In Tokyo, a wooden dog mannequin has a Japanese-style smog mask over its face. In his Paris boutique the 19th-century portraits of aristocrats have collie and bulldog heads."[3]

Internal Impressions Internally, a store's image can be created, in part, by the use of various sizes, shapes, and colours; the layout of departments and traffic aisles; the arrangement of store displays; the application of store lighting and signage; and the selection of store fixtures and equipment. In designing the internal image-creating features of the store, the retailer must work with a particular target consumer in mind. Recently, Sears Canada opted to spend over $240 million in remodelling to "feminize and energize" the interior of many of its stores across Canada.[4]

Neither the retailer nor the store can be all things to all people. Likewise, neither can a single store image be created that will appeal to all consumers. Therefore, a store's facilities should be tailored to the psychological and physical needs of a selected customer group by creating a focused collection of sensory impressions and shopping experiences.

Store Atmospherics

To create a store atmosphere conducive to buying, a retailer should establish in the consumer a frame of mind that promotes a buying spirit.[5] Pleasure induced by store environments is a strong reason that consumers spend extra time in the store and spend more money than intended.[6] Even the economy-minded consumer wants something more than a shopping atmosphere with only the bare essentials. **Store atmosphere** is the overall aesthetic and emotional effect created by the store's physical features; it is the total sensory experience created by the store. Today's shoppers, regardless of their principal shopping motives, are drawn to safe, attractive, and comfortable shopping environments. The store's atmosphere should be an agreeable environment for both the consumer and the retailer.[7]

The retailer wants to influence the consumer's mood by creating an atmosphere that will positively influence buying behaviour. "People are looking for something that will make it easier, more pleasant, more positive and that is what a store mood has to evoke."[8] An appealing buying atmosphere uses cues that appeal to the consumer's senses of sight, hearing, smell, touch, and taste. Sensory cues can be strongly reinforced if they are structured around shopping themes that unify and organize the store's atmosphere. Indigo Books and Music, a new book megastore in Ontario, has developed an interior which emphasizes roominess and has comfortable chairs designed to appeal to those wishing to spend time browsing and reading before they buy.[9]

The following discussion describes how a retailer can use sensory appeals to effect a favourable store image and a pleasant shopping environment.

Sight Appeal The sense of sight provides people with more information than any other sensory mode and therefore must be classified as the most important means by which retailers can appeal to consumers. For present purposes, and for the sake of simplicity, **sight appeal** can be viewed as the process of imparting stimuli, resulting in perceived visual relationships. Size, shape, and colour are three primary visual stimuli a retailer can use to arouse the consumer's attention. Perceptions based on these three visual stimuli are discussed in depth in the "Store Aesthetics" section of this chapter, p. 236.

Visual relationships are mental interpretations made from visual stimuli consisting of harmony, contrast, and clash. Harmony is visual agreement; contrast, visual diversity; and clash, visual conflict. These elements can occur among the many parts of any display, layout, or physical arrangement. In any given situation, either harmony, contrast, or clash may be the best way to create an appealing shopping atmosphere. Harmonious visual relationships are generally associated with a quieter, plusher, and more formal shopping setting, whereas contrasting and clashing visual relationships can promote an exciting, cheerful, or informal atmosphere.

Sound Appeal Sound can either enhance or hinder a store's buying atmosphere. In planning store facilities, it is as important to avoid undesirable sounds as it is to create desirable ones, or **sound appeal**. Disturbing noises detract from a store's appeal, whereas pleasant sounds can attract customers. Obtrusive sounds distract consumers, interrupting the buying process. Whether these sounds originate inside or outside the store, they must be either controlled or eliminated.

Noise avoidance is a problem tailor-made for physical facilities planning. Careful use of architectural design, construction materials, equipment, and interior decor can eliminate or at least substantially reduce most obtrusive sounds. For example, clicking heels can be eliminated by heavy, durable carpeting, humming air conditioners can be strategically positioned away from selling areas, and rattling jackhammers and undesirable external music can be neutralized by proper insulation. Lower ceilings and sound-absorbing partitions and fixtures reduce unwanted sounds even further.

To create an atmosphere that encourages buying, the retailer can use sound appeal in a variety of ways. Sound can be a mood setter, an attention getter, and an informer. Music can relax the customer, promote a buying spirit, set the stage for a particular shopping theme, or remind the customer of a special season or holiday (particularly Christmas), as well as provide a generally pleasant background of familiar sounds. Different kinds of background music can have different effects on customers. A store might use adult contemporary tunes to make customers feel comfortable; but modern rock might be used to create some excitement. Victoria's Secret hires the London Symphony Orchestra to record classical pieces, and then collects them in CDs with such titles as "Passion and Pleasure." The music is used as background for the stores and offered for sale to its customers.[10] The Nature Company, a chain of specialty stores, records and sells its collection of the sounds of nature.[11] Music must complement the selling scene, though, and not detract from it.[12] The type (for example, rock, classical, soul) and volume of music must be suitable to the retailer's consuming public.

Sound has been employed as an attention getter under a variety of circumstances. It can draw customers to a particular display or department. Noise-making toys are effective in attracting both children and adults to the toy department.

Finally, fast, convenient, and pleasurable shopping requires that the customer have sufficient information about the store, its merchandise, and its operations. Frequently, the retailer must inform the consumer about where to go, when to go, how to get there, and what is available. Because this basic information is a prerequisite to the buying process, the informer role of sound is a key element in creating a buying atmosphere.

Scent Appeal The creation of **scent appeal** is a problem similar in scope to the sound-appeal problem—how to avoid unpleasant odours and create pleasant scents. Stale, musty, and foul odours offend everyone and are sure to create negative impressions. Inadequate ventilation, insufficient humidity control, and poorly placed and maintained sanitation facilities are frequent causes of undesirable odours. Store facilities should be designed to minimize these problems or eliminate them entirely.

Pleasurable scents, on the other hand, are key ingredients in creating atmospheric conditions that induce the customer to buy. Research suggests that customers also perceive merchandise in a scented shop to be better than identical goods sold in an unscented shop.[13] A well-placed fan in a bakery shop, candy store, or delicatessen attracts the passer-by to these almost unavoidable pleasurable scents of products frequently bought on impulse. Retailers of foods, coffee, tobacco, flowers, perfumes, and other scented products know the value of exposing their customers' noses to the scents.[14] A store should smell like it is supposed to smell. Some stores, such as a drugstore, should smell clean and antiseptic. For others, such as an antique store, a dusty, musty smell could enhance the buying atmosphere.

Touch Appeal At one point in the history of retailing, the vending machine was considered the retailing store of the future. Today, although the vending machine is admittedly an important retailer of some standardized products, it is still an unacceptable way to sell most goods. The vending machine's lack of acceptance is, to a large extent, the direct result of its inability to provide **touch appeal**. For most products, personal inspection—handling, squeezing, and cuddling—is a prerequisite to buying. Before buying a product, the average consumer must at least hold it, even if it cannot be removed from its package.

Store layouts, fixtures, equipment, and displays encourage and facilitate the consumer's sense of touch. The chances of a sale increase substantially when the consumer handles

Retail Strategies and Tactics

Aromatherapy: The Power of Scents

A growing number of marketers are recognizing that the sense of smell can also be a powerful motivator for sales—and it is not just perfume that is winning by a nose. Businesses are sniffing out the connection between the sense of smell, memory, and mood. They are using this link to sell everything from body lotion to car wax. More remarkable is a line of products lumped under the new-age name of "aromatherapy." Its promoters claim that certain fragrances released into the air have the potential to change the ambiance and mood of both work and home life.

Why is fragrance so important to the buying public? The key is a mixture of biological responses, psychology, and memory. The limbic system is the most primitive of our brain and the seat of immediate emotions. Certain odours elicit elementary emotional reactions because some fingers of the olfactory bulb dip directly into the limbic system. Smell, more than any other sense, is a straight line to feelings of happiness, hunger, disgust, and nostalgia—the same feelings marketers want to tap.

The mind has a strong memory for important smells that remind us of good or bad times, and these associations make up each individual's personal smell palate.

Source: Maxine Wilkie, "Scent of a Market," American Demographics *(August 1995): 40–49.*

the product. The expression "I just could not put it down" underscores the importance of getting the consumer to pick up a product. Many stores allow free demonstrations and in-store use of products to enhance sales.

Taste Appeal For some food retailers, offering the consumer **taste appeal** might be a necessary condition for buying. This is often the case with specialty foods such as meats, cheeses, and bakery and dairy products. Hickory Farms and Yogen Fruz are two specialty food retailers that use taste appeal as part of their selling operations. In designing in-store displays, such retailers provide potential customers with a sample of the product under clean and sanitary conditions.

Store Theatrics

Retailing is more than just the sale of merchandise; in part, it is an exhibition, an event, or an enactment involving the process of shopping. This notion of "retailing as theatre," or **store theatrics**, has become a powerful weapon for a host of different retailers as they seek to gain a competitive advantage in an over-stored and undifferentiated market of "me-too" merchandisers. Musicland, North America's largest record chain, features in-store appearances by well-known artists to juice up sales, motivate store employees, build store loyalty, and enhance store image.[15]

The idea that a store or mall visit is something more than just a shopping trip in which the sole purpose is to purchase goods and services has gained favour in recent years. For retailing formats whose merchandising emphasis is on something other than price and convenience, the store's capabilities to provide recreation and entertainment opportunities, as well as occasions for socialization, can be important store patronage reasons. West Edmonton Mall, long known for its entertainment and attractions, has recently embarked on an effort to attract even more entertainment retailers to its mix of stores by adding such stores as the Hard Rock Café, Hooters, and Kaos.[16] Land Rover dealerships are erecting multimillion-dollar boutiques known as Land Rover Centres. Luxury sport-utility vehicles are displayed on slate-and-wood floors accented with compass markings. Nearby shelves display Land Rover Gear, a branded line of shirts, gloves, sweatshirts, and coats. Videotapes of Rovers taking on the wilds of Africa play on a large-screen television. The decor is pure fantasy.[17] Store theatrics is accomplished through the use of decor themes and store events.

Decor Themes Many retailers find that one or more themes help provide a focus in planning the decor of the store. Shopping themes are a useful vehicle in creating both exterior and interior decor that appeal to the customer's five senses. Any number of decorating themes might be appropriate. Common themes centre around natural (summer or winter) or holiday (Canada Day or Christmas) seasons, historic periods (colonial or Renaissance), current issues (energy or environment), real or imaginary people (Wayne Gretzky or Batman), lifestyles (traditional or outdoor), brands and designers (Nike or Ann Klein), nations and cultures (China or France), and special events (anniversaries or graduation). Theme decor makes the store a more interesting, entertaining place to shop.

Themes assist the merchandiser in gaining the initial attention and maintaining the continued attention of the consumer during the store shopping experience. Kenny Rogers Roasters restaurants are jammed with Rogers paraphernalia, like copies of such gold records as "Lucille" and "Through the Years," photos of the performer in concert with other country stars like Dolly Parton, and videos of his classic hits.[18] Decor themes can be organized on either a chain-wide, store, department, or product line basis.

Store Events Store events are special occasions (for example, merchandise displays, entertainment events, merchandise demonstrations, community affairs, promotional programs, public service events, celebrations) staged by the store's management to attract potential consumers to the store in hopes of achieving the following goals: (1) creating store awareness, (2) providing consumer information, (3) building a favourable store image, and (4) encouraging store patronage. The attainment of these goals requires a stage on which these noteworthy happenings can be produced effectively. That stage is the theatrical qualities of the store and the surrounding area. Like decor themes, special events can be organized around any type of person, place, or thing.

Exterior Store Design

First impressions are important because they are often the swing factor in a consumer's decision to stop at one store or another. The store's exterior is a key factor in stopping and attracting new customers and retaining existing customers.

> In retailing, both research and practice suggests that physical environmental cues such as exterior design . . . will play a major role in helping consumers to categorize the type of place they are in or approaching. How consumers categorize a place should be important to marketers because it prompts a set of inferences about the type of services and products to be found there, and these inferences lead to behavioural consequences such as going in, leaving, staying for a length of time, spending money, and so on.[19]

For example, ChemLawn helps retailers "dress for success" by providing a complete exterior lawn and landscaping service; they work with retailers to make the store's appearance a marketing tool. The major considerations in exterior store design are the store's position, architecture, marquee, and frontage. The focus of our discussion on store exteriors is outlined in Figure 7–3.

Store Position

How and where the store is positioned on the site affects the retailer's ability to attract customers. In evaluating existing store facilities or planning future site layouts, the retailer should consider at least three questions: (1) How visible is the store? (2) Is the store compatible with its surroundings? (3) Are store facilities placed for consumer convenience?

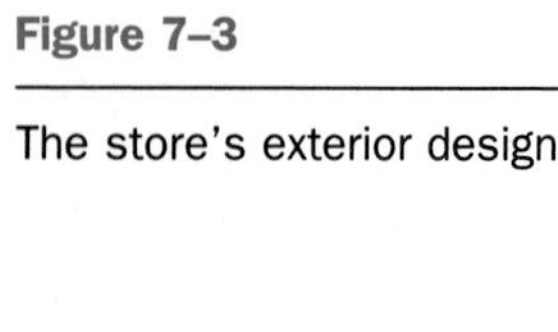

Figure 7–3

The store's exterior design

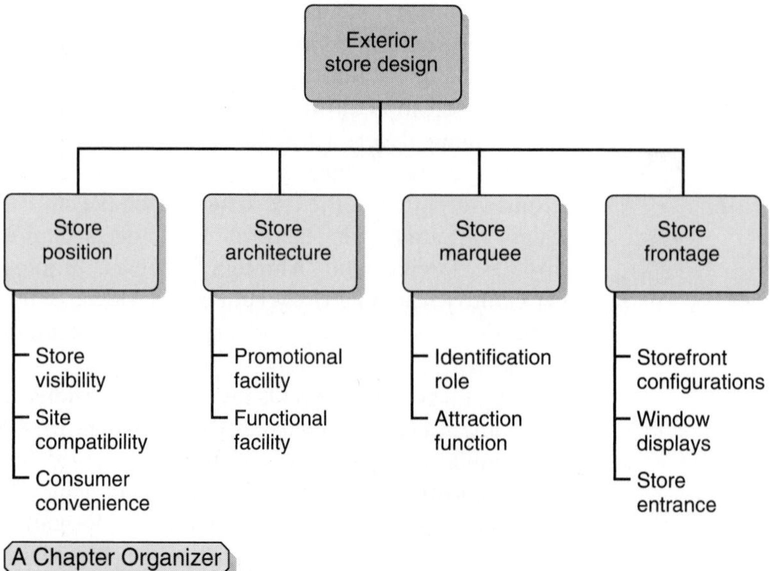

Store Visibility For the physical exterior to accomplish its goals of stopping, attracting, and inviting customers to shop, customers must see it. A visible store becomes part of the consumer's mental map of where to shop for a certain product or service. Simply put, people shop more frequently at stores they are aware of, and **store visibility** is an important factor in developing that awareness. Ideally, a store should be positioned so that it is clearly visible from the major traffic arteries (foot and/or vehicle) adjacent to the site. The retailer improves the store's visibility by using the three interacting factors of setback, angle, and elevation to advantage.

Ideally, a store should be set back far enough to give passersby a broad perspective of the entire store but close enough to let them read major signs and see any window displays. Visual impressions can also be enhanced or hindered by the angle of the store relative to a traffic artery. In positioning the store, a retailer should place the building at an angle to the traffic artery that maximizes exposure. The elevation of a site can place the retailer's store above or below the main traffic artery level. Most consumers do not see stores that are too high or too low. These stores are also perceived as having accessibility problems.

Site Compatibility Fitting the store to the natural lay of the land and the natural habitat can reap substantial benefits for the retailer in terms of visual impressions. In designing for **site compatibility**, the retailer should ensure that the size of the facility be appropriate to the size of the site. Placing an oversized building on a small site produces a distorted sense of proportion. Also, architectural design and construction materials should demonstrate a harmonious relationship with the immediate environment.

Consumer Convenience In planning the store's on-site position, the retailer should consider how the position affects consumer convenience. The retailer might ask several questions: Does the store's position allow enough parking spaces and permit easy access to them? Can cars and trucks turn around in the parking lot? Does the position permit safe, convenient pedestrian traffic? Does the position enhance or hinder pedestrian access to the store?

Store Architecture

Architecture is a major factor in both making the right impression on the consumer and developing an efficient retail operation. In most cases the store's architecture is a compromise between these two objectives.

Promotional Facility The store's architectural motif can be a powerful promotional tool, conveying different impressions as well as a considerable amount of information. A certain architectural style can indicate the size and prestige of the retailer's operation, the nature of the retailer's principal product line (for example, the adobe-style architecture found at Taco Bell), and the retailer's affiliation (for example, store designs). In addition, architectural design can support a central theme or focal point for the retailer's merchandising activities. Exterior store design requires regular "updating" to convey to the consumer a contemporary image. Recently Eaton's, the Bay, and Sears have all begun renovating their stores to avoid an out-of-date look.[20]

Functional Facility The impression-creating elements of the architecture must be balanced against the functional needs of retailer and consumer. Functional considerations that are paramount in the store's design are costs, energy efficiency, security, operational efficiency, and customer convenience. Rapidly rising land, construction, and material costs have made the retailer's attempt to differentiate a store from the competition increasingly difficult. In addition, architectural freedom is limited by the costs associated with maintenance; conversely, architectural designs that reduce maintenance costs often limit customer convenience and store attractiveness.

With increasing energy prices, the retailer has an overriding obligation to minimize energy costs. Energy-saving construction methods include lower ceilings, less window space, proper air circulation, controlled entrances and exits, proper insulation, and energy-efficient lighting. Because of the rising crime rate, modern retailers have had to design facilities that increase store security, including such features as reduced window space, elimination of unexposed areas, controlled entrances and exits, proper lighting, limited exposure of high-value products, and security devices such as television monitors, two-way mirrors, and observation areas.

Another architectural design consideration is operational efficiency. The best allocation of store space for operational activities is one that facilitates movement of customers, sales personnel, and merchandise and gives the retailer maximum product exposure. Maximizing selling areas and creating the highest possible level of product exposure are the chief concerns here. The final architectural design consideration is customer convenience. For example, new government regulations and public pressure require the retailer to ensure that all possible physical barriers to consumers with disabilities are removed.

Store Marquee

A store's sign or marquee is often the first "mark" of the retailer that a potential customer sees. It serves the key purposes of identifying the store and attracting the consumer's attention.

Identification Role Marquees provide the potential customer with the "who, what, where, and when" of the retailer's offering. Signs identify who the retailer is by a name, logo, or some other symbol. Sears, Safeway, and Holiday Inn are immediately recognized by most consumers. Signs also inform consumers about what the retailer's operation is. They transmit information regarding the type of retail operation (for example, department store, supermarket, catalogue showroom), the nature of the product line (for example, food, hardware, clothing, gifts), the extent of the service offering (for example, full-service bank, self-service gasoline station), and the character of the pricing strategy (for example, discount prices, family prices). Signs inform the consumer where the retailer is located and in some cases how to get there (for example, "Located at 5th and Main"). Finally, some retailers use signs to inform the consumer when they are willing to provide service or when they are open (for example, 24 hours).

Attraction Function The store's sign should create awareness, generate interest, and invite the consumer to try the store. The size, shape, colour, lighting, and materials all contribute to the sign's distinctiveness and its ability to create awareness and interest. The special design of McDonald's golden arches has helped it become one of the most highly recognized signs in North America.

Store Frontage

A store's front should clearly communicate to the consumer what he or she can expect to find in the store's interior. As an all-day, everyday promotional vehicle, store frontage must capture the consumer's attention and generate some initial interest (curiosity) as to what the retailer has to offer. As shown in Figure 7–3, the three primary design elements in a store's façade are storefront configuration, window displays, and store entrances.

Storefront Configurations The basic storefront configurations are the straight, angled, and arcade fronts. Each type is illustrated in Figure 7–4.

Straight Front. The **straight front** is a store configuration that runs parallel to the sidewalk, street, mall, or parking lot. Usually the only break in the front is a small recess for an entrance. This storefront design is operationally efficient because it does not reduce interior selling space. It lacks consumer appeal, however, because it is monotonous and less attractive than the other configurations. Reflective glare from windows can inhibit window-shopping. When retailers use the straight-front configuration, window-shoppers can inspect only a small part of any display from any one position.

Figure 7–4

Storefront configurations: straight, angled, and arcade

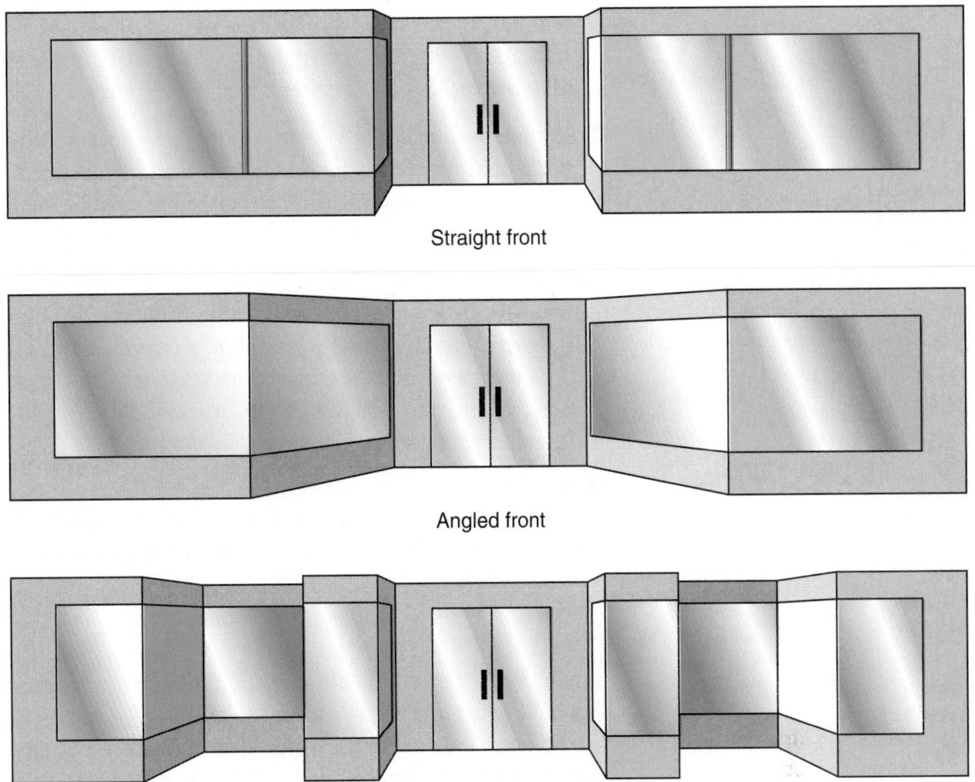

Angled Front. The **angled front** configuration overcomes the monotony of the straight front by positioning the store's front at a slight angle to the traffic arteries. To create a more attractive and interesting front, retailers that use the angled front approach place windows and entrances off-centre or at one end of the store's front. Angled fronts also give the window-shopper a better viewing angle of the merchandise in the window and reduce window glare. The entrance in an angled front is usually located at the most recessed part, to funnel and direct consumers into the store. It provides more protection for the window-shopper than does the straight front. The main limitation of the angled front is that it reduces the interior space the retailer can devote to selling.

Arcade Front. The **arcade front** is characterized by several recessed windows and/or entrances. Its advantages are that it (1) increases the store's frontage exposure and display areas; (2) provides the shopper with several protected areas for window shopping; (3) increases the privacy under which the shopper can inspect window displays; (4) creates an attractive, relaxing atmosphere for the shopper; and (5) reduces glare for a substantial part of the store front. Its disadvantages are that it (1) considerably reduces interior space for selling and displaying merchandise, (2) requires a substantial investment in construction and materials, and (3) needs a professional display staff to make full use of the arcade concept.

Window Displays The number, size, depth, and type of windows a store has can substantially alter its exterior appearance and general impression. To create the desired impression, the retailer can use one or a combination of the following displays:

- **Elevated windows** are display windows with floor elevations from 30 to 90 cm above sidewalk level. The choice of floor height depends on the kind of merchandise and the elevation necessary to place the display at the typical shopper's eye level. Small merchandise such as shoes, jewellery, books, and cosmetics normally are displayed in windows with a floor elevation of 90 cm, whereas large merchandise such as clothing displayed on mannequins usually appears in windows with a floor elevation of 30, 45, or 60 cm. Elevated windows give consumers an excellent visual perspective of the retailer's merchandise.

- **Ramped windows** are standard display windows with a display floor higher in back than in front. The floor ramp is either wedged or tiered, and the backing can be either open, partially opened, or closed. The principal advantage of the ramped display window is the greater visual impact of merchandise displayed in the rear.
- **Shadow box windows** are small, boxlike display windows set at eye-level heights. They are usually completely enclosed and focus the shopper's attention on a selected line of merchandise. Jewellery stores use this type of window display extensively. Tiffany & Co. uses small vaultlike window displays to reinforce the value of its displayed jewellery.[21]
- **Island windows** are four-sided display windows isolated from the rest of the store. Used in conjunction with the arcade storefront configuration, the island window can effectively highlight merchandise lines from all angles. This display advantage can become a disadvantage, however, if the retailer does not carefully select and position merchandise.

Store Entrance Retailers should design store entrances for the customer's safety, comfort, and convenience, as well as for guiding the customer into the store. The store entrance can be used as an attraction and as an invitation to the customer to enter the store. Champs Sports, a new superstore concept from Kinney Shoe, is designed around a sports arena theme that starts at the store entrance with a curved wall featuring a frieze of full-scale athletic figures set against the store's logo.[22] Design considerations for store entrances include (1) good lighting; (2) flat entry surfaces (no steps); (3) nonskid materials; (4) easy-to-open doors (slide away or air curtains); (5) little or no entrance clutter, such as merchandise tables; and (6) doors wide enough for people carrying large parcels. In addition, store entrances must meet all access regulations for people with physical disabilities.

Interior Store Design

The store's interior must contribute to the retailer's basic objectives of minimizing operating expenses while maximizing sales and customer satisfaction. To accomplish these goals, the store's interior must not only be inviting, comfortable, and convenient for the customer but also permit the retailer to use interior space efficiently and effectively.[23] Figure 7–5 identifies the issues discussed in this section.

Store Aesthetics

Store aesthetics involves how the store's physical facilities create sensory experiences. The aesthetic qualities of the store's interior are responsible for shaping the consumer's perceptions of the store's shopping environment, how the store looks and feels to the customer. As shown in Figure 7–5, the aesthetic qualities of the store are created by the consumer's perceptions of sizes, shapes, and colours.

Size Perceptions The sheer physical size of a store, display, sign, or department can communicate many things to many people. Size can communicate relative importance, success, strength, power, and security. Some consumers feel more secure when they buy from large stores because they believe that large stores are more capable and willing to fix, adjust, or replace faulty merchandise. Other consumers prefer larger stores because of the

Figure 7–5

The store's interior design

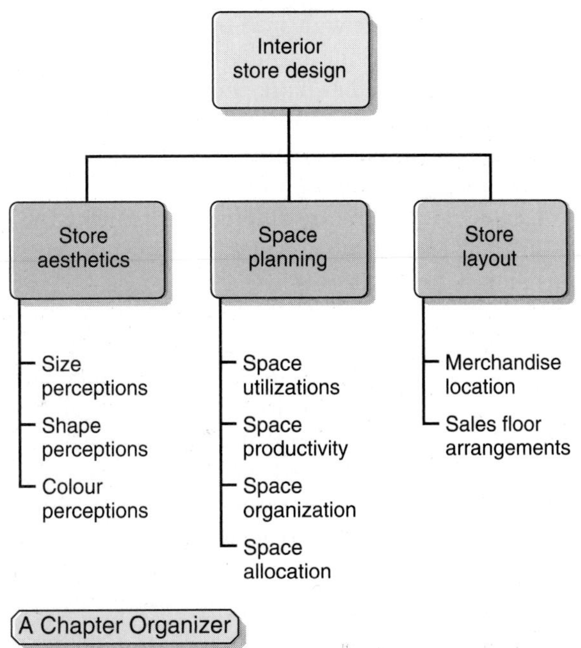

Retail Strategies and Tactics

Spectacular Sobeys

The day before the official opening of Sobeys' Clayton Park store in Halifax, N.S., Store Manager Brian Perro was scouring the community to find some last-minute workers who were willing to finish off his store. There was still plenty of painting to be done, both on the outside of the store, and on the inside. When the store opened on June 24, 1991, some 25 000 people jammed the store and the parking lot for the opening celebration.

That's how life started at this 52 755 sq. ft. [4900 m^2] (gross area) supermarket located in the Park West Centre, a strip plaza at a busy intersection in one of the fastest-growing neighbourhoods in Halifax. The store showcases Sobeys' newest design (although not the only one to share that design), and it has been exceeding the chain's average growth rate in sales. "We have a manager who has great people skills and a tremendous staff that has worked hard and well to make the store a success," says Sobey President Douglas Stewart.

For Perro, whose idea of customer service includes opening every checkout (and there are 15) from 10 a.m. each day until store closing, limiting operating hours is unfair to customers. "We do 80% of our business on Thursday, Friday, and Saturday," he says. Despite the opening restrictions, he makes sure that customers never have to wait in line. "Even on the other days, I believe all checkouts should be available," he says. His store is equipped with NCR registers and NCR scanners. And even though he has 300 shopping buggies, Perro has many days when the store is so busy that all the shopping carts are being used.

Cross merchandising is common: free cabbage packaged with the corned beef in the butcher shop, for example. Flower arrangements and party trays can be arranged jointly by the deli and the floral departments. The store's extensive wedding cake program can tie in as well. This works through the cooperation of each department's manager contacting the others, and introducing customers to them as soon as the customer's interest has been confirmed.

Sampling is also a regular feature. On this particular Tuesday, a cheery young woman is standing over a hibachi in front of the meat department, grilling Sobeys' beef burgers . . . a central product in Sobeys' new line of boxed meat, poultry and seafoods.

Perro calls his store a one-stop shopping service. The customer service counter, positioned at the front of the store, cuts keys, offers Western Union money services, operates a lottery centre, rents carpet cleaners, and sells cigarettes. Beyond the checkouts at the front of the store there is a banking machine, a one-hour photo centre that also sells cameras and film, the exit to the parcel pickup and a rack of warehouse shelves to hold oversize, heavy products like the jumbo-size bags of pet food.

Source: Staff, Canadian Grocer, *August 1993, 14–18.*

prestige they associate with such operations. A smaller store, display, or department may not be perceived as being as important, successful, or powerful as its larger counterparts, but it could be viewed as more personal, intimate, or friendly.

Size is a key element in creating harmony, contrast, and clash. To achieve a harmonious atmosphere in a store department or display, the retailer should maintain a consistent size relationship among its various elements. Using moderately different size elements can create contrast among different departments within the store or different displays within the department. Clashing relationships can be created by using substantially different size elements.

Shape Perceptions Shapes arouse certain emotions in buyers. In planning store layouts and designing store displays, the retailer should recognize that the vertical line gives "a rigid, severe, and masculine quality to an area. It expresses strength and stability . . . gives the viewer an up-and-down eye movement . . . tends to heighten an area, gives the illusion of increased space in this direction."[24] Horizontal lines are used to promote a feeling of rest, relaxation, and repose, while diagonal lines connote action and movement and sometimes give the illusion of instability.[25] Curved lines suggest a feminine atmosphere and add a flowing movement that directs the eye to a display or department. Rampage, a chain junior apparel store, uses curvilinear forms to add a note of quiet sensuality.[26] Equally important in facilities planning is the similarity or dissimilarity of shapes. "For the creation of perfect harmony in a display, shapes that correspond exactly to one another are used exclusively. Inharmonious or dissimilar shapes may be used in a display to create contrast and, in some instances, a point of emphasis."[27]

Colour Perceptions Colour makes the first impression on someone looking at an object. It is often what catches customers' eyes, keeps their attention, and stimulates them to buy. The Canadian consumer is becoming increasingly colour-conscious. "According to psychologists, certain colours consistently evoke the same feelings in human beings. In fact, there is some evidence that colours actually cause psychological reactions."[28] For most customers, if the colour is wrong, all is wrong. The psychological impact of colour is the result of hue, value, and intensity. Hue is the name of the colour. Value is the lightness or darkness of a hue; darker values are referred to as shades, and lighter values are called tints. The brightness or dullness of a hue is its intensity. For the retailer, colour psychology is important not only in selling merchandise but also in creating the proper atmosphere for selling that merchandise.

Hue Considerations. The impact of colour psychology becomes apparent as soon as we classify hues into "warm" and "cool" tones. The warm colours (red, yellow, and orange) and the cool colours (blue, green, and violet) symbolize different things to different consumer groups (see Figure 7–6). Warm colours give the impression of a comfortable, informal atmosphere. Cool colours, on the other hand, project a formal, aloof, or icy impression. When used properly, however, both warm and cool colours can create a relaxing yet stimulating atmosphere in which to shop.

Red is one of the most stimulating colours and should be used with considerable care. Too much red can be overpowering; it should thus be used as an accent colour rather than a basic background colour (except in restaurants and cocktail lounges, where red is thought to stimulate people's appetites). To attract attention and stimulate buyer action, red frequently appears in building signs, fixtures, and displays. Christmas and Valentine's Day are two holiday seasons when red is an appropriate display colour. Shades of red are also appropriate for certain decorative themes, such as carnivals and sports. Men respond strongly to yellow-based red, whereas women prefer reds that are blue-based.[29]

Yellow, like red, is a stimulating colour. Its principal asset is its visibility at long distances, which makes shades of yellow a logical colour selection for signs, walls, and poorly lit areas. Although yellow is a real attention-getter, it can also induce visual stress and should be used with caution.[30] The time to use yellow is in the spring, particularly around Easter. Yellow is also considered a colour for children, so it is appropriate for decorating infants', children's, and toy departments.

Figure 7–6

Perceptions of colours

Warm colours			Cool colours		
Red	Yellow	Orange	Blue	Green	Violet
Love	Sunlight	Sunlight	Coolness	Coolness	Coolness
Romance	Warmth	Warmth	Aloofness	Restful	Retiring
Sex	Cowardice	Openness	Fidelity	Peace	Dignity
Courage	Openness	Friendliness	Calmness	Freshness	Rich
Danger	Friendliness	Gaiety	Piety	Growth	
Fire	Gaiety	Glory	Masculine	Softness	
Sinful	Glory		Assurance	Richness	
Warmth	Brightness		Sadness	Go	
Excitement	Caution				
Vigour					
Cheerfulness					
Enthusiasm					
Stop					

Orange is used sparingly because of its high intensity and its tendency to clash with other colours. Most often thought of as a fall colour (fall foliage, harvest, and Halloween), orange is used primarily for accent and not as a basic decorative colour. Orange, like yellow, is a children's colour and livens up a children's department by evoking warm, cheerful surroundings. One interesting association that most consumers have with the colour orange is that it denotes "cheapness"; therefore, its use is limited to situations in which the goal is to communicate the inexpensive nature of the retailer's product line (for example, fast-food restaurants).[31]

Blues are associated with the cool, blue sky and the calm, blue sea. As a result, retailers use blues to create a peaceful, relaxing shopping atmosphere. Different shades of blue are often used in men's departments because this colour also connotes masculinity. Dark blue conveys respect and responsibility and can be used to upgrade the status of an in-store area or display. Blue-green is viewed as a classy colour with the highest indicator of success.[32] Blue works well as a trim and as a basic background colour for display areas and fixtures. Most studies show that blue is North Americans' favourite colour.[33]

Like blue, *green* suggests many pleasant associations—the newness and freshness of spring and the peace and restfulness of the great outdoors. Many experts believe that green is probably the single most popular and accepted colour. Its soft and relaxing qualities make it an ideal choice for many uses. Green is perceived as a spacious colour and is therefore useful for making small areas appear larger. Its softness also helps accentuate displayed merchandise.

Violet is little used in retail displays, except to achieve special effects. Too extensive use of this hue is thought to dampen shoppers' spirits. Although various shades and tints of violet have been used in carpeting and wall coverings, it has become a gender-neutral colour.[34]

Value Considerations. The lightness and darkness of colours create optical illusions that retailers can use to modify the store's physical characteristics. Experts believe that the shade or tint of a room is an emotional trigger; hence, store planners take value decisions very carefully. Generally, lighter colours make a room or an object appear larger, whereas darker colours create an illusion of smallness. Light neutral tones (for example, beige) are popular as fixture colours because they are perceived as warm and soft and do not detract from the displayed merchandise. On the other hand, darker colours have attention-grabbing ability; for example, by using darker colours at the back of a store, a retailer can draw consumers' attention to that area and increase the flow of customer traffic throughout the store.

Intensity Considerations. The brightness and dullness of different physical facilities also affect the buying atmosphere. As with colour value, colour intensity can create illusions. Bright colours make the facilities appear larger than do duller colours. A bright colour tends to create an illusion of hardness, however, whereas a dull colour appears softer. As a rule, children react more favourably to brighter colours—hence, these colours' widespread use in children's departments. Adults, on the other hand, prefer softer tones, which may explain why so many retailers use pastels.

Space Planning

We now turn to how retailers utilize the store's total space to achieve acceptable levels of productivity from each unit of space. The organization and allocation of space are also discussed here (see Figure 7–5).

Space Utilization

A store's interior can be divided into two general areas according to usage: nonselling and selling areas. The amount of space devoted to each varies depending on the retailer's operating format, size, and philosophy. In most cases, retailers try to maximize the amount of productive selling space while minimizing that area devoted to nonselling activities. The general ratio of nonselling to selling space is 1:4; that is, the store's selling area generally accounts for about 80 percent of the space available. By developing sophisticated inventory logistic systems, Wal-Mart has been able to reduce its nonselling area to about 10 percent of each store's total space; the result has been increased sales volume and improved space productivity.[35] In its renovation program, Sears has increased shopping space by converting in-store warehouses and office space through a more efficient inventory system and centralization of back-office duties.

Nonselling Areas. A nonselling area (sales support area) is space devoted to customer services, merchandise processing, or management and staff activities. Figure 7–7 identifies some of the common sales support activities found in the nonselling area. The four general approaches to locating nonselling areas capable of satisfying both customer convenience and employee productivity needs are the **sandwich**, **core**, **departmentalized**, **peripheral**, and **annex approaches**. Figure 7–8 characterizes each of these placement strategies.

Selling Areas. **Selling space** is that area of the store devoted to the display of merchandise and the interaction between customers and store personnel. The utilization of selling space typically takes one of three forms: (1) wall areas, (2) stock areas, and (3) feature areas. As seen in Figure 7–9, each area plays a unique role in the effective and efficient merchandising of a retailer's product offering.

Space Productivity

Because store space is both limited and expensive, retailers must make effective and efficient use of the entire physical facility. **Space productivity** involves achieving a profitable return per unit of space for various departments or merchandise lines.[36] In planning space productivity, retailers must (1) select those space productivity measures that are appropriate to their particular operating formats and (2) arrange store productivity areas by recognizing that the value of store space varies greatly depending on its location within the store.

Store Productivity Measures. Productivity measurements of store space are directed at determining the cost-effectiveness of the store's layout and design. Stated differently, store productivity measurements involve obtaining a defined financial return per unit of space. The most commonly used space productivity measures include the following:

Figure 7–7

Examples of sales support areas

Customer service areas	Merchandise service areas	Management staff areas
Checkout areas	Receiving area	Offices
Dressing rooms	Checking areas	Lounges
Wrapping desk	Marking areas	Locker rooms
Complaint desk	Stocking areas	Conference rooms
Credit desk	Merchandise control areas	Classrooms
Catalogue desk	Alterations and workrooms	Training areas
Repair counter		
Return desk		
Rest rooms		
Restaurants		

Figure 7–8

Location decisions for nonselling areas

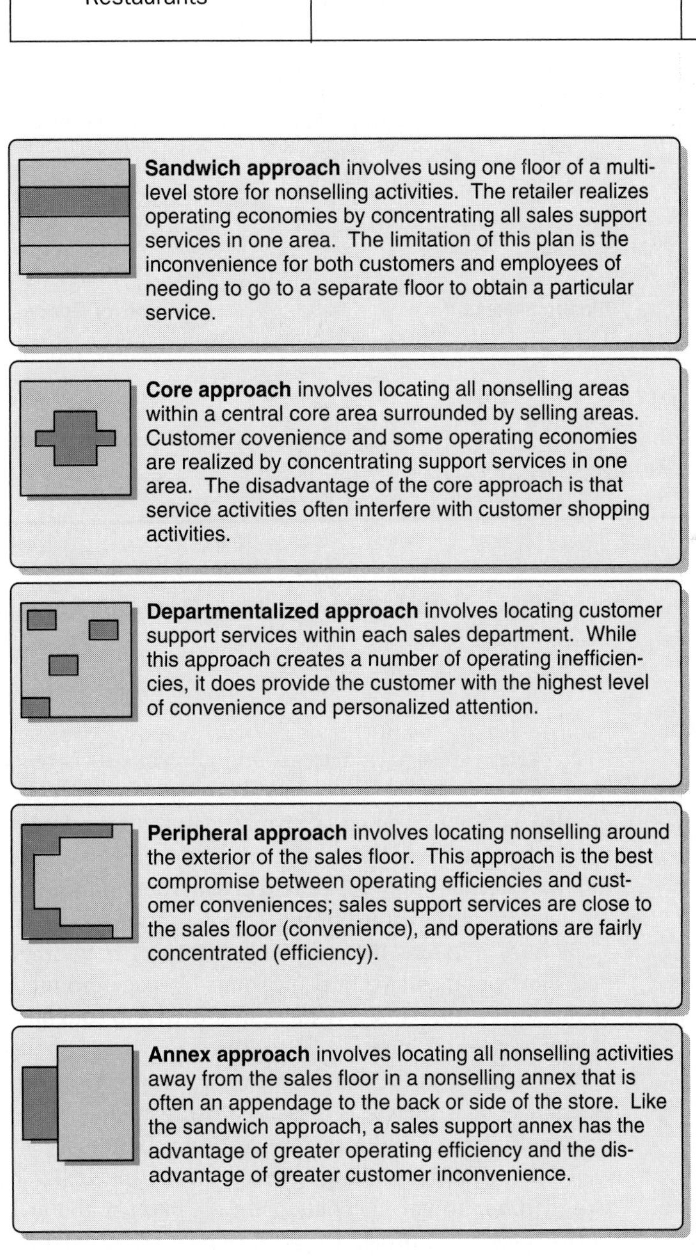

Sandwich approach involves using one floor of a multi-level store for nonselling activities. The retailer realizes operating economies by concentrating all sales support services in one area. The limitation of this plan is the inconvenience for both customers and employees of needing to go to a separate floor to obtain a particular service.
Core approach involves locating all nonselling areas within a central core area surrounded by selling areas. Customer covenience and some operating economies are realized by concentrating support services in one area. The disadvantage of the core approach is that service activities often interfere with customer shopping activities.
Departmentalized approach involves locating customer support services within each sales department. While this approach creates a number of operating inefficiencies, it does provide the customer with the highest level of convenience and personalized attention.
Peripheral approach involves locating nonselling around the exterior of the sales floor. This approach is the best compromise between operating efficiencies and customer conveniences; sales support services are close to the sales floor (convenience), and operations are fairly concentrated (efficiency).
Annex approach involves locating all nonselling activities away from the sales floor in a nonselling annex that is often an appendage to the back or side of the store. Like the sandwich approach, a sales support annex has the advantage of greater operating efficiency and the disadvantage of greater customer inconvenience.

Figure 7–9

Types of selling areas

Wall areas (shaded) are used to improve the vertical productivity of the store by providing extra space for displaying and storing merchandise. Effective utilization of wall space allows the retailer to improve such productivity measures as sales or gross margin per cubic foot. Wall areas are also instrumental in creating store atmospherics that are conducive to favourable consumer shopping behaviour.

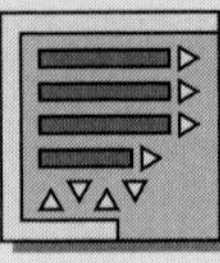

Stock areas (shaded) are used to stock and display the bulk of the retailer's merchandise selection. Stock areas are characterized by parallel aisles of gondolas that promote customer self-service and self-selection. By varying the length of the display, the retailer can increase horizontal productivity (sales per square foot or sales per linear foot) as well as vertical productivity (sales per cubic foot).

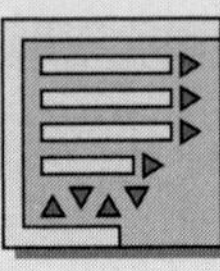

Feature areas (shaded) are attention-getting areas that are designed to promote and highlight carefully selected merchandise. End-of-aisle displays, freestanding displays, audiovisual displays, and other special displays are used to create areas that are capable of building customer traffic, exposing special merchandise, encouraging product inspection, and creating a buying atmosphere.

Financial Return	**Unit of Space**
Net sales per:	Square foot or metre
	Linear foot or metre
	Cubic foot or metre
Gross margin per:	Square foot or metre
	Linear foot or metre
	Cubic foot or metre
Contribution margin per:	Square foot or metre
	Linear foot or metre
	Cubic foot or metre

Net sales (gross sales returns and allowances) is the most commonly used measure of the productive use of store space; it reflects the retailer's ability to generate a certain level of sales within a given space. Gross margin (net sales – cost of goods sold) and contribution margin (net sales cost of goods sold – expenses) are preferred measures of space productivity because they better reflect the true productivity of space—its contribution to the profitability of the entire store.

Because a store is three-dimensional (length, width, and height), retailers must obtain both horizontal and vertical measures of space productivity. The **horizontal productivity** of the store's floor space is measured by using square feet or metres (length × width); to gain a horizontal measure of the productivity of shelf space retailers use linear feet or metres (length) as the unit of measure. The **vertical productivity** of the store's space (for example, wall displays) is measured using cubic feet or metres (length × width × height). As a multidimensional measure, vertical productivity is a more complete measure of how well the retailer is utilizing the store's total space. "Vertical merchandising is more effective than horizontal merchandising . . . because the focus of horizontal images fades out to the sides. By contrast, the eyes (which are responsible for 90% of the brain's imagery) can take in an entire vertical image with one glance."[37]

Computerized planogramming now enables the retailer to experiment with efficient space use based on financial evaluations, product movement, and profit yields. **Planograms** are shelf layout plans that allow the retailer to allocate space vertically and horizontally to product lines based on identified objectives. (See Retail Strategies and Tactics, for a profile of planograms.)

Store Productivity Areas. Not all the interior space is of equal value when judged against its revenue-producing capabilities. The consumer's in-store shopping responses to different interior arrangements vary substantially. Specifically, the value of any unit of store space will vary with the floor location, the area position within each floor, and its location relative to various types of traffic aisles. Many retailers recognize these variations in the value of store space and allocate total store rent to sales departments according to where they are located and how valuable each space is.

The value of space in multilevel stores decreases the farther it is from the main or entry-level floor. Although experts have different opinions on exactly how to allocate rental costs to each floor, they all agree that sales areas on the main floor should be charged a higher rent than sales areas in the basement or on the second, third, and higher floors. The additional customer exposure associated with entry-level floors justifies both the greater sales expectations (value of space) and the higher allocation of total store rent by floors.

The value of space also varies depending on where customers enter and how they traverse the store. In assigning value to interior store areas (and in making rent allocations), the retailer should consider the following: First, the most exposed area of any floor is the immediate area surrounding the entrance; second, most consumers tend to turn right when entering the store or floor; and third, a general rule of thumb is that only one-quarter of the store's customers will go more than halfway into the store. On the basis of these

Retail Strategies and Tactics

Planograms

Planning Efficient Space Utilization

Two important assets that every retailer has are inventory and space. Retailers must actively manage their store space as an asset. Strategic and effective use of store space requires the integration of planogramming information with store planning systems, merchandise planning systems, and inventory control systems.

A planogram is a visual diagram or plan detailing how much space is to be allocated to each product item, or SKU (stock keeping unit), and the location of each item relative to other SKUs. As a planning and control device, planograms assist the retailer in making decisions regarding the effective merchandising and efficient operational use of both vertical space (for example, shelf facings—linear feet) and horizontal space (for example, sales floor area—square feet). In creating standardized presentations of product items, the retailer uses a computer-generated plan for (1) grouping products into sales compatibility units, (2) allocating space to each product grouping, and (3) locating product groupings within well-conceived store and display designs. Planograms use a host of criteria in developing plans, including sales levels, gross margins, product compatibility, package size and shape, storage requirements, display needs, and inventory turnover rates. Planograms are typically generated by corporate merchandising and facility planners and distributed to individual stores.

Target, the Minnesota-based retailer, maintains a computer database of more than 3400 planograms in any running length from 16 to 24 ft. for its standardized gondola sections and display platforms. The discount retailer uses a computer assisted design (CAD) system to customize the merchandise presentation of each outlet. When Target needs a plan for a store, space analysis is performed to determine which and how much area is needed and which product adjacencies are appropriate. The CAD system then indicates which planogram(s) are appropriate for that individual store. Merchandise flexibility is the major benefit Target receives from its store-planning infrastructure.

Source: Adapted from R. Lee Sullivan, "Target's Customized Store Design," Discount Merchandiser *(February 1990): 32; "Computerized Planograms: An Enterprise Tool,"* Chain Store Age Executive *(September 1995): 10–11; and "Computerized Planograms Making Inroads, but Not Entrenched,"* Chain Store Age Executive *(September 1995): 12–13.*

three considerations, Figure 7–10 provides one of several variations for allocating store rents to a floor area. Another rule of thumb in assigning rent allocations is the **4-3-2-1** rule, in which the front quarter of the store is assigned 40 percent of the store's rent, and the second, third, and fourth quarters are assigned 30, 20, and 10 percent of the store's rent, respectively.

Because merchandise located on primary traffic aisles greatly benefits from increased customer exposure, the retailer should assign a higher value and a higher rent to space along these aisles than to that along secondary aisles. To illustrate, Figure 7–11 classifies interior store space into high-, medium-, and low-rent areas on the basis of their position relative to primary and secondary traffic aisles. As illustrated, a high-rent area is one exposed to two primary traffic aisles, whereas a low-rent area is exposed only to secondary aisles. Medium-rent areas are exposed to one primary and one secondary aisle.

Space Organization Better merchandise planning, greater merchandise control, and a more personalized shopping atmosphere are three important reasons for assembling merchandise into some type of natural grouping. A logical grouping of merchandise also helps customers find, compare, and select merchandise suited to their needs.[38] The most common grouping criteria used by retailers include the following:

1. **Functional groupings**—The categorizing of products on the basis of their end uses. For example, a discount store might group merchandise into the following categories: menswear, women's wear, children's wear, housewares, domestics, automotive, lawn and garden, electronics, and home improvement.
2. **Consumer groupings**—The organizing of in-store merchandise on the basis of its appeal to a targeted group of consumers who share common interests and opinions that impact their buying behaviour. For example, a bookstore might be organized by such subject area as fiction, business, spiritual, computers, romance, history, art, and so forth.
3. **Vendor groupings**—The arranging of a merchandise by brands or fashion labels. For example, all or part of an apparel store might feature different national brands or designer labels.
4. **Lifestyle groupings**—The assembling of merchandise assortment that meets the needs of consumers who have similar characteristics and living patterns. A department store, for example, might organize its women's apparel into such lifestyle departments as contemporary, updated, transitionalist, classic, moderate, traditionalist, and conservative.

Figure 7–10 (left)

Rent allocation by floor area

Figure 7–11 (right)

Rent allocation based on traffic flow

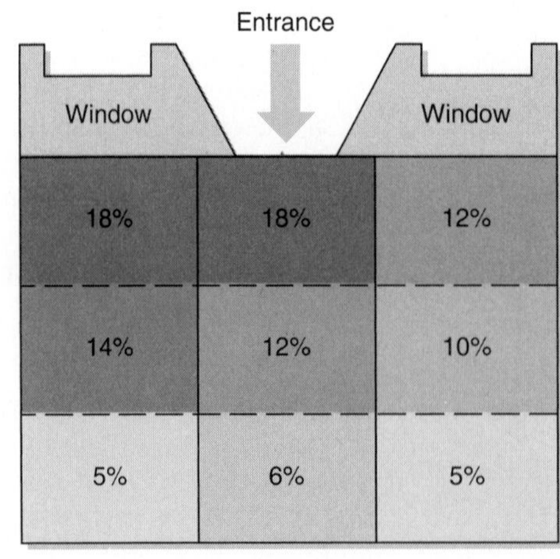

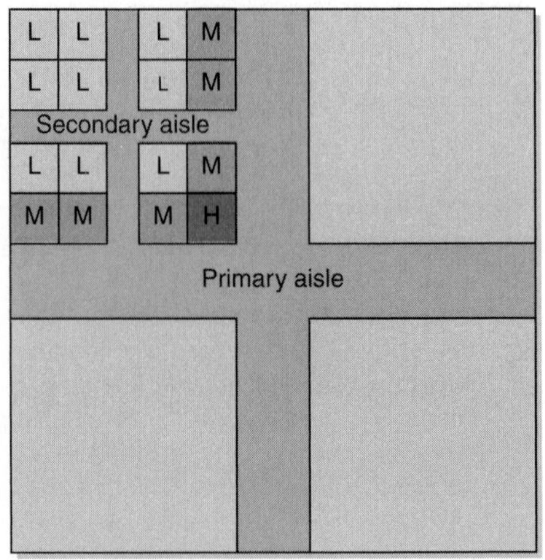

5. **Display groupings**—The arranging of merchandise areas on the basis of each product's display and storage requirements and/or preferences. For example, a supermarket might group its products into dry, refrigerated, or frozen lines.

6. **Product item groupings**—The development of product collections on the basis of their sizes, colours, materials, and prices. Some off-price retailers group all their product lines into a few pricing points (for example, $3.99, $5.99, $7.99, $9.99).

In grouping merchandise, retailers must ensure that the customer understands and appreciates the organization and that merchandise groupings are consistent with efficient operating principles.

Space Allocation After a retailer has grouped merchandise according to some logical criteria, selling space must be allocated to each merchandise group.[39] Given that each store has a limited amount of space, the retailer must select some method of allocating selling space to product lines that meet both customer shopping needs and space productivity needs. Two commonly used space allocation procedures are the model stock and sales productivity methods.

Model Stock Method. Using the model stock method, the retailer determines the amount of floor space needed to stock a desired assortment of goods for each merchandise grouping. For the more important merchandise groupings, the retailer allocates a sufficient amount of space to achieve the desired assortment. Merchandise groupings of lesser importance are allocated space on the basis of their assortment needs and the remaining available space.

Sales Productivity Method. The sales productivity ratio method allocates selling space on the basis of sales per unit of space for each merchandise group. As discussed earlier, some retailers prefer to use gross or contribution margin return per unit space as the basis of space allocation. Merchandise groups are assigned floor, shelf, display, or wall space depending on their level of productivity. Highly productive merchandise lines receive the bulk of the available space, and the less productive products receive minimal space allocations.

Store Layout

Effective store layouts encourage shoppers to buy. Efficient store layouts make good use of all the store's space. Designing a retail store requires the creation of a careful balance between meeting consumer shopping needs and generating acceptable financial returns. To accomplish both effectiveness and efficiency in facilities management, the store designer must construct merchandise location strategies and design sales floor arrangements.

Merchandise Location Where on the sales floor to put each merchandise group is a factor in planning the sales floor. Criteria that retailers consider are rent-paying ability, consumer buying behaviour, merchandise compatibility, seasonality of demand, space requirements, and display requirements.

Rent-paying ability is the contribution that a merchandise group can generate in sales to pay the rent for the area to which it is assigned. Other things being equal, merchandise groups with the highest rent-paying ability are located in the most valuable space.

Consumer buying behaviour criteria are based on the recognition that consumers are willing to spend different amounts of time and effort in searching for merchandise. For example, the retailer should place impulse and convenience goods in areas with high exposure (major aisles, checkout stands, and so on) because customers will not exert much effort to find them. In contrast, the retailer should locate shopping and specialty goods in less accessible areas, because consumers' purchase intents are well established and they will exert the necessary effort to find them.

The degree of relationship between various merchandise groups is termed *merchandise compatibility*. This concept states that closely related merchandise should be located together to promote complementary purchases. For example, the sale of a men's suit will increase the chances of selling men's ties and shirts if those products are located close to and are visible from the men's suit department. One supermarket study showed that by placing a pyramid of neatly stacked crackers next to the soup display the sales of crackers could jump as much as 20 percent, even if the crackers were not on sale—consumers just assume that the price is a sale price.[40]

Merchandise characterized by *seasonality of demand* is often accorded highly valuable, visible space during the appropriate season. In addition, merchandise groups with different seasonal selling peaks are often placed together to enable the retailer to expand or contract these lines without major changes in the store's layout. Examples are Christmas toys adjacent to lawn and garden equipment or women's coats adjacent to women's dresses.

Space requirements for each merchandise group must also be considered in making in-store location decisions. For example, merchandise groups that require large amounts of floor space (for example, a department store's furniture department) use less valuable space either at the rear of the store, on an upper floor, in the basement, or in an annex. Normally, the bulky nature of such products cannot justify their placement in higher-rent locations.

Display requirements also influence where the retailer places a particular group of merchandise. For example, merchandise such as clothing, which must be hung for display, probably is located along the sides of walls or at the rear of the store, where it will not interfere with the customer's needs for convenience and comparison shopping and the retailer's selling and operating needs. Effective display can increase impulse sales substantially as studies show that over 50 percent of purchases are impulse purchases.[41]

Sales Floor Arrangements When designing sales floor layouts, retailers must consider the arrangement of merchandise, fixtures, displays, and traffic aisles so that they can accommodate the spatial and location requirements of different merchandise groups. Selling floor layouts are extremely important because they strongly influence in-store traffic patterns, shopping atmosphere, shopping behaviour, and operational efficiency. Some of the factors the retailer must consider in designing the sales floor layout include the following:

- *Type of displays* (shelves, tables, counters) and fixtures (stands, easels, forms, platforms)
- *Size and shape* of fixtures
- *Permanence* of displays and fixtures
- *Arrangement* (formal or informal balance) of displays and fixtures
- *Width and length* of traffic aisles
- *Positioning* of merchandise groups, customer services, and other customer attractions

Three basic layout patterns are the grid, free-form, and boutique layouts. The **grid layout** is a rectangular arrangement of displays and aisles that generally run parallel to one another. Figure 7–12 is a supermarket that is utilizing a grid layout for the interior of the store; some modifications have been made to accommodate perishable products. The grid layout represents a formal arrangement in which the size and shape of display areas and the length and width of the traffic aisles are fairly homogeneous throughout the store. Although the retailer can develop various modifications to create variety and respond to operational needs, this grid pattern essentially retains its formal arrangement.

Used most frequently by supermarkets and convenience, variety, and discount stores, the grid layout offers several advantages. First, it allows the most efficient use of selling space of any of the layout patterns. Second, it simplifies shopping by creating clear, distinct traffic aisles. Third, it promotes the image of a clean, efficient shopping atmosphere. Fourth, it facilitates routine and planned shopping behaviour as well as self-service and self-selection

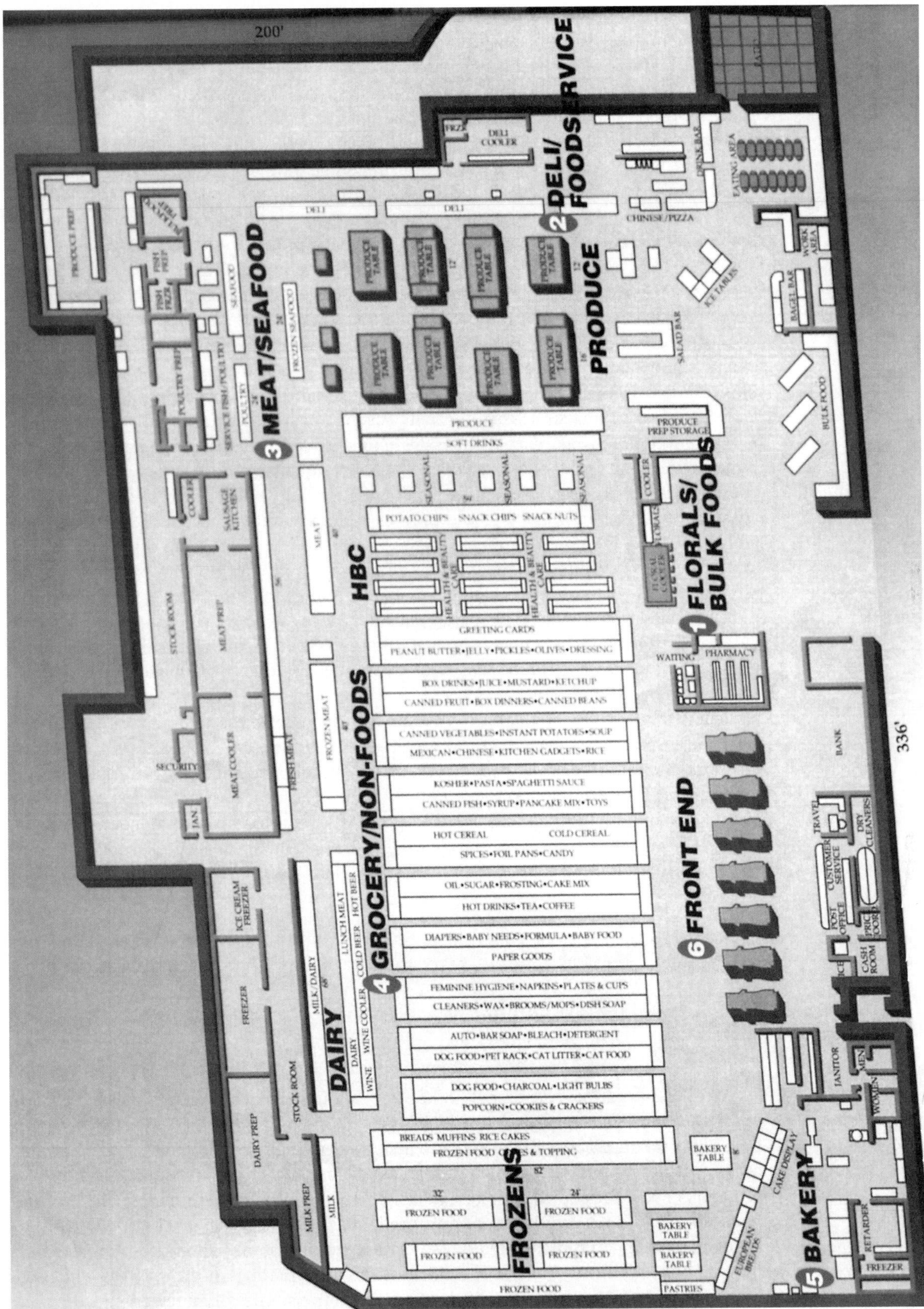

Figure 7–12

The grid layout

by creating a well-organized environment. And, finally, it allows more efficient operations by simplifying the stocking, marking, and housekeeping tasks and reduces some of the problems involved with inventory and security control. The major disadvantage of the grid layout is the sterile shopping atmosphere it creates. For this reason, the grid pattern is simply inappropriate for most shopping and specialty goods retailers.

The **free-form layout**, on the other hand, arranges displays and aisles in a free-flowing pattern. This layout employs a variety of different sizes, shapes, and styles of displays, together with fixtures positioned in an informal, unbalanced arrangement. The supermarket layout shown in Figure 7–13 represents a more free-form layout than the grid pattern illustrated in Figure 7–12.

The main benefit retailers derive from the free-form layout is the pleasant atmosphere it produces—an easygoing environment that promotes window-shopping and browsing. This comfortable environment increases the time the customer is willing to spend in the store and results in an increase in both planned and unplanned purchases. These benefits of a superior shopping atmosphere are partially offset by the increased cost of displays and fixtures, high labour requirements, additional inventory and security control problems, and the wasted selling space that normally accompany a free-form layout.

The **boutique layout** arranges the sales floor into individual, semiseparate areas, each built around a particular shopping theme. The boutique layout illustrated in Figure 7–14 shows the sales floor divided into several small specialty shops, thereby creating stores within stores.[42] By using displays and fixtures appropriate to a particular shopping theme and by stocking the boutique according to this theme, the retailer can create an unusual and interesting shopping experience. Boomers, an adult toy and gift shop, resembles a film set more than a traditional retail outlet. "Boomers is divided into 10 moveable departments or sets. Each one is completely experiential and is delineated by backdrop, lighting, audio, video, and targeted merchandise. Merchandise is arranged by theme of subject rather than by product category."[43] Boutique layouts have essentially the same advantages and disadvantages as free-form layouts.

Retailers employ several variations or modifications of these three layout patterns. A Y-shaped layout allows the retailer to divide its store on the basis of its three major merchandise groupings: sporting goods and apparel, automotive and hardware, and seasonal merchandise (for example, ski items in the winter). Kids R Us uses a circular layout with each merchandise grouping and area being clearly identified by colour-coded signs, fixtures, and carpets: blue for boys, purple for girls, and green for infants.[44] Figure 7–15 illustrates some of the more common layout variations utilized by retailers.

Visual Merchandising

Advertising may attract consumers to the store, but it is either the retailer's visual displays or sales personnel that make the sale after the consumer is in the store. "Marketing experts figure (supermarket) consumers make as many as two-thirds of all buying decisions while looking at the products on the shelves."[45] **Retail displays** are nonpersonal, in-store presentations and exhibitions of merchandise together with rated information. In practice, retail displays are used to (1) minimize product exposure, (2) enhance product appearance, (3) stimulate product interest, (4) exhibit product information, (5) facilitate sales transactions, (6) ensure product security, (7) provide product storage, (8) remind customers of planned purchases, and (9) generate additional sales of impulse items.

Retail displays are essential ingredients in creating the store's shopping atmospherics, because the sight, sound, touch, taste, and scent appeals are largely the result of in-store displays. To compete with the fashion forward presentation of specialty stores, even price-oriented retailers are stressing the need for superiority of presentation. The retailer's visual merchandising program is conceptualized in Figure 7–16.

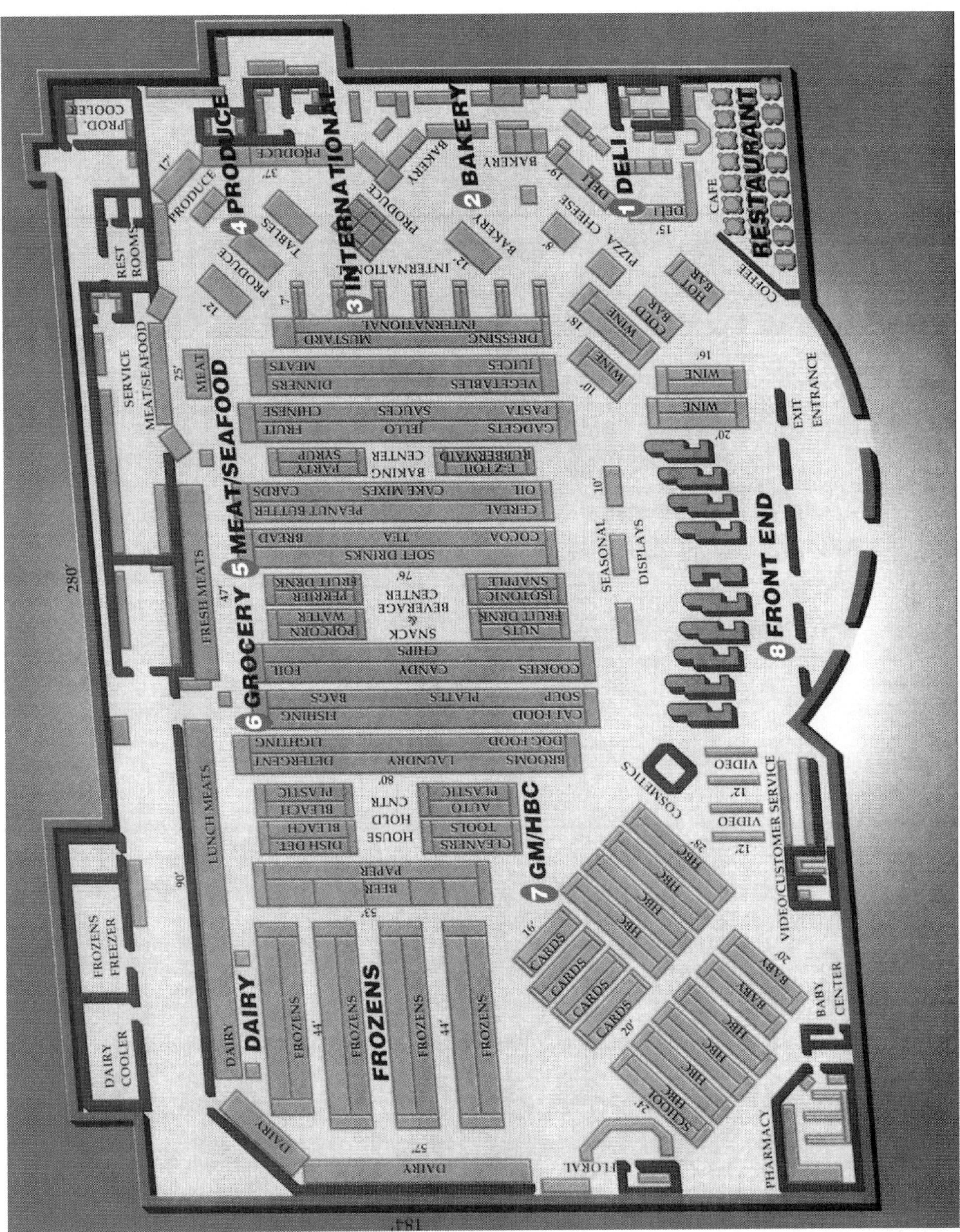

Figure 7–13

The free-form layout

Figure 7–14

The boutique layout

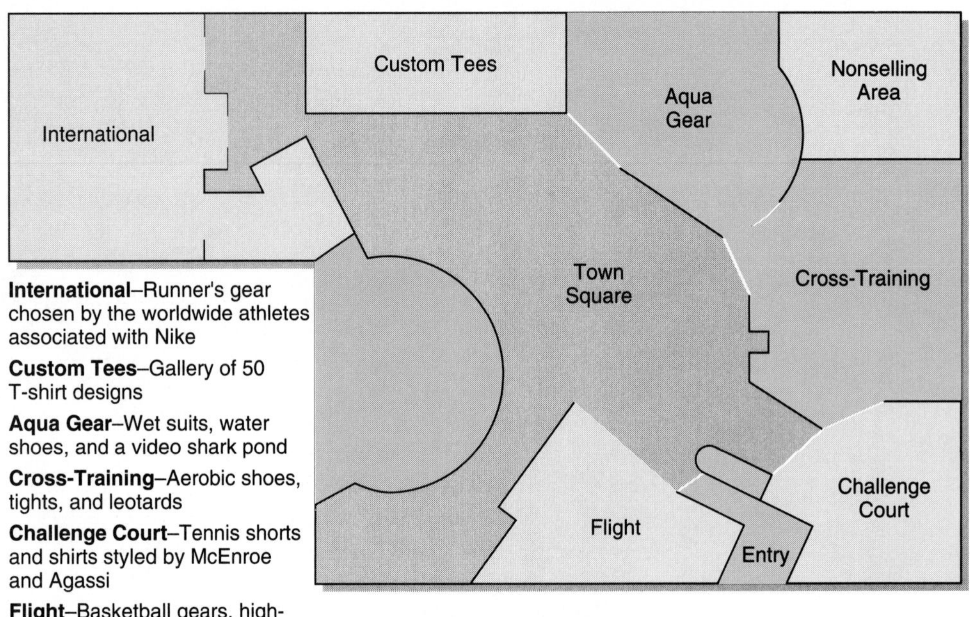

International
Custom Tees
Aqua Gear
Nonselling Area
Town Square
Cross-Training
Flight
Entry
Challenge Court
International–Runner's gear chosen by the worldwide athletes associated with Nike
Custom Tees–Gallery of 50 T-shirt designs
Aqua Gear–Wet suits, water shoes, and a video shark pond
Cross-Training–Aerobic shoes, tights, and leotards
Challenge Court–Tennis shorts and shirts styled by McEnroe and Agassi
Flight–Basketball gears, high-tops, and sleeveless jerseys

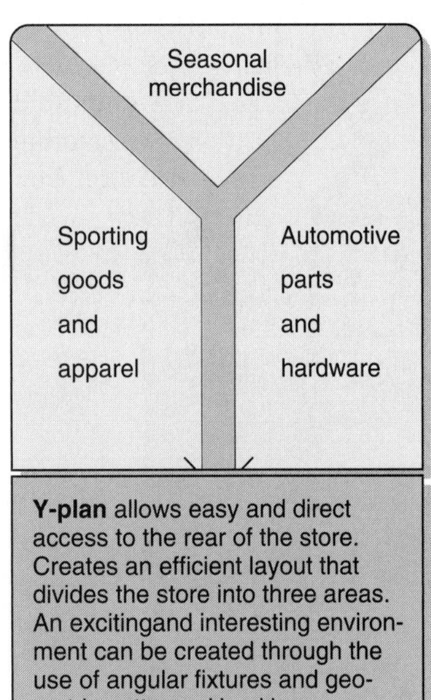

Seasonal merchandise
Sporting goods and apparel
Automotive parts and hardware
Y-plan allows easy and direct access to the rear of the store. Creates an efficient layout that divides the store into three areas. An excitingand interesting environment can be created through the use of angular fixtures and geometric patterns. Used by many department stores

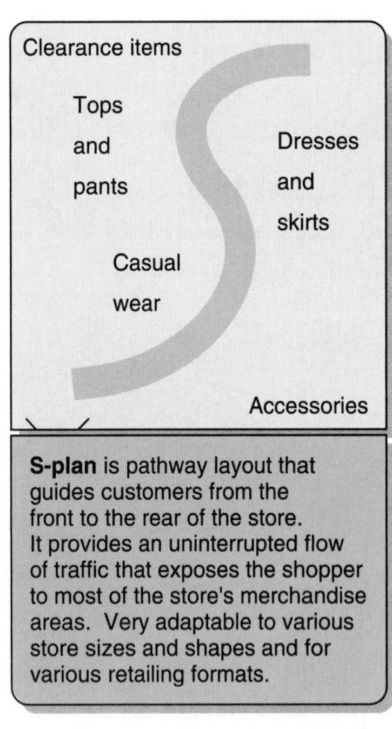

Clearance items
Tops and pants
Dresses and skirts
Casual wear
Accessories
S-plan is pathway layout that guides customers from the front to the rear of the store. It provides an uninterrupted flow of traffic that exposes the shopper to most of the store's merchandise areas. Very adaptable to various store sizes and shapes and for various retailing formats.

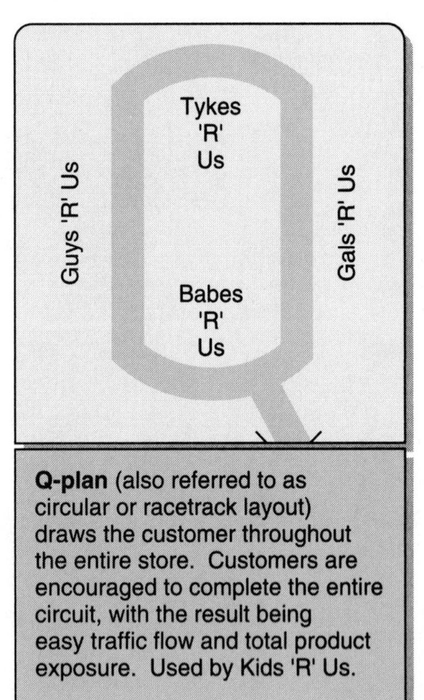

Tykes 'R' Us
Guys 'R' Us
Gals 'R' Us
Babes 'R' Us
Q-plan (also referred to as circular or racetrack layout) draws the customer throughout the entire store. Customers are encouraged to complete the entire circuit, with the result being easy traffic flow and total product exposure. Used by Kids 'R' Us.

Figure 7–15

Additional layout patterns

Display Types

Store interiors are the sums of all the displays designed to sell the retailer's merchandise. Retail displays can be classified in various ways; we identify four general types: selection, special, point-of-purchase, and audiovisual.

Selection Displays Nearly all the merchandise for which retailers rely on self-service and self-selection selling is presented to the consumer in the form of **selection displays**. These mass displays typically occupy rows of stationary aisle and wall units (that is, shelves, counters, tables, racks, and bins) designed to expose the complete assortment of merchandise to the consumer. Selection display units are generally "open" to promote merchandise inspection. Their primary functions are to provide customer access to the store's merchandise and to facilitate self-service sales transactions. As a rule, retailers use selection displays to exhibit their normal, everyday assortments of convenience and shopping goods.

Effective selection displays should present the merchandise in (1) logical selling or usage groupings; (2) a simple, well-organized arrangement; (3) a clean, neat condition; (4) an attractive, informative setting; and (5) a safe, secure state. Customer convenience and operational efficiency are the watchwords for good selection displays.

Special Displays **Special displays** are notable presentations of merchandise designed to attract special attention and make a lasting impression on the consumer. Special displays use highly desirable in-store locations, special display equipment or fixtures, and distinctive merchandise. "Shoppers may come into the store with a shopping list, but they are more likely to grab a product off an eye-catching display than to scout out a brand on the shelves. And while manufacturers are paying retailers more and more for the privilege of mounting special displays, the cost can be well worth it."[46]

Placing special displays in highly desirable locations ensures maximum exposure for the display and its merchandise, thereby significantly affecting the number of units sold. Ends of aisles, countertops, checkout stands, store entrances and exits, and freestanding units in high-traffic areas are all preferred locations for attracting special attention from shoppers. Unique combinations of display equipment (for example, counters, tables, racks, shelves, bins, mobiles) and display fixtures (for example, stands, easels, millinery heads, forms, set pieces) help create a dramatic setting that will attract consumer attention

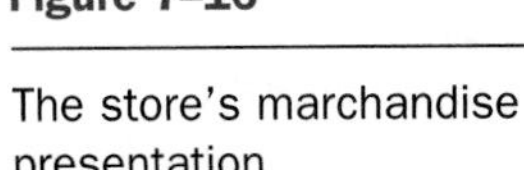

Figure 7–16

The store's marchandise presentation

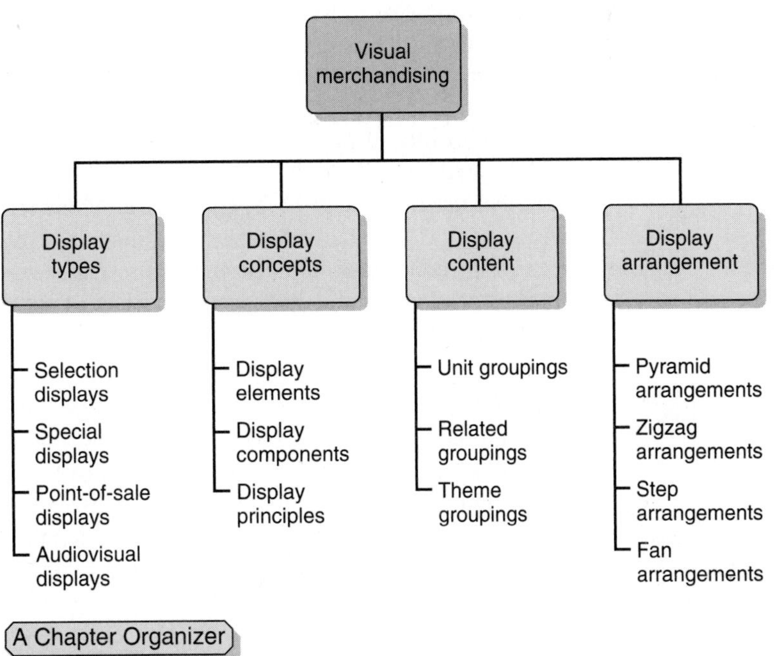

and build shopper interest. The choice of display equipment and fixtures depends on the merchandise, the amount of space available, and the effect sought.

Special displays highlight merchandise that can attract customers into the store, build the store's image, improve sales volume, or increase net profits. Special displays therefore are reserved for advertised, best-selling, high-margin, and high-fashion merchandise, together with product items suitable to impulse and complementary buying behaviour. Merchandise selected for special displays should also lend itself to good display techniques, which create favourable sight, sound, taste, touch, or scent appeal.

Point-of-Purchase Displays Retailers make heavy use of **point-of-purchase (POP)** displays to stimulate immediate purchase behaviour. They are often the first and last chance retailers and manufacturers have to tell customers about merchandise. Point-of-purchase displays include items such as counter displays, window displays, shelf extenders, grocery cart ads, floor-stand displays, dump bins, end-of-aisle stands, banners, shelf talkers, clocks, counter cards, sniff teasers, and video-screen displays.[47] They are designed to attract customer attention and interest, reinforce the store's creative theme, and fit in with the store's interior decoration.

One POP trend is toward lifestyle merchandising, which is manifesting itself as an emerging class of displays called **concept shops**. These displays create a store-within-a-store and establish an image for the brand that matches the lifestyle of the consumer. Some leading retailers are dramatically restaging their stores to address the interests of various consumer segments better, adjusting and redesigning displays by size, location, and style on the basis of research into how shoppers respond.

Translating lifestyles into displays, however, is not a simple process. Although POP displays are well suited to lifestyle marketing because they reach the consumer at the moment a decision is being made, POP has not traditionally been designed to build a brand's image. The primary purposes are to prompt an impulse purchase and reinforce an established image.

Concept shops are becoming the method of choice to achieve lifestyle marketing objectives at the retail level among a variety of trade categories. Currently, concept shops are mostly found in the domain of fashion retailing businesses. This should come as no surprise, because fashion is so integrally entwined with consumer lifestyles. The shopper is coaxed into a comfortable setting amid the general marketplace of a department store. The shopping experience becomes more directly related to the product, helps build the brand's image, and creates a relaxed atmosphere conducive to a favourable purchasing decision.

Audiovisual Displays Another trend in fashion retailing is to make a video statement by applying current technology to stimulate consumer purchases. Retailers now use visual merchandising, audio merchandising, and/or audiovisual merchandising to sell their products. Three key applications of **audiovisual merchandising** are (1) to display the depth and breadth of product lines; (2) to use kiosks to explain the benefits of different products; and (3) to provide customers with basic price information. These display approaches use technology to "speak" to and "show" the consumer available merchandise. Devices include shelf talkers (tape recordings describing the merchandise audibly); rear-screen projections (slide projectors that present wide-screen colour pictures of the merchandise and its use); and audiovisual displays (a combination of sound and videotape or slides to present the product's story).

Display Concepts

To communicate the desired message effectively, the retailer must carefully conceptualize and plan each display. Conceptually effective displays result from the blending of key display elements and components using proven display principles. Figure 7–17 illustrates all the ingredients of this blending process. The Retail Strategies and Tactics box entitled "Merchants of Boom" illustrates the importance of display.

Figure 7–17

The ingredients of a successful retail display

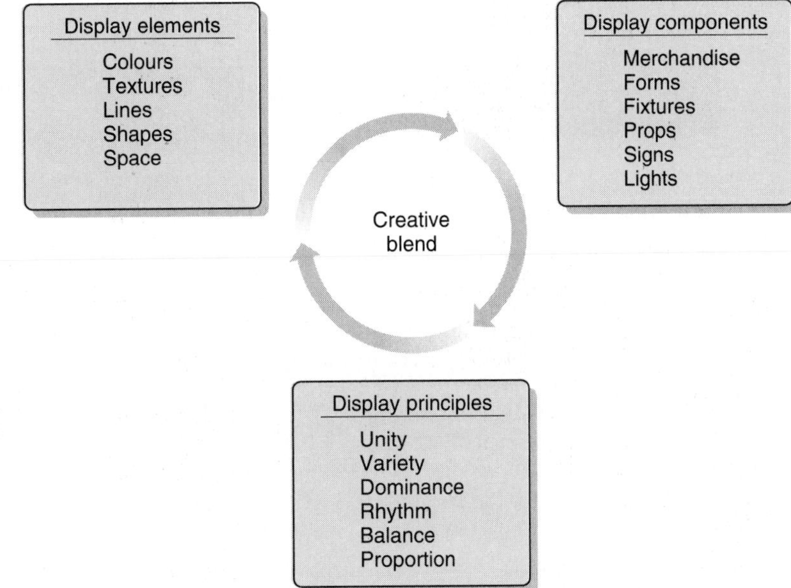

Display Elements Creating attractive displays that sell merchandise involves the careful orchestration of colour, texture, line, shape, and space. Each of these display elements are an integral part of creating the store theatrics and atmospherics discussed previously. (A review of those discussions, p. 228–232, would be useful.) Because *colour* is the first element we notice when we look at a display, it is a powerful element in creating both physical (for example, visibility) and emotional (for example, comfortable feeling) reactions. Colour is an inexpensive, versatile means of visually creating mood and drama in the presentation of merchandise. "Warm colours (reds, oranges, and yellows) physically attract customers to shop. On the other hand, cool colours (blues, greens, and violets) are more appropriate for areas where customers will be deliberating over a big-ticket purchase such as a fur coat. Colour used properly can attract the eye of the potential customer, create the desired mood, and stimulate the viewer to make a purchase decision."[48]

Texture is the basic scheme or structure of the materials that make up the display itself or the merchandise being displayed. Texture is two-dimensional in that it appeals to both the senses of touch and sight. Marble, iron, oak wood, cut glass, plastic, and fabric can be used to create an attractive backdrop for merchandise that has its own texture. For example, the smooth texture of marble combined with the rough, multifaceted character of cut glass can set a rich and interesting textural context within which to display high-end merchandise. Although texture is less dominant than colour when it comes to attracting the customer's attention, its subtle nature is a key element in cultivating the shopper's continuing interest and inspection of the display and its merchandise.

Straight and curved *lines* are instrumental in guiding the viewer's eye and creating a variety of perceptions. Effective displays have a dominance of one type of line (for example, straight diagonal line) yet use other types of lines as well to add interest through a hint of diversity. *Shapes* (circles, ovals, triangles, rectangles, squares, and so on) are the result of connected lines, and each shape has the ability to evoke certain emotions and perceptions. *Space* is the area or distance between displays or the objects within a display. Consumers tend to associate open space with greater freedom and richer environments. Spacious displays and in-store display areas are thought to be more appropriate when merchandising expensive merchandise to upscale consumers who want more privacy in making their selections. Cluttered displays and crowded display areas are perceived as being more exciting and aggressive environments; therefore, the belief is that this type of closeness is suited to creating a buying atmosphere for such price-oriented formats as discount stores and off-price retailers. There is a point, however, when cluttered displays and cramped shopping areas will discourage even the most aggressive bargain hunter. (See

Retail Strategies and Tactics

Merchants of Boom

Some of Canada's best retailers are regional players who specialize in niche markets, yet understand the benefits of large-format locations. Mountain Equipment Co-operative (MEC) is a case in point. The Vancouver-based outdoor equipment and clothing supplier has a mailing list of 925 000 loyal customers, all of whom have bought a mandatory $5 share in the co-op for the privilege of buying its products. MEC's sales have skyrocketed by 285% in the past five years. The co-op sells a large array of goods aimed at the weekend adventurer, everything from $4 polypropylene socks to $4600 folding kayaks. The typical MEC shopper is likely to be any one of the following: young, well-educated and affluent, with an average household income of more than $100 000.

Although the co-op has decided against moving into new territory, it has embarked on some major improvements to its existing network. Anyone who has ever shopped at MEC during the peak Christmas holiday season can probably recall standing in a long lineup at the cash register. After years of waffling, MEC recently opened brand new, large format stores in Vancouver and Calgary, each featuring 30 000 square feet [approximately 2800 m^2] of showroom space and larger storerooms equipped with modern inventory-tracking technology, which has helped eliminate the problem of being caught out of stock. Its five-year-old Ottawa store is likely to be moved to a better location when the current lease expires at the end of the decade. And relief is finally in sight for MEC shoppers in Toronto, who have been bumping elbows in its crowded, 18 000 sq. ft. [approximately 1700 m^2] store on Front Street since the location opened for business in 1985. A new, 30 000-sq.-ft. [approximately 2800 m^2] store, to be built just a stone's throw from the SkyDome, will also feature the added benefit of underground parking.

Source: Brian Hutchinson, Canadian Business, *May 1997, 40.*

"Store Aesthetics," p. 236, for a discussion on size perceptions in conjunction with store aesthetics.)

Display Components Display elements come to life with the selection of each component. Display components include the merchandise to be displayed, the forms or fixtures on which the merchandise is to be displayed, and the props, signs, and lights that enhance the display's effectiveness.

The focus of any display is the merchandise. Every aspect of a display should be designed to complement, not compete with, the presentation of the merchandise. The colours, sizes, and shapes of the display's forms, fixtures, props, and signs must be selected to demonstrate the best features of the products to be highlighted in the display.

Forms consist of various types of human-shaped presentation vehicles, including the following:

- **Mannequins**—Presentation vehicles made in a variety of human forms based on age, sex, race, body type, and so on. Used individually or in groups, mannequins display apparel and accessories often within a theme setting.
- **Partial forms**—Presentation vehicles that consist of certain parts of the human body (for example, upper body, heads, arms, legs). Partial forms are used in displays with limited space and that are focused on a specific apparel item.
- **Body forms**—Presentation vehicles made from a variety of materials (for example, rattan, chrome, plastic, wood) that are general representations of the body. Body forms range from wood stickmen to chrome T-bars to plastic clothes-hanger shapes.

Fixtures are physical structures designed to display and hold merchandise. They are also used to direct customer store traffic, provide sales floor storage, and partition the sale floor into merchandise areas. Store fixtures are grouped into two categories: hanging and non-hanging.[49]

To enhance the store theatrics, retail displays use several types of *props*—any object that enhances the visual presentation, decorates the display, and accents the merchandise. Props might include flowers or fruit, furniture or wall hangings, sporting equipment or luggage, books or records, and anything else that is appropriate to the display's theme.

Signs use words, symbols, and graphics as a means of in-store communications. Signs (1) give directions, (2) identify locations, (3) provide information, (4) create images, and (5) announce events.[50] To make their menu boards more readable, McDonald's has colour-coded them: Breakfast items are signed in yellow, lunch and dinner sandwiches in red, and beverages in blue.[51] Professionalism and creativeness in the design and construction of store signage as well as appropriateness and compatibility with the other aspects of the store's internal design are all part of a successful signage program.

Store *lighting* involves controlling and balancing the degree of lightness or darkness of both the display area and the display itself; it can be categorized into three distinct phases: primary, secondary, and atmospheric.[52] *Primary lighting* supplies the bare essentials of store illumination; typically fluorescent lighting is used. Too much primary lighting frequently creates a harsh visual environment, whereas a store that is poorly lit begets a gloomy atmosphere. *Secondary lighting* is used to attract customer attention to a display and highlight selected merchandise features within a display; it involves the use of spotlights and floodlights to brighten shelves, cases, counters, wall units, and racks. *Atmospheric lighting* involves playing light against shadow to create special effects. For example, it is used to (1) alter the size or shape of the store or display area, (2) hide undesirable store features, (3) focus attention on one feature area, and (4) distinguish one merchandise area (for example, intensely lit toy department) from another (for example, muted menswear department). Store designers use atmospheric lighting to create a sense of theatre. In fact, many of the lighting techniques (such as colour filters, pinpoint spotlights, black lighting) used in live theatrical performances are employed by the store planner in creating the right mood for each merchandise department or display.

Display Principles

Effective blending of the display elements and components is accomplished through the application of several proven principles of display: unit, variety, dominance, rhythm, balance, and proportion.

Unity. Unity is the right combination or ordering of elements and components within a display that promotes an undivided total effect. Displays are more effective when there is a certain level of unification among all display elements (colour, line, texture, shape, and space) and components (merchandise, forms, fixtures, props, signs, and lighting). Display themes based on times, people, places, causes, events, styles, or any other idea are the most effective means for building unity into the retailer's displays. Repetition of a display element (for example, the colour red, a slanted line) and/or component (for example, a certain style mannequin) helps strengthen the display's unity.

Variety. To avoid too much unity, the store planner introduces **variety** by using different elements and/or components in the display. Variety adds interest by creating some contrast. Although the principle of unity must prevail throughout the display so that the viewer understands the organizational structure, variety is necessary to attract and hold the viewer's attention. For example, a repetition of seven black blazers on partial body forms with gray undershells could be contrasted with a few white blouses displayed on tubular body forms. Displaying one small merchandise item with several large items or a single round shape with numerous square shapes is another variety-creating idea.

Dominance. Attractive displays have a centre of attention, or **dominance**, to which the viewer's eye is drawn and held.[53] Without a dominant display feature, the shopper's eye will be attracted elsewhere, and the display does not communicate its sales message effectively. A display element (for example, red) or component (for example, merchandise) is made dominant by subordinating all other elements and components. A red shirt could become the dominant focus of the display by placing it over several black shirts. An accessory (such as a tie) becomes the dominant item on a dressed mannequin if a spotlight is used to pinpoint the item. Dominance within a display enables the retailer to emphasize a single promotional message or focus on a direct purchase incentive.

Rhythm. **Rhythm** refers to the path that the viewer's eye follows when viewing a display. Displays that have good rhythm are those that can hold eye contact until the entire display is inspected. Display rhythm is created by (1) repetition of shapes, (2) progression of sizes, (3) continuous line movement, and (4) radiation. The "lay of interrupted patterns" states that in any situation in which there is a disruption of a prevailing pattern, the eyes move immediately to the break in that pattern.[54] Hence, by breaking the rhythm of a display, the retailer can call attention to a particular product item or items. Figure 7–18 illustrates each of these four means for creating rhythm within a retail display.

Balance. To be an attractive and comfortable experience, a retail display should exhibit a sense of equilibrium, or **balance**, among all elements and components of the display. A balanced display is one in which each part has equal visual weight. Balance can be achieved in either a formal or informal sense. Formal balance is created when both sides of a display are exactly alike in terms of type, size, colour, shape, and placement of objects; each side is a mirror image of the other side. Formal balance creates a restrained, traditional, and conservative atmosphere. Such displays are a comfortable visual experience. A formal balance would be appropriate for a display of men's suits and accessories or fine china settings in the table setting department. Informal balance gives equal visual weight to both sides of the display through the use of objects that are different in terms of type, size, colour, shape, and placement. These displays tend to be more interesting because of the variety in the visual experience. They also convey more action and so can better attract the customer's attention. However, if the display is too informal or unbalanced, it will become confusing and create visual discomfort that discourages continued shopper inspection.

Proportion. **Proportion** is the relative share of each display element or display component with respect to other elements and components and to the display as a whole (for example, how much red is used in the display as opposed to black, what the display

Figure 7–18

Creating rhythm within a retail display

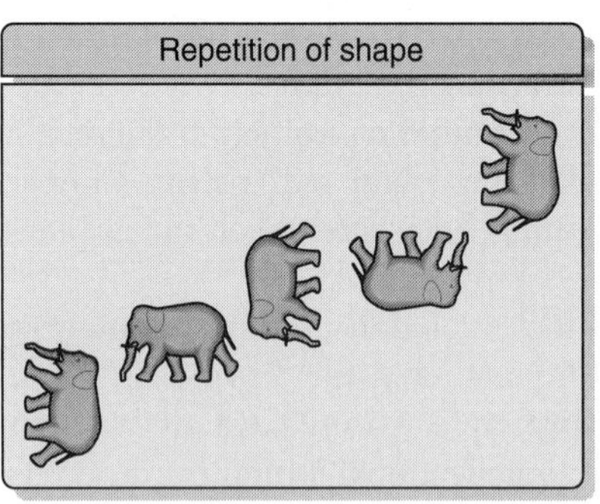

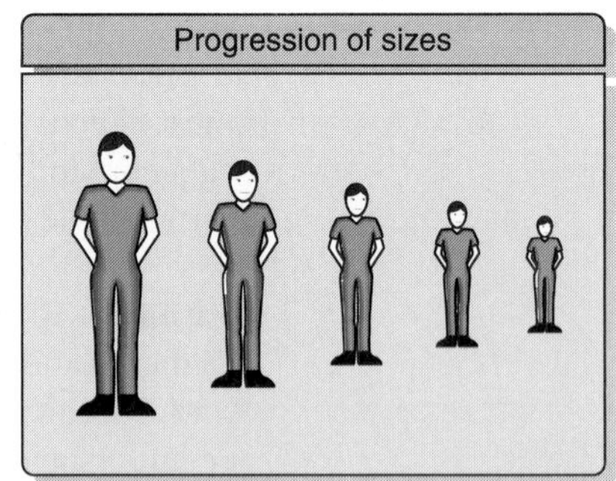

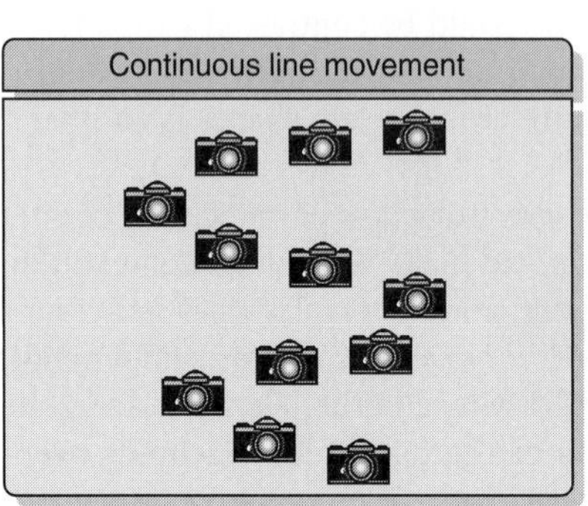

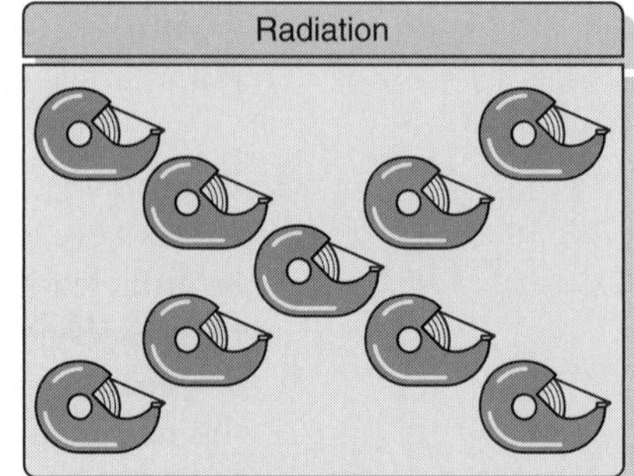

merchandise/display props ratio is). Expressed differently, proportion is the effective arrangement of parts of the display in terms of

- space—the amount of open space relative to closed space;
- shape—the number of round objects relative to square objects;
- colour—the extent of dark shades relative to light shades;
- size—the quantity of small objects relative to large objects;
- texture—the area of rough surface relative to the area of smooth surface;
- forms—the number of full-figure mannequins relative to the number of partial forms; and
- light—the degree of lighted area relative to the degree of shadowy area.

As is the case with displays that have formal balance, well-proportioned displays create a formal, quiet atmosphere. Disproportional displays are used to create interest in the display itself or to some part of the display; it is an effective means of directing and focusing the shopper's attention.

Display Content

Display content is the type and amount of merchandise to be set off. Consumers do not judge a product just on the basis of its intrinsic properties; they also judge it in relation to the context in which it was found.[55] Cluttered displays of unrelated merchandise attract little attention and are ineffective in stimulating customer interest. To ensure good display content, many retailers confine their efforts to one of three groupings: unit, related, or theme.

Unit Groupings **Unit groupings** of merchandise highlight a separate category of product items (for example, shoes, shirts, cocktail dresses, handbags). They contain merchandise that is almost identical (such as, five black leather handbags of different sizes) or closely related (such as three red leather handbags and five brown suede bags). If a single vendor is featured in unit grouping displays, it is often referred to as a *vendor statement*.

Related Groupings **Related groupings** are ensemble displays that present accessory items along with the featured merchandise. For example, a mannequin may be dressed in a matching tennis outfit with a tennis racket and bag. The principal idea behind the inclusion of accessory items is to remind the customer of a need for more than the featured item; in other words, the retailer is using suggestive selling. In its renovation program supporting the "Softer Side of Sears" theme, Sears' new display fixtures are designed to carry a complete outfit and some accessories.[56] A display of either unit or related groupings should contain an odd number of product items. Consumers perceive an odd number of items as more intriguing; hence, the items attract more attention and create a more dramatic setting. When displaying an even number of merchandise items (for example, a set of eight stemmed glasses), it is recommended that one item be set apart from the rest or differentiated in some other way (such as elevated).

Theme Groupings Merchandise displayed in **theme groupings** or settings is sometimes referred to as "presentational theatre." Themes provide a focus in planning displays and are useful vehicles around which the five sensory appeals can be employed. The number of possible display themes is unlimited. For example, there are product themes ("Shoes complete the appearance"), seasonal themes ("Swing into spring"), patronage themes ("Cheaper by the dozen"), usage themes ("Mealtime magic"), occasion themes ("Along the bridal path"), colour themes ("Pastel softness"), lifestyle themes ("The swinging singles set"), holiday themes ("Santa approved") as well as themes based on historic, current, and special events. IKEA's concept store is organized around thematic displays of merchandise—for example, "IKEA cooks" and "IKEA plays."[57]

Display Arrangement

Display arrangement is organizing display merchandise into interesting, pleasing, and stimulating patterns. Haphazard arrangement of merchandise items can substantially reduce a display's effectiveness. Selection displays are simply arranged in some well-organized fashion, but special-display merchandise frequently is presented in one of four definite arrangement patterns: the pyramid, zigzag, step, or fan arrangement (see Figure 7–19).

Pyramid Arrangements The **pyramid arrangement** is a triangular display of merchandise in vertical (stacked) or horizontal (unstacked) form. "The pyramid begins at a large or broad base and progresses up to an apex, or point, at the highest level."[58] The vertical pyramid can be two- or three-dimensional and is well suited to displaying boxed and canned merchandise; it also represents efficient use of space. The base of a horizontal pyramid is placed in the rear of the display to achieve the proper visual perspective. When displaying different-sized merchandise items, larger items are positioned at the base, and the smallest item occupies the apex. Figure 7–19a illustrates the use of pedestal displayers arranged in a pyramid fashion—an effective arrangement pattern for window, counter, and table displays.

Zigzag Arrangements The **zigzag arrangement** is a modified pyramid that zigzags its way to the apex of the display. No two display levels are at the same height. This arrangement is less monotonous than the pyramid; it is perceived to be more fluid, graceful, and perhaps more feminine. A zigzag pattern of pedestal displayers (such as the one shown in Figure 7–19b) is especially appropriate for displaying women's jewellery, cosmetics, small apparel items, and shoes.

Step Arrangements A **step arrangement** is constructed as a series of steps. "Step arrangements lead the eye in a direct line; they begin at a low point on one side of a display area and progress directly to a higher point on the opposite side of that area."[59] Typically, step displays are constructed so that the base of each step increases in area (see Figure 7–19c); the larger base area is used for displaying accessory items, while the steps are used for the featured merchandise. The step arrangement is well suited for a wide variety of merchandise.

Figure 7–19

A gallery of display arrangements: (a) pyramid, (b) zigzag, (c) step, and (d) fan

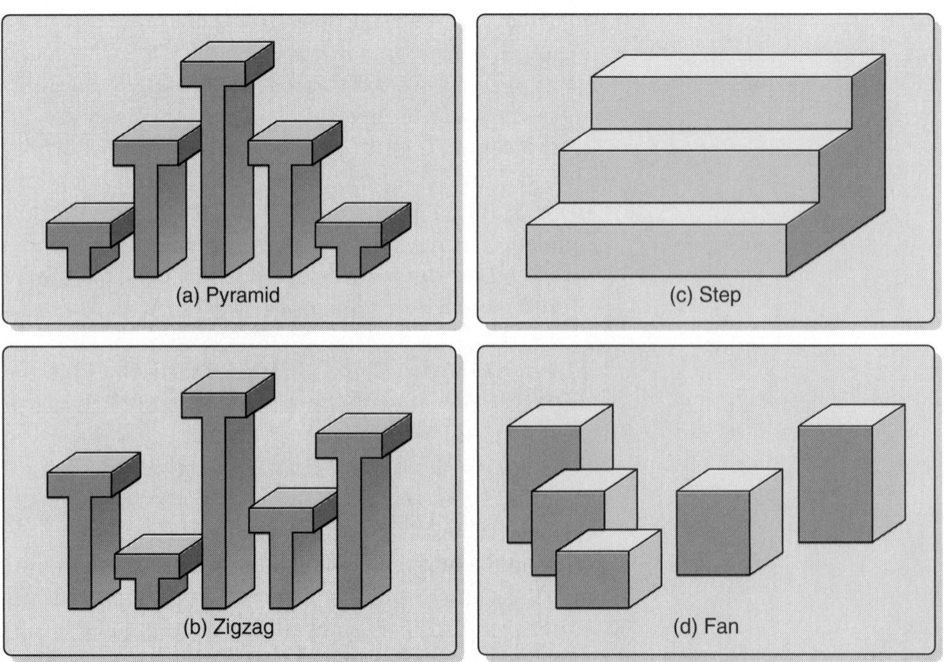

Fan Arrangements A **fan arrangement** is spread up and out from a small base, like an inverted pyramid, thereby directing the viewer's eyes upward and outward (see Figure 7–19d).[60] The fan pattern is appropriate for displaying merchandise ranging from clothing goods to sporting goods.

Store Security

Customer theft, customer fraud, employee theft, supplier theft, and felony theft are everyday facts of life that every retailer must face and protect itself against. It is estimated that Canadian retailers lost $4 billion in 1996 to these causes.[61] Collectively, protective measures against these acts are called *store security*, which must include not only the store and its merchandise but also its customers and employees. This section describes how a retailer can detect and prevent many of the losses resulting from criminal activities such as shoplifting by customers, pilferage by employees and suppliers, passing of bad cheques and credit cards, and thefts by burglary and robbery. Although estimates vary greatly, about five cents out of every dollar spent in a retail store goes to cover the losses resulting from these criminal activities and the security measures used to prevent them. Figure 7–20 outlines the issues discussed in this section. The Retail Strategies and Tactics box looks at how some Canadian retailers deal with the security issue.

Customer Theft

Shoplifting is the act of pilfering merchandise from a store display by customers and individuals posing as customers. To *pilfer* is to commit or practise petty theft. This can account for over 40 percent[62] of all stock losses the retailer suffers. Unfortunately for the store's customers, retail prices must be set high enough to cover these losses. Triggering increases in pilferage are larger store formats, lower staffing levels, higher employee turnover, and less employee training and supervision; each of these trends contributes to a greater opportunity to steal.

Shoplifting occurs in three basic ways: (1) outright theft of merchandise, (2) alteration of the retailer's price tag to reflect a lower price, and (3) switching or substituting a lower price tag for the original tag. Shoplifters fall into two general categories: the amateur who steals to satisfy physical or psychological needs and the professional who steals for a living.

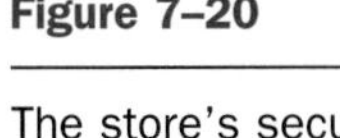

Figure 7–20

The store's security

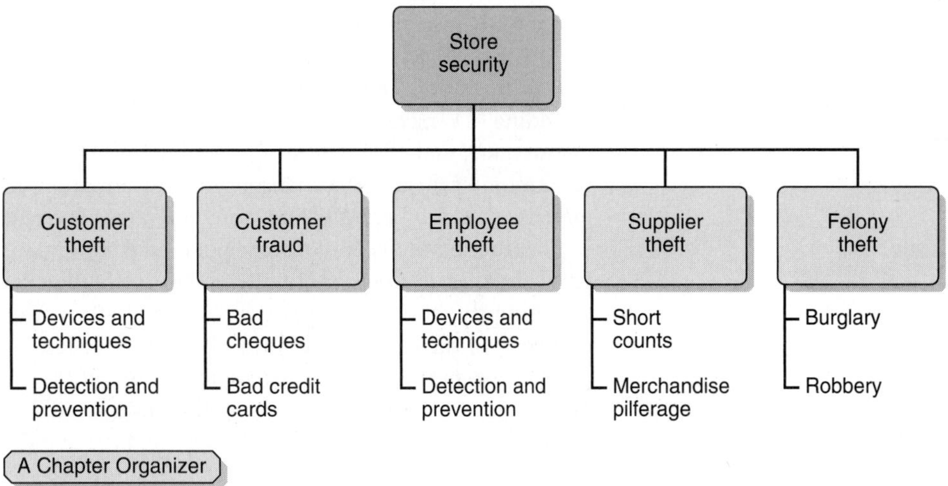

Retail Strategies and Tactics

More Humane Than Cutting Off Hands

The Retail Council of Canada says shoplifting cost its members slightly more than $2 billion in 1995. That's bad news for consumers too, since most retailers build a proportion of their losses into the prices they charge. But several more retailers, including the Hudson's Bay Co. and its offshoot Zellers Inc., are making a determined effort to turn back the tide by adopting a policy now widely accepted in the U.S.—making shoplifters pay civil damages.

Since 1994 the Bay has been demanding financial compensation from people accused of shoplifting from its stores, threatening to take shoplifters to civil court if they refuse. While a large number have paid up, hundreds have not. The first among the latter group are now being hauled before small-claims courts across Canada in what amounts to a series of test cases for the policy. Brian Lawrie, president of ACLAiM Civil Loss Recovery Systems Inc., the company hired as the Bay's civil loss recoverer, is optimistic. "Our lawyers are confident we can win," he says.

Repeated requests for comment from the Bay and Zellers went unanswered. But Lawrie, a former Metro Toronto police officer, says making shoplifters pay helps to defray his clients' security costs and, according to U.S. data, effectively deters repeat offenders. The process begins when a store calls police in, Lawrie says. A letter is sent to offenders—or parents, if the shoplifters are kids—telling them they can prevent a civil action by paying a "settlement amount." This is usually $325, but may be higher if the initial fine isn't paid; in cases where several children are involved, the firm demands $225 from each family. If shoplifters don't pay up, they get a second letter warning of court action, which is followed by a statement of claim.

Source: Canadian Business, *June 1996, 34.*

Retail Council of Canada
www.retailcouncil.org/welcome/welcome.html

Devices and Techniques The amateur and the professional use a variety of devices in shoplifting. The main purpose of shoplifting devices is to conceal both the actual act of stealing and the merchandise after it has been stolen. Shoplifting devices include various types of clothing (for example, coats, "booster" panties, wide-top boots, other loose-fitting garments) and parcels (for example, booster boxes; purses; umbrellas; newspapers; magazines; shopping, school, and knitting bags).

Shoplifters use several techniques in their pilfering activities. The **booster** is a shoplifter who shoves merchandise into concealed areas of parcels and/or clothing. Booster boxes are carefully constructed boxes that appear to be authentic, tightly wrapped packages but contain trap doors that enable the shoplifter to slip merchandise into the box quickly and easily. Other booster devices are *booster hooks and bags* securely fastened to the inside of a large, bulky coat; the shoplifter simply slips merchandise onto the hooks or into the bags and walks away. Some shoplifters use *booster coats* constructed to conceal merchandise. Still others wear *booster panties*, loose-fitting bloomers that are fastened tightly around the knees and worn under bulky clothing. The shoplifter drops merchandise into them at the waist.

The **diverter** is one member of a team of shoplifters who attempts to divert the attention of the store's personnel while a partner shoplifts. Diverters use several techniques, including (1) engaging the salesperson in conversation, (2) creating an attention-grabbing disturbance, and (3) requesting merchandise that requires the salesperson to go to the stockroom. If the diverter manages to draw attention, the shoplifter partner can obtain the merchandise and be out of the store before anyone realizes what has happened.

Obstructing the vision of store personnel while they or a partner shoplift is the principal technique of **blockers**. In a team effort, the blocker simply stands between the salesperson and a shoplifting partner. Working alone, the blocker might employ a topcoat draped over the arm to shield the shoplifting activities of the other hand.

The **sweeper** simply brushes merchandise off the counter into a shopping bag or some other type of container. Typically, sweepers reach over a counter, apparently to examine a piece of merchandise, but in the process of bringing the arm back, sweep merchandise off the counter and into the container.

Other shoplifters have perfected the technique of walking naturally while carrying concealed merchandise between their legs. The **walker** is usually a woman. Shoplifters who have developed this skill are capable of carrying, in a completely natural way, both small items such as jewellery and large items such as small appliances.

The **wearer** tries on merchandise, then wears it out of the store. The *open wearer* is a bold shoplifter who tries on a hat, coat, or some other piece of clothing, removes the tags, and then openly wears it while shopping and exiting the store. It is the boldness of this technique that makes it successful. *Under-wearers* steal clothing items by wearing them under their own loose outerwear. The most common technique is to take several items into the fitting room but return fewer to the racks.

Several other shoplifting techniques also are used by both amateur and professional shoplifters. The **carrier** walks in, picks up a large piece of merchandise, removes the tags, affixes a fake sales slip, and walks out. **Self-wrappers** use their own wrapping paper to wrap store merchandise before removing it from the store. The **price changer** pays for the merchandise but only after taking a shoplifter's reduction by altering or switching the store's price tag or removing the store tag and substituting a realistic fake. The **spoiler** is an individual who purposely damages merchandise, then takes it to the store manager to obtain a markdown; in essence, the customer is attempting to steal the difference between the full price and the customer-induced markdown price. Finally, the **returner** is a shoplifter who uses the store he or she shoplifts from as a fence; that is, they steal the merchandise then return it for a refund. The returner's activities are why a "no receipt, no refund" policy makes good security sense for most retailers.

Detection and Prevention The retailer's security program should include both shoplifting detection and shoplifting prevention measures. Detecting shoplifters is largely a matter of good observation. Training store employees to be better observers increases the chances of not only detecting actual shoplifting activities but also discouraging potential shoplifters. To facilitate observation and detection, many retailers use devices such as mirrors, observation towers, closed-circuit television, and electronic bugs. A recent study found that 18 percent of Canadian retailers use EAS (electronic article surveillance) and an increasing number are utilizing CCTV (closed-circuit television) to apprehend shoplifters.[63]

Prevention is the best way to control losses from shoplifting.[64] While some retailers employ door guards, floor walkers, and mechanical detection devices, the best prevention measures are well-trained, observant employees. Store employees should (1) be aware of all individuals in their areas of responsibility, (2) maintain a high profile in terms of visibility, (3) be alert to the actions of others in the department, (4) be available to assist customers, and (5) keep displays neatly organized so that theft detection is made easier. There are several mechanical and electrical devices that assist store personnel in their theft prevention responsibilities. One such device is "micro locks," which allow the customer to inspect the merchandise (for example, sunglasses and watches) but discourages theft by interfering with thieves' ability to use the product.[65]

Approaching, apprehending, and prosecuting an individual for shoplifting is a tricky business. Provincial and local laws differ regarding the apprehension and prosecution of shoplifters. Store personnel should be trained in the correct policies and procedures for handling shoplifting situations.

Customer Fraud

Customer fraud is an act of deceiving the retailer by misrepresenting oneself for purposes of obtaining money or merchandise. Bad cheques and credit cards are the most common forms of customer fraud.

Bad Cheques A retailer security program must include safeguards against accepting worthless cheques and appropriate procedures for recovering losses resulting from such exchanges. Bad cheques can be stolen and falsely endorsed, written on bank accounts with insufficient funds, and written on nonexistent or closed bank accounts.

It is virtually impossible to avoid some bad checques. Through proper detection and prevention measures, however, the retailer can keep bad-cheque losses at a minimum. By carefully examining each check for not only fraudulent information but simple, honest mistakes in writing, the retailer can help avoid accepting cheques that are intentionally or unintentionally bad. After determining that the cheque is OK, it is then necessary to determine whether the customer offering the cheque is the right person. No cheque should be accepted without proper identification. Many retailers require at least two pieces of acceptable identification, such as driver's licences, automobile registration cards, credit cards, and employment identification cards.

The retailer should establish a system that clearly states cheque-cashing policies. Employees and customers alike should be informed of the types of cheques that are acceptable and the conditions under which the retailer will accept them. With a registration system, retailers request that their customers register identification information at some prior time with the store's credit or customer service office. When registered, the customer receives a cheque-cashing ID card. All pertinent information regarding the customer is gathered at the time of registration and verified by the central office. When paying by cheque, the customer simply shows the ID to the salesclerk, who records the ID number on the cheque and compares the cheque signature with the ID signature.

The increase in cheque writing (and cheque fraud) has caused a miniboom for cheque verification and guarantee companies (such as Electronic Transaction Corporation, Computer Cheque). By sharing bad-cheque information, retailers and others create an electronic network through which the retailer can check on or verify the status and acceptability of an individual presenting a cheque for payment.[66]

Bad Credit Cards Sales charged to stolen, fictitious, cancelled, and expired credit cards cause substantial losses for retailers each year. To reduce these costs, a good policy for retailers is to exercise as much care in accepting credit cards as in cashing cheques. In accepting both third-party credit cards (bank cards, entertainment cards, and so on) and the store's own credit cards, retailers are now using various commercial electronic credit card verification systems.[67]

Employee Theft

The Retail Council of Canada estimates that employee theft represents serious losses for many retailers, accounting for approximately 30 percent of all inventory shortages.[68] It is not uncommon for losses from employee theft to exceed those from all other forms of theft. Perhaps the single most important factor contributing to these losses is the retailer's belief that trusted employees do not and will not steal. Employee pilferage takes one of three forms: theft of merchandise, property, or money. Opportunity and need are the two most commonly cited factors responsible for the dishonesty of employees.

Devices and Techniques Like most thieves, the employee who pilfers money and/or merchandise develops definite patterns or modes of operation. Using these operational modes, profiles can be developed that characterize the typical methods of employee pilferage.

The **eater** is the employee who samples the retailer's food and beverage lines or supplements his or her lunch with a soft drink or dessert. Unfortunately, what starts out as a free snack often leads to a six-course feast. For the food store, restaurant, and cocktail lounge, the eater (or drinker) can literally eat up the profits.

The **smuggler** is the employee who takes merchandise out of the store by whatever means are available. Many retailers might be surprised to learn how much merchandise is carried out the back door in trash cans and bags. The smuggler also uses coats, lunch boxes, purses, and various other types of bags and packages to conceal and transport merchandise from the store's premises.

The **discounter** feels entitled to give unauthorized discounts to friends and relatives. By charging $10 for a $16 pair of slacks, the employee may satisfy a "special" customer but certainly not at a profit for the retailer. Other employees give their friends and relatives unauthorized discounts with free merchandise or "two for one" sales. The friend or relative who receives two for the price of one is sure to spread the word among other friends and relatives. Before long, the employee is in a compromising position with few alternatives other than to quit the job.

The **dipper** is the store employee who steals money by dipping into the cash register or mishandles cash in some other way, such as making short rings, fraudulent refunds, or false employee discounts. A *short ring* occurs when the employee fails to ring a sale on the cash register or rings less than the purchase amount. In either case, the employee pockets whatever money is left over from the transaction. The *fraudulent refund* involves writing up refund tickets for merchandise that has not been returned and pocketing the entire amount of the refund. To use this method the dipper must have access to refund slips and the authority to issue refunds. False *employee discounts* also allow the dipper to pilfer cash; the employee simply rings up a regular customer sale as an employee discount sale and pockets the difference.

The **embezzler** is most often a highly trusted employee who takes advantage of that trust to divert the retailer's funds for either permanent or temporary use. Some of the simpler embezzlement schemes are (1) adding the names of relatives or fictitious employees to the payroll and collecting "their" multiple paycheques; (2) creating dummy suppliers and falsifying purchase orders, then collecting for fictitious shipments; (3) accepting kickbacks from suppliers for inflated purchases; (4) padding expense accounts; (5) falsifying overtime records; and (6) using company supplies and facilities for personal use.

The **partner** is a store employee who does not actually pilfer the merchandise or money but supplies outside individuals with information (such as security procedures) or devices (such as keys) that increase the likelihood of successful theft. In return, the store employee receives a cut of the pilfered merchandise.

The **stasher** is the store employee who hides merchandise in a secure place inside the store. Later in the selling season, when the merchandise is marked down for clearance, the employee removes the stashed merchandise from its hiding place and purchases it at the discount price. Essentially, the store employee has pilfered the difference between the original price of the merchandise and the discounted price.

Detection and Prevention To combat employee pilferage, the retailer's security program should include (1) creating a high-security atmosphere, (2) using security personnel, and (3) establishing security policies.

High-Security Atmosphere. One of the most effective methods of controlling employee theft is to create a general store atmosphere in which not even the slightest degree of dishonesty is tolerated and honesty and integrity are rewarded. The first step in creating a high-security atmosphere is to stop employee theft before it starts by carefully screening employees before they are hired and properly training them after they are employed. The second step is for management to set the example. By engaging in dishonest or questionable behaviour, the manager sets the tone for an atmosphere that can lead to employee pilferage. A third step is to create a work environment that is free from unnecessary temptation. Establishing and enforcing good security policies can substantially reduce opportunities for employee theft. Finally, an important step toward creating a security atmosphere is to establish an environment that makes employees feel like trusted and respected members of a team. Recently, the BiWay chain, which is part of the Dylex group of companies, embarked on an improved security and surveillance system in order to reduce a shrinkage problem which was at 4 percent of sales—twice the industry average. This system included a better security store atmosphere.[69]

Bi Way
www.biway.com

Security Personnel. To detect, discourage, and prevent employees from pilfering, some retailers use several types of security personnel. Stationing **uniformed guards** at employee entrances/exits and requiring employees to check in and out of the store reduce opportunities for removing merchandise from the store. The threat of search on a random basis can serve as a major deterrent to employee theft. Retailers also use **undercover shoppers** to check on the honesty of employees. Posing as a legitimate customer, an undercover shopper can often detect the activities of the eater, the discounter, and the dipper. By informing store employees that such undercover security personnel are present in the store, the retailer has activated an effective preventive measure. Additional security measures include **silent witness programs**, which reward employees with cash for anonymous tips on theft activities of other employees. Tips are transmitted to a third party, who relays the information to the employer.

Security Policies. Retailers have established a variety of store security policies to control employee theft, including the following examples:

1. All packages, bags, trash cans, and other devices for concealing merchandise are subject to unannounced random inspection.
2. All customer discounts or refunds and employee discounts must be specifically approved by the store manager.
3. All sales must be registered, and each customer must be given a sales receipt.
4. All cash registers and cash boxes are subject to regularly scheduled checks as well as random unscheduled checks.
5. All records (sales, purchase, expense, and so on) are audited regularly and randomly.

The same rules apply in approaching, apprehending, and prosecuting employee pilferers as apply for shoplifters.

Supplier Theft

When developing a store security program, the retailer must remember that suppliers have some of the same security problems with dishonest employees as does the retailer. The retailer is very vulnerable to pilfering activities of delivery personnel, which include (1) **short counts**—delivering fewer items than were listed on the purchase order and signed for on the invoice—and (2) **merchandise removal**—stealing merchandise from receiving, checking, stocking, and selling areas. In the latter case, dishonest delivery personnel have readily accessible concealment devices, such as empty boxes, delivery carts, and bulky work clothes. There are numerous security requirements and procedures to reduce and eliminate pilferage by supplier personnel, some of which are listed here:

1. Establish a receiving area for accepting all incoming merchandise, and supervise all deliveries.
2. Control entry and exit to the receiving area.
3. Randomly inspect delivery personnel while they are on the store's premises.
4. Check and document all incoming shipments as to contents, weight, size, condition of shipment, and any other pertinent information.

Felony Theft

Felony theft includes the serious crimes of burglary and robbery. Retail stores are prime targets for these crimes because they are less secure than most other businesses. This lack of security results from carelessness as well as from the general nature of the retailing business (which often requires some isolated locations, evening hours, exposed cash in registers, and so on). Although retailers can do little to alter the nature of their business, they can initiate security measures to make their stores a less desirable target for burglary and robbery and reduce their harmful impact.

Burglary **Burglary** is defined as any unlawful entry to commit a felony or a theft, even though no force is used to gain entrance. Burglars usually operate under cover of darkness, after the store is closed. They gain entry by picking locks, forcing doors or windows open, using duplicate keys, or hiding in the store until it closes. Most security measures are directed at (1) preventing the burglar from gaining entry to the store, (2) securing all high-value merchandise, and (3) informing police and other security personnel of all successful and unsuccessful attempts at entry. Most retailers use locks and lights to discourage attempts at entry, safes to secure valuables, and alarms to warn police.

Robbery **Robbery** is stealing or taking anything of value by force, violence, or use of fear. Robbery is far more serious than burglary because it always holds the potential of loss of life as well as property. By definition, robbery is a violent crime in which one person uses force, or the threat of it, against another individual. Training employees to cope with robbers and limiting the opportunities for robbery helps ensure the well-being of store personnel and reduce property losses.

Antirobbery defence systems are directed at discouraging and apprehending the robber; some of the more common include panic buttons, till traps, video systems, and cash-control devices. Panic buttons are hidden alarm devices that silently alert the police or security company that a robbery is in progress. Till traps are devices installed in cash register drawers that trigger a silent alarm when the last dollar bill is removed from the till. In-house video systems are highly visible closed-circuit TV monitors trained on the cash register. They serve the dual purpose of discouraging potential robbers and providing police with pictures of an actual robbery.[70]

Summary

One of the most valuable ways the retailer can attract customers is by the appearance of the store and its immediate surroundings. The store's environment has both physical and psychological repercussions in the battle for the customer's attention and efficient operations. By identifying the desired image, targeting the right consumer, and communicating the right impression, the retailer creates a store image that is right for shopping and working. Sight, sound, smell, touch, and taste appeals have an obvious influence on the consumer's buying behaviour.

Communication with the consumer is facilitated by the store's exterior. How and where the store is positioned on the site affect the retailer's ability to attract customers. The store should be positioned so that it is visible to the consumer, compatible with the natural environment, and convenient for on-site movement of people and vehicles. The store's architecture should incorporate features that make a good impression while remaining functionally efficient. The store's sign serves two purposes: identifying the store and attracting consumer attention. Because the store's façade often creates the consumer's first impression, an appropriate configuration, attractive window displays, and accessible store entrances are essential.

The store's interior should minimize operating expenses while maximizing sales activities and customer satisfaction. In planning store layouts, the retailer must consider that all space is not equal in sales-producing potential. Also, wise use of nonselling space helps the retailer meet consumers' service needs.

As in-store visual presentations of the merchandise, retail displays assume a key role in creating a shopping atmosphere and enhancing the consumer's buying mood. Depending on their objectives, retailers use a variety of methods to present merchandise, including selection, special, point-of-purchase, and audiovisual displays. To ensure effective displays, retailers should plan merchandise exhibits by controlling content (unit, related, and theme groupings) and arrangements (pyramid, zigzag, step, and fan patterns).

Store security calls for developing the necessary safeguards for the store and its merchandise by initiating programs for detecting and preventing losses resulting from shoplifting by customers, pilfering by employees and suppliers, bad cheques and credit cards, and burglary and robbery.

Shoplifting is the theft of merchandise by customers or individuals posing as customers. There are basically two types of shoplifters: those who steal for need or psychological reasons (amateurs) and those who steal for a living (professionals). Several shoplifting devices and techniques can be identified: the booster, the diverter, the blocker, the sweeper, the walker, and the wearer. The best means of detecting shoplifters is good observation—knowing what to look for and where to look. In addition to well-trained personnel, retailers use convex mirrors, one-way mirrors, observation towers, closed-circuit television, and electronic "bugs" to aid in the detection process. Retailers should apprehend shoplifters in full compliance with the law and prosecute them when conditions warrant.

Store employees do steal; losses from employee pilferage sometimes exceed those from shoplifting. Opportunity and need are the two most critical causes for this type of theft. The eater, the smuggler, the discounter, the dipper, the embezzler, the partner, and the stasher all are types of dishonest employees who pilfer merchandise and money. The retailer can reduce this form of theft by creating an atmosphere of honesty, using security personnel, and establishing strict security policies.

Student Study Guide

Key Terms and Concepts

angled front *p. 235*
annex approach *p. 240*
arcade front *p. 235*
audiovisual merchandising *p. 252*
balance *p. 256*
blockers *p. 260*
booster *p. 260*
boutique layout *p. 248*
burglary *p. 264*
carrier *p. 261*
concept shops *p. 252*
core approach *p. 240*
departmentalized approach *p. 240*
dipper *p. 263*
discounter *p. 262*
diverter *p. 260*
dominance *p. 255*
eater *p. 262*
elevated windows *p. 235*
embezzler *p. 263*
fan arrangement *p. 259*
4-3-2-1 rule *p. 244*
free-form layout *p. 248*
grid layout *p. 246*
horizontal productivity *p. 242*
island windows *p. 236*
merchandise removal *p. 264*
partner *p. 263*
peripheral approach *p. 240*
planograms *p. 243*
point-of-purchase (POP) displays *p. 252*
price changer *p. 261*
proportion *p. 256*
pyramid arrangement *p. 258*
ramped windows *p. 236*
related groupings *p. 257*
retail displays *p. 248*
returner *p. 261*
rhythm *p. 256*
robbery *p. 265*
sandwich approach *p. 240*
scent appeal *p. 230*
selection displays *p. 251*
self-wrapper *p. 261*
selling space *p. 240*
shadow box windows *p. 236*
shoplifting *p. 259*
short counts *p. 264*
sight appeal *p. 229*
silent witness programs *p. 264*
site compatibility *p. 233*
smuggler *p. 262*
sound appeal *p. 229*
space productivity *p. 240*
special displays *p. 251*
spoiler *p. 261*
stasher *p. 263*
step arrangement *p. 258*
store aesthetics *p. 236*
store atmosphere *p. 228*
store image *p. 227*
store theatrics *p. 231*
store visibility *p. 233*
straight front *p. 234*
sweeper *p. 260*
taste appeal *p. 231*
theme groupings *p. 257*
touch appeal *p. 230*
undercover shoppers *p. 263*
uniformed guards *p. 263*
unit groupings *p. 257*
unity *p. 255*
variety *p. 255*
vertical productivity *p. 242*
walker *p. 261*
wearer *p. 261*
zigzag arrangement *p. 258*

Review Questions

1. What is store image? How is it created?
2. Define store atmospherics. Provide some nontext descriptions.
3. What role does sight, sound, scent, touch, and taste appeal have in creating a buying atmosphere?
4. What is store theatrics? How is it accomplished?
5. In evaluating a store's physical position on a site, the retailer considers which three issues? Briefly discuss each issue.
6. Identify the factors that the retailer considers in designing a functional facility. Explain.
7. Describe the who, what, where, and when functions of a retail store marquee.

8. Compare and contrast the three basic storefront configurations.
9. Depict the various options for creating window displays.
10. How are size and shape used to create the visual perceptions of harmony, contrast, and clash?
11. Relate how hue considerations affect the store's aesthetics.
12. How does the retailer measure space productivity?
13. Catalogue and characterize the six means for grouping store merchandise into meaningful collections.
14. Compare and contrast the model stock and sales productivity methods of allocating selling space.
15. How can seasonality of demand affect the in-store location of merchandise?
16. Describe the three basic layout patterns. What are the strengths and weaknesses of each?
17. Describe the four general types of in-store displays.
18. Creative displays are the result of various display elements and components. Name and define each of these elements and components.
19. Display elements and components are blended together using six display principles. What are they?
20. The content of a display is organized around various types of product grouping. What are they?
21. Identify and describe the types of shoplifters on the basis of their techniques.
22. Describe the major devices retailers use in observing and detecting shoplifters.
23. Profile the seven different types of employee pilferers.
24. What are the two most common methods of supplier pilferage?

Review Exam

True or False

______ 1. The sense of sight provides people with more information than any other sense mode.

______ 2. For the creation of perfect harmony in display, dissimilar shapes should be used.

______ 3. A retailer using the 4-3-2-1 rule of store rent allocation would assign 1 percent of the store's rental cost to the back quarter of the store.

______ 4. Using the sales-productivity ratio, the retailer allocates selling space on the basis of sales per square foot or metre generated by a given merchandise group.

______ 5. The most effective method of controlling employee theft is to create a general store atmosphere in which not even the slightest degree of dishonesty is tolerated and honesty and integrity are rewarded.

______ 6. Short counts involve delivering fewer items than were listed on the purchase order and signed for on the invoice.

Multiple Choice

______ 1. Visual relationships are those interpretations made by the "mind's eye" from visual stimuli that consist of ______.
a. harmony, melody, contrast
b. melody, contrast, clash
c. clash, melody, harmony
d. harmony, clash, contrast
e. all of the above

______ 2. Restfulness, peacefulness, freshness, and growth are all perceptions normally associated with the colour ______.
a. red
b. yellow
c. blue
d. green
e. violet

______ 3. Which of the following is not one of the three interacting factors that a retailer uses to improve a store's visibility?
a. setback
b. angle
c. colour
d. elevation

_____ **4.** The _____ storefront configuration is characterized by several recessed windows and/or entrances.
a. straight
b. arcade
c. angled
d. closed
e. open

_____ **5.** If the retailer is interested in achieving the most efficient use of selling space, then it should use the _____ layout.
a. free-form
b. grid
c. square
d. boutique
e. shoppe

_____ **6.** _____ refers to the path that the viewer's eye follows when viewing a retail display.
a. Dominance
b. Balance
c. Rhythm
d. Proportion
e. Trail

Student Application Manual

Investigative Projects: Practice and Application

1. Compare and contrast the image created by the physical facilities of a local Sears store with that of a local Zellers store. Identify similarities and differences. How does each store communicate the right impression and the wrong impression? Provide specific examples.
2. Evaluate the sight, sound, scent, touch, taste, and theme appeals for a major supermarket chain in your community. Identify specific examples of both positive and negative appeals. What changes would you recommend to create a more desirable atmosphere?
3. Draw a comprehensive diagram of the store layout of a local discount store. Redesign the store's layout using the boutique approach. Should a discount store consider using a boutique layout? Explain your reasoning.
4. Retail loss prevention programs could be severely hampered by federal legislation. Some legislation would severely restrict retailer's ability to use electronic monitoring technology for security and data collection purposes. It is designed to prevent the abuse of electronic monitoring in the workplace. For example, it would limit the use of telephone monitoring and hidden video cameras as security measures. Are the individual privacy rights of workers and shoppers more important than retailers' rights to ensure the security of their businesses and employees? Why or why not?

Endnotes

1. Robert Spector and Patrick D. McCarthy, *The Nordstrom Way, The Inside Story of America's #1 Customer Service Company* (New York: John Wiley & Sons, Inc., 1995), 138–39.
2. Wendy Zellner, "Sticky Fingers Are Rifling through Retail," *Business Week*, March 28, 1994, 36.
3. Richard C. Morais, "We're Finally Ready . . ." *Forbes*, April 24, 1995, 104.
4. Sean Silcoff, "The Emporiums Strike Back," *Canadian Business*, September 26, 1997, 54.
5. See Barry J. Babin and William R. Darden, "Good and Bad Shopping Vibes: Spending and Patronage Satisfaction," *Journal of Business Research*, 35 (March 1996): 201–6.
6. Robert J. Donovan, John R. Rossiter, Gilian Marcoolyn, and Andrew Nesdale, "Store Atmosphere and Purchasing Behavior," *Journal of Retailing*, 70 (Fall 1994): 291.
7. See Steven J. Greenland and Peter J. McGoldrick, "Atmospherics, Attitudes and Behaviour: Modeling the Impact of Designed Space," *The International Review of Retail, Distribution and Consumer Research* (January 1994): 1–16.
8. Walter K. Levey, "Making a Difference," *Retail Control* (January 1992): 10.
9. John Heinzl, "Books, Bach and Beer," *Globe and Mail*, September 4, 1997, B10.
10. Louise Lee, "Background Music Becomes Hoity-Toity," *The Wall Street Journal*, December 22, 1995, B1.

Retail Vignette

The Ghermezians—West Edmonton Mall

Once among the largest distributors of Persian rugs in North America, the Ghermezian family has become a major landowner in Alberta. Father Jacob and sons Eskandar, Nader, Raphael, and Bahman emigrated to Canada from Iran in the 1950s. Initially the Ghermezian family continued to be rug merchants in Montreal while they learned about their new country and the sons obtained business education and experience.

Jacob's sons eventually wanted to get into the land development business in a region with a resource-based economy. It wasn't long before they had moved to Edmonton, Alberta, and began to purchase land suitable for development.

West Edmonton Mall
www.westedmall.com

During the late 1970s, the Ghermezians began the planning and negotiations for what has become the largest shopping mall in the world. Phase I of the monster mall was opened in September, 1981, with over 200 retail outlets covering 106 000 m^2. Many predicted the mall's failure and Alberta's sluggish economy in the early '80s was not expected to help. Sales in year one, however, exceeded $133 million and the Ghermezians proceeded with Phase II which included another 105 000 m^2. Phase II was completed in 1983 and comprised an indoor amusement park, an N.H.L.-sized skating rink, and over 200 more stores. Sales continued to rise as tourists and locals flocked to the mall.

By 1985, the Ghermezians had completed Phase III, by far the most ambitious, which brought the total size of the mall to 483 000 m^2, much larger than any other mall in the world. Phase III included a 5-acre water park, four authentic submarines, a life-sized Spanish galleon, an 18-hole miniature golf course, and many other exciting attractions. Because there is so much to see, the Ghermezians added the 354-room Fantasyland Hotel and Resort to facilitate longer visits for tourists and even locals. For the serious shopper and diner, the mall contains over 800 stores and services and over 110 eating establishments. It is estimated that the total economic impact of the mall to the Alberta economy is approximately $1.2 billion. It is also estimated that the mall captures about 49 percent of Edmonton shoppers and 47 percent of the tourist shopping dollar spent in Edmonton. The mall is estimated to receive 20 million visitations annually and provide employment opportunities for 23 500 people.

The West Edmonton Mall is much more than a mall. It is capable of providing a complete lifestyle experience with shopping, recreation, entertainment, amusements, and other amenities for the whole family. The idea, according to the Ghermezians, is to turn shopping into a recreational family experience. All early results indicate that they have been successful at accomplishing this objective.

Printed with permission of West Edmonton Mall.

Location Strategy: War Games

Home Depot faces the same problems as an army in a war of conquest: seizing the right territory, maintaining the supply lines, controlling occupied terrain, and planning offensives. Home Depot assaults new fronts in distinct waves. The first wave plants the flag—putting three or four stores on the perimeter of a designated city. Each store typically serves 100 000 households which have median incomes of $45 000. And 75% of those households are owner occupied. When the initial stores reach combined sales of about $50 million a second wave fills in the territory with new outlets designed to make Home Depot dominant over three to five years.[1]

It's Not Location, It's Destination

In fast food, where the average Joe does not much care if he has a Whopper or a Big Mac, a great location is a marketing imperative. But if you can be the best at something—the only great rib joint in town, the best craft and hobby store in town, or the peerless Western gear shop—then people will find your store wherever you locate it. It will become a destination. If a company positively differentiates itself from its competitors, in terms of product offering, positioning, service, or some other motivating attribute, customers—especially frequent shoppers—will go out of the way to find it.[2]

The Shopping Mall: A Consumer Habitat

The mall has become a natural gathering place and part of the cultural fabric of [North] America. The automobile allows individuals to easily reach a destination where they may safely consume more than goods. Indeed, this expansive habitat fosters interaction with other members of the species, distribution of community information, promotion of for- and non-profit events, climatic shelter for exercising, and an assortment of services ranging from food to dental care.[3]

Retail Location Decisions

Competitive pressures on retailers are leading to a more careful consideration and use of location as a source of competitive advantage. "Increasingly, locational decisions involve not only the evaluation of potential new sites, but also the management of existing ones."[4] The importance of location decisions cannot be overstated. A retailer that selects a poor location will always be at a competitive disadvantage. To overcome a poor location (a struggle that is not always successful), the retailer must make substantial adjustments in the product, price, and promotional mixes. Because adjustments usually are expensive to implement, they adversely affect the firm's profits. On the other hand, selecting a good location enhances the chances of success because it allows greater flexibility in developing the product, price, and promotional mixes. Given the long-term commitment, substantial financial investments, and effects on all retailing operations, the retailer must consider the location problem carefully. This problem consists of identifying, delineating, evaluating, and selecting (1) retail markets, (2) trading areas, and (3) retail sites (see Figure 8–1).

Retail Markets

Geographically, a **retail market** is defined as that area or place where consumers and retailers meet for the purposes of exchange. As described in earlier chapters, a retail market is a buying population and its buying behaviour at any given time and place (see Chapters 3 and 4). Retail markets come in all sizes, shapes, and descriptions; hence, there is no single definition or depiction that covers the range of retail market areas. Figure 8–2 outlines the many issues of retail market analysis to be reviewed in this section.

Figure 8–1

The retail location problem

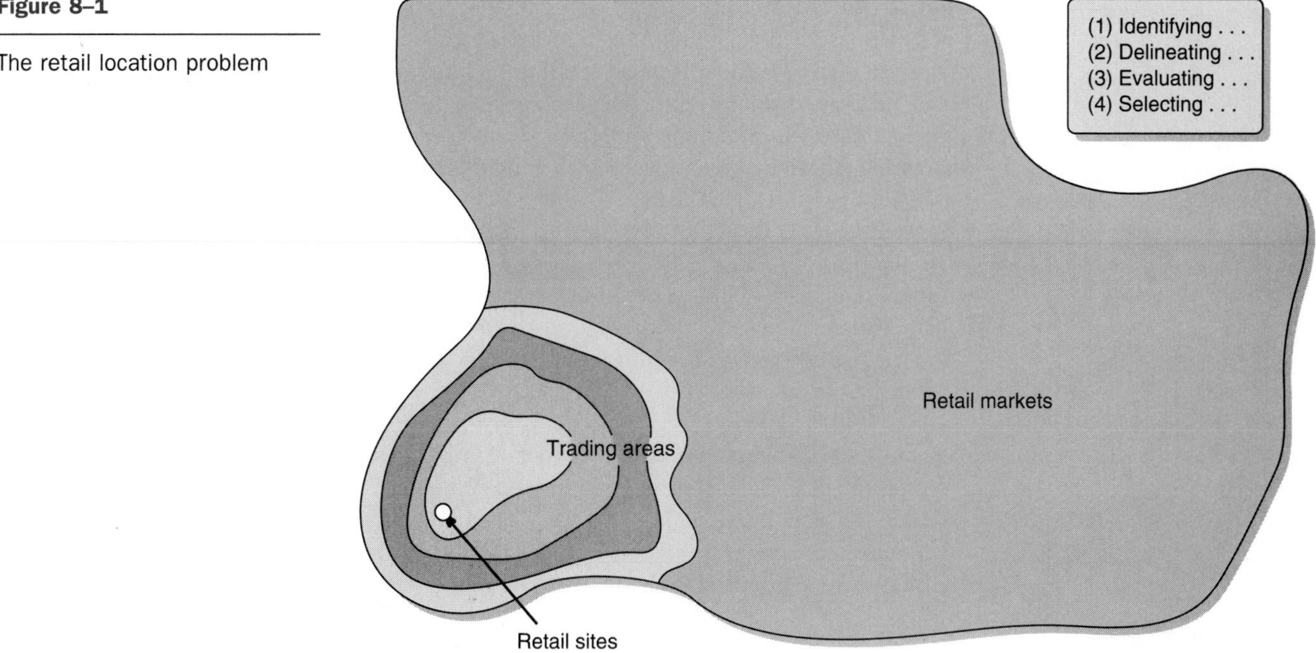

Figure 8–2

Retail market analysis

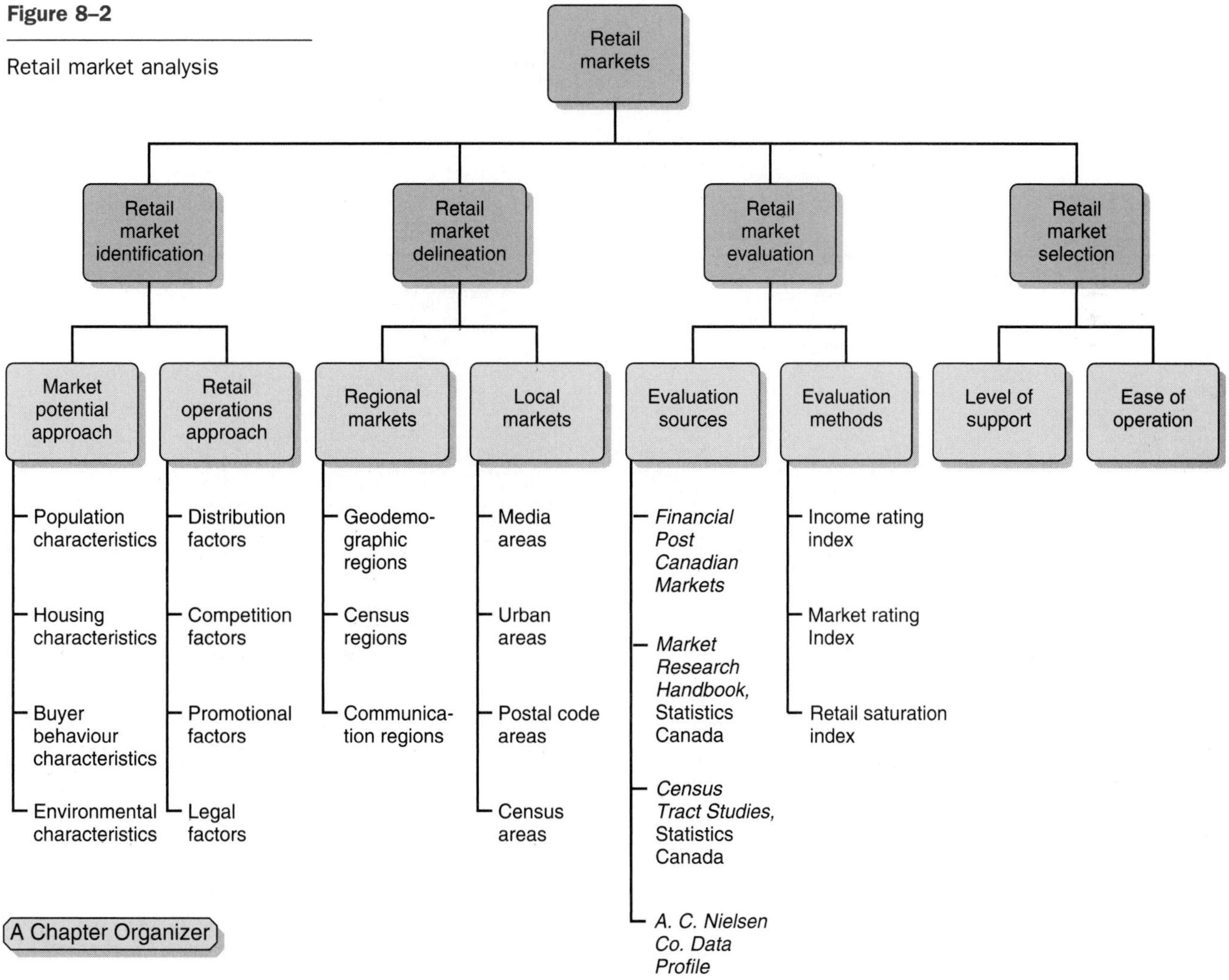

- Retail markets
  - Retail market identification
    - Market potential approach
      - Population characteristics
      - Housing characteristics
      - Buyer behaviour characteristics
      - Environmental characteristics
    - Retail operations approach
      - Distribution factors
      - Competition factors
      - Promotional factors
      - Legal factors
  - Retail market delineation
    - Regional markets
      - Geodemographic regions
      - Census regions
      - Communication regions
    - Local markets
      - Media areas
      - Urban areas
      - Postal code areas
      - Census areas
  - Retail market evaluation
    - Evaluation sources
      - *Financial Post Canadian Markets*
      - *Market Research Handbook,* Statistics Canada
      - *Census Tract Studies,* Statistics Canada
      - *A. C. Nielsen Co. Data Profile*
    - Evaluation methods
      - Income rating index
      - Market rating Index
      - Retail saturation index
  - Retail market selection
    - Level of support
    - Ease of operation

A Chapter Organizer

Retail Market Identification

Retailers use two general groups of criteria to identify retail market areas. Using the **market potential approach**, retailers select criteria that reflect the support (in sales, number of customers, and so on) that a geographic area will provide a given type of retail operation. Using the **retail operations approach**, the retailer examines factors that might enhance or limit the efficiency or competency by which retail operations can be conducted.

Market Potential Approach In utilizing the market potential approach, the retailer uses criteria specific to its class of goods (that is, retailer-specific criteria) to identify market areas. Whereas certain criteria are useful to one retailer, the same criteria may be of little or no use to another retailer. Commonly employed retail market identification criteria include those based on population, housing, buyer behaviour, and physical environment.

Population Characteristics. The most commonly used retail market identification criteria are measurements of total population and its demographic structure. As discussed in Chapter 3 and illustrated in Figure 8–3, a retailer can describe any geographic area (province, county, city, and so on) by any combination of population characteristics. Although total population figures and population densities are of primary importance, the

Figure 8–3

Using population characteristics as criteria in identifying retail markets

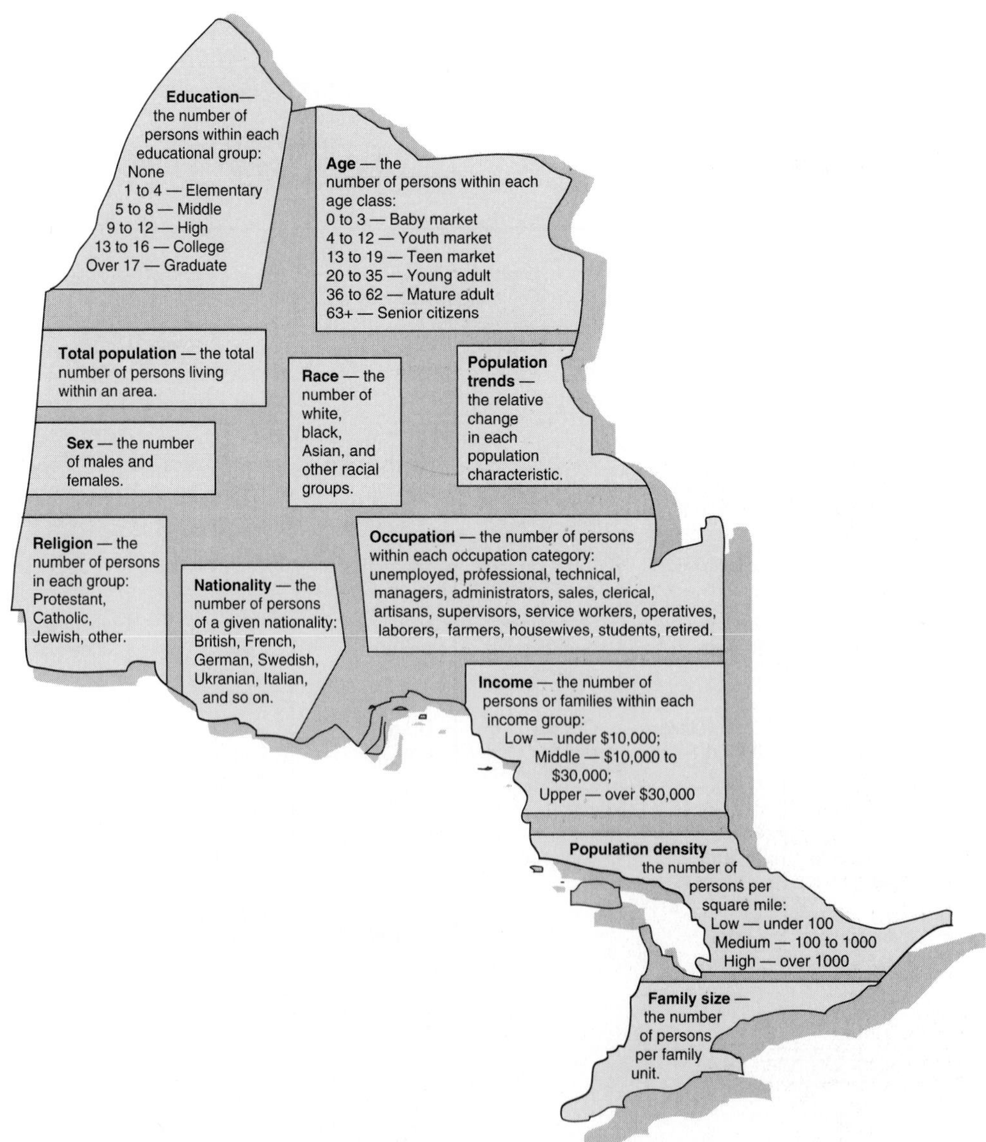

retailer can get a more detailed profile of a market by examining the demographic characteristics of education, age, income, sex, occupation, religion, race, nationality, and family characteristics data. The retailer's purpose is to match a market's population characteristics to those of the people who desire the type of goods and services offered by the retailer. Retailers can get population and demographic data from the Chamber of Commerce, city planning departments, economic development agencies, *The Canadian Census* and other publications, tapes, and materials offered by Statistics Canada.

Housing Characteristics. Housing characteristics are an important criterion for some retailers in determining profitable markets, such as hardware retailers, home improvement centres, and home furnishings stores. Home Depot, the Atlanta-based operator of the home centre chain, continues to push into new market areas, where millions of aging suburban houses and apartments will need huge amounts of remodelling supplies. An aging housing stock is the prime target for this "do-it-yourself" retailer. Figure 8–4 illustrates some of the more important housing characteristics that retailers use to identify lucrative retail markets. To locate this data, retailers can turn to the Census of Population and the Census of Housing. Both of these studies are carried out every five years and contain information on Canadian population and housing. Statistics Canada also has a number of publications on population and housing. Additional information may be obtained from provincial and municipal governments.

Figure 8–4

Using housing characteristics as criteria in identifying retail markets

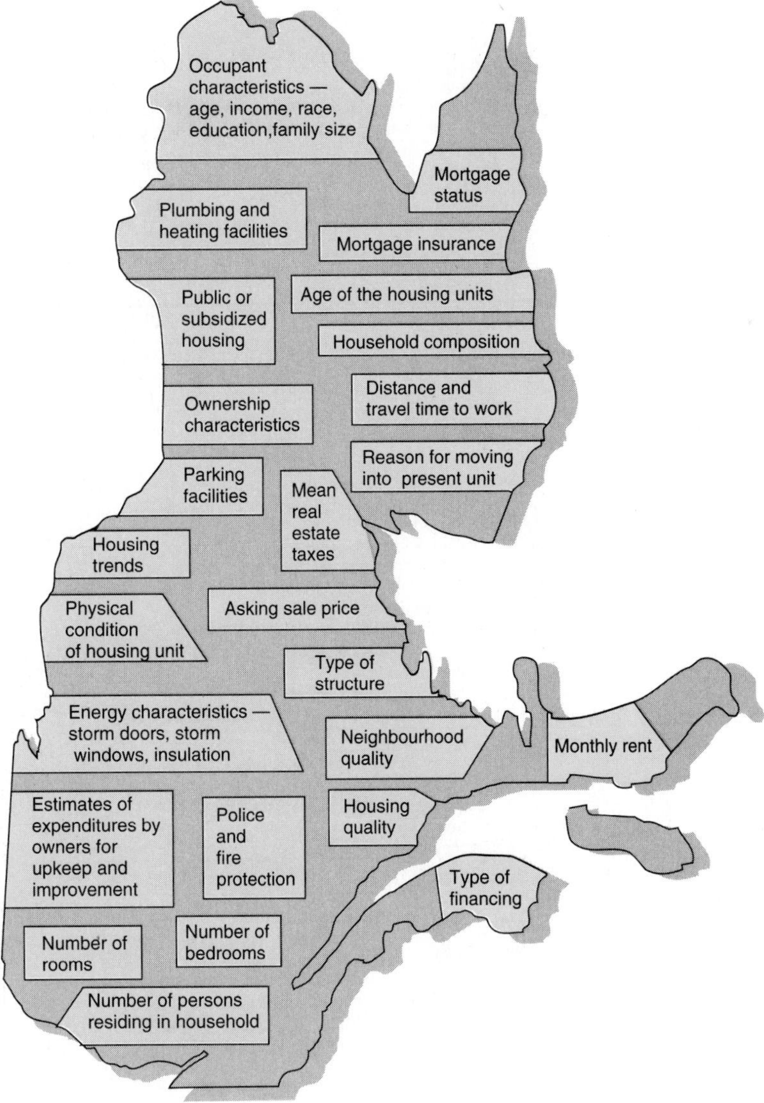

Buyer Behaviour Characteristics. Knowing what, when, where, how, and why consumers buy is extremely useful buyer behaviour information in identifying and segmenting retail markets, as Figure 8–5 illustrates. Among such characteristics are store loyalty, consumer psychographics, store-patronage reasons, usage rates, lifestyles, benefits sought, and purchase situations. Although buyer behaviour characteristics provide retailers with the most useful information to make location decisions (see Chapter 4), the data are not easy to obtain or measure.

Environmental Characteristics. Another way retailers measure market potential is to examine an area's physical environment. Differing characteristics of their physical environments influence people's choices of clothing, housing, foods, and forms of recreation, as well as their preferences among many other products, services, and activities. "What goes on outside determines what sells inside the stores, and it also determines how customers use products."[5] Lawn and garden shops, apparel retailers, sporting goods stores, and recreational vehicle dealers are but a few of the different types of retailers that plan their merchandising effort with an eye to the environment.

Retail Operations Approach

Using the retail operations approach, the location specialist must take into account the nature of the retailer's operations. A profitable retail

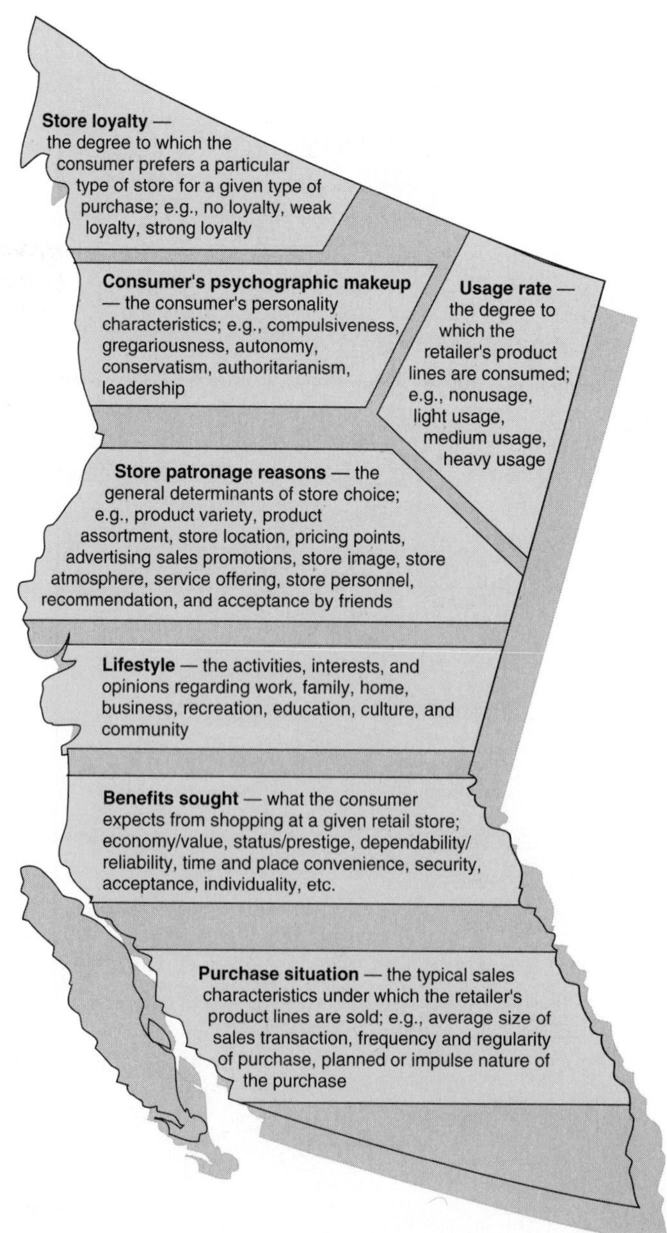

Store loyalty — the degree to which the consumer prefers a particular type of store for a given type of purchase; e.g., no loyalty, weak loyalty, strong loyalty
Consumer's psychographic makeup — the consumer's personality characteristics; e.g., compulsiveness, gregariousness, autonomy, conservatism, authoritarianism, leadership
Usage rate — the degree to which the retailer's product lines are consumed; e.g., nonusage, light usage, medium usage, heavy usage
Store patronage reasons — the general determinants of store choice; e.g., product variety, product assortment, store location, pricing points, advertising sales promotions, store image, store atmosphere, service offering, store personnel, recommendation, and acceptance by friends
Lifestyle — the activities, interests, and opinions regarding work, family, home, business, recreation, education, culture, and community
Benefits sought — what the consumer expects from shopping at a given retail store; economy/value, status/prestige, dependability/reliability, time and place convenience, security, acceptance, individuality, etc.
Purchase situation — the typical sales characteristics under which the retailer's product lines are sold; e.g., average size of sales transaction, frequency and regularity of purchase, planned or impulse nature of the purchase

Figure 8–5

Using buyer behaviour characteristics as criteria in identifying retail markets

store is one that not only serves a consumer market of high potential but also operates in a market that allows for efficiency and competitiveness. Several items that directly influence the retailer's chances to operate successfully are (1) distribution, (2) competition, (3) promotional, and (4) legal factors.

Distribution Factors. A crucial problem for all retailers is to get the product into the store. This involves inventory control—overstocks increase carrying costs, whereas stock-outs cause lost sales and customer ill will. The retailer must consider transportation and handling costs, delivery time, and reliability of delivery services. To identify potential market areas, the retailer also must consider the location and delivery practices of suppliers and the market area's ability to support distribution facilities. When Wal-Mart could not find distributors to supply its scattered network of stores located in small rural communities, the firm established a network of eighteen regional distribution centres and supported each centre with a major trucking company. Retailers must achieve adequate regional clustering to enjoy some of the benefits associated with economies of scale.

Competition Factors. It is imperative that the retailer take into account the reality of the competition when identifying retail markets. Competition varies from one area to another according to the type, number, and size of competitors. Types, levels, and competitive strategies of various retailing formats are discussed in Chapter 2. As a quick review of that chapter would indicate, retail competition is very complex; hence, the market area specialist must carefully audit all competitors, regardless of their form.

Promotional Factors. A retailer that depends heavily on promotional activities can identify market areas by analyzing the advertising media in each market area and the behaviour of competitive retailers. Media selectivity and coverage are both important. With respect to **media selectivity**, the retailer should look at **geographic selectivity** (the ability of a medium to target a specific geographic market area such as a city or a part of a city) and **class selectivity** (the ability of a medium to target specific kinds of people who have common characteristics). In other words, most advertising media are "targeted" to serve certain geographic areas and to appeal to certain groups of consumers. For example, a radio station serves only the geographic area defined by its transmitting power, antenna system, frequency on the dial, and other local conditions. If the station happens to follow a pop format, certain listeners will be attracted by the format. **Media coverage** is the number of people an advertising medium reaches in a given market area. For example, a newspaper might provide excellent coverage in one county by reaching 90 percent of the homes but cover only 30 percent of the homes in a distant county.

Legal Factors. The final group of criteria that retailers use to identify market areas are provincial and local legal requirements. Land use regulation in the form of *zoning restrictions, building codes*, and *signing requirements* has a direct bearing on the success of a retailer's operation. Provincial and local taxes on the firm's *real estate, personal property*, and *inventory* can have an equally important impact on the cost of operation. Retailers must also meet certain licensing requirements to conduct a business. Licence availability and cost are necessary considerations.

Retail Market Delineation

Regionally, retail market analysis consists of delineating the "right region" of the country and the "right part of the region." The geographic extent of a regional market is not fixed and could include either one or several provinces. For many small, independent retailers, the regional market problem is not a concern. They often have narrowed their choice of regions to the ones in which they currently live or work. For the chain organization or the retailer that intends to expand, however, the starting point in the location–decision process is to delineate and identify regional and subregional markets. The next step is to delineate local markets within a regionally defined market. The local market area problem is how to find the "right town" and the "right part of town." For our purposes, "town" refers to any size urban centre that can be associated with a particular regional or subregional market. For Wal-Mart Discount Stores, the right town might be a medium-size metro area like Kitchener, Ontario, or a small rural market like Lethbridge, Alberta.

Overwaitea
www.overwaitea.com

Save-On-Foods
www.sof.com

Regional Markets Most business organizations have categorized Canada in some way into **regional markets**. Regional classification schemes suggest that there are perceived social, cultural, and economic differences among people in various parts of the country. Retailers should identify these perceived differences and determine what impact these differences have on their business. Although regional department store chains have not fared well in Canada, regional supermarket chains (such as Sobeys in Atlantic Canada, and Overwaitea/Save-On in the West) and some regional specialty chains have been successful.[6]

Presented in this section are three samples of regional market area delineations: geodemographic regions, census regions, and communication subregions. In addition, there are many other regional classifications that have been developed by private market research firms. A review of the last several years of *Marketing News*, published by the American Marketing Association, will allow you to identify a large number of marketing research agencies and their service offering.

Geodemographic Regions: The Right Nation. **Geodemography** is the practice of linking demographic data (for example, age, sex, race, occupation of the population) with various geographic locations (for example, regions, counties, cities, postal code areas, census

World of Retailing

International Retailing

How Many McDonald's Can He Build?

CANTALUPO'S THEOREM: If nearly 15 000 McDonald's already sounds like plenty, just wait. James Cantalupo, president of McDonald's International, uses a formula to guesstimate how many stores he can build. He divides a country's population by the number of people per store in the U.S. and adjusts for differences in per capita income. Of course it does not account for factors like competition and eating habits. FORTUNE calculated the potential number of McDonald's that could be built worldwide. Answer: 42 000.

$$\frac{\text{POPULATION OF COUNTRY X}}{\text{NO. OF PEOPLE PER MCDONALD'S IN U.S. (25 000)}} \times \frac{\text{PER CAPITA INCOME OF COUNTRY X}}{\text{PER CAPITA INCOME OF U.S. (\$23 120)}} = \text{POTENTIAL PENETRATION OF MCDONALD'S IN COUNTRY X}$$

MCDONALD'S BIGGEST MARKETS	Current number of restaurants	Minimum market potential	SOME UNDERPENETRATED MARKETS	Current number of restaurants	Minimum market potential
JAPAN	1 070	6 100	CHINA	23	784
CANADA	694	1 023	RUSSIA	3	685
BRITAIN	550	1 794	COLOMBIA	0	79
GERMANY	535	3 235	INDIA	0	489
AUSTRALIA	411	526	PAKISTAN	0	90
FRANCE	314	2 237	SOUTH AFRICA	0	190

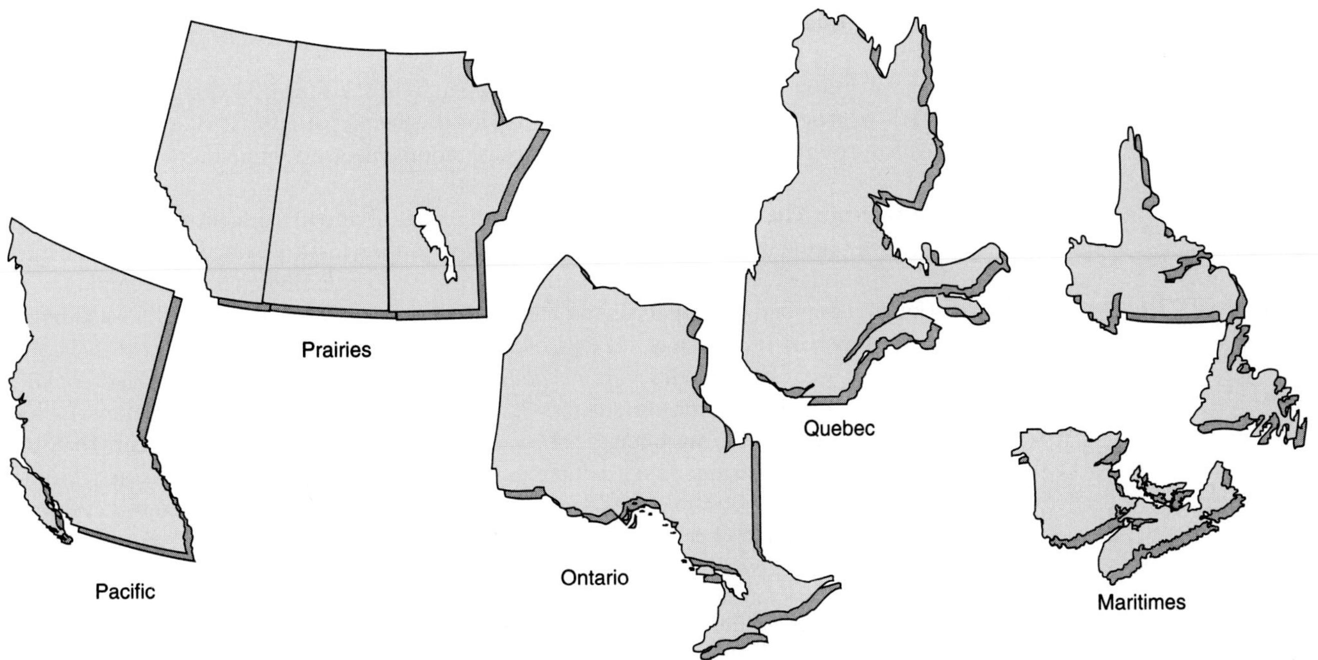

Figure 8–6

Census regions: The right region

tracts, census blocks). "The idea behind all geodemographic cluster systems is the same. Each system divides neighbourhoods into groups based on similarities in income, education, and household type, as well as attitudes and product preferences."[7] Geodemography attempts to identify geographic lifestyles that have a direct influence on consumer attitudes and beliefs, which in turn have a direct impact on consumer buying behaviour and retail store patronage. Many commercial market research firms have developed their version of a geodemographic marketing tool.

Census Regions: The Right Region. Perhaps the most widely used regional classification system is one developed by Statistics Canada. As shown in Figure 8–6, Statistics Canada divides Canada into five census regions. The relative importance of this census market classification scheme is evident from the fact that many public and private organizations use this system as the organizational framework for their information and analyzing process.

Communication Regions: The Right Subregion. Regional markets can be identified on the basis of various types of media coverage—communication markets. In the case of broadcast media, a 50 000 watt radio station like CHUM in Toronto is capable of providing the retailer with multi-area regional coverage. On the other hand, a 10 000 watt station like CJOR in Vancouver covers only a subregional market because its output is restricted to the western portion of British Columbia. The large-area coverage by CHUM is appropriate to a multi-unit retailer (such as Zellers) that has operations in each of the cities CHUM covers.

Local Markets

Faced with an array of thousands of urban centres, the retail location specialist must use some organized method to identify local markets. As shown in Figure 8–2, the local market area delineation problem is a series of locational refinements that requires the location specialist to determine the right county, the right city, the right neighbourhood, and the right block. Market analysts can use media area, urban area, postal code area, and/or census area delineations in defining local retail market areas.

Media Areas: The Right County. Because local print and broadcast advertising is a key merchandising variable for most retailers, one of the simplest ways to delineate local retail market areas is to use data that have been generated by a commercial media research organization, such as The Arbitron Company and the A.C. Nielsen Company. Both these firms have established media market borders that assign a county to only one television market.

The Arbitron Company has delineated what it terms **areas of dominant influence (ADIs)**—a geographic market area based on local viewing patterns. It is an area that consists of all counties in which the home market stations receive a preponderance of viewing.

Urban Areas: The Right City. One method of classifying urban centres is to group or rank them on the basis of population, retail sales, employment levels, disposable income, number of households, and a host of other factors.[8] Many retailing operations employ population and demographic analysis to determine each market's sales potential for a particular line of merchandise or a given type of retail operation.

On the basis of their sales volume potential, urban centres can be classified as **ABC markets**, that is, in descending order as A, B, or C markets. The exact definition of what constitutes an A, B, or C market varies from one retailing organization to another. The purpose of identifying various sized markets is to help the retailer adjust the business format to meet the consumption needs of a particular market. Wal-Mart uses different sizes of its Supercenter format depending on the market's sales potential. Briefly, ABC markets might be described as follows:

- **A markets** have the sales potential to support large and/or multiple operating units. A markets provide retailing environments that can support strategies ranging from discount to prestige pricing, mass to direct advertising, and store to in-home selling.
- **B markets** are second-tier markets that are often medium-size cities offering adequate sales potential for a wide variety of retailing activities. B markets are adequate for most types and sizes of store operations.
- **C markets** are basically small-town markets that have increasingly become targets for expansion by large national chains. As urban markets become more saturated with competing retail formats, C markets offer less competitive retailing environments and good market opportunities for domestic expansion.

Postal Code Areas: The Right Neighbourhood. For most retailers, there are literally "right" and "wrong" parts of town. An urban centre is not simply a homogeneous mass; rather, it is a heterogeneous grouping of people and activities, making up **intraurban markets** that can have a profound effect on a retailer's operations. The internal structure of urban centres is composed of many recognizable areas; one of the more important urban delineations is the local neighbourhood. Ideally, retailers should seek a location that includes the maximum number of choice neighbourhoods within the retailer's local market area. Using postal codes is one of the easiest and most readily available means for delineating neighbourhood market areas.

The Census of Population conducted by Statistics Canada provides information by postal code level for both urban and rural areas in Canada. Continuing shifts to and from urban and suburban areas suggest that classifying population by arbitrary city and county boundaries has its limitations. Marketers are more interested in the size of homogeneous marketing areas than in the number of people within political boundaries. To meet this need, Statistics Canada developed a separate population classification, the **census metropolitan area (CMA)**. The CMA is the "main labour market area" of a continuous built-up area having 100 000 or more population. It's a zone in which a significant number of people are able to commute on a daily basis to their workplaces in the main built-up area.

In other words, CMAs are integrated economic and social units with a large population. They're usually known by the name of their largest city. In 1994, there were 25 CMAs in Canada with a total population of just under 20 million. This represents almost 61.4 percent of the 1994 Canadian total.

These CMAs are major target markets. Toronto, Montreal, and Vancouver are Canada's largest metropolitan areas. Together they comprise approximately 9.4 million people, or 32.1 percent of Canada's 1994 population.

The World of Retailing

Retail Technology

Geographic Information Systems (GISs) Locating Customers and Competitors

Geographic Information Systems (GISs) are computer-based technologies that allow the marriage of a spatial database with traditional alphabetic and numeric databases. For example, retailers can locate their stores and distribution centres on a map overlaid with population figures and other demographic data that are strong indicators of success; potential expansion locations can be identified by finding desirable demographic areas that are not currently being served by existing stores. A GIS needs specialized hardware for input (digitizers, map scanners) and output (plotters and graphic displays), and specialized techniques for storing the coordinates of complex geographic objects, including network of lines (roads) and reporting zones. A GIS enables the user to obtain visual answers to such questions as "What are the income or age characteristics of a given area?" or provide a visual representation (dot map) of all the store's credit customers. The capabilities of GIS enable the retailer to establish the geographic relationship between any set of points (for example, customer's residence), lines (for example, street pattern), and areas (for example, customer's ZIP or postal code). In creating a map, GIS use three basic axes: X for latitude, Y for longitude, and Z for elevation. By using a demographic characteristic for elevation and combining it with the latitudinal and longitudinal reference points, the retailer creates a commercial GIS. A typical GIS assignment is to produce a "retail gravity" model, which weights demographic data according to the needs of a particular retailer. For instance, a do-it-yourself home centre would weight the analyses toward low- and middle-income owners of older houses. The result is a contour map of the patronage probabilities for the home centre.

Source: Adapted from David Churbuck, "Geographics," Forbes, *January 6, 1992, 262–64, 266–67; and Michael F. Goodchild, "Guest Commentary: Geographic Information Systems,"* Journal of Retailing, *67 (Spring 1991), 3–15; Rick Tetzeli, "Mapping for Dollars,"* Fortune, *October 18, 1993, 91–96; Sharen Kindel, "Geographic Information Systems,"* Financial World, *January 19, 1993, 44; and Gary Robins, "Retail GIS Use Growing,"* Stores, *January 1993, 44–50.*

While the CMAs during the past 10 years have grown faster than the overall population, the growth pattern has been uneven across the country. The big winner was Oshawa, with a population growth of 42.8 percent, followed by Vancouver with 39.9 percent, and then by Toronto, Ottawa-Hull, and Kitchener. Note, however, the very low growth rates of Chicoutimi-Jonquiere in Quebec, of Thunder Bay and Sudbury in Ontario, and of Saint John in New Brunswick.

Census Areas: The Right Block. Statistics Canada also provides census area profiles which are designed to provide small area information for a wide range of census variables in limited detail. Figure 8–7 illustrates an example of the type of information available in these reports.

Additional trade area information may be provided by such industry associations as the Retail Council of Canada. An example of what such a report includes is found in the Retail Strategies and Tactics box entitled "Site Analysis Has Never Been So Easy."

Retail Market Evaluation

After identifying and delineating potential regional and local markets, the retail location specialist must evaluate each area. Each of these processes should have provided considerable insight into the various capabilities of each area to support a given type of retail organization. The evaluation process involves collecting (that is, sources) and analyzing (that is, methods) data pertinent to a particular retailer's operation.

Evaluation Sources In addition to the aforementioned sources of geographic market data, the retail market analyst can turn to the following standard commercial sources of information: *The Financial Post Canadian Markets, Market Research Handbook, Census Tract Studies*, and *A.C. Nielsen Co. Data Profile.*

Figure 8–7

Selected characteristics for a census area

Source: Statistics Canada, Census Division, Custom Table.

Selected characteristics for a census area
Total population
Age
Home language
Ethnic origin
Citizenship
Marital status
Education
Employment status
Occupation
Income level

Financial Post
www.canoe.ca/FP/home.html

The Financial Post Canadian Markets. This is an annual publication compiled by the editors of *The Financial Post*. It includes information about population, media sources, retail sales, and demographic data for cities across Canada. This report also compares the profiled centres to the Canadian average for income level and retail sales. Figure 8–8 provides an illustration of a sample page from Canadian markets.

Market Research Handbook. This is an annual compilation of Statistics Canada reports which are relevant to marketers. Categories of information include: (1) selected economic indicators; (2) government revenue, expenditure and employment; (3) merchandising and services; (4) population characteristics; (5) personal income and expenditures; (6) housing, motor vehicles, and household facilities and equipment; (7) metropolitan area data; and (8) census agglomeration data.

Statistics Canada Census Tracts. This provides useful information for retailers in that much of the information compiled by Statistics Canada is prepared visually in the form of maps for the largest metropolitan areas in Canada. Census tract reports include plotted information for a range of population, housing, and socio-economic data for these cities. An example of a census tract report for Toronto is shown in Figure 8–9.

A.C. Nielsen Co. Data Profile. The *A.C. Nielsen's Data Profile* provides a wide range of interesting facts involving each of its DMAs. In addition to population and demographic descriptions, each DMA is profiled in terms of major retail outlets, lifestyle dimensions, retail sales, and population growth estimates.

Evaluation Methods Now we turn to the standard methods used in conducting a retail market evaluation. Retail market evaluation can be accomplished through the use of any number of commercial or proprietary indices, norms, averages, profiles, or standards that compare the potential of one regional or local retail market area with all other market areas. A selected sample of retail market evaluation methods are presented next, including the buying power index, the sales activity index, the quality index, and the retail saturation index.

Retail Strategies and Tactics

Site Analysis Has Never Been So Easy!

Retail Council now offers you DISCOUNT PRICES on TRADAREA™—The inside story on your market area!

A TradArea analysis gives you detailed and accurate market information that will help you determine your market potential for any site, anywhere in Canada. The reports will pinpoint new sales promotion opportunities, provide guidelines for assortment planning and allow you to locate areas for potential expansion sites. And now, membership in Retail Council entitles you to receive this valuable information at a special member price.

Retail Council, in conjunction with Compusearch, can now provide you with a customized analysis of your exact trade area (no matter what the size or shape), which is typically available for under $250. And, you receive a 20% discount when you order your reports through Retail Council.

TradArea will provide you with information previously only available through expensive and time-consuming market research. You can order a variety of market information for your trade area including:

Consumer Spending Potential™ for:

- Women's, Men's and Children's Clothing stores
- Shoe stores
- Hardware stores
- Drug and Sundry stores
- Sporting Goods stores
- Book and Stationery stores
- Camera and Photography stores
- Furniture and Appliance stores
- and many other retail outlets

Census Demographics such as:

- Size of Population
- Number of Households
- Household Income
- Education Level
- Dwelling Characteristics
- Age of Population
- Family Size
- Age of Children
- Own vs Rent Status
- LIFESTYLES™ market segments
- and many more variables

Why Use TradArea?

If your business operates from a fixed location, TradArea is an invaluable tool for determining its market potential, and provides actionable insights about the area where you are located. Many retailers already use it to:

- compare one expansion site to another;
- identify new sales promotion opportunities;
- determine the number of potential customers in an area;
- discover whether a particular area is growing in population or on a decline;
- determine what demographic characteristics are unique to the area;
- segment target groups by the various LIFESTYLES types;
- determine what products or services the households in your trade area are buying; or
- discover hidden market potential.

For more information, contect that TradArea desk at the Council offices (598-4684). Or to get started on an analysis of your current or prospective location, simply tell us the address and nearest cross streets, and the size and shape of your trade area, and within days you will receive the most comprehensive analysis of your market available today.

Source: Retail Council of Canada. TradArea, Consumer Spending Potential and LIFESTYLES are trademarks of COMPUSEARCH Market and Social Research Limited. All Rights Reserved.

Figure 8–8

An example of secondary data—a sample page from *The Financial Post Canadian Markets*

Edmonton CMA

Income:
3% Above National Average

Pers'l Income, 1992	$16,269,488,800
% Canadian Total	3.13
Per Capita	$19,800

Population:

June 1, 1992	*821,400*
% Canadian Total	3.03
% Change, '86–'92	4.57
Average Annual Growth Rate	0.45%

Market:
4% Below National Average

Retail Sales, 1992	$6,826,882,000
% Canadian Total	2.93
Per Capita	$8,300

POPULATION

1986 Census:

Total		*785,465*
Male		*392,810*
Female		*392,655*
Age Groups:	*Male*	*Female*
Under 4	34,145	32,365
5–9	30,075	28,350
10–14	28,105	26,725
15–19	30,360	29,585
20–24	38,735	40,360
25–29	44,345	43,305
30–34	39,315	37,925
35–39	32,740	31,690
40–44	24,245	23,700
45–49	19,690	19,055
50–54	17,856	16,970
55–59	16,140	15,625
60–64	12,810	13,770
65–69	9,030	10,875
70–74	6,705	8,785
75 +	8,505	13,575

MOTHER TONGUE

	1986 Census	*% Total*
English	611,495	81.46
French	18,615	2.48
Dutch	5,960	0.79
Chinese	16,000	2.13
German	22.715	3.03
Greek	1,055	0.14
Hungarian	1,815	0.24
Indo-Pakistani	4,635	0.62
Itilian	5,970	0.80
Japanese	425	0.06
Korean	1,265	0.17
Polish	6,095	0.81
Portuguese	3,175	0.42
Scandinavian Languages	2,380	0.32
Ukranian	24,265	3.23
Vietnamese	3,335	0.44
Other	21,515	2.87

HOUSING

1986 Census:

Occupied Private Dwellings, Total	283,365
Owned	161,750
Rented	121,395
Single detached	163,490
Apartment, 5 or more storeys	20,225
Movable dwellings	3,905
Other dwellings	95,745

CONSUMER PRICE INDEX

(1981 = 100)

1991 (Apr.)	158.3
1990 (Apr.)	148.9
1989 (Apr.)	141.6
1988 (Apr.)	137.3
1987 (Apr.)	132.0

MARITAL STATUS

1986 Census: (Age 15+)

Single (never married)	169,800
Married (includes separated)	379,405
Widowed	28,435
Divorced	28,055

PRIVATE HOUSEHOLDS

1966 Census:

Private Households, Total	283,365
Population in private households	772,005
Average number per household	2.7

RADIO STATION DATA

Station	Market	Format	Mon-Sun 5a.m.-1a.m. All Persons 12+ Wkly. Reach%	Aver. Hrs. Tuned
All Stations			96	22.1
CHED	Edmonton	Contemp.	22	7.0
CJCA	Edmonton	Adult Contemp. News, Talk	22	10.0
CIRK-FM	Edmonton	AOR	27	10.6
CISN-FM	Edmonton	Contemp. Country	19	11.8
CHQT	Edmonton	Easy Listening	16	15.0
CKRA-FM	Edmonton	Album Light Rock	21	7.7
CBX	Edmonton	Multi-format	14	9.7
CJKE-FM	Edmonton	MOR	8	7.4
CFRN	Edmonton	Oldies, Adult Contemp.	29	6.4
CBX-FM	Edmonton	Multi-format	6	6.6
CHFA	Edmonton	Multi-format	1	10.5
CKNG-FM	Edmonton	Adult Contemp.	10	3.8
CKER	Edmonton	Multicultural	n.a.	n.a.
CHMG	Edmonton	Classic Gold	11	13.2
CFCW	Camrose	C & W	17	10.2
CKRD	Red Deer	Adult COntemp.	1	10.7

Source - BBM Spring 1991 Radioi Reach Surveys; area coverage.

TV STATION DATA

Station	Market	Network Affiliation	Mon-Sun 6a.m.-2a.m. All Persons 2+ Wekly. Reach%	Aver. Hrs. Tuned
All Stations			96	21.0
CFRN	Edmonton	CTV	82	6.0
CITV	Edmonton	Ind.	82	5.0
CBXT	Edmonton	CBC	72	3.9
CBXFT	Edmonton	CBC	2	4.3
KREM	Spokane WA	CBS	45	2.2
KHQ	Spokane WA	NBC	48	2.6
KXLY	Spokane WA	ABC	57	2.7
KSPS	Spokane WA	PBS	17	1.7
WDIV	Detroit MI	n.a.	5	3.2
WTVS	Detroit MI	n.a.	9	1.4
VCR	n.a.	n.a.	21	4.0
A&E	n.a.	n.a.	11	1.9
ACCESS	Edmonton	n.a.	15	1.7
CNN	n.a.	n.a.	16	3.5
CABLE	n.a.	n.a.	4	2.7
MUCH	n.a.	Specialty	7	2.1
SUPER	Toronto	Pay TV	7	4.6
TSN	n.a.	Ind.	17	2.8
YTV	n.a.	Ind.	19	1.9

Source - BBM Spring 1991 TV Reach Surveys; CMA coverage.

Figure 8–9

Census tract map for part of Toronto

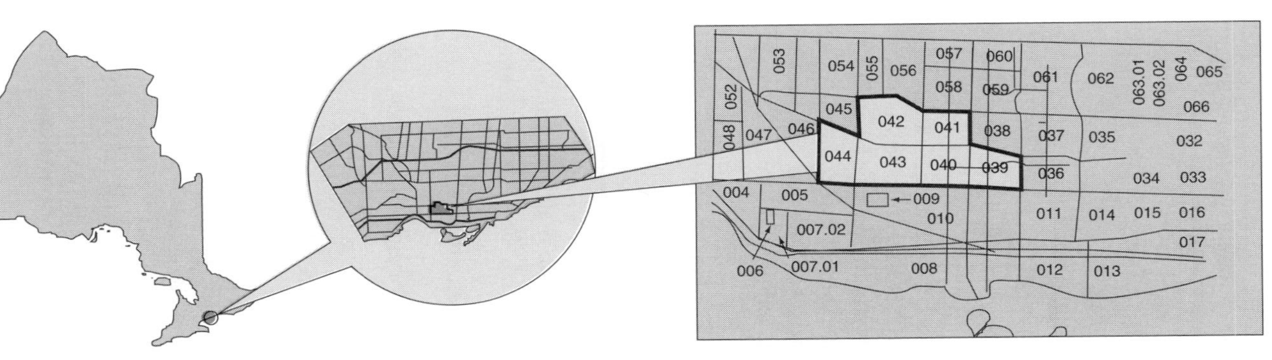

No.	Characteristics	Toronto 039	Toronto 040	Toronto 041	Toronto 042	Toronto 043	Toronto 044
	Population						
1	Population, 1986 (1)	3,840	5,078	3,902	5,916	4,561	5,966
2	Population, 1991 (2)	4,233	4,992	3,875	5,623	4,341	5,811
3	Population percentage change, 1986–1991	10.2%	–1.7%	–0.7%	–5.0%	–4.8%	–2.6%
4	Land area in square kilometres, 1991	0.31	0.36	0.31	0.47	0.54	0.49
	Population Characteristics						
5	Total population	4,235	4,990	3,875	5,620	4,340	5,810
	by sex and age						
6	**Male, total**	2,020	2,625	1,915	2,850	2,250	2,925
7	0–4 years	130	130	105	165	125	175
8	5–9 years	125	135	100	155	125	150
9	10–14 years	140	115	90	160	110	180
10	15–19 years	160	165	150	185	155	205
11	20–24 years	210	345	195	325	205	285
12	25–29 years	230	340	225	340	275	375
13	30–34 years	200	250	200	295	215	305
14	35–39 years	145	220	140	205	210	225
15	40–44 years	115	135	135	175	160	195
16	45–49 years	80	115	80	135	115	150
17	50–54 years	75	100	85	150	105	120
18	55–59 years	80	155	100	155	115	130
19	60–64 years	100	135	115	130	110	130
20	65–74 years	125	190	130	195	145	185
21	75 years and over	95	85	75	75	75	120
22	**Female, total**	2,215	2,370	1,965	2,775	2,090	2,880
23	0–4 years	130	105	100	135	125	175
24	5–9 years	115	95	90	135	105	165
25	10–14 years	135	100	125	155	120	150
26	15–19 years	150	145	130	175	125	170
27	20–24 years	220	260	220	295	215	260
28	25–29 years	190	275	235	345	235	330
29	30–34 years	190	220	170	280	195	250
30	35–39 years	150	160	130	210	180	220
31	40–44 years	135	155	120	155	140	175
32	45–49 years	105	110	90	150	95	155
33	50–54 years	125	140	100	145	105	110
34	55–59 years	100	140	120	145	85	135
35	60–64 years	120	130	90	135	105	140
36	65–74 years	180	205	150	195	125	255
37	75 years and over	175	130	95	130	120	200
	by legal marital status, persons 15 years of age and over						
38	Single (never married)	1,470	1,785	1,240	1,735	1,365	1,615
39	Legally married (and not separated)	1,295	1,985	1,670	2,480	1,790	2,495
40	Legally married and separated	150	90	60	120	110	130
41	Widowed	360	310	200	255	225	405
42	Divorced	185	140	90	130	135	170
	by mother tongue						
43	Single responses	3,925	4,735	3,620	5,230	4,090	5,420
44	English	1,560	1,390	960	1,315	1,455	1,660
45	French	45	25	15	40	35	35
46	Non-official languages	2,330	3,320	2,650	3,880	2,605	3,720
47	Italian	30	100	465	430	55	50
48	Chinese	1,280	1,130	540	415	250	225
49	Portuguese	290	1,600	1,365	2,450	1,815	2,940
50	Polish	55	125	20	60	75	80
51	Spanish	15-	25	90	165	70	100
52	Other languages	520	350	170	360	330	320
53	Multiple responses	310	255	255	395	255	390
54	English and French	15	10	10	15	10	20
55	English and non-official language(s)	255	235	225	355	220	355
56	French and non-official language(s)	5	–	5	5	–	5
57	English, French and non-official language(s)	–	–	5	5	5	5
58	Non-official languages	20	15	10	15	5	15

Income Rating Index. The **income rating index** is calculated by comparing the trading area's per capita income to the Canadian average in the following formula:

$$\frac{\text{per capita income for trading area}}{\text{per capita income: Canadian average}}$$

The resulting number indicates the buying potential of the area relative to the Canadian average and could be used to provide comparison with other trading areas in question. The information required to make this calculation can be obtained from Statistics Canada or *The Financial Post Canadian Markets*, which actually provides the index for most trading areas in Canada.

Market Rating Index. The **market rating index** is similar to the income rating index in that it compares the trading area's per capita retail sales to the Canadian average in the following formula:

$$\frac{\text{per capita retail sales for trading area}}{\text{per capita retail sales: Canadian average}}$$

The market rating index is an effective indicator of the retail potential of a trading area and is also calculated in *The Financial Post Canadian Markets*.

Retail Saturation Index. The **retail saturation index (RSI)** is a measure of the potential sales per unit of store space for a given product line within a particular market area.[9] As a market area evaluation tool, it incorporates both consumer demand and competitive supply. Essentially, the index is the ratio of a market area's capacity to consume to its capacity to retail. The formulation of the index of retail saturation is expressed as the following:

$$RSI = \frac{(C)\ (RE)}{RF}$$

where

RSI = retail saturation index for a given product line(s) within a particular market area,

C = number of customers in a particular market for a given product line,

RE = retail expenditures—the average dollar expenditure for a given product line(s) within a particular market area, and

RF = retail facilities—the total units of selling space allocated to a given product line(s) within a particular market area.

To illustrate, assume that a retail operation needs sales of $450 per square metre of selling space for a given product line to operate profitably. Also assume that the retailer is currently examining three potential market areas (see Figure 8–10). Market area A can be eliminated from further consideration because it does not meet the $120 minimum sales per square metre criterion. Both markets B and C meet the minimum sales criterion. If all other location considerations are equal, however, market B would be preferable to C because it offers the retailer more ($33.34 higher) sales potential per unit of selling space.

The retail saturation index enables the retailer to classify market areas on the basis of their competitive situation—understored, overstored, or saturated.[10] **Understored market areas** are those in which the capacity to consume exceeds the capacity to retail. In other words, there are too few stores and/or too little selling space devoted to a product line to satisfy consumer needs. **Overstored market areas** occur when the capacity to retail

Figure 8–10

Market area evaluation using retail saturation index

	Market area A	B	C
Number of customers (C)	40 000	50 000	70 000
Retail expenditures (RE)	$10	$12	$10
Retail facilities (RF)	1000	1200	1500
Index of retail saturation (IRS)	$400.00	$500.00	$466.66

exceeds the capacity to consume. In this situation, retailers have devoted too much space to a particular product line. The fact is that Canada is overstored in most of its larger urban markets. Finally, **saturated market areas** are places in which the capacity to retail equals the capacity of buyers to consume a product line. In this case, demand for and supply of a given product line are in equilibrium. The understored market area obviously offers the best opportunity for the retailer seeking a new location.

Retail Market Selection

After completing the market area identification and evaluation processes, the retailer must select regional and local markets. There are no simple decision rules to aid the retailer in selection. The basis of the location decision varies with types of retailers, operational characteristics, and stated objectives. At this point, the retailer's judgment is the critical factor. Ultimately, the retailer should select the regional and local markets that provide sufficient sales potential (level of support) and that are conducive to the firm's operational needs (ease of operation). Generally, the market area a retailer selects represents a compromise among several promising but different market situations.

Trading Areas

A **retail trading area** is broadly defined as that area from which a store attracts its customers or obtains its business. Depending on the kind of retail operations, a retail trading area can be described more specifically in the following terms:

- **Drawing power**—The area from which a shopping centre could expect to derive as much as 85 percent of its total volume.
- **Per capita sales**—The area from which a general merchandise store can derive a minimum annual per capita sale of $10.
- **Patronage probability**—The area from which potential customers come who have a probability greater than zero of purchasing a given class of products or services offered by a group of retailers.
- **Retail operations**—The area within which a retailer operates economically in terms of the relative relationship between sales volume and the cost of operations (for example, selling and delivery costs).

Two characteristics common to these definitions are that (1) they identify an area to which retailers draw customers over a specific period of time and (2) they identify a single focal point (such as a town, a shopping centre, or a single retail outlet) around which

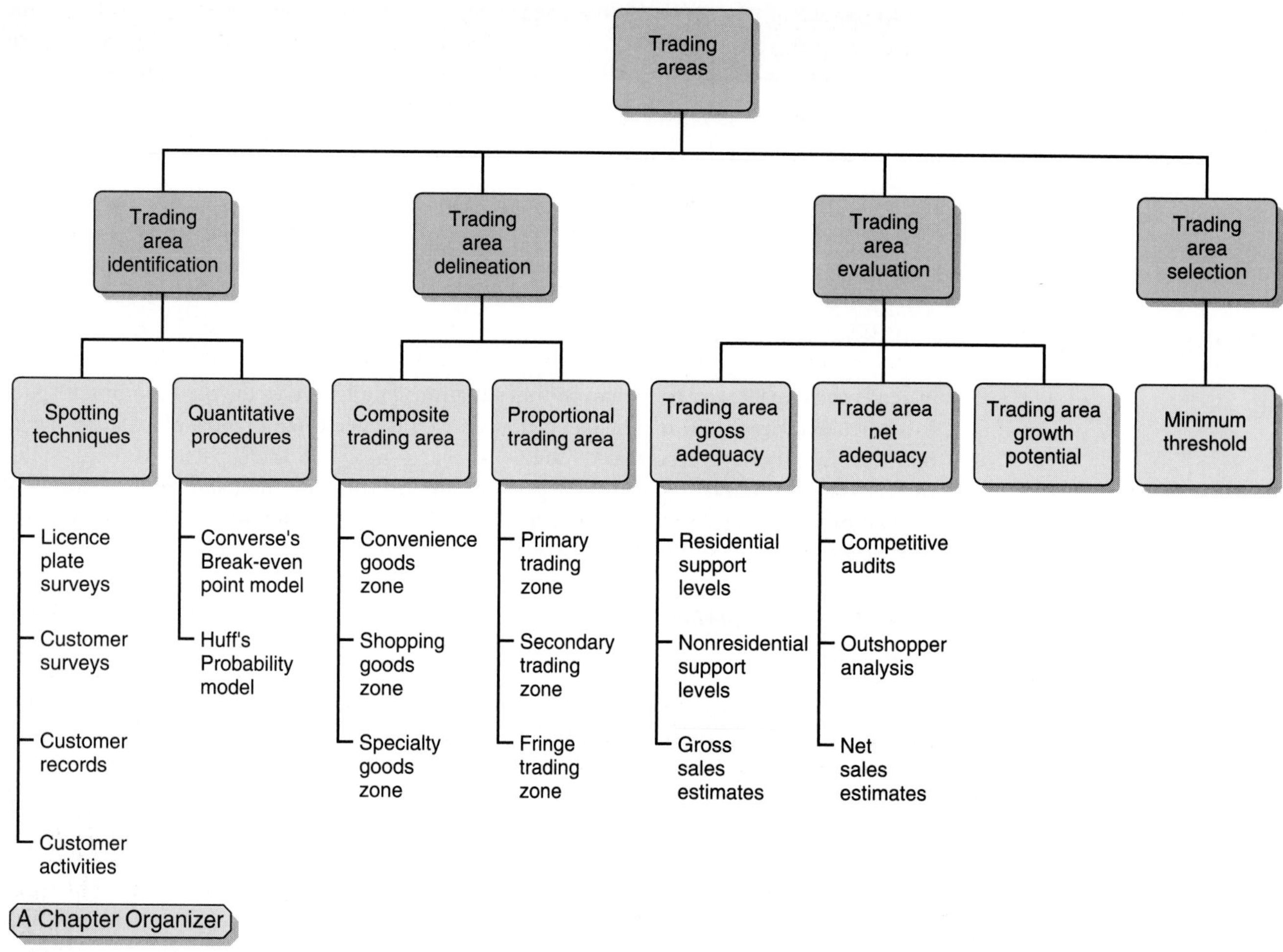

Figure 8–11

Trading area analysis

the trading area develops. Essentially, then, retail trading areas are "gravity areas"—retail sites to which consumers will gravitate or be pulled from an identifiable area.

As is the case with regional and local retail markets, analysis of retail trading areas is a four-stage process involving the identification, delineation, evaluation, and selection of those areas from which retailers plan to attract the majority of their customers. Figure 8–11 outlines the specifics of this four-stage process.

Trading Area Identification

Two general approaches for identifying trading areas are spotting techniques and quantitative procedures. The latter approach is more appropriate for new or expanding retail operations, and the latter technique is typically used by an existing retailer seeking to determine the extent of its present trading area.

Spotting Techniques

Spotting techniques include several methods by which the retailer attempts to "spot" customer origins on a map. By carefully observing the magnitude and arrangement of these origins, the retailer can identify the dimensions of the trading area. Retailers normally define customer origins by home addresses, although customers' places of employment also are important. Some of the more common spotting techniques include surveys of customers' license plates, customer surveys, analyses of customer records, and studies of customer activities.

Licence Plate Surveys. By recording the license plate numbers of automobiles in the store's parking lot, retailers can obtain customer home addresses. Sampling should include checking licence plates at different times of the day, days of the week, and weeks of the month to ensure a representative sample. The primary advantage of this technique is that it is relatively inexpensive to administer. Licence plate surveys have several limitations, however, including the following: (1) there is no way to determine who actually drove the car to the store or whether that car represents a regular customer or someone who just happened to be in the neighbourhood; (2) a survey of licence plates reveals no information on the shopping behaviour of customers, such as what they bought, how much they bought, where they bought, why they bought, or if they bought anything at all; and (3) the number of purchasers in each car cannot be determined.

Customer Surveys. A personal interview, mail questionnaire, or telephone survey can provide information on who lives or works in a given area and who are either current or potential customers. Actual customers can be surveyed on the premises (within a particular store or shopping mall) by either personal interviews or take-home/mail-back questionnaires. Good surveying techniques must be employed to ensure an unbiased, representative sample. Customer surveys can provide a significant amount of information regarding demographics and shopping behaviour; their limitations are cost, time, and the skill required to conduct them efficiently and effectively.

Customer Records. Retailers have several ways to obtain addresses of current customers as well as additional valuable information. Customer credit, service, and delivery records contain a great deal of information if properly developed and maintained. From their records, retailers can find customer addresses and places of employment, ages, sex, family status, telephone numbers, and types and amounts of purchases. Although customer credit, service, and delivery records are a fast, inexpensive means of obtaining information, they are biased because cash customers, who require no services or delivery, are omitted from the analysis.

Customer Activities. Any method that asks or requires customers to provide their names and addresses can help identify an existing or proposed trading area. One popular approach is to request the customer's postal code when ringing up the sale; generally this approach gets good results because consumers do not perceive the request as being intrusive into their private affairs. It is also a quick and easy process to implement. Promotional activities such as contests and sweepstakes can also be effective in obtaining names and addresses. Unfortunately, they tend to be biased toward the consumer who is willing to participate (for example, the high-income consumer would not think it worth the time).

Quantitative Procedures Retailers use several quantitative procedures to delineate retail trading areas,[11] most commonly **retail gravitation**, which provides a measure of the potential interaction between various locations by determining the relative drawing power of each location.[12] On the basis of the relative drawing power of a location within an area, each area can be identified as being part of a trading area (in some cases, trading areas can be shared by more than one location). Two of the more widely recognized gravity formulations are Converse's break-even point and Huff's probability model.

Converse's Break-Even Point Model. Converse developed a formula that enables the retailer to calculate the **break-even point** in miles or kilometres between competing retail centres (stores, shopping centres, or cities).[13] In essence, the break-even point is computed as the point between the competing retailing centres where the probability of a consumer patronizing each retailing centre is equal. This break-even point identifies the trading-area boundary line between competing retail trade centres. By identifying the break-even point between one retail centre and all competing centers, the retailer can determine the trading area. The formula is expressed as follows:

$$BP = \frac{d}{1 + \sqrt{\frac{P_1}{P_2}}}$$

Figure 8–12

Converse's break-even point model

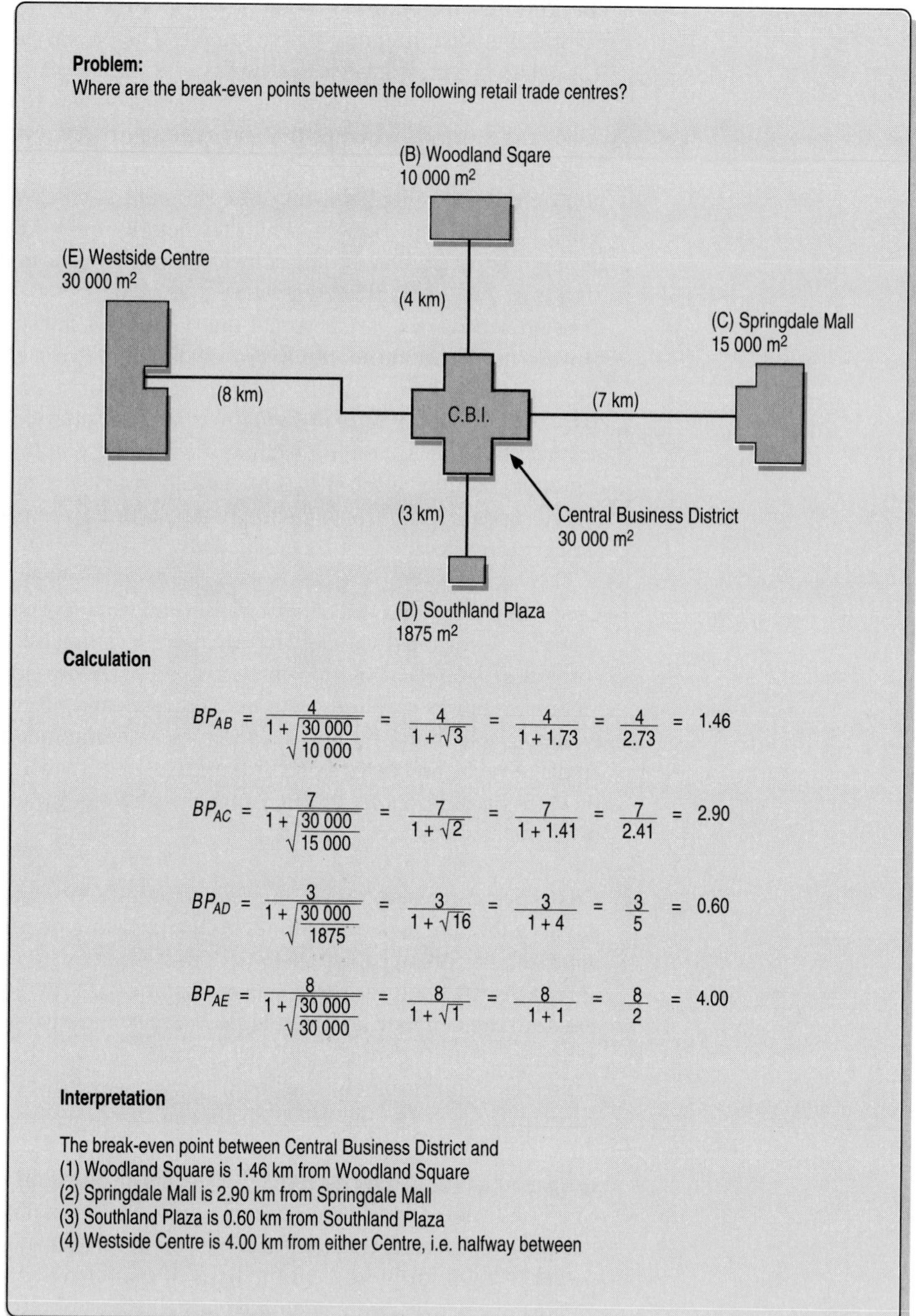

where

BP = break-even point between the competing retail centres in miles or kilometres from the smaller centre,

d = distance between the two competing retail centres,

P_1 = population of the larger retail centre, and

P_2 = population of the smaller retail centre.

Problem:
Where are the break-even points between the following retail trade centres?
(B) Woodland Sqare
10 000 m2
(E) Westside Centre
30 000 m2
(4 km)
(C) Springdale Mall
15 000 m2
(8 km)
C.B.I.
(7 km)
(3 km)
Central Business District
30 000 m2
(D) Southland Plaza
1875 m2
Calculation
$BP_{AB} = \frac{4}{1+\sqrt{\frac{30\,000}{10\,000}}} = \frac{4}{1+\sqrt{3}} = \frac{4}{1+1.73} = \frac{4}{2.73} = 1.46$
$BP_{AC} = \frac{7}{1+\sqrt{\frac{30\,000}{15\,000}}} = \frac{7}{1+\sqrt{2}} = \frac{7}{1+1.41} = \frac{7}{2.41} = 2.90$
$BP_{AD} = \frac{3}{1+\sqrt{\frac{30\,000}{1875}}} = \frac{3}{1+\sqrt{16}} = \frac{3}{1+4} = \frac{3}{5} = 0.60$
$BP_{AE} = \frac{8}{1+\sqrt{\frac{30\,000}{30\,000}}} = \frac{8}{1+\sqrt{1}} = \frac{8}{1+1} = \frac{8}{2} = 4.00$
Interpretation
The break-even point between Central Business District and
(1) Woodland Square is 1.46 km from Woodland Square
(2) Springdale Mall is 2.90 km from Springdale Mall
(3) Southland Plaza is 0.60 km from Southland Plaza
(4) Westside Centre is 4.00 km from either Centre, i.e. halfway between

Both the distance and population expressions require further explanation. Although distance is normally measured in miles or kilometres, studies show that many people think of distance in terms of travel time. Retail analysts can use travel time to replace miles or kilometres for the distance between competing retail centers. Populations (P_1 and P_2) can be expressed in several different ways. The total population in each centre is the most common measurement. Another approach is to use the centre's total number of retailers or the total retail space in the centre as the population measurement. Any measurement that reflects a retail centre's ability to attract customers can be used as an expression of population. Figure 8–12 illustrates the identification of shopping centre trading areas using Converse's break-even point method.

Huff's Probability Model. The consumer choice of a retail store or shopping cluster is a complex decision-making process. The number and importance of store and cluster attributes used in the selection process vary with each shopper. Huff's model "was the first to suggest that market areas were complex, continuous, and probabilistic rather than the nonoverlapping geometrical areas of central place theory."[14] The basic premise of Huff's "shopper attraction" model is based on the following empirical regularities:

1. The proportion of consumers patronizing a given shopping area (cluster) varies with distance from the shopping area.
2. The proportion of consumers patronizing various shopping areas (clusters) varies with the breadth and depth of merchandise offered by each shopping area.
3. The distance that consumers travel to various shopping areas (clusters) varies for different types of products purchased.
4. The "pull" of any given shopping area (cluster) is influenced by the proximity of competing shopping areas.[15]

The Huff's model computation is shown in Figure 8–13.

Figure 8–13

Huff's probability model for identifying retail trading areas

The model developed by D. L. Huff to measure the probability of consumers expected to be attracted to a particular shopping cluster can be formally expressed as follows:

$$\frac{\dfrac{S_i^k}{(Tij)^\lambda}}{\displaystyle\sum_{j=1}^{n} \frac{S_j^k}{(tij)^\lambda}} \qquad (1)$$

$i = 1, 2, \ldots, m$

$j = 1, 2, \ldots, n$

$k = 1, 2, \ldots, p$

where

p_{ij}^k = the probability of a consumer at a given origin i travelling to a particular shopping cluster j for a type k shopping trip

S_j^k = the size of the shopping cluster j devoted to shopping trip k (measured in units of retail selling area devoted to shopping trip k items)

T_{ij} = the travel time involved in getting from a consumer's point of origin i to a given shopping cluster j

λ = a parameter which is to be estimated empirically to reflect the effect of travel time on various kinds of shopping trips

m = the number of origins in the marketing area

n = the number of shopping clusters in the marketing area

p = the number of different types of shopping trips defined

Trading Area Delineation

Trading areas range in size from a few square blocks to a radius of many kilometres. The size of a trading area is a function of the following items:

- The type of goods and services offered by the retailer. Specialty goods retailers draw from a larger trading area than do convenience goods outlets because consumers are willing to travel greater distances to buy specialty goods. One Canadian study found that consumers will travel one kilometre to save 1 percent on the cost of an item. The travelling time was increased for specialty goods, however.[16]
- The size of the store and the extent of its mix of merchandise. Large physical facilities (for example, a wholesale club) that offer a broader and deeper selection of products have greater drawing power than do smaller stores with less selection.
- The number, size, and format of neighbouring competitors. Many large compatible retailers that cluster together and create a one-stop comparative shopping opportunity (for example, large destination stores in a shopping centre) will create a greater attraction than smaller, noncompatible retail clusters.
- The type and character of the transportation network serving the store and its surrounding area. Multilane thoroughfares with controlled intersections, crossable medians, and attractive speed limits create greater accessibility, hence more extensive trading areas.

As suggested, the structure of retail trading areas can be delineated by a variety of factors. Two representative structures are reviewed in this discussion: composite and proportional trading areas.

Composite Trading Area A **composite trading area** is a set of trading areas, each of which is structured according to the type of goods the retailer sells. Figure 8–14a illustrates the composite trading area for a store (or shopping centre) selling convenience, shopping, and specialty goods. In this case, the retailer draws from a larger trading area for

Figure 8–14

Trading area delineation: (a) composite trading area and (b) proportional trading area

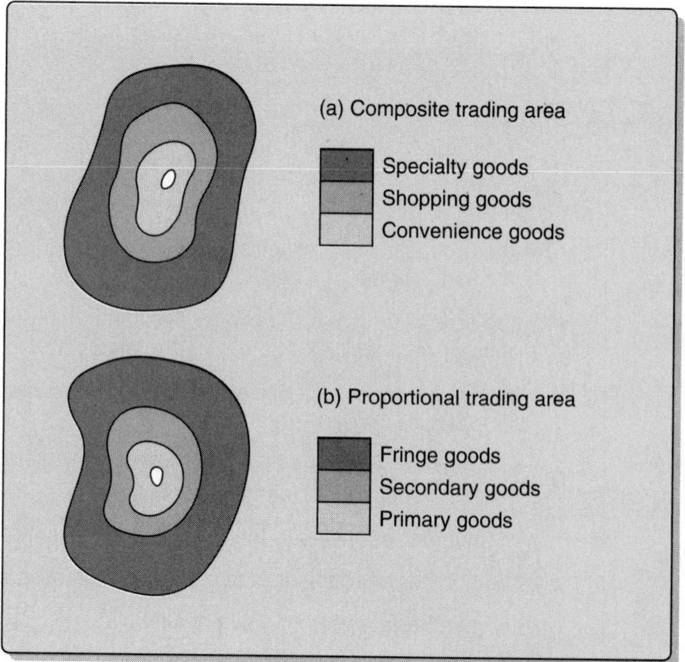

specialty goods than for shopping and convenience goods. The consumer's willingness to exert shopping effort, as described earlier, accounts for the composite area boundary lines.

Proportional Trading Area A **proportional trading area** is based on the distance customers are from the store. The farther customers are from the retail store, the less likely they are to patronize it, and vice versa. This statement defines what retailers call the "distance decay function"; that is, the number of customers attracted to a given store decreases as their distance from the store increases. As illustrated in Figure 8–14b, three distance zones—primary, secondary, and fringe—constitute the proportional trading area.

The *primary trading zone* is the area around which a retailer can expect to attract 50–70 percent of its business. The primary trading area can be defined in one of three ways: (1) the area closest to the store; (2) the area in which the retailer has a competitive advantage, such as customer convenience and accessibility; and (3) the area from which the retailer produces the highest per capita sales. The *secondary trading zone* surrounds the primary zone and generally represents 20–30 percent of the retailer's total sales volume. From the secondary zone, consumers usually select the store as their second or third shopping choice. The fringe trading zone is that area from which the retailer occasionally draws customers (5–10 percent of the business). Retailers generally attract customers from this zone either because they "just happened to be in the vicinity" or because they are extremely loyal to the store or its personnel.

Trading Area Evaluation

A basic trading area evaluation involves two questions: (1) What is the total amount of business that a trading area can generate now and in the future? and (2) What share of the total business can a retailer in a given location expect to attract? Although there is no standard trading area evaluation process, most procedures use the concepts of trading area adequacy and trading area potential to predict total trading area business and the share of business a particular retailer can expect.[17]

Trading area adequacy is the capability of a trading area to support proposed and existing retail operations, in terms of gross or net form (see Figure 8–15). **Gross adequacy** is the capability of a trading area to support a retail operation without any consideration of

Figure 8–15

Elements of trading area adequacy

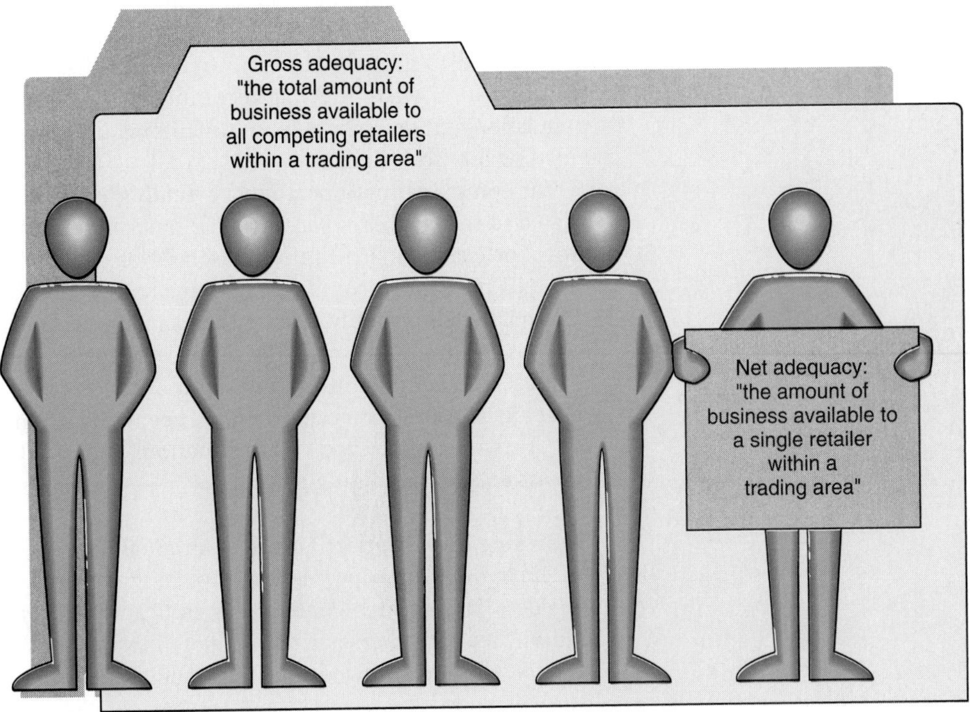
Gross adequacy:
"the total amount of
business available to
all competing retailers
within a trading area"
Net adequacy:
"the amount of
business available to
a single retailer
within a
trading area"

retail competition, that is, the total amount of business available to all competing retailers within a defined trading area. On the other hand, **net adequacy** is the capability of a trading area to provide support for a retailer after competition has been taken into account. Finally, **trading area potential** is the predicted ability of a trading area to provide acceptable support levels for a retailer in the future.

Trading Area Gross Adequacy Measuring gross adequacy determines a trading area's total capacity to consume. The capacity of a retail market to consume is a function of the total number of consumers within a trading area at any given time and their need, willingness, and ability to purchase a particular class of goods. Chapter 4 provides an in-depth discussion of this equation and its impact on store patronage behaviour. Unfortunately, it is not easy to determine consumers' need, willingness, and ability to buy a certain class of goods. To determine gross adequacy, the retailer must first consider appropriate consumption units (such as people, homes, businesses) to count for a general class of goods. Second, the retailer must find an appropriate measure of a consumption unit's need, willingness, and ability to buy. To feel confident in their analyses, retailers must use one or more indicators of their potential buyers' behaviour. Finally, the support capabilities of a trading area depend to some extent on sources outside the gross trading area.

Residential Support Levels. After sufficiently delineating the gross trading area, a retailer must concentrate on the most important source of business: the area's residents. To measure a trading area's potential consumers, the retailer must analyze both population/demographic and household/residential variables.

A trading area's total capacity to consume is partly a function of the total number of people who reside in that trading area. It is important to obtain an accurate population count, because the total population figure plays a part in several quantitative estimates of gross and net adequacy. Although total population figures are informative, a trading area's capacity to consume may not be directly related to its total population; instead, it may be a function of the number of people who have a certain demographic makeup—such as age, sex, income, occupation, and family status. For example, measurements such as the number of children (bike store), the number of women (women's clothing store), or the number of high-income homeowners (expensive home furnishings) indicate a population count that should produce more reliable gross adequacy estimates.

Evaluating gross adequacy is a matter of identifying demographic characteristics that best indicate the consumer's need, willingness, and ability to buy and of obtaining a reliable count of the number of people who have the desired demographic makeup. The location specialist's goal should be to figure out the basic customer demographics and then seek locations where they are plentiful. At the local trading area level, a good source of population and demographic information is the census tract and census area reports provided by Statistics Canada.

For some retailing operations, a trading area's capacity to consume is more directly related to the *number of households* or *residential units* than to the number of people in the area. For example, a count of household or residential units is probably more indicative than is a population count of a trading area for hardware, furniture, and appliance goods. This relationship simply reflects the fact that the household unit purchases many goods, and the consumer's home is the prime determinant of the need for certain product lines. A household unit count by tracts and areas can be obtained from Statistics Canada. To reflect its consumption capacity more accurately, each residential unit can be weighted by average value, size, type of construction, and characteristics noted in housing census reports and local building permits.

Nonresidential Support Levels. Although the majority of a trading area's consumption capacity comes from people who live in that area, some do not. Consumers who reside outside a trading area contribute significantly to that area's capacity to consume. Most trading areas are characterized by daily inward, outward, and through migration of consumers who are attracted into the trading area for work, recreation, and other reasons, such as the need for professional services. Although these consumers might live far away, they do represent a significant portion of trade customers who visit the area. Some of these customers visit frequently and regularly (work trip); others visit infrequently and irregularly (recreation trip). Nevertheless, this external consumption capacity should be included in assessing a trading area's gross adequacy.

Although it is impossible to count accurately the number of consumers that make up the external consumption capacity, it is possible to count the number of nonresidential units likely to attract consumers to the trading area (for example, retailers, wholesalers, manufacturers, offices, schools, churches). Because not all nonresidential units have equal consumption-generating abilities, each must be weighted according to its capability to generate traffic. Because some nonresidential units are more compatible with a retail enterprise than are others, the weights a retailer assigns to each nonresidential unit should reflect the degree of consumer-retailer compatibility.

Gross Sales Estimates. Of the several methods available to estimate trading area sales, the two most widely used are the corollary data method and the per capita sales method. The **corollary data method** assumes that an identifiable relationship exists between sales for a particular class of goods and one or more trading area characteristics (such as population, residential units). Knowledge of these relationships helps retailers estimate total sales. The **per capita sales method** estimates trading area sales for a general product line and is a function of the per capita expenditures for that product line times the total population of that trading area. Retailers can obtain reliable population counts from census materials and per capita expenditure figures from consumer surveys and trade source estimates.

Trading Area Net Adequacy To answer the question, "What is my slice of the pie?" a retailer must estimate the net adequacy of the trading area. Net adequacy has been defined as the proportion of sales volume a retailer can expect to receive from the total sales in a trading area—that is, the percentage of gross adequacy (or market share) a retailer can expect to get. To determine net adequacy, a retailer must consider the trading area's *capacity to consume* and its *capacity to sell.*

The capacity to consume is the gross adequacy measurement. Having obtained a gross estimate of the trading area's sales volume capabilities, the retailer's next problem is to find a method of allocating total sales volume to each of the trading area's existing and proposed competitors. This allocation process consists of (1) analyzing the competitive environment and (2) estimating each retailer's sales and market share.

To determine net adequacy, a retailer must first identify the competitive environment. To analyze the competitive environment, the retailer examines the types of competition, the number and size of competitors, and the marketing mix of competitors. To gain a clearer picture of the competitive environment, a retailer can use two methods: (1) a competitive audit and (2) an outshopper analysis.

Competitive Audits. A **competitive audit** is an arbitrary, composite rating of each competitor's product, service, price, place, and promotion mixes. An audit covers a wide range of activities, including eyeballing competitors' floor space, checking ad results, getting information from media people and vendors, checking competitors' prices, and evaluating the competition's merchandise mix. The purpose of a competitive audit is to assess the ability of competitors to provide a marketing mix that consumers desire within the trading area. The sum of all audits is a measurement of total competition.

Outshopper Analysis. Not all consumers who live within a trading area shop exclusively in that area. A group of consumers known as *outshoppers* frequently and regularly shop outside their local trading area. These consumers spend a considerable amount of time, money, and effort in making inter–trading area shopping trips. To obtain an accurate estimate of total expected sales, the retailer must perform **outshopper analysis**, subtracting outshopping sales, referred to as *sales leakage*, from the trading area's gross sales to arrive at a more realistic total sales volume for the trading area. To estimate sales leakage that results from outshopping behavior, a retailer can either conduct consumer surveys or use standard adjustments. In using consumer surveys, the retailer asks trading area consumers to estimate how much they spend locally on a particular class of goods as a percentage of their total expenditures for those goods. The retailer then can use this percentage to adjust the gross sales figure for the trading area. A simpler and less expensive method is the standard adjustment, which depends on prevailing trading area conditions. For example, if the trading area contains a large number of consumers who are similar to the demographic and psychographic profile of outshoppers, the retailer should make a standard downward adjustment (for example, 5 percent) in gross sales.[18]

Net-Sales Estimates. After evaluating the competitive environment, a retailer can estimate each competitor's sales. To calculate the net adequacy figure (that is, the trading area market share), the retailer can use either the total sales method or the sales per unit of space method. Both methods use a ratio of trading area capacity to consume (gross adequacy) to trading area capacity to sell.

With the *total sales method*, a retailer allocates an equal share of the trading area's total sales for a specific product category to each competing retailer. This calculation is shown in Figure 8–16. The advantage of this method is that it is simple and quick to calculate. A limitation, however, is the assumption that all competing retailers are equal and can generate an equal share of the trading area sales. Because competing retailers devote different amounts of time, money, space, and effort to sales, the analyst must make adjustments to the "all are equal" assumption. The competitive audit, discussed earlier, can be used to make this adjustment.

Another method for allocating trading area sales to competitors is the *sales per unit of space method*, in which the retailer computes a ratio of each retailer's floor space devoted to a specific product category to the total of all retail floor space for the product category in the trading area. The calculation procedure is illustrated in Figure 8–17. This method assumes that selling space is a good predictor of a retailer's competitiveness. Variations of this method substitute amounts of shelf space (linear, square, or cubic metres or feet), sales per employee, or sales per checkout counter for sales per square metre or foot.

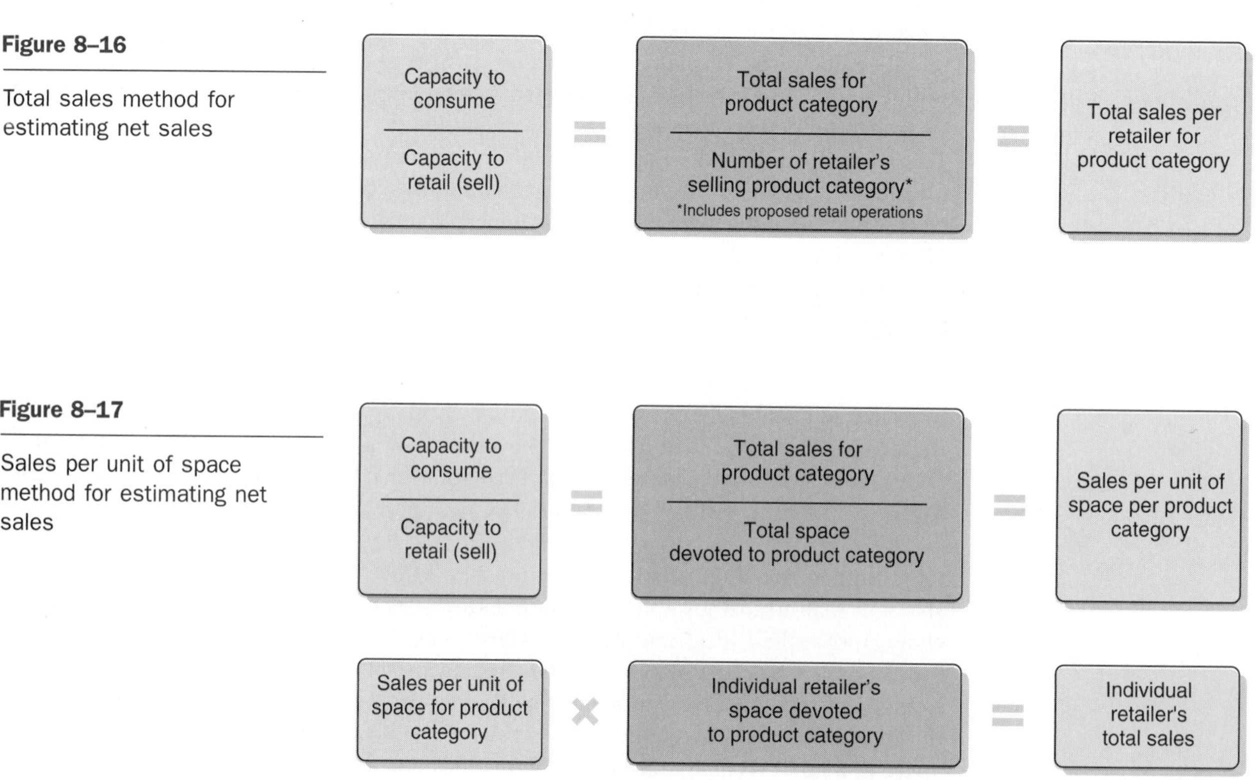

Figure 8–16

Total sales method for estimating net sales

Figure 8–17

Sales per unit of space method for estimating net sales

Trading Area Growth Potential Before completing the trading area evaluation process, the retailer must answer an additional question: What does the future hold for the trading area? Because marketing opportunities can change quickly, dynamically growing trading areas often become either static or declining markets. Visual observation of an area is a simple method of looking into the future. Although lacking scientific methodology, visual inspection of current activities can produce a useful picture of the future. A retailer should consider several factors:

1. New and expanding residential areas combined with older, stable neighbourhoods provide a solid base for future growth.
2. An expanding commercial or industrial base signals growth opportunities.
3. A good balance between items 1 and 2 reflects a stable growth rate that avoids overdependence on limited economic activity.
4. A well-developed transportation network as well as proposed future transportation networks in the trading area contribute to a trading area's growth.
5. An involved local government that takes an interest in residential and business development is a great asset.
6. A progressive social and cultural environment (theatres, museums, zoos, and so on) is a healthy climate for business.

Trading Area Selection

To make the final selection of a trading area, the retailer must evaluate the alternatives in accordance with the goal measurements established by management for each store's performance. Performance standards are often expressed as a minimum threshold; following are three commonly cited ones:

1. A stated minimum population having the desired demographic characteristics (such as 10 000 persons);
2. A stated minimum sales volume (such as $300 000/year);
3. A stated minimum daily traffic count (such as 5000 vehicles per day).

If a trading area does not meet at least one or a certain combination of these minimums, the retailer excludes it from further consideration.

Retail Sites

A **retail site** is the actual physical location from which a retail business operates. Unlike many retailers that focus on one type of location (for example, regional mall locations), The Gap has expanded its choice of physical locations to include downtown sites, main street locations in midsize cities, freestanding sites in urban neighbourhoods, as well as key positions within community, regional, and specialty malls.[19]

Specialists in the retailing field comment that a retailer's site is one of the principal tools for obtaining and maintaining a competitive advantage through spatial monopoly. A given site is unique when its "positional qualities" serve a particular trading area consumer in a way that no other site can match. Obviously, competing sites are also uniquely situated. The *retailer's site problem*, therefore, is how to identify, delineate, evaluate, and select the best available site alternative to serve the needs of consumers profitably within an identified trading area (see Figure 8–18).[20]

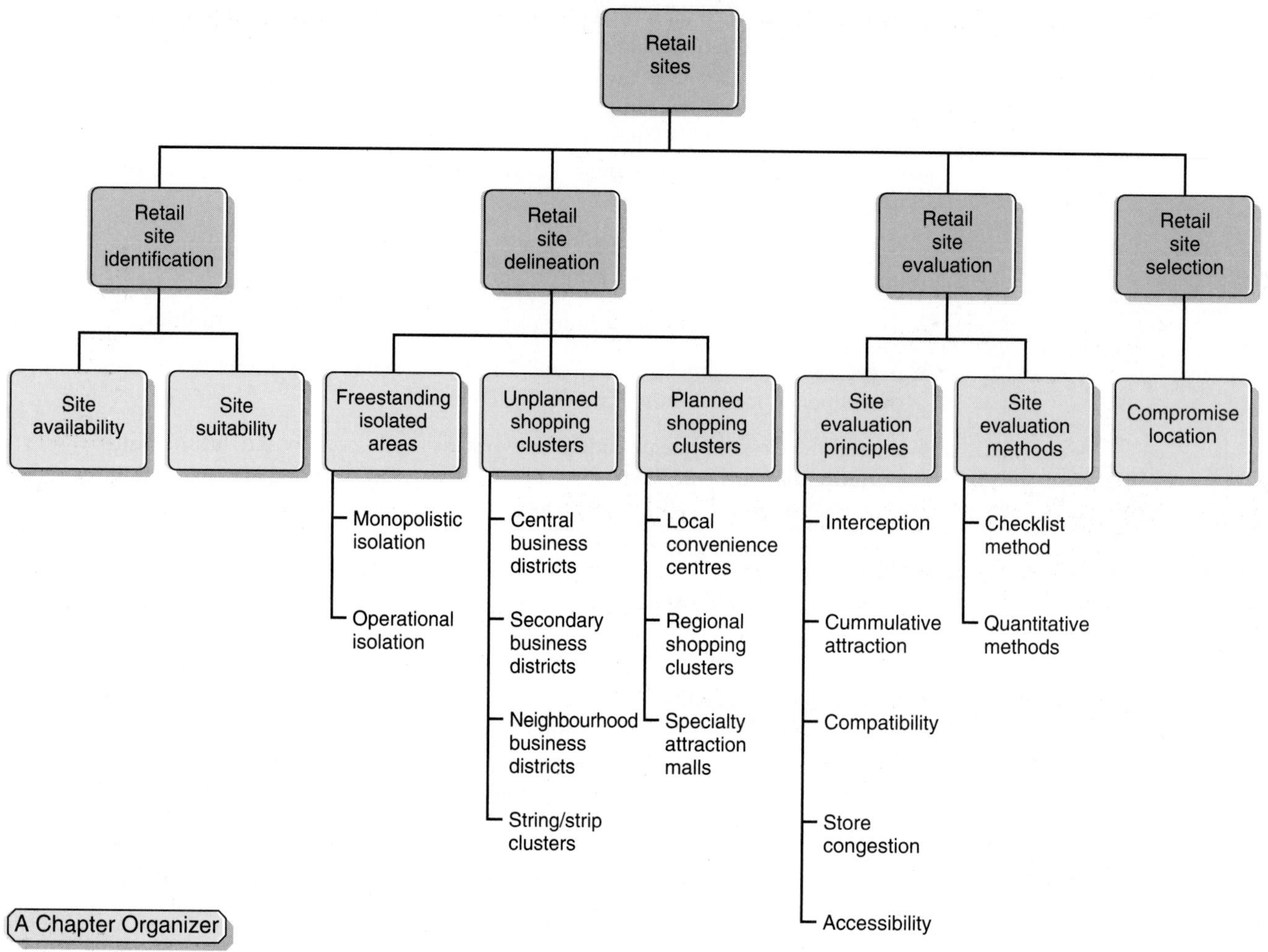

Figure 8–18

Retail site analysis

Retail Site Identification

The first step in appraising retail site locations is to identify all potential site alternatives, which can range from a few to a lot. Before attempting any formal evaluation, the retailer should screen the alternatives as to their availability and suitability.

Site Availability Having completed a retail market and trading area analysis, the location specialist has now narrowed the problem to locating individual commercial properties available within each trading area slated to be served. Practical considerations deem it necessary to find and appraise the merits of those sites that are available for rent, lease, or purchase. Site availability can be determined by scanning the commercial real estate sections of the newspaper or by using the services of a commercial real estate broker. Recently the expansion of Loblaw Stores to Quebec was stalled due in part to an inability to find adequate sites.[21]

Site Suitability Prior to conducting a full-scale site analysis, the retailer must screen the available alternatives in terms of their general suitability. Because comprehensive site analysis programs are costly, sites should be qualified before the retailer assumes those expenses. In determining site suitability, the retailer should ask the following questions:

- Are the site and facilities of a suitable size, shape, and structure?
- Are the site and facilities consistent with the retailer's image and mode of operation?

What constitutes the right **activities mix** can be vastly different for different types of malls. The local convenience centre is largely devoted to in-and-out shopping activities. Power strips offer more recreational and entertainment activities in the form of fast-food and dine-in restaurants, sports bars and nightclubs, and movie theatres. Regional and superregional malls offer food courts, walking circuits, entertainment events, health clubs, product and service demonstrations, and a host of other shows and exhibits. Megamalls add amusement parks, recreational facilities, and numerous other personal and social amenities to those activities commonly found in regional malls. Recently the West Edmonton Mall has found the need to add even more entertainment with the addition of such retailers as the Hard Rock Café, Hooters, Planet Hollywood, and Kaos.[33] Finally, for historic and restoration malls, entertainment and socialization often has equal billing with shopping in the capability of the mall to attract shoppers and other visitors. The list of additional services and activities provided by mall management is expected to grow as intermall competition heats up for the turn of the century.[34]

The structure of a planned shopping cluster's **tenant mix** is very important; as described in Figure 8–19, a different combination of specialty, shopping, and convenience goods and services retailers is appropriate for each shopping cluster.[35] Depending on mall type and size, each developer must find the right blend of (1) general merchandise lines (for example, apparel, shoes, gifts, food); (2) pricing points (for example, exclusive, upper, middle, value); (3) lifestyle and demographic specialties; (4) large anchor/destination stores and small specialty/interceptor stores; (5) full- and limited-service establishments; (6) goods and services retailers; and (7) national chains and local establishments.

A recent trend in planning a centre's tenant mix is to lease to temporary retail tenants. These retail alternatives include kiosks, pushcarts, showcase modules, and electronic catalogue machines. For a limited time they add merchandise variety, marketplace atmospherics, and a sense of the unusual to the centre's normal operational mode. Perhaps the most important consideration involving tenant mix is that it represents the best collection of goods and services for those consumers constituting the centre's trading area.

Mall Layout. Shopping centres are designed in a variety of shapes and arrangements. A given configuration must conform to the site's terrain and the tenants' space requirements and cost restrictions, as well as provide ease of customer movement. The layout of neighbourhood, community, and power strips is, as the name implies, a straight line strip adjacent to a traffic artery. Strip centres are also constructed with a courtyard or L- or U-shaped layout. Specialty attraction malls are configured to support its special feature or, as in the case of restoration malls, to reflect the original structure.

Although any number of configurations are possible, Figure 8–21 illustrates four basic shopping centre configurations. The "I" plan is the simplest and most common regional shopping centre configuration (see Figure 8–21a). Although the I plan is efficient for retailer space requirements and customer movement, it does not create an interesting and exciting shopping environment. For superregional centres containing three or more major anchors, retailers can use either the "Y" plan (Figure 8–21b) or the "L" plan (Figure 8–21c). The "X" plan serves as the basic configuration for the four-anchor, superregional centre (Figure 8–21d).

Regardless of the configuration, a key feature of most superregional and regional shopping centres is a central court. Some superregional centres, megamalls, and specialty centres have several smaller secondary courts, each with its own character and decor. The importance of courts lies in their image-creating role; the central court is what consumers remember most often and most vividly. Another layout and design consideration involves planning various mall areas. Mall areas are the centre's traffic arteries; as such, they must facilitate movement and exchange of customers throughout the entire complex. The length and width of mall areas are prime considerations in planning for movement and exchange. To overcome the "tunnel effect" commonly associated with long mall areas, several design features have been used to create a more comfortable psychological environment. The most common is a "break" in the mall approximately midway between major attractions, such as the central court; however, if the distance between the central court

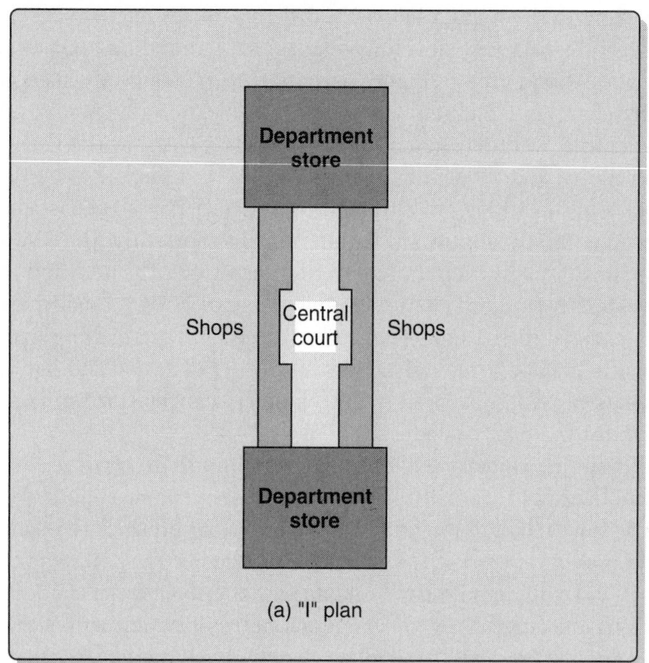

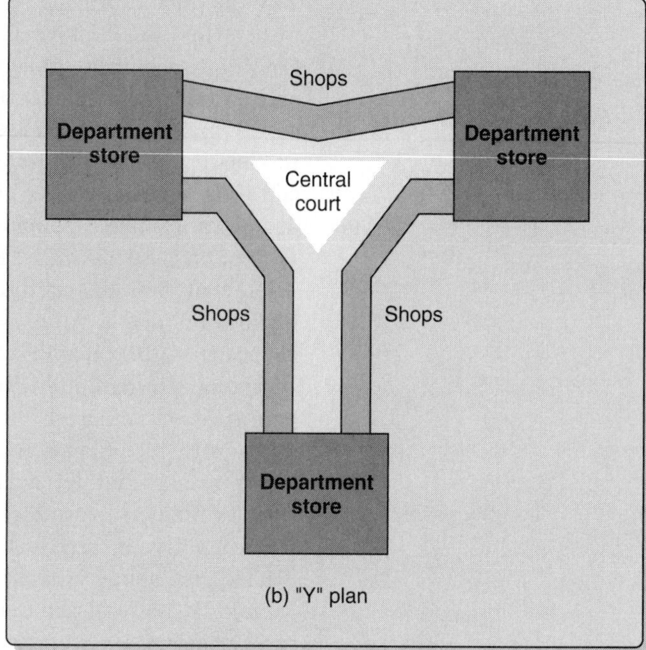

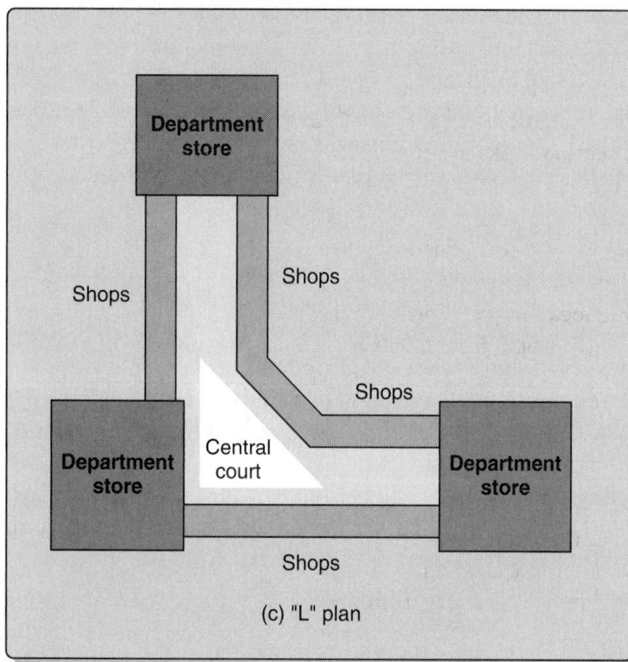

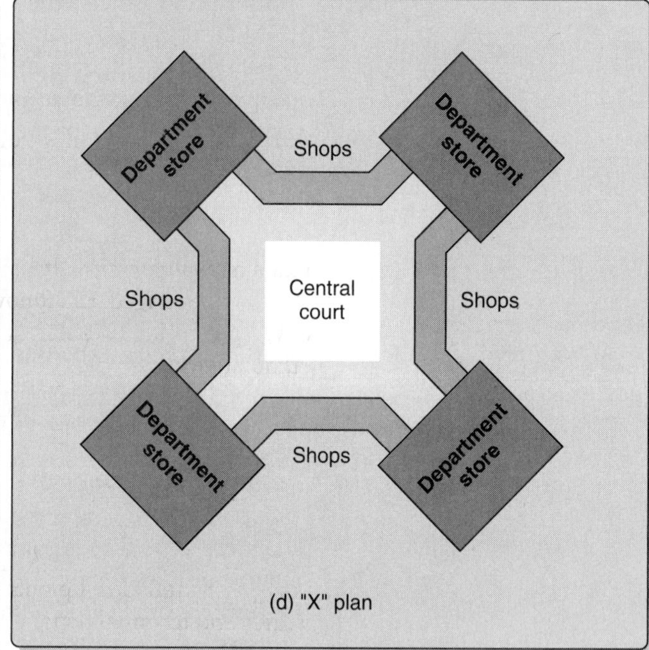

Figure 8–21

Basic regional shopping centre configurations: (a) the "I" plan, (b) the "Y" plan, (c) the "L" plan, and (d) the "X" plan

and each department store is too long, additional breaks may be required. Secondary court areas and slight angles in the mall that require shoppers to make short turns before they can see the remainder of the mall can be extremely effective in reducing the tunnel effect.

Besides customer movement and exchange, mall areas should facilitate shopping. Storefronts should afford the consumer some privacy for window-shopping without jostling from passing pedestrian traffic. Some mall designs incorporate kiosks to create the happy and busy atmosphere of an open marketplace. These freestanding booths with highly specialized product lines (greeting cards, cutlery items, T-shirts, candy) and services (minibanks, snack bars, utility cashiers) add a new dimension to the mall's shopping atmosphere and contribute substantially to profitability.

Mall Location. For retailers, their location within the mall has a considerable impact on their success. Traditionally, malls and centers were built around the "attractor/intercepter" strategy. **Attractors** are large anchor retailers positioned at each end of the centre; their extensive merchandise selection and advertising muscle are used to attract customers to the centre. **Interceptors** are smaller retailers located on the mall area between the centre's anchors; the basic premise of the interception is that people walking up and down the malls going from one anchor to another will be exposed to the offerings of the specialty retailers and engage in impulse or complementary buying.

A retailer's position relative to major anchors, mall intersections, activity areas, comparable retailers, and entrances/exits all are extremely important site decisions that must be judged on an individual basis. With consumer markets becoming more segmented, shopping centres and areas within shopping centres (wings) are being planned as a collection of stores with a purpose and a target market rather than an unrelated positioning of stores offering undefined impulse shopping to random passersby.

"The reliance of larger centres on department stores and mass merchandisers, although a strength in earlier periods, is becoming a liability in the 1990s."[36] Although the traditional department store and mass merchandiser anchor will continue as a major element in the shopping centre's tenant mix, new and different anchors are becoming more important. In some areas, category killers (aggressive, high-volume specialty superstores such as Toys 'R' Us and Future Shop, are assuming the role of anchors as a result of their ability to generate high traffic volumes and attract consumers from considerable distances.

Retail Site Evaluation

The following sections discuss the site evaluation process in two phases. The first section explains several principles of site evaluation and how retailers use them to assess the value of alternative sites. The second section looks at several methods by which retailers evaluate alternative site locations (see Figure 8–18).

Site Evaluation Principles Several consumer-oriented location principles help retailers evaluate site alternatives. Although there are no standard criteria by which all sites can be judged, the following location principles provide the necessary framework for developing practical solutions to the problem of retail site evaluation: (1) interception, (2) cumulative attraction, (3) compatibility, (4) store congestion, and (5) accessibility.

Interception. The principle of **interception** covers a site's positional qualities that determine its capability to "intercept" consumers as they travel from one place to another (see "Mall Location" discussion). Interception has two distinct elements: a source region, from which consumers are drawn; and a terminal region, or consumer destination, to which consumers are drawn. Examples of source and terminal regions are residential areas, office complexes, industrial plants, business districts, and shopping centers. Any point between source and terminal regions can be considered a point of interception. New shopping malls in airports survive by intercepting the traveling public as they wait for departures or arrivals.[37]

In considering a site's interceptor qualities, the evaluator has both an identification and evaluation problem. The identification problem involves determining (1) the location of source and terminal regions, (2) the lines connecting those regions, and (3) appropriate points (sites) along the connection line. The evaluation problem is one of measuring the magnitude and quality of these regions, lines, and points. Thus, the evaluator's problem is how to determine whether a site is an efficient "intervening opportunity" between known source and terminal regions. One common practice is to locate coffee and doughnut shops on the workbound side of a traffic artery and grocery stores and other service outlets on the homebound side of the street.[38]

A different perspective of the interception principle is often expressed as the concept of *location vulnerability*. In this case, the evaluator's job is to determine the source of a competitor's business and then locate a site that intercepts the competitor's customer flow. If such a location exists, the firm's competitor is vulnerable in terms of location, at least regarding one or more source regions.

It is difficult to measure interceptor qualities because of the numerous potential source and terminal regions, connecting lines, and interceptor points (sites) along these lines of movement. Location specialists often use traffic volume as a surrogate measurement of interception.

Cumulative Attraction. According to the principle of **cumulative attraction**, a cluster of similar and complementary retailing activities will generally have greater drawing power than will dispersed and isolated stores engaging in the same retailing activities. Retail location literature often refers to the cumulative attraction effects of the familiar "rows," "cities," and "alleys." In many large cities, certain types of retailing establishments tend to cluster in specific areas. Examples are the familiar automobile rows, mobile home cities, and restaurant alleys. The evaluator's problem in this case is how to determine whether the retail operation can benefit from the cumulative drawing power of a site's immediate environment.

Compatibility. Retail **compatibility** refers to the "degree to which two or more businesses interchange customers."[39] As a rule, the greater the compatibility among businesses located in close proximity, the greater the interchange of customers and the greater the sales volume of each compatible business.[40] Compatibility among retailers occurs when their merchandising mixes are complementary, as in the case of an apparel shop, shoe store, and jewellery store that are located close to one another. If there are several apparel, shoe, and jewellery stores located in the same cluster, all the better! They are not only complementary, they also provide a healthy competitive situation that satisfies the customers' need for comparison shopping and thus provide greater customer interchange for the retailer. Sometimes shopping centre managers reduce cross-shopping (that is, customer exchange) because they spread "like establishments" (intratype competitors like shoe stores) throughout the mall, rather than concentrating them in one area of the mall. As a rule, however, good comparative shopping opportunities benefit all concerned.

A high degree of compatibility is more likely to occur when the pricing structures of neighbouring businesses are complementary. Other things being equal, there will be a greater interchange of customers between one high-margin retailer and another than between a high-margin and a low-margin retailer.

Equally important in site evaluation is determining whether neighbouring businesses are compatible. An exclusive dress shop would be incompatible with a pet shop, for example, because of the odour and noise produced by the pets.

Store Congestion. At some point, the advantages of cumulative attraction and compatibility end, and the problems of site congestion begin. The principle of **store congestion** states that as locations become more saturated with stores, other business activities, and people, they become less attractive to additional shopping traffic. High retail store densities create the perception of crowding, an uncomfortable feeling that will discourage shoppers from visiting a retail shopping cluster.[41] This phenomenon results from the limited mobility of people and cars in the area.[42] Retailers should have learned this lesson from the original congested CBDs. Although the excitement of the crowd can be a positive factor, the aggravation of a mob can be a limiting factor, discouraging customers from visiting the site. Thus, in the site evaluation process, the retailer should estimate at what point the volume of vehicle and foot traffic would limit business, both in the present and the near future. In measuring store congestion, the retailer should recognize that the shopper's tolerance for retail crowding may differ across types of retail establishments (for example, discount stores versus department stores) and shopping times (for example, Christmas season, weekends, lunch hour).

Accessibility. Perhaps the most basic of site evaluation principles, the principle of **accessibility** states that the more easily potential consumers can approach, enter, traverse, and exit a site, the more likely they will visit the site to shop. Accessibility is a function of both physical and psychological dimensions. The physical dimensions of accessibility are tangible site attributes that either facilitate or hinder the actual physical movement of potential consumers in, through, or out of a site. Psychological dimensions of accessibility include how potential customers perceive the ease of movement toward and away from a site. If consumers believe that it is difficult, dangerous, or inconvenient to enter a site, then a psychological barrier has been created equal to any physical barrier. Retailers should consider both real and apparent barriers to accessibility:

1. **Traffic arteries**—The number of traffic arteries adjacent to a site has a profound effect on the consumer's ability to approach and enter the site. Other things being equal, a corner site that is approachable from two traffic arteries is more accessible than a site served by a single traffic artery. Traffic arteries are not all equal, though. Major thoroughfares provide greater accessibility to trading areas than do secondary, feeder, or side streets.

2. **Traffic lanes**—The more lanes in a traffic artery, the more accessible the site located on this artery. Multilane arteries are the consumer's first choice in selecting routes for most planned shopping trips. Multilanes often reduce the consumer's access to a site, however, especially with left turns. Given some drivers' hesitancy to turn left across traffic, wide roads create a psychological barrier, especially when consumers must cross two or more lanes of oncoming traffic.

3. **Directional flow**—The accessibility of any site is enhanced if the site is directly accessible from all possible directions. Any reduction in the number of directions from which the site can be approached has an adverse effect on accessibility. Usually, several traffic arteries adjacent to the site enhance accessibility. The location analyst should examine local maps to determine directional biases.

4. **Intersections**—The number of intersections in the site's general vicinity has both positive and negative effects on accessibility. A large number of intersections offers consumers more ways to approach a site but may also reduce accessibility because of slower speeds and the consumer's increased risk of an accident. Where intersections are plentiful, the role of traffic control devices (such as traffic lights and stop signs) becomes critical. Consumers generally perceive a site located on a three- or four-corner intersection as very accessible because these kinds of intersections are fairly standard; consumers are familiar with them and with negotiating them. When there are more than four corners at an intersection, consumers are often confused by the "unstandardized" configuration.

5. **Medians**—The type of median associated with each of the site's adjacent traffic arteries strongly influences accessibility. Some medians are crossable, others are not. Generally, crossable medians increase accessibility, although in varying degrees. Medians that provide a "crossover lane" are more encouraging to potential consumers attempting site entry than are those without a crossover lane. Crossable medians that force consumers to wait in a traffic lane until crossover is possible create a perceived danger.

   Uncrossable medians are both a physical and psychological barrier to site entry. Elevated and depressed medians serve to separate traffic physically, but they also separate traffic psychologically. Potential consumers travelling on the right side of an uncrossable median tend to feel isolated from left-side locations and become more aware of right-side locations, where access is substantially easier.

6. **Speed limit**—The speed limit on a traffic artery influences a site's accessibility, because it determines the amount of time potential customers have in which to make a decision about entering a site. Expert opinions vary over what constitutes an ideal speed limit. The limit must be high enough to encourage consumers to use the route but low enough to allow them a safe and easy approach to the site.

7. **Traffic control devices**—In terms of accessibility, traffic lights have an enormous effect at crossovers because of the protection left-turn arrows allow. Traffic lights may be more important for their psychological value than for their physical value. Consumers perceive retail sites with controlled crossovers as more accessible. "Free left turn" lights are extremely important to site accessibility. *Stop signs* can increase accessibility in two ways. First, the chances of creating consumer awareness of the retailer's location and product offering are higher if traffic "stoppers" force consumers to halt and look around. Second, stop signs help to space the flow of traffic. Psychologically, these breaks in traffic are extremely important to the potential customer attempting to cross over from a left-hand lane. *Traffic rule signs* prohibiting U-turns and left turns can reduce site accessibility.

   Finally, one effective way to reduce traffic confusion and increase the actual and perceived safety and ease of entering a site is to employ guidance lines (turn- and through-arrows and traffic lines) to direct traffic.

8. **Site dimensions**—The proposed site should be large enough to facilitate all four components of accessibility. Sufficient space should be available to allow ease of parking as well as turning and backing in and out without interfering with consumers who are entering and exiting the site. The shape of the site also can affect accessibility. The wider the site, the greater the exposure to passing traffic, which thereby increases consumer awareness of the retailer's location and activities.

Site Evaluation Methods Analysts use several methods to evaluate retail site alternatives. Some of these methods are subjective, verbal descriptions of a site's worth; others provide objective, quantitative measurements. The subjective methods lack the qualities for good scientific decision making, and the latter methods require specialized skills and equipment. Certain methods, however, incorporate both simplicity and objectivity without the need for specialized training or equipment. One such method of site evaluation is the checklist.

Checklist Method. The checklist method provides the evaluator with a set of procedural steps for arriving at a subjective yet quantitative expression of a site's value. First, the evaluator enumerates the general factors that are usually considered in any site evaluation. A typical list of factors includes all or most of the site evaluation principles: interception, cumulative attraction, compatibility, and accessibility. Second, for each general factor, the evaluation identifies several attribute measurements that reflect the location needs of the proposed retail operation. For example, interception, which is a key location attribute for most convenience retailers, can be divided into the volume and quality of vehicular and pedestrian traffic.

Third, each location attribute receives a subjective weight on the basis of its relative importance to a particular type of retailer. A common weighing system assigns 3 to very important, 2 to moderately important, 1 to slightly important, and 0 to unimportant attributes. The fourth step is to rate each site alternative in terms of each location attribute. Any number of rating scales can be constructed; one possible scale might range from 1 to 10, with 1 as very poor and 10 as highly superior. To illustrate, a site alternative located on a major thoroughfare with a high volume of traffic throughout the day might be rated a 9 or a 10; another located on a traffic artery characterized by high volumes of traffic only during the morning and evening rush hours could be rated 5 or 6.

Fifth, a weighted rating is calculated for each attribute for each site alternative. The weighted rating is obtained by multiplying each attribute rating by its weight. Sixth, the weighted ratings for all attributes are added to produce an overall rating for each site alternative. The last step is to rank all evaluated alternatives in order of their overall ratings. Figure 8–22 illustrates the checklist method for evaluating one site alternative for a fast-food restaurant. If, for example, the numerical value of 236 is the highest of all evaluated

Figure 8–22

The checklist method

Evaluation factor*	Rating	Weight	Weighted rating
Interception			
Volume of vehicular traffic	8	3	24
Quantity of vehicular traffic	8	3	24
Volume of pedestrian traffic	3	3	9
Quantity of pedestrian traffic	2	3	6
Cumulative attraction			
Number of attractors	4	1	4
Degree of attraction	5	1	5
Compatability			
Type of compatability	6	2	12
Degree of compatability	7	1	7
Accessability			
Number of traffic arteries	8	3	24
Number of traffic lanes	10	3	30
Directional flow of traffic	7	2	14
Number of intersections	7	2	14
Configurations of intersections	4	3	12
Type of medians	2	3	6
Speed limit of traffic arteries	5	3	15
Number/type of traffic control devices	6	2	12
Size and shape of site	6	3	18
Overall site rating			236

*For definitions of evaluation factors, see the text discussion of site-evaluation criteria.

alternatives, then from the standpoint of site considerations this alternative would be rated as the retailer's first choice.

The checklist method has the advantages of being (1) easy to understand, (2) simple to construct, and (3) easy to use. In addition, it gives considerable weight to the opinions of location experts who know the firm and its locational requirements.

Quantitative Methods. Several quantitative models can be used to evaluate retailer sites, but only two are detailed here.[43] **Analogue models** are used to make sales projections for new stores on the basis of the sales performance of existing stores.[44] The chain retailer can approach the evaluation problem by finding the best "match" between the characteristics of new site alternatives and those of successful existing sites. This matching process is usually quantified into a statistical model. Ease of implementation is the principal advantage of an analogue approach. This model, however, suffers from two important drawbacks:

> One problem is that the results are dependent on the particular stores chosen as analogues and therefore rely heavily on the analyst's ability to make judicious selection of analogous stores. The second, and perhaps more important difficulty,

is that the method does not directly consider the competitive environment in evaluating the sites. The competitive situation is brought into consideration only through the selection of analogue stores.[45]

Regression models are a more rigorous approach to the problem of site location; hence, they offer certain advantages over checklist and analogue approaches. First, a regression model allows "systematic consideration of both trading area factors as well as site-specific elements in a single framework. Further, regression models allow the analyst to identify the factors that are associated with various levels of revenues from stores at different sites."[46] The basic multiple regression model for analyzing determinants of retail performance is expressed as a linear function of location (L), store attributes (S), market attributes (M), price (P), and competition (C):

$$Y = f\,(L,S,M,P,C)$$

Retail Site Selection

The final selection of a retail site is essentially a process of elimination. By analyzing regional and local markets, assessing retail trading areas, and appraising retail site locations, the retailer has narrowed the range of choices to site alternatives consistent with the firm's objectives, operations, and future expectations. If markets, trading areas, and sites have all been carefully evaluated, the retailer should be able to arrive at the final location decision. Normally, the retailer will not select the optimal location but rather a compromise location that has most of the desirable attributes.

In the end, no steps, procedures, or models can totally quantify the final site selection process. Nevertheless, with the data generated and the analysis completed in the market, trading area, and site evaluations, the retailer has sufficient information to make a good site selection.

Summary

Retail location decisions involve the process of identifying, delineating, evaluating, and selecting retail markets, trading areas, and retail sites. A retail market is defined geographically as that area or place where consumers and retailers meet for the purposes of exchange. Retail markets are identified using the market potential approach (capability of a market to supply enough sales to ensure the success of the store) and the retail operations approach (the market factors that might enhance or limit the efficiency of the store). Retail market areas are delineated into regional markets (geodemographic, census regions, and communication subregions) and local markets based on media areas, urban areas, postal code areas, and census areas. Retail market evaluation relies on various standard sources of information (for example, *The Financial Post Canadian Markets, Statistics Canada Census Tracts, Market Research Handbook* and *A.C. Nielsen Co. Data Profile*) and standard evaluation methods (for example, income rating index, market rating index, and the retail saturation index).

The area from which a store attracts most of its customers is referred to as a retail trading area. Spotting techniques (locating customer origins on a map) and various quantitative methods (break-even point and probability models) are used in identifying the retailer trading area. Trading area structure is delineated into composite trading areas based on the type of goods sold (convenience, shopping, or specialty) or proportional trading zones (primary, secondary, or fringe) based on the distance decay function.

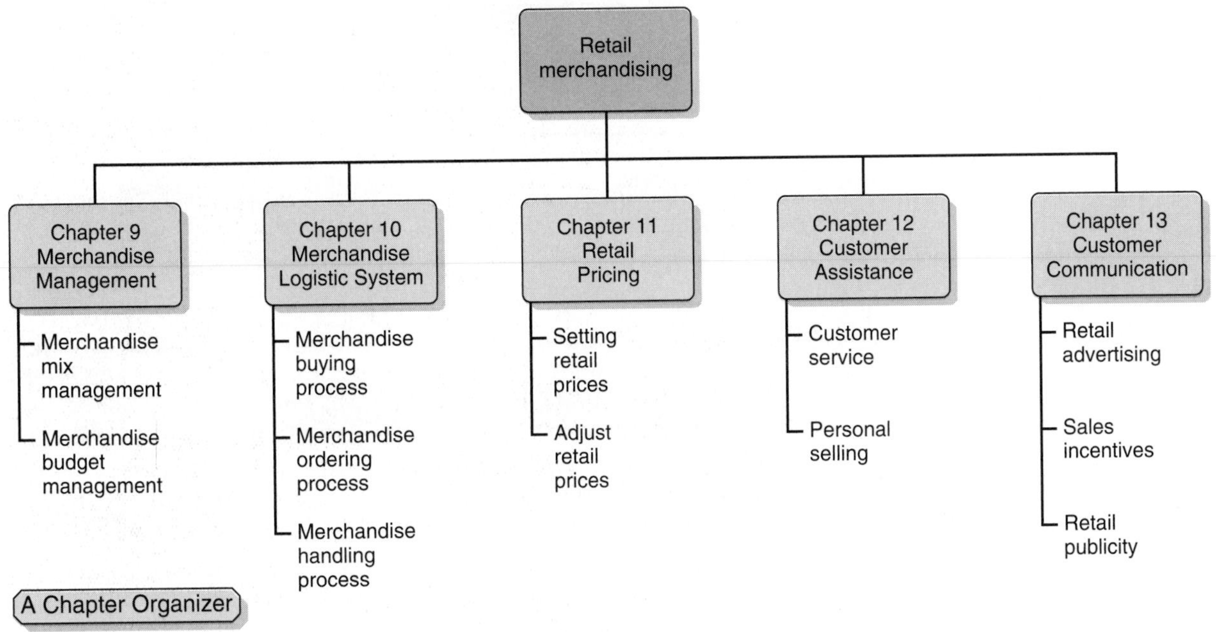

Figure 9–1

Retail merchandising

profit margins. Customer support services and the retailer's personal selling effort are reviewed in Chapter 12. Customer services and personal attention are some of the product "extras" that help build customer loyalty. The last merchandising functions to be discussed are the retailer's advertising, sales incentive, and publicity programs; effective customer communication is the subject of Chapter 13.

Retail Merchandise Management

Merchandise management focuses on planning and controlling the retailer's merchandise mix and its corresponding merchandise *budgets* (see Figure 9–2). **Merchandise planning** consists of establishing objectives and devising plans for obtaining those objectives. **Merchandise control** involves designing the policies and procedures for collecting and analyzing merchandise data to determine whether the stated objectives have been achieved. Planning is the process of establishing performance guidelines, whereas control is the process of checking how well management is following those guidelines.

The **merchandise mix** represents the full range or mixture of products the retailer offers to consumers. The merchandise mix represents appropriate combinations of products to meet customers' specific needs. The number of appropriate mixes is nearly unlimited. As such, success often depends on whether the retailer can identify and operationalize a new and appropriate mix. In making merchandise mix decisions, the retailer must also recognize the degree of perishability of many products. What is an appropriate mix today might not be an appropriate mix tomorrow.

Developing the merchandise mix provides the retailer with one means of dividing the total market and appealing to a select group of consumer segments. By buying, stocking, and selling a select combination of products, the retailer can appeal to particular demographic segments, certain lifestyles, or specific buyer-behaviour patterns.

The **merchandise budget** is a financial tool for planning and controlling the retailer's merchandise inventory investment. While the planning and control of the merchandise mix is directed at meeting consumer-based objectives, equally important in the

Figure 9–2

Retail merchandising management

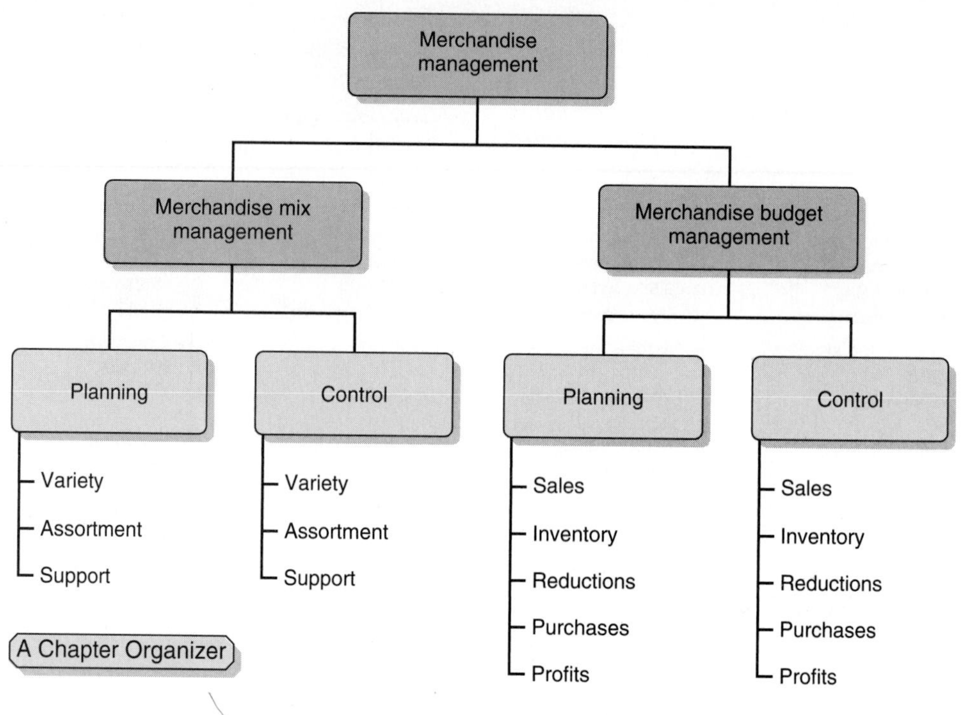

merchandising process is the firm's financial objective of profitability. To ensure profitable operations, the retailer must use a merchandise budget in which sales volumes, stock levels, retail reductions, purchase orders, and profit margins are carefully planned and controlled. The importance of a well-executed budget becomes obvious when one realizes that retailers have millions of dollars invested in inventories at any given time; fractional improvements in the planning and controlling of the merchandise budget can net thousands or perhaps millions of dollars in extra profits.

Merchandise Mix Management

Before proceeding with an examination of management issues involved with the merchandise mix, it is necessary to fully delineate and characterize this multidimensional concept. If the merchandise mix represents appropriate combinations, the obvious question becomes "Appropriate combinations of what?" The answer is "Appropriate combinations of product lines, product items, and product units." A **product line** is any grouping of related products in which the relationship is important to the consumer. A **product item** refers to a specific product within a product line that is unique and clearly distinguishable from other products within and outside the product line. "**Product units**" is an expression used to describe the total number of a particular product item that a retailer has in stock. For example, 100 six-packs (product units) of Coca-Cola (product item) in the soft drink section (product line) describes one part of a supermarket's total merchandise mix. The relationship among product lines, items, and units is shown in Figure 9–3.

To plan and control this collection of product lines, items, and units, the retailer structures the merchandise mix on the basis of (1) merchandise variety, (2) merchandise assortment, and (3) merchandise support. **Merchandise variety** is the number of product lines the retailer stocks in the store. The retailer can engage in variety strategies ranging from a narrow variety of one or a few product lines to a wide variety encompassing a large number of product lines.

Figure 9–3

The relationship among product lines, product items, and product units

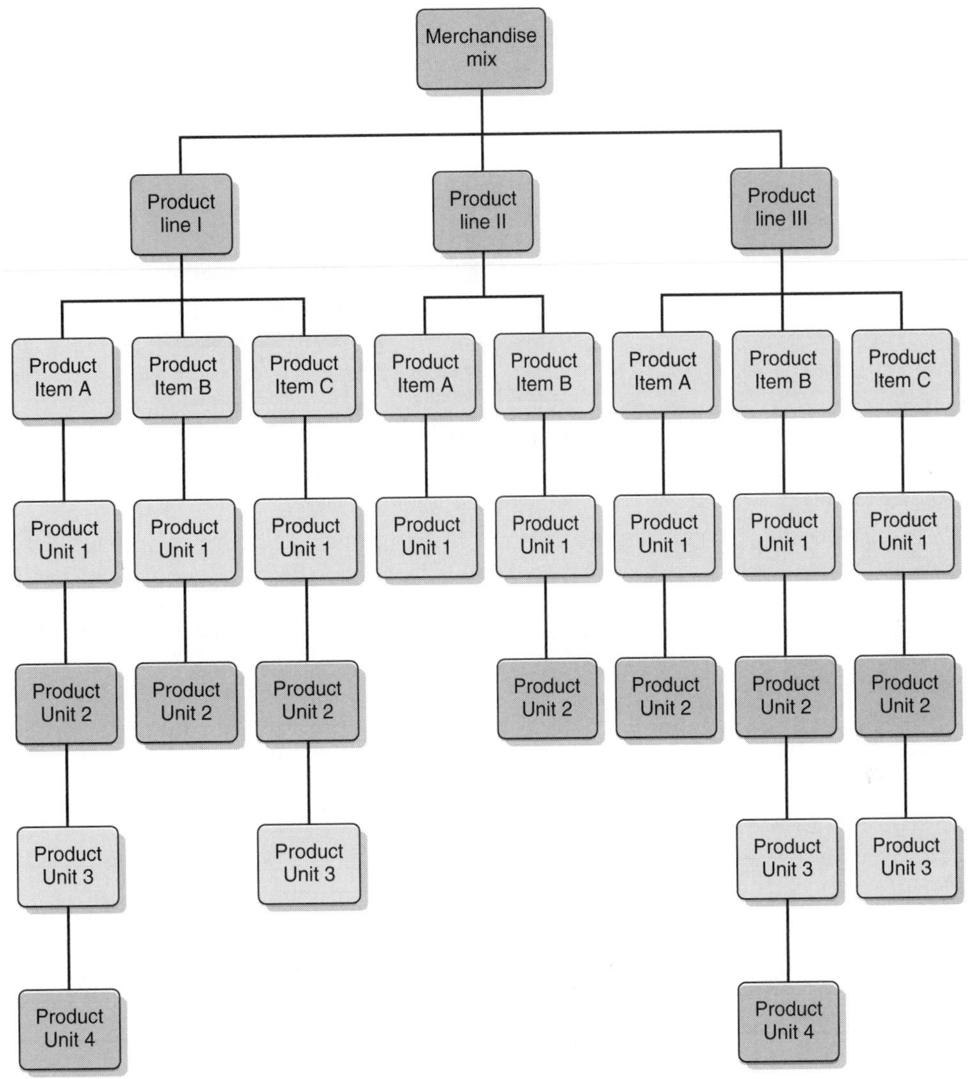

Merchandise assortment refers to the number of different product items the retailer stocks within a particular product line. Assortment strategies vary from shallow assortments of one or a few product items within each line to deep assortments having a large selection of product items within each line. Nikon offers retailers a deep assortment of sunglass lenses differentiated by type of activity. Nikon's wardrobe of sunglasses include specific models for skiing, driving, hiking, flying, shooting, and swimming.[4] **Merchandise support** deals with the planning and controlling of the number of units the retailer should have on hand to meet expected sales for a particular product item. Merchandise support strategies range from low (one or two units) to high (many units of a particular item) support levels.

The interrelated structure of the merchandise mix is illustrated in Figure 9–4. Variety, assortment, and support strategies are discussed more fully later in this section. Having defined the components of the merchandise mix, our discussion now turns to the many management issues involved with planning and controlling the appropriateness of this collection of products. Figure 9–5 outlines each planning and control issue as it pertains to developing and executing the retailer's merchandise variety, assortment, and support strategies.

Figure 9–4

The components of the merchandise mix

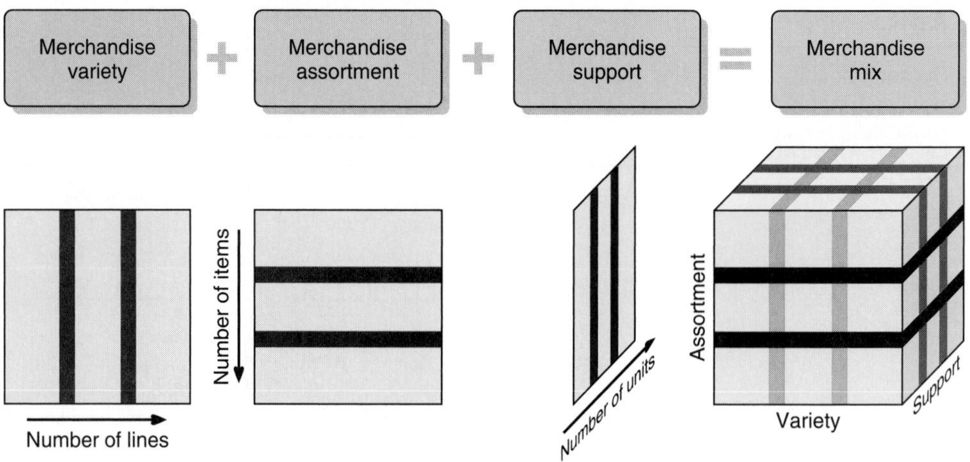

Figure 9–5

Merchandise mix management

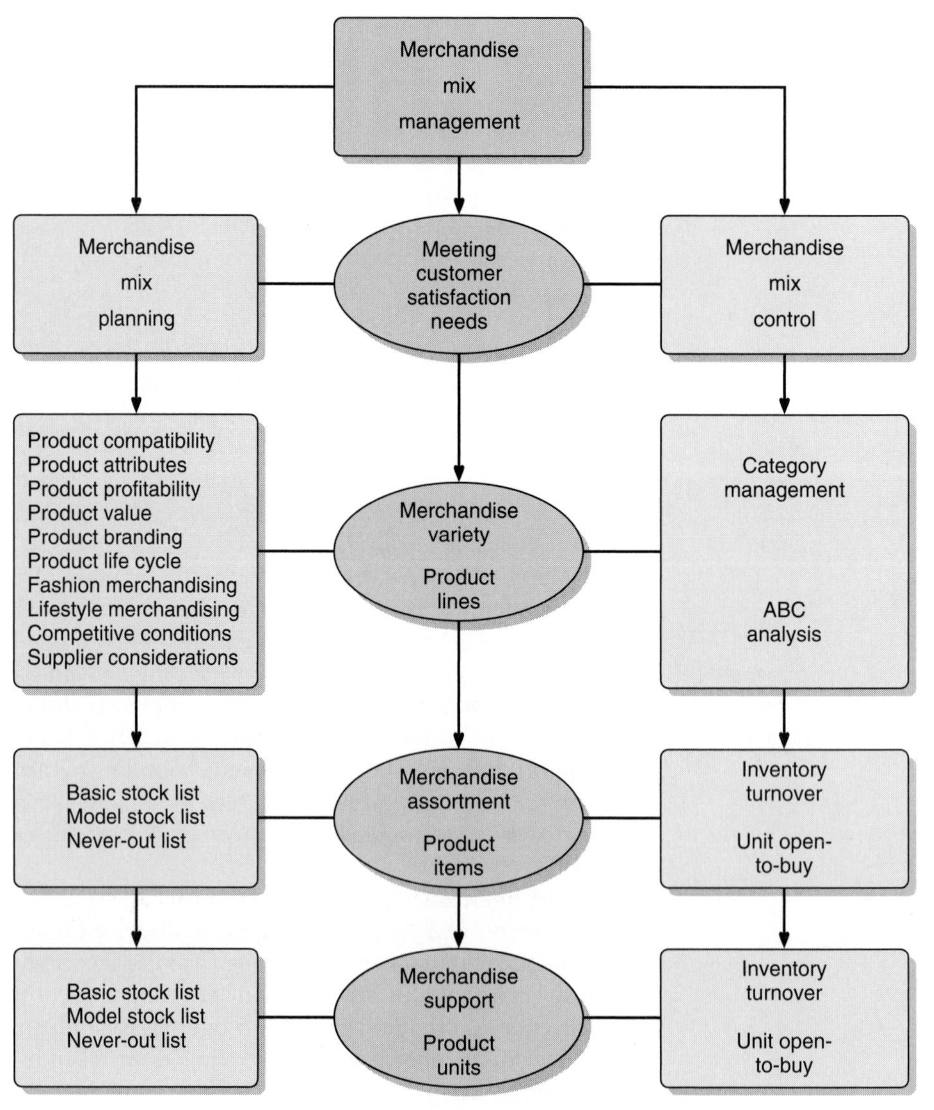

Planning Merchandise Variety

Merchandise variety involves the problems of product line planning and control. On the basis of type and degree of relationship, product lines are grouped to facilitate the retailer's planning of an appropriate merchandise mix. Products can be classified or combined in terms of (1) satisfying a particular need (for example, health or beauty aids); (2) being used together (for example, pieces of living room furniture); (3) being purchased or used by a similar customer group (for example, women's, men's, or children's wearing apparel); or (4) vendor or manufacturer (Nike, Reebok, or Converse). The degree to which products are related also can vary greatly. For illustration in this text, product lines are classified into three groupings: merchandise group, merchandise category, and merchandise class or classification.

A **merchandise group** is a broadly related line of products that retailers and consumers associate together according to end use. Examples of merchandise groups include such wide product combinations as furniture and appliances; home furnishings and housewares; casual and sports apparel; footwear and sporting goods; cosmetics and jewellery; food and health care products; and lawn, garden, and automotive products. Single-line retailers often are identified on the basis of these broad product groupings (for example, hardware store, clothing store). Mass merchandisers frequently use merchandise groups to identify operating divisions. General or divisional merchandise managers are responsible for managing the merchandise mix at this level.

A **merchandise category** is a closely related line of products within a merchandise group. This level more clearly distinguishes consumer need, usage pattern, or behaviour. It often corresponds to the operating departments of a traditional department store and serves as a way to identify many specialty retailers (for example, men's, women's, or children's apparel). Ethan Allen, the bastion of traditional furniture, has refashioned its product lines to appeal to a wider range of customers. Four styles create the basic product categories around which each store is merchandised. They include American Impressions (sturdy wooden pieces inspired by Shaker designs), Country Crossings (a rustic line of maple furniture), American Dimensions (modern look that accents geometric shapes), Legacy (styles that reflect an Italian architectural influence), and Radius (sleek designs reminiscent of the 1960s).[5] The increasing importance of merchandise categories as a product line grouping is evident in the rapidly expanding retail format known as the "category killer."

Sunglass Hut
www.sunglasshut.com

Japan Camera
www.japancamera.com

A **merchandise classification** is a specific line of products within a merchandise category; for example, sport and dress shirts within men's wearing apparel, lipstick and eye shadow within cosmetics, and sofas and end tables within living room furniture. These subdivisions are important because products within merchandise classification are directly comparable and substitutable. It is the level in a product line at which consumer comparison shopping occurs. The superspecialist (for example, Sunglass Hut) and the niche specialist (for example, Japan Camera) are two retailing formats whose merchandise mix is focused on one or a few merchandise classifications.

An example of a product's three subdivisions (merchandise groups, categories, and classifications) is illustrated in Figure 9–6. As shown, subdividing a product line is essentially a refinement process that helps simplify the retailer's problem of how to (1) target certain consumer groups, (2) allocate store space and locations, (3) develop efficient inventory control systems, and (4) create a unique store image.

Retailers continually are besieged with a barrage of "new" and "improved" products and must evaluate each of these products before making any merchandise mix decision. Some product selection decisions require more extensive evaluation than do others. In planning the right combination of product lines, retailers consider each of the following factors:

- The compatibility among product lines,
- The physical attributes of each product line,
- The product lines' potential profitability,
- The role branding plays in the success of product lines,

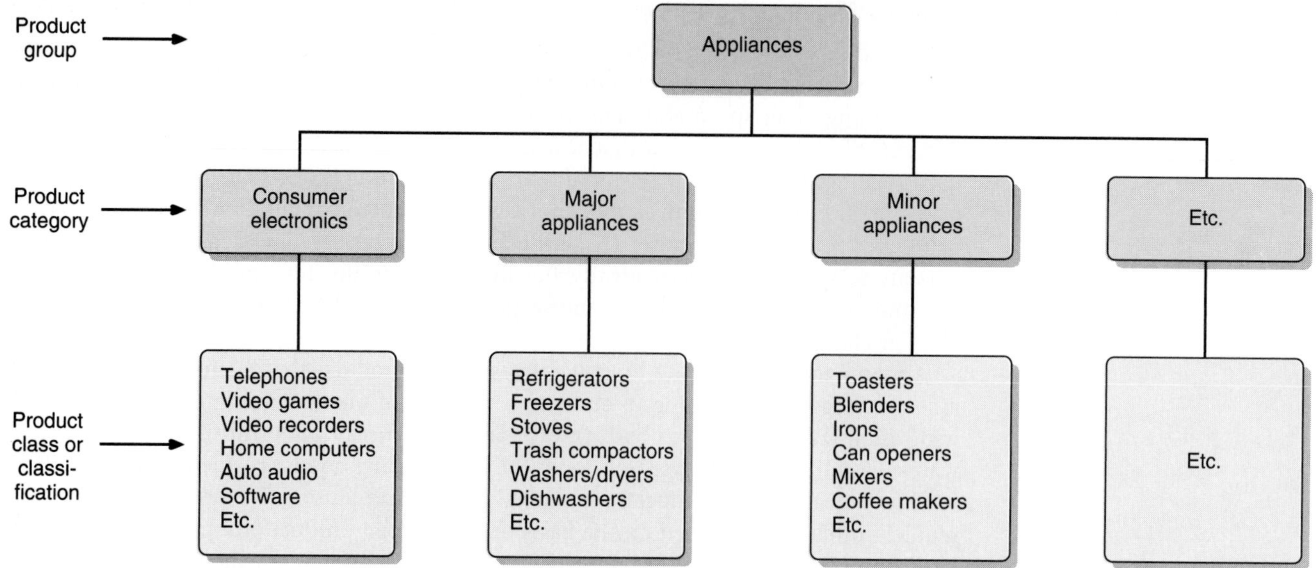

Figure 9–6

Product line subdivisions

- The age of each product within the product life cycle,
- The fashionable nature of each product line,
- The market appropriateness of each product line,
- The impact of lifestyle on product line acceptance, and
- The competitive threat facing each product.

Product Line Compatibility In planning a merchandise mix and deciding which products should be included in it, the retailer should consider **product compatibility**—the nature of the relationships among various product lines and among various product items within them. Depending on the type of compatibility, retailers classify products as (1) substitutes, (2) complements, or (3) unrelated. The degree of product compatibility ranges from a perfect to a general relationship.

A **product substitute** is a product consumers use for the same general purpose as another product; it has the same basic functional attributes and meets the same basic consumer needs. A *perfect substitute* is a product consumers perceive as being essentially the same as another product. In this case, the consumer is completely indifferent about which product to buy and use. A *general substitute* is a product consumers perceive as being different from another product but that serves the same general purpose. Fruit juice can be substituted for milk as a breakfast beverage, for example. In deciding which products to sell, the retailer usually should avoid perfect substitutes. They divert sales from other products without adding anything in return. General substitutes represent an increase in the selection a retailer offers consumers; as such, they can increase total sales. The retailer must realize that many "new" products offered by manufacturers are often nothing more than "me-too" substitutes that add little, if anything, to the store's total sales.

A **product complement** is a product that is bought and used in conjunction with another product. A *perfect complement* is a product consumers must purchase because their original product purchase cannot function immediately or effectively without it (for example, film is a perfect complement to a camera). *General complements* are products sold in conjunction with other products because they enhance or supplement the original purchase in some way. Apparel accessories that are coordinated with the colour and style of a suit or dress are excellent examples of general complements. In supermarkets, researchers have found that rearrangements of product lines can have surprising results. Both perfect and general complements are highly desirable additions to the retailer's merchandise mix because they often represent additional, unplanned sales beyond the original, planned purchase. Also, consumers tend to be less sensitive about the price of complements; hence, retailers often sell them at above-average markups.

Unrelated products are neither substitutes nor complements, but retailers seriously consider them for adding greater variety to their product mix because they represent potential additional sales, theoretically at low risk and reasonable profit. Some impulse goods fit this description. Normally, unrelated products are not stocked in depth; rather, retailers often follow a strategy of "creaming"—stocking and selling only the best-selling items.

Product Line Attributes The attributes of the product itself strongly influence which products are brought into the retailer's total collection of product lines. Four **product attributes** to consider are product bulk, standardization, service requirements, and required selling method.

Product bulk is the weight or size of a product in relation to its value. Bulky products usually require substantial space, both on the sales floor and in the stockroom, and often require special handling. If only limited space is available, the retailer may have to forego stocking bulky products or limit the depth of selection. Furniture, appliances, lawn and garden equipment, and some home improvement products are examples of bulky products. In addition, many bulky products typically are weak space productivity performers; sales per square metre or foot of floor space are comparatively low.

Retailers should also consider *product standardization* in evaluating product attributes. Generally, standardized products fit into the retailer's routine operating procedures, whereas nonstandardized products often require special buying, stocking, and handling. Few products offer enough potential to the retailer to justify developing specialized merchandising skills.

Because products vary noticeably regarding required *service levels*, retailers should evaluate each product individually. If a required customer service (for example, home delivery, home repair, long-term credit) is not part of the retailer's normal service offering, the retailer should seriously consider the product's service requirements before adding it to the merchandise mix. It is seldom possible to add a new service for a new product line and expect that line to be profitable.

Required *selling methods* are particular selling skills needed to sell a product. Some products call for a personal selling approach, whereas others can be sold on a self-service basis. Generally, self-service retailers should not attempt to sell merchandise that requires personal selling. Likewise, an upscale retailer that stocks too many self-service items risks the prestige and product-quality image of the store.

Product Line Profitability In determining the merits of a product, *product profitability* is one of the most important and complex criteria retailers use, because it can be expressed and measured in so many different ways.[6] Figure 9–7 identifies the relative importance of various profitability measurements as judged by merchandising executives for different retailing formats. As seen in Figure 9–7, gross margin percentage and gross margin dollars are viewed as the most valuable performance measures of profitability. It is sufficient to state here that each product should make some contribution to profit; the contribution can be direct, by enhancing per-unit profit, or indirect, by creating customer traffic and additional sales on other products.

Product Branding What is in a name? A great deal! Most consumers rely on **brand** names to distinguish among the massive selection of products offered by competing marketers; in essence, consumers use brand names to help them define their product choices and clarify their preferred merchandise mix.[7] Retailers depend on brand names to help create merchandise collections that distinguish their stores from competitors. The selection or creation of product brands to be included in the retailer's merchandise mix is also an important consideration in building customer loyalty to both the store's products and the retailer. Assuming the retailer's name(s) and brand(s) are associated with positive images created by user satisfaction, the store can position itself on the consumer's quality

Figure 9–7

How profitability measurements differ in different retailing formats (1 = most important; 5 = least important)

Source: Adapted from "Inventory Management: The Focus Increases," (Prepared by Coopers and Lybrand L.L.P.) Chain Store Age, December 1995, 6–16. Reprinted by permission. Copyright Lebhar-Friedman, Inc., 425 Park Ave., New York, NY 10022.

	Type of Profitability Measurement				
Type of retailer	Gross margin percent	Gross margin pollars	Inventory turnover rate	Gross margin return on investment	Sales per unit space
Specialty soft goods retailers	1	2	3	4	5
Specialty hard goods retailers	5	4	1	3	2
Drug stores	2	1	3	4	5
Department stores	2	1	5	3	4
Supermarkets	2	1	3	5	4
Home centres	1	2	3	4	5
Discounters	1	2	3	4	5

continuum (that is, establish a reputation). Although branding can be viewed from several perspectives, this section examines the retailer's efforts at planning brand strategies from the perspective of:

- no-names or nonbrands,
- vendor brands or labels,
- private brands or labels,
- retail store brands or labels,
- licensed merchandise.

No-Names or Nonbrands. A no-name or nonbrand is a **generic** product line to which consumers attach no significant identity, awareness, or meaning.[8] These nonbranded items are typically unadvertised, lower-grade, no-frill product lines offered as low-cost alternatives to brand-name merchandise. These plain-packaged, starkly labelled products (that is, list of contents) achieve their best sales records during inflationary or recessionary periods. Generics are an expected part of the merchandise mix in most supermarkets and drugstores. Therefore, the major decision involves how many generic product lines to stock. Typically, food and drug retailers tend to increase the selection of generic products in stores located in market areas comprising price-oriented consumers and during times of high inflation and economic recession when everyone's buying power is reduced. Given the somewhat questionable and unreliable quality of generic products, consumers tend to be more cautious with food than with nonfood products; hence, the selection of nonfood generics can be increased with lower selling risks.

Vendor Brands or Labels. A **vendor brand** is a label to which consumers attach a specific meaning in terms of a certain image, quality level, and price-point range.[9] Vendor brands are product lines that are produced, owned, controlled, and distributed by such vendors as manufacturers or designers, who supply retailers with their collection of branded or labelled merchandise. Manufacturers such as Ford Motor Company, General Electric, Kellogg, IBM, Hanes, and Levi Strauss and designers such as Liz Claiborne, Anne Klein, Donna Karan, and Ralph Lauren provide retailers with instant name recognition for their collection of product lines.

Name brands are also referred to as *national brands* because many of them have countrywide recognition created through national advertising programs and national distribution systems. The national status of these manufacturer labels creates the image of better and more consistent quality; to consumers they represent a "sure thing" with little or no purchase risk.[10] "An interesting characteristic of the best-managed brands is that the companies that own them have focused their attention on promoting the brand name (Microsoft, Budweiser, Gillette, and Coca-Cola), instead of individual products."[11] Manufacturers reinforce consumer perceptions of consistent quality by developing different brands for different retailers. Sara Lee, the Chicago conglomerate, markets its L'eggs and Just My Size pantyhose in drugstores, supermarkets, and discount outlets. To service its specialty and department store customers, the company offers its Hanes and premium Donna Karan brands.[12] In a similar fashion, VF Corporation markets different brands of jeans through different types of retailers who target different consumer groups. "In jeans, consumers can buy the Tony Girbaud line in higher-priced department stores, while they look to mass marketers for Lee, Wrangler, and Rustler, VF's lowest-priced jeans, are pitched at discount stores. In lingerie, VF's Eileen West line is aimed at upscale department stores, while Vanity Fair (VF) goes to midrange shops and the Vassarette brand to discount stores."[13]

Recently Sears Canada has made a conscious effort to upscale and move into soft goods and fashion apparel to a greater degree. They are increasing their selection of such brand name labels as Liz Claiborne, Jones Studio, and Dockers.[14]

The best insurance for continued success for manufacturers is to build their brand franchise; products rapidly become just commodities if the manufacturer loses its brand identities. Strong brand recognition makes it more difficult for the retailer to replace the branded product with their own private-label "knockoffs."[15] Another problem facing retailers that rely on brand merchandise to differentiate their merchandise mix is the fact that many competitive retailers are stocking the same items and using the same resources. Brand names like Liz Claiborne and Levi's Dockers are almost becoming generic items because every retailer in the marketplace is carrying these popular brands. The results of this "me-too" approach is that many retailers' merchandise mixes have a sameness, a redundancy that does not contribute to any effort at gaining a competitive advantage.

Private Brands or Labels. A **private brand** or label is a product line that is owned, controlled, merchandised, and sold by a specific retailer in its own stores. Supermarkets typically have at least one private label for each product category.[16] On the other hand, Loblaws utilizes the President's Choice private label to cover several categories of merchandise. Soft goods retailers also are very involved with developing private labels in key merchandise categories.[17] For example, Sears has developed its Canyon River Blues label, Kmart's Jaclyn Smith apparel line is enjoying considerable success, and Wal-Mart has introduced its Kathie Lee Collection.[18] Historically, consumers often considered private labels as somewhat lower-quality, lower-status, and lower-priced merchandise, and many retailers directly or indirectly promoted this perceptional difference between their private and national brands. For example, many department stores have traditionally stocked the lower price points within a merchandise category with private-label product lines, the middle price points with national brands (for example, Farrah, Hagger, Hanes, Fruit of the Loom), and the prestige price points with designer labels (for example, Christian Lacroix, Karl Lagerfeld, Geoffrey Beene) and bridge lines (for example, Anne Klein II, Calvin Klein Classics, Perry Ellis Portfolio). In recent years, some department store chains have restructured this relationship by pricing house brands and labels at middle price points and using national brands as fighting brands in lower competitive price points. Although designer labels continue to occupy most of the top spots in the pricing hierarchy, some department store chains are introducing private labels to compete with national designer labels. The primary objectives the retailer must achieve in building private labels are (1) differentiate from competition, (2) maximize profits, (3) enhance quality image, (4) give customers more choice, and (5) maximize sales.[19]

Retail Store Brands or Labels. A **retail store brand** or label is the name of the retail chain or catalogue house as well as an exclusive label on some or all of the items sold in the store.[20] Some of the more successful store labels are The Gap, L.L. Bean, Victoria's Secret, Talbots, Old Navy, Eddie Bauer, and Lands' End. "The battle of the brands" (manufacturer versus store) is a never-ending process. In every merchandise category and classification, manufacturers and retailers are continuously changing strategies in an attempt to find the right collection of products for their chosen markets. For example, in the cosmetic/fragrance category, national labels such as Chanel, Coty, and Revlon are "expanding their retailer lists to include more chain drugs, more specialty stores . . . if for no other reason, to defend against the incursions into the fragrance/cosmetic business of Benetton, Victoria's Secret, and other store brands that are picking off their potential customers."[21]

The "which product lines" (manufacturer or store brand) decision will vary considerably with the different retailers' individual merchandising formats; however, the retail manager should consider the pros and cons of stocking manufacturer and private-label merchandise (see Figure 9–8).

Licensed Merchandise. A product's greatest asset is often the intangible benefits and psychological symbols associated with its name. **Licensed merchandise** include product lines that are designed and sold through identification with a famous individual or corporate name, title, logo, slogan, or fictional character; the owner of the name, logo, or character develops contractual arrangements permitting licensees to use that identification on products they make and sell. Cartoon characters (Teenage Mutant Ninja Turtles), sports organizations (National Football League), corporate logos (Caterpillar workwear), fashion designers (Yves Saint Laurent), and celebrities (Air Jordan) are just a few of the licensed

Figure 9–8

Retailer's viewpoint: the pros and cons of manufacturer and private-label brands

Manufacturer brands: Pros	Manufacturer brands: Cons
Presold to target consumers	Lower gross margins
Lower selling costs	Selling restrictions
Attracts new customers	Pricing restrictions
Helps create assortments	Advertising restrictions
Enhances store image	Create more brand loyalty than store loyalty
Allows comparison shopping	

Private-label brands: Pros	Private-label brands: Cons
Greater price flexibility	Higher selling costs resulting from demand stimulation
Higher gross margins	Greater financial risk resulting from greater involvement
No advertising restrictions	Expanded buying and procuring responsibilities and costs
Enhance store and store brand loyalty	
Better product quality control through specification buying	
Promotes distinctive store	
No direct brand competition	

merchandise categories that retailers can consider for inclusion in the merchandise mix. In choosing from the vast array of licensed merchandise, retailers and their buyers should be increasingly selective. The days of the almost guaranteed licensed product line success have disappeared as the number of lines has increased and their novelty has diminished.

Though licensed names with widespread media exposure can do very well, especially in the short run, most experts today recommend that a retailer evaluate licensed goods as it would any other merchandise, looking first for quality, design, price, and compatibility with current store image and consumer wants with or without the name. If those criteria are met, sales can be greatly enhanced as a result of the extremely fast customer recognition factor and personal identification with the image projected by the licensed name. Thus, for example, though the licensed Coca-Cola clothing line has enjoyed enormous retail success, retail executives attribute its popularity primarily to its quality, stylishness, and reasonable price. The Coke example also illustrates the principle that retailers should look for an appropriate marriage between name and product; Coca-Cola's casual, good-times, active image and lifestyle associations provide an exceptional match with its licensed line of beach towels, sweat shirts, and other active wear.

Despite retailers' best efforts to carry only the right mix of licensed lines, the enormity of the product selection and the basic uncertainty of exactly which licensed names will catch on make these choices difficult. The desire of some image-conscious retailers to be the first in an area to merchandise hot new licenses adds pressure by emphasizing quick decisions. In response to these problems, some large department stores test-market a licensed product item or product line in a few stores before deciding whether to carry it throughout the entire chain. Another problem to consider when choosing which licences to carry is the often accelerated product life cycles of licensed goods. The retailer must be especially alert to timing the introduction and discontinuation of sales of a licensed product line. Many licensed products, such as designer clothing and Disney items, remain strong sellers for years, but others (for example, those tied to currently popular celebrity names or one-time events like Halley's Comet) can have sales that peak within months and then fall precipitously.

Several other licensing strategies are also available. One is called direct licensing, in which a retailer (usually a large chain) signs an exclusive agreement to carry licensed products and often takes an active role in their design and manufacture. Kmart's Jaclyn Smith apparel line has proved very successful. Another popular technique is in-store boutiques, in which all goods of a given licence are merchandised together within a store, often using innovative visual displays and special promotions. Wal-Mart has Better Homes & Gardens Centers in 2000 of its outlets to sell garden tools and supplies.[22] The boutique strategy can both increase sales of the licensed goods and generate store traffic. The final technique involves an entire store devoted exclusively to licensed merchandise bearing logos and emblems of a single college or professional team. Recently, entertainment companies have opened their own retail operations; Disney Stores, Warner Brothers Studio Stores, Turner Broadcasting stores, Hanna-Barbara Cartoon Studios stores, and Ringling Bros., Barnum & Bailey outlets are some of the major examples of this licensed store format.[23]

Product Life Cycle Products pass through several stages in their lifetime, each identified by its sales performance characteristics. This series of stages is called the **product life cycle (PLC)**. Knowing which stage a product is in helps the retailer judge both its existing and future sales potential. Also, the PLC stage suggests a particular retailing strategy. The four stages of the product life cycle are introduction, growth, maturity, and decline. Figure 9–9 illustrates one basic shape of the PLC as defined by sales performance levels.

Introductory Products. The typical supermarket must review and evaluate about 3000 new product items each year. One of the most difficult problems retailers have is keeping up with new products. In the introductory stage, products are characterized by low sales and losses, high risk, and high costs. Many products never make it out of the introductory stage. In the perfume industry, the failure rate of new fragrances is 90 percent.[24]

Figure 9–9

The product life cycle

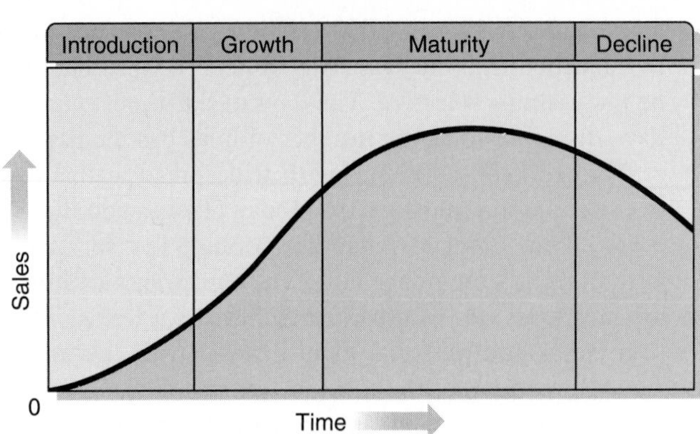

Goodyear's strong promotional support for its Aquatred tire made it the most successful introduction of a tire in the history of the industry.[25] Goodyear hopes to repeat that success with its new Infinitred tire and its lifetime guarantee.[26]

For many retailers, new products are essential to their avant-garde image, and the necessary merchandising skill is to select only introductory products that are truly innovative. Another consideration for retailers is that the manufacturer may decide to limit distribution of the product to a few exclusive or several selective outlets. Faced with this situation, the retailer must decide to get in at once or be shut out permanently. A retailer that stocks introductory products should limit selection to a few key items until primary demand for the product has been established.

Growth Products. Almost without exception, the most desirable products for retailers are those in the growth stage. Products in the growth stage are characterized by accelerating sales, the highest profit levels of any stage in the PLC, limited competitors in the market, and lower relative costs and risk. To satisfy the growing number of customers, retailers usually stock an extensive variety of growth products. Audio books have entered the growth stage of their life cycle. As time-pressed consumers have less reading time, audio books have gained in popularity with commuters, joggers, and workers.[27] Wide-screen television, Internet services, 401(k) retirement plans, and health foods are some other product lines that are currently in the growth stage.

Mature Products. In the maturity stage, sales increase at a slower rate and finally begin to level off. In 1992, the peak of the casual apparel cycle was reached; North Americans had had five years of filling closets with T-shirts, jeans, and sweats. With the levelling off of the casual trend, such casual-based retailers as The Gap saw their markets mature and their growth rate slow dramatically.[28] Personal computers (PCs) are in the early maturity stage of the product life cycle. Because PCs have been able to absorb more functions of other consumer-electronics devices, they continue to experience some sales growth. The market penetration rate of PCs is about 50 percent of North American homes, well beyond the levels at which sales of electric typewriters and video game machines began to slow.[29]

Characteristics of this stage are (1) a highly competitive market, (2) falling prices and margins, (3) more intensive advertising, and (4) lower profits. In most markets, video sales and rentals have already reached the mature stage of their life cycle. Wal-Mart and Zellers now sell videos at attractive prices and use them to pull consumers into their stores. Most retailers should include or continue to include mature products in their merchandise mix because consumers expect them.

Declining Products. As a rule, retailers do not include products that are in the decline stage of the PLC in their merchandise mix. Normally, retailers drop these products, if they have not done so already, because products in the decline stage are high-risk, low-reward items. This stage is characterized by rapidly declining sales and profits (or even losses) and little, if any, manufacturer support in promotion. Retailers that continue to stock declining products should only do so in limited quantities and only if demand is sufficient to yield a reasonable profit.

Fashion Merchandising Style, design, and fashion are related yet different concepts. **Style** incorporates those special characteristics or specific features that distinguish one product from another of a similar type. For example, the specific style features that help distinguish one skirt from another include length (floor, ankle, knee, mini), cut (wraparound, accordion-pleated, bias), and fabric (denim, gabardine, chiffon, seersucker).[30] Individual interpretations or versions of the same style are called **designs** (see Figure 9–10). "Within a specific style, there can be many variations in trimmings, texture, decoration, or other details."[31] Donna Karan succeeds on the premise that customers want their clothes comfortable and flattering as well as fashionable. Joining Karan are other women designers such as Adrienne Vittadini, Linda Allard, Andrea Jovine, and Nicole Miller, who have a sense of which designs are most appropriate for women to work, entertain, and relax in—designs that are comfortable, wearable, and last from season to season.[32] Calvin Klein manages to stay on top of the fashion scene with aggressive and often controversial advertising. "His designer collection of sportswear keeps the high-end customer wanting more, while other categories such as his bridge CK line, jeanswear, unisex fragrances CK One and CK Be, and underwear lines have the same effect on younger consumers."[33] Fashion is all about designer image and customer perception. Other unique designer images have been created by Gucci, Ralph Lauren, Bill Blass, Christian Dior, Pierre Cardin, and Oscar de la Renta.[34]

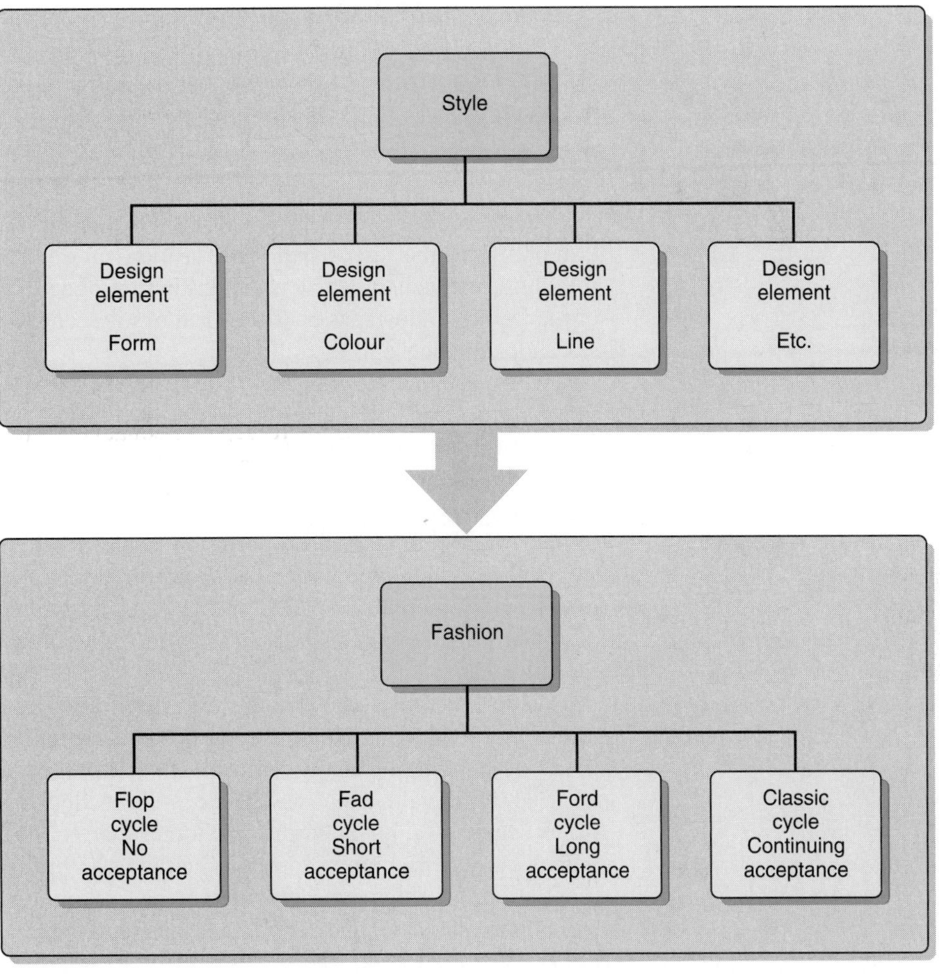

Figure 9–10

The relationship among style, design, and fashion

A **fashion** is a product with distinctive attributes that are currently appropriate and represent the prevailing style. A style becomes a fashion only when it gains consumer acceptance, and it remains a fashion as long as it retains acceptance (see Figure 9–10). Fashion is a sign of the times; it frequently reflects what a culture is feeling, thinking, and doing in all walks of life.

Major fashion houses frequently distinguish between their premium-priced collections, displayed at the New York and Paris fashion shows and sold to a limited number of wealthy clients (high fashion),[35] and their classification merchandise, which is priced lower, has a broader appeal, and incorporates the features of last year's collections (mass-fashion). Profits derived from classification sales subsidize the development of collections, which cast a premium halo over the classification merchandise, for which, in turn, a premium price can be charged. Fashions represent great opportunities for retailers but also substantial risks. Fashionable products include the following:

- High-margin items that can provide above-average profits;
- Shopping and specialty goods that consumers will spend time, money, and effort to find;
- Products that enhance the retailer's general image and help generate consumer traffic; and
- A means of distinguishing a retailer's operation from the competition.

Fashion-conscious consumers can be characterized as follows:

- Oriented toward the social world;
- Gregarious and likable;
- Active participants in society;
- Self-assertive, competitive, and adventuresome;
- Attention seekers and self-confident; and
- Aesthetic-, power-, and status-oriented individuals.[36]

Like the product life cycle, the fashion life cycle is a conceptualization of the "life of a fashion." The risk associated with fashion products comes from the uncertainty surrounding both consumers' level and duration of acceptance of the fashion. The lifeblood of the fashion industry is psychological obsolescence—that driving force and continuous search for the new and the different.

One management tool retailers use to reduce the risks of including fashion products in their product mix is the **fashion cycle**. During its lifetime, a fashion passes through three stages: introduction, acceptance, and decline. From its beginning in the introductory stage to its obsolescence in the decline stage, the fashion innovation struggles to obtain customer acceptance and customer adoptions. The secret to success in the fashion industry is in knowing where customers are in the fashion cycle, getting in early enough to build a store's news-making reputation, being prepared for big-volume selling, and realizing when to get out. Sometimes fashions are recycled. For example, Hush Puppies, those fuddy-duddy bright-coloured suede shoes last in vogue during the 1950s, are back in vogue in the late 1990s.[37]

Customer acceptance of fashion varies significantly according to level of acceptance (as measured by sales) and the duration of that acceptance (as measured by weeks, months, years). Depending on the two acceptance factors, four types of fashion cycles occur: the flop, fad, ford, and classic (see Figure 9–11). A **flop** is a fashion cycle rejected by all consumer segments almost immediately. Other than for a few fashion innovators who try and then discard the fashion, a flop gains neither a significant level nor duration of acceptance. Flops are fashion items most retailers hope to avoid; they not only represent the financial loss of obsolete merchandise, but they also tend to tarnish the retailer's image as a fashion leader. "Victorian funk," the clingy, ankle-grazing crushed velvet dress with droopy ruffled

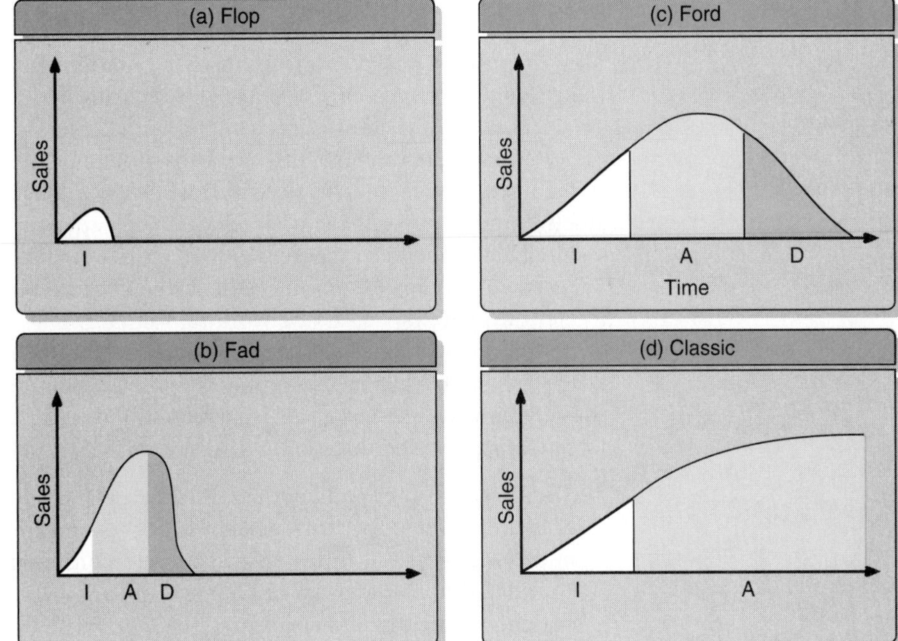

Figure 9–11

Types of fashion cycles: (a) flop, (b) fad, (c) ford, and (d) classic

blouses and high button shoes, was a cheap and flimsy look that was a nightmare on anybody who was not tall and thin. It was a fashion flop that failed to meet customer needs.[38] Some flops are inevitable—they are the realization of the risks that go with fashion merchandising.

A **fad** is a fashion that obtains a relatively high level of customer acceptance for a short time. It is quickly accepted but rejected with the same quickness (see Figure 9–11).[39] Typically, the lifetime of a fad ranges from a few weeks to several months. Because a relatively large number of these items can be sold at substantial markups (consumers are somewhat price insensitive regarding fads) in a short period of time, fads are extremely profitable. They are also highly risky, however, because of the short duration of the cycle. To capitalize on a fad, the retailer must stock the item at the introductory or early part of the cycle. Although the rewards for successfully merchandising fads can be substantial, the problems can be equally considerable. For example, Merry-Go-Round, a specialty retailer that catered to fashion-conscious youth, needed a constant supply of new, funky merchandise to maintain its higher price points. During recessionary times, designers became more conservative because they did not want to be stuck with faddish merchandise that will become quickly outdated; hence, Merry-Go-Round found it hard to procure enough merchandise to retain its cutting-edge image during economic downturns.[40]

A best-seller in fashion merchandising is referred to as a **ford**. A ford is also referred to as a "runner" or "hot item." Fords gain wide customer acceptance over extended periods of time. Because of their wide acceptance, long-term salability, and stable demand, fords usually are produced by many different manufacturers in a variety of price lines. For the same reasons, nearly every retailer must include fords in the merchandise mix or suffer loss of profits and loss of a fashion image. The miniskirt is an excellent example of a ford, lasting from 1965 to 1971; however, its reintroduction in the 1980s resulted in a fashion fad that soon flopped. It was re-introduced in the early 1990s and gained a fair level of acceptance among some fashion-forward consumers. A more recent example is the "sweater set"—a cardigan worn over a matching short-sleeved shell—which has been reborn as the "twin set." The twin set is "a textbook example of that all too rare fashion: a look that the full spectrum of marketers can wring for profits over several seasons."[41] What accounts for its resurrection? It can be a dressy or casual look, it looks equally good on grandmothers and teenagers, it is comfortable and easy to take care of, and it looks good in a wide range of colour combinations.

The "classic look," the "classic cut," and the "classic shape" describe a style trend that endures for many years (see Figure 9–11). The **classic** fashion has both a high level and a long duration of acceptance. Although a classic might undergo minor changes, it essentially looks the same. Currently, the "classic suit" is out of favour; the "new suit" tends to be a less starchy version often blended with tie-less shirts and casual accessories.[42] The classic, even more than the ford, is an absolute must in the retailer's merchandise mix. The decision relative to the classic is not whether to stock it but rather which price line to stock from which supplier with which product features.[43] The pantsuit, introduced as a fashionable women's garment in 1966, retains a high level of acceptance in almost all market segments. It has become a classic fashion because it fits the needs and lifestyles of the modern woman, especially the working woman.

Several theories have been proposed to explain the process by which consumer groups adopt fashionable products. An understanding of this consumer adoption process provides the retailer with one more tool by which to judge the appropriateness of a fashion to the targeted market. The three basic theories of fashion follow.

1. **Trickle-down theory** hypothesizes that new innovative fashions and styles originate in the upper socioeconomic classes and are passed down through the middle class to the lower socioeconomic consumer. European designers are considered to be the usual origin for a given fashion cycle; however, American designers are more often becoming the original source. Figure 9–12a illustrates and describes this theory.

2. **Trickle-up theory** states that some unusual fashions or styles are developed in the lower socioeconomic classes, picked up by the upper class, and finally adopted by the middle class (see Figure 9–12b). Blue jeans, the funky look, and the leather look are examples. The Harley-Davidson collection of "hog fashion" items have had an influence on style for decades, and that impact has been recognized by the Council of Fashion Designers.[44] Dr. Martens boots are currently stomping through North American malls; "Docs" or "DMs" have for decades been standard gear for Britain's skinheads and neo-Nazis.[45]

3. **Trickle-across theory** recognizes that a fashion or style can originate within any social class. Fashions and styles are marketed to opinion leaders within one or more social class levels; these opinion leaders are then instrumental in getting other members of the same social class to adopt the fashion or style. Hence, the fashion spreads horizontally through the population within the upper, middle, and/or lower social class. Generation X, the baby busters, had an impact on fashion with their post-industrial thrift-shop look known as "grunge"—a fashion that celebrated the ill-kept, lumberjack look. Flannel shirts, baggy or ripped jeans, Dr. Marten boots, Teva sandals, reversed baseball caps, wool caps, pierced noses, and tattoos are part of the grunge look.[46]

Market Appropriateness Retailers should evaluate new-product candidates on their chances for success in the marketplace, that is, market appropriateness—how well the new product matches the consumption and buying needs of targeted consumers. Recent problems experienced by Eaton's resulted in part from a failure to understand consumer demand.[47] It is important that retailers stay close to the consumer to identify the products the market wants. The Retail Strategy and Tactics box on page 342 illustrates how Home Depot altered its organization to better meet consumer needs.

Several characteristics that serve as good indicators of how well a product might be received by the retailer's current and potential customers are relative advantage, affinity, trialability, observability, and complexity.

Relative advantage is the extent to which the new product is perceived to be better than existing products. A product that offers clear-cut advantages or a more satisfying benefit package is more likely to attract the interest and patronage of the store's customers. SnackWell cookies have gained wide customer acceptance because the cookie is not only

Figure 9–12

Fashion adoption theories: (a) trickle-down theory and (b) trickle-up theory

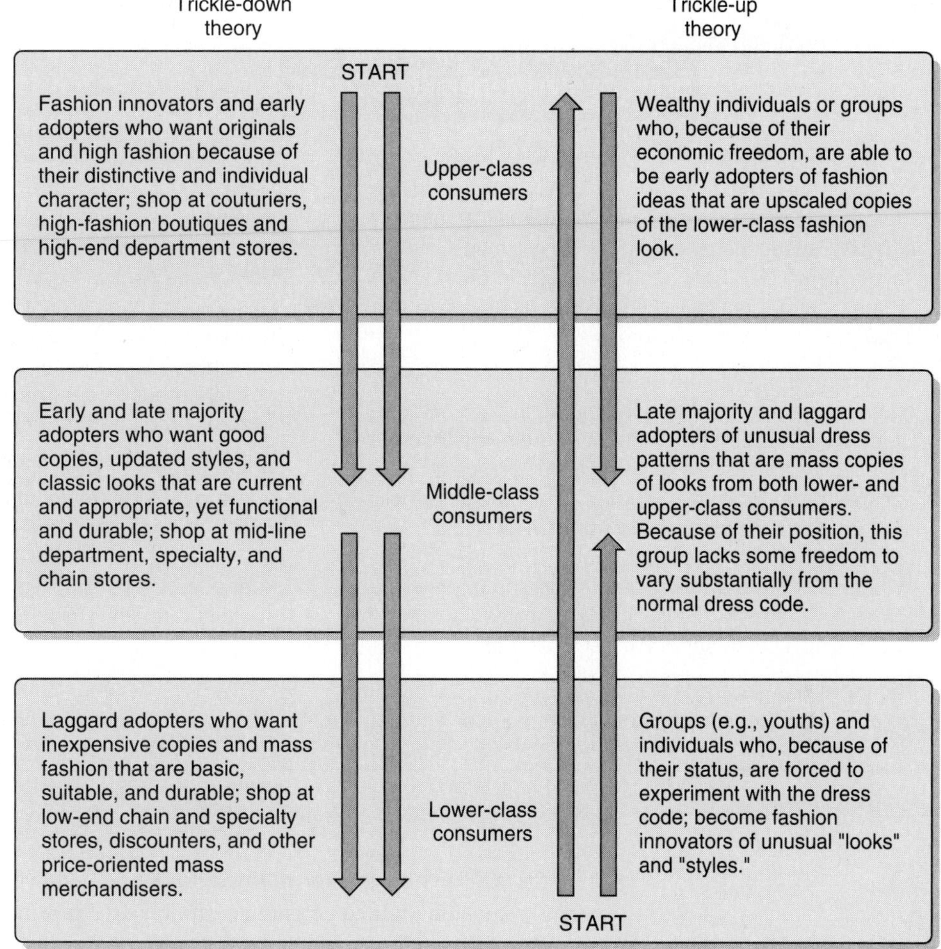

(a)
Trickle-down theory
(b)
Trickle-up theory
START
Fashion innovators and early adopters who want originals and high fashion because of their distinctive and individual character; shop at couturiers, high-fashion boutiques and high-end department stores.
Upper-class consumers
Wealthy individuals or groups who, because of their economic freedom, are able to be early adopters of fashion ideas that are upscaled copies of the lower-class fashion look.
Early and late majority adopters who want good copies, updated styles, and classic looks that are current and appropriate, yet functional and durable; shop at mid-line department, specialty, and chain stores.
Middle-class consumers
Late majority and laggard adopters of unusual dress patterns that are mass copies of looks from both lower- and upper-class consumers. Because of their position, this group lacks some freedom to vary substantially from the normal dress code.
Laggard adopters who want inexpensive copies and mass fashion that are basic, suitable, and durable; shop at low-end chain and specialty stores, discounters, and other price-oriented mass merchandisers.
Lower-class consumers
Groups (e.g., youths) and individuals who, because of their status, are forced to experiment with the dress code; become fashion innovators of unusual "looks" and "styles."
START

fat-free, it also tastes good.[48] As more women enter the workforce, women's shoes are being restyled to ensure that they are as comfortable as they are fashionable.[49]

Affinity is the extent to which the new product is consistent with the consumer's current buying and usage behaviour. An emerging category of products are the so-called organizational goods, product items designed to tidy up the home, office, and any place else that requires organization. Hold Everything, a retail and catalogue seller of organizing goods, is enjoying rapid expansion because it appeals to the space-conscious and time-sensitive consumer who believes everything has a place and should be in it. Consumers often view products that require noticeable behavioural modification as being incompatible with their needs. A product that is consistent with the consumer's beliefs, values, and experiences is more likely to gain consumer acceptance and a faster and higher rate of adoption.

Trialability is the extent to which a new product can be tested on a trial basis. All new-product purchases involve some risk to the purchaser. Anything that substantially reduces the risk improves the chances for initial and subsequent purchases. A product that can be physically divided into small quantities and given as free samples or sold in trial sizes benefits from good trialability. If division is not possible, demonstrations and guarantees can reduce perceived risks.

Observability is the extent to which the consumer can see a new product's favourable attributes. If relative advantages are easily visible and can be easily described to others, the new product's probability of market success is greatly enhanced.

Complexity is the extent to which a new product can be easily understood or used. Products that require the consumer to invest considerable time and effort to reap any

Retail Strategies and Tactics

Economy Hammering Home Depot

Ask Steven Bebis how the economy is treating his home improvements chain, and the president of Home Depot Canada Inc. seems to sink into despair. "It's rough. Very difficult. The economy has had a major impact on our sales. Major," Mr. Bebis acknowledged in an interview. "Housing and remodelling is not in a recession in our industry. It's in a depression."

In addition to tight-fisted consumers, more concerned about keeping their jobs than upgrading their homes, Home Depot faces stiff competition from rivals such as Revy stores in Western Canada. Home Depot is fighting back with a multipronged strategy that includes more aggressive advertising, better staff training and lower prices. To help accomplish the latter objective, the company announced the opening of a 25-person buying office, effective October 1, 1995, in the Vancouver suburb of Coquitlam, B.C., to serve Western Canada.

The move has several advantages. First, it puts the buyer in touch with the local market, which is important for knowing when to stock seasonal items. Second, it will free up buyers from the Toronto office who have been racking up monstrous airline bills with regular trips out west. Third, and perhaps most important, buying directly from manufacturers in Western Canada will allow Home Depot to cut the amount of product it must ship from Eastern Canada, reducing transportation costs. This amounts to a challenge to suppliers in Eastern Canada to open distribution centres in Western Canada. Some have agreed to do just that but others have resisted.

Home Depot is investing $1 million in the new buying office, which will be located within a store to open [in 1995] in Coquitlam. The office will also include a handful of marketing people. By the end of 1996, Home Depot hopes to buy $100 million of merchandise annually from suppliers in Western Canada.

Source: John Heinzl, Globe and Mail, *September 14, 1995, B3.*

benefits will involve greater selling efforts and a slower rate of consumer adoption. With today's time-constrained consumer, anxiety-free products without lots of fancy extras and complex instructions are generally more appropriate. Sony's point-and-click home entertainment centre is designed to overcome the frustration many customers have in trying to use their home entertainment systems.[50]

Lifestyle Merchandise A *lifestyle* is a pattern of living shaped by psychological influences, social experiences, and demographic makeup. For example, the country and western lifestyle has spread beyond its traditional southern and western boundaries and is having an effect on a wide range of retailing activities. Knowing targeted consumers' activities, interests, and opinions enables retailers to select product lines that are consistent with both the consumers' lifestyle and the retailer's image. Developing product lines in accord with consumer living patterns is referred to as **lifestyle merchandising**. This method of product evaluation requires the retailer to do the following:

1. Identify target markets on the basis of consumers' lifestyles and their product, place, promotion, and price preferences.
2. Determine which lifestyle markets are consistent with the retailer's image and mode of doing business.
3. Evaluate which and how many products to carry on the basis of the retailer's ability to satisfy certain lifestyle markets.

Many fashion retailers go to trade shows and producer markets looking for merchandise suited for their targeted consumers' lifestyle. One illustration of how retailers can characterize consumers' lifestyles appears in Figure 9–13. Using this lifestyle scheme and others like it, retailers can select, purchase, and stock merchandise that matches their target consumers' lifestyles.

Figure 9–13

Lifestyle merchandising

"Perfectionist"

- Age: 25–45
- Size: Misses 4–14
- A woman who is *first* in a fashion trend; has the most advanced taste of all customers—the "Fashion Leader"
- Active, worldly; career-oriented; involved; free-spirited; energy abounding
- Inherently understands fashion; incorporates fashion into aspects of her lifestyle.
- Uniqueness and individuality are her two main concerns—she depends on clothes as a means of self-expression.
- She is governed by her emotions. For an adventurous mood, she seeks the most advanced fashions . . . always avant-garde, nonconforming, often impractical. For a classic mood, her taste level is pure, clean, and sophisticated.
- She combines a mix of fashion looks to cover her variety of emotional and active lifestyle needs.
- She is extremely conscious of her body; chooses clothes to complement her figure.
- Demands and appreciates quality.
- Impressed by designers who style for her contemporary lifestyle.
- Not necessarily price conscious; buys what she desires.
- She is influenced by her surroundings when shopping.
- Does not respond well to markdowns or price promotions.
- Needs little salespeople attention.
- Expects new arrivals often.
- Buys impulsively.
- Loyal to a store wherever she feels her *mood runs free.*

"Updated"

- Age: 25–60
- Size: Misses 4–16
- Desires fashion after it has been modified from its pure, advanced stages. Very often *this season's updated styles were last season's perfectionist styles.*
- Demands smart-looking items; stylish, yet not extreme.
- Working woman; housewife; mother.
- Desires clothes that are functional additions to her wardrobe—multipurpose.
- Desires high degree of quality, practicality, and value for the price.
- Not necessarily label conscious.
- Will buy regular stock markdowns; responds only moderately to price promotions.
- Loyal to store that separates her look, supports her type, and puts her look together for her.
- Fastest-growing misses customer type.

"Young Affluent"

- Age: 25–50
- Size: Misses 4–14
- Career woman, wife.
- Leads active social life; involved.
- Often attracted to designer labels.
- Ruled by current designer trends.
- Respects fine merchandise.
- Demands quality.
- Is an investment buyer; designer wardrobe builder.
- Taste level similar to updated customer, but not price conscious.

"Traditionalist"

- Age: 26–65
- Size: Misses 8–20
- The conformist . . . likes fashion only after it is accepted.
- Less career-oriented; more job-oriented. Oftentimes office worker, teacher, housewife.
- Does not react to, or desire, fashion extremes.
- Extremely label conscious—loyal to those she has worn and liked in the past.
- Price conscious; quality aware.
- Very practical; demands ease of care.
- Very insecure about fashion in general—must have fashion put together for her.
- Fashion influenced by peers.
- Loyal to stores and salespeople who service her needs.
- Responds exceptionally well to price promotions and markdowns.
- Replacement customer; conservative taste.

"Establishment"

- Age: 45+
- Size: Misses 8–20
- Older, refined woman—dignified.
- Active in community; holds prestigious position.
- An investment buyer; wardrobe builder.
- Loves fine workmanship, fabrics, and detail.
- Concerned with quality and value.
- Appreciates designer merchandise.
- Limitless buying ability.
- Seeks clothes that fill her needs.

Competitive Conditions To decide which product lines to include or exclude from the merchandise mix, the retailer must consider the competitive conditions under which the product line is available. Two aspects of competitive conditions are type and degree of competition. *Type of competition* refers to whether the product is available to direct or indirect competitors. A **direct** or **intratype competitor** is one whose merchandising program is about the same as another retailer's. An **indirect** or **intertype competitor** is one whose merchandising program is noticeably different from that of a retailer of similar products.

A product that is available to direct competitors has no "distinctive" advantage to any retailer. In some cases, however, it might help a retailer to establish that the store's image is on par with its competitors'; under such conditions the retailer would want to promote comparison shopping. Adopting a product that is available to indirect competitors might either help or hurt the store's image. If upscale, indirect competitors stock the product, the retailer's image can be enhanced; but if downscale, indirect competitors stock the product, the retailer's image could be damaged.

The *degree of competition* refers to the number of competitors that are or will be stocking the product. Competitive conditions can be either *exclusive* (no competitors), *selective* (few competitors), or *intensive* (many competitors). Exclusive rights to a product line offer several advantages. First, they help build an exclusive image by distinguishing the retailer's merchandise mix from that of competitors. Second, they permit greater freedom in merchandising products, because the retailer can worry less about what competitors are doing. Suppliers, however, do not grant exclusive rights to their products without expecting something in return, so retailers must have a clear understanding of the requirements they must meet to handle the product line exclusively.

Selective competition is generally not as desirable as an exclusive arrangement. For retailers that want some limit on competition but still need comparable products to facilitate customer comparison shopping, a selective arrangement is the best alternative. Retailers normally have little incentive to stock the product when there is intense competition; however, they are often "forced" to carry intensively distributed products that are readily available in competitive outlets because consumers expect them to be in stock. For intensively distributed products, retailers must resort to one of two strategies: (1) stock only a limited selection of a best-selling line to satisfy customers whose preferred line is not available and who will accept a substitute or (2) stock a wide variety of these ubiquitous product lines to satisfy most customers and thereby create a store image of having a "complete selection." Many Canadian retailers have found that they need to be focused with their merchandise line in order to be competitive. This is illustrated with the Retail Strategy and Tactics box entitled "Kmart Fights for Survival."

Supplier Considerations In planning the variety of product lines to be included in the merchandise mix, the retailer should examine the conditions under which each product line will be procurable. Two such conditions are the availability and the reliability of various suppliers.

Availability of Supply. Before making a decision to stock a product, the retailer should study the product's availability of supply by asking the following basic questions:

1. Is the product line readily available through the retailer's normal channels of distribution?
2. Are alternative backup sources of supply available?
3. Will the product line be available on a continuing basis?
4. What are the terms and conditions of sale under which the product line is available?[51]

Ideally, for the retailer to make a positive decision on a product candidate, the product line should be available from normal channels, with sufficient alternative supply sources, and under terms and conditions consistent with the product line's sales and profit potential.

Retail Strategies and Tactics

Kmart Fights for Survival

Kmart Canada Ltd. has poured millions of dollars into revamping its stores, with better financial results to show for the work. Still, the improvements haven't stopped doubters from questioning the discounter's future. Indeed, shopping at many of the 123 Kmart outlets has become a better experience. A year ago, shoppers who rushed to Kmart to get those paper towels on sale were often met with empty shelves—spotty inventory controls meant the retailer was constantly running out of popular items. Those problems have largely been solved. Stores are now stocking more of the high-demand items and fewer slow moving goods. As well, main aisles are getting less cluttered and displays are tidier.

"We tried to be too much to everybody," says Michael Lynch, who took over as president of the money-losing discount chain in Canada a year ago after its U.S. parent tried unsuccessfully to sell it. "It turned out we were incomplete in what people came in for anyway, and it was kind of discouraging for the customer." Still, despite a more encouraging performance, industry watchers continue to question how long the chain—and its 12 000 employees—will survive.

"My guess is that they're gone by summer," says retail analyst George Hartman at Eagle & Partners Inc. in Toronto. "I have a feeling that they're winding it down, and they'll probably just sell the real estate."

Kmart's dilemma is that it is the weak cousin among the three major discount department stores in Canada. The two others, Zellers Inc., owned by Toronto-based Hudson's Bay Co., and Wal-Mart Canada Inc. of Toronto, are vying for the top spot, each with roughly 43 percent of the market. That leaves Kmart trailing, with about 14 percent. It isn't only the discounters that have chewed away Kmart's business, although the arrival of giant Wal-Mart Stores Inc. of Bentonville, Ark., almost three years ago made a major dent. Kmart also faces stiff competition from specialty "big-box" retailers that sell everything from sporting goods to home improvement products at low prices. To add to that, consumers have been stingy, demanding bargains and better service.

Source: Marina Strauss, Globe and Mail, *January 27, 1997, 1.*

Reliability of Supplier. In deciding whether to include a product line in its merchandise mix, a retailer should also evaluate the reliability of the supplier. The ease of getting the product line into the store at the right time, in the right quantities, and in good condition is a necessary consideration. Criteria that describe a supplier's reliability include (1) shipping on time, (2) filling orders adequately, (3) maintaining adequate stocks (avoiding stockouts), and (4) adjusting orders to meet the retailer's changing needs.

Controlling Merchandise Variety

Creating merchandise variety is as much of an art as it is a science. There are no hard and fast rules that control what should be included in any given merchandise mix and what should be excluded. Nevertheless, retailers still need some general decision guidelines and management tools for regulating the merchandise mix composition. Presented here are two of the many management methods that might be used in controlling merchandise variety: category management and ABC analysis.

Category Management In recent years, retailers have placed greater emphasis on category management as a preferred means for controlling their many diverse product lines.[52] **Category management** is the process of "managing product categories as individual business units and customizing each category's product mix, merchandising and promotions according to customer preference on a store-by-store basis."[53] It is an attempt by retailers to focus their attention on product categories as opposed to individual brands. The goal is to manage a closely related line of products (category) by analyzing sales performance to see what improvements can be made in the product mix and to identify market niches not currently being reviewed by the retailer.[54] Rather than concentrate on what the manufacturer wants to produce or what the retailer wants to sell, any good category management plan ought to start and stop with the customer.[55]

Under a category management arrangement, retail buyers are responsible for a specific merchandise category and work with all the vendors for that category. Vendors are asked to forego their own brand-specific sales programs. Substitute sales (replacing Brand A with Brand B) is not an acceptable product line strategy. Additional sales of the entire merchandise category is the objective; the vendor that contributes the most to this objective is most likely to benefit the most from increased sales to the retailer.

ABC Analysis Retailers must make many merchandise decisions regarding which product line and how many product lines should be included or excluded from the merchandise mix. To control this decision process, retailers can employ a rank ordering procedure known as **ABC analysis**, which groups product lines according to their actual performance records or potential performance capabilities. Using the "eighty-twenty" principle—80 percent of the retailer's sales and/or profits are derived from 20 percent of the product lines that make up the retailer's merchandise mix—ABC analysis attempts to control merchandise variety by focusing the retailer's attention on high-performance product lines.[56] Recently, Eaton's has embarked on a plan to improve its assortment of merchandise in response to the competition from U.S. retailers.[57]

An application of ABC analysis involves the following steps: (1) a rank ordering of all product lines using some performance criterion (for example, sales or profits); (2) an examination of the ranking to determine what percentage of total sales is accounted for by what percentage of all product lines on the rank-order list (for example, 60 percent of total sales is generated by the top 10 percent of the product line on the rank-order list, 20 percent of total sales is produced by those product lines that make up the next 10 percent of the rank order list, and the remaining 20 percent of total sales is derived from the rest of the retailer's merchandise mix); and (3) the classification of product lines into A, B, C, and sometimes D categories. The result of the analysis is productivity classification of the product lines that compose the retailer's merchandise mix and a merchandising tool for controlling the relative representation of different product lines that determines merchandise variety. The productivity classes follow:

- **A Lines**—The limited number of high-performance product lines that are responsible for a majority of the retailer's sales. These lines are carefully managed with respect to their merchandise assortment and support; that is, the retailer will ensure both complete selection of product items within these lines and a never-out stock position by maintaining an extra safety stock. Typically, A lines get preferred display space and additional advertising support.

- **B Lines**—Second-tier but successful product lines that are essential to the overall success of any retail operation. Retailers provide adequate if not complete assortments and support levels for each of these product lines. Although the frequency and detail of merchandising attention (displaying, pricing, and promoting) given to B lines is less than that afforded to the top A lines, this second tier of product lines must be carefully controlled to ensure continuing success of the merchandise mix.

- **C Lines**—As third-tier product lines, C lines are still important to round out the retailer's total selection of merchandise. However, as weaker performers the retailer must carefully monitor sales and control expenses to maintain the profitability of these lines. Hence, if sales falter or expenses expand, these lines require immediate corrective measures—perhaps deletion from the retailer's merchandise mix.

- **D Lines**—A group of product lines whose sales and/or profit contribution is insignificant or nonexistent. D lines should be dropped from the retailer's merchandise mix. They add no variety to the product offering because they are not part of the customer's product choice set.

ABC analysis provides retailers with a set of general guidelines that can be used to control which and how many product lines will compose the total selection of merchandise to be offered in each store.

Planning Merchandise Assortment and Support

Merchandise assortment planning involves organizing the merchandise mix as to the type and number of different product items (such as brands, sizes, colours, materials, models, styles, price points) the retailer should stock within each of the product lines identified in the merchandise variety planning process discussed in the previous section. A *brand* is a distinctive grouping of products identified by name, term, design, symbol, or any combination of these markings. Used to identify the products of a particular manufacturer or seller, brand is a common criterion in distinguishing both product lines and product items within lines.[58] *Style* refers to the characteristic or distinctive form, outline, or shape of a product item. As a unique mode of expression or presentation, style can be the principal criterion by which consumers distinguish one product item from another (for example, clothing). Products also come in various sizes. *Size* can refer to the product's actual size (for example, 42-long or X-large) or to the size of its package (for example, family size). The physical magnitude, extent, and bulk of a product are not only distinguishing features that influence the consumer's purchase decision, but also important factors in the retailer's decision to buy, stock, display, and shelve the product. Colours, materials, and prices are also important features in distinguishing one product item from another.

Assortment planning is directed at the goal of ensuring that the product item choice is sufficient to meet the merchandise selection needs of the firm's targeted consumers.[59] VF Corporation (which makes Lee and Wrangler jeans), for example, "worked with Wal-Mart buyers to create model assortments of its wares for each store. VF's new artificial intelligence system can automatically adjust the models, so if a particular outlet sells more large sizes than the norm, VF changes the assortment accordingly."[60] Toys 'R' Us banks on an extensive assortment strategy to better serve customers and compete with discount retailers that are moving wholeheartedly into the toy market. With 18 000 toy items as compared with 3500 items stocked by discount stores, Toys 'R' Us has a competitive advantage with its product assortment.[61]

Merchandise support planning deals with devising systems for determining the number of product units the retailer should have on hand for each product item in order to meet expected sales for that brand, size, and colour combination. The purpose of support planning is to safeguard against the possibility of not having a particular product item when and where the customer needs it. In other words, merchandise assortment support planning focuses the retailer's attention on discovering the amount of inventory the retailer should carry by item and by units and answers the inventory questions of how many product items (assortment) and how many units of each item (support) to stock. One of the reasons for Consumers Distributing's recent failure was their frequent out-of-stock conditions caused by errors in sales projections and problems with suppliers.[62]

Assortment and support planning involves the use of several *merchandise lists*—a set of operational plans for managing total assortment and support of merchandise. Depending on the type of merchandise the retailer carries, one or more of the following merchandise lists will apply:

1. Basic stock list—for planning staple merchandise,
2. Model stock list—for planning fashion merchandise, and
3. Never-out list—for planning key items and best-sellers.

Merchandise lists essentially represent the "ideal" stock for meeting the consumer's merchandise needs in terms of assortment and support.

Basic Stock List The **basic stock list** is a planning instrument retailers use to determine the assortment and support for staple merchandise. **Staples** are product items for which sales are either very stable or highly variable but very predictable. In either case, estimates of the required assortment of merchandise items and the number of support units for each item can be made with a relatively high degree of accuracy. Thus, in planning for staple merchandise, the retailer can develop a very specific stocking plan. The basic stock list is a schedule or listing of stock-keeping units for staple merchandise. A **stock-keeping unit (SKU)** is a merchandise category for which separate records (sales and stock) are maintained; an SKU can consist of a single merchandise item or a group of items. The basic stock list usually identifies each SKU in precise terms. A retailer can use the following product characteristics to clearly distinguish an SKU of staple merchandise: (1) brand name, (2) style or model number, (3) product or package size, (4) product colour or material, (5) retail and/or cost price of the product, and (6) manufacturer's name and identification number.

In addition to a complete listing of SKUs, the basic stock list also contains a detailed description of the stock position for each SKU by stock levels (merchandise support, or the total number of units). Also, this description of stock support normally identifies (1) a minimum stock level to be on hand, (2) actual stock on hand, (3) amount of stock on order, (4) planned sales, and (5) actual sales. Stock support information is recorded on a standardized form at regular and frequent intervals (for example, quarterly, monthly). Figure 9–14 illustrates one of several possible forms for recording the information contained in a basic stock list.

The importance of carefully maintaining a basic stock list cannot be overstated. Most merchandise departments, including those that are fashion oriented, contain at least some product items that are basic staples. Examples are black nylon socks and white cotton briefs in the menswear department. Given the "essential" character of staple merchandise in the consumer's buying behaviour patterns, close supervision over the stock position of staples is absolutely necessary. A stockout of a particular staple forces the consumer to look elsewhere for the item. By not meeting the consumer's need for a basic staple, the retailer not only loses the sale but also damages the store's assortment image and strains the customer's goodwill.

Model Stock List Stock planning for fashion merchandise is accomplished through use of the **model stock list**—a schedule or listing of SKUs for fashion merchandise. The

Figure 9–14

A basic stock list form

Key:
R = Retail price
C = Cost price
MS = Minimum stock
PS = Planned sales
AS = Actual sales
OH = Stock on hand
OO = Stock on order

Stock keeping unit		Vendor description			Merchandise description						Stock description				
Number	Name	Manuf. Name	Manuf. I.D.	Brand	Style/ Model	Material	Colour	Size	Price R	Price C		Quarters 1	2	3	4
											MS				
											PS				
											AS				
											OH				
											OO				
											MS				
											PS				
											AS				
											OH				
											OO				
											MS				
											PS				
											AS				
											OH				
											OO				
											MS				
											PS				
											AS				
											OH				
											OO				

model stock list differs from the basic stock list because it defines each SKU in general rather than precise terms. Common criteria in identifying a model SKU are *general price lines* ("better dresses" at $100, $150, and $200 or "moderate dresses" at $40, $60, and $80); distribution of sizes (misses 8, 10, 12, 14, and 16); certain *basic colours* (black cocktail dresses or navy-blue blazers); *general style features* (long and short-sleeve dresses or crew neck, V-neck, and turtleneck sweaters); and product materials (wool, cotton, and polyester dresses). The more general character of each SKU in a model stock plan reflects the transience of fashion merchandise, which represents only the current prevailing style. The likelihood of style changes within a short period and the high probability that market demand (sales) will fluctuate considerably within any selling season require a more general approach to stock planning. If the model stock list calls for 300 "better dresses" equally distributed among the $100, $150, and $200 price lines, the retailer is still free to adapt to specific fashion trends that are currently stylish.

In the initial planning of model stock lists, desired support quantities for each SKU are established on the basis of past sales experience. The exact distribution of those quantities among the various assortment features (for example, colours, styles, materials) is left to the buyer's judgment about what is and will be appropriate for the store's customers. In essence, the model stock list provides general guidelines on the size and composition of an ideal stock of fashion merchandise without specifying the exact nature of the merchandise assortment or support.

The form used to plan the model stock list differs somewhat from the basic stock list form. First, the vendor description is usually absent or abbreviated. Second, the merchandise description is more generalized. Finally, the stock description is frequently more detailed, breaking down each season (quarter) into desired stock levels at various times within the season: beginning of the season, seasonal peak, and end of the season.

Never-Out List The **never-out list** is a specifically created list of merchandise items that are identified as key items or best-sellers for which the retailer wants extra protection against the possibility of a stockout. Product items on the never-out list are those often associated with the A product lines identified by the ABC analysis discussed earlier. As a result of the high level of demand for these items, many retailers establish rigid stock requirements. For example, a retailer might specify that 99 percent of all items on the never-out list must be on hand and on display at all times. Stockouts of these key items result in permanent loss of sales. Typically, the consumer will simply not wait to purchase best-sellers. Never-out lists can include fast-selling staples, key seasonal items, and best-selling fashion merchandise. The integrity of the never-out list is preserved through regular and frequent revision.

Controlling Merchandise Assortment and Support

Controlling merchandise assortment involves both monitoring and adjusting the types of product items that are added and dropped from the merchandise mix. Merchandise support control regulates the flow of product units within the retailer's inventory system. Inventory turnover and open-to-buy are two of the most widely used procedures for controlling the assortment and support components of the merchandise mix.

Inventory Turnover **Inventory turnover** is the rate at which the retailer depletes and replenishes stock. Specifically, inventory turnover is defined as the number of times during a specific period (usually annual) that the average stock on hand is sold. The typical discount store turns inventories four times a year, whereas twenty-five turns is the norm in the supermarket business. The formula for figuring stock turnover rates follows:

$$\text{Inventory turnover} = \frac{\text{Number of units sold}}{\text{Average stock on hand (units)}}$$

Average stock on hand for any time period is defined as the sum of the stock on hand at the beginning of the period, at each intervening period, and at the end of the period divided by the number of stock listings. For example, the average stock at retail for the summer season of June, July, and August would be calculated as follows:

June 1	1000 units
July 1	700 units
August 1	400 units
August 3	1100 units
Total inventory	3200 units

$$\text{Average Stock} = \frac{\text{Total Inventory}}{\text{Number of listings}}$$

$$\text{Average Stock} = \frac{3200}{4} = 800$$

(June–August)

If the net unit sales for the three-month summer season were 4000 units, then the inventory turnover rate would be as follows:

$$\text{Inventory turnover in units} = \frac{\text{Net unit sales}}{\text{Average stock on hand}}$$

$$\text{Inventory turnover in units} = \frac{4000}{800} = 5.0$$

June–August)

Benefits of High Turnover. High inventory turnover rates generally reflect good merchandise planning and control. Several benefits accrue to retailers with a high rate of inventory turnover:

1. **Fresher merchandise**—With a rapid inventory turnover there is more frequent replacement of merchandise and, therefore, a continuous flow of new and fresh merchandise into the store.

2. **Fewer markdowns and less depreciation**—A fast inventory turnover is associated with a fast rate of sales and, therefore, reduced losses resulting from style or fashion obsolescence and soiled or damaged merchandise.

3. **Lower expense**—A quick inventory turnover helps to reduce total inventories and, therefore, reduce such inventory expenses as interest and insurance payments, storage costs, and taxes on inventory. It also helps to reduce promotional costs, because a new and fresh selection of merchandise tends to sell itself more easily.

4. **Greater sales**—A rapid inventory turnover allows the retailer to adjust the merchandise assortment and support according to the changing needs of the target market and, therefore, to generate more customer interest and a greater sales volume.

5. **Higher returns**—A rapid inventory turnover resulting in an increase in sales and a corresponding decrease in inventories will generate a higher return on inventory investment and, hence, a more productive and efficient use of the retailer's capital.

Increasing the rate of inventory turnover requires the retailer to control the size and content of its inventory. Strategies for increasing inventory turnover include (1) limiting merchandise assortment to the most popular brands, styles, sizes, colours, and price lines; (2) reducing merchandise support by maintaining a minimum reserve or safety stock; (3) clearing out slow-moving stock through price reductions; and (4) increasing the promotional effort in an attempt to increase sales.

Limitations of High Turnover. A high rate of inventory turnover is not without its problems. Excessively high stock turns can mean the retailer is buying in too small quantities. If so, then the retailer is (1) not taking full advantage of available quantity discounts, (2) adding to the costs of transportation and handling, and (3) increasing accounting costs by processing too many orders. Another potential problem with high inventory turnover is the danger of losing sales because of stockouts.

Unit Open-to-Buy

Open-to-buy is one of the retailer's most important tools for controlling future merchandise inventories; it helps the retailer decide how much to buy. **Unit open-to-buy** is the amount of new merchandise the retailer can buy during a specific time period without exceeding the planned purchases for that period. Open-to-buy represents the difference between what the retailer plans to buy and what it has already bought—planned purchases minus purchase commitments.

For the retailer engaged in item and unit control, unit open-to-buy is a necessary tool in preventing stockouts and overstocking. Unit open-to-buy is most frequently used to control inventories of staple merchandise. This method lends itself to formal and systematic procedures for reordering merchandise that has well-established and predictable sales trends. Unit open-to-buy calculations involve two steps: (1) determining maximum inventory and (2) computing the unit open-to-buy quantity.

Step 1: Determine Maximum Inventory. **Maximum inventory** is the number of product units that the retailer needs to cover expected sales during the reorder and delivery periods plus a safety stock for either unexpected sales or problems in obtaining the product item. The formula for determining maximum inventory is shown in Figure 9–15.

As an illustration, a hardware retailer reorders a staple item of merchandise every six weeks, expecting that delivery will take three weeks. On the basis of past experience, the hardware retailer expects to sell approximately forty units a week and considers a two-week safety stock necessary. The maximum inventory (MI) for the merchandise is 440 units. It is calculated as follows:

$$\text{MI} = [(6 \text{ weeks} + 3 \text{ weeks}) \times 40 \text{ units}] + 80 \text{ units}$$
$$= 440 \text{ units}$$

The hardware retailer therefore must stock 440 units to cover the reorder and delivery periods and ensure a safety stock capable of covering two weeks' sales if the reorder is delayed or sales are higher than expected.

Figure 9–15

Computing maximum inventory and unit open-to-buy

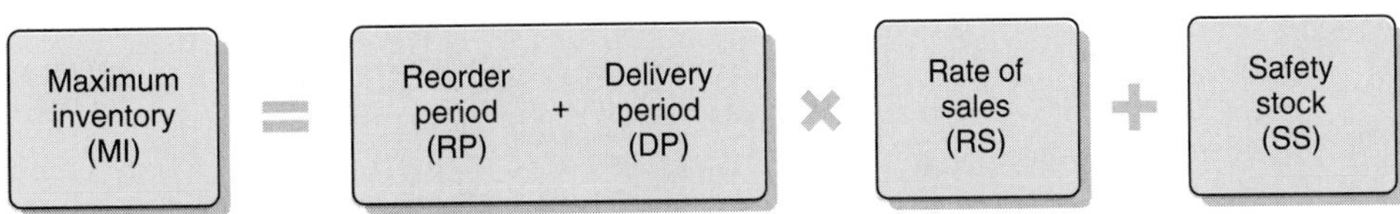

Where RP = the time interval between the scheduled place of orders (e.g., number of weeks)
DP = the amount of time between placement of an order and its arrival in stock ready to be sold (e.g., number of weeks)
RS = the number of units expected to be sold during a specified time period (e.g., on a weekly basis)
SS = the number of reserved units needed to cover any unexpected sales or delivery delays (e.g., a three-week supply)

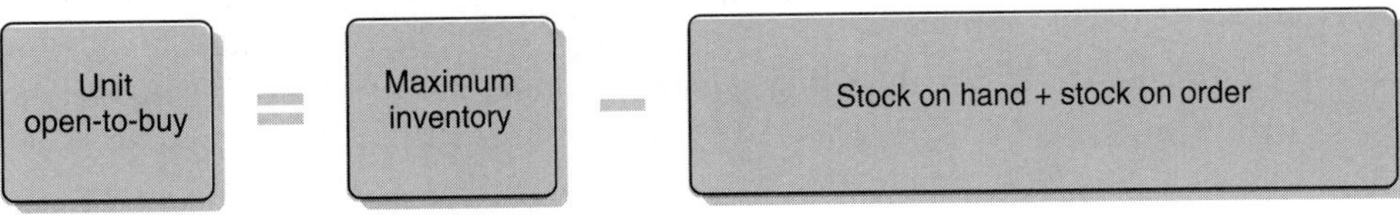

Step 2: Compute Unit Open-to-Buy. Maximum inventory represents the number of merchandise units the retailer is open to buy if there is no stock on hand or on order. Unit open-to-buy is defined as maximum inventory minus stock on hand plus stock on order. The computation formula is shown in Figure 9–15. Suppose our hardware dealer determines that it had 210 units on hand (obtained from the inventory-information system) and 90 units on order (obtained from purchase orders). Then,

open-to-buy = 440 (210 + 90) = 140 units.

Merchandise Mix Strategies

The basic objective in planning and controlling merchandise mixes is to offer consumers an optimum number of product lines and an optimum number of product items within each line supported by an optimum number of units for each product item. Several different optimal variety and assortment strategies are possible, depending on the retailer's circumstances. Figure 9–16 illustrates the four basic variety/assortment combination strategies: (1) narrow variety/shallow assortment, (2) wide variety/shallow assortment, (3) narrow variety/deep assortment, and (4) wide variety/deep assortment.

Narrow Variety/Shallow Assortment A **narrow variety/shallow assortment** strategy offers consumers the most limited product selection (lines and items) of any of the combination strategies. Vending machines that hold only two or three choices of soft drinks, door-to-door sales representatives who sell only one product line, and the newsstand that offers only one or two newspapers are examples of a narrow variety/shallow assortment strategy. The key to merchandising this limited product mix strategy successfully is place and time conveniences—making its offering readily available where and when consumers want it. Generally, the narrow variety/shallow assortment strategy suffers from

Figure 9–16

Merchandise mix strategies

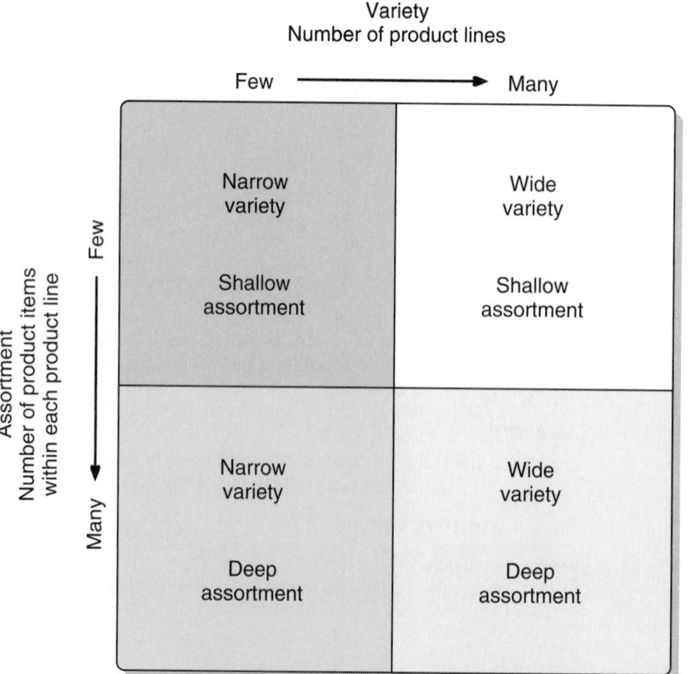

a poor image and little, if any, customer loyalty other than that generated by convenience. A limited merchandise mix, however, simplifies operations, makes inventory control problems insignificant, minimizes facility requirements, and limits inventory investment.

Wide Variety/Shallow Assortment The basic philosophy behind the **wide variety/shallow assortment strategy** is "stock a little of everything." The retailer offers a wide selection of different product lines but limits the assortment of brands, styles, sizes, and so on within each line. Most variety stores (five and dime stores), general stores, convenience stores, and some discount houses follow this product-mix philosophy. A wide and shallow product mix offers the advantages of appealing to a broad market, satisfying the consumer in terms of product availability if not product selection, promoting one-stop shopping, and permitting reasonable control over inventories. Costco Companies Ltd. stocks only the top-selling two or three brands in each category of merchandise.[63] The disadvantages of this merchandise mix strategy are lost sales and customer disappointment with the lack of selection within lines, low inventory turnover rate on slow-moving product lines, weak store image, and limited store loyalty.

Flag Shops
www.flagshops.com

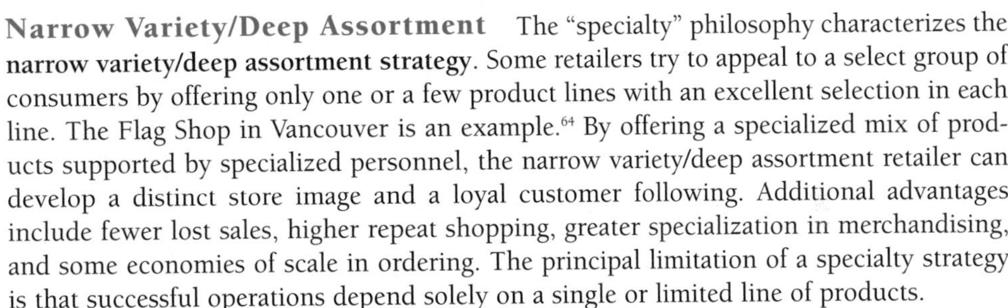

Narrow Variety/Deep Assortment The "specialty" philosophy characterizes the **narrow variety/deep assortment strategy**. Some retailers try to appeal to a select group of consumers by offering only one or a few product lines with an excellent selection in each line. The Flag Shop in Vancouver is an example.[64] By offering a specialized mix of products supported by specialized personnel, the narrow variety/deep assortment retailer can develop a distinct store image and a loyal customer following. Additional advantages include fewer lost sales, higher repeat shopping, greater specialization in merchandising, and some economies of scale in ordering. The principal limitation of a specialty strategy is that successful operations depend solely on a single or limited line of products.

Wide Variety/Deep Assortment The full-line department store best typifies the **wide variety/deep assortment strategy**. One-stop shopping is the basic philosophy of this all-inclusive merchandise mix strategy. A large number of product lines with supporting depth in each line enables the retailer to make a broad market appeal while satisfying most of the product needs of specific target markets. Few sales are lost as a result of an inadequate variety or assortment. Generally, satisfied customers develop store loyalty, leading to a high level of repeat shopping. The most common problems are (1) the necessarily high level of investment in inventory to support such a diverse merchandise mix; (2) the low stock-turnover rate associated with many marginal product lines; and (3) the amount of space, fixtures, and equipment the retailer must have to merchandise such a wide range of products properly.

Merchandise Budget Management

The merchandise budget is a financial management tool that retailers use to plan and control the total amount (in dollars) of inventory carried in stock at any one time. It answers the inventory question of how much the retailer should invest in merchandise during any specified period. Whereas the merchandise mix is planned and controlled in terms of units, the merchandise budget involves dollar planning and control. As an inventory investment model, the merchandise budget is directed at helping the retailer to realize its financial objectives of profitability. The merchandise budgeting and controlling process consists of five stages (see Figure 9–17): (1) planning and controlling retail sales, (2) planning and controlling inventory levels, (3) planning and controlling retail reductions, (4) planning and controlling retail purchases, and (5) planning and controlling profit margins.

To facilitate merchandise planning and merchandise budget preparation, most retailers use a form that summarizes basic budgetary information for a given merchandise grouping during a specified time period. Figure 9–18 illustrates a common form for preparing the merchandise budget.

Figure 9–17

Merchandise budget management

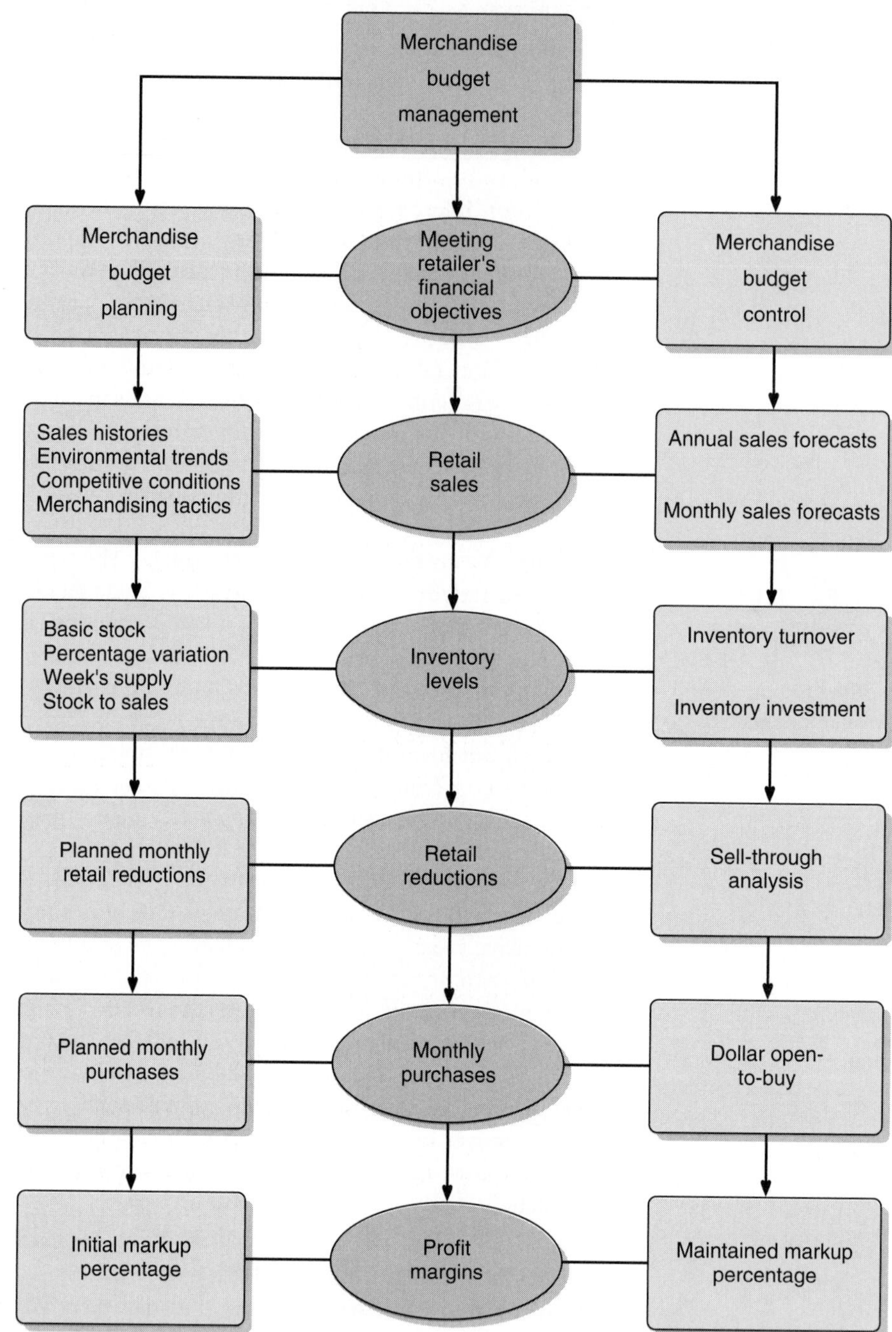

Planning and Controlling Retail Sales

The starting point in developing the merchandise budget is sales planning and control. If future sales are incorrectly estimated during this initial stage, then all other aspects of the merchandise budget (stock levels, reductions, purchases, profit margins) will reflect this initial error and require the retailer to adjust the budget throughout its application.

As shown in Figure 9–17, sales planning steps consist of (1) selecting a control unit, (2) reviewing sales histories, (3) critiquing environmental trends, (4) studying competitive conditions, and (5) scrutinizing proposed merchandising tactics. When sufficient information has been gathered and analyzed, the retailer can then proceed with the complementary process of controlling sales by making annual and monthly sales forecasts.

Figure 9–18

Form for preparing a merchandise budget

Six-month merchandise budget

Date ____________ Department ____________

		Aug.	Sept.	Oct.	Nov.	Dec.	Jan.	Total
Sales	Last year							
	Planned							
	Adjusted							
	Actual							
BOM stock levels	Last year							
	Planned							
	Adjusted							
	Actual							
Reductions	Last year							
	Planned							
	Adjusted							
	Actual							
Purchases	Last year							
	Planned							
	Adjusted							
	Actual							
Initial markup %	Last year							
	Planned							
	Adjusted							
	Actual							

Control Unit Before making sales estimates, the retailer must select the control unit for which the projections will be made. The *control unit* is the merchandise grouping that serves as the basic reporting unit for various types of information (for example, past, current, future sales). The retailer can elect to gather information and estimate future sales for an entire store, a merchandise division or department, or an individual product line or item. Using merchandise categories (specific lines of products that are directly comparable and substitutable, such as blenders) as the basic control unit is recommended because it is generally much easier to aggregate information (summing merchandise categories into merchandise classes and groups) than it is to disaggregate information (breaking down merchandise groups into classes and categories).

Sales Histories Examining sales histories and gathering sales information is the starting point for making sale forecasts. The most widely used internal source of product information is the sales records for various product lines and items. *Past sales records* are especially useful for deciding about staple merchandise. As a result of the regular demand for staples, past demand often is the key to predicting future sales. On the other hand, cyclical demand patterns for fashion goods limit the usefulness of past sales for estimating future demand. In making sales predictions, it is sometimes as important to find out what customers do not want as it is to find out what they do want. Store data on customer returns provide the retailer with valuable information on product lines that failed to provide customer satisfaction.

Want books include several different means (for example, notebooks) by which sales associates systematically record customer inquiries and comments regarding various product lines. *Sales associates* are an excellent source of information regarding the past performances of products; they are in a position to observe what, why, and how consumers buy. Retailers can also use *in-store testing* (test marketing within their stores) to gain sales experience with a product line for projecting future sales. Testing is often the only way to reduce the risk of a four-out-of-five failure rate. Products are pretested by stocking a sample order and observing customer responses. "Whatever the business, really staying in touch with customers often involves a lot more than merely running marketing surveys and the odd focus group. Smart managers increasingly zero in on key customers who no longer want their product or service. The theory behind such exit polling is that you can learn more from your mistakes than from your successes."[65]

Environmental Trends Previous discussions in Chapters 3, 5, and 8 all focus on the extremely important role and the high level of impact that environmental trends have on the success of a retail operation. Monitoring both the general and business press is an effective means for gaining a realistic perspective on current and emerging trends.

Competitive Conditions As outlined in Chapter 8, the sales potential for any given retailer for any given product is limited by the type and degree of competition that exists in the marketplace for that product. In other words, a given retailer only gets a piece of the total product action within a defined market (that is, market share). A good outside source of information on what consumers want is what other stores sell them. Through **comparison shopping** at both competing and noncompeting stores, a retailer can often discover the general sales experience that other retailers have had with a line of products. Comparative checks should include examining the competitor's window and store displays, advertisements, promotions, featured products, prices, shelf quantities, and product appeals.

Perhaps the most effective methods for determining consumer preferences are to ask and observe. Asking consumers their opinions and observing their behaviour yield first-hand information on which products consumers want now and in the future. Three common methods for soliciting consumer opinions and observing consumer behaviour are consumer surveys, consumer panels, and consumer counts. Being in contact daily with large numbers of retailers, vendors and their representatives have a wide range of experiences on which to base their opinions about current and future product successes. They are thus excellent sources of sales information, although retailers must be somewhat wary of their reliability. Attending trade shows and scanning trade publications also afford the retailer the opportunity to gain the collective wisdom of those individuals in the trade as to which products are "hot" and which are not.

Retailers subscribe to numerous *specialized reporting services*. Frequently, these services offer sales information on certain product lines and merchandising activities (for example, advertising, store displays, facings) used to market the line successfully. These private sources provide retailers with information periodically (daily, weekly, monthly) in the form of newspapers, special reports, or flash reports, but the cost can be substantial.

Merchandising Tactics How the retailer plans to merchandise a product line must be reviewed prior to making judgments on the potential sales for that product. Obviously, the retailer can influence a product's rate of sale by providing or withholding merchandising effort. Some factors to consider in planning annual sales include changes in (1) the amount and location of shelf or floor space devoted to the merchandise category; (2) the amount, type, and duration of planned promotional support; (3) basic operating policies (for example, longer store hours, higher levels of service); and (4) the competitiveness of the basic pricing structure used to sell the product.

Annual Sales Forecasting The most commonly followed procedure in forecasting retail sales is first to obtain an annual sales estimate, then allocate those sales to each of the twelve months. When planned monthly sales estimates have been made, retailers have a control mechanism in place that guides the merchandise budgeting process. Time-series and judgmental forecasting are two of the more popular sales estimating procedures discussed here.[66]

Time-Series Forecasting. By plotting the actual sales for each control unit over the past few years, the retailer can identify past sales patterns and gain some insight into possible future sales trends. This approach to sales estimates is generally referred to as *time-series forecasting*. It represents a simple, inexpensive, and widely used method for obtaining reasonably reliable estimates of sales in the near future. Time-series forecasting is generally quite appropriate for staple merchandise, somewhat less appropriate for fashionable merchandise (only for those fashions in a ford or classic life cycle), and completely inappropriate for faddish merchandise.

For purposes of illustration, Figure 9–19 presents a department store's six-year sales experience (1992–1997) with automatic-drip coffee makers and electric blenders. Past sales for these two merchandise categories reveal some interesting patterns. Although both have experienced sales increases, the amount and stability of the increases are noticeably different. The store's past blender sales reveal a small yet steady increase in dollar sales. Looking at changes in the percentage increase in sales per year, we see that sales are increasing but at a decreasing rate. These figures suggest that the blender is in the maturity stage of its product life cycle and that sales are fairly stable and predictable, at least in the near future. The past sales pattern for coffee makers shows both large and small dollar and percentage increases, together with drastic changes from one year to the next. Viewing the overall pattern of coffee maker sales, the retailer could conclude that this product has passed through the growth stage of its product life cycle, and done so fairly erratically at that. (Look at the percentage increase in sales; sales increasing at an increasing rate is indicative of a product in the growth stage of the product life cycle.) In 1997, however, sales of coffee makers began to show increasing sales at a decreasing rate—a possible sign that the product is entering its maturity stage. Thus, because of the erratic changes in the rate of sales of coffee makers and the data's suggestion that the product might be entering its maturity stage, the retailer's 1998 sales estimates for coffee makers are very likely to be much less accurate than sales estimates for blenders.

Judgmental Forecasting. Annual sales estimates for each merchandise category can also be estimated using the experienced judgment of the forecaster. Two such judgment methods are the fixed and variable adjustment procedures. Both procedures are an extension or variation of the time-series forecasting method.

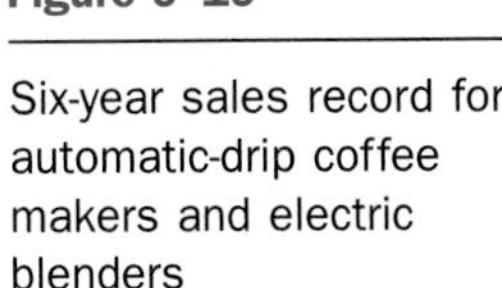

Figure 9–19

Six-year sales record for automatic-drip coffee makers and electric blenders

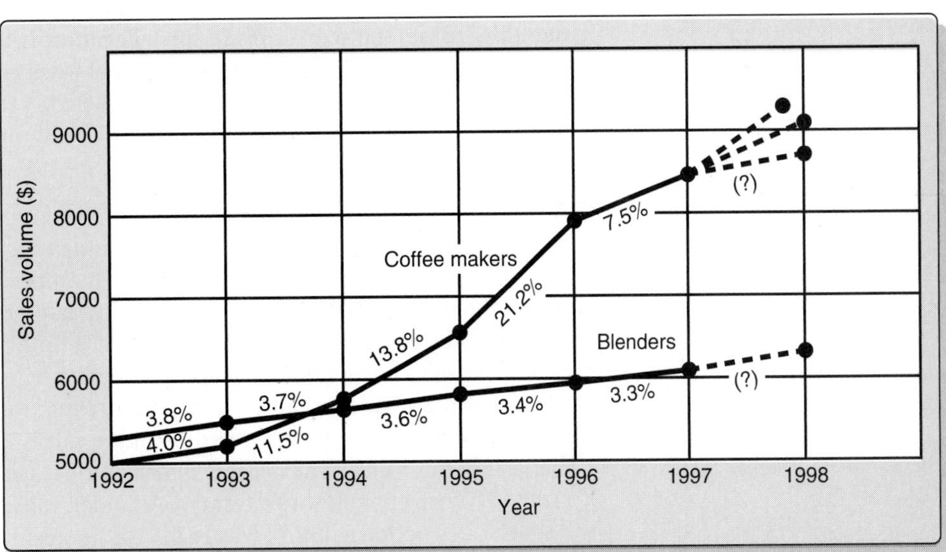

With the **fixed adjustment method**, the retailer adjusts the past year's sales by some fixed percentage to estimate the coming year's sales. The direction (plus or minus) and the size (the exact percentage) of the adjustment are based on the retailer's past sales experience with each merchandise category. For example, on the basis of the past sales trend for electric blenders shown in Figure 9–19, the department store's forecaster might well expect a 3.2 percent increase in sales for 1998 in the absence of extenuating circumstances that might strongly influence the sale of blenders. The fixed adjustment method usually works reasonably well in estimating future sales if a clear and stable sales trend has been established. When past sales patterns are erratic, however, a fixed percentage adjustment is inappropriate.

Equally inappropriate is the "beat last year's sales" approach for calculating next year's sales estimates. Some retailers simply estimate future sales by using a fixed percentage (for example, 4, 6, 8 percent) that will yield sales estimates higher than last year's sales performance. This approach does not recognize that various merchandise categories are in different stages of their product life cycles. Although some are in the growth stage (accelerated sales growth), others may be in the maturity (declining sales growth) or decline (decreased sales) stages. It also fails to take into consideration all the information gathered (for example, environmental trends, competitive conditions) in the sales planning process. Beating the past year's sales may be an appropriate sales goal for the store as a whole, but it is not an appropriate sales-estimating method for an individual category of merchandise.

The second method for estimating annual sales is the **variable adjustment method**. As with the fixed adjustment method, the forecaster usually starts with an examination of the past sales history of the merchandise category. Using the sales history, the forecaster determines a percentage change (for example, 6 percent) that appears reasonable. The figure is then adjusted upward or downward by a degree that depends on the nature of the merchandise and its exposure and sensitivity to environmental influences.

In summary, the **annual sales estimate** for a particular merchandise category equals the previous year's sales plus or minus a fixed or variable percentage adjustment. The adjustment factor is a blend of forecaster judgment, experience, and analytical skill.

Monthly Sales Estimates Retail planning periods typically are based on one-month or several-month periods; for example, some retailers estimate sales for products for the three-month winter season or the six-month fall/winter season. The best operational estimate for budgetary planning purposes is **monthly sales estimates**. Estimating monthly sales involves three steps:

1. **Making annual sales estimates**—To make monthly sales estimates, the forecaster starts with annual sales estimates, as discussed in the previous section.

2. **Determining average estimated monthly sales**—The second step in estimating monthly sales is to allocate the annual sales estimate derived in step 1 on a monthly basis. One way to make this allocation is to determine average estimated monthly sales by dividing the annual sales estimate by the number of months in a year. This figure would be a reasonably reliable estimate of monthly sales if we could assume that sales were evenly distributed over the twelve months of the year.

3. **Adjusting average estimated monthly sales**—Average estimated monthly sales are adjusted according to a monthly sales index based on past monthly sales records. The purpose of this adjustment is to obtain a planned monthly sales figure, the final estimate of each month's sales that the retailer will use throughout the budgetary process. By indexing past monthly sales, the forecaster can establish a sales norm for an average represented by an index value of 100. Any month with an index below 100 represents monthly sales below the norm; above-average sales are represented by index values exceeding 100. For example, a monthly sales index of 76 indicates that sales for that month are 24 (100 – 76) percent below the average. An index value of 181 denotes an above-average sales performance of 81 (181 – 100) percent.

Endnotes

1. Don Taylor and Jeanne Smalling Archer, *Up Against the Wal-Marts* (New York: American Management Association, 1994), 15.
2. Kenneth E. Store, *Competing with the Retail Giants* (New York: John Wiley & Sons, 1995), 100–101.
3. Al Ries & Jack Trout, *The 22 Immutable Laws of Marketing* (New York: HaperBusiness, 1994), 120–21.
4. Suzanne L. Jennings, "Niches within a Niche," *Forbes*, April 25, 1994, 122.
5. Chris Roush, "Rearranging the Furniture at Ethan Allen," *Business Week*, July 11, 1994, 102.
6. Robin Lewis, "What's a Brand Worth?" *Women's Wear Daily*, November 8, 1995, 10–11.
7. Robin Lewis, "A Brand Is a Brand Is a Brand . . . Or It Is Not: The Strategic Implications and What To Do," *Women's Wear Daily* (November 1995): 30–31.
8. "Stagnant Industry Escalates PL Chase," *Women's Wear Daily* (November 1995): 3.
9. *Ibid.*
10. See Alexandra Ourusoff, "Brands, What's Hot. What's Not," *Financial World*, August 2, 1994, 40.
11. Kurt Badenhausen, "Brands: The Management Factor," *Financial World*, August 1, 1995, 52–53.
12. See "The Fairchild 100," *Women's Wear Daily* (November 1995): 7–9. Also see Lois Therrien, "This Marketing Effort Has L'eggs," *Business Week*, December 23, 1991, 51.
13. Janet Bamford, "After Careful Re-tailoring, VF Is Looking Smart," *Business Week*, June 22, 1992, 66.
14. Sean Silcoff, "The Emporiums Strike Back," *Canadian Business*, September 26, 1997, 54.
15. Zachary Schiller and Wendy Zellner, "Clout! More and More, Retail Giants Rule the Marketplace," *Business Week*, December 21, 1992, 72. Also see "Manufacturers Say: Brands Still King, Private Labels Fill In," *Women's Wear Daily* (November 1995): 28–29.
16. See Lore Croghan, "What the Hare Told the Tortoise," *Financial World*, April 25, 1995, 33, 35.
17. "Store Strategies: Bank on Best Lines," *Women's Wear Daily*, November 8, 1995, 12, 20.
18. See "Private Label Jeans, Mount Aggressive Attack on Market," *Stores* (February 1996): 68–69; "Private-Label Apparel, Clothes by Any Other Name," *Consumer Reports* (November 1994): 718; and Raj Sethuraman, "Price Competition Between National and Store Brands: Who Hurts Who?" *Retailing Review*, a quarterly section of Stores (January 1996): RR6–RR7.
19. Susan Reda, "Private Label Transformation," *Stores* (January 1995): 30.
20. See "Retailers Say: Build Own Brands for Profit, Control, Distinction," *Women's Wear Daily* (November 1995): 26–27. Also see Ryan Mathews, "Branding the Store," *Progressive Grocer* (November 1995): 4–28.
21. "Marketing Goes through Series of Profound Changes," *Drug & Cosmetic Industry* (February 1990): 24.
22. Richard A. Melcher, "Home, Gardens—And a Tidy Turnaround," *Business Week*, August 22, 1994, 55–56.
23. David P. Schulz, "Entertainment Goes Retail," *Stores* (June 1992): 46–48.
24. Nancy Rotenier, "Flower Girl Makes Good," *Forbes*, September 11, 1995, 172.
25. See Alison L. Sprout, "Products of the Year," *Fortune*, December 28, 1992, 65.
26. Emily Nelson, "Goodyear Hopes to Drive Home Lifetime Guarantee on New Tires," *The Wall Street Journal*, March 7, 1996, B12.
27. Bob Ortega, "Audio Book Boom Sounds Like a Trend," *The Wall Street Journal*, March 15, 1994, B7–B8.
28. See Susan Caminiti, "Will Old Navy Fill The Gap?" *Fortune*, March 18, 1996, 59–62. Also see Kathleen Morris, "The Thrill Is Gone," *Financial World*, December 8, 1992, 34.
29. Gary McWilliams, "PCs: The Battle for the Home Front," *Business Week*, September 25, 1995, 114.
30. Jeannetta A. Jarnow, Miriam Guerreiro, and Beatrice Judelle, *Inside the Fashion Business* (New York: Macmillan, 1987), 28. Also see Richard C. Morais, "Welsh Couture," *Forbes*, July 20, 1992, 100.
31. *Ibid.*
32. Gretchen Morgenson, "The Feminization of Seventh Avenue," *Forbes*, May 11, 1992, 116.
33. Janet Ozzard, "Designer Collections," *Women's Wear Daily* (November 1995): 34.
34. See Anne D'Innocenzio, "From Grunge to Grand: Young Shoppers Find New Life in Old Guard," *Women's Wear Daily*, October 26, 1995 1, 6–7.
35. See Teri Agins, "Fashion Shows Sashay into the Realm of Superfluity," *The Wall Street Journal*, May 25, 1995, B1, B9.
36. Miriam Tatzel, "Skill and Motivation in Clothes Shopping: Fashion-Conscious, Independent, and Apathetic Consumers," *Journal of Retailing*, 58 (Winter 1982): 91–92.
37. Keith Naughton, "Don't Step on my Blue Suede Hush Puppies," *Business Week*, September 11, 1995, 84, 86.
38. Teri Agins, "Retailers Trip on the Frilly Velvet Look," *The Wall Street Journal*, October 8, 1993, B1, B3.
39. Kathleen Deveny, "Anatomy of a Fad: How Clear Products Were Hot and Then Suddenly Were Not," *The Wall Street Journal*, March 15, 1994, B1, B5. Also see Rick Marin, "Clear Crazy," *Worth*, February 1993, 25.
40. Nanette Byrnes, "Merry-Go-Round: Time to Get Off?" *Financial World*, January 19, 1993, 15–16.
41. Teri Agins, "Twin Sets Redux: There's No Fad Like an Old Fad," *The Wall Street Journal*, January 16, 1996, B1.
42. See Joshua Levine, "A Stitch in Time," *Forbes*, July 31, 1995, 96; Graham Button, "Soft Sell," *Forbes*, December 4, 1995, 252; William Nabers, "The New Corporate Uniform," *Fortune*, November 13, 1995, 132; Cyndee Miller, "A Casual Affair," *Marketing News*, March 13, 1995, 1; and "Casual Clothes Are Workplace Trend," *Brandweek*, July 18, 1994, 17.
43. See Dan McGraw, "Designing for Dollars," *U.S. News & World Report*, November 14, 1994, 103–6.
44. See Lore Croghan, "Customers for Life—How to Hang on to your Core Market the Harley-Davidson Way," *Financial World*, September 26, 1995, 26–31; and Mary Talbot, "From Biker Chic to Biker Cheek," *Newsweek*, March 23, 1992, 66.
45. Richard C. Morais, "What's Up, Doc?" *Forbes*, January 16, 1995, 42.

46. See Christie Brown, "Dressing Down," *Forbes*, December 5, 1994, 155–59; and Laura Zinn, "Move Over, Boomers—The Busters Are Here—And They're Angry," *Business Week*, December 14, 1992, 75, 77.

47. Donald M. Thompson, "Eaton's, A Cautionary Tale," *Business Quarterly*, Summer 1997, 35.

48. James M. Clash "Hit 'em First," *Forbes*, August 28, 1995, 102–3.

49. See John Pierson, "Man Walked on Moon, Why Can't Man Make a Women's Dress Shoe that Doesn't Hurt?" *The Wall Street Journal*, January 10, 1996, B1; and Carolyn T. Geer, "Sensible and Chic," *Forbes*, December 7, 1992, 222.

50. "Entertainment Systems for Idiots," *Forbes*, May 22, 1995, 238.

51. See Bill Pearson, "Chargebacks and Allowances," *Stores* (October 1995): 78.

52. See "Category Management Gains, but Confusion Still Reigns," *Chain Store Age* (January 1996): 112, 116, 118; "The Power of Category Management," *Progressive Grocer* (August 1995): 12–14; and "Toward a Revised Theory of Category Management," *Progressive Grocer* (August 1995): 57–62.

53. "Category Management: Marketing for the '90s," *Marketing News*, September 14, 1992, 12.

54. Susan Reda, "Category Management: Who Wins? Who Loses?" *Stores* (April 1995): 16–19.

55. Ryan Mathews, "Category Management Is a Strategy for All Seasons, yet Fully Realized and Practiced in None," *Progressive Grocer* (August 1995): 4; and Ryan Mathews, "Moving from the Category to the Consumer," *Progressive Grocer* (October 1995): 79–81, 86.

56. Leah Rickard and Jeanne Whalen, "Retail Price Wars Endanger Clout of Brands," *Advertising Age*, February 20, 1995, 36.

57. John Heinzl and Marina Strauss, "Eaton's Sales Job," *Globe and Mail*, September 13, 1997, B4.

58. See Chip Walker, "How Strong Is Your Brand?" *Marketing Tools* (January/February 1995): 47–53.

59. See Barbara E. Kahn and Donald R. Lehmann, "Modeling Choice among Assortments," *Journal of Retailing*, 67 (Fall 1991): 274–99.

60. Schiller and Zellner, "Clout!" 69.

61. See Kate Fitzgerald, "Competitors Swarm Powerful Toys 'R' Us," *Advertising Age*, February 27, 1995, 4; Ellen Neuborne, "Retailer Battles to Remain atop Tough Market," *USA Today*, November 9, 1995, B1; Susan Reda, "1995 NRF Gold Medal Award Winner, Charles Lazarus, Chairman of Toys 'R' Us," *Stores* (January 1995): 131–44; Seth Lubove, "The Growing Gets Tough," *Forbes*, April 13, 1992, 69; and Mark Maremont, "Brawls in Toyland," *Business Week*, December 21, 1992, 36–37.

62. John Lorinc, "Would You Buy This?" *Canadian Business*, December 1996, 119.

63. Jeff Keller, "Born To Buy," *Costco Connection*, July/August 1993, 18.

64. D. Wesley Balderson, *Canadian Entrepreneurship and Small Business Management* (Toronto: McGraw-Hill Ryerson, 1998), 314.

65. Kenneth Labich, "Why Companies Fail," *Fortune*, November 14, 1994, 64.

66. See John B. Mahaffie, "Why Forecasts Fail," *American Demographics* (March 1995): 34–40.

67. See Daniel J. Sweeney, "Improving the Profitability of Retail Merchandising Decisions," *Journal of Marketing*, 37 (January 1973): 60–68.

68. "How Much Is That Dress?" *Consumer Reports* (November 1994): 718.

69. J. Mathews and G. Boyd, "The March of the Retail Market," *Canadian Business* (December 1990), 34.

Merchandise Logistics System
Buying and Handling the Merchandise Mix

Outline

Objectives

To describe the components of a merchandise logistics system

To identify alternative sources of supply and channel options for procuring the merchandise mix

To explain the methods and procedures for initiating and maintaining supply contacts

To discuss the criteria for evaluating and the methods for negotiating with sources of supply

To discuss the strategies for deciding how many sources of supply should be used in obtaining merchandise and describe the buying methods used in the actual purchasing of merchandise

To compare and contrast a traditional purchase order system and a quick-response replenishment system

To design and explain an effective in-store system for receiving, checking, marking, and stocking incoming merchandise

Retail Vignette

Wal-Mart

Samuel Moore Walton began his retail career in Des Moines, Iowa, as a management trainee with the J.C. Penney Company in 1940. Mr. Walton opened the first Walton's Ben Franklin store in Newport, Arkansas, in September, 1945. After losing the lease on his Newport store, Sam Walton relocated to Bentonville, Arkansas, in 1950, and opened Walton's 5 & 10. During the 1950s, the number of Walton-owned Ben Franklin franchises increased to nine.

Merchandising and operation systems were refined. By the end of the 1960s, there were 18 Wal-Mart stores and 15 Ben Franklin stores in operation throughout Arkansas, Missouri, Kansas, and Oklahoma. The company became incorporated as Wal-Mart Stores, Inc., on October 31, 1969.

Wal-Mart
www.wal-mart.com

In 1970, Wal-Mart opened its first distribution centre and home office, a 6700 m^2 complex in Bentonville, Arkansas. Today, the home office totals about 54 000 m^2, and the company's 17 distribution centres often average over 90 000 m^2. By the end of 1979, there were 276 Wal-Mart stores located in eleven states. Stores were primarily located in towns of 5000 to 25 000 population. The stores' sizes ranged from about 3000 to 6000 m^2.

In the 1980s, Wal-Mart expanded its trade territory to 24 states. The company ended the year with 276 stores in 1980, 330 in 1981, 491 in 1982, 551 in 1983, 642 in 1984, 745 in 1985, 859 in 1986, 980 in 1987, 1114 in 1988, 1259 in 1989 and 1402 in 1990, bringing the total to 1573 in 36 states as of January 31, 1991. Today, standard store sizes range from approximately 3000 to 12 000 m^2, with 7000 m^2 being the average size.

Wal-Mart continues to be innovative. Technology designed to expedite the customers's shopping trip is also a major part of the Wal-Mart program. Wal-Mart was the first retail chain to be equipped with scanner cash registers in all facilities. Hand-held computers assist Wal-Mart associates ordering merchandise in all stores. Backroom computers link each store with the Bentonville, Arkansas-based home office and various distribution centres for communications and quick replenishment of merchandise.

Wal-Mart's "quick response" inventory management and ordering system is a model for the retail industry and brings supplies into a close relationship with the retailer to provide excellent stock replenishment. Supplies receive information about movement of their merchandise through computer technology immediately allowing for more timely replenishment and reduction of stock-outs.

In 1994, Wal-Mart purchased the Woolco discount department store chain in Canada. Conversion to full scale Wal-Mart stores was completed in a number of months. By 1997, share for Wal-Mart in the Canadian department store market was approximately 24 percent up from 16 percent when the chain was acquired. As a result of this success Wal-Mart is planning to add new stores in Canada as part continued expansion which now includes retail outlets in six countries besides the U.S.

By mid 1997, Wal-Mart operated 1946 Wal-Mart stores, 362 Supercenters, and 438 Sam's Club discount outlets in the U.S., as well as 136 stores in Canada and 153 in Mexico. Total sales amounted to $9.6 billion. Wal-Mart employs over 675 000 people.

Source: Mark Stevenson, "The Store To End All Stores," Canadian Business, *May 1994, 23;* Wal-Mart Annual Report, *1996.*

Retailing: A Game with New Rules

Look around. There is a new sense of team spirit pervading the relationship between retailers and suppliers. Why? Because, quite simply, retailing in the 1990s is a game that has new rules. It is being played on a game board that has too many stores, too many products, and too few customer dollars to go around. On this playing field, adversarial ways of doing business do not meet anybody's goal of productivity and profit growth. Why? Because they are not focused on meeting the consumer's definition of satisfaction. Developing strong, mutually interdependent relationships is critical in achieving consumer satisfaction. It is needed to remove unnecessary time and costs from the distribution pipeline.[1]

Retail supply chains are complex and strewn with pitfalls. Goods must travel from manufacturers to warehouses to distribution centres to stores or, in some cases, into the homes of customers. All along the way, people are making decisions about how much merchandise must travel, what it should travel in, how quickly it must be moved and how it will be stored. The problem, said Arthur C. Martinez, chairman and chief executive of the Sears Merchandise Group, is that usually each of these decisions is made independent of the others. He calls it "stovepipe" management. Logistics seeks to link the pieces of the supply line.[2]

The Merchandise Logistics System

The **merchandise logistics system** is the process of managing the integrated flow of merchandise and other materials from buying, through distribution, into the retail store, and ultimately into the hands of the customer. This system comprises three subprocesses that are essential to the retailer's quest for obtaining the right products in the right quantities at the right time at the right price (terms and conditions of sale): buying, ordering, and handling merchandise. The **merchandise buying process** involves all the activities necessary for establishing a successful relationship with various sources of supply.

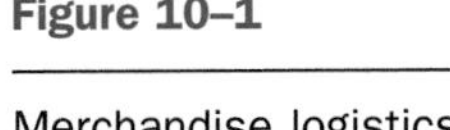

Figure 10–1

Merchandise logistics

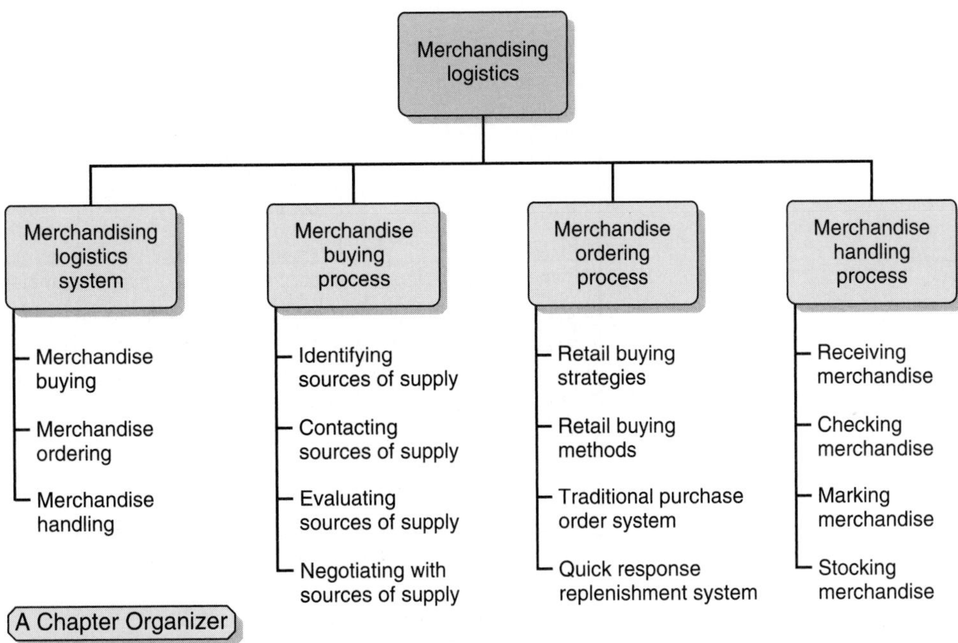

The **merchandise ordering process** entails the efficient obtaining of the retailer's merchandise inventories. The **merchandise handling process** involves all the activities of physically getting the merchandise into the store and onto the shelves. The sequential activities (buying, ordering, and handling) of the retail "prolistics" (combination of procurement and logistics) system are illustrated in Figure 10–1.

The Merchandise Buying Process

Retail buying can be viewed as the decision-making process through which the retail buyer identifies, evaluates, and selects merchandise for resale to the consumer.[3] The merchandise buying process is the retailer's first step in getting merchandise into the store. Primary concerns are determining (1) what sources of supply are available and under what terms and conditions; (2) how to contact and evaluate various suppliers; and (3) how, when, and where to negotiate with and buy from alternative supply sources. The buying process should follow, in sequence, the four steps outlined in Figure 10–2. To complete the buying task in an efficient and timely way, a retailer must establish a buying organization. The major structural dimensions in developing a retail buying organization are given in Figure 10–3.

As Figure 10–3 illustrates, one of the dilemmas for chain organizations is determining the extent of decentralization allowed in purchasing. The Retail Strategies and Tactics box entitled "Bay and Zellers Drop Joint Buying Strategy" illustrates the problems associated with centralizing buying for diverse retail operations.

Figure 10–2

The merchandise buying process

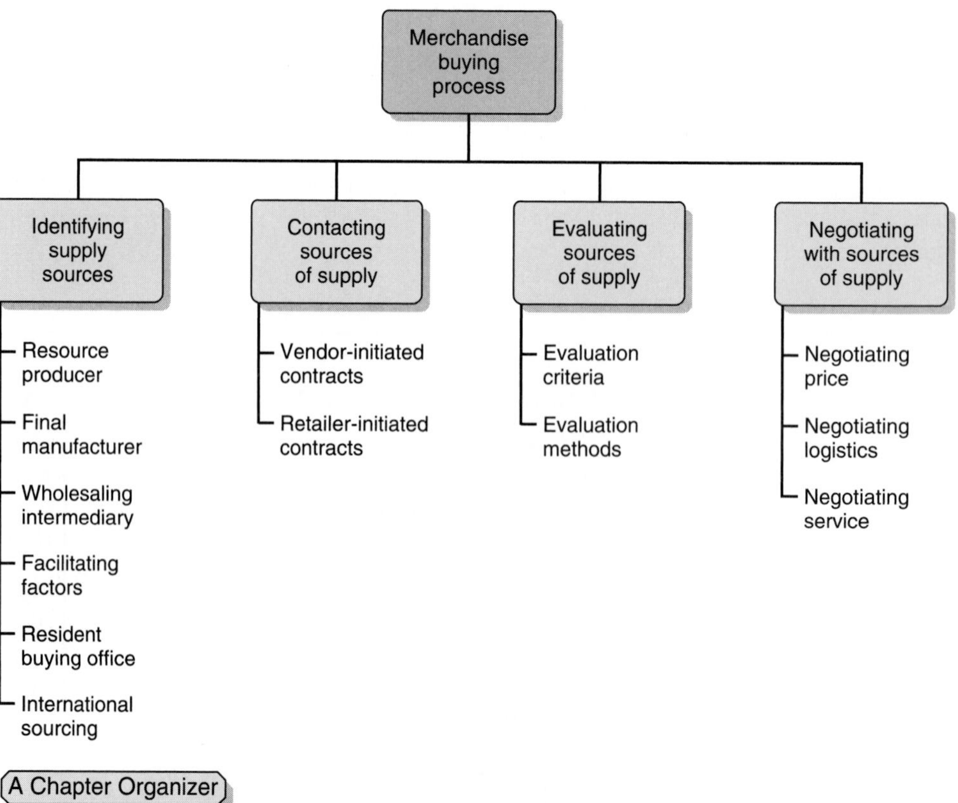

Figure 10–3

Major structural dimensions of a retail buying organization

Formality

A **formal buying organization** has a separate department or division to handle the buying function and related merchandising activities. Used by large retailers, the formal structure presents a clear definition of the department's authority and permits greater use of personnel trained in the buying process. Formal buying structures, however, are generally more costly to establish and to maintain. **Informal buying organizations** incorporate the buying process into the existing organizational structure, where the task of buying is handled by existing store personnel. Because of their lower costs and greater flexibility, informal buying organizations are used mainly by smaller retailers. Shortcomings of informal buying structures include lack of clearly defined authorities and responsibilities and lack of coordination between various activities and personnel.

Centrality

In **centralized buying,** the retailer gives a central office the authority and responsibility to buy merchandise, rather than leaving the decision to each individual store in the multiunit chain. A central buying office allows the retailer to take advantage of discount structures through volume purchases, coordinate and control the buying process for the entire chain, use full-time buying specialists, gain preferential treatment from suppliers, and maintain a consistent customer image of the store's merchandise and quality. On the other hand, central buying hinders adapting to local market needs. Additional problems include information lags, time delays, and poor morale because of the distance between the buying office and the local units and the formal nature of the buying organization.

Decentralized buying is structured and conducted at the local level. Each store or group of stores within a certain geographic market is responsible for the buying process. Adaptability to local market needs is the major advantage in this type of buying organization. Lack of control, inconsistency between stores, and loss of some economies of scale in purchasing are the main shortcomings of buying structures developed around local autonomy.

Specialization

Some retailers prefer to have each buyer specialize in one or a few related merchandise lines—**specialized buying;** others find it necessary to have a few buyers secure all the merchandise lines—**generalized buying.** Higher costs are the principal disadvantage of specialized buying, whereas lower costs are the primary benefit of generalized buying. In turn, greater buying skills and product and market knowledge are associated with specialization, while less-developed skills and less knowledge are found in a generalized buying organization.

Identifying Sources of Supply

The first step in the buying process is to identify the available sources of supply. From these sources, the retailer must decide which channel to use in procuring each merchandise line. In some cases, a direct channel to the manufacturer or original producer (for example, farmer) is preferred. For example, House of Fabrics purchases its fabrics directly from mills, buys in bulk, and then cuts and repackages (break-in-bulk) the fabrics for shipment to individual stores.[4] In other cases, an indirect or extended supply channel using one or more intermediaries is desired. Specifically, the retailer can select from any one or a combination of the following sources of supply:

- Resource producers,
- Final manufacturers,

Retail Strategies and Tactics

Bay and Zellers Drop Joint Buying Strategy

Hudson's Bay Co. Is reversing [1996's] controversial decision to combine the merchandise buying of its two department store chains, the Bay and Zellers—a signal that the cost-saving measure didn't work.

William Fields, who took over as Toronto-based Hudson's Bay president and chief executive officer in June 1997, said in an interview that consolidating the purchasing didn't allow buyers to focus properly on each chain's distinct customers, despite the savings.

Zellers, with 296 stores, is a discount retailer that caters to people shopping for low prices, while the Bay, with 101 outlets, is a traditional department store chain that targets a higher-income consumer.

"They're basically two separate businesses with two separate priorities," Mr. Fields said in a brief interview. "They just couldn't focus on either business to the level that they needed to."

He said it is important for Zellers and the Bay to carve out distinct niches and identities. "There's no sense competing with yourself. We should define the strengths and market segments that each division wants to go after, and go after them aggressively."

The consolidation raised eyebrows when it was unveiled because it is "highly unusual to combine the buying of a discounter with that of a traditional department store," said retail analyst George Hartman of Eagle & Partners Inc. in Toronto. "It's generally not the practice . . . Bill Fields feels that it just muddies the waters."

Source: Marina Strauss, Globe and Mail, *July 19, 1997, B1.*

- Wholesale intermediaries,
- Buying offices, or
- International sources.

The Resource Producer Under certain circumstances, the retailer may elect to obtain supplies directly from a raw resource producer. Large food retailing chains frequently bypass traditional supply sources in their efforts to obtain fresh fruits and vegetables and raw materials for their private-label brands. Buying food products directly from the raw resource producer offers a retailer the advantages of increased speed and reduced handling, both of which are important in getting these perishables to the store fresh and with minimal damage. Other products that retailers buy directly from raw resource producers include lumber, construction materials, and other bulky materials. Recently, Canadian general merchandise retailers have even been advised to bypass wholesalers and purchase directly from producers in order to compete with the "big box" retailers which are expanding into Canada.[5]

The Final Manufacturer With the emergence of large retailing organizations, direct purchases from manufacturers are becoming the rule and not the exception. Where direct buying is available and feasible, several advantages can accrue to the retailer: fresher products, quicker delivery, lower prices, better information regarding product attributes, more lenient adjustment policies on customer returns, and greater opportunity to obtain made-to-specification goods.

The Wholesaling Intermediary The third alternative source of supply is wholesaling intermediaries that position themselves in the distribution channel between the manufacturer and the retailer. Their role in facilitating the transfer of goods between manufacturers and retailers varies, depending on the nature of their operations as well as the functions and services they are willing to provide. Most intermediaries do not provide the full range of wholesaling functions—buying, selling, breaking bulk, assortment creation, stocking, delivery services, credit extension, information and consultation, and title transfer (see Figure 10–4). Instead, they tend to specialize in one or a limited number

Figure 10–4

Wholesaling functions

Buying tasks. Wholesalers act as purchase agents when they anticipate the merchandise needs of retailers and their customers. By locating appropriate sources of supply and securing merchandise that is suitable to the retailer's needs, the wholesaler greatly enhances the retailer's buying and procurement processes.

Selling tasks. Wholesalers help simplify buying procedures by having salespersons calling at the retailer's place of business. Wholesaling intermediaries help reduce the retailer's cost of securing goods by (1) eliminating some trips to the market and (2) assuming some of the responsibilities (e.g., order follow-up, self-stocking), for getting the merchandise onto the retailer's displays.

Credit-extending tasks. Many wholesaling intermediaries finance part or all of a retailer's inventory. The most common credit extension is the setting of the date when the net price of an invoice is due in full. By providing thirty, forty-five, sixty, or more days to pay an invoice without charges, the wholesaler is in effect financing the retailer's inventory. Consignment and memorandum selling wherein the retailer does not pay for the merchandise until it is sold is still another form of extending credit. In addition, many wholesalers make available to retailers short-, intermediate-, and long-term loans that can be used as working and fixed capital.

Informing tasks. Marketing research and source information are two important functions provided by the wholesaler. Many large wholesaling operations engage in an ongoing effort to determine marketplace needs and conditions. By passing this information on, retailers have reference points for examining their market performances and adjusting their marketing programs. On the source side, the wholesaler's unique position within the channel allows him or her to provide useful information on products, manufacturer's programs, supply sources, and activities of competitors.

Consulting tasks. Wholesalers offer their customers a host of advisory services. The more common consultant services deal with accounting, advertising, personnel training, financial and legal advice, location analysis, inventory control, and facilities planning.

Title-transferring tasks. Free-and-clear title to products is essential to the exchange process. Merchant wholesalers that own the goods they deal in assume the responsibility for transfer of payments and the management of title exchange. Agent wholesalers that do not take title to the goods facilitate the exchange of title by providing or arranging for the services necessary to the title-exchange process.

Bulk-breaking tasks. A quantity gap occurs between a manufacturer's need to produce and sell in larger quantities and the retailer's need to buy in smaller quantities. Wholesaling intermediaries help bridge this quantity gap by: (1) buying in car- or truckload quantities, (2) performing break-in bulk activities, and (3) selling smaller quantities (e.g., case lots) to retailers. This bulk-breaking function helps reduce the cost of doing business by reducing inventory carrying and handling costs.

Assortment-creating tasks. An assortment gap exists between manufacturers that need (manufacturing economies of scale) to provide and sell a limited line of identical or nearly identical products and retailers that offer a wider selection of products. Wholesalers can fill this gap by buying the limited product lines and items of different manufacturers and combining these lines and items into appropriate assortments. The retailer's quest for either mass- or target-market appeal is enhanced by the availability of diversified product assortments.

Stocking tasks. Retailers often have limited stockroom space and inventory investment capital. Wholesalers provide an invaluable service by reducing the space and capital needed for retail stock. This reduces the need for facilities and inventory carrying costs for the retailer. The local nature of wholesalers also enhances the time and place availability of products for restocking purposes.

Delivery tasks. Quick and frequent deliveries by the wholesaler help avoid or replenish stockout conditions that result in lost sales. A timely delivery system is one service a wholesaler provides that aids the retailer in holding down in-store inventories that are required to meet customer expectations. Reliable deliveries are also an integral part in reducing safety stock and the risk and investment associated with such stock.

Figure 10–5

Types of wholesaling intermediaries

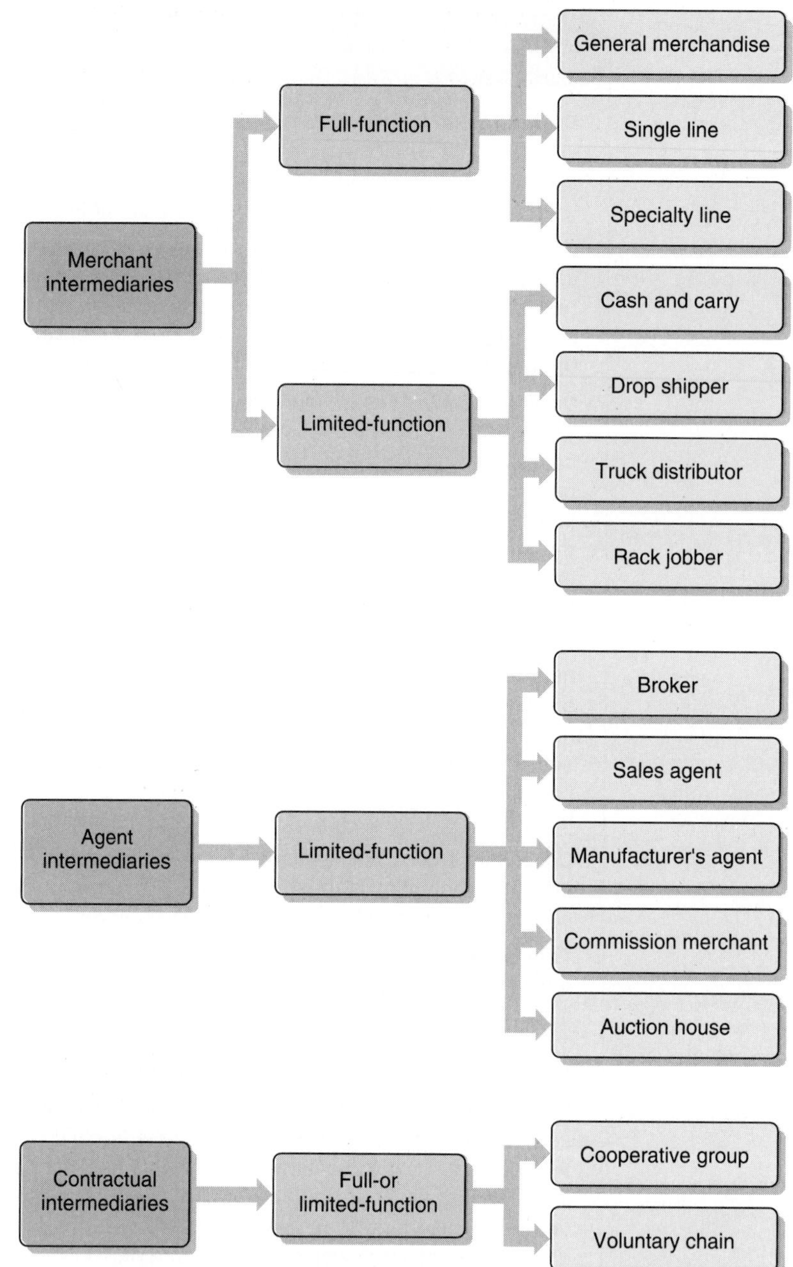

of these functions. Depending on the number and type of functions, wholesaling intermediaries fall into several groups. Figure 10–5 identifies these groups of wholesalers.

Merchant Intermediaries. Wholesalers that are directly involved in the purchase and sale of goods as they move through the channel of distribution are categorized as **merchant intermediaries**. These wholesalers take title to the goods they deal in. As illustrated in Figure 10–5, merchant intermediaries can be classified as full-function and limited-function operations. For many small and medium-size retailers that do not have the volume of sales to buy directly from the manufacturer, merchant intermediaries represent the most important source of supply.

Full-function merchant intermediaries generally perform a full range of wholesaling functions. On the basis of their product lines, three types of full-function merchant intermediaries can be identified. **General merchandise wholesalers** handle a number of different and often unrelated product lines, of which no one is dominant (for example,

supplier receives the entire discount chain (40 percent, 20 percent, 10 percent), whereas the buyer that performs a limited number of services is offered only part of the chain (40 percent).

Quantity Discounts. Suppliers offer **quantity discounts** to retailers as an inducement to buy large quantities of merchandise. Large order quantities help reduce the supplier's costs. However, buying large quantities normally increases the retailer's operating expenses, ties up operating capital, and creates additional inventory control problems. The retail buyer must also be aware of the potential risk of overbuying and then having to mark down the overstocked merchandise.

Quantity discounts can be expressed and calculated in several different ways. They can be based on either the dollar value of the total order or the number of units (or cases) in the order. Quantity discounts can also be handled as a percentage reduction from list price or simply expressed in some form of a schedule with unit or dollar sales corresponding to a particular dollar discount amount. A different approach to quantity discounts is to quote a carload or truckload price. The price of any order less than a carload or a truckload is adjusted proportionally upward by a system of "add-ons."

Three types of quantity discounts—noncumulative, cumulative, and free merchandise—are common. A **noncumulative quantity single discount** is based on a single order or shipment. The supplier uses this type of discount to encourage the retailer to increase the size of an order—the bigger the order, the bigger the absolute discount. Quantity discounts that apply to several orders or shipments placed with the supplier over an extended period (usually a year) are referred to as **cumulative quantity discounts**. The amount of the discount increases as the total (accumulated) order size increases. The supplier's purpose for applying cumulative discounts is to encourage return trade by reducing the price of merchandise on subsequent orders. **Free merchandise** is also a form of quantity discount. The "thirteen" dozen, whereby the supplier offers one free dozen for every twelve dozen ordered, is a common way to give the retailer free merchandise instead of a price reduction or a cash payment.

Seasonal Discounts. Price reductions given to buyers who are willing to order, receive, and pay for goods during the "off season" are referred to as **seasonal discounts**. Although the retailer can realize a savings in the cost of the merchandise by taking seasonal discounts, the savings must be viewed in light of (1) additional inventory costs and problems; (2) greater risks resulting from price changes, style changes, and merchandise depreciation; and (3) restricted use of investment capital already tied up in the merchandise.

Cash Discounts. A **cash discount** is one given for making prompt payment. To encourage retailers to pay their bills before the due date, the supplier sometimes permits the retailer to deduct a certain percentage discount from the net invoice price. When negotiating cash discounts and related payment terms, the retailer must consider three factors: net invoice price, discount amount, and dating terms.

The first consideration in negotiating cash discounts is to establish what constitutes the net invoice price. The **net invoice price** is the net value of the invoice or the total invoice minus all other discounts (trade, quantity, seasonal, and so on). An exception may occur when the supplier allows the transportation charges to be included in the net invoice figure. Depending on trade practices, the inclusion of transportation charges may be open for negotiation; if so, it is obviously to the retailer's advantage to have them included.

The second factor the retailer must consider is the **discount amount**. Although a 2 percent cash discount is common in many trades, the rate ranges from no cash discounts to whatever the supplier is willing to allow. Some retailers insist on a cash discount and automatically deduct a standard discount if payment is made within a specific time period (usually ten days).

Dating terms are important in negotiating cash discounts and payment conditions because they (1) determine the cash discount period or the amount of time the retailer has to take advantage of the cash discount and (2) provide the invoice due date or the amount of time the retailer has to pay the net invoice price in full. Ten days is the most common cash discount period, and thirty days from the dating of the invoice is a fairly standard invoice due date.

The two general classes of dating terms are immediate and future. Sometimes suppliers insist on **immediate dating**, allowing no time for the cash discount or extra time for the invoice payment. Prepayment and cash on delivery (COD) are two examples of immediate dating. **Prepayment dating** means the retailer must make payment when the order is placed. **Cash on delivery (COD)** terms are enforced when the retailer is either unknown or unreliable, and when the merchandise can be easily sold if returned to the supplier.

Future dating is the practice of allowing the retailer more time to take advantage of the cash discount or to pay the net amount of the invoice. In essence, it encourages the retailer to delay payment and helps in short-term financing of inventory. Figure 10–8 describes several types of future dating.

One additional negotiation issue is anticipation—the practice of taking an extra cash discount for paying the net invoice before the cash discount period expires. It is an amount the retailer takes in addition to the cash discount. The anticipation amount depends on the number of days the invoice is paid before the last day of the discount period; for example, paying the invoice on the fourth day of a ten-day cash discount period entitles the retailer to deduct six days of anticipation at a previously agreed-on daily discount rate.

Most experts recommend that retailers take every cash discount available, because most cash discounts yield an equivalent annual interest rate far in excess of the yield most other investments produce. Also, the yield on most cash discounts is more than enough to cover the interest on funds borrowed to meet the time requirement of the cash discount period.

Promotional Allowances. To gain the retailer's cooperation in promotional activities, the supplier frequently offers a promotional allowance. **Promotional allowances**, which reduce the price retailers pay suppliers for merchandise, include advertising allowances, preferred selling space, free display materials, and merchandise deals.[20] *Advertising*

Figure 10–8

Types of future dating terms

Future dating terms	Selected examples	Explanation of examples: Cash discount terms	Explanation of examples: Net invoice terms
Net	Net, 30	No cash discount allowed	Net amount due within 30 days of invoice date
Date of invoice (DOI)	2/10, net 30	2-percent discount within 10 days of invoice date	Net amount due within 30 days of invoice date
End of month (EOM)	2/10, net 60, EOM	2-percent discount within 10 days of the first day of the month following the invoice date	Net amount due within 60 days of the first day of the month following the invoice date
Receipt of goods (ROG)	4/10, net 45, ROG	4-percent discount within 10 days after receiving the goods at the retailer's place of business	Net amount due within 45 days after receiving the goods at the retailer's place of business
Extra	3/10-60 extra, net 90	3-percent discount within 70 days of invoice date	Net amount due within 90 days of invoice date

allowances are discounts retailers earn by advertising the supplier's products in the local media. Retailers give vendors *preferred selling space* in return for a price reduction. The recognition that store space is extremely valuable has led retailers to divert some of their overhead costs to the manufacturer in the form of various fees. Some of the more common fees include the following:

- **Presentation fees**—Payments required by the retailer of the vendor to listen to a sales presentation.
- **Slotting allowance**—Admission fees paid by manufacturers to get their product on the retailer's crowded shelves.
- **Failure fees**—Penalty payments by the vendor to compensate the retailer for displayed products that fail to generate an agreed-upon unit volume.
- **Renewal fees**—Annual charges paid by the vendor to retain the product in its shelf position for a specific time period.[21]

Preferred sales areas include (1) a freestanding display in a high-traffic aisle, (2) an end-of-aisle display, (3) a high-exposure area near a checkout counter, or (4) a special window display. Retailers also use free display materials in the form of counter, window, and floor displays; signs; banners; and shelf strips, as well as various types of giveaways. These materials help to increase sales, reduce selling costs, and earn allowances from suppliers.

Promotional allowances also can take the form of merchandise deals, in which the supplier substitutes free merchandise for monetary allowances as compensation for performing promotional functions. For example, a retailer might get a free case of the displayed product after it purchased and displayed a certain number of cases. By controlling the store and shelf space, retailers are starting "to realize that they are in the real estate business and the price of that real estate is going up."[22]

Negotiating the Logistics The retailer's actual laid-in cost of merchandise also depends on which party assumes the transportation charges and handling responsibilities. In negotiating logistics (transportation and handling) terms, the retailer must consider all of these issues: Who pays transportation charges? Who bears transportation charges? Where does the title exchange hands? Who is responsible for filing claims? The payer and the bearer of transportation charges may or may not be the same thing; for example, to facilitate delivery speed, the supplier may pay transportation charges when the goods are loaded at the factory but charge them back to the retailer on the invoice. In such cases the retailer ultimately bears the cost of transportation. Equally important is the point at which title to the merchandise is transferred from the supplier to the retailer. The party that has title while the goods are in transit is responsible for bearing any insurance costs that might be needed above the liability of the carrier to cover loss. The location where title exchange occurs also influences which party is responsible for filing and collecting any damage claims against the carrier. Figure 10–9 illustrates the six most common expressions of transportation and handling terms. As a note of caution, transportation terms are characterized by a variety of expressions; therefore, retailers should not hesitate to ask for clarification of any expression they do not fully understand.

Negotiating the Service In addition to price, the various types and levels of services the supplier provides are also subject to negotiation. In some cases, a service is fairly standard with only minor adjustments allowed; in other cases, certain services are totally negotiable. The discussion on evaluating sources of supply identifies ten supplier services (see p. 384). Although services may be available, the retailer may not receive some or any of them without actively seeking them as part of the buying process. The terms and conditions for any one of these ten services must be detailed before purchase if the retailer expects the supplier to provide them.

Figure 10–9

Transportation terms and conditions

Source: Adapted from Murrary Krieger, Practical Merchandising Math for Everyday Use *(New York: National Retail Federation, Inc., 1980), 4.*

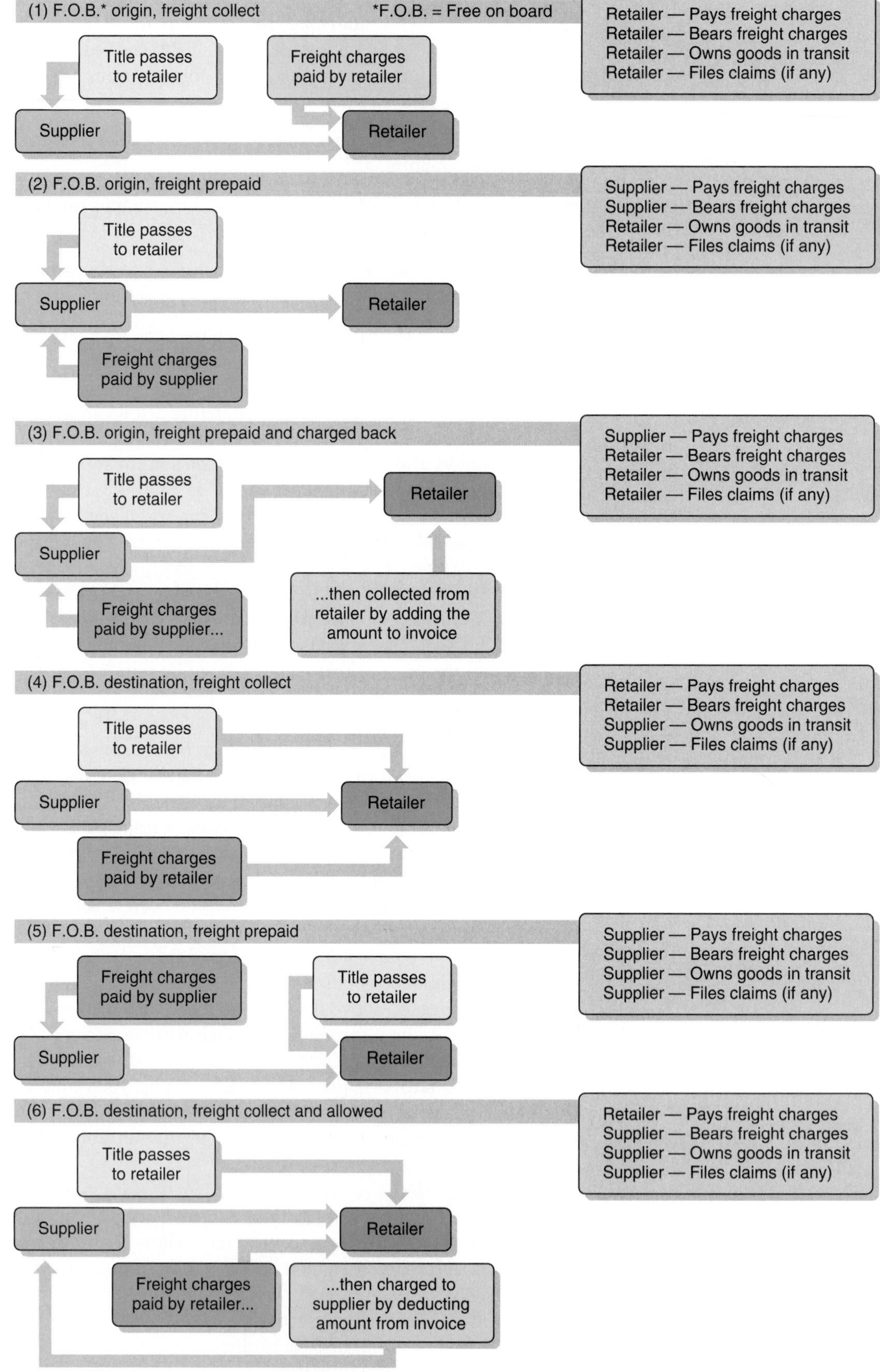

The Merchandise Ordering Process

After the negotiation stage is completed, the retailer is in a position to initiate the ordering process. As seen in Figure 10–10, the merchandise ordering process is the logical extension of the buying process and involves three issues: (1) Should purchase orders be concentrated with a few vendors or spread out among many suppliers? (buying strategies); (2) What type of buying procedures should be used under what type of circumstances? (buying methods); and (3) What type of vendor relationships and order processing arrangements should the retailer establish or become involved in? (traditional purchase order systems and/or quick-response replenishment systems).

Retail Buying Strategies

In deciding how many different sources of supply to use in obtaining the store's merchandise, the retailer can elect to pursue one of two buying strategies: concentrated or dispersed.[23]

Concentration Strategy With a **concentration strategy**, the retailer decides to use a limited number of suppliers, believing it leads to lower total costs and preferential treatment. Canadian department stores, such as Eaton's, Sears, and the Bay, are reevaluating their buying strategies by limiting suppliers in order to remain competitive.[24] Many smaller vendors are unable to compete because they cannot meet the onerous logistic demands.[25] By concentrating purchases, the retailer can lower the laid-in cost of the merchandise by taking advantage of quantity discounts and lower transportation rates. Operating expenses can be lower, because ordering, receiving, and processing of merchandise are more efficient with fewer suppliers. Equally important, many retailers

Figure 10–10

The merchandise ordering process

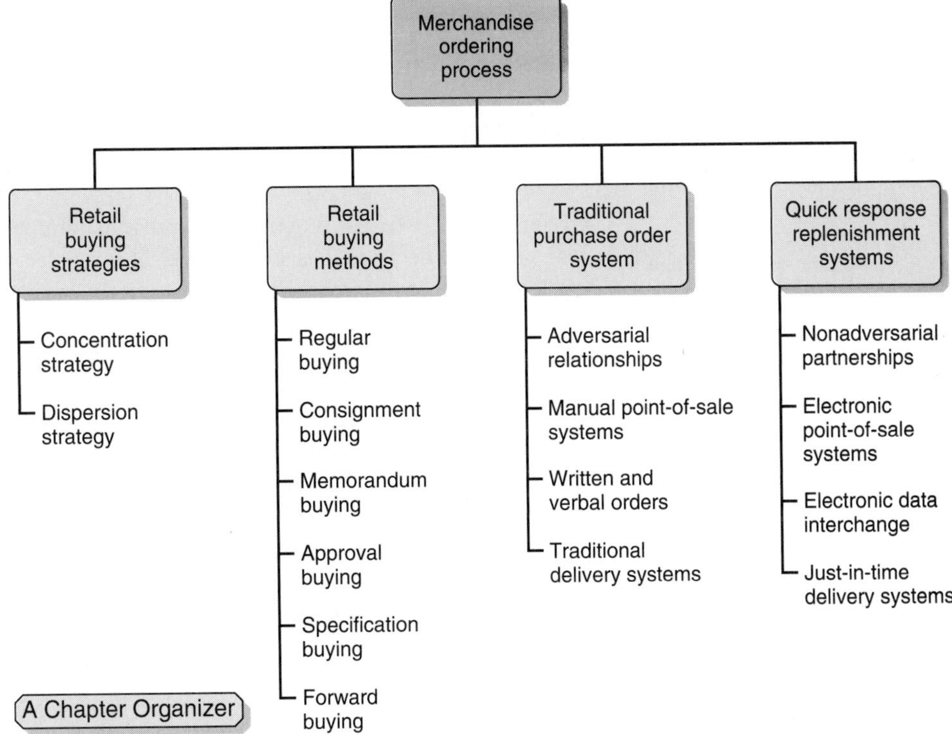

believe that if they become preferred customers by concentrating their purchases, they can expect to receive special considerations for merchandise and supplier services.

Dispersion Strategy Proponents of the **dispersion strategy** believe that concentrated buying is "concentrated risk," because it is dangerous to "put all your eggs in a few baskets." By spreading orders over many suppliers, these retailers believe they can (1) obtain a greater variety of merchandise, (2) be made aware of "hot" items, (3) ensure backup sources of supply, and (4) promote competitive services from different supply sources. Generally, retailers of staple merchandise tend to concentrate their purchases, whereas retailers of fashion merchandise usually elect a less concentrated approach.

Retail Buying Methods

Retailers use several buying methods, depending on their circumstances. They include regular, consignment, memorandum, approval, specification buying, and foreword buying.

Regular Buying Retailers use regular buying to obtain the vast majority of their merchandise lines. **Regular buying** involves the systematic cutting and issuing of purchase orders and reorders. The entire buying process is conducted in conjunction with the merchandise budget and the inventory control process. Purchases are mechanical and automatic. For example, "computerized monitoring of sales data and inventory levels . . . allows Procter & Gamble to automatically replenish Kmart's stock of Crest toothpaste when needed."[26] Most staple goods and many fashion goods can be handled by this method. LeviLink, an automated inventory system provided by Levi Strauss, is capable of automatically replenishing all of its core product items.

Kmart
www.kmart.com

Consignment Buying Retailers prefer to use **consignment buying** when dealing with high-risk products. It involves an arrangement in which the supplier retains ownership of the merchandise shipped to the retailer, and the retailer (1) displays the merchandise, (2) sells it to the final consumer, (3) deducts an agreed-on percentage commission, and (4) remits the remainder to the supplier. Merchandise not sold within a prescribed time is returned to the supplier. This method of buying is usually used when the merchandise is expensive, new, or of such a high-risk nature that the extent and duration of demand is relatively unknown.

Memorandum Buying As a variation of consignment buying, **memorandum buying** is different in that the title to the merchandise exchanges hands when it is shipped to the retailer. The retailer retains the right to return to the supplier any unsold merchandise and to pay for the merchandise after it has been sold. The retailer's purpose for assuming title is to gain more control in setting the selling price to the final consumer.

Approval Buying When merchandise is shipped to the retailer's store before the final purchase decision has been made, the retailer is buying on approval. Before the retailer can sell the merchandise it must obtain ownership. **Approval buying** enables the retailer to inspect the merchandise before making the purchase decision and postpone any purchase until physical possession has been obtained.

Specification Buying Many large retail organizations want some of their merchandise made to their specifications. Specifications can range from minor changes in existing lines of merchandise to complete specifications covering raw materials, design, quality, labelling, and packaging. Through **specification buying**, the retailer can acquire merchandise that is unique and distinct from that of competitors and thus personalized. The Gap, for instance, designs its own clothes, chooses its own materials, and monitors all manufacturing of its apparel lines.[27]

Forward Buying The practice of stocking up on a manufacturer's promotional items at a deep discounted price at the tail end of the designated promotional period is referred to as **forward buying**. Both retailers and wholesalers that have large-scale operating economies often take advantage of their size and build inventories with bulk orders when producer prices are reduced via promotional programs. In a market in which retail prices are increasing, forward buying can make a considerable contribution to the bottom line. However, risks and costs of carrying additional inventory must also be considered.

Traditional Purchase Order System

The basic dimensions of a **traditional purchase order system** are shown in Figure 10–11. As illustrated, this system comprises a series of functions within each organization (receiving, selling, and buying for the retailer and sales, production, and distribution for the vendor) and between organizations (ordering and delivery).

Adversarial Relationships Although a certain level of cooperation and coordination is a necessary part of any distribution system, the interaction between buyers and sellers in a traditional purchase order system is essentially an adversarial relationship. "Research has found that 55 percent of manufacturers distrust retailers and 46 percent of retailers do not trust manufacturers."[28] In this traditional system, both the vendor and the retailer attempt to obtain the best possible terms and conditions for their organization during each purchase transaction. Strong negotiation skills are vital in this adversarial relationship if the retailer is to obtain desired merchandise under favourable terms.

Manual Point-of-Sale Systems A traditional purchase order system starts with the retailer obtaining sales data through manual (for example, point-of-sale tallies, price-ticket or cash register stubs) or automatic (for example, point-of-sale terminal keys) inventory information systems. The sales data are then provided to the retailer's buying office, which uses the information in preparing buying plans and purchase orders.

Written and Verbal Orders Retailers can place merchandise orders verbally or in writing. Because verbal agreements in some jurisdictions are legally binding only up to some stated limit and are subject to vastly different interpretations, retailers should

Figure 10–11

Traditional purchase order system

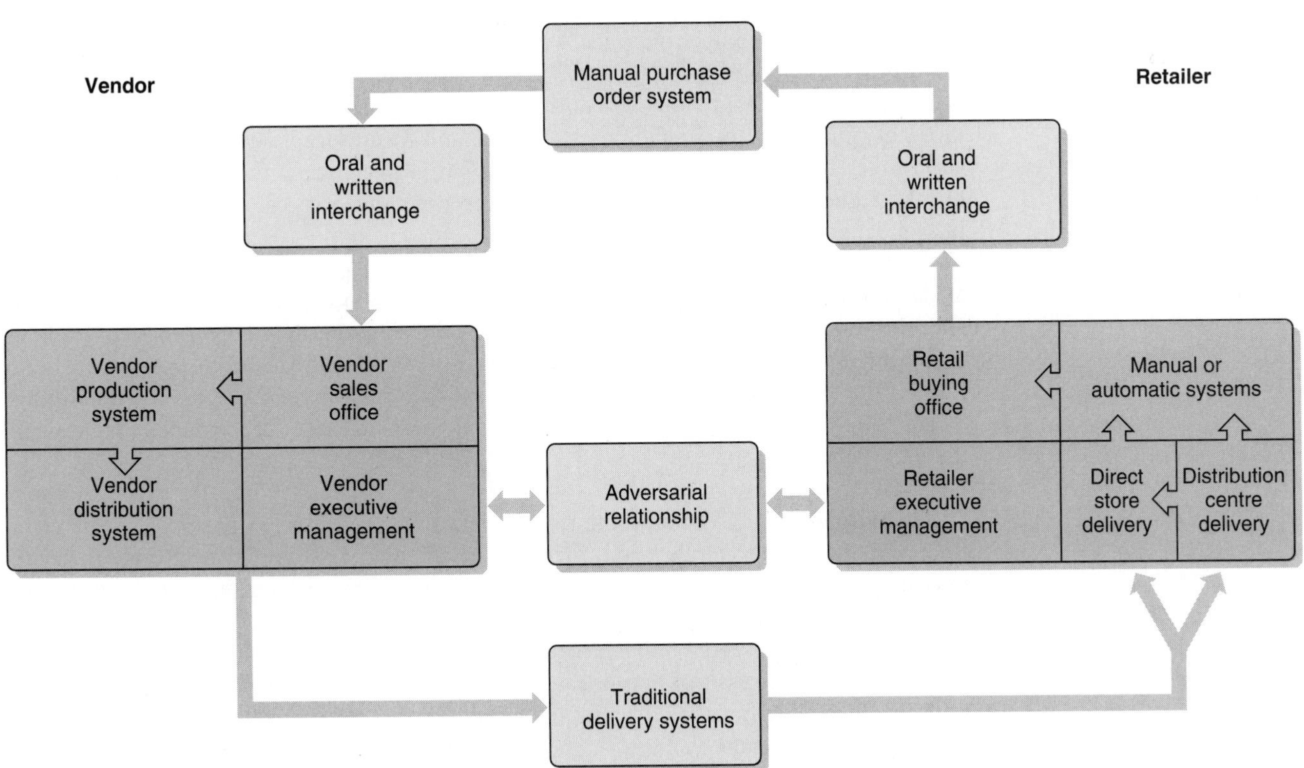

Figure 10–12

Types of orders

Regular order: Orders placed by the buyer directly with the vendor, involves ordering regular stock items with complete specifications as to terms and conditions of sale and delivery.

Reorders: Orders placed with existing supplier for previously purchased goods, usually under terms and conditions specified by the original order.

Advance orders: Orders placed in advance of both the normal buying season and the immediate needs of the retailer. Involves ordering regular stock items in anticipation of receiving preferred treatment.

Back orders: Orders placed by the buyer for merchandise that was ordered but not received on time. Involves orders that the supplier intends to ship as soon as goods are available.

Blanket orders: Orders placed with suppliers for merchandise for all or part of a season. Involves ordering merchandise without specifying such assortment details as sizes, colours, and styles and such delivery details as when and how much to ship. Requisitions against the blanket order will be placed as the need for the merchandise arises.

Open orders: Orders placed with central market representatives (e.g., resident buyers) to be filled by whatever supplier the representative considers best suited to fill the order.

Special orders: Orders placed with suppliers for merchandise not normally carried in stock or for specially manufactured merchandise. May involve specification buying.

have them accurately transcribed into written form at the earliest possible time. When placing a written order, the buyer can use a form provided by the vendor or one provided by the retailer. It is generally recommended that retailers use their own forms whenever possible.

Order Types. The buyer often faces a variety of circumstances that determine which of many different types of orders must be placed. Ordering procedures might involve placing orders (1) with different suppliers at different levels in the channel of distribution; (2) at different times to accommodate past, present, and future needs; (3) for either regular or special merchandise; and (4) with complete or partial specification of terms and conditions of sale. Figure 10–12 identifies and briefly describes seven types of orders that might be placed depending on the circumstances.

Order Forms. The **order form**, a legally binding contract when signed by both parties, specifies the terms and conditions under which the transaction is to be conducted. These terms and conditions usually are stated on both the front and back of the order form. The front of the order form usually contains standard information on the terms and conditions of sale. The back side usually contains a standardized statement of the general conditions under which the supplier will be held legally responsible if it accepts the order.

Order Follow-Up. To be sure the right order is received in the right place at the right time, the retailer needs follow-up procedures. Following up an order is also necessary to make a purchase contract legally binding. In most cases, the original copy of the purchase order, which is sent to the vendor, constitutes a *legal offer* to buy. No purchase contract exists, however, until the seller accepts the buyer's offer. Therefore, the first step in following up an order is to determine whether the supplier has accepted the order. Follow-up procedures also include checking the supplier's acceptance to determine whether the supplier has made any changes in the order. *Routine follow-up* procedures (letters and telephone calls) are used to check for order acceptance and discrepancies between the retailer's original order and the supplier's acceptance. There are *special follow-up procedures* if the importance of the order merits them. They usually involve the use of a field expediter (for example, resident buyer) who personally visits the vendor.

Traditional Delivery Systems When the order has been received and verified by the vendor's sales office, it is processed through production according to purchase order specifications. Final delivery of the merchandise is handled by the vendor's distribution system according to the terms and conditions set forth in the purchase order. Scheduled deliveries can be made to either the retailer's individual store outlets or a centralized distribution centre (see Figure 10–11).

Quick-Response Replenishment System

Quick response (QR) is "a strategy of customer service that uses technology to make possible an industrial pipeline so flexible and efficient that, ideally, retailers can forecast today what they will sell tomorrow and have the merchandise in the stores on time, in the right quantities, colours, sizes, and styles."[29] Quick response is a short-cycle merchandise replenishment (reorder) system that involves an automatic restocking of the retailer's inventories within a matter of days; this shorter cycle is in contrast to the more extended restocking cycles (weeks or months) associated with traditional purchase order systems. The goals of a QR system include (1) higher inventory turnover rates, (2) lower inventory carrying costs, (3) fewer out-of-stock situations, (4) reduced storage space requirements, and (5) better customer service through more finely tuned merchandise assortments. Additional goals include (1) increased sales through quicker reaction to sales trends and customer demands; (2) fewer markdowns by careful monitoring of what is selling and what is remaining on the shelf or rack; (3) reduced merchandising expenses by lessening the amount of time required to create, communicate, and track purchase orders; and (4) lower administrative costs as a result of electronic data processing. The Retail Strategies and Tactics box illustrates the growing use and value of quick response replenishment systems by Canadian retailers.

Retail Strategies and Tactics

Cutting Your Response Time

By no means has the reaction been speedy to Quick Response (QR). But Canadian companies are beginning to embrace the new means of inventory management between retailers and manufacturers.

One of the biggest advocates is Wal-Mart Stores Inc., the retail colossus based in Bentonville, Ark., which shocked the retail scene in Canada by buying 120 Woolco locations. A pioneer in integrated supply chain management, the U.S. giant discount retailer spends only 1.7 percent of its cost of sales on distribution, in contrast to the industry average for discount retailers of 3.5 percent. To appreciate the magnitude in savings, Wal-Mart pushes more than $40 billion worth of goods through its supply pipeline each year.

How does Wal-Mart do it? The retailer works closely with its suppliers to shorten the logistics chain. A shorter supply chain is more responsive, flexible and economical. And the bonus—it offers a higher level of service to customers.

Wal-Mart has entrusted key suppliers to stock its store shelves. In effect, sales forecasting is no longer the domain of Wal-Mart store managers. It has become the responsibility of suppliers such as Procter & Gamble Co., which have 100 percent electronic access to Wal-Mart's merchandising activities through point-of-sale (POS) data. Procter & Gamble, for instance, has an open purchase order to move products as needed to Wal-Mart distribution centres for just-in-time delivery to individual stores.

Whatever the definition, the common attribute of the QR quest is technology. Cycle times are shrinking thanks to recent advances in information networks. Electronic data interchange (EDI), bar coding, and POS systems are some of the hi-tech ways that allow progressive companies to accurately monitor and communicate their changing distribution demands.

Source: Andrew Tausz, Canadian Retailer, *January/February, 1994.*

Although the basic organizational structure of a QR system is essentially the same as a traditional purchase order system (compare Figure 10–11 and Figure 10–13), the QR system possesses four operating characteristics not commonly associated with a more traditional ordering system:

- A nonadversarial partnership between the retailer and the vendor,
- A point-of-sale (POS) system capable of realizing the full benefits of UPC scanning,
- An electronic data interchange (EDI) system that permits the use of electronic purchase orders (EPO), and
- A just-in-time (JIT) delivery system that allows either direct store delivery (DSD) or distribution centre delivery (DCD).

Nonadversarial Partnerships Quick response "centres on a new relationship between retailers and vendors. For both, the 'partnership' requires new business practices, starting with a cooperation that stems from a knowledge of each other's business objectives, opportunities, and constraints."[30] "In the future, strategies to increase cooperation in channel relations will become more important to retailers as the balance of power shifts to retailers."[31] The QR system demands a high level of cooperation and trust between the participating parties. "Black & Decker Corp., for example, has divisions with a dozen or so staffers from a variety of functions, from logistics to finance, dedicated to serving such customers as Home Depot."[32] To build closer relationships between it and its dealers, Agco Corp., the farm implement maker (Allis Chalmers and Massey Ferguson tractors), pays its salesperson commission only after his or her customer—the dealer—has moved the equipment off the lot and onto the field. That tends to unify the Agco salesperson's interest with that of the dealer.[33]

For the QR system to work, a great deal of proprietary information must be shared and used for the benefit of both parties. Management for both the retailer and the vendor must view the relationship as a partnership, one in which each transaction is a win-win situation

Figure 10–13

Quick-response replenishment system

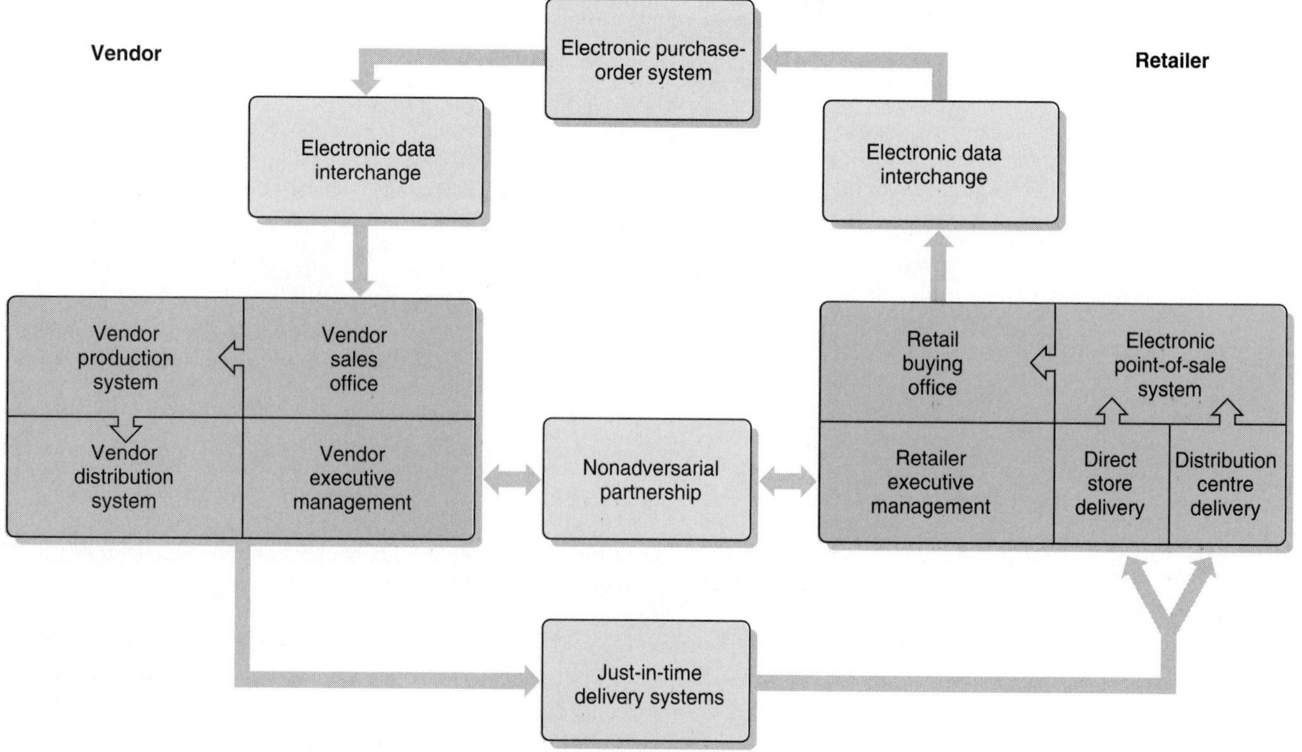

for both partners. Wal-Mart is altering its buying practices to accommodate QR programs; as described by Wal-Mart management, "We want to win at everything we do, and it has been ingrained in our buyers that we want to buy as well as possible."[34] However, with Procter & Gamble, Rubbermaid, and General Electric, "Wal-Mart is trying a nonadversarial approach in which it shares sales projection data through computer links, hoping the vendor can anticipate needs."[35] Wal-Mart's Retail Link program now enables company vendors to have actual access to Wal-Mart's point-of-sale terminals in order to track the retail movement of their own products instantly.[36]

Point-of-Sale Systems Technological advancements in electronic (computer-controlled) equipment have generated a wave of new marking procedures that are compatible with various **point-of-sale (POS)** systems. **Electronic marking** devices can code prices onto tickets and tags that can be quickly and automatically read and processed by optical scanning equipment or **optical character recognition (OCR)** systems. Optical scanners usually are employed at checkout counters, where they read all information on the ticket or tag and transmit it to the store's computer system for further processing (for example, for inventory control and accounting records). The checkout counter wand is the most common type of optical scanner used in general merchandise retailing, and fixed-slot scanners (checkout counters with built-in laser beams that read tags as the merchandise is passed over the beam) are the predominant system used in the supermarket industry. Scanning provides both the retailer and consumer with faster, more accurate information than does any other form of checking. In addition to itemized receipts, some POS registers allow customers to receive rain cheques and refund slips right at the checkout stand.[37]

With the installation of optical scanners, many retailers have elected to use a standardized marking system. These universal vendor marking (UVM) systems involve coding merchandise tags with a machine-readable code that is sponsored by one or more trade associations. The most commonly used code is the **universal product code (UPC)**; the UPC is a bar code system that identifies both the product and the manufacturer (see Chapter 3). A recent development is a two-dimensional bar code, which can store about 100 times more information; it can tell the retailer where the product came from, where it is supposed to go, and how to handle it in transit.[38] The net result of using a scanner-type bar code system is the tremendous amount of detailed information (for example, brand, style, size, model, colour of item) that is available to the retailer's buying office and that can be shared with the product item's vendor.

Electronic Data Interchange **Electronic data interchange (EDI)**, the sharing of data between retailer and vendor electronically, is an important technological development for improving purchase order management through computer linkages (see Chapter 3).[39] "Standard electronic transactions include price/sales catalogues, purchase orders, advanced shipping notices, order status, invoices, and remittance advice."[40] Vanity Fair (VF), the diversified apparel manufacturer (maker of Lee and Wrangler jeans), "is now linked with many of its retailers' computers (e.g., Wal-Mart), which sort out VF sales data from checkout scanners and beam it via satellite direct to VF divisions every night. VF can then replenish stocks sometimes in as little as 72 hours."[41] VF's "market response system (MRS)" helps the company tailor its manufacturing to reflect what the stores are selling. This POS system enables VF to ship merchandise directly to a retailer instead of holding inventory at its own warehouse.[42] As part of Eaton's restructuring, it is insisting that suppliers be able to communicate electronically, deal with just-in-time ordering, and meet the demands of their highly automated warehouse procedures.[43] Using EDI systems, retail managers now have a variety of options for structuring their **electronic purchase order (EPO)** systems. Figure 10–14 illustrates the most common structures retailers and vendors use in exchanging electronic purchase orders and invoice data. The options follow.

Mail Linkages. Purchase order and invoice data are transcribed onto magnetic tape or diskettes and transmitted between retailers and vendors through the mail. This is a practical option for communicating a large volume of information when time is not critical.

Figure 10–14

Electronic purchase order system

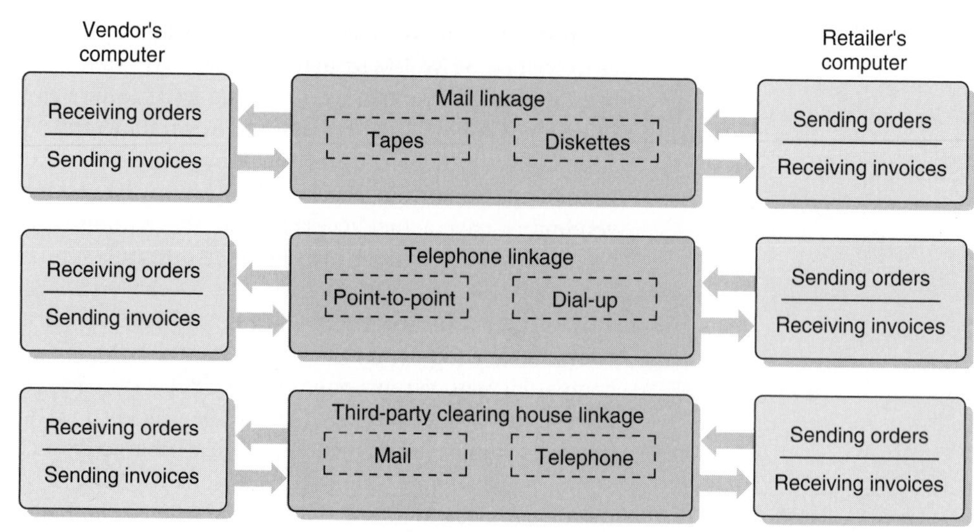

Telephone Linkages. Purchase order and invoice data are communicated between the retailer's computer and the vendor's computer over the telephone. The *point-to-point* option involves arranging transmission schedules and common protocols to allow direct computer-to-computer interchange of data. The *dial-up option* involves the storage of retailer orders and vendor invoices in on-line files and allows each party dial-up access to these files. The Brown Shoe Company provides small independent shoe stores the opportunity to become part of its Direct Access network. For stockout items and items not part of the retailer's assortment, the sales associate can dial up Brown's inventory system to check on the availability of any of its thousands of SKUs. Requested items can be sent directly to the customer or to the store. This dial-up capability greatly expands the potential merchandise assortment for these smaller independent retailers.[44]

Third-Party Clearinghouses. A third-party data processing company makes arrangements to (1) receive orders and invoices, (2) sort them by addressees, (3) store them on-line, and (4) allow subsequent access by authorized addresses. This method allows use of a standardized machine language to establish a bridge for common communication, thereby eliminating the need for separate and distinct methodologies among various vendors and retailers.

To the retailer, the advantages of the EPO system include more effective inventory management, more effective open-to-buy systems, and reduction of ordering lead times, which thereby improve in-stock positions and stock turnovers while reducing inventory carrying costs.

Just-in-Time Delivery Systems The just-in-time (JIT) delivery system involves scheduling merchandise delivery dates to the retailer that coincide exactly with the day inventory levels reach a critical stage. The objective of JIT systems is to have the right merchandise variety and assortment in the exact quantities needed at the precise time needed at the lowest total delivery cost. By shipping smaller quantities on a more frequent basis, the vendor can help reduce a retailer's average stock on hand, thereby increasing inventory turns while lessening inventory costs. The JIT delivery system is the retailer's payback for providing real-time POS data through the electronic purchase orders.

A further enhancement of the QR system is the ability to utilize **direct store delivery (DSD)** or **distribution centre delivery (DCD)**. Depending on the nature of the retailer's merchandise handling process (see "The Merchandise Handling Process," p. 401), efficiencies of distribution can be realized by having merchandise delivered directly to either the store[45] or the distribution centre. "Unlike most food companies, Nabisco runs a 'direct store delivery' operation. There's no dropping shipments at central warehouses for retailers to pick up and cart to their stores. Company rigs show up at the back doors of 105 000 stores about three times a week and then Nabisco's 2800 sales reps manhandle the products from the storage areas onto the shelf or display rack."[46]

Standard bar code shipping container marking and electronic shipment notification are two technological and operational advancements that are contributing to the further development and acceptance of JIT systems. Shipping Container Marking (SCM) is

> the bar code that facilitates the identification and processing of containers. It must be used with an *Advanced Shipping Notice* (ASN). Within the retail industry, code 128 is standard. The vendor marks the containers to speed receipt and verification by the retailer. The SCM code 128 cross-references to an ASN that identifies the vendor, the order number, carton content, the store destination. Each carton in a shipment also has a unique identifier. The hardware required to generate bar codes is a bar code laser printer. Scanner hardware can include hand-held laser guns, wands, flat-bed scanners, or in-line conveyor systems.[47]

Home Depot, the giant of the home improvement industry, is able to receive thousands of bulk cartons in automatic distribution centres and reship them to store locations in a matter of hours.[48]

The Merchandise Handling Process

The merchandise handling process deals with the physical processing of incoming merchandise. Efficient processing of incoming shipments is necessary to ensure their timely arrival on the sales floor. As pressure increases to get products from the vendor into the impatient consumer's hands, the importance of handling cycle times has increased substantially.[49] Figure 10–15 compares and contrasts the traditional and QR systems as to their average handling cycle time. Figure 10–16 identifies the four processing concerns when handling incoming goods: receiving, checking, marking, and stocking merchandise.

Receiving Merchandise

Receiving is the actual physical exchange of goods between the retailer and the supplier's transporting agent. Generally, the retailer should avoid front-door receiving. The typical back-door receiving operation consists of an unloading area and a receiving area. The area devoted to unloading should permit easy manoeuvrability and facilitate careful handling. The receiving area should be large enough to allow inspection of incoming shipments and

Figure 10–15

Response cycle times

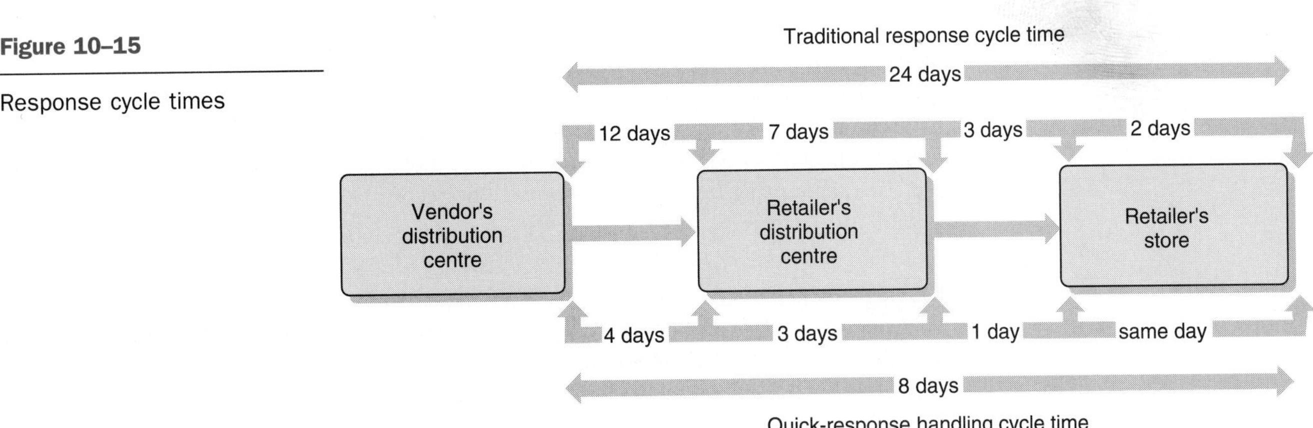

Figure 10–16

The merchandise handling process

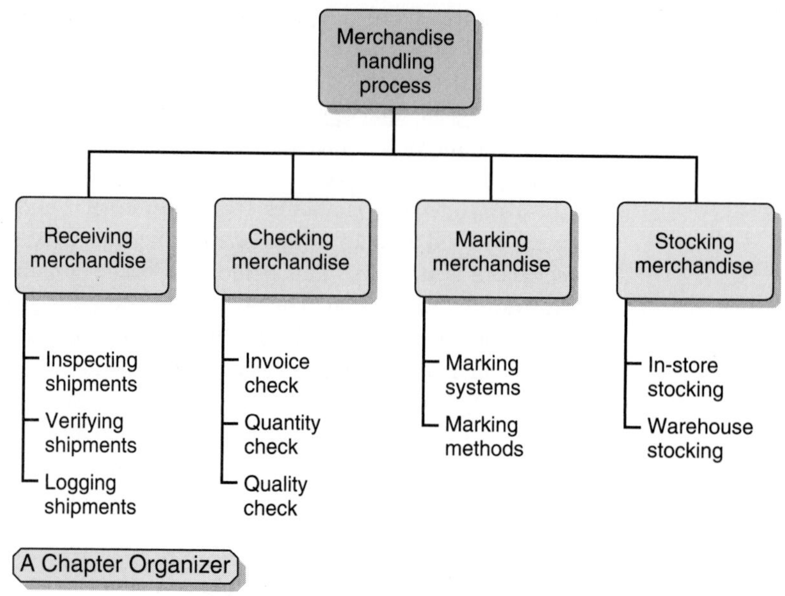

to act as a holding area for merchandise awaiting transfer to the checking room. Proper processing involves inspecting, verifying, and logging incoming shipments.

Inspecting Shipments The first step in inspecting incoming merchandise is a visual inspection of the exterior of each package to determine whether the package has been damaged (crushed, punctured) or opened (broken seal). If a package has been badly damaged or opened, the receiving clerk should refuse to accept the shipment unless the carrier's employee agrees to witness the visual inspection of the contents of the package. Packages that are slightly damaged may be accepted, but before signing for the shipment, the receiving clerk should make a notation of the damage on all transportation and receiving documents.

Verifying Shipments After inspecting the shipment for visual damage, the receiving clerk should make several verifications. First, he or she must verify that the shipment was ordered by consulting the receiving department's file of purchase orders or a log (schedule) of incoming shipments. Second, the completeness of the shipment must be verified; sometimes suppliers ship only partial orders. Third, the receiving clerk should verify that the actual makeup of the shipment is the same as that described on the *bill of lading* (a transportation document between the shipper and carrier that serves as a receipt for the goods tendered to the carrier). The number of cartons in the shipment and the weight of each carton should also be checked. Fourth, freight charges are verified by comparing the total weight of the shipment with various rate schedules.

Logging Shipments To facilitate and organize the processing of incoming shipments, each shipment is logged in a receiving record and assigned a receiving number. The **receiving record** and number follow the shipment through the checking, marking, and stocking steps of the handling process and serve as a quick reference should problems arise. The accounting department also uses the record to verify shipment before invoices are paid.

Checking Merchandise

Checking is the process of determining whether the supplier has shipped what the retailer ordered and whether the shipment has arrived in good condition. Checking involves opening each package, removing the merchandise, and examining it. The retailer can make three checks to ensure it has received what was ordered: an invoice, a quantity, and a quality check.

Invoice Check In the **invoice check**, the retailer compares the invoice with the purchase order. The invoice is the supplier's bill and is the document that itemizes particulars of the shipment in terms of merchandise assortment, quantity, and price. It also identifies the terms of the sale, delivery terms, and the amount due for payment. Checking personnel must determine whether the retailer's purchase order exactly matches the supplier's invoice.

Quantity Check During the **quantity check**, the checking personnel unpack and sort each package to check the actual physical contents of each package against the purchase order, the invoice, or both. Essentially, the checker sorts each package by style, size, and colour (or other assortment factors) and makes a physical count to determine whether the package contains the same number of units as listed on the invoice and purchase order. Any shortages, overages, or substitutions are noted and reported to the buyer or merchandise manager.

Quality Check The **quality check** actually involves two separate checks. First, the merchandise is examined for any damage that is obviously the result of shipping. This kind of damage is the responsibility of the carrier and the insurer of the shipment. The second check is for imperfections in the merchandise and for lesser-quality merchandise than what the retailer ordered.

The retailer can use one of four methods to check the quantity of incoming shipments. In the **direct check**, the retailer checks off from the invoice, which lists all the ordered and shipped items, each group of items as they are counted. Speed and simplicity are the principal advantages of the direct check. The **blind check** is a procedure in which the checker lists and describes each merchandise group on a blank form and then counts and records the number of items in each group. Next, a comparison is made between the checker's list and descriptions with the invoice or purchase order to determine whether there are any discrepancies. Generally, the blind method is the most accurate, but it is also the most expensive. The **semiblind check** is a checking technique that provides the checker with a list and description of each merchandise group in the shipment but not the quantities for each group. The checker must physically count and record the number of items in each merchandise group.

Marking Merchandise

Marking is affixing to merchandise the information necessary for stocking, controlling, and selling. Customers want information on the price, size, and colour of merchandise before they are willing to buy, and the retailer needs to know when and from where the merchandise was obtained, its cost, and where it goes to maintain proper inventory and record controls.

Marking Systems The three most common marking systems are source marking, preretailing, and store marking. **Source marking** is the system by which the retailer authorizes the manufacturer or supplier to mark the merchandise before shipping it to the store.[50] Source marking reduces both in-store marking expenses and the time it takes to get the merchandise onto the sales floor. A standard tag code and format enables the retailer to make very effective use of electronic data processing equipment. **Preretailing** is a retail buying practice of deciding the selling price of merchandise before it is purchased and recording that price on the store's copy of the purchase order so the store's "markers" can put the selling price on the merchandise as soon as it comes through the doors. **Store marking** is the practice of having store personnel mark all merchandise after the store has received it.

Marking Methods Merchandise must be marked before it reaches the sales floor. **Hand marking** is accomplished by using grease pencils, ink stamps, and pens to mark the merchandise, package, label, tag, or ticket directly. **Mechanical marking** involves producing tags and tickets in both printed (human-readable language) and punched (machine-readable language) forms. Retailers frequently elect to use **bulk marking** on merchandise that is characterized by low unit value, high turnover, and suitable size and shape for bin, rack, or table displays. Bulk marking involves simply placing similar merchandise with the same price in a display and attaching one price card to the display. Technology is also coming to bulk marking procedures—**electronic shelf labels (ESLs)** involve small liquid crystal display labels that are attached on the edge of the shelf and can display new prices instantly on command. These ESLs receive information from the database used by a store's POS system. By enabling price changes to be made from a single point automatically, retailers can cut labour costs and attack the problem of display prices not matching prices charged at the checkout counter.[51]

Stocking Merchandise

After the merchandise has been marked, the retailer must decide where to stock the merchandise. **Stocking** includes all the activities associated with in-store and between-store distribution of merchandise. Stocking can involve moving merchandise to the sales floor for display or to the reserve or stocking rooms for storage. The retailer can use an in-store or warehouse stocking plan or some combination of the two plans.

In-Store Stocking The primary goal in stocking is to move the merchandise as close as possible to its selling point. To accomplish this goal, most retailers follow the policy of **in-store stocking**, maximizing the amount of display and forward stock and minimizing the amount of stock in reserve. **Display stock** is stock placed on various display fixtures that customers can directly examine. **Forward stock** is backup stock that is temporarily stored on the sales floor near its selling department. Forward stock may be carried in perimeter storage areas around the department or in drawers or cupboards beneath the sales floor display fixtures. **Reserve stock** is backup stock held in reserve, usually in a central stockroom. Reserve stocks are converted to forward or display stocks as quickly as possible.

Warehousing Stocking **Warehouse stocking** is used for certain types of merchandise or under certain operating conditions.[52] Bulky products such as furniture and appliances usually require warehouse stocking, because the retailer must limit the amount of display stock on the sales floor. Forward stocking is generally prohibitive for such products. Disassembled products that are sold in their cartons are usually picked up by the consumer at a warehouse delivery door or delivered to the customer's home. Seasonal products typically are held in warehouses until the appropriate selling season.

Many retailers prefer using central warehouse and distribution centres that serve several stores because of the operating conditions associated with chain store operations.[53] The receiving, checking, marking, and stocking functions are initially accomplished at these regional facilities, then the merchandise is distributed to individual stores. Wal-Mart's distribution objective is to make sure that every Wal-Mart store is within one day's drive of its distribution centre. This short cycle time from distribution centre to retail store enables the firm to keep merchandise in stock for its customers.[54]

Central facilities often are more efficient, based on the economies of scale that large retailers can realize in ordering, transporting, and processing incoming merchandise and in using modern, expensive facilities and equipment. The key to an effective distribution centre is to move merchandise, not store it. "At its computerized warehouses, many goods enter at one loading dock and leave from another without ever resting on a shelf."[55] Eaton's has reduced the length of time its merchandise is stored in its warehouses to 1.75 days from 8 days in the early 1990s.[56] And Wal-Mart's policy of using **cross docking** ensures that no product sits in any of its distribution centres for more than 72 hours.[57]

Retail Vignette

Costco Companies Inc.

Costco Companies Inc. operates an international chain of Costco and Price Club wholesale membership warehouses that carry quality name-brand merchandise at substantially lower prices than are typically found at conventional wholesale or retail sources.

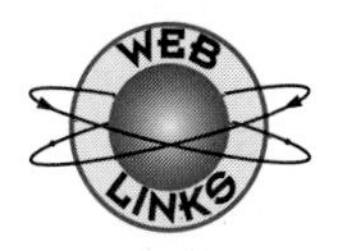

Costco Companies Inc.
www.costco.com

The company opened its first Price Club in San Diego in 1976 and its first Costco in Seattle in 1983, and now has 272 locations in 23 states, nine Canadian provinces, six Mexican states, and five sites in Great Britain. The company also operates a Price Club warehouse in Korea, through a licensing agreement, and has just recently opened it's first unit in Kaohsiung, Taiwan.

"The company's growth has been stimulated by the overwhelming acceptance of the warehouse club merchandising concept which Costco pioneered," says Costco President Jim Sinegal.

Costco's warehouses present one of the country's largest product category selections to be found under a single roof. A few of the categories include groceries, candy, appliances, television and audio, automotive supplies, tires, toys, hardware, sporting goods, jewellery, watches, cameras, books, computer hardware and software, housewares, apparel, health and beauty aids, tobacco, furniture, office supplies, and office equipment. Costco is known for carrying top-quality national and regional brands, 100 percent guaranteed, at prices consistently below traditional wholesale or retail operations.

Members can also shop for private label products of equal or better quality than national brands, including diapers, photographic film, cookies, coffee, soft drinks, clothing, and detergent.

Additionally, Costco Wholesale Industries, a division of the company, operates manufacturing businesses including candy and nut packaging facilities, optical lenses laboratories, photo-processing, and meat processing. These businesses have a common goal of providing members with high-quality, exclusive products at dramatically low prices.

According to Sinegal, "Costco is able to offer lower prices and better value by eliminating virtually all the frills and costs historically associated with conventional wholesalers and retailers, including salespeople, fancy buildings, delivery, billing and accounts receivable systems. We run a tight operation with extremely low overhead, which enables us to pass on dramatic savings to our members."

Costco warehouses generally are open seven days per week for all members, with special hours reserved for business members. With more than 25 million Costco card-holders and 52 700 employees, the company's yearly sales exceed $20 billion.

Printed with permission of Costco Companies Inc.

It's Very Simple, It's Better Value

Companies that do well tend to employ simple strategies; they identified real customers and give those customers what they want to buy. These firms recognize that customers choose one product or service over another for a very simple reason; they believe it is a better value than they could expect to get from the alternative. Many Canadian consumers want low prices and big-store convenience. They also want value as they have less money than their parents did. This, in part, explains the success of Wal-Mart and Costco in Canada.[1]

Value Strategy: A Strong Benefits-to-Burdens Ratio

Stores with a future compete on value, not solely on price. One of the biggest mistakes many retailers make is assuming that value and price mean the same thing to consumers. Price is a part of value, but it is not the equivalent of value. To customers, value is the benefits received for the burdens endured. Benefits may include merchandise quality, personal service, store atmosphere, convenience, and peace of mind. Burdens include both monetary and nonmonetary costs. Examples of the latter might be long waits in checkout lines, unattractive or uninteresting stores, poorly trained sales personnel, and too few sales personnel. Retailers become—and stay—successful with a strong benefits-to-burdens offer. They maximize the most important benefits to targeted customers and minimize the most critical burdens.[2]

Retail Pricing Perspectives

Is price a merchandising decision? A sales decision? A profit decision? A financial decision? Highly effective pricing decisions must take into account all these perspectives. Price is a marketing tool that can be used creatively to help attract consumer traffic, create consumer satisfaction, and build consumer loyalty.[3] To gain a better perspective on retail pricing, we examine both the concept of price and its logical extension, the concept of value.

The Concept of Price

A **retail price** is a monetary expression placed on the value of an actual or proposed exchange (for example, money for goods and/or services) between a retailer and a customer. Price is but one representation of the value of a product or service. The right price is the amount of money that the consumer is willing and able to pay and the retailer is willing to accept in an exchange for merchandise and/or services. The right price enables the retailer to make a fair profit while providing the consumer with value satisfaction before, during, and after the sale.

From the consumer's viewpoint, price can act as a forceful attraction or as an absolute repellent in the consumer's store selection process. It can also serve as either an incentive or a deterrent in the decision to buy. Some consumers consider price the most important criterion in selecting stores and products; others are far less sensitive to price. One expert believes that in today's marketplace, "price is neutralized as a real purchase motivator because everyone focuses on it. Therefore, it is not as powerful and compelling."[4]

Certainly, the fact that so many retailers have focused on the goal of being the consumer's low-cost provider has diminished price's ability to distinguish one retailer from its competitors or to gain a competitive differential advantage.[5] Retailers view price in terms of (1) profitability, or how much they will have left after covering the merchandise cost and operating expenses; (2) sales volume, or how many merchandise units they can sell at various prices; (3) consumer traffic, or how many consumers they can attract to the store using various pricing strategies and tactics; and (4) store image, or what type of image they will project to consumers through different pricing levels, policies, and strategies. Industry analysts estimate that average gross margins have dropped in Canada

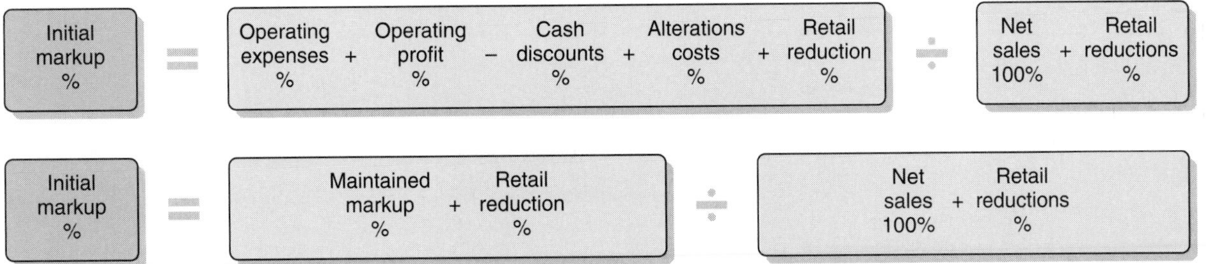

Figure 11–10

Calculating initial markup percentage

To determine the actual percentage markup realized after the foregoing computations are completed, the retailer can use the maintained markup percentage formula expressed in Figure 11–11. For example, if the retailer had originally planned for an initial markup of 40 percent, and retail reductions amount to 8 percent actually occurred:

$$\text{maintained markup \%} = 0.40 - [0.08(1.00 - 0.40)]$$
$$= 0.352 \text{ or } 35.2\%$$

The retail reduction percentage is adjusted because it is based on net sales, whereas the initial markup percentage is based on the original retail price.

Gross Margin **Gross margin** refers to the difference between net sales and total merchandise costs. As such, it is closely related to maintained markup (net sales minus gross merchandise costs). The differences between gross margin and maintained markup or between total merchandise cost and gross merchandise costs are adjustments for cash discounts and alteration costs. This difference can be illustrated as follows:

gross margin = maintained markup + cash discounts − alteration costs

maintained markup = gross margin − cash discounts + alteration costs

If there were no cash discounts or alteration costs, then gross margin would equal maintained markup. The retailer's gross margins represent the amount of money available to the retailer to cover operating expenses and realize operating profits. Because it represents the parameters for successful operations, gross margin is one of the most closely watched measures used by retailers in developing operational and financial plans. For example, one reason that supermarkets push private-label merchandise is that it has a gross margin of 25 to 30 percent, nearly twice as high as gross margins for national brands. The relationship of gross margin to retail price, retail costs, and operating expenses is illustrated in Figure 11–12.

Competitive Pricing

A competitive pricing method means the retailer sets prices in relation to competitors' prices; the basic decision rules are to price below, at, or above competitors' price levels. It is largely a judgmental price-setting method in which the retailer uses competitive prices as reference points for price-setting decisions.

Maintained markup % = Initial markup % − Retail reduction % × (100% − Initial markup %)

Figure 11–11

Calculating maintained markup percentage

Figure 11–12

Understanding gross margin

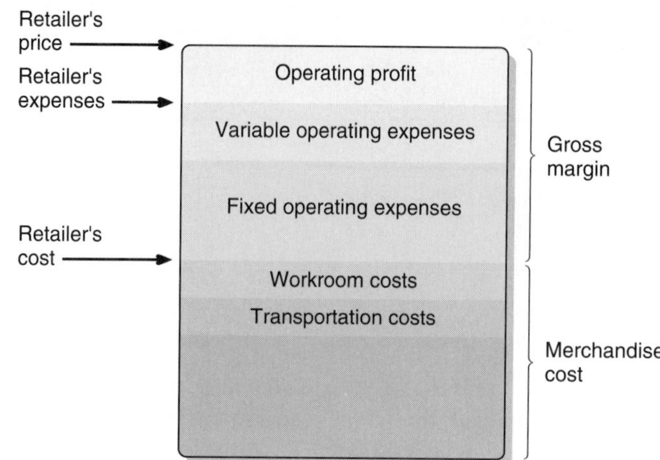

Below Competition One price-setting alternative is **pricing below competition.** Mass merchandisers, such as hypermarkets, superstores, and discounters try to undersell competitors. Pricing below competition is a price-setting policy aimed at generating large dollar revenues to achieve a desired dollar target return. In other words, these retailers practice a low-price, high-volume, high-turnover pricing strategy. The Retail Strategies and Tactics box illustrates the success of the below-competition policy for one Canadian retailer.

To price below competition, the retailer must not only obtain merchandise at a lower cost but also keep operating expenses as low as possible. The lower-price retailer usually stocks and sells "presold" or "self-sold" merchandise, thereby reducing advertising and personal selling expenses. Typically, these retailers sell name brands at the lowest prices to build traffic and promote a low-price image. Low-price retailers stock private brands of many standard items that consumers cannot easily compare with other retailers' private brands and on which they can receive high margins at the lower prices.[27] These retailers keep their service offerings at the minimum levels necessary to sell the merchandise. Physical facilities are spartan and the structure of the store's management organization is generally flat. Generally speaking, the profit strategy of the retailer that elects to price below competition is to keep expenses low to keep prices low; this in turn attracts consumers and generates a profitable sales level through rapid inventory turnover rates.

With Competition The second alternative method of competitive price setting open to the retailer is selling a merchandise item at the "going" or traditional price within the store's general trading area. **Pricing with competition** implies that the retailer has, in general, elected to de-emphasize the price factor as a major merchandising tool and instead decided to compete on a location, product, service, or promotion basis. Competitive price parity does not necessarily imply that the retailer matches every price exactly. Usually, this policy involves setting prices that are within an acceptable range of the competitive standard. Small price discrepancies, especially if they reflect proportional variances in service levels, either go unnoticed or are accepted by consumers. For example, supermarkets, which are typically more convenient for more consumers, do not have to be as sharp on price as supercentres and warehouse clubs. One expert believes that supermarket prices "just have to stay within 5 to 7%. A 15% differential would be too much."[28]

Above Competition Some retailers attempt to differentiate themselves by setting prices above the going trade area price. Although the higher-priced stores do not expect to achieve the turnover rates of their lower-priced competitors, they do expect their products to make a substantially *greater per-unit profit* than the lower-priced retailer's products. Strategically, if the retailer chooses **pricing above competition**, then it must include several of these consumer benefits: (1) many free services, (2) higher-quality

Retail Strategies and Tactics

Merchants of Boom

You won't find Dale Gillespie sampling many of the products he sells. The plain-talking president of Calgary-based Liquidation World Inc. admits that "there's nothing we sell in our stores that you couldn't live without." Canada's premier purveyor of unattractive items has built a fast-growing, cross-border empire by feeding off the misfortune of others.

Last year, Liquidation World turned a record $3.5 million profit after racking up sales of almost $72 million. The company liquidates products it acquires dirt cheap from bankruptcy sales, receiverships, insurance claims or any other type of unfortunate circumstance. Some of the goods it snaps up have been damaged by floods, fires, tornadoes and hurricanes. Goods come from as far away as the Caribbean and even Asia. Disaster-prone California is an especially rich source of product. "We're not retailers in the strictest sense of the word," Gillespie points out. "We don't have a regular list of items for sale all the time."

Nevertheless, Liquidation World has tapped deep into the discount-store boom, a boom which has taken a huge bite out of North America's retail market. The publicly traded company offers all kinds of low-priced goods, everything from flimsy metal spatulas to sturdy, albeit homely, furniture. Haggling with a store clerk over an item is not encouraged, but isn't unheard of either. If a product isn't sold within a certain time frame, the price will be slashed until it finally leaves the store.

Surprisingly, however, high margins, not heavy volume, account for Liquidation World's success. "Most warehouse stores do a high-volume, low-margin business," says the company's Chief Financial Officer, Andrew Searby. "We're just the opposite. We maybe turn our product around two-and-a-half times a year. But our net margins are just under 5 percent." Net margins among normal chain discounters, such as Zellers and Kmart Corp., usually hover at about 2 percent.

In 1994, Liquidation World expended operations into the U.S. Gillespie admits that cracking the U.S. market has been tough, but adds that the opportunities are enormous. "There's just so much retail there," he says. "Everyone is building newer and bigger stores. That means there's a whole bunch of 15-year-old buildings sitting empty. They're perfect for us."

Source: Brian Hutchinson, Canadian Business, *May 1997, 48.*

Liquidation World Inc.
www.liquidationworld.com

merchandise, (3) exclusive merchandise, (4) personalized sales attention, (5) a plusher shopping atmosphere, (6) full staffing in all functional areas of store operations, (7) a prestigious image, (8) superconvenient locations, and (9) longer store hours. In other words, the retailer of higher-priced merchandise must provide consumers with a total product having functional, aesthetic, and service features that give consumers the psychological benefits they expect from buying, using, and possessing the product. Many exclusive specialty shops and some department stores engage in price-setting strategies that establish prices above those of less prestigious competitors.[29]

Regardless of which of the three approaches are taken, the retailer needs to monitor the competitor's prices. Problems can arise when retailers price-shop their competitors' stores, as was the case with Future Shop and A&B Sound.[30]

Vendor Pricing

A third price-setting alternative is **vendor pricing**—letting the manufacturer or wholesaler determine the retail price. This type of price setting assumes the form of a "suggested retail price." Vendors suggest retail prices by supplying the retailer with a price list, printing the price on the package, or affixing a price tag to the merchandise. Although the vendor method of setting prices does relieve the retailer of that difficult task, it is not appropriate for many products and many retailers. As guidelines for retailers, the vendor's suggested price is not appropriate when (1) it fails to provide a sufficient margin to cover merchandise costs, store operating expenses, and an adequate profit; (2) it does not stimulate sufficient sales; (3) it is simply not competitive with merchandise of a similar quality; or (4) it fails to provide the retailer's customers with the value they deserve.

Retail Pricing Policies

Retailers are also guided by several price-setting policies that supplement and modify price-setting methods. For example, a retailer may set prices by using the markup method. The established retail price (for example, $40) is then modified to accommodate an odd-pricing policy (for example, $39.95). This section discusses several retail pricing policies (see Figure 11–13). In reviewing these policies, the reader should bear in mind that (1) they are not mutually exclusive policies, (2) they are commonly used in conjunction with one another, and (3) they can often come into conflict with one other.

Single Pricing

Most Canadian retailers follow a **single pricing** policy, charging all customers the same price for the same product under similar circumstances. In contrast to many foreign consumers, most Canadian consumers are accustomed to paying the established price marked on the merchandise. Price "haggling" or "bargaining" has traditionally been limited to big-ticket items such as homes, cars, appliances, and used merchandise. Part of the revolution that is occurring on showroom floors of many automotive dealerships is a no-haggle, one-price policy. This sale lot revolt is an outgrowth of the fact that buying an automobile is the typical consumer's least favourite shopping experience.[31] A single-price policy facilitates the speed at which each transaction can be made, helps simplify the retailer's various accounting records, and reduces the need for sales personnel and makes a self-service strategy possible.

Some retailers have carried the **one-price policy** to the ultimate limit; that is, all products in the store are priced at one or a few set prices.

Flexible Pricing

A **flexible pricing** policy enables the customer to negotiate the final selling price. The best bargainers receive the lowest prices. Retailers that use a **variable-price policy** deal in merchandise with one or more of the following characteristics: (1) high initial markups, (2) need for personal selling, (3) unstandardized or specialized product features, (4) service requirements, and (5) infrequent purchase rates. Flexible pricing gives the retailer

Figure 11–13

Retail pricing policies

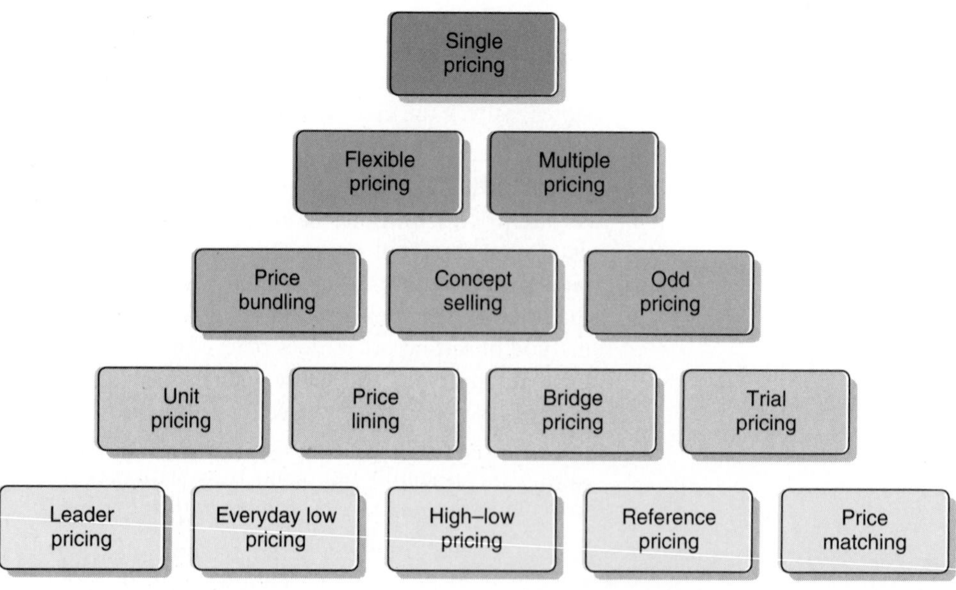

the ability to adjust to the consumer's purchase motivations, but it can increase the retailer's labour costs and selling time and cause dissatisfaction among any customers who were unable to negotiate the same low price as some other customers.

Multiple Pricing

A **multiple-price policy** attempts to increase both unit and dollar sales volume. This pricing strategy gives customers a discount for making quantity purchases; that is, the retailer offers a reduced price if consumers are willing to purchase several units at the multiple-unit price. For example, the retailer can price a can of peas at $0.50 each or three for $1.37. Essentially, multiple-unit pricing is a form of psychological pricing, in that many consumers have been conditioned to expect a bargain price if they buy in multiple quantities. Retailers commonly use multiple-unit pricing with products purchased regularly and frequently and characterized by a low per-unit price.

Price Bundling

A variation of multiple pricing is **price bundling**—the practice of selling products and/or services together as a package deal. Price bundles can be identified in terms of (1) product plus product, (2) product plus service, (3) service plus products, or (4) service plus service. A *product plus product* bundle involves offering one price for a product package (for example, a stereo set) or individual prices on each item of the package (for example, each component of a stereo set).[32] To enhance its BJC-610 Bubble Jet printer, Canon bundles it with a Hallmark cardmaker, Crayola Art drawing program, Pattern Maker, and Sticker and Label Store.[33] Fast-food chains that offer combination meals—a sandwich, fries, and drink—at what are perceived to be bargain prices are engaging in a product plus product price bundle. Establishing the price of a product at a high enough level to cover both the cost of the product (for example, a kitchen appliance) and additional support services (delivery, installation, guarantees) constitutes a *product plus service* bundle pricing policy. One example of a service plus products bundle is the hotel that offers fruit baskets, drinks, and meals as part of visitor's room rates.[34] A *service plus service* bundle might involve a hair salon that offers its clients the opportunity to purchase hair care services priced individually or a complete hairstyling and beauty treatment priced collectively. Several large child care chains have solved parents' transportation problems by providing pickup and delivery to their before- and after-school programs.[35] In each of these practices, the intent of bundle pricing is to generate additional profitable sales from current customers by offering them a price break. Selling more to existing customers is one of the most effective ways to increase the retailer's volume of profitable sales.

Still another variation of bundling is **captive pricing**—the practice of locking in your customer by selling the basic product item at a reduced pricing, then selling consumables at higher prices. An example is an office supply store that sells a leather daily planner notebook at an attractive price but charges notably higher prices for notebook refills (for example, calendars, things-to-do lists, project planning sheets, address files). Sony's approach to marketing its PlayStation video machine is taken from the razors and razorblades chapter. Priced at $299, PlayStation is sold at a loss, the idea being to get the machines into the hands of the consumers and then make the money on sales of compact disc games (at $49–$69 a copy) that work with the PlayStation.[36]

Concept Selling

A further extension of the price bundling practice is **concept selling**—establishing a higher price for a product or service and justifying that price by convincing the customer the total set of benefits (the concept) is worth the extra cost.[37] For example, the full-service brokerage firm sells the concept that the additional financial information, personal investment advice, and faster transactional services provided to its customers is more than enough to offset its higher commission rates.[38]

The selling concept can be based on the premise that the retailer offers a greater selection of unique merchandise, a better-quality product, a more prestigious store image, a higher level of support services, a larger number of convenience locations, or some other combination of buyer benefits. Some consumers are willing to pay more if there are additional benefits to be realized; however, the retailer must be sure that this value-added pricing practice is real and not just promotional fluff.

Odd Pricing

Odd pricing is the strategy of setting prices that end in odd numbers (for example, $0.49, $1.99, $9.95). By setting prices below even-dollar amounts, the retailer is relying on a psychological ploy that consumers perceive odd prices as substantially below even prices (for example, $2.95 is perceived to be considerably less than $3.00).[39] Although nine and five are the most common odd-price endings, retailers also use three and seven to project a bargain-price image. If the retailer wants to project a prestigious image, general retail wisdom suggests the use of **even pricing** (prices ending in even dollar amounts).

Unit Pricing

Given the multiplicity of package sizes and shapes together with the diversity of price tags and product labels, many consumers cannot determine which purchase is the best value for the money. As a result, some retailers have initiated a unit pricing system to eliminate this uncertainty. **Unit pricing** is the retailing practice of posting prices on a per-unit measurement basis. By stating the price per kilogram, litre, or metre for each brand, the retailer helps the consumer compare prices among products of different sizes, shapes, and quantities. Per-unit price tags are usually posted on shelf facings directly above or below the product. Maintaining a unit price system usually means that the retailer will incur additional time, labour, equipment, and material expenses.

Price Lining

The objective of a **price lining policy** is to direct retail prices at a targeted consumer group. The idea of price lining is to identify and offer an acceptable range of prices for a specific group of customers. Toyota's RAV4 is a recreational vehicle targeted to fit a price range ($15 000–$20 000) between the lower-end utility vehicles (for example, Suzuki S-90 and Geo Tracker) and the bigger utility vehicles that sell for $25 000–$30 000 and higher.[40] To accomplish this objective, the retailer must perform two tasks. First, the retailer must identify the appropriate pricing zone for each targeted consumer group. A **pricing zone** is a range of prices that appeals to a particular group of consumers. For example, Bombay Co., a chain specializing in reproductions of English-style furniture, keeps its prices less than $500, thereby focusing its efforts on a select group of consumers who want good antique "knockoffs" at a fair price.[41] Restaurants are often classified on the basis of pricing zones, including (1) low price, fast food; (2) modest price, family dining; (3) moderate price, casual dining; and (4) high price, fine dining.[42] Usually, retailers identify price zones in broad terms; for example, economy price range, intermediate or family price range, and prestige or luxury price range. Although most retailers tend to focus on one broadly defined price range, some retailers try to cover more than one range (for example, middle to high).

Pricing lines are specific pricing points established within pricing zones. Assume, for example, that a specialty store retailer has identified three pricing zones for men's suits: (1) the low-range suit (less than $100), (2) the middle-range suit ($100–$200), and (3) the high-range suit (more than $200). Also suppose the retailer has targeted the middle-price-range consumer as the one to whom it wishes to appeal. Then, the retailer might establish price lines at $119.95, $159.95, and $189.95. The use of price lines is commonly associated with shopping goods and in particular with wearing apparel. In highly competitive product categories, manufacturers often develop "fighting brands" at "combat prices" that are used to compete with private labels and discount brands in the lower price "war zones." Examples of fighting brands targeting the lower price lines include Eastman Kodak and Funtime film, Procter & Gamble and Luvs disposable diapers, and Miller Brewing and Miller High Life beer.[43]

A price lining policy has several advantages for both consumer and retailer. Advantages for the consumer are that it (1) facilitates comparison among merchandise items and (2)

Retail Strategies and Tactics

Merchandise Suitability

Different Strokes for Different Folks

Merchandise suitability is determined by the consumer. In judging whether an item is appropriate for their needs, consumers consider (1) assortment factors such as brand, style, sizing, and price point; (2) individual factors such as uniqueness, originality, and durability; (3) aesthetic factors such as colour, fabric, and print; and (4) quality factors such as construction, material, and crafting. San Francisco–based Gap Inc. utilizes three retailing formats to target different consumer groups. From top to bottom they are Banana Republic, Gap, and Old Navy Clothing Company. Store atmospherics, site locations, and merchandise assortments reflect the different markets to be served by each of the Gap's formats. What constitutes suitable merchandise varies appropriately with each format. One of the "signature items" for the Gap organization is the T-shirt. The following comparison provides an excellent insight into what Gap management believes is suitable for each of these highly successful formats.

Banana Republic T-Shirt

Made in northern Mariana Islands

Cotton weight: 200 grams per square metre

Double-needle stitching around neck to hold shape

Preshrunk

Retail price: $15.00

Gap T-Shirt

Made in the United States

Cotton weight: 180 grams per square metre

Ribbed neck will give, snap back into shape

Will shrink

Retail price: $10.50

Old Navy Clothing Company

Made in the United States and Hungary

Cotton weight: 160 grams per square metre

Shrinks slightly more than the Gap T-shirt

Retail price: $7.50

Source: Adapted from Susan Caminiti, "Will Old Navy Fill The Gap?" Fortune, *March 18, 1996, 59–62.*

reduces shopping confusion and frustration and so helps the consumer make purchase decisions. For the retailer, price lining (1) simplifies the personal selling effort, (2) makes advertising and sales promotion more effective, (3) increases the chances of trading up the customer to the next price, (4) creates an image of good merchandise depth and support, and (5) simplifies the buying process, because the buyer obtains only merchandise that can be profitably priced at a given pricing point.

Bridge Pricing

An extension of the price lining policy is **bridge pricing**—a price that spans or connects two distinctively different price lines or points. The most common form of bridge pricing is found in the fashion industry. To bridge the considerable pricing gap between their high-fashion, designer lines (Yves Saint Laurent and Givenchy) and the mass fashion, national, or store labels (Levi and Gap), most top designers have created bridge lines that are both considerably cheaper than designer outfits but substantially more expensive than off-the-rack fashion at department stores and specialty chains. Anne Klein II and Calvin Klein Classifications are two designer labels that have successfully targeted this price niche and implemented this form of pricing. Donna Karan's DKNY (Donna Karan New York) secondary line of sporty, casual clothes also illustrates a bridge pricing zone with various pricing points.[44]

Trial Pricing

Overcoming the customer's perceived risk in buying a good or trying a service can be a challenging pricing problem. One means of reducing these risks is offering a **trial price**—a low price for buying a limited amount of the product or a low price for trying the service

World of Retailing

Retail Technology

Source-Tags and Store Security

Source tagging for electronic article surveillance (EAS) has become a prime strategy in retailers' war on shrinkage. But retail loss prevention executives are shaking their heads over which technology for source-tagged EAS—and which purveyor—they should choose. The choices include magnetic technology, which is championed by Knogo North America of Hauppauge, New York; "acousto-magnetic" technology promoted by Deerfield Beach, Florida–based Sensormatic; and radio-frequency–based system, as advocated by Checkpoint Systems of Thorofare, New Jersey.

The primary difference among the radio frequency, magnetic, and acousto-magnetic technologies lies in how the EAS tags transmit alarm signals to exit sensors. Following are summaries of how each method works, as well as the benefits claimed by advocates.

Magnetic

A magnetized strip is applied to a product, inserted into packaging or "source-imbedded," a method in which the strip is actually built into the product during manufacturing. Knogo describes source tagging as "the transition stage between do-it-yourself tagging and future source imbedding," and markets its product under the name Super Strip.
Benefits:

- Inexpensive to apply on a per-unit basis;
- Can withstand the heat and pressure of modern manufacturing and shipping; and
- Applicable to a broad range of products.

Acousto-Magnetic

This technology uses interactive electro-magnetic fields between product tags containing a vibrating coil and sensors, which produce an audible alarm when they come within range.

The tags are essentially three-dimensional, thanks to the vibrating coil. Sensormatic technicians are continually miniaturizing both the footprint and depth of their Ultra-Max exterior tags, the latest of which are 0.03 in. thick. They are also creating a tiny new capsule tag that can be inserted within a product such as an aspirin bottle.
Benefits:

- High-speed label application;
- Contact deactivation not necessary; and
- Exit sensors can detect tables in any orientation.

Radio Frequency

Checkpoint's RF tags are essentially labels with a foil-embossed mini-circuit that transmits a radio alarm signal to a receiver in the exit sensor. Their relative flatness makes them fairly easy to integrate into packaged goods displays.

Checkpoint technicians are also working to reduce tag footprint size. The company expects to have a new "origami" tag available by the end of the summer, which analysts say will give superior false-alarm performance.
Benefits:

- Quicker label application;
- Contact deactivation not required; and
- Lower costs.

Source: Paul W. Cockerhan, "Source-tag Shoot-Out," Stores *(March 1995): 39–41.*

for a limited time. Low or break-even trial or sample-size units are used by some retailers to seduce the customer through risk reduction pricing for products. Service trials might be induced by offering a two-month membership fee in a health club or a small preview fee for cable television services on a one-month trial basis.

Leader Pricing

Leader pricing is the strategy of selling key merchandise items below their normal markup or, in some cases, even below the retailer's merchandise costs (negative markup). As with other promotional prices, the main objective of leader pricing is to attract consumers to the store in the hope that they also will purchase other merchandise that has normal markups.[45]

Although leader merchandise contributes very little profit on a per-unit basis, its indirect contribution to total dollar profit can be substantial if the retailer makes anticipated additional sales on high-profit items. In using a leader price strategy, the retailer aims to make money on the mix of products, not on every single item in the mix. To be effective, leader merchandise should include well-known (frequently national brands), widely used items priced low enough to attract most income groups and be easily recognized as a bargain.[46] Supermarkets, in weekly advertised specials, often use meat, dairy, and bakery products as leader merchandise. There are three types of leaders.

Low-leaders are prices set below the customary selling price but above the retailer's actual cost of the merchandise. Customer attraction is the principal objective of the low-leader strategy: low-leaders do generate some profit. **Loss-leaders** are prices reduced to at or below the retailer's cost of the merchandise. Such drastic price cuts aim substantially to improve the store's customer traffic. To build customer traffic, pet store "category killers" are using a high-quality pet food brand such as Science Diet (formerly available only through veterinarians) as a loss-leader.[47] To make loss-leaders work, sales of regular-priced merchandise must be great enough to more than offset the losses generated by the sale of loss leaders.

Bait-leaders are extremely attractive advertised prices on merchandise that the retailer does not intend to sell; the attractive advertised price is "bait" to get the customer into the store. Having accomplished this, the retailer attempts to switch the customer from the merchandise featured in the advertisement to merchandise priced at full markup—hence the common description for this pricing strategy as "bait and switch." Retailers use numerous ploys to switch the customer to more expensive merchandise. In the first step, called the trade-off, the retailer tries to disinterest the customer in the advertised bait merchandise by convincing him or her that the bait merchandise is of inferior quality and a poor value.

The second task is trading up the customer to more expensive merchandise by stressing the higher quality of the substitute merchandise, the better services the customer will receive (delivery, installation, wrapping, repairs, and so on), the easy availability of credit, and any other appeal judged to be effective in convincing the baited customer.

Everyday Low Pricing

Everyday low pricing is the pricing policy of maintaining price points at the same low level year-round. By avoiding the pricing yo-yo of markups and markdowns, the retailer establishes greater price credibility through a more consistent and understandable price program. Adoption of the everyday low price policy involves cutting prices 20–40 percent—in other words, dropping prices permanently to at or near the retailer's former sale and promotional prices. It represents a permanent markdown.[48]

Toys R Us
www.toysrus.com

The success of this type of price policy has been clearly established by such retail success stories as Wal-Mart, Toys R Us, and Canadian Tire.[49] However, everyday low pricing is not for every retailer. Low-end outlets such as warehouse clubs and department stores (such as Eaton's and Sears) that emphasize fashion and service have moved away from this particular pricing practice because it did not fit into their strategic formats.[50] In fact, it has been concluded by Canadian retail industry analysts that Canadian consumers are attracted by sales rather than everyday low pricing.[51] In response to this, Wal-Mart has adjusted its policy and Canadian Tire offers "everyday low prices made better," which allows it to offer more sales along with everyday low pricing.[52]

The popularity of everyday low pricing is an outgrowth of customer frustrations with sale and promotional pricing. Customers have lost the ability to judge whether a sale price is a real bargain or if it is based on a fictitious high price so that the sale can be justified. In general, many customers are fed up with constantly changing prices; it is hard for them to recognize a fair deal, let alone a good deal.

Everyday low pricing requires that the retailer be able to achieve everyday low costs. Additional benefits associated with this type of pricing policy include less ill will resulting from stockout of sale items, higher perceived price credibility, improved image due to fair value pricing, and reduced customer haggling resulting in freed-up clerks for providing other customer services.

High–Low Pricing

A high–low pricing policy is in sharp contrast to everyday low pricing. **High–low pricing** is the practice of buying manufacturer's promotional items in large quantities (forward buying) in order to take advantage of significantly lower cost structures. Then, part of the order is used to support weekly sales specials in which customers are offered low-leader prices. The other part of the order is sold at higher markups during nonsale periods. This promotional pricing practice is directed at attracting both price-conscious consumers looking for good value and bargain hunters who like to shop sales. Some supermarkets and drugstore chains make extensive use of this form of peak-and-valley pricing. It does appear that more educated consumers are rejecting this highly variable-price scheme in favour of the more stable everyday low price practice.

Reference Pricing

To assist consumers in making buying decisions, retailers often provide a point of comparison for judging the price competitiveness of the store's products. **Reference pricing** is the practice of marking products with the retailer's selling price together with one or

Retail Strategies and Tactics

Is This Any Way to Run a Discount Store?

Owned entirely by Hudson's Bay Co. of Toronto, Zellers is the nation's biggest department store, with 300 outlets from coast to coast. It sells more merchandise than any other retailer in the country. But Zellers is in trouble. Intense competition from discount giant Wal-Mart Stores Inc. of Arkansas has had a devastating effect on its bottom-line.

In 1993, a year before Wal-Mart purchased Woolworth Canada Inc. for US $352 million and jumped into the Canadian retail scene, Zellers posted a juicy profit of $256 million. In 1994 Zellers's earnings dipped for the first time in a decade, to $216 million, and its market share began to erode. Last year [1995] was brutal. Zellers's bottom-line was hammered during a price war with Wal-Mart. Profit fell more than 50 percent to $107 million, the lowest since 1987.

Zellers is continuing the price war, although not with the same intensity. But that hasn't turned things around—at least, not yet. The retailer must develop a bold new strategy, it is argued, if it's going to stop Wal-Mart from becoming Canada's top retail chain. What is needed is some serious adjustments, more dramatic than the few changes the company has made to date. "What's happened at Zellers is no mystery," says one Toronto-based retail analyst. "There was a deep reluctance [at Zellers] to make drastic moves. It didn't react quickly enough to the Wal-Mart invasion. But the past two years in the battle between Wal-Mart and Zellers were nothing. What we've seen so far is just the tip of the iceberg."

George Kosich [President of the Hudson's Bay Co.] doesn't buy that, but he does admit that Wal-Mart has stolen away a large share of his profits. "We got into a price war," he says with a shrug. "Wal-Mart's strategy in the US is to have the lowest price in the marketplace. We decided it was not going to establish that in Canada. We had the lowest prices. We weren't going to let it have it. It dropped prices, and so we dropped prices, and we both just kept dropping prices lower and lower. Our margins slipped by 3.5 percent."

The new Zellers president [Millard Barron] will have one priority: "Improve profitability. Period," says Kosich.

Inevitably, that means higher prices. Although Zellers continues to bill itself as the place "where the lowest price is the law," sharp consumers may have already noticed a bit of a jump at the checkout counter. "We're more conservative in pricing," Kosich says. "We're trying to get a little more margin."

Zellers's push for improved margins will focus primarily on so-called "soft goods" such as clothing. Women will bear most of the brunt. Kosich notes that 75 percent of Zellers shoppers are female. "We expect to get a little more out of them," he says. "Take blouses: we didn't used to sell any for more than $29.99; this year we will. We'll upgrade our assortments."

Source: Brian Hutchinson, Canadian Business, *September 1996, 36–41.*

more of the following comparative prices: (1) the retailer's normal retail selling price, (2) the vendor's suggested retail selling price, (3) a competitor's retail selling price, or (4) a market's average selling price. Allowing customers to make price comparisons quickly and conveniently can be a strong selling tool, provided the customer has confidence in the price comparison offered by the retailer.[53] To demonstrate their price prowess, supercentres often provide shelf markers that identify their selling price relative to a local supermarket.

Price Matching

A promise to match the lowest advertised price a customer can find is at the heart of **price matching**. Essentially, a price-matching policy is a price insurance policy that assures consumers they will not miss out on the price breaks offered by other retailers. Although the practice itself can help retain the loyalty of existing customers and attract the patronage of new ones, retailers should take considerable care in implementing a price-matching policy in order not to favour one group of consumers (aggressive bargain hunters) over another consumer group (passive loyal shoppers). Zellers's long-standing and successful slogan "The lowest price is the law" is an example of price leadership of this type. The Retail Strategies and Tactics box illustrates the difficulty of maintaining such a policy over the long term.

Price matching started in the highly competitive consumer electronics industry; it has since spread to a large sector of the retail business. To offset the everyday low pricing strategy of discount stores, Toys R Us has switched to a new policy: "Bring in a rival's ad and we will match the lower price."[54]

Retail Pricing Adjustments

One retail expert suggests that "20 percent of the merchandise in any retail store is excess and obsolete, while another 20 to 25 percent sells only slowly . . . 45 percent of stuff that does not do anything in the store."[55] If these numbers are anywhere close to accurate, it suggests that retail pricing adjustments are a major merchandising activity for any retailer. Retailers make mistakes when setting retail prices. Retail price adjustments are a fact of life for all retailers. Figure 11–14 outlines the issues to be addressed in making price adjustments.

Figure 11–14

Retail pricing adjustments

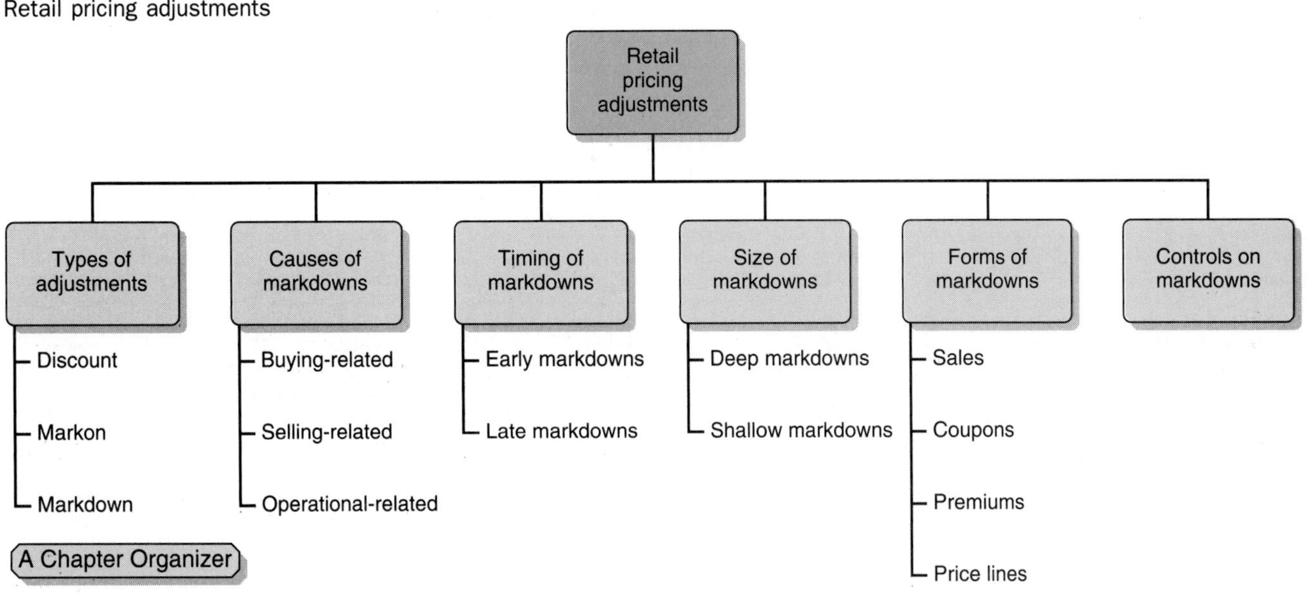

Types of Adjustments

Price adjustments are one means for the retailer to adapt to changing external and internal environmental conditions. Retailers often find it necessary to adjust prices either upward or downward. The three basic types of adjustment are discounts, markons, and markdowns.

Discount Adjustments **Discounts** are defined as reductions in the original retail price; they represent price reductions granted to store employees as special fringe benefits and to special customers (for example, clergy, senior citizens, some disadvantaged consumers) in recognition of their special circumstances. Regardless of the reason for granting the discount, each discount given represents a downward adjustment in price and as such has a direct impact on profit margins. Employee discounts are a customary privilege in many retail organizations. They represent a supplementary means of compensating employees and are frequently used as a motivational tool. Customer discounts are granted to special consumer segments for a number of reasons. Drugstores frequently give "golden-ager" discounts to customers over the age of sixty-five.

Markon Adjustments Retailers use the term "markon" in a variety of ways. Here, however, **markon** refers to markups taken after the initial selling price has been established. In essence, a markon represents an additional markup and an upward adjustment in the initial selling price. Upward adjustments are needed to cover increases in wholesale prices and operating expenses as well as to correct consumers' quality perceptions of merchandise. When consumers believe the quality of a product is questionable because of its low price, retailers sometimes can correct this misconception by increasing the price, thereby taking advantage of the perceived price-quality relationship. Retailers also take additional markons when the demand for an item is high and consumer price sensitivity for the item is low.

Markdown Adjustments A **markdown** is a downward adjustment in the original selling price of a merchandise item. A markdown represents the difference between what the merchandise was originally valued at and what it actually sells for. Estimates are that 75 percent of all department store items are markdowns; this compares with 40 percent a decade ago. Markdowns, together with shortages and employee and customer discounts, are the three major factors retailers consider in planning retail reductions. Retailers use both dollars and percentages to express markdowns. "All men's slacks reduced $5!" is a typical dollar markdown expression. Per-unit **markdown percentages** are computed as a percentage of the reduced selling price or a percentage of the original selling price. The latter expression is generally referred to as the **off-retail markdown percentage**. The formula used for computing per-unit markdowns as a percentage of the reduced price is shown in Figure 11–15. For example, a dress originally priced at $30 is reduced to $20; the markdown as a percentage of the reduced price would be ($30 – $10)/$20, or 50 percent. This procedure is generally preferred for expressing reduced prices. The off-retail markdown percentage formula is also shown in Figure 11–15. The off-retail markdown percentage on the same dress would be ($30 – $20)/$30, or 33.33 percent.

Figure 11–15

Calculating markdown percentage

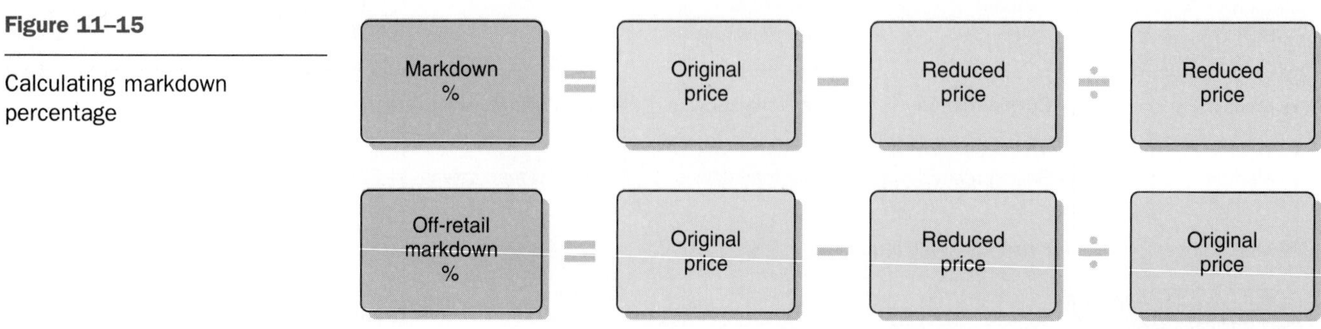

Causes of Markdowns

Retailers must take markdowns for several reasons, some of which are beyond their control. In other cases, markdowns are caused by errors in the retailer's judgment.

Buying-Related Causes

Many markdowns result from retailers' errors in buying or procuring merchandise. Price reductions are often necessary to adjust for errors in the assortment, support, and quality of merchandise the retailer purchased, as well as for mistakes in timing of purchases and selection of suppliers.

Assortment Errors. Assortment errors occur when the retailer buys brands, styles, models, sizes, colours, and materials that do not match what consumers want to buy. Assortment errors are serious not only because they necessitate markdowns but also because they can require major price reductions to move the merchandise. Very attractive prices are typically the only way to sell merchandise the consumer does not really want.

Support Errors. Support errors are quantity errors that result when the retailer buys too much merchandise. Overbuying and overstocking certain merchandise items cause the retailer to tie up capital that could be invested in more profitable merchandise. Support errors occur when the retailer fails to plan sales, stocks, and purchases adequately or fails to execute the plans.

Timing Errors. Timing errors occur when retailers obtain merchandise at the wrong time; they fail to match retail inventories with what their consumers want when they want it. In these cases, markdowns become necessary because the retailer faces surplus merchandise at the end of a selling season. Reordering at the height of a selling season and late shipments are two common causes for surplus merchandise.

Quality Errors. Misjudging the quality of merchandise consumers expect is another reason retailers take markdowns. To move merchandise with unacceptable materials or workmanship, retailers must reduce prices.

Vendor Errors. The final buying-related cause of markdowns is the retailer's selection of suppliers. The retailer should evaluate the service performance levels of each supplier. Late, incorrect, and damaged shipments all contribute to the retailer's need to take price reductions.

Selling-Related Causes

Selling-related causes of markdowns include errors in pricing, attempts to stimulate sales or gain competitive price parity, and various policies and practices relating to the sale of merchandise.

Pricing Errors. A pricing error is any set price that does not create customer interest in the merchandise. Initial prices can be set too high or too low. High prices result in lost sales because consumers' perceptions of value are not satisfied. Low prices result in customer concern over quality. In either case, price adjustments are needed to match customers' perceptions of value and quality.

Sale Stimulation. Retailers frequently use markdowns to stimulate sales. They may use this purposeful reduction of prices to attract additional consumer traffic into the store, introduce a new line of merchandise, boost customer interest during a slack sales period, reduce inventories on slow-moving merchandise, or for a host of other reasons. Sales stimulation markdowns can take the form of loss or low-price leaders, special or promotional prices, a multiunit pricing scheme, or the use of coupons and premiums.

Competitive Parity. Sometimes retailers use markdowns to achieve competitive parity. Direct and indirect competitors that sell the same (or similar) merchandise at lower prices have a comparative shopping advantage over other retailers in their trading areas. Retailers take markdowns to achieve competitive price parity when they cannot justify the price differential.

Selling Policies. Selling policies also can create conditions that lead to markdowns. A policy of "aggressive selling" (for example, trading the customer up to higher priced merchandise, selling the customer more than is desired, making false or misleading claims about product performance) can lead to an above-average rate of merchandise returns. It may be late in the selling season by the time the merchandise makes it back to the sales floor, and the retailer must reduce prices to clear the merchandise out by the end of the season.

Some retailers engage in umbrella merchandising—stocking a limited number of high-fashion merchandise items, such as designer clothing and limited editions, to display merchandise that creates or enhances the store's contemporary image. Retailers often stock this promotional merchandise knowing that much of it will require drastic price reductions to be sold. Another policy that leads to markdowns is assortment maintenance—the image-building policy of carrying a complete selection until late into the selling season—which requires markdowns in the form of clearance sales. Finally, a selling policy that encourages customers to take home merchandise and is supported by a liberal return policy increases the likelihood of taking markdowns.

Operation-Related Causes In a retail store's day-to-day operations, both internal and external circumstances arise that create the need for some type of corrective action in the form of a price reduction. Two such circumstances are market shifts and distressed merchandise.

Market Shifts. Market shifts are changes in demand levels for a particular merchandise line. Faddish and fashion merchandise often have fast and sometimes unexpected changes in both the level and duration of customer acceptance. Introduction of a new product or a new brand can have unsettling effects on the demand for existing products already in stock.

Distressed Merchandise. By its very nature, distressed merchandise requires price reductions. Merchandise that becomes damaged, dirty, or shopworn must be marked down to compensate the purchaser for the obvious reduction in value. Odd lots (a set with one or more pieces missing) also require markdowns.

Timing of Markdowns

An important issue for every retailer is when to take markdowns. Opinions differ, some retailers prefer to take early markdowns, but others believe that a policy of late markdowns is the more profitable strategy.

Early Markdowns **Early markdowns** reduce the selling price of a merchandise item when either of two conditions is present: (1) there is a notable slack in the rate of sales for that item, or (2) the item has been in stock for a specific time period (for example, six weeks). Proponents of early markdowns cite several advantages: (1) *fresher stock*—by weeding out slow movers; (2) *smaller markdowns*—by capturing the remaining demand in the selling season; (3) *reduced selling expenses*—by reducing the need for additional advertising and personal selling expenses; (4) *increased customer traffic*—by encouraging customers to shop now; (5) *reduced selling risks*—by permitting sufficient time to take a second and possibly third price reduction in one selling season; and (6) *heightened market appropriateness*—by preventing repetitive showing of dated merchandise at regular prices.

Early markdowns are most frequent among large department stores and medium-priced specialty retailers that are promotion oriented. "Swimwear has long been one of the biggest profit makers for department stores. As discount chains and catalogues have grabbed market share, the department stores have retaliated by starting to discount their swimsuits much earlier than in the past."[56] Some retailers have an early markdown policy that takes markdowns on a routine basis. **Automatic markdown** policies reduce prices by a fixed percentage at regular intervals. Automatic markdowns are generally taken without regard to how well the merchandise is selling.

Late Markdowns **Late markdowns** maintain the original selling price until late in the selling season, when a major clearance sale is held. A policy of taking late markdowns is most common with smaller specialty retailers and the more prestige- or status-oriented stores. Late-markdown advocates stress these advantages:

1. **Preserved exclusive image**—By not mixing sale priced goods with regular-priced merchandise and regular, prestige-oriented customers with bargain seekers during the normal course of the selling season;
2. **Creative selling encouraged**—By allowing sufficient time for the retailer to experiment with different selling and merchandising approaches;
3. **Allowance for "late bloomers"**—By allowing each merchandise line a trial sales period of sufficient duration to realize the line's full potential;
4. **Reduced purchase postponement**—By discouraging customers from waiting until the merchandise item is placed on sale before making a purchase; and
5. **Creation of the "big event"**—By accumulating large quantities of regularly stocked merchandise for a major clearance sale.

Size of Markdowns

The purpose of a markdown is to increase the customer's incentive to buy the merchandise. Each markdown, therefore, should be large enough to attract customers' attention and induce them to buy. At the same time, unnecessarily deep markdowns will adversely affect the retailer's profit margins. There are no hard and fast rules for determining the size of a markdown. Some retailers believe in making the first "bath" count; that is, they take deep initial markdowns, thereby reducing the need for later, more drastic markdowns. Other retailers think taking several shallow markdowns is the best approach to clearing merchandise with the least negative impact on profit margins.

Highly perishable merchandise (for example, a particular fashion near the end of its cycle or a seasonal product approaching the end of the season) typically requires substantial markdowns as part of the clearance effort. The original retail selling price of the merchandise also influences the size of the markdown needed to generate customer interest. For example, a $5 markdown on a $100 item would hardly be sufficient to attract additional buyers. On the other hand, that same $5 markdown on a $20 item is perhaps more than enough to clear the item out of stock. Early in the selling season the retailer can take smaller markdowns knowing that, if the merchandise fails to sell at the reduced price, there is still time to take additional markdowns. Late markdowns must usually be deeper to stimulate sales. A retailer facing a drastic overstock may decide that the only way to correct the situation is to take deep markdowns. Finally, old merchandise represents a major source of funds for many retailers. To gain immediate use of these funds, the retailer will need to take substantial markdowns.

Forms of Markdowns

Retailers use many pricing strategies that incorporate markdowns either directly or indirectly. Clearance sales are examples of direct markdowns. Indirect price reductions are best exemplified by the retailer's use of coupons, premiums, and trading stamps. Typical strategies are sale prices, prices with coupons and premiums, leader prices, and special-purchase prices.

Sales With many shoppers' zeal for the deal, "sales" are an everyday occurrence in most retail markets. All sales promotions have at least one thing in common: They are designed to draw consumers into the store where, it is hoped, they will purchase not only reduced merchandise but also regularly priced merchandise. To this end, retailers use a variety of sales promotions.[57]

Retailers cite many reasons for holding sales, such as promotions, clearances, liquidations, and closeouts. Promotional sales are short-term price reductions in which markdowns are typically in the 20–30 percent range. Clearance, liquidation, and *closeout sales* are reductions that generally last until the goods are gone and typically result in markdowns ranging from 30 to 50 percent.

"With that four-letter word 'sale' hanging from every retailing rafter, shoppers scarcely think about the 'real' price of anything anymore. [R]etailers have just about destroyed their pricing integrity."[58] Overuse of "sales" is making it increasingly difficult for retailers to get off the price-cutting merry-go-round. Retailers unwittingly have taught consumers that they should not buy something until it is placed on sale unless it is an emergency.

Coupons **Coupons** are sales promotion devices in the form of redeemable cards (for example, direct mail) or cut-outs (for example, newspapers) that allow the customer to purchase specific merchandise at a reduced price. Coupons issued by the manufacturer do not represent a markdown for the retailer; however, coupons issued by the retailer do represent markdowns because the retailer bears the cost of the difference between the original and reduced selling price.

Premiums **Premiums** are price reductions in the form of free or drastically reduced merchandise. Retailers normally offer premiums to consumers after they have completed some requirement (such as test-driving an automobile, filling out a form, or buying a certain dollar amount of merchandise).

Special Purchases A **special-purchase price** is a low advertised price on merchandise the retailer has purchased at reduced prices. Because these promotional prices are initially set below the retailer's customary price for such merchandise, indirectly they represent a markdown pricing strategy. The purpose for special-purchase pricing is the same as for most promotional pricing: to generate customer traffic.

Price Lines For the retailer whose original price-setting strategies include pricing zones (a range of prices) and pricing lines (at specific pricing points), markdown adjustments create a slightly different price reduction problem. Shallow markdowns usually involve reducing the price of an item from one point within a pricing zone to a lower point within the same zone and may be adequate for small clearance sales to dispose of a limited number of units. Deep markdowns are taken by moving a merchandise line from a pricing point in one zone to a pricing point in a lower pricing zone. Deep markdowns become necessary when the retailer considers the merchandise inappropriate for the targeted customer within the original pricing zone.

Controls on Markdowns

Some markdowns are inevitable, the natural result of the risks retailers assume in going into business.[59] An extremely low markdown percentage could indicate that the retailer is not assuming sufficient risks to take advantage of emerging market opportunities. On the other hand, excessive markdowns are often indicative of poor planning and control procedures. By carefully planning sales, stock levels, purchases, and profit margins, the retailer can control to a reasonable extent both the amount and the timing of markdowns.

Summary

Price is one representation of the value of a good or service; as such, it is an essential ingredient in the retailer's customer exchange process. Retailers view prices in terms of their capability to generate profits, sales, and consumer traffic, as well as how they affect the store's image. Value is the interactive relationship between product utility, quality, price, services, conveniences, and intangible benefits. Consumers can view value differently within different shopping experiences.

In setting retail prices, the retailer can elect to be guided by profit, sales, or competitive objectives. Several factors influence the retailer's price-setting decisions, including demand issues (price elasticity and cross elasticity), customer perceptions (psychological pricing), competitive actions (price wars and pricing freedom), cost (total merchandise costs), product (physical, style, and seasonal perishability), and legal considerations.

Retail price-setting methods include those that are cost oriented (markups), competition oriented (above, with, and below competitive prices), and vendor oriented (suggested retail price). Retailers often use numerous pricing policies in refining their price-setting tactics. For example, retailers can elect to employ such pricing structures as single pricing, flexible pricing, multiple pricing, price bundling, concept selling, odd pricing, unit pricing, price lining, bridge pricing, trial pricing, leader pricing, everyday low pricing, high–low pricing, reference pricing, and price matching.

Retailers use price adjustments as adaptive mechanisms to accommodate changing market conditions and operating requirements. Both upward and downward adjustments are needed from time to time to adapt to the dynamic retailing environment. Three common types of price adjustments are discounts, markons, and markdowns. The three general causes for markdowns are buying, selling, and operation related. Some retailers prefer to take early markdowns, whereas others believe late markdowns are more profitable. The size of the markdown depends on the type of merchandise, the price of the item, and the time in the selling season. Markdown pricing strategies include promotional strategies (sales, coupons, premiums, and special-purchase prices) and price-line adjustment tactics.

Student Study Guide

Key Terms and Concepts

automatic markdown *p. 439*
bait-leaders *p. 433*
bridge pricing *p. 431*
captive pricing *p. 429*
competitive parity objectives *p. 417*
competitive price objectives *p. 416*
concept selling *p. 429*
coupons *p. 440*
cumulative markup *p. 423*
discounts *p. 436*
dollar markup *p. 423*
early markdowns *p. 438*
even pricing *p. 430*
everyday low pricing *p. 433*
flexible pricing *p. 428*
gross margin *p. 425*
high–low pricing *p. 434*
initial markup *p. 424*
initial markup percentage *p. 424*
late markdowns *p. 439*
law of demand *p. 418*
leader pricing *p. 432*
loss-leaders *p. 433*
low-leaders *p. 433*
maintained markup *p. 424*
markdown *p. 436*
markdown percentages *p. 436*
market share objectives *p. 416*
markon *p. 436*
markup *p. 423*
multiple-price policy *p. 429*
nonprice competition objectives *p. 417*
odd pricing *p. 430*
off-retail markdown percentage *p. 436*
one-price policy *p. 428*
percentage markups *p. 423*
premiums *p. 440*
price bundling *p. 429*
price elasticity of demand *p. 418*
price leadership objectives *p. 416*
price lining policy *p. 430*
price matching *p. 435*
price wars *p. 419*
pricing above competition *p. 426*
pricing below competition *p. 426*
pricing lines *p. 430*
pricing with competition *p. 426*
pricing zone *p. 430*
profit maximization objectives *p. 416*
psychological pricing *p. 419*
reference pricing *p. 434*
retail price *p. 412*
sales volume objectives *p. 415*
single pricing *p. 428*
special-purchase price *p. 440*
target return objectives *p. 416*
trial price *p. 431*
unit pricing *p. 430*
value *p. 413*
variable-price policy *p. 428*
vendor pricing *p. 427*

Review Questions

1. Describe the concept of value.
2. When might the retailer prefer a market-share maintenance objective over a market-share growth objective?
3. How are two target return-pricing objectives expressed? Explain each expression.
4. Describe the relationship between price leadership and competitive parity objectives.
5. What does price elasticity of demand measure?
6. On what is psychological pricing based? Why is it important?
7. From a product perspective, when are competitive price levels a more important pricing consideration?
8. Discuss how merchandising costs are determined.
9. Identify and discuss the several forms of product perishability.
10. Compare and contrast the initial and maintained markups.
11. Which merchandising strategies are essential to a successful below-competition pricing strategy?
12. When is the vendor's suggested selling price not appropriate?
13. Compare and contrast the following pricing policies: (a) single and flexible pricing, (b) multiple pricing and price bundling, (c) odd and even pricing, and (d) everyday low and high–low pricing.
14. Distinguish pricing zones and pricing lines. Discuss each.
15. What are the advantages to the consumer and to the retailer of a price-lining policy?
16. Describe the two methods for computing markdowns.
17. Briefly describe the four selling-related causes of markdowns.
18. What are the advantages of early markdowns?
19. Describe typical promotional pricing strategies used by the retailer.

Review Exam

True or False

_____ 1. Market-share growth is an appropriate pricing objective in expanding product markets.

_____ 2. Maintained markup equals initial markup minus all retail reductions.

_____ 3. Price lining makes it easier for competitors to develop successful competitive pricing strategies.

_____ 4. A liberal return policy is one method a retailer should use to help reduce the need for taking price markdowns.

_____ 5. A policy of late markdowns usually means the retailer must take deep markdowns to stimulate sales.

_____ 6. Loss-leaders are prices set below the retailer's customary selling price but above the retailer's actual merchandise cost.

Multiple Choice

_____ 1. An appliance dealer purchases a toaster for $14 and sells it for $24. What is the retailer's percentage markup on cost?
a. 71.43
b. 58.33
c. 41.66
d. 171.42
e. 100.00

_____ 2. The difference between gross merchandise cost and the actual selling price of the merchandise is referred to as:
a. initial markup
b. cumulative markup
c. gross margin
d. maintained markup
e. markdown

_____ **3.** Which pricing policy is directed at giving the customer a discount for making quantity purchases?

a. one-price
b. variable-price
c. multiple-price
d. odd pricing
e. unit pricing

_____ **4.** Which odd-price ending(s) is (are) most commonly used by retailers?

a. 9
b. 1
c. 5
d. 3
e. a and c

_____ **5.** The practice of _____ will often lead to additional markdowns because the retailer knowingly stocks for display image purposes a limited number of high-fashion merchandise items that are unlikely to sell at their full markup prices.

a. aggressive selling
b. assortment maintenance
c. umbrella merchandising
d. support maintenance
e. none of the above

_____ **6.** Advantages of late markdowns include all of the following, except _____.

a. preserving exclusive images
b. encouraging creative selling
c. reducing selling risks
d. allowing late bloomers
e. creating the "big event"

Student Application Manual

Investigative Projects: Practice and Application

1. Are retailers "free" to set whatever prices they feel are necessary to make a profit? Explain your answer.

2. Develop a model of your concept of value. List the criteria that you use in defining value. Does your concept of value change with the type of purchase you are making? Check this notion out by describing what constitutes value in the purchase of a hamburger, T-shirt, vacation, and computer.

3. Some retailers prefer to avoid price competition; they prefer to engage in nonprice competition. Why? Identify and describe a retailer who is successful by engaging in nonprice competition.

4. Visit the following types of retailers and observe what price-setting policies are employed: (a) a major chain department store, (b) a major discount chain, (c) a franchised fast-food restaurant chain, and (d) a major shoe chain. Provide specific examples.

Endnotes

1. Mark Stevenson, "The Store To End All Stores," *Canadian Business*, May 1994, 22.

2. Leonard L. Barry, "Stores with a Future," *Retail Issues Letter* (copublished by Center for Retailing Studies, Texas A&M University and Arthur Andersen, March 1995), 2.

3. Michael D. Mondello, "Naming Your Price," *Inc.* (July 1992): 80.

4. Walter K. Levy, "Making a Difference," *Retail Control* (January 1992): 6.

5. Kathleen M. Berry, "How to Regain Control over Retail Prices," *Investor's Business Daily*, July 24, 1994, 1.

6. Donald M. Thompson, "Eaton's, A Cautionary Tale," *Business Quarterly*, Summer 1997, 34.

7. Chad Rubel, "Create Value—or Else," *Marketing News*, April 24, 1995, 17.

8. Jonathan Friedland, "Shoppers Talk, Black & Decker Listens, Profits," *The Wall Street Journal*, January 9, 1995, B1.

9. Teri Agins, "Many Women Lose Interest in Clothes, To Retailers' Dismay," *The Wall Street Journal*, February 28, 1995, A8.

10. See Lasker M. Meyer, "The Customer Won't Pay Regular Price," *Retailing Issues Letter* (copublished by the Center for Retailing Studies, Texas A&M University, and Arthur Andersen & Co. September 1992), 1–2.

11. Stratford Sherman, "How to Prosper in the Value Decade," *Fortune*, November 30, 1992, 91.

12. Marybeth Nibley, "Retailing: What's in Store," *Akron Beacon Journal*, January 17, 1993, B1.

13. "The Discipline of Retail Market Leaders," *Chain Store Age Executive* (April 1995): 40.

14. Jaclyn Fierman, "Americans Can't Get No Satisfaction," *Fortune*, December 11, 1995, 186.

15. See Ruth N. Bolton, "The Robustness of Retail-Level Price Elasticity Estimates," *Journal of Retailing*, 65 (Summer 1989): 193–219. Also see Kathleen Madigan, "The Latest Mad Plunge of the Price Slashers," *Business Week*, May 11, 1992, 36.

16. David S. Lituack, Roger J. Calantone, and Paul R. Warshaw, "An Examination of Short-Term Retail Grocery Price Effects," *Journal of Retailing*, 61 (Fall 1985): 10.

17. Ronald B. Lieber, "Turns Out This Critter Can Fly," *Fortune*, November 27, 1995, 111.

18. Joshua Levine, "It's about Chewing, it's about Salt, it's about Fat," *Forbes*, December 5, 1994, 262.

19. Amey Stone, "Will Consumers Take a Hike?" *Business Week*, August 21, 1995, 27.

20. Less Smith, "Rubbermaid Goes Thump," *Fortune*, October 2, 1995, 100.

21. Paul Brent, "Office Superstores To Merge," *The Financial Post*, September 5, 1996, 3.

22. Bill Saporito, "David Glass Won't Crack under Fire," *Fortune*, February 8, 1993, 80.

23. Andrew E. Serwer, "How to Escape a Price War," *Fortune*, June 13, 1994; Also see Peter R. Dickson and Joe Urbany, "Retailer Reactions to Competitive Price Changes," *Journal of Retailing*, 70 (Spring 1994): 1–21.

24. Marina Strauss, "Bay, Zellers Drop Joint Buying Strategy," *Globe and Mail*, July 19, 1997, B1.

25. Rita Koselka, "Tall Story," *Forbes*, December 18, 1995, 46.

25. Thomas T. Nagle, *The Strategy of Tactics of Pricing* (Englewood Cliffs, NJ: Prentice-Hall, 1987), 59.

27. See "Private Label Jeans Mount Aggressive Attack on Market," *Stores* (February 1996): 68–69.

28. Michael Garry, "Showdown—Standing Up to Supercenter," *Progressive Grocer* (February 1993):

29. See Nancy Rotenier, "Tie Man Meets Queen of England," *Forbes*, September 13, 1993, 46–47.

30. Ian Edwards, "Electronics Retail Secrets," *Profit*, October/November, 1996, 8.

31. Keith Naughton, "Revolution in the Showroom," *Business Week*, February 19, 1995, 70–76.

32. See Jared Sandberg, "High-End Audio Entices Music Lovers," *Wall Street Journal*, February 12, 1993, B1, B6.

33. Damon Darlin, "Here's One for Your Xmas List," *Forbes*, September 25, 1995, 190.

34. Barbara Marsh, "Troubled B&Bs Do Some R&D to Woo Guests," *Wall Street Journal*, March 1, 1993, B1, B2.

35. Theresa Monsour, "Kiddie Rides," *Working Mother* (January 1995): 25.

36. Nina Munk, "Once More into the Breach," *Forbes*, September 11, 1995, 158.

37. See Joshua Levine, "Entertainment Systems for Idiots," *Forbes*, May 22, 1995, 238.

38. See Michael Siconolfi, "Deep Discount Brokers Cut Fees, Frills," *Wall Street Journal*, September 18, 1992, C1, C13.

39. See Robert M. Schindler and Thomas Kibarian, "Do Consumers Underestimate 9-Ending Prices?" *Retailing Review*, a quarterly section of Stores (January 1995): RR10–RR11.

40. Jerry Flint, "The Next Wave," *Forbes*, December 4, 1995, 134–35.

41. Kevin Helliker, "Bombay Co.'s Line of Furniture, Bric-a-Brac Fills a Void," *Wall Street Journal*, October 28, 1992, B4.

42. See Sally Goll Beatty, "Denny's Bites Back with Lower Prices," *The Wall Street Journal*, January 6, 1996, B5; and Howard Rudnitsky, "Indigestion Ahead," *Forbes*, February 1, 1993, 44–45.

43. Jonathan Berry and Zachary Schiller, "Attack of the Fighting Brands," *Business Week*, May 2, 1994, 125.

44. Susan Caminiti, "The Pretty Payoff in Cheap Chic," *Fortune*, February 24, 1992, 73.

45. See Rockney G. Walters and Heikki J. Rinne, "An Empirical Investigation into the Impact of Price Promotions on Retail Store Performance," *Journal of Retailing*, 62 (Fall 1986): 237–66.

46. See Gerard J. Tellis, "Beyond the Many Faces of Price: An Integration of Pricing Strategies," *Journal of Marketing*, 50 (October 1986): 146–60.

47. Jason Vogel, "How Hills Pet Nutrition Became One to the aa-Time Stars in the Colgate Stable," *Financial World*, June 20, 1995, 58–60.

48. See Michael Garry, "Protecting Its Turf," *Progressive Grocer* (November 1995): 84–87.

49. Marina Strauss, "Everyday Low Prices—The New Improved Version," *Globe and Mail*, March 30, 1996, B1.

50. Thompson, "Eaton's, A Cautionary Tale," 38.

51. John Lorinc, "Road Warriors," *Canadian Business*, October 1995, 42.

52. Strauss, "Everyday Low Prices—The New Improved Version," B1.

53. See Anthony D. Cox and Dena Cox, "Compelling on Price: The Role of Retail Price Advertising in Shaping Store Price Image," *Journal of Retailing*, 66 (Winter 1990): 428–445. Also see Tridib Mazumdar and Kent B. Monroe, "Effects of Interstore and In-store Price Comparisons on Price Recall Accuracy and Confidence," *Journal of Retailing*, 68 (Spring 1992): 66–89.

54. Mark Maremont, "Brawls in Toyland," *Business Week*, December 21, 1992, 36.

55. Lornet Turnbull, "Stores in Trouble; Inventories Iffy," *Akron Beacon Journal*, January 16, 1996, B6, B10.

56. Christie Brown, "The Body-Bending Business," *Forbes*, September 11, 1995, 200.

57. See Erica Betts and Peter J. McGoldrick, "The Strategy of the Retail 'Sale': Topology, Review, and Synthesis," *The International Review of Retail, Distribution and Consumer Research* (July 1995): 303–32.

58. Paul B. Brown, "Retailing," *Financial World*, January 5, 1992, 78.

59. See "New Reclamation Systems Turn Returns into Profits," *Stores* (January 1996): 74–76.

Customer Assistance

Building and Providing Customer Service and Personal Selling Support

Outline

Objectives

To appreciate the increased importance of the retailer's service offering in providing customer satisfaction

To recognize the need for customer service quality in all aspects of the retailer service program

To identify the principal objectives in a retail service program

To name and profile the major features of a customer service program

To discuss the five stages in creating positive customer service actions

To explain why the basis for personal selling is good communication

To identify the attributes, traits, and skills of an effective sales associate

To list and describe the seven steps of the retail selling process

Retail Vignette

United Furniture Warehouse

John Volken spent his early childhood in the former Soviet-occupied East Germany. Under that system, because his father was a professional, the young John was not allowed a high school education. This injustice of the totalitarian system left a lasting impression on him. At the age of 14 he moved on his own to West Germany, and for the next 4 years worked during the day and obtained an education at night. In September of 1960, at the age of 18, he moved to Canada with just $20. Upon arriving, he took what work was available, starting as a farm labourer, then as a dishwasher, and then in construction. As soon as he became comfortable with the English language, he moved into sales. During the next few years he lived and worked in Ontario, Quebec, and Nevada. In 1969 he moved to B.C. and operated a door-to-door frozen-food business and mail-order business for the next 12 years.

In 1981 he started United Buy and Sell Service. The original intent was to bring sellers and buyers of used commodities together. However, some of the first merchandise he bought and sold was furniture and he saw the potential in this industry. Furniture soon became the only commodity and after four years "used" furniture was discontinued. By 1995 his furniture chain mushroomed to over 100 stores in Canada and the United States.

John Volken's business philosophy for success is customer appreciation and commitment to employees. "We value our customers not as statistics, but with a warm sense of appreciation," he says. Though financing is available, he refuses to offer any of the popular "no payments till the year 2000" loans because he feels they're not in his customers' best interests. He is also proud of the fact that his customers always know where they stand. "With the ever-increasing competition for people's disposable income, you have to go the extra mile for customers if you want to stay in business," says Volken. "We try to bend over backward for the customer." In its 15 years, United Furniture Warehouse has never offered a sale. When a piece of furniture is assigned a price, it remains at a price that undercuts all competitors. However in keeping with Volken's religious beliefs—he joined the Mormon Church some 20 years ago—all of his stores are closed on Sunday. "Sunday is a family day and our employees are happier and more motivated."

United Furniture Warehouse continues to grow, with over 600 employees and annual sales now at $140 million. In 1995 Volken was selected as Entrepreneur of the Year for the Pacific Canadian Region.

Used with the permission of John Volken.

The Service Edge

The obvious conclusion is that those organizations willing to commit to superior customer service profit on the bottom line. Those unwilling or unable to meet that standard do not and will not thrive—and possibly may not even survive.[1] Many industry analysts are of the opinion that Canadian retailers have room for improvement in this area, as the Retail Strategies and Tactics box illustrates.

Three Times the Sales

At leading retail organizations the world over corporate culture particularly esteems the sales force and their work. The best organizations treat both customers and sales people well, and do so consistently. Sales associates are given the power to deal with customers and make decisions regarding those shoppers' needs as valuable members of the store's team. And indeed they are. Outstanding performance by a sales associate can translate into as much as three times the sales of an ordinary salesperson.[2]

Fire a Buyer and Hire a Seller

Management has to get interested in the problem and consider that the process of selling is of equal importance to the process of buying. Management today is too busy doing other things to remember the simplicity of my definition of retailing: Take good care of your customers, and they will come back. Take good care of your merchandise, and it does not come back. Management can employ a lot of people to take care of the things that are not as important as selling.[3]

Customer Assistance

If the 1990s is the "decade of the customer," then customer assistance is the "strategy of the decade." Business futurists are ascribing to customer assistance the key role in creating customer satisfaction. **Customer assistance** is just that—helping customers find

Retail Strategies and Tactics

Customer Service: A Waiting Game

The recession is not the only culprit responsible for slumping sales in the retail sector. New evidence fingers another villain—retailers themselves.

A national telephone survey conducted by the Angus Reid Group of Toronto suggests retailers' problems go much deeper than the troubled economy.

The poll, which asked 1501 Canadian adults about their best and worst shopping experiences, paints a worrying picture of a consuming public that has become increasingly dissatisfied:

- More than one in four Canadians (27 percent) said they purchased a product or service in the last three months or so where the customer service was so bad they would not buy that product or service again—or at least not from the same company.
- More than half (56 percent) said they had not had a recent experience where the customer service was excellent.
- Only two in five (42 percent) said they had excellent customer service in the last few shopping trips.
- Customers "no longer seem to expect much. They're both cynical and demanding, and they say they're so disgusted in some cases that they'll go elsewhere."
- Front-line staff (salesclerks, tellers, waiters, and so on) provide "the pivotal factor in whether customers are happy or not."

A researcher for Angus Reid Group said there are six keys to good customer satisfaction:

- Follow McDonald's example and strive for consistency.
- Give authority to staff to handle customer problems and complaints without having to go to a manager.
- Be proactive. If you know there is going to be a problem—for example, a late delivery—let the customer know as soon as possible.
- Reward good customers to foster loyalty. The airline industry's frequent-flyer strategy is a good example.
- Be a responsible corporate citizen, especially when it comes to environmental issues. Customers will spend more money for green products and will think better of you.
- Lip service is out. Sincerity is in.

Source: Adapted from Randy Scotland, "Customer Service: A Waiting Game," Marketing, *March 11, 1991.*

satisfaction with the retailer's total offering of goods and services by enhancing the value of that offering through personal attention and the provision of service extras. Canadian retailers have been criticized in the past for offering substandard service.[4] However, new competition from the U.S. has caused most large Canadian firms, such as the Bay,[5] Eaton's,[6] and Canadian Tire,[7] to invest more resources in improving the level of customer assistance.

What customer assistance translates into is **relationship retailing**—any set of customer-oriented activities that attracts, holds, and builds long-term individualistic relationships between the retail firm and its customers. Future survival and growth of many retail formats will require an ongoing personal relationship with loyal yet demanding customers. If the relationship with a customer is to be a marriage and not a one-night stand, the retailer must design the service and sales functions around the customer rather than the retail store or product offering.[8] Customer assistance can no longer be a promotional slogan; for all retailers it must be an operational practice. Why? First, it costs five times more to attract a new customer than to generate additional sales of existing customers. Second, customers who have a good experience with a company tell an average of five other people, whereas dissatisfied customers talk to two to three times more people than satisfied customers do.

Harry Rosen
www.hookup.net/_acecan/sprosen.html

The enhanced role of customer assistance can be explained in part by the partial neutralization of some of the other elements in the retailer's strategic arsenal. Technological advances have resulted in a slew of products of similar quality; hence, product quality differentiation becomes more difficult. New technology has also made it possible to enhance customer service. The management of consumer databases by firms such as Zellers, the air miles participants, and the department stores have helped to increase sales. Even smaller firms such as Wear Else and Harry Rosen maintain database files on their customers.[9] These same technologies have made it possible to locate, communicate, duplicate, and distribute new product concepts, thereby limiting the retailer's ability to create unique product assortments for extended periods of time. New, expanded retailer formats (for example, superspecialty stores and mega-general merchants), with their expanded assortments, further complicate the problem of developing either a better customer-focused merchandise mix or a one-stop shopping opportunity. Competitive pricing strategies such as sales promotional pricing, everyday low pricing, and price

Figure 12–1

Customer assistance

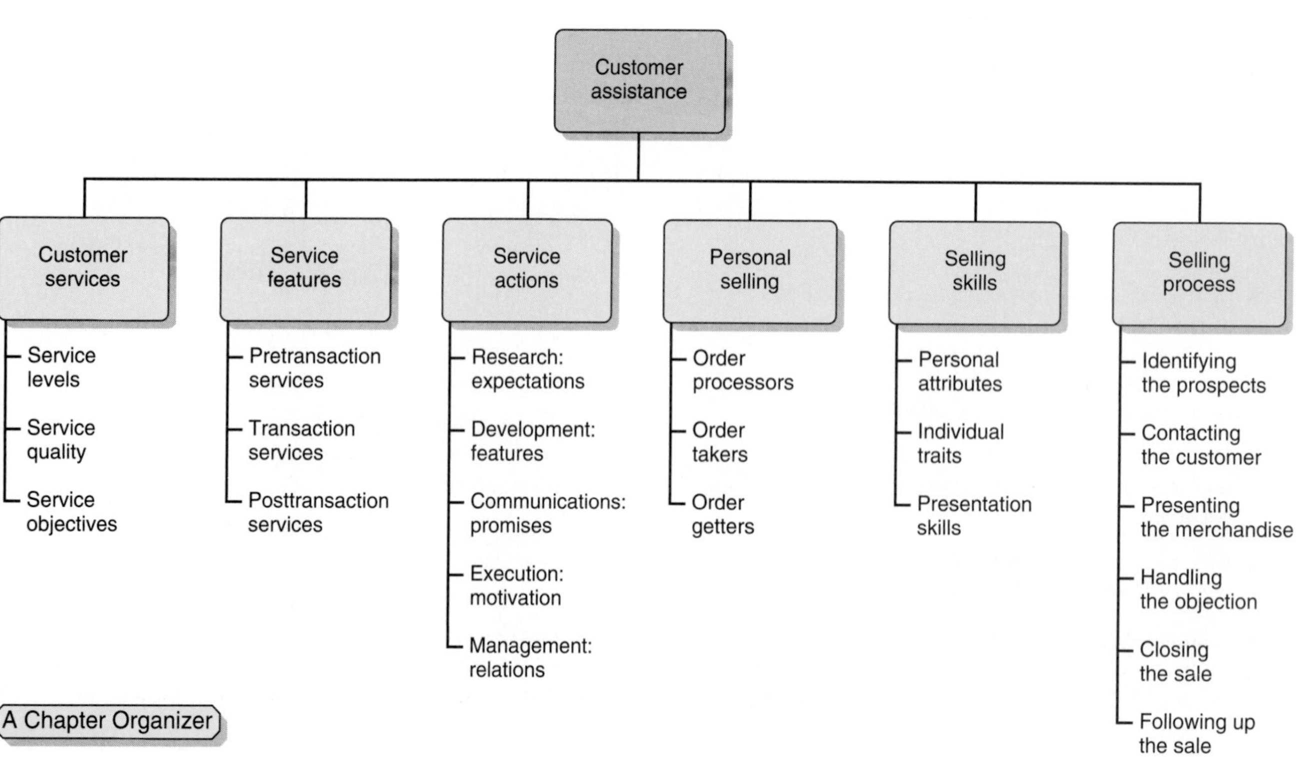

matching have all contributed to the problem of trying to differentiate on the basis of price. Finally, many market areas are overstored; this market saturation hampers the retailer's efforts at finding trading areas and site locations that will provide a locational advantage. So, what's left? Customer assistance is the remaining merchandising area that is lacking or underdeveloped in many retail organizations.

In this chapter, providing customer assistance is viewed from the perspective of the two central means by which customers are assisted: customer service and personal selling. Figure 12–1 outlines the issues as they pertain to each of these customer assistance efforts.

Customer Services

For both the product retailer and the pure service retailer, competitive success is now and will continue to be driven to a large extent by customer perceptions of the quality of the services provided by the retailer.[10] In other words, "performance quality" is quality as retail customers and the retail marketplace see it and define it.[11] To develop a high-quality service program, retail management must first have an understanding and appreciation for the complexities of the service issue.[12] "World-class customer service organizations listen continually to consumers and employees and seek out both compliments and complaints. The successful customer-oriented company measures, tracks, and rewards customer satisfaction."[13]

Customer service can be defined as all the "features, acts, and information that augment the customer's ability to realize the potential value of a core product or service."[14] It involves what extras the retailer should provide in support of the firm's primary offering of goods and/or services. For example, special service extras might include contacting customers about upcoming sales or new merchandise that meets their specific needs, delivering merchandise to their home, pulling merchandise for customers ahead of time, and shopping for complementary items for the customer throughout the store.[15] This definition suggests that a customer service program should take into account each of the following concerns:

- **Level of service features**—Customer service entails what augmenting service extras the retailer should provide. Such customer service features as delivery and installation, alteration and repairs, wrapping and packaging, returns and adjustments, credit and layaway, parking and toting, information and complaint resolution, and store hours are all complementary services that enhance the customer's perceived value of the original purchase of a core product or service.
- **Quality of service actions**—Customer service is equally concerned with how all these extra service features are performed. Customer service acts deal with the friendliness, politeness, willingness, trustworthiness, dependability, reliability, security, and approachability of the service provider.
- **Types of service objectives**—Customer service must be guided by a carefully crafted set of service objectives that focus the retailer's efforts on those service features and actions deemed important by customers. Adding form, time, place, and possession utility; establishing images, positions, and security; or building traffic, sales, and demand are all valid goals around which to focus the firm's service efforts. The Harry Rosen chain of upscale men's clothing stores has an in-store information system that gives salespeople on-the-spot information about customers, so repeat customers get personal treatment at any store.[16]

Figure 12–2 provides an overview of the subject matter discussed in this section.

Figure 12–2

Customer services

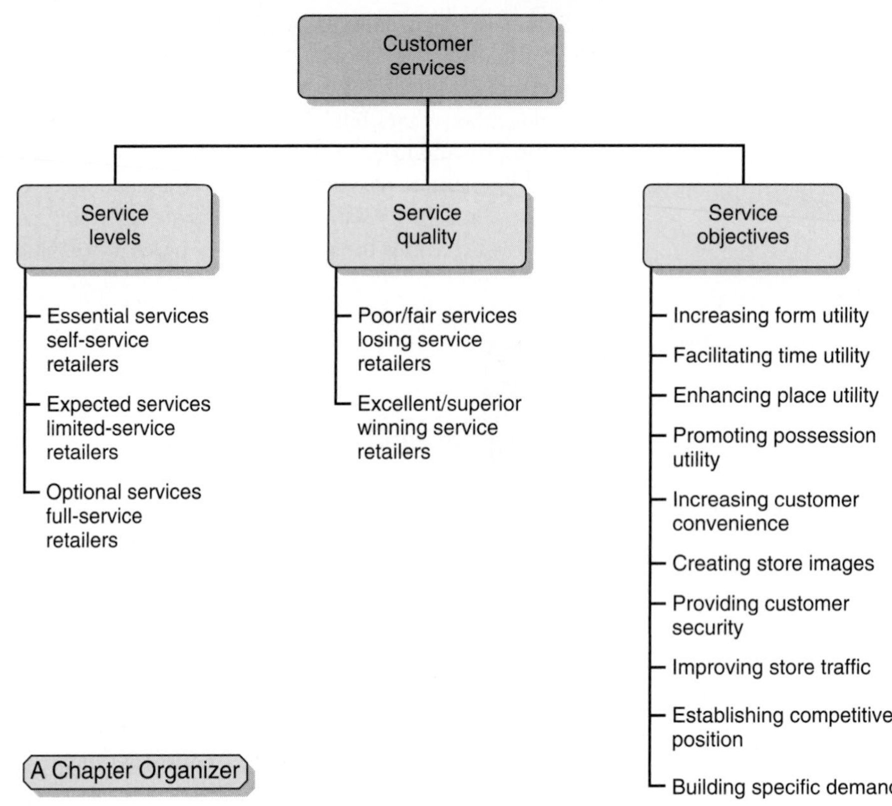

Service Levels: Customer Service Features

Service levels for customer service features can be described in terms of customer expectations regarding the retailer's service offering (optional, expected, essential) or the extent of the retailer's service assortment (full-service, limited-service, or self-service); Figure 12–3 illustrates these two classification schemes.

Essential Services: Self-Service Retailers **Essential services** are basic and necessary to the retailer's merchandising and operational activities; without them, the retailer could not meet the basic transactional needs of the customer. Without essential services, the retailer could not operate. Although essential services vary from one type of retail operation to another, the following services are essential to most retail formats: (1) maintaining store hours, (2) providing parking facilities, (3) supplying information and transactional assistance, (4) furnishing merchandise displays, and (5) handling customer complaints.

Retailers that restrict their service offering to essential services are typically **self-service** operations that are pursuing a *price-oriented retail strategy* (see Figure 12–3b). Warehouse retailers, wholesale clubs, box supermarkets, and some discount stores selling staple merchandise are the most common proponents of this low-price, low-service strategy.

Expected Services: Limited-Service Retailers **Expected services** are not essential for the retailer to operate but are expected by consumers. Failure to offer expected services is failure to meet customer expectations. Delivery, credit, and alterations are three services that consumers expect from appliance, furniture, and clothing stores, respectively. Consumer surveys and competitive analysis are the best ways to determine what is expected and what is not.

Retailers that offer all essential and expected services are following a **limited service** strategy. By offering a moderate level of service at middle-price points, this retailer targets the value-oriented consumer. Some chain stores, variety stores, and limited-line specialty

Figure 12–3

Customer service levels classified by (a) customer expectations and (b) service assortment

Source: From "How to Position for Retail Success" by George H. Lucas, Jr., and Larry G. Gresham, Business *(April–May–June 1988). Copyright © 1988 by the College of Business Administration, Georgia State University, Atlanta. Reprinted by permission of* Business *magazine.*

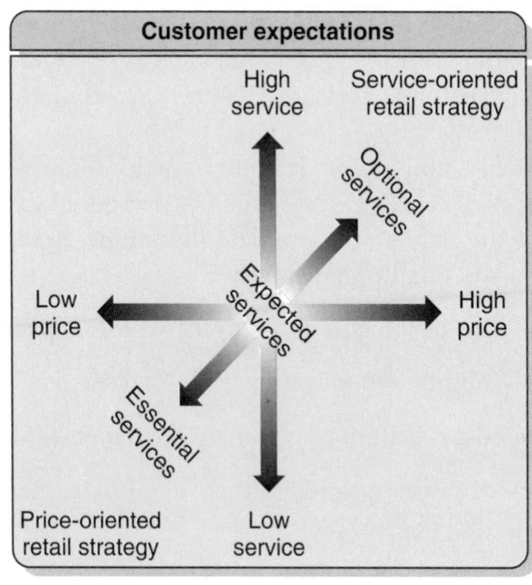

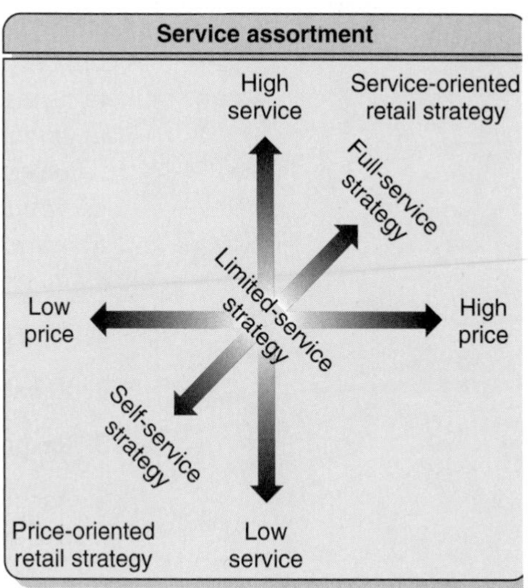

retailers are the most common fence sitters. In recent years, these middle-of-the-road operations have been caught in a competitive squeeze between high- and low-end retailers.

Optional Services: Full-Service Retailers **Optional services** are neither necessary to the retailer's operation nor expected by the customer. Nevertheless, optional services are used by retailers to develop a unique service offering and thereby distinguish themselves from other less service-intense retailers. For example, McDonald's added stock repeater boards in selected restaurants where businesspeople make up most of the morning trade. Along some highway locations, McDonald's provides travellers with maps, tourist information, and automatic teller machines.[17] The distinctive optional service mix offered by Nordstrom, the Seattle-based specialty department store, includes (1) a no-questions-asked return policy backed by a full refund or exchange practice; (2) a formally dressed piano player in each store who provides soothing background music; (3) a "personal book" on each regular customer that profiles the customer's preferences, needs, and buying history, together with important dates (birthdays) and other information that helps sales associates in providing individualized service; (4) a shopping service that will find a needed product at a competitive store if it cannot be found at Nordstrom; (5) home, office, or anywhere delivery; (6) prompt and courteous service at all times under all conditions; and (7) a free shopping environment that allows almost unlimited customer freedom in their involvement with the merchandise (for example, no electronic security tags or limitations on the number of garments a customer can take into the fitting room). With essential, expected, and optional services, the retail firm becomes a **full-service retailer** pursuing a service-oriented retail positioning strategy (see Figure 12–3).

Service Quality: Customer Service Actions

Service quality can be defined as the difference between customer expectations of service and the customer's perception of the service actually received.[18] Customer service expectations are derived from comments of other customers, the retailer's promotional claims, and the customer's past shopping experiences with the retailer. In forming perceptions of the services actually received, customers are as concerned with how services are performed as they are with what services are provided.[19] For example, to have an unconditional merchandise return policy and then to hassle customers when they return merchandise is a completely inappropriate action that will create the impression of low-quality service. Any service feature (for example, delivery and installation) is only as good as the service actions (for example, courtesy and reliability) that support it. One writer describes service quality as delighting the customer by exceeding their expectations. What makes customer satisfaction so difficult to achieve is that firms constantly raise the bar and extend the finish line. They never stop. As the firm's customers get better treatment, they expect better treatment.[20] U.S. retailers expanding into Canada have raised expectations regarding customer service. This has caused many Canadian retailers to respond by upgrading service levels.[21]

Service quality ratings for customer service actions can range from unacceptable to exceptional. Using a rating scale (such as 1 = poor, 2 = fair, 3 = good, 4 = excellent, and 5 = superior), the retailer can evaluate the following list of service actions that might be appropriate to the retail organization:[22]

1. **Tangibles**—Physical facilities, equipment, and appearance of personnel;
2. **Reliability**—Ability to perform the promised service dependably and accurately;
3. **Responsiveness**—Willingness to help customers and provide prompt service;
4. **Assurance**—Knowledge and courtesy of employees and their ability to inspire trust and confidence; and
5. **Empathy**—Caring, individualized attention the firm provides its customers.[23]

Poor/Fair Services: Losing Service Retailers Poor or fair service quality is unacceptable in today's value-oriented marketplace. With overstored markets, consumers no longer are willing to overlook the lack of personal attention and poor service. **Losing service retailers** are characterized by (1) dehumanizing customer interactions and plastic professionalism, (2) inappropriate offerings and unkept promises, (3) inattentive listening and poor communications, (4) disorganized and inefficient policies and practices, (5) slow recognition of and reaction to problems, (6) wasting customer's time and disdaining the customer's opinions.[24]

Excellent/Superior Services: Winning Service Retailers A retailer's actions are judged as being of an *excellent* or *superior quality* when they meet and exceed the expectations of the consuming public. **Winning service retailers** are noticeably more friendly and courteous, and they care about satisfying the customer. They go out of their way to understand customer needs and handle small service details. Winning service is that which is accomplished quickly, accurately, and honestly. Superior-quality service requires the retailer to have a genuine appreciation for the customer's patronage and a strong desire to retain that patronage.[25] In support of its no-hassle policy, Lands' End empowers its phone clerks by granting them the power to solve problems on the spot.[26]

Service Objectives: Customer Service Efforts

To guide their customer service efforts, retailers must establish and follow clearly defined service objectives (see the Retail Strategies and Tactics box). In the following discussion of customer service objectives, the focus is on primary-good retailers and the supplementary service offering. The operations of service retailers are discussed in Chapter 17.

Increasing Form Utility Retailers often receive products from suppliers that require final adjustments and assembly. Additional form-creating services that retailers offer include altering and tailoring for clothing products, installing appliances and home furnishings, engraving and personalizing jewellery, and assembling lawn and garden equipment. Busy consumers often do not have time to fool around with getting a product ready to use. Getting products into a marketable state is a common service provided by such firms as food retailers and automobile dealers.

Facilitating Time Utility For some consumers the right time is now; they want immediate gratification. Consumer credit and extended store hours are two services retailers offer to create time utility. Other consumers are more concerned with saving time; for them, retailers can add time utility to their product mix by accepting telephone and mail orders or by providing carry-out services. L.L. Bean catalogue operations allow shoppers to shop when the mood strikes them; their phone lines are open 24 hours a day,

Retail Strategies and Tactics

How to Keep Customers

Too many companies are creating huge databases filled with customer information without any notion of how they will use it, says Don Peppers, a leading advocate of relationship marketing. Mr. Peppers, a U.S. management consultant and author, has been calling on businesses to stop simply pitching products to the masses and start selling to one customer at a time.

In addition to mindlessly collecting data, companies also remain wedded to programs such as frequent-customer rewards and special cards, which are really just forms of discounting. "All the competition has to do is replicate the program and presto—your clients are gone," Mr. Peppers says. He argues that marketers have to go one step further and give people something that no one else is offering—customized service. "You can create loyalty virtually forever as long as you don't screw it up," Mr. Peppers told a conference sponsored by the Strategic Leadership Forum.

"Companies have to stop focusing on selling as much as they can of one product and start to focus on selling as many products as they can to one customer," Mr. Peppers explains. That's not to say mass marketing is dead. On the contrary, he thinks companies should continue to seek new customers, but they must also identify good existing ones and hang on to them.

In an age of big-box stores and deep discounts, Mr. Peppers says the ticket to success is customization, served up at a premium price. That means listening to what valuable clients want and delivering products designed for them. Once you start providing that unique service—be it remembering a customer's coffee order, her reading tastes, or the way a company likes to receive its shipments—it becomes a lot harder for clients to run to the competition.

Source: Elizabeth Church, Globe and Mail, *February 27, 1997, 13–14.*

365 days a year.[27] Layaway services also add time utility by permitting the consumer to reserve a purchase for some future time when payment is more convenient. Prompt and efficient service is quickly becoming a must for the full-service retailer. The standards for photo processing have shifted from seven days to overnight to one hour. The same thing is occurring with mail delivery, eyeglass service, furniture delivery, automobile maintenance, and medical treatment.

Enhancing Place Utility The best way to add place utility to goods and services is through convenient locations. For example, some supermarkets and supercentres have created "service courts" that house such services as postage and mail, dry cleaning, photocopying, movie rental and entertainment ticket booth, and repair services. Delivery services also form an essential part of some retailers' total offering. Without home deliveries, most bulky products (for example, furniture, appliances) would have no value to consumers without the means to transport them. Some retailers offer catering services to enhance their products' place value.

Promoting Possession Utility Possession utility is the satisfaction consumers receive from owning and using a product. To promote it, retailers must provide consumers with information to facilitate the exchange of ownership process. Personal selling, fashion shows, information booths, complaint desks, bridal registries, and consultants are some of the informational services retailers offer. Auto Zone salespeople can punch the make and year of a car into a store computer and get information and options for thousands of parts and accessories.[28] In addition, retailers accept credit and debit cards, cash personal cheques, and tender itemized receipts.

Increasing Customer Convenience Services that provide customer convenience and comfort include packaging, bagging, free parking, cheque cashing, restaurants, snack bars, rest rooms, lounges, parcel checking, push carts, water fountains, and complimentary coffee. By adding calculators to grocery carts, some supermarket chains provide the means for customers to compute their purchases, coupon discounts, and price per unit. By providing help phones and self-scanners throughout the store, retailers can add considerably to the customer's convenience.[29] Any service that helps customers get into, travel around, and stay in the store not only enhances customers' convenience but also increases the likelihood of planned purchases as well as additional, unplanned purchases.

Creating a Store Image A retailer can use the service mix to pursue one of several image strategies. By offering a *full range of services*, the retailer can promote the image of being a full-service store with high-quality merchandise and prestige prices. For example, at Indigo Books and Music Inc., a newly established book superstore, customers find not only a large supply of books but comfortable chairs, CDs, and a café that serves, among other things, liquor.[30] Conversely, the retailer can choose to offer only services that are essential to the exchange process, thereby creating a no-frills, low-price image. Wal-Mart is adept at striking the delicately balanced need to convince customers that its prices are low while still retaining an edge in customer service. To create its service image, Wal-Mart uses many little touches that enhance its image (for example, a greeter, uniformed store personnel). In its supercentres, Wal-Mart has installed panic buttons throughout the store that, when pressed, quickly dispatch a salesperson on roller skates.[31]

Providing Customer Security Rest room attendants, properly lighted stores and parking facilities, and security guards all enhance the customer's feeling of a safe and secure environment. Perhaps equally important to most customers is product security, provided by such services as warranties, return privileges, allowances, and maintenance contracts. L.L. Bean promises 100 percent satisfaction or your money back, while other catalogue operations offer only limited guarantees on merchandise. Extended warranties are still another service offering to reduce the customers' perceived risk of purchasing certain goods such as automobiles, appliances, and home electronics.

Improving Store Traffic Retailers frequently incorporate into their mix services intended solely to generate additional traffic through their stores. For example, some stores provide (1) rooms for public and private meetings; (2) space for various types of exhibits; (3) rental services for products that might not be related to their product mix; (4) post office, utility bill collection, and entertainment ticket facilities; (5) licence bureaus; and (6) various types of professional services (for example, tax, health, personal care). All these services tend to draw the customers who might not otherwise be attracted. Recently Harry Rosen and Levi Strauss distributed catalogues illustrating clothes-buying tips with the intention of improving store traffic for their merchandise.[32]

Establishing a Competitive Position Retailers can use services either to establish competitive parity or to create a competitive edge. To remain competitive, retailers offer many services because they are essential to the retailer's operation, competitors offer them, or customers expect them. To gain a competitive edge, some retailers offer services that are not essential to their operations or expected by consumers. A distinctive service mix can create competitive benefits that are long-lasting and reasonably difficult to imitate. In the battle for the well-heeled traveller, small luxury cruise ship lines offer gourmet meals and seven-course dinners, special diets and health foods, spacious accommodations with special comfort features, unusual destinations, supervised land excursions, lectures and demonstrations, social events and live entertainment, as well as a variety of recreational and exercise opportunities.[33] In recent years, many Canadian retailers have been forced to improve customer service as a means of competing with the superstores.[34]

Building Specific Demand Although most services contribute either directly or indirectly to the total demand, retailers often build demand for a particular product line or item by offering services that focus consumers' attention on that product. Many cosmetic companies, including Elizabeth Arden and Shiseido, use computer simulation to provide their customers with high-tech information about skin and hair needs. Because of the tremendous increase in the number of "do-it-yourselfers," some home centres offer instructional services and classes on how to repair plumbing, hang a light fixture, and so on, to promote related product lines.

Service Features

Service features consist of any set of "extras" that the retailer offers to customers to assist them before, during, and after the sale (see Figure 12–4).

Pretransaction Services

Before any sales transaction can be completed, the retailer must provide customers certain essential **pretransaction services**, typically including customer parking, store hours, and prepurchase information services.

Parking Facilities Close and convenient parking facilities are an essential part of the service mix for a majority of the nation's retailers. As discussed in Chapter 8, accessible parking dictates that the shopper can easily approach, enter, transverse, and exit parking facilities. Equally important is the security of the facility, good lighting, unobstructed vision, patrolling security personnel, security surveillance, and open space help create the reality and perception of a safe and inviting environment.

Store Hours With a customer attitude of "I want to do what I want to do when I want to do it," the retailer must provide store hours that are convenient to the customer.[35] Evening hours from Monday through Saturday have become commonplace for most retailers. Many supermarkets are now open twenty-four hours a day; many are staffed all

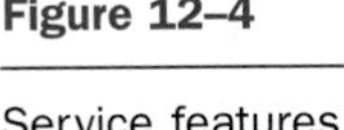

Figure 12–4

Service features

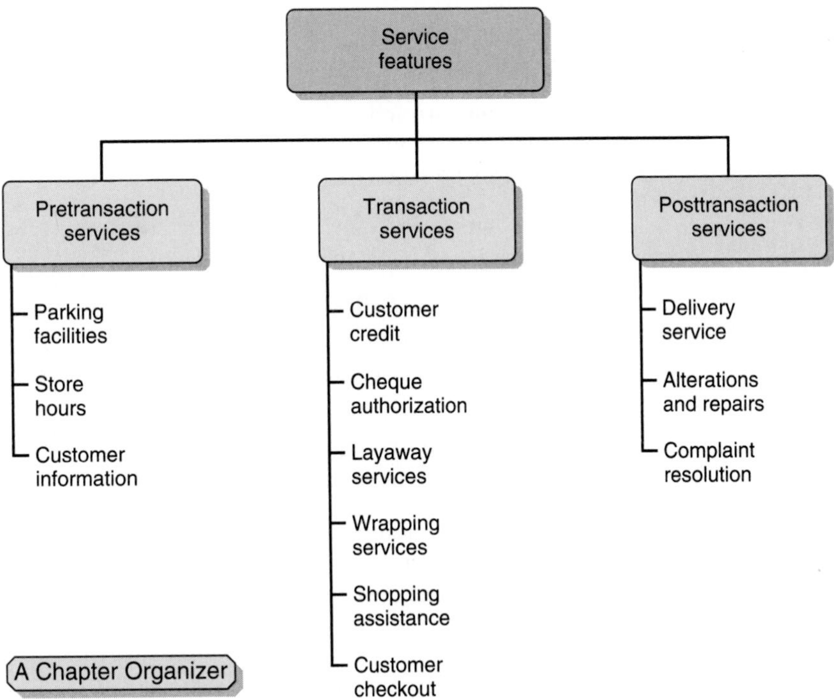

night with stocking personnel, so around-the-clock openings can be accomplished within reasonable cost constraints. In part, night openings are the retailer's response to changing lifestyles of consumers who find it more convenient and enjoyable to shop at night.

The issue of Sunday hours is similar to night hours in all respects except for the social, religious, and legal restrictions imposed in some parts of the country. Many local governments have enacted laws, often referred to as "blue laws," that determine (1) whether Sunday openings are allowed, (2) what types of products can be sold on Sundays (necessities versus nonnecessities), and (3) when and how many hours stores can be open (for example, from 1 p.m. to 6 p.m.).

Customer Information Well-informed shoppers become buying customers. Shoppers must be informed about when the store is open, what goods and services are available, where to find sales items, how to check out, what credit cards the store accepts, how a product works, whether the store carries a particular size or colour—and the list goes on. Given that two out of three shoppers make buying decisions while in the store, providing useful information at the point of sale is a possession-enhancing service of considerable value to the customer. In recent years, retailers and various vendors have developed point-of-sale devices that provide customers with both informative and persuasive information.

Transaction Services

To complete the exchange process, that is, to successfully conclude a sales transaction, retailers offer several **transaction services**, including credit, cheque authorization, layaway, wrapping, shopping assistance, and checkout services.

Consumer Credit To a substantial majority, credit has become either an essential or an expected part of the retailer's service mix. The question for most retailers is not whether to offer credit but what type of credit to offer.

Credit Systems. The retailer can elect to use one of several different credit systems: in-house credit, third-party credit, and private-label credit. An **in-house credit system** (also referred to as proprietary credit) is owned, operated, and managed by the retail firm. Sears has one of the more successful in-house credit cards.[36] Retailers offer credit services for a variety of reasons: (1) consumers expect the service, (2) store image will be enhanced, (3) many consumers cannot afford the retailer's assortment of merchandise unless they are offered credit, (4) competitors offer credit arrangements, and (5) market and economic conditions dictate the need for credit. Offering an in-house credit plan has advantages and disadvantages for most retailers. Advantages include the following:

- **Customer attraction**—Stores that offer credit services tend to attract customers who are more interested in product quality, store reputation, and service offerings and less interested in prices.
- **Customer loyalty**—Credit-granting stores more easily build repeat business, because credit customers tend to be more loyal than are cash customers.
- **Customer goodwill**—Credit-granting stores generally have a more personal relationship with their customers and therefore become the first place the customer shops for a particular purchase.
- **Increased sales**—Credit services increase total sales volume because credit customers tend to buy more goods and pay higher prices than do customers who do not use credit.
- **Sales stabilization**—Credit sales are more evenly spread throughout the month, whereas cash sales correspond more closely with those times immediately following paydays.

- **Market information**—Credit applications provide considerable amounts of information (age, sex, income, occupation, and so forth) on the credit consumer; credit records can reveal a history of what, when, and where (which department) the customer bought.
- **Promotional effort**—Because credit customers are known to be customers of the store, they are an excellent foundation on which to build a mailing or telephone list for special promotions; also, the monthly statement credit customers receive is an effective vehicle for promotional literature.

In addition to these advantages, retailers realize the disadvantages associated with offering credit services, the most commonly cited being those related to the higher costs of developing and managing a credit business.

As an alternative to offering in-store credit services, many retailers use **third-party credit systems**, accepting one or more of the credit cards issued by outside institutions. Often referred to as third-party cards, the most common types are those issued by banks (MasterCard and VISA) and entertainment-card companies (American Express, Diner's Club, and Carte Blanche).

MasterCard
www.canadatrust.com/ct/credit/index.html

VISA
www.visa.com/cgibin/vee/main.html

Major advantages to accepting third-party cards are that retailers (1) do not have the problems of establishing and maintaining a credit department; (2) are relieved of the unpleasant tasks of investigating credit applications, billing customers, and pursuing collections; (3) can offer credit to consumers who otherwise would not qualify (for example, out-of-town consumers); and (4) can maintain a steady cash flow, because financial institutions convert credit card sales quickly and regularly into cash minus agreed-on service charges.

The chief disadvantage for retailers that accept credit cards is the cost of the service. Credit agencies charge rates varying with the retailer's potential credit sales volume and several market and competitive conditions.

A **private-label credit system** is one that retailers offer under their name but that a bank operates and manages. The retail firm realizes most of the benefits associated with in-house credit systems while avoiding many of the problems associated with credit management. Typically, the cost of this type of system is comparable to most in-house systems.

Affinity cards and cobranding credit cards are two additional credit systems available to the retailer. **Affinity cards** are based on a relationship between an affinity group or organization (for example, American Marketing Association, McGill University), a third-party credit system (for example, VISA, MasterCard), and the individual customer and credit user. **Cobranding cards** involve a relationship among a retailer, a third-party credit system, and the individual customer and card user. Typically, the credit card looks like the retailer's proprietary card but has a VISA or MasterCard logo on it that enables the cardholder to use it not only in the retailer's store but anyplace else where VISA or MasterCard are accepted.

Credit Plans. Depending on the type of credit system, one or more of three types of credit plans will be available to the consumer: the open account, the installment plan, and revolving credit.

Often referred to as the "regular charge" or "open book credit," the **open account credit** plan enables customers to buy merchandise and pay for it within a specific time period without finance charges or interest. Usually, the customer is expected to pay the full amount within thirty days of the billing date, although some retailers extend the due date (**deferred billing**) to either sixty or ninety days to promote special occasions or to distinguish their credit services from the thirty-day services their competitors offer. The retailer usually grants an open account without requiring the customer to make a down payment or to put up collateral to obtain the purchase.

Most customers would find it impossible to purchase large-ticket items such as automobiles, furniture, and appliances if they could not make small down payments and spread the additional payments over several months or years. The **installment credit** plan allows consumers to pay their total purchase price (less down payment) in equal monthly installment payments over a specified time period. Retailers prefer to receive a down payment on installment purchases that equals or exceeds the initial depreciation of the product. Some retailers require only a minimal down payment or no down payment to make the sale. Retailers carry installment accounts in one of three ways:

1. **Conditional sales agreement**—The title of the goods passes to the consumer conditional on full payment. The retailer can repossess the product and obtain a judgment against the consumer for any lost product value and expenses resulting from repossession.

2. **Chattel mortgage agreement**—The title passes to the customer when the contract is signed, but the product is secured by a lien against it for the unpaid balance.

3. **Lease agreements**—A contract in which the customer rents a product in the present with the option to buy in the future. Consumers usually pay periodic rent, which is applied toward the purchase price.

Revolving credit incorporates some of the features of both the open account and installment plans. Of the several variations of revolving credit plans, the two most common are the fixed-term and the option-term.

- **Fixed-term revolving credit** requires the customer to pay a fixed amount on any unpaid balance at regularly scheduled intervals (usually monthly) until the amount is paid in full. Under this plan, customers have a credit limit, such as $500, and may make credit purchases up to this limit as long as they continue to pay the agreed-on fixed payment (for example, $50) each month.

- **Optional-term revolving credit** gives customers two payment options. They can either pay the full amount of the bill within a specified number of days (typically thirty) and avoid any finance charges, or they can make at least a minimum payment and be assessed finance charges on the unpaid balance. As with the fixed-term account, a credit line is established and customers are free to make purchases up to the established limits.

Credit Management. A retailer that decides to offer in-store credit must establish applicant creditworthiness by evaluating each individual on the basis of the **three C's of credit**: character, capacity, and capital.

Character in a credit sense refers to attributes (for example, maturity, honesty) that distinguish one individual from another in meeting obligations. Personal interviews, reference checks, and the applicant's credit history help the retailer evaluate this attribute. *Capacity* is the measure of an individual's earning power and ability to pay. A credit applicant's income is important in deciding not only whether to extend credit but also how much credit to extend. The third indication of creditworthiness is *capital* (that is, the applicant's tangible assets). Accumulation of capital suggests that the applicant is capable of managing financial affairs.

Cheque/Credit Authorization For obvious security reasons, few shoppers carry sufficient cash to pay for all of the merchandise that is purchased on a given shopping trip. Credit and personal cheques are the two other means of payment. (The problems of bad cheques and credit cards are discussed in Chapter 7.) For the retailer, the problem becomes how to offer cheque-cashing and card-accepting services without hassling the customer. Cheque and card authorization procedures must provide customer service as well as operational security.

Layaway Services Layaway services afford customers an opportunity to place merchandise on hold until they are ready to complete the transaction. The customer is permitted to guarantee the availability and the price of a merchandise item by making a minimum deposit (typically 20 percent) and paying for the item at a later date. Payments are made either at regular intervals or in full at one time. In either case, the retailer retains possession of the merchandise until full payment is received. For customers who do not have charge cards or some other form of credit and are unwilling or unable to pay cash immediately, layaway services are a valued convenience and accommodation.

Wrapping Services The three basic types of wrapping services retailers perform are bagging or sacking, store wrap, and gift wrap. **Bagging** (1) facilitates handling (especially when multiple purchases are involved); (2) protects purchases from inclement weather; and (3) preserves the privacy of the customer purchase. **Store wrap** is the wrapping of customers' purchases in a standard (colour and design) wrapping paper or box. Most department and specialty stores offer this service free of charge. The retailer that incorporates its prestige name with store wrap can provide additional purchase incentives for customers who seek a prestige gift. **Gift wraps** normally incorporate additional wrapping features such as bows and ribbons to distinguish them clearly from store wraps. Due to increased costs of materials and labour, the customer normally is charged an additional fee for gift-wrapping services.

Shopping Assistance For many time-starved consumers, shopping is an unwelcome chore, not a pleasurable diversion. Still other individuals feel they need assistance in selecting the right merchandise. A valuable addition to the retailer's mix of services is the **personal shopper**—a store employee who manages all or part of a customer's shopping needs. The services of a personal shopper include selecting an entire wardrobe, assembling a grocery order, filling a telephone or mail order, scheduling an early morning or late evening shopping opportunity, and/or escorting the customer around the store and advising him or her on selections. Completing the sales transaction, arranging alterations or installations, and scheduling home or office delivery are additional services provided by a personal shopper. Gift registry is another valuable shopper assistance program.

Customer Checkout Fast and efficient transaction is a service almost every customer values. To the no-nonsense shopper and many time-pressed consumers, good service is defined as efficiency in locating merchandise and transaction speed. When one realizes that the checkout transaction is the last impression that the customer has before exiting the store, the importance of managing this process is self-evident. Retailers who satisfy the customer by having the right merchandise at the right price can still fail to create customer satisfaction if that customer has to stand in long checkout lines, wait for price lookups or cheque authorization, or deal with rude and indifferent checkout personnel. With modern point-of-sale cash register terminals, most mechanical problems can be sharply reduced or eliminated.[37] Employee training and motivation are needed to handle customer-employee relationship problems. Some retailers are experimenting with self-scanning and checkout in order to speed the flow of customers through this bottleneck.[38]

Posttransaction Services

After the sale the retailer should continue to serve. Continued customer satisfaction and store loyalty depend on such **posttransaction services** as delivery, alteration and repairs, and a complaint resolution process.

Delivery Service Delivery service is one of the most controversial aspects of a service mix. In general, delivery service is difficult to plan, execute, and control. Before including delivery service in the service mix, the retailer must have a clear understanding of when to offer it, what problems it entails, under which terms and conditions it can be offered, and what type of delivery system is most appropriate to the operation. Delivery is practically indispensable when (1) retailing such bulky products as furniture, appliances, and building materials; (2) travelling by public transportation is a common mode of transportation; (3) soliciting telephone and mail orders; (4) selling emergency goods (for example, prescription drugs) is part of the product mix; (5) engaging in institutional sales; and (6) protecting a high-service store image.

Retailers can elect to use either an in-store system or an independent system. **In-store delivery** systems can be wholly owned and operated by an individual store (private store systems) or partially owned and operated with other stores (cooperative store systems). They provide the retailer with a higher level of control over delivery operations and greater flexibility in adjusting services to customer needs.

Independent delivery systems are owned and operated independently from the retailer. They offer their services on either a contractual basis (consolidated systems) or an open-to-the-general-public basis (parcel post and express services). Consolidated systems are independent firms that, for a fee, will deliver a store's packages.

Alterations and Repairs Many retailers offer alterations and repairs as both a supplement to the sale of products and an income-producing service. Consumers expect retailers of expensive clothing to provide alteration services, and retailers of appliances, television sets, automobiles, and other durable goods to provide repair services. Retailers have experimented with various types of alteration charges ranging from no charge for minor alterations to partial or full charge for major alterations. Retailers usually charge customers for repairs on durable goods according to the terms and conditions of product warranties and established store policies. Normally, consumers bear no charge (or at most a minimum charge). To increase their income from repair services, many chain retailers (such as Sears) offer maintenance contracts on a fixed-fee basis. Several other Canadian department stores have also added home services to their list of service options. Home service is a growing market in Canada.[39]

In-store alteration and repair services give the retailer all the advantages associated with direct control of such activities; however, this alternative also presents numerous management problems and requires substantial capital investments. Out-of-store alterations are subcontracted to private-service retailers specializing in tailoring services.

Complaint Resolution In 1962, U.S. President John F. Kennedy identified four basic consumer rights: "the right to safety, the right to be informed, the right to choose, and the right to be heard." Two of these rights, the right to be heard and be informed, are key factors in the customer complaint process. Customers expect to be informed of all operating policies that affect their patronage, and they expect to be heard when they want to register a complaint. Customer complaints can be viewed positively. First, a customer who complains gives the retailer a chance to identify and correct a problem.[40] Second, customer complaints serve as a major source of information regarding the retailer's products, services, and other merchandising activities.[41] Dell, a successful direct marketer of computers, has all of its employees memorize the "Dell Vision," which states in part that a customer "must have a quality experience, and must be pleased, not just satisfied. To ensure that the vision is followed, the company holds a weekly Customer Advocate Meeting, 'The Hour of Horror.' Employees from top managers down to assembly workers pore over customer complaints and employee suggestions."[42]

Causes of Complaints. Most customer complaints result from one of two general causes: product- and service-related difficulties. Product-related causes include (1) *poor-quality products*—inferior workmanship and materials; (2) *damaged products*—chipped, stained, or soiled; (3) *incorrect products*—mislabelled or mismatched; and (4) *insufficient selection*—out-of-stock or discontinued.[43]

Service-related causes involve customer dissatisfaction with sales personnel and services such as checkout, delivery, workroom, and customer accounts. Complaints about sales personnel usually centre on the salesperson's (1) *disposition*—indifferent, discourteous, unfriendly; (2) *incompetence*—lack of product knowledge, poor selling skills; (3) *dishonesty*—unfulfilled promises, false information; or (4) *selling methods*—selling them too much of an item or trading them up to a product they cannot afford. Complaints about delivery services include late, lost, and incorrect deliveries. Improper alterations, lengthy delays, and overcharges are the chief causes of complaints stemming from workroom services. Finally, improper handling of accounts irritates customers. Errors in billing, receipt of a bill after it has already been paid, and delays in receiving account statements, are some of the more irksome problems.

Handling of Complaints. The retailer has several alternatives in handling consumer complaints.[44] They include offering returns and refunds; making product, price, and service adjustments; and practising good customer relations.

1. **Returns and Refunds**—Retailers that guarantee satisfaction must decide whether to refund the customer's money in the form of cash or as a credit slip. Some retailers prefer to give cash refunds because they feel this policy creates greater customer satisfaction. Proponents of the credit-slip refund believe this method is better because it maintains contact with the customer and ensures a future sale.[45]
2. **Product Adjustments**—Complaints about incorrect products can easily be handled by allowing customers to exchange the incorrect product for a correct one. By offering to clean, repair, alter, or exchange products, retailers can satisfy most customers' complaints about damaged products. One way to handle consumer complaints about poor-quality products is to substitute a higher-quality product. Complaints involving insufficient selection can be handled by (1) agreeing to stock the product, (2) offering an appropriate substitute, or (3) directing the customer to a store that stocks the desired product.
3. **Price Adjustments**—Price adjustments can be given as either an allowance or a discount on the purchase price of the product. Because it is not always possible to exchange or adjust a product that has been damaged, the retailer often can satisfy customers by reducing the price of the product to compensate for the damages. Price adjustments also can include free merchandise and discount coupons.
4. **Service Adjustments**—Retailers can handle service adjustments in much the same way as price adjustments. For example, if a consumer says that a garment alteration is unsatisfactory, the retailer should make the additional alteration free of charge. Or if a billing error shows the customer paid a bill late, any late charges or interest penalties the retailer would normally charge should be dropped.
5. **Customer Relations**—Some situations generate customer complaints for which none of the preceding adjustments are appropriate. A rude salesperson is one example. In such cases, the customer may just want to be heard or blow off steam. Whether the complaint is justified or not, good customer relations dictate that the retailer listen carefully and politely, reassure the customer, and apologize for the situation. By allowing the customer to register the complaint and handling that complaint professionally, the retailer keeps a good customer.

Customer complaints in small stores usually are handled by the store owner or manager; large stores, however, must develop a system for handling complaints. The two alternatives are centralized or decentralized systems. All customer complaints are referred to a central office or complaint desk under a **centralized complaint system**. The advantages of this arrangement are that it allows the retailer to use trained personnel to implement a more uniform policy for handling complaints and to receive more accurate information regarding complaints. Also, complaints are handled privately and are not aired in public.

A **decentralized complaint system** handles customer complaints at the department level. Department salespersons usually handle minor complaints and adjustments, and the department manager is responsible for major complaints. Customers generally prefer this type of system.

Service Actions

Retailers must develop an action plan to ensure that their customer service actions are sufficient to provide the quality of service appropriate to the retailer's operations. Superior customer service does not just happen—it must be planned and managed just like all other aspects of the retailer's business. In developing a system for customer service, the "emphasis is on the value of pleasing a customer, not the cost. And it empowers front-line employees to use their judgment in creating satisfaction."[46] The following five steps should be part of any action plan to promote high-quality customer service.

Research: Expectations and Desires

What do customers expect? What do customers want? The best research approach for finding the answers to these and other questions involving service quality is to ask consumers and, above all, to listen to them carefully. Formal customer surveys; focus group studies; complaint resolution analysis; evaluation of returns and allowances; suggestion boxes; the recording (mental or otherwise) of informal customer comments; and observation of customer reaction to the store, merchandise, promotions, and personnel can reveal substantial useful information.[47] There is a wealth of information in every retail store if the retailers will organize to obtain and process that information. Embassy Suites conducts over three hundred interviews with its guests each day to identify and resolve problems.

Development: Features and Actions

Decisions regarding what services are to be offered and how they are to be performed are discussed previously. It is sufficient to say that each customer service feature and corresponding service action must be carefully considered in light of customer expectations and retailer resources. It is far better to provide a few high-quality services than to provide a wide variety of low-quality services.

Communication: Promises and Offers

Both the retailer's service mix (features) and service quality (actions) should be carefully communicated to the customer. Poor communication that leads to misunderstandings is itself a bad service. The retailer's service offerings can be communicated through carefully posted signs, in-store announcements, information booths, informed sales associates, available managers, and printed matter such as brochures. It is extremely important that retailers do not promise or appear to promise a service or service level that they cannot live up to. Promising customers more than the firm can deliver can be disastrous. It is the retailer's responsibility to ensure clear and concise communication regarding the store's service offerings.

Execution: Motivation and Evaluation

Quality customer service does not just happen. Friendly, courteous, responsive, honest, and reliable store personnel do not simply materialize out of store fixtures. Retail employees at all levels must be motivated. Although financial motivation (for example, commissions, bonuses) is an important part of the encouragement process, the retail organization must develop a "service culture" in which all store employees recognize their responsibilities to customer service. Training sessions, motivation seminars, employee recognition programs, material and nonmaterial rewards, and many thank-yous are all part of the employee motivation program.

Management: Relationships and Partnerships

Retail managers must be accessible to customers and employees. Good customer service starts in the executive suite. Bernard Marcus, CEO of Home Depot, the home improvement chain, "teaches management training courses, and his managers in turn teach employees to help customers to choose the best and least expensive product suitable to their purpose."[48] If an effective customer service program is to be developed, top executives must support the program financially, operationally, and personally. But for all the inspirational efforts of CEOs, the nitty-gritty of the customer service program falls to sales associates and front-line managers. "Companies that excel at managing frontline workers understand that excellent service is more than just a transaction. It is an experience, one that ought to satisfy the employee as well as the customer."[49]

Successful service programs have typically emerged from management–employee relationships that can best be described as partnerships. When employees see themselves as partners in the organization, they become stakeholders who have an invested interest in seeing that the team succeeds. The chances that a stakeholding partner will take care of providing high-quality customer service is much greater than the efforts one could expect out of an employee.

Personal Selling

Personal selling is direct, face-to-face communication between a retail sales associate and a retail customer. Salespeople are usually the first people in the store to interact with customers on a face-to-face basis; thus, they have tremendous influence on how consumers perceive a store and play a significant role in enhancing or detracting from the consumer's total favourable impressions of the retailer.[50] Retail selling is a special kind of selling in which the customer comes to the store with a general or specific need in mind. It is the responsibility of the sales associate to transform that felt need into a final sale for the retailer and a satisfied need for the customer.

> Retailers must teach associates that when a stranger walks through the door they are first a visitor, then a customer, and finally a client. Sales associates need to learn how to develop clients, not just customers. A visitor may buy, a customer buys and a client returns to buy again and again. The best sales associates practise psychotherapy all day long; they uncover hidden desires, determine emotional needs, discover problems and offer solutions.[51]

The basis for all personal selling is personal communications. Communication is not something you do *to* someone but something you do *with* someone. **Personal communication** is the process of exchanging ideas and meanings with other people. Although one person is listening, even that person is active, not passive, in every communication situation. Figure 12–5 shows the basic elements of the communication interaction between a customer and a salesperson. The model also illustrates that both customer and salesperson are simultaneously sending and receiving information. The transmission and reception of information comes in many forms, such as words, objects, fragrances, colours, gestures, appearances, music, and voice qualities, to name but a few. With all these communications channels occurring at the same time, a good salesperson must be a good listener and observer and adapt quickly to each moment in the selling situation.

Whether a salesperson is an order processor, getter, or taker, certain qualities or characteristics are needed to be effective. **Order processors** are essential behind-the-counter clerks who ring up the sale and bag the merchandise. Typically, the order processor does not get involved with the personal selling process. Nevertheless, the order processor

Figure 12–5

The communication process

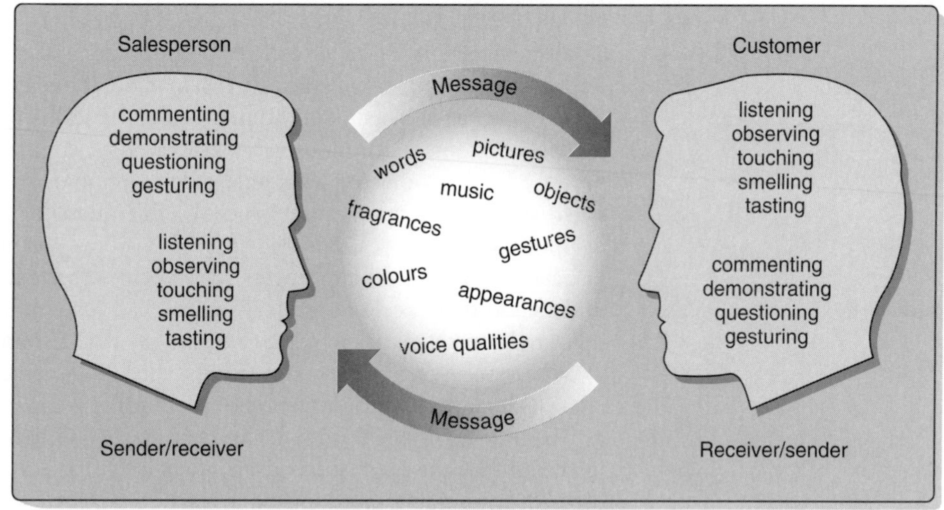

can contribute to creating customer satisfaction by providing speedy checkout service and thanking customers for their patronage. **Order takers** are sales associates involved in the selling process to a limited extent. Providing information and advice, locating merchandise, ringing up the sale, and bagging the merchandise are all part of their role as efficient service providers. The most difficult job (and most rewarding) is order getting. **Order getters** are sales personnel actively involved in the selling process; they play a key role in obtaining a buy decision from the customer. Order takers employ creative problem solving and persuasion in helping customers meet their goods and services needs.

Selling Skills

Although most of the personal characteristics and selling skills described in this section apply mostly to the order getter, they are characteristics and skills that can also help order processors and order takers be successful. As illustrated in Figure 12–6, personal attributes, individual traits, and presentation skills are all instrumental in determining the selling success that a particular individual will enjoy in the retail selling experience.[52]

Personal Attributes

Appropriate grooming is essential to successful selling. What is appropriate depends on the type of retailer and its targeted consumer base. How one is dressed and groomed appropriately when working for a casual apparel retailer targeting the youth market is considerably different than when employed by a men's clothing store that serves a high-end business clientele. However, in most cases such *physical attributes* as clean clothing, shined shoes, well-groomed hair, fresh breath, manicured fingernails, a close shave, and a pleasant smile are essential basics in creating the right first impression.

Good salespeople have developed personality traits of sociability, curiosity, imagination, creativity, enthusiasm, sincerity, ambition, and reliability. Successful sales associates get along with people, want to know more about everything, are willing to try new ways and do something different, have great interest in their work, desire to achieve certain self-imposed goals, are self-starters who strive to reach established goals, and, finally, are truthful about themselves and the products they sell.

are daily and weekly activities, including learning which merchandise is currently in stock; which items are on sale; changes that have occurred in new styles, fashions, and models of merchandise; and dozens of other day-to-day store happenings.

Prospecting for Customers Prospecting is the process of finding people who are *willing* to buy the merchandise a store has to offer and able to pay for it. Surveys have shown that more than anything else, salespeople dislike approaching strangers in a sales situation. Why? They fear rejection. All the more reason that salespeople must learn through experience how to spot good prospects. Good prospects generally display more intense interest in the merchandise than poor prospects who are "just browsing." A variety of behavioural cues set good prospects apart from the poor prospects; for example, carrying several bags of merchandise from other stores is often a clue to a shopper's interest in making additional purchases.

Contacting the Customer

Initial impressions are important determinants in successfully making a sale. A warm smile and the appearance of genuine interest in customers and their needs are part of a good initial impression. Sam Walton used to ask all Wal-Mart associates to make the following pledge: "From this day forward, I solemnly promise and declare that to every customer that comes within ten feet of me, I will smile, look them in the eye, and greet them, so help me Sam." At the beginning of the contact, the salesperson should make an opening comment that quickly captures the buyer's attention and arouses interest. Further, the first words should be positive and stimulate any needs the customer might be displaying. If a woman is holding up a blouse to examine, the salesperson might open by saying, "That blouse certainly would look nice on you. Would you like to try it on?" This opening compliments the woman's taste in clothing, stimulates her need to "look nice," and requests her to take an action (try it on). A simple "May I help you?" is a routine, worn-out phrase that almost invites the customer to turn down the request.

Openings should be original and appropriate to the situation. Consider the following examples of customer situations and potential salesperson responses.

Situation 1: Customer looking at a home video game

- *Preferred opening:* "Press this button like this [salesperson turns game on], and the game's all set to go. Why don't you try your luck?"
- *Nonpreferred opening:* "Do you need some help in how to operate this thing?" Customer: [Gads, he thinks I'm stupid or something.] "No, I was just looking."

Situation 2: Woman looking at a coat in an exclusive, high-fashion women's clothing store

- *Preferred opening:* "That's 100 percent mink. Please let me help you on with it to see how it looks and feels."
- *Nonpreferred opening:* "Want some help?" Customer: [She thinks I don't know how to put on a coat!] "No, thank you."

Situation 3: Shopper looking at a telephone in a phone centre store

- *Preferred opening:* "That phone will make a call for you if simply one button is pressed. Look how easy it is to operate."
- *Nonpreferred opening:* "Are you interested in a phone?"

In summary, a salesperson's opening statement at the point of initial contact can determine whether conversation will continue and, therefore, whether the sale can be made. A good opening should attract the customer's attention, arouse interest, stimulate a customer need, and be original to the situation. A poor opening is generally one that can be answered with a yes or no.

Presenting the Merchandise

After making initial contact, the salesperson is in a position to present the merchandise and the sales message. How the salesperson should present the merchandise depends on the customer. Because customers are not identical, the salesperson's presentations should not be identical; instead, they should be tailored to the individual circumstances. Toyota trains its sales associates to tailor a presentation to the customer's specific interest—or "hot button"—for example, aerodynamics and styling. In making sales presentations consider the following guidelines.

Learn Needs and Wants To know what merchandise to show, the salesperson must learn what the customer needs and wants. Asking key questions and listening attentively help the salesperson determine what merchandise the store has that might meet those needs and wants. Questions allow the salesperson to (1) discover important information that is useful in closing the sale, (2) demonstrate genuine interest in the customer, (3) move the customer toward active involvement in the sales process, (4) correct any misconceptions about the product or the store, and (5) develop rapport with the customer. Figure 12–8 provides guidelines in how to ask questions. The salesperson must closely observe the customer's reactions to each piece of merchandise shown to determine the level of product interest; that is, whether the product is a "must have," "should have," or "would be nice to have" item. Because customer need satisfaction is a goal of the retailer, determining customer needs and wants is a logical first step in presenting and selling merchandise.

Reduce Risks and Uncertainties Customers run the risk that the product they buy might not perform correctly, might fall apart or break down, might embarrass them in a social setting (a "gold" necklace chain turns the neck green), or might be unsafe. These concerns are particularly strong for high-cost items; refrigerators, washers, cars, sets of tires, houses, and television sets represent substantial outlays of money and therefore risk. Perceived risk takes the form of financial, physical, or social risk. Therefore,

Figure 12–8

How to ask questions

Source: Nido R. Quebein, "The Power of Asking Questions," Personal Selling Power *(January/February 1988): 20–21.*

1. Start with broad questions and move toward narrower questions. Broad, open-ended questions are less threatening than narrow, specific questions.
2. Listen to everything the customer says.
3. Keep questions simple and focused. Use one idea at a time.
4. Ask sensitive questions in a nonthreatening way (e.g., "How much were you planning to spend? not "How much can you afford?"). If you must ask a very personal question, always explain why.
5. Always ask questions that are easy to answer! Studies show that people would rather answer a question when they agree than voice their objections.
6. Turn the statements your customer makes into questions to clarify or reinforce feelings, "So, Tuesday would be best for you, is that right?"
7. Use questions to develop the presentation! "You mentioned that your present car needs repairs. What types of repairs does it need?" Explain the advantages of a new car.
8. Use caution when leading clients with questions. Always respect the intelligence of your prospect.
9. Use questions to give information. "Are you aware of our 90-days same as cash policy?"

products with high perceived risk must be accompanied by assurances of satisfactory performance. The salesperson should stress the manufacturer's warranty, the retailer's money-back guarantee, the retailer's in-house repair facilities, the dependable brand name, and so on. This selling situation might also be an opportunity for the salesperson to trade up the customer to higher-quality merchandise to reduce perceived risk and thus make the sale.

Demonstrating Products and Features Some products lend themselves to demonstration better than others, but virtually all products can be demonstrated somehow. Demonstrating the merchandise means the customer sees the product in action—its features, benefits, and possible advantages.

While demonstrating the product, the salesperson should point out the unique features and benefits to reinforce what the customer is seeing. A product can often sell itself, particularly if the salesperson helps a little. Demonstrations can also help reduce some customers' perceived risk in purchasing the product. BMW is currently experimenting with saving prospective buyers time by dropping off demonstrator cars for test drives at the prospect's home or office.

Selling Benefits and Solutions What all manufacturers, retailers, and salespeople must realize is that they do not sell physical products but the physical, social, and psychological *benefits* they provide consumers. People do not buy lawn mowers—they buy trim lawns. People do not buy 1/4-in. drill bits—they buy 1/4-in. holes. Customers buy, in effect, the end result (the benefit), not the product for the product's sake. Therefore, salespeople should sell benefits.

Invoking Feelings and Senses Get customers actively involved with the product! Have them touch, smell, taste, hear, and feel it. Chances of persuading customers to buy a product improve greatly when they actively interact with it. A good salesperson points out how the product affects the customer's five senses. ("Smell the manly scent of this cologne." "Taste the rich flavour of this coffee." "Feel the softness of this sweater.") The more of the customer's senses a salesperson can stimulate, the greater the chance of a sale.

Promoting Understanding and Comprehension Too often salespeople present merchandise in technical terms and phrases that the average customer does not understand. As a result, many customers are frightened off or confused and a sale is lost. Good salespeople present the product message in words that are clear and understandable to the customer. The salesperson must be ready to adapt quickly to each consumer's level of understanding and sophistication. Sometimes the salesperson must use analogies and speak simply; for other customers, the salesperson might engage in technical conversation. The sales message level should be geared to the customer's product knowledge level. Thus, a "golden rule" is to communicate the message at the customer's level of understanding and knowledge.

Handling the Objection

Consumers who do not purchase a product immediately after the merchandise presentation are likely to have perceived "stumbling blocks," objections to buying the product. Sales associates must anticipate objections and know how to handle each type. Handling objections requires that the associate first identify the basis of the objection and then attempt to overcome the customer's objection.

Identifying the Objection Customer objections are a natural part of the retail selling process. The retail sales associate should not be put off by these natural reservations to buying; instead, these concerns should be viewed as an additional opportunity to sell. But before continuing on the selling process, the associate must first clearly understand the nature of the customer's objection.

Product Objections. Some consumers think the product is just not right for them. It is too big, too small, too heavy, too light, does not look right on them, is too simple, too complex, or one of a host of other objections. The salesperson must be creative and adaptable in handling objections. If the customer says, "This does not look right on me," he or she probably means, "My friends (family, coworkers, boss, and so on) would not like it." A creative salesperson counters with reasons why the customer's reference groups might well approve of this merchandise. This approach reinforces the customer's self-image and gives supporting approval from others for making the purchase.

Price Objections. Price is a common customer objection that takes two forms. First, the customer really wants the product but does not have the cash to pay for it. In this case, the salesperson can emphasize the store's easy credit terms. In other cases, the customer does not consider the product worth the price; for these customers, the salesperson must emphasize the product value, perhaps by mentioning that competitors' prices are about the same even though their products do not have comparable features, warranties, or guarantees.

Store Objections. Customers might not like the store itself. An advertisement or a display caught their eye, they came into the store and saw something they liked, but they usually do not shop in this store or "a store like this" and therefore feel uncomfortable buying here. To meet this kind of objection, the salesperson must assure customers of the integrity of the store, its management, and its merchandise.

Figure 12–9

Objection handling techniques

Source: Ronald B. Marks, Personal Selling *(Boston: Allyn & Bacon), 326.*

Method	When to use	How to use
Head-on	With objections arising from incorrect information	Salespeople directly, but politely, deny the truth of the objection; to avoid alienating prospects, it is helpful to offer proof
Indirect denial	With objections arising from incorrect information	Salespeople never directly tell prospects that they are wrong, but still manage to correct the mistaken impression
Compensation	With valid objections, but where compensating factors are present	Salespeople agree with prospects initially, but then proceed to point out factors that outweigh or compensate for the objection (for this reason, it is often called the "yes, but" technique)
"Feel, felt, found"	With emotional objections, especially when prospects have retreated from their adult ego states, and when the prospect fails to see the value of a particular feature and benefit	Salespeople express their understanding for how prospects feel, indicate that they are okay since others have also felt that way, but have found their fears to be without substance
Boomerang	When the objection can be turned into a positive factor	Salespeople take the objection and turn it into a reason for buying
Forestalling	With any type of objection	From prior experience, salespeople anticipate an objection and incorporate an answer into the presentation itself, hoping to forestall the objection from ever coming up

Timing Objections. Putting the purchase off (timing) is another objection salespeople frequently encounter. Customers might not know exactly why they do not want to buy now; they just do not. Customers usually use the "timing" objection to conceal their real objections. Thus, this type of objection is difficult for salespeople to handle, because they do not understand its underlying motives. Handling this objection is "groping in the dark." Nevertheless, the salesperson can emphasize the need to buy immediately ("The sale ends today at this extraordinarily low price," or "There are only a few left in stock"). Any statement indicating the urgency to buy now might overcome this objection.

Salesperson Objection. One last possible customer objection can be to the salesperson. Shifty eyes, long hair, short hair, conservative dress, wild dress, garlic on the breath, or any number of other "faults" may turn away a customer. Whatever the reason, the salesperson is often unlikely to detect it. If the salesperson guesses that this is the objection, he or she should direct the customer's attention to the product—its benefits, its advantages, or its need-fulfilling capacities—or turn the sale over to another salesperson.

Overcoming the Objection Overcoming a customer objection should be a natural, nonconfrontational process that permits customers to reduce the risk and uncertainty of making a buying decision while increasing the sales associate's chances of closing the sale. The right technique for offsetting customer reservations will depend on the type of objection, the nature of the selling situation, the personalities of the parties involved, and the chemistry of their relationship. Figure 12–9 summarizes techniques for handling customer objections in terms of what method to use, when to use it, and how to use it.

Closing the Sale

Timing the Close Closing the sale (suggesting that the customer make the purchase) is the "natural" conclusion to the selling process. Timing in the closing stage, however, is critical. Customers often provide verbal or physical (body language) cues that suggest

Figure 12–10

Customer closing cues

Physical cues provided by customers

1. The customer closely re-examines the merchandise under consideration.
2. The customer reaches for his or her wallet or purse.
3. The customer samples the product for the second or third time.
4. The customer is nodding in agreement as the terms and conditions of sale are explained.
5. The customer is smiling and appears excited as he or she admires the merchandise.
6. The customer intensely studies the service contract.

Verbal cues provided by customers

1. The customer asks "Do you offer free home delivery?"
2. The customer remarks "I always wanted a pair of Porsche sunglasses."
3. The customer inquires "Do you have this item in red?"
4. The customer states "This ring is a real bargain."
5. The customer exclaims "I feel like a million bucks in this outfit!"
6. The customer requests "Can you complete the installation by Friday?"

they might be ready to make a purchase. Figure 12–10 identifies several physical and verbal cues for potential closing opportunities. In timing the closing, the salesperson must adapt to the individual customer and circumstances. Some customers do not want to be rushed into making the final decision; others do not want to wait too long to have the salesperson begin to close. Still other customers do not know how to make the decision or will not make the decision without help. These people need someone to make decisions for them. In other cases, customers definitely make up their own minds and do not want to be pushed. In dealing with customers like these, the salesperson can remind them of their need and of how the merchandise meets that need, restate the advantages and benefits of the merchandise, and explain why they must buy now and not put off the decision.

Figure 12–11

Customer closing techniques

Technique	Definition	Example
Direct close	The salesperson asks the customer directly for the order	"Can I write this order up for you?"
Assumptive close	The salesperson assumes the customer is going to buy and proceeds with completing the sales transaction	"Would you like to have this gift wrapped?"
Alternative close	The salesperson asks the customer to make a choice in which either alternative is favourable to the retailer	"Will this be cash or charge?"
Summary/ agreement close	The salesperson closes by summarizing the major features, benefits, and advantages of the product and obtains an affirmative agreement from the customer on each point	"This dishwasher has the features you were looking for"—YES "You want free home delivery"—YES "It is in your price range"—YES "Let's write up the sale."
Balance-sheet close	The salesperson starts by listing the advantages and disadvantages of making the purchase and closes by pointing out how the advantages outweigh the disadvantages	"This dishwasher is on sale; it has all the features you asked for, you have 90 days to pay for it without any financial charges, and we will deliver it free. Even though we cannot deliver it until next week, now is the time to buy."
Emotional close	The salesperson attempts to close the sale by appealing to the customer's emotions (love, fear, acceptance, recognition)	"The safety of your children could well depend on this smoke alarm. Now is the time to get it installed."
Standing-room-only close	The salesperson tries to get the customer to act immediately by stressing that the offer is limited	"The sale ends today." "This is the last one we have in stock."

Attempting the Close Skilled salespeople have developed several closing techniques that move the customer toward the purchase decision. After the customer has examined several pieces of merchandise, for example, the salesperson usually can determine which one or two items the customer prefers. To avoid confusing the customer and aid in drawing the final decision, the salesperson should put away the less preferred items. If the customer has tried on seven rings, the five or six least preferred rings should be put back in their cases. "I can tell this is the one you really like the most," the salesperson might say. "May I wrap this for you? Will this be cash or charge?" Figure 12–11 identifies seven of the more common closing techniques.

Enhancing the Sale Another aspect of closing a sale is to show customers other merchandise that complements the item they are going to buy. This technique is called **suggestive selling**. If the customer is buying a sport coat, the salesperson can suggest a shirt and tie that are a "perfect" match for the coat. Suggestive selling is a service to customers who might not have thought of purchasing complementary items to enhance the appearance or use of their intended purchase. Both customers and salespeople can benefit from suggestive selling when the additional items represent true benefits for the customer.

Developing Goodwill Next, the salesperson must perform several *administrative* tasks in closing the sale, such as ringing up the sale on the cash register, checking the accuracy of the customer's address; verifying the customer's credit card; and boxing, bagging, or wrapping the merchandise. Finally, closing the sale is not complete until the salesperson has said thank you, asked the customer to come back, and said good-bye. This phase in closing the sale is called "developing goodwill," and repeat business depends on it.

Following Up the Sale

A good salesperson continues to sell the customer after the sale. The sale is not over after the customer has walked out the door. Many customers are happy about their purchases at the time they buy them but later begin to doubt the wisdom of their buying decision. The "doubt" phase usually affects consumers who have made a substantial investment of time, effort, and money. A salesperson might follow up the sale by assuring customers they have made the right decision, the merchandise is of good quality, their friends and relatives will approve, and the store and manufacturer back the merchandise.

Summary

High-quality customer service is vital to the success of any retail operation in the 1990s. Customer service involves all the features, acts, and information that augment the customer's ability to realize the potential value of a core product or service. Service quality is the difference between customer service expectations and what service the customer actually received. Retailers must not only be concerned with what services to offer but equally with how well each service is provided.

Customer service levels for service features (for example, returns, deliveries) can be described as essential, expected, or optional. Low-service level retailers (for example, self-service) provide only essential services, while high-service level retailers (for example, full-service) offer all three types of service: essential, expected, and optional. Customer service actions (for example, friendliness, reliability) can be evaluated on a rating scale of unacceptable to exceptional.

Customer service objectives direct the efforts of the retailer's service program. Some common service objectives include increasing form, time, place, and possession utility; enhancing customer convenience and security; improving store image, traffic, and competitive positions; as well as building specific demand for the retailer's core products and services.

Customer service features include all those "extras" that enhance the core product and service offering. Store hours, credit, delivery, alterations and repairs, wrapping, and complaint resolution are the more common service features in most retail service programs. The five actions to ensure exceptional customer service actions are research, development, communication, execution, and management.

Personal selling is a communication process between salesperson and customer. Retail sales personnel can be classified as order processors, order takers, or order getters, depending on the degree of their involvement with the selling process. Effective communication is a two-way process in which both members actively exchange ideas and meanings. Successful salespeople exhibit certain personal attributes (physical and personality) and individual traits (expertise, credibility, positive attitude, listening skills, similarity, and adaptability). In addition, they are capable of making effective presentations with the right message strategy, positioning, and appeal that ensure customer participation and decision.

Steps in the retail selling process are (1) identifying the prospects, (2) contacting the customer, (3) presenting the merchandise, (4) handling objections, (5) closing the sale, and (6) following up the sale. A good salesperson prepares well for the sale even before greeting the customer, then adapts throughout the sale to each customer and set of store circumstances as they arise at the time.

Student Study Guide

Key Terms and Concepts

affinity cards *p. 457*
bagging *p. 459*
centralized complaint system *p. 461*
cobranding cards *p. 457*
customer assistance *p. 447*
customer service *p. 449*
decentralized complaint system *p. 461*
deferred billing *p. 457*
essential services *p. 450*
expected services *p. 450*
fixed-term revolving credit *p. 458*
full-service retailer *p. 451*
gift wraps *p. 459*
in-house credit system *p. 456*
in-store delivery *p. 460*
independent delivery *p. 460*
installment credit *p. 457*
limited service *p. 450*
losing service retailers *p. 452*
open account credit *p. 457*
optional services *p. 451*
optional-term revolving credit *p. 458*
order getters *p. 464*
order processors *p. 463*
order takers *p. 464*
personal communication *p. 463*
personal selling *p. 463*
personal shopper *p. 459*
posttransaction services *p. 459*
pretransaction services *p. 455*
private-label credit system *p. 457*
relationship retailing *p. 448*
revolving credit *p. 458*
salesperson–customer similarity *p. 466*
self-service *p. 450*
service features *p. 455*
service quality *p. 451*
store wrap *p. 459*
suggestive selling *p. 475*
third-party credit system *p. 457*
three C's of credit *p. 458*
transaction services *p. 456*
winning service retailers *p. 452*

Review Questions

1. Distinguish between a customer service feature and a customer service action.
2. Describe the various types of service levels for customer service features.
3. List some examples of customer service actions.
4. Identify the services the retailer should offer to increase form utility.
5. Provide an example of how a retailer builds specific demand using a service.
6. What are pretransaction services? List and briefly describe them.
7. Identify the two chief disadvantages for retailers that accept third-party credit cards.
8. Does a private-label credit system differ from in-store and third-party systems? How?
9. Briefly describe the three types of credit plans.
10. List the three C's of credit and describe each.
11. Characterize the three basic types of wrapping services.
12. Identify the major product-, service-, and customer-related causes of complaints.
13. How are personal selling and personal communications related?
14. How do order processors, order takers, and order getters differ?
15. Describe the role of salesperson expertise and credibility in the selling process.

16. How can a salesperson improve listening skills?

17. Does salesperson–customer similarity affect the selling process? How?

18. When should a salesperson use a one-sided sales message? When is a two-sided sales message appropriate?

19. Where should the strongest selling points be positioned within a sales message?

20. Should the salesperson draw conclusions for the customer? Are there any exceptions?

21. What should the retail salesperson sell?

22. What are the most common methods for handling customer objections? Give an original (non–textbook) example of each technique.

23. When should a salesperson attempt to close a sale?

24. Describe the various types of closing techniques available to the salesperson, with an original example of each.

Review Exam

True or False

_____ 1. Expected services are basic and necessary to a particular retail operation.

_____ 2. Consumer credit, layaway, and extended store hours are all services directed at the service objective of increasing form utility.

_____ 3. One acceptable alternative for handling customer complaints about insufficient selection of merchandise is to direct the customer to a store that stocks the desired product.

_____ 4. Customers are persuaded more by a salesperson they perceive to be similar to themselves.

_____ 5. When consumers are not knowledgeable about the product, the general rule is to present them with a two-sided message.

_____ 6. "The sale ends today" is a good example of the standing-room-only close.

Multiple Choice

_____ 1. Customer service _____ deals with the issue of how well a retailer is providing a given service.
a. feature
b. optional
c. quality
d. weapon
e. none of the above

_____ 2. Product warranties, return privileges, and maintenance contracts are all services directed at _____.
a. enhancing place utility
b. increasing form utility
c. increasing store traffic
d. facilitating time utility
e. providing customer security

_____ 3. Close rapidly, avoid oversell, avoid over-talk, and note key points is what salespersons should say or do when dealing with a(n) _____.
a. doubting Thomas
b. look around
c. impulsive
d. procrastinator
e. hesitant

_____ 4. In selling merchandise, salespeople should place their strongest selling points at the _____.
a. beginning
b. middle
c. end
d. a and b
e. a and c

_____ 5. Retail salespeople should use the indirect denial method for handling objections _____.
a. arising from incorrect information
b. arising from valid objections but where compensation factors are present
c. that can be turned into a positive factor
d. that are largely emotional
e. of any type

_____ 6. In following up a sale, the more effective method in reducing a customer's post-purchase doubt is:
a. writing a letter to the customer
b. telephoning the customer
c. making a personal visit to the customer
d. all of the above are equally effective

Student Application Manual

Investigative Projects: Practice and Application

1. Develop a comprehensive list of potential customer service features for each of the following retailers: (a) a chain discount store, (b) a supermarket, and (c) a high-fashion boutique. For each retailer and list of features, classify each service on the basis of its importance (essential, expected, or optional) to the retailer's typical customer. Justify your classification.
2. Review the retail service objectives; then, for each of the following retailer firms, rank the objectives in order of their importance to the retailer success: (a) a Canadian Tire store, (b) a Radio Shack electronics store, (c) a 7-Eleven convenience store, and (d) a Sears department store. Justify your rankings.
3. Interview three local retailers, and profile their customer complaint resolution system. Compare and contrast the three systems. Which system is the most effective? Why?
4. Salespeople can make a sales presentation using either a one- or two-sided message. Select a specific product (that is, a specific brand, style, model, and size), and develop a sales presentation using a two-sided message.
5. Discuss the statement "Retail selling is essentially a problem-solving situation; that is, customers are looking for solutions to problems, not products." If this problem-solving theory of retail selling is true, how should a retail salesperson approach the selling situation?

Endnotes

1. Dick Schaaf, *Keeping the Edge, Giving Customers the Service They Demand* (New York: Dutton, 1995), 87.
2. Craig Hamilton, "Best Practices—Fast Track to Results," *Retailers on Retailing, Lessons from the School of Experience* (Arthur Andersen & Co., 1994), 156.
3. Stanley Marcus, "Fire a Buyer and Hire a Seller," *Retailers on Retailing, Lessons from the School of Experience* (Arthur Andersen & Co., 1994), 62.
4. David Estok, "Trouble in Store," *Maclean's*, August 12, 1996, 30–32.
5. Sean Silcoff, "The Emporiums Strike Back," *Canadian Business*, September 26, 1997, 58.
6. John Heinzl, Patricia Lush, "Shoppers' Views Vary On Eaton's," *Globe and Mail*, March 1, 1997, B4.
7. John Lorinc, "Road Warriors," *Canadian Business*, October 1995, 36.
8. Patricia Sellers, "How to Remake Your Sales Force," *Fortune*, May 4, 1992, 98–103.
9. Diane Lucklow, "Better Selling Through Technology," *Profit*, December 1994, 43.
10. James M. Carman, "Consumer Perceptions of Service Quality: An Assessment of the SERVQUAL Dimensions," *Journal of Retailing*, 66 (Spring 1990): 33–56.
11. Brian S. Lunde, "When Being Perfect Is Not Enough," *Marketing Research: A Magazine of Management & Applications* (Winter 1993): 24.
12. See Syed Saad Andaleeb and Amiya K. Basu, "Technical Complexity and Consumer Knowledge as Moderators of Service Quality Evaluation in the Automobile Service Industry," *Journal of Retailing*, 70 (Winter 1994): 367–81.
13. Michael Silverstein, "World-Class Customer Service Builds Consumer Loyalty," *Marketing News*, August 19, 1991, 11.
14. William H. Davidow and Bro Uttal, *Total Customer Service—The Ultimate Weapon* (New York: Harper & Row, 1989), 22. Also see Debbie Withers, "Customers Define Customer Service," *Marketing News*, April 24, 1995, 8.
15. Sharon E. Beatty, "Relationship Selling in Retailing," *Retailing Issues Letter* (copublished by the Center for Retailing Studies, Texas A&M University and Arthur Andersen, November 1993), 2. Also see Duane L. Davis, Joseph P. Guiltinan, and Wesley H. Jones, "Service Characteristics, Consumer Search, and the Classification of Retail Services," *Journal of Retailing*, 55 (Fall 1979): 3–23.
16. See Harry Rosen Stores Homepage: www.cipa.com.win.win08.htm; Susan Reda, "Seven Keys to Better Service," *Stores* (January 1996): 34.
17. Richard Gibson, "Location, Luck, Service Can Make a Store Top Star," *Wall Street Journal*, February 1, 1993, B1.
18. A. Parasuraman, Valarie A. Zeithaml, and Leonard L. Berry, "SERVQUAL: A Multiple-Item Scale for Measuring Customer Perceptions of Service Quality," *Journal of Retailing*, 64 (Spring 1988): 12–40.
19. See J. Joseph Cronin, Jr., and Steven A. Taylor, "Measuring Service Quality: A Reexamination and Extension," *Journal of Marketing*, July 1992, 55–68; Terence A. Oliva, Richard L. Oliver, and Ian C. MacMillan, "A Catastrophe Model for Developing Service Strategies," *Journal of Marketing* (July 1992): 83–95; Ahmed Taher, Thomas W. Leigh, and Warren A. French, "Augmented Retail Services: The Lifetime Value of Affection," *Journal of Business Research*, 35 (March 1996), 217–28; and Steven A. Taylor and Thomas L. Baker, "An Assessment of the Relationship between Service Quality and Customer Satisfaction in the Formation of Consumers' Purchase Intentions," *Journal of Retailing*, 70 (Summer 1994): 163–78.
20. Thomas A. Stewart, "After All You've Done for Your Customers, Why Are They Still Not Happy?" *Fortune*, December 11, 1995, 180.
21. Ric Swihart, "U.S. Parent Firms Pushing Retail Service," *Lethbridge Herald*, September 5, 1995, B4.

22. A. Parasuraman et al., "SERVQUAL," 12–40.

23. A. Parasuraman, Leonard L. Berry, and Valarie A. Zeithaml, "Refinement and Reassessment of the SERVQUAL Scale," *Journal of Retailing*, 67 (Winter 1991): 420–50.

24. George A Rieder, "Show Me: The Secret to Building a Service-Minded Culture," *Retailing Issues Letter* (Center for Retailing Studies, Texas A&M University, June 1986), 1.

25. *Ibid.*

26. Kristan Davis, "How to Get the Service You Deserve," *Kiplinger's Personal Finance Magazine* (February 1992): 48.

27. *Ibid.*

28. William Stern, "Trading Celery for Oil Filters," *Forbes*, January 17, 1994, 69. Also see Gary Robins, "AutoZone System Puts Focus on Customer Service," *Stores* (October 1995): 65–66.

29. Faye Brookman, "Clover Grabs Commuters with Snappy New Design," *Stores* (October 1995): 49–50.

30. John Heinzl, "Books, Bach, and Beer," *Globe and Mail*, September 4, 1997, B1.

31. Bill Jacobs, "Operating Stores," *Chain Store Age Executive* (January 1994): 23MH.

32. Ijeome Ross, "Harry Rosen Adds A New Page To Fashion Pitch," *Globe and Mail*, August 26, 1997, B12; Ijeome Ross, "Levi Strauss Companies Relax Their Dress Codes," *Globe and Mail*, August 26, 1997, B12.

33. See Anne Kalosh, "The Love Boats Are Brawling," *Business Week*, May 1, 1995, 140; Matt Walsh, "You Gotta Believe," *Forbes*, November 21, 1994, 68–70; Ian P. Murphy, "Cruise Lines Float Hopes on First-Time Customers," *Marketing News*, January 1, 1996, 2; and Jeffery D. Zbar, "Cruise Ships Eye First-Timers," *Advertising Age*, January 22, 1996, 12.

34. Richard Wright, "Battle Plan," *Profit*, March 1994, 26.

35. Chad Rubel, "Longer Closing Hours Are Here to Stay," *Marketing News*, January 2, 1995, 22. Also see Carol Felker Kaufman and Paul M. Lane, "Shopping 24 Hours a Day: A Consumer Need or a Losing Strategy?" *Journal of Shopping Center Research*, 1 (Fall 1994): 81–160.

36. Patricia A. Murphy, "Sears Revives Credit Card Business," *Stores* (February 1996): 57.

37. Robert E. Calem, "Coming to a Cash Register Near You: Multimedia," *The New York Times*, July 31, 1994, 7.

38. Tara Parker-Pope, "New Devices Add Up Bill, Measure Shoppers' Honesty," *The Wall Street Journal*, June 6, 1995, B1.

39. Silcoff, "The Emporiums Strike Back," 56.

40. Michael D. Richard and C. Mitchell Adrian, "A Segmentation Model of Consumer Satisfaction/Dissatisfaction with the Complaint-Resolution Process," *The International Review of Retail, Distribution and Consumer Research* (January 1995): 79–98.

41. See Roland T. Rust, Bala Subramanian, and Mark Wells, "Making Complaints a Management Tool," *Marketing Management* 1 (No. 3, 1992): 40–45.

42. Stephanie Anderson Forest, "Customers Must Be Pleased, Not Just Satisfied," *Business Week*, August 3, 1992, 52.

43. See J. Patrick Kelly, Hugh M. Cannon, and H. Keith Hunt, "Guest Commentary: Customer Responses to Rainchecks," *Journal of Retailing* 67 (Summer 1991): 122–37.

44. Dagdip Singh, "A Typology of Consumer Dissatisfaction Response Styles," *Journal of Retailing*, 66 (Spring 1990): 57–100.

45. See Timothy L. O'Brien, "Unjustified Returns Plague Electronics Makers," *The Wall Street Journal*, September 26, 1994, B1; and "Retailers Strengthen Defenses Against Return Fraud," *Stores* (November 1995): 48–49.

46. J. Barry Mason, "The Art of Service Recovery," *Retailing Issues Letter* (co-published by the Center for Retailing Studies, Texas A&M University, and Arthur Andersen & Co., January 1993), 1.

47. See Rahul Jocob, "Why Some Customers Are More Equal Than Others," *Fortune*, September 24, 1994, 218.

48. Nanette Byrnes, "1993 CEO of the Year—Silver Award Winners," *Financial World*, March 30, 1993, 54.

49. Ronald Henkoff, "Finding, Training, & Keeping the Best Service Workers," *Fortune*, October 3, 1994, 116.

50. See Arun Sharma and Michael Levy, "Categorization of Customers by Retail Salespeople," *Journal of Retailing*, 71 (1, 1995), 71–81.

51. Terri Kabachnick, "Is Salesmanship the Dinosaur of the 90's?" *Retailing Issues Letter* (co-published by Arthur Andersen & Co. and the Center for Retailing Studies, Texas A&M University, May 1991), 3.

52. See Jaclyn Fierman, "The Death and Rebirth of the Salesman," *Fortune*, July 25, 1994, 81.

53. See Willian R. Swinyard, "The Impact of Shopper Mood and Retail Salesperson Credibility on Shopper Attitudes and Behavior," *The International Review of Retail, Distribution, and Consumer Research* (October 1995): 488–503.

54. See William Weitzel, Albert B. Schwarzkopf, and E. Brian Peach, "The Influence of Employee Perceptions of Customer Service or Retail Store Sales," *Journal of Retailing*, 65 (Spring 1989): 27–39.

55. Jennifer M. George, "The Importance of Positive Mood and Its Effects on Customer Service," *Retailing Review*, 1 (2): 7.

56. Harry J. Friedman, *No Thanks, I'm Just Looking* (Dubuque, IA: Kendall/Hunt Publishing Company, 1992); Gregory L. Will, *. . . and It Tastes Just Like Chicken—Endless Retail Sales and Management Success* (Burr Ridge, Il: Irwin Professional Publishing, 1994); and James E. Dion, *Retail Selling Ain't Brain Surgery, It's Twice As Hard* (Toronto: J.C. Williams Group Limited, 1995).

Customer Communications
Creating and Directing Advertising
Sales Incentives Programs

Outline

Retail Promotions
Communication Process
The Promotion Mix

Retail Advertising
Purposes of Advertising
Types of Advertising

The Functional Advertising Plan
Advertising Objectives
Advertising Budget
Advertising Organization

The Creative Advertising Approach
Designing the Advertising Message
Selecting the Communications Approach
Creating the Retail Advertisement
Evaluating the Retail Advertisement

The Media Selection Process
Media Characteristics
Media Alternatives

The Sales Incentive Program
Coupons
Sampling
Premiums
Contests and Sweepstakes
Specialty Advertising
Tie-Ins

The Retail Publicity Program

Summary

Student Study Guide
Key Terms and Concepts
Review Questions
Review Exam

Student Applications Manual
Investigative Projects: Practice and Application

Endnotes

Objectives

To describe the communication process and discuss its impact on retail promotions

To identify and define the three major components of the retailer's promotion mix

To discern the role of retail advertising in attracting, informing, and motivating consumers

To discuss how advertising objectives, budgets, and organizations affect the development of an effective advertising plan

To outline the four stages involved in conceptualizing and implementing a creative advertising approach

To evaluate and select appropriate media alternatives for retail advertisements

To describe how sales incentives attract customers and stimulate consumer purchases

To explain how publicity affects retail operations

Retail Vignette

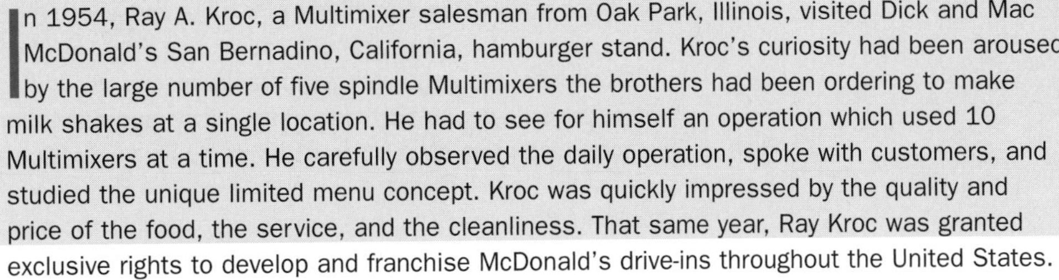

McDonald's Restaurants of Canada Limited

In 1954, Ray A. Kroc, a Multimixer salesman from Oak Park, Illinois, visited Dick and Mac McDonald's San Bernadino, California, hamburger stand. Kroc's curiosity had been aroused by the large number of five spindle Multimixers the brothers had been ordering to make milk shakes at a single location. He had to see for himself an operation which used 10 Multimixers at a time. He carefully observed the daily operation, spoke with customers, and studied the unique limited menu concept. Kroc was quickly impressed by the quality and price of the food, the service, and the cleanliness. That same year, Ray Kroc was granted exclusive rights to develop and franchise McDonald's drive-ins throughout the United States.

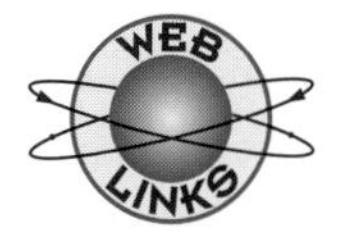

McDonald's
www.mcdonalds.com/main

On April 15, 1955, Ray Kroc opened his first McDonald's in Des Plaines, Illinois. Over six years and 300 restaurants later, Ray Kroc purchased the rights to the McDonald brothers quick service restaurant system and trade name. Kroc had come to realize that there was much more to McDonald's than Multimixers. Today, over 12 000 McDonald's are located in 55 countries, with a new restaurant opening somewhere in the world every 17 hours.

A dedication to a single standard, QSC&V—Quality, Service, Cleanliness, and Value—has made McDonald's the largest food service organization in the world.

Continuing a rapid growth pace, the first McDonald's outside of the U.S. opened in 1967 in Richmond, British Columbia. George A. Cohon, the McDonald's franchise holder for Eastern Canada, soon became convinced McDonald's could flourish in Canada and implemented aggressive marketing programs to develop a strong public profile for McDonald's. In 1972 the East and West operations were amalgamated under McDonald's Restaurants of Canada Limited, with Cohon as President. The Canadian management was given total autonomy to develop the market.

McDonald's soon became the benchmark in the business of franchising; in fact, many people say McDonald's spurred the growth of the industry. By 1990, McDonald's Restaurants of Canada Limited grew to a $1.3 billion business, employing more than 60 000 Canadians and serving an estimated 1.5 million customers a day.

Restaurant design, decor, unique locations, and menu enhancements have evolved along with consumer needs, tastes, and changing lifestyles. McDonald's has always been committed to the communities where they do business and develops restaurants which fit in with local communities' architecture, style, and even history.

Since opening for business in 1955, the driving principles behind McDonald's growth have been good food, served quickly in a clean, friendly environment at a good value. Since then, McDonald's has been keeping pace with the way the world eats. When McDonald's first opened, the limited menu featured hamburgers, fries, soft drinks, and milk shakes. McDonald's innovations over the years reflect changes in customers' tastes and lifestyles. In 1965, Filet-o-Fish was added to the menu, followed by the Big Mac and hot apple pie in 1968. In 1973, McDonald's introduced a quick-service breakfast, in 1984 Chicken McNuggets, and fresh tossed salads in 1988. McDonald's latest menu enhancements include the McLean Deluxe sandwich, low-fat apple bran muffins, whole-grain cereals, low-fat milk shakes and frozen yogurt, and McDonald's pizza.

In 1990, McDonald's Restaurants of Canada and their Soviet Joint Venture partner opened the first McDonald's restaurant in the Soviet Union. A result of almost 14 years of persistent negotiation, planning, and market development, Moscow's McDonald's now serves approximately 50 000 customers a day. The Joint Venture agreement with the food services arm of the Moscow City Council will eventually open 20 McDonald's restaurants.

Because of McDonald's high standards in quality, cleanliness, and value, they are the leader in the quick-service food industry. Quality advertising and marketing programs have been successful in reinforcing McDonald's image. McDonald's ranks as one of the world's largest single-brand advertisers and is one of the five most recognized brand names in the world.

Through local store marketing programs specifically designed to appreciate customers of all ages, advertising, public relations, publicity, and promotions, McDonald's works hard to ensure customers always know they come first at McDonald's.

McDonald's believes putting something back into the communities they serve is good business. Programs such as the Ronald McDonald House, Ronald McDonald Children's Charities, Muscular Dystrophy fund-raisers, and McHappy Days provide McDonald's with opportunities to develop positive community relations with local charities, schools, recreational centres, and civic and business leaders. The spirit of giving back and an unyielding desire to help children in need have become a hallmark for McDonald's along with world-famous hamburgers, french fries, and milk shakes.

Retailers of all types can look to McDonald's for leadership in many facets of retailing as it continues to dominate the quick-service restaurant industry in Canada.

In 1997, McDonald's had Canadian sales of $1.7 billion and employed over 68 000.

Source: Canadian Business Performance 500, June 1997, 154; D. Wesley Balderson and William A. Basztyk, Retailing in Canada, *Prentice Hall Canada Inc., 1994, 374–75.*

More Promotion, Less Advertising

Welcome to the new world of marketing. As recently as a decade ago, selling products was simpler. Companies that wanted to boost sales could drop a few million coupons into local newspapers and watch revenues rise. Or they could buy more advertising time on television and tell themselves that they were building brand equity. No more. Conventional advertising and marketing channels are becoming clogged, and companies are desperately searching for better ways to communicate the value of their products to customers, without going broke in the process. As a result, the art of selling goods is changing faster than the blue-light special at Kmart.[1]

Communications: A Dialogue, Not a Monologue

Communication is a dialogue. When communication is effective both parties gain something. Communicating with customers in the new marketing involves listening as much as talking. It is through dialogue that relationships are built and products are conceived, adapted, and accepted. As all markets begin to look like niche markets with clear infrastructures, the communication process becomes more direct.[2]

Unlike most other businesses, retailers do not generally take their product to market. Instead, they rely on consumers to take the initiative of visiting their stores or placing an order by phone or mail. Most consumers will not take this initiative unless they are in some way motivated to do so. Before consumers will visit a particular store, however, they must be aware of its existence, know its location, and have some idea of what is available inside. They may also want information about prices they must pay, terms of sale they can expect, services available, and store hours in effect. In addition, consumers need to be persuaded that a particular retailer's offering is best suited to their needs. Effective

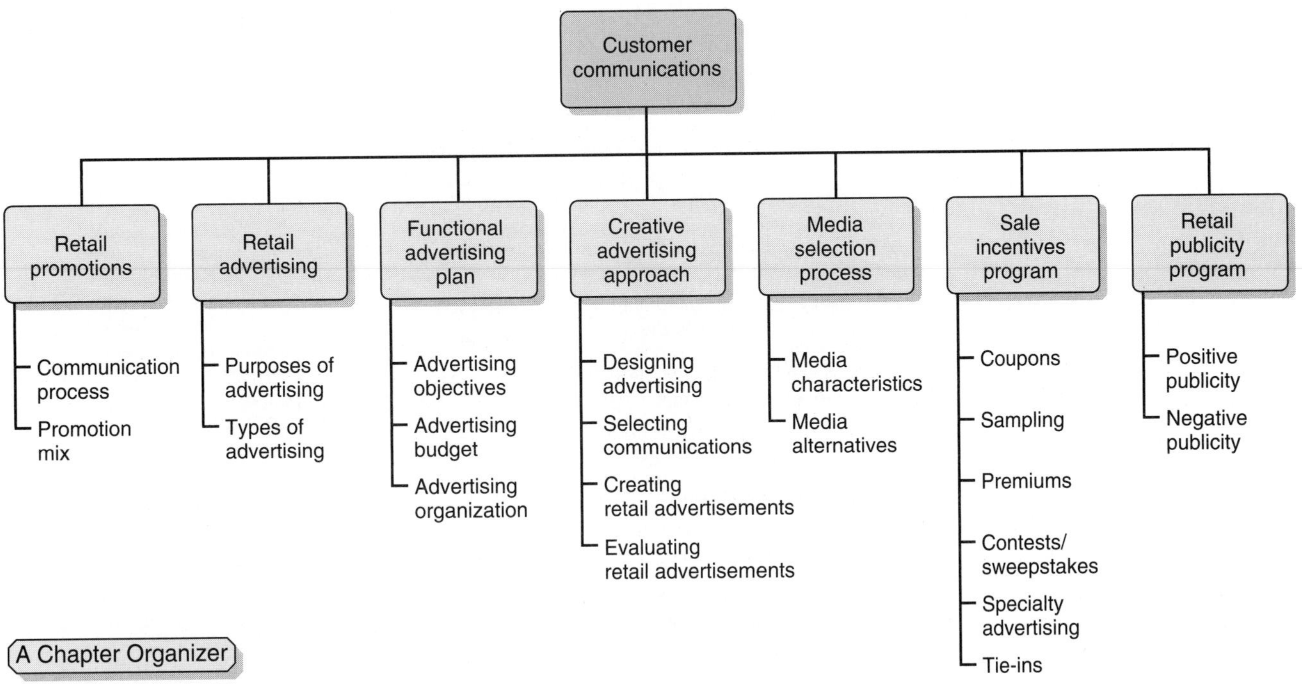

Figure 13–1

Customer communications

retailers supply this information and persuasion, generally through their customer communications program. The basics of that program are outlined in Figure 13–1.

Retail Promotions

Retailers communicate with their customers on a continuous basis, and central to that interaction are the retailer's promotional efforts. **Retail promotions** involve a series of activities that provide consumers with information regarding the retailer's store and its product-service offering; those same activities are also directed at influencing consumer perceptions, attitudes, and behaviour toward the store and what it has to offer. As implied in the definition, promotion is both an informative and persuasive communication process; therefore, it is useful to view the retailer's promotional efforts from the standpoint of the communication process. An understanding of retail promotions requires an examination of both the communication process and the retail promotion mix.

Communication Process

The **communication process** involves transmitting meaningful messages between senders (that is, retailers) and receivers (that is, target consumers). Figure 13–2 illustrates the communication process and its participants (senders and receivers), processes (encoding and decoding), and acts (transmission and feedback).

The source of the communication process is the **sender**—a retailer that wants to inform or persuade a select group of consumers (**receivers**) about the benefits of an idea (for example, lower prices, quality merchandise, high fashion, fast service, contemporary image). Given that the typical consumer encounters an estimated 3000 marketing messages daily, communicating effectively is a difficult and involved task.[3] To be effective, the message must be **encoded** into messages using signs and symbols (for example, words, displays, pictures, gestures) that (1) promote understanding of the idea, (2) attract the

Figure 13–2

The communications process

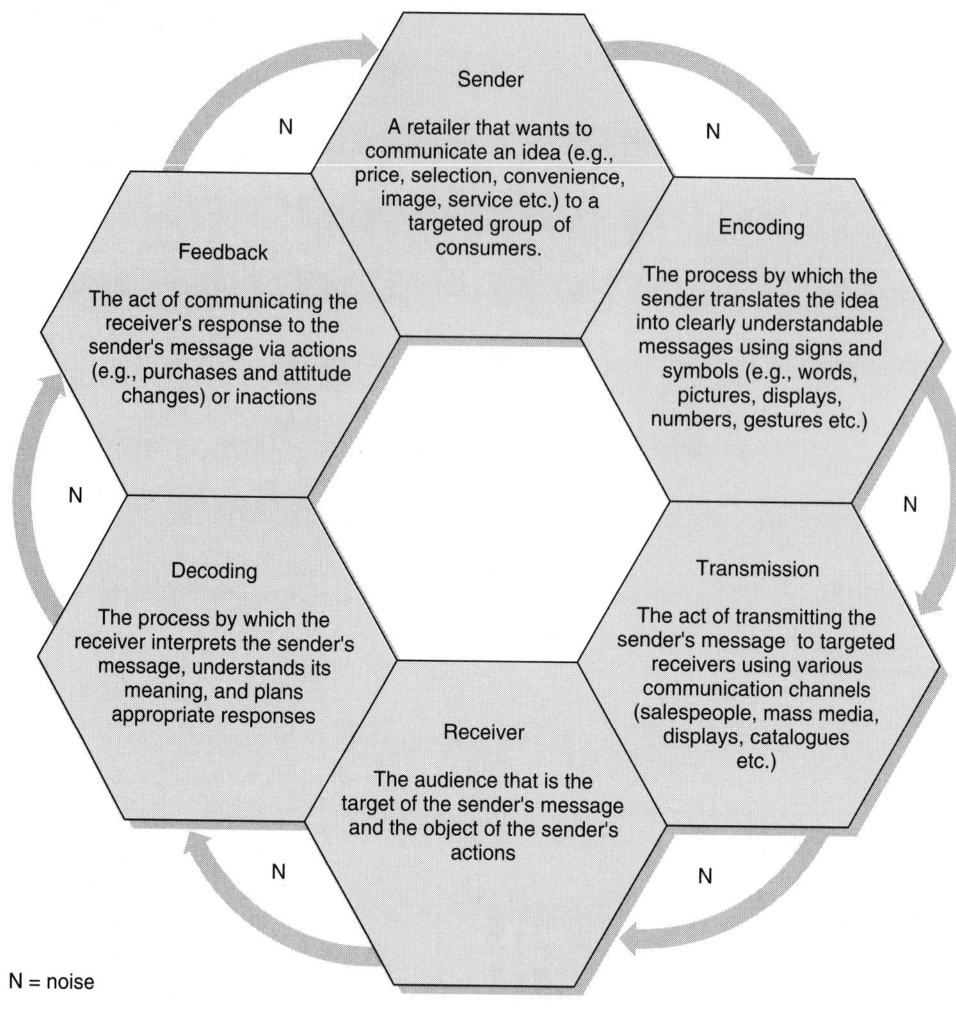

attention of the intended audiences, (3) stimulate needs felt by intended audiences, and (4) suggest a course of action for need satisfaction. Having developed an effective message, the sender must then select the most appropriate communication channel or medium (for example, salespeople, newspapers, magazines, radio, television, direct mail, in-store displays, sales promotions) for **transmitting** the message to consumers targeted as the most suitable recipients of the message. The receiver or target audience is the intended destination of the sender's message and the object of the sender's promotional efforts (for example, creating awareness, generating interest, initiating behavioural change).

The receiver **decodes** the message and interprets its meaning either correctly or incorrectly, depending on how well the message was encoded and the decoder's experience and skill with the communication process. After the decoding process has been completed, the receiver may or may not react (that is, visit the store, phone in an order, or do nothing). The nature of the receiver's response or lack of it is then communicated back to the sender as **feedback**. The information gained through the feedback mechanism is vital in developing and encoding new ideas for future promotions.

A final element in the communication process is **noise**, which is anything that occurs during the communication process that distracts senders or receivers, interferes with the encoding and decoding activity, or interrupts the transmission or feedback process (see Figure 13–2).

The Promotion Mix

The retailer's **promotion** mix blends various combinations of the three basic promotional programs: advertising, sales promotions, and publicity. Personal selling (Chapter 12) and store displays (Chapter 7) also have important promotional implications and are often treated as part of the retailer's promotion mix. (The reader might wish to review those chapters with respect to their promotional impact.)

To develop and implement the promotion mix, retailers use some combination of the following programs together with the retailer's personal selling and store display elements:

- **Advertising**—indirect, impersonal communication carried by a mass medium and paid for by an identified retailer
- **Sales promotions**—direct and indirect impersonal inducements that offer an extra value to consumers
- **Publicity**—indirect, impersonal communication (positive or negative) carried by a mass medium that is neither paid for nor credited to an identified sponsor

Retail Advertising

Retail advertising includes all paid forms of nonpersonal communications about stores, merchandise, service, or ideas by an identified retailer. Its purpose is to favourably influence consumers' attitudes and perceptions about the store, its merchandise, and its activities and to induce sales directly or indirectly. To distinguish it from publicity, advertising is described as a paid form of communication. Advertising is impersonal because the message is delivered through the public medium to many consumers simultaneously, which distinguishes it from personal selling.

Purposes of Advertising

Functionally, advertising has three basic purposes: to inform, persuade, and remind target audiences of the retailer's offering. For the retailer to be effective, consumers must have sufficient information as to what and who the retailer is. *Informative advertising* provides necessary information on the retailer's product mix, operating characteristics, and pricing strategies. *Persuasive advertising* is directed at convincing the consumer that the retailer has the right offer, that it is the best alternative in meeting the consumer's individual needs. Finally, it is important not only to inform and persuade the customer that the retailer has what the consumer needs, but also to communicate continuously the message that the retailer's offering is the most appropriate solution to the consumer's shopping needs—*reminder advertising.*

The Consumer Adoption Model Consumers go through a series of steps, at varying rates, before they are motivated to accept something such as a store or a product and take the action to patronize the business or buy the product they have accepted. Communications theorists have proposed several models of this personal "adoption" process, most of which are similar. The model presented here is known as **DAGMAR** (defining advertising goals for measured advertising results). Developed by Russell Colley, the model describes a sequence of steps through which prospective customers move from total unawareness of a store and its offering to store patronage and purchase (action).

As Figure 13–3 illustrates, several steps intervene between unawareness and action (or store selection). Through advertising, the retailer can help consumers move to *awareness* of the store and its offerings; to *comprehension* or understanding of the store and its image, price structure, services, and so on; to *conviction* or favourable attitudes toward the store.

Figure 13–3

The DAGMAR consumer adoption process

Source: Adapted from Russell H. Colley. Defining Advertising Goals for Measured Advertising Results *(New York: Association for National Advertisers, Inc., 1961), 46–69.*

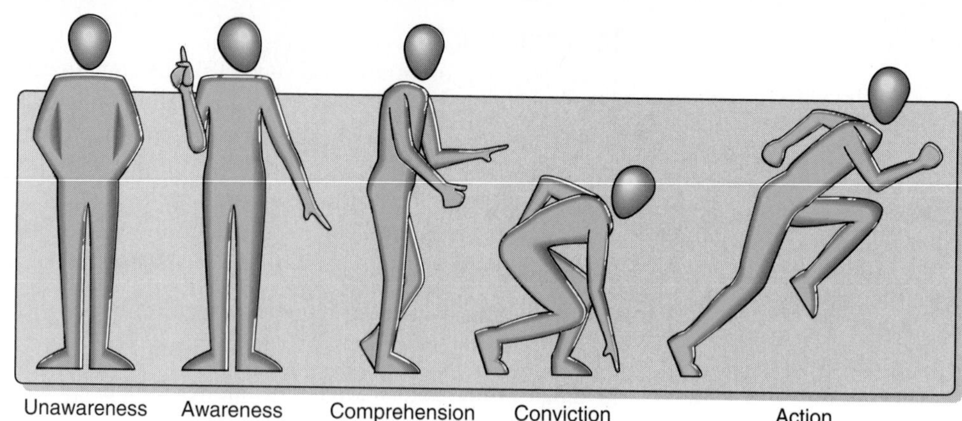

To build awareness and comprehension, each time Wal-Mart enters a new market, it precedes the opening with a "pre-awareness campaign" using television and print advertisements one month before the doors open. When an outlet opens, Wal-Mart does monthly direct mailings and weekly newspaper inserts to obtain continuing favourable consumer response.

The Two-Step Flow of Communication Model Advertising affects a large number of people simultaneously with a single message because of the mass media it uses. Although it is itself a mass form of communication (and therefore impersonal), the ultimate effects of advertising are often magnified by personal communications among consumers. This phenomenon, known as the **two-step flow of communication**, is illustrated in Figure 13–4.

The first step in the process is the communications flow from the media to opinion leaders. **Opinion leaders** are persons whose attitudes, opinions, preferences, and actions affect others. These influentials are a group of trendsetters whose activism and expertise make them the natural source for word-of-mouth referrals. About 10 percent of adults aged 18 years and older can qualify as opinion leaders in one area or another. Opinion leaders (1) are the first to try new products out of curiosity, (2) are activists in their communities, on their jobs, and in the marketplace, (3) are more educated and have higher incomes, (4) are more interested in buying something special, (5) are more likely to study new things, and (6) are in contact with a broad network of people through work, personal life, and community involvement. In short, these influentials are "marketing multipliers" who expand the customer base for products and retailers.[4] The second step is word-of-mouth communications from opinion leaders to others (followers). This communication may occur through personal conversations (a "fashionable" woman tells her friends where she bought her new coat) or through nonverbal personal communications (the friends notice the label in her coat). Word of mouth has a huge potential for spreading the word about a retailer. That word can be either positive or negative.[5]

An implication of the two-step flow theory is that retail advertising should reach opinion leaders. Some methods of working with opinion leaders include (1) creating opinion leaders out of certain persons by supplying them with free merchandise and information; (2) working through influential persons in the community, such as disk jockeys, television personalities, and class presidents; and (3) creating advertising that depicts people having conversations about one's store or products.

Types of Advertising

Retail advertising has two basic purposes: to get customers into the store and to contribute to the store's image. The first purpose is immediacy: today's advertising brings buyers into the store tomorrow. To accomplish this, the store must give buyers some specific reason to come to the store now. Retailers also want long-run, or delayed, results from advertising.

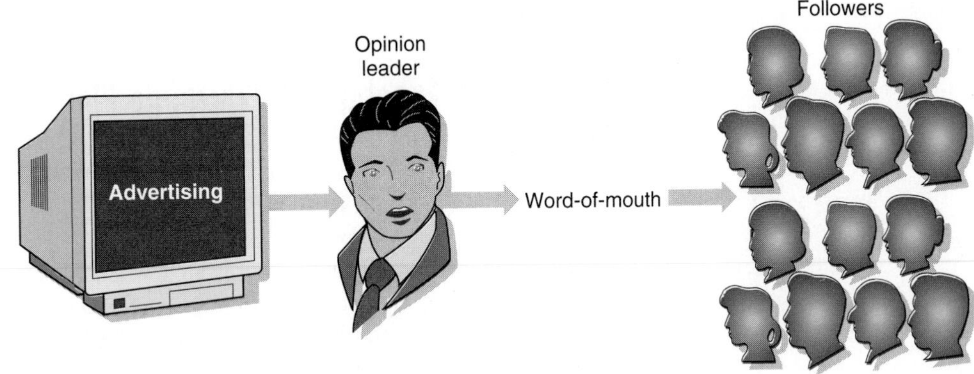

Figure 13–4

The two-step flow of communication

They want customers to know "who" the store is in relation to competitors and the community as a whole. They also want customers to be favourably inclined to shop at the store because of its image. Finally, the retailer must utilize a limited advertising budget in the most efficient manner possible; stretching the ad budget is a goal common to all advertising managers. Accordingly, retailers undertake three kinds of advertising: product, institutional, and cooperative.

Product Advertising **Product advertising** presents specific merchandise for sale and urges customers to come to the store immediately to buy. This indirect form of advertising helps create and maintain the store's reputation through its merchandise. Product advertising themes centre around promoting merchandise that is new, exclusive, and of superior quality and design. With the introduction of the new Infinitred tire, product advertisements for Goodyear tire stores focused on the quality of the tire and its lifetime guarantee.[6] It is often centred around themes relating to complete assortments, good value, and merchandise events. Announcements of sales, special promotions, or other immediate-purpose advertising are other types of product advertising. To force retailers to stock their products, manufacturers build demand by advertising their products so loudly that consumers will ask for the product by name.[7]

Institutional Advertising **Institutional advertising** sells the store generally as an enjoyable place to shop. Lands' End has spent millions to build a brand identity for the term *Lands' End*. Their advertisements rarely feature a product; rather, they sell Lands' End as a retailer with a high-quality image, as an organization that is a good neighbour, and as a company that you would want to do business with. Through institutional advertising, a store helps establish its image as a leader in fashion, prices, wide merchandise selection, superior service, or quality. One study suggests that "companies that put more money behind image advertising are more likely to be market dominators, ranking first in their categories."[8] To "neutralize" the junk food misconception about its food, McDonald's ran a series of magazine ads stressing the nutritional value of its food, as well as several public service spots containing animated lessons in good eating.[9] In reality, practically all of a store's product advertising should communicate its institutional image as well. The art, copy, typography, and logotype of product advertising all help convey store image.

Cooperative Advertising One way a retailer might economically undertake product advertising is to take advantage of **cooperative advertising**.[10] Manufacturers prepare print and broadcast advertising material of their own products and allow the retailer to insert its store name and address in the ad; then the manufacturer and retailer split the cost of media space or time to run the ad. Usually the cost split is 50:50, although the proportions vary.

The Functional Advertising Plan

Like all other retail mix operations, advertising, to be effective, must be done within the framework of an overall plan. The retailer must (1) determine what it wishes to accomplish with its advertising efforts, (2) ascertain the costs of realizing stated objectives, and (3) establish the structure necessary for implementing stated objectives. Figure 13–5 illustrates the key tasks to be completed in developing the functional aspects of an advertising plan.

Advertising Objectives

Objectives—statements of results the retailer wishes to achieve—are the most essential requirement for effective advertising planning. Effective planning is next to impossible

Figure 13–5

The functional advertising plan

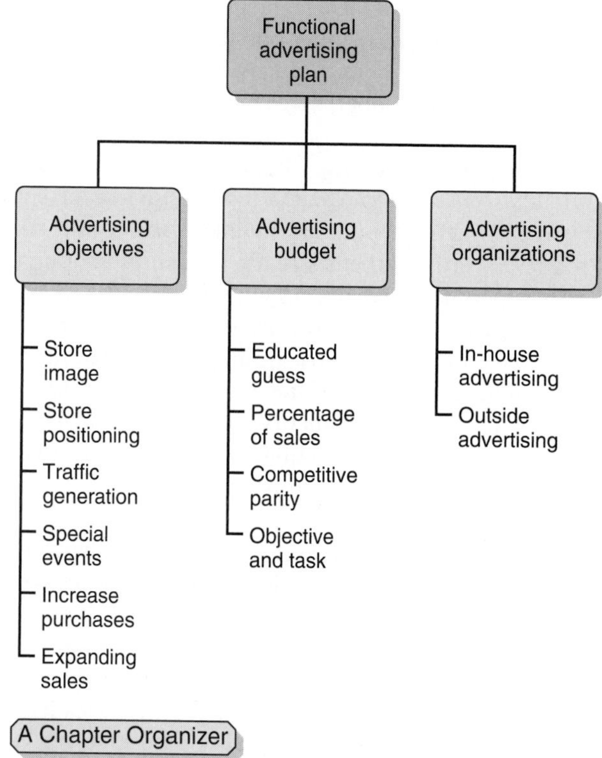

Retail Strategies and Tactics

Advertising Messages by Canadian Retailers Promoting Image

- "The Lowest Price Is the Law"—Zellers
- "Give like Santa. Save like Scrooge"—Canadian Tire
- "Everything You Want in a Store and a Little Bit More"—Sears
- "Scratch and Win"—The Bay
- "You Don't Have to Wait for Sales—We Price It Right the First Time"—Eaton's
- "Satisfaction Guaranteed or Money Refunded"—Eaton's

Source: Collected from the retailers indicated.

without established goals of desired end results. One possible list of advertising objectives might include creating a store image, establishing a store position, generating store traffic, promoting a store event, increasing average purchases, and expanding total sales. The Retail Strategies and Tactics box entitled "Advertising Messages by Canadian Retailers" gives examples of the advertising slogans of some Canadian retailers which illustrate various objectives.

Creating a Store Image To acquire and keep regular customers, every store must be thought of as unique in some way by its target market. The retailer may wish to establish an image by size (large), merchandise specialization (antique furniture store), clientele ("designer" lines for "discriminating" shoppers), fashion leadership or merchandise quality (always presenting fashion "news"), or price levels (not being undersold on products with well-known prices). Marriott Hotels' advertising slogan "We make it happen for you" is an attempt to portray an image of a service retailer committed to giving guests an outstanding experience.[11] Eddie Bauer, the very successful catalogue retailer, effectively utilizes its outdoor image to attract customers and move merchandise.[12] To reinforce its casual image, Eddie Bauer has opened stores and developed promotions that cater specifically to the causal businesswear customer.[13] Recently Zellers moved to alter its image in the wake of Wal-Mart's entry into Canada through its advertising program (see the Retail Strategies and Tactics box, "Zellers Amends Its Price Law"). Eaton's is also spending heavily on advertising designed to alter its image and set a new direction for the future.[14]

Midas
www.midasfran.com

Establishing a Store Position *Positioning* is a term advertisers use in reference to attempts to get the market to think of the store in a certain way in relation to its competition. Midas has traditionally been viewed by the consuming public as a chain of muffler shops. A new advertising campaign is directed at repositioning Midas as an "auto systems expert" that uses high-tech computers to care for its clients' automobiles.[15] Domino's advertising campaign "For hot and wow call Domino's Pizza now" is a dual strategy designed to position itself as the pizza chain that has the best-tasting pizza with the best delivery system.[16]

Retail Strategies and Tactics

Zellers Amends Its Price Law

When people shop for paper towels or sneakers, they often check out the Wal-Mart or Zellers promotions to find out who's offering the best prices. Such fierce competition has been the law among Canada's major discount department stores. Now it has prompted Zellers Inc. to reconsider—and broaden—its marketing strategy, which is moving ever so subtly upscale.

The chain hopes to establish a niche to differentiate itself from Wal-Mart, while improving profit margins with slightly higher prices on items that Wal-Mart doesn't carry, observers say. One striking signal of the new strategy is Zellers' latest ad campaign, which taps the slogan: "More for less is the law." It's a variation on Zellers' long-running campaign tagline: "The lowest price is the law," which veteran ad man Rick Padulo calls "the best positioning statement in retail by a mile."

The discounter's fall [1996] television spots tell us that "real value means more than a low price." The commercials spotlight such Zellers' assets as the More card and Club Z—with its rewards for frequent purchases—as well as weekly sales. The variety of goods, from women's clothes to sporting goods, are also featured.

Analyst William Chisholm noted that Zellers has always focused more than Wal-Mart on fashion and housewares, such as towels and linens. Now Zellers seems to be shifting a little more to these so-called soft goods, which serve up higher margins. And the chain is offering some products that are not identical to those sold at Wal-Mart. This approach allows Zellers more freedom in its pricing, Mr. Chisholm says.

Source: Marina Strauss, Globe and Mail, *September 12, 1996, B14.*

Generating Store Traffic *Traffic* refers to the number of people who visit the store and how often they visit. In general, the more consumers who visit the store, the greater the store's sales. Retailers generate traffic by providing customers with a special purpose for visiting the store. Traffic builders include sales, "theme" promotions (for example, a bridal seminar), special merchandise showings, and demonstrations. In an attempt to build guest traffic during slow weekends, Hilton Hotels launched its "Bounce Back" ad campaign, in which weekend guests are offered special prices, complementary meals and drinks, and special amenities (for example, free newspapers). The concept behind the program is that pampered guests will be rested and ready for a productive work week.[17] Occasionally Canadian retailers target their competitors' customers with their advertising in an effort to increase store traffic (see the Retail Strategies and Tactics box entitled "Consumers' Customers Wooed"). With better-educated consumers and tighter pocketbooks, apparel retailers in general have focused more on fashion function and less on fashion fluff to build traffic in their stores.[18] Price advertisement is another method for generating customer traffic. Caught between casual-dining chains and fast-food chains (for example, McDonald's, Taco Bell, Burger King), Denny's (a midscale eatery) has resorted to price advertising (for example, Breakaway Values campaign) to build customer counts.[19] The retailer can measure the efforts to produce traffic by actually counting the number of people who enter the store.

Promoting a Store Event Sales-promotion events are planned in advance, oriented around some theme, and coordinated through merchandising, store decoration, and advertising. The event induces a large number of customers to visit the store out of curiosity, many of whom make purchases totally unrelated to the special advertised event. Measurable objectives might be evaluated by head counts or the average number of purchases during the course of the promotion. "Event marketing" is an attempt to integrate the retailer's advertising and promotional efforts with consumer lifestyles.[20] Sears, for example, in its efforts to target the female head of households, promoted women's equality in sports with its "Legends of the Final Four" campaign that ran equally during men's and women's NCAA national championships. The advertising campaign was coordinated with in-store merchandising efforts.[21]

Retail Strategies and Tactics

Consumers' Customers Wooed

Some major retail chains are trying to turn rival Consumers Distributing Inc.'s woes into a windfall. T. Eaton Co. Ltd., one of the country's largest department stores, and People's Jewellers Corp., the biggest jewellery chain, each have launched aggressive advertising blitzes in a bid to lure customers of the bankrupt Consumers with special offers. Canadian Tire Corp. Ltd. of Toronto also plans to appeal to Consumers' shoppers in ads and other promotions, spokesman Alan Goddard said. "We certainly see Consumers Distributing customers as an opportunity."

"Unfortunately another Canadian retailer, Consumers Distributing, is closing its doors," Eaton's president George Eaton says in an open letter that ran as a full-page ad in weekend newspapers across the country. "This is sorry news indeed for the Canadian retail industry. And while Consumers was a competitor of ours, we are saddened to see the loss of a store that tried to offer real value to its customers."

Marketing experts take their hats off to these Toronto-based retailers' initiatives to drum up business, but some question whether the advertising investment—at least \$100 000 in each of the two cases—will pay off, particularly for Eaton's. Retail consultant Richard Talbot noted Eaton's has positioned itself as more of an upscale retailer. "It almost goes against the image they're trying to project," he said of its bid to draw Consumers' customers.

Source: Marina Strauss, Financial Post, *September 25, 1996, B8.*

Increasing Average Purchases Many retailers believe the most fruitful method for expanding sales is to induce present customers to buy more. Retailers can identify present customers by reviewing charge account records, asking customers to register, recording names and addresses from personalized cheques, and other ways. These people have already demonstrated a measure of favour toward the store by buying, so concentrated efforts to induce them to buy more may be one of the greatest potential payoffs to advertising. Most retailers attempt to accomplish this objective by direct-mail invitations to sales or by new merchandise showings.

Expanding Total Sales Advertising is intended to contribute to expanded sales.[22] Some retailers therefore express advertising objectives in terms of sales (for example, increase average monthly sales for the shoe department by 10 percent over last year). In an attempt to generate additional sales from cross-shoppers (for example, a man who buys his suits at a high-end specialty store like Harry Rosen and goes to Wal-Mart for his underwear), Kmart uses ads that depict prosperous-looking women reacting with disbelief when one tells the other she bought her smart outfit from Kmart. The major limitation of such a broad sales objective for advertising is that many factors (for example, prices, merchandise quality) affect sales besides advertising.

Advertising Budget

Executing the advertising campaign requires spending money. Therefore, determining the advertising appropriation is the next step in developing a comprehensive advertising plan. Although many retailers use the terms appropriation and budget synonymously, appropriation refers to the total expenditure for advertising undertaken in a time period, whereas budget refers to the allocation of the total expenditure across departments, merchandise lines, advertising media, and planning periods such as weeks, months, and seasons. Figure 13–6 identifies the five largest national retail advertisers.

Advertising budget allocations are made on the basis of departments, merchandise lines, media, and time periods. At different times, the store will want to feature different items in its product line and de-emphasize promotion of other items. Sears has traditionally supported its hard lines with hefty advertising budgets but has switched its focus to the "softer side of Sears" by advertising apparel, home fashion, and other soft-line goods.[23] Some stores choose to promote high-markup, low-turnover items heavily and de-emphasize lower-markup, high-turnover items. Others may elect to either introduce a new line or achieve a higher market penetration in a given line. The retailer must also determine how much of the total advertising appropriation to devote to each of the media (for example, radio, newspapers) to make those expenditures more efficient. Finally, most retailers advertise more at certain times and less at others. Some advertise extensively before and during heavy buying periods, while others attempt to offset slack periods with heavier advertising.[24] Retailers use the following methods to determine their advertising budgets.

Figure 13–6

Leading Canadian retail advertisers (1993)

Source: Stanley J. Shapiro, William D. Perreault Jr., E. Jerome McCarthy, Basic Marketing, *Eighth Canadian Edition, Times Mirror Professional Publishing Ltd., Toronto, 1996, 515.*

	Firm	Ad spending ($ millions)
1	Eaton's of Canada Ltd.	47.1
2	Sears Canada	46.5
3	McDonald's Restaurants of Canada	35.4
4	Cineplex Odeon Corp.	28.8
5	Canadian Tire Corp. Ltd.	28.5

Educated-Guess Method Some small sole proprietors depend on intuition and practical experience to develop an advertising budget—the **educated-guess method**. The retailer simply looks at the past year's sales and advertising expenditures, determines what it hopes to accomplish this year, considers other necessary expenditures, and chooses an amount to spend on advertising the next year.

Percentage-of-Sales Method Using the **percentage-of-sales method**, the retailer takes a predetermined percentage of either the previous year's sales or the estimated sales for the coming year to calculate how much to spend on advertising. The percentage figure is based on either the "traditional" figure the company has taken in the past, personal "insight," or an industry average. After determining the total advertising budget, the retailer allocates the budget according to sales by departments, merchandise lines, and time periods.

Competitive Parity Method Some retailers set their advertising appropriation as the amount they estimate their most important competitors are spending—the **competitive parity method**. By monitoring the amount of advertising Retailer B is doing and estimating its costs, Retailer A may determine its appropriation and even allocate the appropriation across time periods, media, and merchandise in the same proportions as B. The problem is, the advertising programs and budgets of competitors often have little or no bearing on the advertising needs of another retailer.

Objective and Task Method One of the most logical and appropriate methods of advertising appropriation and budgeting is the **objective and task method**, by which retailers follow a four-step process:

1. Establish the objectives for advertising.
2. Determine the type and amounts of advertising necessary to accomplish these objectives.
3. Determine the overall cost of the advertisement.
4. Schedule the advertisements day by day.

The last step allows for budgeting the total appropriation across media, product lines, and time periods.

Advertising Organization

Day-to-day advertising functions include deciding which products to promote, developing copy and artwork, and scheduling and placing ads in the media. How the store is organized to execute these functions depends on its size and the funds available for specialized personnel to perform the functions. In general, the retailer can handle the advertising function by operating an in-house advertising department or hiring an outside advertising specialist.

In-House Advertising Department Most small and midsize retailers do not have an advertising department. They rely on one or two individuals within the organization to work with media representatives to develop, produce, and schedule advertisements. In contrast, large retail chains are likely to have a complete advertising and sales promotion department. A **sales promotion director** usually is responsible for supervising and coordinating the activities of an advertising manager, a display manager, and a special events, publicity, or public relations coordinator. The **advertising manager** performs all the advertising activities described and supervises an art director, copy chief, and production manager. The **sales promotion manager** works with merchandise managers to develop and coordinate advertising, promotion, and displays with sales and special promotions. Even in the largest chains, in-house advertising production is likely to be print oriented; however, large chains contract with advertising agencies to develop broadcast advertising campaigns.

Outside Advertising Specialists Most large retailers outsource the advertising function to freelancers, advertising agencies, and media representatives. An **advertising freelancer** might be an artist, copywriter, or photographer who produces advertising on a contractual basis. **Media representatives** are the employees of newspapers and radio or television stations whose principal job it is to sell advertising space and time. These specialists also can arrange to produce the retailer's advertisements. Usually, newspapers do not charge for production and take compensation only for the space they sell. Radio stations normally do not charge for production. Television stations generally charge a fee for producing commercials in addition to the air time. Although **advertising agencies** produce the majority of national advertising, all but the largest retail chains make limited use of them.

The Creative Advertising Approach

Few retailers become directly involved in creating advertising. Nonetheless, all must be able to distinguish good, effective advertising from poor, ineffective advertising. This section introduces the basic process of creating advertising. For simplicity, we limit discussion to newspaper advertising, the most common kind of retail advertising.

There are as many processes for creating ads as there are creators of ads. In general, though, the creator of an effective advertisement must take into account the following steps in its development: (1) design the basic message, (2) select the communications approach, (3) create the retail advertisement, and (4) evaluate the retail advertisement.

Two basic elements in persuasive communications such as advertising are *what is said* and *how it is said*—substance and style. Too many advertisers concentrate on style and forget about substance, but the substance must be clear before advertising can be effective.

Designing the Advertising Message

Stipulating the basic **advertising message** is determining what to say. Most retail advertising messages are quite simple: "Ours is a high-fashion store"; "Our women's coats are of highest quality"; "Our meat selection is the best in town." The message should be based on the target customer's wants and needs and the ability of the advertised product to satisfy those wants and needs.[25] If, for example, the advertiser thinks its target customers are concerned not with the quality of a coat but with its social acceptability, then the basic appeal of the message should be "Fashionable women wear this coat," not "This coat will last for five years." Note that both messages stress the *benefit* consumers derive from buying, not the *features* of the coat from which they derive the benefit. Although the retailer's advertisement can point out that a coat has a double-stitched lining (a product feature), the resulting benefit (the lining is unlikely to separate from the coat) is the basic message the retailer should stress. Software retailers have found that advertising that focuses on the usefulness of a program is much more effective than ads that attempt to dazzle the customer with their technical merits.[26]

Selecting the Communications Approach

In determining the **communications approach**, the advertiser turns attention from *what to say* to *how to say it*. Most messages can be effectively communicated by either a rational or an emotional approach. The *rational* approach uses facts, narrative, and logical reasoning to persuade the consumer. The *emotional* approach appeals to the consumer's sense of aesthetics, ego, or feelings. For example, a tire dealer may effectively use a rational

Retail Strategies and Tactics

"New Kid"

The Right Message: How to Say It

Developmental psychologists tell us that the values of narcissism, hedonism, and materialism begin to ebb at the onset of middle age. This does not mean that people begin to spend less. They may spend more, but they do it more selectively and thoughtfully. And they will be turned off by advertising that appeals blatantly to narcissism, hedonism, and materialism.

Target consumers by using emotional cues appropriate to their life stages. Research shows that as people grow older, they are less motivated by emotionally neutral information such as commercials that focus on product attributes and benefits. Commercials that tell mini-stories with gentle humour or human interest are often more effective with older viewers, even if they make no mention of what the product can do.

One of the most successful commercials ever aimed at the mature market was a spot for McDonald's called "New Kid." The commercial showed a white haired, grandfatherly man preparing for his first day at a new job. His wife checks his appearance. He squares his shoulders and walks down a small-town sidewalk to meet his new colleagues—a group of fresh-faced teenagers at the local Golden Arches. The commercial makes older people feel good about visiting McDonald's without telling them anything about a Big Mac.

Source: Vicki Thomas and David B. Wolfe, "Why Won't Television Grow Up?" American Demographics *(May 1995): 29.*

approach to promote snow tires ("You can get there on time—even if you wake up to snow") or it may arouse a husband's fear and protective instincts by depicting a solemn wife and two wide-eyed children under the headline, "Are you sure they'll get home tonight?" Although both approaches can be effective, advertising practitioners believe the emotional approach is more effective.

Creating the Retail Advertisement

After the retailer determines the message and approach, it must develop the retail advertisement. A retail ad generally consists of several components: layout, headline, illustration, copy, and logo or "signature." Although each component has a specific purpose, they work together to accomplish the ad's basic purpose: to motivate the consumer to action. An advertisement's layout, headline, and illustration all work to capture the consumer's attention and to create awareness, and copy is written to gain conviction.

Ad Layout The principal purpose of an ad's **layout** is to capture attention and guide consumers through all parts of the advertisement. Several other layout considerations merit attention. For example, one old advertising rule of thumb is that the principal focal point of the layout should fall five-eighths from the top. Sparse illustrations with lots of white space suggest quality and prestige, whereas cluttered ads suggest discounting and a price appeal.

Ad Headline An ad's **headline** performs several functions besides getting attention. It should motivate the reader to review the remainder of the ad by providing news (Eaton's "After much deliberation we decided we needed to change a little" sale), selecting readers ("Now You Can Get Organized"), and arousing curiosity ("Colour TV for a Dollar a Day! Want to Know More?"). Sears's successful advertising campaign the "softer side of Sears" was followed by the "many sides of Sears" and the "merry side of Sears" for Christmas.[27] In general, the more original or unique the headline, the better. The headline must be coordinated, however, with the remainder of the advertisement's basic message. In fact, the headline condenses the basic advertising message, telling the reader essentially what is to come. McDonald's "You Deserve a Break Today" campaign was designed to communicate the price rollback on many menu items and give the customer more value.[28]

Ad Illustration An **illustration** helps build consumer comprehension. The most common illustration is a drawing or a photograph of the product. The illustration can depict the product alone, isolate certain product features or details, demonstrate how a consumer can derive a benefit from the product, or show the product in context (such as illustrating a sofa in a completely furnished living room) or in use.

Ad Copy The **copy**—what is actually said in the advertisement—helps develop consumer comprehension, conviction, and action. In brief, good advertising copy should be simple and readable yet vivid in word selection; it should be conversational in tone, interesting, enthusiastic, and informative; point out benefits; and suggest action. Effective copy can be either brief or lengthy; however, the chance that anyone will read long copy is remote.

Ad Logo The **logotype**, or logo in common usage, is the store's distinctive "signature" that appears in all advertising. It usually is coordinated with the store's sign, point-of-purchase advertising, labels, shopping bags, and so forth. Done in a distinctive style, script, or type, the logo identifies the store in the consumer's mind in much the same way that a trademark identifies a product or company. A logo is effective when it suggests the store's "character" or the nature of the retailer's merchandise. For example, a women's sportswear store might use a "lazy" script for a logotype, whereas an antique furniture store might choose a gothic-looking script. A good logo communicates the store's personality and product offerings.

Evaluating the Retail Advertisement

To establish some measure of control over its advertising effort, the retailer must evaluate the effects of advertising. The effectiveness of advertising has been called into question in light of the fact that many people who have been brought up on a steady diet of commercials view advertising with cynicism. Advertising appeals are becoming less effective because potential consumers are indifferent to their message and presentation. The retailer must measure results against stated objectives.

Meaningful measurements of **advertising effectiveness** are difficult to make.[29] Assuming that external and internal factors remain relatively stable, the retailer can make a gross measurement of its advertising sales effectiveness in two ways. First, for all advertising messages designed to stimulate immediate sales (such as coupons, half-price sales, and so on), the retailer can measure dollar sales increases, increases in number of purchases, increases in store traffic, and so on, against those for a comparable period (for example, last year at the same time or last week). Second, for any direct-advertising campaign, the retailer can measure in-store and out-of-store inquiries, sales increases, or traffic increases. Increases in sales, consumer traffic, and number of purchases are all important success measurements for advertising. An even more appropriate measure of the success of a retail promotion, however, is to compare the gross profits from additional sales generated by the promotion to the cost of the promotion.[30] One method for obtaining this measurement is shown in Figure 13–7.

Advertising designed to achieve communications objectives should be measured over the long run. Changes in customer awareness, attitudes, perceptions, and behavioural intentions toward the store should be measured by either personal interviews or mail surveys. In this case, the retailer must use both pretest and posttest measurements to establish possible changes in consumers' opinions of the store.

Figure 13–7

The effectiveness of advertising

Source: Irwin Broh, "Measure Success of Promotions with In-Store Customer Surveys," Marketing News, *May 13, 1983, 17.*

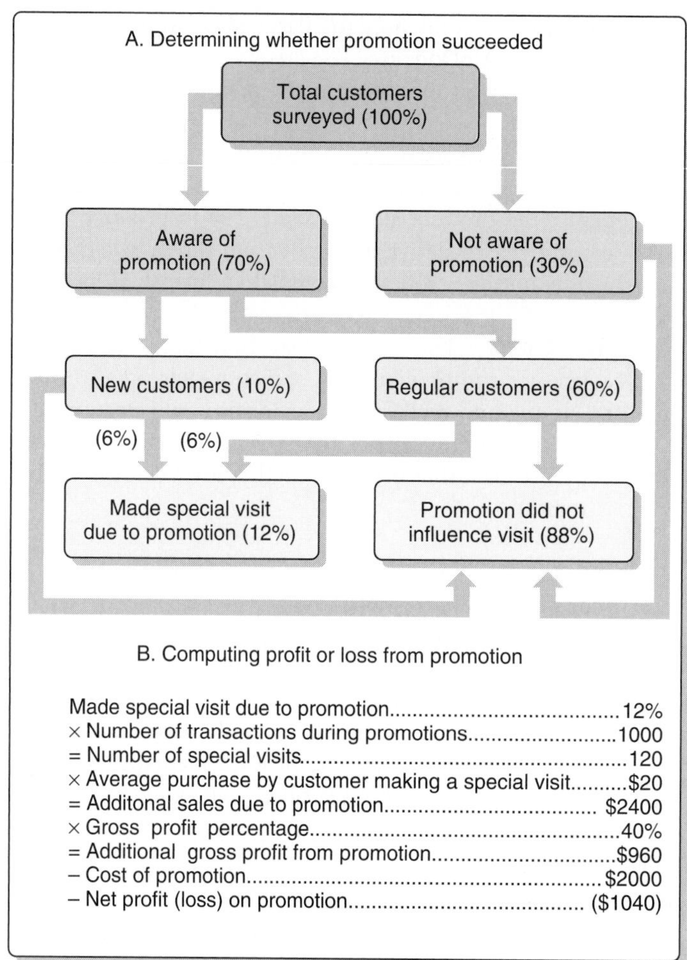

The Media Selection Process

The retailer's advertising messages are carried to the market by communications vehicles called advertising media. The retailer must carefully evaluate which medium is capable of delivering its messages most effectively. The retailer can select from among print media, such as newspapers, shopping publications, and magazines; broadcast media, such as radio and television; sign media, such as outdoor and transit; and miscellaneous media, including point-of-purchase media and advertising specialties. The retailer also can choose to use *in-store advertising* or become its own medium and use *direct advertising* to the consumer through mailed or hand-delivered letters, circulars, and catalogues. The diversity of media characteristics and alternatives is portrayed in Figure 13–8.

Media Characteristics

There are many characteristics to consider in choosing advertising media. Some media are costly, some inexpensive; some communicate a given message well, others poorly; some present the message continuously, others instantaneously. The following checklist of media characteristics provides the retailer with one tool in selecting media alternatives.

Figure 13–8

The media selection process

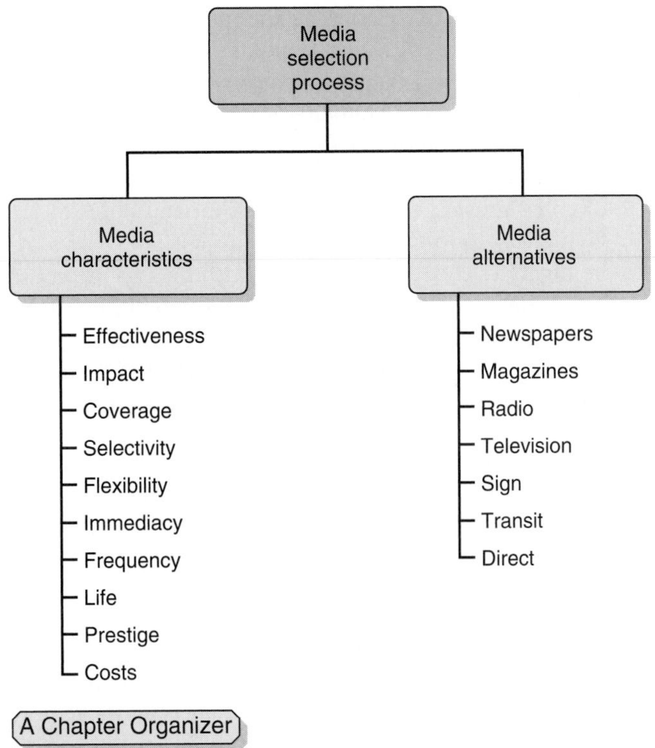

Effectiveness **Communication effectiveness** refers to a medium's capability to deliver the desired impact to the target market. Print media show consumers pictures and words they can see and read. With radio, consumers can only listen to the message, whereas television allows them to both see and hear the retailer's communication. The print media are generally thought to be effective with an intelligent audience, whereas the broadcast media are more effective with a less intelligent audience. Newspapers and radio stimulate quick attention to a retailer's current offering, whereas television and magazines create long-term images in the consumer's mind.

Impact **Impact** refers to how well a medium stimulates particular behavioural responses within the target market. Television and magazines are better than other media in building store images, for example, whereas newspapers and the yellow pages of a telephone directory are better at generating immediate purchase behaviour. The creation of visual impact is an important factor for each of these media alternatives because studies have found that "a picture really is worth a thousand words."

Coverage The percentage of a given market that a medium reaches is referred to as **coverage**. A newspaper might be read by 70 to 90 percent of adults in a certain city, whereas only a fraction of the same market may be reached by a hard-rock FM radio station. Although coverage is often an important criterion in reaching a market, it must be considered in light of audience selectivity.

Selectivity The capability of a medium to target a defined geographic location or a targeted customer group is termed *selectivity*. **Geographic selectivity** is a medium's capability to hone in on a specific geographic area such as a city and its surrounding area. This is an important media characteristic to a retailer, because most customers live in the local area. A medium that delivers the message to many people outside the retailer's market has a high degree of "wastage" circulation, viewership, or listenership, because these people are unlikely to buy from that retailer. Of the major media, local newspapers and local radio and television stations offer the retailer reasonably good geographic selectivity.

Audience selectivity refers to the medium's capability to present the message to a certain target audience within a population. Most magazines appeal to people with special interests, such as antique collectors, golfers, and electronics hobbyists. Radio stations also have a high degree of audience selectivity because their programming format (for example, country and western music, classical music, rock) appeals to distinct groups of consumers. The "old catch-all 'urban contemporary' format that included a wide range of black-oriented musical styles—from rhythm and blues to jazz to gospel to rap to hip hop—is giving way to formats that focus on just one or two of those types."[31] Television can also be highly selective when individual programs are considered. On the whole, people who watch *Hockey Night in Canada* have different interests from those who watch *Days of Our Lives*. Newspapers appeal to groups with a wide array of interests and socioeconomic profiles. Audience selectivity can be increased by placing ads in strategic locations within a newspaper (for example, an ad for a sporting goods store in the sports section).

Flexibility **Flexibility** refers to the number of different things the advertiser can do in the medium. Direct mail, for example, allows the advertiser to enclose money, coupons, pencils, postage-paid envelopes—in fact, practically anything, limited only by the advertiser's ingenuity. Radio, on the other hand, can provide words, music, and sound, but nothing more.

Immediacy A medium's capability to present a timely or newsworthy message describes the idea of **immediacy**. Radio announcements, for example, can be prepared today and aired tomorrow, whereas magazines require one to three months' notice in advance of the issue date. Newspapers also need very little lead time (usually twenty-four hours) to place a retailer's ad. If a snow or ice storm hits a city one day, knocking out electrical power, retailers can advertise oil lamps and butane-burning stoves the next day. A medium's capability to deliver a retailer's message immediately helps the retailer when external events present instant opportunities to the business.

Frequency **Frequency** refers to the number of times the same viewer or reader may be exposed to the same advertisement. A consumer might pass an outdoor poster twice daily for ninety days, whereas a radio spot might be broadcast a dozen times before a person hears it once. Similarly, consumers are likely to read newspapers only once per day but see a magazine ad in one issue several times.

Life The length of time the announcement continues to "sell" determines its **life** span. Broadcast announcements are gone in an instant and must be repeated to be effective, but a newspaper ad may "live" for several hours while people read the paper. Ads in magazines, which people read leisurely, may continue to "live" for several weeks, because consumers leave them in their homes and reexpose themselves to them over a long period of time. Print ads can be clipped, shared, posted, filed, and reviewed.[32]

Prestige **Prestige** is the amount of status consumers attach to a medium. In general, consumers attribute more prestige to advertising in print media than in broadcast media. Naturally, the prestige of print media varies with the individual publication (for example, *Maclean's* versus *Mad* magazine). Broadcast media are thought to be less prestigious in general because of the typically "low-brow" nature of most programming.

Cost **Cost** should be viewed in both absolute and relative terms. Absolute cost is the amount of money a retailer must pay to run an advertisement in a medium; for example, the cost of a full-page ad in a newspaper might be $2000 for one day. *Relative cost* is the number of dollars the retailer spends to reach a specific number of people; for example, if the full-page newspaper ad reaches 300 000 people, then the relative cost is $6.67 per 1000 readers. If, on the other hand, the retailer spends $250 on a radio ad, much less money is spent in absolute terms, but if the message is heard by only 25 000 people, then the relative cost would be $10 per 1000 listeners. Therefore, retailers should compare relative costs as well as absolute costs in selecting media. Once again, audience selectivity and wastage are among the criteria to consider in making final media selections.

Media Alternatives

Selecting advertising media is not easy. It is increasingly difficult to "touch" the consumer with an effective sales message. In the past ten years, network television viewership has declined 6 percent, daily newspaper readership is down 10 percent, and consumer magazine readership is down 25 percent.[33] The retailer must choose the medium or media that will best communicate the advertising message to the greatest number of consumers in the retailer's target market at the lowest cost. To accomplish these tasks, large retailers usually employ several media over a given time and must select the best media for their purposes on the basis of an understanding of the strengths and weaknesses of each medium. Different media have different capabilities to accomplish various communication tasks.

Newspaper Advertising **Newspaper advertising** has always made up the bulk of retail advertising, probably because a newspaper's local nature fits the retailer's desire for geographic coverage, prestige, and immediacy. In addition, newspapers are a "participative" medium that people read partly for the advertising; in fact, many consumers use newspapers as a shopping guide.[34] Retailers gain some measure of audience selectivity by advertising in specific sections of the paper, such as the sports, society, and financial sections. The cost of newspaper advertising is mid-range in terms of the available media.

By size and format, newspapers are classified as either standard or tabloid. Most large newspapers are standard; that is, they are 23.5 in. (59.7 cm) deep and eight columns wide, with each column about 2 in. (5 cm) wide. Tabloid newspapers are smaller "booklet" papers, five columns wide by about 14 in. (35.5 cm) deep.

Newspapers can also be classified as dailies or weeklies. Metropolitan newspapers are circulated daily over an entire metropolitan area (for example, *The Toronto Star*), whereas community newspapers are published weekly for a portion of a city or a suburb. Shopping newspapers are composed mostly of weekly retail and classified advertising.

Newspapers sell two kinds of advertising space: classified and display. Classified advertising is carried in a special section and used only by certain kinds of retailers, such as automobile dealers. Most retailers, however, use display advertising, which is spread throughout the newspaper. The basic unit of space the retailer buys from the newspaper is agate line (or line in common use). An agate line is one column wide and 1/14 in. deep. Fourteen lines of space thus equal one column inch, the basic space unit for smaller papers. One full page of advertising equals about 2400 lines, or approximately 172 column in., depending on the size of the paper.

Newspapers publish their rates on rate cards that they make available to customers. A retailer that buys newspaper space one time with no stipulations would pay the paper's *open rate*. Few retailers, however, actually pay the open rate, because the cost of newspaper space generally decreases with the quantity bought and increases as the retailer improves the "quality" of its advertising by specifying a particular position in the paper or using colour.

Most retailers that advertise regularly make *space contracts* with the newspaper, by which the retailer agrees to use a certain amount of space over the year and pay a certain amount per line that is lower than the paper's open rate for the same space. The lower rate is simply a quantity discount. A retailer that advertises heavily in a newspaper can receive up to 40 percent off the open rate in a large space contract. Unless otherwise specified, newspaper rates are ROP (run of the paper), meaning the paper will put the ad wherever it sees fit in composing the paper. Newspapers do the best they can to make up an attractive paper and place advertising where it fits best. A retailer that is willing to pay a premium called a *position charge* can, however, specify a position in the paper. The retailer can then specify the first three pages, the sports, society, or financial section, or even a specific page. Some retailers even rent a certain space permanently.

Most newspapers can print in colour, which is becoming more common. Needless to say, the retailer pays more for colour, and the more colour used, the more the retailer pays. Many newspapers can also insert preprinted colour advertisements.

Newspaper rate structures are determined by circulation: The greater the circulation, the higher the rates, and vice versa. A paper's paid and unpaid circulation is audited by the Bureau of Printed Measurement (BPM), which publishes a report of circulations throughout the paper's city and its retail trading zone, the area beyond the city proper for which the city is a trade centre. To compare newspapers' advertising rates, which vary widely, advertisers commonly use a calculation called the *milline rate*, which is the paper's cost of getting a line of advertising to a million people. The formula for the milline rate follows:

$$\text{milline rate} = \frac{\text{line rate} \times 1\,000\,000}{\text{circulation}}$$

Magazine Advertising Few retailers use **magazine advertising**. Although magazines do offer a high degree of prestige, audience selectivity, and impact, they generally lack geographic selectivity, which is what the vast majority of retailers require. Because magazines' advertising rates, like newspapers', are based on total circulation, a retailer that places an ad must pay for wasted circulation outside its trading area. Thus, an Ontario retailer that advertises in a nationally circulated magazine pays to advertise not only to Ontario residents but also to readers in British Columbia and Nova Scotia. To offset this disadvantage, many magazines publish regional editions (same editorial matter, different advertising) for certain geographic areas and major cities (for example, Toronto). City and regional magazines have grown in both number and circulation, and the greater geographic selection of these magazines makes them a more feasible advertising medium for some retailers.

Magazines also require a considerable period of time between publication date and the date advertising materials must be available. Magazines therefore do not accommodate the immediate-response advertising that makes up the majority of retail business. Most retailers that use magazines are either nationwide chains or stores with branches in several nearby cities.

Magazine advertising is usually bought in pages and fractions, such as half page, one-third page, or two-thirds page. Generally, the only premium positions are inside the front cover, the inside and outside of the back cover, opposite the table of contents, and the centre spread. Magazine rates, like newspaper rates, are based on circulations, and the rate structures, circulations, facts of publication, and publication requirements are published in *Maclean Hunter's Advertising Rates Book*. Magazines' rates are compared by a calculation known as *cost per thousand (CPM)*, computed as follows:

$$\text{CPM} = \frac{\text{cost of page} \times 1000}{\text{circulation}}$$

If a full-page black-and-white advertisement in a magazine costs $5000 and the circulation is 750 000, then CPM = $5000 × 1000/750 000 = $6.67. As with newspapers, one magazine may have a higher cost per page but a lower CPM than another, depending on their relative circulations.

Radio Advertising North Americans own about five radio receivers per household, and retailers have used **radio advertising** extensively almost since its inception. Among its advantages are low cost and a high degree of geographic and audience selectivity. Although radio broadcasters claim otherwise, sound alone is not a very good communication medium. Therefore, advertisers should stick with a simple message, make it easy to remember (hence the radio "jingle"), and repeat the message frequently.

Like other media advertising rates, radio rates are based on audience sizes. *Coverage* is the geographic area over which the station's signal can be heard; audience refers to the number of people who actually listen. Some 50 000-watt "clear-channel" radio stations broadcast over a broad geographic area, including many areas outside the retailer's market area. Regional stations cover geographic areas that are much larger than a typical city. Local stations (1000 watts or less) broadcast a signal that usually does not carry farther than about twenty-five miles, and most listeners are clearly in the retailer's market area.

Figure 15–1

Retailers often develop merchandising and operating strategies that support a particular store image. What is the essential image that is being promoted in this advertisement?

Figure 15–2

What do each of these retailers have in common? They are both of the same organization and an example of concentric diversification.

a

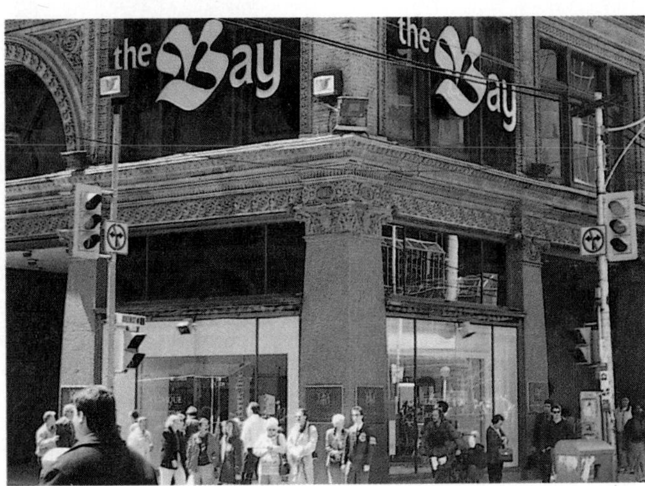

b

Figure 16–1

Warehouse club stores are examples of retailers in the trading-up phase, as described by the wheel of retailing. With the addition of fresh bakery and meat departments, some warehouse clubs might be in the process of moving into the trading-up phase of this theory.

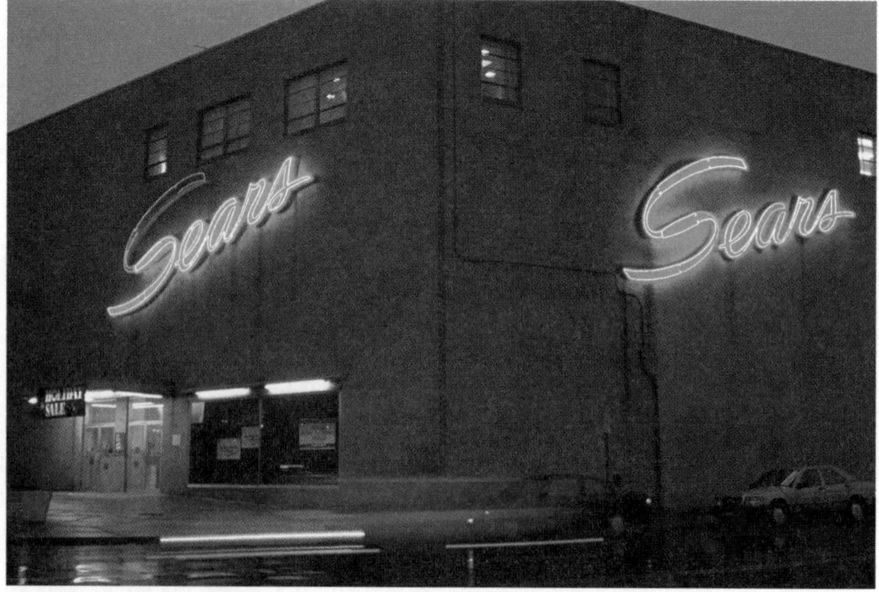

Figure 16–2

Judging from this photo and your personal experience, do you think that Sear's repositioning strategy has been effetive? Why or why not?

Figure 16–3

Which of these retailers are in the innovation, development, and maturity stages of the retail life cycle?

a

b

c

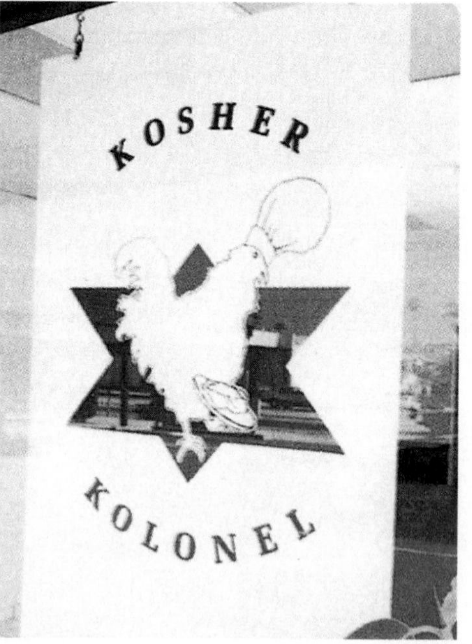

Figure 16–4

Offering product lines that appeal to a particular religious tradition is an excellent way for a retailer to establish a market position.

Figure 16–5

Niche retailers like Tilley Endurables are specialty retailers that occupy a polar position in the continuum of retailing formats.

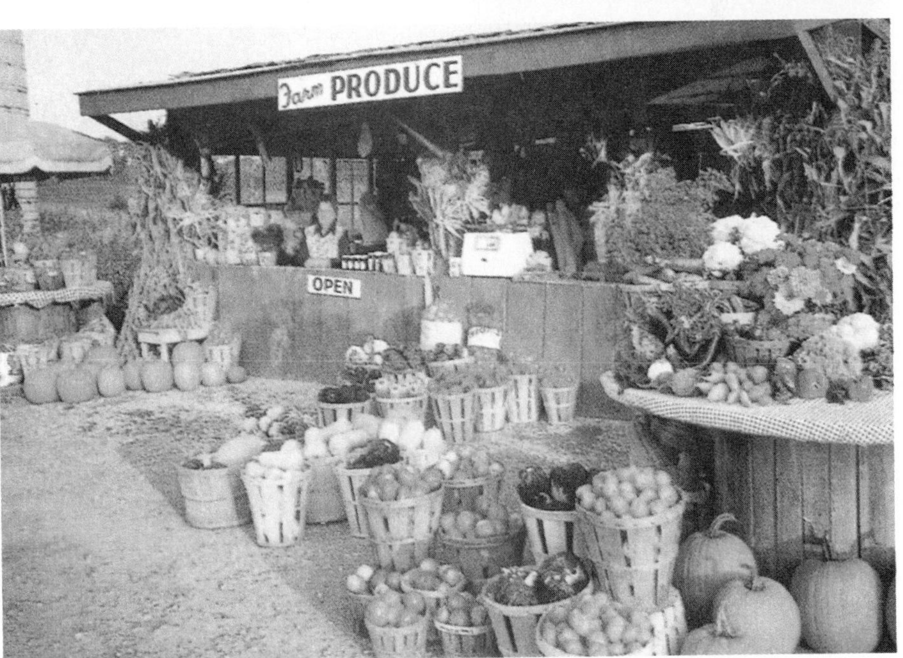

Figure 17–1

The roadside vegetable stand typifies the pure goods retailer that provides no services whatsoever.

Chapter eighteen 18

Figure 18–1

Each country has its own retailing customs that retailers must respect if they hope to be successful.

a

b

Figure 18–2

How are retailers in Japan different from those in Canada?

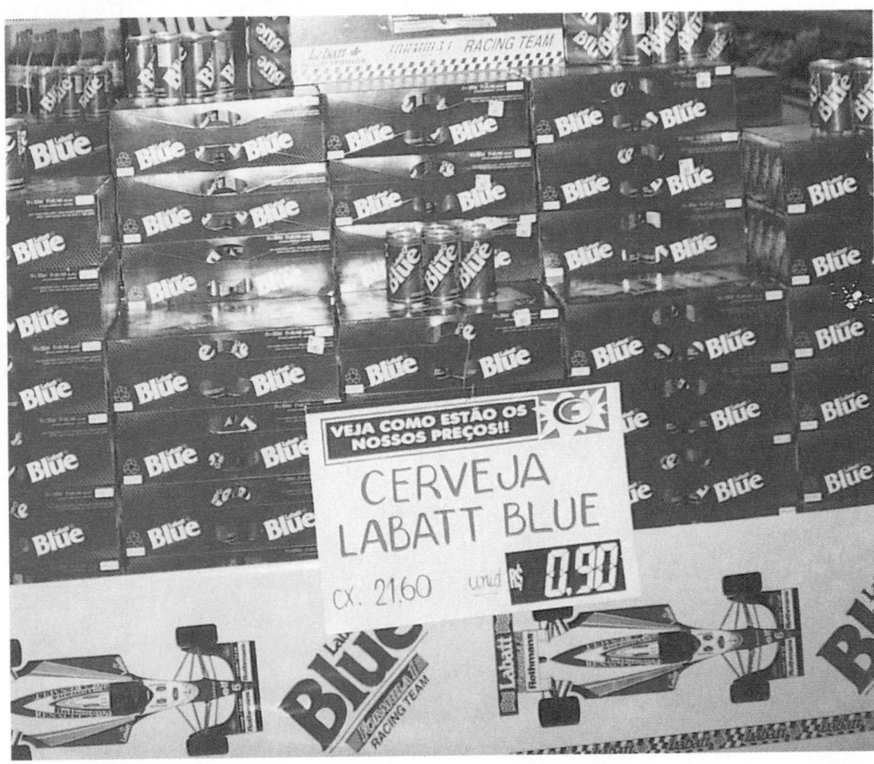

Figure 18–3

Many popular Canadian brands are sold under licensing agreements in several foreign countries.

Figure 18–4

These international retailers have both found success in the Canadian market.

a

b

Radio stations appeal to highly specialized audiences because of their programming: rock and roll, easy-listening, classical music, all-news, or talk-show stations. Moreover, radio listeners are much more station loyal than are television viewers, who switch freely from one channel to another. Radio is particularly important to drivers, who have their radios tuned in about 62 percent of their "drive time"; peak drive times are 7 to 9 a.m. and 4 to 6 p.m.

Radio advertising is sold as either network radio (buying from several stations that air joint programming) or spot radio (bought from individual stations). Because most retailers want to advertise in one city only, most buy spot radio announcements. Stations divide their total air time into classes, usually labelled as AAA, AA, A, B, and C, with the best times being early morning (6 to 10 a.m.) and late afternoon (3 to 7 p.m.). Generally, the fewest people listen at night, so this time is the cheapest. Spot announcements usually are sold in one-minute, thirty-second, and ten-second periods for a certain number of repetitions (for example, 15, 50, 150 times). Retailers often buy weekly "package plans" for a number of repetitions of a message of a certain duration over a certain time class; for example, retailers can select 20 thirty-second announcements in class AA time for a week. They also can buy joint sponsorship of certain programs, such as the daily stock market report. *Maclean Hunter's Advertising Rates* lists radio stations' packages and rates and describes their programming.

Radio rates are based on audience size. Estimates of the number and characteristics of listeners at certain times of the day are made by companies like Bureau of Broadcast Measurement. These statistics are sold to radio stations, which in turn make them available to potential advertisers. The retailer, as an advertiser, can write its own radio copy and have the station "produce" it, provide the announcer, and develop a musical background and whatever sound effects are needed. Normally, the station does not charge for this service if the retailer runs the message on the producing station.

Television Advertising **Television advertising** is the most glamorous and conspicuous advertising medium in Canada. Reaching about 99 percent of all Canadian homes, TV garners a large amount of advertising dollars—but not from retailers. Typically, only the larger chain organizations have the budgets to support television advertising. However, some direct retailers like K-tel (makers of such products as the Veg-O-Matic, Fishin' Magician, Slice-O-Matic)[35] and informercial sellers (for example, Nissan, Sony, Lexus, Apple)[36] have found a means of meeting the higher costs of television advertising by carefully selecting local time slots.

Although television is an excellent communication medium, its high cost constraints eliminate all but the largest retailers from using it regularly. Moreover, preparing television commercials requires expertise that store advertising departments do not usually have, so most retailers depend on advertising agencies to produce and place their television commercials. Television stations also will produce commercials for a fee.

Like radio time, television time is sold as network or spot time. Unlike radio, the majority of television programming originates from the networks. Again, most retailers' markets are localized, and only the largest nationwide chains can buy network television time. Most retailers buy spot announcements from local stations. McDonald's splits its $450 million television advertising budget between national ($300 million) and spot TV ($150 million).[37] In contrast to the number of radio stations, only a few television stations operate in each city.

Television time rate structures and measurements of audience size on which rates are based are quite complex. A complete discussion is beyond the scope of this book; the reader is referred to any standard advertising text. In general, television stations divide their time into classes on the basis of the size of audience at a given time. The larger the audience, the higher the cost of advertising time. Advertising rates are lowest during the times with few viewers and highest during prime time, which normally attracts the most viewers.

Local stations sell spot announcements in and around programming at certain times, as well as packages of announcements much like radio packages. As in almost all media, television stations allow advertisers a quantity discount; the greater the number of repetitions, the lower the cost per repetition. The retailer can buy one-minute, thirty-second, and ten-second spots (or combinations of these), or it can buy partial sponsorship of the station's local programming.

A.C. Nielsen Co.
www.nielsenmedia.com

The sizes of local stations' television audiences are measured by firms such as the A.C. Nielsen Company and the Bureau of Broadcast Measurement. By means of diaries, electronic recording devices, and interviews, these companies estimate the number of people in the station's market area who watch various television programs. With these figures, station managers can compute a CPM figure in much the same way that magazines compute their CPMs. Television and radio stations have a special problem, however; viewership and listenership figures vary with the same program on a day-to-day and week-to-week basis and also from one program to another. Thus, for any one program, it is sensible to calculate an average audience size. A way to calculate CPM for a television station is shown here:

$$\text{CPM} = \frac{\text{average of a minute's advertising} \times 1000}{\text{average audience size}}$$

Sign Advertising Retailers use outdoor advertising media extensively, especially posters, bulletins, and spectaculars.[38] **Sign advertising** gives retailers impact, coverage, frequency, geographic selectivity, and a long life for a relatively low CPM. Out-of-home advertising permits geographic targeting of specific groups. Because it has the advantage of not only reaching target audiences but also frequently exposing them to the ad message, it has the lowest cost per thousand impressions of any medium. Outdoor signs, however, are good for presenting only a short reminder message, perhaps the store name, an illustration, and a few words of copy.[39]

Outdoor signs are owned or leased by local "plant operators," which install the advertisers' messages and are responsible for maintaining the signs and the surrounding areas. The three basic outdoor signs are the thirty-sheet, 12 × 25-ft. (3.7 × 7.6 m) poster that most people call a *billboard*, painted bulletins, and outdoor spectaculars. *Painted bulletins* are signs that measure approximately 14 × 48 ft. (4.3 × 14.6 m) on which the advertising message is actually painted in sections by an artist working from a miniature. When the advertisement is painted in sections, the advertiser can move the message to another location. *Outdoor spectaculars* are nonstandardized, custom-made signs that use elaborate lighting, falling water, rising steam, billowing smoke, and other techniques to attract consumers' attention. Although these signs have higher attention value, they are

World of Retailing

Politically Correct Retailing

Pulling the Plug on Trash Television

How far is too far? Many big retail advertisers on daytime television are carefully considering their advertising associations with many talk shows that many in the viewing public believe have gotten out of control. Talk shows under scrutiny include the Jerry Springer Show, The Ricki Lake Show, The Jenny Jones Show, Sally Jessy Raphael, Geraldo, and others. With such topics as "I'm Having Your Man's Baby," "I'm a 13-Year-Old Prostitute," "Wild Teens," "I Want You To Be The Father Of My Baby," "Makeovers For Transvestites," and "Jenny, Fix Me Up With Your Hottest Guest," many retailers and other business organizations are thinking about joining Procter & Gamble Co. and Pillsbury in either pulling their advertising support for the most offensive shows or supporting only those episodes whose topics are acceptable to the tastes of the general viewing public. Is this a case of buckling under public pressure to act as sensors of public morality or is it just plain politically correct retailing?

Sources: Adapted from Joe Mandese, "Talk Show Stalwart P&G pans 'trash,'" Advertising Age, *November 20, 1995, 1; and Laurie Freeman, "Pillsbury re-evaluates ads on violent shows,"* Advertising Age, *January 15, 1996, 6.*

quite costly to produce. A new outdoor sign system uses satellite technology to feed updated information to LED displays. Messages are displayed 24 hours a day and can be updated (for example, interest rates, stock quotes, program changes) on a hourly basis.[40]

Outdoor signs usually are bought in "showings" for periods of ninety days and longer. A number 100 showing is a number of signs sufficient for a daily exposure of the message to a population equal to that of the market area. Other showing sizes are 75, 50, 25, and 150; a showing size of 75, for example, means that the number of signs will expose the advertiser's message to 75 percent of the market area. The number of signs in a showing is not fixed. Fewer signs are necessary if they are exposed to heavy traffic, whereas more signs are needed if they are exposed to light-traffic areas.

Transit Advertising **Transit advertising** includes car cards, exterior displays, and station posters. *Car cards* are the posters displayed on interior wall racks in buses, subway trains, and the cars of rapid transit systems. *Exterior displays*, which vary in size, are the advertisements shown on the outside of buses, cars, and taxis. *Station posters* are signs displayed in the interiors of subway, railroad, and rapid transit stations.

Advertisers buy transit advertising from transit advertising companies, also known as *operators*, which function in much the same way as outdoor plant operators. Car cards normally are sold in runs. A full run is two cards in every bus, car, and so forth in the market. Half runs and quarter runs are also possible. The rate structure in transit advertising is similar to that of outdoor advertising, because it is based on the volume of traffic passing through bus and train routes. The rates for exterior or travelling displays and station posters are not standardized but, as for outdoor showings, are based on the number of people who view them. The CPM for transit advertising is calculated in the same way as for outdoor media. Like outdoor advertising, transit advertising is relatively inexpensive.

In-Store Advertising The explosive growth of in-store advertising is based on the behavioural buying practices of consumers—more than 70 percent of final consumer purchase decisions are made in the store.[41] This fact suggests that it makes good sense to deliver a promotional message at the last minute when customers are at the point of purchase and are face-to-face with product and service decisions.[42] "Market Growth Resources, an in-store consulting group, defines **in-store advertising** (also referred to as place-based medium) as marketing activities in the store that carry a creative message unit of some type, but with no directly actionable incentive to buy the product. Examples are four-colour ads on shopping carts; aisle, shelf and checkout lane signs; electronic communications; and window banners."[43]

Another emerging in-store advertising form is soundless television commercials that are tailored for a particular retailing environment.[44] NBC On-Site scatters colour television sets throughout a store and features video-only shopping tips (for example, how to select fresh fruits and vegetables) together with commercial messages.[45] McDonald's is testing *McMagazine* in its restaurants as an in-store advertising vehicle. They are also testing McDTV—a format in which closed-circuit monitors entertain restaurant patrons with a combination of cartoons, news, sports, and original programs interspersed with advertising.[46] Place-based advertising now includes television monitors in United Artist theatre lobbies that broadcast short features together with commercial messages.

Direct Advertising **Direct advertising** is a medium that retailers use extensively to communicate their product offerings to a select group of consumers. The retailer creates an advertisement and distributes it directly to consumers through either the mail or the personal distribution of circulars, handbills, or other printed matter, or for a growing number of retailers, the Internet. Increasingly, direct marketing of advertisements is becoming the vehicle of choice for many retailers. Although direct advertising is expensive in terms of CPM, it is the most selective medium, because the ads are read only by people the retailer selects. It also is a personal form of advertising and is extremely flexible. Direct advertising can include pictures, letters, records, pencils, coins, coupons, premiums, samples, and any other gifts the retailer chooses to include.

Retailers can choose to distribute direct advertising to their charge customers or other known or potential customers, or they can buy a mailing list from "mailing-list houses," which sell lists for a certain charge per thousand names. The variety of these lists is astonishing, ranging from magazine subscribers to professional groups, from hobbyists to owners of certain products. The retailer never sees these lists; instead, advertising pieces are sent to the mailing-list house, which addresses and mails them. Some retailers prepare their own direct advertising, whereas others choose agencies to prepare it and arrange for distribution. The cost of direct-mail advertising is also measured by the CPM criterion:

$$\text{CPM} = \frac{\text{cost of preparing and distributing advertising} \times 1000}{\text{total number of recipients}}$$

Unlike most other advertising media, the effectiveness of direct advertising can be directly measured if the advertisement calls for a response or an order. By dividing the total sales resulting from customer responses by the total cost of preparing and distributing the direct-advertising materials, the retailer can establish a measure of the cost per sale or response for this promotion.

The Sales Incentive Program

Retailers use the term *sales incentive* in many ways. A common usage includes all promotional activities other than advertising, personal selling, and publicity as sales incentives or sales promotions. This text defines **sales incentive** as any direct or indirect nonpersonal inducement that offers extra value to consumers. Retailers use these "extras" to supplement advertising, personal selling, and other merchandising activities. Typically, sales incentives are temporary offers extended to the customer to stimulate an immediate response—the purchase of a good or service. Sales incentives are targeting activities in that they are directed at triggering particular customer actions.[47] In the 1990s, retailers have been resorting to more short-term demand stimulants as consumers look for enhanced value for their money. Figure 13–9 identifies the primary sales incentive choices that the retailer might emphasize.

Coupons

Coupons are manufacturer or retailer certificates that give consumers a price reduction on specific kinds of merchandise. Consumers obtain coupons from newspapers, magazines, mail; on and in packages; door-to-door; and from in-store advertising supplements. Figure 13–10 illustrates the trends of distribution and redemption among these types of coupons in Canada. Catalina Marketing has developed a coupon-dispensing system that provides customers with coupons at the checkout stand. "As a clerk passes groceries over

Figure 13–9

The sales incentive program

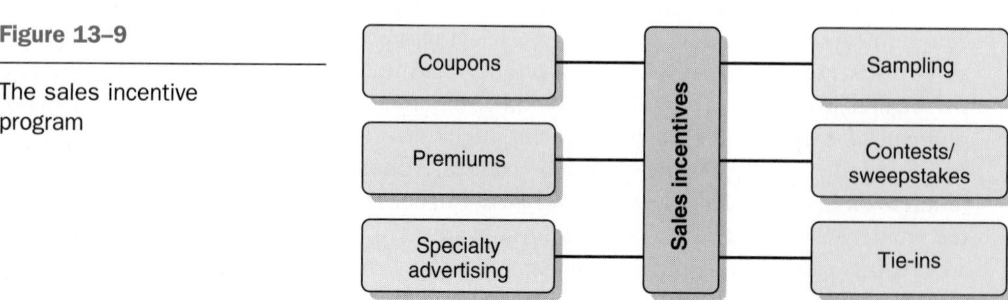

Figure 13–10

Trends in coupon distribution and redemption in Canada

Source: NCH Promotional Services.

Share of coupons distributed and redeemed*	1992	1993	1994
Freestanding inserts	49 (22)	47 (20)	46 (17)
In/on package	13 (27)	13 (28)	18 (34)
In store	9 (30)	12 (35)	13 (38)
Cooperative direct mail	13 (7)	11 (4)	8 (2)
Selective direct mail	3 (8)	5 (8)	5 (6)
Newspaper (run of press)	4 (1)	4 (1)	5 (1)
Magazine	6 (2)	6 (1)	4 (1)
Other—unclassified	3 (3)	2 (3)	1 (1)

Total coupons distributed (billions)	1992	1993	1994
Consumer directed	3.9	3.8	3.3
Retailer initiated	17.8	15.7	12.0
Total	21.7	19.5	15.3

Average coupon face values	1992	1993	1994
Average face value	$0.67	$0.68	$0.68

*Percentage of coupons redeemed by media in parentheses

the checkout scanner, bar codes trigger Catalina's automatic printer, which promptly spits out coupons based on the customer's purchases. The coupons, handed over with the customer's change, can be for competing or complementary products: a six-pack of Coke might yield a coupon for Pepsi, a bag of potato chips, or a larger bottle of Coke."[48] Couponing attracts customers to the store. Shoppers come into the store to purchase the "bargain" but usually end up buying other merchandise as well.

Optical card coupons are currently being tested in a number of stores. Consumers receive optical cards that contain "cents-off" coupons by mail. When consumers buy featured items, they present optical cards at checkstands. Cents-off offers that are specified on the card are matched with purchase data obtained by scanners. When validated, savings are deducted from the bill, and the cents-off offer is marked as used.

Couponing is popular with consumers and is a relatively low-cost sales incentive program;[49] however, it also has its problems. First, everyone is into the act. Canadian manufacturers distributed 3.3 billion coupons in 1996, of which consumers saved an estimated $100 million through redemption.[50] With so many coupons distributed each year, it becomes more difficult to gain customer attention and to get "one up" on competitors. A second problem is in coupon distribution. In-pack coupons create repurchases by current users, not new users. Frequent coupon redeemers use coupons for brands they already use—hence, retailers get few new sales. Third, misredemption (illegal redemption) is a major problem. Fourth, complex coupons (for example, self-destruct, sticky, multiple purchase, size-specification coupons) add significantly to handling time and create customer confusion.

Sampling

Sampling involves giving the customer a free trial or sample of the product; it gets the customer involved with the product through hands-on experience. Trial use invites active participation, which can quickly lead to a customer purchase decision. The kinds of products retailers can sample have low unit cost, are small in size, and are subject to high repeat sales. Supermarkets hand out samples of sausage; bakeries provide sample pastries; Hickory Farms places cheese and crackers at convenient points throughout its stores so customers can sample them. Sampling is generally quite expensive, but because it gives customers direct experience and involvement with the product, it is a powerful tool to induce purchases. How is this for a sample? To build its casual businesswear business, Levi invited human-resource managers to visit a Dockers shop for an in-store fashion show and seminar. For their efforts, attendees received a free Dockers outfit.[51]

Premiums

A **premium** is a merchandise item given to the consumer free of charge or at a substantial price reduction as an inducement to purchase another product, participate in an activity, or both. Essentially, a premium is an extra bonus or gift given to a qualified customer. A customer purchase is the most common way to qualify for a premium; however, premiums are sometimes given for visiting the store or participating in an activity (for example, taste-testing a new product). Store visits and participation events are often referred to as "traffic-building premiums." Several types of premiums involve retailers with manufacturers in this kind of effort to create sales incentives: self-liquidating, direct or value pack, mail-in, and continuing premiums.

Self-liquidating premiums require the consumer to pay something for the premium; typically, the consumer must pay an amount sufficient to cover the costs associated with the premium. Successful self-liquidating premiums are merchandise items that usually cannot be obtained elsewhere, and their uniqueness makes them valued gifts that consumers perceive to be worth considerably more than what they have to pay for them. The cosmetic industry, in concert with many department and specialty store retailers, provides an excellent example of self-liquidating premium offers. These offers take the form of purchase with purchase (PWP) and gift with purchase (GWP) premiums. These PWP and GWP premiums might consist of garment bags, overnight totes, sunglasses, billfolds, ties, and other apparel items complete with the insignias of the company or designer (for example, Calvin Klein, Ralph Lauren). The customer had to make several trips to McDonald's to get a full set of cups because a different cup was available each week for four weeks.

Direct premiums or value packs are free gifts given to the customer at the time of purchase. The gift can be (1) attached to the product package—"on packs"; (2) contained in the product package—"in packs"; (3) found adjacent to the product package—"near packs"; or (4) provided in special decorator packages with the product—"container packs." To the extent that these direct premiums generate store traffic and ensure rapid product turnover, they are desirable additions to both the retailers' and manufacturers' sales incentive program.

Mail-in premiums require the customer to send in a proof of purchase to receive a free gift. This type of premium encourages first-time or repeat purchases; however, given the extra effort required of the customer, it has limited acceptance on the part of the general consuming public. But if the retailer does not have to get involved with processing and handling the mail-in offer, this type of premium is still another weapon in a successful sales incentive arsenal.

Continuity premiums require the customer to make repeat purchases of products and services to benefit from the premium offer. This kind of premium is offered as part of a continuous, ongoing sales incentive program. The customer's length and degree of involvement usually determines the value of the gift; longer and greater involvement results in bigger and better gifts. The most common type of continuity premiums are trading stamps.

Competing with trading stamps is a new type of continuity premium—the **frequent buyer program**.[52] This format gives customers bonus points for each purchase, with the number of points corresponding to the amount of purchase. It also provides retailers with an excellent means for collecting information on consumers and their buying behaviour. A newsletter informs customers of specials, and a monthly statement informs them how many promise points they have earned and offers a money voucher to use toward future purchases. One of the most successful Canadian retail promotions in recent years has been that of Zellers' Club Z. Club Z combined all elements of retail promotion in a coordinated effort that Zellers officials say generated a 55 percent increase in sales, a 30 percent increase in store traffic, a 99 percent awareness level, 4 000 000 active members (45 percent of Canadian households), and the 1987 Retail Council of Canada Communication Award for retail promotion.

The Club Z promotion uses television, direct mail, newspapers, public relations, credit card staffers, store signs, public address announcements, cash register receipts, and shopping bags that carried the message. In addition, store employees were encouraged to generate members through a special training program and reward system.

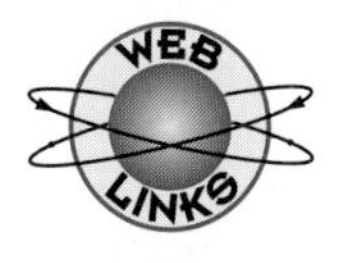

Air Miles
www.airmiles.com

Club Z was a result of extensive focus group research and the observation of the success of other North American frequent-shopper programs. It is a good example of how a well-planned and executed program can lead to improved performance.[53]

Another recent successful Canadian continuity program is the Air Miles Program developed by Loyalty Management Group of Toronto. Sales have grown to over $100 000 000 in 1997.[54]

Contests and Sweepstakes

Contests and sweepstakes are theme-based sales incentive programs designed to create a special event that generates customer involvement with the store and its merchandise. **Contests** are promotional activities in which participants compete for rewards; successful participants are selected on the basis of their skill in completing a particular task (for example, designing a store advertisement or completing a puzzle). McDonald's/NBA TwoBall promotion is a skills competition for 9- to 17-year-olds that is designed to mould young fans into future players and consumers of programming and licensed merchandise.[55]

Sweepstakes are promotions in which customers win prizes on the basis of chance. For the sweepstakes to be legal, however, the customer cannot be required to risk money for a chance; the major requirement is that the customer fill out an entry form to have a chance to win. Sweepstakes involve pure chance and minimal effort for entrants.

Specialty Advertising

The Specialty Advertising Association defines **specialty advertising** as a useful article of merchandise that is imprinted with an advertisement and given to the customer without obligation. Specialty items can range from inexpensive key chains to expensive travel bags. To be successful, a specialty item should be useful, fashionable, and appropriate for the targeted consumer. A good rule for the retailer to remember about a specialty item is that the store's name will be on the item; hence, the item should be consistent with the store's image.[56]

Tie-Ins

Sales incentive **tie-ins** (taking advantage of a specific event, place, person, or thing to promote the store or its products) are another approach to attracting attention to a store's offerings. Successful tie-ins can generate excitement, enthusiasm, and sales, but if the tie-in (such as a movie) bombs, the retailer can suffer.

Besides a tie-in with an entertainment event, tie-ins can occur in conjunction with national holidays, special occasions, sporting events, local celebrations, annual conventions, unusual events, and other products, to name but a few ways. The purpose of tie-ins is to capitalize on the excitement generated by momentary trends or events (for example, Lion King, Mighty Morphin Power Rangers, Pocahontas).[57] They are by definition transient—how many people today would buy a coffee mug with a 1988 Calgary Winter Olympics decal on it?

Tie-ins of complementary merchandise have several advantages:

- **Increased awareness**—By promoting two or more compatible pieces of merchandise, the retailer can attract more attention than by promoting a single piece of merchandise.
- **Increased readership**—Readership of advertising sales promotion literature will increase, particularly if there is a logical tie-in between the merchandise.
- **Reinforced image**—Where there are natural "go-togethers," the image of the store's merchandise can be reinforced because of the combined benefits the consumer will derive from using both pieces of merchandise together.
- **Cross-brand trial**—If customers are loyal to one brand of a store's merchandise, they are likely to try the complementary merchandise because of the "promotional marriage."
- **Cost efficiency**—Retailers can save money by promoting tie-ins; that is, two or more pieces of merchandise can be promoted together, achieving a synergistic effect.

The Retail Publicity Program

Publicity is one of the tools of public relations. It can be defined as positive or negative communication that is indirect, nonpersonal, carried by a mass medium, and neither paid for nor credited to an identified sponsor. A key concern to the retailer regarding publicity is that the firm has no control over what is said (the message), how it is said (the presentation), to whom it is said (the audience), and how often it is said (the message frequency). Nevertheless, publicity plays an important supportive role in enhancing and augmenting product and store advertising. Hence, it behooves the retailer to appreciate both the positive and negative results of good and bad publicity.

Although retailers cannot control publicity, they can take steps to gain favourable publicity and decrease the impact of negative publicity. Safeways in Alberta miscalculated the negative publicity which they received during the 1997 lockout of union workers.[58] Negative publicity requires fast and decisive action on the part of the retailer in order to contain and correct unfavourable impressions.

Publicity can be either planned or unplanned. Planned publicity means the retailer exercises some control over the news item. Regarding unplanned publicity, the retailer simply responds to the uncontrollable events as they occur. Planned publicity includes press releases, press conferences, photographs, letters to the editor, editorials, and special events. Large retailers will typically send out dozens of news releases about their stores and activities. Further, they use press conferences to describe major news events that might be of interest to the public. Pictures and drawings are useful devices for showing store-expansion plans, new equipment to better serve customers, and so forth; these are generally newsworthy items that bring attention to the retailer. These approaches to gaining favourable publicity are subject to the whims of the news media, because they select what they consider newsworthy. The media, however, do have space or time to fill, and persistence and continually disseminated media releases increase the likelihood of favourable coverage.

To develop a publicity story, the retailer first must identify the kinds of stories the media accepts and the criteria they use to make decisions. This step gives retailers basic ideas on which to develop stories. Stories that depict new and unusual events, store innovations, improvements in working conditions, new store openings, and stories that are currently important to the public often attract the interest of the news media. Publicity must also be newsworthy, somewhat unusual, truthful, and appeal to a broad cross-section of the public. Publicity stories are more effective if they are dramatic or emotional and if they show action or human interest through photographs and illustrations.

Summary

Retail promotion involves providing consumers with information about the retailer's store and its offerings and influencing their perceptions, attitudes, and behaviours. Promotion is also closely related to the communication process because transmitting meaningful messages through the retailer's promotion mix involves the three components of advertising, sales promotion, and publicity. The purpose of advertising is to inform, persuade, and remind consumers that the retailer's market offering is best suited to their needs. Advertising works for the retailer by prompting individual consumers to move through the adoption process and by stimulating the two-step flow of mass communications. Retail advertising can be classified as (1) product advertising, which presents merchandise for sale and urges customers to act immediately, (2) institutional advertising, which sells the store as the right place to shop, and (3) cooperative advertising, in which the retailer and the vendor share the creation and costs of advertising.

In developing functional advertising plans, the retailer sets advertising objectives (for example, store image, store position, store traffic, store event, increased purchase size, expanding sales), develops advertising budgets (for example, educated-guess, percentage-of-sales, competitive parity, objective and task methods), and obtains the services of an advertising organization (in-house department or outside specialist). The retailer's approach to creative advertising involves designing the basic message (advertising substance), selecting the communications approach (advertising style), creating the retail advertisement (layout, headline, illustration, copy, logotype), and evaluating the effectiveness of the advertisement. The media selection process involves the use of media characteristics (for example, effectiveness, impact, coverage, selectivity, flexibility, immediacy, frequency, life, prestige, cost) to evaluate media alternatives. Retailers use newspapers, consumer magazines, radio, television, sign media, direct advertising, and numerous other miscellaneous media.

Coupons, sampling, premiums, contests, sweepstakes, specialties, and tie-ins are among the many devices retailers use to communicate with customers about their store and their merchandise. Sales incentive approaches are limited only by the retailer's imagination. Publicity is an important part of a retailer's public relations program. Good publicity can bring attention to a retailer and its merchandise and help build a good store reputation and sales. Bad publicity can ruin a retailer. A retailer therefore must learn how to manage its publicity.

Student Study Guide

Key Terms and Concepts

advertising agencies *p. 493*
advertising budget *p. 491*
advertising effectiveness *p. 495*
advertising freelancer *p. 493*
advertising manager *p. 492*
advertising message *p. 493*
audience selectivity *p. 498*
communication effectiveness *p. 497*
communication process *p. 483*
communications approach *p. 493*
competitive parity method *p. 492*
contests *p. 507*
continuity premiums *p. 506*
cooperative advertising *p. 487*
copy *p. 495*
cost *p. 498*
coupons *p. 504*
coverage *p. 497*
DAGMAR *p. 485*
decodes *p. 484*
direct advertising *p. 503*
direct premiums *p. 506*
educated-guess method *p. 492*
encoded *p. 483*
feedback *p. 484*
flexibility *p. 498*
frequency *p. 498*
frequent buyer program *p. 507*
geographic selectivity *p. 497*
headline *p. 494*
illustration *p. 495*
immediacy *p. 498*
impact *p. 497*
institutional advertising *p. 487*
in-store advertising *p. 503*
layout *p. 494*
life *p. 498*
logotype *p. 495*
magazine advertising *p. 500*
mail-in premiums *p. 506*
media representatives *p. 493*
newspaper advertising *p. 499*
noise *p. 484*
objective and task method *p. 492*
opinion leaders *p. 486*
percentage-of-sales method *p. 492*
premium *p. 506*
prestige *p. 498*
product advertising *p. 487*
promotion *p. 485*
publicity *p. 508*
radio advertising *p. 500*
receivers *p. 483*
retail advertising *p. 485*
retail promotions *p. 483*
sales incentive *p. 504*
sales promotion director *p. 492*
sales promotion manager *p. 492*
sampling *p. 506*
self-liquidating premiums *p. 506*
sender *p. 483*
sign advertising *p. 502*
specialty advertising *p. 507*
sweepstakes *p. 507*
television advertising *p. 501*
tie-ins *p. 507*
transit advertising *p. 503*
transmitting *p. 484*
two-step flow of communication *p. 486*

Review Questions

1. Identify and briefly describe the various participants, processes, and acts of the communication process.
2. List and define the three elements of the promotion mix.
3. How is product advertising different from institutional advertising?
4. What is the purpose of an advertising objective aimed at store positioning?
5. What considerations should the retailer take into account when allocating advertising budgets?
6. Describe the four-step objective and task method of determining the retailer's advertising budget.
7. In developing the basic advertising message, the retailer is concerned with which two issues?
8. List the five components of a retail advertisement, and define each component.
9. Which media characteristics do retailers consider when selecting the most appropriate types of media for communicating with their consumers?
10. Newspapers sell two kinds of advertising space. What are they? How is newspaper space measured?
11. Explain the following newspaper advertising concepts: open rate, space contract, ROP, and position charge.
12. How are newspaper rate structures determined?
13. Identify the positive and negative aspects of magazine advertising from the retailer's viewpoint.
14. How is radio advertising sold?
15. From the retailer's perspective, what are the positive and negative characteristics of television advertising?
16. What are the three types of outdoor advertising? Describe each type.
17. What is a sales incentive?
18. What is the primary purpose of sampling?
19. Compare and contrast the various types of premiums.
20. Identify the advantages of tie-in promotions.
21. What does the retailer have no control over in publicity-related stories?

Review Exam

True or False

_____ **1.** The difference between advertising and publicity is that advertising refers to television media and publicity refers to print media.

_____ **2.** The percentage-of-sales method of setting advertising expenditures is generally accepted as the best means to determine an advertising budget.

_____ **3.** Copy is the store's distinct signature, which appears in all advertising.

_____ **4.** Direct advertising is one of the least expensive methods of advertising.

_____ **5.** Sweepstakes are sales incentives that involve pure chance and a minimal effort on the part of the customer.

_____ **6.** One advantage of publicity is that the public perceives news stories as having higher credibility than advertising.

Multiple Choice

_____ **1.** Establishing favourable attitudes toward the store is an achievement that is associated with the _____ stage of the DAGMAR model.

a. unawareness
b. awareness
c. comprehension
d. conviction
e. action

_____ **2.** The communications approach focuses on _____.

a. what the retailer is saying
b. how the message is conveyed
c. to whom the message is directed
d. the choice of media to convey the message

_____ **3.** A lot of white space in an advertisement suggests _____.

a. quality and prestige
b. limited product line
c. discounting and a price appeal
d. that the retailer wanted to minimize costs of the ad
e. none of the above

_____ **4.** Retailers that wish to purchase a specific area in the paper will pay a(n) _____.

a. position charge
b. open rate
c. short rate
d. ROP rate
e. space rate

_____ **5.** A medium's capability to present a timely or newsworthy message is referred to as _____.

a. geographic selectivity
b. audience selectivity
c. impact
d. immediacy
e. life

_____ **6.** The _____ type of sweepstakes are those in which the entrant is required to give back some information from a label, package, or advertisement, with winners chosen from the correct entries.

a. straight
b. matching
c. instant winner
d. programmed learning
e. contest

Student Application Manual

Investigative Projects: Practice and Application

1. By surveying your local newspaper, identify advertisements directed toward the objectives of (a) building store image, (b) positioning the store in the market, (c) generating store traffic, and (d) creating special events. Which of your advertisements is most effective in accomplishing its objective? Why?
2. Discuss the pros and cons of participating in cooperative advertising. Under which circumstances should a retailer agree to cooperative advertising?
3. List four major radio stations that serve your community. Interview each station manager and determine the audience selectivity of each station. Identify the types of retailers that would best be served by each station. Explain.
4. Explain why coupon promotions tend to work better with consumers who can be profiled as being older, married, more affluent, better educated, and living in urban areas. Why would these more upscale consumers have a higher coupon redemption rate than younger, single consumers who are less affluent and less educated?
5. The effectiveness of any sales incentive tool varies according to the operational and merchandising characteristics of a given type of retailer. Identify the most and least effective sales incentive tools for each of the following retailers: (a) a small gift shop, (b) a hardware store, (c) a fast-food restaurant, and (d) a cosmetic department. Explain your selection.

Endnotes

1. Stephen Kindel, "Cutting through the Clutter," *Financial World*, April 13, 1993, 36, 38.
2. Rigis McKenna, *Relationship Marketing* (Reading, MA: Addison-Wesley Publishing Company, 1991), 119.
3. Erik Larson, "Attention Shoppers: Don't Look Now but You Are Being Tailed," *Smithsonian* (January 1993): 71.
4. This discussion of influentials was based on "Maximizing the Market with Influentials," *American Demographics* (July 1995): 42–43.
5. Chip Walker, "Word of Mouth," *American Demographics* (July 1995): 38.
6. Emily Nelson, "Goodyear Hopes to Drive Home Lifetime Guarantee on New Tires," *The Wall Street Journal*, March 7, 1996, B12.
7. See Phyllis Berman, "The Spray Lingerie," *Forbes*, November 7, 1994, 102.
8. Kenneth A. Banks, "Does Anyone See Our Ads?" *Retailing Issues Letter* (published by the Center for Retailing Studies, Texas A&M University, and Arthur Andersen & Co., November 1992), 3.
9. Laura Bird, "McDonald's Slates Nutrition-Advice Spots," *Wall Street Journal*, September 23, 1992, B8. Also see Scott Hume, "When It Comes to Burgers, We Crave Beef, Not McLean," *Advertising Age*, March 1, 1993, 3, 48.
10. G.A. Marken, "Firms Can Maintain Control over Creative Co-op Programs," *Marketing News*, September 28, 1992, 7, 9.
11. Christy Fisher, "Marriott Chief Gets Personal in Ads," *Advertising Age*, March 15, 1993, 12.
12. Christopher Palmeri, "Indoor Outdoorsman," *Forbes*, March 29, 1993, 43.
13. Linda Himelstein, "Levi's vs. The Dress Code," *Business Week*, April 1, 1996, 58.
14. Marina Strauss, "Eaton's Pouring $25 Million Into Its Biggest Ad Blitz," *Globe and Mail*, September 19, 1997, B1.
15. Leah Haran, "Midas Wants Motorists to Look beyond Mufflers," *Advertising Age*, March 11, 1996, 3.
16. Judann Pollack, "Taste, Delivery Inspire Domino's Ads," *Advertising Age*, March 18, 1996, 2.
17. Kevin Goldman, "Hotel Chains Now Turn to Sniping in Ads," *Wall Street Journal*, March 12, 1993, B5.
18. Calmetta Y. Coleman, "Apparel Firms Plan Blitz to Lure Shoppers," *The Wall Street Journal*, January 29, 1996, B8.
19. Sally Goll Beatty, "Denny's Bites Back with Lower Prices," *The Wall Street Journal*, January 6, 1996, B5.
20. See Stephen Kindel, "Gentlemen, Flash Your Logos," *Financial World*, April 13, 1993, 46–48. Also see Stephen Kindel, "Anatomy of a Sports Promotion," *Financial World*, April 13, 1993, 49–50.
21. "Sears Links to NCAA Women," *Advertising Age*, March 11, 1996, 1, 35.
22. See Kiram W. Karande and V. Kumar, "The Effect of Brand Characteristics and Retailer Policies on Response to Retail Price Promotions: Implication for Retailers," *Journal of Retailing*, 71, (Fall 1995): 249–78.
23. Kate Fitzgerald, "Sears Looks to Coasts for $25M Review," *Advertising Age*, March 1, 1993, 44.
24. "It's Not Looking Like Christmas to Retailers," *The Wall Street Journal*, December 18, 1995, B1.
25. See Jeffery D. Zbar, "Fear," *Advertising Age*, November 14, 1994, 18.
26. Judy Ward, "Soft Sell," *Financial World*, April 11, 1995, 43.
27. Robert Berner, "Sears's Softer Side Paid Off in Hard Cash This Christmas," *The Wall Street Journal*, December 29, 1995, B4.

28. "McDonald's New Theme Sounds Like Old Theme," *Marketing News*, March 27, 1995, 5.

29. See C.B. Bhattacharya and Leonard M. Lodish, "A System for Evaluating Retail Advertising Effectiveness," *Retailing Review*, A quarterly section of *Stores* (October 1995): RR10–RR11.

30. Irwin Broh, "Measure Success of Promotions with In-Store Customer Surveys," *Marketing News*, May 13, 1983, 17.

31. Wendy Brandes, "Black-Oriented Radio Zeroes in on Narrowly Defined Audiences," *The Wall Street Journal*, February 13, 1995, B8.

32. "Fast Forward To 2045," *Advertising Age*, July 31, 1995, 32.

33. Ryan Mathews, "In-Store Media: Past Its Prime?" *Progressive Grocer* (October 1995): 59.

34. Kevin Goldman, "Consumers Prefer Print Ads, Study Says," *The Wall Street Journal*, June 6, 1995, B8.

35. See Christopher Palmeri, "Veg-O-Matic Does Europe," *Forbes*, March 15, 1993.

36. Kathy Haley, "In the Changing '90s market, the Informercial 'Here to Stay'," *Advertising Age*, March 11, 1996, 2A.

37. Chuck Ross and Judann Pollack, "McD's Turns Back to Local TV," *Advertising Age*, March 25, 1996, 1.

38. See Cyndee Miller, "Outdoor Advertising Weathers Repeated Attempts to Kill It," *Marketing News*, March 16, 1992, 1, 6. Also see Riccardo A. Davis, "New Advertisers Limit Outdoor Loss," *Advertising Age*, March 15, 1993, 6.

39. Sallie Hofmeister, "Advertisers Discover Great Outdoors," *The New York Times*, August 9, 1994, C1.

40. Cyndee Miller, "Outdoor Gets a Makeover," *Marketing News*, April 10, 1995, 1, 26.

41. Adrienne Ward Fawcett, "Listening to the In-Store Ad Song," *Advertising Age*, October 23, 1995, 34.

42. Mathews, "In-store Media: Past Its Prime?" 59–67.

43. Charles D. Peebler, Jr., "In-Store: Where Advertising Isn't Considered Advertising," *A.N.A./The Advertiser* (Spring 1992): 42.

44. "Turner Checks Out," *Advertising Age*, March 1, 1993, 16.

45. Kevin Goldman, "Turner Bags Checkout Channel, but Rivals Remain Undeterred," *Wall Street Journal*, March 4, 1993, B5.

46. Sidney Roslow, J.A.F. Nicholls, and Lucette B. Comer, "Measuring Place-Based Media—The Cooperation Challenge," *Marketing Research—A Magazine of Management & Applications* (Winter 1993): 34–39.

47. See Corliss L. Green, "Differential Responses to Retail Sales Promotion among African-American and Anglo-American Consumers," *Journal of Retailing* 71 (Spring 1995): 83–92.

48. See Matt Walsh, "Point-of-Sale Persuaders," Forbes, October 24, 1994, 232–34; Richard S. Teitelbaum, "Catalina Marketing," *Fortune*, November 18, 1992, 128; and Bradley Johnson, "Catalina Takes Shopping List to Stores," *Advertising Age*, November 2, 1992, 24.

49. Kelly Shermach, "Coupons, In-Store Promotions Motivate Consumer Purchasing," *Marketing News*, October 9, 1995, 6.

50. Louise Leger, "Keen on Coupons," *Grocer Today*, September 1997, 71.

51. Himelstein, "Levi's vs. The Dress Code," 58.

52. Murray and Neil Raphel, "Something for Everyone," *Progressive Grocer* (January 1996): 21.

53. D. Wesley Balderson and William Basztyk, *Retailing in Canada* (Scarborough, ON: Prentice Hall, 1994): 364.

54. Ijeoma Ross, "Loyalty Program Rewards Firm," *Globe and Mail*, July 24, 1997, B10.

55. Jeff Jensen, "NBA and McDonald's Shoot for the Future," *Advertising Age*, February 5, 1996, 26.

56. See John R. Hayes, "As Long as It's Free," *Forbes*, January 30, 1995, 72.

57. Jonathan Berry, "Wilma! What Happened to the Plain Old Ad?" *Business Week*, June 6, 1994, 54, 58; and Cyndee Miller, "Movie deals galore!" *Marketing News*, June 5, 1995, 1.

58. Andrew Nikiforuk, "Why Safeway Struck Out," *Canadian Business*, September 1997, 27–31.

Video Case for Part 5

Consumers Distributing

Consumers Distributing was established by Jack Stupp in the late 1950s, when he opened a small store (about 100 m^2) in his basement to sell cookware. He put together a small catalogue of his products to take along on sales calls. Initially his customers were companies who bought the products as gifts for employees and customers. Increasingly, however, employees bought these items for themselves. The first Consumers Distributing outlet opened in 1960. Sales and store outlets expanded and in 1968 Consumers Distributing became a publicly traded company.

Consumers' operation included the consumer filling out an order from a catalogue at the front of the store and then having the sales clerk retrieve the merchandise from the attached warehouse. The Consumers philosophy—that of providing brand-name merchandise at a lower price, albeit little service—was readily accepted by Canadian consumers concerned about inflation and recessions. Consumers grew rapidly by adding stores across Canada and the United States. Sales exceeded $1 billion in 1988 with profits of close to $11 million. The future looked bright for this unique catalogue retailer whose slogan read "suffer a little, save a lot."

However, by the early 1990s there were hints that the retail environment was changing and that Consumers was in trouble. Canadian consumer buying habits were changing—reflecting a greater desire to obtain value for their money. This "value" included quality merchandise, service, and assortment, as well as low prices. Canadians were also choosing to increase their savings accounts instead of spending due to uncertainty over the economy. In contrast, Consumers shoppers complained about the high number of "out-of-stock" items and the long waits to receive merchandise. The ordering system was viewed as archaic and inefficient.

During this time, strong new competitors were moving into Canada from the United States. These "warehouse" stores, such as Home Depot, Wal-Mart, and Office Depot, offered the same low prices which Consumers advertised but with a higher level of service and availability of merchandise.

Consumers' new management team responded in 1994 by countering with its own "big box" stores and computerized its consumer ordering system in an effort to provide a better level of customer service. Unfortunately, Consumers' expansion coincided with Wal-Mart's purchase of Woolco Stores. The ensuing price war between Wal-Mart and some of Canada's other discount department stores severely crippled Consumers' new stores' chance of success.

Furthermore, this new division was undercapitalized, sending the company into debt to a total of $250 million. A considerable portion of the required financing came at the expense of the company's merchandise suppliers. Consumers' supplier relationships were already strained due to a "compliance program" in which suppliers received a "fine" for late delivery of merchandise, a program which many thought was unfair. Some suppliers quit dealing with Consumers as a result of what they felt was a "heavy-handed" approach. This further contributed to the number of "out of stock" situations, and more consumers moved to other retailers.

On July 29, 1996, Consumers' lawyers appeared in a Toronto courtroom to seek creditor protection for the chain while it attempted to restructure. The first move of this restructuring included liquidating 130 stores. While liquidation brought in some needed cash, it was not enough, and it also angered many suppliers who could see that they were about to lose heavily. Within a few months it was evident that the restructuring was not going to be successful and the company declared bankruptcy with outstanding debts exceeding $243 million.

Questions

1. Discuss the advantages and disadvantages of the Consumers Distributing type of "catalogue retailing."
2. How could Consumers have competed more successfully with the big box retailers such as Wal-Mart and Home Depot?
3. What can be learned about supplier-retailer relationships from the Consumers experience?

Source: "Consumers Distributing," Venture *608 (September 15, 1996; 9:45).*

Retail Information and Control Systems
Enhancing and Managing the Firm's Decisions

Outline

Objectives

To prepare a basic income statement for a retailing enterprise

To prepare a basic balance sheet for a retailing enterprise

To analyze and evaluate the operational and financial performance of a retail firm

To describe the procedures for managing the retailer's operating expenses

To outline the methods for collecting and the procedures for processing merchandise data

To discuss the methods and procedures for valuing the retailer's inventories

To use information productively in retail problem-solving and decision-making situations

To recognize the key considerations in effective management of the retailing information system

To design, implement, and manage a retail research project

Retail Vignette

Eaton's

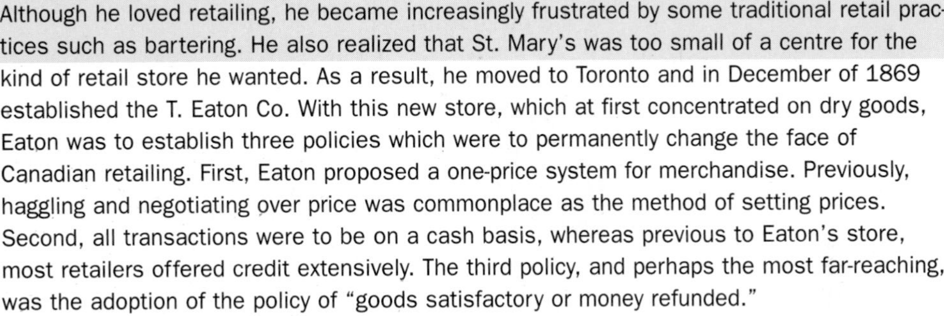

Timothy Eaton came to Canada from Ireland in 1854 and settled north of Toronto. For several years, he worked in various general stores and learned the retail industry, and then became a partner with his brothers in a general store in the small town of St. Mary's, Ontario.

Eaton's
www.eatons.com

Although he loved retailing, he became increasingly frustrated by some traditional retail practices such as bartering. He also realized that St. Mary's was too small of a centre for the kind of retail store he wanted. As a result, he moved to Toronto and in December of 1869 established the T. Eaton Co. With this new store, which at first concentrated on dry goods, Eaton was to establish three policies which were to permanently change the face of Canadian retailing. First, Eaton proposed a one-price system for merchandise. Previously, haggling and negotiating over price was commonplace as the method of setting prices. Second, all transactions were to be on a cash basis, whereas previous to Eaton's store, most retailers offered credit extensively. The third policy, and perhaps the most far-reaching, was the adoption of the policy of "goods satisfactory or money refunded."

These new policies proved to be successful and Eaton's began to grow and prosper. By 1880 it had become a full-fledged department store and by 1929 had expanded to include several stores accounting for almost half of Canada's retail sales. In addition to the policies previously cited, Eaton is also given credit for inaugurating the following concepts in retail selling:

- The Eaton's catalogue, named the "Wishing Book"
- The reduction of store hours
- Emphasis on advertising and public relations with the annual Santa Claus parade in downtown Toronto
- The installation of elevators and escalators for customer convenience

The T. Eaton Co. has remained in the family over the years, and Timothy Eaton's great grandsons currently operate the business as one of Canada's largest private companies. In 1977, Eaton's opened a major nine-storey Eaton Centre store in downtown Toronto, which contains 300 departments. This type of development which Eaton's has participated in has helped refurbish the inner city core of several cities in Canada. In 1978 Fredrik Eaton accepted the prestigious International Retailer of the Year Award on behalf of Eaton's. Many of the innovative ideas and attention to quality and detail which Timothy Eaton was known for remain with the organization and identify Eaton's as a major high-class Canadian retailer.

The 1990s ushered in a new era for the environment of Canadian retailing. The lingering recession curbed consumer spending, and strong competition from the U.S. (with the purchase of Woolco stores by Wal-Mart in 1994) caused sales to fall. These external forces and a high debt load have caused Eaton's to restructure its operations in an effort to remain competitive. Several stores were closed in 1997 and industry analysts predict that a new slimmer Eaton's will emerge from its current difficulties.

Sources: D. Wesley Balderson and William A. Basztyk, Retailing in Canada, *Prentice Hall Canada Inc., 8–9.; Ian McGugan, "Eaton's on the Brink,"* Canadian Business, *May 1994, 46–69.; Jennifer Wells, "The Empire Strikes Out,"* Maclean's Magazine, *March 10, 1997, 32–35.; Donald N. Thompson, "Eaton's, A Cautionary Tale,"* Business Quarterly, *Summer, 1997, 31–39.*

Information. Now!

Research tools have changed radically in the last decade. New geographic software, CD-ROM databases, and high-performance workstations have become inexpensive and widely available. More significantly, the nature of market research has changed. As consumer markets move faster, the people who follow consumer trends need more current sources of information. The leisurely pace of the past has given way to overnight survey results, same-day reports of scanner data, and instant analysis of other marketing databases.[1]

Bigger Than Gutenberg?

Gutenberg probably had no idea what he was starting when he invented the moveable printing press in the early 15th century. Modern technology mavens are not so modest, however. Today's technology is making it possible to find, retrieve, manipulate, and send information almost instantly. These changes are going to be at least as big as Gutenberg. But a true information revolution cannot live by technology alone. People must recognize it and make it happen.[2]

Retail Information Systems

Because successful retailing starts with the possession and proper use of business information, many retailers have developed and implemented some form of a **retailing information system (RIS)**. An RIS is an interacting organization of people, machines, and methods designed to produce a regular, continuous, and orderly flow of information necessary for the retailer's problem-solving and decision-making activities. The RIS is a planned, sequential flow of information tailored to the needs of a particular retail operation. The reason for this careful gathering and processing of information is so that the retailer will have sufficient information on hand to control and coordinate all of its operations adequately. Successful retailers are those that possess and effectively use the best information systems.[3]

The fundamental purpose of the RIS is to provide a framework for gathering and processing information from both the retailer's external and internal environments so that the retailer can develop the best possible output ("correct" decisions and "solved"

Figure 14–1

Retail information system

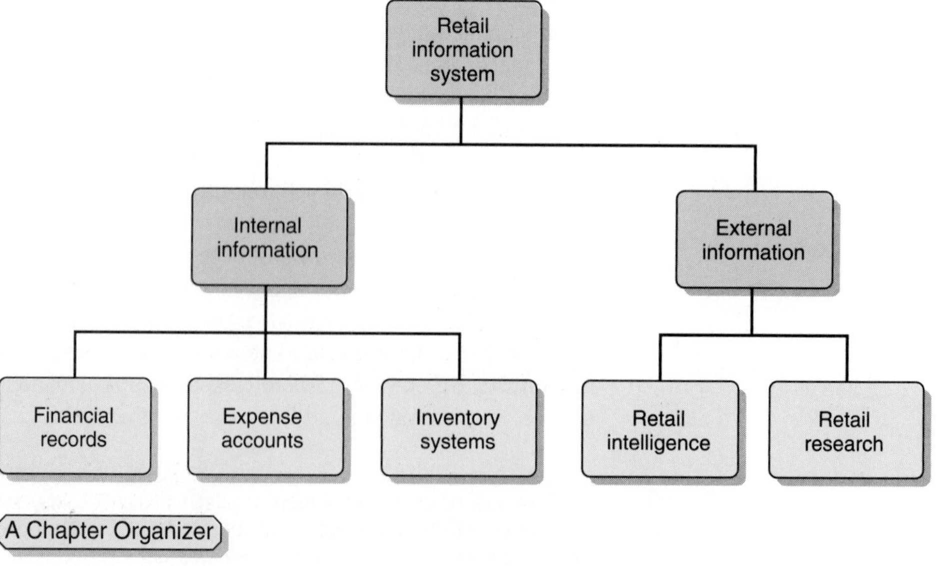

Figure 14–8

Examples of Operating statements for selected Canadian retailers

Source: (1) Adapted from Statistics Canada, Small Business and Special Surveys Division; (2) Adapted from Canadian Grocer 1997 Executive Report, *27. (Statistics Canada Information).*

	Sporting Goods Stores —Alberta Industry Average, Alberta 1991 (1)	Supermarket and Grocery Stores Canada 1994/1995 (2)
	% of total operating revenue	
Revenues	**100**	**100**
Expenses		
Cost of goods sold	**64.8**	**78**
Opening inventory	20.8	5
Purchases and materials	68.4	78
Closing inventory	24.4	5
Gross margin	**35.2**	**21.9**
Wages, salaries, and benefits	12.6	11.6
Other operating expenses	14.8	7.7
Total expenses	**96.6**	**97.3**
Net profit/loss	**3.4**	**2.6**

assets divided by net worth. This ratio is a measure of the relative owner/creditor contributions in the firm's capital structure. **Return on net worth** is net profit (after taxes) divided by net worth. This ratio measures the return on funds invested in the firm by its owners.

Profitability goals can be established by setting a target rate of return on net worth. Profit performance can be judged by how well the firm achieves its targeted return. What constitutes a high performer in the retail industry has varied considerably over the last few decades; currently, return on net worth ratios of high performance retailers are in the range of 15 to 35 percent.[10] To improve its return on net worth ratio, a retailer can strive to improve profit margins, increase asset turnover rates, or seek higher leverage ratios.

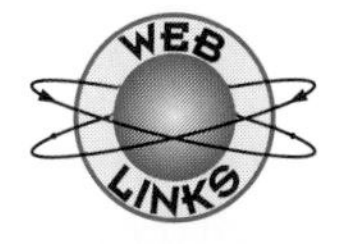

Dun & Bradstreet
www.dbisna.com

A widely used source of financial ratios are those reported by Dun & Bradstreet in its publication *Industry Norms and Key Business Ratios.* An example of these ratios is shown in Figure 14–8. These key performance measurements help the retailer make meaningful comparisons between the firm's financial performance and the median performance of similar retailers. They also are useful in establishing realistic financial objectives.

Expense Accounts

Expense management is the planning and control of operating expenses. To ensure an operating profit, operating expenses must be less than the retailer's gross margin. The retailer that fails to plan and control operating expenses risks losing financial control over an important segment of the business. Many Canadian retailers have carried out extensive cost-cutting recently to maintain their competitiveness.[11] Expense management entails

Figure 14–9

Expense accounts

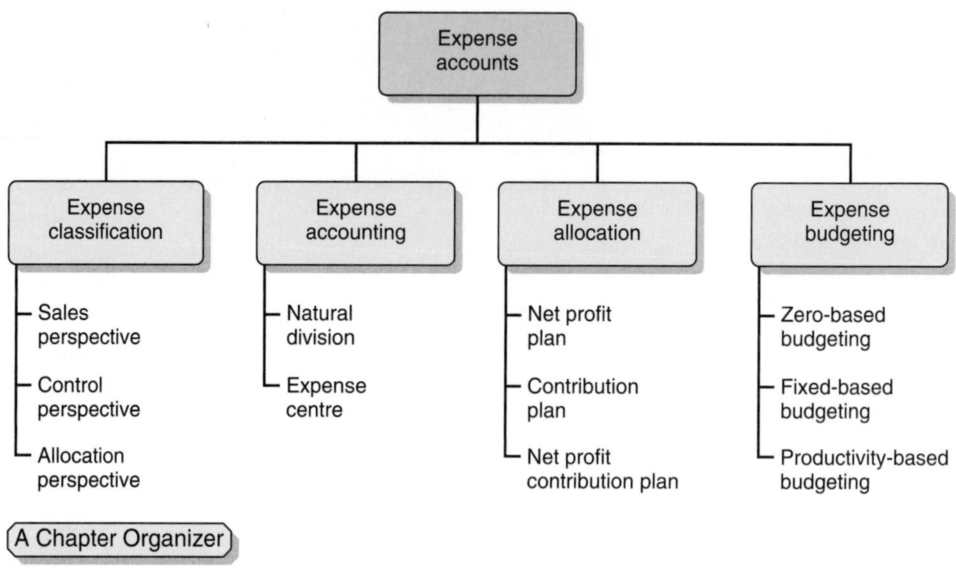

four basic planning and control activities: expense classification, accounting, allocating, and budgeting (see Figure 14–9).

Expense Classification

All planning and control activities require careful identification and classification of every relevant factor. Hence, the first step in expense management is to recognize the various costs of doing business and classify these costs into logical groupings based on some common feature. In retailing, there are three fundamental perspectives on operating expenses: sales, control, and allocation.

Sales Perspective One way to look at operating expenses is to see how such expenses are affected by sales. From a sales perspective, operating expenses are classified as fixed and variable. **Fixed expenses** are usually fixed for a given period of time (for example, the life of a contract or a planning or operating period). Expenses are classified as fixed when they remain the same regardless of the sales volume. As sales increase or decrease, fixed expenses remain constant.

Expenses that vary with the volume of sales are called **variable expenses**. As sales increase or decrease, variable expenses also increase or decrease. Although the relationship between sales and expenses is not always directly proportional, they are sufficiently related so that the retailer can reasonably predict changes in operating expenses. By being attentive to specific relationships between a variable expense and sales, the retailer can identify opportunities for increasing profits. For example, initial increases in advertising expenditures could increase sales to such a degree that profit increases are greater than the advertising expense.

Control Perspective The second way to look at operating expenses is to see whether a particular expense is controllable. As the name implies, **controllable expenses** are those over which the retailer has direct control. Retailers can adjust these expenses as warranted by operating conditions. For example, part-time help can be reduced during slack sales periods. **Uncontrollable expenses** are outlays over which retailers have no control and that, in the short run, they cannot adjust to current operating needs. Expenses incurred as a result of long-term contractual arrangements are uncontrollable over the short run. Given their adaptability, controllable expenses should be the focus of the retailer's attention. Daily or weekly monitoring of these expenses helps maintain operating expenses at acceptable levels.

Allocation Perspective In using the allocation perspective, the retailer looks at operating expenses to see whether they can be directly attributed to some operating unit. Many retailers find it useful for purposes of analysis and control to allocate operating expenses to various operating units, such as store units or departmental units. Under this approach, retailers classify operating expenses as either direct or indirect expenses. **Direct expenses** are those directly attributable to the operations of a department or some other defined operating unit. If the retailer eliminated a department or unit, then the direct expenses associated with that department would also be eliminated. Salaries and commissions of departmental sales personnel are examples of direct expenses. Expenses not directly attributable to the operations of a department are classified as **indirect expenses**. These costs cannot be eliminated if a particular department is dropped. Indirect expenses are general business expenses a retailer incurs in running the entire operation.

Expense Accounting

Retail expense accounting categorizes expenses into well-defined groups that the retailer can use to identify year-to-year trends for each expense class and make comparisons with trade averages of similar retailers. Expense accounting helps the retailer identify, analyze, and initiate controls for expenses that are out of line with either the previous year's figures or those of similar retailers. Using this accounting approach, the retailer can classify operating expenses using either a natural division of expenses or expense centre accounting.

Natural Division Using the **natural division of expenses**, the retailer groups expenses on the basis of the kind of expense each is, without regard for (1) which store functions (for example, selling, buying, receiving) incurred the expense or (2) where (for example, store, department) the expense was incurred. The natural division method of expense classification is used primarily by small and medium-sized retailers looking for simple yet acceptable means of classifying expenses (see Figure 14–10).

Expense Centre The second accounting method for classifying operating expenses is **expense centre accounting**. An expense centre is a functional centre within the store's operation or a centre of a certain store activity. The centre incurs expenses in the process of providing its assigned functions or performing its required activities. Expense centre accounting is a system of classifying operating expenses into such functional or activity classes as management, direct selling, customer services, and so on. The National Retail

Figure 14–10

Natural division of expenses

Source: Adapted from Retail Accounting Manual, *rev. ed. (New York: Financial Executive Division, National Retail Federation, Inc., 1978), iii–3.*

01 Payroll	13 Depreciation
02 Allocated fringe benefits	14 Professional services
03 Media costs	16 Bad debts
04 Taxes	17 Equipment rentals
06 Supplies	18 Outside maintenance and equipment service contracts
07 Services purchased	20 Real property rentals
08 Unclassified	90 Expense transfers in
09 Travel	91 Expense transfers out
10 Communications	92 Credits and outside revenues
11 Pensions	
12 Insurance	

Figure 14–11

Major expense centres

Source: Retail Accounting Manual, *rev. ed. (New York: Financial Executives Division, National Retail Federation, Inc., 1978), iii–3.*

010 Property and equipment
- 020 Real estate, buildings, and building equipment
- 030 Furniture, fixtures, and nonbuilding equipment

100 Company management
- 110 Executive office
- 130 Branch management
- 140 Internal audit
- 150 Legal and consumer activities

200 Accounting and management information
- 210 Control management, general accounting, and statistical
- 220 Sales audit
- 230 Accounts payable
- 240 Payroll and time-keeping department
- 280 Data processing

300 Credit and accounts receivable
- 310 Credit management
- 330 Collection
- 340 Accounts receivable and bill adjustment
- 350 Cash office
- 360 Branch store selling location offices

400 Sales promotion
- 410 Sales promotion management
- 420 Advertising
- 430 Shows, special events, and exhibits
- 440 Display

500 Service and operations
- 510 Service and operations management
- 530 Security
- 550 Telephones and communications
- 560 Utilities
- 570 Housekeeping
- 580 Maintenance and repairs

600 Personnel
- 610 Personnel management
- 620 Employment
- 640 Training
- 660 Medical and other employee services
- 670 Supplementary benefits

700 Merchandise receiving, storage, and distribution
- 710 Management of merchandise receiving, storage, and distribution
- 720 Receiving and marking
- 730 Reserve stock storage
- 750 Shuttle services

800 Selling and supporting services
- 810 Selling supervision
- 820 Direct selling
- 830 Customer services
- 840 Selling support services
- 860 Central wrapping and packing
- 880 Delivery

900 Merchandising
- 910 Merchandising management
- 920 Buying
- 930 Merchandise control

Figure 14–17

Inventory systems

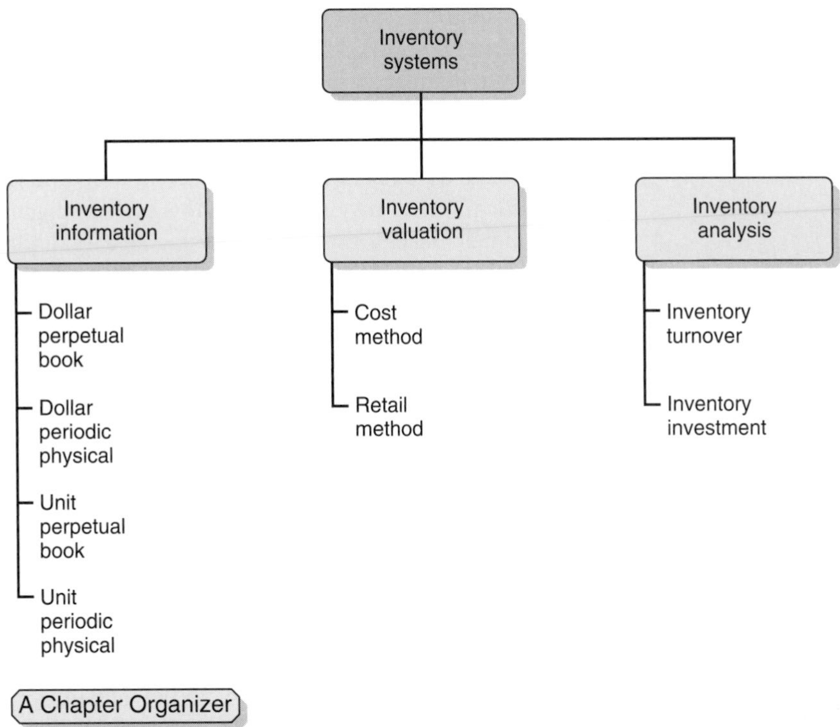

system includes methods for evaluating the retailer's past merchandising performance and decision-making tools for controlling future merchandising activities. Merchandise planning (see Chapter 9) and merchandise logistics (see Chapter 10) rely on the retailer's inventory information, valuation, and analysis systems to control inventory investment as well as inventory assortment and support.

Inventory Information

To control their inventories effectively, retailers must have an efficient means of obtaining information on the inventories' past and current status. Inventory control focuses on the issues of where it is and where it went. An adequate inventory information system is a prerequisite to planning and controlling future merchandising activities. As discussed in Chapter 9, merchandise investment and merchandise assortment and support are the principal elements the retailer wants to control. To complement merchandise planning, the retailer's inventory information system must be capable of providing both dollar control and unit control. Recalling the discussion in Chapter 9, dollar control considers the "value" of merchandise and attempts to identify the dollar amount of investment in merchandise. Dollar control requires the retailer to collect, record, and analyze merchandise data in terms of dollars. Unit control involves the number of different product items (assortment) and the number of units stocked within each item (support). It is the number of physical units (sales, purchases, and stock levels) recorded and analyzed. Both dollar and unit control are essential for the retailer that needs investment information for profit control and assortment information for stock control.

The retailer's source of inventory information is the inventory system. Inventory systems differ depending on when (perpetually or periodically) inventory is taken and how (book or physical) it is taken. On the basis of these two factors, inventory procedures can be classified as either perpetual book inventory systems or periodic physical inventory systems.

Perpetual book inventory refers to a system of inventory taking and information gathering on a continuous or ongoing basis using various accounting records to compute stock on hand at any given time. The purchase, sales, and markdown figures needed to calculate stock on hand are derived from internal accounting records that must be kept current if the computed book inventory is to reflect correctly the retailer's true stock position. In summary, a perpetual book inventory represents an up-to-the-minute, -day, or -week accounting system in which all transactions that affect inventory are considered as they occur or shortly thereafter. Its major advantage is that the retailer can determine stock on hand as required by operating conditions and the need for inventory information.

Periodic physical inventory refers to a system of gathering stock information intermittently (usually once or twice a year) using an actual, physical count and inspection of the merchandise items to compute sales for the period since the last physical inventory. Limitations of a periodic physical inventory system are the time-consuming process of making an actual, physical count of each merchandise item and the fact that most retailers have faster, easier methods for obtaining sales information. Nevertheless, a physical inventory must be taken at least once a year for income tax purposes. A physical count of the retailer's inventory also is necessary to determine stock shortages (book inventory minus physical inventory). Finally, for the small retailer that can afford neither the electronic data processing equipment nor the accounting personnel to maintain a sophisticated accounting system, a periodic physical inventory is the only alternative. Figure 14–17 identifies the major types of inventory information systems.

Dollar/Perpetual/Book Inventory

Dollar control using a **dollar/perpetual/book inventory** system provides the retailer with continuous information on the amount of inventory (dollars) that should be on hand at any given time as determined by internal accounting records. The basic procedures for calculating a perpetual book inventory in dollars are as follows:

beginning stock on hand
+ purchases
= total stock handled
– sales
– markdowns
= ending stock on hand

Dollar control systems express values either in terms of retail prices or cost prices. To simplify the discussion of dollar control, all values are considered here at retail price.

In the preceding formulation, the beginning stock-on-hand value is the ending stock-on-hand value from the preceding accounting period. Merchandise data involving purchases, sales, and markdowns are obtained from the appropriate internal accounting records. The computed ending stock on hand is the dollar value of the retailer's inventory, provided no shortages have occurred as a result of customer shoplifting, employee pilfering, or other causes that would reduce the value of the merchandise on hand. To determine actual stock shortages, the retailer would have to check the book inventory by taking a physical inventory. Many retailers use an estimated shortage percentage (for example, 2 percent) based on past experience to adjust the ending stock-on-hand value perpetually. A final adjustment is then made at the end of the season or year by conducting a physical count and valuation of the merchandise.

Dollar/Periodic/Physical Inventory

A **dollar/periodic/physical inventory** system for dollar control provides the retailer with periodic information on the amount of inventory (dollars) actually on hand at a given time as determined by a physical count and valuation of the merchandise. It permits the retailer to compute the dollar amount of sales since the last physical count. A periodic physical inventory usually is computed at designated intervals (monthly, quarterly, or semiannually) using the following basic procedure:

beginning stock on hand
+ purchases
= total stock handled
– ending stock on hand
= sales and markdowns
– markdowns
= sales

The beginning stock on hand is the value of the ending stock on hand brought forward from the previous accounting period. Internal purchases and markdown records are used to determine the dollar amount of purchases and markdowns since the last accounting period. The ending stock-on-hand figure is derived from a physical count and valuation of the merchandise inventory. The sales figure is computed as shown and incorporates the value of whatever shortages have occurred. Most retailers have easier and more timely means to obtain sales information.

Unit/Perpetual/Book Inventory A perpetual book inventory system for unit control—a **unit/perpetual/book system**—involves continuous recording of all transactions (for example, number of units sold or purchased), which changes the unit status of the retailer's merchandise inventory. Each unit transaction is posted as it occurs or shortly thereafter (for example, on a daily basis). Perpetual unit control provides a running total of the number of units of a given type that are flowing into and out of the store or department and helps the retailer continuously control the balance between units on hand and unit sales. Perpetual unit control systems are maintained manually or through various automatic recording systems.

Manual Systems. A manual system of perpetual unit control is maintained by the retailer's accounting personnel, who continuously record merchandise data on standard forms. To determine stock on hand, the accountant simply adds the number of units received during the accounting period and subtracts the number of units sold. The number of units received into stock is obtained from records furnished by the receiving department or clerk. Information on the number of units sold can be gathered by means of a number of manual systems, such as (1) point-of-sale-tallies; (2) price-ticket stubs; and (3) cash-register stubs.

Automatic Systems. Computer-based electronic data processing equipment allows the retailer to automatically convert merchandise data on sales, purchases, and stocks into useful information for planning and controlling merchandise assortment and support. Automatic systems include (1) *tag systems*, which use prepunched merchandise tags that are collected when the item is sold; (2) *card systems*, which involve sales personnel recording assortment information directly onto punch cards or scanner cards; or (3) *point-of-sale (POS) systems*, which use cash registers or terminals capable of transmitting assortment information directly to the central data processing facility as the sale is being recorded. Several methods can be used to record sales and assortment information in a point-of-sale system. Two common methods are (1) *optical scanners*, which read codes (for example, Universal Product Code) that have been premarked or imprinted on the merchandise item or package, and (2) *terminal keys*, which transmit data directly to the computer when sales personnel depress them.

Unit/Periodic/Physical Inventory A **unit/periodic/physical system** involves making a periodic physical check on the status of the retailer's inventory. Stock levels are monitored by a visual inspection or a physical count. For a **visual inspection**, stock-control personnel visually examine the stock of each item to determine whether sales have depleted the stock to the point of reordering. A *physical count* is the actual counting and recording of the number of units on hand at regular intervals. The retailer attempts to determine the number of units sold since the last physical count by adding purchases during the intervening period to the beginning stock on hand and then subtracting the ending stock on hand obtained from the current physical count.

Inventory Valuation

A major financial concern of every retailer is determining the actual worth of the inventory on hand. How the retailer establishes the value of the inventory can have a profound effect on the outcome of various financial statements (for example, the income statement, the balance sheet). Retailers can value their inventories at cost (what they paid for the merchandise) or at retail (what they can sell the merchandise for). This section examines the cost and retail methods of inventory valuation and reviews the relative strengths and weaknesses of each method.

The Cost Method Some retailers prefer the **cost method of inventory valuation** because it is easy to understand and implement and requires a limited amount of record keeping.[12] The retailer simply values merchandise inventory at the original cost to the store each time a physical inventory is taken. One of two procedures is typically used in computing the cost value of merchandise items: (1) The original cost can be coded on the price tag or merchandise container, or (2) the retailer can imprint a serialized reference number on each price tag corresponding to an itemized merchandise stock-control list containing the per-unit cost of each item.

A major problem of the cost method occurs when the retailer procures various shipments at different times during inflationary periods. Although the rate of inflation can vary significantly, the mere fact that inflation exists creates a problem (the extent of the problem depends on the rate of inflation), with different shipments of identical products being purchased at different wholesale prices (cost to retailer). The retailer then must decide which cost value to use. FIFO (first-in, first-out) and LIFO (last-in, first-out) are two inventory costing methods used to resolve this dilemma.

The **FIFO (first-in, first-out) method** assumes that merchandise items are sold in the order in which they are purchased; that is, older stock is sold before newer stock that was purchased at a later date. The cost of the oldest units in stock determines the retailer's cost of goods sold. From an operational viewpoint of maintaining the freshness of merchandise in stock, FIFO makes good sense and is the operating practice of most retailers. From a financial accounting viewpoint, however, during inflationary periods the FIFO method results in an overstatement of profits, thereby increasing the firm's tax liability.

Under **LIFO (the last-in, first-out method)**, recent acquisition costs are used to price inventory (even though in actuality, the inventory bought last is not sold first). The cost of the newest units in stock determines the retailer's cost of goods sold.

Although the cost method is simple, it does have several disadvantages. First, a cost valuation of inventory requires a physical count of the merchandise, and the need to count and decode prices is both time-consuming and costly. Second, the cost method does not provide a book inventory of which merchandise ought to be on hand. Therefore, the retailer has no means to determine shortages. (Remember, shortages equal book inventory minus physical inventory.) Finally, the cost method is often untimely, because physical inventory is usually taken only once or twice a year. As a result, the retailer cannot prepare weekly, monthly, and quarterly financial statements. "The growth of computer capacities is aiding the transition from the retail method to the cost accounting system. But deeply ingrained traditions within retailing and concerns over the expense of the change are slowing the transition."[13]

The Retail Method The **retail method of inventory valuation** enables the retailer to estimate the cost value of an ending inventory for a particular accounting period without taking a physical inventory. Essentially, the retail method is a book inventory system in which the cost value for each group of related merchandise (for example, a department) is based on its retail value (selling price). By determining the percentage relationship between the total cost and the total retail value of the merchandise available for sale during an accounting period, the retailer can obtain a reliable estimate of the ending inventory value at cost. To use the retail method, the retailer must make the following calculations: (1) the total merchandise available for sale, (2) the cost complement, (3) the total retail deductions, and (4) the ending inventory at retail and cost values.

Total Merchandise Available. The total merchandise available for sale is illustrated in the following example:

	Cost ($)	Retail ($)
beginning inventory	120 000	200 000
+ net purchases	80 000	140 000
+ additional markons		2 000
+ freight charges	4 000	
= total merchandise available	204 000	342 000

As shown, beginning inventory and purchase figures are kept at both cost and retail values. The beginning inventory is the ending inventory brought forward from the previous accounting period, obtained from the stock ledger that the accounting department maintains. Net purchases represent all purchases the retailer made during the accounting period minus any returns to the vendor. A purchase journal is used to record all purchase transactions. Any additional markons taken since setting the original retail price are added to the retail value of the inventory to reflect the market value of the merchandise. A price-change journal is maintained to keep track of additional markons as well as markdowns and other changes in the original retail selling price. Finally, freight charges obtained from the purchase journal are added to portray the true cost of the merchandise.

Cost Complement. The cost complement is the average relationship of cost to retail value for all merchandise available for sale during an accounting period. In essence, it is the complement of the cumulative markup percentage. The cost complement is computed as follows:

$$\text{cost complement} = \frac{\text{cost value of inventory}}{\text{retail value of inventory}}$$

Using the previous example, in which the value of the total merchandise available for sale equals \$204 000 at cost and \$342 000 at retail, then

$$\text{cost complement} = \frac{\$204\ 000}{\$342\ 000} = \Delta\ 0.5965$$

In this example, the retailer's merchandise cost is, on the average, equal to 59.65 percent of the retail value of the merchandise.

Retail Deductions. The third step in the retail method of inventory valuation is to determine the total merchandise available for sale. Retail deductions include merchandise that has been sold, marked down, discounted, stolen, and lost. Total retail deductions are obtained by adding all the deductions, reducing the retail value of the merchandise that is available for sale. To continue our illustration,

sales for period	$160 000
+ markdowns	30 000
+ discounts	10 000
+ shortages (estimated)	2 000
= total retail deductions	$202 000

The sales figure for the accounting period represents both cash and credit sales and is obtained from the retailer's sales journal. The amount of markdowns taken during the accounting period and the amount of the discounts granted to employees and special customers can be obtained from the price-change journal. Because shortages resulting from shoplifting, employee pilfering, and lost merchandise cannot be determined without a physical inventory, the retailer usually estimates the shortage figure on the basis of past experience.

Ending Inventory Value. The final step in implementing the retail method is to determine the value of ending inventory at retail and at cost. The retail value of ending inventory is computed by subtracting total retail deductions from total merchandise available for sale at retail. In our example,

total merchandise available at retail	$342 000
– total retail deductions	202 000
= ending inventory at retail	$140 000

The cost value of ending inventory is calculated by multiplying the ending inventory at retail by the cost complement in the following manner:

ending inventory at cost = ending inventory at retail × cost complement

ending inventory at cost = $140 000 × 0.5965 = $83 510

Although $83 510 is only an estimate of the true cost value of the ending inventory, the figure is sufficiently reliable to enable the retailer to estimate both the cost of goods sold and gross margin for the accounting period. To complete our example:

total merchandise available at retail	$204 000
– ending inventory at retail	$ 83 510
= cost of goods sold	$120 490

sales for the period	$160 000
– cost of goods sold	$120 490
= gross margin	$ 39 510

Although the retail method has the disadvantages of requiring the retailer to keep more records (stock ledger and sales, purchases, and price-change journals) and use averages to estimate cost values, its advantages are numerous. The retail method forces the retailer to "think retail" in that it highlights both retail and cost figures. Second, frequent and regular calculations of various financial and operating statements are possible as a result of the availability of cost and retail information. These statements are essential to good financial planning and control and enable the retailer to adjust more quickly to changing market conditions. Third, when the retail method is used, physical inventories are taken in retail prices, thereby eliminating the costly, time-consuming job of decoding cost prices. Recording physical inventory in retail prices greatly simplifies the process and encourages a more frequent physical count of stock. Fourth, the retail method facilitates planning and control on a departmental basis. Sales, purchases, inventories, and price-change information are recorded by department and can be used to evaluate each department's performance. Fifth, by providing a book figure on what inventory should be on hand, the retail method enables the retailer to determine shortages each time a physical inventory is taken. Sixth, the retail method facilitates planning for insurance coverage and collecting insurance claims by providing an up-to-date valuation of inventory.

Given the many advantages of the retail method of inventory valuation, it is not surprising that it is used extensively by large department and chain store retailers to gain tighter control over their various operating units.

Inventory Analysis

Inventory information is only useful when it provides the retailer with insights into past mistakes and with foresight for future planning. Merchandise data collected and processed by the inventory information system can be used to evaluate past performances and plan future actions. A determination of stock turnover and return on inventory investment are the principal methods for evaluating the retailer's past performance in controlling merchandise inventories. The dollar and unit open-to-buy methods (extensively reviewed in Chapter 9) are two of the more important tools for controlling future merchandising activities.

Retail Intelligence

Retail intelligence is any method or combination of methods used to obtain external secondary information. To keep the firm's decision makers current, the retailing information and control system must be able to monitor the daily developments of the marketplace. Retail intelligence involves search procedures to comb libraries and government and trade sources for pertinent information regularly and systematically. For a fee, additional retail intelligence can be obtained from various commercial organizations that specialize in monitoring certain aspects of the marketplace.

Gathering retail intelligence from library, government, association, and commercial sources provides the retailer with information about legal, political, social, economic, and technological environments. For any one of these sources, the information can be published or reported in the form of books, monographs, reports, periodicals, bulletins, disks, tapes, films, or several types of special publications.

Library Sources

The library not only is a source of information on a wide variety of subjects but also frequently serves as a means for locating other sources of retail intelligence. For the retailer seeking external secondary information, the library is a good starting point. Library research skills are developed by using the library and becoming familiar with its information retrieval systems (for example, card catalogues, visual display terminals, computer search technologies). Also, many libraries have specialized personnel (for example, government documents librarian) trained in finding specific information.

Government Sources

The most prolific compilers of external secondary information are federal, provincial, and local governments. Although government sources collect and disseminate an enormous amount of information on a wide variety of subjects, the types of information retailers use most often are census and registration data.

Census Information Statistics Canada collects data every five years as part of the census of population. This information can be valuable to a retailer. Information on population demographics, ethnic origin, household expenditures, and many other areas may prove helpful for several purposes. A special application of the census is the *Census Tract Reports* prepared for the larger cities in Canada. These reports can be very helpful to retailers in selecting locations in urban areas. Provincial government agencies in many provinces also provide information valuable to retailers. This information is often more specific and may include smaller centres than the Statistics Canada data.

American Marketing Association
www.ama.ca

Registration Information All levels of government at various times require individuals and organizations to register and report activities in which they are engaged. These routinely collected data can provide the retailer with a tremendous amount of useful information if the retailer knows how and where to obtain it. Some of the more common forms of registration include public records on (1) births, (2) deaths, (3) marriages, (4) school enrollments, (5) income, (6) sales tax payments, (7) automobile and recreational vehicle registration, and (8) general and special business licences and crime statistics.

Retail Strategies and Tactics

Association Sources of Retail Information

Trade and Professional Associations

American Marketing Association
Association of Canadian Franchisers
Association of Canadian Advertisers
Automotive Parts Manufacturers Association of Canada
Canadian Apparel Manufacturers Institute
Canadian Association of Marketing Research Organization
Canadian Booksellers Association
Canadian Council of Better Business Bureau
Canadian Council of Furniture Manufacturers
Canadian Federation of Independent Grocers
Canadian Hardware and Housewares Manufacturers Association
Canadian Jewellers Association
Canadian Research Management Association
Canadian Restaurant and Food Services Association
Canadian Retail Building Supply Council
Canadian Retail Hardware Association
Canadian Shoe Retailers' Association
Canadian Sporting Goods Association
Canadian Wholesale Druggists Association
Chamber of Commerce
Retail Council of Canada

Trade and Professional Publications

American Fabrics and Fashions
Auto Merchandising News
Business Marketing
Canadian Grocer
Canadian Hotel and Restaurant
Canadian Markets
Canadian Retailer
Chain Store Age
Curtain, Drapery and Bedspread Magazine
Dealerscope (appliances)
Discount Merchandiser
Drug Topics
Floor Covering Weekly
Florist
Furniture News
Hardware Age
Journal of Retailing
Juvenile Merchandising
Luggage and Leather Goods
Merchandising Week
Modern Jeweller
Office Products News
Retail Advertising Week
Retail Directions
Sports Merchandiser
Stores Magazine
Visual Merchandising
Volume Retail Merchandising
Women's Wear Daily

Source: D. Wesley Balderson and William A. Basztyk, Retailing in Canada, *Prentice Hall Canada Inc., 1993, 44.*

Association Sources

A third major source of external secondary information is the large group of trade and professional associations that collect and publish highly specialized information. It would be difficult to find a subject on which one or more of these organizations could not provide information. For instance, retailers might turn to the Canadian Federation of Independent Business, Retail Council of Canada, a relevant industry association, or the Canadian Chamber of Commerce for information and assistance on a wide range of business problems. Their charges for information range from free to various organization membership fees and publication subscription rates. A brief summary of some of these associations is found in the Retail Strategies and Tactics box entitled "Association Sources of Retail Information." Most associations publish a magazine, journal, or newsletter; they usually issue special reports, maintain files of information, and send out promotional literature as well.

Canadian Federation of Independent Business
www.cfib.ca

Commercial Sources

Many retailers are turning to **outsourcing** (contracting with firms that specialize in one or more information gathering or processing services) for their retail intelligence.[14] With the restructuring of many retail organizations, outsourcing is often the only way to obtain some forms of retail intelligence.[15] Commercial sources make a business out of collecting, tabulating, analyzing, and reporting information. The *Financial Post Canadian Markets* provides information on a variety of topics of interest to the retailer. This source provides estimated values for population, retail sales, household expenditures, and personal income for all census subdivisions in Canada. The *Canadian Business Index, Canadian News Index*, and *Business Periodicals Index* are sources of information which could also be useful to retailers. *Bradford's Directory* lists more than 350 firms engaged in the commercial gathering and selling of information. The *Directory of Marketing Information Companies*, the *Directory of Focus Group Facilities & Moderators*, and the *Directory of Customer*

Retail Strategies and Tactics

Selected Examples of Standardized Information Sources

- *Consumer Attitudes and Buying Plans (Conference Board of Canada)*
  Information on consumer confidence regarding business conditions, employment, and income, as well as on buying intentions.
- *Financial Post Canadian Markets*
  A compilation of information on households and retail sales as well as personal income for areas across Canada.
- *Handbook of Canadian Consumer Markets*
  Provides consumer market data pertaining to population characteristics, growth, labour force and employment, income, expenditures, production, distribution of goods and services, and consumer and industry price indices.
- *Media Survey (Broadcast Bureau of Measurement [BBM])*
  The BBM conducts and reports on network and TV market surveys as well as the radio broadcast sessions.
- *Media Survey (Print Measurement Bureau [PMB])*
  Provides detailed readership and demographic data for over seventy consumer and business publications, magazines, and other media. It also describes product usage habits nationally and by market.
- *Television Index (A.C. Nielsen)*
  Information on the size of television audience, viewing habits, flow of audience, and cost per 1000 homes reached.
- *Media Survey (Audit Bureau of Circulation)*
  Information on readership of newspapers and magazines.
- *Media Survey (Canadian Advertising Rates and Data)*
  Information on advertising rates for various media.

Source: D. Wesley Balderson and William A. Basztyk, Retailing in Canada, *Prentice Hall Canada Inc., 1993, 43.*

Satisfaction Measurement Firms are three additional, more specialized commercial sources of information.[16] Typically, commercial information sources provide either a standardized information service or a service tailored to the informational needs of a particular customer. Standardized information services provide a prescribed type of information continuously and regularly. *Tailored information services* provide customized information for the specific needs of the retailer. See the Retail Strategies and Tactics box entitled "Selected Examples of Standardized Information Sources" for other sources of retail intelligence.

Retail Research

Retail research is the systematic process of gathering and analyzing primary, external information about consumers, suppliers, and competitors. It is conducted on a project-by-project basis and directed at a particular problem-solving or decision-making situation. The main purpose of research is to obtain specific information on a timely basis in order to reduce the risks of making a decision. Calgary Co-op, for example, undertakes ongoing market studies and customer satisfaction surveys to identify consumer demand and evaluate store performance.[17] Conducting research can be an expensive and time-consuming venture, so each research project must be selected carefully on the basis of its potential for providing meaningful, useful information. To improve chances for success, many retailers are integrating their customer databases (for example, scanning data, credit records) and their retail research projects to help define research problems and guide survey research efforts.[18] Such firms as Canadian Airlines, Zellers, Harry Rosen, and Wear Else are examples of Canadian retailers that are utilizing customer databases to better serve their target market.[19] The Retail Strategies and Tactics box entitled "Sleep Country's Wake-Up Call" illustrates how one Canadian retailer did extensive research prior to establishing the business.

Research projects that have proven to be productive ventures for the retailer in the past include studies on (1) consumer attitudes toward the retailer and its merchandising efforts, (2) consumer purchase motives and preferences, (3) demographic and psychographic profiles of both customers and noncustomers, (4) buyer behaviour patterns and their relationships to the retailer's mode of operations, (5) service and performance records of suppliers, (6) price and cost comparisons among suppliers, (7) merchandising and operational strengths and weaknesses of competitors, and (8) employee perceptions of the company and its dealings with them. As shown in Figure 14–18, research methods, research instruments, and sampling procedures are the key issues to be decided when contemplating a research project.

Research Methods

Retail analysts use three basic methods in collecting external primary information: surveys, observation, and experimentation. The method used typically depends on the nature of the research problem under investigation.

Survey Method Using the **survey method**, the researcher systematically gathers information directly from the appropriate respondents. Generally, in the survey method the researcher uses a questionnaire administered either in person, over the telephone, or by mail. In recent years, the growing number of households owning PCs and the popularity of the Internet has made e-mail surveys a viable vehicle for some survey research projects.[20]

Retail Strategies and Tactics

Sleep Country's Wake-Up Call

In a well-planned assault on two of Canada's biggest markets, mattress retailer Sleep Country Canada opened multiple outlets in Vancouver in October 1994 and in Toronto [in early 1996]. Its stores were all bright and attractive, its staff eager and well-trained. At the same time, it aired a barrage of radio ads, complete with catchy jingle. Indeed, the launch was so smooth that research revealed that after 12 months in the market, most Vancouverites figured the company had been around for five years.

None of that was by accident. SCC's president, Christine Magee, had years of experience in commercial banking. Her partners, merchant bankers Gordon Lownds and Stephen Gunn, had once invested in a mattress manufacturer. But they had another edge: they had found an experienced mentor to make their startup flawless.

The three partners all saw a promising niche for a mattress chain offering value and first-class service. But that concept wasn't enough. To improve their profit potential, they visited mattress dealers across the U.S. to see if they could learn from someone who was already doing what they hoped to do.

In Seattle the partners discovered a 13-store family business called Sleep Country USA. They liked its name, its commitment to service (example: a 60-day exchange guarantee), its bright, airy stores—even its jingle, which asked, "Why buy a mattress anywhere else?" Under president Sunny Kobe Cook, "They were doing exactly the service and marketing program we wanted to do," says Magee. So the Canadians licensed the rights to the concept, including the right to expand into other parts of the U.S.

Today SC Canada has 96 stores, with plans for eight or nine more [in 1997]. Next, it is eyeing a push into the U.S. With her proven formula, Magee should sleep easier than most Canadian retailers trying to grow south of the border.

Source: Rick Spence, Profit Magazine, *April/May 1997, 8.*

Sleep Country Canada
www.sleepcountry.com

Figure 14–18

Retail research

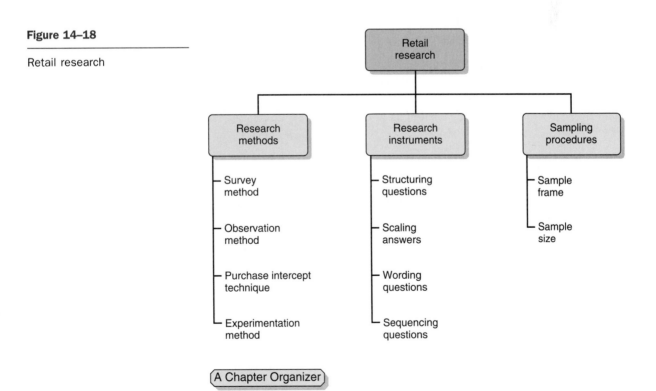

- Retail research
  - Research methods
    - Survey method
    - Observation method
    - Purchase intercept technique
    - Experimentation method
  - Research instruments
    - Structuring questions
    - Scaling answers
    - Wording questions
    - Sequencing questions
  - Sampling procedures
    - Sample frame
    - Sample size

A Chapter Organizer

Personal Interview. The personal interview is a face-to-face question-and-answer session between the interviewer and the respondent. In recent years, computer-assisted interviews have greatly enhanced the effectiveness and efficiency of personal interviews.[21] Interviewers can contact respondents at their homes, places of employment, or public places (for example, street corners, shopping centres, retail stores). Typically, the personal interview consists of these steps: (1) *identification*—a statement of who is conducting the interview, what the survey is about, for whom it is being conducted, and why it is being conducted; (2) *permission*—a request of the respondent for an interview; (3) *administration*—the interviewer asks a predetermined list of questions and records the respondent's answers; and (4) *closure*—the terminating step in which the interviewer thanks the respondent for his or her cooperation.

Telephone Survey. In a telephone survey, retailers phone potential respondents at their homes. Successful telephone interviews take no more than three or four minutes of the respondent's time. The basic survey steps of identification, permission, administration, and closure are essentially the same for telephone surveys as they are for personal surveys.

Mail Surveys. Mail surveys differ from personal interviews and telephone surveys in that the questionnaire is administered in writing. The potential respondent in a mail survey receives and returns the questionnaire by mail. The survey director also can administer the survey by attaching questionnaires to products or packages, passing them out in a store or on the street, or placing them in newspapers. In these cases, respondents are asked to return the questionnaire in a self-addressed, postage-paid envelope. Because the questionnaire is in written form and the interviewer is not available to ask or answer questions, the questionnaire should be short and simple and have complete instructions. To help the retailer select the best survey method, Figure 14–19 summarizes the relative strengths and weaknesses of each method.

World of Retailing

Retail Technology

Kiosks for Retail Research

Traditionally, researchers have used phone and exit interviews, mall intercepts, and mail surveys to study retail shopping experiences. Although these methods have their strengths, there is an alternative: kiosk-based research.

Kiosks are multimedia, touch-screen computers contained in free-standing cabinets. They can be programmed to perform complicated surveys, show full-colour scanned images (store layouts, products), play high-quality stereo sound clips and show video segments.

With little need for instruction, most people enjoy these interviews and "play" them with little reservation. Kiosks have been used at conventions and trade shows, but the technology transfers easily to the retail environment.

Kiosks, like exit interviews, score high in terms of capturing recent experiences and are useful for interviewing low-incidence respondents because they are on site.

At the same time, kiosk-based research tends to be less expensive than exit interviews, allowing a higher number of stores to be included in the survey. A bonus is that people tend to give more honest answers to a computer than to another human being.

Kiosks have several other advantages. Internal control, for example, is much higher with kiosk than with other methods. Because the survey is preprogrammed, the researcher does not have to worry about whether the correct visual stimuli was shown or whether the right skip pattern was followed.

Source: Beth Schneider, "Using interactive kiosks for retail research," Marketing News, *January 2, 1995, 13.*

Observation Method Researchers can obtain significant amounts of primary information simply by observing consumers' behaviour. The **observation method** records some aspect of consumers' overt behaviour by either personal or mechanical means. Shopper-Trak system records every shopper who enters and exits the store, along with the time and the date. "Retailers can monitor how many people come and go, the direction that the individual shopper walks in, and how fast people are moving through the store or a specific department."[22] What the consumer does, not says, is the principal focus of the observation method. The advantages of this method are that it (1) eliminates any interviewer bias associated with the survey method and (2) does not require the respondent's cooperation. The major disadvantage of the observation method is that the retailer cannot investigate the consumer's motives, attitudes, beliefs, and feelings. If the retailer uses this method, it must decide what observation and recording techniques to use, the setting in which to make the observation, and whether to inform consumers that they are being observed (see Figure 14–20).

Purchase Intercept Technique By combining the observation method with the survey (self-report) method, the **purchase intercept technique (PIT)** capitalizes on "the advantages of observation (e.g., accuracy and objectivity) and the significant information gained through self reporting (e.g., information about why the specific behaviour takes

Figure 14–19

Determining which survey method to use

Selection criteria	Survey method: Personal interview	Telephone survey	Mail survey
Cost:[1] What is the most expensive method of collecting information?	Most expensive	Intermediate	Least expensive
Speed: What is the fastest method of collecting information?	Slowest method	Fastest method	Intermediate
Accuracy: What is the most accurate method of collecting information?	Most accurate	Intermediate	Least accurate
Volume: Which method is capable of collecting the most information?	Most information	Least information	Intermediate
Response rate: Which method results in the highest number of completed interviews?	Highest response	Intermediate	Lowest response
Flexibility: What method is most capable of adjusting to changing interviewing conditions?	Most flexible	Intermediate	Least flexible
Sample control:[2] Which method is capable of securing the best representative sample of the total population?	Intermediate	Worst representation	Best representation
Interview control: What method provides the interviewer the greatest amount of control over the interview situation?	Greatest control	Intermediate	Least control
Administrative control: Which method provides the retailer the greatest amount of control over the actions of the interviewer?	Least control	Intermediate	Greatest control

[1]Where the sample is scattered over a wide geographic area.
[2]Assumes an accurate mailing list.

Figure 14–20

Using the observation method

Decision	Description	Example
Observation methods:		
1. Direct	Observing current behaviour	Watching the number of consumers who stop to inspect a store display
2. Indirect	Observing past behaviour	Counting the number of store branded products (e.g., Sears) found in the consumer's home
Recording methods:		
1. Personal	Recording observations by hand	Logging customer reactions to a sales presentation by visually observing and manually recording the process
2. Nonpersonal	Recording observations mechanically or electronically (counters, cameras, sensors)	Measuring television viewing habits using an "audiometer," measuring pupil dilation while an advertisement is viewed using a "perceptoscope," and using an "eye camera" to measure eye movements of consumers as they view a display
Observation setting:		
1. Natural	Observing behaviour in an unplanned and real setting	Observing the customer's natural trip behaviour through the store
2. Artificial	Observing behaviour in a planned and contrived setting	Observing sales personnel reaction to various customer "plants" who dress in various fashions
Observation organization:		
1. Structured	Observing specific behaviour patterns	Observing the actions of only female customers who purchase a particular product
2. Unstructured	Observing general behaviour patterns	Observing all of the actions of all customers regardless of who they are or what they buy
Observation situation:		
1. Disguised	Observing behaviour without the person being aware that he or she is being observed	Using a two-way mirror to observe how customers inspect a display
2. Nondisguised	Observing behaviour in an open fashion, thereby allowing the person to be aware that he or she is being observed	Following the customer around the store to observe shopping patterns

place)."[23] The PIT is an in-store information-gathering technique consisting of the following steps: (1) observe customer in-store shopping behaviour; (2) record pertinent shopping behaviour information; and (3) interview customers immediately about their purchase or shopping behaviour.[24] Revco, a large drugstore chain, used "trackers" who shadowed, recorded, and interviewed shoppers to gain the needed information to redesign and improve store layouts.[25]

Experimentation Method The **experimentation method** is a technique that researchers use to determine a cause-and-effect relationship between two or more factors. An experiment is usually conducted under controlled conditions; that is, the factors under study are manipulated while all other factors are held constant. For example, a retailer might increase the price of a product by $5 to see what effect the price change has on sales and profits, while holding constant all other factors, such as location, amount of shelf space, advertisements, and in-store displays.

The before-after design *without* a control group measures the dependent factor (sales volume) before and after the factor has been manipulated (for example, change from a middle-aisle to end-of-aisle display). The researcher assumes that the difference in sales volume is caused by the change in location, because all other factors affecting the sale of the product are held constant (see Figure 14–21a).

The before-after design with control group is essentially the same as the design just described except that a control group is used to determine whether any changes in sales volume would have occurred regardless of any manipulation. For example, in Figure 14–21b, Store A's sales volume is measured before and after an advertising campaign to determine the effects of advertising. To prove that all changes in sales volume are the result of advertising, any changes in the sales volume of control Store B, which is unaffected by the advertising campaign, are also measured over the same period of time. If control Store B experienced no change in sales volume, then the researcher can more comfortably state that changes in sales volume for Store A are the result of the advertising campaign, everything else being equal.

The after-only with control group design is the most widely used design because of its simplicity and ease of implementation. As shown in Figure 14–21c, it involves measuring the dependent factor (sales volume of Department A in Store A) for one group that has been manipulated (increased size of display area) and comparing it with the same dependent factor (sales volume of Department A in Store B) for the control group that was not manipulated.

Research Instruments

By far the most widely used research instrument in retail research is the questionnaire.[26] This discussion therefore is limited to this particular instrument. The four major factors a researcher must carefully consider are structuring, wording, and sequencing questions, and scaling answers in the questionnaire.

Structuring Questions Questions can be either open-ended (unstructured) or closed-ended (structured). Open-ended questions enable respondents to answer questions in their own words, thereby providing greater freedom in communicating their responses. Used extensively in motivation research, the open-ended question enables respondents to project their feelings about the retailer's merchandising and operational activities. Retailers can use several open-ended or projective techniques.

Word Association Test. The first projective technique is a *word association* test—a set of words or phrases to which respondents must give their immediate reactions. One possible set of words and responses might be the following: (1) store—clean; (2) products—good selection; and (3) prices—low.

Figure 14–21

Experimental research designs: (a) before-after design without control group, (b) before-after design with control group, and (c) after-only with control group

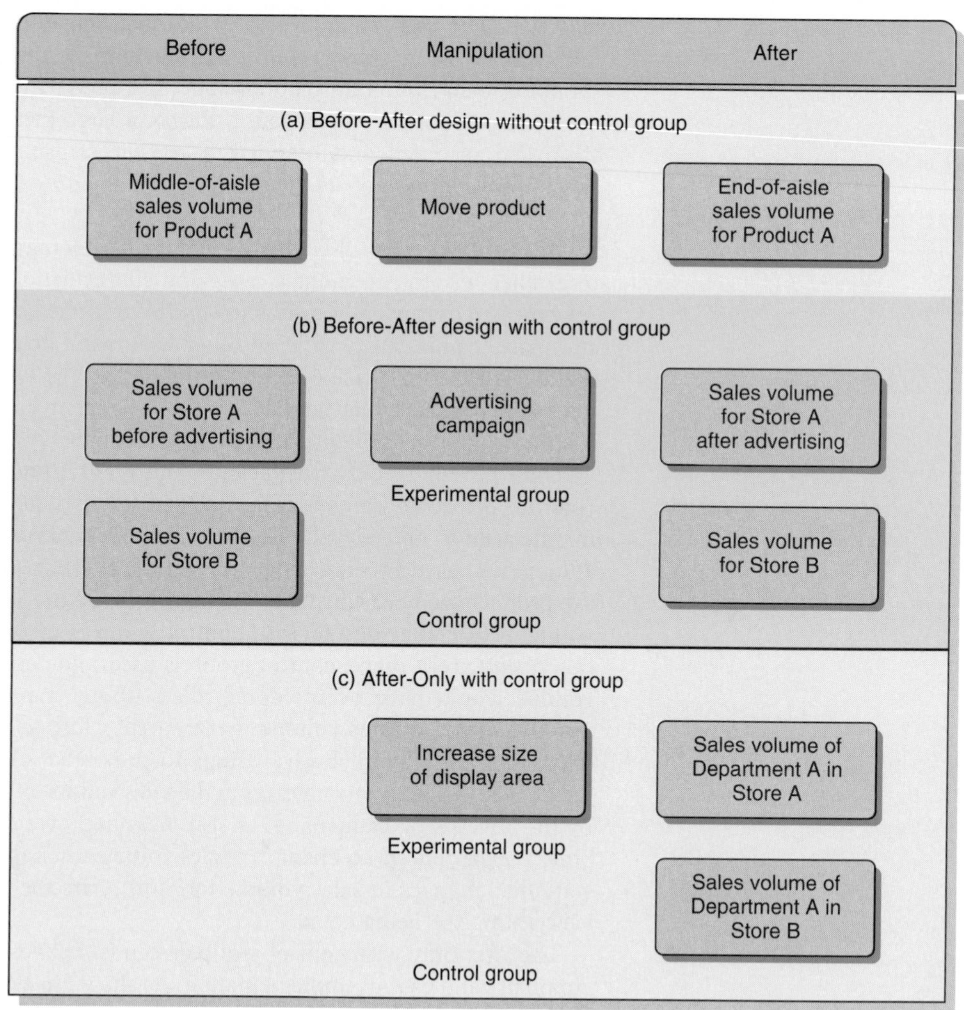

Sentence Completion Test. A second projective technique is the *sentence completion* test, which asks respondents to finish a set of sentences. For example, store personnel should be ______; the best price is one that ______; and private labels are ______.

Narrative Projection Test. A third open-ended questionnaire is the *narrative projection* test, in which the researcher provides respondents with a descriptive situation and asks them to write a paragraph in response.[27] An example of a descriptive situation the researcher might give respondents is the following: "A neighbour asks you what is the best store in town for buying draperies and why you think it is best. What would you tell him or her?" Respondents would then write their reactions to this description.

Thematic Apperception Test. The fourth projection technique is the *thematic apperception test*, during which respondents are shown a cartoon, drawing, or picture and then asked to put themselves into the situation and tell a story about what is happening or what they would do: "A picture showing one customer observing a poorly dressed elderly woman placing merchandise into a pocket." A typical response to this picture might be, "She lives on welfare, has very little money, and must resort to shoplifting."

The major purpose of most **open-ended questionnaires** is to explore and identify potential problems and obtain information that could be included in a structured research study. Because of the numerous difficulties in classifying and interpreting the results of open-ended questions, many retailers prefer to use structured questioning. The closed-ended questionnaire is a highly structured format that gives respondents a set of answers from which to choose. The three most common closed-ended questionnaires are dichotomous questions (answering yes or no, true or false), multiple-choice (selecting correct answers from a list of answers), and rank-ordered questions (ranking a list of factors in order of their importance).

Many researchers prefer structured questions because they are easier to tabulate and analyze and because they eliminate the ambiguity of answers and the interpretation problems of unstructured questions. The major disadvantage of structured questions is that they limit the amount and type of answers the respondent can make.

Scaling Answers To overcome the high cost and interpretation problems associated with unstructured questions and to gain more information than structured questions provide, many researchers prefer to use questions whose answers reflect the relative degree of the respondent's attitudes and opinions on a subject.[28] The two most commonly used scales in retail research are (1) *Likert's Summated Rating Scale*, which measures attitudes and opinions by asking respondents to indicate the extent of their agreement or disagreement (for example, strongly agree, agree, undecided, disagree, strongly disagree) with a list of statements involving the issue being studied;[29] and (2) **semantic differential rating scale**, a set of seven-point, bipolar scales that measure the meanings and attitudes that people have regarding some object. The respondent is asked to mark one of seven positions on a scale with ends identified by opposite descriptive terms. For example, the retailer that wants to obtain information regarding the appearance of its store might use the following scale:

Clean ______ ______ ______ ______ ______ ______ ______ Dirty

Each position of the semantic scale is assigned a numerical value that can be used to calculate arithmetic means for all respondents' answers to each scale. These figures can be used to profile a store's image, as illustrated by the connected lines.

Wording Questions If questions are leading, ambiguous, poorly worded, or use a vocabulary with which respondents are unfamiliar, then the resulting answers will not be especially helpful, perhaps even meaningless. To help the researcher avoid wording problems, the following guidelines should be observed: (1) keep each question as short as possible; (2) limit each question to one idea; (3) use simple, concise language; (4) avoid technical terms and buzzwords; (5) ask questions that have answers the respondent can be expected to know and remember; and (6) ask personal questions in a generalized way.

Sequencing Questions After the researcher has carefully worded the questionnaire, the next step is to order the questions. Order is an important aspect of developing any questionnaire because the sequence can affect the final results. To sequence questions, use the following guidelines: (1) use an attention getter and an interest grabber for the opening question; (2) ask general questions first, specific questions last; and (3) place personal questions at the end of the questionnaire.

Sampling Procedures

After selecting the type of research method and the instrument, the retailer must decide on the sampling procedure to use in collecting information. That is, when the retailer has decided *what* information is needed and *how* it is to be obtained, it must then determine *whom* to ask to obtain the desired information. The *who* in this case is a **sample**, or some portion of a predefined population. A **population** is the total membership of a defined group of individuals or items. For example, a population could be defined as either all potential consumers or all actual consumers of a particular product. Researchers use samples instead of an entire population because it is too costly and time-consuming to observe or survey an entire population. With proper sampling procedures, the researcher can draw valid conclusions about the attitudes, opinions, makeup, and behaviour of the total population without contacting its entire membership.[30]

The retailer's sampling procedures follow three essential steps: (1) identifying the sampling frame, (2) determining the size of the sample, and (3) selecting the sample items.

Sample Frame The first step in sampling is to create or find a list of people or entities included in the defined population being investigated. From this list the sample will be drawn. For example, the list could be the names of retail businesses listed in the phone book, names and addresses of all adults (aged 18 years and older) living within a defined trading area, or a list of a store's credit card holders.

Sample Size Sample size is the number of people the researcher wants to survey. A large sample normally results in greater accuracy and more reliable information; however, as the size of the sample increases, so do the costs of obtaining the sample. If scientific sampling procedures are followed carefully, small samples such as 400 or 500 persons can provide satisfactory results and reliable information.

Sample Item The last sampling procedure is to select the sample, determining how the sample items or persons are to be chosen. There are two general types of samples: probability and nonprobability. In a **probability sample**, each person in the total population has a known and equal chance of being selected. In a **nonprobability sample**, each person in the total population does not have a known and equal chance of being selected, but the researcher controls selection. Whenever possible, the researcher should use a probability sample, because it provides more reliable results and permits the use of more sophisticated analytical techniques. Figure 14–22 identifies and briefly defines the various types of probability and nonprobability samples.

Figure 14–22

Types of probability and nonprobability samples

Probability samples	Nonprobability samples
1. *Simple random:* A sampling procedure in which one sample is drawn from the entire population, with each individual or item having an equal probability of being selected.	1. *Convenience:* A sampling procedure in which each sample individual or item is selected at the convenience of the researcher (e.g., whoever walks into the store).
2. *Stratified random:* A sampling procedure in which the population is first subdivided into groups based on some known and meaningful criteria (e.g., sex, age). Then a simple random sample is drawn for each subgroup.	2. *Judgment:* A sampling procedure in which each sample individual or item is selected by the researcher based on an idea of what constitutes a representative sample (e.g., every seventh person who walks past the display counter).
3. *Cluster or area:* A sampling procedure in which geographical areas (e.g., census tracts or blocks) are randomly selected. Then a simple random sample is used to select a certain number of individuals or items (e.g., houses) from each of the selected geographical areas.	3. *Quota:* A sampling procedure in which the researcher divides the total population into several segments based on some factor believed to be important (e.g., sex and age). Then the researcher arbitrarily selects a certain number (quota) from each segment (e.g., selects five females over age 40, five females under age 40, five males over age 40, and five males under age 40).
4. *Systematic:* A sampling procedure in which the first individual or item of a sampling frame is selected randomly. Then each subsequent individual or item is selected at every *n*th interval (e.g., every fifth item on the list).	

Summary

A key means of gaining retailing success is fiscal control. The retailer must develop a set of financial records that provides a broad picture of the firm's financial condition. A typical set of records includes sales, cash receipts, cash disbursements, purchases, payroll, equipment, inventory, accounts receivable, and accounts payable. The retailer then uses these records to prepare two essential financial statements: the income statement and the balance sheet.

The income statement summarizes the retailer's financial activity for a stated accounting period. It is prepared to show the profit (or loss) a retailer has made during an accounting period. The income statement is a systematic set of procedures that helps the retailer identify five income measurements: gross sales, net sales, gross margin, operating profit, and net profit. The balance sheet is a statement of the retailer's financial condition on a given date. It summarizes the basic relationship among the retailer's assets, liabilities, and net worth.

In performance analysis, the retailer must judge the firm's operating and financial performance. By using several standardized operating and financial ratios, the retailer can compare performance, on a historic or a trade basis, with national norms. Expense allocation is accomplished by using the net profit plan, the contribution plan, and the net profit contribution plan. An expense budget is used to plan and control operating expenditures. The retailer uses one of several budgeting procedures: zero based, fixed based, or productivity based.

An inventory information system is a set of methods and procedures for collecting and processing merchandise data pertinent to planning and controlling merchandise inventories. Depending on the kind of information needed and the available sources of that information, the retailer can elect to use (1) a dollar/perpetual/book system, (2) a dollar/periodic/physical system, (3) a unit/perpetual/book system, or (4) a unit/periodic/physical system. An essential element in dollar control is knowing the true value of inventories. The two methods of inventory valuation are the cost method and the retail method. The inventory analysis system includes methods for evaluating the retailer's past merchandising performance as well as the decision-making tools available for controlling future merchandising activities.

Retail intelligence is any method or combination of methods used to obtain external secondary information. The principal sources of retail intelligence are libraries, government publications (for example, census and registration information), association information (trade and professional organizations), and commercial providers (those that make a business out of collecting, analyzing, and reporting information).

Retail research uses a set of procedures to gather external primary information from consumers, suppliers, and competitors. Collection of primary information is accomplished using research methods such as surveys, observations, purchase intercepts, and experiments. In conducting research, retailers must concern themselves with such issues as the structuring of questions, the scaling of answers, and the wording and sequencing of questions. Sampling procedures are crucial in conducting primary retail research. The retailer must develop the skills for identifying the sample frame, determining the sample size, and selecting the sample item.

Key Terms and Concepts

Review Questions

1. What is the purpose of an income statement? Identify and define the role of the nine elements of an income statement.
2. Why is a balance sheet prepared? Describe the basic balance sheet equation.
3. Distinguish between current and fixed assets and current and long-term liabilities, with specific examples of each.
4. How should the retailer view the concept of net worth?
5. What is ratio analysis?
6. Describe the relationships expressed by operating ratios. Cite examples of these relationships.
7. Compare and contrast the current and the leverage ratios. What does each ratio measure?
8. How can expenses be classified? Describe the various expense classification systems.
9. Expense allocation is accomplished through the use of three allocation methods. Describe each method.
10. Expense budgeting can be accomplished in several ways. Describe the three expense budgeting approaches.
11. What distinguishes perpetual book inventory from periodic physical inventory?
12. How are stock levels monitored in a unit/periodic/physical inventory system? Briefly describe each method.

13. Describe the FIFO and LIFO methods of costing inventories.

14. List the advantages of the retail method of inventory valuation.

15. How do the two general forms of commercial sources of retail intelligence differ?

16. Characterize the personal interview process. How should a personal interview be conducted?

17. How do mail surveys differ from personal and telephone surveys?

18. Develop a graphic presentation of the three experimental designs used by researchers.

19. Describe the four open-ended or projective techniques for collecting primary information.

20. What guidelines should be followed to avoid the many pitfalls in wording questionnaire items?

21. How should questions be sequenced?

22. What is a sample frame?

23. Describe briefly the various types of probability and nonprobability samples.

Review Exam

True or False

______ 1. The income statement is a picture of the retailer's assets, liabilities, and net worth on a given date; the balance sheet is a picture of the retailer's profits or losses over a period of time.

______ 2. Fixed assets are those assets that require a significant length of time to convert to cash.

______ 3. The contribution plan of expense allocation will almost always show a positive contribution. This means the department is contributing its fair share to the store's profit.

______ 4. When the LIFO method of inventory costing is used, the cost of the oldest unit in stock determines the retailer's cost of goods sold.

______ 5. Mail surveys provide the interviewer with the greatest amount of control over an interview situation.

______ 6. The after-only with control group design is the most widely used experimental design because of its simplicity and ease of implementation.

Multiple Choice

______ 1. Gross margin ______.
a. is the dollar difference between net sales and the total cost of goods sold
b. is the dollar difference between gross sales and net returns and allowances
c. represents the funds available for covering operating expenses and generating a profit
d. a and c
e. b and c

______ 2. A(n) ______ ratio measures the relative contribution of owners and creditors in the financing of the firm's operation.
a. leverage
b. current
c. debt
d. liquidity
e. operating

______ 3. Using the natural division of expenses, the retailer classifies expenses on the basis of ______.
a. which store function incurred the expense
b. where (examples: store or department) the expense was incurred
c. fixed or variable
d. kind of expense

______ 4. A ______ inventory system refers to a system in which inventory is taken and information is gathered on a continuous or ongoing basis using various accounting records to compute stock on hand at any given time.
a. perpetual book
b. perpetual physical
c. periodic book
d. periodic physical

_______ **5.** All of the following instruments are open-ended projective techniques except _______.
a. word association tests
b. sentence completion tests
c. thematic apperception tests
d. rank-ordering tests

_______ **6.** When designing a questionnaire, the wording of each question is extremely important. To avoid wording problems, all of the following guidelines should be observed, except _______.
a. limit each question to one idea
b. use concise and simple words
c. avoid technical terms and buzzwords
d. ask personal questions in a specific manner
e. keep each question as short as possible

Student Application Manual

Investigative Projects: Practice and Application

1. Classify the following expenses as either fixed or variable, controllable or uncontrollable: (a) sales commissions, (b) store manager's salary, (c) a weekly newspaper advertisement, (d) a business licence, (e) employees' health insurance payments, (f) the services of an accounting firm, (g) a donation to the United Way, (h) cost of new fixtures, (i) store rent, and (j) a monthly telephone bill. Explain your classification.

2. By making a visual survey of several hardware, variety, and sporting goods stores, identify and describe several examples of the visual inspection method used in a unit/periodic/physical inventory information system.

3. The manager of a specialty furniture accessories shop is considering adding a line of ceiling fans. Before making this product line addition, the manager wants more information involving (a) consumer attitudes regarding product features, preferred brands, and desired price ranges and (b) consumer past purchases of ceiling fans and their future buying intentions. Design an effective, efficient consumer survey research instrument that will obtain the desired information.

4. Consider the problem outlined in question 3. Design a sampling procedure that will enable the retailer to draw valid conclusions about the attitudes, behaviour, and intentions of the total population without contacting its entire membership. Be sure to include in your design a discussion of the sample frame, the sample size, and the procedures for selecting each sample item.

Endnotes

1. Peter Francese, "Managing Market Information," *American Demographics* (September 1995): 56.
2. Thomas E. Miller, "New Markets for Information," *American Demographics* (April 1995): 46.
3. See Philip Z. Dolen, "How Retailers Can Use Information for Competitive Advantage," *International Trends in Retailing* (Arthur Andersen & Co., Spring 1986), 23–38.
4. See Michael J. O'Connor, "How Much to Take and How Much to Leave," *International Trends in Retailing* (Arthur Andersen & Co., Summer 1992), 19–28.
5. See "Retailers Strengthen Defenses against Return Fraud," *Stores* (November 1995): 48–51.
6. Faye Brookman, "Staying Lean and Mean in a Tough Economy," *Stores* (June 1991): 36.
7. See Zina Moukheiber, "Retailing," Forbes, January 4, 1993, 172–75. Also see "The Business Week 1000," *Business Week*, 1993 Special Bonus Issue, 114–200.
8. See Norman M. Scarborough and Thomas W. Zimmerer, *Effective Small Business Management* (New York: Merrfli/Macmillan, 1988): 170.
9. *Ibid*, 171.
10. See Robert F. Lusch and Patrick Dunne, *Retail Management* (Cincinnati: South-Western, 1990), 54–55.
11. Andrew Nikiforuk, "Why Safeway Struck Out," *Canadian Business*, September 1997, 27–31.
12. James R. Larson, "Inventory Accounting: The Cost Method Makes Slow but Steady Gains," *Retail Control* (March 1991): 13–18.
13. "Retailers Consider Switch to Cost Accounting," *Stores*, November 1995, 50.
14. See Bill Kelley, "Outsourcing Marches On," *Journal of Business Strategy*, 16 (July/August 1995): 39–42; and Richard Henry, "Outsourcing Leverage in the Nineties," *Retail Control* (March 1992): 19–26.

15. Alan L. Gilman, "Outsourcing for Competitive Advantage," *Chain Store Age Executive* (May 1992): 214.

16. See *Marketing News Insert*, March 2, 1992, CMSI–CMS12. Also see *Marketing News Insert*, January 6, 1992, FGI–FG16. Also see *American Demographics*: 1992 Directory of Marketing Information Companies 1991, 1–45.

17. Sheila Hansen, "Coop—Celebrating 40 Years," *Calgary Coop Magazine*, April 1997, 35.

18. Phillip Ezop, "Database Marketing Research," *Marketing Research*, 6 (Fall 1994): 34–41.

19. Diane Lucklow, "Better Selling Through Technology," *Profit*, December 1994, 43–44.

20. See Martin Oppermann, "E-mail Surveys—Potentials and Pitfalls," *Marketing Research* 7 (Summer 1995): 29–33.

21. Michael Geurts and David Whitlark, "A Little Inducement Goes a Long Way," *Marketing Research* 6 (Summer 1994): 12–15.

22. Cyndee Miller, "Retail System Keeps Track of Shoppers," *Marketing News*, April 29, 1991, 14.

23. Shelby H. McIntyre and Sherry D. F. G. Bender, "The Purchase Intercept Technique (PIT) in Comparison to Telephone and Mail Surveys," *Journal of Retailing*, 62 (Winter 1986): 364.

24. *Ibid.*

25. See Howard Riell, "Revco Tracks the Customer," *Stores*, April 1995, 35–36.

26. See Andrew C. Bean and Michael J. Roszkowski, "The Long and Short of It," *Marketing Research*, 7 (Winter 1995): 20–27.

27. See Sharon L. Hollander, "Projective Techniques Uncover Real Consumer Attitudes," *Marketing News*, January 4, 1988, 34.

28. See Diane H. Schmalensee, "Finding the 'Perfect' Scale," *Marketing Research*, 6 (Fall 1994): 24–27.

29. See Terry Grapentine, "Dimensions of an Attribute," *Marketing Research*, 7 (Summer 1995): 18–19.

30. Ruth N. Bolton, "Covering the Market," *Marketing Research*, 6 (Summer 1994): 30–35.

Video Case for Part 6

Dylex

The Dylex company has been the leading retail clothing chain in Canada for a number of years. Although its stores do not bear the Dylex name, the company owns controlling interest in several well-known retail chains such as Braemar, Fairweather, Tip Top Tailors, BiWay, Club Monaco, and Thrifty's, with over 700 outlets in Canada. Recently Dylex has returned to profitability following some difficult years which brought it to the brink of bankruptcy.

Dylex was established in 1967 by Wilfred Posluns and James Kay. The Dylex concept was to bring specialty chains into the company, each appealing to a different segment of the market, and allow them to operate in a decentralized way with minimal head office interference. This formula worked well at first but by the 1980s the Canadian retail environment became more competitive, forcing many clothing retailers into financial difficulties. Many of the chains in the Dylex family were affected adversely, causing the chain to lose close to $55 million in 1991.

These difficulties resulted in management changes, the sell-off or close down of several money-losing stores (see Table 1), and a restructuring of operations to make the company more efficient. By 1996 signs that the company had weathered the storm were appearing. In distributing the annual report for 1996, Elliot Wahle, Dylex's new President and CEO, said, "although the Canadian retail sector continues to undergo major upheaval, our results demonstrate our ability to compete in tough times. I am optimistic that these results, plus a growing recognition of Dylex's renewed financial stability, will continue to build confidence in our prospects for the future."

Table 1

Former Dylex Chains

Chain	Stores in 1986	Today
Brooks, T. Edwards (U.S.)	872	Bankrupt (1987)
Ruby's, Feathers, Fantasia, Diva	54	Sold (1988)
Harry Rosen Women	10	Closed (1988)
Foxmoor (U.S.)	609	Bankrupt (1990)
B.H. Emporium	28	Closed (1990)
Town and Country	209	Closed (1991)
Club International (U.S.)	6	Sold (1991)
Suzy Shier, L.A. Express	181	Sold (1993)
Big Steel Man	114	Closed (1993)
Drug World	2	Closed (1993)
NBO	21	Sold (1995)

Financial highlights of the annual report are shown below and on page 562 (with comparisons to the previous year) in Tables 2–4.

Table 2

Statement of Financial Position

	February 1, 1997 ($ thousands)	February 3, 1996 ($ thousands)
Current assets		
Cash and short-term investments	6 384	14 854
Accounts receivable	12 264	9 234
Inventories	161 437	173 370
Other current assets	8 433	10 537
Investment held for resale	—	5 790
	188 518	213 785
Current liabilities		
Accounts payable	111 416	134 178
Notes payable	—	586
Long-term debt due within one year	1 060	10 275
Obligations under capital leases due within one year	1 358	4 438
Other current liabilities	4 241	7 013
	118 075	156 490
Working capital	70 443	57 295
Other assets	88 193	100 421
Assets employed	158 636	157 716
Long-term debt	11 830	37 292
Obligations under capital leases	1 031	9 823
Non-controlling interestin subsidiaries	6 694	17 699
Deferred revenue	10 284	12 678
	28 839	77 492
Shareholders' equity	128 797	80 224
Capital employed	158 636	157 716

Questions

1. What are the advantages and disadvantages of the Dylex concept compared to putting the Dylex name on each store?
2. Calculate the operating ratios for February 1, 1997 and February 3, 1996, and comment on the health of the company as well as the trends.
3. Dylex is concerned with the sales and profit drop of BiWay. What type of research could be carried out to help them make a decision?

Source: Kenneth Kidd, "The Fall of the House of Dylex," Report on Business Magazine, *September 1995, 50–61; Annual Report for Dylex Corporation 1996.*

Video Source: "Dylex," Venture *591 (May 19, 1996; 6:08).*

Table 3

Consolidated Statement of Earnings

	February 1, 1997 ($ thousands)	February 3, 1996 ($ thousands)
Sales		
Retail	1 210 089	1 275 712
Fashion manufacturing	26 339	23 338
	1 236 428	1 229 050
Earnings from operations before the following	48 309	41 801
Depreciation and amortization	19 289	19 186
Interest	7 088	8 810
Earnings before the undernoted	21 932	13 805
Gain on sale of investments	5 839	—
Store closing and related CCAA costs	—	(3 646)
Write-down of investments	—	(2 457)
Earnings before income taxes	27 771	6 702
Income tax expense	2 921	222
	24 850	6 480
Loss from investment in associate companies	—	(3 228)
Non-controlling interest in subsidiaries' earnings	(1 995)	(1 366)
Net earnings	22 855	1 866

Table 4

Consolidated Sales

	February 1, 1997 ($ thousands)	February 3, 1996 ($ thousands)	$ change ($ thousands)
Wholly owned			
Fairweather	124 730	133 604	(8 874)
Braemar	92 018	97 888	(5 870)
Tip Top	163 140	185 007	(21 867)
BiWay	544 186	572 484	(28 298)
Thrifty's	104 520	99 393	5 127
Corporate	—	—	—
	1 028 594	1 088 376	(59 782)
Other operations	207 834	210 674	(2 840)
	1 236 428	1 299 050	(62 622)

Part seven 7

Retail Management

Strategic Retail Management Planning and Targeting the Firm's Actions

Outline

Objectives

To appreciate the need for strategic retail management and planning

To develop an organizational mission statement that can serve as a focus for the firm's current and future activities

To construct the organizational objectives for achieving the organization's mission

To conduct a portfolio analysis and classify and evaluate different business units on the basis of their position within the portfolio

To identify the various types of organizational opportunities and evaluate the appropriate strategies associated with each type of opportunity

Retail Vignette

Provigo

Provigo, with 1996 sales of 5.8 billion, ranks number three in Canada and tenth in North America in the food industry. It has also traditionally been among the most profitable Canadian companies in terms of both return on capital employed and shareholders' equity.

Provigo
www.provigo.com

The company was founded in 1969 by two Montreal families who merged their food wholesaling operations. It achieved extremely rapid growth—both through acquisitions and internal growth. The company bought up regional wholesalers at an extraordinary pace to build a strong position in many regions of Quebec. From that solid Quebec base, the company achieved significant geographic diversification. In 1977, Provigo acquired LOEB, an Ontario company nearly twice its size in terms of sales. That single transaction enabled the company to establish a strong operating base in Ontario, Canada's most populated province. At the same time, this acquisition enabled Provigo to expand its food operations into western Canada (through Horne & Pitfield) and the northern California market (through Market Wholesale). In 1980, Provigo acquired 87 Dominion stores, 71 of which were located in the Montreal region.

The company's core business has always been food distribution. However, along the way, the company added some nonfood operations that required a similar type of management. These were:

- National Drugs (bought with LOEB in 1977)
- Sports Experts (1981) and merger of Collegiate/Arlington (1985)

In 1985, the company intensified the rate of development of both its food and nonfood operations by acquiring such firms as Consumers Distributing, National Drugs (Medis), and C-Corp, a national chain of convenience stores. Provigo also moved into California with the purchase of Petrini's and Alpha Beta stores.

In 1989, sales had almost doubled to close to $8 billion, but the balance sheet was loaded with debt. More importantly and troubling: several of the operations were not performing well. In October 1989, Provigo proceeded to do essentially three things:

- Refocus the business in its core business which is food and upgrading stores.
- Dispose of unprofitable and undesirable operations in both of the nonfood and food sectors. Sports Experts, Consumers Distributing, and California grocers and distribution businesses were sold.
- Refocus attention and effort on the bottom line through cost cutting with increased focus on convenience, selection, low prices, and reduced administration costs.

These three measures resulted in a greatly improved balance sheet, a more focused organization, and a more profitable company. At the same time, Provigo aggressively expanded its most productive units. Today, the company has the fastest market-share growth in the industry.

Provigo now operates Provigo Distribution Inc. in Quebec (164 Provigo supermarkets, 69 Maxi and 4 Maxi & Co.) and LOEB Inc. in Ontario and western Quebec (102 LOEB supermarkets). Its wholesale activities are carried through its Distribution Group which supplies more than 700 smaller independent stores under different banners.

Provigo's share of the total Canadian food market is 16 percent [in 1996] compared with 14 percent [in 1993] (38 percent market share in Quebec and 10 percent in Ontario). In 1996, Provigo introduced a new superstore banner, Maxi & Co. These 8000 m^2 stores contain 4600 m^2 of grocery space with the rest allocated to general merchandising. Four Maxi & Co. were opened in 1996 and another seven are planned in 1997, including three in Ontario.

Printed with permission of Provigo Ltd.

Visualize the Mission

Facing tougher competition and tighter budgets, more companies, cities, schools and even individuals are taking stock of who they are, what they do, and how they plan to do it better. Then they are writing it all down. The result: a proliferation of "missions," "visions," "values," and the like, emblazoned on annual reports, factory walls and—companies hope—the psyches of their workers. It is the new groupthink: If we state our goals, we are more likely to meet them.[1]

Modern Corporate Philosophy

Modern corporate philosophy is not a standardized thing. There is no established format, nor should there be. A corporate philosophy should be as unique as the company that adopts it. However, companies that have adopted a philosophy generally include a clear definition of corporate purpose. A corporate philosophy usually details the contribution the organization expects to make to society, and it outlines the organization's responsibilities to its customers, its employees, its sources of capital, its community, and in some instances, its suppliers and business associates.[2]

Singing from the Same Sheet

Most importantly, is everyone "singing from the same sheet"? Are top management, middle management, and frontline employees in sync with the company's objectives, strategies, and styles? Or do misalignments, mixed signals, and inconsistencies confuse, frustrate, and hamper productivity on all levels?[3]

Reason for Being

Stores with a future are led by executives who can answer the question: "What do we want our stores to be famous for with customers?" Managers know what makes the store special for customers, they know what drives customer loyalty, and they are highly focused on executing this vision. Management has a clear vision of what the business is and, just as importantly, what the business is not.[4]

Organizational Planning

Planning is essential if the retail organization is to survive and prosper in the competitive environment associated with consumer markets. **Strategic retail management** is the process of planning the organization, implementation, and control of all the firm's activities. It involves making both strategic and tactical decisions for different levels within the retail organization. In this discussion, we review the process by which strategic planning is accomplished and the resulting retail strategic plan.

Figure 15–1

Business planning levels

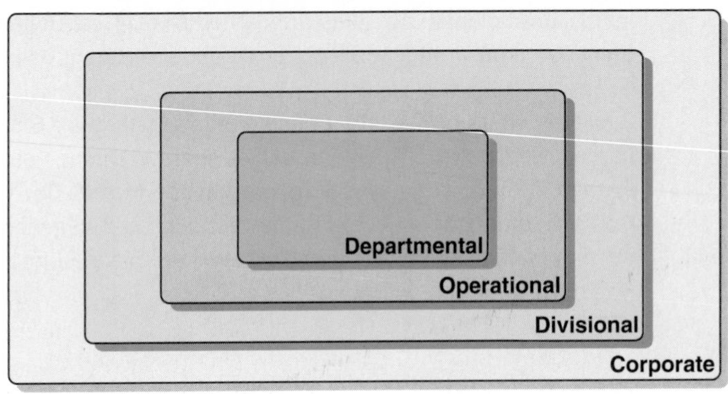

Strategic Planning Process

Before describing the structure of strategic retail plans, it is instructive to examine the issue of strategic versus tactical planning as it relates to the various levels (corporate, divisional, functional, and departmental) within the retail organization. **Strategic planning** involves long-term, broad-based intentions that unfold over a period of time; it is a multifaceted outline of what the retail firm hopes to accomplish now and in the future. **Tactical planning** is a logical outgrowth of the firm's strategic plan; it involves short-term, focused, and operationally based activities that are designed to gain the retailer a competitive advantage on a temporary or permanent basis. Figure 15–1 highlights the relationships among the various levels at which strategies and tactics are planned and executed.

Corporate Level Planning Corporate planning is conducted by the corporate headquarters management team and is directed at developing an overall plan for the entire organization. Planning at the corporate level is the responsibility of the firm's CEO, president, vice presidents, and their support staffs. The corporate planning process is strategic because it establishes the general framework for the firm's actions over an extended period of time. As a broad statement based on experience, intuition, and analytical judgment, the corporate plan outlines the organization's general business intent. Equally important to the firm's success and future direction is the "tone," or general attitude, that is set and transmitted to all levels of the organization. Successful managers practise what they preach.[5]

Divisional Level Planning Business planning at the divisional level involves developing a course of action for each of the **strategic business units (SBUs)** within the retail organization. An SBU is a business division with a clearly identifiable merchandise strategy (retail format) that targets a market segment (customer focus) within a defined competitive environment (market position). Each SBU is typically operated as a separate business with its own competitive strategy. In carrying out the strategic planning process at the divisional level, the retailer must examine both the strategic plans of the individual SBU and the role of each SBU in the overall corporate strategy.

Operational Level Planning The planning process continues with the development of plans for each store or group of stores within each SBU. It is this level at which the directions to the future must be operationalized by actions in the present. It is where strategies are transformed into tactics. At this operational level of the organization each of the functional areas within the store (for example, developing merchandise mixes, establishing merchandise logistics systems, finding favourable retail locations, designing internal store layouts, developing human resource management programs, cultivating customer communications policies) requires tactical plans that are both executable and controllable, as well as consistent with the corporate strategies.

Departmental Level Planning At the department level, planning is mostly tactical. It focuses more on current problems and decisions faced in implementing those strategies and directions identified at the corporate, divisional, and operational levels. Departmental managers are mostly concerned with managing the day-to-day activities of the specific departments within the store. The focus for the department manager is how merchandise plans (see Chapter 9) at the department level are coordinated with operational tactical plans that must be translated into divisional strategic plans to meet the overall corporate goals.

Strategic Retail Plan

Strategic planning aims to develop a long-term course of action that will provide an overall sense of direction for a retail organization's business activities. The **strategic retail plan** is a grand design or blueprint for ensuring success in all the organization's business endeavours. A strategic plan is directed at achieving a strategic fit between the organization's capabilities (present and future) and its environmental opportunities (present and future). A good fit positions the organization to enable it to sustain competitive assets and overcome competitive liabilities, as well as to anticipate external environmental changes and identify needed internal organizational adjustments.

The development of an organization's strategic plan is a process that consists of (1) establishing the organization's mission, (2) identifying the organization's objectives, (3) evaluating the organization's portfolio of SBUs, and (4) assessing the organization's opportunities (see Figure 15–2).

Figure 15–2

Strategic retail plan

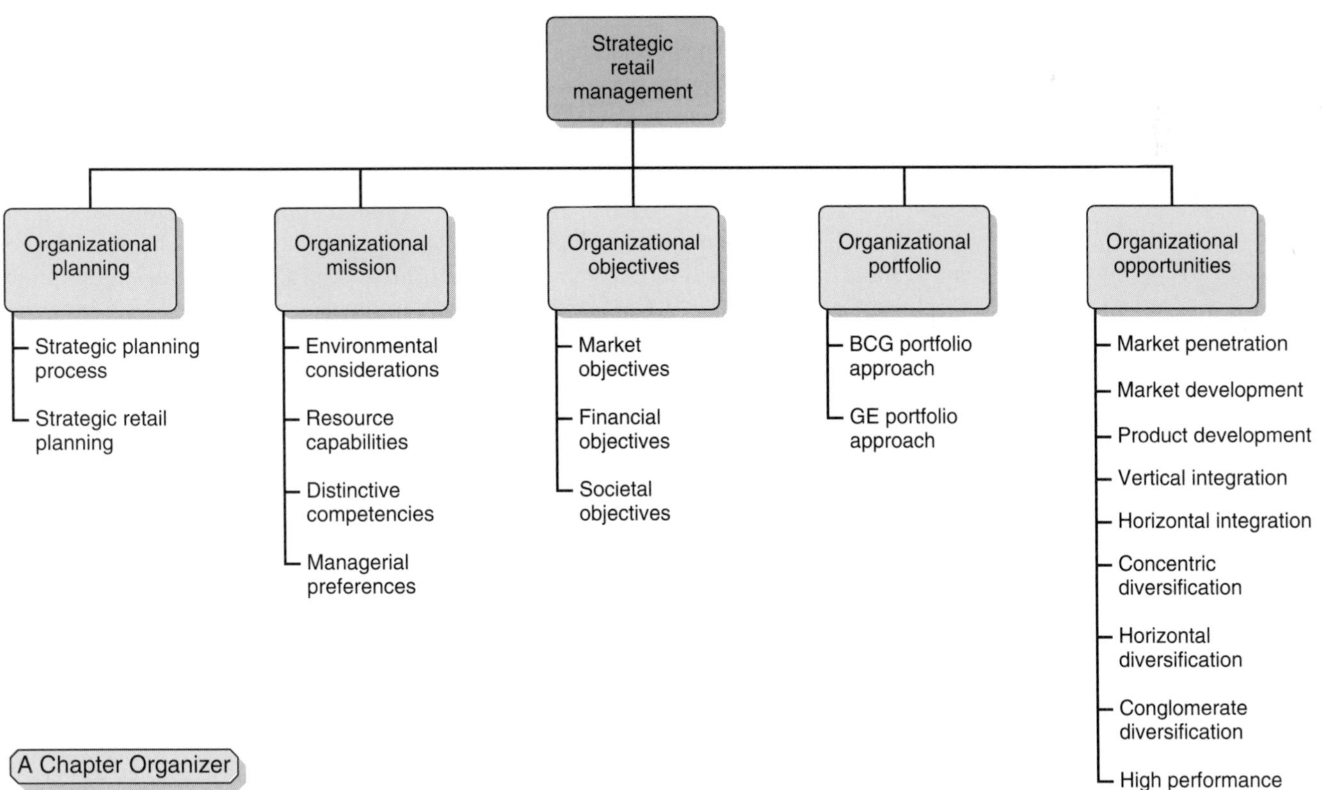

Retail Strategies and Tactics

Industrial Foresight

The vital first step in competing for the future is the quest for industrial foresight. This is the race to gain an understanding deeper than competitors, of the trends and discontinuities—technology, demographic, regulatory, or lifestyle—that could be used to transform industry boundaries and create new competitive space.

Industry foresight gives a company the potential to get to the future first and stake out a leadership position. It informs corporate direction and lets a company control the evolution of its industry and, thereby, its own destiny. The trick is to see the future before it arrives.

We do not believe any company can get along without a well-articulated point of view about tomorrow's opportunities and challenges. Today many companies seem convinced that foresight is the easy part; it is implementation that is the killer. We believe that creating industry foresight and achieving operational excellence are equally challenging.

Source: Gary Hamel and C. K. Prahalad, "See The Future First," Harvard Business School Press, *September 5, 1994, 64.*

Organizational Mission

The **mission statement** is a generalized yet meaningful expression of the organization's future direction. It is a commitment to future actions, citing numerous tasks to perform.

First, a mission statement identifies both the business and customer domains in which the organization operates or plans to operate. A well-defined mission will answer such business domain questions as, What is our business? What will our business be? What should our business be? Corresponding questions in the customer domain are, Who is our customer? Who will our customer be? Who should our customer be? The revised strategic plan for Danforth Lumber, an independent home improvement store located in Toronto, calls for the company to focus on personalized service. This helps the firm to avoid some of the head-to-head competition with Home Depot, the nation's largest home improvement chain.[6] Merry Maid, the housecleaning division of Service Master, revised its customer strategy from focusing on the process of cleaning houses to one of giving the customer peace of mind that not only will the house be cleaned but that nothing will be stolen, broken, or rearranged.[7] As Figure 15–3 illustrates, strategic gaps grow between each of these business and customer domain questions as one moves from the present to the future. These gaps represent the difference between current, expected, and desired performances, and as such, they indicate the possible need for changing the strategic plan of the organization. A good mission statement acts as the ultimate control system by forcing the firm to return to its original intent.

Second, a mission statement identifies the organization's responsibilities toward the people with whom it interacts. Retailing has been described as a people business, and the mission statement should recognize this orientation.

Third, a mission statement provides a general blueprint for accomplishing the organizational mission.

The statement of the organizational mission is developed by taking several factors into account. As seen in Figure 15–2, these factors include environmental considerations, resource considerations, distinctive competencies, and managerial preferences. In developing the mission statement, the retailer should (1) involve everyone (that is, everyone who must live by the statement), (2) allow customization (encourage compatible adaptations to meet departmental conditions), (3) expect and accept resistance (recognize the diversity of the firm's culture), (4) keep it short (thereby keeping it simple and understandable), (5) eschew hokum (take it seriously so others will), (6) challenge it (test the statement by questioning its worth), and (7) live it (actions speak louder than words).[8]

Mission statements of several Canadian retailers are illustrated in Figure 15–4.

Figure 15–3

Fundamental mission statement question

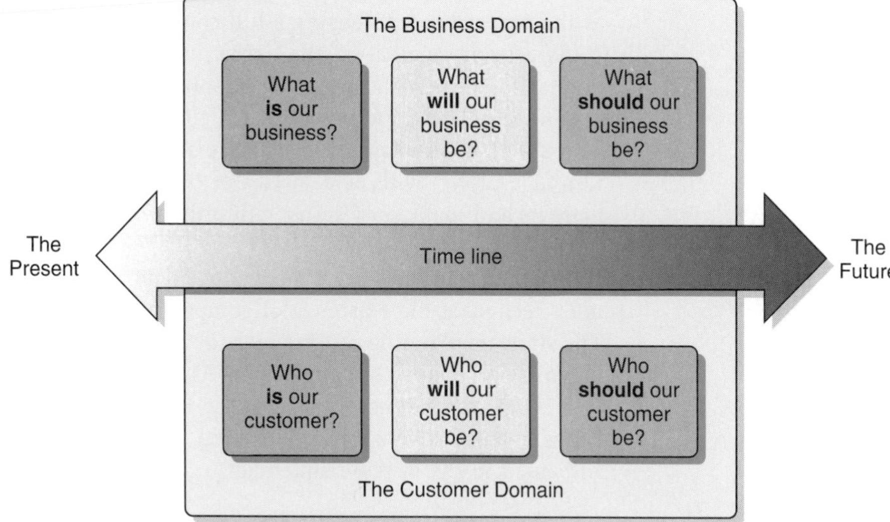

Figure 15–4

Mission statements of some Canadian retailers

Sources: Hudson's Bay Annual Report (1996); Provigo Annual Report (1996); Canadian Tire Annual Report (1996); Sears Canada Annual Report (1996); Home Hardware Stores Limited Annual Report (1996).

Hudson's Bay	"The company aims to develop its human and material resources and capitalize on its experience in merchandising to anticipate and satisfy the needs of customers for the goods and services they seek at fair prices, and thereby earn a satisfactory return for its shareholders."
Provigo	"Our mission is to market and distribute food products and related products in Canada and the United States."
Canadian Tire	"Our mission is to use the resources and business acumen already developed to extend our existing operations to their full potential as well as become a portfolio of well-positioned businesses, diversified with respect to growth and risk, but sharing a common basis on the supply of consumer goods and services in North America."
Sears Canada	"Sears Canada is a full-line, full-service department store and catalogue retailer dedicated to providing its customers with quality merchandise and exceptional service, coast to coast."
Costco	"To provide our members with quality goods and services at the lowest possible prices."
Home Hardware	"To supply Home dealers with quality products and services, assisting them with programs to operate effective and efficient stores at a profitable level allowing them to serve the customer with competitive prices and superior service. We have, over the years, developed a very impressive and efficient infrastructure and systems to get product to the dealers."

Environmental Considerations

The retail organization must accommodate and react to several different environments that present both opportunities and threats. Some of the major components of an organization's environment are suppliers, marketing intermediaries, customers, competitors, and the public. As a marketing intermediary, the retail organization has an internal environment within which the daily operation of the firm must be successfully completed. The strengths and weaknesses of the organization's structure and personnel must be accounted for when developing mission statements. The planning process should involve all levels of the organization to ensure a full commitment from all affected parties.

As a team member in the marketing channel of distribution, the mission statement must also address the needs of suppliers and customers. The retailer's mission should recognize the need for a coordinated effort and a cooperative spirit in conducting channel affairs. Retail organizations that have adopted the marketing concept (customer satisfaction at a profit) will, as a matter of course, consider the expectations of their targeted markets and make provisions within the mission statement for gaining buyer acceptance of the firm's programs.

Retailing activities are not conducted in a vacuum; the mission statement therefore must recognize the existence of competitors and the expectations of the general public. The strategic planning process must devote considerable attention to positioning the retail organization relative to competition. The general public's perception of the retail organization is also vital to acceptance of the firm's activities. The goal of serving the public by being a responsive corporate citizen meeting its social responsibilities also must be addressed in the mission statement.

Resource Considerations

The mission statement must be realistic. The extent of that realism depends on the resources available to the retail organization. Because resources are essential to implement the firm's current and future strategies, the mission statement should recognize the problems associated with acquiring, maintaining, and using resources. The resource base to consider in developing the mission statement consists of (1) the financial assets and liabilities of the firm, (2) the organizational composition and structure of the management

Retail Strategies and Tactics

Totem Battling American Invaders

Remember how almost everyone thought the big fierce American warehouse stores that have invaded Canada were going to drive homegrown businesses into extinction?

Well, almost everyone was wrong.

Consider the case of Calgary's Totem Building Supplies, a company that's proving smart Canadian retailers can thrive in head-to-head competition with anyone.

"One of the keys is our ability to change quickly," says Totem president Jim Thorogood. "That's absolutely essential for a small business."

Totem stood toe to toe with new warehouse stores and quickly changed its business in ways that earned the company recognition as Canadian Retailer of the Year by *Hardware Merchandising* magazine.

Totem was built around an innovation in the first place. The company introduced the cash-and-carry approach to the building supply business more than 25 years ago.

The company was created by Thorogood and his father Cliff.

When the Home Depot opened in Toronto, Thorogood and his employees visited there and also checked out a number of U.S. locations to see how Home Depot operated and how the competition, particularly independent operators like Totem, were trying to compete against the giant.

They came up with a strategy based on the courage to invest a lot of cash.

Source: Barry Nelson, Medicine Hat News, *June 10, 1996, A6.*

team, (3) the human resource component in terms of supporting personnel, and (4) the physical plant—store facilities, fixtures, and equipment.

Distinctive Competencies

A careful assessment of practically any retail organization will reveal certain merchandising and operating capabilities that distinguish it from competing organizations. Distinctive competencies might occur in such areas as visual merchandising, exclusive supplier relationships, customer communications and sales promotions, unique store imagery, inventory planning and control systems, organization integration, product assortments, market coverage, or store atmosphere. The Walt Disney Company, for example, locates its Disney stores in tourist locations (that is, distinctive competency). In any case, distinctive competencies are solid foundations for suggesting future strategies in a mission statement. The Retail Strategies and Tactics box entitled "Totem Battling American Invaders" illustrates the distinctive competency developed by one Canadian retailer.

Managerial Preferences

Additional considerations in developing a mission statement include the merchandising and operating preferences of the organization's cadre of managers. The type and extent of managerial expertise (for example, mass merchandise versus specialty retailing) will vary among retail organizations; therefore, it is both logical and practical to consider management strengths when planning the organization's future directions. Managerial intuition likewise should not be overlooked. Anita Roddick, founder of the Body Shop, believed that trying to seduce women into buying overpackaged, overhyped, and overpriced cosmetics was an insult to their intelligence.[9] Using these intuitive feelings, Roddick was able to build a highly successful global retail chain based on natural ingredients for a wide array of personal beauty aids, as well as bed and bath products.[10]

Body Shop
www.the-body-shop.ca

Organizational Objectives

Organizational objectives can be defined as strategic positions to be attained or purposes to be achieved by the retail organization and/or one of its SBUs. They are aims or end-of-action statements toward which the retail organization's efforts are directed (see Figure 15–5). The two major categories of organizational objectives are the market objectives of customer patronage and competitive position and the financial objectives of profitability and productivity.

Market Objectives

Market objectives are aimed at obtaining customer patronage and achieving competitive positions in the general marketplace. Market objectives are realized by carefully planned merchandising programs that can satisfy the consumer's psychological, social, and personal needs.

Sales Objectives Sales volume increases are a commonly identified objective. A sales growth objective is typically expressed as a certain percentage increase (for example, 15 percent) for a particular SBU (for example, store) over a defined time period (for example, next year). Sales increases are an expansion objective that involves additional commitment of the organization's resources and the foregoing of short-term profits for long-term gains. Increases in total sales volume could be achieved by (1) adding new operating units or (2) increasing sales at existing stores by raising advertising expenditures, improving product/service offerings, lowering prices, or making other merchandising adjustments

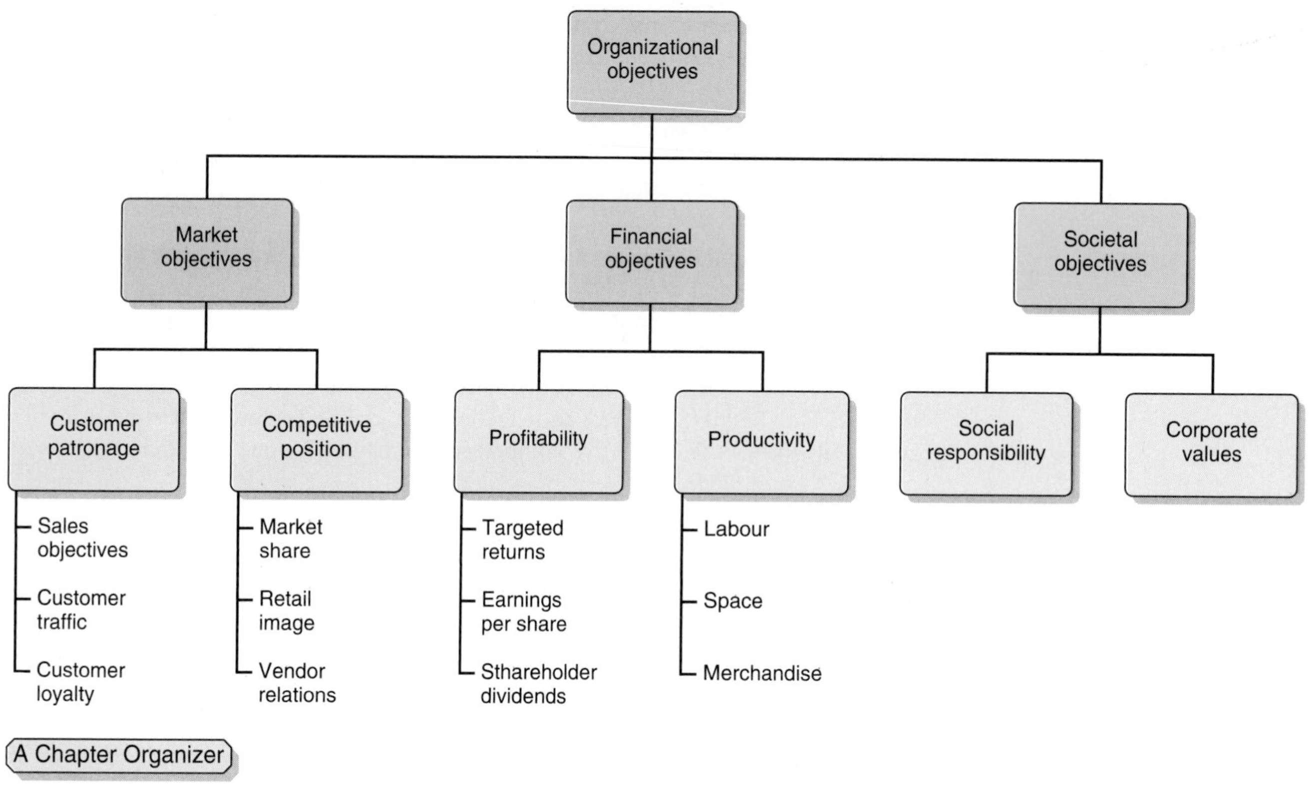

Figure 15–5

A topology of organizational objectives

(for example, added convenience) that can increase customer satisfaction. Successful retailers focus attention on increasing "same-store" sales; they do not fall into the trap of depending on constantly opening new stores to achieve earnings gains.[11] Same-store sales increases are a key indicator used by Wall Street in judging a retail organization.

Another type of sales volume objective is to increase the average customer sale. Increasing the total amount spent by each customer during a store visit should have a direct and positive effect on total sales. A Buck or Two, a Canadian chain of one-price retail stores, may have difficulty growing because it has a low average customer purchase and is unable to notably improve it. With such slim margins at the $1 price point, low earnings potential sharply limits the chain's expansion goals.[12] Personal selling and various sales promotion methods are used to increase the amount of the average sale.

Customer Traffic Many retailers believe that if they can attract customers into the store, then they can obtain desired sales through customer exposure to the direct merchandising efforts of the organization. Their objectives are thus to increase the total number of customers visiting the store during a specific time period. Supermarkets that offer the added convenience of in-store banking to their customers enhance the prospects of increased store traffic and customer patronage.[13]

Possible strategies to increase the total number of customer visits include additional mass advertising, sales promotions, and special-event merchandising. Offering a range of pricing points and a wider selection of merchandise are two additional means by which a firm can expand its appeal to a more extensive customer base. Offering unique services, specialty merchandise lines, and personal selling from sales representatives who have appropriate expertise can increase the traffic of targeted customer groups. Drugstore chains such as Shoppers Drug Mart use prescription drugs as traffic builders and then attempt to sell customers a wide range of convenience goods ranging from health and beauty aids to household products.

Shoppers Drug Mart
www.lifebrand.com

Customer Loyalty A customer loyalty objective is aimed at improving return trade. Repeat business is essential to almost any retail operation because for many it represents store loyalty. The Weather Channel was the object of intense snickering when it was first introduced. Today it is one of the top cable networks because it has become the preferred branded provider of weather information.[14] The average number of store visits or purchases during a defined time period is one means of measuring return trade. Ideally, a worthy objective is to develop a high preference level for the organization and its merchandising programs. Obviously, the key to store loyalty is customer satisfaction. Retailers should understand the realities of customer loyalty—it is something the retailer must earn and keep on earning. Assuming that the old adage that "20% of your customers account for 50% to 80% of your profits" is true, it makes "intuitive sense to focus a company's resources on the best customers rather than on the flighty, fairweather types."[15]

Market Share Market share objectives are the most commonly used form of expressing competitive position. **Market share** is a measure of a retail organization's sales position relative to all competitors within the same market. It is calculated by dividing a retail organization's total sales by total market sales for a defined business type or product line category. In expanding market areas, market share growth could well be an appropriate objective (for example, increase market share by 6 percent over the duration of this planning period). On the other hand, retail organizations operating in mature and stable market areas generally call for the more moderate objective of market share maintenance (for example, protect our current market share against the aggressive actions of all competitors). Retaining market share forced Toys R Us to break one of its cardinal rules—"no periodic sales." A strong believer in everyday low prices, the firm's policy was to mark down only items that were being dropped from inventory. Because of rough competition from discounters that were attempting to cut in on Toys R Us markets, however, in-store sales catalogues are being used to maintain its market share.[16]

Retail Image An image is the mental conception of something held in common by members of a group. A *retail image* is the mental picture of a retail organization as viewed by customers and the general public. Retail image includes both the functional or physical properties of the store as well as its psychological attributes—a sense of belonging or a feeling of friendliness.[17] The term *retail* is used here in its most generalized meaning; to the consumer, **store image** is a symbolic representation of the basic attributes, orientations, and activities of the organization. Service Merchandise is in the process of re-imaging itself by convincing the consuming public that it is a retail store and not a catalogue showroom retailer.[18] Dylex Corporation has strived to develop clear, distinct images for each of its chains.[19]

Retailers establish image objectives because they realize that consumers tend to categorize people, places, and things in relative terms (for example, bigger, better, faster, easier, sooner). By offering wider product selections, higher-quality products, better price values, more convenient locations, easier credit terms, and faster service, retailers can competitively position themselves in the minds of consumers. By careful planning it is possible to position the organization in an imagery niche that clearly distinguishes it from its competitors.

Vendor Relations Carving out a viable competitive position includes a "supply side" that a retail organization's statement of objectives should also recognize. Prudent retail organizations strive to ensure that they are well positioned with respect to both established vendors (for example, to be considered a preferred account by desired vendors) and newly emerging sources (for example, to engage in a systematic search for suppliers of new and innovative products). Retailers must also cooperate and coordinate their activities with other members of the marketing channel of distribution. This type of relationship is an agreement to work together toward a common goal of maximizing sales and profits of both parties and to jointly meet customer expectations.[20] Strong vendor relationships involve an equitable sharing of both the costs and benefits of doing business with one another. Vendor alienation can lead to long-run problems that can be avoided by viewing the retailer–vendor relationship as a partnership to be nurtured.[21]

Financial Objectives

Financial objectives are directed at ensuring that the retail organization operates profitably and productively. Financial objectives provide quantifiable standards by which the organization's performance will be judged. Targeted returns, earnings, and dividends are three common profitability goals. The three most critical resources that require careful management in a traditional retail enterprise are labour, space, and merchandise.

Targeted Returns The monetary return the retail organization desires can be stated in terms of return on sales or assets. These profit-based objectives reflect what management expects in return for its efforts. A return on sales (net profit divided by net sales) objective identifies what percentage of the average sales dollars should be profit. For example, an objective of 20 percent could be the targeted net profit return on net sales. To realize a fair return on the organization's asset investment, a return on assets (net profit divided by total assets) objective is frequently included in the organization's statement of objectives.

Earnings per Share Objectives should also reflect the performance of the organization relative to shareholders' interests. A targeted earnings per share of common stock can be established as an objective to show the amount of earnings available to the owners of common stock. A desired objective of $4 per share of common stock could be the targeted earnings/share ratio. In Sears's remarkable turnaround in 1995, the retailer was able to increase its earnings per share from $2.13 the previous year to $2.53. Wall Street definitely took notice. Sears's stock went from $15 in 1992 to $46 in 1995.[22]

Shareholder Dividends A designated proportion of the earnings that will actually be allocated to shareholders can also serve as an objective. Dividends are a measure of the return to common stock owners representing the return on their investment (this statement does not reflect any increase or decrease in the market value of the common stock). For example, a retailer could set as its objective a $2 dividend yield on each share of common stock.

Labour Productivity Labour is the No. 1 expense in a store and the most controllable line item; it only makes sense that a retailer who can better manage labour is going to see better returns.[23] The productivity of the organization's labour pool can be measured by dividing net sales by the total number of employees or net sales by the total number of worker hours of labour; the latter measure would take into account the productivity of both full- and part-time employees. The average annual sales per retailer employee is $102 900, ranging from $388 100 for new and used car dealers to $29 500 for employees of restaurants.[24] Retailing can be a labour-intensive business; hence, the contribution of human resources must be recognized and productivity performance standards established.[25] Many retailers also recognize that turnover adversely affects labour productivity, and therefore they strive to reduce this phenomenon by setting employee satisfaction objectives aimed at increasing employee retention.

Space Productivity One of the retailer's most important resources is the amount of available merchandising and operating space it has. Most retail organizations attempt to maximize their selling space and productivity. Sales/productivity ratios are established for stores as well as for individual department and product line areas. Space productivity is measured by dividing net sales or gross margin by the most appropriate expression of area. Some examples of sales/space or margin/space productivity ratios are (1) net sales per unit of floor space, (2) net sales per cubic unit of display area, (3) net sales per linear unit of shelf space, and (4) gross margin dollars per square unit of space. Wal-Mart's goal is to continue to get more productivity from its large discount stores where it currently gets sales of about $275 per sq. ft. ($2960 per m^2).[26]

Merchandise Productivity Inventory turnover is the most widely used criterion for measuring the productivity of merchandise; it can be defined as the number of times (for example, four times) during a specific time period (for example, a year) that the average stock on hand is sold. The desired objective is to achieve the highest possible inventory turnover rate for the type of merchandise being sold and the additional resources that must be used to improve turnover rates. Obviously, convenience goods will have higher stock turns than specialty goods; therefore, an annual turnover objective of three turns for specialty goods could be considered as productive as fifteen yearly turns for convenience goods. An objective of increasing the turnover rate by increasing advertising or adding more sales personnel may prove productive if increased expenditures do not exceed the additional profits derived from such a strategy.

Societal Objectives

In addition to market and financial objectives, retail organizations often identify objectives that relate to their social responsibilities (as discussed in Chapter 1). Such social objectives

Retail Strategies and Tactics

Statements of Objectives of Canadian Retailers

Hudson's Bay — "We will:

- Enhance the distinct identity of each of our companies.
- Develop programs to emphasize our image of good quality and low price.
- Strive to improve customer service, both in quality and in understanding customer needs.
- Continue to improve the quality and productivity of management.
- Close, re-utilize, or dispose of under-performing assets.
- Become much more flexible in our use of working capital for inventories to exploit in-season merchandise opportunities.
- Develop new and innovative businesses and new formats within existing franchises."

Provigo — "The Provigo formula combines the efficiency of a large distributor with the flexibility of a decentralized network, a large part of which is operated by affiliated and franchised entrepreneurs. . . . [I]ncrease market share in all regions where the company operates."

Canadian Tire — "The corporation provides a variety of marketing, merchandising, administrative, and ancillary services to its Associate Dealers as well as financial services to both Associate Dealers and their customers. These businesses will be managed in a decentralized style against aggressive profit and growth objectives."

Sears Canada — "To be Canada's most successful retailer by providing our customers with total shopping satisfaction, our associates with opportunities for career advancement and personal growth, and our shareholders with superior returns on their investment."

Costco — "In order to achieve our mission we will conduct our business with the following five responsibilities in mind. (1) Obey the law. (2) Take care of our members. (3) Take care of our employees. (4) Respect our vendors. (5) Take care of our shareholders.

Home Hardware — "Focus on helping the dealers to improve their overall profitability while maintaining Home Hardware's strong financial base. Continue to grow the business, achieving modest sales increases and a minimal bottom line that can be returned to dealers in the form of a surcharge refund."

Source: Hudson's Bay Annual Report (1996); Provigo Annual Report (1996); Canadian Tire Annual Report (1996); Sears Canada Annual Report (1996); Home Hardware Stores Limited Annual Report (1996).

include supporting charitable causes, providing educational opportunities, assuming an equitable tax burden, and participating in professional and social organizations and events. At Residence Inns, Marriott's chain of extended-stay hotels, guests are provided information on how to live a healthy lifestyle while staying at its inns. "Working with the American Heart Association, Marriott has developed recipes (for in-room cooking) and exercises (for in-room workouts)."[27] In its "Gifts in Kind" program, LensCrafter holds annual events in which it distributes free eyeglasses to needy people.[28] The need for being socially responsible is well summarized in a statement by Stanley Gault, chairman, Goodyear Tire & Rubber Co.: "Pursuit of financial results today cannot come at the expense of aid to education, charitable contributions or shortcuts in areas relating to the quality of products or the environment."[29]

Lenscrafters
www.lenscrafters.com

The Retail Strategies and Tactics box on page 575 provides examples of some Canadian retailers' organizational objectives.

Organizational Portfolio

The third stage in developing a strategic plan is to review the organization's portfolio of SBUs. An **organizational portfolio** is the collection of SBUs held and managed by a retail organization. The portfolio approach to retail planning is becoming an increasingly important method used by the diversified retail organization. Portfolio analysis is appealing because it suggests, but does not dictate, specific courses of action to achieve a balanced mix of businesses that will provide the maximum long-run benefits from scarce cash and managerial resources.[30]

Portfolio analysis is not in and of itself a strategy; rather, it is an analytical tool to provide perspective on the organization's current situation (where it is now) and suggest possible courses of action for the future (where it wants to be). Two commonly used portfolio approaches are the growth/share matrix developed by the Boston Consulting Group (BCG) and the market attractiveness/competitive position approach developed at General Electric.

BCG Portfolio Approach

The **BCG portfolio approach** is best illustrated by the use of two matrices: the market growth/market share matrix (see Figure 15–6) and the cash generation/cash usage matrix (see Figure 15–7). The former is used to illustrate current market positions of each SBU, whereas the latter identifies each SBU's net cash flow position.

Market Growth/Market Share Matrix In Figure 15–6, the vertical axis identifies the annual growth rate (percentage) of each SBU's operating market. The sales growth rate ranges from a low of 0 percent to a high of whichever percentage is appropriate (for example, 25 percent). A rate of 8 to 12 percent is generally considered to be quite good in most industries.

The horizontal axis indicates the relative market share of the SBU, a ratio of SBU share of the market to that of the largest competitor. Market share is considered important on the basis of research indicating that profitability of an SBU is directly related to its market share. The size of each square in the matrix shows each SBU's dollar sales, and the location of each SBU square indicates its competitive market share position for various growth rate markets. The size and location of each SBU square simply suggest different financial and marketing needs.

To facilitate analysis of the growth/share matrix, it is arbitrarily divided into four quadrants classifying SBUs as one of four types of businesses: stars, cash cows, question marks, or dogs. **Stars** are SBUs that have a high market share in a high-growth market.

Figure 15–6

Market growth/market share matrix

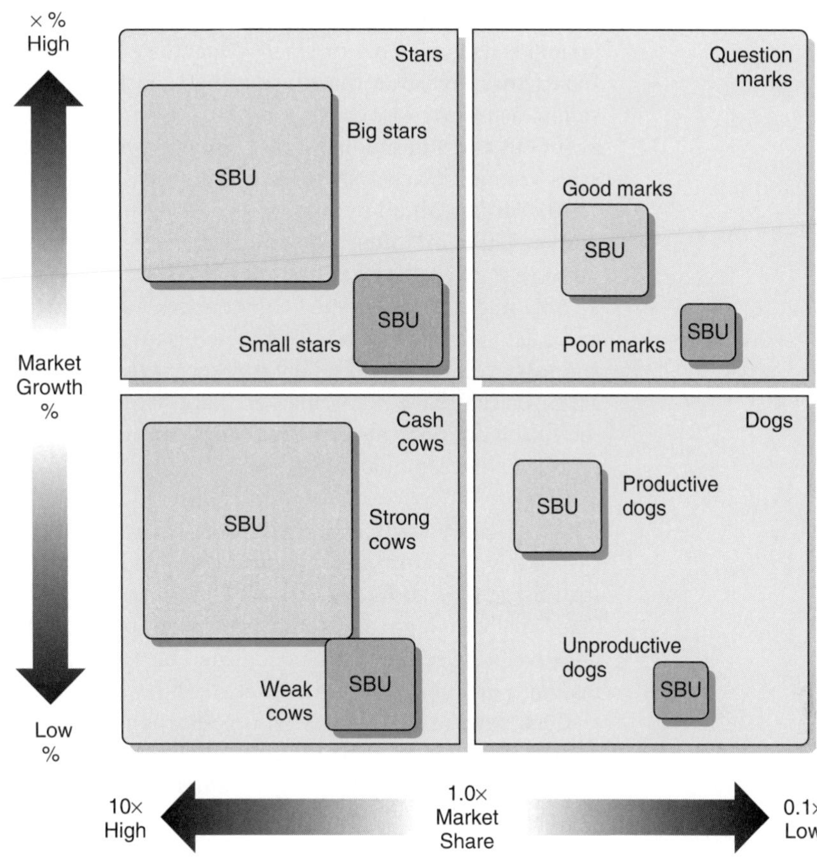

Figure 15–7

Cash generation/cash usage matrix

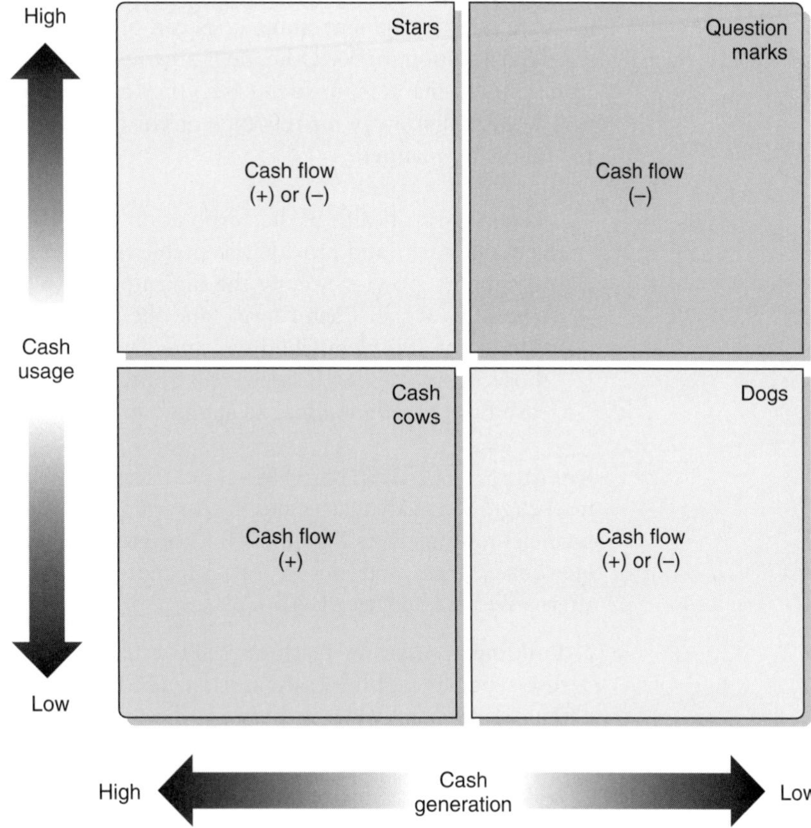

These businesses are market leaders within their respective industries. As Figure 15–6 shows, stars can be big or small, depending on the sales volume and share of the market. **Cash cows** are SBUs that have a high market share within a low-growth market. Like stars, cash cows also have a dominant or leader position; unfortunately, this position occurs in a less desirable market. Some cows are stronger than others on the basis of the sales volume, market share, and the growth characteristics of their market (see Figure 15–6). SBUs with a low market share in a high-growth market are classified as **question marks**. These are often also called *problem children* because they can offer considerable promise if given the attention they need. Depending on the amount of promise it shows, an SBU might be considered a good mark (reasonable chance for increasing market share and sales volume with an acceptable resource investment) or a poor mark (market share and sales volume increases are unlikely within acceptable resources commitments). **Dogs** are SBUs that have a low market share within a low-growth market. Their prospects for the future are dim; nevertheless, dogs can be productive if they find a market niche and produce an acceptable profit level.

Cash Generation/Cash Usage Matrix The net cash flow situation for stars, cash cows, question marks, and dogs is shown in Figure 15–7. The vertical axis shows cash usage (low to high), and the horizontal axis portrays cash generation (low to high). Stars are both high users and generators of cash, but their net cash flow tends to be negative because they require considerable cash to expand with their growing market and maintain or improve their market share.

Cash cows are the key to an organization's cash flow problems. Given the low market growth rate, fewer expenditures are needed to maintain market position; cash cows therefore tend to be net cash generators. The SBU cash cow provides the bulk of the cash to finance stars' and question marks' marketing operations. Tandy has used Radio Shack as a cash cow to finance its expansion of its superstore format—Incredible Universe.[31]

Question marks typically use more cash than they produce. If the organization decides that a question mark is capable of becoming a star, then it must provide the cash needed to capture additional market share.

Dogs can produce either a positive or negative net cash flow. Properly niched within a secure market segment, some dogs can provide some cash that can be used to finance stars and question marks. Other dogs are unproductive because of their vulnerable position in no-growth markets; in such cases, they can become "cash traps" and a lost cause.

The overall strategy for this type of portfolio analysis was described by one author in the following manner:

> The long-run health of the corporation depends on having some businesses that generate cash (and provide acceptable reported profits), and others that use cash to support growth. Among the indicators of overall health are the size and vulnerability of the "Cash Cows" (and the prospects for the "Stars," if any), and the number of "Problem Children" and "Dogs." Particular attention must be paid to those businesses with large cash appetites. Unless the company has abundant cash flow, it cannot afford to sponsor many such businesses at one time.[32]

Resource Allocation Matrix The combined information provided in the market/growth share matrix and the cash generation/usage matrix suggests ways to allocate financial resources. As Figure 15–8 illustrates, for each category of SBU (stars, cash cows, question marks, and dogs), two or more of the five following possible allocation alternatives are suggested:

1. **Building** involves increasing an SBU's market share. The decision to build an SBU typically requires cash infusion. The building alternative is used to expand smaller stars into bigger stars and transform promising question marks into stars.

2. **Holding** involves maintaining an SBU's market share. The decision to hold is a defensive posture by which the organization will protect and reinforce its

Figure 15–8

Resource allocation matrix

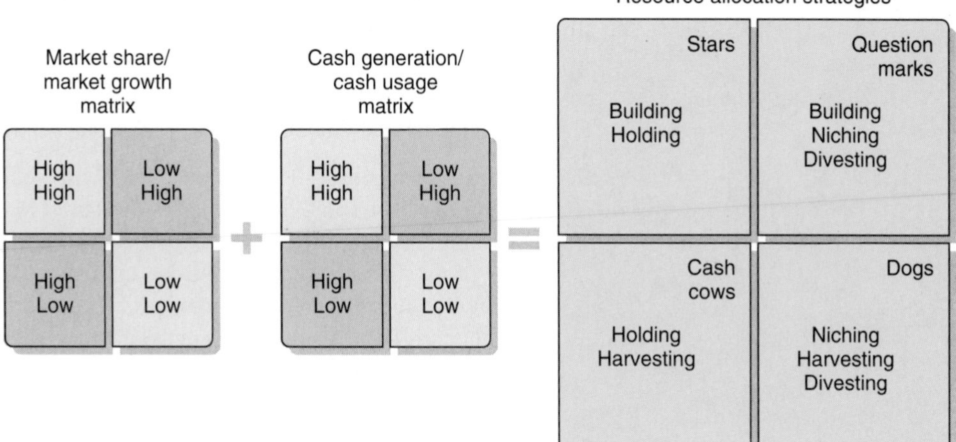

current market share. The goal is to make big stars productive in terms of positive net cash flow and keep strong cash cows producing a large cash flow.

3. **Harvesting** entails milking an SBU of its cash to finance other SBU alternatives that seem to have a brighter future. This cash extraction is often at the expense of the long-run survival of the SBU being harvested. Given the drastic nature of this alternative, it should be used only for weaker cash cows and dogs whose futures are extremely dim, with little hope of maintenance or survival and where additional resource investment is unjustifiable.

4. **Niching** involves moving an SBU into a market niche (segment) in which the fit between resource requirements and available resources is more acceptable. The goal is to find a market niche where the SBU is reasonably well protected from the actions of competitors while allowing it to generate sufficient long-term sales volumes and profits to justify the repositioning costs. Niching is used for some question marks and dogs that demonstrate the potential for a unique and limited market appeal.

5. **Divesting** involves disposing of SBUs that offer little or no hope of improving either their market share or cash flow position. Divestment can be accomplished by selling or liquidating the SBU.[33] Unproductive dogs and poor question marks are both candidates for divestiture. Dylex has sold Rubys, Feathers, and Club International chains to improve its overall profitbility.[34]

GE Portfolio Approach

Research has suggested that the BCG portfolio approach might be too limiting in its assessment of an organization's portfolio.[35] By focusing on market growth and market share, the BCG matrix ignores other factors that could be important in determining either the market attractiveness of existing or potential markets or the competitive position of the retail enterprise relative to other retail formats.

One means of overcoming the limitations of the BCG matrix is to utilize the **GE portfolio approach**, in which opportunities are screened using several variables and their measurements to assess both the attractiveness of the market and the competitiveness of the retailer. The goal of the GE portfolio approach (developed by the General Electric Company) is to assess the overall desirability of the markets currently being served by the retailer and to ascertain the retailer's relative capabilities to serve current markets as compared with the abilities of competitors. To accomplish this task, the retailer constructs a market attractiveness/competitive position matrix.

Market Attractiveness/Competitive Position Matrix The nine-cell market attractiveness/competitive position matrix is illustrated in Figure 15–9. The vertical axis represents the market attractiveness scale (low, medium, and high), and competitive position is shown on the horizontal axis as a scale ranging from weak to medium to strong. The multidimensional character of each axis can be characterized as follows:

- **Market attractiveness**—The overall desirability of a market in terms of its capability to (1) support the retailer as measured by such factors as total market size and market growth rate, (2) generate acceptable profits as measured by historic profit margins and competitive intensity, (3) permit efficient low-cost operations as measured by economies of scale and productivity efficiencies, and (4) offer a friendly operating environment as measured by social and political expectations, legal and environmental regulations, as well as economic and inflationary pressures.
- **Competitive position**—The relative business strengths of the retailer in terms of (1) existing market share and market share growth rate, (2) selection and uniqueness of merchandise offered, (3) number and quality of services offered, (4) efficiency and productivity of the merchandise logistics systems, (5) reach and effectiveness of customer communication, and (6) image and reputation of the retailer.

Each of the market attractiveness and competitive position factors cited can be quantified using a five-point rating scale, ranging from very attractive or highly competitive to very unattractive or highly noncompetitive. If the retailer judges various factors to have a different level of impact, each factor could be weighted by its importance on an appropriate scale (for example, 5 = very important to 1 = unimportant). By multiplying the factor rating by the factor weight, the retailer can construct a weighted-rating evaluation of whichever factors are to be used in the assessment of the attractiveness and competitiveness of an opportunity.

In using the matrix to determine how attractive a given opportunity might be and whether the retailer has the capability to capitalize on the opportunity, each case under consideration is located on the matrix, and on the basis of that location various decisions become appropriate. As seen in Figure 15–9, the nine cells of the matrix fall into three general action zones:

- **Green zone**—The three upper left-hand cells in the grid identify the *growth and investment zone*. It is the "go" zone that represents the best opportunity for continued growth of existing operating units and for future investment for

Figure 15–9

Market attractiveness/ competitive position matrix

Competitive position / Market attractivenenss	Strong	Medium	Weak
High	Green zone "Go"	Green zone "Go"	Yellow zone "Caution"
Medium	Green zone "Go"	Yellow zone "Caution"	Red zone "Danger"
Low	Yellow zone "Caution"	Red zone "Danger"	Red zone "Danger"

expanding operations. For green zone operations, the retailer must protect and consolidate through continuing investments and enhancements of competitive strengths.

- **Yellow zone**—The three middle diagonal cells in the grid identify the *earnings and discerning investment zone*. This "caution" zone represents important opportunities for carefully managing existing store operations for cash generation. It also provides a limited number of opportunities for selective investment by strengthening store operations in those areas where the retailer's competitive position is weak but the market is attractive.
- **Red zone**—The three lower right-hand cells in the grid identify the *harvest and divest zone*. These "danger" zones offer very modest opportunities to (1) harvest existing store operations for the cash that they can generate and (2) reposition a limited number of store operations into protected market niches that could prove to be long-term cash generators. For many store operations in the far lower cell of this zone, the only viable alternative is divestiture.

Matching the right store operation (one with a competitive advantage) with the right market (one whose characteristics are attractive for the retailer's format) is the ultimate task to be accomplished by using the market attractiveness/competitive position matrix. This match is important because a retailer that lacks competitiveness cannot survive in an attractive market, and a strong competitor cannot prosper in an unattractive market.

Organizational Opportunities

Portfolio analysis enables the retail organization to assess its current situation (what its business is) and identify possible future courses of action (what its business should be) for various SBUs. After completion of the portfolio analysis, the decision to target some SBUs for extinction (harvesting) or replacement (divesting) and others for maintenance (holding) and growth (building) often leaves a strategic gap between the current and desired performance of the retail organization. In other words, projected sales will fall short of desired sales. To fill this strategic gap, retail management must take advantage of any opportunities for better growth and/or improved performance.

Market Penetration

One opportunity that is readily available to each retailer is to pursue **market penetration**—the strategy of trying to increase the sales productivity of current SBU stores in existing markets. Several objectives might be identified in pursuit of this strategy:

- Increase patronage level of current customers by increasing the frequency of store visits and the amount of the average sale per customer visit. McDonald's focuses much of its marketing effort on what it calls superheavy users (SHUs)—males 18–24 years of age who eat at McDonald's three to five times per week.[36]
- Stimulate trial visits among nonpatrons who reside in existing trading areas.
- Entice customers who currently patronize competing outlets within existing trading areas.

To achieve stated objectives, retailers employ such tactics as (1) increasing advertising and sale promotion activities, (2) expanding product and service mix, (3) using suggestive selling more aggressively, (4) engaging in trade-up selling, (5) developing special-event

Retail Strategies and Tactics

Harry Rosen Targets Younger Crowd

Harry Rosen invited customers to phone him personally with gripes about his upscale menswear stores. But instead of complaints, his recent full-page newspaper ad elicited a flood of positive calls. Mr. Rosen's personal touch and loyal following have helped carry his 22 stores to more than $100-million in annual sales, a relatively strong showing in today's sluggish retail climate. But profit—estimated at more than $1.2-million—could be a size or two larger, analysts say.

Mr. Rosen, chairman and CEO, acknowledges that he needs to broaden his customer base by reaching out to younger men and telling his story to more people. So he has plucked one of the country's hot-shot ad agencies, Roche Macaulay & Partners Advertising Inc., to try to tailor a fresh image and lure the under-40 crowd into Harry Rosen stores. "But it's time to address a younger customer. We're leaving all doors open for Roche to come in. This is a new ballgame."

Mr. Roche says he'd like to make the Harry Rosen name a "little less stuffy" and try to cash in on the movement to casual Fridays at work. He'd also like to catch the fancy of more women, since they often do men's shopping. He is considering other media beyond print—perhaps. "There are a lot of misconceptions about Harry Rosen that offer us opportunities," Mr. Roche says. Some observers are concerned the retail chain may be dipping into too young a market to generate more in sales. "I think they would be at risk if they tried to go down in age and income," warns merchandising analyst David Brodie at CIBC Wood Gundy, who is impressed with the stores' management.

Source: Marina Strauss, Globe and Mail, *May 23, 1996, B13.*

merchandising programs, and (6) offering lower prices. The Retail Strategies and Tactics box illustrates Harry Rosen's new direction in marketing.

Market Development

Market development is the strategy of increasing sales by expanding existing store operations into new markets. Retailers have three market choices if they elect to engage in market development. First, market development can be achieved by opening new *geographic markets* by identifying new locations and developing new store sites within geographic areas not previously served. Sears Canada plans to expand market coverage in smaller communities and the catalogue market by increasing the number of catalogue outlets.[37]

Second, a retailer's market development strategy might be realized by appealing to *new market segments*—that is, trying to attract different consumer groups by offering a new merchandise mix, enhanced customer service, better value, or any other inducement that the retailer feels is necessary to attract and hold the new customer segment.

Finally, new market sales goals can be reached by expanding into *new market levels*. By offering products and services to other retailers, wholesalers, institutional markets (for example, hospitals, universities, government agencies), and manufacturers, the retailer is capable of serving industrial and commercial markets as well as consumer markets. Beaver, one of Canada's leading home centre chains, attempts to serve two distinct customer bases: professional builders and amateur fixer-uppers. Warehouse club memberships (such as Costco) consist of two groups of buyers at different levels within the channel of distribution: wholesale/business-level members and retail-level consumers. Lands' End, the catalogue retailer, has developed a Corporate Sales Catalog that sells specialty items to corporations that can be used as corporate gifts, sales incentives, or customer premiums.[38]

Product Development

For most retailers, existing markets represent additional market potential due to unmet needs. Product development is one means of serving those unsatisfied needs. To increase sales within existing markets by developing new goods and services is the focus of a product development strategy. Retailers can operationalize a **product development** strategy by either replacing old merchandise lines with new lines or adding new product lines and items. Sears Canada has decided to expand its focus on nationally branded appliances due to stiff competition from other retailers.

Product development usually translates into (1) adjusting merchandise variety and assortment to create a more differentiated merchandise mix and fine-tuning the type and number of services in order to offer a more extensive selection of expected and optional services, (2) adding more desirable merchandise items and service types that are normally associated with another retail format, and (3) developing a general-purpose product mix by combining two or more broad product lines or service offerings.

Retail Strategies and Tactics

Wal-Mart's New Market Development Strategy

Wal-Mart has traditionally limited its domain to rural and middle-income markets where its value merchandise, everyday low prices, and folksy service were highly prized. From its original base in Arkansas, Wal-Mart spread throughout the United States overwhelming one regional discounter after another. As the last [U.S.] regional market, the northeastern United States, becomes Wal-Martilized, the nation's largest retailer is looking for new worlds to conquer. Some of those worlds include international markets. Wal-Mart invaded the Canadian market with the purchase of the Woolco discount chain. The assault on Mexico has been in the form of a joint venture with its Mexican partner Cifra, that country's largest retailer. What new markets are left for this retail juggernaut to conquer?

With its stellar performance over the last couple of decades, Wal-Mart has created high expectations within the company and the financial community. Wal-Mart has used its consistently appreciating stock to motivate its employees with its profit sharing programs. As a perpetual "darling" of Wall Street, Wal-Mart has enjoyed the continuous support of the financial community as it produced 99 consecutive quarters of earnings growth. That record came to an end with the fiscal fourth quarter ending January 31, 1996. Stiffer competition, shifting consumer loyalties, limited discretionary income, and saturated market areas are some of the reasons cited for the end of one of the best runs in the history of retailing. What to do next?

Future growth of Wal-Mart is directed at new geographic markets (upper middle income suburbs), new market segments (value-conscious high-income shopper), and new emphasis on different market levels (small independent business organizations). In order to attract the upscale discount consumers, Wal-Mart is building new conventional discount units and superstores in such high-rent markets as Evergreen, Colorado; Princeton, New Jersey; Germantown, Tennessee; and Scotsdale, Arizona. Improved interior store atmospherics (wider aisles, better signage, more attractive lighting, more in-store specialty boutiques, high-tech kiosks, and more upscaled fixturing) and exterior store appearances (stone-pillar-and-oak exterior, vaulted roof, and landscaped parking lots) are directed at bringing in a more upscale consumer willing to purchase higher margin merchandise. The renewed effort to serve the wholesale market level is being accomplished by focusing Wal-Mart's warehouse club chain (Sam's Club division) on better serving the needs of the office manager, convenience-store operator, and other business people who come to the warehouse club to stock up on products ranging from paper goods to soda. Not only will this refocusing of the warehouse division expand sales at the wholesale level, it will help Wal-Mart to avoid cannibalizing sales from its regular discount stores and its superstore combination units.

Will Wal-Mart's market development strategies be sufficient to re-energize sales growth? Are its choices of new geographic markets, new market segments, and greater emphasis on the wholesale market level the right ones? Check your preferred business news source for the most current information on the results of Wal-Mart's new strategic efforts.

Sources: Adapted from Louise Lee, "Discounter Wal-Mart Is Catering to Affluent to Maintain Growth," The Wall Street Journal, *February 7, 1996, A1, A6; Kevin Helliker and Bob Ortega, "Falling Profit Marks End of Era at Wal-Mart,"* The Wall Street Journal, *January 18, 1996, B1, B11; Bob Ortega, "What Does Wal-Mart Do if Stock Drop Cuts Into Workers' Morale?"* The Wall Street Journal, *January 4, 1995, A1, A8; and Wendy Zeller, "Why Sam's Wants Businesses To Join the Club,"* Business Week, *June 27, 1994, 48–49.*

Vertical Integration

Opportunity growth can take the form of vertical integration. In this integrative growth opportunity, the organization's efforts focus on building or acquiring SBUs related to the organization's current portfolio of SBUs. A **vertical integration** strategy aims to increase sales by incorporating one or more levels of the marketing channel of distribution into the organization's operations. A fully integrated channel is one in which a single channel member (for example, the retailer) is in control of the entire channel and each of its functions. For example, Safeway Supermarkets has equity ownership at both the production and wholesale levels of its distribution channel.

Forward integration is the attempt by manufacturers, designers, and/or wholesalers to ensure entry into the market by acquiring retail organizations or creating new channel opportunities. Many manufacturers (Sherwin-Williams) and wholesalers (Home Hardware) have engaged in forward integration by developing or acquiring retail businesses and operating them as part of their strategic marketing efforts. Shaw Industries, a major producer of carpets, has turned to vertical integration to gain control of its destiny. Its goal is to be involved with as much of the process of making and selling carpet as is practical.[39] Guess Inc., the blue jeans producer, continues to open its jeanswear and sportswear stores.[40] Pendleton Woolen Mills "does not own its own sheep as is rumoured, but it does buy raw wool right off sheeps' backs. Pendleton workers grade, sort, and scour the fibre, spin it into yarn, dye it, weave it into fabric, and ultimately make the garments. Pendleton even retails about 15% of its production in its own 18 stores and its 52 company-affiliated stores."[41] Franklin Mint, the maker and direct marketer of a wide range of collectibles, has developed Franklin Mint Gallery stores, in which it retails its complete line of heirloom dolls, precision-crafted cars, fashion jewellery, collectible plates, luxury edition games, and sculptures.[42]

Backward integration involves seeking ownership and/or control of supply systems (for example, a retailer acquiring a wholesaler or manufacturer). Although developing strategic partnerships and alliances with vendors (to be discussed in more depth in Chapter 16) is the preferred method for retailers to integrate backward, many retailers gain direct control of their sources of supply. For instance, the Bombay Co.'s line of reproductions of English-style furniture is designed, produced, and sold entirely by the firm's highly integrated distribution system.[43] The Gap has also engaged in backward integration by assuming control of the production and procurement processes for many of its lines of merchandise.

Horizontal Integration

A strategy of **horizontal integration** is achieved by seeking ownership and/or control of competitors at the same level within the marketing channel. Examples of horizontal integration include the purchases of Kmart Canada, Woodwards Department Stores of Vancouver, and Simpsons of Toronto by the Hudson Bay Company.

Concentric Diversification

With **concentric diversification**, a retailer tries to attract new customers by adding businesses that possess technological or marketing similarities with existing businesses. Because it represents an opportunity to grow in a familiar and less risky environment, concentric diversification is the most popular of the diversification alternatives. The following examples support this claim:

- **Hudson Bay Co.**—Department stores (The Bay), discount stores (Fields), and discount department stores (Zellers)
- **The Gap Inc.**—Upscale specialty stores (Banana Republic), middle market specialty stores (The Gap), low-end specialty stores (Old Navy Clothing Co.), and children's apparel (GapKids)[44]
- **Dylex Ltd.**—Women's fashion wear (Fairweather, Suzy Shier), men's fashion wear (Tip Top Tailors), and family wear (BiWay, Thrifty's)

Retail Strategies and Tactics

Woolworth Corporation

A Concentric Diversification Strategy

For Woolworth Corporation, shopping malls are like hundreds of laboratories, for it is within these shopping clusters that the company test market merchandising ideas to create national specialty store chains with a merchandise focus that ranges from costume jewellery to kids' clothing to sporting equipment. Today, Woolworth Corporation does business through 40 different retail chains and operates almost 8000 stores. The management complexities of such a diversified portfolio of retailing formats is enormous. The principle strategic issues to be addressed by Woolworth's management include: (1) finding a focus for its chaotic collection of retail formats, (2) divesting itself of underperforming formats and units, (3) meshing the individual operations in order to gain operating economies, (4) developing better organization-wide information systems, (5) improving productivity, and (6) controlling expenses. The portfolio of retailing formats that comprise Woolworth's diversification strategy include:

- Foot Locker: running shoes and sportswear
- Lady Foot Locker: women's athletic footwear
- Kids Foot Locker: children's athletic footwear
- Northern Reflections: women's casual wear
- Kinney Shoes: family shoes
- Afterthoughts: costume jewellery, handbags, and accessories
- Champs Sports: athletic merchandise
- Woolworth Express: down-sized variety stores
- Randy River: men's casual clothing
- Ashbrooks: home furnishings
- San Francisco Music Box Company: musical giftware
- Williams the Shoeman: family shoes
- Silk & Satin: lingerie and sleepwear

In addition to these specialty retail operations, Woolworth is growing other niche specialists in both domestic and international markets. Mathers-Australia and Rubin-Germany are part of Woolworth's international retail operations.

One of the advantages of Woolworth's diversity strategy is that it affords the corporation the ability to adjust to changing economic conditions. For example, during the recession of the early 1990s, Woolworth dropped, sold, or changed over 10 percent of its stores in order to meet the conditions of this economic downswing.

Sources: Based in part on Leah Richard, "Woolworth walking down a new path," Advertising Age, *May 15, 1995, 4; Phyllis Berman and Caroline Waxler, "Woolworth's woes,"* Forbes, *August 14, 1995, 47–48; Lori Bongiorno, "Lost in the Aisles at Woolworth,"* Business Week, *October 30, 1995, 76–77; and Laura Bird, "Woolworth Sets Out to Find New Chief for Retail Giant,"* The Wall Street Journal, *October 12, 1994, B4.*

One of the challenges of such diversification is how the expanded company is managed. The desire to achieve economies of scale often creates problems with diverse corporate missions and objectives. The Bay and Zellers recently abandoned plans to merge certain aspects of their companies due to such differences.[45]

Horizontal Diversification

The objective of **horizontal diversification** is to increase sales by adding SBUs that appeal to the organization's current customers even though they are not technologically related to its current businesses. The joint venture of IBM and Sears in developing a videotex service is a good example of horizontal diversification: computer and information processing by IBM and retailing and merchandising by Sears.[46] U-Haul unsuccessfully tried to diversify into the general rental business, in which it rented everything from motor homes to jet skis.[47]

Conglomerate Diversification

The retail organization can also expand through **conglomerate diversification**—adding new businesses that are totally unrelated to its current SBUs in hopes of appealing to entirely new markets. Examples of conglomerate diversification are Provigo and the

Hudson's Bay Co. Some of these arrangements have led the parent company to divest itself of unrelated retail businesses.[48]

High Performance

Several opportunities exist for improving an organization's profits and productivity through more efficient usage of organizational resources—financial, human, and facility.[49] The previous discussion on organizational objectives identifies the need to achieve acceptable performance in (1) return on sales and assets, (2) earnings per share, (3) labour and space productivity, and (4) inventory turnover. Improved operational and managerial efficiencies are the key to achieving desired performance standards. "Operationally excellent companies deliver a combination of quality, price, and ease of purchase that no one else in their market can match."[50] Toys R Us and Wal-Mart are among an elite group of retailers whose size, market clout, and efficiency have positioned them to succeed. These "power retailers" are fast and focused and have been on the cutting edge of merchandising and operating developments.[51]

Summary

Strategic retail management is the process of planning the organization's survival and growth. Planning is conducted at corporate, divisional, operational, and department levels of the organization. The retail organization's strategic plan is an overall business plan developed for the entire firm that involves (1) identifying the organizational mission, (2) establishing organizational objectives, (3) conducting an organizational portfolio analysis, and (4) evaluating organizational opportunities.

The mission statement is a generalized yet meaningful expression of the organization's future direction. Its three tasks are to identify (1) the business and customer domains within which the organization operates, (2) the organization's responsibilities toward the people with whom it interacts, and (3) the blueprint for accomplishing the organizational mission. Mission statements are developed according to environmental and resource considerations, distinctive competencies, and managerial preferences.

Organizational objectives identify the specific purposes that the firm is to achieve. Most retail organizations identify two general sets of objectives: market and financial. Market objectives aim at obtaining customer patronage (sales volume, customer traffic, and customer service objectives) and achieving competitive positions within the general marketplace (market share, store image, and vendor relations objectives). Financial objectives establish goals for profitability (returns, earnings, and dividends), and productivity (labour, space, and merchandise). Finally, societal objectives are identified to encourage the firm to meet its social responsibilities to its various publics.

Organizational portfolio analysis involves reviewing the SBUs that constitute the total business interests of a diversified retail organization or evaluating the opportunities for growth and investment in existing store operations within existing market areas. The most commonly used portfolio analysis approaches are the market growth/market share matrix developed by the Boston Consulting Group and the market attractiveness/competitive position matrix developed by General Electric. A portfolio analysis enables the retail organization to assess its current situation (what its business is) and identify possible future courses of action (what the business should be).

The final step in developing a strategic plan is to identify and evaluate potential opportunities for continued organizational growth and improved organizational performance. Organizational opportunities can take the form of pursuing such strategies as market penetration, market development, product development, vertical integration, horizontal integration, concentric diversification, horizontal diversification, conglomerate diversification, and high-performance retailing, which includes more efficient use of financial, human, and facility resources.

Key Terms and Concepts

backward integration *p. 584*
BCG portfolio approach *p. 576*
cash cows *p. 578*
competitive position *p. 580*
concentric diversification *p. 584*
conglomerate diversification *p. 585*
dogs *p. 578*
financial objectives *p. 574*
forward integration *p. 584*
GE portfolio approach *p. 579*
green zone *p. 580*
horizontal diversification *p. 585*
horizontal integration *p. 584*
market attractiveness *p. 580*
market development *p. 582*
market objectives *p. 571*
market penetration *p. 581*
market share *p. 573*
mission statement *p. 568*
organizational objectives *p. 571*
organizational portfolio *p. 576*
product development *p. 583*
question marks *p. 578*
red zone *p. 581*
stars *p. 576*
store image *p. 573*
strategic business units (SBUs) *p. 566*
strategic planning *p. 566*
strategic retail management *p. 565*
strategic retail plan *p. 567*
tactical planning *p. 566*
vertical integration *p. 584*
yellow zone *p. 581*

Review Questions

1. What is strategic retail management? Define and describe its two major components.
2. At what level do strategic and tactical planning occur? How is each planning level different from the other?
3. Characterize a strategic plan. Describe its purposes.
4. What are the four elements of the strategic planning process? Define each.
5. Describe the three tasks of an organizational mission.
6. Identify and briefly describe the factors to be considered in developing an organizational mission.
7. There are six types of market objectives. Provide a brief description and example of each.
8. List the six types of financial objectives. Provide a brief description and example of each.
9. Describe the BCG market growth/market share matrix approach to portfolio analysis.
10. What are the five alternatives for the allocation of financial resources as identified in the BCG portfolio approach? Discuss each alternative.
11. Describe the market attractiveness/competitive position matrix and discuss how it is used to evaluate opportunities for existing store operations.
12. Define market penetration, market development, and product development. How are they alike? How are they different?
13. Compare and contrast concentric diversification, horizontal diversification, and conglomerate diversification.

Review Exam

True or False

______ 1. Departmental planning is more tactical than strategic in nature.

______ 2. The mission statement is expressed in very specific terms in order to clearly identify specific actions to be taken.

______ 3. A portfolio analysis is an analytical tool to provide perspective on the organization's current situation (where it is now) and to suggest possible courses of action for the future (where it wants to be).

______ 4. Dogs always produce a negative cash flow.

______ 5. Building involves expanding small stars into big stars and transforming promising question marks into stars.

______ 6. Increasing the patronage level of current customers is one tactic used by retailers as part of their market development strategy.

Multiple Choice

_____ 1. A strategic plan is directed at achieving a strategic fit between _____.
a. the organization's present capabilities and its present environment opportunities
b. the organization's future capabilities and its future environment opportunities
c. the organization's present capabilities and its future environment opportunities
d. all of the above relationships
e. none of the above relationships

_____ 2. _____ is an organizational objective aimed at improving return trade and increasing repeat business.
a. Sales volume
b. Customer traffic
c. Customer loyalty
d. Market share
e. Earnings

_____ 3. _____ provide the bulk of the cash to finance the expansion of other SBUs.
a. Question marks
b. Dogs
c. Problem children
d. Good children
e. None of the above

_____ 4. The goal of _____ is to find a market in which the SBU is reasonably protected from the actions of competitors.
a. building
b. holding
c. harvesting
d. niching
e. divesting

_____ 5. _____ diversification is accomplished by adding new businesses that have technological or marketing synergies with existing businesses.
a. Horizontal
b. Concentric
c. Backward
d. Conglomerate
e. Elliptical

_____ 6. To increase the sales productivity of current SBU stores within existing markets is the objective of _____.
a. product development
b. horizontal integration
c. market development
d. conglomerate diversification

Student Application Manual

Investigative Projects: Practice and Application

1. Strategic distinction in terms of a unique merchandising and/or operating characteristic is essential for success in the 1990s. Choose five of the following retailers from your region and identify the strategies that distinguish them from their competitors now or in the past: (a) Domino's Pizza, (b) The Gap, (c) Toys R Us, (d) Wal-Mart, (e) McDonald's, (f) Future Shop, (g) The Keg, (h) Pier 1, (i) Canadian Tire, (j) Sears, (k) Loblaws, (l) Foot Locker, (m) Bloomingdale's, (n) Zellers, (o) Disney Stores.

2. Develop six specific statements (goals) involving social responsibility that retailers might include in their mission statement.

3. Develop one specific organizational objective (non-text example) for each of the six types of market objectives and the six types of financial objectives.

4. By conducting a literature review in the library, identify current examples of each of the following growth opportunities: (a) market penetration, (b) market development, (c) product development, (d) backward integration, (e) forward integration, and (f) horizontal integration.

Endnotes

1. Gilbert Fuchsberg, " 'Visioning' Missions Becomes Its Own Mission," *The Wall Street Journal*, January 7, 1994, B1.
2. Michael J. O'Connor, "Why Do Some Organizations Do Better and Last Longer Than Others?" *Retailers on Retailing: Lessons from the School of Experience* (Arthur Andersen & Co., SC, 1994), 4.
3. Terri Kabachnick, "Turning the Tide against Turnover," *Retailing Issues Letter*, (copublished by the Center for Retailing Studies, Texas A&M University and Arthur Andersen, September 1995), 5.
4. Leonard L. Berry, "Stores with a Future," *Retail Issues Letter* (copublished by the Center for Retailing Studies, Texas A&M University and Arthur Andersen, March 1995), 1.
5. Kenneth Labich, "Why Companies Fail," *Fortune*, November 14, 1994, 68.
6. Elizabeth Church, "Home Depot Builds Tough Competition," *Globe and Mail*, September 2, 1996, B14.
7. Ronald Henkoff, "Service Is Everybody's Business," *Fortune*, June 27, 1994, 60.
8. Alan Farnham, "State Your Values, Hold the Hot Air," *Fortune*, April 19, 1993, 122, 124.
9. Gary Hamel and C. K. Prahalad, "Seeing the Future First," *Fortune*, September 5, 1994, 67.
10. Charles P. Wallace, "Can the Body Shop Shape Up?" *Fortune*, April 15, 1996, 119–20.
11. Daniel J. Sweeney, "Retailing—An Industry under Siege," *Retail Control* (December 1991): 31.
12. Joseph Epstein, "Dollar Tree Stores, To the Sky?" *Financial World*, September 26, 1995, 18.
13. P. Rajon Varadarajan and Daniel Rajaratnam, "Symbiotic Marketing Revisited," *Journal of Marketing*, 50 (January 1986): 11.
14. Fleming Meeks, "What Brand Is Your Weather?" *Forbes*, October 23, 1995, 320.
15. Rahul Jacob, "Why Some Customers Are More Equal Than Others," *Fortune*, September 19, 1994, 216. Also see "What's A Loyal Customer Worth?" *Fortune*, December 11, 1995, 182.
16. See Kate Fitzgerald, "Competitors Swarm Powerful Toys R Us," *Advertising Age*, February 27, 1995, 4; Susan Reda, "1995 NRF Gold Medal Award Winner," *Stores* (January 1995): 131–44; Susan Caminiti, "After You Win the Fun Begins," *Fortune*, May 2, 1994, 76; and Seth Lubove, "The Growing Gets Tough," *Forbes*, April 13, 1992, 69.
17. David Mazursky and Jacob Jacoby, "Exploring the Development of Store Images," *Journal of Retailing*, 62 (Summer 1986): 146–47.
18. Karen Hsu, "Service Merchandise Turns the Page on Its Catalog Past," *The Wall Street Journal*, August 25, 1995, B3.
19. Kenneth Kidd, "The Fall of the House of Dylex," *Report on Business Magazine*, September 1995, 54.
20. Elaine Pollack, "Partnership: Buzzword or Best Practice?" *Chain Store Age* (August 1995): 11A.
21. See Teri Agins, "Apparel Makers Are Refashioning Their Operations," *The Wall Street Journal*, January 13, 1994, B4; and Christina Duff, "Big Stores' Outlandish Demands Alienate Small Suppliers," *The Wall Street Journal*, October 17, 1995, B1.
22. Debra Sparks, "Arthur Martinez, Financial World's CEO of the Year," *Financial World*, March 25, 1996, 18–19.
23. "Nike 'Just Does It' With Staffworks," *Chain Store Age Executive* (June 1995): C10.
24. Fraglan Du and Ira Apfel, "The Future of Retailing," *American Demographics* (September 1995): 29.
25. Shannon Dortch, "Productive Projections," *American Demographics* (June 1995): 4.
26. Bill Saporito, "And the Winner Is Still . . . Wal-Mart," *Fortune*, May 2, 1994, 64.
27. Paul N. Bloom, Pattie Yu Hussein, and Lisa R. Szykman, "Benefiting Society and the Bottom Line," *Marketing Management* 4 (Winter 1995): 13.
28. See "Retailers Use Charity Program to Cut Logistics Costs," *Stores* (March 1996): 46–47.
29. Don L. Boroughs, "The Bottom Line on Ethics," *U.S. News & World Report*, March 20, 1995, 63.
30. George S. Day, "Diagnosing the Product Portfolio," *Journal of Marketing*, 41 (April 1977): 29.
31. John F. Geer, Jr., "Tandy: Time to Unplug," *Financial World*, May 23, 1995, 18.
32. Day, "Diagnosing the Product Portfolio," 31.
33. See Lori Bongiorno, "Everything Must Go—To the Liquidators," *Business Week*, January 15, 1996, 52.
34. Kidd, "The Fall of the House of Dylex," 54.
35. See Robin Wensley, "Strategic Marketing: Betas, Boxes, and Basics," *Journal of Marketing* (Summer 1981): 173–82.
36. Jeanne Whalen, "McDonald's Shaking Marketing, Agencies," *Advertising Age*, August 12, 1994, 4.
37. *Sears Canada Annual Report*, 1996, 7.
38. "Look What Lands' End Just Cooked Up for Del Monte," *The Wall Street Journal*, February 8, 1996, B7.
39. Andrew E. Serwer, "How to Escape a Price War," *Fortune*, June 13, 1994, 88.
40. "Guess: 2 More Stores," *Women's Wear Daily* (October 1995): 10.
41. Phyllis Berman, "From Sheep to Shirt," *Forbes*, May 22, 1995, 163.
42. Laura Loro, "Nostalgia for Sale at Franklin Mint," *Advertising Age*, May 15, 1995, 33.
43. "Selling Instant Gratification," *Fortune*, June 28, 1993, 102; and Kevin Helliker, "Bombay Co.'s Line of Furniture, Bric-a-Brac Fill a Void," *The Wall Street Journal*, October 28, 1992, B4.
44. "The Gap, Inc.," *Hoover's Handbook of American Companies, 1996*, edited by Patrick J. Spain and James R. Talbot, The Reference Press Inc. 1995, 395.
45. Marina Strauss, "Bay, Zellers Drop Joint Buying Strategy," *Globe and Mail*, July 19, 1997, B1.
46. See Paul M. Eng, "Can Prodigy Keep Pace?" *Business Week*, August 7, 1995, 32; Jeffrey Rothfeder, "How Long Will Prodigy Be a Problem Child?" *Business Week*, September 10, 1990, 75; and Michael W. Miller, "Prodigy Faces Big Shake-Up, New Strategy," *The Wall Street Journal*, January 7, 1992, B1, B3.
47. Seth Lubove, "American Gothic," *Business Week*, November 21, 1994, 120.
48. Annual Reports of Provigo and Hudson's Bay Co., 1996.
49. Jagdish N. Sheth and Rajendra S. Sisodia, "Feeling the Heat—Part 2," *Marketing Management*, 4 (Winter 1995): 19–33.
50. Michael Treacy and Fred Wiersema, "How Market Leaders Keep Their Edge," *Fortune*, February 6, 1995, 90.
51. See Zachary Schiller and Wendy Zellner, "Clout! More and More, Retail Giants Rule the Marketplace," *Business Week* (December 1992): 66–69, 72–73.

Adaptive Retailing Strategies Changing and Surviving in a Dynamic Environment

Outline

Objectives

To appreciate and grasp the contribution that theories of adaptive behaviour make to the understanding of retail institutional change

To utilize and apply the theories of adaptive behaviour in anticipating and adapting to the changes in the competitive nature of the retailing marketplace

To identify and describe the practices used by contemporary retailers in their efforts to adapt to the changes in the retail environment

To adapt and use current retailing practices to meet the challenges of future marketplace dynamics

Retail Vignette

Forzani's

In 1974 John Forzani, his brothers Joe and Tom, and Basil Bark, all former Calgary Stampeder football players, established their first Locker Room store in Calgary with an investment of $9000. It was the right time in the right place with the right name recognition that propelled Forzani's to become one of the most successful retailers in its category in Canada within a short time period.

Their new store coincided with the growing fitness craze and the Forzani name was well known and connected to the Calgary community. Within three years annual sales zoomed to $1 million and the foursome were netting profits of $150 000.

By 1983 Forzani operated 23 Locker Room stores in Alberta and Saskatchewan and had created Jersey City franchise outlets. Success and growth continued with the addition of other chains, such as R&R The Walking Store and Sport Chek. Each store was directed towards a slightly different target market and with the skillful leadership of John Forzani had emerged as a leading Western Canadian retailer.

In 1994, concerned that Forzani's did not have an eastern presence and with the threat of competition from U.S. category killer sporting goods chains moving into Canada, the company spent $20 million to purchase the 180-store Sports Experts chain from Provigo and added 32 Sports Chek stores within a year. Total area increased from 32 000 to 88 000 m^2. Sales jumped 304 percent and markets were still healthy at $7.7 million in 1994. Although they were now the number one sporting goods retailer in Canada, Forzani's was beginning to suffer from such a rapid expansion. The debt loan was too high, some inventory that came with the acquisition was hard to move, and merchandise management problems were compounded with the growth. In addition, two U.S. chains, Sports Authority and Sport Mart, entered the market creating greater competition and further saturating the retail space for sporting goods and accessories. Economic recession coupled with the above conditions resulted in a $20 million loss for the chain in 1995.

In 1996 John Forzani realized some changes were required to ensure the viability of Forzani's. He restructured the inventory system, moved buyers closer to customers, closed unprofitable stores, and brought personnel with rational retail experience into the organization. He is now looking at the possibility of greater involvement in supplying inventory to independent retailers through franchising. Early indications are that this strategy is paying off for the 270-store chain with $300 million in sales. An additional bonus was the withdrawal of Sport Mart from the Canadian market in 1997.

Source: "Final Fumble," Calgary Herald, *1996; "Sport Mart Exit, 'Good News' For Forzani,"* Calgary Herald, *January 1997; "First and Goal,"* Profit Magazine, *April/May 1997, 37–39; "Forzani Builds a New Team,"* Globe and Mail, *January 16, 1997; "Forzani Quietly Restructures,"* Globe and Mail, *April 15, 1997.*

The Wheel of Retailing

The wheel, in sum, is not likely to be rolling off into the metaphorical sunset. The concept may have been deflated at times, but it has not yet been punctured. Some of its former customers may have succumbed to the attraction of imported models, but the wheel has not yet lost its grip upon the imaginations of marketing scholars. Indeed, despite its thirty-year history, the theory remains in virtual showroom condition. Contrary to the contention of some academics, the wheel does not need to be changed, nor does it require retreading, rebalancing, or realignment. In my opinion, it needs to be roadtested more often.[1]

Darwinian Evolution

Retailing is Darwinian evolution—survival of the fittest. New forms evolve. Old forms adapt or die. To try to control this process would be unnatural.[2]

The Age of Sober Realization

Retailers came to realize that the world was changing. Lifestyles were changing. People's incomes were changing, mostly for the worse. A new word crept into their vocabulary—downsizing. Until then, it was a matter of assuming that the good times would roll again. Then retailers realized that the good times would only roll again if they could adapt to the new rules of the game.[3]

What Makes a Retail Market Leader?

Market leaders win not by being everything to everyone, but by focusing their entire operations—management systems, processes, structure, even culture—toward delivering one of three types of value: the best total cost, best product, or best "total solution." Companies that dominate their categories choose one of these dimensions of value and drive it to unmatched levels, thereby creating a unique value proposition to customers—one that differentiates a company from all its competitors and sets the rules for market domination.[4]

Traditional Theories of Adaptive Behaviour

Retailing and the institutions of retailing are continuously adapting in response to numerous environmental trends and the ever-dynamic behaviour of consumers. Innovative merchandising strategies and operational methods are constantly being developed to meet new competitive challenges and evolving customer expectations. What the future will

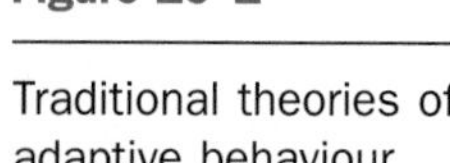

Figure 16–1

Traditional theories of adaptive behaviour

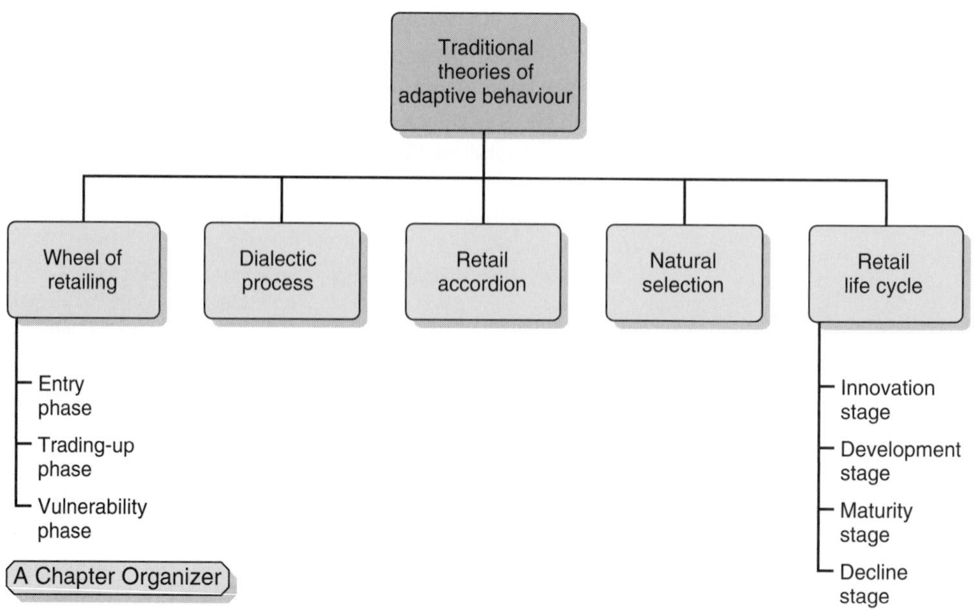

bring to the constantly changing retailing world is a matter of speculation. Given that "the past is the key to the future," however, some retailing experts have identified patterns of competitive change that they express as theories of retail institutional change. Five of the more commonly accepted theories are the wheel of retailing, the dialectic process, the retail accordion, the theory of natural selection, and the retail life cycle (see Figure 16–1).

Wheel of Retailing

One of the most widely recognized theories of retail institutional change is the **wheel of retailing.**[5] First hypothesized by Malcolm P. McNair, the wheel of retailing states that the dynamics of institutional change are a "more or less definite cycle"; the cycle "begins with the bold new concept, the innovation" and ends with "eventual vulnerability . . . to the next fellow who has a bright idea."[6] A careful examination of the wheel theory reveals three distinct phases to each cycle and that a pattern of cycles will develop over a period of time. Figures 16–2 and 16–3 illustrate the three phases of entry, trading up, and vulnerability and how each cycle might be repeated to form a wavelike pattern.

Entry Phase In the first phase of the cycle, an innovative retailing institution enters the market as a low-status, low-price competitor. In recent years, the warehouse club format (for example, Costco) represents one of the most successful entries into the retail marketplace as a value-driven, low-cost operator.[7] By reducing operating expenses to a minimum, the new institution can operate at a gross margin substantially below (30 percent as opposed to 50 percent) the required gross margins of the more established retailers in the market. Operating expenses usually are maintained at low levels by (1) offering minimal customer services, (2) providing a modest shopping atmosphere in terms of exterior and interior facilities, (3) occupying low-rent locations, and (4) offering limited product mixes. Historically, market entry was easier for retailers selling low-margin, high-turnover products. However, in the value-driven decade of the 1990s, offering high-quality branded products can be an integral part of the market entry strategy. Both the warehouse club and category killer formats were successful in gaining a market foothold by offering well-known brand names at substantial savings. Although consumers and competitors consider the innovative institution low-status, it does gain market penetration primarily on the basis of price appeals. When the new form of retailing has become an established competitor, it enters the second phase of the cycle.

Trading-Up Phase Emulators quickly copy the successful innovation because of its success and market acceptance. The competitive actions of these emulators force the

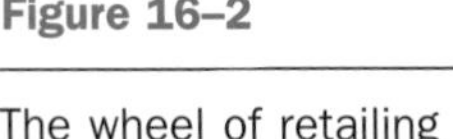

Figure 16–2

The wheel of retailing

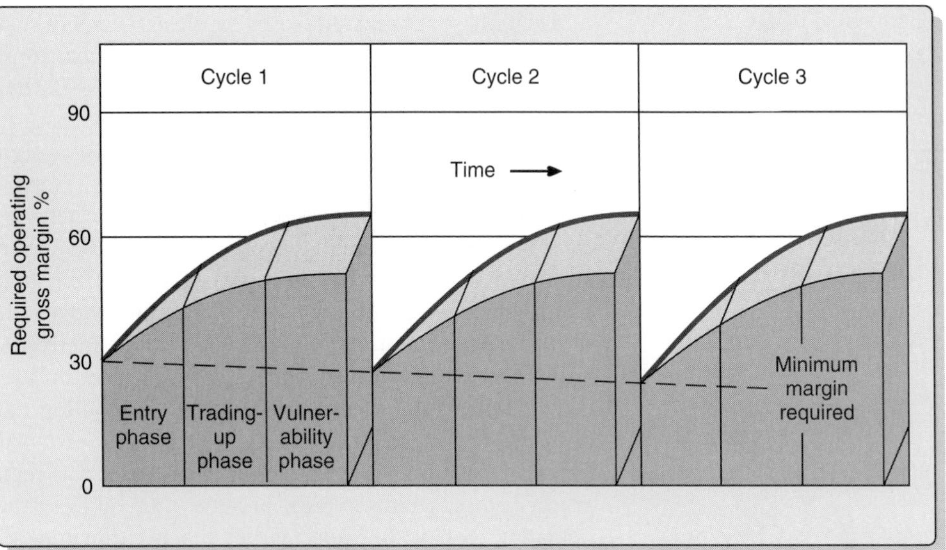

Figure 16–3

The retailer and the wheel of retailing

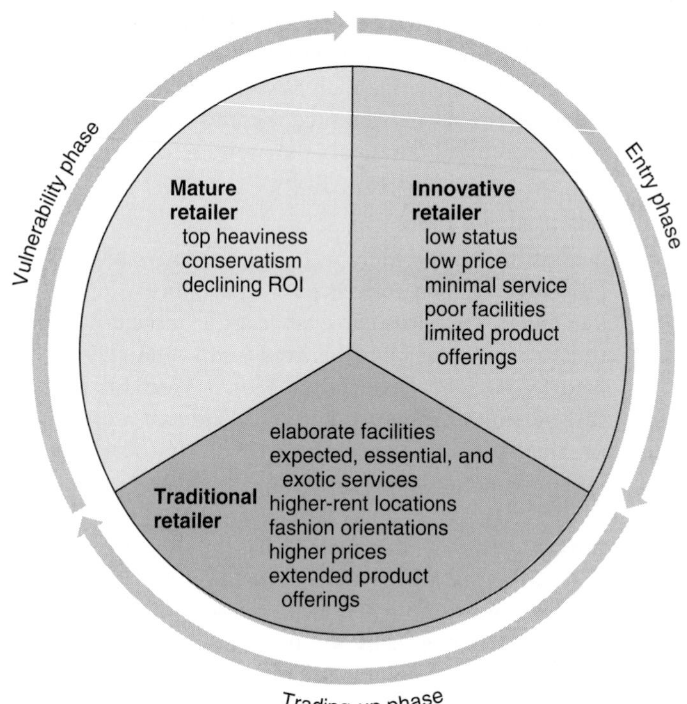

original innovative business to differentiate itself by engaging in the process of trading up. The trading-up phase of the cycle involves various changes to upgrade and distinguish the innovative institutions.[8] Trading up usually takes the form of acquiring more elaborate facilities, offering expected and exotic as well as essential services, and locating in high-rent neighbourhoods. To help distance itself from its former spartan image, Wal-Mart's new prototype store features wider aisles and classy displays as well as better information and enhanced services.[9] Also, product lines frequently are traded up to include high-markup items, often with a fashion orientation.

The end result of the trading-up phase is that the original innovative institution matures into a higher-status, higher-price operation with a required operating gross margin comparable to that of many established competitors. In other words, the innovative institution matures into a traditional retail institution.

Vulnerability Phase With maturity, the now-established innovative institution enters a phase "characterized by top-heaviness, conservatism, and a decline in the rate of return on investments."[10] Eventually, the original innovator becomes vulnerable "to the next fellow who has a bright idea and who starts his business on a low-cost basis, slipping in under the (price) umbrella that the old-line institutions have hoisted."[11] The entry of a new low-price innovator into the retail market signals the end of one cycle and the beginning of a new competitive cycle.

In a general way The Gap fell victim to the wheel process: (1) it entered the market as a lower-price retailer of jeans, T-shirts, and other casual clothing; (2) it attracted emulators of its colourful, well-priced apparel; (3) it upscaled both its merchandise and stores in order to differentiate itself from copycat formats; (4) it became somewhat overpriced with a product line that lacked distinctiveness and good value; and, finally, (5) rolled back prices on many product lines to regain its momentum.

In practice, the theory of the wheel of retailing has been used to explain numerous changes in the general institutional structure of North American retailing. In the food industry, the independent corner grocery store was replaced to a large extent by the chain grocery store, which in turn became vulnerable to the competition of the supermarket operation. Today, the supermarket is being threatened by the success of the supercentres (combination of a supermarket and discount store) and to a lesser extent, the warehouse club. And electronic food shopping is just in the very early stages of the entry phase.

A second commonly cited example of the wheel concept is the emergence of the department store innovation as an alternative to the small specialty retailer and its subsequent vulnerability to discount retailers. Recently, some discount retailers have progressed far enough into the trading-up phase that they, in turn, are also becoming vulnerable to warehouse clubs and supercentres.

Dialectic Process

The **dialectic process** is a "melting pot" theory of retail institutional change in which two substantially different competitive forms of retailing merge into a new retailing institution, a composite of the original two forms (see Figure 16–4). It involves a thesis (the established institutional form), an antithesis (the innovative institutional form), and a synthesis (the new form drawn from the other two). The dynamics of the dialectic process, as outlined by Maronick and Walker, are as follows:

> In terms of retail institutions, the dialectic model implies that retailers mutually adapt in the face of competition from "opposites." Thus, when challenged by a competitor with a differential advantage, an established institution will adopt strategies and tactics in the direction of that advantage, thereby negating some of the innovator's attraction. The innovator, meanwhile, does not remain unchanged. Rather, as McNair noted, the innovator over time tends to upgrade or otherwise modify products and institutions. In doing so, he moves toward the "negated" institution. As a result of the mutual adoptions, the two retailers gradually move together in terms of offerings, facilities, supplementary services, and prices. They thus become indistinguishable or at least quite similar and constitute a new retail institution, termed the synthesis. This new institution is then vulnerable to "negation" by new competitors as the dialectic process begins anew.[12]

Retail Accordion

The **retail accordion** theory (also known as the *general-specific-general process*) is based on the premise that the changing character of retail competition stems from strategies that alter the width (selection) of the merchandise mix.[13] Historically, retail institutions have evolved from general store (offering wide variety of merchandise) to the specialty store

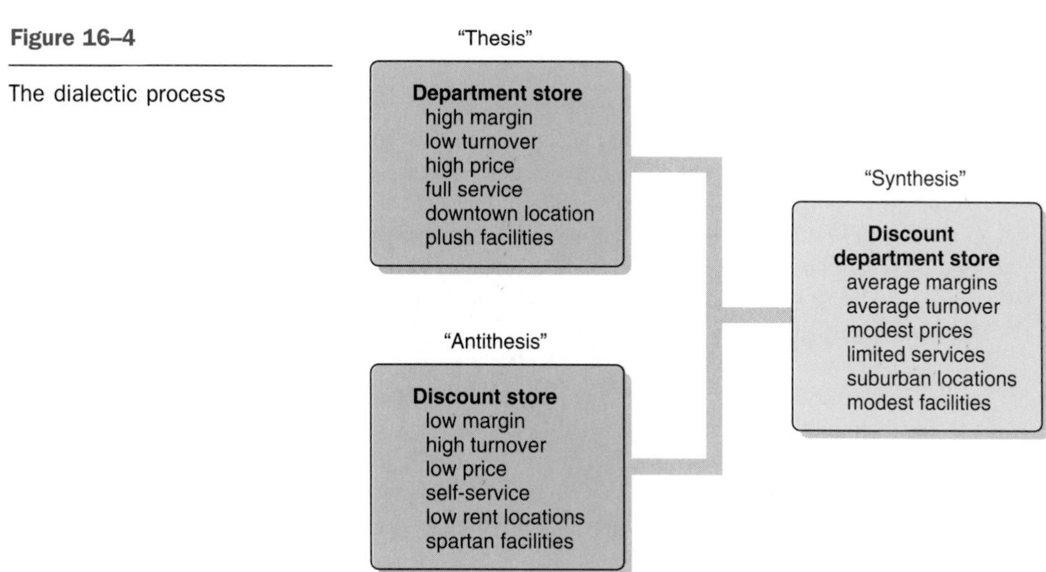

Figure 16–4

The dialectic process

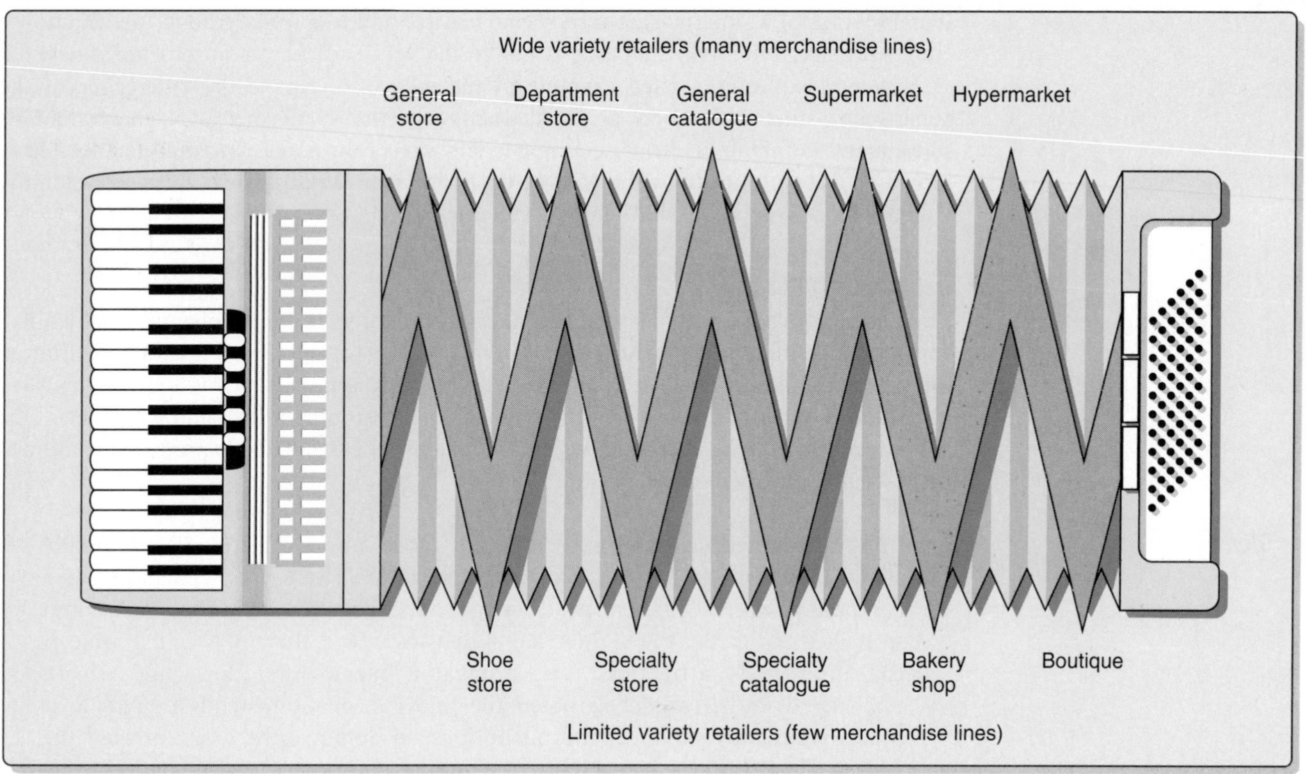

Figure 16–5

The retail accordion theory

(offering a limited variety of merchandise) back to general-line stores and so on (see Figure 16–5). The term "accordion" is used to suggest the alternating expansion and contraction of the retailer's merchandise mix. As described by Ralph Hower in his book *The History of Macy's of New York*:

> Throughout the history of retail trade (as, indeed, in all business evolution) there appears to be an alternating movement in the dominant method of conducting operations. One swing is toward the specialization of the function performed on the merchandise handled by the individual firm. The other is away from such specialization toward the integration of related activities under one management or the diversification of products handled by a single firm.[14]

Natural Selection

The concept of the "survival of the fittest" is the central theme in Darwin's theory of **natural selection**. Environmental suitability and adaptive behaviour are necessary traits for the long-term survival of a species. The species most willing and able to adapt to changing environmental conditions is the one most likely to prosper and grow. A highly fluid or flexible retail organization is necessary to ensure the adaptive behaviour necessary to meet dynamic consumer needs. The demise of Sears as North America's top retailer can be traced to its "caretaker" mentality, dedicated to maintaining the majesty of Sears that management thought was unassailable.

> Sears did not fully realize there was a kind of sea change going on in customer preferences, against which it had no workable strategy. In retailing, it rolled out one strategy after another. But try as it might, Sears could not get back its merchandising magic. A certain reason for this failure is that the company always stayed "encased in time." They never truly caught up with all that was going on.

> Sears seems to be the corporate equivalent of a laboratory "boiling frog"—the hapless creature that sits calmly and unsuspiciously in water whose temperature is gradually raised to the killing point.[15]

Fortunately, Arthur Martinez assumed the role of CEO of Sears in the U.S. and orchestrated a turnaround far beyond anyone's expectations. Since Martinez took over Sears' merchandising, sales have increased 13 percent to $35 billion, while earnings have almost tripled, to $1.25 billion.[16] Sears Canada is currently following the lead of its U.S. parent with its new CEO, Paul Walters.[17]

An unwillingness or inability to change could result in a species' stagnation or possible extinction. As an economic species, competitive retailers are both willing and able to change and adapt to the environmental conditions under which they operate. The potential list of environmental conditions that might require adaptive behaviour on the part of the retailer is almost endless. In general terms, the dynamic environments of retailing include changes in the social, cultural, political, legal, technological, economical, and competitive structure of the marketplace. With consumers becoming more tight-fisted with their pocketbooks, specialty stores are going after the discount store customer. As an adaptive strategy, The Gap is rapidly rolling out its low-end format—the Old Navy Clothing Company.[18] Required adaptation by The Gap and other retailers might involve a number of different alterations in the product, price, place, and/or promotional mix offered to the retailer's targeted customer base.[19]

Retail Life Cycle

The **retail life cycle** hypothesizes that all retail institutions pass through a series of four life stages: innovation, accelerated development, maturity, and decline. At each stage, retailers must be willing to adapt their merchandising efforts and operating methods to meet the environmental (for example, consumer expectations, competitive actions, economic conditions) circumstances of that stage. Some retail formats have gone through a "compressed life cycle," going from birth to maturity in just a few years. Some examples are warehouse clubs, home shopping television networks, and category killers. The life of a retailing format is best sustained by offering consumers an unmatched value proposition as defined by unique product offerings, superior customer service, and intimate customer relationships.[20]

Both risks and opportunities are present at each stage; it is management's responsibility to reduce the risks and to take advantage of the opportunities. Figure 16–6 identifies the basic circumstances found within each life cycle stage.

Innovation Stage A technological, operational, and/or marketing innovation is generally the foundation for the origin of a new retailing institution during the innovation stage. The jumbo size of the supercentre and its food/general merchandise combination is one example of a retail institution in the innovation stage. Video catalogues, Internet, and other electronic retailing formats are also in this origination state of the retail life cycle.[21] Customer acceptance, cost controls, profit margins, operational feasibility, and competitive response to these innovators will determine which institutions have a business format capable of carrying them into the growth stage of the life cycle. One of the best ways to control a market is to invent it by creating an innovative format that is difficult to copy.[22]

Development Stage During the accelerated development stage, sales increase rapidly and profits are high; however, to sustain the growth, the retailer must invest heavily in all aspects of the business. In an attempt to retain their status as growth institutions, specialty retailers (for example, superspecialists, niche specialist, category killers) are opening new stores, refurbishing existing stores, altering merchandise mixes, upgrading service offerings, automating store operations, and developing better management controls. Closeout stores, home shopping networks, warehouse clubs, and catalogue retailers are all growth retailers that are refining their merchandising and operating

	Area or subject of concern	Innovation	Accelerated development	Maturity	Decline
		Stages in the life cycle			
Market characteristics	Number of competitors	Very few	Moderate	Many direct competitors; moderate indirect competition	Moderate direct competition; many indirect competitors
	Rate of sales growth	Very rapid	Rapid	Moderate to slow	Slow or negative
	Level of profitability	Low to moderate	High	Moderate	Very low
	Duration of new innovations	3–5 years	5–8 years	Indefinite	Indefinite
Appropriate retail actions	Investment/growth/risk decisions	Investment minimization, high risks accepted	High level of investment to sustain growth	Tightly controlled growth in untapped markets	Marginal capital expenditures and only when essential
	Central management concerns	Concept refinement through adjustment and experimentation	Establishing a preemptive market position	Excess capacity are "overstoring," prolonging maturity and revising the retail concept	Engaging in a "run-out" strategy
	Use of management control techniques	Minimal	Moderate	Extensive	Moderate
	Most successful management style	Entrepreneurial	Centralized	"Professional"	Caretaker

Figure 16–6

The retail life cycle

Source: Adapted from an exhibit in William R. Davidson, Albert D. Bates, and Stephen J. Bass, the "Retail Life Cycle," Harvard Business Review *54 (November–December 1976): 92. Reprinted with permission of the* Harvard Business Review. *Copyright © by the President and Fellows of Harvard College; all rights reserved.*

methods in an effort to sustain their growth. The current growth enjoyed by warehouse clubs is based on more than fifteen years of work directed at making no-frills shopping not only acceptable but fashionable.[23] But even at this early stage, experts can see signs of the eventual levelling off of growth and the maturity of the format.

Maturity Stage The maturity stage involves increased competition, levelling sales, moderate profits, overstored markets, and more complex operational problems. Chain stores, department stores, and off-price retailers have all entered the maturity stage. The adaptive behaviour of chain stores has been to develop their "store-within-a-store" concept in an attempt to better target more profitable customer segments. Department stores are becoming more focused in their merchandising strategies and are enhancing their service offering in order to better deal with the competitive challenge of specialty retailers. Off-price retailers are trading up by offering more services and sales assistance and improved store atmospherics. Video stores are coping with early maturity by developing the superstore concept as typified by Blockbuster. Extending the retail institution's mature life while retaining acceptable profitability levels are the key institutional goals during this stage of the life cycle.

Decline Stage Variety stores, conventional supermarkets, and some regional discount chains[24] are experiencing market share losses, marginal profitability, and the inability to compete; they are entering the decline stage of the cycle. By finding small marginal and unserved markets (for example, older strip centres, small towns, decaying neighbourhoods), declining institutions can survive for some period of time provided they are willing to accept the weak profit performance of their outlets. For instance, the small general store still exists in sparsely populated areas.

Contemporary Practices of Adaptive Behaviour

To survive in the contemporary world of retailing, retail formats must adapt rapidly and creatively to the dynamics of the marketplace. Past and current winners in the field of retailing have been those that have best identified emerging unsatisfied needs of consumers and developed innovative merchandising and operating strategies and practices to satisfy them. The following discussions of some of the contemporary trends in retailing strategies and practices are not intended to be totally exclusive of one another or of some of the material previously discussed. The purpose of this discussion is to draw upon many of the concepts and practices that you have already been exposed to and use that information to review, understand, and appreciate some of the ways in which retailers are currently adapting to this very dynamic environment. Figure 16–7 identifies each of the contemporary strategies and practices examined in this section.

One-Stop Shopping: Extensions, Additions, and Combinations

One-stop shopping is the marketing strategy of broadening the retail offering to meet consumer's expanding needs. By expanding the number of product options, retailers try to increase the size of their total market by appealing to several submarkets and thereby attempting to satisfy more of the specific shopping needs of several individual market segments. In this expansion process, the one-stop merchandiser attempts to develop a more general-purpose retailing format that will satisfy the needs of most consumers "pretty well."

Merchandisers that elect to employ a one-stop shopping philosophy typically expand their customer appeal by following a sequence of practices (line extension, line addition, and/or format combination) that progressively expands the retailer's one-stop shopping image and its ability to attract new shoppers and hold existing customers.

Line Extensions **Line extensions** are accomplished by extending the selection of product items within one or more of the retailer's existing product lines. The addition or expansion of private labels has been a key strategy of retailers in meeting the expectations

Figure 16–7

Contemporary practices of adaptive behaviour

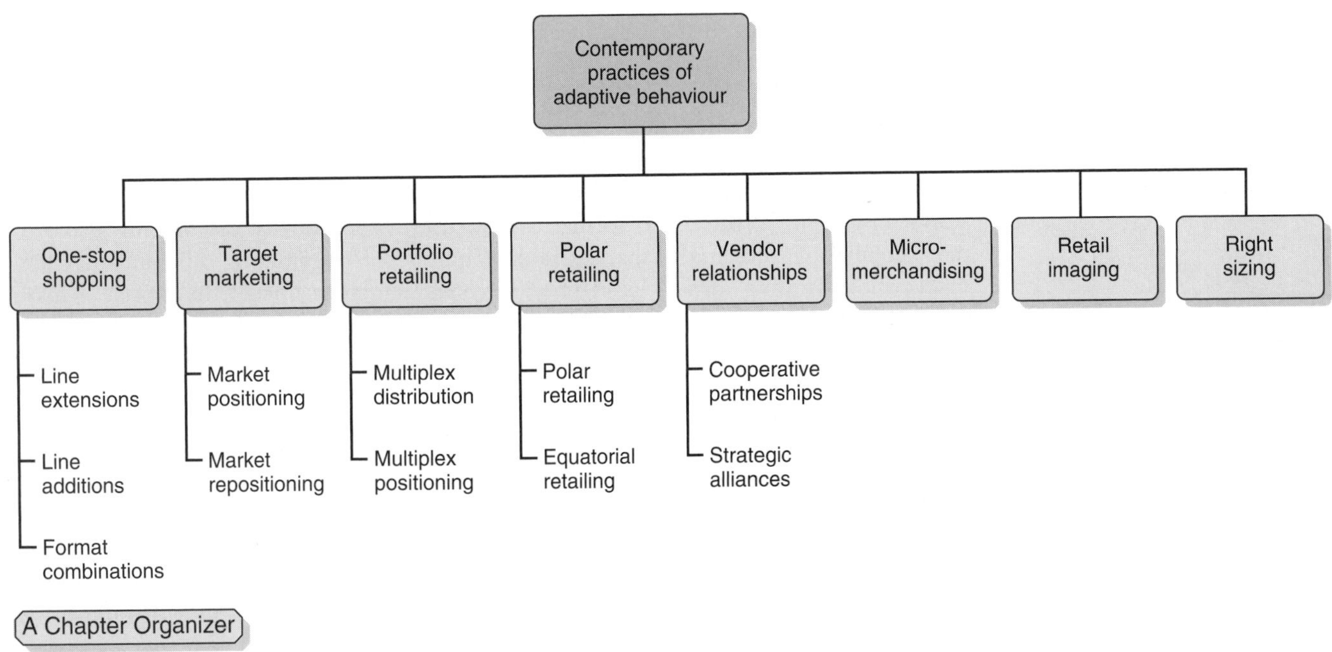

of the value-minded consumer. Loblaw's use of President's Choice and the addition of GREEN products is an example. Wal-Mart's addition of its giant house brand, Great Value, is another example of this form of line extension.[25] Adding totally new product lines or services to the retailer's product mix is another, more elaborate practice of line extension. ChemLawn's original product/service offering was going out to a house to fertilize and weed; it now offers to move trees, plant flower beds, or put in shrubs. Eddie Bauer, the specialty cataloguer, used a line extension strategy when it expanded its outdoor clothing to include lines for the not-so-rugged, broadened its range of women's clothing and footwear, and added home furnishings to its total product mix.[26]

In both cases, line extension involves product items and lines that are closely related to the existing product offering. Supermarkets expanded their meat departments to include such line extensions as a deli, seafoods, and prepared foods. One example of line extension is the practice of Blockbuster Video selling popcorn, candy, frozen yogurt, and soft drinks. Although line extensions are less risky than new product additions, the retailer must carefully judge the risks and benefits associated with this practice.[27]

Line Additions **Line additions** involve adding to one retailer's traditional merchandise mix the more desirable product items normally associated with another type of retail format. Book, magazine, cosmetic, and apparel racks are line additions that have been added to the supermarket's primary product offerings. Computers and computer-related software have been successful line extensions for electronic superstores, office supply superstores, and warehouse clubs.[28] Apparel retailers that expand their product mix to include accessories, shoes, and cosmetics are also practising line addition. Faced with stiff competition with the apparel business, The Gap and Talbots are adding such merchandise lines as toiletries, housewares, kids' gear, and shoes.[29] In the retailing industry, line addition is often accomplished through the process of *cherry picking*—adding product lines that are considered the cream of the crop, the best product line. Characteristics of these product lines are (1) low risk because of reasonably sure sales, (2) relatively high turnover rates, (3) adequate margins for respectable profits, (4) minimal personal selling effort, (5) routine ordering and stocking procedures, and (6) relatively low per-unit prices with high levels of impulse and unplanned purchasing.

Retailers use the practice of line addition on both permanent and temporary bases. Frequently, retailers add products on a trial basis to determine how well customers will receive them and whether the product additions provide sufficient profits with minimal operating difficulties. If these conditions are met, the retailer will add the product permanently. Wal-Mart, Zellers, and other discounters are adding more grocery lines (for example, spaghetti sauces, canned goods, microwavable meals) as they successfully experiment with expanded grocery sections and discover the drawing power of food. In other instances, some retailers engage in the practice of adding seasonal lines. During Christmas, for example, retailers add "hot items" as potential gift selections, although they would not stock these lines during other times of the year.

Format Combinations The next step in the upward progression of providing one-stop shopping opportunities is **format combination**—the practice of combining two or more compatible retailing formats. The principle behind combining different merchandising and operating formats is to provide consumers with one of the most extensive arrays of product selections under one roof. An example of a retail organization that exemplifies this practice is the supercentre. The supercentre combines standard retailing formats of the supermarket and the discount store.[30] Some supercentres also include one or more of the following: a drug store, a variety store, a lawn and garden shop, a dine-in restaurant, and a hardware store. Wal-Mart and Kmart have their versions of the supercentre.[31] With consumers increasingly demanding more convenience and with the desire for one-stop shopping, superstores could be the wave of the future.

The one-stop shopping phenomenon is expected to continue as the retail industry becomes more consolidated and competitive giants (for example, category killers, supercentres, warehouse clubs) collide in their efforts at sustaining growth rates.[32] Are there some limitations on this extension process? Keep on reading.

Target Marketing: Market Positioning and Repositioning

Target marketing is the strategy of focusing the retailer's efforts on a select group of customers. The target marketer employs a penetration strategy in which the retailer's merchandising efforts are concentrated and focused on serving "all" of the individual needs of a given market segment. In targeting markets, retailers tailor their entire merchandising effort (for example, product mixes, service offerings, communication programs, store facilities) to the needs and expectations of the selected group of consumers. By concentrating on a limited market, the target marketer develops a specific-purpose merchandising program that will satisfy most of the targeted consumers' specific needs for a selective offering of products and services. Much of the target marketer's task involves creating a consumer mind-set by engaging in market positioning and repositioning strategies.

Market Positioning The ultimate marketing battleground is in the mind of the consumer.[33] **Market positioning** is the strategy of creating a "position" for a store and its total merchandising effort in the minds of consumers by relating it to other stores and their merchandising efforts or by establishing a perception of being the most appropriate retailer for a select group of customers. Market positions can be established by using the ABCs of positioning:

- **Attributes**—Identify the intrinsic qualities of the retailer's merchandising effort; the characteristics and features that distinguishes one retail format from another.
- **Benefits**—Delineate the comparative advantages that one retail format has over another format on the basis of each format's merchandising and operating attributes.
- **Claims**—Communicate the format's attributes and resulting benefits to existing and potential customers by making specific claims and/or promises.[34]

Market positioning attributes, benefits, and claims are based on some unique combination of product lines and items, service types and levels, communication appeals and programs, price lines and points, store atmosphere and theatrics, and operating practices and policies. "Positioning helps customers know the real differences among competing products (retailers) so that they can choose the one that is of most value to them."[35] True positioning must be based on real merchandising and operating dimensions; otherwise it becomes more illusion than reality, more hype than honesty.[36] Home Depot, the chain of warehouse home centre stores, believes it has defined clearly who and what it is—a specialty chain that focuses on the home. "When people come into a Home Depot store, they do not expect to find sporting goods and toothpaste. They expect to find everything and anything related to home improvement. It helps the customers understand exactly what to expect, . . . and that creates a level of expectation that you can meet."[37] By carefully establishing a market niche or perceived image, the target marketer hopes to achieve dominant position with a targeted market segment. The Retail Strategies and Tactics box entitled "Masters of the Niche" illustrates how Mark's Work Wearhouse has successfully pursued a niche market and is now broadening its market.

Market Repositioning **Market repositioning** is the process of altering the customer's existing image of the retailer by changing how the consumer perceives the retailer relative to other retailers and relative to their individual shopping needs. The Gap repositioned itself to attract an older customer base; the firm changed its image from a teenaged jeans mecca to a purveyor of casual and active sportswear for middle-aged men and women. Several Canadian retailers, due to strong U.S. competition, are in the process of repositioning their stores. Eaton's is expanding its upscale soft goods merchandise.[38] Sears has repositioned itself from its image as a hard goods retailer toward a "softer side" as an apparel retailer.[39] The Bay is also de-emphasizing hardware and highlighting clothing and fashion.[40] Kmart is moving upscale.[41] Even Zellers, the undisputed leading Canadian discount department store for years, is altering part of its discount strategy.[42]

Retail Strategies and Tactics

Masters of the Niche

Even the most optimistic of market watchers will concede that retailing these days is a tough business. And when that retail market is clothing, especially men's clothing, it's particularly true. Yet, despite the stark realities of a harsh marketplace, Mark's Work Wearhouse isn't just holding on; the chain is declaring profits, and showing strong growth in the face of challenging economic times.

John Williams, partner at J.C. Williams Group Ltd. in Toronto, says the company has done a lot of things right. "Its physical presence is not as great as department stores, and yet it has market share close to theirs." According to figures released in 1996 by the retail consultancy that ranks market penetration for men's apparel, Mark's Work Wearhouse placed fourth, following Sears, Zellers and the Bay.

Life hasn't always been so rosy for Mark's Work Wearhouse. Indeed, the company, founded by Mark Blumes in 1977, has battled back from significant financial difficulties earlier this decade. "Through most of the '80s, it had a bit of a roller coaster ride in terms of its profitability," says Mitchell. "It ended up at the very beginning of the '90s being in pretty serious financial trouble."

In 1991, the company set out to put its affairs in order. Says Mitchell: "The biggest requirement we had was obviously to reposition, reorganize and restructure the company so that we provided the right merchandise for our customers and the right returns to our shareholders."

In a society that includes a shrinking number of blue-collar workers, that meant the chain needed to expand its mandate. "We enriched our definition of work wear," Mitchell says. "We broadened our customer base. We wanted to sell apparel to everyone who didn't wear a suit and tie to work."

"I think one of the things they've done well is to understand who the customer is, and focus on that customer," says Richard Talbot, Managing Director of Thomas Consultants International Inc., in Unionville, Ontario.

"They've found a market niche and stuck to it," agrees Joan A. Pajunen, a partner in Service Dimensions Inc., in Mississauga, Ontario. "They don't range very far from the core business."

Meanwhile, the company also overhauled its marketing efforts and buying practices, and has relocated and renovated about 80 percent of its stores. "Our primary goal," says Mitchell, "was to return the company to profitability by providing better merchandise and better stores for our customers."

For example, on the marketing front, Mark's moved to an "event marketing strategy," explains Lambert. The company hosts about seven major events during the year, each with a targeted buying strategy. "That focused the whole organization to plan better around events. We're spending less of a percentage of sales on marketing than we did five years ago and we're getting better bang for the dollar."

Source: "Masters of the Niche," Canadian Retailer, May/June 1997, 8–13.

Other retailers such as Harry Rosen[43] and A&P Supermarkets are expanding their market to include younger shoppers.[44]

Market positioning and repositioning are illustrated in Figure 16–8. As can be seen from the multidimensional surface that represents the almost endless number of ways that market segments can be defined, retailers have ample opportunities for identifying then targeting one or more market segments and creating then establishing one or more competitive positions. Given the dynamic nature of the marketplace, retailers will also have continuous need for repositioning and reimaging their businesses.

Portfolio Retailing: Multiplex Distribution and Positioning

"No single retailing approach is likely to be sufficient in the future simply because markets are diverging more and more with respect to wants, needs, and buying power. Therefore, a single way of doing business is unlikely to appeal to all market segments."[45] An extension of the market positioning strategies discussed previously is portfolio retailing—a blend of the strategy of diversification with the strategy of focus.[46] A **portfolio retailer** is a retail enterprise that operates multiple types of retail formats, each with individually tailored merchandising programs designed to serve the specific needs of a different target market.[47]

Figure 16–8

Market positioning and repositioning

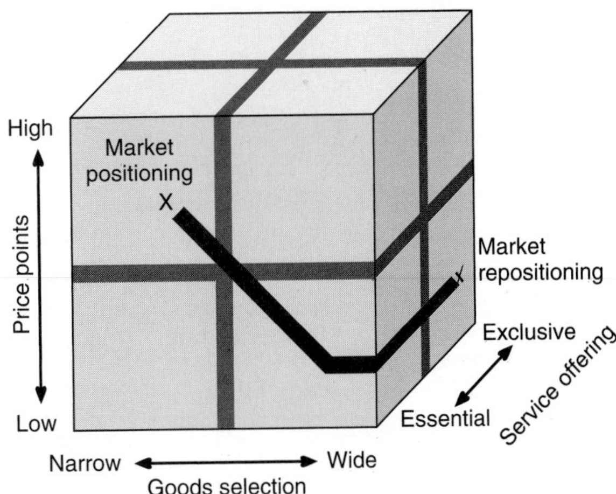

In other words, the portfolio retailer operates a collection of separate and specialized retail businesses specifically suited for and focused on selective consumer segments. This type of "focused diversification" is "precisely the strategy many of America's most respected retailers are using to grow. Portfolio retailing is a growth strategy that, when executed properly and under the right conditions, enables a retail firm to prosper in troubled as well as good times."[48] By the end of the decade, "some lines of trade will be 'owned' by only a handful of the strongest players, each of whom will operate from a portfolio of distinctive store concepts tailored to specific customer segments. The weaker companies will be 'gobbled up' by the stronger and better managed companies."[49]

By managing a collection of retail businesses, the portfolio retailer gains an important competitive advantage, that of flexibility. Some experts believe that merchandising and operating flexibility is equal to quality in its importance for future retailing success. A multiplex distribution system necessitates a multiplex positioning strategy; that is, each separate retail format within the organization's portfolio will require an individualistic image and a uniquely defined market position. The whole purpose of having a retail portfolio is to take aim at many target markets and compete effectively against different formats. This collective type of retailing accomplishes the task of serving several target markets by using a "freeform" organization that permits it to develop specialized merchandising efforts for each market segment support by a unique image and competitive strategies. Sears Canada Inc.'s new growth strategy includes creating specialty offshoot businesses such as automotive and home repair services as a way to grow—rather than adding more traditional department stores.[50]

Polar Retailing: Specialty Stores vs. Mass Merchandisers

The phenomena of **polar retailing** is the tendency for retail organizations to evolve around either the specialty store format (shown as the south pole in Figures 16–9 and 16–10) or formats that employ mass merchandising techniques within a large store facility (shown as the north pole in Figures 16–9 and 16–10). The general merchant that occupies the competitive middle ground tends to experience slower growth and in some cases declining market share. Profitability of polar retailers is usually more rewarding than the profit performance of middle merchandisers. Polarization continues to be an important competitive positioning strategy as retailers struggle to service appropriate markets.

As illustrated in Figure 16–9, to the mega and mass merchandiser, polar retailing involves developing merchandising programs and operational practices that are effective and efficient in serving the mass markets. On the other hand, polar retailing for the category and classification specialist necessitates the development of a highly focused merchandise mix capable of reaching narrowly defined market segment niches. **Equatorial retailing** is the competitive middle position between the polar extremes; it involves a

Figure 16–9

The polarization of retailing

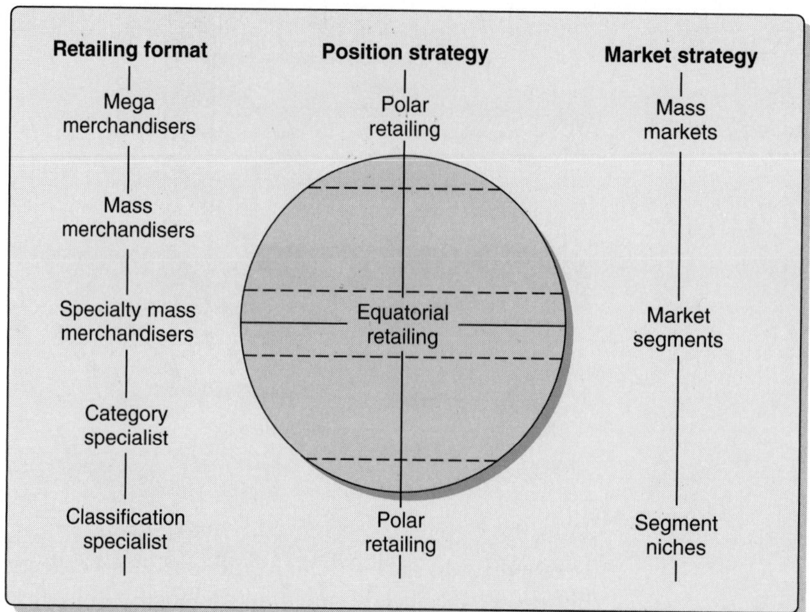

Figure 16–10

Strategical and tactical descriptions of polar retailers

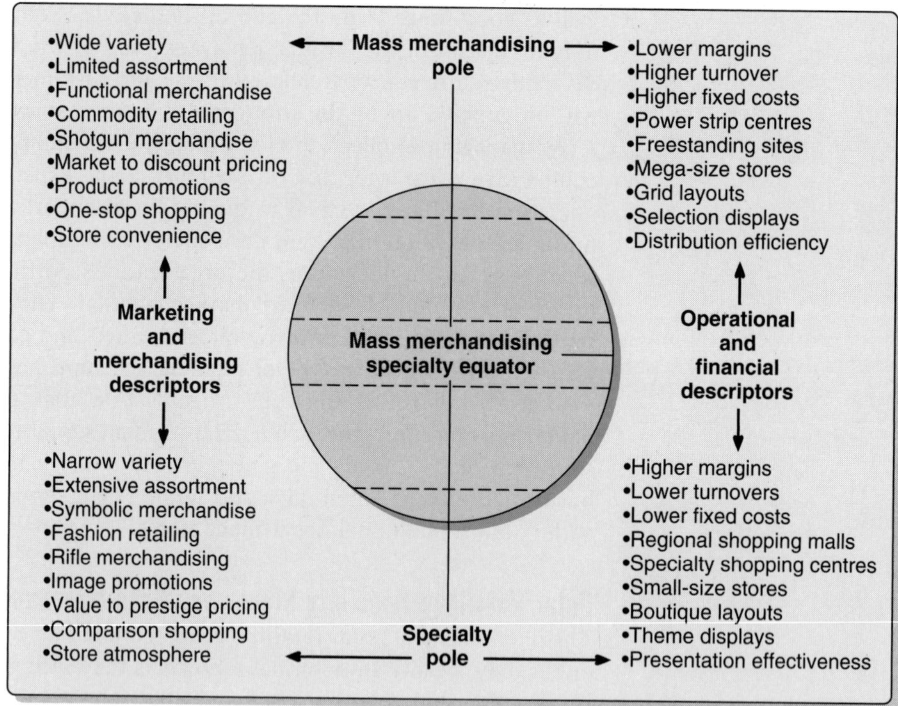

combination of the two polar formats (that is, specialty mass merchandiser) designed to target more broadly defined market segments.

Polar retailing is not limited to just the mass merchandiser/specialist dichotomy. Retail analyst Walter Loeb predicts a major polarization between commodity retailing and fashion retailing, with both types evolving into either convenience or distribution outlets. Eaton's and the Bay are fashion destination stores, whereas supercentres operated by Wal-Mart typify the commodity destination store. Commodity retailers focus their merchandising efforts around convenience, excitement, and bargains. Fashion retailers offer excitement, service, and education (Home Depot). Although some fashion retailers are playing it cautiously (for example, becoming more of a equatorial retailer) with moderate price points and safe but uninspiring fashion assortments,[51] many others are defining a viable and well-differentiated polar niche that should enable them to prosper despite the turbulence in the retail industry.[52]

Polar retailers will continue to refine, restructure, and exploit the specialty and mass merchandising concept; new format developments will typically be extensions of existing polar formats. Customer services, store size and atmosphere, product selection and presentation, and store locations are just a few of the additional dimensions that some experts identify as being used to extend polarization and establish a defensible competitive market position.

As in the past, the key to success in the future will be retailing formats that meet customer needs (satisfaction) while achieving organizational goals (performance). Strategies and tactics for successful marketing and merchandising must be matched with equally viable operational and financial programs. Figure 16–10 identifies the major strategic and tactical elements that have helped polar retailers in their attempts to establish a defined position within the marketplace. At both the mass merchandising and specialty poles, retailers are putting together a large number of unique and competitive retail formats using various combinations of and emphasis on the marketing/merchandising and operational/financial elements identified in Figure 16–10.

So, what is the future of these general merchants that occupy a place within the equatorial zone? Like so many intermediaries, success depends on finding an innovative compromise between two polar extremes. Prior to its purchase by the Bay, Kmart had identified what it felt was a market niche above the discount and traditional department stores.[53]

Historically, institutional change is evolutionary, not revolutionary.[54] Nevertheless, the last two decades have probably witnessed more evolutionary development than any other period in retailing history. The result has been a richness of retailing concepts and formats ranging from hypermarkets to discount department stores to office supply power formats to the superspecialist (review Chapter 2).[55] "The opportunity for evolutionary growth may be waning, however. It is hard to identify a product category in which at least some form of specialty super store does not exist. Similarly, most of the categories in which warehouse operations make economic sense have already been developed. It may be time for the next retail revolution."[56]

Although the next retail revolution may involve several changing scenarios, the scenario being followed by most equatorial retailers is that of a combinative nature. General merchants are exhibiting considerable adaptive behaviour in developing new integrative retailing formats that incorporate various strategic and tactical features of both the mass merchandiser and the retail specialist.

Figure 16–11 illustrates the world of retailing as it relates to the continuum of retailing formats. At the north pole, the dominant retailers are hypermarkets and supercentres, together with warehouse and discount retailers. Polar retailing at the south pole ranges from the single-line specialist to the very narrowly focused niche and superspecialists. In and around the equator are six retailing formats that have or are in the process of developing some type of specialist/mass merchandise combination:

- **Discount department store**—A compromise of the discount store and the department store. The disadvantages of discount retailing that are achieved through mass merchandising are supported by the benefits of specialization that result from store departmentalization. Wal-Mart typifies this type of format.

- **Promotional department store**—A combination of a traditional department store with an aggressive advertising and sales effort supported by highly efficient, technologically based centralized management that maintains tight control over all organizational operations. The Bay and Sears are principal proponents of this retailing concept.

- **Store-within-a-store**—A mall-without-walls concept that incorporates both company-operated stores and leased specialty stores (for example, Toys R Us)

Figure 16–11

The world of retailing

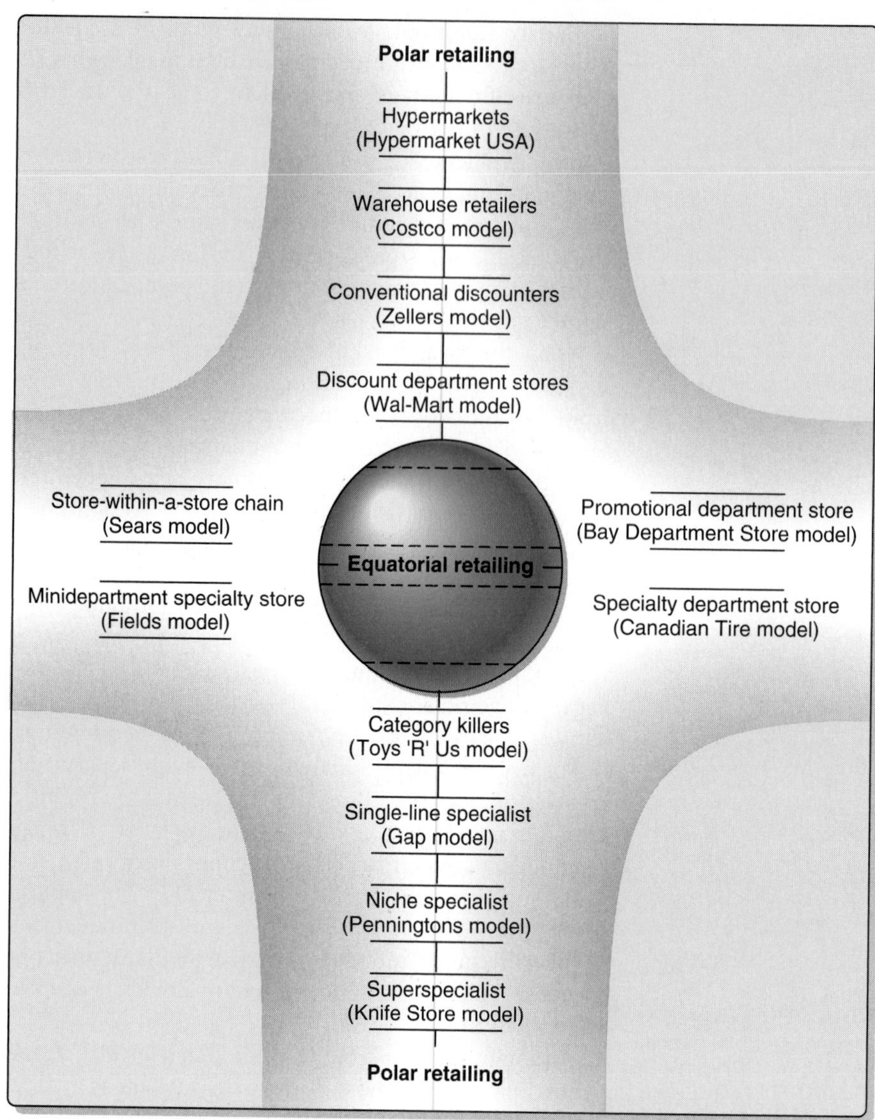

under one roof. The store has both a general store identification and individual store identities.

- **Specialty department store**—A department store that has narrowed its assortment by eliminating all or most hard lines. This format retains the departmental structure of the department store while narrowing its product focus by concentrating on one general merchandise line and related merchandise. Canadian Tire typifies this strategy of boutiquing the department store.
- **Minidepartment specialty store**—A specialty retailer that engages in line extension by adding boutique departments that are logical and tested extensions of existing merchandise lines.
- **Category killer**—A specialty retailer that utilizes such mass merchandising techniques as huge stores, large selection displays, competitive prices, warehouse stocking, centralized checkout and customer service, and computer-based technologies to gain market dominance in a single product category. Killers and would-be killers include Toys R Us, Chapters, and Future Shop.

With every trend there are countertrends; hence, it is not surprising that as more effort was focused on the polar extremes of retailing, someone would rediscover the old but changed opportunities that occupied the middle. Where discrepancies or gaps occur, opportunities emerge; middle-ground opportunities will continue to materialize throughout the 1990s (see Figure 16–11).

Vendor Relationships: Fostering Partnerships and Alliances

The bottom line for many retailers is measured by the strength of the relationships they are able to build with their vendors.[57] **Strategic alliances** are associations formed to further the common interests of vendors and retailers. For retailers and vendors alike, these associations have become "an integral part of contemporary strategic thinking."[58] New partnerships and alliances with vendor resources will play a key role in creating the competitive vertical marketing systems of the future.

Strong retailer/vendor relationships are beneficial to both parties. Some of the more commonly cited benefits associated with partnering relationships are: (1) better communication systems, (2) more competitive prices, (3) better quality products, (4) improved delivery schedules, (5) greater trust and sharing of information, (6) quicker response time, (7) better forecasting and planning, (8) greater operating flexibility, and (9) lower cost structures.[59] With a wealth of information from scanning, retailers have a more active role in the manufacturer's product development, research, and planning processes. The reduced risks associated with new product introduction and old product modification are considerable for both parties; customer satisfaction will also be greatly enhanced. Value-added partnerships are also essential to the effective use of electronic transmission of purchase orders, invoices, and advanced orders, as well as the full utilization of quick-response and just-in-time inventory systems. Adversarial relationships within channels of distribution are being replaced by the cooperative spirit so essential to the totally coordinated distribution system.

One alternative to retailer-vendor cooperation is retailer-vendor competition. In the past, vendors cooperated because they lacked direct access to the market; today, "the best of class resources/designers (Lauren, Claiborne, Coach, Waterford/Wedgewood, Esprit) are opening their own retail chains to insure their growth, create the type of POS environment they seek, and/or gain greater control over their distribution."[60]

Micromerchandising: Individualism and Mass Customization

Micromerchandising (or micromarketing) is the process of identifying the wants and needs of a local trading area, then planning, building, and delivering a store-specific merchandising mix (product selection, price points, support services, promotional campaigns, and store atmospherics) needed to satisfy those individuals who typically patronize a particular store. North American consumers create a diverse marketplace in which local racial, ethnic, and lifestyle differences are important and must be accommodated. "The aim of micromarketing is to turn an individual store, or a cluster of stores, into a separate marketing unit responsive to the demands, and sensitive to the needs, of its own unique consumer block."[61]

The fragmentation of the consumer market means that the individualism of consumer tastes and preferences that emerged as a significant marketing force in the 1980s is equally significant today. Target markets are becoming more defined as market segments become market niches, which in turn are becoming individual markets.

The challenge to retailers today is to develop true retail signatures (unique images) that are product and design driven. The ultimate in target marketing and customer satisfaction is offering a customized product supported by a micromerchandising effort that is carefully tailored to each buyer's expectations. Customized products typically involve mass customization in which computer-assisted operational and merchandising practices are used individually to shape traditional mass market products. Mass customization is often achieved through modularization—a point of sale customization in which standardized parts and components are used to customize a product at the end of the distribution chain (that is, the retail store). For example, a customer might buy one manufacturer's turntable, another's amplifier, and speakers from a third vendor; the final stereo system is tailored to one individual's specific needs, but the parts are standard mass-produced components. IKEA, the Swedish furniture company, allows customization of some of its products (for example, couches) by providing fabric choices and pillow styles.

For successful retailers in the future, product assortment planning will incorporate mass customization to some extent. Competition and the search for new markets are forcing retail companies to develop and manage product assortments at the smallest level of aggregation, be it small groups of highly homogeneous customers or a single individual consumer. Levi's has developed a means for mass-customizing blue jeans that are tailored to the individual shape of a customer's body.

Retail Image: An Identity Crisis in a Cookie-Cutter World

Just as the individualization of consumer tastes and preferences will necessitate the customization of the product/service offering, this same market phenomenon will promote the customization of **retail images**. Retailers that clearly communicate well-established and understandable identities have the best chance of meeting the expectations of consumers. The age of the cookie-cutter store is over. Contemporary retail practices require that the cookie cutters be thrown away and individualistic store formats be developed that project a unique and appropriate image.

Hard Rock Café
www.hardrockcafe.ca

Retailer identity is best created by the use of theme marketing—the use of a theme as a focal point for the retailer's merchandising effort. Theme marketing uses all forms of communication, with strong emphasis on store atmosphere and merchandise presentation. Selling the theme rather than the merchandise can be a powerful force in attracting consumer attention and patronage. Entertainment retailers are nowing popular with consumers by incorporating a specialty entertainment theme along with merchandise. Examples are Planet Hollywood, Hard Rock Café, and Canary Island.[62] Experiences, not merchandise, will be the "hot seller" or "in" product during the remainder of this decade. Therefore, marketing skills, as well as carefully honed merchandising practices, are the tools of preference in this search for identity.[63] Winners are being recognized for their identities; losers are going unrecognized for the lack of it. Indigo Music and Books, the supersize bookstore, attempts to compete with Chapters by creating a distinctive image, which includes lounge chairs, a coffee bar, music, and other cultural features.[64]

"Do Good" Retailing: Marketing Ploys or Social Concerns?

Retailers engage in a wide variety of social activities that are designed to assist society; these activities may or may not be directed at providing direct benefits to the retailer. A retailer's social activities can be classified as social marketing, philanthropic endeavours, cause-related retailing, and social responsibility.[65]

Social Marketing

Social marketing includes any initiatives by a retailer that devotes significant amounts of time and effort toward persuading people to engage in a socially beneficial behaviour. The primary objective of the retailer's social marketing activities is to promote a social benefit. In social marketing, the benefits of the behaviour are intended by the retailer to accrue primarily to the consumer or to the society in general and not to the retailer.[66] Social marketing activities include encouraging people to eat right, exercise on a regular basis, have regular checkups, stop smoking, drive carefully, drink in moderation, and engage in safe sex.

Philanthropic Endeavours

Philanthropic endeavours are those occasions when the retailer gives money or other gifts to a charitable organization. This form of social activity usually is an outright gift and does not involve active participation of the retail firm or its personnel. In addition to monetary contributions, retailers are frequently asked to donate products that can be sold, auctioned off, or given as prizes in a contest held in support of a social issue. When Kmart Canada sells one of its "Marty" stuffed toys (Marty is a cougar mascot who heads Marty's Kids Club at Kmart), one dollar of sales is donated to the Kids Help Line.[67]

Cause-Related Retailing **Cause-related retailing** is an attempt by members of a retail organization or the organization itself to (1) create awareness of a social issue or need, (2) gain acceptance of a particular social idea or cause, and (3) induce favourable behaviour (actions) from its customers or the general public relative to the social cause being promoted. Some cause-related retailing activities are directed at fulfilling a social need without any direct benefit to the retailer. Benetton, the Italian apparel producer and retailer, has used a program of highly controversial ads in order to raise the social consciousness of people with regard to such social issues as racism, violence, and war. Many critics of Benetton's promotional effort believe that the firm has ulterior motives for using this form of shock advertising. The nature of messages are such that it allows Benetton advertisements to cut through all the advertising clutter and be noticed by consumers. Cause-related retailing can also involve a direct tie between the support (for example, money or gifts in kind) given to a social issue and the purchase of the retailer's goods and services.[68] The theory behind this form of cause-related retailing is that politically correct consumers will seek out socially responsible retailers to patronize.[69]

> A program with a strong tie between sought-after social behaviour and sales of the company's products, but without direct personal benefits for the customer engaging in the behaviour is The Body Shop's "Once Is Not Enough" recycling campaign . . . urging customers to bring in their empty cosmetic containers for recycling or reuse. The program is successful, considering that they hand out thousands of dollars in rebates each year for refills on Body Shop cosmetics and personal care products. However, no one has been able to determine how much social impact this campaign has had in reducing solid waste.[70]

The dangers associated with cause-related retailing are evident in both the Benetton and The Body Shop examples.

Social Responsibility **Social responsibility** is the expectation that retailers will act as a good corporate citizens. Being socially responsible means that the retailer seriously considers the impact that the firm's actions might have on other individuals, institutions,

Retail Strategies and Tactics

Community Support

Victoria-based Thrifty Foods has for many years been involved in the community, sponsoring juvenile sports teams and supporting hospital fundraising efforts and other local initiatives for abused women and children. Company president and CEO Alex Campbell Sr. feels that it's his company's responsibility to give back to the community that supports it. In turn, that community support, Campbell says, helps Thrifty Foods. "It helps reinforce that Thrifty Foods is local. Because we've gotten to a size where some people think we're just another big chain with a head office in Toronto. And I think [supporting the community] helps reinforce that we're local, and we care about where we live."

Calgary Co-op, Thrifty Foods, H.Y. Louie, Canada Safeway, the Overwaitea Food Group—these are just a few of the retailers across Canada that are deeply committed to serving their communities, through programs such as Literacy B.C., The Sunshine Foundation, the Variety Club Cash for Kids, Kid's Help Phone, the United Way and many, many others. In fact, there's such an overwhelming number of worthwhile causes out there, that choosing which ones to support can be very difficult.

Some retailers have formed guidelines and corporate strategies for giving, to help narrow the sponsorship focus. "We select priorities to be a sort of guideline for the store," says Canada Safeway's [Vice President of Public Relations and Government Affairs, Toby] Oswald. "Our priorities are health and social services, education, youth, and amateur sport. And over the years, we have concentrated more in the communities in which our stores are operating."

Source: Pat Price, Grocer Today, *April 1997, 14–16.*

and society in general. It means that the retailer will seek to balance the short-term financial and operational needs of the firm with society's long-term interests. Social responsibility requires the retailer to be proactive (support a particular issue—such as voter participation) and reactive (correct a past abuse—such as environmental restoration). Public service by the firm's employees (serving on the United Way Campaign) is one of the most effective means by which retailers can show their commitment to the community.[71]

Right Sizing: How Big Is Too Big?

Is there a limit to how big a store should be? This question is addressed in the issue of **right sizing**. Although stores will tend to get somewhat larger due to the broader variety of products and services that will be required to meet consumer preferences, the "mass" in mass merchandising could well peak out. Larger stores at all levels (for example, supermarket to the hypermarket) are receiving mixed reviews.

From a consumer perspective, larger store formats offer greater one-stop shopping opportunities with certain price advantages (see previous discussion). However, even for the original "shop 'til you drop" consumer, the multihour shopping trip is simply becoming too long. As sizes increase (such as the 180 000 m^2 supercentre), the massiveness of such stores creates tremendous hurdles for the time-constrained consumer who seeks conveniences of time and place. For other customers, the megastore environment is too overwhelming in terms of both its vertical and horizontal space. The mature consumer and the parent-child shopper also find the vastness to be a barrier to an enjoyable, comfortable shopping experience. Crowded parking lots, long checkout lines, packed shopping aisles, and overtaxed service desks are additional problems associated with huge facilities that dampen the advantages of the one-stop shop.

From the retailer's perspective, increased store sizes offer the potential for economies of scale that comes with a large operation. Wal-Mart has suspended its plans for building any more hypermarkets in favour of its supercentre concept. This action represents a downsizing of its big store concept from more than 20 000 m^2 to less than that amount of space. Operational problems that are part of a large-store operation include (1) finding and recruiting enough qualified workers in a scarce labour market, (2) maintaining a secure operation in a sea of merchandise, (3) operating a low-margin business (that is, 15 to 18 percent) with high fixed costs, (4) maintaining a huge physical plant (basic housekeeping chores of cleaning, servicing, and repairing store equipment), and (5) keeping the store shelves stocked and organized.[72]

Are bigger stores better? Retailers at all levels and sizes are finding that more space is not necessarily the answer to greater profitability. As a result, the near future could bring some downsizing or, at the very least, the capping of store size at current levels. Growth in store space will be highly selective.

Cross-Shopping: Cross-Merchandising, Cross-Selling, and Cross-Promotion

The tendency toward larger retail stores has necessitated the effective use of cross-merchandising strategies in displaying, selling, and promoting merchandise.[73] **Cross-merchandising** is the process of selling between and among departments to facilitate larger transactions and to make it more convenient for the customer to do related-item shopping.[74] Cross-merchandising involves creating store layouts in which displays of complementary items are placed in close and visible positions in the hope that when customers see the displays they will cross over from one product line to another.[75] Cross-merchandising also incorporates the tactics of cross-selling and cross-promotions. Sobey's, the Maritime supermarket chain, utilizes cross-merchandising by offering free cabbage with corned beef in the butcher shop, and flower arrangements and party trays arranged jointly by the deli and floral departments, for example.[76] **Cross-selling** is the practice of allowing retail sales associates to work in more than one department; it encourages the associate to build a rapport with the customer by helping in the purchase of any of the store's merchandise lines. Cross-selling is a vital part of the sales strategy employed by some high-end department stores. **Cross-promotions** involve the selling of complementary product items

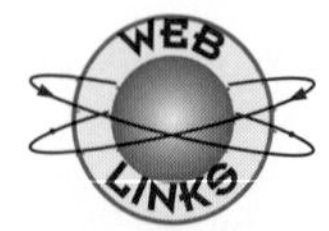

Sobey's
www.sobeysweb.com/english/history/history.html

with an advertisement or within a particular sales promotion program (for example, a tie-in coupon). Like cross-selling, the goal of cross-promotions is to make the consumer aware, interested, and predisposed to buying additional related goods and services.

Cross-merchandising, cross-selling, and cross-promotions are all directed at creating **cross-shopping** by a significant number of those customers who visit the retailer store. Wal-Mart and Kmart have been successful with their supercentre format because they are getting cross-shopping from significant numbers of people who visit their stores. "Cross-shopping is probably at 60 percent or 70 percent level, and it is the ability of supercentre operators to deliver this cross-shopping that attracts people past discount stores and supermarkets about once every second or third shopping trip."[77] Finally, there is also cross-shopping between various types of retail outlets that are quite different.

Cost Leadership: A Strategy for All Seasons

Retailing is a mature and oversaturated industry.[78] Slow growth rates and thin profit margins necessitate tight cost controls. **Cost leadership** is the strategy of gaining a competitive advantage by being the low-cost retailer in broadly defined markets. By offering comparable products at the same price, cost leaders outperform other competitors within the industry because lower cost structures make profit margins higher. McDonald's improved its cost leadership position by reducing the size of its average restaurant. Lower construction, installation, and operational costs have allowed McDonald's to price its products low enough to attract the value-oriented consumer and still have a reasonable profit margin.[79]

Higher cost structures rob a retail organization of the strength to weather market downturns and the flexibility to respond to competitive challenges.[80] Being the No. 1 "cheapo" when it comes to cost structures helps any retail organization define how the industry is going to operate. Wal-Mart's tight-fisted approach to costs of any kind is perhaps the best example of what a cost leadership position can do for an organization.

Summary

Changes in the retail marketplace and adaptations to those changes are part of the natural evolution of retailing formats. Several traditional theories of adaptive behaviour by retail institutions have been developed by retail experts. The wheel of retailing suggests that there is a cycle of change consisting of three phases: the entry phase (innovative retail format enters the marketplace), the trading-up phase (innovative format tries to distinguish itself from copycat formats), and the vulnerability phase (increased cost structures and dated merchandising practice creates a sense of vulnerability to new innovative formats). The dialectic process is the "melting pot" theory of retail format change in which two different competitive formats merge together to create a new, more competitive way of conducting a retail business.

The retail accordion theory states that there is a cyclical pattern (general to specific to general, and so on) that retailers follow in developing appropriate product mixes for changing market conditions. Natural selection is the theory of the survival of the fittest—retailers must adapt to marketplace dynamics or they will not survive. Finally, the retail life cycle hypothesizes that all retail institutions pass through a series of four life stages: innovation (birth), development (growth), maturity, and decline.

As retailers struggle to survive and thrive in today's highly competitive environment, several contemporary operating and merchandising practices have emerged to help retailers to cope and compete. One-stop shopping is an attempt by retailers to satisfy a wide range of customer needs within a single store. Product line extensions, product line additions, and format combinations are three commonly employed practices designed to enhance a retailer's one-stop shopping experience. Target marketing, the focusing of the retailer's efforts on a select group of customers, is accomplished by engaging in market positioning and repositioning strategies. Portfolio retailing is the practice of developing separate business formats for each target market selected to be served. Portfolio retailers operate a collection of different retail businesses designed for different consumer markets.

Polar retailing is the practice by which a retail organization elects to pursue either a highly focused specialty store format strategy or a high-volume mass merchandising strategy. A key success factor for most retailers today is their ability to forge strategic alliances between themselves and key vendors. Partnerships, not adversarial relationships, are survival tactics necessary to a successful marketing channel operation. Micromerchandising is the practice of planning, building, and delivering store- or individual-specific goods and service mixes designed to meet the specific needs of a narrowly defined market. Retailers are what consumers believe they are. Creating the right retail image is the practice of carefully communicating to the consumer the exact impressions the retailer wants to convey. Social marketing, philanthropic endeavours, cause-related retailing, and social responsibility are all ways in which the retailer engages in social activities. Right sizing involves the issue of whether there is a limit to how big a store should be. The right size is the one that is most appropriate to the shopping needs of consumers. Cross-shopping is an attempt to get the customer more involved with the retailer's merchandise; it is accomplished through cross-merchandising, cross-selling, and cross-promotions. In the highly competitive marketplace, it is hard to go wrong with an effective cost leadership strategy.

Student Study Guide

Key Terms and Concepts

cause-related retailing *p. 609*
cost leadership *p. 611*
cross-merchandising *p. 610*
cross-promotions *p. 610*
cross-selling *p. 610*
cross-shopping *p. 611*
dialectic process *p. 595*
equatorial retailing *p. 603*
format combination *p. 600*
line additions *p. 600*
line extensions *p. 599*
market positioning *p. 601*
market repositioning *p. 601*
micromerchandising *p. 607*
natural selection *p. 596*
one-stop shopping *p. 599*
philanthropic endeavours *p. 608*
polar retailing *p. 603*
portfolio retailers *p. 602*
retail accordion *p. 595*
retail images *p. 608*
retail life cycle *p. 597*
right sizing *p. 610*
social marketing *p. 608*
social responsibility *p. 609*
strategic alliances *p. 607*
target marketing *p. 601*
wheel of retailing *p. 593*

Review Questions

1. What is the basic premise of the wheel of retailing theory of institutional change? Characterize the three phases of the wheel.
2. What does the dialectic model of retail institutional change imply?
3. How does the concept of "survival of the fittest" describe the competitive conditions faced by retailers?
4. Profile the four stages of the retail life cycle.
5. Describe the practices used by retailers to expand their one-stop shopping image.
6. What are the ABCs of marketing positioning?
7. Define marketing repositioning.
8. Describe portfolio retailing and its relationship to multiplex distribution and multiplex positioning.
9. What is polar retailing? Describe the merchandising and operating characteristics of each type of polar retailer.
10. Who are the polar retailers? Provide nontext examples. Who are the equatorial retailers? Provide nontext examples.
11. Describe the benefits that retailers receive from a close relationship with vendors.
12. Discuss mass customization and its role in creating customer satisfaction.
13. How is retailer identity created?
14. Are bigger stores better?

Review Exam

True or False

______ 1. The basic premise of the retail accordion theory is that a retail institution facing competition will adopt strategies and tactics of the competitor and will eventually become just like the competitor.

______ 2. Line extensions involve adding to one retailer's traditional merchandising mix the more desirable product items normally associated with another type of retail format.

______ 3. An adversarial relationship between retailers and vendors is a healthy situation because it promotes competition and is essential in the development of vertical marketing systems.

______ 4. Target markets are becoming more narrowly defined as market segments become market niches, which in turn are becoming individual markets.

______ 5. Consumers prefer stores that have a broadly defined identity and a generalized merchandising approach.

______ 6. Bigger stores are not always better stores.

Multiple Choice

______ 1. When a retail institution is operating at gross margins that are substantially below the required gross margins of the more established retailers in the market, the retail institution is in the ______ phase of the wheel of retailing.
a. trading-up
b. trading-down
c. entry
d. vulnerability
e. spoke

______ 2. Increased competition, level sales, moderate profits, overstored markets, and complex operations are all part of the conditions facing retailers when they enter the ______ stage of the retail life cycle.
a. birth
b. death
c. growth
d. decline
e. maturity

______ 3. Retail enterprises that operate multiple types of retail formats are described as ______.
a. portfolio retailers
b. group retailers
c. chain retailers
d. national retailers
e. none of the above

______ 4. The strategy of creating a place for a store and its product mix in the minds of consumers by relating it to other stores and their mixture of products is called ______.
a. multiplex distribution
b. market positioning
c. line combination
d. item addition
e. mind probing

______ 5. A customer who buys one manufacturer's turntable, another's amplifier, and speakers from a third vendor is engaging in ______.
a. bifurcation
b. assortment planning
c. mass merchandising
d. mass customization
e. mass confusion

______ 6. ______ are specialty retailers that engage in line extension by adding boutique departments that are logical and tested extensions of existing merchandise lines.
a. Category killers
b. Minidepartment specialty stores
c. Specialty department stores
d. Store-within-stores
e. Promotional department stores

Student Application Manual

Investigative Projects: Practice and Application

1. Survey retail stores in your local community and find specific examples of line extensions, line additions, and format combinations. Do you believe these retailing strategies are being accepted by the consuming public? Why?
2. Identify three limited-line stores in your community that are engaging in a market positioning strategy. What merchandise and operating tactics are they using to establish a market niche and a particular market image in the consumer's mind?
3. By surveying print advertisements (newspapers and magazines), identify three good examples and three bad examples of retailers that are communicating a clear identity and a unique image. Be specific and support your analysis.
4. Review Chapter 2, then position the following retailers in the world of retailing as shown in Figure 16–11. Describe the relative market position of the following retailers: (a) off-price retailer, (b) convenience store, (c) conventional supermarket, (d) food and drug combo supermarket, (e) catalogue showroom, and (f) a vending machine.

Endnotes

1. Stephen Brown, "Guest Commentary: The Wheel of Retailing: Past and Future," *Journal of Retailing* (Summer 1990): 147.
2. Murray Forseter, "Darwinian Theory of Retailing," *Chain Store Age* (August 1995): 8.
3. Fanglan Du and Ira Apfel, "The Future of Retailing," *American Demographics* (September 1995): 26.
4. "The Discipline of Retail Market Leaders," *Chain Store Age* Executive (April 1995): 38.
5. See Stephen Brown, "Postmodernism, the Wheel of Retailing and Will to Power," *The International Review of Retail, Distribution and Consumer Research* (July 1995): 387–414.
6. Malcolm P. McNair, "Significant Trends and Developments in Post War Period," in *Competitive Distribution in a Free, High-Level Economy, and Its Implications for the Universities*, ed. A. B. Smith (Pittsburgh: University of Pittsburgh Press, 1958), 18.
7. Susan D. Sampson and Douglas J. Tigert, "The Impact of Warehouse Membership Clubs: The Wheel of Retailing Turns One More Time," *The International Review of Retail, Distribution and Consumer Research* (January 1994): 33–59. Also see Louise Lee, "Warehouse Clubs Embrace Marketing to Fill the Aisle," *The Wall Street Journal*, November 11, 1995, B4.
8. Arieh Goldman, "The Role of Trading-Up in the Development of the Retailing System," *Journal of Marketing*, 39 (January 1975): 54–62.
9. See Louise Lee, "Discounter Wal-Mart Is Catering to Affluent to Maintain Growth," *The Wall Street Journal*, February 7, 1996, A1, A6; Kevin Helliker and Bob Ortega, "Falling Profits Marks End of Era at Wal-Mart," *The Wall Street Journal*, January 18, 1996, B1, B11. and Kevin Helliker, "Wal-Mart's Store of the Future Blends Discount Prices, Department-Store Feel," *Wall Street Journal*, May 17, 1991, B8.
10. Arieh Goldman, "Institutional Changes in Retailing: An Updated 'Wheel of Retailing' Theory," in *Foundations of Marketing Channels*, ed. A. G. Woodside, J. T. Sims, D. M. Lewison, and I. F. Wilkinson (Austin, TX: Lone Star, 1978), 193.
11. McNair, "Significant Trends," 18.
12. Thomas J. Maronick and Bruce J. Walker, "The Dialectic Evolution of Retailing," in *Proceedings: Southern Marketing Association*, ed. Burnett Greenburg (1974), 147.
13. See Stanley C. Hollander, "Notes on the Retail Accordion," *Journal of Retailing*, 42 (Summer 1966): 20–40, 54.
14. Ralph Hower, *The History of Macy's of New York 1858–1919* (Cambridge, MA: Harvard University Press, 1943), 73.
15. Carol J. Looniis, "Dinosaurs?" *Fortune*, May 3, 1993.
16. Debra Sparks, "Arthur Martinez, Financial World's CEO of the Year," *Financial World*, March 25, 1996, 48.
17. Sean Silcoff, "The Emporiums Strike Back," *Canadian Business*, September 26, 1997, 52.
18. Ike Lagnado, "New Trends," *Women's Wear Daily* (May 1995): 4; and Mark Tosh, "Old Navy Flagship: A Record Day," *Women's Wear Daily*, November 8, 1995, 21.
19. See Stephanie N. Mehta, "Small Retailers Struggle to Survive the Winter," *The Wall Street Journal*, January 16, 1996, B1.
20. "The Discipline of Retail Market Leaders," 44.
21. Stratford Sherman, "Will the Information Superhighway Be the Death of Retailing?" *Fortune*, April 18, 1994, 106.
22. Damon Darlin, "Thank You, 3M," *Forbes*, September 25, 1995, 88.
23. See Wendy Zellner, "Why Sam's Wants Businesses to Join the Club," *Business Week*, June 27, 1994, 48–49. Also see Julie Liesse, "Welcome to the Club," *Advertising Age*, February 1, 1993, S6.
24. Louise Lee, "More Closings in Store for Retailers in '96," *The Wall Street Journal*, December 17, 1995, A2.
25. Jennifer Lawrence, "Brands Beware, Wal-Mart Adds Giant House." *Advertising Age*, April 7, 1993, 1, 45.
26. Christopher Palmeri, "Indoor Outdoorsman," *Forbes*, March 29, 1993, 43.
27. Judann Pollack, "Role of New Products Puts Scope on SKUs," *Advertising Age*, October 9, 1995, 1.
28. Bruce Fox, "Can the Computer Superstore Survive?" *Chain Store Age Executive* (February 1995): 35.
29. Laura Bird, "Apparel Makers Try to Peddle More Items That Aren't Apparel," *The Wall Street Journal*, June 6, 1995, B1.

30. Stephen Bennett, "Mighty Merchandisers," *Progressive Grocer* (October 1995): 69.

31. See Sharon Edelson, "Supercenters Get Nod in Wal-Mart Expansion Plans for Next Year," *Women's Wear Daily*, October 11, 1995, 1, 13; and Zina Moukheiber, "The Great Wal-Mart Massacre, Part II," *Forbes*, January 22, 1996, 44–45.

32. See Kate Fitzgerald, "Retailers Prescribe Pharmacies," *Advertising Age*, March 15, 1993, 3, 51.

33. Jack Trout, *The New Positioning* (New York: McGraw-Hill, Inc., 1996), ix.

34. See Martin R. Lautman, "The ABCs of Positioning," *Marketing Research* (Winter 1993): 12–18.

35. Edward DiMingo, "The Fine Art of Positioning," *The Journal of Business Strategy* (March/April 1988): 34.

36. *Ibid.*

37. "Blank Fills Out the Niche for Home Depot Growth," *Advertising Age*, February 1, 1993, S5.

38. Ian McGugan, "Eaton's on the Brink," *Canadian Business*, March 1996, 48.

39. Silcoff, "The Emporiums Strike Back," 54.

40. *Ibid*, 58.

41. *Ibid*, 58.

42. Brian Hutchinson, "Is This Any Way to Run a Discount Store?" *Canadian Business*, September 1996, 36–39.

43. Marina Strauss, "Harry Rosen Targets Younger Crowd," *Globe and Mail*, May 23, 1996, B13.

44. Marina Strauss, "A&P Freshens Up Its Image," *Globe and Mail*, June 6, 1996, B15.

45. Jagdish N. Sheth, "Emerging Trends for the Retailing Industry," *Journal of Retailing*, 59 (Fall 1983): 14.

46. Leonard L. Berry and Kathleen Seiders, "Growing through Portfolio Retailing," *Marketing Management*, 2 (3, 1993) 9–10.

47. See Robert J. Kopp, Robert J. Eng, and Douglas J. Tigert, "A Competitive Structure and Segmentation Analysis of the Chicago Fashion Market," *Journal of Retailing*, 65 (Winter 1989): 496–515.

48. Leonard L. Berry and Kathleen Seiders, "Growing Through Portfolio Retailing," 10.

49. John J. Shea, "Retail: Managing in Turbulent Times," *Retail Control* (June/July 1992): 13.

50. Marina Strauss, "Sears Sets Out Growth Strategy," *Globe and Mail*, June 13, 1997, B14.

51. Hooper, "Apparel Specialty Stores: Playing Fashion Defense," 13A.

52. "Is Specialty Apparel Dead?" *Chain Store Age*, October 1995, 134.

53. Marina Strauss, "Kmart Fights for Share," *Globe and Mail*, January 27, 1997, B1.

54. Ronald Savitt, "Looking Back to See Ahead: Writing the History of American Retailing," *Journal of Retailing*, 65 (Fall 1989): 337.

55. Albert D. Bates, "The Extended Specialty Store: A Strategic Opportunity for the 1990s," *Journal of Retailing*, 65 (Fall 1989): 383.

56. *Ibid.*

57. See Ryan Mathews, "A Spirit of Cooperation," *Progressive Grocer* (January 1996): 61–62; and Myron Magnet, "The New Golden Rule of Business," *Fortune*, February 21, 1994, 60–64.

58. Stratford Sherman, "Are Strategic Alliances Working?" *Fortune*, September 21, 1992, 77.

59. See Elaine Pollack, "Partnerships: Buzzword or Best Practice?" *Chain Store Age* (August 1995): 11A–12A; and Eugene H. Fram, "Purchasing Partnerships: The Buyer's View," *Marketing Management*, 4 (Summer 1995): 49–55.

60. Walter K. Levy, "The End of an Era: A Time for Retail Perestroika," *Journal of Retailing*, 65 (Fall 1989): 397.

61. Ryan Mathews, "Micromarketing: A Dream with Strings Attached," *Progressive Grocers* (August 1995): 45.

62. Paul Marck, "West Edmonton Mall Follows Through Toward Entertainment Centre," *Edmonton Journal*, September 12, 1997, 8.

63. See Walter J. Salmon, "Retailing in the Age of Execution," *Journal of Retailing*, 65 (Fall 1989): 368–78.

64. *Globe and Mail*, September 4, 1997, B1 & B11.

65. This discussion is based on Paul N. Bloom, Pattie Yu Hussein, and Lisa R. Szykman, "Benefiting Society and the Bottom Line," *Marketing Management*, 4 (Winter 1995): 8–18.

66. *Dictionary of Marketing Terms*, Second Edition, edited by Peter Bennett, (Chicago: NTC Business Books in conjunction with the American Marketing Association, 1995), 266.

67. *Marketing*, May 3, 1993, 5.

68. See Geoffrey Smith. "Are Good Causes Good Market?" *Business Week*, March 21, 1994, 64; Udayan Gupta, "Cause-Driven Companies' New Cause: Profits," *The Wall Street Journal*, November 8, 1994, B1; and Nelson Schwartz, "Giving—And Getting Something Back," *Business Week*, August 28, 1995, 81.

69. Paul Nolan, "Corporate Heroes," *Potentials in Marketing* (February 1994): 12.

70. Bloom, Hussein, and Szykman, "Benefiting Society and the Bottom Line," 13.

71. Marshall Loeb, "The Big Payoff from Public Service," *Fortune*, March 18, 1996, 135.

72. See Laurie M. Grossman, "Hypermarkets: A Surefire Hit Bombs," *Wall Street Journal*, June 25, 1992, B1.

73. See Ryan Mathews, "Party on . . . and On," *Progressive Grocer* (July 1995); 446.

74. *Dictionary of Marketing Terms*, Second Edition, 71.

75. Jerry M. Rosenberg, *Dictionary of Retailing and Merchandising* (New York: John Wiley & Sons, Inc., 1995), 55.

76. "Spectacular Sobeys," *Canadian Grocer*, August 1993, 14–18.

77. Michael Hartnett, "Studies Probe Appeal of Supercenters," *Stores* (December 1995): 23.

78. Sharon Edelson, "High Retail Mortality Predicted for Last Half of the Nineties," *Women's Wear Daily*, October 30, 1995, 12.

79. Richard L. Papiernik, "Mac Attack," *Financial World*, April 12, 1994, 28.

80. See Kenneth Labich, "Why Companies Fail," *Fortune*, November 14, 1994, 58.

Eaton's

An Irish immigrant by the name of Timothy Eaton has often been referred to as the father of Canadian department store retailing. Eaton came to Canada in 1854 and settled north of Toronto. For several years he worked in various general stores and learned the retail industry. He eventually became a partner with his brothers in a general store in St. Marys, a small town in southern Ontario.

Although he loved retailing, he became increasingly frustrated by some traditional retail practices, such as bartering. He also realized that St. Marys was too small a centre for the kind of retail store he wanted. As a result, Timothy and his wife moved to Toronto and in December of 1869 established the T. Eaton Co. With this new store, which at first concentrated on dry goods, Eaton was to establish three policies that were to permanently change the face of Canadian retailing. First, Eaton proposed a one-price system for merchandise. Previously, haggling and negotiating over price was commonplace as the method of setting prices. Second, all transactions were to be on a cash basis, whereas before Eaton's store, most retailers offered credit extensively. The third policy, and perhaps the most far-reaching, was the adoption of the policy of "goods satisfactory or money refunded."

These new policies proved to be successful and Eaton's began to grow and prosper. By 1880 it had become a full-fledged department store and by 1929 had expanded to include several stores, accounting for almost half of Canada's retail sales.

In 1977, Eaton's opened a major nine-storey Eaton Centre store in downtown Toronto, which contains 300 departments. This type of development has helped refurbish the inner-city core of several cities in Canada. In 1978, Fredrik Eaton accepted the prestigious International Retailer of the Year Award on behalf of Eaton's.

The retail market began to change in Canada during the 1980s. As more and more consumers shopped at discount and specialty stores, the department store was caught in the middle. Eaton's, along with other Canadian department stores, faced decreased sales and rumours about their financial problems began to circulate in the early 1990s. Attempts were being made to shift the company's emphasis from hard goods into soft goods, especially fashion. By emphasizing designer clothes instead of appliances, Eaton's was hoping to sidestep competition from discount chains such as Wal-Mart.

Some retail analysts, however, believe that there is simply one too many department stores in Canada. "The demographics here are different than the U.S.," says James Capel's George Hartman. "There you have the rich, the near rich, the not-so-rich and the poor. The country is big enough that a department store chain can prosper by specializing in any layer of that market. In Canada, you have essentially a middle class market concentrated in a few large and widely dispersed urban centres. So you wind up with three look-alike department-store chains, all pursuing essentially the identical customer." This analysis appeared to have some substance as by 1996 sales were estimated to have dropped by $500 million during the previous five years and the company lost $120 million that year. In February 1997, Eaton's was granted protection from its creditors (whom it owed over $419 million) in order to restructure. The Eaton family then hired George Kosich, retired former CEO of The Bay, to head up the company through the restructuring period. The restructuring plan, which was accepted by creditors in September 1997, called for the closing of 17 underperforming stores, plans to renovate and expand many of the existing stores, and will place over $25 million in a rejuvenated marketing campaign.

Questions:

1. Relate Eaton's history to retail institution life cycles and the wheel of retailing theory.
2. Discuss the relationship of Eaton's current difficulties to the components of a retail strategy.
3. Evaluate Eaton's attempt to "upscale" in light of the retail analysts' opinion. Discuss the consequences of a strategy change.

Source: Adapted from Ian McGugan, "Eaton's on the Brink," Canadian Business, *March 1996, 39–73; Donald M. Thompson, "Eaton's—A Cautionary Tale,"* Business Quarterly, *Summer 1997, 31–39; and D.W. Balderson, "Retailer Spotlight,"* Retailing in Canada, *1994.*

Video Source: "Eaton's Troubles," Venture *635 (March 23, 1997; 5:51).*

Part eight 8

Retail Specialization

Service Retailing
A Growth Opportunity in Retailing

Outline

Objectives

To identify the unique characteristics that distinguish service retailers from goods retailers

To describe the importance of service retailers in our nation's economy

To discuss the various types of service retailers and their operations

To explain the factors involved in offering the right service in the right way in the right place at the right time at the right price by the right appeal

Retail Vignette

Molly Maid International Inc.

There are several trends which have a significant effect on the success of retailing ventures. Those retailers that are aware of these trends and are perceptive enough to develop a retailing concept which responds to changing demand have experienced considerable success in the 1990s. One example of this is the case of Molly Maid International Inc.

Molly Maid International Inc.
www.mollymaid.com

In 1978 Adrienne Stringer, a former nurse, invested $2000 to organize a maid service business. She felt that changing lifestyles and the increasing number of two-income families had created a market for the business. The North American family had changed to the point that many people had no time to clean their houses and were looking for an efficient and inexpensive way to take care of this chore. This would leave families more time for leisure pursuits in their off-work hours.

By 1980 she was grossing about $100 000 and could see further growth possibilities. Because of her lack of finances to accomplish this growth, she decided that equity money was necessary either from new partners or through a franchise system. She therefore sold 80 percent of the company to Jim MacKenzie, a marketing executive and business graduate of Queen's University. MacKenzie immediately began developing a complete franchise system for Molly Maid and awarded the first franchise to Stringer.

Since that time, Molly Maid has grown dramatically and is now the number one maid/cleaning service in the industry. Operating in Canada, the United States, the United Kingdom, and Japan, sales topped $60 million in 1996, and the company provided employment for over 4000 maids.

The success of Molly Maid can be attributed to the recognition by Stringer and MacKenzie of an underdeveloped market and the business acumen to properly organize and administer the franchising system. Thanks to two major economic trends, Molly Maid Inc. is growing faster than the layer of dust gathering on your living room furniture. As corporate downsizing leaves managerial workers with separation cheques in their pockets, many of them have discovered that Molly Maid offers a relatively inexpensive way to own their own business. And with the growing number of working women and busy two-income families, leisure time has become a precious commodity. "We don't believe we're in the cleaning business," said Kevin Hipkins, current vice-president and general manager of the house-cleaning franchise headquartered in Oakville, Ontario. "We believe we're in the business of selling people free time. The further the commute time people have to their jobs, the greater the demand."

A consistent dedication to marketing and consumer research has made the company the dominant maid service in Canada and has allowed to open new markets internationally. Continuing lifestyle changes, both in Canada and internationally suggest that Molly Maid's growth has only just begun.

Printed with permission of Molly Maid International Inc.

The Emotile Economy

The "emotile economy" is a term that combines emotional or focus on personal well-being, with motile, or mobile. The new jobs will be found in service areas that include stimulating the intellect (information, education, entertainment); health (physical and emotional); security (personal safety and financial security); personal service; and spiritual fulfillment (religion and public issue advocacy).[1]

Lack of Attention

Service industries have dominated most Western industrialized economies for more than a quarter of a century. Yet policy makers, economists, and management educators have tended to focus on manufacturing, agriculture, and natural resources. It is only recently that the challenging task of how to manage service organizations more effectively has finally begun to attract the attention that it deserves.[2]

People Are Not Obsolete

So is the juggernaut of technology going to slowly but steadily do away with all human employment, leading to science fiction author Frank Herbert's Butlerian Jihad, a forerunner to the world of Dune in which zealots cleansed the world under a single dictum: "Thou shall not make a machine to counterfeit a human mind?" Probably not. The prospect of a job shortage is very real, and the service sector is going to see lots more automation, displacement, and elimination of jobs as it continues to evolve, but people are not going to go out of style.[3]

The service sector of the economy encompasses a broad array of service industries as well as many government and nonprofit organizations. The North American marketplace is in the process of switching over from a production-oriented economy to a service-based economy. The impact of this change on the North American society will be greater than that experienced when our economy moved from the agricultural to the industrial era. Services have become North America's biggest and broadest business category. With rapid expansion in sales, employment, and number of establishments, services are the brightest spots in the North American economy.[4] New environmental threats and opportunities will continue to be commonplace as the economy evolves. Nevertheless, the retailing of services

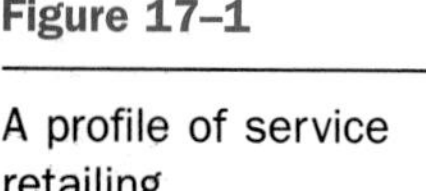

Figure 17–1

A profile of service retailing

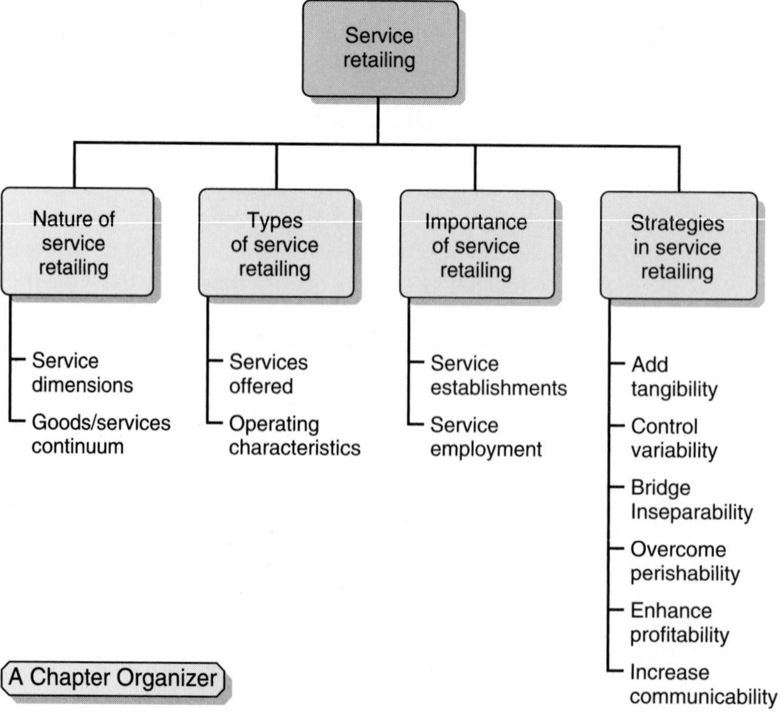

involves most of the same problems and decisions associated with the retailing of goods. Many of the merchandising and operating strategies and tactics discussed in the previous sixteen chapters therefore are equally applicable to service retailers, with appropriate modifications. This chapter describes the nature and types of service retailing, identifies its distinguishing characteristics, and discusses the issues surrounding the development of appropriate service blends and integration of marketing and operating strategies. Figure 17–1 outlines and describes the issues to be covered in this chapter.

Nature of Service Retailing

What is service retailing? How does it differ from goods retailing? **Service retailing** incorporates any business enterprise in which the sale of a service or services represents the core business. The core is that service which is designed to meet the primary demand need of a specific group of consumers; it is the reality of that which is offered and accomplished by the service retailer.[5] As shown in Figure 17–2, service retailing equals the retailer's service mix plus supporting services and/or complementary goods. Remember from Chapter 1, retailing (and that includes service retailing) is only considered to be retailing when the business enterprise derives a majority of its sales from ultimate consumers who utilize the service for their own personal benefit or the benefit of their family.

Service Dimensions

The definition and description of service retailing can be rather elusive because of the concept's multifaceted nature. Depending on the environmental and temporal context, service retailing can be many different activities to different people at different times. Figure 17–3 illustrates the multifaceted, complex, interactive character of retail services. As shown, a retail service can be any of the following:

- An intangible process that is provided to inform a client (for example, a lawyer's advice on what and what not to say in court)
- A variable performance that is orchestrated to entertain a patron or fan (for example, a concert by The Tragically Hip)
- An inseparable procedure that is provided to benefit a patient (for example, an orthodondist who straightens someone's teeth)
- A perishable event that is created to amuse a customer (for example, a water slide at an amusement park)
- A profitable task that is developed to satisfy a traveller (for example, a slot machine in the lobby of a hotel)

Figure 17–2

A definition of service retailing

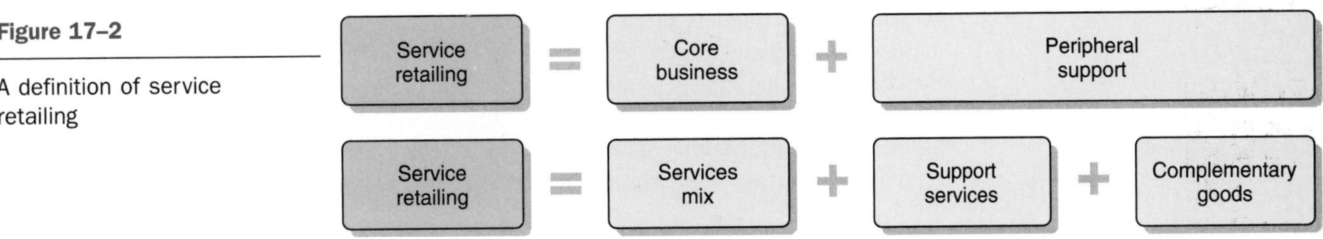

Figure 17–3

A description of service retailing

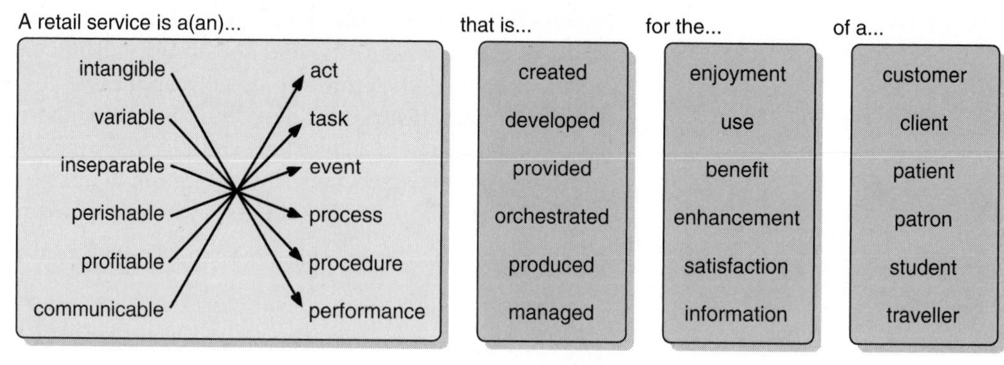

- A communicable act that is produced to educate a student (for example, an interesting lecture by your professor)
- A host of any other combination of elements and examples that you might think of

It is obvious, then, that retail services can be described and characterized along many different dimensions.

Who provides services? Individuals, groups, and organizations are all service providers. Although we tend to think of services as face-to-face interactions between individuals (such as doctor–patient, consultant–client, tutor–student), some services are essentially the collective efforts of a group (for example, jazz quartet, car wash attendants, basketball team) or an organization (for example, hospital, museum, employment agency). The customer's particular situation and need determines whether an individual or collective effort is required to develop the service package.

Goods-Services Continuum

How do service retailers differ from goods retailers? Goods retailers emphasize physical objects; service retailers emphasize "people, ideas, and information instead of things."[6] There is no clear distinction between goods and service retailers; rather, "it is generally accepted that there is a continuous spectrum running from a pure good to a pure service. Many goods companies are building service related benefits into their projects and many service companies deliver goods as part of the bundle of benefits they provide to consumers."[7] Figure 17–4 illustrates the goods-services continuum for the ultimate consumer.

On one end of the continuum is the **pure goods retailer**, which provides no services whatsoever. One example might be the roadside vegetable stand that does not even provide a formal parking area; another example is the farmer's market that requires customers to bring their own containers and harvest their own products. As a point of fact, even retailers that emphasize goods retailing usually provide essential services necessary to the successful operation of a business (for example, parking, bagging, store hours).

At the other end of the continuum is the **primary service retailer**, which concentrates on rendering a service; the core of the business is a service. Southwest Airlines treats its customers to no first class, no food other than snacks, no assigned seats, and no transfer of luggage to other carriers. So what does this very successful service organization offer its customers? Southwest offers the best on-time arrival and departure record in the industry and prices that are significantly less than what its competitors charge.[8] Like goods retailers, primary service retailers often supplement their core service offering with both complementary services and goods (for example, a beautician who also provides hair products for the client). Service (renting time on computer stations) is the core business of Cybersmith, an "online" café where people gather to "surf the net" or sample games, software, and CD-ROMS. Cybersmith supplements its service offering by selling food and coffee, which is served by "technosmiths" who can also offer customers a guided tour of cyberspace.[9]

Figure 17–4

The goods-services continuum

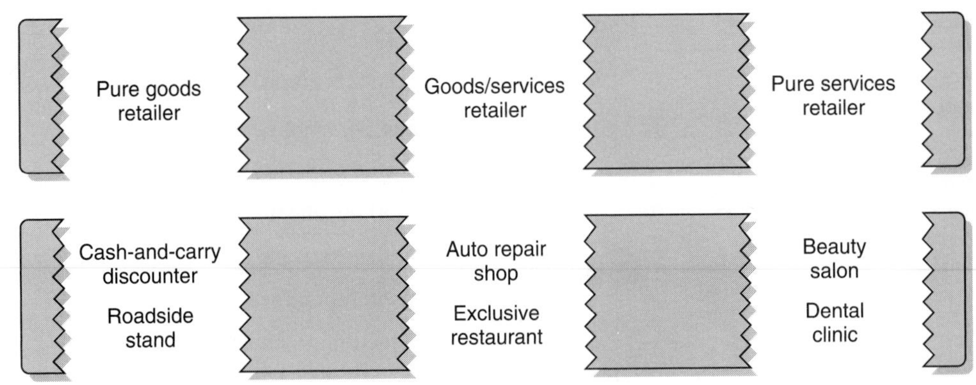

At the midpoint of the continuum (see Figure 17–4) are retail businesses that have an equal or near-equal emphasis on goods and services. A dining occasion is special because of the quality and presentation of the food, the attentiveness and courtesy of the waiter, and the atmospherics and comfort of the room and table. When a person patronizes a fast-food restaurant like McDonald's, is it for good food or fast service? It depends on the circumstances: with or without children, seeking a quick lunch or a leisurely dinner.

Types of Services Retailing

The multifaceted nature of services requires an equally complex classification system. Like goods retailers, service retailers can be classified according to the character of the service, organizational structure and operating characteristics, type of channel relationships and level of integration, size and ownership arrangements, and type and degree of customer contact. By whatever criterion we group and identify service retailers, a mutually exclusive classification system is impossible. For our purposes, this chapter examines two of the more common schemes based on the character of the service offered and the operating characteristics.

Services Offered

The service industry in Canada is divided into four major categories: (1) leisure and personal services; (2) food and beverage services; (3) accommodation; and (4) business services. Industries within each category are shown in Figure 17–5.

Operating Characteristics

Service retailers can be classified on their degree of reliance on equipment in performing the service and on the level of skill required by the service provider.[10] As seen in Figure 17–6, equipment-based service retailers rely heavily on equipment, and skill levels ranging from a totally automated service provider (for example, automated teller machines) to highly skilled airline pilots. AT&T is fundamentally an equipment-based networking company designed to use its highly automated communications, computer-based system to bring people, information, and services together. Today, AT&T uses only a fraction of the people (phone operators) it once did in providing this networking function.[11] People-based service retailers are highly dependent on a person to perform the service; that person may be an unskilled provider (for example, janitor) or a highly skilled professional (for example, surgeon). Unlike equipment-based industries in which technology can give productivity a major boost, in such services as health care and education, people are a limiting factor in future productivity growth.[12]

AT&T
www.att.com

Figure 17–5

Service categories and industries

Source: Adapted from Canada Year Book 1994 *(Ottawa: Ministry of Industry, Science and Technology), 558–560.*

	Revenue ($ billions)
Leisure and personal services	
Amusement and recreation services	7.5
Personal and household services	4.9
Food and beverage services	
Licensed restaurants	8.0
Unlicensed restaurants	4.9
Take-out food services	2.2
Caterers	1.6
Taverns, bars, and nightclubs	1.2
Accommodation services	
Hotels and motels	6.7
Campgrounds, trailer parks, etc.	0.9
Business services	
Primary business services	24.7
Machinery, equipment, auto leasing	6.0
Other service industries	11.3
Total service industry	79.9

Figure 17–6

A classification of service retailing

Source: From an exhibit in "Strategy in Different Service Businesses" by Dan R.E. Thomas, Harvard Business Review, *July/August 1978. Reprinted by permission of* Harvard Business Review. *Copyright 1978 by the President and Fellows of Harvard University. All rights reserved.*

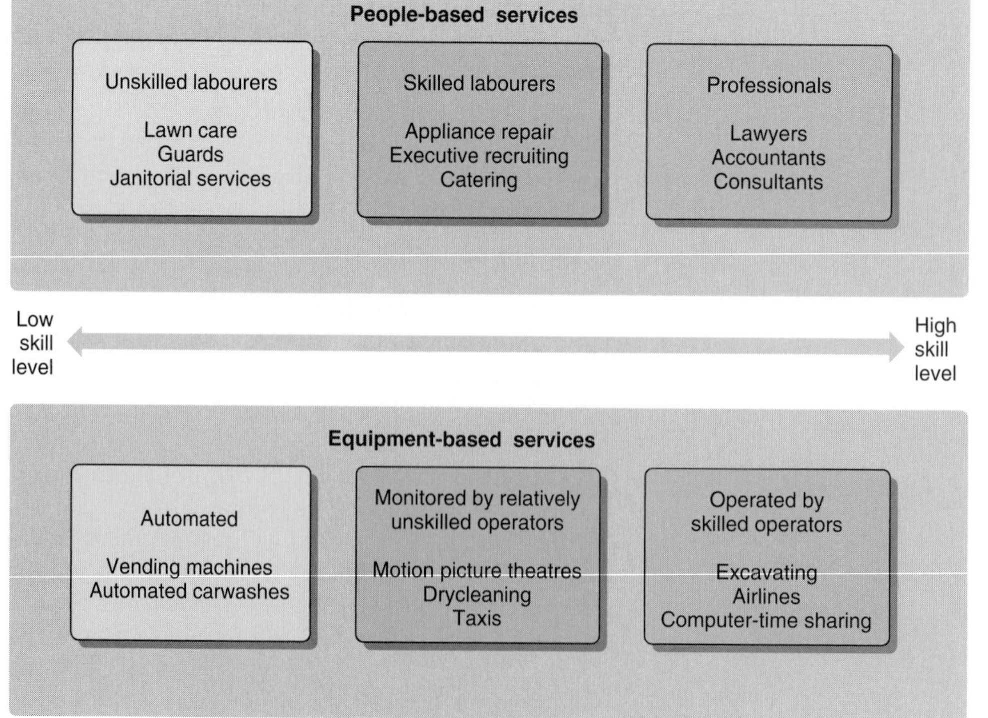

Importance of Service Retailing

How important are services? In many respects, services represent the most important part of our economy, constituting nearly three-quarters of the North American economy.[13] Canadian services growth in terms of sales has far outpaced the growth of tangible goods sales over the past number of years.[14] To gain an idea of the importance of the service industry to our economy, let us examine the service industry with respect to the number of service establishments and the number of people employed by service firms.

Service Establishments

Although consolidation and concentration of the service industry has been a significant trend during the last decade, the service sector is still made up of many small, individually owned and operated establishments. Service-based industries account for 50 percent of all business establishments. Given the economic slowdown of the early 1990s, the retail service sector offers the entrepreneur one of the best opportunities to start a new business.

Service Employment

The service economy in Canada is diverse and includes many of the country's largest corporations. The market encompasses venture-capital firms, investment dealers, banks, trust and insurance companies, software companies, professional firms of accountants and management consultants, real estate companies, advertising agencies, and hotel and food-service businesses. All of these industries, and the companies that compete within them, are actively involved in marketing.

In Canada, the period since the Second World War has been marked by a steady shift away from the production of goods toward more emphasis on services. More than seven out of ten employed Canadians now work in the service industry overall (see Figure 17–7). The growth in services originated in such information-based industries as finance and communications. As well, the growing call for government services means that the government now accounts for about 25 percent of employment.[15] With the exception of government employment, much of Canada's growth in the 1990s is expected to come from service industries. Although there is fear that growth in the service sector will not compensate for the decline in the manufacturing sector, it should be noted that service companies actually invest heavily in plants and equipment and are highly technology-oriented, adding as much value to the economy per worker as manufacturing does.[16]

The service sector's role as North America's principal employer is expected to continue as we drift towards a high-tech future. It is expected that between 80 and 90 percent of all new jobs will be created by the service sector.[17]

Strategies in Service Retailing

American Express
www.americanexpress.com

Understanding the unique characteristics inherent in services is a prerequisite to developing successful marketing strategies. As is the case with goods retailers, each service retailer must develop a service strategy that is right for their targeted group of consumers. American Express's old strategy of delivering an upscale product enabled the company to charge customers and merchants more because it offered great service. What was right for the affluent 1980s, however, is not working very well in the value-oriented 1990s. Today, American Express must compete with a horde of credit card companies offering

Figure 17–7

Employment by detailed industry and sex, 1995

Source: Statistics Canada, Catalogue no. 71F0004XCB.

	Number employed (thousands)		
	Both sexes	Men	Women
All industries	**13 506**	**7 397**	**6 109**
Goods-producing industries	**3 653**	**2 774**	**879**
Service producing industries	**9 852**	**4 622**	**5 230**
Agriculture	**431**	**292**	**138**
Other primary industries	**296**	**255**	**41**
Fishing and trapping	33	29	4
Logging and forestry	91	81	10
Mining, quarrying and oil wells	172	145	27
Manufacturing	**2 061**	**1 477**	**584**
Construction	**724**	**642**	**82**
Transportation, communications and other utilities	**1 033**	**765**	**268**
Transportation and storage	561	455	107
Communications	329	202	127
Other utilities	142	108	34
Trade	**2 307**	**1 271**	**1 036**
Wholesale trade	608	837	862
Retail trade	1 699	837	862
Finance, insurance and real estate	**809**	**330**	**479**
Finance and insurance	541	182	359
Real estate and insurance agencies	268	148	120
Services	**5 036**	**1 911**	**3 126**
Business services	867	479	388
Educational services	944	358	585
Health and social services	1 340	275	1 065
Accommodation, food and beverage industries	861	370	491
Other service industries	1 025	429	596
Public administration	**810**	**453**	**357**

all manner of special deals, discounts, rebates, and other features. To compete, American Express has geared up frequent-flier and other incentives to get cardholders to use the card more often.[18] The hotel industry is coming out with a leaner and cheaper model of lodging for the business traveller whose company is expecting more productive business trips with lower cost structures. The new business hotel prototypes do not have spacious lobbies or fancy restaurants but do have plenty of business centres, in-room fax machines, and personal computers. Hilton Garden Inns is one such chain that Hilton plans to roll out over the next several years.[19] Figure 17–8 identifies six key issues faced by each service retailer and the corresponding appropriate strategy for dealing with the issue. This discussion reviews the major issues facing the service retailer and includes examples of unique and successful applications in the service industry.

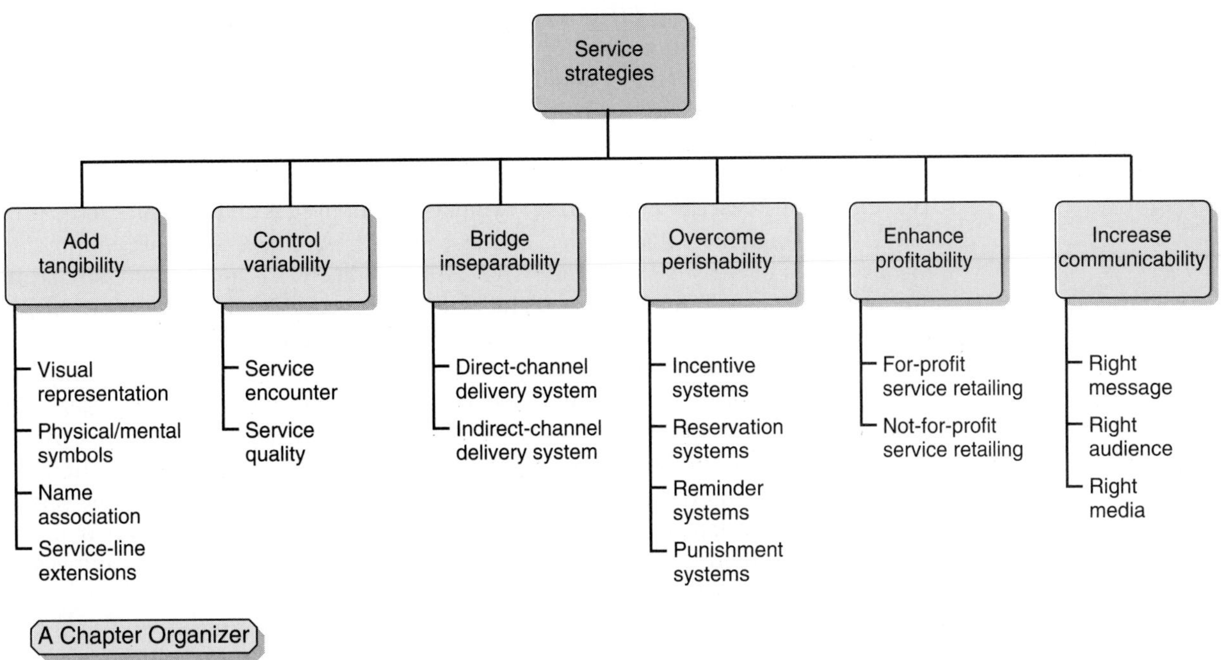

Figure 17–8

Service strategies

Offering the Right Service: Add Tangibility

If you can see, hear, smell, touch, and taste what you have purchased, it is more a good than a service; if you cannot see, hear, smell, touch, and taste your purchase, it is more a service than a good. It is whether the essence of what is being bought is tangible or intangible that determines a product's classification as good or service. **Tangibility** or physical features (size, shape, workmanship, and so on) determine to a considerable extent how well a good will function; one can evaluate these features before making a purchase. A service is not distinguished by physical features; hence, consumers may have a difficult time judging the service before making the purchase, and in many cases, they have little or no tangible evidence to take away with them to show they have made a purchase or gained something of ongoing utility. Memories from a concert, ideas from a lecture, impressions from a funeral, and excitement from a game are not tangible. Thus, a major marketing problem for every service retailer is to add a greater degree of tangibility to the firm's services.

At the centre of every demand for the **right service** is the core benefit or benefits sought by the consumer. In the financial investments industry, for example, the investor at any one time might be looking for investment security, opportunity, direction, convenience, or special treatment. Whatever the benefit sought, the service provider must find some way to "tangibilize" the offer to help the customer visualize and mentally grasp the core service concept. The service offering can be made tangible by (1) providing representations of the service, (2) creating physical and mental symbols for the service, (3) developing name or brand recognition for businesses or service lines, and (4) adding extra peripheral services or supplementary goods.

Visual Representation A visual representation of the service and its positive attributes (benefits) can notably enhance the tangibility of the service offer. An architect who provides a scale model of the proposed building or facility has created a tangible substitution for design ideas and concepts that might not otherwise be appreciated or understood. When that same architect provides a complete set of architectural plans and specifications, the consumer has available sufficient information to make a good judgment and correct decisions before, during, and after the purchase. Other examples of visual concept representations are (1) an information systems analyst's schematic drawing of a proposed information flow, (2) a management consultant's organization chart demonstrating the reporting relationships (line and staff) within an organization, (3) an interior designer's sketches illustrating a room layout, and (4) a professor's diagram (handout) portraying a concept or idea. These examples not only are visual but also provide the customer with something to hold.

Physical and Mental Symbols Symbols, both physical and mental, can be used to show the tangibility of a service and its benefits. A classic example of physical symbolization is the plastic credit card; it represents credit (that is, money and purchasing power) and a whole lot more (status—plain, silver, gold cards; convenience—cash, cheque, charge cards; and security—limited liability and cashless crime target).

Mental symbols can be equally effective in creating service-offering tangibility; for instance, the customer is (1) in the good hands of Allstate, (2) rock solid safe with Prudential, (3) under the protection of the Traveler's umbrella, or (4) covered by the security blanket of Nationwide. Each of these symbols are used to communicate more effectively what insurance can provide people; they are devices used to make the service more easily grasped mentally. The maple leaf, the Christian cross, and the scales of justice are examples of symbols that may be associated with both physical and mental imagery.

Name Association Service identification and differentiation often depend on linking a specific image or concept with a specific brand name. Adding tangibility through name association is the focus of this tactic. Names can be associated with service type, quality, convenience, cost (price), status, and a host of other identities. Consider the associations with these service names and brands: auto care (Jiffy Lube),[20] home care (Molly Maid), health care (MetLife), emergency health care (Med Center), car rental (Budget), automated teller machines (Green Machine), air travel (Canadian Airlines), freight transportation (Overnite)—the potential list of service branding examples is almost endless. "It's Just Lunch" is an excellent descriptive name for a dating service that arranges prescreened lunch dates for busy professionals. Given that a lunch is not much more than a one-hour commitment should the match be less than satisfying, this dating service is a more civilized, less risky, and convenient way to meet potential partners.[21] Developing brand recognition for a service is a major task for many Canadian companies.[22]

Canadian Airlines
www.cdnair.ca

Service-Line Extensions A more tangible service can be created through service-line extensions—adding extra peripheral services or supplementary goods. Weight Watchers International, a division of H.J. Heinz, not only has a line of food products that it markets through supermarkets, the diet firm also has joint ventures with life insurance companies wherein its members receive rebates on their premiums for participating in the Weight Watchers programs.[23]

In the Right Way: Control Variability

Services tend to be people-oriented activities on both the production and consumption sides of the service exchange process. As a result of the people-intensive nature of this process, service providers have considerable latitude in structuring the service encounter and controlling the service quality. The key to offering services in the **right way** is controlling **variability** and thus ensuring service reliability—performing services dependably and accurately.[24]

Service Encounter The **service encounter** is the time and place of interaction between the service provider and buyer. "A service encounter is the event at which a customer comes into contact with a service provider, its people, its communications and other technology, and the services it provides. It is especially the point at which marketing, operations, and human resource management are brought to bear on the process of creating and delivering a service that meets customers' needs, perceived risks, and expectations."[25] (The Retail Strategies and Tactics box entitled "Hired Shopper Born to Buy" illustrates a unique service that meets consumer needs.) This encounter can be crucial because it often

Retail Strategies and Tactics

Hired Shopper Born to Buy

While Christmas shopping can loom like a dark cloud above most mere mortals, Janice Foley is unfazed. For a professional shopper, Christmas gifts are just more of the same. Ms. Foley, who runs Private Shopping Excursion in Toronto, has been shopping for a living for the past 10 years, buying a vast array of items ranging from special shoes for disabled clients to high-end fashions for wealthy socialites. For a $30-an-hour flat fee, she will shop for a client, accompany a shopper looking for advice, or organize shopping excursions in Toronto for groups of tourists. "It's easy for me because I know where to go and I'm used to shopping."

Ms. Foley says her shopping business takes up about half of her working time. She also works part-time as a real estate agent, which occasionally helps her make contacts for her other job, she says.

The secret to success in running a shopping business is highly personalized service, Ms. Foley says. For example, she will start from scratch with a client who has no idea what to buy for a gift, offering suggestions, asking questions, and narrowing down ideas. "We go to them. The clients never come to us. People are calling us because they don't have time. If they have to make time to come to meet me, it defeats the whole purpose. It's very personalized. It's based on what the client needs and on their budget."

Source: Janet McFarland, Globe and Mail, *December 17, 1996, B14.*

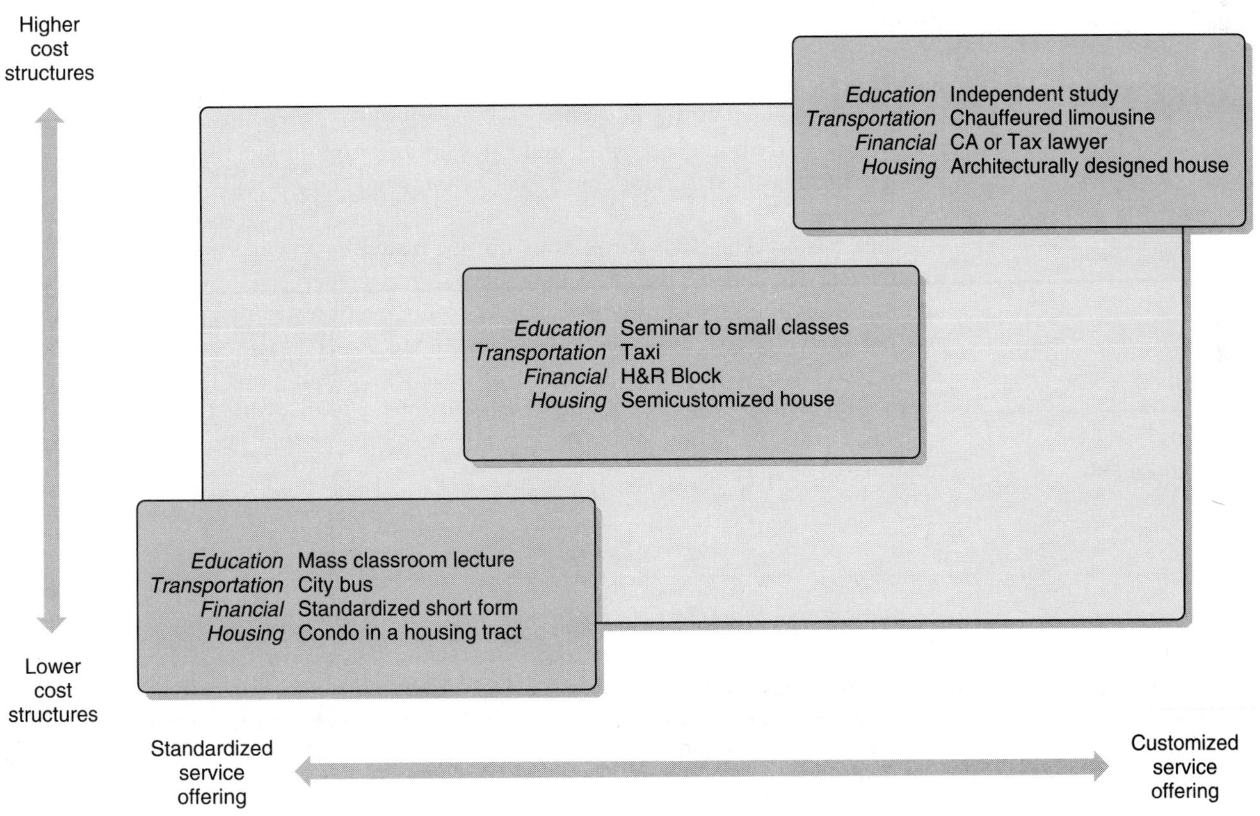

Figure 17–9

Customer service encounters

determines the customer's perception of the service. The service encounter can range from a totally standardized set of actions to a highly customized set of activities. For example, a college course in business administration can range from a highly customized independent study to the totally standardized mass classroom lecture (see Figure 17–9). In planning the service encounter, the education service provider must decide such issues as which is more appropriate as an educational experience: a mass lecture, a regular class format, a seminar, or an independent course? That decision depends partly on what type of cost structures are associated with each element of the service mix. For instance, although students typically prefer the small-class format, they may or may not be willing to cover the higher costs associated with such individual attention.

Service Quality **Service quality** is a function of the nature and level of the retailer's service actions—the manner in which customer services are performed and the way in which the customer is treated, assisted, and served (see Chapter 1). It is determined by comparing the expectations of the customer with the performances of the service provider.[26] When the service performance of the provider meets or exceeds the expectations of the customer, the service quality is perceived to be satisfactory (meeting expectations) or exceptional (exceeding expectations).[27] Current Canadian service firms are attempting to develop service standards for the services they provide. They have been aided by a unique company established by Steve Rogers. His firm, Franchise Company, helps service firms develop greater brand recognition.[28] The Walt Disney Company plans for customer satisfaction at its amusement parks in minute detail, from greeting travel-weary hotel guests at their cars to staffing parking areas with roving rescue teams to assist visitors with car trouble.[29] British Airways (BA) recast its first-class transatlantic service to emphasize what happens on the ground as much as the service in the air. BA gives premium fliers the option of dinner on the ground in the first-class lounge before the flight leaves. After they are in the air, they can slip into BA pajamas, rest their head on real pillows, curl up under a duvet, and enjoy an interruption-free flight. On arrival, they can have breakfast, use comfortable dressing rooms and shower stalls, and even have their clothes pressed.[30]

When customer service perceptions do not match customer service expectations, a negative service gap is created. This **expected service/perceived service gap** must be understood by the service provider in order to discover means for improving both what and how services are provided. As seen in Figure 17–10, the source of the expected service/perceived service gap is essentially a series of four potential gaps or miscues between the service provider and the service customer and/or within the service provider's execution of its marketing and operating practices.[31] These four gaps or miscues can be summarized as follows:

Figure 17–10

The expected service/perceived service gap

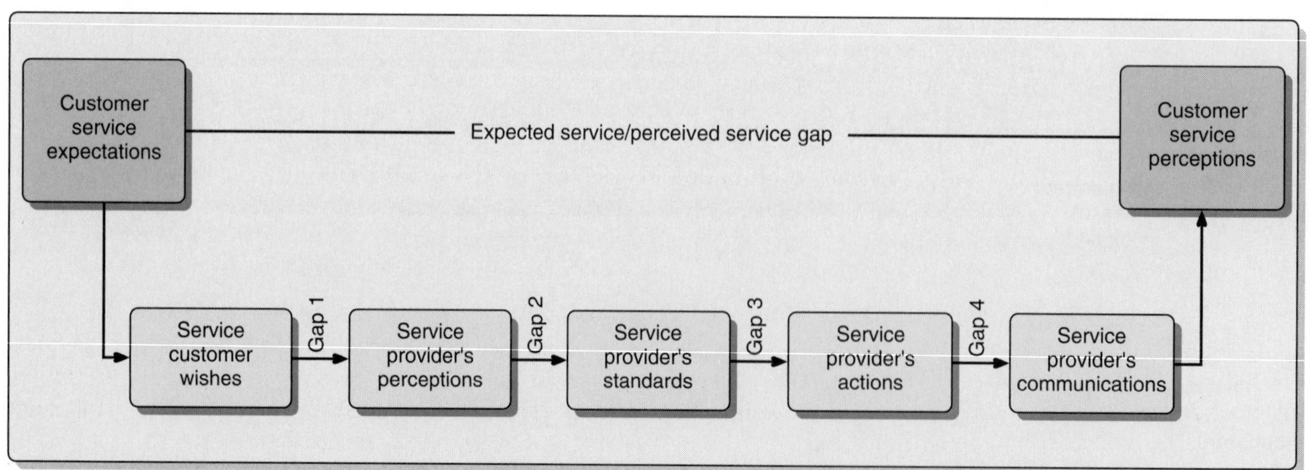

- **Gap 1: Service customer's wishes/service provider's perceptions**—The difference between what the service customer actually wants in terms of services and what the service provider thinks the customer wants. For example, a rental car agency may think that its customers want fast and friendly counter service supported by a choice of clean cars. The customer's wishes, on the other hand, are for a simple and straightforward rental agreement without all of the complex rate structures and insurance options.
- **Gap 2: Service provider's perceptions/service provider's standards**—The difference between what the service provider perceives in terms of customer service expectations and the set of standards or specifications that are established by the provider to ensure adequate service performance. If studies conducted by our rental car agency showed that the expected transaction time at the service counter is five minutes or less and the agency, in a cost control effort, only staffs enough service stations to ensure transaction times of ten minutes, then a service gap is created.
- **Gap 3: Service provider's standards/service provider's actions**—The difference between the standards set by the service provider and the actions taken by frontline personnel. Continuing the car rental scenario, if, due to inadequate training, the ten-minute transaction time standard established by the firm's management is not achieved by those individuals who have face-to-face contact with the customer at the service counter, then the service provider's actual performance is short of its stated performance goal.
- **Gap 4: Service provider's actions/service provider's communications**—The difference between what the service provider promises to do in its advertising and promotion programs and what it actually delivers to the service customer. If the rental car agency promotes a promise of fast and efficient counter service but fails to staff service counters with well-trained service agents, then a false and unrealistic service expectation is created with the service customer.

Both an appreciation and an understanding of why and how customers become dissatisfied with the service retailer's efforts are crucial steps in correcting poor-quality service. By eliminating the four gaps discussed here, the service retailer can ensure a better match between customer service expectations and service perceptions—that is, better service quality.

As suggested previously, the quality and consistency of services can vary considerably because of the differing skill levels and degrees of automation employed in the production and delivery of a service. Adding to the degree of variability are the personal attributes and attitudes of the service provider and how these are conducted in providing service (for example, the courtesy of the hotel bell captain, the efficiency of the bank teller). Controlling service variability in this case requires that management ensure customer satisfaction by first ensuring employee satisfaction through high motivation and constructive training. "The changing nature of customer relationships demands a new breed of service worker, folks who are empathetic, flexible, informed, articulate, inventive, and able to work with minimal levels of supervision."[32] Employee empowerment can also make a major contribution to customer satisfaction.[33] Employees who have the authority to act can correct problems when and where they occur.[34] Good personnel management is critical to successful retail service operations.[35]

In the Right Place: Bridge Inseparability

Inseparability is the typical exchange mode in the service industry; that is, under typical conditions a service is produced and consumed simultaneously (for example, a lecture by a professor, a cleaning by a dental hygienist, an actress's live performance)—the **right place** is anywhere the provider and consumer are together. Day-care services tend to be local mom-and-pop businesses because parents value a provider's personal involvement with their child. Simultaneous production and consumption means that the service provider is often physically present when consumption occurs.[36] In cases in which service production and consumption can be separated, intermediaries (service agents) can facilitate the exchange process. Depending on the degree of inseparability of production and consumption, service retailers can use either a direct- or indirect-channel delivery system (see Figure 17–11).

Direct-Channel Delivery System The direct-channel delivery system is a one-on-one relationship between service producer and service consumer. It is used when the service cannot be separated from the producer. Direct-channel delivery options (see Figure 17–11) include consumer-to-supplier and supplier-to-consumer channels. The consumer-to-supplier channel requires the consumer to (1) go to a single site for the service (for example, hospital for surgery) or (2) select one of several sites (for example, emergency medical care chain). The supplier-to-consumer channel delivers the service (1) to a single site (for example, home lawn care) or (2) at any one of several locations (for example, tailoring service at home, office, or club). Many colleges of business administration are developing long-distance learning systems that will enable them to deliver degree and executive education programs to firms' corporate classrooms.[37] Warner Bros. and other big producers of television programs "are moving rapidly and aggressively toward vertical integration—controlling both the programming content and the distribution system to get the programming to the public."[38] As an inexpensive way to expand their reach, many banks are putting branches in grocery stores and other retail establishments that provide customers with both time and place convenience.

Indirect-Channel Delivery System The indirect-channel delivery system involves a facilitating agent between producer and consumer. It is used when the service can be separated from the producer. Like direct channels, the service-exchange process

Figure 17–11

Types of service delivery systems

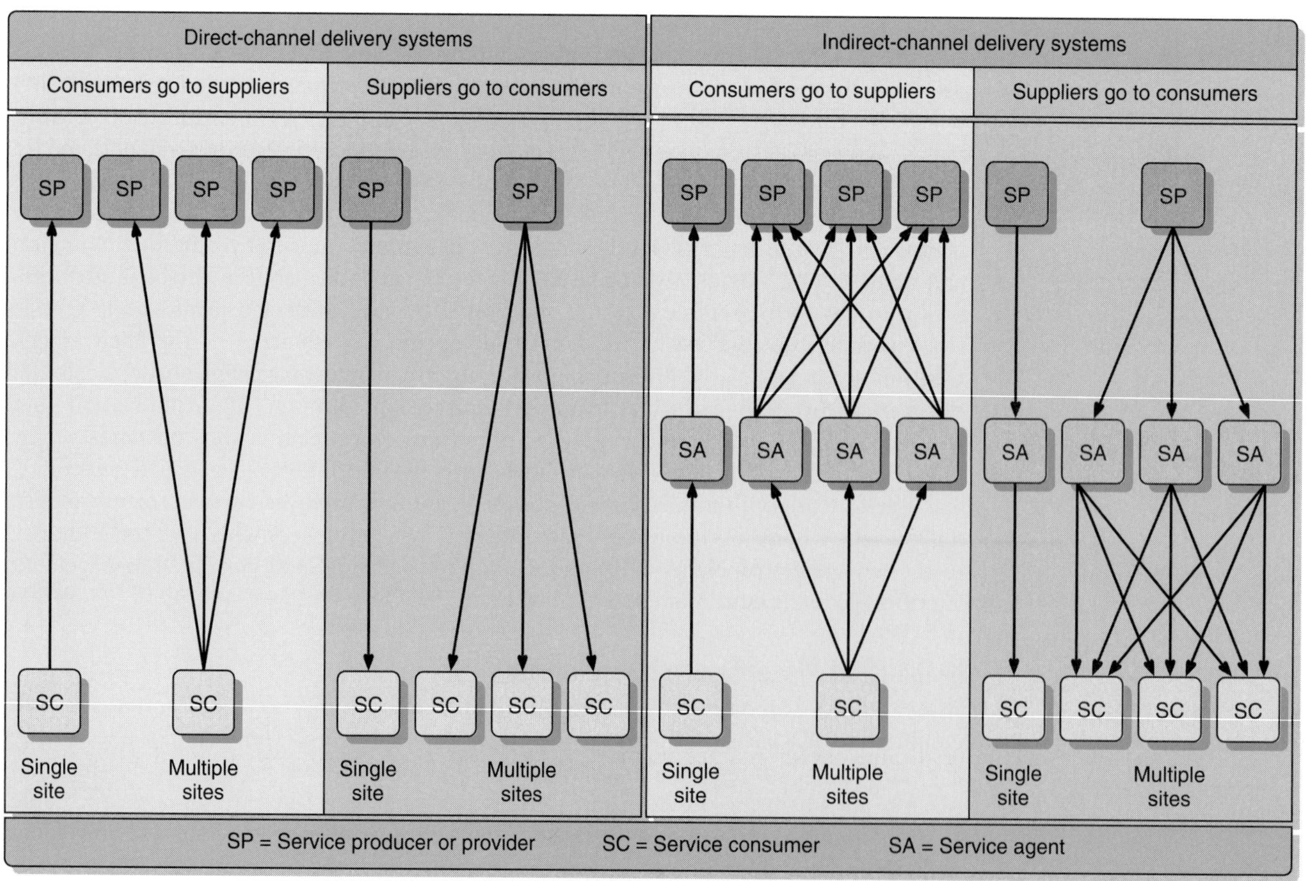

can be initiated by the consumer going to the producer or the producer going to the consumer (see Figure 17–11); single and multiple outlets are also found within the indirect channel option. A representative sample of common service intermediaries associated with indirect delivery systems would include travel, ticket, and employment agents and stock, real estate, and insurance brokers. A travel agent with a single location may have only one option in selecting an airline (for example, a feeder airline) when booking a flight from one small airport to another. The same agent or an agent with several locations has multiple options (airlines), however, when booking flights between Toronto and Montreal. A service supplier (local symphony orchestra) may elect to sell tickets through (1) an exclusive ticket sales agent with one location (such as, downtown), (2) an exclusive ticket sales agent with several ticket outlets, or (3) several ticket sales agents who may have one or more outlets.

At the Right Time: Overcome Perishability

Neither time nor a service can be put into storage and carried as inventory. The value (revenue-producing capabilities) of services is defined temporally; a service is offered at a particular time. After that **right time** has passed without the service being used, the value of that service is lost forever. Classic examples of service **perishability** are described this way: "What is the value of an empty airplane seat on yesterday's flight or the unused appointment time because of a no-show?"[39] Fluctuating demand is a key contributing factor to the high degree of service perishability; when demand stabilizes, the perishable character of services is greatly reduced. Offering the right services at the right time requires service retailers to strive to balance and synchronize their supply of services to the demand for their services.[40] Demand-supply synchronization can be accomplished by adjusting demand, supply, or both demand and supply.

Adjusting and synchronizing the demand for a service retailer's output might be achieved by means of the following: (1) incentive systems, (2) reservation systems, (3) reminder systems, and (4) punishment systems.

Incentive Systems. Incentive systems can shift demand from peak times to off-peak periods. Incentives take the form of (1) lower prices for lower demand periods (for example, afternoon movie, late-night flight); (2) quantity discounts for patronage during off periods (for example, two-nights' lodging for the price of one night during the weekend); (3) product extras for off-peak service (for example, complimentary dessert for the early-bird dinner); and (4) service extras to reshape demand patterns (free late-fall cleanup with each annual summer lawn care program).

Reservation Systems. Reservation systems can schedule supply to meet customer demand to maximize the service provider's output and minimize customer uncertainty and confusion. It promotes good planning on the part of both the service provider and customer. Dentists, hair stylists, and auto care centres are but a few examples of service retailers who schedule their time carefully and fully.

Reminder Systems. Reminder systems are used to contact customers immediately before scheduled service time to verify day and time of appointment and avoid any perishable "downtime" for the service retailer. Some service retailers use both a mail reminder (postcard) and a telephone reminder usually conducted the day before the appointment. Most consumers view reminder systems as an enhancement to quality of service offered by the service retailer.

Punishment Systems. Punishment systems charge customers for missed appointments or appointments that were cancelled too late for rescheduling the service provider's time. Full and partial charges might be levied. There are several tactics for altering supply capacities to better match demand patterns. One service retailing expert recommends the following:

- Use part-time employees performing only essential tasks during peak demand periods.
- Train employees to perform multiple jobs so they can switch from one to another as demand dictates.
- Use paraprofessionals so that professionals can concentrate on duties requiring their expertise (for example, parabankers who do legwork, solve routine problems, and handle clerical duties).
- Substitute equipment for human labour to make the service system more productive (for example, automated car washes, computer-prepared income tax returns).

At the Right Price: Enhance Profitability

Service providers often are divided into profit and nonprofit enterprises. The principal difference between these two forms of service organizations are their goals: profit motives or social motives. Although our focus has been on for-profit service providers, we also briefly look at the nonprofit sector.

For-Profit Service Retailing Services-for-profit retailers seek financial gain. Managing labour, equipment, and facility costs while obtaining the **right price** are the key elements in the service retailer's **profitability** equation. Unlike the goods retailer, cost of goods sold is not a major profit determinant. Controlling labour cost is usually the most important contribution the labour-intensive service retailer can make to ensure satisfactory profits.

The service retailer's price is often not a price; rather, price is expressed in terms of a fee, charge, rent, tariff, contribution, commission, admission, donation, tuition, interest, rate, offering, or retainer. Regardless of what it is called, the service retailer's price is important because it takes on greater emphasis as a result of the intangibility of the service offering. Correctly or incorrectly, price is often used as the most important indicator of the quality of the service.

Price determinants and price-setting methods for service retailers are similar to those of goods retailers. Depending on the circumstances, the service retailer might use demand-based, cost-plus, and/or competitive-oriented pricing strategies and tactics. (A review of these strategies and tactics, discussed in Chapter 12, would be helpful.)

Not-for-Profit Service Retailing Nonprofit businesses (for example, educational, religious, charitable, civic organizations) strive to meet social and public interest goals. For example, the Corporation for Public Broadcasting is a nonprofit organization whose mission is education and cultural enhancement.[41] Often these organizations are involved with **social marketing** in that they direct their activities at promoting social causes, ideas, and behaviours, as well as enhancing the image and involvement of nonbusiness institutions. Contributions, grants, and membership dues are but some of the means by which not-for-profit organizations express their pricing structures. Royalties are a relatively new source of income. Nonprofit organizations earn royalty income by allowing their name and symbol to be used as a brand name for appropriate products. The Arthritis Foundation Pain Reliever is one such example.[42] Monetary goals are typically less important than social outcomes that are measured in such terms as the number of (1) people in attendance, (2) individuals treated, (3) religious conversions, (4) votes, or (5) graduates.

By the Right Appeal: Increase Communicability

Creating the **right appeal** is the same for service retailers as it is for goods retailers; it involves the three-step process of presenting the right message to the right audience through the right media, which add up to **communicability**.

Right Message The right message addresses the concerns of the targeted consumer. Service retailers can make a service, patronage, or price appeal. *Service appeals* emphasize the rightness of the service offering in meeting the consumer's needs. Unfortunately, as a result of the intangible nature of most service offerings, it is often quite difficult to communicate the exact nature, the true value, the extra dimensions, the full benefit, and a host of other attributes that constitute a service offering. The persuasive and informative communication process becomes quite challenging when the object of the promotion is an idea, task, event, process, procedure, or performance. While fitness and wellness are the primary appeals used by health clubs, many clubs are marketing themselves as "the third place" for socializing, after work and home.[43] Developing a service appeal usually centres on building brand-name recognition and creating an image the customer can visualize. *Patronage appeals* are somewhat more tangible messages; they emphasize the rightness of the service provider's facilities, location, and operating hours. *Price appeals* are a major promotional element for some service retailers. For example, an advertised competitive price is essential to the success of auto repair, home cleaning, lawn care, travel, recreational, and entertainment firms. In the professional services field (for example, dental and legal), price appeals were (and in some cases still are) considered unprofessional, unethical, and/or low class. These restrictions on price advertising are rapidly disappearing as more professional services firms become market-oriented chain organizations (for example, The Dental Center at Sears). Service retailers use both "logical" (a factual presentation) and "emotional" (an appeal to feelings) approaches to presenting their message in the right way.

Mountain Quest Adventure Co. Ltd.
www.passageway.com/mtquest/contact.htm

Retail Strategies and Tactics

A Walk on the Wild Side

The president of the highly successful Mountain Quest Adventure Company Ltd. of Calgary is discovering that money really does grow on trees—the trees of western Canada's wilderness. Before Trent Schumann made the discovery that a small ecotourism company could mean big business, the 34-year-old Yukoner with a computer science degree made a great career start in the burgeoning software sector. Then he had a change of heart.

"I did some soul searching and thought about what legacy I would like to leave," says Schumann. "Computer software wasn't it. I decided I want to be remembered for showing people this incredible country we call home. I knew what we have here is so unique on the world scene."

Schumann says he "jumped in with both feet" and started Mountain Quest with his computer software "life savings" in 1993 to see business double every year, full-time staff rise from just himself to eight, and an icing-on-the cake nomination as Entrepreneur of the Year (Entrepreneur of the Year Institute) in 1996.

Lessons learned from his first career are applied to his new business of selling nature experiences every day. Those lessons learned include knowing his market (35 to 55 years old, upper middle and upper income, professional, educated and influential), knowing what works ("hire only the best, most knowledgeable, seasoned guides") and having "the most computerized and automated small adventure company in western Canada."

Mountain Quest's clientele continues to grow with the first quarter results for 1997 outpacing those of 1996. According to its president that's because "we offer an experience that is more real, personal, touching, and soul-expanding than traditional corporate meetings or incentive trips. The ski bus to Whitefish or the golf course doesn't bring the same rewards for a company. Mountain Quest is good for business. Employees learn how to work together and then go back to the office having shared a nature experience that can really affect people."

As for Schumann's career quest, "I love what I'm doing now. As the saying goes, I'm the master of my own destiny. I'm having a terrific time, and I'm making a good living. I see people at their best, interesting people having fun, and I feel I am helping to strengthen people's connection to and understanding of nature. This is a legacy I will be happy to be remembered for."

Source: Elaine Davidson, Alberta Venture Magazine, *May 1997, 45–46.*

Right Audience The highly intangible, variable, personal, and perishable nature of most services requires that service retailers target their promotional appeals. The right audience is the targeted individual or group who can use a particular type of service at a particular time. Few service concepts (for example, freedom, health, salvation, security) can be effectively targeted and promoted to a mass audience. Although general demand for a service concept might be created through promotional appeals to mass markets, specific demand for a particular provider's service must be created through tailored appeals to targeted audiences. The Retail Strategies and Tactics box entitled "A Walk on the Wild Side" illustrates how a service strategy is communicated.

Right Media For-profit service retailers use the full range of media choices. Both print (newspapers, magazines, direct-mail pieces) and broadcast (television and radio) media are used to inform, persuade, and remind customers of the service retailer's total service offering. Nonprofit service organizations also use all of the media choices; however, they tend to rely on public relations and publicity activities rather than paid commercial advertisements. Word of mouth becomes an extremely important vehicle for getting out the messages of the nonprofit organization.[44] "Over 40 percent of North Americans seek the advice of family and friends when shopping for doctors, lawyers, or auto mechanics. Word of mouth is also crucial to restaurants, entertainment, banking, and personal services."[45]

World of Retailing

Politically Correct Retailing

Word of Mouth or Walking Figures

While word of mouth in the form of referrals is still the most important way of finding a lawyer, legal-advice advertising is becoming more commonplace. Often the constitutional rights to free speech and codes of conduct of various state bar associations have clashed over what is legal and professional. With one of the lower rankings in The Gallop Poll's survey of the public's opinions about honesty and ethical standards of practitioners in various fields, many lawyers are very sensitive about the image of their profession. They believe that print and broadcast advertisements which aggressively hawk their services in the public marketplace creates the wrong image and is an inappropriate activity for the legal profession. Those who support aggressive advertisement counter with the fact that advertising provides necessary information for potential clients who have limited information on the legal profession and do not have access to someone who could refer them to qualified lawyers. For others, the issue is not whether or not lawyers should advertise but how they advertise. Which of the following messages and appeals are appropriate?

- Experience, strength, and determination are the qualities I offer my clients when representing them.
- Can personal bankruptcy help you? Bankruptcy can free you of all or most of your debts and give you a new start in life. Contact us to learn how we can solve your debt problem.
- Legal services at very reasonable fees.
- Our highly trained staff offers you prompt, personal attention and immediate action to settle your case.
- No Recovery, No Fee.
- Let our personal injury team fight for your rights!
- If you've been injured . . . I get results!

Source: Based on Jennifer Fulkerson, "When Lawyers Advertise," American Demographics *(June 1995): 54–55.*

Summary

A service is a multifaceted concept involving several activities performed by an individual or group of individuals for the benefit of a customer or group of customers. Service retailers differ from goods retailers in that the former emphasize people, ideas, and information, whereas the latter focus on physical things and objects. The nation's service industry is the most important sector of the economy; it is the principal employer of the nation's work force and accounts for over 50 percent of Canada's business establishments.

Service retailers are classified into four major categories: (1) leisure and personal services; (2) food and beverage services; (3) accommodation; and (4) business services. Services also can be classified according to operating characteristics, such as equipment-based and people-based service retailers.

The right service strategy consists of six issues. Those issues and their associated goals include offering the right service (add tangibility) in the right way (control variability) in the right place (bridge inseparability) at the right time (overcome perishability) at the right price (enhance profitability) by the right appeal (increase communicability).

Student Study Guide

Key Terms and Concepts

communicability *p. 634*
expected services/perceived services gap *p. 630*
inseparability *p. 631*
perishability *p. 633*
primary service retailer *p. 622*
profitability *p. 634*
pure goods retailer *p. 622*
right appeal *p. 634*
right place *p. 631*
right price *p. 634*
right service *p. 627*
right time *p. 633*
right way *p. 628*
service encounter *p. 628*
service quality *p. 630*
service retailing *p. 621*
social marketing *p. 634*
tangibility *p. 627*
variability *p. 628*

Review Questions

1. Develop three original definitions and examples of a retail service.
2. Who provides services?
3. Distinguish service retailers from goods retailers. Give an original example of a pure-goods and a pure-service retailer.
4. Identify two additional examples for each of the various types of equipment-based and people-based service retailers.
5. Outline the issues of concern in offering the right service and adding tangibility.
6. Give additional original examples of physical and mental symbols of service organizations.
7. Discuss the problem of service variability and how the service retailer might control this problem.
8. Describe the channel delivery system available to the service retailer.
9. Why are services perishable? Cite three examples.
10. Identify and describe the systems service retailers use to synchronize demand and supply.
11. Express the concept of price in other terms or language.
12. What is typically the most important factor in determining the price of a service?
13. Describe the process of increasing communicability by the right appeal.

Review Exam

True or False

______ **1.** All services are conducted as face-to-face interactions between one individual and another.

______ **2.** An important marketing principle is that services are distinguished by their physical attributes and these attributes should be fully utilized in service retailers' merchandising strategies.

______ **3.** A professor who utilizes a diagram to portray a concept or idea to students is using a visual representation to add tangibility to his or her service offering.

______ **4.** The "good hands" of Allstate Insurance is an example of using mental symbols to make a service offering tangible.

______ **5.** Because of the variability in the personal attributes and attitudes of the individual service provided, controlling this variability requires that service managers first ensure employee satisfaction through motivation and training before attempting to provide customer satisfaction.

Multiple Choice

______ **1.** Of the following operations, which is not a good example of a pure services retailer?
a. dental clinic
b. employment agency
c. exclusive restaurant
d. massage parlour
e. management consultant

______ **2.** The service offering can be made tangible by ______.
a. providing representation of the service
b. creating physical and mental symbols for the service
c. developing name or brand recognition for businesses or service lines
d. adding extra peripheral services or supplementary goods
e. all of the above

______ **3.** An empty airplane seat on yesterday's flight best represents the ______ problem of a service retailer's offering.
a. perishability
b. communicability
c. variability
d. normalization
e. none of the above

______ **4.** There are several tactics for altering supply capacities to better match service demand patterns. Which of the following actions is not one of those tactics?
a. using part-time employees
b. training employees to perform multiple jobs
c. charging customers for missed or cancelled appointments
d. using paraprofessionals as partial substitutes for professionals
e. substituting equipment for human labour

______ **5.** The service retailer's price is expressed in terms of a(n) ______.
a. fee
b. commission
c. admission
d. retainer
e. all of the above

Student Application Manual

Investigative Projects: Practice and Application

1. Using the multidefinitional model in Figure 17–3, provide a specific service industry example for ten different definitions of a retail service. For example, a concert by the Toronto Symphony Orchestra is a perishable event that is developed for the enjoyment of a patron.
2. Identify five nontext examples of physical or mental symbols used by service retailers to add tangibility to their service offerings.
3. Do you think punishment systems for demand-supply synchronization are fair? Why?
4. By surveying magazines and other print media, find three examples of service retailers that are using a service appeal, a patronage appeal, and a price appeal in an attempt to increase communicability by using the right appeal.

Endnotes

1. Edith Weiner, "The Fast Approaching Future," *Retailing Issues Letter* (copublished by the Center for Retailing Studies, Texas A&M University and Arthur Andersen, July 1994), 4.
2. Christopher H. Lovelock, *Managing Services: Marketing, Operations and Human Resources* (Englewood Cliffs, NJ: Prentice-Hall, 1992), 5.
3. Dick Schaaf, Keeping the Edge, *Giving Customers the Service They Demand* (New York: Dutton, 1995), 268–69.
4. Fanglan Du, Paula Mergenbagen, and Marlene Kee, "The Future of Services," *American Demographics* (November 1995): 30.
5. Jack E. Forrest, "Services Marketing Strategic Planning Models," *Marketing: Foundations for a Changing World* (Proceedings of the Annual Meeting of the Southern Marketing Association, November, 1995) 196.
6. James L. Heskett, "Lessons in the Service Sector," *Harvard Business Review* (March–April 1987): 126.
7. John E. G. Bateson, "Retailing and Services Marketing: Friends or Foes?" *Journal of Retailing*, 61 (Winter 1985): 11.
8. See Ronald Henkoff, "Smartest and Dumbest Managerial Moves of 1994," *Fortune*, January 1995, 94; Richard S. Teitelbaum, "Where Service Flies Right," Fortune, August 24, 1992, 115–16. Also see Andrea Rothman, "The Airlines Get Out the Good China," *Business Week*, February 3, 1992, 66.
9. Paul C. Judge, "Mr. Smith Goes to Cyberspace," *Business Week*, October 30, 1995, 72. Also see Julie Tilsner, "Coffee à la Modem," *Business Week*, September 25, 1995, 64.
10. See Christopher H. Lovelock, "Classifying Services to Gain Strategic Marketing Insights," *Journal of Marketing* (Summer 1983): 9–20.
11. John Huey, "Waking up to the New Economy," *Fortune*, June 27, 1994, 38.
12. See G. Pascal Zachary, "Service Productivity Is Rising Fast—and So Is the Fear of Lost Jobs," *The Wall Street Journal*, June 18, 1995, A1; and Myron Magnet, "Good News for the Service Economy," *Fortune*, May 3, 1993, 50.
13. *Ibid.*
14. Statistics Canada, *Service Industry Bulletin*, 63-105.
15. *Canada Year Book 1994* (Ottawa: Ministry of Industry, Science and Technology): 596.
16. Jay Bryan, "Growth Is in Service Industry," *Whig Standard*, May 12, 1994, 16.
17. See Joseph Cronin, Jr., and Steven A. Taylor, "Measuring Service Quality: A Reexamination and Extension," *Journal of Marketing* (July 1992): 55–68. Also see Joseph Cronin, Jr., and Steven A. Taylor, "Understanding Service Quality in Banking, Fast Food, Dry Cleaning, and Pest Control Industries," *Retailing Review* (Spring 1993): 8.
18. See Gary Levin, "AmEx's Newfound Love of Lending," *Advertising Age*, December 5, 1995, 4; Jon Berry, "Don't Leave Home Without It, Wherever You Live," Business Week, February 21, 1994, 76–77; and Leah Nathans Spiro, "Less-Than-Fantastic Plastic," *Business Week*, November 9, 1992, 100.
19. Jon Bigness and Jonathan Dahl, "Soon, Hotels Only a Boss Could Love," *The Wall Street Journal*, February 2, 1996, B5.
20. See Carrie Goerne, "Car Dealers Try to Dent $5 Billion Quick Lube Market," *Marketing News*, April 13, 1992, 9.
21. Suzanne Oliver, "Yuppie Yenta," *Forbes*, March 25, 1996, 102.
22. John Southerst, "Service Chain Develops Brand Name," *Globe and Mail*, June 7, 1997, B5.
23. Keith L. Alexander, "A Health Kick at Weight Watchers," *Business Week*, March 7, 1994, 36.
24. See Leonard L. Berry and A. Parasuraman, *Marketing Services—Competing through Quality* (New York: The Free Press, 1991), 15–33.
25. James L. Heskett, W. Earl Sasser, Jr., and Christopher W. L. Hart, *Service Breakthroughs Changing the Rules of the Game* (New York: The Free Press, 1990), 2.
26. A. Parasuraman, Valarie A. Zeithaml, and Leonard L. Berry, "Alternative Scales for Measuring Service Quality: A Comparative Assessment Based on Psychometric and Diagnostic Criteria," *Journal of Retailing*, 70 (Fall 1994): 201–30.
27. See Steven A. Taylor and Thomas L. Baker, "An Assessment of the Relationship Between Service Quality and Customer Satisfaction in the Formation of Consumers' Purchase Intentions," *Journal of Retailing*, 70 (Summer 1994): 163–78.

28. Southerst, "Service Chain Develops Brand Recognition," B5.

29. Allan J. Magrath, "Marching to a Different Drummer," *Across the Board*, June 1992, 54.

30. Rahul Jacob, "Why Some Customers Are More Equal Than Others," *Fortune*, September 19, 1994, 220.

31. This discussion is based on A. Parasuraman, Valarie Zeithamil, and Leonard Berry, "A Conceptual Model of Service Quality and Its Implications for Service Quality Research," *Journal of Marketing*, 49 (Fall 1985): 41–50.

32. Ronald Henkoff, "Service Is Everybody's Business," *Fortune*, June 27, 1994, 49.

33. Mary Jo Bitner, Bernard H. Booms, and Lois A. Mohr, "The Employee's Viewpoint of Critical Service Encounters," *Retailing Review*, A quarterly section of Stores magazine (January 1995): RR4–RR5.

34. See James S. Hirsch, "Now Hotel Clerks Provide More Than Keys," *Wall Street Journal*, March 5, 1993, B1, B2.

35. See J.A.F. Nicholls, Sydney Roslow, and John Tsalikis, "Bank Transactions: Satisfaction and Customer Attributes," *The Journal of Marketing Management*, 5 (Spring/Summer 1995): 39–45.

36. See Scott W. Kelley, James H. Donnelly, Jr., and Steven J. Skinner, "Customer Participation in Service Production and Delivery," *Journal of Retailing*, 66 (Fall 1990): 315–35.

37. John A. Byrne, "Virtual B-School," *Business Week*, October 23, 1995, 64.

38. Elizabeth Jensen, "What's Up, Doc? Vertical Integration," *The Wall Street Journal*, October 16, 1995, B1.

39. See Nikhil Hutheesing, "Keeping the seats warm," *Forbes*, January 1, 1996, 62–63.

40. See Lisa Miller and Garbriella Stern, "Car-Rental Companies Neglect Core Business, Often Skid into Losses," *The Wall Street Journal*, February 15, 1996, A1.

41. Michael Oneal and Richard A. Melcher, "Dead End for Sesame Street?" *Business Week*, June 19, 1995, 66.

42. See Jeff Smyth, "Non-Profits Get Market-Savvy," *Advertising Age*, May 29, 1995, 1; and Pamela Sebastian, "Nonprofit Group's Name to Go For-Profit Pills," *The Wall Street Journal*, July 13, 1994, B4.

43. Chad Rubel, "Health Clubs Add 'Convenience' Services to Please Busy Patrons," *Marketing News*, March 13, 1995, 1–2.

44. See Avery M. Abernethy and Daniel D. Butler, "Advertising Information: Services Versus Products," *Journal of Retailing*, 68 (Winter 1992): 398–419.

45. Chip Walker, "Word of Mouth," *American Demographics* (July 1995): 38.

International Retailing
A Global Perspective on Retailing

Outline

International Retailers
Global Retailers
Multinational Retailers

International Business Environments
The Economic-Financial Environment
The Political-Legal Environment
The Cultural-Social Environment

International Retail Markets
The Americas Alliance
The European Community
The Pacific Rim

International Retail Organizations
Alternative Market Entry Strategies
International Retailing Examples

Summary

Student Study Guide
Key Terms and Concepts
Review Questions
Review Exam

Student Applications Manual
Investigative Projects: Practice and Application

Endnotes

Objectives

To appreciate and understand the trend toward a global economy and an interdependent world

To recognize and describe the distinguishing characteristics of a global retailer as compared with a multinational retailer

To discuss and characterize those environmental issues that affect international retailing activities

To compare and contrast the dimensions of international retail markets

To profile the operations of foreign retail organizations

Retail Vignette

IKEA

For more than 40 years, Scandinavian furniture giant IKEA (pronounced eye-Key-ah) has sold its stylish, low-cost furniture worldwide. Smart targeting, careful attention to customer needs, and rock-bottom prices have made IKEA the world's largest home furnishings company.

IKEA
www.ikea.com

IKEA's first North American store opened in 1976. Like all IKEA outlets in new markets, the company opened this one as a franchise. IKEA's procedure when entering unpredictable or untried markets is to start with a franchise location until they learn the market and decide to expand. At that time, they buy back the franchise rights and operate the stores under the ownership of the IKEA Group. Initially IKEA considered North America a very dangerous market because of the high failure rate experienced by European retailers. Vancouver was chosen as the location for the first store. Interestingly, this is a rare instance of an international retailer opening in Canada ahead of the United States. It was not until 1985 that the first IKEA opened in the United states.

IKEA is one of a new breed of retailers called "category killers." These retailers get their name from their marketing strategy: Carry a huge selection of merchandise in a single product category at such good prices that you destroy the competition. Category killers are striking in a wide range of industries, including furniture, toys, records, sporting goods, housewares, and consumer electronics.

An IKEA store is about three football fields in size. Each store stocks more than 6000 items—all furnishings and housewares, ranging from coffee mugs to leather sofas to kitchen cabinets. IKEA sells Scandinavian-design "knock-down" furniture—each item reduces to a flat-pack kit for assembly at home. Consumers browse through the store's comfortable display area, where signs and stickers on each item note its price, details of its construction, assembly instructions, its location in the adjacent warehouse—even which other pieces complement the item. Customers wrestle desired items from warehouse stacks, haul their choices away on large trolleys, and pay at giant-sized checkout counters. The store provides a reasonably priced restaurant for hungry shoppers and a supervised children's play area for weary parents. But best of all, IKEA's prices are low. The store operates on a simple philosophy: provide a wide variety of well-designed home furnishings at prices that most people can afford.

IKEA has encountered occasional difficulty, however, in managing its huge inventory, sometimes over-promising or inconveniencing customers. The company's expansive stores also require large investments and huge markets. Some consumers find that they want more personal service than IKEA gives or that the savings aren't worth the work required to find products in the huge store, haul them out, and assemble them at home. Despite such problems, IKEA has gained worldwide prosperity beyond its founders' dreams. It now has 95 stores in 23 countries, racking up over $5.1 billion a year in sales. Since opening the initial store in Vancouver, IKEA has expanded to cities such as Calgary, Edmonton, Toronto, and Montreal. In 1996, IKEA added a phone-order business for customers living in British Columbia and Alberta. Canadian annual sales are in the range of $40 million and overall, North American sales account for 14 percent of IKEA's total sales. IKEA is in the North American market for the long run. Over the next 25 years, the company plans to add 60 new stores.

Most retailing experts predict great success for stores like IKEA. One retailing analyst, Wallace Epperson, Jr., "estimates IKEA will win at least a 15 percent share of any market it enters and will expand the market as it does so."

Source: Adapted from Bill Saporito, "IKEA's Got 'Em Lining Up," Fortune, *March 11, 1991, 72; Laura Loro, "IKEA,"* Advertising Age, *July 14, 1994, 52.*

The Global Economy

A truly global economy is emerging, and with it, a truly global corporation. The advent of these two will affect where you live, what job you hold, and even what hours you sleep.[1]

Retailing: Going Global

Retailing traditionally has been "local" because it required knowledge of the needs and habits of specific groups of customers. However, with more trade barriers dropping, retailing has been added to the list of businesses that must sell globally to stay competitive. More businesses are tapping into other countries' markets and learning how to succeed overseas.[2]

What a Market!

The earth, which already is teeming with 5.5 billion people, is expected to double its population to reach a stable level somewhere between 10 billion and 14 billion humans by the mid-twenty-first century. About 95 percent of this growth will occur in the less developed countries (LDCs).[3]

International retailing consists of the management of merchandising and operating activities across national boundaries in order to satisfy the particular needs of various foreign and/or domestic markets. Globalization of retailing is fast becoming a marketing and operating reality for both domestic and foreign retailers; this process is reshaping the international retail marketplace. "Globalization of markets is [a] very real, inevitable force. By the year 2000, big retailers will either be global or they will be gone."[4] Retail globalization involves many interactions that cross international boundaries. For example, international sourcing has become a common practice for many retailers; it involves domestic retailers obtaining merchandise from offshore sources of supply (see Chapter 10). Most

Figure 18–1

International retailing

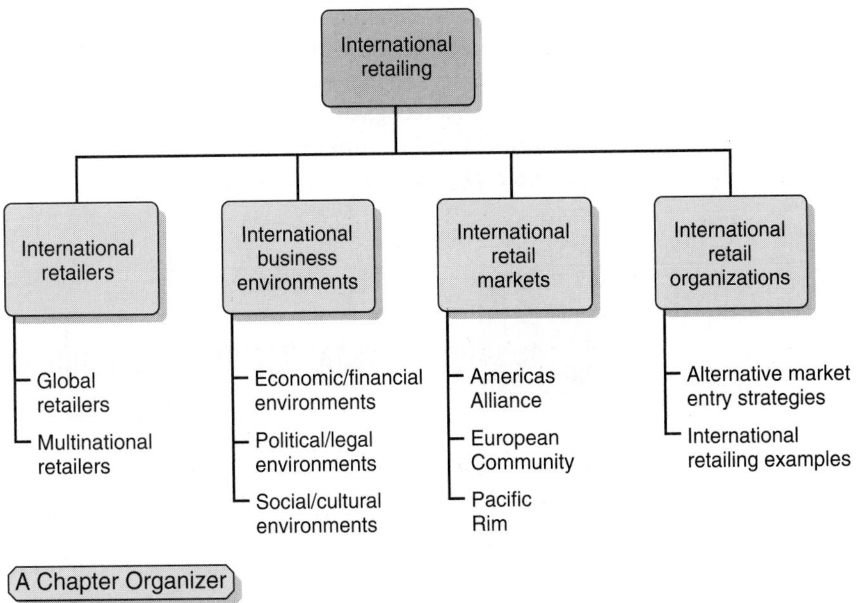

domestic retailers are also feeling the competitive heat of retailing formats that had their origins in foreign markets. As domestic markets become saturated for a particular retail organization or format, the pursuit of a growth strategy necessitates the entrance into foreign markets. Our approach to the study of international retailing is presented in Figure 18–1.

International Retailers

International retailers assume the organizational and operational structure of either a global retailer or a multinational retailer. A quick review will reveal some subtle but important differences between these two forms of international retailers.

Global Retailers

Global retailers are highly integrated and fairly standardized retailing formats that direct their efforts at finding similar customers in each of the foreign markets targeted by the organization. By taking a world view and developing an international strategy, the global retailer becomes a highly adaptive retail format that views the world as a stateless market without national boundaries; yet this retailer is capable of responding to the unique nuances of various domestic cultures. Centralized management and control is used to gain operating economies and consistencies. McDonald's and Toys R Us from the United States and the Europe-based IKEA, Benetton, and Laura Ashley exemplify retailers that pursue a global retailing strategy. Merchants such as "Marks & Spencer, Disney, and Toys R Us are seeking to differentiate themselves from one another by transforming their store names into global brands, much like Coke and Pepsi. This lets them sell higher-margin private-label goods, protects them from price wars, and gives them more leverage with their suppliers."[5] Ford and its worldwide network of retail dealerships are working toward the goal Ford 2000—the idea of creating and using the same systems and processes around the world to design products that can be built, distributed, and sold in different places with only modest local variations.[6]

Multinational Retailers

Multinational retailers are international retailing organizations that either adapt existing or develop new retailing formats designed to meet the special needs of each targeted country or market. Essentially, the multinational retailer pursues a quasi-portfolio approach to international retailing by developing a collection of national or local retail businesses that recognizes the real or perceived needs of local cultures and markets. Local management and control over merchandising efforts enhances the firm's ability to reflect local market preferences.

International Business Environments

Taking a world view, business environments become a complex maze of nationalistic markets and business practices. This section is designed to acquaint you with some of the issues faced by retailers of all nations as they consider expansion into international markets. Figure 18–2 profiles the environments of international retailing.

World of Retailing

International Retailing

Norway: Retailing Within a Mixed Economy

The Norwegian market consist of about 4.3 million people who tend to be concentrated around its capital Oslo in the southern part of the country. Almost one-third of Norway's rugged mountainous terrain lies within the Arctic Circle. Land distribution to difficult-to-reach regions of the country are often supplemented by water routes along Norway's extensive coastline. The Norwegian economy is healthy with one of the highest Gross Domestic Product rates in Europe, a real disposable income that is growing, a low unemployment rate, and a low rate of inflation. With a constitutional monarchy, Norway's political climate tends to be socialistic in nature.

Norway's retailing trade is a highly regulated industry. National and local government officials strongly influence operating hours, radio and television commercials, and the sale of many products such as wine and liquor. As a nation that needs to be very active in international trade in order to meet its needs for a wide array of products, the level of government involvement in this area of trade is also quite extensive.

Different channels of distribution are used in the Norwegian food industry. Four large retail food chains serve much of the Norwegian market. Each of the chains are vertically integrated with their own dedicated wholesalers. The four chains are:

- Norges Kooperative Landsforening (NKL) or Coop Norway is a cooperative purchasing, distribution, and service organization with 1200 stores and a 25 percent market share.
- Hakon Gruppen is a privately held chain of 1000 food outlets with 24 percent market share.
- Reitan Gruppen is a franchise food system with more than 400 stores and a 11 percent market share.
- Norges Detalj is a chain owned and operated by participating retailers. It is Norway's largest retail food organization with 2300 stores and 37 percent market share.

Nonfood retailers are dominated by the specialty store format. Department store retailing in Norway is relatively unimportant and is not expected to gain market share in the near future. The discount retailing format has not made inroads into the Norwegian retailing structure. Norway's specialty stores consist largely of independent retailers who can be found in one of the nation's large shopping malls. International specialty retailers who have become part of the Norwegian retailing scene include IKEA, Hennes & Mauritz, Benetton, Laura Ashley, and Marks & Spencer. While mail order retailing accounts for about 2 percent of total domestic trade, a majority of Norwegian shoppers do make purchases by mail. This retail format is popular with consumers living in one of Norway's many remote and isolated communities.

Source: Adapted from Arne H. Ramstad, "Now Only Nordic Nation Outside EU, Norway's Economy Grows Record 6.4%," International Trends in Retailing, *(Arthur Andersen & Co., December 1995) 19–24.*

only at home but abroad. Food retailing in the United Kingdom is dominated by the big four: J. Sainsbury, Tesco, Argyll, and ASDA.[42] With the formation of the European Community, British retailers are becoming more international in their outlook and are developing extensive overseas operations on both the continent and in North America. On the flip side, attracted by fat profit margins, U.S. discounters, warehouse clubs, category killers, and superstores are invading the markets of the United Kingdom.[43]

Germany The reunification of East and West Germany created Europe's largest economy.[44] With a combined population of more than 81 million people, unified Germany has become the single largest retail market within the European Community. More than seventy percent of the German population lives in urban centres. The largest markets are in the northern and central sectors of the country; they include Berlin (3.5 million), Hamburg (1.6 million), Cologne (1 million), and Frankfort (647 000). The major southern market is Munich (1.2 million). Although Germany is still experiencing the transitional strife brought on by reunification in 1990, the former East Germany and its neighbouring nations of Central Europe are viewed as the best expansion opportunity for German retailing conglomerates. The largest of these conglomerates include the following:

- **Metro Holding AG**—a portfolio of diversified retailing formats with operations in fifteen countries
- **Tenglemann**—a portfolio of different retailing formats that operate in ten countries
- **Aldi**—a supermarket operator and food retailer with stores in ten countries
- **Karstadt Group**—a portfolio of department stores, specialty stores, and mail order operations in six countries
- **Otto Versand GmbH**—a mail order retailer that serves fifteen countries[45]

Germany's retail structure consists of the full complement of retailing formats: department stores, specialty shops, discounters, and mail order retailing. Cooperatives and voluntary groups also are important in German retailing because they help small variety stores compete against the larger chain store operations. As is the case in Canada and the United Kingdom, the market share held by German department stores is declining, while the more price-aggressive retail formats (for example, discounters and hypermarkets) are increasing. Mail-order retailing in Germany is lead by Otto Versand (which owns Spiegel and Eddie Bauer). Because the German retail market is quite saturated, new market entries will have to displace existing retailers if they are to be successful. Smaller variety stores and some department stores look the most vulnerable to new cost-efficient competitors.

The short-term outlook for Germany is clouded by a higher unemployment level, the aging of the population, declining birth rates, and elevated immigration levels. Nevertheless, Germany remains a driving force in Europe and the world. "German retailers are expected to continue their march around the world and will continue to be a factor in the ongoing globalization of the retail landscape."[46]

Spain Spain became one of Europe's fastest-growing economies during the 1980s; it was during this decade that the nation was transformed from an agricultural to an industrial and service economy. Although Spain's population of 40 million consumers

Retail Strategies and Tactics

Pit Stop in Germany

Germany is renowned throughout the world for its standards of quality and craftsmanship. Now, however, a Canadian company is giving Germany a lesson in the ways of a consumer-driven economy. Pit Stop, Germany's leading chain of auto service centres, is wholly owned by Speedy Muffler King Inc. of Toronto.

The Pit Stop quickly made a name for itself by providing something Germans don't get very often: good service. Customers are given detailed explanations of what work needs to be done and exactly how much it will cost, just as they are in Speedy outlets in Canada. They can also watch the work being done and be out of the shop, usually, within a few hours. No appointments are necessary.

Although customer-friendly service like this is almost unknown in Germany, it didn't take long for the concept to catch on. In contrast, the typical German service station demands that customers make an appointment at least 24 hours in advance, takes at least a day to do the work, and can charge more than the estimate without consulting the customer first.

Pit Stop is now the largest company of its kind in Germany, with 90 outlets. Speedy also has 231 shops in France and another 18 in Belgium. Business is booming! Pit Stop's decidedly un-German name comes from the original owners who opened the first outlet in 1970. Tenneco Inc., an automobile parts supplier, eventually bought them out and they in turn sold Pit Stop to Speedy in 1988. Whether the German outlets change their well-established name of Pit Stop to Speedy remains a topic of discussion in the company. Very likely Speedy will not tamper with a successful formula. Next pit stop, eastern Germany!

Source: Adapted from Karen Nickel, "Canadian Muffler Company Makes Pit Stop in Germany," Financial Post, *June 18, 1994, 16.*

creates the base for a major retail market, the potential of the Spanish market is limited by the fact that the nation's per capita income is 25 percent lower than the average for the European Community.[47] Spain's unemployment rate (about 23 percent) is one of the highest in Europe.[48] Nevertheless, Spain's association with the European Community is expected to provide the technology and investments required to realize the nation's growth potential.

The most populous and prosperous areas of Spain are the coastal tourist areas, the industrial areas of the northeast, and the urban areas of Madrid and Barcelona.[49] Sparse populations and low standards of living characterize the remaining areas of Spain. "This geographical diversity inevitably gives rise to sharply differing economic situations: the purchasing power of the richer parts of the country is three times higher than in the poorer areas."[50] Although essential goods and services are available to most Spanish consumers, the ownership of such luxury goods as VCRs is relatively low. In sum, the Spanish market offers attractive opportunities for many different retailing formats and many nonessential goods and services.

Traditional forms of retailing (small, family-run shops) have dominated Spanish retailing for decades. Ninety-five percent of all retail outlets are of the traditional format; however, they account for only 54 percent of total sales. In contrast, new forms of retail distribution (for example, hypermarkets, supermarkets) account for only 5 percent of total retail outlets, and they generate 46 percent of sales. The inefficiencies of the traditional Spanish retail structure make it very vulnerable to the more efficient supermarkets and hypermarkets. Survival of these family businesses will require them to become more focused in product offering (for example, becoming bakeries, delicatessens, cheese shops, or apparel boutiques) and develop value-enhancing services such as credit, home delivery, and longer hours (evening and Sunday openings are not a common practice for most retailers). Traditional shops will have to improve operating efficiencies by associating themselves with purchasing organizations, voluntary chains, or cooperatives.

The hypermarket is very popular in Spain, and practically every region in Spain has at least one of these huge retailing formats. Supermarkets have been successful because they have been able to combine the positive features of the traditional store (convenience and personal service) with those of the hypermarket (selection, novelty, and technology). With the recent development and expansion of the shopping centre concept, specialty retailing is starting to gain ground as a preferred shopping format. In Spain, middle-class shopping centres located on the edge of cities tend to be anchored by hypermarkets and department stores or general merchandise stores and supermarkets. High-end shopping tends to be located on prime shopping streets within the city centres of Madrid and Barcelona.

The Pacific Rim

The **Pacific Rim** is generally delineated as the eight newly industrialized economies (NIEs)—South Korea, Taiwan, Philippines, Hong Kong, Thailand, Malaysia, Singapore, and Indonesia—plus Japan and China. Developing nations such as Vietnam, Laos, and Cambodia also have the potential to join the NIEs of the Pacific Rim. The emerging Asian economies along the Pacific Rim are in a new growth phase. The Asia-as-No. 1 thesis suggests:

> Sometime early in the next century, Asia will eclipse North America as the world's most powerful region. With a population ten times that of North America and six times that of Europe, and with faster growth rates than either North America or Europe, Asia at some point would inevitably overtake the other two regions economically, in total output if not in per-capita terms. And that point may be coming sooner than perhaps most Americans and Europeans realize.[51]

Whether or not this imminent Asia century thesis has merit, one thing is certain: The NIEs of the Pacific Rim will play an increasingly important world role economically and politically.[52]

The international retailing implications of the Pacific Rim to Canada are enormous. This area is a major source for a wide range of products made to the specifications of many North American manufacturers and retailers. With respect to international marketing in the Pacific Rim, everything from fast-food franchises (McDonald's and KFC in most nations) to fine jewellery and apparel (Tiffany & Co. and Brooks Brothers in Japan)[53] has been successful when markets have been carefully identified and local cultures accommodated.

Our sample of the Pacific Rim nations is limited to an examination of the Japanese and Chinese retailing systems.

Japan Japan represents one of the greatest economic success stories in modern history. Since World War II, Japan has transformed itself from a defeated nation to one of the world's economic superpowers. The huge Japanese market is based on its population of more than 125 million and a per capita income similar to that found in Canada. Japanese population trends are also quite similar to those found in Canada. With a rapidly aging population that has a traditionally high savings rate, the "silver market's" demand for high-quality goods and services will be tremendous.

"In [North America], the customer is king. In Japan, the saying goes, the customer is god."[54] Japanese customers have historically been demanding in their expectations of product quality, product variety, and customer service. Expensive foreign labels (for example, Polo, Christian Dior, Saint Laurent) have traditionally been highly prized because they represent prestige and quality. Higher prices are an accepted part of the Japanese shopping experience.

The sharp slowdown in Japan's economy during the early 1990s led to a profound structural change in the consumption patterns of the Japanese consumer. In contrast to the excessive consumption behaviour of the 1980s, Japanese consumers are spending their money differently. Shopping smarter and cheaper is becoming more accepted for most Japanese consumers, especially younger customers.[55] Too many gadgets, too many models, and too much service have led the Japanese consumer in search of simpler products that people can use. Japanese juniors (ages 18–21), for example, are looking for casual fashions that represent simplicity and good value. American retailers such as L. L. Bean, J. Crew, and The Gap are perceived as delivering on these attributes.

L.L. Bean
www.llbean.com

Although shopping for value is all the rage in Japan these days, price consciousness, which is second nature to many Canadians, is a startling change for most Japanese consumers.[56] During the spending boom of the 1980s, Japanese consumers were willing and eager to spend more money for high-quality products. Today, conspicuous consumption is a bit rich for Japan's sobered consumer. People are now willing to make price comparisons, hunt for bargains, and shop at discount stores.[57] Figure 18–6 demonstrates the sharp contrast between department store and discount store prices and the potential rewards that a value-conscious consumer might reap by shopping around and making price comparisons. For the once almost invincible Japanese department stores and the three-tier distribution system (manufacturer, wholesaler, and retailer) that supplies them, shifting consumer behaviours will require major adaptations of traditional retail operations. Let us examine the Japanese retailing system in greater detail.

Japanese Distribution System. "The Japanese distribution system is widely perceived as inefficient, and terms such as premodern, archaic, Byzantine, outdated, anachronistic, or maze are often used to describe it."[58] This system, which protects and promotes manufacturers, wholesalers, and small shopkeepers at the expense of the Japanese consumer, is coming under unprecedented pressure for reform. The retailing system in Japan has traditionally been burdened by too many wholesalers and small retailers that add unnecessary and substantial increases to the costs of distributing goods. When one considers that Canada's retail market is considered saturated and that the number of retail establishments per capita in Japan is double that found in Canada, the burdensome structure of the Japanese distribution system becomes quite evident.

The most restrictive characteristic of the Japanese retailing system is the *Large Scale Retail Stores Law*, which protects small, inefficient retailers by regulating the location and

Figure 18–6

Consumer price differentials between traditional Japanese department stores and emerging Japanese discount stores

Source: Emily Thornton, "Revolution in Japanese Retailing," Fortune, *February 7, 1994, 144.*

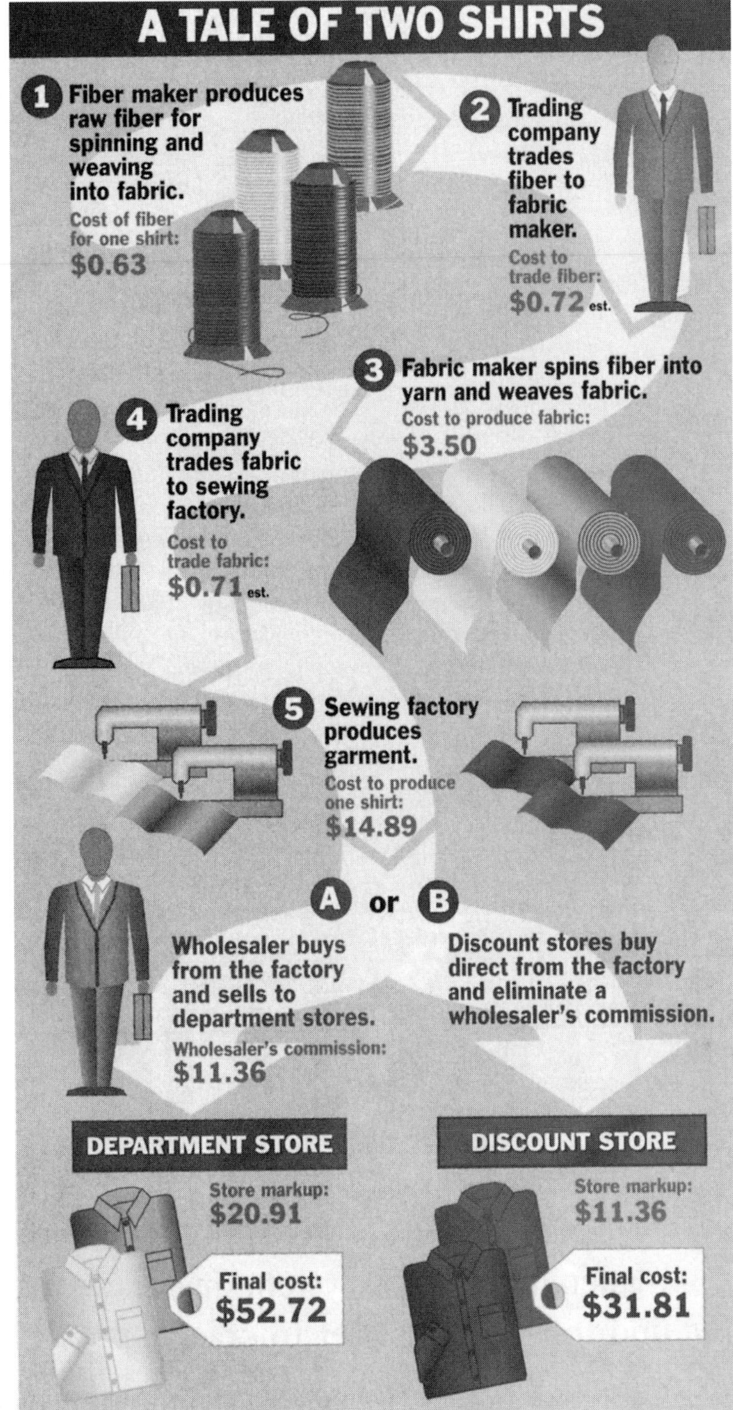
A TALE OF TWO SHIRTS
1 Fiber maker produces raw fiber for spinning and weaving into fabric.
Cost of fiber for one shirt:
$0.63
2 Trading company trades fiber to fabric maker.
Cost to trade fiber:
$0.72 est.
3 Fabric maker spins fiber into yarn and weaves fabric.
Cost to produce fabric:
$3.50
4 Trading company trades fabric to sewing factory.
Cost to trade fabric:
$0.71 est.
5 Sewing factory produces garment.
Cost to produce one shirt:
$14.89
A or B
Wholesaler buys from the factory and sells to department stores.
Wholesaler's commission:
$11.36
Discount stores buy direct from the factory and eliminate a wholesaler's commission.
DEPARTMENT STORE
Store markup:
$20.91
Final cost:
$52.72
DISCOUNT STORE
Store markup:
$11.36
Final cost:
$31.81

opening of larger stores (larger than 500 m^2). Other restrictive practices include the following:

- A complicated rebate system involving secret, individually negotiated rebates based on nontransparent, ad hoc criteria;
- Long-term and close, personal relationships among all channel members;
- Exclusive arrangements between manufacturers and wholesalers and manufacturers and retailers, and the prevalence of vertical arrangement;

- Emphasis on noneconomic aspects in the relationships between participating channel parties; and
- Administrative prices resulting in high prices to consumers and lack of price competition.[59]

Japanese Retailing Formats. In reality, retail distribution in Japan is a two-part system consisting of either (1) traditional retailing formats, established channel relationships, and customary business practices or (2) contemporary retailing formats, expanding channel relationships, and modern business practices. As the wheel of retailing turns in Japan, the traditional retailing formats are slowly losing market share to the larger, more modern members of the Japanese system of distribution.

Traditional Retailing Formats. Traditional small-store Japanese retailers can be classified as either marginal or specialized.[60] *Marginal small-store retailers* operate from their homes and carry a shallow assortment of goods for neighbourhood shoppers. This family-owned marginal operator is often looking to supplement a salary income and help cover the high rents that prevail throughout Japan. *Specialized small-store retailers* carry a deep assortment of a narrow product line. Located in neighbourhood shopping districts, near train and subway stations, and along major streets, the small specialty store provides a convenient interceptor opportunity for those Japanese customers desiring personal service, product freshness, and convenient locations. Although numbers are declining, the traditional small-store format accounts for more than half of the retail establishments in Japan. Plagued by high rent, weak management, and increasing competition, the downward trend in the number of small, traditional stores is expected to continue.

Contemporary Retailing Formats. A large and modern retail sector exists in Japan. Many of the current formats were transplanted from the United States during the last three decades. Amway, the U.S. direct sales company, has become the second most profitable foreign company in Japan. "Through its network of 1.2 million distributors who sell directly to customers in their homes, Amway delivers everything from Paul Newman's spaghetti sauce to cosmetics."[61] Contemporary Japanese formats range from specialty to department stores, from mass-selling stores to discounters, and a range of food stores. In recent years, mail-order retailers and category killers have been added to that list of retailers seeking to gain favour with the Japanese consumer. It should be stressed that each of these formats has undergone considerable adaptation in order to be appropriate for the Japanese consumer and the business practices of the Japanese retailer.

Japan's department stores are the most backward among the more contemporary retailing formats. The main reason for this backwardness is the dependence of department stores on the industry's traditional consignment system.

> The stores neither buy nor even select much of the merchandise they display. Instead, they are essentially real estate operations: They rent space to individual apparel companies, and these suppliers select the products, dispatch sales staff, and even take back unsold items. Department stores make money largely by taking a cut of the tenant's sales. On the surface, it sounds like a great deal for the stores. The suppliers get stuck with any slow-selling products and write the paycheques for nearly half of the stores' omnipresent sales clerks. But that buffer adds to the cost of the goods the stores sell, and to keep the product moving, they have to shave their margins razor-thin. Their high prices also make them vulnerable to competition.[62]

Department stores in Japan can be classified into the following four categories:

1. **City department stores**—Huge "warship" stores (50 000 to 90 000 m^2) located in major urban business districts; Mitsukoshi and Takashimaya are examples.

2. **Train terminal department stores**—Huge stores (20 000 to 90 000 m^2) located on top of or adjacent to major subway terminals or train stations; Umeda Hankyu and Ikebukuro Seibu are examples.
3. **Suburban department stores**—Large stores (20 000 to 50 000 m^2) located along major suburban streets or in shopping malls; Tamagawa Takashimaya and Tama Sogo are examples.
4. **Local department stores**—Large stores (15 000 to 80 000 m^2) located in smaller urban areas and branch locations; Tokiwa and Okajima are examples.[63]

All Japanese department stores are huge compared with their North American counterparts. The larger stores are essentially vertical malls with eight to ten floors, offering an enormous variety of goods ranging from foodstuffs to luxury items. "Japanese department stores are more than just stores. They act as public institutions promoting culture, the arts, and other interests through exhibitions, shows, and events that are open to the public. The lavishly decorated stores provide additional in-store amenities, such as theatres, museums, restaurants, and beauty shops. Many of these stores feature a top floor 'exhibit' that serves as a major promotional draw."[64] One interesting tactic employed by Japanese department stores is the use of an outside sales staff that calls on businesses and goes door to door selling merchandise using catalogues, videos, and personal presentations. Because they make a significant contribution to sales and profits, outside sales have become an important part of the total merchandising strategy.

Mass-selling stores are self-service stores that sell a wide variety of merchandise at low prices. Although food products dominate the product mix, these mass merchandisers also sell consumer durables, household goods, and clothing. Mass-selling stores range in size from 4000 to 16 000 m^2. The largest of the mass-selling stores are compound stores, which attract customers by incorporating sports and cultural facilities as in-store operations. As would be expected, the lower prices and convenient locations appeal to Japan's middle- and lower-income consumers.

Discount stores are low-price retailers of general merchandise that are in the process of dumping the strategy of cheap low-quality goods and adopting the North American practice of offering better-quality goods at low prices; that is, they are embracing the value strategy. A new format that is being introduced by American retailers is the category killer. Toys R Us has successfully overcome the Large Scale Retail Store Law and introduced its category killer format into the Japanese retailing scene.[65] The Japanese have also jumped onto the category killer bandwagon. Step, a Tokyo-area home electronics retailer, has enjoyed success by offering low prices and essential services.[66]

Specialty store retailers are stores that deal in a limited range of merchandise, offer a considerable assortment within each line, tailor their product selection to the specific needs and tastes of their consumers, and use specialized knowledge to meet customer expectations and complete the sale. Specialty retailing in Japan includes apparel and accessories retailers, household appliances and furniture, stationery and books, jewellery and collectibles, tapes and CDs, as well as sporting goods and automotive supplies. One recent American specialty store chain that is currently enjoying success in Japan is The Gap; its array of value-priced casual wear is grabbing the attention of Japanese consumers.[67] The establishment of large-scale roadside stores is the most current trend in Japanese specialty retailing.

Food stores include formats that range from small food specialty stores (for example, confectionery, meat) to convenience stores, to large supermarkets. Given the high density of residential areas, most market areas for food stores tend to be rather small and localized. Longer hours, personal services, prepared foods, lower prices, and better selections are the competitive tactics used to hold or gain market share. Thanks to a world-class inventory management system, 7-Eleven, the convenience store chain, can deliver fresh food three times daily to each of its 6163 outlets.[68] Although small and localized food retailers still dominate, the trend toward lower prices and better value is encouraging the development of both supermarkets and hypermarkets. The construction of these food superstores is proliferating.[69]

World of Retailing

International Retailing

South Korea

South Korea is in the process of transforming itself from a low-wage economy where workers churned out low-tech products into an advanced industrial power where workers produce high-tech goods. South Korea's population is over 45 million and is growing at an annual rate of 1.5 percent. With a per capita income of over $10 000 and a total GNP (gross national product) of $440 billion, South Korea ranks 11th among the world's top economic powers. The transformation of the South Korea economy has also transformed the nation socially and culturally. As wealth has filtered into broader segments of the population, middle-class Koreans are demanding greater choice in terms of products and the type of retailers who sell them.

Traditionally, the South Korean government has protected its domestic producers and retailers by restricting foreign competition. The nation's distribution system is characterized by marketing channels that typically have five levels with multiple tiers of wholesalers and retailers. This cumbersome distribution system has the effect of greatly increasing retail prices and substantially reducing product quality through additional handling and less freshness resulting from shipping delays. Responding to consumer pressure, the Korean government is beginning to open up Korean markets to foreign retailers. In the fast-food business, McDonald's, KFC, Pizza Hut, and Subway have successfully penetrated the South Korean Market. Price/Costco, Wal-Mart, Tower Records, and T.G.I. Fridays are additional U.S.-based retailers who have set up shop in South Korea.

Korean food retailing is dominated by small independent retailers that operate their local food stores following traditional Korean business practices. The supermarket concept has not yet become a part of the domestic food retailing system. American and Korean convenience store chains are slowly making inroads in the market and now create some competition for local independents. Dry goods retailing in South Korea is dominated by department store chains. Lotte, Hyundai, and Shinsegae are the nation's largest chain organizations. There are also several single-unit department stores that provide additional alternatives. Recently, mail order retailing has emerged as a growing retailing format as major credit card companies expand their operations to include product promotions with monthly statements.

South Korea's retailing industry is expected to change significantly over the next decade as the government permits greater impact of foreign retailers. Stores will become larger, better stocked, and more efficient. Korean customers will experience an explosion of different retailing formats.

Sources: Adapted from William J. Holstein and Laxmi Nakarmi, "Korea" Business Week, *July 31, 1995, 56–63; Gale Eisenstodt, "Park Gui-Sook's reading list,"* Forbes, *September 11, 1995, 72–73; and Bumcoo Cho, "Restrictions on Foreign Investment Eased, As South Korea's Economic Growth Slows,"* International Trends in Retailing, *(Arthur Andersen & Co., Winter 1993), 47–50.*

China With a population of 1.3 billion, the People's Republic of China is the most populous nation in the world.[70] In land area, China is the third largest nation. China's economy is in transition. The communist government of China is in the process of liberalizing its control, and the economy is transitioning between a centrally planned economy to a more market-oriented economy. The intended outcome is a middle-of-the-road "socialist market economy." China represents a wellspring of pent-up consumer demand for both domestic and foreign retailers. "With the population steadily shifting to the cities, it seems like all roads lead directly to the urban centres."[71] Guangzhou (south), Shanghai (central), and Beijing (North) are three of the most important urban markets.

All the world's industrial nations are competing for an opportunity to operate within Chinese markets.[72] For any global retailer looking to enter the Chinese market, the potential rewards are enormous but the risks are equally challenging. Some of the more common pitfalls are (1) a sometimes corrupt and hidden bureaucracy that must give its approval to any retailing enterprise, (2) the chances of becoming involved with unreliable partners due to the inability to adequately check their credentials, (3) the difficulty of getting or conducting reliable market research projects, (4) the scarcity of qualified business managers and professional workers, (5) a very archaic distribution and transportation system that is overwhelmed by the rapidly expanding economy, (6) a tendency of local officials to strongly favour local businesses, (7) the lack of a reliable judicial system that will adequately and quickly resolve disputes, and (8) the complications in obtaining foreign exchange in a straightforward manner.[73]

The retailing sector of the Chinese economy is still largely controlled by the state. The range and category of products sold by a retail enterprise must be approved by the government. Retail businesses in China can be classified on the basis of ownership; there are state, collective, individual, and joint ownership retail businesses.[74] Let us briefly preview China's principle retailing formats. State-owned department stores have traditionally been a major player in China's retailing industry. Serving major urban markets, these state-operated retail enterprises are now held accountable for their own performance. The government also operates in urban and rural markets various types of state-owned specialty stores and central open markets (a kind of shopping centre that sells products ranging from foodstuffs to housewares). State-owned businesses account for 40 percent of total retail sales.

Collectively owned shops are retail shops within a particular county that has cooperative arrangements to sell the output of local factories, farmers, or other producers within the same county. The 1.2 million collectively owned retail enterprises account for about 32 percent of total retail sales.

Individually owned enterprises are retail businesses that are privately owned by unemployed youths and retired workers who are registered residents of cities or towns in which they operate. This ownership group is the small business sector of China's retailing economy and is the largest in terms of total number of units (more than 7 million). These entrepreneurs account for 19 percent of total sales.

Joint ownership retailing are joint ventures between (1) a Chinese retailer and a foreign investor or (2) various types of domestic retailers (for example, a state-owned enterprise and collectively owned businesses). This form of retailing is the smallest in terms of total sales (less than 10 percent), but it is the fastest growing (60%) sector of the Chinese retail economy.

International Retail Organizations

The decision to "go international" is a major decision for any retail organization.[75] How a retail organization does this will depend on a host of complex factors, including the following:

- **Cost**—What is the most cost effective way to conduct business in terms of both fixed and variable cost structures?
- **Risk**—What entry strategies pose acceptable financial, political, and social risks to all parties involved?
- **Legal**—What are the legal requirements of both the host and entering countries in establishing and operating the enterprise, and which entry strategy affords all parties the most legal protection against known risks?
- **Expertise**—What level of expertise (for example, in terms of knowledge of customs, business practices, market conditions) does the retailer possess regarding the host country?
- **Competition**—What type and level of competition can the retailer expect to encounter in the host country?
- **Control**—What level of control does the retail firm want to exercise over foreign operations?

Alternative Market Entry Strategies

Conducting international retailing operations can be accomplished in a variety of ways. Alternative entry strategies that a retailer might use to set up retail operations in a foreign country include (1) licensing, (2) franchising, (3) management contracts, (4) joint ventures, and (5) wholly owned subsidiaries.

Licensing **Licensing** is a market entry agreement in which a retailer (the licensor) grants a foreign entity (the licensee) the right to an intangible property (for example, design, trademark, brand name, program, system). For instance, a retailer might grant a foreign concern the right to use its name. The licence may be an exclusive or nonexclusive right to use the intangible property for a prescribed period of time in return for initial licensing fees and continuing royalty payments. For the licensor it is an opportunity to generate additional revenues without any additional costs. The licensee benefits by gaining recognition through association with a known design, name, or program.

Franchising **Franchising** is an extension of the licensing strategy. Under such a system, the retailer (franchiser) not only grants the right to use its trademarks and brand names, it also provides the foreign franchisee with the methods and procedures for operating the retailer's business format in a successful way. Initial franchising fees, royalty payments on sales, and management consultant fees are the principal means by which the franchiser is compensated for the use of its retailing format. Because of the high level of involvement, franchising enables the retailer to retain more control over the foreign operation than is possible under a licensing agreement. For many fast-food retailers facing a saturated market in North America, entry into foreign markets is their best opportunity to retain their historic high growth rates. McDonald's, KFC, and Pizza Hut are three such firms actively pursuing foreign markets through the entry strategy of franchising. The hotel and car rental industries are two more examples of service retailers following the foreign franchising strategy.

Management Contracts **Management contracts** involve retail organizations that use their retailing knowledge and personnel to manage foreign retail operations. This "rent-a-retailer" approach provides the foreign concern with the expertise needed to start a new enterprise, rescue a troubled operation, or expand an existing format. Management contracts are quite common in such retail service businesses as the travel and hotel industries.

Joint Ventures The fourth type of foreign market entry strategy is the **joint venture**—a business arrangement in which a retailer joins together with a foreign entity (usually a business or group of businesses) to establish a new retailing enterprise (new startup) or purchase an established retail concern (acquisition) within the host nation. Depending on the legal requirements of the host country, joint ventures involve joint but not necessarily equal ownership of the retail business. It allows both parties to share the costs and risks of the venture, as well as any rewards or profits from the common effort. These foreign and domestic partnerships are often looked upon with considerable favour by the government of the host country, which is interested in developing its economy. Like any cooperative partnership, conflicts are common if the expectations and relationships are not fully defined and decision-making authority is not clearly established.

Wholly Owned Subsidiaries As suggested by its name, a **wholly owned subsidiary** is a strategy in which a retail organization enters a foreign market by either starting a new operation from scratch or acquiring an existing operation. In either case, the retailer has complete ownership over the retail business. The chief advantage is the total control the retailer enjoys in both merchandising and operations. Complete ownership has the additional benefit of not having to share profits but the limitation of assuming all the risks. Those risks can be reduced if the retailer elects to acquire an established retailer with a known and proven track record of meeting the needs of the local market. Depending on the track record, acquisitions can be costly—the better the track record, the higher the acquisition costs.

International Retailing Examples

Global retailing activities expanded rapidly during the 1980s, and that growth is expected to continue into the next century. Retailers in all industrialized nations, as well as many developing nations, will have to change the way they think about and act toward international competitors. Figure 18–7 is a listing of the world's fifty largest retailing companies. An examination of the list reveals both the size and international character of the retailing community. Each of these retailing powers are either currently involved with international retailing activities or in the process of expanding into international markets. Although the United States, Germany, Japan, and the United Kingdom have the dominant position in the international community of retailers, several other European nations, together with Canada and Australia, also are major players focusing on international markets.

Figure 18–7

Top 50 global powers

Source: Adapted from Global Powers of Retailing, Study Organized by Coopers & Lybrand, Chain Store Age *(December 1995): 4, 6. Reprinted by permission. Copyright Lebhar-Friedman, Inc., 425 Park Ave., New York, NY 10022.*

Sales Rank	Company	Country of Origin	1994 Sales (US$)
1	Wal-Mart Stores, Inc.	United States	82 494
2	Metro Holding AG	Switzerland/Germany	52 000
3	Kmart Corporation	United States	34 025
4	Sears, Roebuck and Co.	United States	33 099
5	Tenglemann Warenhandelsgesellschaft	Germany	32 400
6	The Daiei, Inc.	Japan	29 545
7	Ito-Yokado Co., Ltd.	Japan	28 175
8	Aldi	Germany	24 900
9	Carrefour SA	France	24 577
10	Kroger Company	United States	22 959
11	Dayton Hudson Corporation	United States	21 311
12	JC Penney Company, Inc.	United States	21 082
13	Jusco Co., Ltd.	Japan	19 586
14	American Stores Company	United States	18 355
15	J Salnsbury pic	United Kingdom	17 398
16	Promodès SA	France	17 072
17	Auchan	France	16 750
18	Price/Costco, Inc.	United States	16 481
19	Koninklijke Ahold, NV	Netherlands	15 931
20	Safeway	United States	15 627
21	Tesco pic	United Kingdom	15 474
22	Karstadt Group	Germany	14 912
23	Otto Versand GmbH	Germany	14 800
24	Nichil Co., Ltd.	Japan	14 545
25	Kaufhof Group	Germany	13 620

continued

Figure 18–7 (continued)

Sales Rank	Company	Country of Origin	1994 Sales (US$)
26	SHV Holdings	Netherlands	13 556
27	Selyu, Ltd.	Japan	13 009
28	Casino Guichard-Perrachon	France	12 929
29	Pinault Printemps-Redoute	France	12 765
30	Home Depot, Inc.	United States	12 477
31	May Department Stores Company	United States	12 223
32	Albertson's Inc.	United States	11 895
33	Asko Deutsche Kaufhaus AG	Germany	11 667
34	Coles Myer Ltd.	Australia	11 648
35	Takashimaya Co., Ltd.	Japan	11 618
36	Groupe Delhaize "Le Lion"	Belgium	11 393
37	Lidl & Schwarz Stiftung & Co. KG	Germany	11 300
38	Melville Corporation	United States	11 286
39	Winn-Dixie Stores, Inc.	United States	11 082
40	Marks & Spencer pic	United Kingdom	10 427
41	Great Atlantic & Pacific Tea Co., Inc.	United States	10 332
42	Mitsukoshi Ltd.	Japan	9 954
43	Jardine Matheson Holdings	Hong Kong	9 569
44	George Weston Ltd.	Canada	9 516
45	Walgreen Co.	United States	9 235
46	Quelle Schickedanz AG & CO.	Germany	9 036
47	Argyll Group pic	United Kingdom	8 907
48	Toys R Us, Inc.	United States	8 746
49	Publix Super Markets, Inc.	United States	8 665
50	Uny Co., Ltd.	Japan	8 524

Summary

International retailing involves the management of all retailing activities across national boundaries in the pursuit of foreign markets. Global retailers are highly standardized retail formats that appeal to the same market segments in different nations. Multinational retailers have different retail formats for each country they target.

International business environments are a complex maze of nationalistic markets and business practices. The economic environment consists of economic systems that range from market (supply-and-demand) economies to command (state-planned) economies. Financial environments take into account the international monetary system and the role of exchange rates in hindering or facilitating international commerce. The political environment involves how each nation conducts governmental affairs and makes governmental policy. International political systems range from democratic structures to totalitarian systems. International retailers must contend with national, international, and sometimes extraterritorial laws. In assessing the cultural and social environments, retailers must take into account

(1) verbal and nonverbal communications, (2) formal and informal education, (3) religion and faith, (4) ethics and standards, (5) values and attitudes, (6) manners and customs, and (7) material life.

Comparative analysis of international retail markets is based on a sample of nations from the triad market: the Americas Alliance, the European Community, and the Pacific Rim. The Americas Alliance is the conceptual idea of a free-trade zone that incorporates both North and South America. The retail markets and formats of the United States, Mexico, and Argentina are described as a representative sample of retailing in the Americas. The European Community comprises twelve European nations that are in the process of building a common market. With 320 million people, it will rival the Americas Alliance and the Pacific Rim as one of the world's largest consumer markets. The retail industries of the United Kingdom, Germany, and Spain are described. The emerging Asian economies along the Pacific Rim have entered the 1990s in a growth mode. Japan is the undisputed economic leader of this community of nations; therefore, it is detailed as a representative of the retailing scene within this bloc of nations.

Alternative entry strategies into foreign markets are typically accomplished through the use of licensing and franchising agreements, management contracts, joint ventures, and wholly owned subsidiaries.

Student Study Guide

Key Terms and Concepts

acculturation *p. 648*
bilateral treaties *p. 648*
change agent *p. 648*
civil law *p. 647*
command economy *p. 645*
common law *p. 647*
common market *p. 657*
culture *p. 648*
customs *p. 650*
democracy *p. 646*
economic environment *p. 645*
European Community *p. 657*
exchange rate *p. 646*
extraterritorial law *p. 647*
financial environment *p. 645*
franchising *p. 668*
global retailers *p. 644*
international law *p. 647*
international monetary system *p. 646*
international retailing *p. 643*
joint venture *p. 668*
licensing *p. 668*
legal environment *p. 646*
management contracts *p. 668*
manners *p. 650*
market economy *p. 645*
material life *p. 650*
mixed economy *p. 645*
multilateral treaties *p. 648*
multinational retailers *p. 644*
national law *p. 647*
Pacific Rim *p. 661*
political environment *p. 646*
theocratic law *p. 647*
totalitarianism *p. 646*
triad market *p. 651*
wholly owned subsidiary *p. 668*

Review Questions

1. Define international retailing.
2. Compare and contrast global retailers and multinational retailers.
3. How does a market economy differ from a command economy?
4. What effect does exchange rate have on the activities of international retailers?
5. Describe the three types of legal systems that retailers face when engaging in international activities.
6. Identify the seven cultural elements that each retailer encounters when pursuing international market opportunities. How might these elements affect the retailer's operations?
7. Profile the Americas Alliance.
8. Identify and describe the major retailing formats of Argentina.
9. Profile the European Community.
10. Identify and describe the major retailing formats of Spain.
11. Profile the Pacific Rim.
12. Identify and describe the major retailing formats of Japan.
13. What are some of the factors the retailer should consider before going international?
14. List and define the five alternative strategies for entering a foreign market.

Review Exam

True or False

______ **1.** Because of the planning involved, state-planned command economies are more conducive to the expansion activities of retailers.

______ **2.** Retailers should support the separation of church and state; therefore, religious and faith issues of different nations are of no interest to the international retailer.

______ **3.** The North American Free Trade Agreement (NAFTA) is an exclusive trade pact between the United States and Canada.

______ **4.** The most populous and prosperous areas of Spain are the coastal tourist areas, the industrial areas of the northeast, and the urban areas of Madrid and Barcelona.

______ **5.** The Pacific Rim is composed of the countries of South Korea, Taiwan, Philippines, Hong Kong, Thailand, Malaysia, Singapore, Indonesia, Japan, and China.

______ **6.** Unlike the industrial sector, Japan has an open-door policy that encourages foreign retailers to establish retail businesses within the country.

Multiple Choice

______ **1.** International retailing activities are subject to several different legal systems. Which of the following systems is not cited in this chapter as having an impact on the activities of global retailers?
a. national laws
b. international laws
c. extraterrestrial
d. extraterritorial

______ **2.** A ______ is not one of the four general retailing formats that constitute the retailing industry of Argentina.
a. hypermarket
b. category killer
c. supermarket
d. self-service store
e. traditional shop

______ **3.** A list of the nations that have joined the European Community would include all of the following countries except ______.
a. Norway
b. Greece
c. Germany
d. Spain
e. the Netherlands

______ **4.** Department stores in Japan are classified into one of four categories. Which one does not represent one of the four categories?
a. city department stores
b. specialty department stores
c. train terminal department stores
d. suburban department stores
e. local department stores

______ **5.** The market entry agreement in which a retailer grants a foreign entity the right to an intangible property is called ______.
a. subsidiaries
b. joint ventures
c. licensing
d. franchising
e. contracting

Investigative Projects: Practice and Application

1. Conduct a library search of a country under a totalitarian form of government. Develop a list of characteristics that would appear to hinder foreign retail activities. Recommend actions that might overcome these limitations.
2. Develop a list of ten foreign cultural traits or practices that are notably different from how North Americans view the same issue. Describe how a retailer might accommodate each of these traits and practices and still ensure customer satisfaction.
3. Develop a set of strong arguments in support of the North American Free Trade Agreement (NAFTA), then develop one opposing it.
4. Conduct a comprehensive study of a foreign retailer operating within the Canadian market. What mistakes did the firm make? Why has it been successful? How has it had to adapt its retailing format to the Canadian consumer? Will it continue to be successful? Why?

Endnotes

1. Alan Farnham, "Global—Or Just Globaloney?" *Fortune*, June 27, 1994, 97.
2. Kim Howard, "Global Retailing 2000," *Business Credit* (February 1994): 22.
3. Willian E. Hatal, "Global Strategic Management in a New World Order," *Business Horizons* (November/December 1993): 5.
4. Larry R. Katzen, "Retailing—The Global Mandate," *Retailing Issues Letter* (copublished by the Center for Retailing Studies, Texas A&M University and Arthur Andersen, September 1993), 5.
5. Carla Rapoport, "Retailers Go Global," *Fortune*, February 20, 1995, 102.
6. See Jerry Flint, "One World, One Ford," *Forbes*, June 20, 1994, 40–41, and Jerry Flint, "You Know What's in My Heart," *Forbes*, February 13, 1995, 42–44.
7. Andrew Marshall Hamer, "Cashing in on China's Burgeoning Middle Class," *Marketing Management* 4 (Summer 1995): 9–22; and Amy Borrus and Joyce Barnathan, "China's Gates Swing Open," *Business Week*, June 13, 1994, 52–53.
8. See Tony Horwitz, "Europe's Borders Fade, and People and Goods Can Move More Freely," *Wall Street Journal*, May 18, 1993, A1, A10.
9. See Howard Schlossberg, "North American Marketers Await Trade Pact: Canadians Are Cautious, but Hopeful," *Marketing News*, May 10, 1993, 1, 17.
10. See Cyndee Miller, "North American Marketers Await Trade Pact: U.S. Companies Are Eager to Head South," *Marketing News*, May 10, 1993, 1, 10.
11. See "World Retailing Highlights," *International Trends in Retailing* (Arthur Andersen & Co., July 1995), 83–128.
12. Bob Davis, "One American," *Wall Street Journal*, September 24, 1992, R1.
13. *Ibid.*
14. Stephen Baker and Elizabeth Weiner, "Latin America—The Big Move to Free Markets," *Business Week*, June 15, 1992, 52.
15. *Ibid.*
16. Blayne Cutler, "North American Demographics," *American Demographics* (March 1992): 38.
17. See Geri Smith, "NAFTA: A Green Light for Red Tape," *Business Week*, July 25, 1994, 48; and Douglas Harbrecht, William C. Symonds, Elisabeth Markin, and Geri Smith, "What Has NAFTA Wrought? Plenty of Trade," *Business Week*, November 21, 1994, 48–49.
18. "Analysis of Retailing in Latin America," *International Trends in Retailing* (Arthur Andersen & Co., July 1995), 3.
19. Ignacio Galceran and Jon Berry, "A New World of Consumers," *American Demographics* (March 1995): 28.
20. U.S. Census Bureau Information.
21. John Heinzl, "Sporting Goods Departments in Final Innings," *Globe and Mail*, June 16, 1995, B1; Dawn Walton, "It's Dog Eat Dog in Pet Food," *Globe and Mail*, July 21, 1997, B1; Richard Wright, "Battle Plan for the Counter Attack," *Profit*, March 1994, 22–27.
22. Paul Waldie, "Canadai Retailers Warned—Shape Up or Face Extinction," *Globe and Mail*, May 17, 1995, B11; Sean Silcoff, "The Emporiums Strike Back," *Canadian Business*, September 26, 1997, 52.
23. United Nations Data, *Canadian Market Research Handbook*, 1995, Statistics Canada.
24. Canadian Press, "U.S. Parent Firms Pushing Retail Service," *Lethbridge Herald*, September 5, 1995, B4.
25. Arthur H. Good and Stephan Granovsky, *Business Review*, Summer 1995, 31–33.
26. John Heinzl, "Blumes Brothers Differ on Dylex Bio," *Globe and Mail*, August 30, 1997, B7; Mathew Ingram, "A Few Bricks Short," *Alberta Report*, September 25, 1989, 18.
27. Brian Hutchinson, "Merchants of Boom," *Canadian Business*, May 1997, 46; Matt Murray, "Wendy's to Bring Tim Hortons to U.S.," Globe and Mail, April 16, 1997, B10.
28. Henry W. Lane, Donald F. Hunter, and Terry Hildebrand, "How to Survive in U.S. Retail Markets," *Business Quarterly*, Winter 1990, 63.
29. *Ibid.*
30. Juan M. Gras and Walter Fraschetto, "Analysis of Retailing in Mexico," *International Trends in Retailing* (Arthur Andersen & Co. Summer 1993), 9.
31. See Joan Rothman, "The New Sexenio," *Marketing Management* 3 (Spring 1995): 41–48.

32. Matt Moffett, "U.S. Firms Yell Olé to Future in Mexico," *Wall Street Journal*, March 8, 1993, B1.

33. See Geri Smith, Stanley Reed, and Elisabeth Malkin, "Mexico: A Rough Road Back," *Business Week*, November 13, 1995, 104–7.

34. Rapoport, "Retailers Go Global," 103.

35. "Mexico: Peso Devaluation Forces Global Retailers to Stall Plans," *Cooper & Lybrand's Global Powers of Retailing*, published in Chain Store Age, December 1995, 32–34.

36. This discussion of Argentina is drawn largely from Benjamin G. Harriague, "Argentina's Outlook Strong: GNP Up 33%, Retailing 40% Since 1991 Convertibility Plan," *International Trends in Retailing*, (Arthur Andersen & Co., July 1995), 9–13; and Benjamin G. Harriague, Roger Ingold, Mario Olimpio Pontes, and Luis A. Tredicce, "Analysis of Retailing in Brazil and Argentina," *International Trends in Retailing*, (Arthur Andersen & Co., Fall 1990), 3–21.

37. Mike Galetto, "Wal-Mart's Argentine Rivals Cry Foul," *Advertising Age*, September 4, 1995, 11.

38. See David Walters and Derek Knee, "Retailing Strategy: A European Perspective," *International Trends in Retailing* (Arthur Andersen & Co., Fall 1989), 45–56.

39. Madhav P. Kacker, "The Internationalization of European Retailing: Diverse Approaches and Emerging Trends," *Retailing: Reflections, Insights, and Forecasts*, ed. Robert L. King (Richmond, VA: Academy of Marketing Science, 1991), 192.

40. This discussion of the United Kingdom is drawn largely from "United Kingdom: The Cost of Entry Is High but Profit Margins Are Too," Coopers & Lybrand's Global Powers of Retailing, Published in *Chain Store Age* (December 1995): 20–22; and Mark Aston and Richard Wildman, "Analysis of Retailing in the United Kingdom," *International Trends in Retailing* (Arthur Andersen & Co., Spring 1990), 3–14.

41. Kevin Helliker, "Harrods: Grandeur Comes at Grand Cost," *The Wall Street Journal*, December 1, 1993, B1, B6.

42. See Alan G. Hallsworth and John McClatchey, "Interpreting the Growth of Superstore Retailing in Britain," *The International Review of Retail, Distribution and Consumer Research* (July 1994): 315–28; and Steve Burt and Leigh Sparks, "Structural Change in Grocery Retailing in Great Britain: A Discount Reorientation," *The International Review of Retail, Distribution, and Consumer Research* (April 1994): 195–218.

43. See Kevin Helliker, "U.S. Discount Retailers Are Targeting Europe and Its Fat Margins," *The Wall Street Journal*, September 20, 1993, A1, A7.

44. This discussion of German retailing is drawn from George Virnich and Martin Muser, "Analysis of Retailing in Germany," *International Trends in Retailing* (Arthur Andersen & Co., Spring 1991), 5–30. Also see Peter C. Bontinck and Alexander Strempel, "Analysis of Retailing in Germany," *International Trends in Retailing* (Arthur Andersen & Co., Fall 1986), 3–14.

45. "Germany Juggles Ups and Downs of Reunification," in Coopers & Lybrand, Global Powers of Retailing, published in *Chain Store Age* (December 1995): 17.

46. *Ibid*, 19.

47. This discussion of Spanish retailing is drawn largely from Javier del Barrio, Alfonso Gonzalez, and Marian Lopez, "An Analysis of Retailing in Spain," *International Trends in Retailing* (Arthur Andersen & Co., Fall 1989), 3–16.

48. Carmen Sierra, "World Retailing Highlights, Spain," *International Trends in Retailing* (Arthur Andersen & Co., July 1995), 116–17.

49. See Gareth A. Jones, "The Changing Retail Environment in Spain: Restructuring in Madrid," *The International Review of Retail, Distribution, and Consumer Research* (October 1994): 369–92.

50. del Barrio, Gonzalez and Lopez, "An Analysis of Retailing in Spain," 3.

51. Urban C. Lehner, "Belief in an Imminent Asian Century Is Gaining Sway," *Wall Street Journal*, May 17, 1993, A12.

52. David Hage, "Caught in the Undertow," *U.S. News & World Report*, May 17, 1993, 61.

53. Suzanne Costas, "The Ties that Bind," *Worth* (February 1993): 134.

54. Bill Powell, "Japan's Quality Quandary," *Newsweek*, June 15, 1992, 48.

55. Karen Lowry Miller, "You Just Can't Talk to These Kids," *Business Week*, April 19, 1993, 104, 106.

56. Yumiko Ono, "As Discounting Rises in Japan, People Learn to Hunt for Bargains," *The Wall Street Journal*, December 31, 1993, A1.

57. See Larry Holyoke, "What? Everyday Bargains? This Can't Be Japan," *Business Week*, September 6, 1993; and Tumiko Ono, "Japanese Department Stores Fall from 1980s Heyday," *Wall Street Journal*, February 9, 1993, B4.

58. Arieh Goldman, "Evaluating the Performance of the Japanese Distribution System," *Journal of Retailing*, 68 (Spring 1992): 12.

59. Goldman, "Evaluating the Performance," 15. Also see Kathleen Morris, "Adam Smith in Tokyo," *Financial World*, January 4, 1994, 22–24.

60. Arieh Goldman, "Japan's Distribution System: Institutional Structure, Internal Political Economy, and Modernization," *Journal of Retailing*, 67 (Summer 1991): 161–62.

61. Emily Thornton, "Revolution in Japanese Retailing," *Fortune*, February 7, 1994, 146.

62. Ono, "Japanese Department Stores," B4.

63. Shunroku Nishimura and Masaru Yokawa, "Analysis of Retailing in Japan," *International Trends in Retailing* (Arthur Andersen & Co., Fall 1991), 9.

64. Stanley Marcus and Larry R. Katzen, "Contrasts and Similarities: Department Store Retailing in Japan and the U.S." *International Trends in Retailing*, (Arthur Andersen & Co. Fall 1992), 43.

65. See Gale Eisenstodt, "Bull in the Japan Shop," *Forbes*, January 31, 1994, 41–42; and Larry Holyoko, "A Bargain Basement Called Japan," *Business Week*, June 27, 1994, 42–43.

66. Gale Eisenstodt, "In Step," *Forbes*, October 26, 1992, 50.

67. Brian Bremner, " 'Made in America' Isn't the Kiss of Death Anymore," *Business Week*, November 13, 1995.

68. See Ronald Henkoff, "New Management Secrets From Japan—Really," *Fortune*, November 27, 1995, 136; and Gale Eisenstodt, "Information Power," *Forbes*, June 21, 1993, 44–45.

69. "Japan: Value and Convenience Driving Retail," Cooper & Lybrand's Global Powers of Retailing, published in *Chain Store Age* (December 1995): 15.

70. Louis Kraar, "The New Power in Asia," *Fortune*, October 31, 1994, 80–88.

71. Hamer, "Cashing in on China's Burgeoning Middle Class," 9.

72. See Amy Borrus and Joyce Barnathan, "China's Gates Swing Open," *Business Week*, June 13, 1994, 52–53; and Andrew Tanzer, "The Bamboo Network," *Forbes*, July 18, 1994, 138–44.

73. Hamer, "Cashing in on China's Burgeoning Middle Class," 18.

74. Janet Zhang, "Asia: Opportunities Large and Small," Coopers & Lybrand's Assignment Asia, published in *Chain Store Age* (January 1995): 7.

75. See Luca Pellegrini, "Alternative for Growth and Internationalization in Retailing," *The International Retail, Distribution, and Consumer Research* (April 1994): 121–48.

Video Case for Part 8

Magicuts—Premier Salons International Inc.

Brian Luborsky started out his business career as a chartered accountant with Coopers & Lybrand. It didn't take long for him to realize, however, that he wanted to be part of something more growth-oriented and which allowed him to be more entrepreneurial. He still remembers the day he decided to quit. His boss wanted him to write a memo, but Luborsky, who was building and buying houses on the side, was working to save $50 000 on a property to buy. "The deal was worth more than my annual salary," he laughs, "I wasn't doing myself any favours and I wasn't being fair to the company, so I resigned."

Meanwhile he became interested in a new hair salon franchise called Magicuts. Magicuts had been established in 1981 as a discount haircut chain which attempted to bring the McDonald's efficiency principles to hair salons. Luborsky joined Magicuts as a franchisee, purchasing four franchises in 1984. What lured him was the math. "There is such a high ratio of sales to assets in hair-cutting it was hard to go wrong," he says. "Say it costs $50 000 to set up shop. I can do $250 000 in sales in a year out of that store. Now, say I make 10 percent on that: I'm getting a 50 percent return on investment, and that's hard to beat."

With those returns, Luborsky began buying up other franchises. By 1988 he owned all 26 franchises, and following a disagreement between the company's original three principals, Luborsky was asked to become president. He took a minority stake in Magicuts and ran it as president for two years. He bought the rest of the Markham, Ontario-based firm in 1990.

In 1993 Luborsky considered expansion to the United States. He realized the difficulties that Canadian retailers had experienced south of the border but felt with the right approach he could be successful. He became aware of a chain of hair salons which he felt could fit in with the system which he had developed for Magicuts. After difficult negotiations for financing, he was successful in acquiring a large financially troubled Minneapolis-based chain of hair salons—MEI Salons. MEI had 1600 outlets, three times as many as Magicuts, but was in need of financial and management stability which Luborsky could provide.

The success of Premier Salons is evidenced by the fact that the company now has 400 Canadian shops and 650 in the United States. Sales have topped $250 million and Premier now employs over 7000 people. This growth earned Premier the title of fastest growing Canadian company in 1995.

Luborsky's goal for growth is now centred in three areas. First he wants to continue to emphasize superior service in order to compete with the independent mom-and-pop salons which dominate the industry. Because of the size of the company, it can take advantage of economies of scale, and this allows investment in employees. As a result, Premier has invested heavily in extensive employee training. Premier's 76 trainers teach the latest styles and trends, as well as soft skills such as dealing with clients. His second push involves "partnerships" with well-known retailers, most of which are department stores. Magicuts is now installed in more than 100 Zellers stores. "The price fits well with our customers," says

Zeller's Vice-President Garnet Kinch. Luborsky's third growth strategy is to seek out compatible chains and purchase them, similar to what occurred with MEI. Recently, Premier purchased 22 Boscov's salons in Pennsylvania.

Questions:

1. Discuss Luborsky's attempt to standardize the quality of a personal service like hair dressing.
2. Discuss the advantages of franchising compared to company-owned stores in this industry.
3. Evaluate the approach which Luborsky took in expanding into the U.S. market. Why might the hair salon business have better prospects for success in the U.S. than tangible goods retailing? What other potential problems might Luborsky face with such expansion?

Source: "Magicuts," Venture *548 (July 9, 1995; 10:05).*

Figure A–3

Values and beliefs audit

Value/Belief	Rating Scale: Very important	Important	Not important
Directions: Values are core beliefs that shape one's attitudes and guide one's actions. Rate the following values and beliefs in terms of how important they are to you. Check the response that best describes your importance rating. Values and beliefs are important because they have a great deal to do with one's character. Hence, employers are very interested in assessing the values and beliefs of potential employees. Employers are interested in knowing what values are important to you, why they are important, how you live by these values, and what impact these values will have on your work life.			
Achievement	____	____	____
Ambition	____	____	____
Altruism	____	____	____
Autonomy	____	____	____
Courage	____	____	____
Creativity	____	____	____
Equality	____	____	____
Freedom	____	____	____
Happiness	____	____	____
Harmony	____	____	____
Honesty	____	____	____
Imagination	____	____	____
Independence	____	____	____
Justice	____	____	____
Knowledge	____	____	____
Logic	____	____	____
Love	____	____	____
Loyalty	____	____	____
Morality	____	____	____
Physical Appearance	____	____	____
Pleasure	____	____	____
Power	____	____	____
Recognition	____	____	____
Religious Faith	____	____	____
Wealth	____	____	____
Wellness	____	____	____

Figure A–4

A job attributes audit

Directions: Review the following list of job attributes and characteristics and rate each in terms of its degree of importance to you as a decision variable in comparing and evaluating job opportunities. Those attributes you designated as essential, very important, or desirable will make up the key inputs in developing one or more ideal job descriptions. This exercise should provide you with a fairly good idea of what your job preferences are in terms of finding and obtaining a satisfactory position with a firm or organization that is suited to your needs. Use the following scale in rating each job attribute or characteristic.

1. Essential
2. Very Important
3. Desirable
4. Somewhat Important
5. Not Important

Figure A–4 (continued)

_____ Privacy—the opportunity to work independently and with little contact with other people.

_____ Security—The level of certainty of retaining a job or finding a similar one; the longevity associated with a particular job in a particular firm or an industry.

_____ Responsibility—The chance to assume responsibility for set policy and determining course of action.

_____ Competition—The opportunity to pit one's skills and capabilities against others in the pursuit of a goal or an objective.

_____ Creativity—The prospect of using one's own creative skills and talents in meeting the challenges of the job.

_____ Work Aesthetics—The quality of the environment(s) within which one must work; the physical atmospherics of the office, store, or other workplace.

_____ Supervision—The type and level of supervision under which the job's requirements are accomplished. The nature of the organizational chart (that is, vertical or flat) under which the job falls.

_____ Recognition—The manner in which good job performance is acknowledged and appreciated.

_____ Compensation—The manner and forms in which good job performance is rewarded (salary, benefits, and perks).

_____ Velocity—The pace or tempo at which the job must be performed.

_____ Stress—The level of anxiety and tension under which the job is performed.

_____ Variety—The diversity of tasks associated with performing the job.

_____ Authority—The level of authority to accomplish the responsibilities associated with the job.

_____ Specialization—The number of different tasks to be completed in order to successfully complete the job.

_____ Unity of Command—The number of supervisors that one will report to.

_____ Independence—The degree of freedom one has in completing the responsibilities associated with a job.

_____ Morality—The ethical nature of the job and the absence of any unethical or questionable responsibilities.

_____ Geography—The location of the job relative to various parts of the country.

_____ Location—The place where the majority of the job takes place; inside (office) or outside (field) the workplace.

_____ Physical Requirements—The level of physical strength required to successfully handle the job.

_____ Temporality—The freedom of setting and maintaining one's own work schedule.

_____ Status—The relative perceived position of the job within the hierarchy of positions (for example, titles, power, influence).

_____ Affiliation—The desirability of being associated with a particular profession, firm, or group.

_____ Relationships—The opportunity to build close work relationships, develop friendships, and work with people.

_____ Stability—Have regular and predictable job responsibilities and assignments.

_____ Contribution—The opportunity to help others and to contribute to society.

_____ Seniority—The ability to build up security and privileges with years of service.

_____ Proximity—The desirability of being close to family, and friends.

Step 1: Listing Employment Criteria. In the initial stages of an employment search, you must determine the general conditions under which you are willing to accept a job, that is, your **employment criteria**. Although the particulars of any job (for example, salary) are determined during actual employment negotiation, you may have certain preconditions regarding employment. Common preconditions involve location, organization, and position. For personal, professional, and many other reasons, you may prefer or need to work in a particular part of the country or certain province or city. You should also list any preconditions regarding the kind of organization for which you are willing to work. Representative organizational preconditions might include the size of the firm, the type of organization (for example, independent versus chain organization), and nature of the operation (for example, department, specialty, or discount organization). Finally, you should include a list of any preconditions regarding positions you are willing or unwilling to accept. For example, you should consider your interest (or lack of interest) in accepting a position in such areas as merchandising, operations management, sales promotion, or personnel.

Step 2: Ranking Employment Criteria. Not all the criteria identified in step 1 will necessarily be equally important to you. Step 2 of the prospective employer identification process requires that you rank each of the employment criteria according to importance. You may judge some criteria extremely important or essential (for example, for family reasons you must find a job in the Toronto area); others might be preferences but not absolutely essential (for example, you prefer to work in the merchandising area for a large department store). Finally, you might view other criteria as not important but a definite plus (for example, the opportunity to work in a particular merchandising department, say, women's apparel). By ranking employment criteria, you develop a concrete means of judging employment opportunities.

Step 3: Scaling Employment Preferences. The third step in identifying prospective employers is to develop a preference scale of employment opportunities. This step requires developing general job descriptions for first, second, and third preference levels. For example, your most preferred job description might be an assistant manager of a women's apparel department in a major Toronto department store, preferably somewhere in the northwest part of the city. On the other end of the scale your least preferred job description might be the same type of job in an out-of-town location. After you have developed two or three general job descriptions for each preference level, you will be ready for the final stage of your employer identification process.

Step 4: Matching Job Preferences with Prospective Employers. Now that you have listed, ranked, and scaled your preferences, the final step in the employer identification process is to match those preferences with prospective employers. The matching process consists of compiling a list of jobs and screening that list of prospective employers according to your scaled preferences.

It will be to your benefit to explore all possible sources in compiling a **jobs list**. The campus placement office is a logical starting point, as it represents one of the most fruitful sources for good leads for potential employment. It also provides some services (for example, setting up personal interviews) that can greatly facilitate your employment search process. By checking with your placement office frequently and regularly, you will be able to keep your jobs list updated. You also need to systematically check the employment sections of local and national newspapers as well as trade and professional journals, magazines, and newspapers. Commercial employment agencies are still another source. Before making any commitments to one of these agencies, however, be sure you fully understand what services they provide and under what conditions and terms. You can obtain additional job leads by sending inquiries to the personnel departments of retail firms you believe have the potential to offer the kind of employment you desire. Finally, some of the best leads to employment opportunities come through personal contacts. Professors, friends, relatives, and social and professional acquaintances often provide an inside track to opportunities.

Screening a jobs list is a fairly routine procedure if you have carefully completed the previous step in the employment search process—scaling employment preferences. Jobs list screening involves (1) reducing your jobs list to employment opportunities that meet your minimum requirements for employment and then (2) rank-ordering the remaining jobs on the list according to your preferences. This screening results in a list of available and acceptable employment opportunities rank-ordered from most to least desirable.

Obtaining a Personal Interview Personal interviews are a way for retailers to question and observe job applicants in a face-to-face situation. Most retailers consider interviews essential to hiring. One short interview with the store's personnel manager is usually all that is necessary for lower-echelon positions. By contacting the personnel department and completing an application form, qualified applicants normally will be granted a personal interview.

The **personal interview process** for most managerial positions is much more involved. Typically, it involves a series of personal interviews with various managers at different levels. Although it is necessary to be successful at each of these interviews, getting the initial interview is the most crucial step because without it nothing else happens. Obtaining the initial interview can be quite simple or extremely difficult. The method you use to get the first interview depends on the circumstances surrounding the job (for example, type and level of the position) and the firm's employment practices (for example, where and how they recruit). There are several methods for obtaining the initial interview with retailing firms. They include (1) obtaining an on-campus interview schedule from the school placement office and scheduling an interview through that office, (2) contacting the store's personnel office and making arrangements for the initial interview, (3) asking personal contacts to set up a personal interview, and (4) writing brief letters and making telephone calls and personal visits to one or more of the firm's managers to discuss possible employment opportunities.

Preparing for a Personal Interview Lack of preparation is perhaps the most common error applicants make in the personal interview process. It is foolish for anyone to spend several years in college preparing for a career and then fail to spend several hours preparing for the key interview that could very well launch a career with the right firm. Preparing for a personal interview involves getting to know something about the firm interviewing you and helping the firm in its efforts to get to know you.

Before the interview, you should do some research on the firm. Your ability to talk knowledgeably about the firm and its activities will pay substantial dividends during the actual interview. Preparation will not only make a favourable impression on the interviewer but will also enable you to answer and ask meaningful questions. Your information search on the firm should help you discuss the firm's organizational structure, market positions, merchandising strategies, financial positions, and future prospects. Examining various trade magazines, industrial directories, and other reference books can provide a good general picture of the firm and its operations.

To help the firm get to know you, you will need to prepare a résumé, which should include (1) a brief statement of personal data (for example, name, address, and telephone number); (2) a brief outline of educational experience (that is, type of degree, name of school, date of graduation, major and minor fields of study, class ranking, scholarships, honours, awards, and extracurricular activities); (3) a short history of work experience (that is, a list of jobs, positions and responsibilities, names of employers, and dates of employment); and (4) a summary of other activities, interests, and skills that support your professional credentials. Also, you might wish to include a list of references and a short statement of your career objectives. In preparing a résumé, the following guidelines are helpful:

1. Be concise. The purpose of a résumé is to stimulate the interviewer's interest, not to tell your life story. A one-page résumé is sufficient to create this interest. If interviewers want to know more, they will ask for more information and clarification.
2. Be factual. Experienced interviewers will recognize résumé "puffery" and generally take a dim view of it. A statement of a few real accomplishments is received much more favourably than a list of artificial ones.
3. Be professional. A well-organized, neatly produced résumé is an excellent "scene setter" for your personal interview. A poorly organized résumé with confusing layout, typographical errors, misspellings, and blurred or messy photocopying make a definite statement about your abilities to organize and produce good work.

As a final note, you must recognize that it is your responsibility to establish and verify the time and place for each interview. Missing or being late to an interview is rarely excusable, regardless of the reason. You should therefore plan for unforeseen delays to ensure getting to your interview on time.

Taking a Personal Interview The interview situation varies according to the interviewer's personal preferences. Some interview situations are conducted formally in a structured question-and-answer format. Other interview situations are informal, conducted without any apparent structure. Figure A–5 outlines the typical stages and topics of an initial interview. Whether the interview is formal or informal, your ability to read the interview situation and react accordingly will determine your success. All interviews, formal or informal, usually have four parts, with parts 2 and 3 being the most important: (1) rapport building—a few minutes of chit-chat to open the interview; (2) questions and answers—information exchange; (3) the sell—applicant outlines what he or she can do for the retailer while the retailer explains the opportunities available with the organization; and (4) the close—each party, if favourably impressed, tries to end the interview on a positive note.[8] No absolute rules apply in taking a personal interview, but the guidelines that follow are useful in most situations.

Dress Appropriately. The job or position for which you are interviewing will provide you with cues on how to dress. Do not overdress or underdress for the occasion.

Be Prepared for Openers. Many interviewers like to open their interviews with broad questions such as "What do you expect out of life?" "Why do you want to work for our firm?" "Where do you want to be in your career ten years from now?" "What do you think you can do for our company?"

Be Relaxed. Interviewers expect a reasonable amount of nervousness; however, excessive

Figure A–5

Stages and topics covered during the initial interview

Source: Peterson's Business and Management Jobs 1985, *© 1984 by Peterson's Guides, Inc., P.O. Box 2123, Princeton, NJ 08540. Current edition available at bookstores or direct from the publisher.*

Stages	Interviewer topics	Interviewer looks for
1. First impressions	Introduction and greeting Small talk about traffic conditions, the weather, the record of the basketball team	Firm handshake, eye contact Appearance and dress appropriate to the business, not campus, setting
2. Your record	*Education* Reasons for choice of school and major Grades, effort required for them Special areas of interest Courses enjoyed most and least, reasons Special achievements, toughest problems Value of education as career preparation Reaction to teachers *Work Experience* Nature of jobs held Why undertaken Level of responsibility reached Duties liked most and least Supervisory experience Relations with others *Activities and Interests* Role in extracurricular, athletic, community, and social service activities Personal interests—hobbies, cultural interests, sports	Intellectual abilities Breadth and depth of knowledge Relevance of course work to career interests Special or general interest Value placed on achievement Willingness to work hard Relation between ability and achievement Reaction to authority Ability to cope with problems Sensible use of resources (time, energy, money) High energy level, vitality, enthusiasm Leadership ability, interest in responsibility Willingness to follow directions Ability to get along with others Seriousness of purpose Ability to motivate oneself, to make things happen Positive "can do" attitude Diversity of interests Awareness of world outside the laboratory Social conscience; good citizenship
3. Your career goals	Type of work desired Immediate objectives Long-term objectives Interest in this company Other companies being considered Desire for further education/training Geographical preferences and limitations Attitude toward relocation	Realistic knowledge of strengths and weaknesses Preparation for employment Knowledge of opportunities Seriousness of purpose, career-oriented rather than job-oriented Knowledge of the company Real interest in the company Work interest in line with talents Company's chance to get and keep you
4. The company	Company opportunities Where you might fit Current and future projects Major divisions and departments Training programs, educational and other benefits.	Informed and relevant questions Indications of interest in answers Appropriate but not undue interest in salary or benefits

Figure A–5 (continued)

5. Conclusion	Further steps you should take (application form, transcript, references) Further steps company will take, outline how application handled, to which departments it will be sent, time of notification of decision Cordial farewell	Candidate's attention to information as a sign of continued interest

nervousness may well suggest to the interviewer that you are unable to handle pressure situations. Avoid nervous gestures. On the other hand, avoid appearing so relaxed or laid-back that you give the impression of being disinterested in the interview or the job.

Listen Carefully. Let the interviewer guide the interview, at least during the initial stages. Interviewers provide cues as to how they want to conduct the interview and what they want to talk about. Also, by listening carefully, you will be able to understand fully the nature of the questions thus give better responses.

Ask Questions. If you want a job with the interviewer's company, you should be able to show your interest by asking intelligent questions about the firm.

Be Informative. Answer the interviewer's questions fully and quickly but avoid talking too much or too fast. Most of the interviewer's questions will require more than a yes or no answer; however, you should avoid telling your life story, boasting about your accomplishments, and complaining about your problems.

Be Somewhat Aggressive. It is better to be perceived as a little too aggressive rather than too passive. In terms of aggressiveness, the right impression to portray might be that you are a "mover" but not a "shaker."

Be Honest. Answer questions as truthfully as you can. Interviewers recognize that everyone has strengths and weaknesses. Frankly admitting a weakness adds credibility to the statements you make about your strengths. Admitting a weakness also makes you appear more trustworthy to the interviewer.

Following these guidelines greatly improves one's chances for a successful interview. One last point: If you can make the interviewer feel comfortable and at ease, then you have gone a long way toward getting a second interview and possibly a position with that company. To improve your interviewing skills, you should evaluate your performance after each interview. Figure A–6 provides a series of criteria and a means of evaluating interview performance.

The final stage in the job search process is the evaluation of job offers. Those individuals who have carefully conducted both a life audit and a career audit are in the best position to evaluate job opportunities relative to their unique needs, aspirations, and capabilities. To facilitate your analysis of job offers, Figure A–7 provides a fairly detailed methodology.

Ownership Opportunities

Regardless of their income, many people who work for others feel they are living a hand-to-mouth, paycheque-to-paycheque existence. According to one old adage, the only way to get ahead is to get other people to work for you or to get money working for you—the idea is that income and perhaps job satisfaction are limited when you work for someone else. They tend to believe that (1) the best bureaucrats, not the best performers get ahead, (2) it is too easy to get pigeonholed or stuck in a dead-end job with no way out, (3) it takes too long to get enough responsibility, authority, and reward, (4) there is not enough flexibility about where and when you work, and (5) top managers do not really want or reward risk takers and self-starters.[9] Hence, many would-be retailers want to be in a situation in which their growth is limited only by their own talent, energy, and ambition—and that usually means an entrepreneurial situation.[10] Many people find that self-employment is the answer to a better income, greater independence, a more rewarding career, and an improved lifestyle. Many people think that going into business for themselves is the only way they can fully realize their hopes and aspirations. To have a chance at realizing their

Figure A–6

Assessment of personal interview performance

Rating Scale			
+	−	0	Evaluation Criteria

Directions: Practice and evaluation are essential if you are to improve your interview style. The use of mock interviews and the taking of actual interviews will provide necessary interviewing experience. One of the most effective means of improving your interviewing skills is to videotape one or more of your interviews and review the tapes with a professor, an interviewer, or a human resource manager. After each interview, it is instructive to review your performance with others as well as to conduct a self-evaluation of your performance. The following checklist should assist you in conducting such an analysis. Rate your performance on each of the relevant criteria as either positive, negative, or neutral.

Interview Date: ____________________

Position: ____________________

Company: ____________________

Interviewer: ____________________

+	−	0	Evaluation Criteria
____	____	____	Adjusted well to the physical environment of the interview room and facilities.
____	____	____	Executed an effective introduction (smile, handshake, greeting).
____	____	____	Used good nonverbal body language.
____	____	____	Respected the interviewer's personal space.
____	____	____	Acted calm and relaxed yet interested and attentive.
____	____	____	Showed good listening skills by providing relevant answers and asking appropriate questions.
____	____	____	Answered the actual questions and did not give evasive answers.
____	____	____	Avoided answering questions with only a yes or no answer.
____	____	____	Avoided any negative comments and used positive language when answering questions or describing experiences.
____	____	____	Spoke in unruffled voice with the right volume.
____	____	____	Used action words in answering questions and describing experiences.
____	____	____	Used the interviewer's name several times during the interview.
____	____	____	Dressed appropriately for the interview situation.
____	____	____	Presented achievements effectively without appearing to be bragging.
____	____	____	Presented skills and abilities effectively by relating them to the employer's needs and the duties of the position.
____	____	____	Communicated personal values and beliefs by demonstrating how they would affect job performance in a positive manner.
____	____	____	Provided proof of skills and abilities by citing appropriate examples of previous experiences.
____	____	____	Used good grammar throughout the entire interview.
____	____	____	Demonstrated good preparation for interview by using company facts in answering and asking questions.
____	____	____	Focused on the employer's needs and how those needs can be met.

Figure A–6 (continued)

____	____	____	Avoided inappropriate questions, answers, impressions, or actions.
____	____	____	Expressed interest in the position, the company, and the industry.
____	____	____	Attempted closure by asking for some type of commitment, response, or future contact.
____	____	____	TOTAL RESPONSES

Figure A–7

Analysis of job offer

Directions: The final stage in the job search process is the evaluation of job offers. In analyzing any job offer in the very dynamic work environment of today, you need to be equally concerned with how each job affects you now and in the future. A position that offers you security today may not prepare you for future employment opportunities. Employment experts estimate that most of you will have to change jobs and companies six to ten times during your career. Hence, the job you get today must help you prepare for tomorrow's job opportunities. The work component of your life involves a very significant commitment of your total lifetime. Working fifty hours a week for forty years at an occupation and in a job that is unrewarding is not a very pleasant prospect. Analyze and select job offers with extreme care. One effective and efficient means of evaluating job offers is to develop a weighted-rating score for each identified job offer. The process involves the following five steps:

1. From the list below, select those evaluation criteria that you consider to be relevant in defining a good job. To ensure the comparability among offers, use the same list of criteria for job evaluations.
2. Rate each job offer with respect to your selected evaluation criteria by using the following rating scale to express the degree of acceptability of the job offer with respect to your selective list of evaluation criteria:

   3. Very Acceptable
   2. Acceptable
   1. Marginally Acceptable
   0. Unacceptable

3. Not all evaluation criteria you selected are equally important to you when evaluating a job offer. Express your assessment of the relative degree of importance of each job evaluation criterion selected by using the following scale:

   3. Very Important
   2. Important
   1. Marginally Important
   0. Unimportant

4. Calculate weighted-rated score for each evaluation criterion by multiplying the weight by the rating.
5. Determine a composite weighted-rate score for a job offer by summing the individual weighted-rate scores for all evaluation criteria. This value will provide a fairly objective measurement of a highly subjective problem and enable you to effectively evaluate a single job offer or to compare two offers of two or more firms.

Figure A–7 (continued)

Job Identification: ____________________
Position: ____________________
Company: ____________________
Offer: (terms/ conditions of employment) ____________________

Job Evaluation:

Rating	Weight	Score	
____	____	____	Position is compatible with and supportive of my chosen career path.
____	____	____	Position is consistent with my short-term career objectives.
____	____	____	Position will support and help in advancing my long-term career goals and aspirations.
____	____	____	Position responsibilities and duties are clearly defined.
____	____	____	Position responsibilities and duties are manageable with my current skill levels.
____	____	____	Position responsibilities and duties are interesting, challenging, and exciting.
____	____	____	Position responsibilities and duties are consistent with my values and beliefs.
____	____	____	Position responsibilities and duties allow sufficient freedom to use my own creative skills and talents.
____	____	____	Position involves the type of work experiences that will allow me to use and enhance my current skills.
____	____	____	Position offers good opportunities to develop new skills and abilities.
____	____	____	Company provides good opportunities for additional formal training and professional development.
____	____	____	Company encourages the pursuit of advanced degrees and offers financial support.
____	____	____	Organizational culture is consistent with my personality.
____	____	____	Management style will enable me to succeed and advance.
____	____	____	Performance expectations are clearly defined and measurable.
____	____	____	Performance expectations are both reasonable and attainable.
____	____	____	Reward and recognition structures are clearly defined.
____	____	____	Reward and recognition structures are fair and equitable.
____	____	____	Benefits package is adequate and appropriate for the position.
____	____	____	Position comes with meaningful perks (car, office, computers, travel expenses, and so on).
____	____	____	Position provides opportunities for advancement.
____	____	____	Type and degree of supervision seems appropriate; provides guidance but permits freedom and creativity.
____	____	____	Position offers an acceptable level of job security.
____	____	____	Work environments (facilities) are pleasant and conducive to good productivity.
____	____	____	Job location meets my professional, personal, and family needs.
____	____	____	Industry growth prospects within which the company operates appear to be promising.
____	____	____	Company has a strong market position within its industry.
____	____	____	Company has a strong reputation and image within its industry.

Figure A–7 (continued)

____	____	____	Company size is within my preference range.
____	____	____	Company growth aspects appear to be promising.
____	____	____	Position is considered to be an essential element of the firm's operations.
		____	COMPOSITE WEIGHTED-RATE SCORE

Job Ranking:
This job ranks ____ out of ____ job offers.

Job Decision:
____ Job is acceptable, accept offer
____ Job is acceptable, stall offer
____ Job is unacceptable, reject offer

personal, career, and life goals, these individuals are willing to assume the considerable burdens and risks of owning and operating their own businesses.[11]

The preceding chapters fully discuss the factors necessary for a successful retail operation. With that background in mind, consider whether you are the kind of person who could succeed as an independent retailer. To help assess this possibility, take the self-evaluation test in Figure A–8; it should give you some insight into whether you have the personal attributes to become an independent retailer.

If, after taking the self-evaluation test, you decide that you do have what it takes to be an independent retailer, three options are open to you: (1) starting a new business, (2) buying an existing business, or (3) obtaining a franchise. Each option has its advantages and disadvantages that you should fully explore. Figure A–9 compares issues surrounding the decision to start a new business or buy an existing one. The principal concerns associated with obtaining a franchise are outlined in Figure A–10. In addition to the host of merchandising and operating practices discussed previously in this text, studies have shown that there are critical success factors for smaller retail operations that enable them to compete effectively against retail chains. The most commonly cited success factors include the following:

1. A dedication to customer service and a drive to build close customer relationships,
2. An expertise in, and enthusiasm for, the goods and services offered by the business,
3. A sense of social responsibility and community spirit,
4. A hands-on management style and a genuine respect for the well-being of its employees, and
5. A unique merchandising idea and a sense of retail theatre.[12]

To achieve success in today's value-based market, small retail operations must be able to clearly differentiate and position themselves as a unique market offering based on some combination of these critical success factors.[13]

Figure A–8

Do you have what it takes to be an independent retailer?

Source: Checklist for Going into Business, *Small Marketers Aids No. 71 (Washington, D.C.: Small Business Administration, October 1976), 4–5.*

Under each question, check the answer that says what you feel or comes closest to it. Be honest with yourself.

Are you a self-starter?
- ❑ I do things on my own. Nobody has to tell me to get going.
- ❑ If someone gets me started, I keep going all right.
- ❑ Easy does it, man. I don't put myself out until I have to.

How do you feel about other people?
- ❑ I like people. I can get along with just about anybody.
- ❑ I have plenty of friends—I don't need anyone else.
- ❑ Most people bug me.

Figure A–8 (continued)

Can you lead others?
- ❑ I can get most people to go along when I start something.
- ❑ I can give the orders if someone tells me what we should do.
- ❑ I let someone else get things moving. Then I go along if I feel like it.

Can you take responsibility?
- ❑ I like to take charge of things and see them through.
- ❑ I'll take over if I have to, but I'd rather let someone else be responsible.
- ❑ There's always some eager beaver around wanting to show how smart he is. I say let them.

How good an organizer are you?
- ❑ I like to have a plan before I start. I'm usually the one to get things lined up when the gang wants to do something.
- ❑ I do all right unless things get too goofed up. Then I cop out.
- ❑ You get all set and then something comes along and blows the whole bag. So I just take things as they come.

How good a worker are you?
- ❑ I can keep going as long as I need to. I don't mind working hard for something I want.
- ❑ I'll work hard for a while, but when I've had enough, that's it, man!
- ❑ I can't see that hard work gets you anywhere.

Can you make decisions?
- ❑ I can make up my mind in a hurry if I have to. It usually turns out okay, too.
- ❑ I can if I have plenty of time. If I have to make up my mind fast, I think later I should have decided the other way.
- ❑ I don't like to be the one who has to decide things. I'd probably blow it.

Can people trust what you say?
- ❑ You bet they can. I don't say things I don't mean.
- ❑ I try to be on the level most of the time, but sometimes I just say what's easiest.
- ❑ What's the sweat if the other fellow doesn't know the difference?

Can you stick with it?
- ❑ If I make up my mind to do something, I don't let *anything* stop me.
- ❑ I usually finish what I start—if it doesn't get fouled up.
- ❑ If it doesn't go right away, I turn off. Why beat your brains out?

How good is your health?
- ❑ Man, I *never* run down!
- ❑ I have enough energy for most things I want to do.
- ❑ I run out of juice sooner than most of my friends seem to.

Now count the checks you made.

How many checks are there beside the *first* answer to each question? ______

How many checks are there beside the *second* answer to each question? ______

How many checks are there beside the *third* answer to each question? ______

If most of your checks are beside the first answer, you probably have what it takes to run a business. If not, you're likely to have more trouble than you can handle by yourself. Better find a partner who is strong on the points you're weak on. If many checks are beside the third answer, not even a good partner will be able to shore you up.

Figure A–9

To start or to buy?

Source: Norman M. Scarborough and Thomas W. Zimmerer, Effective Small Business Management *(New York: Merrill/Macmillan, 1984), pp. 130–131.*

Should I start my own business from scratch or should I purchase an existing business? These are the two alternatives facing the potential small business manager. If the business is started fresh, there are these advantages:

1. You can create a business in your own image. The business is not a made-over version of someone else's place, but it is formed the way you think it should be.
2. You do not run the risk of purchasing a business with a poor reputation that you would inherit.
3. The concept you have for the business is so unusual that only a new business is possible.

The creation of a new business also has some substantial drawbacks. Some of the disadvantages include:

1. Too small a market for your product or service.
2. High cost of new equipment.
3. Lack of a source of advice on how things are done and who can be trusted.
4. Lack of name recognition. It may take a long time to persuade customers to give your business a try.

Buying an existing business also has advantages and disadvantages. The major advantages are:

1. A successful business may provide the buyer with an immediate source of income.
2. An existing business may already be in the best location.
3. An existing business already has employees who are trained and suppliers who have established ties to the business.
4. Equipment is already installed and the productive capacity of the business is known.
5. Inventories are in place, and suppliers have extended trade credit, which can be continued.
6. There is no loss of momentum. The business is already operating.
7. You have the opportunity to obtain advice and counsel from the previous owner.
8. Often, you can purchase the business you want at a price much lower than the cost of starting the same business from scratch.

Purchasing an existing business can have some real drawbacks, such as the following:

1. You can be misled, and end up with a business that is a "dog."
2. The business could have been so poorly managed by the previous owner that you inherit a great deal of ill will.
3. A poorly managed business may have employees who are unsuited to the business or poorly trained.
4. The location of the business may have become, or is becoming, unsuitable.
5. The equipment may have been poorly maintained or even be obsolete.
6. Change can be difficult to introduce in an established business.
7. Inventory may be out of date, damaged, or obsolete.
8. You can pay too much for the business.

To avoid buying a business that cannot be made profitable, investigate six critical areas:

1. Why does the owner wish to sell? Look for the real reason and do not simply accept what you are told.
2. Determine the physical condition of the business. Consider the building and its location.
3. Conduct a thorough analysis of the market for your products or services. Who are your present and potential customers? You cannot know too much about your customers. Conduct an equally thorough analysis of your competitors, both direct and indirect. How do they operate and why do customers prefer them?
4. Consider all of the legal factors that might constrain the expansion and growth of the business. Become familiar with zoning restrictions.

Figure A–9 (continued)

5. Identify the actual owner of the business and all liens that might exist.
6. Using the material covered in previous chapters, analyze the financial conditions of the business.

The business can be evaluated on the basis of its assets, its future earnings, or a combination of both. Don't confuse the value of a business with its price. Price is determined through negotiation. The bargaining zone represents that area within which agreement can be reached.

Figure A–10

A retail franchise: Is it for you?

Source: Norman M. Scarborough and Thomas W. Zimmerer, Effective Small Business Management *(New York: Merrill/Macmillan, 1984), pp. 101–102.*

The Franchiser and the Franchise

1. Is the potential market for the product or service adequate to support your franchise? Will the prices you charge be in line with the market?
2. Is the market's population growing, remaining static, or shrinking? Is the demand for your product or service growing, remaining static, or shrinking?
3. Is the product or service safe and reputable?
4. What will the competition, direct or indirect, be in your sales territory? Do any other franchisees operate in this general area?
5. Is the franchise international, national, regional, or local in scope? Does it involve full- or part-time involvement?
6. How many years has the franchiser been in operation? Does it have a sound reputation for honest dealings with franchisees?
7. How many franchise outlets now exist? How many will there be a year from now? How many outlets are company-owned?
8. How many franchisees have failed? Why?
9. What services and assistance will the franchiser provide? Training programs? Advertising assistance? Financial aid? Are these one-time programs or are they continuous in nature?
10. Will the firm perform a location analysis to help you find a suitable site?
11. Will the franchiser offer you exclusive distribution rights for the length of the agreement, or may it sell to other franchises in this area?
12. What facilities and equipment are required for the franchise? Who pays for construction? Is there a lease agreement?
13. What is the total cost of the franchise? What are the initial capital requirements? Will the franchisor provide financial assistance? Of what nature? What is the interest rate? Is the franchisor financially sound enough to fulfill all its promises?
14. How much is the franchise fee? **Exactly** what does it cover? Are there any continuing fees? What additional fees are there?
15. Does the franchiser provide an estimate of expenses and income? Are they reasonable for your particular area? Are they sufficiently documented?
16. Does the franchiser offer a written contract that covers all the details of the agreement? Have your lawyer and your accountant studied its terms and approved it? Do **you** understand the implications of the contract?
17. What is the length of the franchise agreement? Under what circumstances can it be terminated? If you terminate the contract, what are the costs to you? What are the terms and costs of renewal?
18. Are you allowed to sell the franchise to a third party? If so, will you receive the proceeds?
19. Is there a national advertising program? How is it financed? What media are used? What help is provided for local advertising?

Figure A–10 (continued)

The Franchisee—You

20. Are you qualified to operate a franchise successfully? Do you have adequate drive, skills, experience, education, patience, and financial capacity? Are you prepared to work hard?
21. Are you willing to sacrifice some autonomy in operating a business to own a franchise?
22. Can you tolerate the financial risk?
23. Are you genuinely interested in the product or service you will be selling?
24. Has the franchiser investigated your background thoroughly enough to decide you are qualified to operate the franchise?
25. What can this franchiser do for you that you cannot do for yourself?

Endnotes

1. Donald Zale, "The Need to Rekindle the Entrepreneurial Spirit," *Retailing Issues Letter* (Center for Retailing Studies, Texas A&M University, September 1986): 2.

2. Figure A–1 shows some of the indicators of entrepreneurial attitudes. The best answers to these questions are (1) c, (2) b, (3) c, (4) a, (5) a, (6) c, (7) a, (8) c, (9) a, (10) c, (11) c, (12) a, (13) b, and (14) c. Score one point for each correct answer. Questions 1, 2, 3, 7, 9, and 12 suggest whether you are a realistic problem solver who can run a business without constant help from others. Questions 5, 6, and 8 probe whether you take calculated risks and seek information before you act. Questions 4, 10, 13, and 14 show whether you, like the classic entrepreneur, find other people satisfying when they help fulfill your need to win. Question 11 reveals whether you take responsibility for your destiny—and your business. If you score between 11 and 14 points, you could have a good chance to succeed. If you score from 7 to 10 points, you had better have a superb business idea or a lot of money to help you out. If you score 7 or less, stay where you are!

3. Kevin Helliker, "Retailing Chains Offer a Lot of Opportunity, Young Managers Find," *The Wall Street Journal*, August 25, 1995, A1.

4. "Store Managers Pay Jumps," *Stores* (December 1995):26–27.

5. Louis S. Richman, "How to Get Ahead in America," *Fortune*, May 16, 1994, 46–56.

6. Keith H. Hammonds, "The New World of Work," *Business Week*, October 17, 1994, 76–87.

7. Lee Smith, "Landing That First Real Job," *Fortune*, May 16, 1994, 58–60.

8. Marilyn M. Kennedy, "How to Win the Interview Game," *Business Week's Careers* 5 (September 1987): 17.

9. Kenneth Labich, "Kissing off Corporate America," *Fortune*, February 20, 1995, 50.

10. *Ibid*, 46.

11. See Andrew E. Serwer, "Paths to Wealth in the New Economy," *Fortune*, February 20, 1995, 56–62.

12. "Critical Success Factors for Small Retailers," *Chain Store Age* (October 1995):5A–7A.

13. See Bill Pearson, "It Is the Worst of Times . . . It Is the Best of Times," *Stores* (February 1996):74–75.

Appendix B Strategic and Tactical Cases

Table of Contents

PART VII: Retail Management

CASE 20: Kinney Canada Inc.: Considering a New Location Strategy.
Shilpa Stocker

CASE 21: Hudson's Bay Company.
D. Wesley Balderson

PART VIII: Retail Specialization

CASE 22: Chipman Roofing: Management of a Service Retailer
D. Wesley Balderson

CASE 23: Roots Canada Ltd.: Expansion to the United States.
D. Wesley Balderson

CASE 1: Packman's Books: Surviving the Onslaught of Category Killers

James Strong and Dale M. Lewison, The University of Akron

Charles Packman's father started Packman's Books shortly after World War II, and Charles took over the business in 1981, when it was grossing $750 000, and built it into an impressive $7 million operation by 1997. Packman's Books, located near the University of Pennsylvania in Philadelphia, has changed locations three times to accommodate this impressive growth.

Part of Packman's growth has been due to good managerial and marketing decisions. For example, Charles has kept the old-world bookshop ambience, while instituting some very current marketing tactics. The publications are displayed on pine bookcases stained with a warm dark finish. The carpet is a deep peaceful green, and scattered throughout the store are comfortable couches and easy chairs that allow patrons to relax while they browse through the store. The salespeople sit at old-fashioned library desks, and even the PCs are painted brown so they blend in with the woodwork. Charles discovered early in his career that allowing customers to browse increased their loyalty, the amount of time they spend in the store, and their purchase size. The small amount of damage and loitering is more than offset by increased sales.

Packman's Books is not a small store, covering 10 000 sq. ft. [930 m^2] of selling area that covers two floors. The city location near a major university is an advantage, and the parking and traffic situation is not a major problem. Approximately 7500 vendors supply the store, and more than 85 000 titles can be found at any given time, with twice that amount in the computer system available for special order. Excellent selection is the hallmark of Packman's Books. New fiction, nonfiction, general fiction, history, travel, sports, and children's books are featured on the ground floor. On the second level customers can find books on psychology, religion, philosophy, science and nature, foreign language, performing arts, cookbooks, and a selection of maps. Clearly such selection and ambience is paying off. Packman's averages 1200 customer transactions per day, and special orders average an impressive 200 to 250 per day.

However, not all the success of Packman's is due to the astute management of Charles Packman—growth in the industry has also supported the store. Books sales have increased every year for the past fifteen years. This attractive sales growth record has resulted in an equally impressive expansion in the number of book stores. The fast-growing segment of the book industry has been in the superstore or category killer format.

Packman's impressive size, selection, relaxed ambience, and large and knowledgeable sales staff have enabled it to easily compete with mall bookstores like B. Dalton and Waldenbooks, which offer 15 000 to 20 000 titles per store. A large portion of Packman's overhead goes toward personnel. The firm has more than 100 full- and part-time employees who keep the operation running smoothly and pride themselves on being able to find any book a customer wants. Charles Packman insists that salespeople spend as much time as necessary with customers and not use any aggressive sales tactics. In fact, salespeople are paid straight salary. The sales staff is diverse and well read and benefits from both veteran personnel and local graduate students who work part-time while pursuing their degrees. This differs greatly from the more aggressive and poorly read salespeople usually found in mall bookstores.

However, some changes in the industry have Charles deeply concerned about his business. Margins for bookstores average among the lowest in retailing. According to trade publications, a very healthy bookstore has a profit margin between 1 and 5 percent. Packman's has a net profit margin of 1.3 percent, which is too low according to Charles's accountant. Prices are largely set by the publisher. Packman's averages a 40 percent discount off the cover price, but that 40 percent must cover an overhead that is quite substantial. The impressive customer service and amenities provided by Packman's are expensive.

Even more worrisome is the growth of book superstores by most of the dominant national bookstore chains, now that the mall market is nearly saturated. In recent years,

Barnes & Noble, Crown Books, Borders Books, and Waldenbooks have all launched and expanded their version of these category killer stores. These superstores are targeted to more serious literary book consumers and have copied the strategy of the large successful independents like Packman's by marketing their stores as a "destination" shop. The superstores offer many of the amenities of Packman's, such as comfortable chairs, wide aisles, and toys and play areas for children. Most superstores are attempting to hire and train more knowledgeable salespeople. Some go even farther, offering in-store theatres and coffee and pastry bars. New York–based Barnes & Noble has a 15 000-sq.-ft. [1400 m^2] Barnes & Noble, Jr., children's bookstore within the superstore, utilizing the store-within-a-store concept. Barnes & Noble is trying to take the service level one step higher, attempting to be more than a bookstore by becoming a cultural resource. For example, book signings have been replaced by presentations on subjects such as Ukrainian egg decorating and Shaker furniture. Besides the advantages of wider coverage and more efficient promotional budgets, the superstores are offering discounted prices that independents will find difficult to match. For instance, Barnes & Noble superstores discount every hardcover book by 10 percent, and best-sellers are reduced 30 percent. The average superstore is 15 000 sq. ft. [1400 m^2] and offers between 100 000 and 150 000 titles. The book categories are similar to Packman's, consisting of best-sellers and expanded sections on history, psychology, philosophy, and literature.

Charles Packman wonders if there is enough room in the marketplace for all these new stores. He also wonders how he can compete with the lower prices of the superstores. Sales for Packman's have been flat for two years, and profits have eroded slightly.

Assignment

1. Can independent bookstores like Packman's compete with superstores owned by dominant national chains? Why?
2. Assuming it can compete, what strategies and tactics should Packman's institute or stress in order to survive this competitive threat? What advantages does a well-managed independent have over chain superstores? What advantages do the superstores have over independents like Packman's? Be creative, and identify some new and different merchandising tactics that might help Packman's differentiate itself from the rest of the industry.
3. Evaluate Barnes & Noble's strategy of reformatting a bookstore into a cultural centre. Identify and describe some merchandising tactics that would support this transformation.

Sources

Laura Bird, "Need a Sitter? Some Parents Use Barnes & Noble," *The Wall Street Journal*, August 17, 1995, B1, B4; Meg Cox, Barnes Noble's Boss Has Big Growth Plans that Booksellers Fear," *The Wall Street Journal*, September 11, 1992, Al, A4; Meg Cox, "Booksellers Put Survival on Top Shelf as Superstores Vie for Tough Customers," *The Wall Street Journal*, May 26, 1992, B4; Carolyn Friday, Lourdes Rosado, and Larry Reibstein, "The Book on Marketing," *Newsweek*, May 18, 1992, 55–56. Carrie Goerne, "Now Book Browsers Can Munch Brownies as They Shop for Browning," *Marketing News*, July 6, 1992, 1, 9; and Linda Dumas, "The Tattered Cover," *Stores* (March 1992): 52–53.

CASE 2: Retailing on the Internet: The Impact of Technology on Retail Strategies and Distribution

Mark R. Freemal, The University of Akron

Yolanda Smith is not your typical retailer. Ms. Smith works in the technology department of a public university and is also an avid antique collector. She is considering starting her own antique mall on the Internet as a way to join her two hobbies and interests.

Ms. Smith, who is in her early 50s, graduated with a B.A. in English from a private midwestern university. She also has master's degrees in both English and Library Science from a large midwestern state university, where she is employed in the computer laboratory of the college of business. Ms. Smith's teaching experience includes two years of English in public high schools and four semesters of managerial skills in the college's graduate MBA program as well as the current "Introduction to the World Wide Web" class. She handles several high-technology issues for the college of business, including the maintenance of its World Wide Web site.

In her spare time, Ms. Smith has become a fixture at local antique auctions. She has been hooked since her first auction over a year ago, finding them to be an excellent way to relax after a week of hard work. Part of the mystique of the auctions has been studying the antique dealers that are always present and learning how they know when to stop bidding on particular items. Besides just attending local auctions, Ms. Smith has started travelling to more rural areas, where better deals are often found. In doing so, she has met and befriended several of the local dealers.

Antiques are a booming business in this country. The value of an item is set only by what someone is willing to pay for it. Because of this, dealers will go to great lengths to expand their market in an attempt to locate the one person who is willing to pay more. Most of the dealers travel to regional shows, which adds to their cost of doing business and their risk of damaging irreplaceable goods. This is also an investment in time that often results in only one chance at selling an item. If a prospective customer changes his or her mind after the show, it is too late to change it back.

Over the past year, Ms. Smith has come to the conclusion that selling antiques over the Internet would create new distribution possibilities as well as bring together two of her passions. Ms. Smith plans on using the local antique auctions as her source of raw materials. In addition, her computer experience and familiarity with the Net will help her in establishing and maintaining her Web site. She can also rely on the support of her friends in both the business and antique communities.

The Internet, or Net, was started by the Pentagon in the 1960s as a computer network that does not rely on any one computer so it would be invulnerable to a nuclear attack. Since then, it has developed into an elaborate international network of other computer networks. No one owns or oversees the Net. It is governed by unwritten codes of conduct known to the users simply as "Netiquette." The World Wide Web, a part of the Internet, is a network comprising more than 10 000 privately owned computers belonging to universities, institutions, businesses, and private individuals in 152 countries. Each of these computers has its own address or home page. Users of the Net jump from site to site on these computers using a series of links. Most sites covering similar topics link to one another as a matter of courtesy. When contacted, each computer displays its home page. A business's Web site can be a catalogue, brochure, sales presentation, interactive ordering system, or even more. The Internet is interactive in that the user scrolls through only the information that interests him or her and can leave messages or even place an order.

In the past, the Net was difficult to use, but this has changed with the introduction of sophisticated graphical interfaces that can show text, pictures, sound, and even video clips. Specific topics can be referenced using one of the several search engines available. The Net can be accessed through online services such as America Online, CompuServe, and Prodigy or through a local service provider. Many cable and phone companies such as AT&T are also starting to offer Internet access, which brings this technology one step closer to mass acceptance.

Already, the use of the Internet has increased phenomenally. The number of Net users has grown from 1 million in 1988 to more than 50 million in 1996. Of these users, more than 20 million are American. The typical Internet user is well educated and upper income. Although most of the population in the past was male, women now account for more than 30 percent of the users. More than 110 000 U.S. companies are now connected to the Net, and there are over 1000 specialty stores and cybermalls established. It is estimated that consumers spent more than $400 million on goods purchased using the Internet in 1995. During the same time, international companies spent more than $80 million on site development and almost $50 million on advertising their Web sites. All of these statistics are increasing daily as the Internet continues to grow at the fastest rate of any media in history.

Obviously, this new technology will have a profound impact on how people conduct business. Industry analysts predict that the Internet and other methods of electronic shopping will change the way that business is done. Already, more consumers are choosing to shop from home because of the convenience that it offers. The creation of this electronic "marketspace" offers several additional advantages to retailers. First, it is an effective way for companies to improve communications with both consumers and suppliers. Another benefit is that the Internet is interactive. Consumers can tailor the flow of information that they receive and respond easily and instantaneously. Companies can monitor this flow of information and see which products or services are generating the most leads and inquiries. Third, the Net is a great equalizer. Here, every company can have a home page, creating a way for smaller companies to compete with industry leaders in markets that require huge investments, personal selling, or large advertising budgets. Also, it is essentially a new channel of distribution that can eliminate both the intermediary and much of the paperwork resulting in lowered overhead and other costs. This has resulted in an explosion of consumer choice that has blurred the lines between custom and mass marketing. Individuals can now access detailed information from manufacturers and use this to place and track their own orders. Several companies are successfully marketing a diverse group of products on the Net, ranging from flower and grocery delivery to airline ticket and new car sales.

As with any new technology, however, the Internet is not without its faults. Perhaps the largest of these is that the Net is not governed or monitored by any one group or individual. This makes it akin to the Wild West, with cases of fraud and other security concerns. The difficulties of marketing are also increased by the fact that there are no established rules, only the loosely defined "Netiquette." Any company that accidentally crosses the lines of acceptance will be the target of "flames," or vicious e-mail messages that can clog a company's computer and crash its Web site. Because the Internet is a large network, it can be difficult to locate specific topics. This creates the unique challenge of letting customers know that you even exist. In addition, consumers must be educated to the methods of conducting business on the Internet.

Previously, one of the unwritten rules of the Internet was no commercialization. Companies who attempted to advertise or sell goods on the Net were subject to flaming and other attacks. As the Internet has become easier to use and its audience has grown, however, commercial ventures have started to appear. Such behaviour is now acceptable as long as it is available by request only and not forced upon everyone on the system. The first businesses on the Internet started to appear only two to three years ago. One of these is Auntie Q's Antique Shop, which is the oldest antique dealer on the Net. Another major competitor among the many others is the Collector's Supermall, a cybermall that logs more than 40 000 "hits" (visits to the site) every month. Cybermalls are simply the Internet version of a normal mall—a location that "leases" space on its page to other dealers. Traffic through Internet sites is measured by the number of hits made to that site over a certain period of time.

One of the more important issues facing Ms. Smith has been whether she should join one of the existing cybermalls or establish her own site. At first, Ms. Smith was planning on joining a cybermall. After examining several of the leading antique sites, however, she could not find one that totally satisfied her needs. Now, Ms. Smith is investigating starting her own antique cybermall on the Internet and leasing out space to other local dealers. This decision has been difficult because costs for both options are highly confusing and often hard to find.

Most cybermalls lease space on a monthly basis, but their exact charges vary drastically. The approximate cost of joining one of the existing locations is between $25 and $500 per month depending on the size of the store and the package selected. In addition to the monthly fee, Ms. Smith would have to pay $20 per month for her own Internet access.

To establish her own site, Ms. Smith would first need her own computer and high-speed modem to run the home page. In addition, the page would have to be designed and created, which would require a colour scanner. Ms. Smith also wants to incorporate her business. The estimated cost for purchasing the additional computer and equipment, filing for incorporation, and developing her home page is $5000. Ms. Smith would also need to contract with a local service provider to get a commercial Internet access account. Orders would be placed over the Internet and confirmed using an 800 number. This way, Ms. Smith would not have to worry about encrypting credit card numbers to protect against fraud. The access charge and 800 number would cost an additional $100 per month.

If Ms. Smith decides to establish her own page, she plans on developing it into a cybermall and leasing out space to some of her dealer friends. For the first eight weeks, she would do this at no cost in order to convince them of the value of the service. After the introductory period, she plans on charging for this. Her rates will be based on a breakdown of the actual costs. Ms. Smith plans on making her site fun and interactive, using such innovative techniques as cyberauctions to draw in customers. Ms. Smith would display pictures and information on the antique that is currently up for auction. As with a live auction, viewers on the Internet would then be able to simultaneously bid on the object until it is sold to the highest bidder. Similar interactive promotions on the Internet have been extremely successful at drawing participants and even spectators.

Ms. Smith is looking forward to starting her antique shop on the Internet for the entertainment even more than for the anticipated profits. She sees this as the perfect opportunity for someone to start a business and not be judged on a personal basis. Neither sex, race, age, religion, nor any other personal characteristic is displayed across the Internet. Ms. Smith also appreciates the irony and challenge of selling antiques over one of the most modern communications channels, the Internet.

Assignment

1. Do you think that the retail potential of the Internet has been overestimated? What about the potential of the Internet as a business tool in general?
2. Develop a list of advantages and disadvantages of conducting business over the Internet.
3. How does retailing on the Internet compare to in-store retailing and other home-based retail formats such as catalogues and home shopping channels?
4. Do you think it would be better for Ms. Smith to join an existing cybermall, or should she establish her own location?
5. Perhaps one of the greatest challenges of doing business on the Internet is developing awareness of your site. What methods would you use to overcome this?
6. How does the Internet help retailers create the different forms of utility (form, place, time, possession) for their customers? Or, how does retailing over the Internet affect the four Ps of marketing (product, place, promotion, price)?

Sources

Personal Interview, Yolanda Smith, March 15, 1996. Arthur Andersen & Company, "The Internet: Web Sites Offer Net Profit," *Arthur Andersen Consumer Products Highlights*, First Quarter 1996. Ernst & Young, "Retail i.t.," *Ernst & Young's 14th Annual Survey of Retail Information Technology*, September 1995. Keith Naughton, "Revolution in the Showroom," *Business Week*, February 19, 1996. Susan Reda, "Interactive Shopping," *Stores* (March 1995). Rosalind Resnick, "Follow the Money," *Internet World* (May 1996). Michael Rollins, "Shopping in the Virtual World," *Arthur Andersen Retailing Issues Letter* (January 1996). Fred Schneider, "Retailing on the Internet," *International Trends in Retailing*, December 1995. John Verity, "The Internet: How It Will Change the Way You Do Business," *Business Week*, November 14, 1994.

CASE 3: Consignment Retailing: A New Retailing Format or a Used Business Concept

Dale M. Lewison and Michael d'Amico, The University of Akron

As Ana Taylor examined her weekly planner she realized that it was already two weeks into the spring semester. This semester was going to be a challenge. With three required and three elective courses, she knew that careful planning and scheduling would be essential if she wants to maintain her rather impressive grade point average. By the end of this term, she would need only six more hours to graduate. Her college career would soon be coming to an end. It had been a great four years. She was pleased with her decisions to major in marketing (emphasis in retail merchandising) and minor in entrepreneurship. With the conclusion of this term, Ana's only remaining degree requirement is to complete a six-credit capstone course for her minor in entrepreneurship. The capstone Venture Management course involves developing a complete business plan for starting a proposed business. She will write the plan this summer and present it to a group of professors and representatives from the business community. There are dozens of horror stories about students who have not been successful in meeting the requirements of this final challenge.

Consulting a weekly "things to do" list, Ana identified the major projects to be launched this week: Select a topic, develop a writing outline, and conduct a literature search for a term paper required in Strategic Retail Management. This assignment accounts for 25 percent of the final grade. As outlined in the course syllabus, the assignment requires each student to write an analytical paper on "the current state and future prospects of a particular retailing format." The assignment permits a considerable degree of latitude. The retailing format can be defined in broad (for example, the department store industry) or narrow (for example, one-price retailing) terms. Page limit guidelines were set at ten to thirty double-spaced pages. Tables, graphs, and art work are to be presented on separate pages. The paper is to be supported by an extensive collection of current references that are properly cited. Each paper's grade is determined on the basis of 70 percent content and 30 percent writing style, grammar, and the professional nature of the written presentation.

Ana had already selected a topic, the less-than-glamorous format of consignment retailing. Although selling used merchandise might appear to be an unlikely business with little or no future prospects, Ana's experience suggested otherwise. Having worked for two years as the assistant store manager for her Aunt Kimmberly's Second Time Around thrift shop, Ana believed that consignment retailing not only has a future, it has a bright one. Admittedly, the merchandising and operating practices of many thrift stores like her aunt's are both amateurish and archaic. However, Ana believes that with careful application of some key merchandising concepts and operating principles learned in her retailing and marketing courses, thrift retailing can become a very viable retailing format in the future.

Consignment retailing has some real competitive advantages that can be used to gain a market position as a very low-cost retailer that offers superior customer value in a store setting that is reasonably comparable with more traditional retailers. A thrift store does not have to be located in a lower-income neighbourhood with used merchandise strewn haphazardly around an unorganized and musty-smelling store in unattractive displays. Nor does the merchandise have to look shopworn or unkept. Ana had tried to implement some of her merchandising ideas in her aunt Kimmberly's store, but it would have required a complete restructuring of the entire store to really get the job done. Aunt Kim was simply not up to this much change at this stage in her life. Starting this type of business from scratch was probably the only way to introduce modern merchandising techniques to this old-fashion retailing format.

One fact that always intrigued Ana was a statement made by her cousin Jack, who acted as his mother's accountant. In that conversation, Jack had speculated that there must be millions of dollars' worth of used merchandise stashed away in peoples' closets, attics, spare rooms, basements, garages, and storage sheds. Most people had no need for that merchandise and would gladly get rid of it if they could get something for it and if it would not be too much bother. As a source of supply, these storage areas represent virtual gold mines. Jack had also told Ana about Grow Biz International, a Minneapolis-based retail organization that develops and franchises value-oriented business concepts for stores that buy, sell, trade, and consign used merchandise. According to what Jack had read, the company's most successful format is Play It Again Sports—a chain of sporting goods stores with 587 units. Some other formats developed by the company include Once Upon a Child (a 129-store chain selling children's apparel, furniture, and accessories); Computer Renaissance (a 24-unit chain selling computer equipment); Disc Go Round (a 69-unit chain dealing in used compact disks) and Music Go Round (a 5-unit chain selling musical instruments). From what Jack could remember, all these formats were enjoying reasonably good success.

As Ana thought about the possibilities of such a business, she realized that starting a consignment retailing shop was something she had had in the back of her head for a long time. Prior to this assignment, she really had not stopped to consider this interest. She decided that starting a consignment retailing enterprise would be the focus of her business plan for the Venture Management Course. By writing her term paper on the current state and future prospects of consignment retailing, Ana knew she could get a big jump on writing a complete business plan.

Consulting her retailing textbook, Ana listed the following questions to be addressed in her analytical term paper:

1. What are the relative strengths and weaknesses of consignment retailing as a retail business format?
2. What are the current and future environmental threats and opportunities that face this form of retailing?
3. What changes and modifications in current merchandising and operating practices will be needed to increase the competitiveness and attractiveness of this retailing format? What constitutes offering the right products, in the right quantities, in the right place, at the right time, with the right appeal and service?

Assignment

Assume the role of Ana and complete her term paper assignment for the Strategic Retail Management course. You are responsible for meeting all of the requirements outlined in the course syllabus.

Sources

Bruce Fox, "The New Momentum in Used Merchandise," *Chain Store Age* (August 1995): 23–32; Mary Ethridge, "Used Goods New Profits," *Akron Beacon Journal*, February 3, 1996, B1, B5; Sacasas Rene, "The Modern Consignment Shop," *Business and Economic Review* (April–June 1996): 10–13; and David R. Gourley, "Second Hand Stores: The Resurgence of an Old Form of Retailing," *Arizona Business* (First Quarter 1983): 16–22.

CASE 4: Canadian Retailing: An Industry in Chaos

Peggy H. Cunningham, Queen's University

"Retailing is like the ocean. It shifts with the tide in and the tide out . . . you're going to have to keep changing all the time." These words, uttered by John Craig Eaton to a *Canadian Business* interviewer, certainly describe the state of the industry today. There may be no industry in Canada experiencing as much turmoil as the retailing sector. However, questions remain about whether the tide is coming in or has gone out for Canadian retailers.

Nineteen ninety-five has been called the bleakest year in Canadian retailing in decades. Part of the reason is consumers' nervousness about the economy and their ability to keep their jobs. Another is that many consumers have "maxed" out their credit cards and are facing a payment crunch. Others suggest that consumers are just becoming more savvy and are increasingly demanding better value for their money. New labels have been developed for 1990s consumers, such as "strident consumers," "cash-strapped shoppers," "value-driven buyers," and "shoppers from hell"—reflecting the attitudes of the retailers who serve them.

Whereas consumers in the 1980s often purchased $1000 suits and $200 scarves, some now seem to be focusing on purchases for their homes when they reluctantly part with their hard-earned dollars. Many shoppers rank convenience as their number-one criteria for store choice, which is not surprising given that 69 percent of mothers with children under 16 years of age also work outside the home. In addition, 1.3 million Canadians are now working extended hours, with an estimated 13.5 percent working more than a 50-hour week.

Paralleling the changes in consumer behaviour, the retailing industry itself has been evolving. Traditional department stores are being challenged on all sides. Whereas once they were the only venue that promised one-stop shopping, now this claim has been made meaningless by the presence of large shopping malls. Department stores like Eaton's and The Bay are being challenged by discounters, like Zellers and Wal-Mart, in a battle more fierce than any fought before. New competitors, known as "category killers,"—stores that offer everything a consumer could want in a limited product market, such as toys or furniture—have taken away share from traditional retailers that offered wide versus deep product assortments. Stores like Toys 'R' Us, Leon's, The Brick Warehouse, and Business Depot fall into this category. New retailing formats, such as televised shopping networks and Internet-based virtual shopping malls, have taken on more traditional venues.

Every lesson in competitive strategy is being played out before the eyes of every Canadian consumer. We see stores vying for the position of cost leader so that they can win consumers over with lower prices. We glimpse at others carving out specialized niches offering product assortments to narrow groups of purchasers. We view the remainder trying desperately to differentiate themselves from the pack by focusing on specific categories of goods that appeal to wider groups of consumers. Let us now examine some of the players in each category.

Discount Department Stores

Three major discounters are operating in the Canadian market: Zellers, Kmart, and Wal-Mart.

Kmart began its Canadian operations in 1963, and today the company operates 123 stores. Even though it began an ambitious store renewal plan in 1990, along with a focus on private-label fashions such as Basic Editions and Jaclyn Smith, it is believed to be doing poorly. It was recently reported to be looking for buyers for some of its outlets. Wal-Mart, on the other hand, stormed onto the Canadian market like a stampede from its American homeland, trampling many others in its path. Bringing with it the know-how gained in the highly competitive U.S. marketplace, its success begins with a superb inventory management and distribution system. It relies heavily on an Electronic Data Interchange system that feeds information from its checkouts via satellite to its suppliers. The technology helps the company to recognize those items that are selling like hot cakes while enabling it to drop those that are slow movers. This system not only explains why Wal-Mart is rarely out of stock, it also enables it to lower costs by two or three percent below the industry average. Its ability to make large-volume purchases in conjunction with its American operations, adds to its ability to keep costs low.

While Wal-Mart claims to be a price discounter, it has developed a strategy of only offering the best prices on about 500 frequently purchased items. These are the items where the consumer recognizes a bargain as soon as he or she sees the price. This creates the impression of great prices throughout Wal-Mart stores, even though the remainder of its stock may actually be sold at the same or even higher prices than at other retailers. This strategy has allowed Wal-Mart to achieve sales of $400/square foot that are the envy of the entire North American retailing industry.

Zellers. Allowing Wal-Mart to purchase the 122 Woolco stores in 1994 was viewed by some analysts as Zellers's biggest mistake. Letting the American giant into its backyard has caused Zellers a number of apparently unexpected problems. It seems ironic that in May 1994, investors and the press alike hung on the words of Hudson Bay's CEO, George Kosich. Decrying the fall in Canadian retail stock prices, Kosich called this "a huge overreaction."

His words were echoed in the next few minutes by another executive who called it an "enormous overreaction"! The phrases reflected the confidence these managers had in Zellers's position as a truly "Canadian" retailer, and in its Club Z programs to weather the onslaught from Wal-Mart.

Zellers's spokespeople are not using these words any longer. The Hudson Bay Co., which owns Zellers, announced in March 1996 that it was closing Zellers's Montreal headquarters and merging it with the Toronto operations in an effort to avoid duplication and cut operating costs. Remember that this was just two years after the speeches described above!

Zellers's 300 stores make it Canada's largest department store and the stores account for approximately 23 percent of the $15-billion discount department-store market. It competes head-to-head with Canada's other two discounters—Kmart and Wal-Mart Canada. Targeting low-income females in the age group 25–49 years of age with children, Zellers has long been known in Canada for its famous slogan, "Where the lowest price is the law." Zellers has used its loyalty program, Club Z, to differentiate itself from other Canadian retailers. Its displays were designed to convey an image of merchandise abundance and to maximize store traffic. While it was behind the industry in terms of incorporating technology such as checkout scanners into its stores, it did have a state-of-the-art distribution centre. However, the mismatch between the two parts of the organization often caused bottlenecks at the store loading ramps.

In the second half of 1995, Zellers began to live its low price slogan with a passion. It entered into a price-matching battle with Wal-Mart. As a result, operating profit fell from $215.6 million to $106.7 million. Although 1995 wasn't a good year for most retailers, many analysts believed it was more than economic conditions that caused Zellers's poor showing. Some thought its single-minded focus on prices blinded it from considering other important factors such as cutting costs, improving its distribution system, reducing stock-outs, and improving forecasting.

Major Department Stores

Three retailers comprise this category in Canada: Sears Canada with 41 percent of this segment, The Bay with a 31 percent share, and Eaton's, which is believed to control 28 percent. Department stores account for approximately $6.5 billion in annual retail sales. These stores have been losing share of market. In 1991, Statistics Canada reported their sales at $7.1 billion.

To try and recover their positions and prevent further loss of share, each retailer is struggling with the question of what it means to consumers in the new world of the 1990s. The Bay has begun renovating its stores and has started re-emphasizing hardware while focusing on fashion and cosmetics. It uses sales and heavy promotion to attract customers. Similarly, Sears, following its U.S. parent's lead of focusing on "the softer side of Sears," is also stressing clothing, but has aimed at a more casual market of slightly lower-income consumers. Building on its traditional roots, it has started developing new freestanding stores called "Whole Home Furniture Stores" to better compete with category killers like the Brick and Leon's.

Eaton's. Founded in 1869, Eaton's is one of Canada's oldest businesses. Today it operates 93 stores across Canada. It is still a family-owned enterprise and management has passed down through four generations of the family. By the 1950s, it was Canada's favourite store, accounting for 50 percent of department-store spending in Canada. Founded by an Irish immigrant, Eaton's revolutionized Canadian retailing with the promise, "Goods satisfactory or money refunded." Such a promise was unheard of in an age when retailing was very much a case of "buyer beware." Integrity and a sense of social responsibility have long marked this veteran business. When its staff members were sent to World War I and II, Eaton's continued to pay their wages. During the Depression of the 1930s, it refused to lay off employees. Not surprisingly, employees have expressed deep loyalty for the company and its owners. The Eaton family is revered as much as Sam Walton was by members of his organization.

Even though tradition has been the backbone of the company, it may also have been part of its downfall. Eaton's clung to traditional parts of the business long after market forces dictated dropping them from the store's portfolio. For example, long after specialty retailers, like Shoppers Drug Mart, took away the majority of the business, Eaton's still refused to drop drug departments from its stores. It refused to shut down many of its small-town operations, even though the economics of maintaining them seemed insurmountable.

Some analysts believe that Eaton's has been the hardest hit of the big retailers. Since Eaton's is a private company, its earnings are not posted, so market share gains and losses in this sector always involve some degree of speculation. However, since the Bay's sales are known to have dropped slightly while Sears have held even, there is reason to believe that Eaton's has suffered. Others suggest, however, that Eaton's bottomed out in 1994, and is now on the rebound.

In an effort to win back consumers, Eaton's has been trimming its staff, modernizing its information systems, and improving its distribution. There is some evidence that it is moving away from its strategy of "everyday low pricing" to one that uses occasional promotions. Its stores now have state-of-the-art systems for tracking goods from supplier to store floor. The company can now move goods from its distribution centre in less than two days, whereas just four years ago, it took eight days. It has begun working more closely with its suppliers and, like discounter Wal-Mart, has demanded more from them. If suppliers do not follow its strict rules on packaging, labelling, and shipment accuracy, they face stiff fines. It is also dealing with fewer suppliers who provide top quality and service rather than the many diverse companies as was its policy previously.

Eaton's is also one of the first retailers to recognize the need for more professional retail managers. It has gone beyond developing its own in-house training program (which was based on the best practices of companies like Motorola and General Electric), to founding the Eaton School of Retailing at Ryerson University (http://www.ryerson.cal-retailed/), which opened in 1994. By forming partnerships with other universities, it now offers courses in Montreal, Edmonton, Winnipeg, and Vancouver, in addition to those offered in Toronto.

Eaton's has begun to focus its merchandising on areas in which it faces no competition from discounters. It features store-within-stores and one has the sense of visiting boutiques full of designer-label apparel like Ralph Lauren, Nautica, and Hugo Boss, as well as Eaton's own brands such as Retreat and Distinction.

Eaton's has begun to renovate its stores, earmarking $300 million for the facelift. The purpose of the renovation is to make shopping easier for its time-pressured consumers. Eaton's pictures its consumers to be mainly women, even for menswear. The company believes that 60 to 70 percent of menswear purchases are made by women. Many of them are struggling to balance hectic lives with careers, husbands, homes, and kids. Thus, Eaton's believes that they must be able to find what they are looking for quickly, and receive rapid customer assistance, both in making their choices and in paying their bills. The new concentric floor plans have been designed with this purpose in mind.

Specialty Retailers

The remainder of Canada's retail industry is made up of specialty retailers. One can find specialty stores that cater to almost every imaginable need or interest of Canadian consumers. There are specialty stores for power-boat and yacht enthusiasts, cooking stores for the would-be gourmet, clothing boutiques for the fashion-conscious, bookstores for those with alternative lifestyles, retailers who cater to swimmers and rowers, cat shops for feline lovers, personal care stores like the Body Shop, and bird-watching stores, just to name a few. One of the biggest categories of specialty goods, however, is the area of sporting goods, a $3-billion market in Canada which is forecast to continue to grow by double digits.

The Forzani Group Ltd. One of the most successful specialty retailers is the Calgary-based Forzani Group Ltd., owners of a number of chains including Sports Experts, Forzani's Locker Room, Jersey City, Sport Chek, and RnR The Walking Store. Its 270 stores rack up annual sales of over $350 million, which equals about 12 percent of this market sector. This chain of stores experienced explosive growth that matched the fitness boom and growing interest in both professional and amateur sports during the 1980s.

As is the case in other sectors of retailing, U.S. superstores are threatening home-grown players. Giants like the Sports Authority and Sportsmart have been setting up shop and are trying to lure the value-conscious sports enthusiast. Sports Authority, a Florida-based company, has been extremely successful in the United States. It attributes its success to its ability to carry extremely deep assortments of products such as 164 types of baseball bats and over 20 000 apparel items. Its entry into Canada hasn't exactly been an effort to quietly sneak in the back door. In Toronto alone, they planned to open 11 stores in 1995. Forzani has no doubt that these giants will be tough competitors.

Sport Chek stores are smaller than some of their American competitors (Sport Chek stores come in formats ranging from 2800 m^2 to 3300 m^2, whereas U.S. rivals are over 3700 m^2). Although the larger, standardized American stores can carry larger amounts of inventory (500 different styles of athletic shoes, for example), the flexible size and format of the Forzani stores enable them to be better designed to meet the needs of the local marketplace. Furthermore, it has allowed the Forzani chain stores to be located in existing shopping malls, easily accessible by consumers, rather than being forced to set up shop in the fringe locations that the American firms have to buy in order to build their megastores. According to Forzani, size will not be the deciding factor in this battle—good service will! While the U.S. entrants will offer huge selection, they are not known for knowledgeable service or, for that matter, any service. Members of the Forzani chain pride themselves on their ability to serve customers. Providing rewards to store personnel who give exceptional service, has long been a policy of the chain.

Another weapon in the chain's sport bag of tricks is its focus on keeping costs low wherever possible. Even the president, former Calgary Stampeder John Forzani, wedges his football player's 120 kg frame into economy class seats when he travels. If managers travel in pairs, they must share rooms. Not only does this save money, but it helps team building as it does in professional sports, Forzani believes. Being able to buy in volume for the entire chain helps the firm get better deals from suppliers. Similarly, the ability to use umbrella advertising for the chain also keeps advertising costs lower than if separate ads had to be formulated for regional markets.

The Future

Turmoil and change seem to be the best words to describe retailing in Canada. While the tide may be coming in for some retailers, there is no doubt that it is going out for others. Many believe that there are currently just too many stores for the size of the Canadian population and that some of the major urban markets are seriously over-saturated. Mergers and acquisitions are expected to consolidate parts of the industry, but the death and decline of players in other sectors will surely occur as the industry shake-out continues. Remember that names like Birks and Woodwards were once well-recognized parts of the Canadian retailing scene.

Assignment

1. Can the concept "the wheel of retailing," be used to describe the current state of retailing in Canada?
2. Develop a profile for the "typical" customer you think regularly shops at a major department store like Eaton's, Sears, or the Bay; another for people who shop discounters like Zellers, Wal-Mart, or Kmart; and a third for those who frequent specialty retailers like Sport Chek, the Body Shop, or Birders World. Which group of stores attracts the most loyal customers? The least loyal? What does this tell you about the way people cross-shop retailers?
3. Some analysts believe that the demographics of the Canadian market are very different from those of the United States. In the United States, they claim, there are four distinct groups of consumers: the rich, the near rich, the not-so-rich, and the poor. In response, there are four classes of retailers that serve these distinct segments. These analysts believe that in Canada there is only a "middle class" market that is fragmented across widely dispersed urban areas. As a result, all retailers in Canada target the same consumer using virtually identical positioning strategies. Give the reasons why you agree or disagree with this analysis.
4. Describe the consumer of the 1990s. Which of the retailers described in this case do you think has best responded to the needs of this consumer?
5. Choose one of the retailers described in this case. If you were hired as a consultant to give them advice on how to improve their operations, what would you recommend they do? Be sure to include a description of the primary target market, the positioning you would recommend, and recommendations for modifications to their marketing mix.

Sources

Taken from *Principles of Marketing*: 3rd Canadian Edition, *Philip Kotler, Gary Armstrong, Peggy H. Cunningham*, and *Robert Warren*, Prentice-Hall Canada Inc., 1996, 482–5. Printed with permission.

Peggy Cunningham wrote this case based on the following sources: Paul Brent, "Bay Shakes Up Zellers," *The Financial Post*, March 15, 1996, 1–2; John Heinzl, "Did Zellers Discount the Wal-Mart Threat?" *Globe and Mail*, March 8, 1996; John Heinzl, "Playoff Pressure," *Report of Business Magazine*, April 1996, 91–98; Ian McGugan, "Eaton's on the Brink," *Canadian Business*, March 1996, 39–73; Mark Stevenson, "The Store to End All Stores," *Canadian Business*, May 1994, 20–24; Wal-Mart Integrated Case Exercise, Wilfrid Laurier University, 1994.

CASE 5: Entertainment Retailing: Creating an Exciting Shopping Experience

Dale M. Lewison and Michael d'Amico, The University of Akron

Traditionally, the monthly meetings of the Table Rock Mall Tenants' Association tended to be rather dull affairs devoted to finding ways in which mall tenants could cooperate in promoting the mall and its businesses. For the last year, however, the meetings have been anything but dull. The causes of this new-found excitement are several unfavourable consumer behaviour trends which have seriously dampened sales and profits of just about every member of the Tenants' Association. The results of a recent consumer survey have confirmed what every mall tenant already knew; that is, consumer shopping frequency and visit duration have declined significantly over the past two years. As revealed by the mall-intercept survey, consumers from Table Rock's primary trading area are coming to the mall less often (2.1 visits per month as compared with 3.4 monthly visits in the past), staying a shorter length of time per visit (about one hour as compared with one hour and forty-five minutes), and visiting fewer stores (three or four stores as compared with seven or eight stores). Given the more limited nature of these shopping trips, it is not surprising that average purchase amounts per shopping trip have declined by about 35 percent.

These disturbing trends have already resulted in numerous business failures and have forced several stores to seek less expensive locations in one of the smaller strip malls that line the traffic arteries leading into the Table Rock Mall. Many of these relocated businesses have found new life as lower-cost operators. If Table Rock's management does not find a way to halt these declines and reverse these trends, many of the mall's tenants will be following those who have already left the mall or gone out of business.

Located in a stable middle to upper-middle class trade area, Table Rock Mall has served as the major shopping complex for the city's entire west side for the past twenty-five years. Trade area demographics are very favourable and represent a cross-section of middle America. Like the national economy, the local economy has shown moderate and steady growth with no major negative trends that would explain the downturn in Table Rock's capability to attract and hold shoppers. One possible explanation is the age of the Table Rock facility. The mall's courtyards and common areas are rather drab and dated after nearly a quarter century of use and neglect. Another explanation advanced by some of the mall's tenants is the rather haphazard nature of the tenant mix in different areas of the mall: Many incompatible businesses are located in close proximity to one another. The tenant mix is quite standardized in that it consists of the same retailers that are found in almost every mall. In the words of one Table Rock shopper: "It's boring, they have the same old stores and same old merchandise as every other mall." As do malls elsewhere, Table Rock also faces stiffer competition from two major "power strip shopping centres" that are located adjacent to the mall. With such "category killers" as Toys Я Us, Office Max, Marshall's, Home Depot, Sears Hardware, and Sports Authority, these power strips have considerable customer drawing power. Judging from the number of cars in their parking lots and the endless trade press articles on their growth and success, it appears that most of Table Rock's surrounding shopping strip centres are not experiencing the same declines in customer traffic. Several of the Association's members believe that these power strips and a host of smaller strip centres are intercepting shoppers before they get to the mall. If that is a correct assumption, a major issue becomes, What can Table Rock Mall do to draw shoppers past the strip centres and into the mall?

The main item on the agenda for the May meeting of the Table Rock Mall Tenants' Association was a discussion of specific actions that might be taken to reverse the declining fortunes of the mall and to build and hold mall traffic. A number of standard actions had already been discussed at the April meeting. Although increasing advertising and promotional events might help, most of the members of the Association believe that something more drastic is needed to correct the rapidly escalating problem of too few customers. As the meeting proceeded, a consensus was formed that a more comprehensive and long-term marketing strategy is essential to the future economic health of the mall and the well-being of its tenants. Equally important is any strategy that has a focus that would create a distinctive image for the mall and enhance its ability to attract shoppers to the mall and hold their attention when they got there. A number of concepts were discussed, but the idea of "entertainment retailing" or "retailing as theatre" seemed to offer the most promise as an integrative theme for the mall and its tenants. The idea is that a trip to the mall should be something more than just an opportunity to buy goods and services. Customers want a more comprehensive experience consisting of socialization, recreation, entertainment, and shopping activities. When a mall and its tenants offer all four of these activities, they give the consumer more reasons to visit the mall and to extend that visit by becoming involved with more of the available activities. As expressed in one trade magazine, "In an overstored environment, where time is precious, price parity is endemic, and non-store shopping options are blossoming, retailers and developers across the country are convinced that entertainment retailing is the way to lure consumers out of their homes and into the mall and stores." To get started, the members of the association agreed to hire a consultant to investigate the causes of the mall's problems and to develop a preliminary analysis of whether an entertainment retailing focus would be a viable strategic marketing focus capable of effectively addressing those problems.

Assignment

Assume the role of the consultant and write a report that addresses the problems faced by Table Rock Mall. Using a variety of different sources of information (for example, literature search, field observation, personal interviews with shoppers, retailers, and mall operators), answer the following questions.

1. Are there any environmental trends that might help to explain why shoppers are making fewer trips to the mall, spending less time in the mall, and visiting fewer stores? Which environmental trends might serve as the bases of a marketing campaign that would help reverse the recent misfortunes of Table Rock Mall?
2. What psychological, personal, and social factors might help explain the deteriorating shopping behaviour of consumers with regard to Table Rock Mall? On the basis of these determinants of consumer buying behaviour, are there any specific recommendations that you can make that would help to build store traffic and to encourage more extensive shopping behaviour on the part of Table Rock patrons?
3. How would you define entertainment retailing? Which forms of entertainment retailing might be more appropriate for Table Rock Mall? Does entertainment retailing offer a viable solution to Table Rock's problems of fewer and shorter customer shopping trips? If the Table Rock Tenants' Association were to endorse an entertainment retailing strategy for the mall, what specific recommendations would you make regarding the implementation of such a strategy for the mall as a whole and for individual retail mall tenants?

Sources

Susan Reda, "That's Entertainment," *Stores* (October 1995): 16–20; Candace Talmadge, "Retailers Injecting More Fun Into Stores," *Advertising Age*, October 30, 1995, 38, 40; Eben Shapiro, "Entertainment Giants Push Playgrounds for Grown-Ups," *The Wall Street Journal*, June 8, 1995, B1; Kim Cleland, "Playgrounds Take a High-Tech Turn," *Advertising Age*, April 24, 1995, 13, 16; Marianne Wilson, "Brand Name, High-Profile Stores Create a Splash," *Chain Store Age Executive* (February 1994): 22–26; Sandra Pesmen, "It's a Mall World After All, Mall of America's Entertainment Mix," *Advertising Age*, December 19, 1994, 3,9; Cyndee Miller, Sony's Product Playground Yields Insight on Consumer Behavior," *Marketing News*, February 3, 1992, 1, 13; Mitchell Pacelle, "Malls Add Fun and Games to Attract Shoppers," *The Wall Street Journal*, January 23, 1996, B1, B5; and Christina Duff, "Megastores that Entertain and Educate May Signal the Future of Merchandising," *The Wall Street Journal*, March 33, 1993, B1, B3.

CASE 6: VideoMania: Using Database Marketing Technologies

Mark R. Freemal, The University of Akron

At first, Mark Roberts could not believe what he was hearing. He looked around at the rest of the executives at the VideoMania board meeting, wondering what their reactions would be. Jana Leigh, the new marketing manager, was proposing the use of sophisticated database marketing techniques to profile the company's current customers. This information would then be used to recommend movies to current customers, tailor special offers, and target new customers. Although these techniques had been used successfully by many companies in diverse industries, Roberts felt that it was an invasion of the customer's privacy.

VideoMania is one of the country's most successful mail-order video catalogues. The company specializes in providing unique films for an upscale clientele. Their selection includes smaller art films as well as the latest foreign releases and documentaries. The company has become extremely profitable by targeting educated and well-to-do young professionals. An important part of the company's growth has been VideoMania's dedication to excellent customer service. The company's operations are centred around a database containing information on all of their current customers and their past orders. When a customer calls, the computerized system automatically pulls up their file and routes it to the first available telephone representative. All transactions are logged and orders are instantly processed. The system enables the telephone representatives to give up-to-the minute information on pricing and availability for all of the movies that VideoMania carries. Roberts, the operations manager, takes pride in the fact that until this point, VideoMania has treated all customer information as confidential and has never used it for any marketing purposes. Also, the customer database has never been sold to another company or traded no matter how outrageous the offer. New customers come solely from referrals and a small advertising campaign.

After several years of strong growth, however, VideoMania's sales and profits have started to erode. Upper management blames this on recent trends, including the nationwide acceptance of large video rental chains, such as Blockbuster, that often carry special interest and foreign films. The company is also concerned about future advances in cable television that will enable viewers to request which movies they would like to see. To combat this, the board of directors hired Leigh, who has a strong background introducing innovative marketing techniques. She has proposed proactively marketing VideoMania's services using the latest in database marketing technology. This includes developing customer profiles that can be used for marketing additional goods and services as well as selling and trading the customer information for new prospects. Roberts is worried that this strategy will backfire and alienate the company's current customers.

The emergence of database marketing is based on the premise that past behaviour is the best indicator of future purchase patterns. The increase in computer power and storage capabilities coupled with decreasing costs now enables companies to deal directly with customers on an individual level. This sophisticated twist to the ancient art of persuasion has been called everything from database marketing, one-to-one marketing, macromarketing, and data mining. Consumers are increasingly leaving more electronic footprints detailing their buying behaviour, which companies are collecting and analyzing to predict buying habits and to create precisely tailored messages.

This technology is extremely attractive to many companies that feel survival in a competitive marketplace depends on strong bonds with current customers and the ability to attract new ones. Firms can use database marketing to figure out who their customers are and what it takes to obtain their loyalty. Creating a detailed profile on each customer is viewed as a method of establishing a collective memory that recreates the close relationship with customers that has been lost in the mass market with the traditional forms of mass media.

The casino industry offers an example of how database marketing is often used. Most casinos now issue cards to gamblers that can be used to track their wagers. This information is fed into a database that compiles a list of heavy gamblers. These preferred customers are then sent special offers, including room discounts, in an attempt to entice them back to the casino. Weaving relationships such as this with customers can make it more inconvenient for them to switch. Most airlines now offer a frequent flier program designed to make travellers think twice about using another airline. A similar example is the proliferation of credit cards offering rebates on everything from travel to gasoline and even new cars. Database marketing has also been embraced by the tobacco industry, whose advertising is extremely regulated. Most of the major companies have attempted to compile a list of all known smokers. The companies can then target the smokers directly with special promotions and offers.

Direct marketing companies were among the first to adopt database marketing and studies have shown that consumers are indeed responding. The use of database marketing techniques usually increases response rates two to three times. Even a single percentage gain in response rate can be crucial for companies because it slashes the amount of mailings required at a time when both mail and production costs are increasing. Direct marketers consider database marketing to be an excellent method of eliminating waste and nonproductive reach, thereby making their efforts more efficient. Simply put, they can now cast their offers more narrowly yet catch more customers.

Database marketing is based on a five-step process. First, companies should start with the customer information that they already have. This can consist of sales records, requests for information, or calls to 800 numbers. The next step is to get customers to volunteer more information. The most common source of this is warranty cards, which request information on everything from income level to hobbies and interests. Other methods include surveys, mail-in coupons, rebates, and sweepstakes. Third, companies can bolster their databases with the glut of information available from a variety of public and private sources. Publicly available information includes driver's licences, automobile registrations, mortgage tax records, and credit reports. Private sources include transaction data from credit card companies, banks, health and life insurance companies, hospitals and clinics, stock brokers and investment firms, and long-distance telephone companies. In the past, credit card companies and other organizations only kept transaction data for a limited time, such as six months. Advances in storage capabilities, however, mean that this information is now stored for an unlimited time. Other third-party sources include other companies that have profiled their customers and companies that specialize in developing profiles. One organization has created records on almost 200 million Americans that include information down to their age and weight. These records can be leased or bought by other firms.

Next, the company must process the information. Sophisticated computers can be used to develop models and predict future behaviour. This lets the marketer see relationships in the data and the variables that effect behaviour and impact purchase. Although computer prices have been steadily decreasing, this stage is often the most expensive. The complex data analysis requires advanced computing techniques, such as parallel processing and neural networks. Also, companies must invest in extensive data storage in order to hold all of the information. Although it can be relatively easy to develop a large database of customer information, the challenge is in analyzing the data and making sense of the results. Computers aid in this process because they can recognize complex patterns and use them to build models. The last step in the database marketing process is using this information to develop a highly specific profile of the company's customers. This step, referred to as "drilling down" the data, is then used to match new customers or create special targeted offers for the current customer.

As can be seen, advances in technology are shaking up the traditional methods marketers use to reach their targets. In the past, marketers became accustomed to working with broad categories of customers. Now, companies can target their efforts down to the individual level. Practitioners of database marketing believe that most companies are sitting on a powerhouse of information in their own records that can and should be tapped. To these marketers, nothing is more powerful than knowledge; specifically, knowledge about a customer's individual behavioural practices and buying preferences.

As with any new technology, though, database marketing is not without its critics. Consumer activists feel that the collection, manipulation, and combination of personal consumer information is an invasion of privacy. Although there is a small threat of unauthorized use, many people are concerned that the larger threat is from companies collecting information for one purpose and using it for another without the consumer's knowledge or consent. There are currently no legal mandates on the use of database marketing, but the practice has started to draw the attention of politicians. In 1995, the Clinton administration's Privacy Working Group published a report directed at database marketing titled, "Privacy and the National Information Infrastructure: Principles for Providing and Using Personal Information." This report did not introduce any new laws, but it did recommend that consumers should always be given knowledge of the use of their information, notice if it is going to be shared, and the chance to say no if they do not consent. Companies using database marketing maintain that they can police themselves by implementing privacy policies similar to this doctrine and giving their employees sensitivity training on privacy issues. An example of this is the establishment of a phone number that consumers can call to be removed from mailing lists, although critics claim that this is ineffective. Companies that decide to implement a database marketing approach must be careful to keep the converging ideas of the power of information and the exploitation of privacy in balance.

At this point, VideoMania has not ventured into database marketing. The company would be in a good position to do so, though, because they already have detailed records on each of their current customers. It would be easy to bolster this with information from third-party sources and develop some profiles.

Leigh has suggested that the results could be used in three ways. First, a system would be developed that would recommend new movies to customers on the basis of their past selections. This is seen as a way to introduce customers that are already satisfied with VideoMania to movies that they otherwise might not have considered.

Second, VideoMania would analyze the movie selections of its current customers and use this information to make special promotional offers in conjunction with other companies. For example, if a couple purchased several European movies, they might receive an offer for a special trip to Paris or a special promotion on international films. Several of the independent video retailers have already found this type of cross-promotion to be extremely lucrative. One of the most profitable areas concerns adult-oriented movies. Many companies sell or trade the names of anyone who rents an adult film to a variety of companies selling similar merchandise.

Last, the information on the company's current customers would be used to develop a detailed profile of the typical or ideal customer that could then be used to target new customers for the company's services. Currently, the company gets new customers through referrals and a limited advertising campaign. All of the advertising is placed using only intuition. Although these methods have been successful in the company's past, Leigh believes that VideoMania needs to market more aggressively if it is to continue to grow in the future. A similar possibility is that there would be a market for the individual customer profiles that VideoMania develops. These profiles could either be sold to a data warehouse or noncompeting company for profit or be traded for additional names that could then be added to the mailing list.

Roberts agrees that the company needs to actively solicit more business. He believes, however, that implementing such a database marketing program would be seen as intrusive by VideoMania's educated customers. He has warned Leigh that if VideoMania takes database marketing too far, it could backfire and actually alienate their customers instead of attracting them. Leigh has argued that if VideoMania does not try these techniques, one of their competitors will.

Both sides agree that there is no more important asset than a happy customer. What Roberts and Leigh must now agree on is whether the concern of violating the customer's privacy is offset by the potential gain to customers from the introduction to new products and special offers.

Assignment

1. Have you ever received an offer for goods or services that made you feel intruded upon? Have you ever felt that a company knew too much about you?
2. The new forms of database marketing are meant to match products better to prospective consumers. If this works correctly, is this really an invasion of the consumer's privacy or is it a service?
3. How responsible are companies to unwritten ethical guidelines when they will negatively affect the company's competitive advantage and profits?
4. Is the company justified in investing in such a program simply because the competition might?
5. There might be reasonable limits to what a company should know about a private citizen. What do you think these limits should be? Do these limits change if the citizen is a prospect or a client?
6. Should the use of sophisticated database marketing techniques be regulated? If so, who should regulate them?

Sources

Jonathan Berry, "A Potent New Tool for Selling: Database Marketing," *Business Week*, September 5, 1994. Mary Culnan, "Fair Game or Fair Play?" *Journal of Business Strategy* (November/December 1995). Mark Lewyn, "You Can Run, But It's Tough to Hide from Marketers," *Business Week*, September 5, 1994. Janet Novack, "The Data Miners," *Forbes*, February 12, 1996. Greg Paus, "Consumers Want Privacy," *Advertising Age*, October 30, 1995.

CASE 7: State College Bookstore: Operating within a Complex Legal and Ethical Environment

James Strong, The University of Akron

While preparing the current goals and objectives report for the president, Claude Landauer was reflecting on the progress that has been made with the State College Bookstore since he arrived seven years ago to revamp the once stodgy operation. Seven years ago the State College Bookstore simply sold books and related supplies and made a modest contribution to the university. Since then, Claude has turned the bookstore into a major profit centre for the university.

The profitability of the bookstore operation has created some conflict within the university community. One of the more significant problems is the growing controversy surrounding the pricing of textbooks. Students are calling for price reductions on all or most textbooks. The average text is $45 to $55, and although book expenditures make up the smallest portion of education expenses, many students believe texts are overpriced. This perception persists even though textbook prices have risen at the same rate as inflation for the last several years. About 35 percent of retail selling price of textbooks is retained by the bookstore to cover operating costs and net profit. Transportation and handling costs average around 5 percent of each sales dollar. The publisher share of each retail sales dollar is 60 percent. From its share, the publisher must produce and market the book, pay royalties to the author, and generate a profit.

Claude has a policy of buying back used textbooks for 50 percent of the original selling price if his inventory needs replenishment and the book is being used at the university the next semester. The purchase price for used books that are current but not needed averages 25 percent. The price is less for these books in order to cover the freight costs of sending them to a central warehouse. Students gripe about the buy-back prices, especially when low amounts are given because the book is not needed. It also happens that a student's book has no value at all because the publisher has brought out a new edition, something they have increasingly done in recent years. Today, new revisions come out every two or three years. Ten years ago, textbooks were revised every three to five years. Shorter revision cycles help reduce the amount of used books in the market. A sale of a used book means no revenues or profits for the publisher and the author.

Claude also purchases "examination copies" of new textbooks for 50 percent of their value and sells them at 15 percent off the regular retail price for new books. These books are very popular with students, and the net profits for the bookstore are substantially higher than when students buy books purchased directly from the producer. Publishing companies routinely send examination copies of new texts at no charge to professors who teach the course. The publisher's logic behind this practice is that the publisher's texts need to be on the professor's shelves when the professor makes his or her text selection for the coming semester. Professors will only consider those texts that they have on hand when selecting for the next semester. And, of course, when most of the competition is engaged in this practice, any one publisher finds it difficult to avoid it. Entrepreneurs have developed a lucrative business by buying these examination copies from some professors for cash, paying anywhere from 5 to 30 percent of the value of the book and reselling them to book distributors, who in turn resell them to college bookstores. In this "gray" market the entrepreneurs, distributors, and bookstore are making above-normal margins, and the publisher and author receive nothing. This practice is roundly criticized by publishers and authors, who contend that the used book buyers are free-riding on their work and investment. However, to date the publishers have not significantly curbed the distribution of examination copies, although they are now printing "examination copy-not for resale" across the books. This has not dried up the supply. Some publishers are considering leaving chapters out of examination copies, rendering them useless in the used book market.

Claude is being pressured by publishers and State College faculty authors not to buy examination copies. These groups consider the practice unethical. Claude has mixed feelings about the issue, but he leans toward continuing to sell the books because they do represent a discount for students, and he sees the problem as something essentially under the control of the publishers.

Assignment

1. Is it unethical for college bookstores to buy examination copies for discounted prices and resell them at a discount? Are the publishers and authors being cheated by this practice? Should this practice be illegal?
2. Is it unethical for publishers to bring out new editions that are only marginally different every two years in order to shrink the used book market? Consider that from an academic standpoint the appearance of new editions every three or four years is acceptable. Should publishing new editions primarily to eliminate the used book market be illegal?
3. Without any help from lawmakers, what could publishers do to solve the "gray market" problem?
4. Are textbooks overpriced? If so, what can/should college bookstores do to address this problem?

CASE 8: Furniture City: Legal Implications in Retailing*

D. Wesley Balderson, University of Lethbridge

Furniture City was a newly established furniture-appliance store located in Edmonton, Alberta. The store stocked a large inventory of medium-quality furniture, stereos, and televisions. Furniture City had a large advertising budget and featured frequent sales and discount prices. The owner of the store, Mr. Brady, felt that this was the only way to compete in the market in Edmonton, which had recently been entered by Future Shop and A&B Sound. It was Furniture City's policy to meet the price of any competitor. Mr. Brady was not too concerned about losing a lot of margin through this practice as Furniture City did not stock the leading brands of appliances and there was not a great deal of brand recognition in the furniture industry.

Despite Furniture City's promotional policies, sales for the first six months of operation, particularly of appliances, were disappointing. Furniture sales reached 80 percent of the projected amounts but TV and stereo sales were about 25 percent of what Mr. Brady thought he could achieve. Mr. Brady realized that something would have to be done to improve the situation. He was already spending a large amount of money on advertising and was hesitant to increase it. He was happy with his current suppliers and felt that the merchandise he stocked was in harmony with the store's overall objectives. Mr. Brady felt that if he could just get more TV and stereo shoppers into the store, he and his two salespeople could convince a large number of them to buy. One of his employees suggested that the way to draw people into the store was through a drastically low price on a line of merchandise. It then might be possible for Brady and his staff to "sell up" the customers to merchandise that was regularly priced. What was lost on the sale items would be more than compensated for with the increased sales. For the sale Brady decided to offer ten 12-inch black and white TVs at $49.99 which was $10 below his cost and $20–$30 below the price at other stores.

Because of the extreme price competition, Mr. Brady realized that the sale would have to feature drastic price cuts to attract attention. Furniture City placed the following ad in the local newspaper on Wednesday, Nov. 23, 1997.

Furniture City
Door Buster TV Sale

NEW TVs PRICED AS LOW AS $49.99

SATURDAY ONLY 9AM–5PM

Furniture City 10533 - 82 Ave.

Mr. Brady and his staff were unprepared for the response. There was a lineup outside the door when he opened up at 9 a.m. on Saturday. Although many customers were upset by the fact that the TVs were small and black-and-white, they quickly sold out. Customers continued to stream in throughout the day. Although this was the situation Mr. Brady wanted, he and his staff were unable to close many sales on the other merchandise. In fact, most customers were irate that they had been drawn into the store and the sale items were already sold out. At the end of the day, Brady and his two clerks decided they wouldn't try that again.

*Although this case is factual, the names and location have been changed.

His troubles were not over, however. A few days later the Consumer and Corporate Affairs Department contacted Brady and after getting details of the sale, informed him that Furniture City would be charged under the Unfair Trade Practices Act for bait and switch advertising. The following months were a nightmare for Brady. The investigation culminated in Furniture City receiving a fine and being required to publish the following ad in the paper.

NOTE OF APOLOGY

On Nov. 23, 1997, Furniture City ran an ad in the *Edmonton Journal* which was deemed to contravene the Alberta Unfair Trade Practices Act. The advertisement was the "Door Buster TV Sale" in which Furniture City offered 12" black and white TV sets at $49.99. Furniture City had an insufficient supply of these items available and apologizes for this error.

In accordance with the terms of an Undertaking under the Alberta Unfair Trade Practices Act, Furniture City has undertaken to abide by the terms of that Act and to provide this notice to you. Further, to show our good faith we have agreed to offer 75 of the televisions at the same "Door Buster" price commencing at 9 a.m. Saturday March 14th, 1998, and continuing until all of the TVs have been sold.

Assignment

1. Suggest possible reasons why appliance sales were not reaching Mr. Brady's projections prior to the "Door Buster" sale.
2. Explain why the Door Buster sale was likely a contravention of the Unfair Trade Practices Act. How was this sale different from using a loss leader?
3. Evaluate the consequence of this situation for Furniture City.

CASE 9: Nelson Hardware Store: Employee Problems*

D. Wesley Balderson, University of Lethbridge

Nelson Hardware is a small hardware store located in Elmira, Ontario, an agricultural community near Guelph. Merchandise stocked includes automotive and farm supplies, furniture and appliances, sporting goods, plumbing and electrical supplies, and giftware. The owner is Donald Nelson, a prominent businessman in the community who also owns another business which occupies a large portion of his time. Because of this, Mr. Nelson has delegated considerable authority to the manager of the store, Mr. Bill Tracy. In July of 1997, Mr. Nelson and Bill Tracy decided that they should hire a new employee to be trained as an assistant manager. They first discussed the possibility of promoting one of the existing employees in the store, but Bill did not feel any of them would be suitable as assistant managers as he felt they were either too old or not interested in the extra responsibility. Bart Harris, Bill's uncle, was already 63 years old and though working full-time had indicated that he wanted to work fewer hours and begin to ease into retirement. Lois Scott, 52, had been with the company for 12 years but had tended to concentrate on the giftware side of the department and Bill did not feel she had an adequate knowledge of the farm supply side of the business, which was the most important to the store in terms of revenue. Rose Barker, 61 years old, had only worked with the company for 6 years (some of which had been part-time) and although very competent and knowledgeable, it was felt she was also too old to fill the position. The only other employees were part-time students who worked Saturdays and summers. As a result of their discussions, it was decided that they should advertise for an assistant manager in the local paper. This resulted in a few enquiries but no applicants who met the two criteria that Bill Tracy and Mr. Nelson felt were important—that of knowing the people in the community and having a knowledge of agriculture.

Mr. Nelson and Bill met again in August to discuss the fact that no prospects had turned up and Mr. Nelson suggested that he might contact Karl Nicol, an acquaintance of his who lived in Elmira, about coming to work for the company. He was currently working in a town some 40 km away and it was thought that there might be a chance he could be attracted to his hometown. Karl was young, only 25, and knew the people in the community. Mr. Nelson approached Karl and found that he was interested in coming to work for him but indicated that he required a salary figure higher than Mr. Nelson and Bill Tracy had planned for this position. If they agreed to pay the salary Karl requested, it would mean Karl would be paid a higher wage than the other hardware department employees except Bill Tracy himself. Although Mr. Nelson and Bill worried about this, they decided to hire Karl and requested that his salary be kept confidential. Karl was informed that he would be in a training position for approximately six months and then assume the position of assistant manager of the store.

Things went smoothly for the first while but after a few months it was evident to Mr. Nelson that some problems were surfacing. Mr. Nelson noticed antagonism between Karl and the other three regular employees that was noticeable to customers. In discussing Karl's progress with Bill Tracy he learned that Karl was frequently late for work, his appearance was unsatisfactory, he was very slow in gaining essential product knowledge, and that Bill had had several complaints from customers about him. In addition to this discouraging report from Bill Tracy, Karl himself had contacted Mr. Nelson directly and expressed his disillusionment with the job and with his supervisor, Bill Tracy. He indicated that Bill was not providing adequate training about the products or authority for ordering inventory, setting prices, and so on, and that when Bill was on his day off several sales were lost because none of the employees knew

* Although the situation described is factual, the names and location have been changed.

the information required by customers. He also mentioned that as assistant manager he shouldn't have to sweep the floors as he had been required to do on several occasions. He further requested of Mr. Nelson that he be granted time off to take a management course at a local college two afternoons a week to help him prepare for the management aspects of his job. Mr. Nelson discussed the problem again with Bill, who said that as soon as Karl proved himself he would be given the requested authority and, of course, he was very opposed to his taking time off for a management course, so this request was turned down. Towards the end of November, Karl contacted Mr. Nelson to see if he could take some of his holidays just before Christmas. When Mr. Nelson mentioned Karl's request to Bill Tracy, Bill was very opposed because, as he indicated, this period was the busiest time of the year for the store and that furthermore, in the past, employees had worked a year before they took their holidays. However, Mr. Nelson allowed Karl to go on the holiday.

They were able to get through the Christmas rush and inventory-taking without serious incident. Things seemed to get progressively worse until finally, nine months after Karl was hired, he handed in his resignation as he was going to go back to university. Mr. Nelson was relieved that the problem employee had left but hoped next time the same thing would not happen.

Assignment

1. Comment on the possible reasons why this situation did not turn out successfully.
2. What lessons can be learned from this case?

CASE 10: Murray Hardware Stores: Designing Layouts and Planning Space Productivity

David Burns and *E. Terry Deiderick*, Youngstown State University

Susan McNally is cofounder of Jones & McNally, an interior design firm specializing in designing both aesthetic and functional retail and service facilities. She recently obtained a contract to design the store interior for a new

Figure B–10–1

Available store alternatives

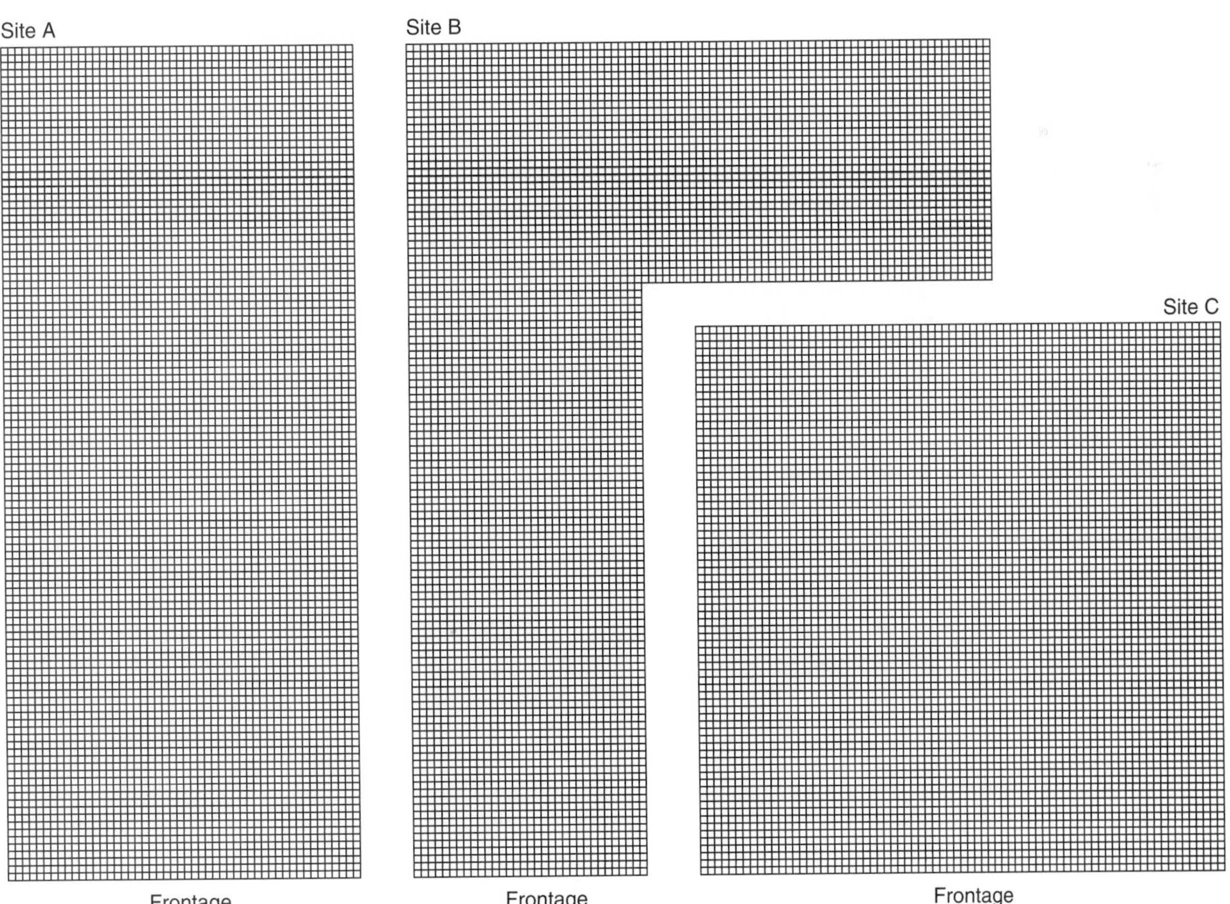

Figure B-10-2

Space requirements, customer convenience/service expectations, and operating margins

Product/use description	Space requirements[1]	Convenience/service levels[2]	Gross margins[3]
Nonselling areas			
Offices	600	Low	
Rest rooms	200	Medium	
Checkout	200	High	
Customer service	600	High	
Selling areas			
Bulk seasonal goods[4]	500	High	Medium
Seasonal goods[5]	1 000	High	High
Paints	1 200	High	Medium
Housewares	500	Low	Medium
Plumbing	800	High	High
Electrical	800	High	High
Auto	150	Medium	Medium
Tools	500	Low	Medium
Hardware	1 200	Low	Medium
Bicycle parts	100	Medium	Medium
Unrelated goods[6]	650	Medium	Medium
Promotional goods[7]	1 000	Medium	Low
Total nonselling and selling areas	10 000		

[1]Space requirements are expressed in square feet; however, space productivity also takes vertical space into account.

[2]Convenience/services levels are classified as: (a) High—Customers view items as specialty goods and are willing to spend time, money, and effort to find the right product; however, customers continually require personal attention for product information and sales support. (b) Medium—Customers view items as shopping goods and are willing to spend a moderate amount of time shopping for the product. Customers occasionally require the personal attention of sales associates. (c) Low—Customers view the items as convenience goods and will not spend time, money, or effort to find these readily available products. Customers purchase these products on a self-service basis; therefore, little or no personal attention is required if the store is properly merchandised.

[3]Gross margins are identified as: (a) High—greater than 75%, (b) Medium—50% to 75%, and (c) Low—less than 50%.

[4]Bulk seasonal goods represent floor displays of the following items: Winter—Christmas trees and snow blowers. Spring—Lawn mowers and fertilizers. Summer—Swimming pools and lawn furniture. Fall—Rakes, leaf blowers, fireplace supplies.

[5]Seasonal goods represent gondola displays of the following items: Winter—Christmas supplies, snow shovels, snow brushes, insulated gloves, hats. Spring—Hand lawn and garden tools, seeds, pruning tools, outdoor flower containers. Summer—Barbecue and pool supplies, lawnmower parts, camping supplies, canning supplies. Fall—Leaf bags, weatherstripping, plant bulbs.

[6]Unrelated products consist of nonhardware items such as gift ideas, clocks, stationery, and candy.

[7]Promotional goods represent advertised specials, sales items, and special purchases that feature extra value.

Murray Hardware Store that will be opening soon in the new Fox Valley Community Shopping Centre. Murray Hardware's primary target market is composed of local "do-it-yourself" residents who want to obtain needed tools, supplies, and advice at a convenient location in a timely manner. Although Murray Hardware cannot compete with market area home centres such as Menard's on price or product selection, Murray prospers by operating smaller stores within close proximity to the residential areas housing its target consumer groups. The store's competitive advantage is the place convenience and the personal attention it offers customers.

What makes this particular contract challenging is that McNally has three sites available to her in the Fox Valley Community Shopping Centre. The consulting contract calls for Jones & McNally to (1) develop preliminary interior store designs for each of the three sites, (2) identify the strengths and weaknesses of each site and its interior store design, and (3) recommend which site and store design offer the best opportunity for Murray's to meet both its space productivity and customer service goals. The three site alternatives are as follows (see Figure B–10–1):

- Site A: 10 000 sq. ft., rectangular shape with 66.8 ft of frontage and 150 ft deep. Rent is $10 per sq. ft.
- Site B: 10 000 sq. ft., L-shaped with 50 ft of frontage and 150 ft deep and 100 ft wide along the back. Rent is $9 per sq. ft.
- Site C: 10 000 sq. ft., square shape with 100 ft of frontage and 100 ft deep. Rent is $11 per sq. ft.

Because the centre is new, the placement and configuration of windows and doors are flexible for each of the sites. Local building codes require (1) 4-ft. clearance between fixtures and (2) 8-ft. clearance for the main traffic aisles. For economic reasons, 3-ft.-wide, two-sided shelving units will be used as the primary display fixture.

The primary products for which customers visit Murray Hardware are hardware, electrical, and plumbing products. Additional sales are in the areas of such seasonal and promotional goods as lawn and garden equipment, auto parts, bicycle parts, and housewares. Customers often purchase unrelated goods as impulse items when in the store for other items. The information in Figure B–10–2, furnished by Murray's management, cites the space requirements for each department and essential information on customer shopping behaviour and financial performance results. The firm's management made it very clear that both customer satisfaction objectives and financial performance objectives play an important role in any of the firm's key decisions.

Assignment

1. Assume the role of Susan McNally and fulfill the terms of the consulting contract. Using graph paper, construct a layout to scale for each of the sites. As you position the various departments, be sure to take adjacencies and potential traffic patterns into account as well as potential store atmosphere. Evaluate each layout, and make a recommendation as to which site offers the best opportunity to meet and balance management's customer and financial objectives.

CASE 11: Sensormatic: Securing the Retail Store

Cristine Braman, The University of Akron

Stallions is a small retail apparel chain specializing in western wear. Its successful Bainbridge Mall store produces annual sales of $1 million with 3000 sq. ft. [280 m^2] of retailing space. Stallions offers casual clothing and accessories for the male 16–40 years of age. The merchandise is composed of jeans, casual pants, shorts, heavy cotton clothing, many types of casual shirts, jackets, long coats, belts, boots, shoes, hats (predominantly cowboy), socks, jockey shorts, and two private collection colognes. The store has been experiencing an increase in security problems in recent years, most especially since JOX, a sporting goods store, moved into an adjacent location. Sporting goods stores have a history of shoplifting problems, which has affected Stallions. This problem of having a shoplifting magnet next door cannot be solved by relocating, because Stallions' lease has six more years to go.

In the retail industry the loss of inventory is referred to as shrink or shrinkage. There are a few causes for this shrink at Stallions. More than half results from employee pilferage, about a third is a consequence of shoplifting by customers, and the rest is from bad cheques written for merchandise and paperwork errors by the retailer. Shrinkage is costing Stallions approximately 1.5 percent of sales, which is a 0.5 percent increase from last year. The loss of inventory is always a concern for retailers, and the management at Stallions has decided to concentrate on controlling one particular area of shrinkage at a time. Shoplifting by customers has increased the most dramatically for Stallions. The previous year it accounted for a quarter of all shrinkage, increasing to a third for this year. Consequently, the current area of concentration is curbing customer theft. When this problem is under control, it should be easier to focus on employee theft.

Seth Kreig, the store manager of Stallions, has been investigating the options involved with retail pilfering. A store can focus on catching shoplifters or preventing shoplifters; if the choice is prevention, there are many devices to choose from. Lauren Broden is a sales representative from Sensormatic, a manufacturer of many shoplifting prevention devices, and she is coming in today for an appointment.

Seth welcomes Lauren and gives her a tour so that she can get an idea of Stallions' operations. This location in Bainbridge Mall was not equipped with many security devices when the mall was first built, and Stallions has not had many problems until recently. The only provisions in the store were locations for two-way mirrors and closed-circuit televisions, but these had never been installed, and the space has not been utilized. Lauren also notes that the entryway from the mall is a wide doorway with a distinct design. She noticed that most of the stores in Bainbridge Mall have elaborate storefronts with wide, open doorways.

This is Seth's first position as a store manager, and he has an aggressive attitude about catching shoplifters. He would like to schedule an employee, during the busiest hours of the week, whose primary duty during that particular shift would be to watch for potential shoplifting. The employee could walk around the store monitoring customers directly, or two-way mirrors could be installed so that the employee could monitor both shoppers and employees.

Seth explains his ideas to Lauren, and she listens patiently. As soon as Seth asks her opinion, Lauren takes the opportunity to explain that "catching" shoplifters will not solve the security problem. This intrigues Seth, and he asks her to explain.

Lauren describes the history of Sensormatic to Seth. The company began selling security items twenty-five years ago. It took a few years for the company to realize that it should be in the business of preventing shoplifting and not "catching shoplifters." Sensormatic discovered that catching shoplifters was only a deterrent for a short time and that it was expensive. Seth interjected at this point that he believed if Stallions became known as a store that caught people stealing, this would be a deterrent.

At this point, Lauren explained that the image of being a difficult store to steal from usually lasts only for a short time. Also, after the shoplifters are caught, prosecuting them is time-consuming and costly. The retailer must pay legal fees and support employees in testifying against the shoplifter. The retailer cannot follow through with every case, which further tarnishes the image of being a difficult store to steal from. In addition, catching shoplifters takes the store's eye off of who should be the focus of attention—the customer.

The people at Sensormatic came to realize that it was more efficient to prevent shoplifting than to catch shoplifters. Security in retail stores can be effective without becoming an unreasonable expense. Paying for security devices to prevent shoplifting is cheaper than paying the legal fees to prosecute each thief. The security devices used to deter shoplifters are effective for the long term and also contribute to the prevention of employee pilferage. When purchased, they are used continually, and the potential thieves, whether shoppers or employees, are aware of this.

At this point, Seth becomes convinced that protection, not prosecution, is the best solution for his store. He asks Lauren if Sensormatic manufactures the plastic tags that many stores attach to merchandise. Seth assumes that this is one of the better prevention devices available to a retailer. Lauren explains that the hard tags are part of a system better known as electronic article surveillance (EAS). This system includes the hard tags on the clothing, the detachers used by the salespeople to take the tags off the clothing, and a monitor at the exit of the store. An EAS system would cost a store the size of Stallions about $7000. A newer item also used on clothing is an ink tack, which splatters ink on the clothing if it is tampered with. This would ruin the garment even if the thief is successful in removing it from the store. Ink tacks are used when a retailer believes that if it cannot sell the merchandise, then the thief should not be able to use it. It would cost Stallions about $500 to employ these, and they could be used in conjunction with another system.

A system that might be more appropriate for the needs of Stallions is the closed-circuit television (CCTV) system. It is used in a larger-than-average mall store and consists of a dome, fixed camera monitors, and video camera recorders (VCRs). This system would cost Stallions approximately $8000 and could be used in conjunction with the ink tacks or the EAS system.

The success of Sensormatic since the company changed its orientation also confirms that prevention is the answer to security problems. The company has had more than 50 percent market share in any market that it has entered, and this success is global. For example, Sensormatic has approximately 70 percent of the market share in the Japanese market, where it competes with three Japanese companies, two European companies, and one other U.S. company.

Assignment

1. You have been hired as the new assistant store manager, and Seth has asked you to investigate which of the alternative systems would be most appropriate for Stallions. Specifically, he has asked you to address the following issues, and knowing Seth as you do, the "whys" of each of these situations will have to be addressed along with the "whats":
    a. What are the benefits and drawbacks of each of the three security alternatives suggested by Lauren?
    b. What type of favourable and/or unfavourable experiences have other retailers had with each of these alternatives?
    c. Which security alternative should Stallions install, if any?

CASE 12: Value Mart Stores: Trading Area Analysis

D. Wesley Balderson, University of Lethbridge

Value Mart Stores is a regional chain of supermarkets located in the northwestern United States. Over the years it has been fairly successful and has grown to 33 outlets in the states of Montana, Idaho, and Washington. Its supermarkets are similar in theme to that of Safeway, emphasizing low prices, quality products, and a pleasant store atmosphere. The long-range plans for Value Mart include continued growth and establishing stores in new geographic markets, as they feel that many of their current locations are getting fairly saturated.

As a result of their growth strategy and the Free Trade Agreement between the U.S. and Canada, Value Mart executives are looking at expanding into Canada. They plan to do so in a careful, systematic way, however, realizing that many retailers have been unsuccessful attempting this in the past. Value Mart is currently examining three cities (to locate their first Canadian store), which are all in close proximity to their present market. They have collected information (See Figure B–12–1) on the cities of Cranbrook, Lethbridge, and Medicine Hat.

Cranbrook is located in the southeast corner of British Columbia. It is only 80 km from the U.S. border and within a four-hour drive of Spokane, Washington, where Value Mart's distribution warehouse is located. Cranbrook's economy depends primarily upon forestry, mining, and agriculture, all three of which have experienced recent economic downturns. The major supermarkets in Cranbrook are

Figure B–12–1

	Cranbrook	Medicine Hat	Lethbridge
Population	18 000	68 000	55 000
Per Capita Income	12 700	13 600	12 900
Retail Sales	100 000 000	400 000 000	320 000 000
Retail Grocery Sales	25 000 000	90 000 000	75 000 000
Number of Direct Competitors	4	15	10
Canadian Averages			
Per Capita Income	14 800		
Per Capita Retail Sales	6 400		

Safeways, Save-On Foods, and Overwaitea, the latter two owned by the Pattison organization. Annual population growth rate is 0.3%.

Lethbridge is service centre for a large agricultural community. It is estimated that an additional 50 000 people live in the small towns and farms within an 80-kilometre radius of the city. Lethbridge is located 80 km from the U.S. border and is only 240 km from Great Falls, Montana, where Value Mart currently has two stores. The major supermarkets in Lethbridge are Safeway, Save-On Foods (which has recently moved to Lethbridge from B.C.), and Food City. There are also a number of fairly successful independent supermarkets in the city. Annual population growth rate for Lethbridge is 1.7%.

The third city, Medicine Hat, is located 160 km east of Lethbridge, close to the Saskatchewan border. Medicine Hat's economy is tied to natural gas as well as agriculture. The major competitors for Value Mart in this city are Safeway and Co-op, a Saskatchewan-based supermarket co-operative. The annual population growth rate for Medicine Hat is 0.7%.

The executives of Value Mart are investigating the income, retail sales, and competitive situations of the three cities in order to help them make their decision about where to locate their first Canadian store.

Assignment

1. Estimate the relative attractiveness of the three centres using the income rating index, market rating index, and index of retail saturation.
2. What other factors should be examined before Value Mart makes a decision?

CASE 13: Starbucks Coffee Company: Location Analysis

D. Wesley Balderson, University of Lethbridge

Starbucks Coffee Company Ltd. is the leading retailer, roaster, and brand of specialty coffee in North America. Starbucks not only supplies its product to many organizations, its specialty retail division is the fastest growing coffee house chain in North America, with over 1270 stores and nearly $1 billion in sales in 1997. Starbucks has also expanded to the Pacific Rim, Latin America, and Europe.

Starbucks began as a take-out coffee roaster in Seattle's Pike Market in 1971. This store was opened for less than $10 000 and was purchased in 1987 for $4 million by current CEO Howard Schultz. Schultz realized that there was opportunity for growth and began rapid expansion of the retail specialty division by opening stores across the United States and Canada shortly after the purchase. In addition, agreements with large corporate entities provided greater exposure for the Starbucks brand name. As part of this program, Starbucks became the official coffee of United Airlines, Barnes and Noble Booksellers, Chicago's Wrigley Field, and scores of other institutions. The company has also co-branded its product and siren logo with Breyer's ice cream, Redhook Ale's Double Black Stout, and a Pepsi-distributed store version of its Frappuccino drink. Starbucks has even unveiled the prototype for an Intel-partnered cybercafé, and begun offering book selections in conjunction with Oprah Winfrey.

In October of 1997, Starbucks announced an agreement with Wells Fargo to create a new retail concept. Full-service banking, Starbucks coffee and products, efficient postal services, quality dry cleaning, copying, and more will soon be available in one convenient, comfortable place. Seven locations will be chosen in late 1997 for the pilot stores and should be ready for business in 1998.

Despite this new type of outlet based on convenience, Starbucks has long emphasized the atmosphere of their

Figure B–13–1

	Red Deer	Lethbridge	Canadian Average
Population	75 000	70 000	
Per Capita Income	$15 000	$14 000	$14 800
Retail Sales	$550 000 000	$500 000 000	$ 6 400
Coffee Outlets	40	35	
Profit Margin for coffee houses			5%

outlets and the high quality and assortment of their products. This emphasis has had the effect of placing Starbucks in the category of a specialty retailer even though the product is generally thought to be a convenience good. Some strong competitors have emerged in Starbucks markets. Second Cup, for example, is a successful Canadian franchise of coffee houses and has provided stiff competition for Starbucks in some of its markets. In addition, numerous independent businesses successfully compete for market share in this growing market.

Starbucks is committed to continued growth (2000 stores by the year 2000) of their traditional retail outlets but is currently concerned that many markets have become saturated with the aforementioned competition and even existing Starbucks stores. As a result, Starbucks is carefully considering expansion into some smaller cities in Western Canada. They have recently decided to add an outlet in *either* Red Deer or Lethbridge, Alberta, in 1998. They have collected some information about the trading areas of these two centres, which is shown in Figure B–13–1.

Whichever centre Starbucks locates its coffee outlet in, it is desirous to locate in a mall to ensure higher traffic. Red Deer and Lethbridge each have two major malls. Starbucks wants to locate its store in the mall which will draw the largest traffic counts, as they know from past experience that they will be able to attract 20 percent of mall visitors to their store with an average sale of $3 per customer. They have collected the following information about the two malls in each city.

The malls in Red Deer are 15 minutes driving time apart. The Red Deer Mall, located on the north side of Red Deer, has 100 stores, while the Parkland Mall on the south side of the city contains 50 stores. It is estimated that each mall achieves a base customer traffic count of 4000 people per day from three directions *plus* a fraction of the population living between the two malls. There is an estimated population of 3000 between the malls and their homes are evenly spaced so that there are 200 people for every one minute of driving time.

The malls in Lethbridge are 10 minutes apart. College Mall contains 60 stores and Lethbridge Centre has 90 stores. Both also have a base daily traffic count of 4000 *plus* a fraction of the market between the two malls. There are 4000 people living between the two malls and their homes are evenly spaced so that there are 400 people for every one minute of driving time.

Assignment

1. Using income rating, market rating, and saturation indexes discuss which of the two centers would be the most attractive for Starbucks to locate in.
2. What other nonquantitative factors in trading area selection would/should apply to this situation?
3. Explain how the classification of consumer goods relates to the specific site decision in the Starbucks situation.
4. Using the gravitational methods, which of the four malls should Starbucks locate in?
5. For the mall you selected, what is the profit potential of that site?

CASE 14: Klawson Electronics: Inventory Management

Shilpa Stocker, University of Lethbridge

Gary Klawson is the sole owner of Klawson Electronics, which is located in Lethbridge, Alberta. Klawson Electronics is locally owned and operated and is one of the two largest electronic stores in Lethbridge, a predominantly agricultural town of 70 000 people. Klawson's major competition is the Electronic Superstore which is a chain operated out of Vancouver, British Columbia, with stores throughout British Columbia, Alberta, and Saskatchewan. Buying for the Electronic Superstore takes place at the central office in Vancouver. Presently, Electronic Superstore carries the same product lines as Klawson Electronics; however, Gary has the opportunity to acquire an exclusive line from Alpine Distributors. Alpine has assured Gary that he'll be the sole carrier of its high-end products in Lethbridge.

Inventory

Klawson Electronics carries radios, compact disc players, television sets, car audio equipment, camcorders, radar detectors, phones, answering machines, and home entertainment systems. Gary places his orders for these products with salespeople from various electronic suppliers (e.g., Pioneer Electronics). The electronic suppliers obtain approval from Ajax Financing Company prior to shipping the goods to Klawson Electronics. Ajax maintains a continual creditworthiness evaluation of Klawson. Gary's payments to Ajax Financing are determined when Ajax sends an inventory auditor to Klawson Electronics. It is important for Gary to maintain a 90-day turnover on his products, since Ajax levies service charges on inventory financed over 90 days. Ajax also demands payment for products as they are sold.

Ajax's inventory auditor is able to identify products and the length of time they've been on Gary's floor by the product's model and serial number. Ajax auditors have accurate computer records of when the product was purchased, the cost, and from which electronic supplier. The auditor has a hand-held computer device which allows him or her to enter model numbers and serial numbers within one or two days. A computer printout is given to Gary at the end of this audit, and payment must be made on the goods sold and the goods remaining in Gary's possession, as well as on the interest due on the amounts borrowed.

Personnel Organization

Although Gary owns the store, his main involvement is in the buying and advertising. He is often able to encourage suppliers to participate in cooperative advertising and, as a result, his buying can focus on obtaining a sizable cooperative advertising allowance from the participating suppliers.

Gary has an office manager who keeps track of receivables, payables, and payroll on the computer. Financial statements are drawn up by a local accounting firm. The accounting firm insists on a physical inventory twice a year.

The warehouse is located next to the store. The warehouse manager is responsible for the shipping and receiving of merchandise within the store. Shipments are stacked in the warehouse, and the salespeople inform the warehouse manager when floor stock needs to be replenished. The warehouse manager also enlists the aid of the salespeople in completing the physical inventories as requested by the accountants.

Gary's selling organization consists of five full-time salespeople with whom he has occasional sales meetings. In addition to the information acquired at these sales meetings, the salespeople have access to the costs of the products as well as the manufacturer's suggested retail prices. They also have a good indication of the lead time required in bringing certain types of products into the store. In most cases, this lead time is nine days from the date of ordering. Once informed by the salespeople, Gary is able to order by phone or fax from the suppliers. These suppliers provide a wealth of information and are current on industry trends and breakthroughs.

June Promotion

It is April, and Gary has just completed the slowest season (February/March) in electronics. He has targeted for \$90 000 worth of sales by planning a car and personal audio promotion in June. Spring and summer are great seasons for car audio (amplifiers, tuners, cassette players, speakers, etc.) and personal audio (radios, discmen, blasters, etc.) sales. He is planning his commitments for the various electronic suppliers. He plans on having approximately \$15 000 worth of car and personal audio left in stock at the end of May. Gary is able to secure cooperative advertising with Pioneer and Kenwood if he places an order of \$35 000 with each company. Gary is certain that he can remain fairly competitive with the Electronic Superstore if his pricing reflects a total of \$7500 worth of discounts during the sale.

In glancing at his personal audio records, Gary has noticed that he was able to move approximately 800 units last June. Since the price of personal audio ranges from \$30 to \$300, he feels fairly comfortable maintaining a safety stock level of 270 units. In choosing this level, he wants to ensure that a customer is accommodated immediately since the Electronic Superstore always has a good selection of personal audio.

Assignment

1. If Gary plans on having \$5000 worth of car and personal audio left at the end of June, how much can he order from his remaining suppliers?
2. In units, what is Gary's maximum inventory level for personal audio?
3. What are some ideas for Gary to ensure that there is reasonable success at turning his stock over within 90 days to avoid interest charges and payments to Ajax Financing?
4. Compared to Electronic Superstore, what advantages and disadvantages does Klawson Electronics face in buying?

CASE 15: King Foods: Evaluating Everyday Low Pricing as an Alternative to High-Low Buying Practices

James Strong, The University of Akron

Albert and Benny King own and operate King Foods, a seven-store supermarket chain located in Canton, Ohio. The firm has a reputation for low prices, loyal employees, and good customer service. King Foods serve consumers who are in the low- to middle-income groups. Store sizes are small compared with modern supermarkets and supercentres, but the firm's conservative financial management has resulted in much lower than average overhead costs. However, some shoppers are dissatisfied with the limited and unstable product assortment that is the result of the stores' limited space and King's extensive use of low-price buying strategies. The King brothers attempt to purchase merchandise only when it is offered at special prices by manufacturers during "deal" periods.

Many supermarket chains, such as Shop 'n Save, Safeway, and Great Atlantic & Pacific Tea Co. (A&P), use a high-low buying strategy. Supermarkets forward-buy months' worth of inventory from manufacturers when the products are being offered at discount prices. The supermarkets then offer consumers discounted pricing for a certain time period. When the sale period is over, the supermarkets realize above-average margins by selling the stockpiled discounted inventory at the regular retail price. Discounts range from 8 to 20 percent; thus the retail price can vary substantially. Low-priced promotional items are advertised to draw customers who will also purchase regularly priced items that have normal and high margins. On the average, supermarkets rely on these trade promotions for 40 percent of their profits. Grocery wholesalers derive 75 percent of their profits from trade promotions. Not all supermarkets use the high-low strategy, although industry analysts estimate that 90 percent of supermarkets follow this approach.

Wal-Mart supercentres, the warehouse clubs, and some deep-discount drug/supermarkets have sought everyday low pricing (EDLP) as a buying practice. Retailers using this buying strategy to negotiate a stable low price devoid of discount periods from the manufacturer and in turn pass the permanent discount on to the customer. In other words, they buy and sell using an EDLP strategy. Whereas the EDLP is not as low as the promotional price, it is lower than the regular price and provides stability to both the wholesale and retail markets. For example, if Product X regularly wholesales for $10 and the promotional price is $7, the EDLP would be $8.

King Foods uses a modified high-low strategy. Albert and Benny attempt to purchase only promotionally priced merchandise and, departing from the traditional high-low strategy, offer the low price until the inventory is depleted. If the product is not being offered at the promotional price at the time of reorder, King Foods will try to purchase a competitive product that is being discounted. The company is somewhat unusual in its willingness not to stock an item considered a standard item by the trade. The King brothers believe that purchasing on special coupled with their low overhead and slimmer margins is the only way they can compete with national and regional chains. To date, they have been willing to accept the limitations this places on their product assortment.

Recently, Procter & Gamble (P&G) concluded that constant price discounting to the trade (retailers and wholesalers) has caused significant inefficiencies in the market and an erosion of manufacturer profitability and power. Manufacturer power has been lost because consumers have been conditioned to search for the best discounted price for an item, and the discounts are so substantial that consumers will quickly switch brands to save money. Thus, brand loyalty has been eroded, weakening the pull strategy that large consumer products firms have traditionally used to control retailers. Consequently, in 1992 P&G announced that it would phase out price and trade promotions and move toward EDLP.

A number of supermarket chains that utilize the high-low strategy have reacted very negatively to P&G's new policy because in the short run it will have a negative effect on the profitability of these firms.

However, stores that understand the hidden costs of forward buying and utilize EDLP, such as Wal-Mart and the warehouse clubs, are very supportive of P&G's new policy and hope other manufacturers follow suit. Some industry analysts state that the use of EDLP by Wal-Mart and warehouse clubs has contributed to their highly efficient distribution systems, helping them gain the competitive advantage of being the low-cost producer. Supercentres and warehouse clubs have grown rapidly in the grocery market and have taken a significant portion of market share away from supermarkets. Supermarkets may be forced to use EDLP and bulk packaging to match prices across their product assortment with supercentres and warehouse clubs or face dwindling market share.

A number of supermarket chains accuse P&G and other manufacturers of offering Wal-Mart and the warehouse clubs better pricing, terms, and support than is offered to supermarkets. Manufacturers uniformly deny this charge, but one supermarket chain reported finding an invoice from a manufacturer to a warehouse club revealing preferential pricing. Manufacturers respond that higher prices to supermarkets are justified because of the greater demands (for example, slotting fees) supermarkets impose compared with these alternative channels. They also contend that supermarkets should concentrate on merchandising and improving the efficiency of their operations rather than continually looking for promotionally priced merchandise.

Albert and Benny King were perplexed regarding how to respond to P&G's EDLP policy. They already were providing the lowest prices possible to their customers, but they were doing so strictly on the basis of buying the lowest price in the market. Albert had read that some supermarkets intended to remain high-low operators and adapt to P&G's EDLP policy by not passing along all of P&G's price cuts but saving them in order to offer periodic sales. Benny pointed out that the instability of their product assortment was already a weakness of the firm and that with promotional pricing they could usually provide the leading brands in the best-selling sizes and packages. If the brothers decided to de-emphasize and reduce the number of

P&G products in their assortment, it could create serious holes in their assortment. On the other hand, perhaps they should maintain their "bargain hunter" strategy that has been quite successful and emphasize manufacturers, such as Lever Brothers, that continue to provide "deal" pricing and promotional support. King's had been able to compete with supermarkets in the past, but Albert wondered if it would continue to be competitive now that the supercentres and warehouse clubs were so dramatically increasing competition and lowering prices.

Assignment

1. What are the relative advantages of EDLP to the manufacturer? What advantages do retailers enjoy from buying EDLP?
2. Which corporate strategy should King Foods employ in order to compete effectively in the grocery market in the 1990s?
3. Which overall buying strategy should King Foods utilize? Which specific tactics should they employ regarding P&G products?
4. What will the short-term ramifications of P&G's EDLP strategy be on P&G, supermarkets, supercentres, and warehouse clubs? Is P&G's EDLP strategy going to be effective in the long term for P&G, supermarkets, supercentres, and warehouse clubs?

Sources

Zachary Schiller, "Value Pricing Pays Off," *Business Week*, November 1, 1993, 32–33; Zachary Schiller, "Ed Artzt's Elbow Grease Has P&G Shining," *Business Week*, October 10, 1994, 84, 86; Jennifer Lawrence, "Supermarket Tug of War," *Advertising Age*, April 19, 1993, 42–43; Zachary Schiller, "Procter & Gamble Hits Back," *Business Week*, July 19, 1993, 20–22; Valerie Reitman, "Eliminated Discounts on P&G Goods Annoy Many Who Sell Them," *The Wall Street Journal*, August 11, 1992, Al, A6; Bradley Johnson, "Retailers Accepting P&G Low Pricing," *Advertising Age*, June 22, 1992, 36; Julie Liesse and Judann Dagnoli, "Supermarkets Foresee 'Era of Tension,'" *Advertising Age*, May 11, 1992, 6; Howard Schlossberg, "Retailers, Manufacturers Urged to Work Together for Profits," *Marketing News*, November 11, 1991, 13; Howard Schlossberg, "Manufacturers Fighting Back with Alternative Retail Outlets," *Marketing News*, August 3, 1992, 9, 11; Patricia Sellers, "The Dumbest Marketing Ploy." *Fortune*, October 5, 1992, 88–94.

CASE 16: Save-On Foods: Implications of a Price War

D. Wesley Balderson, University of Lethbridge

"Save-On Foods to expand to Lethbridge" read the headline in the *Lethbridge Herald* in the fall of 1990. Save-On Foods was one of the companies owned by the Jimmy Pattison Empire. It was showing impressive growth and success in British Columbia and Northern Alberta. It had now decided to expand to Lethbridge, a city of 65 000 in southwest Alberta. Save-On incorporated modern supermarket technology into their operations by providing both traditional grocery products as well as restaurant, deli, and nonfood merchandise. The interior of the store was spacious, contemporary, and unique.

The Lethbridge market for groceries was already very competitive prior to the Save-On entrance. Safeway was the dominant food retailer with three stores and there were 10 other well-established independent supermarkets. There were also numerous small convenience, chain, and corner grocery stores. Lethbridge catered to a fairly large agricultural trading area of approximately 100 000. A significant number of people in these outlying areas purchased their groceries in the city of Lethbridge.

Save-On Foods constructed a large store next to a new shopping mall in downtown Lethbridge. The building was completed in the fall of 1991, and Save-On's grand opening was scheduled for November.

Concern was expressed by the independent supermarkets that Save-On would resort to extreme price cutting in order to draw customers into the store and establish a quick market share. Their fears were well founded as the opening day advertisement by Save-On indicated very low prices on many items. One very noticeable loss leader was a 2-litre carton of milk priced at 98¢. The average price for the equivalent size of milk in Lethbridge prior to this promotion was in the $1.70–$1.80 range. It had only been about a year since the Public Utilities Board of Alberta had dropped minimum milk price legislation, so this drastically reduced price was seen as a real bargain for consumers. It was not long before Safeway responded with their own milk promotion (see Figure B–16–1). The advertising price war escalated with Save-On publishing a price comparison with Safeway (see Figure B–16–2) a week later.

Not to be outdone by Save-On, Safeway countered with the ad in Figure B–16–3 the next day. Although the primary combatants in the price war were Save-On Foods and Safeway, Food City entered the battle directly and most of the other independents stepped up their price and sales promotion advertising considerably. Loss leaders and price comparisons were the order of the day through the winter months. Customer traffic was heavy at Save-On Foods and also appeared to increase at Safeway as well. What appeared to be a very competitive situation for the food retailer was turning out to be a major benefit to grocery shoppers.

Assignment

1. What is likely to be the long-run result of Save-On's entry to the Lethbridge market to food retailers, and to consumers?
2. Discuss the use of milk as a loss leader for the Lethbridge market.
3. If you were one of the 10 independent retailers in Lethbridge, how would you react to Save-On's entry? If you were a convenience store operator what would your reaction be?

Figure B–16–1

A BETTER WAY TO SAVE
FREE
LUCERNE
MILK
Free! one 2 Litre carton LUCERNE MILK
With a $25.00 family purchase
DIVISION COUPON PLU 7027
SAFEWAY
Lucerne 2%
Lucerne
two litres
2% partly skimmed milk pasteurized
With Coupon and a purchase of $25⁰⁰ or More
BONELESS SIRLOIN STEAKS
1 97
Cut From Canada
Grade 'A' Beef
Super Pack, 5lbs or Over
4³⁴ kg/lb
Join us in the
GRAND OPENING
of our newest Safeway store at 2750 Fairway Plaza
ENTER TO WIN
you could win our Grand Prize of a
1992
Cavalier
Courtesy of Safeway and Schneiders
or Win 46" Zenith Digital Big Screen Color TV
or Win Groceries For a Year!
SAFEWAY will meet or beat Save-On-Foods advertised prices.
Safeway will meet or beat all newspaper and flyer advertised prices of Save-On-Foods provided we stock the item. If you wish to purchase an item advertised by Save-On-Foods and our price has not been adjusted to meet or beat their advertised price, then simply bring Save-On-Foods advertisement to our attention.
WE REDEEM ALL GROCERY COMPETITORS' COUPONS*
* Provided it is a regular stocked item.
SAFEWAY
Prices effective in Lethbridge Safeway stores from Tuesday, November 26 until closing Saturday, November 30, 1991. We reserve the right to limit sales to retail quantities. While stocks last.

Figure B–16–2

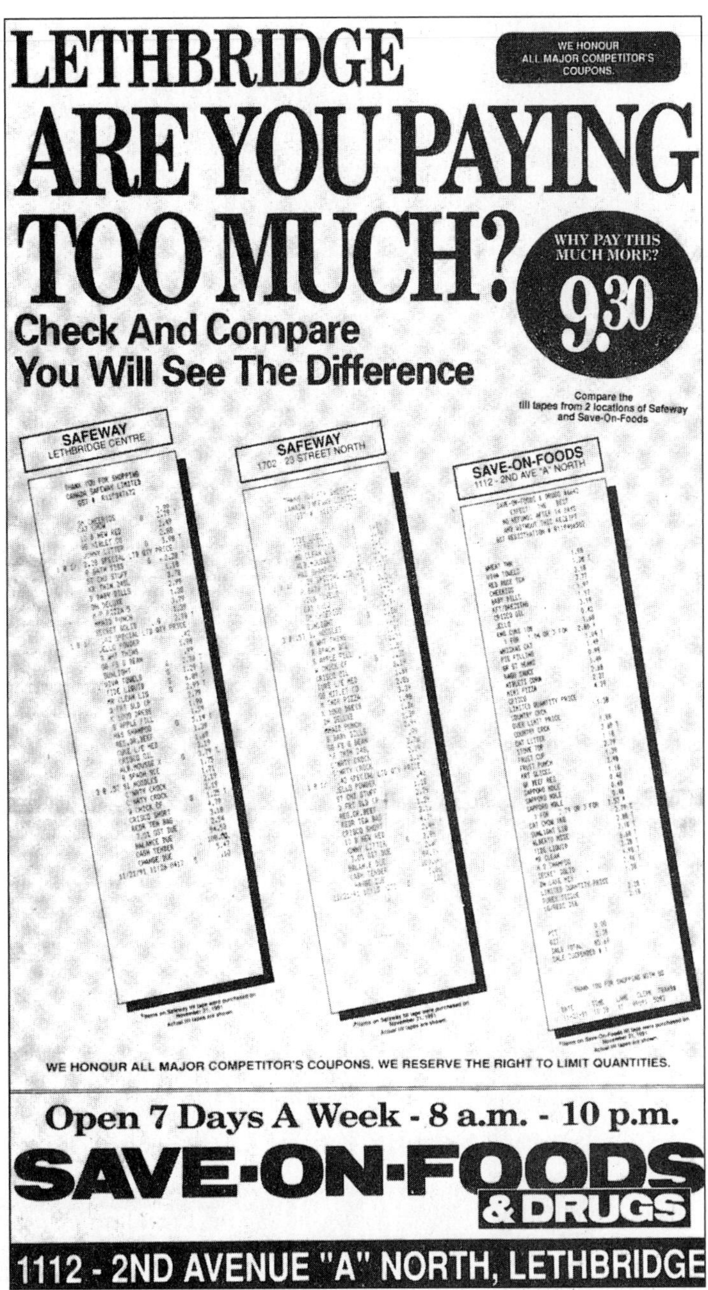
LETHBRIDGE
WE HONOUR ALL MAJOR COMPETITOR'S COUPONS.
ARE YOU PAYING TOO MUCH?
WHY PAY THIS MUCH MORE?
9.30
Check And Compare
You Will See The Difference
Compare the till tapes from 2 locations of Safeway and Save-On-Foods
SAFEWAY
LETHBRIDGE CENTRE
SAFEWAY
1702 23 STREET NORTH
SAVE-ON-FOODS
1112 - 2ND AVE "A" NORTH
WE HONOUR ALL MAJOR COMPETITOR'S COUPONS. WE RESERVE THE RIGHT TO LIMIT QUANTITIES.
Open 7 Days A Week - 8 a.m. - 10 p.m.
SAVE-ON-FOODS
& DRUGS
1112 - 2ND AVENUE "A" NORTH, LETHBRIDGE

Figure B–16–3

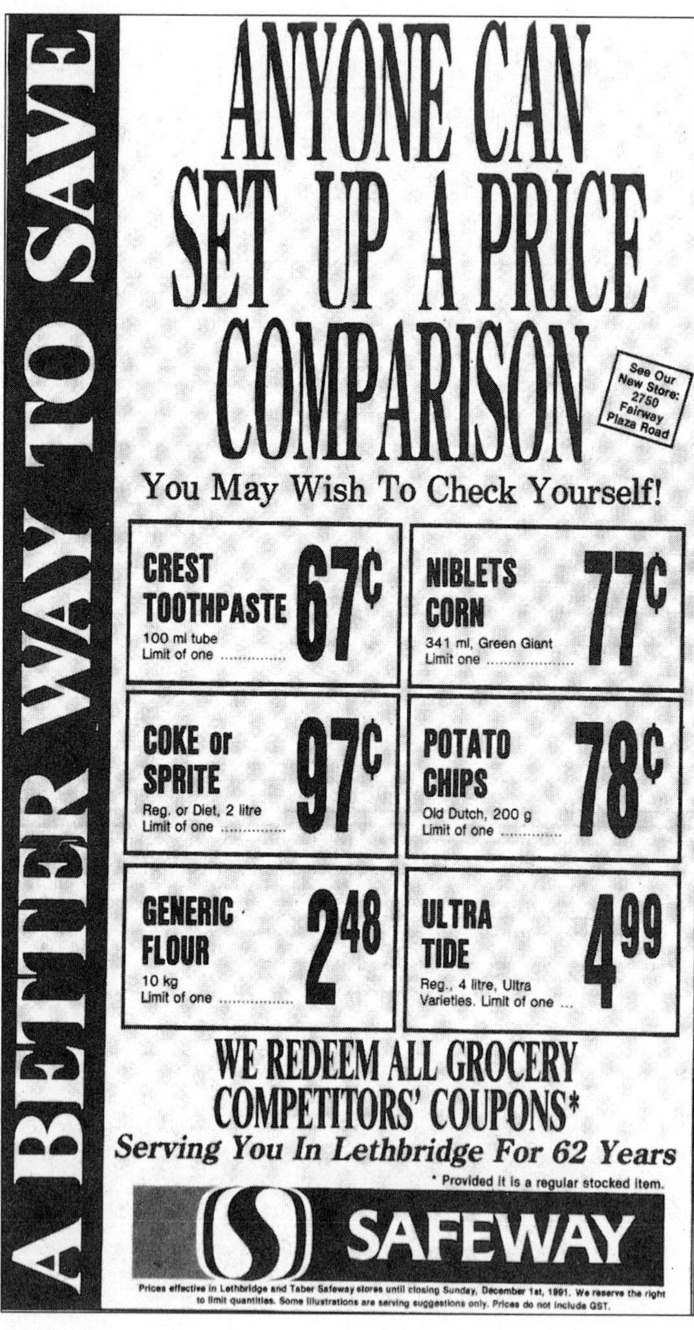

A BETTER WAY TO SAVE
ANYONE CAN SET UP A PRICE COMPARISON
See Our New Store: 2750 Fairway Plaza Road
You May Wish To Check Yourself!
CREST TOOTHPASTE 67¢
100 ml tube
Limit of one
NIBLETS CORN 77¢
341 ml, Green Giant
Limit one
COKE or SPRITE 97¢
Reg. or Diet, 2 litre
Limit of one
POTATO CHIPS 78¢
Old Dutch, 200 g
Limit of one
GENERIC FLOUR 2.48
10 kg
Limit of one
ULTRA TIDE 4.99
Reg., 4 litre, Ultra Varieties. Limit of one
WE REDEEM ALL GROCERY COMPETITORS' COUPONS*
Serving You In Lethbridge For 62 Years
* Provided it is a regular stocked item.
SAFEWAY
Prices effective in Lethbridge and Taber Safeway stores until closing Sunday, December 1st, 1991. We reserve the right to limit quantities. Some illustrations are serving suggestions only. Prices do not include GST.

CASE 17: Hallmark Card Shops: Reshuffling the Deck for a New Card Game

Jon M. Hawes and *Dale M. Lewison*,
The University of Akron

For the last several decades, Hallmark Cards, Inc., a privately held company, has relied on card and gift shops to move its extensive line of greeting cards, gift and entertainment items, stationery and holiday ornaments. Hallmark's network of card shops consists of 20 000 independently owned and operated outlets and 216 company-owned stores. To become a Hallmark dealer, each licensed retailer agrees to display and merchandise a certain amount of Hallmark merchandise.

Hallmark's family image as the premier producer and merchandiser of greeting cards and related items is based on a merchandising formula that calls for (1) an extensive assortment of merchandise (more than 21 000 card designs in 20 languages each year), (2) a high-quality product line that sells at moderate and higher price points with adequate gross margins that allow dealers attractive profit margins, (3) a distribution channel whose structure is almost exclusively made up of specialty retailers that can focus their attention on meeting the very personalized needs of the greeting card customer, (4) an effective program of sales promotions that feature in-store displays and visuals that support product concepts and benefits, and (5) one of the most successful, long-running advertising campaigns involving thrice-yearly "Hallmark Hall of Fame" network television specials. Many of these television specials have become classics and are now hot-selling videocassettes. Hallmark merchandising philosophy might be best summarized by its 50-year-old signature line, "When you care enough to send the very best."

Hallmark management is currently facing somewhat of a paradox. Although sales revenues have continued to increase at a fairly steady rate over the past five years, Hallmark's market share has slipped from an estimated 50 percent market share to 45 percent share. Return on equity (ROE) figures have also sagged in recent years. The company's current ROE of 8 percent is significantly below historical returns of 15 to 20 percent. To maintain its current 45 percent market share in the $5.6 billion greeting card industry, Hallmark must review its current merchandising strategies and market positions.

As reported in *Advertising Age*, "The high-velocity lifestyles of today's dual-career families, plus new competition in retail channels, have put Hallmark on the defensive. Women, who account for 85% to 90% of all greeting card purchases, are spending less time than ever lingering in Hallmark's card stores." Convenience has become a decisive factor in determining where working women buy greeting cards. The 1980s and early 1990s saw a shift in the buying patterns for greeting cards, away from card shops and toward discounters, supermarkets, drugstore chains, and other retail outlets that afford one-stop shopping opportunities. Twenty years ago, North Americans bought more than half of their cards at specialty shops. Today, that number has declined to about 30 percent. As is the case in many other product lines (for example, toys, books, records, and apparel), Hallmark has fallen victim to the one-stop shopping trend that has seen the spectacular rise of the superstore format in both discount and specialty store retailing. For example, in the area of specialty store retailing, the growth format has been "category killer" superstores such as Toys Я Us, Borders Books and Music, Best Buy, and Sports Authority.

Unlike Hallmark, the other two major greeting card companies, American Greetings and Gibson, recognized the shift to mass merchandisers. Although Hallmark retains its position as the No. 1 specialty store retailer of greeting cards, American Greetings has become the leader in such mass retail chains as Wal-Mart, Kmart, and a host of drugstore and supermarket chains. Gibson is the strong player in deep-discount outlets, where price is the deciding factor. To compete in the mass and discount markets, Hallmark created the Ambassador line of greeting cards. Although Ambassador now accounts for about 19 percent of Hallmark's sales, this fighting brand is believed to have cannibalized the Hallmark brand and hammered its gross margins.

Hallmark management has entertained the idea of placing its Hallmark line in selective discount outlets, but loyalty to its current dealer network of specialty shops has prevented any serious effort at opening new channels of distribution for the Hallmark brand. Some retailing experts have suggested that Hallmark would be well advised to abandon the card shop altogether and commit its Hallmark brand to mass marketing channels. For the paternalistic Hall Family (the principle owners of Hallmark), this would be a very difficult decision. It would be like abandoning all of the members of its retailing family.

Actions currently under review by Hallmark management range from developing new store formats to diversifying into new businesses to finding cost-cutting opportunities to introducing new product lines to creating a new company image appealing to new customer segments.

Assignment

Investigate Hallmark's declining fortunes by conducting a search of the literature, interviewing Hallmark retailers and customers, and making field observations of Hallmark stores and their merchandising strategies. List and describe some of the merchandising strengths and weaknesses of Hallmark shops in your area by comparing their product, price, place, and promotion tactics. Make recommendations as to specific actions that Hallmark should take in order to regain its momentum as the premier retailer of greeting cards and related items.

Source

William M. Stern, "Loyal to a Fault," *Forbes*, March 14, 1994, 58–59; Kate Fitzgerald, "Hallmark Alters Focus as Lifestyles Change," *Advertising Age*, October 31, 1994, A3; Susan Chandler, "Can Hallmark Get Well Soon?" *Business Week*, June 19, 1995, 62–63; Debra Sparks, "The Card Game," *Financial World*, July 5, 1994, 28–29; and Glenn Collins, "Hallmark Pulls Its Hip Characters out of Shoebox," *New York Times*, July 16, 1994.

CASE 18: The Lost Weekend: Conducting a Performance Analysis

Dale M. Lewison and *John Thanopoulos*, The University of Akron

It was late Friday afternoon and Mike Showater had been trying to finish up some work before heading off to the lake for a weekend of rest and relaxation when Art Weiss, vice president of finance, stopped by Mike's office. With his usual lack of consideration, Art threw down a set of financials and told Mike that he expected a complete financial analysis by Monday morning. When Mike inquired as to the purpose of the analysis, Art informed him that he had to catch a plane and did not have time to explain any further. So much for a weekend of fun in the sun.

The financial statements consisted of the basic income statement and balance sheet for two respected apparel retail chains—The Apparel Mart and Status Clothiers. Speculating on the reason for the analysis, Mike wondered if Retail Internationale was on the hunt for a new acquisition; surely they would have more information than one year's financials. Nevertheless, having recently joined Retail International, takeover speculation was not in Mike's job description, but financial analysis was. Who knows, maybe this is just the job to keep him from getting bored at the lake. Grabbing the financial statements and his laptop, Mike headed for the door.

Assignment

Using the information in Figures B–18–1 and B–18–2, assume Mike Showater's responsibilities and conduct a complete financial analysis for the two firms. Compare the performance of The Apparel Mart with that of Status Clothiers. Given that the purpose of the analysis is not entirely known, be sure to provide a clear interpretation of your findings.

Figure B–18–1

Financial statement for the Apparel Mart

The Apparel Mart Financial Statement
For The Year Ending January 1, 1994

Income Statement

Gross sales		$123 425 000
−Returns and allowances	$ 700 000	
Net sales		$122 725 000
−Cost of goods sold	$60 872 000	
Gross margin		$ 61 853 000
−Operating expenses	$53 753 000	
Operating profit		$ 8 100 000
+Other income	$ —	
−Other expenses	117 000	
Net profit		$ 7 983 000

Balance Sheet

Assets		Liabilities and net worth	
Current	$52 326 000	Current	$ 22 873 000
Fixed	$24 174 000	Fixed	$ 17 748 000
		Net worth	$ 35 879 000
Total assets	$76 500 000	Total liabilities and net worth	$ 76 500 000

Figure B–18–2

Financial status for Status Clothiers

Status Clothiers Financial Statement
For The Year Ending January 1, 1994

Income Statement

Gross sales		$ 33 811 000
−Returns and allowances	$ 820 000	
Net sales		$ 32 991 000
−Cost of goods sold	$ 16 463 000	
Gross margin		$ 16 528 000
−Operating expenses	$ 14 913 000	
Operating profit		$ 1 615 000
+Other income	$ 74 000	
−Other expenses	10 000	
Net profit		$ 1 679 000

Balance Sheet

Assets		Liabilities and net worth	
Current	$ 5 527 000	Current	$ 3 093 000
Fixed	$ 3 873 000	Fixed	$ 263 000
		Net worth	$ 6 044 000
Total assets	$ 9 400 000	Total liabilities and net worth	$ 9 400 000

CASE 19: Baker Hardware Ltd.: Financial Analysis

D. Wesley Balderson, University of Lethbridge

Baker Hardware Ltd. is a hardware store in the town of Souris, which is located in an agricultural area of southern Manitoba. Souris is about 50 km south of Brandon (population 55 000), which is the major trading centre for many smaller towns within a 100-kilometre radius.

Mr. Baker, the owner of Baker Hardware, is contemplating expanding his merchandise offering to include lumber and building supplies. Currently Baker's, in addition to a standard selection of hardware merchandise, carries paint and building tools; therefore, Mr. Baker thinks this new line would be fairly compatible.

Baker Hardware was a part of the Home Hardware network of dealers, a nationwide group of hardware stores and home centres located primarily in smaller towns and cities. For the past few years, Home Hardware had been encouraging its dealers to expand into building supplies. Concerned that there was another lumber yard in Souris (which happened to be next door to Baker Hardware), Mr. Baker had shown little interest in such a move in the past.

Recently, however, he became aware that this lumber yard, Banner Building Supplies, was for sale or would be closed down. Mr. Baker gathered information from both the owners of Banner as well as from Home Hardware and was in the process of making a decision. As Mr. Baker saw it, he had three choices: (1) purchase Banner Building Supplies, (2) expand into building supplies through Home Hardware on his own premises, or (3) maintain current operations (not expanding into building materials).

The Market

As previously mentioned, Souris was a small town of about 2000 located in an agricultural area of southern Manitoba. The estimated population of surrounding area farms was 500. The town was located 50 km southwest of Brandon, the major trading centre for the area. Over the years, the retail communities in most of the small towns close to Brandon had deteriorated due to the strong competition of retailers there and the increased mobility of consumers. The building supply industry was no exception. Such chains as Canadian Tire and Beaver Lumber, which had outlets in Brandon, had attracted numerous customers from these rural communities.

The population of Souris consisted mainly of farmers, commuters who worked in Brandon, and professionals such as teachers who worked in the town. The town had experienced some growth in recent years because of its relaxed atmosphere and excellent recreational facilities. Projections indicated the population could reach 2500 by the year 2000.

Baker Hardware had operated successfully in Souris for many years. Mr. Baker had purchased the store from his father, and with changes and modernizations, increased sales from $450 000 in 1975 to $800 000 in 1995. Although sales showed a significant increase, profits did not. The strong competition from hardware chains in Brandon in recent years had eroded Mr. Baker's profit margin. Baker Hardware's competitive strength had always been that it catered to the agricultural community. Unfortunately, farm incomes had experienced considerable volatility in recent years, and this trend directly affected Baker Hardware's profit performance.

Baker Hardware currently had 1100 m^2 of selling space and a large (750 m^2) warehouse. Mr. Baker believed that if he went into building supplies he could, with some renovations, free up about half of the warehouse space to house the new merchandise.

Baker Hardware's current financial situation, while not serious, was such that if a capital investment were made, Mr. Baker would have to borrow to finance it. At the current interest rate of 14 percent, this was a concern for Mr. Baker.

Home Hardware. Home Hardware Ltd. is a well-established franchise system of dealer-owners located across Canada. Originating in southern Ontario, it has expanded to become a dominant small-town retailer of hardware merchandise. Recently Home Hardware moved into the building supply industry in an attempt to capitalize on the growth of the home centre concept. Home Hardware has been encouraging its dealers to branch into this area, and many have done so.

Mr. Baker obtained from Home Hardware a list of the recommended product assortment for a home building supply dealer. A summary of this list, along with space requirements and markups, appears in Figure B–19–1. Home Hardware also suggested that Mr. Baker would need a forklift (estimated cost $15 000, used), a delivery truck (estimated cost $10 000, used), and a shed of at least 460 m^2 (estimated cost $5000).

Banner Building Supplies. Banner Building Supplies was a family-owned business that had operated in Souris for over 40 years. It was owned by two brothers, both close to retirement age, who also owned a window and door manufacturing plant. As the manufacturing plant was much larger in size and scope of operations, the Banners had devoted most of their time and energy to this business. The retail building supplies outlet had, over the years, taken second priority in their business interests, although it provided a stable and needed outlet for the town.

Interest in selling the retail outlet resulted from two major factors. First, both brothers wanted to cut back on their work responsibilities, as both were approaching

Figure B–19–1

Recommended home building supply for a full product assortment

Product	Cost	Suggested Markup on Cost	Estimated Turnover	Space Requirement in Square Metres
Insulation	$ 4 000	25%	4.0	60
Doors and mouldings (complete assortment)	6 000	30%	2.5	90
Plywood (complete assortment, two pallets each)	10 000	15%	5.5	210
Drywall (complete assortment, two pallets each)	6 000	15%	4.5	60
Cement	2 000	30%	5.0	18
Roofing materials	5 000	25%	3.5	60
Nails	1 000	30%	5.0	12
Siding, soffit, facia	6 000	30%	2.0	90
Dimensional lumber (2 × 4, 2 × 6, etc.) (complete assortment, two pallets each)	20 000	15%	6.0	300
	$60 000			900

Figure B–19–2

Banner Building Supplies: Estimated Income Statement for 1992

Sales	230 000	
Cost of goods sold (85%)	195 500	
Gross profit		34 500
Expenses		
Wages	22 500	
Taxes and licences	2 000	
Insurance	11 000	
Professional fees and administration	500	
Utilities	2 000	
Fuel for trucks, etc.	1 200	
Bad debts	1 000	
Depreciation	1 800	
Repairs and maintenance	1 000	
Miscellaneous supplies, etc.	500	33 500
Net income before taxes		1 000

Figure B–19–3

Banner Building Supplies: Inventory estimate

Insulation	$ 6 000
Doors and mouldings	24 000
Plywood	12 000
Drywall	7 000
Cement	1 000
Roofing materials	2 000
Nails, etc.	1 200
Siding	2 000
Dimensional lumber	35 000
Paints	2 500
Tools and hardware	2 500
Carpet and lino	1 800
	$97 000

retirement age and had no family members interested in taking over the business. However, one brother had a son-in-law who was interested in the manufacturing part of the business. Second, the profitability of the retail outlet had suffered in recent years due to strong competition from larger hardware chains and home centres in Brandon. Some of these competitors could sell certain types of lumber and other supplies at lower prices than Banner's costs. The estimated profit and loss statement Mr. Baker obtained from Banners for 1995 is shown in Figure B–19–2. Currently Banner Building Supplies has approximately $97 000 in inventory (see Figure B–19–3) and owns a large lot containing some sheds and a showroom next door to Baker Hardware. The estimated value of real estate and buildings is approximately $25 000. The company has no debt.

In looking at the merchandise requirements recommended by Home Hardware, Mr. Baker noted that Banner's inventory levels were different. Mr. Baker discussed this with the previous manager of Banner's and learned that some building supplies did not sell well in Souris. He informed Mr. Baker that the standard types of lumber (plywoods, two-by-fours, etc.) were the steady sellers, although warpage caused considerable waste in dimensional lumber. He also mentioned that it was very difficult to compete with the city building centres for the large contractors' business. The major market for Banner's had been the small contractor (renovators) and the do-it-yourself customer.

Armed with this information, Mr. Baker was determined to make a decision.

Assignment

1. What other information should Mr. Baker obtain before he makes this decision?
2. Using the information provided, evaluate the alternatives Mr. Baker has identified. Be sure to evaluate the attractiveness of the proposed merchandise lines.
3. What other alternatives has Mr. Baker not explored?

CASE 20: Kinney Canada Inc.: Considering a New Location Strategy

Shilpa Stocker, University of Lethbridge

On August 5, 1965, Kinney Canada, Inc., a division of Woolworth Company, moved into the Canadian market. It has now climbed to the successful position of being one of

Figure B–20–1

Kinney Canada, Inc.'s retailing formats

Kinney Shoes. Dubbed as the "Great Canadian Shoe Store," this store specializes in reasonably priced footwear for the entire family. The first Kinney store opened its doors in 1966 and Kinney Shoes now consists of over 1800 stores in major markets in the United States and Canada.

Foot Locker. With eighty percent of its customers being male, Foot Locker offers many styles and popular brand names in athletic shoes and clothing. There are over 1000 stores in the United States, Canada, Germany, and Australia; the average store is 150 m^2 in size.

Lady Foot Locker. More commonly known as the "Sensation in Co-ordination," Lady Foot Locker has 461 stores located across Canada and the United States. Lady Foot Locker is favoured among women who like to shop at a store just for them, especially since it offers a varied selection of styles and colours in athletic leisure wear from head to toe. The target market is basically women between the ages of 25 and 50 years. The average store is approximately 140 m^2 in size.

Sportelle. This specialty store offers accessories as well as funky, casual clothes in fun, comfortable styles appealing to women of all ages. Ninety-eight Sportelle stores are located across the United States and Canada.

Canary Island Adventure & Travel Co. As the name suggests, Canary Island offers travel and vacation apparel for men and women in Canada. The atmosphere denotes adventure, as the store is set up as a tropical cabana. Canary Island appeals to those who like casual clothing and leisure wear made of 100% natural fibres. Clothing comes in a varied range of sizes and adventure styles.

Randy River. Since the opening of the first Randy River store in 1985, the number of Randy River stores has increased to over 65. Randy River sells fashionable clothing for men and appeals to those in their late teens to late twenties.

Raglans. Raglans' casual apparel appeals to men, women, and children between the ages of twelve and thirty-five. The clothing consists of cotton or cotton blends and sizes range from extra-extra small to extra-large, thereby appealing to wide range of people.

the leading forces in Canadian retailing by offering apparel targeted to a varied range of fashion-conscious consumers. By positioning itself as an important specialist in the fashion apparel market through multiple retail formats and efficient distribution centres, Kinney Canada, Inc., has become one of the top achievers across many industries in Canada. A basic operating principle is the firm's pursuit of excellence "to offer the absolute best customer shopping experience anywhere—the best stores—the best merchandise—the best merchandise presentation—the best customer service—the best 'everything' that a customer sees and experiences."

In 1993 Kinney Canada, Inc., was considering a new "cluster location strategy" that would group several or possibly all of its various retailing formats within one shopping mall. For example, within one shopping mall, Kinney Canada, Inc., could create a store cluster comprised of: (1) Kinney Shoes, (2) Foot Locker, (3) Lady Foot Locker, (4) Sportelle, (5) Canary Island Adventure & Travel Co., (6) Randy River, and (7) Raglans. Figure B–20–1 profiles each of Kinney Canada Inc.'s retailing formats.

Assignment

Evaluate the proposed "cluster location strategies." As a location consultant, would you recommend it to the chairperson of Kinney Canada, Inc.? Defend your recommendation. Assume the chairperson wants you to develop two different "cluster" prototypes: (1) for an upscale shopping mall in Toronto catering to upper-income consumers and (2) for a typical middle-class shopping centre in Calgary. Provide supporting rationales for your prototypes.

CASE 21: Hudson's Bay Company

D. Wesley Balderson, University of Lethbridge

The Hudson's Bay Company (HBC) is Canada's oldest corporation and the country's largest retailer. Although originally established as a fur trading company early in this century, HBC turned more of its attention to retailing which has now become its most important activity. HBC built downtown department stores in each of the major cities of western Canada (1913–1968). Expansion into eastern Canada, on the other hand, took place primarily through acquisitions of other retail organizations. HBC began expanding to the suburbs of the larger Canadian cities as the shopping mall concept became more popular during the 1960s.

In the 1970s, with land prices appreciating rapidly, the HBC followed the lead of many expansionary Canadian businesses and added significant real estate assets to its already large holdings in retailing and the resource industry. This allowed HBC to actively participate in shopping mall development which was taking place at a rapid pace in Canada at this time.

It was also during the 1970s that HBC began to pursue a greater market share of the Canadian retail industry. In 1978 HBC purchased Zellers, a successful Montreal discount department store chain of 200 stores for $170 million. This purchase more than doubled HBC's retail space and more than tripled its number of stores in Canada. Because Zellers followed a significantly different format than HBC's retail chain (The Bay), it was allowed to retain much of its identity following the transaction.

In 1979 HBC purchased the upscale Simpsons chain of Toronto in a much publicized takeover that included Simpsons management and Sears Roebuck of the United States. With this purchase HBC surpassed Sears and became the largest retailer in the country with approximately one-third of department stores' sales.

The years following these corporate transactions proved very difficult for the HBC. The acquisitions of Zellers and Simpsons and the expansion of the Bay division had been financed with borrowed money. Total debt reached $2.3 billion by the mid '80s, costing the company $265 million in interest expense in 1986.

Another problem was that HBC had expanded into many other areas besides retailing. Management attention was divided among these activities and a clear focus seemed to be lacking. With the exception of Zellers, HBC's acquisitions were not very profitable and represented a drain of both capital and management resources.

The recession of the early 1980s further compounded HBC's problems. Sales were off and competition forced gross profit down. Many Canadian retailers experienced losses during this period and some were forced out of business as total Canadian retail sales stagnated. HBC was not immune from these conditions, and the company endured five years of losses from 1981 to 1985. Department stores seemed to be affected by this situation more than specialty chains and independents, as department store share of retail sales experienced steady declines.

By 1984 the board of directors at HBC recognized that action had to be taken in both retailing and non-retailing areas to turn the company around. As part of this evaluation, department store retailing was identified to be the core business of the company. Other interests were sold, including HBC's real estate and petroleum subsidiaries, and its wholesale and fur divisions. These transactions netted proceeds of over $500 million, which was applied towards debt reduction and started the company on the road to interest cost reduction.

A new segmented store focus became the positioning policy of the department stores. Simpsons, having lost market share due to an undefined marketing focus, was redesigned to appeal to fashion-conscious, upscale urban markets. This included enlarging soft goods areas, increased advertising, upgrading stores and fixtures, and converting all non-Toronto Simpsons stores to Bay outlets.

The Bay worked at refining the customer profile of each of its stores to target middle-income earners, with a "medium" range of merchandise appealing to urban and suburban shoppers. To accomplish this, the Bay increased its soft goods concentration, increased in-store marketing and advertising, and transferred 18 stores to the Zellers format in areas that were too small to be considered as upscale as the Bay required.

Zellers continued to concentrate on low prices and increased its promotion along two main themes—guaranteeing low prices (the lowest price is the law), and the introduction of a frequent purchase program called Club Z. This program was to become the most successful of its kind in Canadian retail history. Within the first few years the Club Z program generated a 55 percent increase in sales, a 30 percent increase in store traffic, a 99 percent awareness level, over 4 million active members (45 percent of Canadian households), and the 1987 Retail Council of Canada Communication Award for retail promotion.

George Kosich, the president of HBC, tightened control for the remaining units in the retail division by establishing strict computer-aided cost controls. This system was designed to assist in developing and maintaining inventory assortments, to provide automatic replenishment of more basic, non-fashion-oriented items, to monitor sales by department and stock keeping unit (SKU) and to provide related management reports. Retail managers were held accountable for inventory levels and product performance. Advanced computer technology was also incorporated into the distribution facilities to allow for "same day" delivery to individual stores in order to improve customer service.

All non-merchandising activities of the Bay, Simpsons, and Zellers were combined. In addition, while Zellers's merchandising, marketing, and buying remained separate, these activities at the Bay and Simpsons were completely combined. These actions allowed lower-cost volume buying, greater advertising and fixture allowances, and an increased returns allowance. It also allowed for a dramatic reduction in overall staff. Cost savings through the use of new technology and reduction of overlap in administrative activities were estimated at over $100 million annually. With this new focus and acquisitions, HBC had increased overall retail department store market share to 32.9 percent by 1989.

HBC's major competitors were also adjusting their strategies to the new competitive realities during this time. Sears was involved in a massive overhaul of existing stores and was attempting to return its market focus to the middle-income consumer. Internally Sears, like HBC, was devoting more attention to "tracking" merchandise to more effectively manage inventories. Eaton's was attempting to establish itself once again at the upscale end of the department store market and reduce its reliance upon discounting and frequent sales. The establishment of the "everyday low pricing" policy was the result. In the west, Woodwards had taken the opposite approach by attempting to move to the lower scale customer by increasing price promotions and reducing service and overhead. The discount chains of Woolco and Kmart appeared to have relatively stable strategies, but their market share was still behind that of Zellers.

In 1990 HBC continued its divestiture of non-retail activities and further consolidation occurred with the complete merging of Simpsons stores to the Bay. Although HBC had attempted to operate the two companies as separate and later as partially separate entities, it seemed to be too difficult to accomplish.

By the early '90s the previous changes appeared to have been successful. Zellers, whose strategies included everyday low prices, tough expense management, and Club Z, had become the most successful of the Canadian discount department stores. The Bay returned to profitability by emphasizing its flagship downtown stores, and by absorbing Simpsons. Debt and interest costs decreased due to downsizing and strict cost control. Market conditions during this period, however, continued to be adverse for the retail industry. Such things as the recession, increases in cross-border shopping, reduced consumer disposable incomes, and unemployment contributed to financial difficulties for many retailers.

The HBC, however, was financially strong enough to consider retail expansion again. In 1991 HBC purchased the 51-store Towers chain, a discount department store chain located in Ontario, Quebec, and the Maritimes. The purchase increased Zellers's market coverage by one third in those areas. Its merchandise mix and pricing policies were very similar to those of Zellers and as a result, it provided a smooth transition to the Zellers format. The changeover was accomplished in 11 weeks and significantly increased Zellers's market share in eastern Canada.

In 1993 HBC also increased its market share in western Canada with the purchase of Woodwards, a 21-outlet department store chain in Alberta and British Columbia and one of its major competitors in that area. Eleven of these stores were converted to the Bay format and the remaining 10 became Zellers outlets. The Woodwards acquisition reversed a negative trend for retail store growth in the west for HBC, while the Towers acquisition contributed significantly to store growth and market penetration in the east.

A major concern for most retailers in Canada in 1994 was the purchase of the 122-store Woolco chain by Wal-Mart Inc. of the United States. Stock prices of most major Canadian retailers including HBC dropped following the announcement of the sale. The establishment of Wal-Mart in Canada has proved to be a significant development for retailers such as HBC.

Assignment

1. Relate the history of HBC to the wheel of retailing and retail life cycles.

2. The majority of expansion efforts of HBC have been made through acquisition of existing retail chains. Why do you think that HBC chose this course of action as opposed to opening up new outlets?

3. Discuss the possible reasons why the Simpsons acquisition was not successful. Contrast this with the purchase of Towers and Woodwards.

4. Identify the factors which have led to HBC becoming successful in recent years when most other retailers have been struggling.

5. Discuss the implications of Wal-Mart's expansion to Canada upon the operations of HBC.

CASE 22: Chipman Roofing: Management of a Service Retailer

D. Wesley Balderson, University of Lethbridge

Robert Chipman had just completed an entrepreneurial course at a local college as preparation for establishing his own roofing business. One of the main things that he learned in the course was the necessity of preparing a business plan for the enterprise. As a result, Robert went to work and within a few days had put together the following business plan for Chipman Roofing.

Background

I, Robert Chipman will be the sole owner of this proprietorship which will install and carry out roof repairs in the Lethbridge, Alberta, market area. I have completed an entrepreneurial course at the Lethbridge Community College and have had several years experience in the roofing business working for Charles Hill Roofing, the largest roofer in the Lethbridge area.

I am desirous of starting my own business in order to be independent and to obtain a higher financial compensation than I am currently receiving. I want everyone in Lethbridge and surrounding areas to know my company and the quality work we do.

Market Approach

The target market will be every person that owns a house, apartment building, warehouse, condo, or office building. The services we provide will cater to all people who own buildings that need roof repair or construction. I will provide all types of roofing materials, eavestroughing, and services. Quality workmanship will be the building block of the business. I will ensure a one-year guarantee on all workmanship.

Because the service Chipman Roofing will provide is of high quality, I will charge a slightly higher price on our product. I will try to maintain a 20 percent markup over costs to keep our prices fair to every customer.

Chipman Roofing will utilize several forms of promotion. Brochures and pamphlets will be prepared and sent through direct mail to every homeowner in Lethbridge. Newspaper ads and the Yellow Pages will also be used to promote the business.

Physical Facilities

The business will be located in my home at first. This will save a considerable amount of money until the business gets established. Equipment, supplies, and opening inventory will be purchased from local suppliers. The schedule in Figure B–22–1 provides a listing of the equipment and supplies that will be needed to get started.

Financial

To estimate potential revenue for Chipman Roofing for new houses, I have multiplied the average roofing job for new houses ($8000) by the number of new houses constructed in Lethbridge (400) in 1996, for a total of $3 200 000. For repair jobs, I have taken the average dollar expenditure per

Figure B–22–1

Physical Requirements	
1 work truck (used half ton)	$ 5 000
3 ton dump truck	$ 5 000
1 hoist	$ 500
4 ladders (25 foot)	$ 1 500
Roofing tools	$ 1 000
Computer system	$ 3 000
Office equipment and supplies	$ 1 000
Total	$17 000

Figure B–22–2

Chipman Roofing Projected Income—Year 1	
Sales	580 000
Cost of Goods Sold (45%)	261 000
Wages	100 000
Depreciation	2 000
Advertising	2 600
Insurance	1 200
Repairs and Maintenance	5 000
Licences and permits	200
Professional fees	800
Interest (8% on $15 000)	1 200
Net Income	$206 000

household for the Lethbridge area (Urban Family Expenditure Data) of $100 and multiplied it by the number of homes (26 000) for a total of $2 600 000. Of this total of $5 800 000, I estimate that Chipman Roofing will obtain a 10 percent market share for a total revenue of $580 000.

There are currently eight other roofers in the city, but because of my quality workmanship I hope to increase the market share of Chipman Roofing to 20 percent within five years.

Projected income based on these estimates are found in Figure B–22–2.

Chipman Roofing will obtain a loan from a local bank to finance $15 000 of the startup requirement. The remaining $2000 will be supplied by myself, the owner. The financial records of the business will be prepared and maintained by an accountant

Legal Requirements

The necessary business licences and permits will be obtained from the City of Lethbridge. Initially the business will be operated as a proprietorship, and when the business becomes more established I will consider forming a limited company.

Personnel

The personnel required to keep Chipman Roofing operating will vary from season to season. Due the uncertainties of the weather, part-time employees will be utilized. Ads will be placed in the local newspaper to find workers for the business. I will also utilize the government employment agency of Canada Manpower. During the summer months I may also look at hiring students. I estimate that on average I will have about five workers on the payroll. Training will take place on the job which is appropriate for this type of work.

Assignment

1. Evaluate the Chipman Roofing business plan from an investor and lender point of view.
2. Comment on the effectiveness of Robert's service strategy relating to the right service (add tangibility), the right way (control variability), in the right place (bridge inseparability) at the right time (overcome perishability) at the right price (enhance profitability) by the right appeal (increase communicability).

CASE 23: Roots Canada Ltd.: Expansion to the United States

D. Wesley Balderson, University of Lethbridge

Roots co-founders Michael Budman and Don Green became friends while attending summer camp at Camp Tamakwa in northern Ontario. After completing their educations at Michigan State University, they decided to team up to develop products which utilized the Canadian environment. Inspired by the natural beauty and simplicity of the northern woods lifestyle, the entrepreneurial pair nurtured a simple idea for a negative heel "earth" shoe and established Roots Canada in 1973. Since that time, Roots has become Canada's leading independent manufacturer and retailer of high-quality leather products and casual clothing for men, women, and children. Roots has chosen to design, manufacture, and wholesale the products it sells in Canada and employs over 1000 people in its Canadian operations. Roots currently has 95 stores in Canada retailing footwear, natural fibre clothing, leather jackets, and accessories.

Roots products are known for superior quality, enduring style, and outstanding value. Ninety-five percent of Roots goods are made in Canada, of which the majority are manufactured in Roots's own factories in Toronto. Budman and Green have conveyed the Canadian culture and lifestyle through their products. They have also made a commitment to environmental matters, literacy campaigns, Canadian heritage, and the promotion of a healthy and fulfilling lifestyle. The success of this approach is evident by the performance of the company, which has now generated sales of over $100 million.

One of the reasons for this growth in sales has been Roots's expansion into international markets with their retail stores. Budman and Green approached international expansion cautiously, insisting on the right markets and making sure they maintained control of their operations. Roots currently has six stores in the United States and thirteen in the Pacific Rim markets of Taiwan, Korea, Hong Kong, and Japan. At a time when Canadian retailers have had a difficult time breaking into foreign markets, especially in the U.S., Roots seems to have found an effective strategy for doing so. Budman even suggests that Roots's sales could double within five years if the U.S. expansion continues to be successful.

The Canadian wilderness still forms the backbone of Roots's marketing image, particularly in Asia, where the company's products are increasingly popular. "Asians are enamoured with our rugged, natural environment," Budman says. If ever there was a company that focuses on "lifestyle," it's got to be Roots. "That's a very prominent niche, and Roots really caters to it," says Toronto retail analyst Ed Strapagiel. "The lifestyle market has not been encroached upon by the big-box stores."

Budman and Green remain optimistic about the future of Roots. Although consumer expenditures on "extras" such as clothing are not on the rise, they insist that sales of casual clothing such as that found in Roots stores will remain strong for several years, as this style is becoming acceptable for more office workers.

Assignment

Discuss how Roots Canada Ltd. may have been successful with its expansion to the U.S. and other countries where many other Canadian retailers have failed.

Sources

Brian Hutchinson, "Merchants of Boom," *Canadian Business Magazine*, May 1997, 46–48; Roots Profile, "Roots Co-founders—since 1973," http://www.roots.com/founders.html; World-Wide Roots, "Roots Commitment to Social and Environmental Issues, http://www.roots.com/worldroots/html; Roots Factory, "The Roots Factory—A Unique Canadian Facility," http://www.roots.com/factory.html; Roots Profile, "Roots Canada," http://www.com/rootstory.html; *Venture*, CBC Corporation, July 29, 1985.

Appendix C
Glossary

ABC analysis A rank-ordering procedure that groups product lines according to their actual performance records or potential performance capabilities.

ABC markets An urban market classification system based on a given area's sales volume potential; urban centres are classified in descending order as either A, B, or C markets.

Account A record of the increases and decreases in one type of asset, liability, capital, income, or expense.

Achievement test A personnel evaluation instrument involving questionnaires designed to measure a person's basic knowledge and skills.

Adaptive adhocracy A retail organizational structure that limits vertical management while promoting horizontal working relationships in accomplishing the retailer's objectives.

Advertising An indirect, impersonal communication carried by a mass medium and paid for by an identified retailer.

Advertising budget An allocation of advertising dollars made on the basis of departments, merchandise lines, media, and time periods.

Advertising cost The amount of money a retailer must pay to run an advertisement in a medium (absolute); the number of dollars the retailer spends to reach a specific number of people (relative).

Advertising effectiveness The process of establishing specific, measurable advertising objectives, then acquiring or developing instruments and methodologies to determine whether those objectives were met.

Advertising frequency The number of times the same viewer or reader may be exposed to the same advertisement.

Aesthetic features The elements of a product that appeal to the five senses of hearing, seeing, tasting, feeling, and smelling.

Affective component The emotions a consumer feels about a person, place, or thing.

Affinity The extent to which a new product is consistent with the consumer's current buying and usage behaviour.

Agent intermediary An intermediary who specializes in the tasks of buying and selling in order to facilitate the exchange process between manufacturer and retailer by bringing channel members together.

Analogue model A quantitative technique that is used to make sales projections for new stores based on the sales performance of existing stores.

Annual sales estimate A sale forecasting technique that uses the previous year's sales plus or minus a fixed or variable percentage adjustment as an estimate of future sales.

Anticompetitive leasing arrangement An arrangement that limits the type and amount of competition a particular retailer faces within a given area (for example, shopping centre).

Antitrust legislation A set of laws directed at preventing unreasonable "restraints on trade" and "unfair trade practices" to foster a competitive environment.

Approval buying A buying method that allows the retailer to inspect the merchandise before making the purchase decision and postpone any purchase until physical possession has been secured.

Areas of dominant influence (ADIS) A geographic market area based on local viewing patterns; it is an area identified by the Arbitron Company that consists of all counties in which the home market stations receive a preponderance of viewing.

Asset turnover A financial ratio calculated by dividing net sales by total assets.

Assets Anything of value that is owned by a retailer.

At-home retailing The market approach of making personal contacts and sales in the consumers' homes.

Attitude An evaluative mental orientation that provides a predisposition to respond in a certain fashion.

Audience selectivity A medium's capability to present a promotional message to a certain target audience within a population.

Audiovisual display A display type in which current audiovisual technology is employed to stimulate consumer purchases (visual merchandising, audio merchandising, and audiovisual merchandising); a combination of sound and videotape or slides to present the product's story.

Autocratic management A retail management style that relies on centralized authority and control to attain the firm's mission and goals.

Automatic identification system A group of several interacting technologies that enables machines to recognize and enter data into a computer system.

Automatic markdown A price adjustment practice in which prices are reduced by a fixed percentage at a regular interval.

Average stock The sum of the stock on hand at the beginning of the period, at each intervening period, and at the end of the period divided by the number of stock listings.

Backward integration The process of gaining ownership and/or control of supply systems.

Bait and switch The "bait" is an advertised low price on a product that the retailer does not really intend to sell; the "switch" involves personal selling techniques that induce the customer to buy a higher-priced product that will provide the retailer with greater profits.

Bait leader An extremely attractive advertised price on merchandise that the retailer does not intend to sell; the attractive advertised price is "bait" to get the customer into the store.

Balance sheet A picture of the firm's assets, liabilities, and net worth on a given date that summarizes the basic accounting equation of assets equal liabilities plus net worth.

Bar code A series of light and dark bars that constitute a symbol that is typically attached to a product package or shipping carton.

Basic stock list A planning instrument retailers use to determine the assortment and support for staple merchandise.

Basic stock method A stock planning method that begins each month with stock levels that equal the estimated sales for that month plus an additional basic stock amount that serves as a "cushion" or "safety stock" in the event that actual sales exceed estimated sales.

BCG portfolio approach A matrix model used to illustrate the current positions of an organization's strategic business units.

Behaviour component The predisposition to respond in a certain way based on one's beliefs and feelings.

Blue laws A set of local laws that regulate everything from operating hours and days to operating locations.

Borrowed capital The money the firm has obtained from outside sources.

Boutique layout A store layout that arranges the sales floor into individual, semiseparate areas, each built around a particular shopping theme.

Brand A distinctive grouping of products identified by name, term, design, symbol, or any combination of these markings.

Brand-name products Products that are branded or labelled by manufacturers, retailers, or licensors.

Bridge pricing The retail pricing practice of creating a price point that spans or connects two distinctively different price lines at different price levels.

Brochure A form of mail-order retailing that involves preparation of a small booklet or leaflet that is mailed to potential consumers.

Brokers Agent intermediaries whose primary function is to bring prospective buyers and sellers together to complete a transaction.

Building A portfolio strategy that calls for increasing an SBU's market share.

Bulk marking A price marking technique that involves placing similar merchandise with the same price in a display and attaching one price card to the display.

Burglary Any unlawful entry to commit a felony or a theft, even though no force is used to gain entrance.

Buying behaviour The manner in which consumers act, function, and react to various situations involving the purchase of a good or service or the acceptance of an idea.

Buying centre A basic unit of consumption that engages in the buying process.

Buying power The financial resources available to the consumer for making purchases.

Buying scene The actual place where consumers complete a purchase transaction.

Captive pricing The retail pricing practice of locking in the customer by selling the basic product item at a reduced price, then selling consumables at higher prices.

Cash cow A strategic business unit that has a high market share within a low-growth market.

Cash discount A discount given for making prompt payment within a prescribed time period.

Catalogue A retail operation that involves the use of specially prepared catalogues that present the retailer's merchandise both visually and verbally.

Catalogue showroom A warehouse retailer featuring hard goods such as housewares, small appliances, jewellery, watches, toys, sporting goods, lawn and garden equipment, luggage, stereos, televisions, and other electronic equipment at a discount; a merchandise catalogue is combined with the showroom and an adjacent warehouse as part of the retailer's operation.

Category killer A retail format that wants to achieve merchandise dominance in its respective category by creating narrowly focused jumbo-size stores.

Category management The process of managing product categories as individual business units and customizing each category's product mix and merchandising effort to meet customer preferences on a store-by-store basis.

Category retailer A retail operation that sells one or more merchandise categories to one or more market segments.

Central business district (CBD) A downtown retailing cluster located at or near the centre of an urban area.

Central market A geographic area with a concentration of selling offices and merchandise showrooms of a large number of suppliers for a particular line of merchandise.

Centralization The concentration of policy and decision making in one location (central headquarters or home office).

Chain store Any retail organization that operates multiple outlets, offers a standardized merchandise mix, and utilizes a centralized form of ownership and control.

Chain trade discount A series of percentage discounts applied to the list price in successive order and given to the retailer for its role and contributions as a channel member.

Channel integration The process of incorporating all channel members into one channel system and uniting them under one leadership and one set of goals.

Checking The material handling process of determining whether the supplier has shipped what the retailer ordered and whether the shipment has arrived in good condition.

Checklist method A site evaluation process in which the evaluator (1) enumerates the general factors considered in any site evaluation, (2) identifies several attribute measurements that reflect the location needs of the proposed retail operation, (3) selects a subjective weight based on relative importance to the retailer, (4) rates each location attribute, and (5) calculates a weighted-rating score for each site alternative.

Clash The visual conflict among the many parts of any display, layout, or physical arrangement.

Class selectivity The capability of a medium to target specific kinds of people who share certain common characteristics.

Classic A fashion that has a high level and long duration of acceptance.

Classification retailer A retail store that focuses on a single product class or a few product classes that are highly related.

Closeout store An outlet that specializes in the retailing of a wide variety of merchandise obtained through close-outs, retail liquidations, and bankruptcy proceeds.

Clustered site A retail location that is either next to or very near other retail locations.

Coercive buying The retailer's use of financial, distribution, marketing, and other powers to gain lower prices from vendors.

Cognitive component What the consumer believes about an object based on available information and knowledge.

Commission agent An intermediary who takes physical possession of goods, provides storage and handling, and acts as the selling agent for the producer.

Commissionaire An international intermediary that operates either full or limited buying offices within one or more foreign countries.

Communication effectiveness An advertising medium's capability to deliver the desired impact to the target market.

Communication market A retail market identified on the basis of various types of media coverage.

Communication process The process of transmitting meaningful messages between senders.

Communications approach The concept of how a message is expressed; the use of facts, narrative, and logical reasoning to persuade (rational); the act of appealing to the consumer's sense of aesthetics, ego, or feelings (emotional).

Community shopping centre A shopping centre serving a composite of many neighbourhoods within a ten- to fifteen-minute drive from the centre.

Comparison shopping The consumer behavioural process in which a customer compares and/or substitutes products within merchandise classes.

Competitive audit An arbitrary, composite rating of each competitor's product, service, price, place, and promotional mixes.

Competitive parity method An advertising budget-setting method in which the budget is set at the amount that the firm estimates its most important competitors are spending.

Competitive price objectives The price objective of meeting the major competitor's price.

Complexity A new product evaluation criterion based on the concept of how well a new product can be easily understood or used.

Composite trading area A set of trading areas, each of which is structured according to the type of goods the retailer sells.

Computer-based point-of-sale A computerized check-out counter that involves a computerized cash register and terminal connected to a central computer.

Concentric diversification The growth strategy of adding businesses to a firm's portfolio that have technological or marketing similarities with existing businesses.

Concept selling The retail pricing practice of establishing a higher price for a product or service and justifying that price by convincing the customer the total set of benefits (the concept) is worth the extra costs.

Conglomerate diversification The growth strategy of adding new businesses that are totally unrelated to an organization's current SBUs in order to appeal to entirely new markets.

Consignment buying An arrangement in which the supplier retains ownership of the merchandise shipped to the retailer, and the retailer sells the merchandise, deducts an agreed-on percentage commission, and remits the remainder to the supplier.

Consumer buying process The sum total of the sequential parts of problem recognition, information search, alternative evaluation, purchase decision, and postpurchase evaluation.

Consumer market A market composed of individuals and/or households that are the ultimate consumers of goods or services.

Contest A sales incentive consisting of promotional activities in which participants compete for rewards.

Continuity premium A sales incentive that requires the customer to make repeat purchases of products and services to benefit from the premium offer.

Contract warehousing A distribution tactic that involves contracting with third-party warehouse companies to take care of all or part of the retailer distribution needs.

Contrast The visual diversity among the many parts of any display, layout, or physical arrangement.

Control unit The merchandise grouping that serves as the basic reporting unit for various types of information.

Controllable expenses An expense classification over which the firm has direct control.

Convenience products Those products that the consumer is not willing to spend time, money, and effort in locating, evaluating, and procuring.

Convenience store A retailing format that offers customers a convenient place to shop—time convenience (for example, open longer and during inconvenient early morning and late night hours) and place convenience (for example, small, compact, fast-service operations close to consumers' homes and places of business).

Conventional marketing channel A loosely aligned, independently owned and operated channel team.

Cooperative advertising A form of advertising in which manufacturers prepare print and broadcast advertising material of their own products and allow the retailer to insert its store name and address in the ad; the manufacturer and retailer split the cost of media space or time to run the ad.

Copy What is actually said in the advertisement.

Core approach A space allocation approach in which all non-selling areas within a central core are surrounded by selling areas.

Corollary data method A method used to estimate trading area sales that assumes that an identifiable relationship exists between sales for a particular class of goods and one or more trading area characteristics.

Corporation A legal business entity authorized by law to operate as a single person even though it may consist of many persons.

Cost justification defence A legal argument that makes it lawful to charge retailers different prices if the supplier can justify those price differences on the basis of its cost of doing business with each competing retailer.

Cost method of inventory valuation Valuing merchandise inventory at the original cost to the store each time a physical inventory is taken.

Cost of goods sold The value of the merchandise sold during any given accounting period.

Counterfeit good A good that has illegally used a registered trademark to deceive consumers into thinking that the merchandise was produced by the original manufacturer.

Coupon A form of mail-order retailing that involves using magazine and newspaper advertisement to deliver manufacturer or retailer certificates that give consumers a price reduction on specific kinds of merchandise.

Coverage The percentage of a given market that a medium reaches.

Credit The borrowing power of a consumer, an amount of money that is placed at a consumer's disposal by a financial or other institution, and the time allowed for payment for goods and services sold on trust.

Cross docking The distribution method used in retail distribution centres in which merchandise is received, sorted, and routed directly from receiving to shipping without spending any time in storage.

Cross-elasticity of demand A pricing relationship in which a change in the price of one product results in a change in demand for another product.

Cues External stimuli that direct consumers toward specific objects that can satisfy basic needs and reduce drives.

Culture The sum total of knowledge, attitudes, symbols, and patterns of behaviour that are shared by a group of people and transmitted from one generation to the next.

Cumulative markup The markup placed on an item that is based on the weight each item contributes to the total markup of all the items in the merchandise group.

Cumulative quantity discount A quantity discount that applies to several orders or shipments placed with the supplier over an extended period of time.

Current assets All items of value that can be easily converted into cash within a relatively short time.

Current liabilities Short-term debts that must be paid during the current fiscal year.

Current ratio A financial ratio that is computed by dividing current assets by current liabilities; it represents the firm's ability to meet current debt with current assets.

Customer assistance The concept that incorporates all of the features, acts, and information that augment the customer's ability to realize the potential value of a core good or core service.

DAGMAR (defining advertising goals for measured advertising results) A sequence of steps through which prospective customers move from total unawareness of a store and its offering to store patronage and purchase.

Debit card An electronic chequebook that allows the retailer to automatically subtract payments from a customer's chequing account at the time of sale.

Debt ratio A financial ratio that is computed by dividing total debt by total assets.

Deceptive brokerage activity An illegal practice involving the establishment and use of "dummy" brokerage firms to obtain a brokerage allowance from suppliers, thereby giving retailers an unfair purchase-price advantage.

Deceptive price advertising The illegal practice of using price information to mislead consumers into believing that they are receiving a better price or a larger discount than is actually being offered.

Deceptive product advertising The illegal practice of making a false or misleading claim about the physical makeup of the product, the appropriate uses for the product, or the benefits of using the product, as well as using packages and labels that tend to mislead the customer about the exact contents, quality, or quantity of the package.

Decoding A stage in the communication process in which an individual is receiving a message and interpreting its meaning either correctly or incorrectly, depending on how well the message was encoded and the decoder's experience and skill with the communication process.

Democratic management A retail management style that relies on delegated authority to subordinates and voluntary participation by employees in the achievement of mutually beneficial goals.

Demography The study of statistics that are used to describe a population.

Department store A large retailing institution that carries a wide variety of merchandise lines with a reasonably good selection within each line.

Departmentalization A retail organizational principle that calls for the grouping of tasks and employees into departments to achieve the operating efficiencies of specialization for a group performing similar tasks.

Design A fashion term that describes an individual's interpretation or version of a style.

Designated marketing area (DMA) A geographic area that is best served by selected broadcasting stations; it is a commercial product of the A. C. Nielsen Company.

Desires A consumer's conscious impulses toward objects or experiences that hold promise of enjoyment in their attainment.

Dialectic process A "melting pot" theory of retail institutional change in which two substantially different competitive forms of retailing merge together into a new retailing institution, a composite of the original two forms.

Dichotomous questions A survey research tool that limits a respondent's answer to only one of two choices.

Direct-action message An advertising message that urges the consumer to come to the store now to take advantage of a promotion.

Direct advertising A medium that retailers use extensively to communicate their product offerings to a select group of consumers.

Direct channel A channel structure in which the producer eliminates both retailer and wholesaler and markets directly to the final consumer.

Direct expenses Those expenses directly attributable to the operations of a department or some other defined operating unit.

Direct (intratype) competitor A retail competitor whose merchandising program is about the same as another retailer's.

Direct-mail retailer A direct marketer that utilizes only postal services to communicate the merchandising offer to the consumer, who in turn responds by mail or telephone.

Direct marketing An interactive system (between buyer and seller) of marketing that uses one or more advertising media to make customer contact or obtain a customer order.

Direct premium A sales incentive that consists of free gifts given to the customer at the time of purchase.

Direct product profit (DPP) A performance measurement technique that enables the retailer to calculate the profitability of a merchandise category as well as a particular product item.

Direct-response retailer A direct marketer that uses both broadcast and print media to communicate with consumers and is willing and able to accept orders or handle responses from customers.

Direct selling A direct-to-customer marketing practice that involves personal explanation and demonstration of the products and services.

Discount A reduction in the original retail price that is granted to store employees as a special fringe benefit and to special customers in recognition of their status.

Discounter An employee who gives unauthorized discounts to friends and relatives.

Discretionary income That portion of an individual's or family's disposable income that remains after purchasing the basic necessities of life—food, clothing, and shelter.

Display stock Stock placed on various display fixtures that customers can directly examine.

Disposable income The income that remains after taxes and other required payments have been deducted from total income.

Dissatisfiers Employment factors that make workers unhappy with their jobs, leading to high turnover and weak performance.

Diversification growth An organization's adding of SBUs whose business nature and format are dissimilar to the current SBUs held by the firm.

Divesting Disposing of SBUs that offer little or no hope of improving either their market share or cash flow position.

Divisional bureaucracy A retail organizational structure in which a large number of departments operate as autonomous units under a common organizational umbrella.

Dog An SBU with a low market share in a low-growth market.

Dollar control Collecting, recording, and analyzing merchandise data in terms of dollars.

Dollar markup A cost-oriented approach to setting prices in which the retailer adds to the cost of the merchandise a dollar amount large enough to cover related operating expenses and provide a given dollar profit.

Dollar open-to-buy at cost The buyer multiplies open-to-buy at retail by the complement of the initial markup percentage.

Dollar open-to-buy at retail The buyer starts with planned monthly purchases and subtracts purchase commitments already made during the month.

Dollar/periodic/physical inventory system Provides periodic information on the amount of inventory (dollars) actually on hand at a given time as determined by a physical count and valuation of the merchandise.

Dollar/perpetual/book inventory system Provides the retailer with continuous information on the amount of inventory (dollars) that should be on hand at any given time as determined by internal accounting records.

Dollar planning A financial management tool used to plan the amount of total value (dollars) inventory a retailer should carry.

Drawing power The area from which a shopping centre can expect to derive as much as 85 percent of its total volume.

Drive Whatever impels individual behaviour; it arises from a strongly felt inner need that requires action.

Dual distribution A form of vertical competition in which a manufacturer or wholesaler competes directly with a retailer by selling the same merchandise.

Durables Products that are capable of surviving many uses.

Educated-guess budgeting method The use of intuition and practical experience to develop an advertising budget.

Elastic demand A condition in which a change in price strongly influences consumer demand.

Electronic data processing A computer-based system of processing information.

Electronic data interchange A communication system that enables buyers and suppliers to conduct business transactions electronically.

Electronic point-of-sale A point-of-sale system that uses various software packages together with a computerized checkout counter to capture, process, and analyze sales and inventory data.

Electronic retailing A form of retailing over electronic and video systems in the innovation stage of the retail life cycle.

Electronically programmable shelf labels Small liquid crystal display labels that are attached on the edge of the shelf and can display new prices instantly on command.

Emotional approach A presentation that appeals to consumers' feelings.

Encoding Using signs and symbols that promote understanding of the idea, attract attention of the intended audiences, stimulate needs felt by intended audiences, and suggest a course of action for need satisfaction.

Equal-store organization Emphasizes centralization of authority and responsibility.

Equity capital What the firm owns.

Essential services Those services basic and necessary to the retailer's merchandising and operational activities.

Esteem needs Aspirations involving prestige, recognition, admiration, self-respect, success, and achievement.

Ethics A system or code of conduct based on universal moral duties and obligations that indicate how one should behave.

Everyday low pricing The retail pricing practice of maintaining price points at the same low level all the time.

Exclusive market coverage Using one location to serve either an entire market area or some major segment of that market.

Exclusive dealings Arrangements between retailers and suppliers in which the retailer agrees to handle only the supplier's products or no other products that pose direct competition.

Exclusive territories Agreements under which a supplier grants a retailer the exclusive right to sell its products within a defined geographic area.

Executive training programs (ETPS) Educational sessions directed at supervisors, managers, and executives.

Expected services Services not essential for the retailer to operate but expected by customers.

Expense budget A plan or a set of guidelines that a firm uses to control operating expenses.

Experimentation A technique that researchers use to determine a cause-and-effect relationship between two or more factors.

Expert systems Computer programs that have knowledge bases contributed by experts in a particular field and are used to aid in decision making and problem solving.

Expressed warranties Written and verbal statements that the seller makes to consumers about a product and performance and that the retailer is legally obligated to honour.

Extended channel Marketing through both wholesalers and retailers.

External information Information obtained from outside the firm.

Factor A credit company that buys manufacturers' receivables at a discount and then retrieves payment from retailers.

Factory outlet Direct manufacturer's outlet store that sells its own seconds, overruns, and pack-aways from last season.

Factory outlet mall A discount mall whose tenant mix is composed of various manufacturers' factory outlets.

Fad A fashion that obtains a relatively high level of customer acceptance for a short time.

Fashion A product that has distinctive attributes that are currently appropriate and represent the prevailing style.

Fashion cycle The three stages a fashion passes through: introduction, acceptance, and decline.

Fashion mall A shopping centre in which the tenant mix is primarily made up of retailers whose merchandise focus is apparel and accessories.

Fast-food retailer A limited-selection prepared-food retailer that offers quick-response service and low to modest prices.

Feedback The nature of the receiver's response or lack of it communicated back to the sender.

Financial leverage A financial ratio obtained by dividing total assets divided by net worth.

Financial objectives A strategic position directed at ensuring that the organization operates profitably and productively.

Financial ratio A mathematical relationship between elements in the balance sheet or between a balance sheet element and an income statement element to determine a firm's financial performance.

First-in first-out (FIFO) A method of costing inventory in which merchandise items are sold in the order in which they are purchased; older stock is sold before newer stock that was purchased at a later date.

Fixed asset An asset that requires a significant length of time to convert into cash, usually more than one year.

Fixed-based budgeting A budget allocation process in which each expense is budgeted to a specific dollar amount.

Fixed capital Money needed to purchase physical facilities.

Fixed expense An expense classification in which an expense is fixed for a given period of time and remains the same regardless of the sales volume.

Flexibility A media characteristic involving the number of "things" the advertiser can do in the medium.

Flexible pricing A retail pricing policy that enables the customer to negotiate the final selling price.

Flop A fashion rejected by all consumer segments almost immediately.

Ford A best-seller in fashion merchandising that lasts for several seasons.

Format combination The retail strategy of combining two or more compatible retailing formats into a new, single, and more extensive retailing format.

Forward buying The practice of stocking up on a manufacturer's promotional items at a deep discount at the tail end of the designated promotional period.

Forward integration An expansion strategy that involves developing or acquiring retail businesses and operating them as part of the firm's strategic marketing effort.

Forward stock Backup stock that is temporarily stored on the sales floor near its selling department.

4-3-2-1 rule The decline in value of store space from front to back of the shop is expressed by assigning 40 percent of a store's rental cost to the front quarter of the shop, 30 percent to the second quarter, 20 percent to the third quarter, and 10 percent to the final quarter.

Franchising A continuing relationship in which the franchiser provides a licensed privilege to do business, plus assistance in organizing, training, merchandising, and management in return for a consideration from the franchisee.

Freeform layout A store layout plan that arranges displays and aisles in a free-flowing pattern.

Fringe trading zone The surrounding trading area from which the retailer occasionally draws customers and representing 5 to 10 percent of total sales.

Full-function merchant intermediary An intermediary that performs a full range of wholesaling functions; depending on the width of the product lines, identified as a general merchandise wholesaler, single-line wholesaler, or specialty-line wholesaler.

Full-line department store A large-scale retailer offering a wide variety of merchandise categories (usually hard and soft goods) within a departmentalized framework.

Full-line discount store A retailing institution that sells a wide variety of merchandise (fifth-line) at less than traditional retail prices.

Full-line forcing A buying arrangement in which the supplier requires the retailer to carry the supplier's full line of products if the retailer wishes to carry any part of that line.

Full-service retailer A retailer that provides essential, expected, and optional services.

Full warranty A legal agreement in which the producer or retailer agrees to repair or replace a defective product without charge to the consumer.

Functional features The physical aspects of a product that include the tangible elements of size, shape, and weight, together with a product's chemical and/or biological makeup.

Functional objective A specific task objective that identifies a specific function and how it is to be accomplished.

Functional training A program that develops and expands the basic skills and knowledge employees need to perform their jobs successfully.

Future dating The practice of allowing the buyer more time to take advantage of the cash discount or pay the net amount of the invoice.

General business licence A local operating requirement in which the retailer pays a registration fee in order to operate a business.

General partnership A legal form of retail organization in which all partners take part in the control and operation of the partnership; hence, all partners can be held jointly and severally liable for the debts of the partnership.

Generic products A product category consisting of unadvertised, lower-grade, no-frill brands offered as low-cost alternatives to name-brand merchandise.

Geodemography The process of linking demographic data (for example, age, income, sex) with geographic locations.

Geographic selectivity A medium's capability to hone in on a specific geographic area such as a city and its surrounding area.

GE portfolio approach A matrix approach used to assess the overall desirability of the markets currently being served by the retailer and the retailer's relative capability to serve current markets as compared with the abilities of competitors.

Global retailer An international retailer characterized by a highly integrated and fairly standardized retailing format that is used to serve similar customers in each of the foreign markets targeted by its management.

Good-faith defence A legal argument that makes it lawful for a seller to discriminate in price if such action is done in good faith to meet an equally low price of a competitor.

Goods Tangible items defined by their size, shape, and weight together with their chemical and/or biological makeup.

Goods retailer A retailer whose core product is a tangible product.

Gray marketing The selling of branded merchandise by unauthorized retailers that obtain the goods through unauthorized channels of distribution.

Grid layout A store layout plan consisting of a rectangular arrangement of displays and aisles that generally run parallel to one another.

Gross adequacy The capability of a trading area to support a retail operation without any consideration of retail competition.

Gross margin A financial term that expresses the difference between net sales and total merchandise costs.

Gross margin return on inventory (GMRI) The financial ratio of gross margin dollars to the average stock on hand.

Gross sales The total dollar revenues received from the sale of merchandise and services.

Group training methods A set of training techniques that involve the simultaneous training of several employees through lectures, demonstrations, case studies, role-playing activities, computer simulations, and interactive videos.

Hand marking A merchandise marking procedure that involves using grease pencils, ink stamps, and pens to mark the merchandise, package, label, tag, or ticket directly.

Harmony A sight appeal factor involving visual agreement among the many parts of any display, layout, or physical arrangement.

Harvesting An alternative portfolio management option that calls for milking an SBU of its cash in order to finance the growth of other SBU alternatives.

Headline The component of an advertisement that condenses the basic advertising message into a concise statement and tells the reader essentially what is to come.

Historical restoration mall A shopping centre located in places of historic significance, often involving the renovation of interesting structures (for example, old warehouses, factories, train stations).

Holding An alternative portfolio management strategy of maintaining an SBU's market share.

Home centre A warehouse retailing format that combines the traditional hardware store and lumber yard with a self-service home improvement centre.

Horizontal diversification A growth strategy that involves adding SBUs that appeal to the organization's current customers even though they are not technologically related to its current businesses.

Horizontal integration A growth strategy that involves gaining ownership and/or control of competitors at the same level within the marketing channel.

Horizontal price fixing An illegal pricing practice that involves collaboration between two or more competing retailers to establish and charge a fixed retail price for one or more merchandise lines.

Hypermarket A huge superstore format that features a line combination of hard goods, soft goods, and foodstuffs.

Illustration The component of an advertisement consisting of a drawing or photograph of the product.

Immediacy A medium's capability to present a timely or newsworthy message.

Immediate dating A condition of sale that allows no time for qualifying for the cash discount or extra time for the making invoice payment.

Impact A media evaluation terms that expresses how well a medium stimulates particular behavioural responses within the target market.

Implied warranty A warranty statement in which the seller's "intended" promises of product performance are suggested even though not actually expressed in either written or verbal form.

Importer A domestically based commission wholesaler that represents retailers in the buying process.

Income rating index Per capita income of trading area compred to per capita income of Canada.

Income statement A picture of the retailer's profits or losses over a period of time that summarizes the firm's income and expenses.

In-home retailing The direct-seeing approach of making personal contacts and sales in the consumer's home.

In-house credit system A credit system that is owned, operated, and managed by the retail firm.

In-store testing A market research technique involving the conducting of test sales of a products within a store in order to judge customer response (for example, sales) to the product.

Independent off-price outlet A retail operation that buys seconds, irregulars, cancelled orders, overages, or leftover goods from manufacturers or other retailers and offers them to the consuming public at substantially discounted prices.

Index of retail saturation (IRS) A measure of potential sales per unit of store space for a given product line within a particular market area; expresses a relationship between a trading area's capability to consume and its capability to retail.

Indirect-action message An advertising message that attempts to change consumers' attitudes toward the retailer by cultivating its image as the "right" place for the consumer to buy.

Indirect expense An expense classification that contains expenses that cannot be directly attributed to the operations of a department.

Indirect (intertype) competitor A retail competitor whose merchandising program is noticeably different from that of a retailer of similar products.

Individual training method A personnel training program in which employees "train" themselves; the individual is put on the job and expected to learn by trial and error, observation, and asking questions.

Inelastic demand A demand relationship in which a change in price has little or no influence on consumer demand.

Infomercials A mail-order retailing format in which thirty-minute program-length ads mix information and entertainment with sales presentations. Consumers view the infomercials on television and usually place orders by the telephone or mail.

Information flow The two-way communication of useful data between channel participants.

Initial markup The difference between merchandise cost and the original retail price.

Initial markup percentage A price-setting method in which the first retail price is established by summing operating expenses, operating profit, alterations cost, and retail reduction and dividing by the sum of the net sales plus retail reductions.

Institutional advertising A form of advertising that attempts to sell the store as an enjoyable place to shop; the focus is on creating an image based on store attributes, not product dimensions of the retailer's offering.

Intensive market coverage A location strategy in which the retailer selects and utilizes as many retail outlets as are justified to obtain blanket market coverage of an entire market area.

Intermediate-term credit Money that can be borrowed for a term greater than one year but less than five years.

Intertype competition The type of competition between two or more retailers using different types of business formats to sell the same type of merchandise.

Intratype competition The type of competition between two or more retailers using the same type of business format.

Inventory assortment The number of different product items the retailer stocks within a particular product line.

Inventory investment The total dollar amount that the retailer has invested in merchandise inventory at any one time.

Inventory support The number of units the retailer has on hand for each product item to meet sales estimates.

Isolated site A retail location that is geographically separated from other retailing sites.

Job description The first step in the staffing process; contains the following items: job title, job location, job position and relationships, and job description.

Job specification The minimum qualifications a person must have in order to apply for a job.

Joint venture An international business arrangement in which a retailer joins together with a foreign entity to establish a new retailing enterprise or to purchase an established retail concern within the host nation.

Last-in, first-out (LIFO) A method of costing inventories in which recent acquisition costs are used to price inventory (even though in actuality, the inventory bought last is not sold first).

Late markdown A markdown strategy that calls for maintaining the original selling price until late in the selling season, at which time a major clearance sale is held.

Layout The arrangement of each element of a print advertisement that is designed to capture the consumer's attention and guide the reader through all parts of the advertisement.

Leader pricing The strategy of selling key merchandise items below their normal markup or, in some cases, even below the retailer's merchandise costs.

Learning The consumer/buyer behavioural process of acquiring knowledge through past experiences.

Lease agreement A contractual arrangement in which the customer rents a product in the present with the option to buy in the future.

Leased department A contractual retail format in which an independent lessee operates departments (usually in specialized lines of merchandise) under contractual arrangements with conventional retail stores.

Ledger A book in which a number of accounts are kept together.

Leverage buyout A financial integrative strategy in which an acquisition is financed through the sale of high-return bonds junk bonds and the support of a bank loan.

Leverage ratio A measure of the relative contributions of owners and creditors in the financing of the firm's operations.

Licensed merchandise An item that is designed and sold through identification with a famous individual or corporate name, title, logo, slogan, or fictional character.

Licensing An international market entry agreement in which a retailer (licensor) grants a foreign entity (licensee) the right to an intangible property (design, trademark, or brand name).

Life The length of time an advertisement continues to "sell."

Life cycle A description of the changes that occur in an individual's demographic, psychographic, and behaviouristic profile while progressing through a series of stages during his or her lifetime.

Lifestyle A patterned style of living that stems from the individual's needs, perceptions, and attitudes.

Lifestyle merchandising The strategy of developing product lines in accordance with consumer living patterns.

Likert's Summated Rating Scale A method for measuring attitudes and opinions by asking respondents to indicate the extent of their agreement or disagreement with a list of statements regarding the issue being studied.

Limited channel A marketing channel that eliminates wholesalers and uses only retailers to reach the final consumer.

Limited-function merchant intermediaries Wholesalers that limit their offered services; examples include cash-and-carry wholesalers, drop shippers, truck distributors, and rack jobbers.

Limited-line department store A large-scale retailer that stocks a somewhat limited variety of merchandise categories and classifications but functions with a fashion orientation and full markup policy, in stores large enough to be shopping centre anchors.

Limited partnership A legal form of organization with one or more members of the partnership contributing capital to the formation and running of the partnership, but these limited partners do not take part in managing the firm's retail operations.

Limited-service strategy The retail service strategy employed by retailers that offer all essential and expected services.

Limited warranty A legal statement that places limitation on the responsibilities of the producer and seller to correct any product deficiency.

Line additions The merchandising tactic of adding to one retailer's traditional merchandise mix the more desirable product lines normally associated with another type of retailer.

Line relationship The retail organization concept that expresses the affiliations among managers at different organizational levels or between a manager and a subordinate within the same level who are directly responsible for achieving the firm's strategic, operational, and/or functional objectives.

Lines of authority and responsibility The organization principle that each store employee (managerial and nonmanagerial) should be given the authority to accomplish whatever responsibilities have been assigned to that individual.

Liquid capital Money held in reserve for emergency situations.

Liquidity ratio A type of financial ratio that answers the question of the firm's solvency; the two most common liquidity ratios used by retailers are the quick ratio and the current ratio.

Logical approach A factual presentation about a merchandise offering.

Logotype A store's distinctive "signature" that appears in all advertising.

Long-term credit A loan obtained for periods greater than five years.

Long-term liabilities An expression of a retailer's indebtedness that is due at some time after the current year.

Loss-leader A price that is reduced to at or lower than the retailer's cost of the merchandise; used to attract consumers to the store.

Low-leader A price set lower than the customary selling price but higher than the retailer's actual cost of the merchandise; used to attract consumers to the store.

Machine bureaucracy A tall, highly structured and centralized retail organization with precise hierarchical lines of authority and a large number of middle managers with large support staffs.

Machine vision A technology that uses video cameras to read bar codes or identify a product through its signature.

Mail-in premium A sales incentive that requires the customer to send in a proof of purchase to receive a free gift.

Mail-order retailer A direct marketer that communicates its offer of goods and services through television, radio, newspaper, or magazine advertisements and accepts orders by mail or telephone.

Main-store organization The parent organization (the main store) exercises operating and merchandising control over branch stores.

Maintained markup The difference between gross merchandise cost and actual selling price.

Manufacturer brand A product that is produced, owned, controlled, and sometimes distributed by the manufacturer.

Manufacturer's agent The sales agent for several manufacturers within a prescribed market territory.

Markdown A downward adjustment in the original selling price of a merchandise item.

Markdown control The act of maintaining records on the causes or reasons for taking markdowns on a particular merchandise item.

Markdown percentage The expression of the size of a price markdown as a percentage of the reduced selling price or as a percentage of the original selling price.

Market A geographic area where buyers and sellers meet to exchange money for products and services.

Market development A strategy employed by a firm to increase sales of current products through new product uses or selling in new markets.

Market penetration A strategy employed by a firm to increase sales of current products in a current market.

Market positioning The strategy of creating a "position" for a store and its product mix in the minds of consumers by relating it to other stores and their mixture of products.

Market potential A market's total capacity to consume a given good, service, or idea.

Market potential approach A retail location approach in which the firm selects criteria that reflect the amount of support that a geographic area will provide a given retail operation.

Market rating index Per capita retail sales of trading area compared with per capita retail sales for Canada.

Market repositioning The strategy of altering the customer's existing image of the retailer by changing how the consumer perceives the retailer relative to other retailers and to their individual shopping needs.

Market share A measure of an organization's sales position relative to all competitors within the same market.

Market-share objective A goal that expresses a retailer's desire either to increase or maintain its share of the total market.

Marketing channel A team of marketing institutions that directs flow of goods or services from the producer to the final consumer.

Marketing concept The philosophy that the overall goal of every business organization is to satisfy consumer needs at a profit.

Marking The process of affixing to merchandise the information necessary for stocking, controlling, and selling.

Markons The additional markups taken after the initial selling price has been established.

Maximum inventory The number of merchandise units the retailer needs to cover expected sales during the reorder and delivery periods plus a safety stock for either unexpected sales or problems in securing the merchandise.

Mazur plan A retail organization plan that divides the retail organization into four functional divisions: finance, merchandising, promotion, and operations.

Media coverage The number of people an advertising medium reaches in a given market area.

Media representatives Employees of newspapers and radio or television stations whose principal job is to sell advertising space and time.

Megamall The largest type of shopping centre with sizes ranging from 4 million to 5 million sq. ft. [370 000 to 464 000 m^2] or many times the size of the average shopping mall; The West Edmonton Mall is one example.

Memorandum buying A buying method in which the title to the merchandise exchanges hands when it is shipped to the retailer, but the retailer retains the right to return to the supplier any unsold merchandise and to pay for the merchandise after it has been sold.

Merchandise assortment The number of different product items the retailer stocks within a particular product line.

Merchandise budget A financial plan for managing merchandise inventory investments.

Merchandise buying process The activities necessary for establishing a successful relationship with various sources of supply.

Merchandise category A closely related line of products within a merchandise group.

Merchandise classification A specific line of products within a merchandise category.

Merchandise compatibility The degree of relationship among various merchandise groups.

Merchandise control The process of designing the policies and procedures for collecting and analyzing merchandise data in order to determine whether the stated objectives have been achieved.

Merchandise group A broadly related line of products that retailers and consumers associate together according to end use.

Merchandise handling process The activities of physically getting the merchandise into the store and onto the shelves.

Merchandise management The actions of planning and controlling the retailer's inventories.

Merchandise mix The full range or mixture of products the retailer offers to consumers.

Merchandise ordering process The efficient obtainment of the retailer's merchandise inventories.

Merchandise planning The process of establishing objectives and devising plans for obtaining those objectives.

Merchandise support The number of product units the retailer should have on hand to meet expected sales for a particular product item.

Merchandise variety The number of different product lines the retailer stocks in the store.

Merchandising The process of developing, obtaining, managing, and pricing the merchandise mix to meet the firm's marketing and financial objectives.

Merchant intermediaries Wholesalers that are directly involved in the purchase and sale of goods as they move through the channel of distribution.

Merger An organizational strategy in which one firm acquires the stocks or assets of another firm, combines the two organizations, and operates as one organization.

Micromerchandising The process of planning, building, and delivering the store-specific product mix needed to satisfy narrowly defined consumer markets.

Minidepartment specialty retailer A "power format" that utilizes retailers' size, merchandising muscle, and operational efficiency either to dominate the market for a product category or assume at least a market leader position within the product category.

Minimum-cutoff method An evaluation procedure that establishes a minimum standard or cutoff point for each evaluation criterion; choice is made from alternatives that have exceeded the minimum cutoff on all criteria.

Mission statement A generalized yet meaningful expression of the organization's future direction.

Mixed-use centre A commercial centre that combines a shopping centre with such commercial activities as offices, recreation and entertainment facilities, residential units, hotels, transportation facilities, and government offices.

Mobile vendor A travelling retailer that takes goods and services to the point of sale and consumption.

Model stock list A schedule or listing of SKUs for fashion merchandise.

Monopolistic isolation A site that affords the retailer a uniquely convenient and accessible location to serve consumers.

Monthly sales estimates A sales forecasting method that involves three steps: (1) making annual sales estimates, (2) determining estimated monthly sales, and (3) adjusting monthly sales estimates using a monthly sales index.

Motivation The process by which consumers are moved or incited to action.

Multilevel marketing A direct selling format in which a hierarchical network of distributors is created to sell and distribute a wide variety of goods and services. Distributors' efforts are directed at making retail sales of goods and services and recruiting members for their distribution network.

Multinational retailer An international retail organization that either adapts existing or develops new retailing formats designed to meet the special needs of each targeted country or market.

Multiple pricing A retail pricing policy that gives customers a discount for making quantity purchases; the retailer offers a reduced price if consumers are willing to purchase several units at the multiple-unit price.

Multiplex distribution The marketing strategy of serving several target markets using a "freeform" organization that permits it to develop a specialized product mix for each market segment.

Narrative projection test A customer survey technique in which respondents are given a descriptive situation and asked to write a paragraph in response.

Narrow variety/deep assortment A "specialty" philosophy that appeals to a select group of consumers by offering only one or a few product lines with an excellent selection within each line.

Narrow variety/shallow assortment The merchandising strategy of offering consumers a very limited product selection (lines and items).

Natural selection A theory of retail evolution in which adaptive retailers survive and nonadaptive retailers perish; in other words, it is survival of the fittest.

Needs The essential physiological and psychological requirements necessary to the general physical and mental welfare of the consumer.

Neighbourhood business district (NBD) A small retailing cluster that serves primarily one or two residential areas.

Neighbourhood shopping centre A shopping centre that obtains its customers from one or a few neighbourhoods within the immediate vicinity.

Net adequacy The capability of a trading area to provide support for a retailer after competition has been taken into account.

Net invoice price The net value of the invoice or the total invoice minus all other discounts.

Net profit The sum of operating profit and other income minus other expenses.

Net sales The income measurement that results when returns and allowances are subtracted from gross sales.

Net worth A financial expression that represents the store owner's equity in the business.

Never-out list A specially created list of merchandise items that are identified as key items or best-sellers for which the retailer wants extra protection against the possibility of a stockout.

Niche specialist A retailer that targets a narrowly defined consumer market by carefully developing a selective merchandise mix and appropriately designing stores that are tailored to the customer's expectations.

Niching The alternative of adjusting a firm's portfolio by moving an SBU into a market niche in which the fit between resource requirements and available resources is more acceptable.

Noise Anything that occurs during the communication process that distracts senders or receivers, interferes with the encoding and decoding activity, or interrupts the transmission or feedback process.

Nondurable A perishable product that is used up in one or a few uses.

Nonprobability sample A sampling procedure in which each individual in the total population does not have a known and equal chance of being selected.

Objective and task method An advertising budgeting method that consists of (1) establishing the objectives for advertising, (2) determining the type and amounts of advertising necessary to accomplish these objectives, (3) calculating the overall cost of the advertisement, and (4) scheduling the advertisements day by day.

Observability The extent to which the consumer can see a new product's favourable attributes.

Observation method A consumer research method that involves the gathering of primary information by recording some aspect of consumers' overt behaviour by either personal or mechanical means.

Odd pricing A pricing practice of setting prices that end in odd numbers.

Off-retail markdown percentage A markdown formula in which the original price minus reduced price is divided by the original price.

Off-site job training A personnel training method that is conducted in centralized training classrooms away from the employee's work environment.

On-the-job training A decentralized personnel training approach that occurs on the sales floor, in the stockroom, or in some other work environment where employees are performing their jobs.

One-price retailer An off-price retailing format that offers all merchandise (for example, overruns, odd lots, cancelled orders, closeouts) at a single, fixed price.

One-stop shopping The marketing strategy of broadening the retail offering to meet consumer's expanding needs within the context of a single retail operation or store.

Open-to-buy The amount of new merchandise the retailer can buy during a specific time period without exceeding the planned purchases for that period.

Operating expenses Those expenses incurred in operating a business or department.

Operating profit The difference between gross margin and operating expenses.

Operating ratio The mathematical relationships between elements in the income statement used to determine a firm's operating performance.

Operational objectives The general, long-term operational requirements necessary to achieve a strategic objective.

Opinion leader A person whose attitudes, opinions, preferences, and actions affect others.

Optical scanner An electronic device that reads bar codes and feeds information directly into a terminal and onto a computer.

Optional services Those services that are neither necessary to the retailer operation nor expected by the customer.

Order form A legally binding contract when signed by both parties, specifying the terms and conditions under which a transaction is to be conducted.

Order getters Sales personnel who are actively involved in the selling process.

Order takers Sales personnel who simply comply with the customer's requests for certain types of merchandise.

Organization orientation A program that either initiates new employees or updates old employees on the general organization of the firm and its policies, rules, and regulations.

Organizational culture A set of key values shared by all or most members of a retail organization.

Organizational market A type of market that is composed of industrial firms, resellers, and governments that represent intermediate consumers of goods and services.

Organizational objective A strategic position to be attained or a purpose to be achieved by the organization and/or one of its strategic business units.

Organizational portfolio The collection of strategic business units held and managed by an organization.

Outshopper analysis A method to estimate total expected sales by subtracting outshopping sales from the trading area's gross sales to arrive at a more realistic sales volume for the trading area.

Overstored market area A market area in which the capacity to retail exceeds the capacity to consume.

Ownership flow The process of transferring title from one channel participant to another.

Participation The active involvement of the customer in the learning process as it pertains to the acts of shopping and buying.

Partnership A legal form of retail organization in which two or more persons form a business without incorporating.

Patronage appeal A promotional message that emphasizes the rightness of the store, location, and hours.

Patronage probability The area from which potential customers come who have a probability greater than zero of purchasing a given class of products or services that either a retailer or group of retailers offers for sale.

Payment flow The transfer of monies from one channel participant to another as compensation for services rendered and/or goods delivered.

Per capita sales method A forecasting approach that estimates trading area sales for a general product line and is a function of the per capita expenditures for that product line times the total population of that trading area.

Percentage-of-sales method An advertising budget method that involves taking a predetermined percentage of either the previous year's sales or the estimated sales for the coming year to calculate how much to spend on advertising.

Percentage variation method A stock planning method that attempts to adjust stock levels in accordance with actual variations in sales.

Perception The process by which consumers attach meaning to incoming stimuli by forming mental pictures of persons, places, and objects.

Periodic physical inventory A system of gathering stock information intermittently using an actual physical count and inspection of the merchandise items to compute sales for the period since the last physical inventory.

Perishability The process of losing quality, value, and marketability within a short period of time; all products and services are perishable to some extent.

Perpetual book inventory A system of inventory taking and information gathering on a continuous or ongoing basis using various accounting records to compute stock on hand at any given time.

Personal communications The process of exchanging ideas and meanings with other people.

Personal discrimination A situation in which the personal biases of an individual in authority enter the decision-making process in employment matters to the detriment of applicants or employees.

Personal selling A direct, face-to-face communication between a retail salesperson and a retail consumer.

Personality A general response pattern used by individuals in coping with their environment.

Personality traits The individual characteristics people acquire over a lifetime.

Physical flow The actual movement of a physical product from one channel participant to another.

Physiological needs The life-sustaining and creature comforts that must be reasonably satisfied before the search for fulfillment of higher-order needs.

Planned cluster site A purposeful cluster of retail and service establishments at a location designed to serve a specific geographic, demographic, and psychographic market segment.

Planned publicity A type of publicity over which the retailer exercises some control.

Planograms Computer-based shelf management plans that assist the retailer in using their space allocation and control programs.

Point-of-purchase (POP) display A type of display designed to attract customer attention and interest, reinforce the store's creative theme, and fit in with the store's interior decoration.

Population density The number of persons living within a delineated geographic area.

Portfolio retailing Retail enterprises that operate multiple types of retail formats that have individually tailored merchandising programs designed to serve the specific needs of a different target market.

Posttransactional service A service provided after the sales transaction and designed to build store loyalty; delivery, alterations, repairs, and complaint resolution are examples.

Power strip A cluster of destination-type retailers located in a strip shopping centre adjacent to a major traffic artery and generally in close proximity to a regional shopping mall.

Predatory pricing A pricing tactic in which the retailer charges customers different prices for the same merchandise in different markets to eliminate competition in one or more of those markets.

Premium A merchandise item given to the consumer free of charge or at a substantial price reduction as an inducement to purchase another product, participate in an activity, or both.

Prepayment dating A condition of sale that requires the making of payment when the order is placed.

Preretailing A retail buying practice of deciding the selling price of merchandise before it is purchased and recording that price on the store's copy of the purchase order so the store's "markers" can put the selling price on the merchandise as soon as it arrives.

Prestige The amount of status consumers attach to an advertising medium.

Pretransaction service A service provided before any sales transaction; customer parking, store hours, and information are common examples.

Price bundling A retail pricing practice of selling products and/or services together as a package deal.

Price elasticity of demand A measure of the effect that a price change has on consumer demand (that is, the number of units sold).

Price flow An illegal pricing activity in which several retailers establish a fixed retail selling price for a particular product line within a market area.

Price lining The pricing practice of directing a set of retail prices at a targeted consumer group.

Price matching A retail pricing practice in which the retailer promises to match the lowest advertised price a customer can find.

Pricing line A specific pricing point established within a pricing zone.

Pricing zone A range of prices that appeals to a particular group of consumers either for demographic, psychographic, product usage, or product benefit reasons.

Primary trading zone The area around which a retailer can expect to attract 50 to 70 percent of its business.

Principle of accessibility The idea that the more easily potential consumers can approach, enter, traverse, and exit a site, the more likely they will visit the site to shop.

Principle of cumulative attraction The idea that a cluster of similar and complementary retailing activities will generally have greater drawing power than will dispersed and isolated stores engaging in the same retailing activities.

Principle of interception The idea that a site's positional qualities determines its capability to intercept customers as they travel from one place to another.

Principle of store congestion The idea that as store locations become more saturated with stores, other business activities, and people, they become less attractive to additional shopping traffic.

Private-label credit system A credit system that retailers offer under their name but that a bank operates and manages.

Probability sample A sampling procedure in which each individual in the total population has a known chance of being selected.

Problem recognition A stage in the consumer buying process in which a discrepancy is felt between an ideal state of affairs and the actual state of affairs.

Product A bundle of benefits (goods, services, or ideas) capable of satisfying consumer wants and needs.

Product advertising A type of advertising that presents specific merchandise for sale and urges customers to come to the store immediately to buy.

Product appeal A promotional appeal that emphasizes the rightness of a product for consumers.

Product compatibility The nature of the relationship between various product lines and between various product items within them.

Product complement A product that is bought and used in conjunction with another product.

Product developer An offshore source of goods that serves as an international gatekeeper by searching global markets for high-quality goods and unique merchandise that offers good profit potential to clients.

Product development A growth strategy that involves the modification of current products or development of new products in order to appeal to current markets.

Product guarantee A policy statement made by a retailer expressing its general responsibility for the products it sells.

Product item A specific product within a product line that is unique and clearly distinguishable from other products within and outside the product line.

Product liability A legal situation that can result from either failing to inform the customer of the dangers associated with using the product; misrepresenting the product as to how, when, and where it should be used; or selling a product that results in injury as a result of its failure to meet warranty standards.

Product life cycle (PLC) The series of stages a product passes through: introduction, growth, maturity, and decline.

Product line A grouping of related products in which the relationship is important to the consumer when buying, using, and/or possessing the product.

Product mix concept The full range or mixture of products the retailer offers to consumers.

Product profitability The contribution of a product, either directly by generating per-unit profit or indirectly by creating customer traffic and additional sales on other products.

Product substitute A product consumers use for the same general purpose as another product, it has the same basic functional attributes and meets the same basic consumer needs.

Product units The total number of a particular product item that a retailer has in stock.

Productivity-based budgeting A budgeting process in which a series of expense budgets are prepared to correspond to various sales levels.

Professional bureaucracy A retail organization characterized by a flat hierarchical structure with a limited number of middle managers and a large technical support staff that provides administrative tasks.

Profit margin A financial relationship that is computed by dividing net profit after taxes by net sales.

Profit maximization objective A pricing objective that strives for the highest possible profit through pricing and other merchandising activities.

Programmed learning A personnel training program in which employees (1) study a unit of material, (2) respond to a series of questions on the material they read, (3) receive immediate feedback on their performance in answering the questions, and (4) continue to repeat the first three steps until they master the material.

Promotion The merchandising activity of providing the consumer information regarding the retailer store and its product-service offering as well as influencing consumer perceptions, attitudes, and behaviour toward the store and what it has to offer.

Promotion flow The flow of persuasive communication directed at influencing the decisions of consumers and other channel participants.

Promotional allowances Reductions in the price retailers pay suppliers for merchandise, including advertising allowances, preferred selling space, free display materials, and merchandise deals.

Proportional trading area An area based on the distance customers are from the store and their likelihood of patronage.

Psychological benefits The benefits derived from buying, using, and possessing a product.

Psychological tests Personnel evaluation instruments designed to measure an applicant's personality, intelligence, aptitudes, interests, and supervisory skills.

Publicity An indirect, impersonal communication carried by a mass medium that is neither paid for nor credited to an identified sponsor.

Purchase intercept technique An in-store information-gathering technique consisting of observing customer in-store shopping behaviour, recording pertinent shopping behaviour information, and interviewing customers immediately about their purchase or shopping behaviour.

Quantity discount A price reduction given by suppliers to retail buyers of large quantities of merchandise.

Question mark An SBU with a low market share in a high-growth market.

Quick ratio A financial ratio computed by dividing current assets minus inventory by current liabilities; it measures the firm's ability to meet current payments with assets that can be immediately converted to cash.

Quick-response replenishment system A short-cycle merchandise replenishment system that involves an automatic restocking of the retailer's inventories within a matter of days.

Radio frequency data communication The transmitting of data through the airwaves between a hand-held data collection device and a host computer.

Rank-ordered question A customer survey instrument in which the respondent is asked to rank a list of factors in order of their importance.

Ratio analysis An examination of the relationship between elements in the income statement and/or balance sheet.

Receiving The actual physical exchange of goods between the retailer and the supplier's transporting agent.

Reference group A peer group that serves as a model or standard for an individual's behaviour and attitudes.

Reference pricing The retail pricing practice of marking products with the retailer's selling price together with such comparable prices as the retailer's normal price, a competitor's price, the suggested retail price, or the average market price.

Regional mall A shopping centre built around one or two full-line department stores and having 400 000 to 600 000 sq. ft. [37 000 to 55 000 m²] of gross leasable area.

Regression model A quantitative procedure using linear or multiple-regression equations to analyze determinants of retail performance.

Regular buying The systematic cutting and issuing of purchase orders and reorders.

Reinforcement The buyer behaviour postpurchase response of comparing anticipated results with the actual results experienced from a chosen response.

Related grouping An ensemble display that presents accessory items along with the featured merchandise.

Relationship retailing Any set of customer-oriented activities that attracts, holds, and builds long-term individualistic relationships between the retail firm and its customers.

Relative advantage The extent to which a new product is perceived to be better than an existing product.

Repetition The act of repeating a past experience, or the number of times a consumer is exposed to an advertisement.

Resale price maintenance A pricing practice in which manufacturers and wholesalers require retailers to sign contracts agreeing to sell their products at the "suggested" prices.

Reserve stock A backup stock held in reserve, usually a central stockroom.

Resident buying office An organization that specializes in the buying function by locating its buying offices in major wholesaling and producing markets.

Responses The actions taken by consumers to reduce a cue-stimulated drive.

Retail accordion A theory of retail institutional change based on the premise that the changing character of retail competition stems from strategies that alter the width (selection) of the merchandise mix.

Retail compatibility The degree to which two businesses interchange customers.

Retail competition The actions of one retailer against other retailers in obtaining resources and the patronage of consumers.

Retail display A nonperson, in-store presentation and exhibition of merchandise together with related information.

Retail format The total mix of operating and merchandising tactics and practices used by a retail firm to distinguish and differentiate itself from retail competitors.

Retail gravitation concept A retail location theory that provides a measure of the potential interaction between various locations by determining the relative drawing power of each location on the basis of its size and the distance between it and other competing locations.

Retail image The impression, personality, or mental picture a consumer has when asked to describe or characterize a particular retail operation.

Retail intelligence Any method or combination of methods used to obtain external secondary information.

Retail life cycle The theory of retail institutional change that hypothesizes that change occurs in stages of an identifiable life cycle pattern; the four stages of the retail life cycle are innovation, accelerated development, maturity, and decline.

Retail method of inventory valuation A method of estimating the cost value of an ending inventory for a particular accounting period without taking a physical inventory.

Retail operations approach A market evaluation process in which an area is evaluated from the perspective of whether a retail operation can be economically successful and transactionally efficient.

Retail promotions A series of activities that provides customers with information regarding the retailer store and its product and service offering; it also deals with the issues of creating a favourable customer perception regarding the retail store and its operations.

Retail reduction The difference between the merchandise item's original retail value and the actual final sales value.

Retail research The use of a set of scientific procedures to gather external primary information from consumers, suppliers, and competitors.

Retail site The actual physical location from which a retail business operates.

Retail strategy An overall plan to gain competitive advantage through the use of a distinctive retail format to capture the patronage of one or more target markets.

Retail trading area The area from which a store attracts its customers or obtains its business.

Retailer Any business establishment that directs its marketing effort toward the final consumer for the purpose of selling goods or services.

Retailer-sponsored cooperative group A contractual organization formed by many small independent retailers that usually involves the common ownership of a wholesaler; allows the small independent to realize economies of scale by making large-quantity group purchases.

Retailing The business activity of selling goods or services to the final consumer.

Retailing information system An interacting organization of people, machines, and methods designed to produce a regular, continuous, and orderly flow of information necessary for the retailer's problem-solving and decision-making activities.

Return on assets A financial ratio that is computed by dividing net profit after taxes by total assets.

Return on net worth A financial ratio that is computed by dividing net profit after taxes by net worth.

Right message The right thing to say presented in the right manner.

Right price The amount consumers are willing to pay and retailers are willing to accept in exchange for merchandise and services.

Right quantity The exact match between the consumer's buying and using needs and the retailer's buying and selling needs.

Robbery Stealing or taking anything of value by force, violence, or fear.

Safety need The need to feel safe, secure, and stable.

Salary plus bonus plan A compensation plan in which a straight monthly salary is supplemented by either semiannual or annual bonuses for exceeding performance goals.

Salary plus commission plan A compensation plan in which employees receive a salary and a commission on sales over a prescribed level.

Sales agent An intermediary who is independent of the manufacturer but assumes the entire marketing function for a manufacturer.

Sales incentive Any direct or indirect nonpersonal inducement that offers extra value to customers.

Sales per unit of space method A sales forecasting model in which the retailer computes a ratio of each retailer's floor space devoted to a specific product category to the total of all retail floor space for the product category in the trading area. Total trading sales are allocated to each retailer on the basis of its proportion of space devoted to the product.

Sales volume objectives Sales objectives expressed in terms of either sales volume or market share.

Sample Some portion of a predefined population.

Sampling A sales incentive that involves giving the customer a free trial or sample of the product.

Satisfiers Employment factors that produce pleasurable reactions within people's work lives.

Saturated market area An area in which the capacity to retail equals the capacity of buyers to consume a product line.

Scent appeal The process of creating an atmosphere that encourages buying through pleasant scents.

Seasonal discount A price reduction given to buyers who are willing to order, receive, and pay for goods during the "off season."

Secondary business district (SBD) A retailing cluster located at the intersections of major traffic arteries and adjacent to a major economic activity (for example, hospital, university, entertainment complex).

Secondary information Existing information that has been collected for another purpose and is often published.

Secondary trading zone An area surrounding the primary zone and generally representing 20 to 30 percent of a retailer's total sales volume.

Selection display A display consisting of rows of stationary aisle and wall units designed to expose the retailer's complete assortment of merchandise to the consumer.

Selective distortion The act of misinterpreting incoming stimuli to make them consistent with the individual's beliefs and attitudes.

Selective exposure The act of limiting the type and amount of stimuli that is received and admitted to awareness.

Selective market coverage The strategy of choosing enough locations to ensure adequate coverage of selected target markets.

Selective retention The act of remembering only the information that the individual wants to remember.

Self-actualization The desire to reach one's full potential as an individual.

Self-concept The set of perceptions that people have of themselves within a social context.

Self-liquidating premium A sales incentive that requires the consumer to pay something for the premium.

Self-service operation A retailer that restricts its service offering to essential services.

Sell-through analysis A comparison between actual and planned sales; represents a measurement of the amount of merchandise sold within a defined category.

Semantic differential rating scale A set of seven-point, bipolar scales that measure the meanings and attitudes that people have regarding some object.

Sender A retailer that wants to inform or persuade a select group of consumers about the benefits of its retailing format or merchandising concept.

Separate-store organization A retail setup that treats each branch as an independent operation with its own organizational structure of managers, buyers, and sales personnel.

Service features Any "extras" that might include delivery, alterations, installation, repairs, warranties, returns, adjustments, wrapping, telephone and mail ordering, or any other service that consumers want for purchase satisfaction.

Service quality The difference between customer expectations of the service and customer perceptions of the service actually received.

Service retailer A retailer that sells a product that emphasizes people, ideas, and information instead of a tangible object.

Services Largely intangible activities that typically involve the application of human skills within a consumer problem-solving context.

Shoplifting The act of pilfering merchandise from a store display by customers and individuals posing as customers.

Shopping goods Products for which consumers want to make price, quality, suitability, and/or style comparisons.

Short-term credit Money that can be borrowed for less than one year.

Shortages Reductions in the total value of the retailer's inventory as a result of shoplifting, pilfering, and merchandise being damaged and misplaced.

Sight appeal The process of imparting stimuli, resulting in perceived visual relationships.

Silent witness program A store security measure that rewards employees with cash for anonymous tips on theft activities of other employees.

Single-most-important criterion method The evaluation procedure of comparing alternatives and judging one superior according to the single-most-important criterion.

Single pricing A pricing policy in which the retailer charges all customers the same price for all merchandise under the same circumstances.

Single trade discount A single percentage adjustment to the supplier's list price.

Site compatibility The process of fitting the store to the natural lay of the land and the natural habitat.

Site geography The size, shape, and terrain requirements of the retailer operation.

Slotting allowance An admission fee paid by manufacturers to get their products onto the retailer's shelves with better positions and greater shelf facings.

Smart card A plastic identification card embedded with a small microprocessor.

Social needs The desire for love, belongingness, affection, and friendship.

Social responsibility The acceptance of an obligation to consider operating efficiencies, financial returns, customer satisfaction, and societal well-being of equal importance in evaluating the retail firm's performance.

Sole proprietorship A business owned and managed by a single individual.

Sound appeal The process of creating an atmosphere that encourages buying through music or other auditory stimuli.

Source marking The system by which the retailer authorizes the manufacturer or supplier to mark the merchandise before shipping it to the store.

Space productivity The goal or process of achieving a profitable return per unit of space for various departments or merchandise lines.

Span of control A retail organization principle that sets guidelines for the number of subordinates a superior should control, depending on the level within the organization and the nature of the tasks being performed.

Special business license A local legal requirement that applies to either the sale of certain types of products or the operation of a particular type of retail organization.

Special display A notable presentation of merchandise designed to attract special attention and make a lasting impression on the consumer.

Special purchase price A low advertised price on merchandise the retailer has purchased at reduced prices.

Specialization A distinguishing feature of chain store organizations in which employees specialize by task and function.

Specialized reporting service An outsource that offers information on certain product lines and merchandising activities; provides retailers with information periodically in the form of newspapers, special reports, or flash reports, but the cost can be substantial.

Specialties Useful articles of merchandise imprinted with an advertisement and given to the customer without obligation.

Specialty mall A cluster of specialty retailers that tends to be highly focused on its target market. Targeting on the high-income consumer is a common strategic focus.

Specialty products Those products in which the consumer's buying behaviour is directed at obtaining a particular good, service, or idea without regard to time, effort, or expense.

Specialty store A retail format that specializes in the merchandise offered; it varies according to (1) the type, selection, and quality of merchandise; (2) the range of price lines; and (3) the size, design, and location of stores.

Specification buying A retail buying method in which the retailer acquires or produces merchandise that is unique and distinctive from that of competitors.

Sponsor method of training A personnel training method that uses an experienced employee to assume part or all of the responsibility for training a new employee.

Staff relationships Advisory or supportive relationships appearing on organizational charts as broken lines.

Staples Product items for which sales are either very stable or highly variable but very predictable.

Star An SBU with a high market share in a high-growth market.

Stock-keeping unit (SKU) A merchandise category for which separate records (sales and stock) are maintained.

Stock/sales ratio method The stock planning method of maintaining a certain ratio of goods on hand to planned monthly sales.

Stock turnover The rate at which the retailer depletes and replenishes stock.

Stocking The activities associated with in-store and between-store distribution of merchandise.

Store advertising The in-store marketing activities that carry a creative message of some type but with no directly actionable incentive to buy the product. Shopping cart ads, checkout signs, aisle signs, and electronic signs are all examples.

Store atmospherics A store's overall aesthetic and emotional effect created by its physical features; the total sensory experience created by the store.

Store (private-label) brands Items owned, controlled, merchandised, and sold through the retailer's own outlets.

Store displays Direct, impersonal in-store presentations and exhibitions of merchandise together with related information.

Store marking The practice of having store personnel mark all merchandise after the store has received it.

Store outlet A store that serves as a direct outlet for a retailer's overstocks, shopworn goods, and odd-lot sizes and colours.

Store theatrics The notion that retailing is theatre and more than just selling merchandise—it is an exhibition, event, or enactment involving the process of shopping.

Straight-commission plan A compensation plan in which a store employee receives a percentage of what he or she sells at either a fixed or variable rate.

Straight-salary plan A fixed amount of compensation for a specified work period; offers the advantages of easy administration and a high level of employer control.

Strategic alliance An association formed to further the common interests of vendors and retailers.

Strategic business unit (SBU) A business division with a clearly identifiable merchandise strategy that targets a market segment within a defined competitive environment.

Strategic objectives General, long-term goals that the retail firm intends to pursue.

Strategic plan A grand design or blueprint for ensuring success in all of an organization's business endeavours.

Strategic retail management The process of planning the organization, implementation, and control of all the firm's activities.

String/strip cluster A retailing cluster developed along a major thoroughfare, depending on the consumption activity of people who travel these busy thoroughfares.

Style The characteristic or distinctive form, outline, or shape of a product item.

Suggestive selling A closing technique in which the salesperson shows the customer other merchandise that complements the item being bought.

Supercentres Large combination supermarket/discount stores that typically range from 100 000 to 180 000 sq. ft. [9000 to 17 000 m^2].

Supermarket No commonly accepted definition exists because of the wide range of business formulas used in this industry.

Superregional mall A shopping center built around at least three and often four major department stores and having 750 000 to 1 000 000 gross sq. ft. [70 000 to 90 000 m^2] of leasable area.

Superspecialist A retailer that presents a single, narrowly defined classification of merchandise with an extensive assortment of brands, sizes, colours, materials, styles, and prices.

Superstore retailer A huge combination supermarket and discount general merchandise store that stocks and sells a complete selection of food products together with a wide variety of hard and soft goods at deep-discount prices.

Supervision The process of directing, coordinating, and inspecting the efforts of store employees to attain both company and individual goals.

Survey method The systematic gathering of information directly from the appropriate respondents.

Sweeper A shoplifter who simply brushes merchandise off the counter into a shopping bag or some other type of container.

Systematic discrimination The unintentional and inadvertent discrimination resulting from policies, practices, and decision-making criteria that negatively affect protected classes.

Systems competition Competition between two or more vertical marketing systems.

Target return objectives Profit objectives for guiding price-setting decisions.

Taste appeal The act of appealing to consumers' taste by providing potential customers with a sample of an edible product under clean and sanitary conditions.

Technological environment The various improvements in the technical processes that increase the productivity and efficiency of machines and eliminate or reduce manual operations.

Telemarketing The selling of goods and services through telephone contact.

Thematic apperception test Respondents are shown a cartoon, drawing, or picture and then asked to put themselves into the situation and tell a story about what is happening or what they should do.

Theme appeal A display or department centred around natural and holiday seasons, historic periods, current issues, and special events.

Theme groupings Merchandise displayed according to a central theme or setting.

Third-party credit system The acceptance of one or more credit cards issued by outside institutions.

Tie-in An approach to attract attention to a store's offering by associating the offering with an entertainment event, a character, or a person's name.

Total assets The sum of current assets and fixed assets.

Total population The total number of persons or organizations within an area at a given time.

Total-product concept Acknowledges the need for retailers to market every one of a product's dimensions.

Total sales method The retailer allocates an equal share of the trading area's total sales for a specific product category to each competing retailer.

Touch appeal The process of creating an atmosphere that encourages buying through providing the ability to touch the product.

Trade discount A form of compensation that the buyer may receive for performing certain functions for the supplier.

Trade shows Occasions when manufacturers get together to exhibit their merchandise in one place.

Trading area adequacy The capability of a trading area to support proposed and existing retail operations.

Trading area potential The predicted capability of a trading area to provide acceptable support levels for a retailer in the future.

Transaction service A service that is essential or helpful in completing a sales transaction; credit, cheque authorization, layaway, wrapping, and checkout are common examples.

Transmission The process of sending the message to those consumers targeted as the most suitable recipients of the message.

Trial pricing The retail pricing practice of offering a low price for trying a limited amount of a product or a service for a limited amount of time.

Trialability The extent to which a new product can be tested on a trial basis.

Trickle-across theory Recognizes that a fashion or style can originate within any social class.

Trickle-down theory Hypothesizes that new innovative fashions and styles originate in the upper socioeconomic classes and are passed down through the middle class to the lower socioeconomic class consumer.

Trickle-up theory States that some unusual fashions or styles are developed in the lower socioeconomic classes, picked up by the upper class, and finally adopted by the middle class.

Trunk show Merchandise demonstrations by the designer or manufacturer within the retailer's store.

Two-step flow of communication The ultimate effects of advertising magnified by personal communication among consumers.

Tying contracts Conditional selling arrangements between retailers and suppliers in which a supplier agrees to sell a retailer a highly sought-after line of products if the retailer will agree to buy additional product lines from the same supplier.

Ultimate consumers Individuals who purchase goods and services for their own personal use or for use by members of their household.

Uncontrollable expenses Expenses over which the firm has no control and cannot adjust to current operating needs in the short run.

Undercover shopper A person hired to pose as a customer to observe the activities and performance of employees.

Understored market area An area in which the capacity to consume exceeds the capacity to retail.

Unemployment compensation A tax levied by the government on each retailer payroll; employees who are either laid off or fired usually qualify for benefits; employees who simply quit usually do not qualify.

Unfair trade practice acts Laws that regulate the right of retailers to sell either below cost or at cost plus some minimum markup.

Unit control Deals with the number of different product items and the number of units stocked within each item.

Unit grouping A display that highlights a separate category of product items; contains merchandise that is almost identical or closely related.

Unit open-to-buy The number of units that the retailer can buy at any given time and still be within planned limits.

Unit/periodic/physical inventory Making a periodic physical check on the status of the retailer's inventory through visual observation or actual product counts.

Unit/perpetual/book system Involves continuous recording of all transactions, which changes the unit status of the retailer's merchandise inventory.

Unit pricing The retail pricing practice of posting prices on a per-unit measurement basis.

Unity of command States that the organizational structure of the retail firm should ensure that each store employee be directly accountable to only one immediate supervisor at any one time for any given task.

Universal Product Code (UPC) A bar code system that identifies both the product and the manufacturer.

Unlimited liability The sole proprietor assumes total responsibility for all debts stemming from the business, and that responsibility extends to current and future personal as well as business assets.

Unplanned publicity Publicity over which the retailer has no control but simply responds to uncontrollable events as they occur.

Utilitarianism An ethics principle that judges not the act itself but the consequences of the act.

Value The interactive and changing relationship among product utility, product quality, product price, customer service, customer convenience, and intangible benefits.

Value outlet mall A discount mall with a tenant mix of manufacturers' outlets, off-price retailers, and retail clearance stores.

Values Core beliefs or desires that guide or motivate attitudes and actions.

Variable expenses Expenses that vary with the volume of sales.

Variety store A retail format that offers a limited selection of a wide variety of inexpensive merchandise at reasonable prices within a self-service store.

Vending machine retailing A machine-based retailing format designed to meet the fill-in, emergency, and after- or off-hour needs of consumers.

Vertical competition Competition between a retailer and a wholesaler or producer that is attempting to make retail sales to the retailer customers.

Vertical integration The merger of two organizations from different levels within a channel of distribution.

Vertical mall A multilevel shopping complex typically found within the central business districts of major urban centres.

Vertical marketing system A distribution arrangement that integrates the marketing channel to achieve operating economies and common objectives.

Vertical price fixing The collaboration between a retailer and a wholesaler or manufacturer to set retail prices at an agreed-on level.

Videologue A form of direct-mail retailing involving shop-at-home videotapes; a visual catalogue.

Voice recognition Computers responding to the human voice for data input or operating commands.

Warehouse club A huge, no-frills, deep-discount outlet that caters to customers who have joined the club in order to obtain merchandise at 20 to 40 percent less than prices at supermarkets and discount stores.

Warehouse showroom A single-line hard-goods retailer that stocks merchandise such as furniture, appliances, or carpeting.

Warranty A specific statement by the seller of the quality or performance capabilities of the product and the exact terms under which the seller will take action to correct product deficiencies.

Week's supply method A stock plan that determines stock levels in direct proportion to sales.

Weighted-rating method A procedure for evaluating alternatives by assigning weighted values to each of a set of evaluation criteria.

Wheel of retailing The most widely recognized theory of retail institutional change involving a series of adaptations that occur in a cyclical fashion; each cycle is made up of the three phases of entry, trading up, and vulnerability.

Wholesaler-sponsored voluntary chain A contractual arrangement in which a wholesaler develops a merchandising program that independent retailers voluntarily join.

Wholly owned subsidiary The strategy in which a retail organization enters a foreign market by either starting a new operation from scratch or acquiring an existing operation.

Wide variety/deep assortment The strategy of offering a large number of product lines with supporting depth in each line.

Wide variety/shallow assortment The strategy of offering a wide selection of product lines but a limited selection of brands, styles, sizes, and models within each line.

Word association test A set of words or phrases to which respondents must give their immediate reactions.

Workers' compensation An employee accident and disability insurance program required under various state laws; covers the employee who is accidentally injured while working or who is unable to work as a result of a disease associated with a particular occupation.

Working capital The money needed to meet day-to-day operating expenses.

Zero-based budgeting A budgeting process in which each operating department starts with no allocated expenses; to obtain operating funds, each department must justify its need for each expense item on the budget.

Zoning ordinances Controls that local governments place on land use by regulating the type of activities and buildings located in certain areas.

Name Index

Subject Index

Photo Credits

1–1	Prentice Hall Archives/Kathleen Bellesiles
1–2	Atlantic Photo Inc.
1–3	Dick Hemingway
1–4	Gamma-Liaison, Inc.
1–5	Goodwin/Monkmeyer Press
1–6	With the permission of Canadian Tire
2–1	Levinson/Monkmeyer Press
2–2	Pizza Hut
2–3	Bob Daemmrich/Stock Boston
3–1	Benali/Gamma-Liaison, Inc.
3–2	PhotoEdit/Tony Freeman
4–1a	Philip & Karen Smith/Tony Stone Images
4–1b	Michael Newman/PhotoEdit
4–1c	Gregg Mancuso/Stock Boston
4–2	Granitsas/The Image Works
4–3	Dick Hemingway
5–1	Price Costco Canada Inc.
5–2	Dick Hemingway
5–3	Bob Daemmrich/Stock Boston
6–1	Bemsau/The Image Works
6–2	David Young Wolff/PhotoEdit
7–1a	Courtesy of Moneysworth and Best
7–1b	John Lawrence/Tony Store Images
7–1c	Barbara Alper/Stock Boston
7–2	SuperStock, Inc.
7–3a	Tom Carroll/FPG International
7–3b	Kim Golding/Tony Stone Images
8–1	Tower City Development
8–2	Dick Hemingway
8–3	Mall of America
8–4	West Edmonton Mall
8–5	The Forum Shops at Caesar's
9–1	Harry Rosen Inc./Jeff Smith
9–2	PhotoEdit
9–3	Loblaw Brands Limited
9–4a	Shinichi Kanno/FPG International
9–4b	Michael Grecco/Stock Boston
10–1	Bill Sandford/Toronto Sun
10–2	Charles Gupton/The Stock Market
10–3	Ralf-Finn Hestoft
11–1	James Leynse/Saba Press Photos, Inc.
11–2	Ogust/The Image Works
12–1	Tony Page/Tony Stone Images
12–2	Gabe Palmer/The Stock Market
12–3a	Gary Buss/FPG International
12–3b	Dick Hemingway
13–1a	Dick Hemingway
13–1b	Dick Hemingway
13–2a	Marco Shark Images
13–2b	Levy/Gamma Liaison, Inc.
15–1	Radio Shack
15–2a	Prentice Hall Archives
15–2b	Leucar/Bob Carroll
16–1	James Knowles/Stock Boston
16–2	Crandall/The Image Works
16–3a	The Home Depot Canada
16–3b	The Photo Works/Monkmeyer Press
16–3c	1–800–FLOWERS
16–4	Bill Aron/PhotoEdit
16–5	Marco Shark Images
17–1	John P. Andress/The Stock Market
18–1a	S. Kanno/FPG International
18–1b	Guy Marchz/FPG International
18–2	Travelpix/FPG International
18–3	Labatt Breweries of Canada
18–4a	Najilah Feanny/SABA Press Photos, Inc.
18–4b	Rob Crandall/Stock Boston